Chapter 5
519-530
542-647
675-700
Chapter 6
701-712
725-802
816-838

629

CASES AND MATERIALS

BUSINESS ASSOCIATIONS

AGENCY, PARTNERSHIPS, AND CORPORATIONS

FOURTH EDITION

by

WILLIAM A. KLEIN
Maxwell Professor of Law Emeritus
University of California, Los Angeles

J. MARK RAMSEYER
Mitsubishi Professor of Japanese Legal Studies
Harvard Law School

STEPHEN M. BAINBRIDGE
Professor of Law
University of California, Los Angeles

NEW YORK, NEW YORK
FOUNDATION PRESS

2000

 TEXT IS PRINTED ON 10% POST
CONSUMER RECYCLED PAPER

PREFACE

"You should lay off candy bars for a while," Marlene Dietrich once told Orson Welles. Bloated, he was twice the size of his former self and half the man. Bloated, he resembled nothing so much as the typical corporate law casebook.

We try to be different. And toward that end, in editing this book we follow six basic but apparently widely ignored principles. Each principle is one that we think helps produce a book that teaches students the gist of the law they need to know; that trains them to apply it; and that (perish the thought) almost makes them enjoy the process.

First, we give judges one chance—but only one chance—to explain the law. Most judicial opinions are as bloated as any character Welles ever played, but law schools teach students that point marvelously well in the first year. We see no reason to make the point again in the second. More specifically, we see no reason to force students to plow through fifteen pages of bad prose when a disciplined judge could explain the law in three. We edit the law, and edit it ruthlessly.

Second, working within the "give us the facts, ma'm, just the facts" tradition, we include the facts in all their ambiguity. In corporate law as in most of legal practice, the gist is in the application, and for application the facts matter critically. Although we heavily edit discussions of the law, we include most statements of the facts in full. When helpful, we add extra fact-based problems to explore those applications further.

Third, because lawyers plan at least as often as they litigate, we bring a planner's perspective. In the first half of the book, for example, we explore how the parties to a case could have avoided the disputes at stake. At the end of the book, we use corporate debt to ask both how business executives can structure the relationships among their many investors, and what economic consequences follow from those structural possibilities.

Fourth, we believe in agency and partnership law. We believe they matter not just for their own sake, but for understanding corporate legal practice. Consequently, we include materials on agency and partnership that are complete, that cohere within themselves, and that help explain how the corporate enterprise functions.

Fifth, we offer a *case*book, not a treatise. One of us (Klein) has already published a handbook on the subject (*Business Organization and Finance*, with John C. Coffee, Jr., Foundation Press). As that handbook is widely available, we see no need to fill the pages between the cases with long discussions of legal theory and doctrine. Instructors who prefer casebooks without extensive explanatory text will find this the casebook for them; instructors who prefer the explanatory matter should assign *BOF* in conjunction with this casebook.

Last, if a case is no fun, we omit it. There are exceptions, to be sure. Even we could not eliminate some key but dull U.S. and Delaware Supreme Court opinions. In general, however, we include only cases that at least one of us enjoys teaching. Law school drags enough as it is without assigning cases no one wants to read. Corporate law *can* be fascinating. In this book, we do our best to make it so.

The result, we think, is a book that provides simple settings for sophisticated analysis. We offer interesting and challenging cases; we edit them carefully but ruthlessly; we include the necessary statutes; and we add questions and problems where helpful. Through this, we think we offer a book that isolates the basic ideas, eliminates distracting detail, and motivates students to apply those ideas to a world they will soon help shape.

Lean, we think, but not mean. Enjoy the book.

WILLIAM A. KLEIN
J. MARK RAMSEYER
STEPHEN M. BAINBRIDGE

JANUARY, 2000

EDITORIAL NOTE AND ACKNOWLEDGMENT

Footnote numbers in cases are as in the original, with no renumbering to take account of omitted footnotes. Footnotes in editorial text, notes, and other material are consecutively numbered in each chapter.

Citations in cases are generally omitted, except where the authority cited might be familiar to a student or where the citation provides the source of quoted language.

We are grateful for permission to reprint copyrighted material from *Knights, Raiders, and Targets: The Impact of the Hostile Takeover,* edited by John C. Coffee, Louis Lowenstein, & Susan Rose-Ackerman. Copyright © 1988 by the Center for Law and Economic Studies. Reprinted by permission of Oxford University Press, Inc.

*

SUMMARY OF CONTENTS

Sec.

TABLE OF CONTENTS

Sec.

Sec.

TABLE OF CASES

Principal cases are in bold type. Non-principal cases are in roman type. References are to Pages.

xix

*

BUSINESS ASSOCIATIONS

*

CHAPTER 1

AGENTS AND EMPLOYEES

SECTION 1. AN INTRODUCTION TO THE ORGANIZATION OF BUSINESS

We begin with a case, Fowler v. Pennsylvania Tire Co., in which a tire distributor, Martin, has become bankrupt. Martin's business was taken over by a bankruptcy trustee—an individual appointed by the court, in this case, to liquidate the assets of the business and distribute among the creditors the cash realized by the liquidation. Penn Tire was the manufacturer and supplier of certain tires held by Martin at the time the bankruptcy trustee took possession of the business. The question is whether Penn Tire had retained title to the tires (under a "consignment"), in which case it can retrieve the tires, or had transferred title to Martin (under a "conditional sales contract"), in which case (because Penn Tire failed to perfect any security interest) the tires are an asset of Martin, to be sold for the benefit of all creditors.

Part of the usefulness of the case lies in the opportunity it presents, by virtue of its description of the business setting in which it arises, for examining alternative methods of organizing economic activity. Penn Tire can be compared, for example, with Firestone, which sells its tires through its own stores, and with Michelin and Bridgestone, which sell through independent outlets. Different forms of economic organization present different problems to the lawyer as planner. As you read the case, think about how litigation (and the controversy leading to litigation) could have been avoided by proper planning by the parties. "Planning" refers to the process of reaching and drafting agreements, buying insurance, deciding to rely on independent contractors, and using various other techniques for avoiding or solving problems before they arise. A planner thinks of agreements and of cooperation, not of controversy or of adversarial relationships. To do a good job as a planner, a lawyer must understand what the people running the business want to achieve and what their alternatives may be.

Fowler v. Pennsylvania Tire Company

326 F.2d 526 (5th Cir.1964).

■ Before HUTCHESON and BROWN, CIRCUIT JUDGES, and SIMPSON, DISTRICT JUDGE.

■ SIMPSON, DISTRICT JUDGE.

This is an appeal by the trustee in bankruptcy from a judgment of the District Court reversing an Order of the referee in bankruptcy denying the

1

petition for reclamation as filed by the appellee, Pennsylvania Tire Company. The question for decision is whether the agreement by which the appellee delivered its tires to the appellant-bankrupt for resale was a consignment for sale or an absolute sale with a right of return.

On May 27, 1960, Pennsylvania Tire Company and Jeff Martin, Jr. d/b/a Martin's DX, Manly's Associates, Manly's and Martin's Tire & Appliance Co., (hereinafter referred to as Bankrupt), entered into a contract, whereby the former agreed to deliver tires to the latter for resale at prices and terms fixed by the latter. This contract was termed a consignment with the title expressly being reserved with the appellee. While monthly inventory reports were required, there was no provision for any sort of segregating or earmarking of these tires.

On April 17, 1962, bankrupt filed a voluntary petition in bankruptcy, and on the following day, an order of adjudication was entered. On May 1st, Pennsylvania filed its petition for reclamation of these tires still in bankrupt's possession, asserting that this transaction was a consignment, and therefore, the title to the tires did not pass to the bankrupt and consequently could not pass to the trustee under Sec. 70, sub. c of The Bankruptcy Act (Title 11 U.S.C. § 110, sub. c). The outcome of this litigation depends on a determination of who had title to these tires. In addition to the express reservation of title in the contract, it is necessary for the Court to examine the transaction and, if possible, to ascertain the correct intent of the parties.   .   .   .

[The findings of the referee were, in part, as follows:]

"(1) That on April 17, 1962 Jeff Martin, Jr. d/b/a Martin's Tire & Appliance, filed a voluntary petition in bankruptcy and on May 1, 1962, Leon W. Fowler qualified as Trustee of said estate.

"(2) That on the 27th day of May, 1960, the bankrupt and the Pennsylvania Tire Company entered into an agreement called 'POC Warehouse Agreement'.

"(3) That the said POC Warehouse Agreement was not recorded in Texas, nor in the State of Ohio, the law of which latter State the parties agreed to be controlling in construing the said Agreement.

"(4) That no signs were posted as provided for in the Agreement in the bankrupt's place of business which disclosed a relationship between the petitioner Pennsylvania Tire Company and the bankrupt other than being one of a sale to the bankrupt.

"(5) That the tires were not segregated or kept in a separate place from the rest of the merchandise of the bankrupt in accordance with said Agreement.

"(6) That the bankrupt made out the orders for tires which he desired to be shipped to him rather than the company selecting the tires for shipment, and that the tires which were shipped to Martin were for the purpose of resale and that there were no restrictions on the amount of tires the bankrupt could sell or as to the terms of such sale.

. . .

"(8) That the copies of the 'Customer Invoice File' indicated that the tires were 'sold to Martin Tire & Appliance Co., 105 West Commerce St., Gladewater, Texas', and that the tires were 'shipped to Same'.

"(9) That no tires could be returned to the Company or transferred to other Company distributors without prior express authority of the Pennsylvania Tire Company.

"Conclusions of Law:

"That the business transactions between the Pennsylvania Tire Company and Jeff Martin, Jr., d/b/a Martin Tire & Appliance amounted to a sale, and that the said Jeff Martin was obligated to pay for tires that were shipped to him by the said Pennsylvania Tire Company."

. . .

[The terms of the contract were, in part, as follows:]

"TITLE: Title in and to all such stock shall be and remain in Company until disposed of by the Warehouseman in accordance with the provisions hereinafter outlined. The Warehouseman agrees to take all necessary steps to protect and maintain the Company's title in and to such merchandise; to keep such merchandise separate and apart from similar merchandise owned by persons other than the Company; to not permit same to be mingled with any other merchandise; to at all times maintain appropriate signs, labels or other identification clearly designating same as Company's property.

"INVENTORY REPORTS: The Warehouseman shall forward to the Company at Mansfield, Ohio, immediately after the end of each month an actual physical inventory indicating the quantity, size and type of such consigned stock at the beginning and end of the month and a list of transfers to and from such stock. All reports are to be prepared on such forms as the Company may provide. Acknowledgment receipts of all consigned stock received shall be furnished daily. Warehouseman further agrees to maintain such records [and] to make such further and additional reports which the Company may deem necessary from time to time in regard to the consigned stock.

"ACCESS TO STOCK: The Company shall have access to the consigned stock at all times, whether during or after business hours.

"WITHDRAWAL REPORTS: When stock is withdrawn from warehouse stock, invoices or reports on forms furnished by the Company must be issued daily, all copies of which must be mailed either to Mansfield, Ohio, or the Division Office, as Mansfield may direct through the Warehouse Manual of Instruction in effect from time to time. Withdrawal reports issued by Warehouseman shall not be valid until accepted by Company, however, all such reports received by Company shall be deemed to have been accepted unless Company notifies Warehouseman to the contrary within 30 days from their receipt.

. . .

"FIRE INSURANCE: The Company agrees to carry adequate insurance against loss by fire of all merchandise carried in the Warehouse stock, cost of said insurance to be paid to the Company by Warehouseman promptly after receipt of billing.

"TAXES: The Warehouseman will, where and when required, list the stock for taxation in his own name as bailee, showing the merchandise as stock held on consignment. The Warehouseman will pay to the proper authority, as they become due, all taxes or fees on such stock, or by reason of having or selling the stock, or upon billing at any time from Company at the latest available rate, will make such payment to Company, who will then be responsible to the taxing authority. The Warehouseman will furnish Company copies of tax returns and receipts covering such property. Warehouseman will secure and maintain all licenses at his own expense.

"RETURNED GOODS: Except for the provisions as outlined under 'Termination' as set forth below, the following procedure will apply to returned goods:

"1) Any merchandise withdrawn by Warehouseman for his own account shall not thereafter be returned to the consigned stock without prior written approval from the Company.

. . .

"TERMINATION: Breach of this agreement by either party will be considered just cause for immediate termination. This agreement may also be cancelled by either party at any time upon three days' written notice. In either event, Warehouseman agrees to deliver immediately thereafter to location designated by Company and without expense or commission of any nature to Company, all consigned stock in his possession."

[Opinion]

First of all, the appellant contends that this agreement amounted to a sale and not a consignment and secondly, that if this was not an absolute sale, then it was at least a conditional sales contract. [Discussion of the question of choice of law, that of Texas or that of Ohio, is omitted. The court finds that under the law of both states, to protect a security interest in property, a seller under a conditional sales contract must record its interest, but a consignor need not do so.]

Turning to the controlling issue in this case of whether the transaction was a consignment for sale or a sale with the right of return, the trustee persistently contends that notwithstanding the express language in the contract—that the title is reserved with Pennsylvania Tire Company—the agreement is a sale with the right to return any of the tires which the bankrupt does not sell. The basis for this contention is that subsequent to the contract, the actions of the parties indicated that they were treating the tires as belonging outright to the bankrupt. The trustee takes the position that the conduct of the parties finally determines the position of the parties with reference to their intentions, citing Goodyear Tire & Rubber Co. v. Orebaugh, 6 Cir., 79 F.2d 738, to support his argument. But the facts there are distinguishable, which difference results in the application of another principle of law. In the above case, the manufacturer sold tires to the bankrupt, and having some doubt as to the latter's financial ability, attempted to take back title through the issuance of credit memoranda. The bankrupt never gave up possession of the tires and failed to earmark them as the property of Goodyear. The Court held that as to third parties, the transaction was ineffective to divest the bankrupt of his title to the tires. In the instant case, title never passed to the bankrupt by the terms of the agreement, so there is no need to decide whether there occurred sufficient later acts to divest the bankrupt of his title. There is language in the case of Matter of Klein, 2 Cir., 3 F.2d 375, to the effect that a test of the good faith of an agreement purporting to be a consignment for sale is to ascertain whether the parties adhered to the agreement and performed its terms or ignored it and, in violation of its terms, treated deliveries of goods as actual sales. The force of this language relates to discovering the intentions of the parties as to whether they actually intended to effect a consignment or whether the arrangement was only a cloak intended to conceal an actual sale. There is no question here of any bad faith or collusive dealings between the parties which could result in detriment to third parties.

As to determining the intent of the parties, the prevailing view is that it will be determined solely by the words employed in the written instrument, where the meaning of such instrument is clear and unambiguous. . . . But where the contract or agreement is unclear or of doubtful meaning, the Court in interpreting what the parties were called upon to do, may properly consider acts done by the parties in the course of performance. . . . The foundation for this latter principle is that a person's construction of his own language constitutes the highest evidence of his intentions. However, this rule is applicable only if the contract is ambiguous or of doubtful meaning; it does not apply to any agreement that is free of ambiguity. . . .

Here the terms used and their meaning are clear. The agreement is complete and no dispute is present as to the meaning of any language used.

The prime distinguishing factor of a consignment as opposed to a sale is that after the goods have been delivered to the dealer, no obligation arises on the part of the dealer to pay for them.

. . .

In the instant case, neither in the written agreement nor in the facts can there be found any reason to support a claim that the bankrupt was or could be obligated, at any time, to buy or pay for any unsold tires. . . .

The judgment of the District Court was correct; it is

Affirmed.

■ JOHN R. BROWN, CIRCUIT JUDGE (dissenting).

I agree that ultimately "[t]he outcome of this litigation depends on a determination of who had title to these tires," that is, whether the tires were the property of the bankrupt. I also agree that a different result obtains depending on whether the legal relation between the bankrupt and the Pennsylvania Tire Company is that of buyer and seller or consignee and consignor. I cannot agree, however, that in attempting to discover the nature of the relationship we are confined to the 4 corners of the instrument called "POC" Warehouse Agreement. Nor do I think that much is gained in discussing the case in terms of "title" or "consignment" versus "sale." These are not a statement of the reasons *why*. They are, rather, a statement of the problem, or, once it is decided, a statement of the conclusion. Because the broader inquiry which I believe is required yields a conclusion different from that reached by the majority, I respectfully dissent.

As I see it, whether title passed to the bankrupt on delivery of the tires or remained in the Tire Company until the tires were sold to a third-party user-customer depends on the agreement between the bankrupt and the Tire Company as evidenced by both the written "POC" Warehouse Agreement and the long-continued course of dealing. Admittedly several provisions of the Warehouse Agreement are consistent with a relationship of consignee and consignor. But the hard facts are that the bankrupt and the Tire Company did not operate in the manner called for by the Agreement.

The Agreement called for the bankrupt to keep the "merchandise separate and apart from similar merchandise owned by persons other than the [Tire] Company;" to make sure that the merchandise covered by the Agreement was not "mingled with any other merchandise;" and "to at all times maintain appropriate signs, labels or other identification clearly designating same as [Tire] Company's property." These requirements simply were not met by the bankrupt. He kept one common stock of tires on display for sale. Various other brands of tires were mixed with the Pennsylvania tires whose title is here in dispute. No signs or labels were maintained either on the premises or on the Pennsylvania tires which indicated that they were the property of the Tire Company rather than property of the bankrupt.

The Agreement required the bankrupt to forward to the Tire Company "immediately after the end of each month an actual physical inventory indicating the quantity, size and type of such consigned stock at the beginning and end of the month and a list of transfers to and from such stock." Acknowledgment receipts of all consigned stock received were required to "be furnished daily." Finally, the bankrupt was required to "render detailed reports daily reflecting the total amount of merchandise . . . withdrawn from the consigned stock." These reports were not made. The evidence is that the practice was for the bankrupt to fill out a statement of sale whenever, in his opinion, a sufficient number of tires had been sold to justify the making of a report.

Although it is apparent from the face of the Agreement that the Tire Company was attempting to set up an arrangement whereby the bankrupt would act as the agent of the Tire Company for the purposes of delivering merchandise to user-customers and collecting sales proceeds in trust for subsequent transmission to the Tire Company,[1] other provisions of the Agreement and certainly the course of dealing between the parties were inconsistent with an arrangement of this type. Under the Agreement, the bankrupt was responsible for any shortage in the stock whether caused by negligence, theft, fire [2] or otherwise. The bankrupt was likewise liable ultimately for all taxes on the stock.[3] In return for assuming all the risk of loss and for performing the storage and selling function for the Tire Company one would assume that the bankrupt would be allowed some compensation. He was, but it was measured—under the agreement—just as the compensation of retailers is universally measured. The bankrupt was allowed to retain an amount equal to the retail price of tires sold minus the wholesale price. Out of this amount the bankrupt was to pay the service charge of 1 and ½ per cent per month on the wholesale value of the tires not yet sold. This obviously was a charge for the financing of inventory. I need not determine the legal consequences of such arrangements if put into actual operation. The fact is that the bankrupt and the Tire Company never operated in the manner outlined. The tires were invoiced as "Sold To Martin Tire & Appliance, 105 Commerce, Gladewater, Texas," and the Tire Company charged Accounts Receivable when the tires were shipped. As noted above, the tires were not segregated, and the receipt and withdrawal reports were not made. The bankrupt dealt with the public as though the tires were his. He sold tires at prices and terms of his sole discretion. Rather than segregating the sales proceeds in trust in a bank account separate from his general bank account as apparently called for by the agreement,[4] he deposited the receipts in his general bank

1. Presumably this duty would require the bankrupt to segregate the sales proceeds in a trust account in the bank separate from his general bank account.

2. The agreement provided that the Tire Company would purchase fire insurance on the stock. The premium was to be paid ultimately by the bankrupt, however, and in actual practice the bankrupt carried its own fire insurance payable to its order.

3. Under the terms of the agreement, all taxes whether initially paid by the Tire Company or by the bankrupt were to be paid ultimately by the bankrupt. Although the agreement provided for segregation of the Pennsylvania tires for taxing purposes and detailed reporting in the form of tax returns and receipts concerning the Pennsylvania tires, the practice was for the bankrupt to render and pay taxes on all the stock as though it were all his. No renditions, assessments, or returns or receipts indicating taxes paid on Pennsylvania tires were sent to the Tire Company because such tires were simply not rendered or assessed for taxation, and the taxes were not paid in a manner that would make this possible.

4. See note 1, supra and accompanying text.

account. When he made remittances, either in payment of amounts billed on the tires or in payment of the "service charge," he drew a check on his general account. Even the service charge was computed in a manner different from that provided in the agreement. Rather than being computed on the balance of inventory unsold and on hand, it was computed on the total value of tires shipped to the bankrupt during the month, whether sold or not. Finally, both under the contract and in actual practice, the bankrupt could return tires only with the consent of the Tire Company. In short, the relationship in actual practice had every earmark of that of buyer and seller, with inventory financing aid being supplied by the seller, Pennsylvania Tire Company.

I have not set forth this detail with the thought in mind that this alters or varies the terms of the written contract. We do not have that case before us. Whatever the legal consequences of its terms might be if adhered to, the fact is that neither party complied with them. Assuming it controlled absolutely the initial "consignment" of tires, the contract, if ignored as it was throughout all subsequent times, could not extinguish either the fact of actual conduct or the legal significance of it. Moreover, these actual operations in disregard or violation of the terms of the agreement were not concealed, unilateral, unknown actions. The Tire Company made regular inspections and frequent reports of these derelictions were made to the home office. Nevertheless the home office continued to ship and invoice tires to the bankrupt knowing that what the contract prescribed would never be complied with.

In that situation the legal relationship of the parties and to the merchandise should be determined by what was done, not by what they said they would do.

The consequences of this decision in terms of the Texas policy of protecting creditors is ominous. . . .

Whether the dealer is a tire retailer, a dry goods store, general merchandise establishment or automobile dealer, the manufacturer-wholesaler can protect himself absolutely by a simple "warehouse" contract. All he need do to insure that he will always be able to reclaim from his bankrupt dealer goods sold but yet unpaid for is to execute with the dealer at the inception of their business dealings an instrument which on its face creates a consignor-consignee relationship. Then they can deal with each other as sellers and buyers normally do, but with the assurance that should the dealer become bankrupt the supplier—rather than having to share the assets with all the general creditors—will be able to come into the Bankruptcy Court with his "POC" Warehouse Agreement in one hand and a petition for reclamation in the other and reclaim the merchandise.

I therefore dissent.

NOTE

The majority's conclusion is that Penn Tire retained title to the tires and that consequently the tires did not become assets of the bankrupt,

Martin, that could be sold for the benefit of all the creditors. If Penn Tire had lost, it would have been entitled, along with other general creditors, to its pro rata share of the assets (ultimately, cash) available for distribution. Today, under Uniform Commercial Code § 2–326, Penn Tire would lose without regard to whether it had retained title to the tires. U.C.C. § 2–326(3) provides, "Where goods are delivered to a person [Martin] for sale and such person maintains a place of business at which he deals in goods of the kind involved, under a name other than the name of the person making delivery [Penn Tire], then with respect to claims of creditors of the person conducting the business the goods are deemed to be on sale or return[,]" and, under § 2–326(2), are "subject to the claims of the buyer's [Martin's] creditors . . . while in the buyer's possession." Under the U.C.C. there are various ways in which a firm such as Penn Tire can establish a security interest in the goods, including filing certain documents under Article 9.

ANALYSIS

The majority in the *Fowler* case reasoned as follows: The transaction took the form of a consignment; the contract was cast in terms of consignment. Therefore Penn Tire retained title to the tires. Therefore Martin's other creditors have no claim to them; the tires simply do not belong to Martin. The dissent argued that regardless of form, the transaction in practice had the indicia of a sale (with Penn Tire providing financing), and should be treated as a sale, to Martin.

1. What are the facts that the dissent relied upon in finding a sale?

2. How would you frame the argument that these facts, rather than the form of the transaction, should be controlling?

3. How would you frame the argument that the form of the transaction (that is, the terms of the contract) should be controlling?

4. One of the criteria of a good legal rule for this case is fairness—in this case, fairness to Penn Tire and to the other creditors. If you focus on this criterion, how do you decide the case? Why?

5. Another relevant criterion is that the legal system should facilitate useful exchange. Under this criterion, how would you decide the case? Why? (In this connection, think of what the interested persons might reasonably be expected to do to protect themselves.)

BUSINESS SETTING AND ALTERNATIVES

Think of the underlying business setting in *Fowler* from the perspective of Penn Tire. Suppose the owners of Penn Tire think of themselves first as tire makers, then begin to think about how to sell the tires. Consider the various ways in which they might do so.

1. The selling process could be organized "within the firm." That is, Penn Tire could establish its own sales outlets, hire managers and sales people, etc. Think of Firestone tires.

2. The selling process might be organized "across markets." That is, Penn Tire could sell its tires to independent distributors. Think of Michelin or Bridgestone tires.

3. What are the advantages and disadvantages of each method of doing business?

4. What kinds of legal documents would be necessary under each approach?

5. What are the substantive issues—the "deal points"—that must be resolved? Consider (a) duration and termination, (b) control, (c) risk of loss, and (d) sharing of gain.

6. Assume that Penn Tire decides to open its own outlets. How might it modify the pure form of organization within the firm to achieve some of the advantages of organization across markets?

7. Suppose that Penn Tire's executives decide to sell through independent outlets. Then they begin to think about some of the disadvantages of that approach. One problem is of the sort presented in the *Fowler* case: how to protect Penn Tire's financial interest in the tires. How can that problem be solved? Suppose Penn Tire has tried to maintain an image of producing high-quality tires and of backing up that image by providing good service and effective guarantees. What can it do to protect that image? (What do you suppose fast-food franchisors, such as McDonald's, do?)

SECTION 2. EMPLOYEE VERSUS INDEPENDENT CONTRACTOR

The two cases that follow, Humble Oil & Refining Co. v. Martin and Hoover v. Sun Oil Company, again present the issue of organization within the firm versus organization across markets. Here we have large oil companies faced with the business issue of how to sell their principal products, gasoline and oil. One possibility is to sell through independently owned and operated gasoline filling stations. Another possibility is to sell through stations that they own and operate through employees. As the cases illustrate, in practice the arrangements have some characteristics of each of these possibilities.

In the era in which these cases arose, most gasoline stations performed three functions. (1) They sold gasoline, with service. There were no self-serve pumps. (2) They sold tires, batteries, and accessories (TBA). And (3) they performed repair services. The oil companies wanted to supply the gasoline and oil and the tires, batteries, and accessories. The repair services were provided by, or under the direction of, the operator of the station, who generally was himself an automobile mechanic.

The cases involve the liability of the oil companies for personal injuries negligently inflicted by gasoline station personnel. The legal issue turns on whether the operator of the station was an employee—a "servant" in the language of the law—or an independent operator (independent contractor) or, in more modern language, a franchisee. Under the doctrine of respondeat superior, a "master" (employer) is liable for the torts of its servants (employees). A master-servant relationship exists where the servant has agreed (a) to work on behalf of the master and (b) to be subject to the master's control or right to control the "physical conduct" of the servant (that is, the manner in which the job is performed, as opposed to the result alone). See Restatement (Second), of Agency §§ 1 and 2.

Servants are distinguished from independent contractors. The latter are of two types, agents and non-agents. An agent-type independent contractor is one who has agreed to act on behalf of another, the principal, but not subject to the principal's control over how the result is accomplished (that is, over the "physical conduct" of the task). A non-agent independent contractor is one who operates independently and simply enters into arm's length transactions with others. For example, if a carpenter is hired to build a garage for a homeowner, and if it is agreed or understood that the carpenter is simply responsible for getting the job done and is not to take directions from the homeowner, the carpenter is an independent contractor and is not acting as an agent. If the carpenter agrees to buy lumber for the project, on the credit account of the homeowner, the carpenter will still be acting as an independent contractor (assuming again that the homeowner does not have the right to tell the carpenter how to accomplish the task), but, because the carpenter is now

11

acting on behalf of the homeowner in the purchase of the lumber, the carpenter is an (independent-contractor-type) agent of the homeowner.

The two cases are concerned only with the distinction between servants and independent contractors. They need not, and do not, address the distinction between agent-type independent contractors and non-agent-type independent contractors.

These two cases also do not address the issue of "apparent" agency. A person may be liable for the torts of another person even if the other is not a servant if there is an appearance of a master-servant relationship. For example, in Gizzi v. Texaco, Inc., 437 F.2d 308 (3d Cir.1971), the plaintiff, Gizzi, bought a used Volkswagen van from the operator of a Texaco station, Hinman, for $400. Hinman agreed to perform repairs on the van, including work on the brakes. Hinman completed the work and Gizzi drove away in the van. Shortly thereafter, the brakes failed and Gizzi was injured. According to the court, it was plain that in selling the van, Hinman was acting on his own behalf, not as an agent of Texaco. The court did not consider whether in performing the brake repairs (as opposed to selling the van) Hinman acted in fact as a servant-type agent of Texaco. The issue as framed on appeal was only whether Hinman was *apparently* an agent of Texaco for performing the repairs. The court cited Texaco's nationwide advertising, its slogan, "trust your car to the man who wears the [Texaco] star," and the prominent display of Texaco signs and insignia at Hinman's station, and concluded that the evidence of apparent agency was sufficient to permit the case to go to a jury.

We will return to the issue of apparent agency and apparent authority in Section 5. The two cases to be examined here are concerned only with "actual" authority. (Purists argue that "actual" is surplusage.)

Humble Oil & Refining Co. v. Martin

148 Tex. 175, 222 S.W.2d 995 (1949).

Petitioners Humble Oil & Refining Company and Mrs. A.C. Love and husband complain here of the judgments of the trial court and the Court of Civil Appeals in which they were held [liable] in damages for personal injuries following a special issue verdict at the suit of respondent George F. Martin acting for himself and his two minor daughters. The injuries were inflicted on the three Martins about the noon hour on May 12, 1947, in the City of Austin, by an unoccupied automobile belonging to the petitioners Love, which, just prior to the accident, had been left by Mrs. Love at a filling station owned by petitioner Humble for servicing and thereafter, before any station employee had touched it, rolled by gravity off the premises into and obliquely across the abutting street, striking Mr. Martin and his children from behind as they were walking into the yard of their home, a short distance downhill from the station.

The trial court rendered judgment against petitioners Humble and Mrs. Love jointly and severally and gave the latter judgment over against

Humble for whatever she might pay the respondents. The Court of Civil Appeals affirmed the judgment after reforming it to eliminate the judgment over in favor of Mrs. Love, without prejudice to the right of contribution by either defendant under Article 2212, Vernon's Ann.Civ.Stat., 216 S.W.(2d) 251. The petitioners here respectively complain of the judgment in favor of the Martins, and each seeks full indemnity (as distinguished from contribution) from the other.

The apparently principal contention of petitioner, Humble, is that it is liable neither to respondent Martin nor to petitioner Mrs. Love, since the station was in effect operated by an independent contractor, W.T. Schneider, and Humble is accordingly not responsible for his negligence nor that of W.V. Manis, who was the only station employee or representative present when the Love car was left and rolled away. In this connection, the jury convicted petitioner Humble of the following acts of negligence proximately causing the injuries in question: (a) Failure to inspect the Love car to see that the emergency brake was set or the gears engaged; (b) failure to set the emergency brake on the Love car; (c) leaving the Love car unattended on the driveway. The verdict also included findings that Mrs. Love "had delivered her car to the custody of the defendant Humble Oil & Refining Company, before her car started rolling from the position in which she had parked it"; that the accident was not unavoidable; and that no negligent act of either of petitioners was the sole proximate cause of the injuries in question. We think the Court of Civil Appeals properly held Humble responsible for the operation of the station, which admittedly it owned, as it did also the principal products there sold by Schneider under the so-called "Commission Agency Agreement" between him and Humble which was in evidence. The facts that neither Humble, Schneider nor the station employees considered Humble as an employer or master; that the employees were paid and directed by Schneider individually as their "boss," and that a provision of the agreement expressly repudiates any authority of Humble over the employees, are not conclusive against the master-servant relationship, since there is other evidence bearing on the right or power of Humble to control the details of the station work as regards Schneider himself and therefore as to employees which it was expressly contemplated that he would hire. The question is ordinarily one of fact, and where there are items of evidence indicating a master-servant relationship, contrary items such as those above mentioned cannot be given conclusive effect.   . . .

Even if the contract between Humble and Schneider were the only evidence on the question, the instrument as a whole indicates a master-servant relationship quite as much as, if not more than, it suggests an arrangement between independent contractors. For example, paragraph 1 includes a provision requiring Schneider "to make reports *and perform other duties in connection with the operation of said station that may be required of him from time to time by Company.*" (Emphasis supplied). And while paragraph 2 purports to require Schneider to pay all operational expenses, the schedule of commissions forming part of the agreement does just the opposite in its paragraph (F), which gives Schneider a 75%

"commission" on "the net public utility bills paid" by him and thus requires Humble to pay three-fourths of one of the most important operational expense items. Obviously the main object of the enterprise was the retail marketing of Humble's products with title remaining in Humble until delivery to the consumer. This was done under a strict system of financial control and supervision by Humble, with little or no business discretion reposed in Schneider except as to hiring, discharge, payment and supervision of a few station employees of a more or less laborer status. Humble furnished the all important station location and equipment, the advertising media, the products and a substantial part of the current operating costs. The hours of operation were controlled by Humble. The "Commission Agency Agreement," which evidently was Schneider's only title to occupancy of the premise, was terminable at the will of Humble. The so-called "rentals" were, at least in part, based on the amount of Humble's products sold, being, therefore, involved with the matter of Schneider's remuneration and not rentals in the usual sense. And, as above shown, the agreement required Schneider in effect to do anything Humble might tell him to do. All in all, aside from the stipulation regarding Schneider's assistants, there is essentially little difference between his situation and that of a mere store clerk who happens to be paid a commission instead of a salary. The business was Humble's business, just as the store clerk's business would be that of the store owner. Schneider was Humble's servant, and so accordingly were Schneider's assistants who were contemplated by the contract. Upon facts similar to those at bar but probably less indicative of a master-servant relationship, the latter has been held to exist by respectable authority, which seems to reflect the prevailing view in the nation. . . .

The evidence above discussed serves to distinguish the instant case from The Texas Company v. Wheat, 140 Texas 468, 168 S.W.(2d) 632, upon which petitioner Humble principally relies. In that case the evidence differed greatly from that now before us. It clearly showed a "dealer" type of relationship in which the lessee in charge of the filling station purchased from his landlord, The Texas Company, and sold as his own, and was free to sell at his own price and on his own credit terms, the company products purchased, as well as the products of other oil companies. The contracts contained no provision requiring the lessee to perform any duty The Texas Company might see fit to impose on him, nor did the company pay any part of the lessee's operating expenses, nor control the working hours of the station. . . .

Hoover v. Sun Oil Company

58 Del. 553, 212 A.2d 214 (1965).

This case is concerned with injuries received as the result of a fire on August 16, 1962 at the service station operated by James F. Barone. The fire started at the rear of plaintiff's car where it was being filled with gasoline and was allegedly caused by the negligence of John Smilyk an employee of Barone. Plaintiffs brought suit against Smilyk, Barone and Sun Oil Company (Sun) which owned the service station.

Sun has moved for summary judgment as to it on the basis that Barone was an independent contractor and therefore the alleged negligence of his employee could not result in liability as to Sun. The plaintiffs contend instead that Barone was acting as Sun's agent and that Sun may therefore be responsible for plaintiff's injuries.

Barone began operating this business in October of 1960 pursuant to a lease dated October 17, 1960. The station and all of its equipment, with the exception of a tire-stand and rack, certain advertising displays and miscellaneous hand tools, were owned by Sun. The lease was subject to termination by either party upon thirty days' written notice after the first six months and at the anniversary date thereafter. The rental was partially determined by the volume of gasoline purchased but there was also a minimum and a maximum monthly rental.

At the same time, Sun and Barone also entered into a dealer's agreement under which Barone was to purchase petroleum products from Sun and Sun was to loan necessary equipment and advertising materials. Barone was required to maintain this equipment and to use it solely for Sun products. Barone was permitted under the agreement to sell competitive products but chose to do so only in a few minor areas. As to Sun products, Barone was prohibited from selling them except under the Sunoco label and from blending them with products not supplied by Sun.

Barone's station had the usual large signs indicating that Sunoco products were sold there. His advertising in the classified section of the telephone book was under a Sunoco heading and his employees wore uniforms with the Sun emblem, the uniforms being owned by Barone or rented from an independent company.

Barone, upon the urging of Robert B. Peterson, Sun's area sales representative, attended a Sun school for service station operators in 1961. The school's curriculum was designed to familiarize the station operator with bookkeeping and merchandising, the appearance and proper maintenance of a Sun station, and the Sun Oil products. The course concluded with the operator working at Sun's model station in order to gain work experience in the use of the policy and techniques taught at the school.

Other facts typifying the company-service station relationship were the weekly visits of Sun's sales representative, Peterson, who would take orders for Sun products, inspect the restrooms, communicate customer complaints, make various suggestions to improve sales and discuss any problems that Barone might be having. Besides the weekly visits, Peterson was in contact with Barone on other occasions in order to implement Sun's "competitive allowance system" which enabled Barone to meet local price competition by giving him a rebate on the gasoline in his inventory roughly equivalent to the price decline and a similarly reduced price on his next order of gasoline.

While Peterson did offer advice to Barone on all phases of his operation, it was usually done on request and Barone was under no obligation to follow the advice. Barone's contacts and dealings with Sun were many and their relationship intricate, but he made no written reports to Sun and he alone assumed the overall risk of profit or loss in his business operation. Barone independently determined his own hours of operation and the identity, pay scale and working conditions of his employees, and it was his name that was posted as proprietor.

Plaintiffs contend in effect that the aforegoing facts indicate that Sun controlled the day-to-day operation of the station and consequently Sun is responsible for the negligent acts of Barone's employee. Specifically, plaintiffs contend that there is an issue of fact for the jury to determine as to whether or not there was an agency relationship.

The legal relationships arising from the distribution systems of major oil-producing companies are in certain respects unique. As stated in an annotation collecting many of the cases dealing with this relationship:

"This distribution system has grown up primarily as the result of economic factors and with little relationship to traditional legal concepts in the field of master and servant, so that it is perhaps not surprising that attempts by the court to discuss the relationship in the standard terms have led to some difficulties and confusion." 83 A.L.R.2d 1282, 1284 (1962).

In some situations traditional definitions of principal and agent and of employer and independent contractor may be difficult to apply to service station operations, but the undisputed facts of the case at bar make it clear that Barone was an independent contractor.

Barone's service station, unlike retail outlets for many products, is basically a one-company outlet and represents to the public, through Sunoco's national and local advertising, that it sells not only Sun's quality products but Sun's quality service. Many people undoubtedly come to the service station because of that latter representation.

However, the lease contract and dealer's agreement fail to establish any relationship other than landlord-tenant, and independent contractor. Nor is there anything in the conduct of the individuals which is inconsistent with that relationship so as to indicate that the contracts were mere subterfuge or sham. The areas of close contact between Sun and Barone stem from the fact that both have a mutual interest in the sale of Sun products and in the success of Barone's business.

The cases cited by both plaintiffs and defendant indicate that the result varies according to the contracts involved and the conduct and evidence of control under those contracts. Both lines of cases indicate that the test to be applied is that of whether the oil company has retained the right to control the details of the day-to-day operation of the service station; control or influence over results alone being viewed as insufficient.   .   .   .

The facts of this case differ markedly from those in which the oil company was held liable for the tortious conduct of its service station operator or his employees. Sun had no control over the details of Barone's day-to-day operation. Therefore, no liability can be imputed to Sun from the allegedly negligent acts of Smilyk. Sun's motion for summary judgment is granted.

ANALYSIS

1. Important elements of business relationships include duration, control, risk of loss, and return. Which of these becomes the key issue in the two cases? How can the outcomes in the two cases be reconciled?

2. Pretend you know nothing about the legal rules that distinguish between employees (servants) and people working for themselves (independent contractors).

(a) If you were a person like Schneider (the gas station operator in the *Humble Oil* case), which terms or elements of the relationship with Humble Oil would make you feel like an employee? Which terms would make you feel that you were independent, working for yourself?

(b) If you were a person like Barone (the operator in the *Sun Oil* case), would you feel less like an employee and more like an independent business person than a person like Schneider? Why?

(c) Focus on those terms of each relationship that suggest that the operator is independent. Assume that the oil companies could have changed those terms to make them consistent with an employment relationship. What would the new terms be? Why do you suppose the oil companies chose what may be thought of as a hybrid set of terms?

PLANNING

1. In *Humble Oil* the court states, "The hours of operation were controlled by Humble." In *Sun Oil* the court states, "Barone independently determined his own hours of operation." What do you suppose is the practical difference in the control of each of the oil companies over hours of operation? What do you suppose would happen to Barone if the people at Sun Oil concluded that he was not staying open late enough and that, as a result, Sun Oil was losing sales?

2. If you were advising Humble Oil and wanted to improve the prospects of avoiding liability for personal injuries, what changes would you suggest in the manner in which Humble Oil structured its relationship with its operators? What would be the likely substantive effect of these changes?

POLICY QUESTIONS

In the *Sun Oil* situation, presumably Sun Oil could have insisted that Barone take out a policy of liability insurance, protecting both him and Sun

Oil, or that he agree to indemnify Sun Oil for damages and show that he had enough assets to meet his obligation.

1. Do you think that it was irresponsible for Sun Oil to fail to do that?

2. Assume that your answer to part 1 was yes. What if Barone had operated ten gas stations, under his own name (but still bought most of his gasoline and oil and tires, batteries, and accessories from Sun Oil)?

3. Should the law somehow impose an obligation on Sun Oil to ensure that Barone is able to pay his debts?

4. Assume your answer to part 3 was yes. How would you frame the law?

5. What is your general theory of when people who do business with one another should and should not be liable for each other's tort, or contract, damages?

Section 3. Franchises

Murphy v. Holiday Inns, Inc.

216 Va. 490, 219 S.E.2d 874 (1975).

On August 21, 1973, Kyran Murphy (plaintiff) filed a motion for judgment against Holiday Inns, Inc. (defendant), a Tennessee Corporation, seeking damages for personal injuries sustained on August 24, 1971, while she was a guest at a motel in Danville. Plaintiff alleged that "Defendant owned and operated" the motel; that "Defendant, its agents and employees, so carelessly, recklessly, and negligently maintained the premises of the motel that Plaintiff did slip and fall on an area of a walk where water draining from an air conditioner had been allowed to accumulate"; and that as a proximate result of such negligence, plaintiff sustained serious and permanent injuries.

Defendant filed grounds of defense and a motion for summary judgment "on the grounds that it has no relationship with regard to the operator of the premises .   . other than a license agreement permitting the operator of a motel on the same premises to use the name 'Holiday Inns' subject to all the terms and conditions of such license agreement." That agreement, filed as an exhibit with defendant's motion for summary judgment, identifies defendant's licensee as Betsy–Len Motor [Hotel] Corporation (Betsy–Len).

Upon a finding that defendant did not own the premises upon which the accident occurred and that "there exists no principal-agent or master-servant relationship between the defendant corporation and Betsy–Len Motor Hotel Corporation", the trial court entered a final order on April 25, 1974, granting summary judgment in favor of defendant.

Plaintiff's sole assignment of error is that the trial court erred "in holding that no principal-agent or master-servant relationship exists."

On brief, plaintiff argues that the license agreement gives defendant "the authority and control over the Betsy–Len Corporation that establishes a true master/servant relationship." .   .   .

Actual agency is a consensual relationship.

"Agency is the fiduciary relation which results from the manifestation of consent by one person to another that the other shall act on his behalf and subject to his control, and consent by the other so to act." Restatement (Second) of Agency § 1 (1958).

.   .   .

19

"It is the element of continuous subjection to the will of the principal which distinguishes the agent from other fiduciaries and the agency agreement from other agreements." Id., comment (b).

. . .

When an agreement, considered as a whole, establishes an agency relationship, the parties cannot effectively disclaim it by formal "consent." "[T]he relationship of the parties does not depend upon what the parties themselves call it, but rather in law what it actually is." Chandler v. Kelley, 149 Va. 221, 231, 141 S.E. 389, 391–92 (1928). . . . Here, plaintiff and defendant agree that, if the license agreement is sufficient to establish an agency relationship, the disclaimer clause [1] does not defeat it.

Plaintiff and defendant also agree that, in determining whether a contract establishes an agency relationship, the critical test is the nature and extent of the control agreed upon.

The subject matter of the license defendant granted Betsy–Len is a "system." As defined in the agreement, the system is one "providing to the public . . . an inn service . . . of distinctive nature, of high quality, and of other distinguishing characteristics." Those characteristics include trade names using the words "Holiday Inn" and certain variations and combinations of those words, trade marks, architectural designs, insignia, patterns, color schemes, styles, furnishings, equipment, advertising services, and methods of operation.

In consideration of the license to use the "system," the licensee agreed to pay an initial sum of $5000; to construct one or more inns in accordance with plans approved by the licensor; to make monthly payments of 15 cents per room per day (5 cents of which was to be earmarked for national advertising expenditures); and "to conduct the operation of inns . . . in accordance with the terms and provisions of this license and of the Rules of operation of said System".

Plaintiff points to several provisions and rules which he says satisfy the control test and establish the principal-agent relationship. These include requirements:

That licensee construct its motel according to plans, specifications, feasibility studies, and locations approved by licensor;

That licensee employ the trade name, signs, and other symbols of the "system" designated by licensor;

That licensee pay a continuing fee for use of the license and a fee for national advertising of the "system";

That licensee solicit applications for credit cards for the benefit of other licensees;

1. That clause provides that "Licensee, in the use of the name 'Holiday Inn' . . . shall identify Licensee as being the owner and operator [and] . . . the parties hereto are completely separate entities, are not partners, joint adventurers, or agents of the other in any sense, and neither has power to obligate or bind the other".

That licensee protect and promote the trade name and not engage in
any competitive motel business or associate itself with any trade association designed to establish standards for motels;

That licensee not raise funds by sale of corporate stock or dispose of a
controlling interest in its motel without licensor's approval;

That training for licensee's manager, housekeeper, and restaurant
manager be provided by licensor at licensee's expense;

That licensee not employ a person contemporaneously engaged in a
competitive motel or hotel business; and

That licensee conduct its business under the "system," observe the
rules of operation, make quarterly reports to licensor concerning operations, and submit to periodic inspections of facilities and procedures conducted by licensor's representatives.

The license agreement of which these requirements were made a part
is a franchise contract. In the business world, franchising is a crescent
phenomenon of billion-dollar proportions.

> "[Franchising is] a system for the selective distribution of goods and/or
> services under a brand name through outlets owned by independent
> businessmen, called 'franchisees.' Although the franchisor supplies
> the franchisee with know-how and brand identification on a continuing
> basis, the franchisee enjoys the right to profit and runs the risk of loss.
> The franchisor controls the distribution of his goods and/or services
> through a contract which regulates the activities of the franchisee, in
> order to achieve standardization." R. Rosenberg, *Profits From Fran-
> chising* 41 (1969). (Italics omitted).

The fact that an agreement is a franchise contract does not insulate
the contracting parties from an agency relationship. If a franchise contract
so "regulates the activities of the franchisee" as to vest the franchisor with
control within the definition of agency, the agency relationship arises even
though the parties expressly deny it.

Here, the license agreement contains the principal features of the
typical franchise contract, including regulatory provisions. Defendant
owned the "brand name," the trade mark, and the other assets associated
with the "system." Betsy–Len owned the sales "outlet." Defendant
agreed to allow Betsy–Len to use its assets. Betsy–Len agreed to pay a fee
for that privilege. Betsy–Len retained the "right to profit" and bore the
"risk of loss." With respect to the manner in which defendant's trade
mark and other assets were to be used, both parties agreed to certain
regulatory rules of operation.

Having carefully considered all of the regulatory provisions in the
agreement, we are of opinion that they gave defendant no "control or right
to control the methods or details of doing the work," Wells v. Whitaker,
207 Va. 616, 624, 151 S.E.2d 422, 429 (1966), and, therefore, agree with the
trial court that no principal-agent or master-servant relationship was

created.[2] As appears from the face of the document, the purpose of those provisions was to achieve system-wide standardization of business identity, uniformity of commercial service, and optimum public good will, all for the benefit of both contracting parties. The regulatory provisions did not give defendant control over the day-to-day operation of Betsy–Len's motel. While defendant was empowered to regulate the architectural style of the buildings and the type and style of furnishings and equipment, defendant was given no power to control daily maintenance of the premises. Defendant was given no power to control Betsy–Len's current business expenditures, fix customer rates, or demand a share of the profits. Defendant was given no power to hire or fire Betsy–Len's employees, determine employee wages or working conditions, set standards for employee skills or productivity, supervise employee work routine, or discipline employees for nonfeasance or misfeasance. All such powers and other management controls and responsibilities customarily exercised by an owner and operator of an ongoing business were retained by Betsy–Len.

We hold that the regulatory provisions of the franchise contract did not constitute control within the definition of agency, and the judgment is

Affirmed.

Parker v. Domino's Pizza

629 So.2d 1026 (Fla. Dist. Ct. of Appeal, 4th Dist., 1993).
Rehearing, Rehearing En Banc and Certification Denied, 1994.

.   .   .   The complaints filed in those consolidated actions alleged that Jeffrey Todd Hoppock (Hoppock), while within the course and scope of his employment delivering pizza for J & B Enterprises, Inc., d/b/a Domino's Pizza (J & B Enterprises), operated a vehicle in a reckless, negligent and careless manner, causing it to strike another vehicle. The Parkers, who were both pedestrians at the time of the incident, allege that they were injured when a third vehicle hit them while they were helping the victims of the accident caused by Hoppock. .   .   .   It was further alleged that at the time of the accident J & B Enterprises and Hoppock, employer and employee, were operating as the agents, apparent agents, servants and/or employees of Domino's Pizza, Inc. (Domino's), and that Domino's exercised control over all of the activities of its franchisee, J & B Enterprises, and thus was vicariously liable for the negligence of J & B Enterprises and Hoppock.

Domino's moved for summary judgment based upon its position that at the time of the accident Hoppock was an employee of J & B Enterprises, not Domino's, and that neither J & B Enterprises nor Hoppock were employees of Domino's nor acting within the scope of any employment or agency relationship with Domino's. .   .   .

2. Because defendant had no such control or right to control, the distinction between a principal-agent and a master-servant relationship is not relevant here. .   .   .

The trial court determined that, as a matter of law, J & B Enterprises was an independent contractor, as provided in paragraph forty-five of the franchise agreement between the parties. Consequently Domino's could not be held vicariously liable for the negligence of J & B Enterprises, its agents and employees. . . .

. . .

Whether one party is a mere agent rather than an independent contractor as to the other party is to be determined by measuring the right to control and not by considering only the actual control exercised by the latter over the former. . . .

. . .

The relationship between Domino's and J & B Enterprises is established by a franchise agreement and an operating manual. We have summarized the requirements that best seem to illustrate the extent of control Domino's retains over the performance of its franchisees.

The "preambles" section of the franchise agreement states in relevant part:

Franchisee has applied to the Company for a franchise to operate a Domino's pizza store selling the products and services authorized and approved by the Company and utilizing the Company's business format, methods, specifications, standards, operating procedures, operating assistance, advertising services and the Marks.

The franchise agreement itself contains, *inter alia*, the following:

(1) Sales quotas;

(2) Franchise renewal dependent upon compliance with Domino's specific prescriptions;

(3) Location sites and guidelines for changing locations;

(4) Domino's approval of site and architectural plans, including the dimension requirements for all furniture, fixtures, and equipment;

(5) Specific rules for pizza and beverage preparation, including the minimum standards for delivery, performance, appearance;

(6) Specific signage and decorating requirements;

(7) Guidelines for a mandatory training program completion of which is a precondition to employment;

(8) A reservation of the rights Domino's retains to advise the franchisee on improvements, food preparation, hiring, advertising and general operational procedures;

(9) Company inspections;

(10) A prohibition on selling any products or services other than those authorized by Domino's;

(11) A requirement that delivery service zones may not extend to areas where pizza could not feasibly be delivered within 30 minutes;

(12) Specifications and quality standards by which every single item in the restaurant must abide, including though not limited to the

pizza ingredients, packaging, uniforms, cleaning supplies and advertisements;

(13) That each store must contribute 3% of its weekly royalties to
a fund administered by Domino's for its advertising and promotions;

(14) Strict advertising restrictions and requirements;

(15) Strict Domino's prescribed book-keeping requirements;

(16) That each franchisee submit weekly, monthly and annual
reports of their sales and profits, all which are open to audit by
Domino's to check for understatements in earnings;

(17) Specifications for operating procedures including but not limited to employee grooming, delivery techniques, advertising, signage,
handling of customer complaints, etc.

(18) That the franchisee will abide by the Domino's operating
manual;

(19) That all new ideas or improvements in products or services
conceived by franchisee must be divulged to Domino's without compensation;

(20) Managers must spend no less than 40 hours per week at the
store;

(21) The franchisee is responsible for obtaining motor vehicle and
comprehensive general liability insurance naming Domino's as an
additional insured;

(22) That Domino's has control over the use of trademarks, and
may prohibit a franchisee from using them provided the franchisee is
compensated for costs;

(23) The franchisee must pay Domino's a 5 ½ royalty fee of the
store's weekly net sales (the franchisee is, however, given the freedom
to determine the prices for the products and services it sells);

(24) Random inspections of the inventory, records and assets
which may be conducted any time during business hours.

The second item of documentary evidence demonstrating Domino's
control over its franchisees is its operations manual. As "Domino's Concept
and Objectives," the manual states:

Our phrase depicts the Domino's concept, "The Domino's People are
Pizza People, Period." Thus, the Domino's purpose is: make the finest
pizza possible and deliver it fast, hot, and free. . . . Specifically,
every pizza is hot, tasty, and good-looking. Ingredients are in the
proper proportion to insure a balance of flavor. They are also in the
proper amounts to insure a fair value. The product is consistant (sic)
throughout the chain. Service is fast and courteous. Specifically, a
Domino's pizza is delivered within 30 minutes after the order is taken.
Pick-up pizzas are ready in 10 minutes. At all times, the customer
receives courteous service . . . [and the] customer is assured that his
pizza is prepared only from wholesome ingredients, in sanitary facilities, by clean personnel.

The manual which Domino's provides to its franchisees is a veritable bible for overseeing a Domino's operation. It contains prescriptions for every conceivable facet of the business: from the elements of preparing the perfect pizza to maintaining accurate books; from advertising and promotional ideas to routing and delivery guidelines; from order-taking instructions to oven-tending rules; from organization to sanitation. The manual even offers a wide array of techniques for "boxing and cutting" the pizza, as well as tips on running the franchise to achieve an optimum profit. The manual literally leaves nothing to chance. The complexity behind every element of the operation gives new meaning to the familiar slogan that delivery is to be, "Fast, Hot and Free."

The foregoing leads us to the self-evident conclusion that it was error to determine as a matter of law that Domino's does not retain the right to control the means to be used by its franchisee to accomplish the required tasks. At the very least a genuine and material question of fact is raised by the documentation. We reverse and remand for such other and further proceedings as may be appropriate.

ANALYSIS AND PLANNING

1. According to the court in *Holiday Inns*, "Plaintiff and defendant agree that, in determining whether a contract establishes an agency relationship, the critical test is the nature and extent of the control agreed upon." Is it possible for a franchisor to have a degree of control consistent with the master-servant relationship without that master-servant relationship arising as a matter of law? What other requirement, if any, must be satisfied? See Restatement (Second) of Agency § 1, quoted by the court. To put the issue another way, in either the *Holiday Inns* case or the *Domino's Pizza* case, does it seem to you that the defendant might have prevailed even if it had lost on the control issue? In other words, did the defendant have another, unused, string to its bow?

2. How do firms like Holiday Inns, Inc. and Domino's Pizza make their profit? What are their risks? In their relationships with franchisors, what legal rights are likely to be important to them?

3. How do the franchisees make their profit? What are their risks? In their relationship with the franchisors, what legal rights are likely to be important to them?

4. How much freedom does a franchisee like Betsy–Len have to run its business? Suppose that a field representative of Holiday Inns, Inc. visits the Betsy–Len motor hotel and finds that the desk clerk, who is a son of one of the owners of the franchise, is surly and inefficient, and that the restaurant, managed by the other owner, is badly run, with poor food and slow service. What are the various steps that Holiday Inns, Inc. can take to induce its franchisee to improve its performance? What do your answers to these questions tell you about drafting a franchise contract? Would your answers to these questions be significantly different for the Domino's Pizza franchise?

SECTION 4. CONTROL AND THE LIABILITY OF CREDITORS

In the next case, A. Gay Jenson Farms, Co. v. Cargill, Inc., the legal focus, once more, is on control, but the context is that of a creditor exercising control over its debtors after the debtor has experienced financial difficulties. The plaintiffs were farmers who sold their grain crops to Warren Grain & Seed Co. (Warren). Warren was a local firm that operated a grain elevator (a storage facility). Cargill is a large, worldwide dealer in grain. On Cargill's view of the facts, Warren bought grain from the farmers and sold it to Cargill. On the farmers' view of the facts, Warren bought grain as an agent for Cargill. Warren became insolvent without having paid the farmers for their grain and they sued Cargill. The case offers a nice illustration of a legal issue of considerable importance to business firms like Cargill that provide trade credit to other firms, as well as to banks and other financial intermediaries.

A. Gay Jenson Farms Co. v. Cargill, Inc.
309 N.W.2d 285 (Minn.1981).

Plaintiffs, 86 individual, partnership or corporate farmers, brought this action against defendant Cargill, Inc. (Cargill) and defendant Warren Grain & Seed Co. (Warren) to recover losses sustained when Warren defaulted on the contracts made with plaintiffs for the sale of grain. After a trial by jury, judgment was entered in favor of plaintiffs, and Cargill brought this appeal. We affirm.

This case arose out of the financial collapse of defendant Warren Seed & Grain Co., and its failure to satisfy its indebtedness to plaintiffs. Warren, which was located in Warren, Minnesota, was operated by Lloyd Hill and his son, Gary Hill. Warren operated a grain elevator and as a result was involved in the purchase of . . . grain from local farmers. The cash grain would be resold through the Minneapolis Grain Exchange or to the terminal grain companies directly. Warren also stored grain for farmers and sold chemicals, fertilizer and steel storage bins. In addition, it operated a seed business which involved buying seed grain from farmers, processing it and reselling it for seed to farmers and local elevators.

Lloyd Hill decided in 1964 to apply for financing from Cargill. Cargill's officials from the Moorhead regional office investigated Warren's operations and recommended that Cargill finance Warren.

Warren and Cargill thereafter entered into a security agreement which provided that Cargill would loan money for working capital to Warren on "open account" financing up to a stated limit, which was originally set as $175,000.[2] Under this contract, Warren would receive funds and pay its

---

2. Loans were secured by a second mortgage on Warren's real estate and a first chattel mortgage on its inventories of grain and merchandise in the sum of $175,000 with 7% interest. . . .

expenses by issuing drafts drawn on Cargill through Minneapolis banks. The drafts were imprinted with both Warren's and Cargill's names. Proceeds from Warren's sales would be deposited with Cargill and credited to its account. In return for this financing, Warren appointed Cargill as its grain agent for transaction with the Commodity Credit Corporation. Cargill was also given a right of first refusal to purchase market grain sold by Warren to the terminal market.

A new contract was negotiated in 1967, extending Warren's credit line to $300,000 and incorporating the provisions of the original contract. It was also stated in the contract that Warren would provide Cargill with annual financial statements and that either Cargill would keep the books for Warren or an audit would be conducted by an independent firm. Cargill was given the right of access to Warren's books for inspection.

In addition, the agreement provided that Warren was not to make capital improvements or repairs in excess of $5,000 without Cargill's prior consent. Further, it was not to become liable as guarantor on another's indebtedness, or encumber its assets except with Cargill's permission. Consent by Cargill was required before Warren would be allowed to declare a dividend or sell and purchase stock.

Officials from Cargill's regional office made a brief visit to Warren shortly after the agreement was executed. They examined the annual statement and the accounts receivable, expenses, inventory, seed, machinery and other financial matters. Warren was informed that it would be reminded periodically to make the improvements recommended by Cargill.[3] At approximately this time, a memo was given to the Cargill official in charge of the Warren account, Erhart Becker, which stated in part: "This organization [Warren] needs *very strong* paternal guidance."

In 1970, Cargill contracted with Warren and other elevators to act as its agent to seek growers for a new type of wheat called Bounty 208. Warren, as Cargill's agent for this project, entered into contracts for the growing of the wheat seed, with Cargill named as the contracting party. Farmers were paid directly by Cargill for the seed and all contracts were performed in full. In 1971, pursuant to an agency contract, Warren contracted on Cargill's behalf with various farmers for the growing of sunflower seeds for Cargill. The arrangements were similar to those made in the Bounty 208 contracts, and all those contracts were also completed. Both these agreements were unrelated to the open account financing contract. In addition, Warren, as Cargill's agent in the sunflower seed business, cleaned and packaged the seed in Cargill bags.

---

3. Cargill headquarters suggested that the regional office check Warren monthly. Also, it was requested that Warren be given an explanation for the relatively large withdrawals from undistributed earnings made by the Hills, since Cargill hoped that Warren's profits would be used to decrease its debt balance. Cargill asked for written requests for withdrawals from undistributed earnings in the future.

During this period, Cargill continued to review Warren's operations and expenses and recommend that certain actions should be taken.[4] Warren purchased from Cargill various business forms printed by Cargill and received sample forms from Cargill which Warren used to develop its own business forms.

Cargill wrote to its regional office in 1970 expressing its concern that the pattern of increased use of funds allowed to develop at Warren was similar to that involved in two other cases in which Cargill experienced severe losses. Cargill did not refuse to honor drafts or call the loan, however. A new security agreement which increased the credit line to $750,000 was executed in 1972, and a subsequent agreement which raised the limit to $1,250,000 was entered into in 1976.

Warren was at that time shipping Cargill 90% of its . . . grain. When Cargill's facilities were full, Warren shipped its grain to other companies. Approximately 25% of Warren's total sales was seed grain which was sold directly by Warren to its customers.

As Warren's indebtedness continued to be in excess of its credit line, Cargill began to contact Warren daily regarding its financial affairs. Cargill headquarters informed its regional office in 1973 that, since Cargill money was being used, Warren should realize that Cargill had the right to make some critical decisions regarding the use of the funds. Cargill headquarters also told Warren that a regional manager would be working with Warren on a day-to-day basis as well as in monthly planning meetings. In 1975, Cargill's regional office began to keep a daily debit position on Warren. A bank account was opened in Warren's name on which Warren could draw checks in 1976. The account was to be funded by drafts drawn on Cargill by the local bank.

In early 1977, it became evident that Warren had serious financial problems. Several farmers, who had heard that Warren's checks were not being paid, inquired or had their agents inquire at Cargill regarding Warren's status and were initially told that there would be no problem with payment. In April 1977, an audit of Warren revealed that Warren was $4 million in debt. After Cargill was informed that Warren's financial statements had been deliberately falsified, Warren's request for additional financing was refused. In the final days of Warren's operation, Cargill sent an official to supervise the elevator, including disbursement of funds and income generated by the elevator.

After Warren ceased operations, it was found to be indebted to Cargill in the amount of $3.6 million. Warren was also determined to be indebted to plaintiffs in the amount of $2 million, and plaintiffs brought this action

---

4. Between 1967 and 1973, Cargill suggested that Warren take a number of steps, including: (1) a reduction of seed grain and cash grain inventories; (2) improved collection of accounts receivable; (3) reduction or elimination of its wholesale seed business and its speciality grain operation; (4) marketing fertilizer and steel bins on consignment; (5) a reduction in withdrawals made by officers; (6) a suggestion that Warren's bookkeeper not issue her own salary checks; and (7) cooperation with Cargill in implementing the recommendations. These ideas were apparently never implemented, however.

in 1977 to seek recovery of that sum. Plaintiffs alleged that Cargill was jointly liable for Warren's indebtedness as it had acted as principal for the grain elevator.

. . .

1. The major issue in this case is whether Cargill, by its course of dealing with Warren, became liable as a principal on contracts made by Warren with plaintiffs. Cargill contends that no agency relationship was established with Warren, notwithstanding its financing of Warren's operation and its purchase of the majority of Warren's grain. However, we conclude that Cargill, by its control and influence over Warren, became a principal with liability for the transactions entered into by its agent Warren.

Agency is the fiduciary relationship that results from the manifestation of consent by one person to another that the other shall act on his behalf and subject to his control, and consent by the other so to act. . . .

In order to create an agency there must be an agreement, but not necessarily a contract between the parties. . . . An agreement may result in the creation of an agency relationship although the parties did not call it an agency and did not intend the legal consequences of the relation to follow. The existence of the agency may be proved by circumstantial evidence which shows a course of dealing between the two parties. . . . When an agency relationship is to be proven by circumstantial evidence, the principal must be shown to have consented to the agency since one cannot be the agent of another except by consent of the latter. . . .

Cargill contends that the prerequisites of an agency relationship did not exist because Cargill never consented to the agency, Warren did not act on behalf of Cargill, and Cargill did not exercise control over Warren. We hold that all three elements of agency could be found in the particular circumstances of this case. By directing Warren to implement its recommendations, Cargill manifested its consent that Warren would be its agent. Warren acted on Cargill's behalf in procuring grain for Cargill as the part of its normal operations which were totally financed by Cargill.[7] Further, an agency relationship was established by Cargill's interference with the internal affairs of Warren, which constituted de facto control of the elevator.

A creditor who assumes control of his debtor's business may become liable as principal for the acts of the debtor in connection with the business. Restatement (Second) of Agency § 14 O (1958). It is noted in comment a to section 14 O that:

> A security holder who merely exercises a veto power over the business acts of his debtor by preventing purchases or sales above

---

7. Although the contracts with the farmers were executed by Warren, Warren paid for the grain with drafts drawn on Cargill. While this is not in itself significant . . . it is one factor to be taken into account in analyzing the relationship between Warren and Cargill.

specified amounts does not thereby become a principal. However, if he takes over the management of the debtor's business either in person or through an agent, and directs what contracts may or may not be made, he becomes a principal, liable as a principal for the obligations incurred thereafter in the normal course of business by the debtor who has now become his general agent. The point at which the creditor becomes a principal is that at which he assumes de facto control over the conduct of his debtor, whatever the terms of the formal contract with his debtor may be.

A number of factors indicate Cargill's control over Warren, including the following:

(1) Cargill's constant recommendations to Warren by telephone;

(2) Cargill's right of first refusal on grain;

(3) Warren's inability to enter into mortgages, to purchase stock or to pay dividends without Cargill's approval;

(4) Cargill's right of entry onto Warren's premises to carry on periodic checks and audits;

(5) Cargill's correspondence and criticism regarding Warren's finances, officers salaries and inventory;

(6) Cargill's determination that Warren needed "strong paternal guidance";

(7) Provision of drafts and forms to Warren upon which Cargill's name was imprinted;

(8) Financing of all Warren's purchases of grain and operating expenses; and

(9) Cargill's power to discontinue the financing of Warren's operations.

We recognize that some of these elements, as Cargill contends, are found in an ordinary debtor-creditor relationship. However, these factors cannot be considered in isolation, but, rather, they must be viewed in light of all the circumstances surrounding Cargill's aggressive financing of Warren.

It is also Cargill's position that the relationship between Cargill and Warren was that of buyer-supplier rather than principal-agent. Restatement (Second) of Agency § 14K (1958) compares an agent with a supplier as follows:

One who contracts to acquire property from a third person and convey it to another is the agent of the other only if it is agreed that he is to act primarily for the benefit of the other and not for himself.

Factors indicating that one is a supplier, rather than an agent, are:

(1) That he is to receive a fixed price for the property irrespective of price paid by him. This is the most important. (2) That he acts in his own name and receives the title to the property which he thereafter is to transfer. (3) That he has an independent business in buying and selling similar property.

Restatement (Second) of Agency § 14K, comment a (1958).

Under the Restatement approach, it must be shown that the supplier has an independent business before it can be concluded that he is not an agent. The record establishes that all portions of Warren's operation were financed by Cargill and that Warren sold almost all of its market grain to Cargill. Thus, the relationship which existed between the parties was not merely that of buyer and supplier.

. . .

The amici curiae assert that, if the jury verdict is upheld, firms and banks which have provided business loans to county elevators will decline to make further loans. The decision in this case should give no cause for such concern. We deal here with a business enterprise markedly different from an ordinary bank financing, since Cargill was an active participant in Warren's operations rather than simply a financier. Cargill's course of dealing with Warren was, by its own admission, a paternalistic relationship in which Cargill made the key economic decisions and kept Warren in existence.

Although considerable interest was paid by Warren on the loan, the reason for Cargill's financing of Warren was not to make money as a lender but, rather, to establish a source of market grain for its business. As one Cargill manager noted, "We were staying in there because we wanted the grain." For this reason, Cargill was willing to extend the credit line far beyond the amount originally allocated to Warren. It is noteworthy that Cargill was receiving significant amounts of grain and that, notwithstanding the risk that was recognized by Cargill, the operation was considered profitable.

On the whole, there was a unique fabric in the relationship between Cargill and Warren which varies from that found in normal debtor-creditor situations. We conclude that, on the facts of this case, there was sufficient evidence from which the jury could find that Cargill was the principal of Warren within the definitions of agency set forth in Restatement (Second) of Agency §§ 1 and 14 O.

NOTE

Warren, Minnesota was a town with a population of about 2,000 at the time this case was tried. Warren is located in Marshall County, which is in the northwest corner of Minnesota, on the North Dakota border, with a population of about 15,000. The plaintiffs were local farmers and the defendant was a corporate giant. The case was tried to a jury.

ANALYSIS

1. Why do you suppose Cargill kept extending more and more credit to Warren?

2. What could the farmers have done to protect themselves from the risk of nonpayment?

3. What could Cargill have done to ensure that the grain it bought from Warren was paid for?

4. In light of your answers to questions 2 and 3, does the result in the case place responsibility for avoiding loss on the person with the lower cost of doing so?

5. If Peter says to Amy, "Go out and buy a thousand bushels of corn for me and I'll pay you the usual commission," Amy is Peter's nonservant agent (that is, she acts on behalf of Peter but is not subject to his control over how the objective is achieved). Peter is bound to contracts made by Amy to buy the corn. Control of the manner in which Amy accomplishes the assignment is not an issue. In the *Cargill* case, however, there seems to have been no evidence to support that kind of ordinary nonservant principal/agent relationship. Presumably that is why the court focuses on control and on the Restatement (Second) of Agency § 14 O. Examine the nine factors listed by the court as supporting a conclusion that Cargill exercised control over Warren. How, if at all, does each of these factors tend to establish a principal/agent relationship rather than a relationship of creditor to debtor or buyer to supplier?

PLANNING

Suppose you are Cargill's lawyer. The chief executive officer (CEO) of the company, after hearing about the decision in the case involving Warren Grain & Seed Co., asks for your recommendations about how Cargill should change the way it does business to avoid liability in the future. She also wants your views on whether, with a supplier like Warren, at the time that its financial condition became desperate, it would have been advisable for Cargill to (a) call in its loans and force the supplier into bankruptcy or (b) notify all other potential creditors that Cargill would not be liable for any purchases by the supplier. What would you say? Bear in mind that you are expected to exercise sound business, as well as legal, judgment, but that your role is to offer alternatives, not to make decisions.

Section 5. Apparent Authority and Apparent Agency

Lind v. Schenley Industries, Inc.

278 F.2d 79 (3d Cir.1960) (en banc).

■ Biggs, Chief Judge.

This is a diversity case. Lind, the plaintiff-appellant, sued Park & Tilford Distiller's Corp.,[1] the defendant-appellee, for compensation that he asserts is due him by virtue of a contract expressed by a written memorandum supplemented by oral conversations as set out hereinafter. Lind also sued for certain expenses he incurred when moving from New Jersey to New York when his position as New Jersey State Manager of Park & Tilford terminated on January 31, 1957. The evidence, including Lind's own testimony, taking the inferences most favorable to Lind, shows the following. Lind had been employed for some years by Park & Tilford. In July 1950, Lind was informed by Herrfeldt, then Park & Tilford's vice-president and general sales-manager, that he would be appointed assistant to Kaufman, Park & Tilford's sales-manager for metropolitan New York. Herrfeldt told Lind to see Kaufman to ascertain what his new duties and his salary would be. Lind embarked on his new duties with Kaufman and was informed in October 1950, that some "raises" had come through and that Lind should get official word from his "boss," Kaufman. Subsequently, Lind received a communication, dated April 19, 1951, signed by Kaufman, informing Lind that he would assume the title of "District Manager." The letter went on to state: "I wish to inform you of the fact that you have as much responsibility as a State Manager and that you should consider yourself to be of the same status." The letter concluded with the statement: "An incentive plan is being worked out so that you will not only be responsible for increased sales in your district, but will benefit substantially in a monetary way." The other two district managers under Kaufman received similar memoranda. Lind assumed his duties as district sales manager for metropolitan New York. . . .

In July 1951, Kaufman informed Lind that he was to receive 1% commission on the gross sales of the men under him. . . . Lind was also informed by Herrfeldt in the autumn of 1952 that he would get a 1% commission on the sales of the men under him. Early in 1955, Lind negotiated with Brown, then president of Park & Tilford, for the sale of Park & Tilford's New Jersey Wholesale House, and Brown agreed to apply the money owed to Lind by reason of the 1% commission against the value

1. Park & Tilford Distiller's Corp. was merged into Schenley Industries, Inc., a Delaware corporation, before the commencement of this action, with Schenley assuming all of Park & Tilford's obligations. Schenley was substituted in this action on March 31, 1958, by order of Judge Wortendyke.

33

of the goodwill of the Wholesale House. The proposed sale of the New Jersey Wholesale House was not consummated.

Notice to produce various records of Lind's employment was served on Park & Tilford but one slip dealing with Lind's appointment as district manager was not produced and is presumed to have been lost. The evidence was conflicting as to the character of the "incentive compensation" to be offered Lind in connection with his services as a district manager. Herrfeldt designated the incentive an "added incentive plan with a percentage arrangement." Kaufman characterized the plan as "bonuses and contests." Weiner, Park & Tilford's Secretary, said that the incentive was a "pension plan." Kaufman testified, however, that the pension plan had nothing to do with the bonus incentive he referred to.

The record also shows that Lind commenced his employment with Park & Tilford in 1941, that from 1942 to 1950 he worked on a commission basis, that on August 31, 1950, he became an assistant sales manager for the New York metropolitan area at $125 a week, which was raised to $150 a week on October 1, 1950, plus certain allowances. After Lind became district manager on April 19, 1951, he continued to receive the same salary of $150 a week but this was increased to $175 in January 1952. On February 1, 1952, Lind was transferred from New York to New Jersey to become state manager of Park & Tilford's business in New Jersey. He retained that position until January 31, 1957, when he was transferred back to New York.

Park & Tilford moved for but was denied a directed verdict at the close of all the evidence. . . . However, the court . . . submitted the case to the jury subject to a later determination of the legal questions raised by Park & Tilford's motion to dismiss. The court then requested the jury to answer [certain] questions. . . .

The answers provided by the jury amounted to a determination that Kaufman did offer Lind a 1% commission on the gross sales of the men under him; that the agreement commenced April 19, 1951; that the agreement terminated February 15, 1952, the date of Lind's transfer to New Jersey; that Park & Tilford did cause Lind to believe that Kaufman had authority to offer him the one percent commission; and that Lind was justified in assuming that Kaufman had the authority to make the offer. [The jury found in favor of Lind in the amount of $37,000, but the trial court entered a judgment notwithstanding the verdict and, in the event of a reversal, an order for a new trial.]

The Judgment for Defendant

The decision to reverse the verdict for Lind with respect to the 1% commission was based on two alternative grounds. First, the court found that Lind had failed to prove a case of apparent authority in that the evidence did not disclose that Park & Tilford acted in such a manner as to induce Lind to believe that Kaufman had been authorized to offer him the 1% commission. Also the court concluded that the issues of "actual" and "implied" authority had somehow been eliminated from the case. Second, the court reasoned, that even if the jury could find apparent authority, the alleged contract was not sufficiently definite nor specific to be enforceable against Park & Tilford. The trial judge rejected a contention by Park & Tilford that a document signed by Lind on January 31, 1957, upon receiving his last pay check as New Jersey State Manager, should be construed as a release of his claims for commissions.

. . .

The problems of "authority" are probably the most difficult in that segment of law loosely termed, "Agency." Two main classifications of authority are generally recognized, "actual authority," and "apparent authority." The term "implied authority" is often seen but most authorities consider "implied authority" to be merely a sub-group of "actual" authority. . . . An additional kind of authority has been designated by the Restatement, Agency 2d, §§ 8A and 161(b) as "inherent agency." Actually this new term is employed to designate a meaning frequently ascribed to "implied authority."

"Actual authority" means, as the words connote, authority that the principal, expressly or implicitly, gave the agent. "Apparent authority" arises when a principal acts in such a manner as to convey the impression to a third party that an agent has certain powers which he may or may not actually possess. "Implied authority" has been variously defined. It has been held to be actual authority given implicitly by a principal to his agent. Another definition of "implied authority" is that it is a kind of authority arising solely from the designation by the principal of a kind of agent who ordinarily possesses certain powers. It is this concept that is called "inherent authority" by the Restatement. In many cases the same facts will support a finding of "inherent" or "apparent agency." Usually it is not necessary for a third party attempting to hold a principal to specify which type of authority he relies upon, general proof of agency being sufficient. . . .

In the case at bar Lind attempted to prove all three kinds of agency; actual, apparent, and inherent, although most of his evidence was directed to proof of "inherent" or "apparent" authority. From the evidence it is clear that Park & Tilford can be held accountable for Kaufman's action on the principle of "inherent authority." Kaufman was Lind's direct superior, and was the man to transfer communications from the upper executives to the lower. Moreover, there was testimony tending to prove that Herrfeldt, the vice-president in charge of sales, had told Lind to see Kaufman for information about his salary and that Herrfeldt himself had confirmed the 1% commission arrangement. Thus Kaufman, so far as Lind was concerned, was the spokesman for the company.

It is not necessary to determine the status of the New York law in respect to "inherent agency" for substantially the same testimony that would establish "inherent" agency under the circumstances at bar proves conventional "apparent" agency. The Restatement, Agency 2d § 8, defines "apparent agency" as "the power to affect the legal relations of another person by transactions with third persons, professedly as agent for the other, arising from and in accordance with the other's manifestations to such third persons." There is some uncertainty as to whether or not the third person must change his position in reliance upon these manifestations of authority, but this is of no consequence in the case at bar since Lind clearly changed his position when he accepted the job of district manager with its admittedly increased responsibilities.

The opinion of the court below and the argument of the appellee here rely heavily on Gumpert v. Bon Ami Co., 2 Cir., 1958, 251 F.2d 735, a diversity case decided under New York law, upholding the lower court's reversal of a jury verdict for the plaintiff. The facts in that case showed that Gumpert had been hired by Rosenberg, a director and member of the executive board of the Bon Ami company for a salary of $25,000 in cash plus $25,000 worth of the company's common stock. The Court of Appeals found that the jury could not properly find that the Bon Ami company had clothed Rosenberg with apparent authority to offer Gumpert $25,000 in common stock. This decision is inapposite for here we deal with an offer made by an employee's immediate superior, the man who represented the company to those under him, not a contract offered by one not an officer of a corporation to prospective employee. Furthermore a salary of $25,000 in cash and $25,000 in common stock might well be deemed unusual enough to put the prospective employee on notice as to a possible lack of authority in the director to make the offer but the same may not be said of an offer of a commission to a salesman who had been habitually working on that basis, in a corporation that confined itself to selling others' products. It should be borne in mind also that a director, even if he be a member of the executive board, does not ordinarily hire employees. Moreover in the case at bar there was evidence by an employee of Schenley that at least some state managers received 1% commissions.

Testimony was adduced by Schenley tending to prove that Kaufman had no authority to set salaries, that power being exercisable solely by the president of the corporation, and that the president had not authorized Kaufman to offer Lind a commission of the kind under consideration here. However, this testimony, even if fully accepted, would only prove lack of actual or implied authority in Kaufman but is irrelevant to the issue of apparent authority.

The opinion below seems to agree with the conception of the New York agency law as set out above but the court reversed the jury's verdict and the judgment based on it on the conclusion, as a matter of law, that Lind could not reasonably have believed that Kaufman was authorized to offer him a commission that would, in the trial judge's words "have almost quadrupled Lind's then salary." But Lind testified that before he had become Kaufman's assistant in September 1950, the latter position named being that which he had held before being "promoted" to district manager in April 1951, he had earned $9,000 for the period from January 1, 1950 to August 31, 1950, that figure allegedly representing half of his expected earnings for the year. Lind testified that a liquor salesman can expect to make 50% of his salary in the last four months of the year owing to holiday sales.   Thus Lind's salary two years before his appointment as district manager could have been estimated by the jury at $18,000 per year, and his alleged earnings, as district manager, a position of greater responsibility, do not appear disproportionate.   On the basis of the foregoing it appears that there was sufficient evidence to authorize a jury finding that Park & Tilford had given Kaufman apparent authority to offer Lind 1% commission of gross sales of the salesmen under him and that Lind reasonably had relied upon Kaufman's offer.

. . .

The judgment of the court below will be reversed and the case will be remanded with the direction to the court below to reinstate the verdict and judgment in favor of Lind.

■ HASTIE, CIRCUIT JUDGE, with whom KALODNER, CIRCUIT JUDGE, joins (dissenting).

I agree that the order granting judgment for the defendant notwithstanding the verdict for the plaintiff must be set aside.   However, I think the majority make a serious mistake when they take the extraordinary additional step of reversing the alternative order of the trial judge, granting a new trial because he considered the verdict against the weight of the evidence.

. . .

The present record discloses a sharp conflict of testimony whether Kaufman, the metropolitan sales manager, ever promised plaintiff, his subordinate district manager, a 1% commission on all gross sales of agents working under plaintiff.   There are several remarkable aspects of this alleged promise which could reasonably have influenced the trial judge on this decisive issue.   This commission would have more than quadrupled plaintiff's salary of $150 per week, making him much higher paid than his immediate superior, Kaufman, or any other company executive, except the president.   No other sales manager or supervisor received any such commission at all.   Moreover, after the alleged promise was made, month after month elapsed with no payment of the 1% commission or indication of any step to fulfill such an obligation.   Yet plaintiff himself admits that he made no formal demand for or inquiry about the large obligation for several years, and said nothing even informally about it to anyone for many months save for an occasional passing verbal inquiry said to have been addressed to Kaufman.   . . .

NOTE

This case introduces two theories of liability of principals for the acts of their agents: inherent agency (also referred to as inherent agency power) and apparent authority.   These are both theories under which the principal may be held liable for the acts of an agent where (as in the present case) there is no (actual) authority. Inherent agency is a puzzling doctrine that is used to impose liability on the principal when there is neither authority nor apparent authority. As the court says, it arises "solely from the designation by the principal of a kind of agent who ordinarily possesses certain powers." The primary focus here will be on apparent authority. Subsequent cases will focus on the doctrine of inherent agency power.

ANALYSIS

The court quotes the Restatement (Second) of Agency § 8, which makes the issue of apparent authority turn on the principal's "manifestations." (a) What were the manifestations by Park & Tilford that led Lind to believe that Kaufman had authority to enter into the contract for his (Lind's) services? (b) If the contract had been for ten years, would Park & Tilford still have been liable? What if it had been for Lind's lifetime?

PLANNING

1.   What should firms like Park & Tilford (Schenley) do to avoid the problem that gave rise to this decision?

2.   What could Lind have done to avoid the problem?

Three–Seventy Leasing Corporation v. Ampex Corporation

528 F.2d 993 (5th Cir.1976).

Three–Seventy Leasing Corporation (370) seeks damages from Ampex Corporation (Ampex) for breach of a contract to sell six computer core memories. The district court, sitting without a jury, found that there was an enforceable contract between 370 and Ampex.   . . .

The Contract

Three–Seventy Leasing Corporation was formed by Joyce, at all times its only active employee, for the purpose of purchasing computer hardware from various manufacturers for lease to end-users. In August of 1972, Kays, a salesman of Ampex and friend of Joyce, initiated discussions with Joyce regarding the possibility of 370 purchasing computer equipment from Ampex. A meeting was arranged between Kays, Joyce, and Mueller, Kays' superior at Ampex. Joyce was informed at this meeting that Ampex could sell to 370 only if 370 could pass Ampex's credit requirements. Joyce informed the two that he did not think this would be a problem.

At approximately the same time, Joyce began negotiations with Electronic Data Systems (EDS), which resulted in EDS's verbal commitment to lease six units of Ampex computer core memory from 370. Desiring to close the two transactions simultaneously, Joyce continued negotiations with Kays. These negotiations resulted in a written document submitted by Kays to Joyce at the direction of Mueller. The document provided for the purchase by Joyce of six core memory units at a price of $100,000 each, with a down payment of $150,000 and the remainder to be paid over a five year period. The document specified that delivery was to be made to EDS. The document also contained a signature block for a representative of 370 and a signature block for a representative of Ampex.

Joyce received this document about November 3, 1972, and executed it on November 6, 1972. The document was never executed by a representative of Ampex. This document forms the core of the present controversy. 370 argues that the document was an offer to sell by Ampex, which was accepted upon Joyce's signature. Ampex contends that the document was nothing more than a solicitation which became an offer to purchase upon execution by Joyce, and that this offer was never accepted by Ampex. 370 counters by arguing in the alternative that even if the document when signed by Joyce was only an offer to purchase, the offer was later accepted by representatives of Ampex.

The district court, in concluding that there existed an enforceable contract, made no determination as to whether the document described above was an offer to sell accepted by Joyce's signature, or an offer to purchase when signed by Joyce which was later accepted by Ampex.

We reject the first alternative as being without evidentiary support. Elemental principles demand that there be a meeting of the minds and a communication that each party has consented to the terms of the agreement in order for a contract to exist. . . . There is no evidence, either written or oral, other than the document itself, which shows that Ampex had the requisite intent necessary to the formation of a contract prior to November 6, 1972, the date the document was executed by Joyce. And the document on its face does not supply that intent. Rather, the fact that the document had a signature block for a representative of Ampex which was unsigned at the time it was submitted to Joyce, in the absence of other evidence, negates any interpretation that Ampex intended this to be an offer to Joyce, without any further acts necessary on the part of Ampex.

Thus, the document, when signed by Joyce, at most constituted an offer by him to purchase. In order for there to be a valid contract, we must therefore find some act of acceptance on the part of Ampex.

On November 9, 1972, Mueller issued an intra-office memorandum which stated in part that "[o]n November 3, 1972, Ampex was awarded an Agreement by Three–Seventy Leasing, Dallas, Texas, for the purchase of six (6) ARM–3360 Memory Units", to be installed at EDS. This memorandum further informed those concerned at Ampex of Joyce's request that all contact with 370 be handled through Kays. On November 17, 1972, Kays sent a letter to Joyce which confirmed the delivery dates for the memory units.[2] We conclude, in light of the circumstances surrounding these

---

2. That letter stated:

Dear John:

With regard to delivery of equipment purchased by Three–Seventy Leasing:

negotiations, that the district court was not clearly erroneous when it found that Kays had apparent authority to accept Joyce's offer on behalf of Ampex, and we further conclude that the November 17 letter, in these circumstances, can reasonably be interpreted to be an acceptance.

An agent has apparent authority sufficient to bind the principal when the principal acts in such a manner as would lead a reasonably prudent person to suppose that the agent had the authority he purports to exercise. . . . Further, absent knowledge on the part of third parties to the contrary, an agent has the apparent authority to do those things which are usual and proper to the conduct of the business which he is employed to conduct. . . .

In this case, Kays was employed by Ampex in the capacity of a salesman. It is certainly reasonable for third parties to presume that one employed as salesman has the authority to bind his employer to sell. And Ampex did nothing to dispel this reasonable inference. Rather, its actions and inactions provided a further basis for this belief. First, Kays, at the direction of Mueller, submitted the controversial document to Joyce for signature. The document contained a space for signature by an Ampex representative. Nothing in the document suggests that Kays did not have authority to sign it on behalf of Ampex.[3] Second, Joyce indicated to Kays and Mueller that he wished all communications to be channeled through Kays. Mueller agreed, and acknowledged this in the November 9 intracompany memorandum. Neither Mueller, nor anyone else at Ampex ever informed Joyce that communication regarding acceptance would come through anyone other than Kays. In light of this request and Ampex's agreement, Joyce could reasonably expect that Kays would speak for the company.

Various individuals in the Ampex hierarchy testified at trial that only the contract manager or other supervisor in the company's contract department had authority to sign a contract on behalf of Ampex. However, there is no evidence that this limitation was ever communicated to Joyce in any manner. Absent knowledge of such a limitation by third parties, that limitation will not bar a claim of apparent authority.

Thus, when Joyce received Kays' November 17 letter, he had every reason to believe, based upon Ampex's prior actions, that Kays spoke on behalf of the company. We thus agree with the district court's finding that Kays had apparent authority to act for Ampex.

Ampex will ship three (3) million bytes of ARM–3360 magnetic core in sufficient time to install 1½ million bytes the weekend of December 16, 1972. The remaining balance of 1½ million bytes will be installed by the weekend of December 30, 1972.

The equipment will be installed in Camphill, Pennsylvania at a predetermined site by Electronic Data Systems.

Regards,

Thomas C. Kays

Sales Representative

3. It would have been an easy matter to provide in the document that only certain officers of Ampex had authority to sign on its behalf. Any inference to the contrary resulting from Ampex's failure to specify such a limitation must weigh against Ampex.

Having determined that Kays had apparent authority to bind Ampex, we further conclude that his letter of November 17, in light of the pattern of negotiations, could reasonably be interpreted as a promise to ship the six memory units on the dates specified in the letter and on the terms previously set out in the document executed by Joyce and submitted to Ampex. The district court's finding that a contract was formed is therefore not clearly erroneous.

ANALYSIS

1. What was Joyce's function? Was he a sales representative of Ampex? A purchasing agent of EDS? Neither?

2. What was Kays's position and function?

3. Kays did not have authority to enter into the contract. Do you find this surprising as to (a) the agreement to sell the core memory units or (b) the agreement to extend credit, or both?

4. What were the defendant's manifestations that supported a finding of apparent authority?

PLANNING AND ECONOMIC EFFICIENCY

1. What should Ampex have done to protect itself against the problem that arose in this case?

2. What could Joyce have done to protect himself?

3. In light of your answer to questions 1 and 2, does the result in the case place responsibility for avoiding loss on the person with the lower cost of doing so?

Billops v. Magness Construction Co.

391 A.2d 196 (Del.Sup.1978).

Plaintiffs brought suit in Superior Court against Magness Construction Co., t/a Brandywine Hilton Inn, Inc. (the franchisee), Hilton Inns, Inc., Hilton Hotels Corporation, Hilton International Co. (collectively denominated as franchisors), and Gray Magness, charging false imprisonment, invasion of privacy, intentional and negligent infliction of emotional distress, battery, assault and defamation. The incident which led to the suit occurred at the defendant Brandywine Hilton Inn when the banquet director of the Inn wrongfully attempted to extort funds in addition to those previously paid by plaintiffs for the use of one of the Inn's ballrooms. The suit was dismissed as to defendant Gray Magness, and that ruling is not challenged. The motion of the corporate franchisors for summary judgment was granted after the Superior Court determined that no actual or apparent agency relationship existed between the franchisors and the franchisee, and that, therefore, no legal basis existed for holding the franchisors vicariously liable for the torts of the franchisee or its employees. We reverse.

I

Viewing the facts in the light most favorable to plaintiffs, the party opposing the motion for summary judgment, . . . we find the following:

Ronald Billops, on behalf of certain of the plaintiffs, entered into a written contract for the rental of one-half of the Regency Ballroom of the Brandywine Hilton Inn for a social event consisting of an art exhibit, fashion show and dance. Billops paid the entire rental fee in advance, and received a receipt as evidence of the payment. On the day of the event the Brandywine Hilton banquet director wrongfully requested an additional rental payment which was refused. Thereafter, the director and other Hilton personnel harassed plaintiffs and their guests by loudly demanding the additional money, refusing to adequately heat the ballroom, impounding the art exhibit, failing to provide an adequate dance floor, summoning the State Police, and threatening to have plaintiffs arrested. The complaint alleged that the wrongful acts caused serious injury to the reputation of the plaintiffs, and their association, and also caused physical injury to several plaintiffs resulting from stress created by the incident.

The banquet director responsible for the allegedly wrongful conduct resigned his position with the Brandywine Hilton Inn six weeks after the event. Further facts concerning plaintiffs' reliance on the name Hilton, and concerning the legal and actual relationship between the various corporate defendants are developed in the body of this opinion as necessary for the application of the appropriate legal principles.

II

Plaintiffs allege the theories of actual and apparent agency for their contention that the franchisors may be held liable for the torts of the franchisee. We address each *seriatim*.

A.

Actual authority is that authority which a principal expressly or implicitly grants to an agent. Lind v. Schenley Industries, Inc., 3 Cir., 278 F.2d 79 (1960). A franchisor may be held to have an actual agency relationship with its franchisee when the former controls, or has the right to control, the latter's business. Hoover v. Sun Oil Company, Del.Super., 212 A.2d 214 (1965). . . . The vicarious tort liability of a master, or franchisor, flows from an actual agency relationship. . . .

Franchise agreements, in general, attest to the skill of corporate counsel in reserving as many rights in the franchisor as is possible to maintain control and to protect the product and service covered by the trademark or tradename. If, in practical effect, the franchise agreement goes beyond the stage of setting standards, and allocates to the franchisor the right to exercise control over the daily operations of the franchise, an agency relationship exists. . . .

It is our opinion that there are sufficient facts of record which, along with the reasonable inferences therefrom, show day-to-day control of the business of the Brandywine Hilton Inn by the franchisors so that the latter's motion for summary judgment should have been denied leaving the issue of actual agency to be resolved at trial.

Franchisors have issued to the franchisee a detailed and in parts mandatory, operating manual which is incorporated into the franchise agreement. The manual regulates such matters as identification, advertising, front office procedures, cleaning and inspection service for guest rooms and public areas, minimum guest room standards, food purchasing and preparation standards, requirements for minimum supplies of "brand name" goods, staff procedures and standards for soliciting and booking group meetings, functions and room reservations, accounting, insurance, engineering and maintenance, and numerous other details of operation. The franchisee is required to keep detailed records in order for the franchisor to insure compliance with the manual guidelines. In addition, by an express provision of the franchise agreement, the franchisor retains the right to enter the premises of the hotel "to inspect the hotel so as to maintain the high standards and reputation of the system, the good will of the public, and compliance with the provisions of this Agreement [the franchise contract] and the Operating Manual . . .". The apparent strength of the enforceability of the requirements set by the franchising agreement and the Operating Manual lies in the right of unilateral termination for violation given the franchisor in the following section of the franchise agreement:

> If Licensee violates any provision of this Agreement or of the Operating Manual and such violation continues for a period of twenty (20) days after written notice from Licensor, . . ., then the Licensor without further demand or notice, may declare this License Agreement and all of Licensee's rights hereunder terminated, ...

While we make no judgment as to whether, in this case, an actual agency relationship exists, we cannot say that it does not. The facts of record reveal a triable issue on the question of actual agency, and defendants were not entitled to summary judgment.   . . .

B.

The concept of apparent agency or authority focuses not upon the actual relation of a principal and agent, but the apparent relationship. Manifestations by the alleged principal which create a reasonable belief in a third party that the alleged agent is authorized to bind the principal create an apparent agency from which spring the same legal consequences as those which result from an actual agency.   . . . The manifestations may be made directly to the third party, or may be made to the community in general, for example, by way of advertising.   . . . In order to establish a chain of liability to the principal based upon apparent agency, a litigant must show reliance on the indicia of authority originated by the principal, . . . and such reliance must have been reasonable.   . . .

The record presents ample evidence of indices of authority suggesting that franchisees are the agent of the franchisor. The Hilton logo and sign are required to be displayed to the exclusion of all others. The franchise agreement forbids the mention of any name other than Hilton to the customers of the hotel as management of the Brandywine Hilton Inn. The franchisee is required by the franchising agreement to identify itself completely with the Hilton "system," including the color schemes and design of the Inn which must be consistent with the "system." In fact, defendants admitted in their answer to plaintiff's interrogatories that there is no reasonable basis which can be derived from the method of operation or the physical environment of the Brandywine Hilton Inn from which an ordinary person would have reason to know that he or she was dealing with anyone other than the Hilton Corporation.

Plaintiffs have presented evidence of their reliance on Hilton as a "quality enterprise." Depositions of several of the plaintiffs produced the following testimony:

By Mr. Billops: ". . . we did go to the Hilton Hotel for the evening and the people paid $10.00 for the event and not this shabby treatment. . . ."

By Mr. Naylor: "We received letters from the Hilton, signed by Parker [the banquet director] that they were happy that we had picked their hotel to have our affair in. And we said now we have got a first class hotel with a first class affair. That is why we charged $10.00 in advance." ". . . that night the treatment of Parker and the attitude of the personnel at that point, it so alarmed me that it broke my heart because I put a lot of faith and trust into the Hilton, because it was a major hotel. . . ."

These are statements of express reliance on the Hilton name, and the quality it represents.

. . .

Material issues of fact appearing, we are of the opinion that the Superior Court incorrectly granted summary judgment in favor of the franchisor defendants, and that ruling is, therefore,

REVERSED and the case is REMANDED for proceedings consistent with this opinion.

ANALYSIS

1. What's going on here? Why is the franchisor fighting this case? Isn't it in the franchisor's interest to ensure that plaintiffs like Billops will not have to worry about finding a solvent defendant?

2. What are the plaintiff's theories of liability here? In its theory of "actual" agency, what is the nature and function of the agency relationship? (Compare the cases in Section 2 of this Chapter.) Who is supposed to

be representing whom and for what purpose? In the theory of apparent agency, what must the plaintiff prove on remand?

PROBLEM

Suppose that the owners of twenty-five motels in a certain state decide that in order to compete they need a trade name and some statewide advertising. They realize that in order to benefit from the trade name they must ensure that each motel maintains high standards and that all the motels set room rates at a figure that is consistent with their intended image. They agree that they will remodel their lobbies to create a common attractive appearance and will require their employees to wear an agreed-upon uniform. They form a corporation called Finest Motels Corp., in which they share ownership. They are required to make periodic payments to Finest Motels Corp. to pay for advertising and for policing compliance with standards. They hire a former executive of Hilton Inns, Inc. and tell her that they want their motels to live up to Hilton standards. Each of the motels is to change its name, with the new name beginning with the location, followed by "Finest Motel"—for example, "Anaheim Finest Motel." If any of the motels become insolvent, is Finest Motel Corp., or any of the other motels, liable for its debts? What suggestions would you offer to protect against that outcome?

SECTION 6. INHERENT AGENCY POWER

Watteau v. Fenwick

[1893] 1 Queen's Bench 346 (1892).

From the evidence it appeared that one Humble had carried on business at a beerhouse called the Victoria Hotel, at Stockton-on-Tees, which business he had transferred to the defendants, a firm of brewers, some years before the present action. After the transfer of the business, Humble remained as defendants' manager; but the licence was always taken out in Humble's name, and his name was painted over the door. Under the terms of the agreement made between Humble and the defendants, the former had no authority to buy any goods for the business except bottled ales and mineral waters; all other goods required were to be supplied by the defendants themselves. The action was brought to recover the price of goods delivered at the Victoria Hotel over some years, for which it was admitted that the plaintiff gave credit to Humble only: they consisted of cigars, bovril, and other articles. The learned judge allowed the claim for the cigars and bovril only, and gave judgment for the plaintiff for 22*l*. 12*s*. 6*d*. The defendants appealed.

1892. Nov. 19. *Finlay, Q.C.* (*Scott Fox,* with him), for the defendants. The decision of the county court judge was wrong. The liability of a principal for the acts of his agent, done contrary to his secret instructions, depends upon his holding him out as his agent—that is, upon the agent being clothed with an apparent authority to act for his principal. Where, therefore, a man carries on business in his own name through a manager, he holds out his own credit, and would be liable for goods supplied even where the manager exceeded his authority. But where, as in the present case, there is no holding out by the principal, but the business is carried on in the agent's name and the goods are supplied on his credit, a person wishing to go behind the agent and make the principal liable must show an agency in fact.

[Lord Coleridge, C.J. Cannot you, in such a case, sue the undisclosed principal on discovering him?]

Only where the act done by the agent is within the scope of his agency; not where there has been an excess of authority. Where any one has been held out by the principal as his agent, there is a contract with the principal by estoppel, however much the agent may have exceeded his authority; where there has been no holding out, proof must be given of an agency in fact in order to make the principal liable.

Boydell Houghton, for the plaintiff. The defendants are liable in the present action. They are in fact undisclosed principals, who instead of carrying on the business in their own names employed a manager to carry it on for them, and clothed him with authority to do what was necessary to u02 carry on the business. The case depends upon the same principles as *Edmunds v. Bushell,* where the manager of a business which was carried on in his own name with the addition "and Co." accepted a bill of exchange, notwithstanding a stipulation in the agreement with his principal that he should not accept bills; and the Court held that the principal was liable to an indorsee who took the bill without any knowledge of the relations between the principal and agent. In that case there was no holding out of the manager as an agent; it was the simple case of an agent being allowed to act as the ostensible principal without any disclosure to the world of there being any one behind him. Here the defendants have so conducted themselves as to enable their agent to hold himself out to the world as the proprietor of their business, and they are clearly undisclosed principals: *Ramazotti v. Bowring.* All that the plaintiff has to do, therefore, in order to charge the principals, is to show that the goods supplied were such as were ordinarily used in the business—that is to say, that they were within the reasonable scope of the agent's authority.   . . .

Dec. 12. Lord Coleridge, C.J. The judgment which I am about to read has been written by my brother Wills, and I entirely concur in it.

■ WILLS, J. The plaintiff sues the defendants for the price of cigars supplied to the Victoria Hotel, Stockton-upon-Tees. The house was kept, not by the defendants, but by a person named Humble, whose name was over the door. The plaintiff gave credit to Humble, and to him alone, and had never heard of the defendants. The business, however, was really the defendants', and they had put Humble into it to manage it for them, and had forbidden him to buy cigars on credit. The cigars, however, were such as would usually be supplied to and dealt in at such an establishment. The learned county court judge held that the defendants were liable. I am of opinion that he was right.

There seems to be less of direct authority on the subject than one would expect. But I think that the Lord Chief Justice during the argument laid down the correct principle, viz., once it is established that the defendant was the real principal, the ordinary doctrine as to principal and agent applies—that the principal is liable for all the acts of the agent which are within the authority usually confided to an agent of that character, notwithstanding limitations, as between the principal and the agent, put upon that authority. It is said that it is only so where there has been a holding out of authority—which cannot be said of a case where the person supplying the goods knew nothing of the existence of a principal. But I do not think so. Otherwise, in every case of undisclosed principal, or at least in every case where the fact of there being a principal was undisclosed, the secret limitation of authority would prevail and defeat the action of the person dealing with the agent and then discovering that he was an agent and had a principal.

But in the case of a dormant partner it is clear law that no limitation of authority as between the dormant and active partner will avail the dormant partner as to things within the ordinary authority of a partner.

The law of partnership is, on such a question, nothing but a branch of the general law of principal and agent, and it appears to me to be undisputed and conclusive on the point now under discussion.

The principle laid down by the Lord Chief Justice, and acted upon by the learned county court judge, appears to be identical with that enunciated in the judgments of Cockburn, C.J., and Mellor, J., in Edmunds v. Bushell, the circumstances of which case, though not identical with those of the present, come very near to them. There was no holding out, as the plaintiff knew nothing of the defendant. I appreciate the distinction drawn by Mr. Finlay in his argument, but the principle laid down in the judgments referred to, if correct, abundantly covers the present case. I cannot find that any doubt has ever been expressed that it is correct, and I think it is right, and that very mischievous consequences would often result if that principle were not upheld.

In my opinion this appeal ought to be dismissed with costs.

Appeal dismissed.

NOTE

The Restatement (Second) of Agency § 194 states that an undisclosed principal is liable for acts of an agent "done on his account, if usual or necessary in such transactions, although forbidden by the principal."

Under the Restatement (Second) of Agency § 195, "An undisclosed principal who entrusts an agent with the management of his business is subject to liability to third persons with whom the agent enters into transactions usual in such business and on the principal's account, although contrary to the directions of the principal."

As the court points out, the law of partnership is a branch of the law of agency. Partners are considered to be agents of the partnership, with power to incur obligations on behalf of the partnership. All partners are liable, as principals, for partnership obligations. Since the agency rules relating to undisclosed principals, and to the power of agents to bind their principals, apply to partnerships, a person who becomes a partner cannot escape liability for partnership debts by concealing his or her membership in the partnership and any partner can incur debts for which the other partners will be liable, even if forbidden by the partnership agreement to do so.

ANALYSIS

1. Is there any basis in this case for holding the defendants liable on a theory of apparent authority?

2. Humble had authority to buy "ales and mineral waters" from third parties but not "cigars, bovril, and other articles." (Bovril is a nonalcoholic drink.) The court claims that "mischievous consequences" would result

from a decision for the defendants. What are those mischievous consequences? In responding to this question, ask yourself if there is any basis
for distinguishing between ales and mineral waters, on the one hand, and
cigars and bovril, on the other hand. Bear in mind that the plaintiffs seek
recovery from the personal assets of the defendants, not just the assets (if
any) invested by the defendants in the Victoria Hotel.

Kidd v. Thomas A. Edison, Inc.

239 Fed. 405 (S.D.N.Y.1917).

At Law. Action by Mary Carson Kidd against Thomas A. Edison,
Incorporated. On defendant's motion to set aside, on exceptions, a verdict
for plaintiff. Motion denied.

This is a motion by the defendant to set aside a verdict for the plaintiff
on exceptions. The action was in contract, and depended upon the authority of one Fuller to make a contract with the plaintiff, engaging her without
condition to sing for the defendant in a series of "tone test" recitals,
designed to show the accuracy with which her voice was reproduced by the
defendant's records. The defendant contended that Fuller's only authority
was to engage the plaintiff for such recitals as he could later persuade
dealers in the records to book her for all over the United States. The
dealers, the defendant said, were to agree to pay her for the recitals, and
the defendant would then guarantee her the dealers' performance. The
plaintiff said the contract was an unconditional engagement for a singing
tour, and the jury so found.

The sole exception of consequence was whether there was either any
question of fact involved in Fuller's authority, or a fortiori whether there
was no evidence of any authority. In either event the charge was erroneous, and the defendant's exception was good. The pertinent testimony was
that of Maxwell, and was as follows: He intrusted to Fuller particularly the
matters connected with the arranging of these "tone test" recitals. He
told him to learn from the artists what fees they would expect, and to tell
them that the defendant would pay the railroad fares and expenses. He
also told Fuller to explain to them that the defendant would book them,
and act as booking agent for them, and would see that the money was paid
by the dealers; in fact, the defendant would itself pay it. He told him to
prepare a form of contract suitable for such an arrangement with such
artists as he succeeded in getting to go into it, and that he (Maxwell) would
prepare a form of booking contract with the dealers. He told him to
prepare a written contract with the artists and submit it to him (Maxwell),
which he did. He told him that he was himself to make the contracts with
the artists by which they were to be booked, that he was not to bring them
to him (Maxwell), but that he should learn what fees they would demand,
and then confirm the oral agreement by a letter, which would serve as a
contract.

This is all the relevant testimony.

■ LEARNED HAND, DISTRICT JUDGE (after stating the facts as above).

The point involved is the scope of Fuller's "apparent authority," as distinct from the actual authority limited by the instructions which Maxwell gave him. The phrase "apparent authority," though it occurs repeatedly in the Reports, has been often criticized (Mechem, Law of Agency, §§ 720–726), and its use is by no means free from ambiguity. The scope of any authority must, of course, in the first place, be measured, not alone by the words in which it is created, but by the whole setting in which those words are used, including the customary powers of such agents. . . . This is, however, no more than to regard the whole of the communication between the principal and agent before assigning its meaning, and does not differ in method from any other interpretation of verbal acts. In considering what was Fuller's actual implied authority by custom, while it is fair to remember that the "tone test" recitals were new, in the sense that no one had ever before employed singers for just this purpose of comparing their voices with their mechanical reproduction, they were not new merely as musical recitals; for it was, of course, a common thing to engage singers for such recitals. When, therefore, an agent is selected, as was Fuller, to engage singers for musical recitals, the customary implication would seem to have been that his authority was without limitation of the kind here imposed, which was unheard of in the circumstances. The mere fact that the purpose of the recitals was advertisement, instead of entrance fees, gave no intimation to a singer dealing with him that the defendant's promise would be conditional upon so unusual a condition as that actually imposed. Being concerned to sell its records, the venture might rightly be regarded as undertaken on its own account, and, like similar enterprises, at its own cost. The natural surmise would certainly be that such an undertaking was a part of the advertising expenses of the business, and that therefore Fuller might engage singers upon similar terms to those upon which singers for recitals are generally engaged, where the manager expects a profit, direct or indirect.

Therefore it is enough for the decision to say that the customary extent of such an authority as was actually conferred comprised such a contract. If estoppel be, therefore, the basis of all "apparent authority," it existed here. Yet the argument involves a misunderstanding of the true significance of the doctrine, both historically (Responsibility for Tortious Acts: Its History, Wigmore, 7 Harv.L.Rev. 315, 383) and actually. The responsibility of a master for his servant's act is not at bottom a matter of consent to the express act, or of an estoppel to deny that consent, but it is a survival from ideas of status, and the imputed responsibility congenial to earlier times, preserved now from motives of policy. While we have substituted for the archaic status a test based upon consent, i.e., the general scope of the business, within that sphere the master is held by principles quite independent of his actual consent, and indeed in the face of his own instructions. . . . It is only a fiction to say that the principal is estopped, when he has not communicated with the third person and thus misled him. There are, indeed, the cases of customary authority, which perhaps come within the range of a true estoppel; but in other cases the principal may properly say that the authority which he delegated must be judged by his directions, taken together, and that it is unfair to charge him with misleading the public, because his agent, in executing that authority, has neither observed, nor communicated, an important part of them. Certainly it begs the question to assume that the principal has authorized his agent to communicate a part of his authority and not to disclose the rest. Hence, even in contract, there are many cases in which the principle of estoppel is a factitious effort to impose the rationale of a later time upon archaic ideas, which, it is true, owe their survival to convenience, but to a very different [one] from the putative convenience attributed to them.

However it may be of contracts, all color of plausibility falls away in the case of torts, where indeed the doctrine first arose, and where it still thrives. It makes no difference that the agent may be disregarding his principal's directions, secret or otherwise, so long as he continues in that larger field measured by the general scope of the business intrusted to his care. . . .

The considerations which have made the rule survive are apparent. If a man select another to act for him with some discretion, he has by that fact vouched to some extent for his reliability. While it may not be fair to impose upon him the results of a total departure from the general subject of his confidence, the detailed execution of his mandate stands on a different footing. The very purpose of delegated authority is to avoid constant recourse by third persons to the principal, which would be a corollary of denying the agent any latitude beyond his exact instructions. Once a third person has assured himself widely of the character of the agent's mandate, the very purpose of the relation demands the possibility of the principal's being bound through the agent's minor deviations. Thus, as so often happens, archaic ideas continue to serve good, though novel, purposes.

In the case at bar there was no question of fact for the jury touching the scope of Fuller's authority. His general business covered the whole tone test recitals; upon him was charged the duty of doing everything necessary in the premises, without recourse to Maxwell or any one else. It would certainly have been quite contrary to the expectations of the defendant, if any of the prospective performers at the recitals had insisted upon verifying directly with Maxwell the terms of her contract. It was precisely to delegate such negotiations to a competent substitute that they chose Fuller at all.

The exception is without merit; the motion is denied.

ANALYSIS

1. What is a better legal theory for liability in Kidd v. Thomas A. Edison, Inc., apparent authority or inherent agency power? As to apparent authority, what manifestations did the defendant make to the plaintiff?

2.   What could each of the parties have done to avoid the problem that arose in this case and how does that bear on the wisdom of the decision?

Nogales Service Center v. Atlantic Richfield Company
126 Ariz. 133, 613 P.2d 293 (1980).

The trial below was on Nogales Service Center's (NSC) claim for breach of contract against Atlantic Richfield Company (ARCO). This is an appeal from the judgment entered on a jury verdict in favor of ARCO. NSC contends the trial court erred in denying certain instructions and in the admission and rejection of evidence.

Prior to June 1969, Albert F. Cafone and Angus McKenzie were produce brokers in Nogales, Arizona. They decided that profits could be derived from the operation at Nogales of a facility to sell fuel to the great number of trucks which seasonally came to Nogales, loaded with produce to be transported to points in the United States and Canada. No such enterprise was operating in Nogales at that time.

Before contacting ARCO, Cafone and McKenzie approached Texaco and Shell. They were looking for a supplier to lend them a large sum of money to be applied towards the construction and equipment of a suitable facility. They finally contacted ARCO, which was itself looking for a truck stop in the area. Cafone and McKenzie organized a corporation, Nogales Service Center, and entered into an agreement with ARCO for construction of the facility. The total estimated cost of the facility, which was to include an auto/truck service station, coffee shop, motel and brokerage offices, was $508,000. ARCO lent the corporation $300,000 to help finance construction.

Construction of the truck stop began in 1969 and was finished in early 1970. Operations began in April or May of 1970. As originally built, the facility did not include the motel and restaurant, a factor which created a definite problem. The funds which ARCO lent to NSC were not put in escrow and some were spent for a cantaloupe crop which failed, therefore the restaurant was not constructed.

NSC and ARCO also entered into a products agreement on November 4, 1969. It was to be effective for a period of 15 years, subject to termination by mutual agreement after the 10th year, and provided for the sale of fuel at prices to be fixed by ARCO, subject to change by the latter at any time without notice. It called for the purchase of at least 50 percent of NSC's fuel from ARCO.

NSC's operation was in financial difficulty from the beginning of its operation. Among other things, its price for diesel fuel was not competitive with truck stops in the Tucson area. In May of 1972, Cafone's brother-in-law, William Terpenning, bought out McKenzie and assumed his liability on the $300,000. In July and August, Cafone and Terpenning met in Los Angeles, California with Joe Tucker who was then ARCO's manager of truck stop marketing. The problem of competitive pricing was discussed.

It was at these meetings that, according to Terpenning, NSC and ARCO entered into an oral agreement which formed the basis of NSC's claim. Terpenning testified that Tucker told him that the construction of a motel and restaurant at the truck stop was a "must"; that if NSC constructed these facilities, which were estimated to cost $400,000, it would lend $100,000; that ARCO would give NSC a 1 cent per gallon across the board discount on all diesel fuel; and that it would keep NSC "competitive." In reliance on Tucker's promise, Terpenning bought out Cafone, borrowed money and used his own funds to construct the motel and restaurant. ARCO approved the loan application after the construction was commenced and lent the $100,000 but the 1 cent per gallon discount was disapproved. According to Terpenning, ARCO never made NSC "competitive."

Terpenning and NSC defaulted on the original note and on the $100,000 note. ARCO then brought a foreclosure action and prevailed. This suit involves a counterclaim filed by NSC which was tried after the foreclosure judgment. For convenience in the trial court, NSC, the counterclaimant, was designated the plaintiff and the original plaintiff, ARCO, was designated the defendant.

At trial ARCO contended that Tucker never agreed to make NSC competitive or to give it an across-the-board 1 cent discount; that if such an agreement were made by Tucker it was outside his authority and that the statute of frauds barred any action on the alleged oral contract.

The trial court, *without objection* [emphasis supplied], gave the following instructions relating to the authority of an agent:

> An employee-agent has apparent authority to make an agreement binding on his employer-principal, if, but only if, the latter through officers or other agents authorized to do so has held out that [the] employee-agent . . . has such authority. In this case, in order to find Joe Tucker had apparent authority to make an agreement for ARCO, you must find that ARCO had actually or by necessary implication, represented to the officers of Nogales Service Center that Tucker had such authority; and you must find further that such representations were made by officers or other agents of ARCO having authority from the company to make them.

> If you find by a preponderance of all the evidence that such an agreement was made, then you shall consider whether those making it were authorized by their respective companies to do so. An employee-agent can legally bind his employer-principal only when he has actual or apparent authority to do so. Authority of either type, actual or apparent, can be derived only from acts of the employer-principal. An employee-agent cannot confer authority upon himself merely by claiming it for himself. If you find that Joe Tucker had no actual authority to enter into any agreement for ARCO, then he could do so in such a way as to bind ARCO if, but only if, you find that he had apparent authority to make an agreement.

The trial court refused to give the following instruction offered by the appellant:

Requested Jury Instruction No. 21:

ARCO's employees who dealt with Service Center in the claimed oral agreements made ARCO responsible for any such agreements if they are acts which usually accompany or are incidental to transactions which the agent is authorized to conduct, even if the employees were forbidden to make such agreements, if persons from Nogales Service Center reasonably believed that ARCO's employees were authorized to make them, and has no notice that ARCO's employees were not so authorized.

. . .

Appellee contends that No. 21 was covered by the instructions which were given. We do not agree. The instructions given covered only actual or apparent authority. Inherent authority depends upon neither of these concepts since it may make the principal liable because of conduct which he did not desire or direct, to persons who may or may not have known of his existence or who did not rely upon anything which the principal said or did. . . .

The Restatement (Second) of Agency Sec. 8A (1957) defines inherent agency power:

Inherent agency power is a term used in the restatement of this subject to indicate the power of an agent which is derived not from authority, apparent authority or estoppel, but solely from the agency relation and exists for the protection of persons harmed by or dealing with a servant or other agent.

The rationale of inherent agency power is explained in Comment b to Sec. 8A:

The other type of inherent power subjects the principal to contractual liability or to the loss of his property when an agent has acted improperly in entering into contracts or making conveyances. Here the power is based neither upon the consent of the principal nor upon his manifestations. There are three types of situations in which this type of power exists. First is that in which a general agent does something similar to what he is authorized to do, but in violation of orders. In this case the principal may become liable as a party to the transaction, even though he is undisclosed. As to such cases, see Sections 161 and 194. Second is the situation in which an agent acts purely for his own purposes in entering into a transaction which would be authorized if he were actuated by a proper motive. See §§ 165 and 262. The third type is that in which an agent is authorized to dispose of goods and departs from the authorized method of disposal. See §§ 175 and 201.

In many of the cases involving these situations the courts have rested liability upon the ground of 'apparent authority,' a phrase which has been used by the courts loosely. If the meaning of the term is restricted, as is done in Section 8, to those situations in which the principal has manifested the existence of authority to third persons, the term does not apply to the above situations. No theory of torts, contract or estoppel is sufficient to allow recovery in the cases. But because agents are fiduciaries acting generally in the principal's interests, and are trusted and controlled by him, it is fairer that the risk of loss caused by disobedience of agents should fall upon the principal rather than upon third persons.

Appellant's offered Instruction No. 21 is a paraphrase of Sec. 161 of the Restatement (Second) of Agency which states:

A general agent for a disclosed or partially disclosed principal subjects his principal to liability for acts done on his account which usually accompany or are incidental to transactions which the agent is authorized to conduct if, although they are forbidden by the principal, the other party reasonably believes that the agent is authorized to do them and has no notice that he is not so authorized.

As explained in Comment b to Sec. 161, inherent power is to be distinguished from apparent authority:

The Rule stated in this Section applies to cases in which there is apparent authority, but includes also cases in which there is no apparent authority. Thus, the principal may be liable upon a contract made by a general agent of a kind usually made by such agents, although he had been forbidden to make it and although there had been no manifestation of authority to the person dealing with the agent.

The rule set forth in Sec. 161 was apparently followed by the court in Lois Grunow Memorial Clinic v. Davis, 49 Ariz. 277, 66 P.2d 238 (1937) although the court at times used the term "implied authority" for inherent authority and confused "apparent authority" with inherent authority.

Sec. 161 uses the term "general agent." The Restatement (Second) of Agency defines a "general agent" as an agent authorized to conduct a series of transactions involving a continuity of service. Restatement (Second) of Agency Sec. 3 (1957). Tucker dealt with the various truck stops accounts in the area of special problems, on matters of investment and discounts. Although the evidence was that he did not have authority to grant the alleged across-the-board discount, he did have authority to grant certain discounts such as volume discounts, gasoline merchandising discounts and dealer temporary aid discounts. On the subject of an agent disobeying the principal it was observed by Judge Learned Hand in the case of Kidd v. Thomas A. Edison, Inc., 239 F. 405 (S.D.N.Y.1917), aff'd, 242 F. 923 (2d Cir.1917) that:

It makes no difference that the agent may be disregarding his principal's directions, secret or otherwise, so long as he continues in that larger field measured by the general scope of the business intrusted to his care.

239 F. at 407. However, there are two reasons why there was no error in refusing [Instruction 21]. First, [this instruction] conflict[s] with and contradict[s] the instruction given, without objection, which told the jury

the agreement was binding only if there was actual or apparent authority. The second reason is the form of objection [was insufficiently specific].

.   .   .

Affirmed.

ANALYSIS

1.   Is the distinction between apparent authority and inherent agency power a useful one in a case such as *Nogales Service Center*?

2.   What proof might the plaintiff have offered in support of each theory?

3.   What can reasonably be expected of a person like Terpenning to assure himself that the person with whom he was dealing had authority to make the deal that Tucker offered?

PROBLEMS

1.   Suppose Professor Paula Potter has a student research assistant, Allie.   Allie is about to graduate and Paula asks her to hire a successor. Paula says that she is willing to pay $9 per hour for 100 hours of work. Allie finds another student, Zelda, who wants the job but points out that the going rate is $10 per hour.   Allie says, "Well, if that's the going rate, that's O.K.   You have the job."   Thereafter Paula tells Zelda that she will pay only $9 and Zelda (who has turned down other job offers) seeks to enforce the contract that she thinks she has for $10 per hour.   Who wins? Why?   Suppose Paula had said to Allie, "Find the best available person, tell that person what the job is and how much I am willing to pay, and send her or him to me so I can offer the job if I am satisfied with your choice." Same result?

2.   Suppose you are the lawyer for M/M Records, a small record company with good management and exciting prospects.   The head of the company, Millie Mogul, has just hired a woman named Sheena Swiftie, who is friendly with a number of leading recording stars and hopes some day to establish herself as an independent agent in the entertainment industry, but wants to start out as an employee (largely because she needs a steady income).   Sheena's job is to line up recording stars to make records for M/M Records.   Sheena will be paid a salary plus bonuses based on what she produces.   Millie tells you, "Sheena seems a bit flaky, but I think she can deliver."   In recent years, in the recording business, it has become common for record companies to offer substantial guarantees to star performers, but M/M Records does not do so, because it cannot afford to take the risk. Instead, it offers higher royalties than its competitors do.   Millie wants Sheena to have authority to pin artists down to contracts when the moment is right, but has emphasized to Sheena the M/M Records policy of no guarantees.   Millie asks you if she has anything to worry about and, if she does, what suggestions you might have.   You are aware that Millie tends to resent lawyers in general because she thinks they are "deal breakers."   What is your response to her?

SECTION 7. FIDUCIARY OBLIGATION

We now shift our attention to the fiduciary obligation, or duty of loyalty, owed by agents to their principals. Three of the four cases to be examined involve agents of corporate principals. They are included in this chapter, rather than in Chapter 4, which covers corporate-law issues, because the fact that the principal is a corporation, rather than an individual, is unimportant. Chapter 4 examines problems relating to the relationships of shareholders among themselves and the relationships between shareholders and the people who manage their businesses for them. In Chapter 4 we will return to the problem of fiduciary obligation, but the issues will relate mainly to the exercise of basic control of the corporation by its agents (specifically, by top executives and members of the board of directors). In the cases that follow in this chapter, the alleged violations of the fiduciary obligation do not involve exercise of general control of the corporation.

General Automotive Manufacturing Co. v. Singer

19 Wis.2d 528, 120 N.W.2d 659 (1963).

Action commenced by General Automotive Manufacturing Company, hereinafter referred to as "Automotive", against John Singer, a former employee, to account for secret profits received while in its employ. Trial was to the court without a jury, which found defendant liable to plaintiff for $64,088.08 and costs. Appeal is from that judgment.

Automotive, plaintiff-respondent, is a Wisconsin corporation engaged in the machine shop jobbing business and has about five employees. Louis Glavin controlled Automotive and was its secretary.

John Singer, defendant-appellant, is a machinist-consultant and manufacturer's representative. Singer has worked in the machine shop field for over thirty years. He is adept at machine work and had ability not only as a machinist but also as to metal treatment, grinding techniques and special techniques. He enjoys this reputation in machine shop circles. None of Automotive's employees has defendant's ability to handle these machines. He is also known to be qualified in estimating the costs of machine-shop products and the competitive prices for which such products can be sold.

. . .

We have carefully reviewed the evidence and have ourselves reached conclusions as stated by the trial court and set forth in its Findings of Fact, as follows:

"3. That heretofore and on or about the 28th day of March 1953, the plaintiff hired and employed the defendant as general manager of its business and affairs and the defendant accepted such employment under and pursuant to a written contract.

. . .

"6.   That in and by said contract as aforesaid, the plaintiff promised and agreed to pay to the defendant as compensation, a fixed monthly salary together with a sum equal to 3% of the gross sales of the plaintiff.

. . .

"8.   That in and by said contract, in consideration of compensation to be paid by the plaintiff to the defendant, the defendant promised and agreed:

"A.   To devote his entire time, skill, labor and attention to said employment, during the term of this employment, and not to engage in any other business or vocation of a permanent nature during the term of this employment, and to observe working hours for 5½ days.

"B.   Not to, either during the term of his employment, or at any time thereafter, disclose to any person, firm or corporation any information concerning the business or affairs of the Employer which he may have acquired in the course of or as incident to his employment hereunder, for his own benefit, or to the detriment or intended or probable detriment of the Employer."

. . .

Although stated as a Finding of Fact, Finding No. 10 is mainly a conclusion of law. It produces the principal issue in the case and deserves further discussion. It reads:

"10.   That the defendant breached his contract of employment with the plaintiff and violated the duty of loyalty which he owed to the plaintiff and his fiduciary duty of general manager thereof during the existence of such employment by engaging in business activities directly competitive with the plaintiff, to-wit by obtaining orders from a customer for his own account."

The record leaves no room for doubt of the correctness of Finding 11, as follows:

"11.   That thereafter, instead of turning such orders over to the plaintiff the defendant turned such orders over to other concerns to be filled, collected the proceeds thereof from the customers for his own account and kept the profits accruing therefrom."

Finding 12 is: "That such activities of the defendant were carried on in secret and without the knowledge of the plaintiff."

The evidence on which Finding 12 is based is in dispute. It is not against the great weight and clear preponderance of the evidence and the finding should not be disturbed.

. . .

Study of the record discloses that Singer was engaged as general manager of Automotive's operations. Among his duties was solicitation and procurement of machine shop work for Automotive. Because of Singer's high reputation in the trade he was highly successful in attracting orders.

Automotive is a small concern and has a low credit rating. Singer was invaluable in bolstering Automotive's credit. For instance, when collections were slow for work done by Automotive Singer paid the customer's bill to Automotive and waited for his own reimbursement until the customer remitted. Also, when work was slack, Singer set Automotive's shop to make parts for which there were no present orders and himself financed the cost of materials for such parts, waiting for recoupment until such stock-piled parts could be sold. Some parts were never sold and Singer personally absorbed the loss upon them.

As time went on a large volume of business attracted by Singer was offered to Automotive but which Singer decided could not be done by Automotive at all, for lack of suitable equipment, or which Automotive could not do at a competitive price. When Singer determined that such orders were unsuitable for Automotive he neither informed Automotive of these facts nor sent the orders back to the customer. Instead, he made the customer a price, then dealt with another machine shop to do the work at a less price, and retained the difference between the price quoted to the customer and the price for which the work was done. Singer was actually behaving as a broker for his own profit in a field where by contract he had engaged to work only for Automotive. We concur in the decision of the trial court that this was inconsistent with the obligations of a faithful agent or employee.

Singer finally set up a business of his own, calling himself a manufacturer's agent and consultant, in which he brokered orders for products of the sort manufactured by Automotive,—this while he was still Automotive's employee and without informing Automotive of it. Singer had broad powers of management and conducted the business activities of Automotive. In this capacity he was Automotive's agent and owed a fiduciary duty to it. . . . Under his fiduciary duty to Automotive Singer was bound to the exercise of the utmost good faith and loyalty so that he did not act adversely to the interests of Automotive by serving or acquiring any private interest of his own. . . . He was also bound to act for the furtherance and advancement of the interest of Automotive. . . .

If Singer violated his duty to Automotive by engaging in certain business activities in which he received a secret profit he must account to Automotive for the amounts he illegally received. . . .

The present controversy centers around the question whether the operation of Singer's side line business was a violation of his fiduciary duty to Automotive. The trial court found this business was conducted in secret and without the knowledge of Automotive. . . .

The trial court found that Singer's side line business, the profits of which were $64,088.08, was in direct competition with Automotive. However, Singer argues that in this business he was a manufacturer's agent or consultant, whereas Automotive was a small manufacturer of automotive parts. The title of an activity does not determine the question whether it was competitive but an examination of the nature of the business must be made. In the present case the conflict of interest between Singer's business and his position with Automotive arises from the fact that Singer received orders, principally from a third-party called Husco, for the manufacture of parts. As a manufacturer's consultant he had to see that these orders were filled as inexpensively as possible, but as Automotive's general manager he could not act adversely to the corporation and serve his own interests. On this issue Singer argues that when Automotive had the shop capacity to fill an order he would award Automotive the job, but he contends that it was in the exercise of his duty as general manager of Automotive to refuse orders which in his opinion Automotive could not or should not fill and in that case he was free to treat the order as his own property. However, this argument ignores, as the trial court said, "defendant's agency with plaintiff and the fiduciary duties of good faith and loyalty arising therefrom."

Rather than to resolve the conflict of interest between his side line business and Automotive's business in favor of serving and advancing his own personal interests, Singer had the duty to exercise good faith by disclosing to Automotive all the facts regarding this matter. . . . Upon disclosure to Automotive it was in the latter's discretion to refuse to accept the orders from Husco or to fill them if possible or to sub-job them to other concerns with the consent of Husco if necessary, and the profit, if any, would belong to Automotive. Automotive would then be able also to decide whether to expand its operations, install suitable equipment, or to make further arrangements with Singer or Husco. By failing to disclose all the facts relating to the orders from Husco and by receiving secret profits from these orders, Singer violated his fiduciary duty to act solely for the benefit of Automotive. Therefore he is liable for the amount of the profits he earned in his side line business.

. . .

During the trial the parties stipulated that in the event the court should find that Automotive was entitled to recover profits realized by Singer in his side line business, Singer should be given a credit equal to three percent of the gross sales of that business. Based upon this stipulation the sum of $64,088.08 would be reduced by $10,183. . . .

Judgment . . . affirmed.

LEGAL ANALYSIS

1. The court says that when Singer received an order that he thought the corporation could not fill, he was supposed to tell someone higher up about it. What's the point of that observation?

2. Paragraph 8A of the employment contract has two parts: "devote his entire time . . ." and "not to engage in any other business. . . ." What is the relationship between these two parts? Are they redundant? What is the effect of the phrase "of a permanent nature"?

3. Finding of Fact 10 states that Singer "breached his contract of employment" and "violated [his] duty of loyalty." Would either legal theory be sufficient to support the result (Singer's liability)? What difference would it have made if the court had rested its decision on one or the other of the two theories? Would it have been possible to conclude that Singer had breached his contract without violating his duty of loyalty, or vice versa?

4. Suppose that before Singer was hired, he and the owner of General Automotive had consciously and expressly addressed the possibility that Singer would receive offers of work that he would consider beyond General Automotive's capability. Suppose further that it was clear that it would not have been feasible for Singer to consult with the owner, or any representative of the owner, on what to do with such offers. It is conceivable that the parties might have agreed that Singer would simply turn down these offers. It is also conceivable that they would have agreed that Singer could act as broker, as he did in the actual case, and keep all the profit. Which of these two alternatives seems more likely? Which is more likely to lead to optimal results for both parties? What other solution might you suggest and why?

5. The rule applied by the court is a default rule that is, one that applies in the absence of agreement. Some default rules reduce the costs of contracting, and achieve fairness, by approximating as closely as possible the provision that the parties would have adopted had they addressed the matter. Other default rules do not have this characteristic but instead are calculated to induce one or the other party to reveal his or her wishes to the other and seek agreement. Into which category does the rule in this case fall?

Bancroft–Whitney Company v. Glen

64 Cal.2d 327, 49 Cal.Rptr. 825, 411 P.2d 921 (1966).

■ MOSK, JUSTICE.

[The plaintiff in this case, Bancroft–Whitney Company, was a lawbook publisher with its headquarters in San Francisco. The defendants were Judson B. Glen, formerly president of Bancroft–Whitney; Matthew Bender & Co., another lawbook publisher, with headquarters in New York; and John T. Bender, the president of Matthew Bender & Co. In 1961, Matthew Bender & Co. began an ultimately successful effort to set up a west coast division. As part of this effort, it hired Glen to head that division. Glen, in turn, assisted Matthew Bender & Co. in various ways in hiring away some of Bancroft–Whitney's key people. The plaintiff's claim, described more fully below, is that while Glen was free to quit his job at Bancroft–Whitney and go to work for Matthew Bender, he breached his fiduciary duties to Bancroft–Whitney when, while still working for Bancroft–Whitney, he helped Matthew Bender line up Bancroft–Whitney employees who defected to Matthew Bender. The trial court, sitting without a jury, found in favor of the defendants. The Supreme Court reverses.]

The Employment of Glen and Baker by Bender Co.

The majority of the stock of plaintiff corporation is owned by the Lawyer's Co–Operative Publishing Co. (LCP), whose principal place of business is Rochester, New York. Glen was employed by the parent company as an editor from 1938 until 1949, and in 1949 he became the editor-in-chief of plaintiff. From 1958 until his resignation on December 15, 1961, he was also president of plaintiff, chairman of the executive committee of plaintiff, and chairman of the product planning committee of LCP. In April 1960, Thomas Gosnell became president of LCP and exercised direct control and domination over much of the actual business operations of plaintiff. Glen and Baker [sales manager of Bancroft–Whitney] thereafter became dissatisfied with their employment.

Prior to 1961, Bender Co. desired to expand its operations in California. In May of that year Bender directed William Vanneman, a vice president of Bender Co., to attempt to verify circulating reports that Glen was unhappy in his position with plaintiff. On May 12, 1961, Vanneman reported orally and in writing to Bender that he had not been able to confirm the rumors of dissatisfaction in his discussions with Glen, but stated that he had heard from the president of another subsidiary of LCP that Bender could create a substantial western operation using plaintiff's personnel. Bender testified that he discarded this suggestion.

Nevertheless, on July 10, 1961, Bender instructed his assistant, Joseph Billo, to contact Glen in San Francisco privately to explore further the possibilities covered in the Vanneman report. After a meeting with Glen at his office in San Francisco, Billo reported to Bender that Glen had reached retirement age, that his pension had vested and he was open to offers, that he would consider a change of employment if he could build up his estate and direct the new operation himself, that he had been asked to stay on in plaintiff's employ for five to seven years, and that, despite feelings of loyalty to plaintiff, he could be swayed. Bender wrote Glen at his home, arranged to meet him in San Francisco on September 19, and there they discussed the possibility that Glen might head a new western division of Bender Co. following his retirement. They also discussed the need for a sales manager for the new organization, and Glen suggested that Bender contact Gordon Baker, who was the Los Angeles regional sales manager and a director of plaintiff. Glen called Baker and arranged a meeting between Bender and Baker in Los Angeles. At that meeting Baker indicated that he might be interested in serving as sales manager for the new organization, but only if Glen also became associated with it. On October 10 the fact that Bender was interested in hiring Glen and Baker (and a number of editors employed by plaintiff, as will be discussed later) came to the attention of Gosnell, the president of LCP, and other LCP officers.

Gosnell met Glen in San Francisco in a series of meetings beginning on October 23, 1961, to discuss the situation with him. Glen testified that at these meetings Gosnell did not ask him about his personal plans, but Gosnell claimed that he asked Glen whether he and Baker had been approached about employment by Bender and that Glen had replied he and Baker were not interested in going to work for Bender Co. More of this meeting is discussed hereinafter.

On November 17, 1961, after further negotiations between Glen, Baker, Bender, and other employees and officers of Bender Co., Glen and Baker signed employment contracts with Bender Co., requiring them to commence work on January 1, 1962. Glen's contract provided that he would share in the profits of the new enterprise. On December 15, 1961, Glen resigned as president and director of plaintiff and as a director of LCP. Baker resigned on the same day, and both men commenced employment with Bender Co. in January 1962.

Before November 16 Glen had personally discussed negotiations concerning his probable future employment by Bender Co. with at least two other directors at LCP, and they did not indicate any objection or reproval of Glen's activities. Glen had no written contract of employment with plaintiff, his employment was terminable at will by either plaintiff or himself, and he was not required by the terms or particular circumstances of his employment to resign from or give notice to plaintiff or its remaining officers, directors, or shareholders before negotiating for or signing an employment contract with Bender Co. for the purpose of establishing a western division.

Defendants rely on evidence showing that Glen was discontented with his employment, that a number of plaintiff's officers and employees knew of Glen's discontent and were aware of his negotiations with Bender, and that Glen would have been required to retire from his position with plaintiff because he had reached the age of 65. The evidence regarding these matters is not set forth in detail because it is tangential to the primary issues in the case as described above.

The Hiring of Employees Other Than Glen and Baker

. . .

From the first meeting on September 19, 1961, between Glen and Bender, Glen had mentioned that a dozen editors might accompany him to the new organization. In subsequent contacts this figure fluctuated between 10 and 15 editors. Indeed, at one point Glen suggested to Bender that he might "take" practically all the personnel in plaintiff's organization, but Bender replied that he did not want them all. . . .

On or before October 10, 1961, Glen spoke with two of plaintiff's four managing editors about the possibility of their coming to work with the new organization, and both of them expressed interest. Jules Kalisch testified that Glen had offered him a salary of $15,000, a five-year contract, and a percentage of the profits, but that Kalisch felt $15,000 was not enough and Glen then offered him $18,000.   .   .   .   Kalisch's salary with plaintiff was $12,750. Allan Solie, the second managing editor, testified that he was asked by Glen if he was interested in joining the new organization and that Glen offered him a salary of $15,000 a year, a profit-sharing arrangement, and an opportunity to be a member of the board of directors. Solie was earning $11,000 a year. About the middle or the end of November, Glen approached the treasurer of plaintiff, a man named Lahti, and asked him if he was interested in leaving. He was offered a salary of $17,500, representing a $2,500 increase, a five-year contract, and a position as controller of the new organization.

.   .   .

As mentioned above, when Gosnell, the president of LCP, became aware in early October that Bender Co. might be interested in employing Glen, Baker, and editorial personnel of plaintiff, he came to San Francisco to discuss the matter in a series of meetings with Glen. There is a sharp conflict in the evidence as to whether Gosnell asked Glen at these meetings whether there was a danger of a raid by Bender Co. on plaintiff's editors. Gosnell testified that he asked Glen if there was any danger that Bender might be taking a group of editors from plaintiff and that Glen replied he didn't think there was any danger of this and thought everyone in the editorial department was happy and pleased. Glen denied that Gosnell asked him specifically about a raid by *Bender Co.* but admitted that the subject of a raid by another company was discussed and that he told Gosnell that if there should be a raid on plaintiff's editorial staff he (Glen) would be the first to know about it and "presumably" he would report the matter immediately. Glen testified that his statements did not refer to a raid by a company with which he, Glen, would become associated, because in that case he would not be there to notify anyone. He stated that he knew at the time that if things worked out for him with Bender he would be seeking editors from plaintiff.   .   .   .

Another matter Gosnell discussed with Glen during his visit to San Francisco was salary raises for plaintiff's editors. Although editorial salaries had been under review since the beginning of 1961, Gosnell had ordered another analysis to be made so that he could propose to Glen that increases in salary be given to the editors. The purpose of the suggestion was to head off any Bender Co. raid of plaintiff's editorial staff by maintaining salaries close to the prevailing market rate.

In his meetings with Glen, Gosnell suggested that the salaries of managing editors be raised $2,000 per year, that of assistant managing editors raised $1,500 per year, and that other editors be given raises of $300, $500, or $700 a year, depending upon their experience and competence. Glen told Gosnell that he wished, for purposes of internal administration of plaintiff, to "not make quite such a large jump at this time" but to cut the $2,000 raises for three of the four managing editors to $1,500 and give the full $2,000 raise only to Solie. He also suggested to Gosnell that the salary raises be given in two stages, half immediately, and the other half after January 1, 1962.

Gosnell agreed to the two-step arrangement, and he testified that he was satisfied with the assurances given by Glen before he returned to Rochester. The first-step raises for some of the editors went into effect in November. There is no evidence that Bender knew of the portion of Glen's conversation with Gosnell relating to the raises.

On November 14, Glen flew to New York to attend a directors' meeting of LCP in Rochester. While in Rochester, he told two LCP directors that he might go to work for Bender Co. and stated to one of them that if he decided to leave, Kalisch and Lahti would go with him. . . .

At the meeting in New York Bender and Glen discussed the two managing editors who were to be hired. Bender testified he knew that Glen had definite people in mind for the jobs, but could not recall if Glen mentioned the names of Kalisch and Solie. However, Glen indicated that the salary range for the persons he wanted would run between $15,000 and $17,000 or $17,500. . . .

At this meeting Glen suggested that Bender come to Carmel, where he could meet the two or three people he had in mind as employees and where these persons could meet Bender.

Glen returned to San Francisco, made hotel reservations in Carmel for the meeting, and informed Kalisch, Solie and Lahti about it. Baker learned of the proposed meeting when he was in New York to sign his contract. On November 27 Bender wrote Glen telling him when he expected to arrive for the meeting and assuring Glen that adequate financing for the new organization would be forthcoming. This letter also stated: ". . . the very first thing is to take immediate steps to put together an editorial organization in the following respects: A) Managing Editors B) Experienced Editors C) Selected Trainees. As to group (A) above, Carmel is for that purpose. Then, thereafter, it is your judgment as to when I should be in the picture and when I should be left out of the picture, having in mind that until you actually resign from your present position and the fact of the new organization is known, we will have to be very deft and at least not overlook the possibility of a Fifth Columnist. . . ."

. . .

Bender explained that the reference to a "Fifth Columnist" meant that he didn't want anyone to come to Carmel who wouldn't want to join the new organization because he felt that potential employees would be embarrassed if they attended the meeting and word got back to LCP about it. He also stated he wanted to keep the meeting secret from another competitor.

Bender and his attorney arrived in San Francisco on Friday afternoon, December 1. Glen met them at the airport and drove them to Carmel, taking Solie along. In Carmel they met Kalisch, Baker, and Lahti. Friday night was devoted to the social amenities. On Saturday morning Lahti, Solie, and Kalisch were sitting in the lobby of the hotel when Glen handed them each a copy of an employment contract . . . Lahti, Solie, and Kalisch read their contracts, Bender and his attorney reviewed them, and they were signed with only minor alterations, Bender signing on behalf of Bender Co.   .   .   .

After the contracts were signed, Glen, Solie, and Kalisch proceeded to choose the other editors employed by plaintiff who would be invited to join the new organization.   To facilitate this procedure, Glen had brought with him 56 3 × 5 cards, each designating the name of one of the editors employed by plaintiff, and the editor's salary.   Prior to leaving for Carmel, he had requested a record of the editors' salaries from plaintiff's personnel department and had entered the amounts on the cards.   At the Carmel session, Glen would read the name of an editor and his salary from a card, the three men would discuss his qualities among themselves, and, if it was decided that he should be invited to join, Kalisch would enter his name on a list, place beside it the salary paid to him by plaintiff, and, after a discussion among the three men, a suggested salary to be offered by the new organization.

There is some dispute as to how the suggested salaries were determined.   One witness testified that they were 10 per cent higher than the salaries paid by plaintiff, and another that the salaries were determined "by guess and by golly."   In each case, however, the suggested salary was higher than the editor was receiving from plaintiff.   Glen testified that, in making the selection, he wanted competent candidates.   In some cases, an editor was known to only one of the men.   Glen recommended that two of the four indexers employed by plaintiff be invited to join, and he suggested one or two other persons unknown to the others.   Solie tried to pick some of the younger men to avoid the necessity of offering high salaries.   In some cases capable editors were rejected because of purportedly undesirable personal habits or because of a record of absenteeism.   In one instance a man was passed over because it was reported he had a good chance for advancement with plaintiff.   Kalisch testified that there was no discussion about choosing the "cream of the crop" of editors and that editors from one of the departments of plaintiff were deliberately passed over because that group was working on a national publication and they did not want to interfere with its work.   At the conclusion of the meeting, Glen, Kalisch, and Solie had compiled a list of 14 prospects who were to be invited to join.   The list also contained the present and the suggested salaries for each candidate.

Bender and his attorney were in the room during a part of the selection process.   Bender informed Glen that he (Bender) wished the choice of editors to be made on the basis of their capabilities and their willingness to come to work for Bender Co., and he believed that the selections made followed these requirements.   .   .   .

After the selection process concluded, there was a discussion as to the method of contacting the candidates.   Bender's attorney advised that if persons employed by plaintiff solicited the candidates there was a possibility that a lawsuit would result and that they should keep their "hands off." He advised that the actual contacts be made by someone from Bender Co.   .   .   .

Billo [assistant to Bender] arrived [in San Francisco] on December 9. He did not testify, but his deposition was read at the trial. He could not find the list [prepared at the Carmel meeting] at the time his deposition was taken but when he left New York he had with him the list of candidates, their present salaries, and a suggested salary for each. He met Glen before he contacted the editors, and they discussed some of the persons on the list. . . . Billo called each of the editors, told them briefly about the new organization, and invited them to be a part of it. Glen had provided a picture of the building which had been leased for the western division, and Billo showed it to each editor. Billo had been given absolute discretion as to salaries by Bender and had offered salaries "comparable" to the Bender Co. editorial salary scale. In most cases he offered more than the amount suggested on the list.

One of the editors contacted by Glen, who did not accept employment with Bender Co., testified that in his meeting with Billo the latter had stated that several editors who worked for plaintiff were being contacted for employment, that "they" considered these editors to be the cream of the legal editors on the West Coast, and that Billo was in a position to offer the editor $900 per year more than he was receiving from plaintiff. Another editor testified that Billo had told him that "they were selecting all producers," that they were "the cream of the editors on the West Coast," and that the position he would have with Bender Co. would mean an increase in salary of $1,100.

During the period that Billo was soliciting the editors Glen wrote Bender, "I met with Joe Billo last night and he is starting today on his recruiting program. He will keep in touch with us so that he and we here can cooperate to full advantage." On the 11th, the second day of solicitation, Bender telegraphed Billo as follows: "Stengel and Maris eh! The Yanks need you. Tell Jud we'll settle for a championship western division." Bender testified that he did not know what these references meant, but that he thought the telegram was intended to be congratulatory. On December 12 Glen wrote Bender, "We are making fine progress in getting editors. Eleven have committed themselves in our favor. Two will not come with us. We have not heard from the others. It is now my estimate that we will end up with fourteen editors—not bad for a start."

. . .

On December 15, Glen, Kalisch, Solie, Lahti, Baker, and 12 editors resigned from plaintiff's employ. . . .

At noon the departing editors met at a restaurant for lunch and executed tax information forms previously sent out by Bender for them.

Each of the persons (with the exception of Glen) who resigned from plaintiff's employ was contacted personally before he commenced working for Bender Co. by representatives of plaintiff, who invited him to return to plaintiff's employ. Plaintiff had every opportunity it desired to rehire these employees and utilized this opportunity without interference from any defendant. Plaintiff presented each resigning employee with the most favorable terms it was willing to offer in order to induce him to return to its employ, but it did not offer higher salaries than Bender Co. as an inducement. As a result of the meetings, Solie and two of the editors decided to remain with plaintiff. Subsequently, a number of other employees of plaintiff accepted positions with Bender Co.

In analyzing the legal principles applicable in this case, it should be repeated that we are not concerned with the simple right of one competitor to offer the employees of another a job at more favorable terms than they presently enjoy or the right of an employee (or an officer of a corporation) to seek a better job. The question here is whether the president of a corporation is liable for the breach of his fiduciary duty because of the conduct described above relating to other employees of the corporation and whether, under these facts, those who hire the employees are guilty of unfair competition for acting in concert with the president.

The general rules applicable to the duties of a corporate officer have been frequently stated. In the leading case of Guth v. Loft (1939) 23 Del.Ch. 255, 5 A.2d 503, 510, these obligations were cogently described as follows: "Corporate officers and directors are not permitted to use their position of trust and confidence to further their private interests. While technically not trustees, they stand in a fiduciary relation to the corporation and its stockholders. A public policy, existing through the years, derived from a profound knowledge of human characteristics and motives, has established a rule that demands of a corporate officer or director, peremptorily and inexorably, the most scrupulous observance of his duty, not only affirmatively to protect the interests of the corporation committed to his charge, but also to refrain from doing anything that would work injury to the corporation, or to deprive it of profit or advantage which his skill and ability might properly bring to it, or to enable it to make in the reasonable and lawful exercise of its powers." Section 820 of the Corporations Code provides that an officer must exercise his powers in good faith, with a view to the interests of the corporation.

. . .

The mere fact that the officer makes preparations to compete before he resigns his office is not sufficient to constitute a breach of duty. It is the nature of his preparations which is significant.[10] No ironclad rules as to

---

10. Comment e of section 393 of the Restatement Second of Agency provides that an agent can make arrangements to compete with his principal even before the termination of the agency, but that he cannot properly use confidential information peculiar to his employer's business and acquired therein. "Thus, before the end of his employment, he can properly purchase a rival business and upon termination of employment immediately compete. He is not, however, entitled to solicit customers for such rival business before the end of his employ-ment nor can he properly do other similar acts in direct competition with the employer's business. The limits of proper conduct with reference to securing the services of fellow employees are not well marked. An employee is subject to liability if, before or after leaving the employment, he causes fellow employees to break their contracts with the employer. On the other hand, it is normally permissible for employees of a firm, or for some of its partners, to agree among themselves while still employed, that they will

the type of conduct which is permissible can be stated, since the spectrum of activities in this regard is as broad as the ingenuity of man itself.

. . .

There is broad language in some cases to the effect that protection of the corporation's interest requires full disclosure of acts undertaken in preparation for entering into competition. . . . An analysis of these cases indicates, however, that the liability for breach of fiduciary duty was not predicated on the officer's mere failure to disclose such acts, but upon some *particular circumstance* which rendered nondisclosure harmful to the corporation or upon the officer's wrongful conduct apart from the omission.

There is no requirement that an officer disclose his preparations to compete with the corporation in every case, and failure to disclose such acts will render the officer liable for a breach of his fiduciary duties only where particular circumstances render nondisclosure harmful to the corporation. . . . Conversely, the mere act of disclosing his activities cannot immunize the officer from liability where his conduct in other respects amounts to a breach of duty. The significant inquiry in each situation is whether the officer's acts or omissions constitute a breach under the general principles applicable to the performance of his trust.

In our view, the conduct of Glen in the present case, when assessed by the standards set forth above, amounts to a breach of his fiduciary duties to plaintiff as a matter of law. The undisputed evidence shows a consistent course of conduct by him designed to obtain for a competitor those of plaintiff's employees whom the competitor could afford to employ and would find useful. If Glen while still president of plaintiff had performed these acts on behalf of Bender Co. without also obligating himself to join the company, there could be no doubt that he would have violated his duties to plaintiff. Surely his position in this regard cannot be improved by the fact that he was also to be employed by Bender Co. and was to share in the profits of the new western division. In carrying out his design, Glen misled Gosnell into believing there was no danger that Bender Co. would attempt to hire plaintiff's personnel, suggested a two-step salary increase without informing Gosnell that he had solicited some editors and that he or Bender Co. would solicit others if they successfully consummated their negotiations, and disclosed confidential information regarding salaries to Bender in order to facilitate the solicitation. Ultimately, positions at higher salaries than plaintiff was paying were offered either by Glen or

engage in competition with the firm at the end of the period specified in their employment contracts. However, a court may find that it is a breach of duty for a number of the key officers or employees to agree to leave their employment simultaneously and without giving the employer an opportunity to hire and train replacements."

The illustration given by the Restatement is as follows: "A is employed by P as manager for a year. Before the end of the year, A decides to go into business for himself; in anticipation of this and without P's knowledge, he contracts with the best of P's employees to work for him at the end of the year. At the end of the year, A engages in a competing business and employs the persons with whom he has previously contracted. A has committed a breach of his duty of loyalty to P."

Bender Co. to the treasurer of plaintiff, three of its four managing editors, one or two of the four assistant managing editors, three of the four indexers, and approximately 10 other editors. We need not decide whether any of these acts would constitute a breach of fiduciary duty, taken alone, since there can be little doubt that, in combination, they show a course of conduct which falls demonstrably short of "the most scrupulous observance" of an officer's duty to his corporation.

Misleading Gosnell

The conclusion is inescapable that Glen deliberately misled Gosnell regarding the possibility of a raid by Bender Co. on plaintiff's editorial staff and that his suggestion to Gosnell that half of the proposed salary increases for the editors be postponed until after January 1, 1962, without informing Gosnell of his plan to offer them positions, directly or indirectly, with Bender Co. at higher salaries if his own negotiations with Bender were successful, amounts at the very least to a deliberate and inexcusable failure to inform Gosnell of a matter of vital interest to plaintiff.

Disclosing the Salaries of Plaintiff's Employees

Another significant aspect of Glen's activities on behalf of Bender relates to the list of employees and their salaries compiled at Carmel. It is beyond question that a corporate officer breaches his fiduciary duties when, with the purpose of facilitating the recruiting of the corporation's employees by a competitor, he supplies the competitor with a selective list of the corporation's employees who are, in his judgment, possessed of both ability and the personal characteristics desirable in an employee, together with the salary the corporation is paying the employee and a suggestion as to the salary the competitor should offer in order to be successful in recruitment. This conclusion is inescapable even if the information regarding salaries is not deemed to be confidential. . . .

Assisting the Solicitation of Plaintiff's Employees

The assistance given by Glen to the solicitation of the editors on the list is also to be condemned as a breach of his fiduciary duty. As we have seen, Glen not only provided the list on which the recruiting was based, but he suggested certain tactics to be followed in discussions with the editors, supplied a picture of the new organization's quarters for use by Billo, discussed the persons on the list with Billo during the recruiting campaign, and, in Glen's own words in his letter to Bender, Billo was to keep in touch with him so that "he and we here can cooperate to full advantage." In addition, Glen personally approached Lahti, Kalisch, Solie, Keesey, and Marquis and offered them employment.

. . .

Another matter relied upon by defendants relates to a letter written by Bender on October 10, 1961, to a man named Briggs, who was a director of LCP but was seeking employment with Bender Co. In this letter, Bender stated that he was interested in employing Glen and Baker and that although he had no intention of conducting a raid on plaintiff's personnel, he would not turn his back on any opportunities offered. Briggs showed this letter to Gosnell, and defendants argue that Bender knew Briggs would do so and that therefore Gosnell had been fully informed by Bender of his plans.

However, *after* seeing this letter Gosnell came to San Francisco and received assurances from Glen that he would report to Gosnell any attempt to raid plaintiff's editorial staff, and Glen told Bender he had assured Gosnell that Bender Co. did not intend such action. Thus, any effect of the notice was dissipated by Glen's deception of Gosnell, a matter of which Bender had knowledge. Moreover, the basis underlying the action against Bender and Bender Co. is their cooperation in Glen's breach of fiduciary duty. Since Glen committed many disloyal acts with Bender's knowledge and cooperation, notice of Bender's interest in plaintiff's employees would have been of little significance, and the letter to Briggs does not materially affect the liability of Bender and Bender Co.

. . .

It is clear from the evidence set forth above that Bender was aware of or ratified Glen's breach of his fiduciary duties in all but a few respects, that he cooperated with Glen in the breach, and that he received the benefits of Glen's infidelity.

Damages

Defendants argue that even if we conclude that Glen breached his fiduciary duty and that the other defendants are guilty of unfair competition, we cannot award any damages for this wrongdoing because plaintiff has failed to show that the departure of the employees was proximately caused by defendants' actions. They admit that the primary reason the employees left was that they were offered higher salaries by Bender Co. As recounted above, it was Glen's breach that enabled Bender to determine the amount of salary which would induce these persons to leave plaintiff's employ. Under these circumstances there is no merit in defendants' contention. The causal relationship between Glen's violation of duty and Bender's persuasive inducement to the plaintiff's personnel is crystal clear.

Defendants urge that plaintiff itself bears responsibility for the ultimate departure of its employees because it failed to offer higher salaries in order to induce them to return after they had reached agreement with Bender Co. We cannot indulge in an assumption that such offers would have been accepted under the circumstances. In any event, the question of plaintiff's conduct subsequent to the successful recruitment campaign of defendants relates to the question of damages rather than to proximate cause. To hold otherwise would suggest that a corporation could not protect itself against an officer's breach of fiduciary duties in this regard, no matter how flagrant his conduct, since it could always be said that the corporation which lost its employees might have offered them additional salary to return and that the departing employees might have accepted these offers.

. . .

The trial court found that plaintiff was not damaged in any amount by any tortious acts of defendants, that by the end of 1962 it had fully recovered from the adverse effects "if any" caused by the loss of personnel, and that the only adverse effect "if any" on plaintiff from this loss was a contribution to a delay in 1962 in the preparation and shipment of its work. The undisputed evidence shows that plaintiff suffered other adverse effects as well, and the trial court's findings in this regard are not supported by the evidence. At the very least, it was shown without contradiction that plaintiff had incurred certain expenses in attempting to persuade the persons who had resigned to return to its employ.

. . .

The judgment is reversed with directions to the trial court to retry the issue of general damages and enter judgment for plaintiff.

■ TRAYNOR, C.J., McCOMB, PETERS, TOBRINER, PEEK, and BURKE, JJ., concur.

ANALYSIS

Suppose you had been Bender's lawyer just before Bender approached Glen and had been asked what Glen could and could not do and what the likely costs (in damages) would be if he violated his obligations. With the benefit of the decision you have just read, what would you have said, specifically with respect to the following?

(a) Whether Glen has an obligation to his employer to notify his superiors of (i) the offer to him or (ii) the broader "raid" on LCP employees.

(b) Whether Glen may provide information about the salaries and the capabilities of his subordinates.

(c) Whether Glen may talk to his subordinates about going to work for Bender.

PROBLEM

Suppose you are a senior associate in the ABC law firm. You are well thought of by the partners of ABC and have good reason to believe, and do believe, that you will soon be asked to become a partner in the firm. You are approached by a partner, Paula, in the XYZ law firm about the possibility of becoming a partner in that firm. The partners in ABC have a strong commitment to the idea of loyalty to the firm; your position at ABC would be undermined if it were known that you were giving serious consideration to the possibility of joining XYZ, but in fact you are doing so.

(a) Do you have a legal obligation to ABC to reveal the possibility of your moving to XYZ? What about a moral obligation? What if one of the senior partners of ABC is your mother?

(b) Suppose Paula says that XYZ also has an interest in two or three of the associates working under your direction. You feel that you would be more likely to want to join XYZ if they went with you. What, if anything, can you say to them?

(c) Your secretary at ABC does an outstanding job and your decision to join XYZ will to some degree depend on whether she will go with you. What can you say to her?

(d) A number of the clients whose work you have been doing might follow you to XYZ. Can you ask them whether they will do so?

Town & Country House & Home Service, Inc. v. Newbery

3 N.Y.2d 554, 170 N.Y.S.2d 328, 147 N.E.2d 724 (1958).

This action was brought for an injunction and damages against appellants on the theory of unfair competition. The complaint asks to restrain them from engaging in the same business as plaintiff, from soliciting its customers, and for an accounting and damages. The individual appellants were in plaintiff's employ for about three years before they severed their relationships and organized the corporate appellant through which they have been operating. The theory of the complaint is that plaintiff's enterprise "was unique, personal and confidential," and that appellants cannot engage in business at all without breach of the confidential relationship in which they learned its trade secrets, including the names and individual needs and tastes of its customers.

The nature of the enterprise is house and home cleaning by contract with individual householders. Its "unique" quality consists in superseding the drudgery of ordinary house cleaning by mass production methods. The house cleaning is performed by a crew of men who descend upon a home at stated intervals of time, and do the work in a hurry after the manner of an assembly line in a factory. They have been instructed by the housewife but work without her supervision. The householder is supplied with liability insurance, the secrets of the home are kept inviolate, the tastes of the customer are served and each team of workmen is selected as suited to the home to which it is sent. The complaint says that the customer relationship is "impregnated" with a "personal and confidential aspect."

The complaint was dismissed at Special Term on the ground that the individual appellants were not subjected to negative covenants under any contract with plaintiff, and that the methods and techniques used by plaintiff in conducting its business are not confidential or secret as in the case of a scientific formula; that house cleaning and housekeeping "are old and necessary chores which accompany orderly living" and that no violation of duty was involved in soliciting plaintiff's customers by appellants after resigning from plaintiff's employ. The contacts and acquaintances with customers were held not to have been the result of a confidential relationship between plaintiff and defendants or the result of the disclosure of secret or confidential material.

By a divided vote the Appellate Division reversed, but on a somewhat different ground, namely, that while in plaintiff's employ, appellants conspired to terminate their employment, form a business of their own in competition with plaintiff and solicit plaintiff's customers for their business. The overt acts under this conspiracy were found by the Appellate Division to have been that, in pursuance of this plan, they formed the corporate appellant and bought equipment and supplies for their operations—not on plaintiff's time—but during off hours, before they had severed their relations as employees of plaintiff. The Appellate Division concluded that "it is our opinion that their agreement and encouragement to each other to carry out the course of conduct thus planned by them, and their consummation of the plan, particularly their termination of employment virtually en masse, were inimical to, and violative of, the obligations owed by them to appellant as its employees; and that therefore appellant was entitled to relief." . . .

Although the Appellate Division implied more relief than we consider to have been warranted, we think that the trial court erred in dismissing the complaint altogether. The only trade secret which could be involved in this business is plaintiff's list of customers. Concerning that, even where a solicitor of business does not operate fraudulently under the banner of his former employer, he still may not solicit the latter's customers who are not openly engaged in business in advertised locations or whose availability as patrons cannot readily be ascertained but "whose trade and patronage have been secured by years of business effort and advertising, and the expenditure of time and money, constituting a part of the good will of a business which enterprise and foresight have built up" (Witkop & Holmes Co. v. Boyce, 61 Misc. 126, 131, 112 N.Y.S. 874, 878, affirmed 131 App.Div. 922, 115 N.Y.S. 1150,. . .). . . . .

The testimony in the instant record shows that the customers of plaintiff were not and could not be obtained merely by looking up their names in the telephone or city directory or by going to any advertised locations, but had to be screened from among many other housewives who did not wish services such as respondent and appellants were equipped to render, but preferred to do their own housework. In most instances housewives do their own house cleaning. The only appeal which plaintiff could have was to those whose cleaning had been done by servants regularly or occasionally employed, except in the still rarer instances where the housewife was on the verge of abandoning doing her own work by hiring some outside agency. In the beginning, prospective customers of plaintiff were discovered by Dorothy Rossmoore, wife of plaintiff's president, by telephoning at random in "sections of Nassau that we thought would be interested in this type of cleaning, and from that we got directories, town directories, and we marked the streets that we had passed down,

84-89
93-100
105-114

and I personally called, right down the list." In other words, after selecting a neighborhood which they felt was fertile for their kind of business, they would telephone to all of the residents of a street in the hope of discovering likely prospects. On the first day Mrs. Rossmoore called 52 homes. If she enlisted their interest, an appointment would be made for a personal call in order to sell them the service. At the end of the first year, only 40 to 50 customers had thus been secured. Two hundred to three hundred telephone calls netted 8 to 12 customers. Moreover, during the first year it was not possible to know how much to charge these customers with accuracy, inasmuch as the cleaning requirements of each differed from the others, so that special prices had to be set. In the beginning the customer usually suggested the price which was paid until some kind of cost accounting could demonstrate whether it should be raised or lowered. These costs were entered on cards for every customer, and this represented an accumulated body of experience of considerable value. After three years of operation, and by August, 1952, when the individual appellants resigned their employment by plaintiff, the number of customers amounted to about 240. By that time plaintiff had 7 or 8 crews doing this cleaning work, consisting of 3 men each.

Although appellants did not solicit plaintiff's customers until they were out of plaintiff's employ, nevertheless plaintiff's customers were the only ones they did solicit. Appellants solicited 20 or 25 of plaintiff's customers who refused to do business with appellants and about 13 more of plaintiff's customers who transferred their patronage to appellants. These were all the people that appellants' firm solicited. It would be different if these customers had been equally available to appellants and respondent, but, as has been related, these customers had been screened by respondent at considerable effort and expense, without which their receptivity and willingness to do business with this kind of a service organization could not be known. So there appears to be no question that plaintiff is entitled to enjoin defendants from further solicitation of its customers, or that some profits or damage should be paid to plaintiff by reason of these customers whom they enticed away.

For more than this appellants are not liable.   . . .

ANALYSIS

1. Just what could the defendants have done to lure away Town & Country customers, without incurring liability to the plaintiffs?

2. Assume (reasonably) that the law would allow a competitor with no prior relationship with Town & Country to follow Town & Country trucks and thereby discover the addresses, and then the names and telephone numbers, of Town & Country customers, and then to solicit those customers. Is there any good reason why the defendants should not be permitted to hire a detective to do the same sleuthing and then use the list put together by the detective as a basis for telephone solicitation?

Corroon & Black–Rutters & Roberts, Inc. v. Hosch

109 Wis.2d 290, 325 N.W.2d 883 (1982).

■ CECI, JUSTICE.

The question presented is whether it is unfair competition for an insurance agent to use his former employer's customer lists to direct clients to the agent's new insurance agency.

A jury found that the defendant, Jack Hosch, had unfairly used confidential information to compete with the plaintiff, Corroon & Black–Rutters & Roberts, Inc. The court of appeals reversed and remanded for judgment notwithstanding the verdict, holding that the verdict was not supported by credible evidence and was contrary to public policy. We conclude that the information gleaned by the defendant from the plaintiff's files does not constitute a trade secret under Wisconsin law and, therefore, affirm the decision of the court of appeals.

Jack Hosch has been an agent licensed to sell insurance since 1958. In that year, he began his employment with the Roberts Company, a general insurance agency. In 1973, the business and assets of Roberts, including all of its insurance accounts, were acquired by Corroon & Black through an exchange of the stock of Roberts with the stock of Corroon & Black.

During his employment, Hosch was responsible for procuring and servicing insurance accounts for a large number of Corroon & Black's customers. Hosch himself brought about half of these accounts to Corroon & Black. Servicing an account involved, among other things, contacting a customer when the policy was about to expire and reviewing and updating the coverages before renewing the policy.

When the two agencies merged in 1973, Hosch and other employees of Roberts who joined Corroon & Black were required to sign a covenant not to compete. Hosch's covenant not to compete terminated on December 31, 1977. He entered into no other such agreement.

When the term of the covenant not to compete ended, Hosch left Corroon & Black to work for a competitor. Shortly thereafter, in January of 1978, Corroon & Black's president learned that numerous agent-of-record letters had been issued in favor of Hosch and his new agency. These letters notified insurance companies that certain accounts were being switched to a different agency. This resulted in substantial losses of commissions for Corroon & Black, since approximately two-thirds of Hosch's Corroon & Black customers changed to his new agency.

It is clear that Hosch actively solicited his former Corroon & Black clients. That he utilized information gained during his employment with Corroon & Black is not in dispute. This information was of help to him in contacting former customers. Corroon & Black presented testimony that Hosch may have taken detailed information in the expiration lists. Such lists contain names and addresses of policyholders, key personnel to contact, renewal dates and amounts of coverage. . . . .

Corroon & Black's customer files were kept in filing cabinets, which were never locked. Expiration lists were kept in cabinets which were locked on rare occasions. There were approximately 75 employees, all of whom had access to these files.

. . .

The jury determined that it was unfair competition for Hosch, an insurance agent, to use customer lists of his former employer to divert clients to his new insurance agency. Corroon & Black emphasizes the unfairness of this situation and asserts that Hosch was untrustworthy. The plaintiff in Gary Van Zeeland Talent, Inc. v. Sandas, 84 Wis.2d 202, 267 N.W.2d 242 (1978), made a similar argument. However, any perceived unfairness should not be the determining factor. As we stated in *Van Zeeland* :

> "[S]o long as a departing employee takes with him no more than his experience and intellectual development that has ensued while being trained by another, and no trade secrets or processes are wrongfully appropriated, the law affords no recourse." Id. at 214.

We also feel compelled to point out that there was no covenant not to compete in effect when Hosch began working for a competitor of Corroon & Black.

Since the protection of a covenant not to compete is not available to Corroon & Black, the outcome in this case necessarily turns on the question of whether the information taken by Hosch was a trade secret.

. . .

[Our] conclusion that an insurance agency's customer list is not a trade secret is consistent with current Wisconsin law, as enunciated in our decisions in Abbott Laboratories v. Norse Chemical Corp., 33 Wis.2d 445, 147 N.W.2d 529 (1967), and Gary Van Zeeland Talent, Inc. v. Sandas, 84 Wis.2d 202, 267 N.W.2d 242 (1978).

In *Abbott*, an employee took, among other things, a customer list for artificial sweeteners and used it to compete against his former employer. In the *Abbott* opinion, we noted that the law concerning trade secrecy features two basic themes. Some courts have emphasized the breach of confidence aspect of the law of unfair competition. Usually, however, such cases also involve an assumed trade secret. The second theme is the requirement of the existence of an actual trade secret as the *sine qua non* of a cause of action for unfair competition. The emphasis is on the nature of the ideas and concepts which employees take with them to their new jobs.

Corroon & Black's analysis in the instant case bears close resemblance to the first theory in trade secret law discussed in *Abbott*. As mentioned previously, Corroon & Black emphasizes the alleged confidentiality of its customer lists and apparently equates confidentiality of information with trade secret status. We find this to be an inaccurate statement of existing law. This court in *Abbott* adopted the Restatement view of the law of trade secrets, finding that it:

> " . . . gives proper balance to the two factors that have cropped up throughout the development of the law of trade secrets." Id. at 456.

In discussing the definition of a trade secret, we quoted with approval the following language from Restatement, 4 *Torts*, § 757, comment b (1939):

> "Some factors to be considered in determining whether given information is one's trade secret are: (1) the extent to which the information is known outside of his business; (2) the extent to which it is known by employees and others involved in his business; (3) the extent of measures taken by him to guard the secrecy of the information; (4) the value of the information to him and to his competitors; (5) the amount of effort or money expended by him in developing the information; (6) the ease or difficulty with which the information could be properly acquired or duplicated by others." Id. at 463–64.

Applying the Restatement definition, this court held that Abbott's customer list was not a trade secret, because it was not sufficiently secret or confidential and because it contained only the names and addresses of the individual to be contacted, rather than complicated marketing data concerning the customer's projected market needs or the customer's market habits.

We also noted that customer lists are the periphery of the law of unfair competition. This is because legal protection would not provide the incentive to compile such lists; most are developed in the normal course of business, anyway.

. . . .

We are not unmindful of the fact that the Corroon & Black list may have contained more detailed information than the "bare bones" customer lists in *Abbott* and *Van Zeeland*. However, we do not agree with Corroon & Black's contention that this should be a deciding factor. Even though it contains more than just names and addresses of customers, an insurance agency customer list, such as the one in this case, is not entitled to trade secret protection under Wisconsin law.

Corroon & Black contends that the six Restatement elements are not requirements for trade secret status, but rather are factors under which the defendant must show that a trade secret does not exist. It is argued that the expiration lists qualify as trade secrets under this interpretation of the Restatement definition.

We hold that an insurance agency expiration list does not meet the six-factor Restatement definition of a trade secret. Each of the six factors should indicate that a trade secret exists if the information is to be afforded legal protection.

Corroon & Black asserts that considerable time and money were expended in the development of the information on the expiration lists. In

Abbott and *Van Zeeland*, we stated that the customer lists in those cases were "merely the outgrowth of normal marketing endeavors" and were "nothing unique or confidential that should be protected in order to prevent competition." *Van Zeeland*, 84 Wis.2d at 217. The court of appeals below correctly determined that the time and money expended by Corroon & Black were spent on the development of the market which the customer list represents, rather than on the compilation of the information. Thus, the fourth and fifth elements of the Restatement definition are lacking. To afford protection to insurance agency customer lists, which are developed in the normal course of business anyway, would be contrary to public policy.

Corroon & Black's president testified that the files were, in his opinion, confidential. However, the evidence shows that most, if not all, of Corroon & Black's employees had access to this information. On this basis, the customer lists fail to meet the Restatement definition under the second and third elements.

Finally, there is some evidence which indicates that the information on many of the larger insurance clients could have been obtained by Hosch and others even without the customer lists.

Aside from the Restatement definition of a trade secret, this court also considered the route-nonroute distinction in *Abbott* and *Van Zeeland*. As we explained in *Abbott*, a nonroute customer is likely to purchase from several suppliers. Courts are less likely to afford protection against "unfair" competition by a former employee, because there is no particular relationship developed between a customer and a salesman (the employer) which is enduring. 33 Wis.2d at 467. In *Van Zeeland* we pointed out that certain professionals, for example, dentists, doctors, attorneys and accountants, may be considered to be covered by the route sales rationale, even though they do not meet the traditional definition of "route salesman."[6]

Corroon & Black asserts that insurance agents are in the route salesman category. We disagree. To the extent that the route-nonroute rationale applies[7] in this situation, it appears that insurance agents are nonroute salesmen. It seems clear to us that many insurance customers do not depend on one agency for all of their insurance needs. Moreover, many persons change companies and agents quite frequently in order to save a few dollars in premium.

. . .

---

6. "The typical and classical case of a route customer is the relationship between a householder and a milk delivery salesman. In that situation, the householder, during the course of the relationship, typically buys exclusively from the particular salesman; and it is assumed that, therefore, a special personal relationship will develop which will continue even though the salesman should commence his own enterprise or switch employers." Gary Van Zeeland Talent, Inc. v. Sandas, 84 Wis.2d 202, 215, 267 N.W.2d 242 (1978).

7. Apparently the route-nonroute rationale is most often employed in cases where there is a covenant not to compete and the enforceability of the covenant is being questioned. See, Trade Secrets, Customer Contacts and the Employer–Employee Relationship, 37 Ind. L.J. 218, 230 (1961–62).

The decision of the court of appeals is affirmed.

■ ABRAHAMSON, JUSTICE (dissenting).

I dissent because the majority has departed, without justification or explanation, from the well-accepted legal principles which this court has previously adopted in trade secret cases and because the majority has not given proper deference to the jury verdict.

I.

In order to evaluate the majority's departure from precedent and the majority's new standard of appellate review of jury verdicts, I will set forth the factual dispute which the jury in this case was called upon to resolve and the jury instructions which provide the legal framework for the jury to use in deciding the issues presented to it.

Corroon & Black presented evidence that Hosch had unlawfully taken and used three types of information:

(1) "Customer lists," that is, lists containing names and addresses of 85 commercial and 113 personal customers that Corroon & Black had assigned to Hosch;

(2) "Expiration lists," that is, lists of the customer policies showing their expiration date; and

(3) Information contained in "insurance agency files," such as:

(a) names of key personnel to contact regarding particular insurance policies;

(b) type and amount of coverage under each policy;

(c) name of insurer providing each type of coverage;

(d) summaries of calls made to customers and information discussed during those calls;

(e) suggestions concerning information that might be discussed with the customer on the next call;

(f) memoranda regarding a customer's problems that would affect the customer's insurance coverage,

(g) the names of insurance companies with which Corroon & Black had placed the customer's insurance business;

(h) the premium charge for each policy;

(i) the commissions on the policies;

(j) the customer's claims history and loss experience;

(k) whether any other insurer had refused to write a particular type of policy for the customer;

(*l*) engineering surveys and information on structures insured;

(m) evaluations of the customer's business indicating potential for additional insurance.

Hosch acknowledged that he had access to all of this information when he worked for Corroon & Black and that the information had value to an insurance agent or agency because it gave the agent or agency a competitive advantage over others in the business. He denied that he took either the expiration lists or the information in the insurance agency files.

. . .

The jury found, by special verdict, that the insurance files of Corroon & Black were of a confidential nature and that Hosch had made unauthorized use of the information in the insurance files.

On appeal, the court of appeals remanded the case to the trial court to enter a judgment notwithstanding the verdict, and the majority here has, to a great extent, adopted the reasoning of the court of appeals. The majority concludes that the trial court erred in failing to find, as a matter of law, that the information in issue does not constitute a trade secret. In reaching its conclusion, the majority alters significantly the substantive law of trade secrets and undermines the established standard used to review jury verdicts.

II.

The majority departs in two significant ways from this court's prior cases which analyze trade secrets. First, the majority fails to follow our prior case law which recognizes that a wide spectrum of information may be protected as a trade secret and that the decision to protect information as a trade secret in a particular case must be determined on the basis of the facts of the case. Second, the majority, contrary to this court's interpretation of the *Abbott* –Restatement test, holds that the information sought to be protected must fulfill each prong of the six-factor test.

This court has consistently reviewed each trade secret case on its own facts, refusing to create "generic" categories of information which are or are not trade secrets.

. . .

The *Abbott* –Restatement formulation of trade secrets does not categorically deny trade secrets protection to information generated in the normal course of business. The Restatement describes a trade secret as "any formula, pattern, device or compilation of information which is used in one's business and which gives him [or her] an opportunity to obtain an advantage over competitors who do not know or use it." (Id. at p. 5, emphasis added) In addition, the six factors all relate to business information. 4 Restatement of Torts, sec. 757, comment b, p. 6 (1939). Since business information and information used in business are often generated in the normal course of business, I do not construe either *Abbott* or the Restatement as precluding protection for information generated in the normal course of business.

Similarly, the Wisconsin legislature's definition of a "trade secret" includes business information used or for use in business. The legislature does not exclude from the definition of "trade secret" information generated in the normal course of business. Sec. 943.205, Stats. 1979–80, which applies to both civil and criminal cases, defines trade secret as follows:

> " 'Trade secret' means the whole or any portion or phase of any scientific, technical, laboratory, experimental, development or manufacturing information, equipment, tooling, machinery, design, process, procedure, formula or improvement, or any business information used or for use in the conduct of a business, which is manifestly intended by the owner not to be available to anyone other than the owner or persons having access thereto with the owner's consent and which accords or may accord the owner a competitive advantage over other persons." Sec. 943.205(2) (a), Stats. 1979–80 (emphasis added).

If the legislature authorizes punishment as a felony for the theft of information which might have been generated in the ordinary course of business, the majority's enunciation of public policy should not preclude civil protection of information generated in the ordinary course of business.

. . .

The evidence in this case did not necessitate the majority's conclusion that the protection of Hosch's mobility outweighs the protection of Corroon & Black's business. There was no evidence that protecting Corroon & Black's information would have had any impact at all on Hosch's employability in another insurance agency. There was much evidence that eliminating trade secret protection for this information resulted in Corroon & Black's loss of the competitive advantage it had built up through its efforts. The jury made this balance, and the majority opinion gives no adequate explanation for the court's substitution of its conclusion for the jury's.

. . .

ANALYSIS

1. How, if at all, can one rationalize the difference in outcomes in *Corroon & Black* and *Town & Country* ?

2. Why is a lawyer like a milk-delivery person? (See footnote 6 and related text of the majority opinion in *Corroon & Black*.)

3. The majority in *Corroon & Black* opined that "the outcome in this case necessarily turns on the question of whether the information taken by Hosch was a trade secret." Is that correct? Was there a viable alternative theory of liability?

4. Is the rule in *Corroon & Black* a "default" rule—that is, one that applies only in the absence of an agreement to the contrary? If so, is it the right default rule? Why?

5. The majority in *Corroon & Black* relies on a definition of trade secrets from the Restatement of Torts. The dissent quotes a Wisconsin statute that makes theft of trade secrets a felony and that contains a

definition of trade secrets. The Uniform Trade Secrets Act, which has been adopted in a number of jurisdictions (e.g., Ind. Code §§ 24–2–3–1 to 24–2–3–8) contains the following definition:

"Trade secret" means information, including a formula, pattern, compilation, program, device, method, technique, or process, that:

(1) derives independent economic value, actual or potential, from not being generally known to, and not being readily ascertainable by proper means by, other persons who can obtain economic value from its disclosure or use; and

(2) is the subject of efforts that are reasonable under the circumstances to maintain its secrecy.

Would the majority have reached the same result using the definitions in the Uniform Trade Secrets Act or in the Wisconsin felony statute?

6. The majority states,

customer lists are the periphery of the law of unfair competition. This is because legal protection would not provide the incentive to compile such lists; most are developed in the normal course of business, anyway.

This implies that legal protection would not affect economic incentives and, thus, would not affect anyone's behavior. Does that seem plausible?

7. What should the outcome in *Corroon & Black* have been if Hosch had solicited customers for his rival business before leaving Corroon & Black's employment?

PLANNING

Suppose that you were practicing law in Wisconsin at the time *Corroon & Black* was decided. Corroon & Black has just fired its lawyer (for good reason?) and seeks your advice on what, if anything, it might do to protect its customer lists and files in the future. What do you say?

CHAPTER 2

PARTNERSHIPS

SECTION 1. PARTNERS COMPARED WITH EMPLOYEES

Fenwick v. Unemployment Compensation Commission
133 N.J.L. 295, 44 A.2d 172 (1945).

This is an appeal from a judgment of the Supreme Court reversing a determination of the Unemployment Compensation Commission. The question involved is whether one Arline Chesire was, from January 1, 1939, to January 1, 1942, a partner or an employee of the prosecutor-respondent, John R. Fenwick, trading as United Beauty Shoppe. If she was an employee, then she was the eighth and deciding employee for the purpose of determining the status of the respondent for the year 1939 as an employer subject to the terms of the statute. N.J.S.A. 43:21–1 et seq. [requiring employer payments for unemployment compensation fund]. It is not the contention of the appellant commission that there was a fraudulent intent to avoid the act but the case is submitted as one of legal construction of the relation between Mrs. Chesire and the respondent.

Respondent Fenwick commenced operation of the beauty shop in Newark in November, 1936. In either 1937 or early 1938 he employed Mrs. Chesire as a cashier and reception clerk. Apparently her duties were to receive customers, take their orders for services to be performed by the operators, and collect the charges therefor. The shop did not work on an appointment basis but on a "first come-first served" plan. Mrs. Chesire was employed at a salary of $15 per week and continued at that salary until December, 1938, when she requested an increase. Respondent expressed a willingness to pay higher wages if the income of the shop warranted it. Thereupon an agreement was entered into by the parties. This agreement was drawn by a lawyer who had offices nearby and provided:

1.   That the parties associate themselves into a partnership to commence January 1, 1939.

2.   That the business shall be the operation of the beauty shop.

3.   That the name shall be United Beauty Shoppe.

4.   That no capital investment shall be made by Mrs. Chesire.

5.   That the control and management of the business shall be vested in Fenwick.

6.   That Mrs. Chesire is to act as cashier and reception clerk at a salary of $15 per week and a bonus at the end of the year of 20% of the net profits, if the business warrants it.

7.   That as between the partners Fenwick alone is to be liable for debts of the partnership.

8.   That both parties shall devote all their time to the shop.

9.   That the books are to be open for inspection of each party.

10.   That the salary of Fenwick is to be $50 per week and at the end of the year he is to receive 80% of the profits.

11.   That the partnership shall continue until either party gives ten days' notice of termination.

The relationship was terminated on January 1, 1942, at the request of Mrs. Chesire who desired to cease work and remain at home with her child.

The Commission held that the agreement was nothing more than an agreement fixing the compensation of an employee. The Supreme Court held that the parties were partners. The court apparently gave great weight to the fact that the parties had entered into the agreement, had called themselves partners, had designated the relationship one of partnership, and held that the surrounding circumstances, the conduct of the parties, etc., were not such as to overcome the force and effect to be given the declaration of the agreement.

Most of the cases wherein the courts have undertaken to determine whether or not a partnership existed, or whether certain persons were members of existing partnerships, have been those in which creditors have sought to impose liability upon alleged partners. In most cases, too, there have been no written partnership agreements to assist in fixing the status. However, the principles of law to be applied are the same. We think there can be no doubt of the right of the Commission, in the circumstances of this case, to raise the question and have a determination of the question of whether a partnership exists in law even though there is this agreement which is called a partnership agreement. We need not consider here what the effect of the agreement on the parties inter sese would be, but only its effect on the application of the unemployment compensation law.

There are several elements that the courts have taken into consideration in determining the existence or non-existence of the partnership relation. The first element is that of the intention of the parties and here, of course, the agreement itself is evidential although not conclusive. Light on the intent of the parties is shed by the testimony of the respondent as follows:

"Q.   When was she first hired by you? A. That is what I said, either 1937 or 1938, I can't say definitely what it was without looking it up: I couldn't give you the exact date. And she felt as though she was not getting enough money. Well, we were doing a lot of business, but the prices were very low at the time; it was in the depression and you had to bring your prices down to get business. And I told her I did not want to lose her because she was a very very good girl to me in that office, she was what I needed. I told her I couldn't see where I could afford to give her any more. And I did not want to lose her. So it went back and forth, back and forth. Finally I said, 'I will tell you what I will do: If we make any more money I will pay you more, if you want to go along on that agreement.' And that is where the partnership thing came in; that is how we started to be on the partnership concern at that time; that is when that was all discussed and arranged."

That statement is persuasive that the intention of the parties was to enter into an agreement that would provide a possibility of increase of compensation to Mrs. Chesire and at the same time protect Fenwick from being obliged to pay such increase unless business warranted it. The whole thing was prompted and instigated by the demand of the employee for an increase. The employer valued her services and did not wish to lose her. He wished to retain her in the exact same capacity as before but was afraid to promise a straight increase for fear it might mean loss to him. There is no suggestion that anything but the financial relation between the parties, with respect to compensation for services, was the thing they had in mind. After January 1st, 1939, the date the alleged partnership became effective, the operation of the business continued as before. Mrs. Chesire continued to serve in precisely the same capacity as before and Fenwick continued to have complete control of the management of the business. It would seem that, as far as the intention of the parties is concerned, the effect of the statements in the agreement has been met and overcome by the sworn testimony of Fenwick and by the conduct of the parties.

. . .

Another element of partnership is the right to share in profits and clearly that right existed in this case. However, not every agreement that gives the right to share in profits is, for all purposes, a partnership agreement. . . . Therefore, this point is not conclusive.

Another factor is the obligation to share in losses, and this is entirely absent in this case because the agreement provides that Mrs. Chesire is not to share in the losses.

Another is the ownership and control of the partnership property and business. Fenwick contributed all the capital and Mrs. Chesire had no right to share in capital upon dissolution. He likewise reserved to himself control.

The next is community of power in administration, and the reservation in the agreement of the exclusive control of the management of the business in Fenwick excludes this element so far as Mrs. Chesire is concerned. In Wild v. Davenport, Mr. Justice Depue, speaking for this court, said [48 N.J.L. 129, 7 A. 297]:

"In Voorhees v. Jones [29 N.J.L. 270], the decision that a servant or agent who had a share of profits simply as compensation for services was neither a partner, nor liable for partnership debts, was placed by Chief Justice Whelpley on the ground that such a person had no control over the operation of the firm, and could not direct its investments, nor prevent the contracting of debts; in other words, had none of the prerogatives of a principal in the management and control of the business.''

.   .   .

Another element is the language in the agreement, and although the parties call themselves partners and the business a partnership, the language used excludes Mrs. Chesire from most of the ordinary rights of a partner.

The conduct of the parties toward third persons is also an element to be considered and the conduct of the parties here does not support a finding that they were partners. They did file partnership income tax returns and held themselves out as partners to the Unemployment Compensation Commission, and Fenwick in his New York state income tax return reported that his income came from the partnership. But to no one else did they hold themselves out as partners. They did not inform the persons they purchased materials from, although Fenwick says this was not necessary since all purchases were for cash and they neither sought nor gave credit. The right to use the trade name had apparently come to Fenwick from one Florence Meola, by lease, and the partnership was given that name by Fenwick. There is no evidence that the trade name was ever registered as that of the partnership.

Another element is the rights of the parties on dissolution and apparently in this case the result of the dissolution, as far as Mrs. Chesire is concerned, was exactly the same as if she had quit an employment. She ceased to work and ceased to receive compensation and everything reverted to the condition it was in prior to 1939, except that Fenwick carried on with a new receptionist.

Under all these circumstances, giving due effect to the written agreement and bearing in mind that the burden of establishing a partnership is upon the one who alleges it to exist, . . ., we think that the partnership has not been established, and that the agreement between these parties, in legal effect, was nothing more than one to provide a method of compensating the girl for the work she had been performing as an employee. She had no authority or control in operating the business, she was not subject to losses, she was not held out as a partner. She got nothing by the agreement but a new scale of wages.

.   .   .

The Uniform Partnership Act defines a partnership as an association of "two or more persons to carry on as co-owners a business for profit." N.J.S.A. 42:1–6. Essentially the element of co-ownership is lacking in this case. The agreement was one to share the profits resulting from a business owned by Fenwick. He contributed all the capital, managed the business and took over all the assets on dissolution. Ownership was conclusively shown to be in him.

The Act further provides that sharing of profits is prima facie evidence of partnership but "no such inference shall be drawn if such profits were received in payment . . . as wages of an employee," R.S. 42:1–7, N.J.S.A., and it seems that is the legal inference to be drawn from the factual situation here.

The judgment is reversed.

■ For affirmance: The CHIEF JUSTICE and JUSTICES CASE, BODINE, COLIE, and OLIPHANT—5.

■ For reversal: The CHANCELLOR, JUSTICE DONGES, and JUDGES WELLS, RAFFERTY, DILL, FREUND, and McGEEHAN—7.

ANALYSIS

1. Near the end of its analysis, the court refers to Mrs. Chesire as "the girl." Fenwick, in his testimony, uses the same description. How might the attitude that may be reflected in this usage affect the decision in a case such as this?

2. What were the "deal points" (that is, the important terms of the economic relationship) between Mr. Fenwick and Mrs. Chesire?

3. Section 18 of the Uniform Partnership Act provides, "The rights and duties of the partners in relation to the partnership shall be determined, *subject to any agreement between them,* by the following rules: . . . (e) All partners have equal rights in the management and conduct of the partnership business." (Emphasis added.) A key finding of the court in the present case seems to have been that "Fenwick continued to have complete control of the management of the business." How might a lawyer draft a "partnership" agreement to make it appear that Chesire had control consistent with the UPA, without in fact depriving Fenwick of the dominant position that he would no doubt insist upon as a matter of business judgment?

4. UPA § 31 provides, in part:

Dissolution is caused: (1) Without violation of the agreement between the partners, . . . (b) By the express will of any partner when no definite term or particular undertaking is specified.

That leaves the problem of what happens to the partnership property upon dissolution. Presumably Fenwick would want to ensure that upon dissolution he would be entitled to take back all the partnership property needed in the business. How might his lawyer provide for this outcome? UPA § 18 provides, in part, "(a) Each partner shall be repaid his contributions . . . and share equally in the profits and surplus."

5. The court states, "Another factor is the obligation to share losses, and this is entirely absent in this case. . . ." How might the agreement be drafted to weaken this argument?

6.   Another possibility that Fenwick might want to consider would be to engage Chesire as an "independent contractor." How would you draft an agreement to achieve this result (without significant change in the substance of the relationship)?

Frank v. R.A. Pickens & Son Company

264 Ark. 307, 572 S.W.2d 133 (1978).

Appellant brought this action seeking an accounting and liquidation of the partnership affairs of appellee R.A. Pickens and Son Company, a farming partnership which leases and farms some 13,000 acres of land owned by another partnership, R.A. Pickens & Son. The partnership in question has existed in one form or another since 1925. Appellee R.A. Pickens has managed the firm since 1937. At the close of business on December 31, 1975, there were 22 partners of which R.A. Pickens & Son owned the largest interest, 31%. R.A. Pickens is not a partner in R.A. Pickens & Son Company but is a partner of R.A. Pickens & Son. Appellant employee was brought into the farming partnership on January 1, 1968, initially acquiring a 2% interest and eventually acquiring a total interest of 3%. His initial investment ($21,600) was made by giving his note to the partnership with the understanding that his share of the profits would apply to its payment. He remained an active partner until May 31, 1976, when appellee Pickens, as manager of the partnership, terminated appellant's partnership interest and tendered him a check in the amount of $35,805.97. This sum represented 3% of the partnership capital account of $1,950,000 as of December 31, 1975, or $58,500 plus 10% interest on this amount from January 1, 1976, until May 31, 1976, less a $17,000 note and 5 months interest owed by appellant to the partnership and less $7,706.53 owed by appellant to the partnership store account. Appellant refused to accept the check. That sum has, to date, been retained by the partnership as part of the partnership capital and carried on the books as a credit due appellant and a partnership liability. Appellant has had no active duties in the partnership affairs since May 31, 1976.

About a month thereafter, appellant filed a petition seeking an accounting of the partnership affairs, alleging that he had been wrongfully excluded. This petition was later amended to seek judicial dissolution and liquidation of the partnership assets. Appellees filed a counter-complaint seeking judicial recognition of the dissolution assertedly effected by appellee R.A. Pickens' notification to appellant on May 31, 1976, of his election to dissolve the partnership, which was a partnership at will. The counter-complaint also alleged the existence of an oral agreement for the purchase and termination of an interest in the partnership. The purchase of an interest in the partnership was based upon book value. Upon termination or dissolution, the value of the outgoing partner's interest was based upon the book value of such an interest as of December 31 of the year preceding such dissolution, plus 10% interest per annum from December 31 of that year to the date of dissolution. As previously indicated, appellees computed the amount due appellant at his partnership termination to be $35,-805.97, after reduction of appellant's indebtedness to the partnership.

The trial court found that a partnership existed between the parties; that appellant purchased his 3% interest at book value; that Pickens, as managing partner, had the contractual right to terminate appellant's interest at will; that under the terms of the agreement appellant's contractual interest at termination was 3% of the book value of the partnership, or $58,500 as of December 31, 1975; that termination occurred on May 31, 1976, and the 10% interest on that amount, as alleged in the counter-complaint, was not included within the proved contractual terms relating to the calculation of appellant's partnership interest at termination; that appellant's capital and services were used by the partnership until the date of his termination; and therefore he was entitled to $13,843.48 which was $\frac{5}{12}$ths of his 3% interest of the net profit for 1976, plus interest. These amounts were to be reduced by appellant's indebtedness to the partnership on his note and store account which were also ordered to bear interest.

Appellant contends that the court erred in not finding that he was entitled to a full share of the profits of the partnership so long as the partnership retained and used his capital contribution, the court erred in finding that R.A. Pickens had a contractual right to terminate appellant's partnership interest and erred in not ordering a termination and winding up of the partnership affairs. As we understand the thrust of appellant's argument, the Uniform Partnership Act is applicable here and therefore appellant has the right to a forced sale and liquidation of the partnership assets and his proper share of the net proceeds.

We first emphasize:

> The business association that is known in the law as a partnership is not one that can be defined with precision. To the contrary, a partnership is a contractual relationship that may vary, in form and substance, in an almost infinite variety of ways.

Zajac v. Harris, 241 Ark. 737, 410 S.W.2d 593 (1967). Further the Uniform Partnership Act provides that the rights and duties of parties are "subject to any agreement between" the partners. Ark.Stat.Ann. § 65–118 (Repl. 1966). The Act also contains a provision that "settling accounts" between partners after a dissolution shall be "subject to any agreement. . . ." § 65–140. The partners here could agree, as the court found, that Pickens had exclusive control over the terms of admission and expulsion of the partners.

Pickens testified that appellant, upon becoming a partner, understood that he purchased his interest at book value. Upon leaving, he would be paid the book value and his status as a partner was dependent upon Pickens' willingness for him to continue in that status. It appears undisputed that at the conclusion of each year Pickens conferred with each partner about their individual equity or earnings in the profit sharing venture.

Numerous past and present partners testified. According to them the understanding was they bought their interest in the partnership at book value. The length of their membership was at the will and pleasure of Pickens, the general manager, and upon leaving the company they would be paid at book value. Although appellant denies the oral agreement asserted by Pickens, he admits he acquired his interest at book value based upon a loan of the purchase funds to him by the company as evidenced by a note. Appellant is a college graduate with a business degree. It appears his duties as an employee with the partnership consisted of general office work and bookkeeping a short time before acquisition of his interests and during the 8½ years he was a partner. He was familiar with transactions at book value with respect to incoming and outgoing partners. As indicated, upon termination he refused a tender of payment of his interest after a settlement of accounts.

Here the chancellor had the advantage of seeing and hearing the witnesses and at the same time studying the exhibits to their testimony. We do not reverse a chancellor's finding unless it is against the preponderance of the evidence. Here the chancellor's finding is clearly supported by the preponderance of the evidence. Therefore, in view of the agreement, the Uniform Partnership Act is not applicable and consequently appellant cannot force a liquidation and sale of the appellee partnership.

Affirmed.

ANALYSIS AND PLANNING

1. On your view of the facts, was the plaintiff, Frank, a partner or an employee?

2. UPA § 9 provides in part, "(1) Every partner is an agent of the partnership for the purpose of its business, and the act of every partner, including the execution in the partnership name of any instrument, for apparently carrying on in the usual way the business of the partnership of which he is a member binds the partnership, unless the partner so acting has in fact no authority to act for the partnership in the particular matter, and the person with whom he is dealing has knowledge of the fact that he has no authority." Suppose that you had been R.A. Pickens's lawyer and he had asked you whether he should be concerned about people like Frank incurring obligations on behalf of the partnership. What would your response have been?

3. To what extent was Frank entitled to share in increases in the total value of the farming business of the partnership?

4. Could the relationship of Frank to the other people involved in the business have been cast in terms of employment, rather than partnership, without changing the basic terms of the economic arrangement?

5. The court states that "there were 22 partners." The rule of partnership control, in the absence of an agreement to the contrary, is that

each partner has one vote. Assume that there was no provision in the partnership agreement assuring Pickens of his position as managing partner. Frank and eleven other minor partners could have formed a coalition, demanded a meeting of the partners, and voted to fire R.A. Pickens as manager and replace him with Frank. What power did Pickens have that would have made such a plan futile? What does this tell you about partnership control, legal and de facto, in this case? In a law firm?

6. "Book value" is an amount on the books of the firm, reflecting the original cost of assets, less depreciation (an allowance for decline in value of an asset by virtue of the passage of time and wear and tear), plus profits that have not been distributed to the partners. What are the advantages and disadvantages to Frank in the use of book value to determine the amount of his buy-out entitlement, as opposed to, say, appraised value? What other methods of setting the amount might be worth considering? What are their advantages and disadvantages?

Remitted then, as we are, to the documents themselves, we refer to circumstances surrounding their execution only so far as is necessary to make them intelligible. And we are to remember that although the intention of the parties to avoid liability as partners is clear; although in language precise and definite they deny any design to then join the firm of K.N. & K.; although they say their interests in profits should be construed merely as a measure of compensation for loans, not an interest in profits as such; although they provide that they shall not be liable for any losses or treated as partners, the question still remains whether in fact they agree to so associate themselves with the firm as to "carry on as co-owners a business for profit."

In the spring of 1921 the firm of K.N. & K. found itself in financial difficulties. John R. Hall was one of the partners. He was a friend of Mr. Peyton. From him he obtained the loan of almost $500,000 of Liberty bonds, which K.N. & K. might use as collateral to secure bank advances. This, however, was not sufficient. The firm and its members had engaged in unwise speculations, and it was deeply involved. Mr. Hall was also intimately acquainted with George W. Perkins, Jr., and with Edward W. Freeman. He also knew Mrs. Peyton and Mrs. Perkins and Mrs. Freeman. All were anxious to help him. He therefore, representing K.N. & K., entered into negotiations with them. While they were pending a proposition was made that Mr. Peyton, Mr. Perkins, and Mr. Freeman, or some of them, should become partners. It met a decided refusal. Finally an agreement was reached. It is expressed in three documents, executed on the same day, all a part of the one transaction. They were drawn with care and are unambiguous. We shall refer to them as "the agreement," "the indenture," and "the option."

We have no doubt as to their general purpose. The respondents [Peyton, Perkins, and Freeman] were to loan K.N. & K. $2,500,000 worth of liquid securities, which were to be returned to them on or before April 15, 1923. The firm might hypothecate them to secure loans totaling $2,000,000, using the proceeds as its business necessities required. To insure respondents against loss K.N. & K. were to turn over to them a large number of their own securities which may have been valuable, but which were of so speculative a nature that they could not be used as collateral for bank loans. In compensation for the loan the respondents were to receive 40 per cent. of the profits of the firm until the return was made, not exceeding, however, $500,000, and not less than $100,000. Merely because the transaction involved the transfer of securities and not of cash does not prevent its being a loan . . .. The respondents also were given an option to join the firm if they, or any of them, expressed a desire to do so before June 4, 1923.

Many other detailed agreements are contained in the papers. Are they such as may be properly inserted to protect the lenders? Or do they go further? Whatever their purpose, did they in truth associate the respondents with the firm so that they and it together thereafter carried on as co-owners a business for profit? The answer depends upon an analysis of these various provisions.

As representing the lenders, Mr. Peyton and Mr. Freeman are called "trustees." The loaned securities when used as collateral are not to be mingled with other securities of K.N. & K., and the trustees at all times are to be kept informed of all transactions affecting them. To them shall be paid all dividends and income accruing therefrom. They may also substitute for any of the securities loaned securities of equal value. With their consent the firm may sell any of its securities held by the respondents, the proceeds to go, however, to the trustees. In other similar ways the trustees may deal with these same securities, but the securities loaned shall always be sufficient in value to permit of their hypothecation for $2,000,000. If they rise in price, the excess may be withdrawn by the defendants. If they fall, they shall make good the deficiency.

So far, there is no hint that the transaction is not a loan of securities with a provision for compensation. Later a somewhat closer connection with the firm appears. Until the securities are returned, the directing management of the firm is to be in the hands of John R. Hall, and his life is to be insured for $1,000,000, and the policies are to be assigned as further collateral security to the trustees. These requirements are not unnatural. Hall was the one known and trusted by the defendants. Their acquaintance with the other members of the firm was of the slightest. These others had brought an old and established business to the verge of bankruptcy. As the respondents knew, they also had engaged in unsafe speculation. The respondents were about to loan $2,500,000 of good securities. As collateral they were to receive others of problematical value. What they required seems but ordinary caution. Nor does it imply an association in the business.

The trustees are to be kept advised as to the conduct of the business and consulted as to important matters. They may inspect the firm books and are entitled to any information they think important. Finally, they may veto any business they think highly speculative or injurious. Again we hold this but a proper precaution to safeguard the loan. The trustees may not initiate any transaction as a partner may do. They may not bind the firm by any action of their own. Under the circumstances the safety of the loan depended upon the business success of K.N. & K. This success was likely to be compromised by the inclination of its members to engage in speculation. No longer, if the respondents were to be protected, should it be allowed. The trustees therefore might prohibit it, and that their prohibition might be effective, information was to be furnished them. Not dissimilar agreements have been held proper to guard the interests of the lender.

As further security each member of K.N. & K. is to assign to the trustees their interest in the firm. No loan by the firm to any member is permitted and the amount each may draw is fixed. No other distribution of profits is to be made. So that realized profits may be calculated the existing capital is stated to be $700,000, and profits are to be realized as promptly as good business practice will permit. In case the trustees think this is not done, the question is left to them and to Mr. Hall, and if they differ then to an arbitrator. There is no obligation that the firm shall continue the business. It may dissolve at any time. Again we conclude there is nothing here not properly adapted to secure the interest of the respondents as lenders. If their compensation is dependent on a percentage of the profits, still provision must be made to define what these profits shall be.

The "indenture" is substantially a mortgage of the collateral delivered by K.N. & K. to the trustees to secure the performance of the "agreement." It certainly does not strengthen the claim that the respondents were partners.

Finally we have the "option." It permits the respondents, or any of them, or their assignees or nominees to enter the firm at a later date if they desire to do so by buying 50 per cent. or less of the interests therein of all or any of the members at a stated price. Or a corporation may, if the respondents and the members agree, be formed in place of the firm. Meanwhile, apparently with the design of protecting the firm business against improper or ill-judged action which might render the option valueless, each member of the firm is to place his resignation in the hands of Mr. Hall. If at any time he and the trustees agree that such resignation should be accepted, that member shall then retire, receiving the value of his interest calculated as of the date of such retirement.

This last provision is somewhat unusual, yet it is not enough in itself to show that on June 4, 1921, a present partnership was created, nor taking these various papers as a whole do we reach such a result. It is quite true that even if one or two or three like provisions contained in such a contract do not require this conclusion, yet it is also true that when taken together a point may come where stipulations immaterial separately cover so wide a field that we should hold a partnership exists. As in other branches of the law, a question of degree is often the determining factor. Here that point has not been reached. . . .

The judgment appealed from should be affirmed, with costs.

■ CARDOZO, C.J., and POUND, CRANE, LEHMAN, KELLOGG, and O'BRIEN, JJ., concur.

Judgment affirmed, etc.

NOTES

1. According to the lower court opinion, K.N. & K. was a large, prominent firm, with substantial foreign banking operations, 300 employees, and total transactions of over $100 million a year. 219 A.D. 297, 220 N.Y.S. 29. Hall had "been indebted to Peyton in [sic] a substantial sum of money since 1913" and Peyton had helped Hall in various business matters. The reason for the loan of securities rather than cash was to avoid

the usury laws. (If Peyton, Perkins, and Freeman had not had ready access to cash, presumably they could have used their securities as collateral for a bank loan of cash, which they could then have loaned to K.N. & K.) The losses that gave rise to the litigation resulting in the present decision arose from speculative investments in foreign exchange, which were prohibited by the agreement between K.N. & K. and Perkins and the other investors. Though Hall was not directly involved in making these investments, he knew about them and apparently did not tell his friends Peyton, Perkins, and Freeman.

2. There is an important economic principle relating to risk that may have been at play in the situation described in Martin v. Peyton. Crudely stated, the principle is that you should not allow other people to gamble with your money for their own profit. At the very least, the facts of the case offer a nice opportunity for describing that principle. Suppose that K.N. & K. has suffered losses and has reached a point where its assets have a value of $12 million, including $1 million in a bank account, and its liabilities are $20 million. After about two more weeks of normal operations K.N. & K. will not be able to pay its bills and its creditors will shut it down. K.N. & K. has an opportunity to invest $1 million in a foreign exchange transaction. The expectation is that if the transaction turns out as the K.N. & K. partners hope, the payoff will be $20 million, but the probability of that happening is only one in forty. If the transaction does not turn out as hoped, the entire $1 million will be lost. A one in forty chance of a return of $20 million is worth only $500,000, so the investment appears to be a bad one. But suppose it is K.N. & K.'s last chance. If the investment pays off what is the financial effect for the partners of K.N. & K.? If it does not pay off, what do they lose? If you think this is a rare or trivial phenomenon, consider the story of the billions of dollars of losses in the savings and loan industry in recent years—a classic case of people (managers of insured savings and loan institutions) gambling with someone else's money (mostly, as it turns out, the taxpayers').

3. The risk of liability for Peyton, Perkins, and Freeman would have been avoided if K.N. & K. had been organized as a corporation. Under that form of organization, the equity investors (the counterparts of partners) enjoy "limited liability"—that is, they are not personally liable for the debts of the firm and therefore stand to lose only the amount they have invested in it. Thus, even if the purported lenders had been treated as shareholders, they would have been shielded from the personal liability that the creditors sought to enforce.

At the present time, another organizational alternative for K.N. & K. would be the Limited Liability Company (LLC), which is now available in almost all the states. In an LLC the investors are called "members." Like the traditional corporation, the LLC provides a liability shield for its members. It allows somewhat more flexibility than the corporation in developing rules for management and control. The LLC may be managed by all its members (as in a partnership) or by managers, who may or may not be members (as in a corporation). The LLC also offers advantageous tax treatment as compared with a corporation. A corporation pays tax on its profits as earned and the shareholders (the equity investors) pay a second tax when those profits are distributed to them. Investors in an LLC are taxed, like partners, only once on its profits, as those profits are earned. Moreover, the investors in an LLC can take account, on their individual tax returns, of any losses of the LLC as those losses are incurred; the losses are said to "pass through." A corporation's losses can be carried forward to offset any future profits but cannot be used by its shareholders. In addition, the LLC allows greater freedom than a corporation in allocating profit and loss for tax purposes.

The formation of an LLC, like the formation of a corporation, requires some paperwork and filings with a state agency. Some states impose fees and taxes (generally modest) on LLCs that are not imposed on partnerships.

Another recent development is the Limited Liability Partnership (LLP), which is now available in about half the states. Limited liability is achieved by filing a document with a state official. See, e.g., Del.Code Ann. tit. 6, § 1515 (1994); La.Rev.Stat.Ann. §§ 9:3431–35 (Supp.1994); Tex. Rev.Civ.Stat.Ann. Art. 6132b, § 15 (Supp.1995). These three statutes, like most of the others, provide limited liability only for partnership debts arising from negligence and similar misconduct (other than misconduct for which the partner is directly responsible), not for contractual obligations. (The Delaware law requires liability insurance, or segregated funds, of $1 million, id. § 1546, while the Texas law requires insurance or segregated funds of $100,000.) The provisions in Maryland, Minnesota, and New York provide protection for both contract and tort liabilities. Md.Code Ann., Corporations and Associations, § 9–307(c)(1) (1995); Minn.Stat.Ann. § 323.14, Subd. 2 (1995 Supp.); N.Y. Partnership Law § 26(b) (McKinney 1995 Supp.). The principal impetus for the enactment of the first LLP legislation, in Texas in 1991, was the concern of lawyers for malpractice liability, following the collapse of the savings and loan industry and the potentially devastating effect of the collapse of one such institution on a leading Dallas law firm. See Robert W. Hamilton, Registered Limited Liability Partnerships: Present at the Birth (Nearly), 66 U.Colo.L.Rev. 1065, 1069 (1995). Professor Hamilton notes that "more than 1,200 law firms, including virtually all of the state's largest firms, elected to become LLPs within one year after . . . enactment" of the Texas LLP legislation. Id. at 1065.

The LLP legislation raises a number of interesting questions. For example, why would a state require substantial insurance or segregated funds for an LLP when limited liability can be achieved by forming a corporation with minimal capital? Why should limited liability be available to partners, without incorporation, but not to sole proprietors? Would it be wise to dispense with the filing requirement and make limited liability the default rule?

ANALYSIS

1. What amount of loss were Peyton, Perkins, and Freeman (PPF) prepared to risk? Why were they willing to take a substantial risk? What is the moral of the story of their investment in K.N. & K.?

2. What were the various elements of return on their investment that PPF bargained for? What does their potential return tell you about the degree of risk that they believed they were accepting?

3. Given the degree of risk to which PPF were exposed, and given the fact that they did not want to be involved in running the business, what kinds of protections would you expect them to want? What protections did they in fact bargain for?

4. As stated above, K.N. & K. violated their agreement with PPF by speculating in foreign exchange and this produced the losses that led to K.N. & K.'s downfall. Why do you suppose PPF did not enforce the agreement and prevent the speculation? What was the value of the prohibition?

5. Apparently PPF relied heavily (and, as it turned out, foolishly) on their friend Hall to protect their interests. Yet the court concludes that Hall was not their agent for the purpose of exercising control over the K.N. & K. operations. Why?

6. Can the outcome in this case be reconciled with the outcome in the *Cargill* case (supra page 23)?

PLANNING

The court did not reach its decision in the case without difficulty. It seems fair to say that PPF had a close call with financial disaster. What changes in the agreement might have been made to strengthen their legal position (that is, their claim that they were not partners) without depriving them of important protections?

PROBLEM

It is your first day of law school. You are sitting in Professor Kingsfield's Contracts class. Your reading assignment for the day began: "Assumpsit against a surgeon for breach of an alleged warranty of the success of an operation." The case then proceeded to detail the travails of one George Hawkins, who when eleven years old had been scarred on his right hand by an electrical burn. Once he reached 18, he had turned to a Dr. Edward McGee who had promised him: "I will guarantee to make the hand a hundred percent perfect hand or a hundred percent good hand." Unfortunately, McGee grafted skin from Hawkins' chest. After the operation Hawkins found himself with a hand that could make only greatly restricted movements and was covered by a dense clump of hair.

You read on, and find that the court holds McGee liable for "the difference between the value to him of a perfect hand or a good hand . . . and the value of his hand in its present condition. . . ."

Kingsfield has called your name. You have heard what he does to students who try to pass, and have no intention of passing. He asks you about the contract law issues, but you have not a clue. Instead, you ask yourself, what kind of idiot promises his patients 100 percent perfect results? Was McGee part of a group practice? How dumb would the other doctors have had to be to let a man like McGee join their group? Surely they knew he was a wild card. Were they insured? If he goes broke and the group has no assets, are they personally liable for the judgment? Why is the recovery for contract damages rather than tort damages?

Rather than answer Kingsfield, you ask him how McGee and his colleagues organized their practice. Kingsfield asks, with a sneer on his face, how that can possibly be relevant. You tell him that it is reasonable to suppose that Dr. McGee and his partners, if they were setting up their practice today, would have tried to obtain limited liability.

Kingsfield, outraged by your audacity and content with the thought that he can still manage to humiliate you, invites you to tell the class what the various organizational possibilities might be, taking account not only of liability but also of tax consequences and control. You stutter. You know he is winding up to tell you to call your mother and tell her you will never be a lawyer. Rather than reenact an opening scene in a bad movie, you decide you must respond. What do you say?

Kaufman–Brown Potato Co. v. Long

182 F.2d 594 (9th Cir.1950).

[This is a decision in a bankruptcy proceeding. Horton and Althouse were partners in the business of growing and of distributing potatoes, under the names of Gerry Horton Company and Gerry Horton Farms. They entered into an agreement with Kaufman and Brown, who were partners in the business of produce distribution, under the name of Kaufman–Brown Potato Co. Horton and Althouse became bankrupt and Kaufman–Brown filed a claim in the bankruptcy proceeding. The rights of Kaufman–Brown turned on whether it was a creditor of Horton and Althouse or a partner of theirs. The lower court ruled against Kaufman–Brown and this is the decision on its appeal.]

Appellants rely mainly upon these arguments: The dealings between Gerry Horton, J.D. Althouse, Charles H. Kaufman, and Albert H. Brown could not constitute [as is claimed they must under California law to constitute a partnership] an association for the purpose of *jointly* carrying on a business together. The word "partner" used twice in each of the written agreements was inadvertent and is not conclusive. The written contracts or agreements themselves in certain particulars and the conduct of the parties under such written agreements negative both any intent to form a partnership or that a partnership in fact was formed or existed.

It appears from the evidence that Horton and Althouse, prior to any association with Kaufman–Brown Potato Company, were doing business in partnership both as Gerry Horton Company and Gerry Horton Farms, under the former name as farm produce distributors and under the latter name as producers. In 1944 they held two parcels of California farm land under lease. As to each parcel separately Horton and Althouse as Gerry Horton Farms contracted in writing with Kaufman and Brown doing business as Kaufman–Brown Potato Company, who were distributors, relative to planting, raising, and harvesting potatoes on such land.

It was agreed in each contract that Kaufman and Brown would purchase from Horton and Althouse for a certain amount an undivided interest [50% as to one parcel; 40% as to the other parcel] in all potato crops to be planted, raised and harvested upon such leased land during the year 1944. Horton and Althouse agreed to pay all costs and expenses of planting and raising in excess of the amount above mentioned to be paid in by Kaufman and Brown for the above undivided interests. The net proceeds after repayment to Kaufman and Brown of the amount they paid in and of any amounts paid by Horton and Althouse in addition thereto for the expenses of planting and raising were to be divided "between the partners" [quoting from such contracts] in like manner. The over-all losses sustained in the venture were to be borne by the parties in their interest ratio. It was also provided that Horton and Althouse would keep full and accurate accounts of the enterprise at their place of business. The written contracts provided for an option to Kaufman and Brown Potato Company to purchase the crop raised and harvested on each parcel of land for a price equal to the prevailing market price but if there were no prevailing market price upon harvest Kaufman and Brown agreed to handle all the potatoes as agents for Horton and Althouse for a stated commission "for said services rendered on behalf of the partners hereto" and pay to Horton and Althouse all money received from the sale thereof "subject to accounting and distribution as hereinbefore set forth." [Quotations are from each contract.] In the event that Kaufman and Brown exercised their option to purchase, Horton and Althouse could add to the purchase price any markups allowed by O.P.A. regulations but the total amount of such markups [was to] be divided between the parties in the ratio of their interests. Horton and Althouse were to furnish all the necessary farming equipment. The contracts also provided for the execution of a crop mortgage as security for faithful performance by Horton and Althouse and for a promissory note also to be executed in an amount which as above mentioned Kaufman and Brown were to pay in. After each contract had been fully complied with, the mortgage and note were to be surrendered and cancelled. It was declared that the mortgage and note were executed solely as security for performance and that Horton and Althouse were not to be held liable for any losses resulting from causes beyond their control. The contracts did not provide for a firm bank account nor for a firm name of the business to be conducted under the provisions of the contracts. Both agreements were prepared by Horton and Althouse's attorney pursuant to Horton's instructions.

As to their farming activities, during the year 1944 Horton and Althouse devoted themselves solely to operations under and in conformity with the written agreements. Potatoes were farmed, harvested and sold and Kaufman–Brown Potato Company, exercising its option, purchased some and paid to Horton and Althouse the prevailing market price therefor. In the aggregate [as to both leases] Kaufman and Brown in fact advanced to Horton and Althouse some $43,000 and had been repaid $20,000. The latter had issued bank checks for the balance of such advances not repaid but they were not honored for lack of sufficient funds. The total of such dishonored checks represents the amount of the claim asserted by Kaufman and Brown in the instant involuntary petition in bankruptcy. It was testified that such checks were accepted in payment of the mortgages and notes executed by Horton and Althouse pursuant to each contract. Appellants assert their claim here as unsecured.

No assignments of the leases held by Horton and Althouse were ever made to the purported partnership with Kaufman–Brown Potato Company. No bank account was maintained separate from those kept in the names of each of the partnerships of which Horton and Althouse were the sole members. There was no evidence that any of the creditors of the 1944 farming enterprise were told or knew that Kaufman–Brown Potato Company was a partner in the farming of the leased ground or that any of them knew anything about Kaufman–Brown's association or interest.

Section 2400 of the California Civil Code [now § 15006 of the California Corporations Code] defines a partnership in the language of the Uniform Partnership Act as an "association of two or more persons to carry on as co-owners a business for profit." Rules for determining the existence of a partnership are stated in section 2401 of the California Civil Code [now section 15007 of the California Corporations Code].[4]

A partnership may be formed for a single venture. . . . Whether or not a partnership relationship exists is determinable by the intent of the

---

4. California Civil Code section 2401 [California Corporations Code section 15007] reads as follows:

"In determining whether a partnership exists, these rules shall apply:

"(1) Except as provided by Section (2410) persons who are not partners as to each other are not partners as to third persons.

"(2) Joint tenancy, tenancy in common, tenancy by the entireties, joint property, common property, or part ownership does not of itself establish a partnership, whether such co-owners do or do not share any profits made by the use of the property.

"(3) The sharing of gross returns does not of itself establish a partnership, whether or not the persons sharing them have a joint or common right or interest in any property from which the returns are derived.

"(4) The receipt by a person of a share of the profits of a business is prima facie evidence that he is a partner in the business, but no such inference shall be drawn if such profits were received in payment:

"(a) As a debt by installments or otherwise.

"(b) As wages of an employee or rent to a landlord.

"(c) As an annuity to a widow or representative of a deceased partner.

"(d) As interest on a loan, though the amount of payment vary with the profits of the business.

"(e) As the consideration for the sale of a goodwill of a business or other property by installments or otherwise."

parties to do things which constitute a partnership.   . . . It is immaterial that the parties deign not to call their relationship, or believe it not to be, a partnership, especially where as here the rights of third persons are involved. It is true that a mere agreement to share profits and losses does not make a partnership but both the sharing of profits and losses are usual in partnership agreements and practices.

It is plain that the contracts in question were drawn with some of the usual covenants and conditions both of a straight financing contract with options and of a partnership agreement. Appellants point especially to the provisions for crop mortgages as supporting the former relation but their argument is offset by the proviso that such were to be security only for performance on the part of Horton and Althouse and that Horton and Althouse would not be liable for any losses occasioned by causes beyond their control. The non-mention of capital contribution of each of the parties is stressed, but all partners need not contribute capital in the strict sense of the word; some may invest their labor and skill.   . . . These contracts provide that Kaufman and Brown were to put up so much money for initial expense but note that all of it was to be returned out of the product as expense before division of sales returns. Horton and Althouse were to devote themselves to the farming aspect using their own equipment, and Kaufman and Brown were to use their sales organization and experience if necessary to effect distribution of the crop. However, the provision that the amounts paid in by Kaufman and Brown were to be repaid before division of sales returns is consistent with a partnership relationship.   . . . There is a provision in each of the contracts that in certain circumstances Kaufman and Brown would act as agents for Horton and Althouse to dispose of the potatoes upon harvest through Chicago markets for a stated commission and would pay to Horton and Althouse money obtained from sales. This provision appears to be more unusual in a partnership contract than inconsistent with one, for Horton and Althouse were to keep the accounts and all such provisions were stated to be "subject to accounting and distribution as hereinbefore set forth." The use of the word "partner" in each agreement could have been but a handy word to include personnel without naming them but the fact-finder, on analyzing the complicated contracts, would not be justified in rejecting its possible bearing on the issue entirely. The contracts also provide that Horton and Althouse keep the "books of account and all other records" of the enterprise at their place of business and that each of the partners hereto "shall at all times have access to and may inspect and copy any of them." The latter quoted language is taken verbatim from California Civil Code section 2413 [California Corporations Code section 15019], which relates to "partnership books".

It is evident that Kaufman and Brown advanced more than was required by the contracts. This fact could be accounted for by their desire to protect their interests in either relation. Further, there is testimony to the effect that both Messrs. Kaufman and Brown came to California and made recommendations relative to operations under the contracts. Of course, their interest in the contracts could have justified their personal presence on the ground, either as partners or joint venturers, but it is consistent with partnership interest.

We are of the opinion that the record contains the essentials of a partnership and also substantial proof that such was the intention at least of Horton and Althouse, the authors of the contracts. Upon a review of the record as a whole we do not find that a mistake has been made.   . . .

FACTUAL AND LEGAL ANALYSIS

1.   What seem to have been the motivations of Kaufman–Brown in entering into the arrangement with Horton and Althouse? How did Kaufman and Brown expect to gain?

2.   Why did not Kaufman and Brown simply hire Horton to run the farm, as an employee of Kaufman–Brown?

3.   What degree of control did Kaufman–Brown have? Was this consistent with the role of a lender?

4.   How can this case be reconciled with Martin v. Peyton, supra page 83?

PLANNING

What should Kaufman–Brown have done to protect its rights as a creditor?

Section 3. Partnership by Estoppel

Young v. Jones

816 F.Supp. 1070 (D.S.C.1992).

. . . Plaintiffs are investors from Texas who deposited over a half-million dollars in a South Carolina bank and the funds have disappeared.

PW–Bahamas [Price Waterhouse, Chartered Accountants, a Bahamian partnership] issued an unqualified audit letter regarding the financial statement of Swiss American Fidelity and Insurance Guaranty (SAFIG). Plaintiffs aver that on the basis of that financial statement, they deposited $550,000.00 in a South Carolina bank. Other defendants, not involved in the motions herein, allegedly sent the money from the South Carolina Bank to SAFIG. The financial statement of SAFIG was falsified. The plaintiffs' money and its investment potential has been lost to the plaintiffs and it is for these losses that the plaintiffs seek to recover damages.

. . .

The letterhead [used for the SAFIG audit] identified the Bahamian accounting firm only as "Price Waterhouse." The audit letter also bore a Price Waterhouse trademark and was signed "Price Waterhouse."

Plaintiffs assert that it was foreseeable to the accounting firm that issued the letter that third-parties would rely upon the financial statement, the subject of the audit letter. According to the plaintiffs, the stamp of approval created by Price Waterhouse's audit letter of SAFIG's financial statement lent credence to the defrauders' claims so that plaintiffs were induced to invest to their detriment.

. . .

Plaintiffs assert that PW–Bahamas and PW–US [the Price Waterhouse partnership in the United States] operate as a partnership, i.e., constitute an association of persons to carry on, as owners, business for profit. In the alternative, plaintiffs contend that if the two associations are not actually operating as partners they are operating as partners by estoppel.

Defendants PW–US and PW–Bahamas flatly deny that a partnership exists between the two entities and have supplied, under seal, copies of relevant documents executed which establish that the two entities are separately organized. Counsel for plaintiffs admits that he has found nothing which establishes that the two entities are partners in fact. The evidence presented wholly belies plaintiffs' claims that PW–Bahamas and PW–US are operating as a partnership in fact. Thus, the court finds that there is no partnership, in fact, between PW–Bahamas and PW–US.

. . . [T]he argument for estoppel seems to be that if the two partnerships are partners by estoppel then PW–US can be held liable for the negligent acts of its partner PW–Bahamas, so the claim against PW–Bahamas operates as a claim against PW–US. . . .

As a general rule, persons who are not partners as to each other are not partners as to third persons. S.C.Code Ann. § 33–41–220 (Law. Co-op 1976) [U.P.A. § 7(1)]. However, a person who represents himself, or permits another to represent him, to anyone as a partner in an existing partnership or with others not actual partners, is liable to any such person to whom such a representation is made who has, on the faith of the representation, given credit to the actual or apparent partnership. S.C.Code Ann. § 33–41–380(1) [U.P.A. § 16(1)]. . . .

Generally, partners are jointly and severally liable for everything chargeable to the partnership. . . . In South Carolina, a partnership is an entity separate and distinct from the individual partners who compose it. . . . Therefore, plaintiffs' argument is that if the court would find that PW–Bahamas and PW–US are partners by estoppel, PW–US would be jointly and severally liable with PW–Bahamas for everything chargeable to the partnership of the two firms. Moreover, if the two partnerships are partners by estoppel, the individual partners of PW–US would then be jointly and severally liable for the negligent acts of the PW–Bahamas partnership.

Plaintiffs maintain that Price Waterhouse holds itself out to be a partnership with offices around the world. According to the plaintiffs, the U.S. affiliate makes no distinction in its advertising between itself and entities situated in foreign jurisdictions. The foreign affiliates are permitted to use the Price Waterhouse name and trademark. Plaintiffs urge the conclusion of partnership by estoppel from the combination of facts that Price Waterhouse promotes its image as an organization affiliated with other Price Waterhouse offices around the world and that it is common knowledge that the accounting firm of Price Waterhouse operates as a partnership.

Plaintiffs offer for illustration that PW–Bahamas and PW–US hold themselves out to be partners with one another, a Price Waterhouse brochure, picked up by plaintiffs' counsel at a litigation services seminar, that describes Price Waterhouse as one of the "world's largest and most respected professional organizations." The brochure states: "[O]ver 28,-000 Price Waterhouse professionals in 400 offices throughout the world can be called upon to provide support for your reorganization and litigation efforts." Plaintiffs assert that assurances like that contained in the brochure cast Price Waterhouse as an established international accounting firm and that the image, promoted by PW–US, is designed to gain public confidence in the firm's stability and expertise.

However, the plaintiffs do not contend that the brochure submitted was seen or relied on by them in making the decision to invest. In addition, plaintiffs point to nothing in the brochure that asserts that the affiliated entities of Price Waterhouse are liable for the acts of another, or that any of the affiliates operate within a single partnership.

To bolster their argument, Plaintiffs sought to discover certain documents filed in a 1980 suit, entitled Cross v. Price Waterhouse, which resulted in a September 27, 1982, order. The court in *Cross* allegedly found that the U.S. partnership of Price Waterhouse was vicariously liable for negligence of the Bahamas firm of Price Waterhouse.

Defendant PW–US supplied copies of the relevant Cross documents which showed that the order of Judge Pratt was later vacated. Furthermore, PW–US informs the court that during the period in question in the *Cross* case, there were licensing agreements between the U.S. partnership and the Bahamian partnership for use of the name and trademark on which the decision was based. Such licensing agreements are no longer in existence.

PW–US points out that the South Carolina statute, which was cited by plaintiffs in support of their argument for partnership by estoppel, speaks only to the creation of liability to third-persons who, in reliance upon representations as to the existence of a partnership, "[give] credit" to that partnership. . . . There is no evidence, neither has there been an allegation, that credit was extended on the basis of any representation of a partnership existing between PW–Bahamas and the South Carolina members of the PW–US partnership. There is no evidence of any extension of credit to either PW–Bahamas or PW–US, by plaintiffs. Thus, the facts do not support a finding of liability for partners by estoppel under the statutory law of South Carolina.

Further, there is no evidence that plaintiffs relied on any act or statement by any PW–US partner which indicated the existence of a partnership with the Bahamian partnership. Finally, there is no evidence, nor is there a single allegation that any member of the U.S. partnership had anything to do with the audit letter complained of by plaintiffs, or any other act related to the investment transaction.

The court cannot find any evidence to support a finding of partners by estoppel. Therefore, the allegations of negligence against PW–Bahamas cannot serve to hold individual members of the PW–US partnership in the suit. . . .

ANALYSIS

1. Price Waterhouse is, and long has been, a leading accounting firm in the United States. Its name would be recognized by anyone with any knowledge of business or finance. How does the Bahamian firm become entitled to use the same name? Why would it want to use the name? Should the answers to these questions be relevant to the outcome of the case?

2. What is the difference in proof required for the two separate theories on which the plaintiff relied?

3. Might the plaintiff also have relied on an agency theory?

SECTION 4. THE FIDUCIARY OBLIGATIONS OF PARTNERS

Meinhard v. Salmon

249 N.Y. 458, 164 N.E. 545 (1928).

■ CARDOZO, CH.J.   On April 10, 1902, Louisa M. Gerry leased to the defendant Walter J. Salmon the premises known as the Hotel Bristol at the northwest corner of Forty-second street and Fifth avenue in the city of New York.   The lease was for a term of twenty years, commencing May 1, 1902, and ending April 30, 1922.   The lessee undertook to change the hotel building for use as shops and offices at a cost of $200,000.   Alterations and additions were to be accretions to the land.

Salmon, while in course of treaty with the lessor as to the execution of the lease, was in course of treaty with Meinhard, the plaintiff, for the necessary funds.   The result was a joint venture with terms embodied in a writing.   Meinhard was to pay to Salmon half of the moneys requisite to reconstruct, alter, manage and operate the property.   Salmon was to pay to Meinhard 40 per cent of the net profits for the first five years of the lease and 50 per cent for the years thereafter.   If there were losses, each party was to bear them equally.   Salmon, however, was to have sole power to "manage, lease, underlet and operate" the building.   There were to be certain pre-emptive rights for each in the contingency of death.

The two were coadventurers, subject to fiduciary duties akin to those of partners.   .   .   .   As to this we are all agreed.   The heavier weight of duty rested, however, upon Salmon.   He was a coadventurer with Meinhard, but he was manager as well.   During the early years of the enterprise, the building, reconstructed, was operated at a loss.   If the relation had then ended, Meinhard as well as Salmon would have carried a heavy burden.   Later the profits became large with the result that for each of the investors there came a rich return.   For each, the venture had its phases of fair weather and of foul.   The two were in it jointly, for better or for worse.

When the lease was near its end, Elbridge T. Gerry had become the owner of the reversion.   He owned much other property in the neighborhood, one lot adjoining the Bristol Building on Fifth avenue and four lots on Forty-second street.   He had a plan to lease the entire tract for a long term to someone who would destroy the buildings then existing, and put up another in their place.   In the latter part of 1921, he submitted such a project to several capitalists and dealers.   He was unable to carry it through with any of them.   Then, in January, 1922, with less than four months of the lease to run, he approached the defendant Salmon.   The result was a new lease to the Midpoint Realty Company, which is owned and controlled by Salmon, a lease covering the whole tract, and involving a huge outlay.   The term is to be twenty years, but successive covenants for renewal will extend it to a maximum of eighty years at the will of either party. The existing buildings may remain unchanged for seven years. They are then to be torn down, and a new building to cost $3,000,000 is to be placed upon the site. The rental, which under the Bristol lease was only $55,000, is to be from $350,000 to $475,000 for the properties so combined. Salmon personally guaranteed the performance by the lessee of the covenants of the new lease until such time as the new building had been completed and fully paid for.

The lease between Gerry and the Midpoint Realty Company was signed and delivered on January 25, 1922. Salmon had not told Meinhard anything about it. Whatever his motive may have been, he had kept the negotiations to himself. Meinhard was not informed even of the bare existence of a project. The first that he knew of it was in February when the lease was an accomplished fact. He then made demand on the defendants that the lease be held in trust as an asset of the venture, making offer upon the trial to share the personal obligations incidental to the guaranty. The demand was followed by refusal, and later by this suit. A referee gave judgment for the plaintiff, limiting the plaintiff's interest in the lease, however, to 25 per cent. The limitation was on the theory that the plaintiff's equity was to be restricted to one-half of so much of the value of the lease as was contributed or represented by the occupation of the Bristol site. Upon cross-appeals to the Appellate Division, the judgment was modified so as to enlarge the equitable interest to one-half of the whole lease. With this enlargement of plaintiff's interest, there went, of course, a corresponding enlargement of his attendant obligations. The case is now here on an appeal by the defendants.

Joint adventurers, like copartners, owe to one another, while the enterprise continues, the duty of the finest loyalty. Many forms of conduct permissible in a workaday world for those acting at arm's length, are forbidden to those bound by fiduciary ties. A trustee is held to something stricter than the morals of the market place. Not honesty alone, but the punctilio of an honor the most sensitive, is then the standard of behavior. As to this there has developed a tradition that is unbending and inveterate. Uncompromising rigidity has been the attitude of courts of equity when petitioned to undermine the rule of undivided loyalty by the "disintegrating erosion" of particular exceptions (Wendt v. Fischer, 243 N.Y. 439, 444). Only thus has the level of conduct for fiduciaries been kept at a level higher than that trodden by the crowd. It will not consciously be lowered by any judgment of this court.

The owner of the reversion, Mr. Gerry, had vainly striven to find a tenant who would favor his ambitious scheme of demolition and construction. Baffled in the search, he turned to the defendant Salmon in possession of the Bristol, the keystone of the project. He figured to himself beyond a doubt that the man in possession would prove a likely customer. To the eye of an observer, Salmon held the lease as owner in his own right, for himself and no one else. In fact he held it as a fiduciary, for himself and another, sharers in a common venture. If this fact had been proclaimed, if the lease by its terms had run in favor of a partnership, Mr. Gerry, we may fairly assume, would have laid before the partners, and not merely before one of them, his plan of reconstruction.   The pre-emptive privilege, or, better, the pre-emptive opportunity, that was thus an incident of the enterprise, Salmon appropriated to himself in secrecy and silence. He might have warned Meinhard that the plan had been submitted, and that either would be free to compete for the award.   If he had done this, we do not need to say whether he would have been under a duty, if successful in the competition, to hold the lease so acquired for the benefit of a venture then about to end, and thus prolong by indirection its responsibilities and duties.   The trouble about his conduct is that he excluded his coadventurer from any chance to compete, from any chance to enjoy the opportunity for benefit that had come to him alone by virtue of his agency.   This chance, if nothing more, he was under a duty to concede.   The price of its denial is an extension of the trust at the option and for the benefit of the one whom he excluded.

No answer is it to say that the chance would have been of little value even if seasonably offered.   Such a calculus of probabilities is beyond the science of the chancery.   Salmon, the real estate operator, might have been preferred to Meinhard, the woolen merchant.   On the other hand, Meinhard might have offered better terms, or reinforced his offer by alliance with the wealth of others.   Perhaps he might even have persuaded the lessor to renew the Bristol lease alone, postponing for a time, in return for higher rentals, the improvement of adjoining lots.   We know that even under the lease as made the time for the enlargement of the building was delayed for seven years.   All these opportunities were cut away from him through another's intervention.   He knew that Salmon was the manager. As the time drew near for the expiration of the lease, he would naturally assume from silence, if from nothing else, that the lessor was willing to extend it for a term of years, or at least to let it stand as a lease from year to year.   Not impossibly the lessor would have done so, whatever his protestations of unwillingness, if Salmon had not given assent to a project more attractive.   At all events, notice of termination, even if not necessary, might seem, not unreasonably, to be something to be looked for, if the business was over and another tenant was to enter.   In the absence of such notice, the matter of an extension was one that would naturally be attended to by the manager of the enterprise, and not neglected altogether. At least, there was nothing in the situation to give warning to anyone that while the lease was still in being, there had come to the manager an offer of extension which he had locked within his breast to be utilized by himself alone.   The very fact that Salmon was in control with exclusive powers of direction charged him the more obviously with the duty of disclosure, since only through disclosure could opportunity be equalized.   If he might cut off renewal by a purchase for his own benefit when four months were to pass before the lease would have an end, he might do so with equal right while there remained as many years.   .   .   .   He might steal a march on his

Sec. 31.   Dissolution is caused: (1) Without violation of the agreement between the partners, .   .   .

(d) By the expulsion of any partner from the business bona fide in accordance with such a power conferred by the agreement between the partners.

Lawlis was expelled in accordance with the partnership agreement on February 23, 1987.   Thus, dissolution occurred on that date, not when he was notified of the proposal to expel him.   Lawlis has no claim for damages under IC 23–4–1–38(a)(2) [UPA § 38(a)(2)].

Lawlis next argues his expulsion contravened the agreement's implied duty of good faith and fair dealing because he was expelled for the "predatory purpose" of "increasing [the firm's] lawyer to partner ratio," as evidenced by the Finance Committee's proposal contained in its November 25, 1986, memo to partners regarding the 1986 year end meeting.   The partnership, however, posits Indiana does not recognize a duty of good faith and fair dealing in the context of an at will relationship.

It would be a simple matter to extrapolate the principle that an employer may terminate an at will employee for any cause or no cause without liability and apply it to the roughly comparable at will business relationship we find here, namely, the relationship existing between the partnership as an entity and its individual partners.   The Indiana Uniform Partnership Act, however, prevents us from so doing.

As noted above, when a partner is involuntarily expelled from a business, his expulsion must have been "bona fide" or in "good faith" for a dissolution to occur without violation of the partnership agreement.   IC 23–4–1–31(1)(d).   Said another way, if the power to involuntarily expel partners granted by a partnership agreement is exercised in bad faith or for a "predatory purpose," as Lawlis phrases it, the partnership agreement is violated, giving rise to an action for damages the affected partner has suffered as a result of his expulsion.

Lawlis finds a predatory purpose in the Finance Committee's November 25, 1986, memo to the partners by quoting portions of the memo's section "4.   FIVE YEAR PLAN, Firm Growth and Financial Goals."   He states:

> The five-year plan stated that, "The goal is to increase the top partners to at least $150,000 within the next two to three years.   .   .   .   In order to achieve the goal, we need to continue to improve our lawyer to partner ratio."

Appellant's Brief, at 17.   From that quote Lawlis reasons:

> Obviously, the easiest way for the Partnership to improve its lawyer to partner ratio, and thus increase the top partners' salaries, was to eliminate a senior partner.   Lawlis' position in the Partnership had been weakened by his absences due to illness.   The remaining partners knew this and pounced upon the opportunity to devour Lawlis's partnership interest.

Appellant's Brief, at 18.   The undisputed facts demonstrate the total inaccuracy of the final sentence quoted from appellant's brief.

From the time Lawlis's addiction to alcohol became known to the partnership's Finance Committee, it sought to assist and aid him through his medical crisis, even though he was taking substantial amounts of time off from his work to attempt cures in sanatoriums and had concealed the fact of his alcoholism from his partners for many months.   The firm permitted him to continue drawing on his partnership account even though he became increasingly unproductive in those years, as reflected by the continuing yearly drop in the number of units assigned him.   After signing the Program Outline in August, 1983, which structured his business life by providing among other things for the monitoring of his work product by the firm for a period of one year, recommending he attend Alcoholics Anonymous meetings, setting the specific times he would arrive at and remain in the office, and containing a provision "3.   .   .   .   there is no second chance," Lawlis "resumed the consumption of alcohol" in March, 1984.   Instead of expelling Lawlis at that time, the partnership acting through its Finance Committee continued to work with Lawlis by drawing up yet another set of conditions he was to meet to remain with the firm.   Clearly, these undisputed facts present no "predatory purpose" on the firm's part, nor does the Finance Committee's Five Year Plan when that proposal is read in full.

In essence, the proposal was to change the manner in which the firm valued its performance, and to obtain more production, i.e., billable hours from the attorney associates working for the firm in its various departments to achieve its goal of increased income to the partners.   There is no proposal that the number of partners be reduced to accomplish the Five Year Plan's stated goals, nor any reasonable inference arising therefrom to that effect.

Also, in the same memo .   .   ., the Finance Committee, instead of recommending Lawlis's immediate expulsion as a method of increasing its lawyer to partner ratio, proposed he remain a partner for a maximum total of an additional eight months to give him time to find other employment and retain insurance coverage while so engaged.   During that period it proposed he be permitted one participation unit upon which to draw up to $25,000 while he sought other employment.   Such proposal again clearly negates a partnership "predatory purpose" for Lawlis's expulsion.   Thus, there is no "genuine" issue as to whether the partnership acted in good faith when it expelled Lawlis because it can be foreclosed by reference to the undisputed facts here.   .   .   .

Lawlis next argues the firm's act of expelling him was constructively fraudulent because it constituted a breach of the fiduciary duty owed between partners which requires each to exercise good faith and fair dealing in partnership transactions and toward co-partners.   .   .   .   While we agree with Lawlis's bald statement of that concept, it has no application to the facts of this case.

The fiduciary relationship between partners to which the terms "bona fide" and "good faith" relate

> . . . concern the *business aspects or property of the partnership* and prohibit a partner, to wit a fiduciary, from taking any personal advantage touching those subjects. . . . Plaintiffs contend there was substantial evidence indicating the individual partner's breach of fiduciary duties they owed to plaintiffs as members of the bar. In view of our holding that the executive committee *had the right to expel plaintiffs without stating a reason or cause pursuant to the Partnership Agreement, there was no breach of any fiduciary duty.* (Emphasis supplied.)

Holman v. Coie (1974), 11 Wash.App. 195, 522 P.2d 515, 523–524. *Holman* concerned the expulsion of two partners from a law firm for no stated cause, but there was evidence a political speech by one of them had disgruntled the chief executive of one of the firm's major clients, the Boeing Corporation. Substantially the same consideration present in *Holman,* i.e., potential damage to partnership business, is present in this case.

. . .

All the parties involved in this litigation were legally competent and consenting adults well educated in the law who initially dealt at arm's length while negotiating the partnership agreements here involved. At the time the partners negotiated their contract, it is apparent they believed, as in *Holman,* the "guillotine method" of involuntary severance [that is, immediate termination by partnership vote without notice or hearing] would be in the best interests of the partnership. Their intent was to provide a simple, practical, and above all, a speedy method of separating a partner from the firm, if that ever became necessary for any reason. We find no fault with that approach to severance.

Where the remaining partners in a firm deem it necessary to expel a partner under a no cause expulsion clause in a partnership agreement freely negotiated and entered into, the expelling partners act in "good faith" regardless of motivation if that act does not cause a wrongful withholding of money or property legally due the expelled partner at the time he is expelled. . . . Clearly, the senior partners acted in the belief they had the legal right to do so under the partnership agreement, as they did. That they recommended a step-down severance over six months rather than the "guillotine" severance permitted them under the agreement demonstrates a compassionate, not greedy, purpose. If we were to hold otherwise, we would be engrafting a "for cause" requirement upon this agreement when such was not the intent of the parties at the time they entered into their agreement. Mere lapse of time, however long, does not alter that initial intent. Lawlis's constructive fraud argument is without merit.

. . .

Affirmed.

ANALYSIS

1.   What would the result have been if Lawlis had been expelled in July 1983 when his partners first discovered that he was suffering from alcoholism?

2.   What if he had been expelled in August 1984?

3.   Suppose you had been a client of the partnership. What approach would you have wanted it to take?

Bohatch v. Butler & Binion

977 S.W.2d 543 (Tex.1998).

█ ENOCH, JUSTICE, delivered the opinion of the court, in which GONZALEZ, OWEN, BAKER, and HANKINSON, JUSTICES, join.

Partnerships exist by the agreement of the partners; partners have no duty to remain partners. The issue in this case is whether we should create an exception to this rule by holding that a partnership has a duty not to expel a partner for reporting suspected overbilling by another partner. The trial court rendered judgment for Colette Bohatch on her breach of fiduciary duty claim against Butler & Binion and several of its partners (collectively, "the firm"). The court of appeals held that there was no evidence that the firm breached a fiduciary duty and reversed the trial court's tort judgment; however, the court of appeals found evidence of a breach of the partnership agreement and rendered judgment for Bohatch on this ground. We affirm the court of appeals' judgment.

I. FACTS

[The following statement of the facts is taken from the concurring opinion. It is more complete than the majority's statement, but otherwise the two statements are consistent with one another.]

John McDonald, an attorney licensed to practice in the District of Columbia and managing partner of the Washington, D.C. office of Butler & Binion, a Houston-based law firm, hired Colette Bohatch, also a D.C. lawyer, as a senior associate in January 1986. The firm's Washington office had only one other lawyer—Richard Powers, also a partner in the firm—and represented essentially one client—Pennzoil—before the Federal Energy Regulatory Commission. Bohatch, who had been deputy assistant general counsel of the FERC when she left to join Butler & Binion, worked for McDonald and Powers on Pennzoil matters.

In January 1989, Bohatch was made a partner in the firm on McDonald's recommendation, and as a partner she began receiving internal firm reports showing the number of hours each attorney worked, billed, and collected for. Reviewing these reports, Bohatch questioned how McDonald could bill as many hours as he reported, given her personal observations of his work habits. She and Powers discussed the subject on several occasions and even went so far as to look through McDonald's daily time diary surreptitiously and make a copy of it.

Bohatch never saw the bills to Pennzoil, which McDonald prepared and sent, so she did not know what fees Pennzoil was actually charged, or even what Butler & Binion's fee arrangement was with Pennzoil. Nevertheless, from monthly internal reports consistently showing that McDonald billed far more hours than she saw him working, Bohatch concluded that McDonald was overbilling Pennzoil. Convinced that she was obliged by the District of Columbia Code of Professional Responsibility governing lawyer conduct to report her concerns to the firm's management, she discussed them with Butler & Binion's managing partner, Louis Paine, on July 15, 1990. Paine assured her that he would look into the matter.

Bohatch told Powers of her meeting with Paine, and Powers told McDonald. The next day, McDonald informed Bohatch that Pennzoil was dissatisfied with her work. Bohatch feared that McDonald was retaliating against her, and in fact, from that point forward neither McDonald nor Powers assigned Bohatch any other work for Pennzoil. McDonald also insinuated to other partners that Bohatch had complained of him because Pennzoil found her work unacceptable, even though Bohatch had contacted Paine before she was aware of any criticism of her work.

Bohatch called Paine to tell him of McDonald's retaliation, and Paine assured her that he was still investigating. Paine reviewed the firm's bills to Pennzoil and found that in all but one instance fewer hours were billed than were shown on internal computer printouts as having been worked. However, since the printouts merely reflected the time reported by attorneys, and Bohatch was claiming that McDonald reported more time than he actually worked, Paine determined that Pennzoil must be told of Bohatch's assertions so that it could itself evaluate the amounts charged.

Robert Burns, a member of Butler & Binion's management committee, told John Chapman, the Pennzoil in-house attorney who dealt most directly with Butler & Binion's Washington office, of Bohatch's assertions and asked him to review the firm's bills. Chapman confirmed to Burns that he had complained to McDonald several months earlier about the quality of Bohatch's work, and Burns intimated that Bohatch's assertions might have been in response to such complaints. Chapman discussed the matter with his immediate superior and with Pennzoil's general counsel. The three of them reviewed Butler & Binion's bills for the preceding year and concluded that they were reasonable. After Chapman's superior discussed their conclusions with Pennzoil's president and chief executive officer, Chapman told Burns that Pennzoil was satisfied that the firm's bills were reasonable.

Bohatch expected that Paine would ask her for additional information, and when he did not do so, she wrote him that she believed McDonald had overcharged Pennzoil $20,000 to $25,000 per month for his work. In fact, in the preceding six months McDonald had billed Pennzoil on average less than $24,000 per month for his work, so that if Bohatch had been correct, McDonald should have billed Pennzoil almost nothing. On August 23, 1990, a few weeks after their initial meeting, Paine told Bohatch that he had found no evidence of overbilling. Since he did not see how Bohatch could continue to work for McDonald or Pennzoil under the circumstances, given the rifts her allegations had caused, Paine suggested that she begin to look for other employment.

For more than nine months Butler & Binion continued to pay Bohatch a partner's monthly draw of $7,500 and allowed her to keep her office and benefits while she sought other employment. So as not to impair her prospects, the firm did not immediately expel her as a partner, but it did not pay her any partnership distribution other than her draw. . . . Bohatch left to join another firm in September, and Butler & Binion formally expelled her as a partner in October.

Bohatch sued Butler & Binion, Paine, Burns, and McDonald for breach of the firm partnership agreement and breach of fiduciary duty. A jury found [for her on both counts].

. . . The court of appeals held that defendants' only duty to Bohatch was not to expel her in bad faith. " 'Bad faith' in this context," the court of appeals wrote, "means only that partners cannot expel another partner for self-gain." Finding no evidence that defendants expelled Bohatch for self-gain, the court concluded that Bohatch could not recover for breach of fiduciary duty. . . .

[The majority opinion follows.]

II. BREACH OF FIDUCIARY DUTY

We have long recognized as a matter of common law that "[t]he relationship between . . . partners . . . is fiduciary in character, and imposes upon all the participants the obligation of loyalty to the joint concern and of the utmost good faith, fairness, and honesty in their dealings with each other with respect to matters pertaining to the enterprise." Fitz–Gerald v. Hull, 150 Tex. 39, 237 S.W.2d 256, 264 (Tex.1951) (quotation omitted). Yet, partners have no obligation to remain partners; "at the heart of the partnership concept is the principle that partners may choose with whom they wish to be associated." Gelder Med. Group v. Webber, 41 N.Y.2d 680, 394 N.Y.S.2d 867, 363 N.E.2d 573, 577 (N.Y. 1977). . . .

[A]s provided by the partnership agreement, Bohatch's expulsion did not dissolve the partnership. . . . [T]he partnership agreement contemplates expulsion of a partner and prescribes procedures to be followed, but it does not specify or limit the grounds for expulsion. Thus, while Bohatch's claim that she was expelled in an improper way is governed by the partnership agreement, her claim that she was expelled for an improper reason is not. Therefore, we look to the common law to find the principles governing Bohatch's claim that the firm breached a duty when it expelled her.

Courts in other states have held that a partnership may expel a partner for purely business reasons. . . . Further, courts recognize that a law firm can expel a partner to protect relationships both within the firm and with clients. See Lawlis v. Kightlinger & Gray, 562 N.E.2d 435, 442 (Ind.App.1990) (holding that law firm did not breach fiduciary duty by expelling partner after partner's successful struggle against alcoholism because "if a partner's propensity toward alcohol has the potential to damage his firm's good will or reputation for astuteness in the practice of law, simple prudence dictates the exercise of corrective action . . . since the survival of the partnership itself potentially is at stake");. . . . Finally, many courts have held that a partnership can expel a partner without breaching any duty in order to resolve a "fundamental schism."

The fiduciary duty that partners owe one another does not encompass a duty to remain partners or else answer in tort damages. Nonetheless, Bohatch and several distinguished legal scholars urge this Court to recognize that public policy requires a limited duty to remain partners—i.e., a partnership must retain a whistleblower partner. They argue that such an extension of a partner's fiduciary duty is necessary because permitting a law firm to retaliate against a partner who in good faith reports suspected overbilling would discourage compliance with rules of professional conduct and thereby hurt clients.

While this argument is not without some force, we must reject it. A partnership exists solely because the partners choose to place personal confidence and trust in one another. . . . Just as a partner can be expelled, without a breach of any common law duty, over disagreements about firm policy or to resolve some other "fundamental schism," a partner can be expelled for accusing another partner of overbilling without subjecting the partnership to tort damages. Such charges, whether true or not, may have a profound effect on the personal confidence and trust essential to the partner relationship. Once such charges are made, partners may find it impossible to continue to work together to their mutual benefit and the benefit of their clients.

We are sensitive to the concern expressed by the dissenting Justices that "retaliation against a partner who tries in good faith to correct or report perceived misconduct virtually assures that others will not take these appropriate steps in the future." However, the dissenting Justices do not explain how the trust relationship necessary both for the firm's existence and for representing clients can survive such serious accusations by one partner against another. The threat of tort liability for expulsion would tend to force partners to remain in untenable circumstance—suspicious of and angry with each other—to their own detriment and that of their clients whose matters are neglected by lawyers distracted with intrafirm frictions.

Although concurring in the Court's judgment, Justice Hecht criticizes the Court for failing to "address amici's concerns that failing to impose liability will discourage attorneys from reporting unethical conduct." To address the scholars' concerns, he proposes that a whistleblower be protected from expulsion, but only if the report, irrespective of being made in good faith, is proved to be correct. We fail to see how such an approach encourages compliance with ethical rules more than the approach we adopt today. Furthermore, the amici's position is that a reporting attorney must be in good faith, not that the attorney must be right. In short, Justice Hecht's approach ignores the question Bohatch presents, the amici write about, and the firm challenges—whether a partnership violates a fiduciary duty when it expels a partner who in good faith reports suspected ethical violations. The concerns of the amici are best addressed by a rule that clearly demarcates an attorney's ethical duties and the parameters of tort liability, rather than redefining "whistleblower."

We emphasize that our refusal to create an exception to the at-will nature of partnerships in no way obviates the ethical duties of lawyers. Such duties sometimes necessitate difficult decisions, as when a lawyer suspects overbilling by a colleague. The fact that the ethical duty to report may create an irreparable schism between partners neither excuses failure to report nor transforms expulsion as a means of resolving that schism into a tort.

We hold that the firm did not owe Bohatch a duty not to expel her for reporting suspected overbilling by another partner.

. . .

■ Hecht, Justice, concurring in the judgment.

The Court holds that partners in a law firm have no common-law liability for expelling one of their number for accusing another of unethical conduct. The dissent argues that partners in a law firm are liable for such conduct. Both views are unqualified; neither concedes or even considers whether "always" and "never" are separated by any distance. I think they must be. The Court's position is directly contrary to that of some of the leading scholars on the subject who have appeared here as amici curiae. The Court finds amici's arguments "not without some force," but rejects them completely. I do not believe amici's arguments can be rejected out of hand. The dissent, on the other hand, refuses even to acknowledge the serious impracticalities involved in maintaining the trust necessary between partners when one has accused another of unethical conduct. In the dissent's view, partners who would expel another for such accusations must simply either get over it or respond in damages. The dissent's view blinks reality.

. . .

This case does not force a choice between diametrically opposite views. Here, the report of unethical conduct, though made in good faith, was incorrect. That fact is significant to me because I think a law firm can always expel a partner for bad judgment, whether it relates to the representation of clients or the relationships with other partners, and whether it is in good faith. I would hold that Butler & Binion did not breach its fiduciary duty by expelling Colette Bohatch because she made a good-faith but nevertheless extremely serious charge against a senior partner that threatened the firm's relationship with an important client, her charge proved groundless, and her relationship with her partners was destroyed in the process. I cannot, however, extrapolate from this case, as the Court does, that no law firm can ever be liable for expelling a partner for reporting unethical conduct. Accordingly, I concur only in the Court's judgment.

. . .

II

A

. . .

At least in the context of professional partnerships, the courts have uniformly recognized that a partner can be expelled to protect relationships both inside the firm and with clients. . . .

[I]n Heller [v. Pillsbury Madison & Sutro, 58 Cal.Rptr.2d 336 (Cal. App. 1996)] the court held that a law firm was not liable for expelling Heller, a partner, who was not as productive as the firm expected and who was offensive to some of the firm's major clients. . . . The court [stated]:

> More importantly, even with evaluating the evidence in the light most favorable to Heller, the evidence shows that the Executive Committee expelled Heller because of a loss of trust in him. "The foundation of a professional relationship is personal confidence and trust. Once a schism develops, its magnitude may be exaggerated rightfully or wrongfully to the point of destroying a harmonious accord. When such occurs, an expeditious severance is desirable. . . . " Id. (quoting Holman [v. Coie, 11 Wash. App. 195, 522 P.2d 515, 524, review denied, 84 Wash.2d 1011 (1974), cert. denied, 420 U.S. 984 (1975)).

. . .

Despite statements in these cases that partners cannot expel one of their number for personal profit, in each instance the expelling partners believed that retaining the partner would hurt the firm financially and that the firm—and thus the partners themselves—stood to benefit from the expulsion. It is therefore far too simplistic to say, as the court of appeals held, that partners cannot expel a partner for personal financial benefit; if expulsion of a partner to protect the firm's reputation or preserve its relationship with a client benefits the firm financially, it perforce benefits the members of the firm. If expulsion of a partner can be in breach of a fiduciary duty, the circumstances must be more precisely defined.

. . .

Scholars are divided over not only how but whether partners' common-law fiduciary duty to each other limit expulsion of a partner. . . . Nine distinguished law professors—Professor Richard L. Abel of the University of California at Los Angeles School of Law, Professor Leonard Gross of the Southern Illinois University School of Law, Professor Robert W. Hamilton of the University of Texas School of Law, Professor David J. Luban of the

University of Maryland School of Law, Professor Gary Minda of the Brooklyn Law School, Professor Ronald D. Rotunda of the University of Illinois College of Law, Professor Theodore J. Schneyer of the University of Arizona College of Law, Professor Clyde W. Summers of the University of Pennsylvania School of Law, and Professor Charles W. Wolfram of the Cornell Law School, the Reporter for the Restatement (Third) of Law, The Law Governing Lawyers—have argued in amicus curiae briefs that expulsion of a partner in bad faith is a breach of fiduciary duty, and that expulsion for self-gain is in bad faith, but so is expulsion for reporting unethical conduct. . . .

B

. . .

[I] am troubled by the arguments of the distinguished amici curiae that permitting a law firm to retaliate against a partner for reporting unethical behavior would discourage compliance with rules of conduct, hurt clients, and contravene public policy. . . .

This very difficult issue need not be finally resolved in this case. Bohatch did not report unethical conduct; she reported what she believed, presumably in good faith but nevertheless mistakenly, to be unethical conduct. . . .

Even if expulsion of a partner for reporting unethical conduct might be a breach of fiduciary duty, expulsion for mistakenly reporting unethical conduct cannot be a breach of fiduciary duty. At the very least, a mistake so serious indicates a lack of judgment warranting expulsion. No one would argue that an attorney could not be expelled from a firm for a serious error in judgment about a client's affairs or even the firm's affairs. . . . Reporting unethical conduct where none existed is no different. . . .

Butler & Binion's expulsion of Bohatch did not discourage ethical conduct; it discouraged errors of judgment, which ought to be discouraged. . . .

III

. . .

B

The dissent would hold that "law partners violate[ ] their fiduciary duty by retaliating against a fellow partner who ma[kes] a good-faith effort to alert her partners to the possible overbilling of a client." In fact, the dissent would adopt the broader proposition that a partner could not be expelled from a law firm for reporting any suspected ethical violation, regardless of how little evidence there might be for the suspicion. . . .

Bohatch was expelled not because she insisted on reporting admitted unethical actions, but because she insisted on complaining of actions that were not unethical.

. . . .

■ SPECTOR, joined by PHILLIPS, CHIEF JUSTICE, dissenting.

.   .   .

The issue in this appeal is whether law partners violate a fiduciary duty by retaliating against one partner for questioning the billing practices of another partner. I would hold that partners violate their fiduciary duty to one another by punishing compliance with the Disciplinary Rules of Professional Conduct. Accordingly, I dissent.

.   .   .

The majority views the partnership relationship among lawyers as strictly business. I disagree. The practice of law is a profession first, then a business. Moreover, it is a self-regulated profession subject to the Rules promulgated by this Court.

.   .   . As attorneys, we bear responsibilities to our clients and the bar itself that transcend ordinary business relationships.

Certain requirements imposed by the Rules have particular relevance in this case. Lawyers may not charge unconscionable fees.   .   .   .

.   .   .

I believe that the fiduciary relationship among law partners should incorporate the rules of the profession promulgated by this Court.   .   .   . Although the evidence put on by Bohatch is by no means conclusive, applying the proper presumptions of a no-evidence review, this trial testimony amounts to some evidence that Bohatch made a good-faith report of suspected overbilling in an effort to comply with her professional duty. Further, it provides some evidence that the partners of Butler & Binion began a retaliatory course of action before any investigation of the allegation had begun.

.   .   .

.   .   . [R]etaliation against a partner who tries in good faith to correct or report perceived misconduct virtually assures that others will not take these appropriate steps in the future. Although I agree with the majority that partners have a right not to continue a partnership with someone against their will, they may still be liable for damages directly resulting from terminating that relationship.

.   .   .

The Court's writing in this case sends an inappropriate signal to lawyers and to the public that the rules of professional responsibility are subordinate to a law firm's other interests.   .   .   . Accordingly, I respectfully dissent.

ANALYSIS

1.   Although employment relationships at common law were regarded as "at will" in the absence of contrary agreement between the parties, and thus could be terminated at any time without cause, some courts have recently created a public policy-based exception to this rule forbidding firms from firing whistleblowers who call public or law enforcement attention to misconduct at the firm. If Bohatch had been an associate, rather than a partner, would the case for creating such a public-policy-based rule forbidding her termination have been stronger? What about a public-policy-based rule allowing her to be terminated, but imposing damages for doing so if her termination was done to retaliate against her for "blowing the whistle"? Would any of the three judges who wrote opinions in this case agree with you?

2.   Partnership agreements sometimes permit expulsion of a partner only for "cause." If the partnership agreement in this case had contained such a limitation, would Bohatch's conduct have constituted "cause" for this purpose? Would any of the three judges who wrote opinions in this case agree with you?

3.   Suppose Pennzoil had "fired" the law firm as a result of the turmoil surrounding Bohatch's charges. Should Bohatch be liable to her fellow partners for making good faith but erroneous charges?

4.   Richard Powers was the third partner in Butler & Binion's Washington office. The dissent relates the following additional facts: Bohatch and Powers had each independently observed McDonald working only three to four hours a day. Powers approached Bohatch with his suspicions that McDonald might be over-billing Pennzoil. When Bohatch agreed that there was cause for concern, Powers urged Bohatch to "do something." When Bohatch did so, she was fired, but Powers was not. Given the emphasis in both the majority and concurring opinions on intra-firm trust, why wasn't Powers fired too? Given that Powers wasn't fired, does Butler & Binion's explanation for Bohatch's firing seem plausible?

5.   The dissent states: "The practice of law is a profession first, then a business." Do you agree? If so, what implications does that statement have for the doctrinal duties of lawyers? Would any of the cases studied so far have come out differently if they had involved law firms instead of "ordinary" businesses?

6.   If you had been in Bohatch's position, what would you have done?

7.   What suggestions would you offer to a law firm to prevent the kind of problem that arose in this case?

8.   Suppose that the managers of the firm had not expelled Bohatch; that McDonald had then quit in a huff and had taken the client, Pennzoil, with him; and that since the Washington office then had virtually no business, the firm decided to close it. Would the dissenters allow the firm to expel Bohatch without subjecting itself to an action for damages? Would the dissenters hold that Bohatch had a good cause of action against McDonald? Would the firm have a good cause of action against McDonald?

Section 5. Partnership Property

Putnam v. Shoaf

620 S.W.2d 510 (Ct. App. of Tenn., Western Section, at Jackson, 1981).

This dispute is over the sale of a partnership interest in the Frog Jump Gin Company.

The Frog Jump Gin had operated for a number of years showing losses in some years and profits in others. In the time immediately preceding February, 1976, it appears that the gin operated at a loss. Originally, the gin was operated as an equal partnership between E. C. Charlton, Louise H. Charlton, Lyle Putnam and Carolyn Putnam. In 1974 Mr. Putnam died and Mrs. Putnam, by agreement, succeeded to her husband's interest. The gin operated under that control and management until February 19, 1976, when Mrs. Putnam desired to sever her relationship with the other partners in Frog Jump Gin. At that time the gin was heavily indebted to the Bank of Trenton and Trust Company, and Mrs. Putnam desired to be relieved of this liability. John A. and Maurine H. Shoaf displayed an interest in obtaining Mrs. Putnam's one-half interest in the partnership. An examination by the Shoafs of the financial records of the gin, evidenced by a statement from the gin bookkeeper, indicated a negative financial position of approximately $90,000.00. The Shoafs agreed to take over Mrs. Putnam's position in the partnership if Mrs. Putnam and the Charltons would each pay $21,000.00 into the partnership account. The Shoafs agreed to assume personal liability for all partnership debts, including Putnam's share of any partnership debts made prior to their coming into the partnership, although the Uniform Partnership Act would only make him personally liable for debts made after his entry into the partnership unless he agreed to more.   .   .   . Both the Charltons and Mrs. Putnam paid their respective amounts into the partnership account, and Shoaf assumed all partnership obligations as aforesaid.

At the time of his agreement the known assets of the Frog Jump Gin consisted primarily of the gin, its equipment, and the land upon which they were located. All gin assets, including the land, were held in the name of the partnership. Mrs. Putnam conveyed her interest in the partnership to the Shoafs by means of a quit claim deed. Upon Shoaf's assumption of the position of a partner, the services of the old bookkeeper were terminated and a new bookkeeper was hired.

In April, 1977, with the assistance of the new bookkeeper, it was learned that the old bookkeeper had engaged in a scheme of systematic embezzlement from the Frog Jump Gin Company from the time of Mr. Putnam's death until the bookkeeper's services were terminated. This disclosure led to suits being filed by the gin against the bookkeeper and the

139

banks that had honored checks forged by the bookkeeper. There is no need to go into the details of all that litigation. Suffice it to say that Mrs. Putnam was allowed to intervene claiming an interest in any fund paid by the banks and the upshot of it all was a judgment paid into Court by the banks in excess of $68,000.00. One-half of that sum, by agreement, has been paid to the Charltons as owners of a one-half interest in the gin, and the other half is the subject of this dispute between the Shoafs and Mrs. Putnam's estate. She has died pending this litigation and the case revived.

. . .

The conveyance between Mrs. Putnam and the Shoafs is evidenced by what is styled a "Quitclaim Deed" executed by Mrs. Putnam on February 19, 1976, which is as follows:

"FOR AND IN CONSIDERATION of the sum of One Dollar ($1.00), cash in hand paid, the receipt of which is hereby acknowledged, and the assumption by Grantees of all Grantor's obligations arising or by virtue of her partnership interest in the Frog Jump Gin Company, including three notes to Bank of Tenton and Trust Company, I, CAROLYN B. PUTNAM, a widow, have this day bargained and sold and by these presents so hereby sell, transfer, convey and forever quitclaim unto JOHN A. SHOAF and wife, MAURINE H. SHOAF, their heirs and assigns, all the right, title and interest (it being a one-half (1/2) undivided interest) I have in and to the following described real and personal property located in the 25th Civil District of Gibson County, Tennessee, and described as follows; to-wit:"

(The legal description of the real property follows.)

"PERSONAL PROPERTY:

"All of the personal property and machinery in said Frog Jump Gin Company's buildings and on said properties described and used in the operation of its cotton gin plant on the above-described parcel of land, including two Moss Gordin 75 saw gin stands; one Overhead incline cleaner; stick and green leaf machine; two Moss Gordin lint cleaners; two Mitchell Feeders; two Mitchell burners; one Hardwick Etter all steel press; condensers; fans; motors; pulleys; shafting; all piping; belting and machinery and appliances and other personal property, including all cotton trailers, on said parcel of land and used in connection with the operation of said cotton gin, accounts receivable, inventory and all other assets of Frog Jump Gin Company.

"TO HAVE AND TO HOLD the said real and personal property with the appurtenances, estate, title and interest thereto belonging unto the said John A. Shoaf and wife, Maurine H. Shoaf, their heirs and assigns, forever.

"Witness my signature this the 19 day of February, 1976."

On the same day Mrs. Putnam and the Charltons executed the following agreement:

"This Agreement made and entered into on this the 19th day of February, 1976, by and between E. C. Charlton and wife, Louise H. Charlton, party of one part, and Carolyn B. Putnam, party of the other part, all of Trenton, Gibson County, Tennessee;

"WITNESSETH: THAT WHEREAS, the parties have heretofore been conducting a business, as partners, under the firm name and style of Frog Jump Gin Company; and

"WHEREAS, Carolyn B. Putnam has agreed to pay into the partnership the sum of Twenty-one Thousand Dollars ($21,000.00), the receipt of which is hereby acknowledged, and has sold and conveyed her interest in the partnership to John A. Shoaf and wife, Maurine H. Shoaf.

"NOW, THEREFORE, it is mutually agreed that the partnership be and hereby is dissolved. It is further mutually agreed that the parties do hereby release and forever discharge each other from any and all claims and demands on account of, connected with, or growing out of the said partnership, or the division of the assets thereof; and it is expressly understood and agreed that Carolyn B. Putnam is completely released and discharged from any and all liability, debts, or causes of action of the Frog Jump Gin Company, presently existing, contingent, or otherwise, including notes owed to Bank of Trenton and Trust Company, and that E. C. Charlton and wife, Louise H. Charlton assume all liability and indebtedness of the said partnership and covenant to indemnify and save harmless the said Carolyn B. Putnam in the premises.

"In Witness Whereof, the parties have hereunto set their signatures, this day and date first above written."

At approximately the same time, Mrs. Putnam obtained from the Bank of Trenton a complete release from all personal liability for note indebtednesses to the Bank in the face amount of $105,000.00 in consideration of the Shoafs' assumption of all obligations of the Frog Jump Gin.

. . .

First, we must discover the nature of the ownership interest of Mrs. Putnam in that which she conveyed. Under the Uniform Partnership Act, . . . her partnership property rights consisted of her (1) rights in specific partnership property, (2) interest in the partnership and (3) right to participate in management. . . . The right in "specific partnership property" is the partnership tenancy possessory right of equal use or possession by partners for partnership purposes. This possessory right is incident to the partnership and the possessory right does not exist absent the partnership. The possessory right is not the partner's "interest" in the assets of the partnership. . . . The real interest of a partner, as opposed to that incidental possessory right before discussed, is the partner's interest in the partnership which is defined as "his share of the profits and surplus and the same is personal property." . . . Therefore, a co-partner owns no personal specific interest in any specific property or asset of the partnership. The partnership owns the property or the asset. . . . The partner's interest is an undivided interest, as a co-tenant in all partnership property. . . . That interest is the partner's pro rata share of the net value or deficit of the partnership. . . . For this reason a conveyance of partnership property held in the name of the partnership is made in the name of the partnership and not as a conveyance of the individual interests of the partners. . . .

This being true, all Mrs. Putnam had to convey was her interest in the partnership. Accordingly, she had no specific interest in the admittedly unknown choses in action to separately convey or retain. Therefore, the determinative question is: Did Mrs. Putnam intend to convey her interest in the partnership to the Shoafs? There can be no doubt that such was the intent of Mrs. Putnam, as she had no other interest to convey. . . . If we would say otherwise, that is that she intended to convey less, and thereby retain a partnership interest, Mrs. Putnam would have remained a partner unknown to the other parties and, in reality, unknown to herself. It is abundantly evident that the last thing Mrs. Putnam wanted was to remain a partner. She wanted out, and out she got.

. . . This situation is no different from a hypothetical oil discovery on the partnership real property after transfer of a partnership interest with neither party believing oil to be present at the time of the conveyance. The interest in the real property always was and remained in the partnership. Of course, the transferor would not have transferred his partnership interest had he known of the existence of oil on partnership property; but, mutual ignorance of the existence of the oil would not, in our opinion, warrant a "reformation" of the contract for sale of the partnership interest, or warrant a decree in favor of the transferor for a share of the value of the oil.

. . . We wonder what would be the position of Mrs. Putnam, or the estate, had the Frog Jump Gin failed, leaving a sizeable deficit, even after the influx of the bank's refund. Would she accept a partner's share of the Frog Jump Gin's liabilities for a share of the bank's refund? The question answers itself and we pose it only to show that she did not have a specific interest in any specific assets of the Frog Jump Gin, either to retain or convey. All she had was a partner's interest in a "share of the profits" (and losses) which she certainly intended to convey.

ANALYSIS

1. A partnership might be thought of as an entity—like a corporation, which is conceived of as a separate entity, in which individuals may own shares. Alternatively, it might be thought of as an aggregation of assets each of which is owned pro rata by the partners—just as, for example, an individual owning a hardware store might be thought to own directly and personally each and every item in the store's inventory. Does the court in

the present case treat the partnership as an entity or an aggregate? Would it matter?

2. Suppose that after the change of ownership it was discovered, much to everyone's surprise, that an underground stream had undercut the land on which the gin was located and it was necessary to abandon the property. Could the Shoafs have recovered their loss from Ms. Putnam?

SECTION 6. RAISING ADDITIONAL CAPITAL

Business firms often need additional funds to finance their activities and generally are confronted only with the question of what is the lowest-cost method of doing so. In some circumstances, however—especially where the need arises from a failure of the business to meet expectations—there may be virtually insurmountable barriers, arising not from the nature of the investment but rather from the financial relationships among the investors. It may be clear, for example, that additional funds can only be raised from the equity investors and that all such investors would be better off if each provided a pro rata share of the amount needed. Yet each investor, acting out of self interest, may decline to invest, and all may lose. This kind of self-destructive stalemate can arise in large businesses as well as small ones. Generally it can be avoided by proper planning, but often it is not. The hypothetical facts in the following problem illustrate one form of the phenomenon in a small-scale context.

PROBLEM

A real estate developer formed a partnership for the construction of an apartment building. Initially, 40 partners invested $25,000 each (a total of $1,000,000) and $9,000,000 was borrowed. Each partner received a 2.5 percent interest in the partnership. For bookkeeping purposes, each partner was assigned 25 "points," for a total of 1,000 points, initially worth $1,000 each. The developer represented that it would cost $10,000,000 to build the building and reach the point where the net cash flow from rents would be sufficient to meet all cash needs. In fact, it has turned out that all the money is gone and the project is not yet quite complete. No more money can be borrowed, except possibly from the partners. An outside expert has represented that the value of what is completed will be $9,500,-000, but if it were necessary to sell, the selling costs would be $500,000, leaving only $9,000,000. That would mean that after paying off the loan there would be nothing left for the partners. They would lose their entire investment. The outside expert has also represented that if an additional $500,000 could be raised, it could be used to complete the project and reach the point where rents are sufficient to meet cash needs, and the value of the investment would be $10,000,000 (subject to the $9,000,000 debt). These facts may be summarized as follows:

Original cost of project	$10,000,000
Debt	$9,000,000
Equity	$1,000,000
Number of partners	40
Investment per partner ($1,000,000/40)	$25,000
Total points	1,000
Initial value of one point ($1,000,000/1,000)	$1,000

Points per partner (1,000/40)	25
Present value of project	$9,500,000
Equity if retained	$500,000
Selling cost	$500,000
Net Proceeds if sold ($9,500,000–$500,000)	$9,000,000
Equity if sold ($9,000,000–$9,000,000)	0
Money needed to retain	$500,000
Amount needed, per partner ($500,000/40)	$12,500
New value if $500,000 is invested in project	$10,000,000
New equity value if $500,000 is invested in project ($10,000,000–$9,000,000)	$1,000,000

Unfortunately, there is no provision in the partnership agreement covering the need for additional capital. This means that no partner can be forced to contribute anything. Moreover, no new partner can be added without the consent of all the existing partners and no partner's share in the partnership can be changed without her or his consent.

1. The managing partner sends out a letter to each of the partners, explaining the situation and asking that each partner contribute $12,500 as a loan to the partnership, without interest. The letter of solicitation states, "if you contribute $12,500, and everyone else does, we will have our needed $500,000 and your investment will be worth $25,000 (2.5 percent of the equity of $1,000,000). If you do not contribute, and we cannot raise the needed $500,000, your investment will be worthless. In other words, I am asking that you spend $12,500 to make $25,000, which is a good deal." Suppose you are a partner; you are not personally acquainted with any of the other partners; you could easily afford to invest the $12,500; you accept the projections of the outside expert, but you have a sour attitude toward the partnership and would prefer not to put any more money into it; you think that if you do not contribute, but just about everyone else does, the managing partner will somehow find a way to make up the shortfall. What are you likely to do? What are the other partners likely to do?

2. Some partnership agreements do address the issue of a possible need for additional capital. A commonly used provision permits the managing partner to issue a call for additional funds and provides that if any partner does not provide the funds called for, her or his share is reduced, according to the existing formula. This is sometimes referred to as pro rata dilution. In the context of our problem, it would mean that additional points would in effect be sold at the original price of $1,000 per point. Imagine the letter of solicitation from the managing partner: "I urge each of you to buy 12.5 points for $1,000 per point, a total of $12,500. If you and all of the other partners do this, you will have an investment worth $25,000. If some partners do not invest, the new points allocable to that partner will be offered to the other partners." Suppose you think that half of the partners are inclined to contribute and half are not. Thus, each of the partners who do contribute will be required to invest $25,000 and each will receive 25 new points. There will be 500 new points and a total of 1,500 points. Each point will be worth $667. Each of the partners

making a new contribution of $25,000 will have 50 points, worth a total of $33,333. Each of the noncontributing partners will have 25 points worth $16,666. What do you do?

3. Imagine a time before the managing partner has raised the money for the project. She comes to you and urges you to invest. You have had no experience in real estate investments. You ask, "Are you sure that the $1,000,000 in equity will give you enough money to complete the project?" The managing partner says, "No problem." You ask, "Are you absolutely certain?" The reply is, "Absolutely." At this point, you mumble to yourself, "Gotcha." You are ready to ask for a provision in the partnership agreement covering the possible problem (or, as the managing partner purports to see it, nonproblem) of meeting the need for additional funds. What provision do you think you might be able to insist upon?

4. Another approach that is sometimes used is called "penalty dilution." To illustrate, in the context of our problem, the partnership agreement might provide that if the managing partner determines that additional funds are needed, new points will be offered to the partners at a price of $250 each. (This would be called 4 to 1 dilution, since the original points were sold for $1,000 each and $1,000 will now buy 4 points.) You receive a letter from the managing partner offering you (and each of the other partners) 50 points at $250 each, a total of $12,500. The total number of new points being offered to the 40 partners at $250 each is 2,000, so the total number of new and old points will be 3,000. The equity value will be $1,000,000, so each point will be worth $333. Thus, you can invest $12,500 and have 75 points (25 original and 50 new) worth a total of $25,000. Or you can refuse to invest, in which case (assuming that the other partners buy all the points being offered), you will have 25 points worth $8,333. What are you (and each of the other partners) likely to do? In what circumstances do you think that investors, at the outset, might be willing to accept a partnership agreement providing for penalty dilution? (You may assume that the penalty dilution described here would not be regarded as a penalty for purposes of the rule of contract law that makes penalties unenforcible.)

5. An approach that bears some similarity to penalty dilution requires partners to make loans to the partnership, pro rata, when called upon by the managing partner to do so. The loans might bear interest at, say, three percent above the prime rate, with no distributions to be made to the partners until the full amounts of the loan and interest are paid. The tough problem is to specify the consequences of a failure of a partner to comply with a request for loan money. One possibility is to allow the nondefaulting partners to make the loan and compensate them for doing so by providing for repayment of, say, 150 percent of the amount loaned, plus interest. What do you think of this approach? In what circumstances would you be willing to invest in a partnership that had adopted such an approach in its partnership agreement? (For our purposes, ignore any possible problems of usury or of the nonenforcibility of penalty clauses.)

6. Another approach is to provide in the partnership agreement that the managing partner can sell new partnership shares to anyone at whatever price can be obtained. This is comparable to a corporation selling new shares of its common stock on the stock market, in order to raise new equity funds. In what circumstances might this approach be objectionable in the case of a partnership?

SECTION 7. THE RIGHTS OF PARTNERS IN MANAGEMENT

In many, perhaps most, small partnerships, each of the partners expects to play a role in conducting the business of the partnership. The right of each partner to participate in the operation of the business in some way will be an implicit term of the partnership agreement. At the same time, disagreements may arise over various business decisions. Section 18(e) of the UPA provides that in the absence of an agreement to the contrary, "all partners have equal rights in the management and conduct of the partnership business," and § 18(h) provides that "any difference arising as to ordinary matters connected with the partnership business may be decided by a majority of the partners." (To the same effect is UPA (1996) §§ 103, 401(f) and (j).) Thus, if there are three partners and they disagree as to an "ordinary" matter, the decision of the majority controls. For example, if the partnership operates a grocery store, and two of the partners, for business reasons, want to stop buying bread from a certain supplier, their decision is binding on the third partner. The majority can deprive the minority partner of the authority to buy bread from that supplier. If the supplier is made aware of the limitation, an order for bread from the minority partner would not bind the partnership or the other partners. If, however, there are only two partners, there can be no majority vote that will be effective to deprive either partner of authority to act for the partnership. Similar stalemates can, of course, arise in any partnership with an even number of partners.

National Biscuit Company v. Stroud

249 N.C. 467, 106 S.E.2d 692 (1959).

C.N. Stroud and Earl Freeman entered into a general partnership to sell groceries under the firm name of Stroud's Food Center. There is nothing in the agreed statement of facts to indicate or suggest that Freeman's power and authority as a general partner were in any way restricted or limited by the articles of partnership in respect to the ordinary and legitimate business of the partnership. Certainly, the purchase and sale of bread were ordinary and legitimate business of Stroud's Food Center during its continuance as a going concern.

Several months prior to February 1956 Stroud advised plaintiff that he personally would not be responsible for any additional bread sold by plaintiff to Stroud's Food Center. After such notice to plaintiff, it from 6 February 1956 to 25 February 1956, at the request of Freeman, sold and delivered bread in the amount of $171.04 to Stroud's Food Center.

In Johnson v. Bernheim, 76 N.C. 139, this Court said: "A and B are general partners to do some given business; the partnership is, by operation of law, a power to each to bind the partnership in any manner legitimate to the business. If one partner go to a third person to buy an article on time for the partnership, the other partner cannot prevent it by writing to the third person not to sell to him on time; or, if one party attempt to buy for cash, the other has no right to require that it shall be on time. And what is true in regard to buying is true in regard to selling. What either partner does with a third person is binding on the partnership. It is otherwise where the partnership is not general, but is upon special terms, as that purchases and sales must be with and for cash. There the power to each is special, in regard to all dealings with third persons at least who have notice of the terms." There is contrary authority. 68 C.J.S. Partnership § 143, pp. 578–579. However, this text of C.J.S. does not mention the effect of the provisions of the Uniform Partnership Act.

The General Assembly of North Carolina in 1941 enacted a Uniform Partnership Act, which became effective 15 March 1941. G.S. Ch. 59, Partnership, Art. 2.

G.S. § 59–39 is entitled "Partner Agent of Partnership as to Partnership Business", and subsection (1) reads: "Every partner is an agent of the partnership for the purpose of its business, and the act of every partner, including the execution in the partnership name of any instrument, for apparently carrying on in the usual way the business of the partnership of which he is a member binds the partnership, unless the partner so acting has in fact no authority to act for the partnership in the particular matter, and the person with whom he is dealing has knowledge of the fact that he has no such authority." G.S. § 59–39(4) states: "No act of a partner in contravention of a restriction on authority shall bind the partnership to persons having knowledge of the restriction."

G.S. § 59–45 provides that "all partners are jointly and severally liable for the acts and obligations of the partnership."

G.S. § 59–48 is captioned "Rules Determining Rights and Duties of Partners." Subsection (e) thereof reads: "All partners have equal rights in the management and conduct of the partnership business." Subsection (h) hereof is as follows: "Any difference arising as to ordinary matters connected with the partnership business may be decided by a majority of the partners; but no act in contravention of any agreement between the partners may be done rightfully without the consent of all the partners."

Freeman as a general partner with Stroud, with no restrictions on his authority to act within the scope of the partnership business so far as the agreed statement of facts shows, had under the Uniform Partnership Act "equal rights in the management and conduct of the partnership business." Under G.S. § 59–48(h) Stroud, his co-partner, could not restrict the power and authority of Freeman to buy bread for the partnership as a going concern, for such a purchase was an "ordinary matter connected with the partnership business," for the purpose of its business and within its scope, because in the very nature of things Stroud was not, and could not be, a majority of the partners. Therefore, Freeman's purchases of bread from plaintiff for Stroud's Food Center as a going concern bound the partnership and his co-partner Stroud. The quoted provisions of our Uniform Partnership Act, in respect to the particular facts here, are in accord with the principle of law stated in Johnson v. Bernheim, supra; same case 86 N.C. 339.

In Crane on Partnership, 2d Ed., p. 277, it is said: "In cases of an even division of the partners as to whether or not an act within the scope of the business should be done, of which disagreement a third person has knowledge, it seems that logically no restriction can be placed upon the power to act. The partnership being a going concern, activities within the scope of the business should not be limited, save by the expressed will of the majority deciding a disputed question; half of the members are not a majority."

Slayden, Fakes & Co. v. Lance, 151 N.C. 492, 66 S.E. 449, is distinguishable. That was a case where the terms of the partnership imposed special restrictions on the power of the partner who made the contract.

At the close of business on 25 February 1956 Stroud and Freeman by agreement dissolved the partnership. By their dissolution agreement all of the partnership assets, including cash on hand, bank deposits and all accounts receivable, with a few exceptions, were assigned to Stroud, who bound himself by such written dissolution agreement to liquidate the firm's assets and discharge its liabilities. It would seem a fair inference from the agreed statement of facts that the partnership got the benefit of the bread sold and delivered by plaintiff to Stroud's Food Center, at Freeman's request, from 6 February 1956 to 25 February 1956. . . . But whether it did or not, Freeman's acts, as stated above, bound the partnership and Stroud.

The judgment of the court below is

Affirmed.

ANALYSIS

What could Stroud have done to protect himself from liability for obligations incurred by Freeman?

PLANNING

Suppose that you are practicing law (with a license) and that Stroud and Freeman come to you before forming their partnership and ask you to draft a partnership agreement for them. What terms might you propose to avert or mitigate the problem that gave rise to the litigation in this case?

PROBLEM

Alison, Bill, and Charles formed a partnership about two years ago to open and operate a grocery store. In accordance with their initial understanding, Alison has served as general manager, Bill has served as assistant general manager and produce manager, and Charles has run the meat department. About six months ago, Charles hired his son Don to work in the meat department. Alison and Bill believe that Don is surly and slow and that he is driving customers away. They have asked Charles to fire him, but Charles has refused to do so. He thinks Don is brash but lovable and that many customers like his style, and he is satisfied that he works fast enough to get his job done. The relationship of Alison and Bill with Charles and Don is unpleasant.

Alison and Bill come to you for advice. They ask whether they can fire Don and, if so, how they should go about it. What do you say?

Day v. Sidley & Austin

394 F.Supp. 986 (D.D.C.1975), affirmed sub nom. Day v. Avery, 548 F.2d 1018 (D.C.Cir.1976), cert. denied, 431 U.S. 908 (1977).

This case involves a dispute between a former senior partner of Sidley & Austin (S & A), a Chicago law firm, and some of his fellow partners. The controversy centers around the merger between that firm and another Chicago firm, Liebman, Williams, Bennett, Baird and Minow (Liebman firm), and the events subsequent to the merger which ultimately led to plaintiff's resignation. Plaintiff seeks damages claiming a substantial loss of income, damage to his professional reputation and personal embarrassment which resulted from his forced resignation.

The matter is now before the Court on defendants' motion for summary judgment. After consideration of the pre- and post-hearing memoranda of counsel, answers to interrogatories, affidavits, and oral arguments, this Court concludes that defendants' motion for summary judgment should be granted.

The Factual Background

The basic and material facts in this controversy may be briefly detailed.

Mr. Day was first associated with Sidley & Austin in 1938. His legal career was interrupted by World War II service in the Navy and by his tenure with both the Illinois state government and as Postmaster General of the United States. Upon leaving the federal government, he was instrumental in establishing a Washington office for the firm in 1963. As a senior underwriting partner, he was entitled to a certain percentage of the firm's profits, and was also privileged to vote on certain matters which were specified in the partnership agreement. He was never a member of the executive committee, however, which managed the firm's day-to-day business. He remained an underwriting partner with Sidley & Austin from 1963 until his resignation in December 1972.

At some time between February 1972 and July 12, 1972, S & A's executive committee explored the idea of a possible merger between that firm and the Liebman firm. S & A partners who were not on the executive committee were unaware of the proposal until it was revealed at a special meeting of its underwriting partners on July 17, 1972. At that meeting, each partner present, including plaintiff, voiced approval of the merger idea and favored pursuing further that possibility in such manner as the executive committee of S & A might think proper or advisable, with the understanding that any proposed agreement would first be submitted to all partners for their consideration before any binding commitments were made. The merger was further discussed at meetings of the underwriting partners held on September 6, September 22, September 26 and September 28. The plaintiff received timely notice of the meetings but did not attend.

The final Memorandum of Understanding dated September 29, 1972 and the final amended Partnership Agreement, dated October 16, 1972 were executed by all S & A partners, including plaintiff. The Memorandum incorporated a minor change requested by plaintiff.

At a meeting of the executive committee of the combined firm on October 16, 1972, it was decided that the Washington offices and the Washington office committees of the two predecessor firms would be consolidated. The former chairmen of the Washington office committees of the two firms were appointed co-chairmen of the new Washington Office Committee.

In late October of 1972, the new Washington Office Committee recommended to the Management Committee that a combined Washington office be set up at 1730 Pennsylvania Avenue, thus eliminating the old S & A Washington office in the Cafritz Building. A decision was then made to move to the new location despite plaintiff's objections.

Mr. Day resigned from Sidley & Austin effective December 31, 1972 claiming that the changes which occurred after the merger in the Washington office—the appointment of co-chairmen and the relocation of the office—made continued service with the firm intolerable for him.

. . .

Mr. Day contends that he had a contractual right to remain the sole chairman of the Washington office, and that the maintenance of this status was a condition precedent for his rejoining the firm in 1963 and opening the Washington office. According to plaintiff, the decision to appoint co-chairmen was made prior to the merger and defendants' concealment of that decision was a material omission and without that prior information his vote of approval for the merger would not have been given.

He further alleges that certain active misrepresentations about the results of the proposal also had the effect of voiding the approval of the merger. These other alleged misrepresentations were:

(1) that no Sidley partner would be worse off in any way as a result of the merger, including positions on committees;

(2) that two senior partners of the Liebman firm would soon be leaving law practice;

(3) that the merged firm would drop representation of a certain Liebman client whose interests might conflict with some Sidley clients;

(4) that the merger with Liebman would be advantageous to the Sidley partners and would add to the standing and prestige of the firm;

(5) that all aspects of the merger had been exhaustively investigated by defendants; and

(6) that there were good, sound, objective reasons which made the merger highly desirable.

Plaintiff also alleges that the fact that the Liebman firm had been shopping around for a merger partner for 10 years was concealed.

Events after the merger, allegedly void because of the mentioned omissions and misrepresentations, inevitably led to plaintiff's resignation. The loss of his status as sole chairman of the Washington office was viewed by plaintiff as a humiliating experience, especially as it was accompanied by harassment by the defendants. Day points to the method of handling the relocation of the consolidated firm as the most obvious manifestation of the defendants' intent to force his resignation. In an affidavit submitted by plaintiff, he asserts that the process of approving the office move entailed a series of meetings held and decisions made without consulting him, all in derogation of his former status as the final decision maker for the S & A Washington office.

Defendants do not concede that misrepresentations or omissions tainted the approval of the merger, nor do they admit engaging in harassment techniques intended to force plaintiff to resign. The thrust of defendants' argument for summary judgment is that plaintiff's factual allegations are not material because they fail to state a cause of action. Defendants contend that any possible taint of plaintiff's vote in favor of the merger is of no consequence because only a majority, and not unanimous consent, was required for the merger under the provisions of the partnership agreements. Defendants also contend that any diminution of status as perceived by plaintiff cannot have any legal consequences because he had no vested contractual right to remain the sole chairman. They rely on the terms of the partnership agreements to support this defense. Under the agreements, the Executive Committee had the authority to govern the composition of all other firm committees and no special provisions had been made as to plaintiff's vested right in the Washington office.

An analysis of the adequacy of each of plaintiff's causes of action follows.

Fraud

.   .   .

The key misrepresentation which forms the basis of plaintiff's complaint is that no Sidley partner would be worse off as a result of the merger. Plaintiff interpreted this to mean that he would continue to serve as the sole chairman of the Washington office and that he would wield the commanding authority regarding such matters as expanding office space.

It was the change in plaintiff's status at the Washington office which directly precipitated his resignation.

This misrepresentation regarding plaintiff's status cannot support a cause of action for fraud, however, because plaintiff was not deprived of any *legal* right as a result of his reliance on this statement. The 1970 S & A Partnership Agreement, to which plaintiff was a party, sets forth in some detail the relationships among the partners and the structure of the firm. No mention is made of the Washington office or plaintiff's status therein, whereas special arrangements are specified for certain other partners. If chairmanship of the Washington office was of the importance now claimed, the absence of such a provision from the partnership agreement requires a measured explanation which Mr. Day does not supply. Plaintiff's allegations of an unwritten understanding cannot now be heard to contravene the provisions of the Partnership Agreement which seemingly embodied the complete intentions of the parties as to the manner in which the firm was to be operated and managed.

Nor can plaintiff have reasonably believed that no changes would be made in the Washington office since the S & A Agreement gave complete authority to the executive committee to decide questions of firm policy,[8] which would clearly include establishment of committees and the appointment of members and chairpersons. Having read and signed the 1970 and 1972 S & A partnership agreements which implicitly authorized the Executive Committee to create, control or eliminate firm committees, plaintiff could not have reasonably believed that the status of the Washington Office Committee was inviolate and beyond the scope and operation of the Partnership Agreements. Thus, since plaintiff had no right to remain chairman of the Washington office, a misrepresentation regarding his chairmanship does not form the basis for a cause of action in fraud.

Breach of Contract, Conspiracy and Wrongful Dissolution or Ouster of Partner

As shown above, plaintiff had no contractual right to maintain his authority over the Washington office, and therefore he has not made out a

8. Both the 1970 and 1972 S & A Partnership Agreements contained the following language:

1. All questions of Firm policy, including determination of salaries, expense, Partners' participation, required balances of Partners, investment of funds, designation of Counsel, and the admission and severance of Partners, shall be decided by an Executive Committee . . . provided, however, that the determination of participation, admission and severance of Partners, shall require the approval of Partners (whether or not members of the Executive Committee) then holding a majority of all voting Percentages. The Committee shall advise and consult with other Partners to such an extent as the Committee may deem advisable and in the best interest of the Firm.

Any amendment of this Agreement or any subsequent agreement, if signed or initialed by Partners then holding a majority of all voting Percentages, shall be as effective as though signed or initialed by all Partners; provided, however, that any agreement providing for the incorporation of the Firm shall be signed by Partners then holding seventy-five percent (75%) of all voting Percentages. . . .

case for breach of contract. Since he did not have a legal right to maintain his status in the firm, the conspiracy charge amounts to no more than an internal power sweep, executed and permitted under the provisions of the partnership agreement for which there is no legal remedy.

Similarly, there was no wrongful dissolution or ouster of plaintiff from the partnership because the merger of the two firms was authorized under the terms of the S & A partnership agreement. By the terms of the agreement, the executive committee was entrusted with "all questions of Firm policy." [10] Additionally, partners could be admitted and severed from the firm and the partnership agreement could be amended by majority approval by the partners. The merger of S & A with the Liebman firm could be considered either as the admission of new partners or the making of a new or amended agreement, and thus majority approval was all that was required, and a post facto change in plaintiff's vote would be of no effect.

Plaintiff contends that the merger was such a fundamental change in the nature of the partnership that unanimous approval was required and that had he known the personal consequences of the merger, he would have exercised a "veto" and the events which forced him to resign would not have occurred. This theory, however, runs counter to the prevailing law of partnership. Generally, common law and statutory standards concerning relationships between partners can be overridden by an agreement reached by the parties themselves. The Uniform Partnership Act (adopted both in Illinois and the District of Columbia) specifically provides that statutory rules governing the rights and duties of the partners are "subject to any agreement between them."

Nor do the cases cited by plaintiff support the proposition that unanimous consent is needed for the merger of partnerships. In McCallum v. Asbury, 238 Or. 257, 393 P.2d 774 (1964), a partner sued to dissolve a partnership of medical doctors. Plaintiff challenged the amendment of the agreement by majority vote which provided for management by an executive committee. The court held that a majority could approve this change, even though the agreement provided that all partners were to have an equal share in management. Likewise, Fortugno v. Hudson Manure Co., 51 N.J.Super. 482, 144 A.2d 207 (1958), affords little support.

Fortugno basically held that a partner could not be effectively changed into a stockholder in a corporation without his consent. In that case, there had been no prior contract that the partnership agreement could be amended by majority vote. The S & A agreement, however, dealt specifically with incorporation of the firm, providing that incorporation would be effective if approved by three-fourths of the partners. Merger was a less dramatic change than incorporation, which would have eliminated the partnership entity. It cannot reasonably be argued, therefore, that the merger fell outside the purview of the Agreement, requiring unanimous

---

10. *See* note 8, *supra.* Management by an executive committee elected by a majority of the partners is a legally acceptable contractual arrangement. . . .

consent for its approval. Amendments to the Agreement and admission of partners required only majority approval, and plaintiff's proposed "veto power" is nothing more than an expressed hope, incompatible with and contrary to the overall scheme and provisions of the S & A Agreement.

Breach of Fiduciary Duty

Plaintiff also alleges that defendants breached their fiduciary duty by beginning negotiations on a merger with the Liebman firm without consulting the other partners who were not on the executive committee and by not revealing information regarding changes that would occur as a result of the merger, such as the co-chairmen arrangement for the Washington office. An examination of the case law on a partner's fiduciary duties, however, reveals that courts have been primarily concerned with partners who make secret profits at the expense of the partnership. Partners have a duty to make a full and fair disclosure to other partners of all information which may be of value to the partnership. . . . The essence of a breach of fiduciary duty between partners is that one partner has advantaged himself at the expense of the firm. . . . The basic fiduciary duties are: 1) a partner must account for any profit acquired in a manner injurious to the interests of the partnership, such as commissions or purchases on the sale of partnership property; 2) a partner cannot without the consent of the other partners, acquire for himself a partnership asset, nor may he divert to his own use a partnership opportunity; and 3) he must not compete with the partnership within the scope of the business. . . .

A typical case of breach of fiduciary duty and fraud between partners cited by plaintiff is Bakalis v. Bressler, 1 Ill.2d 72, 115 N.E.2d 323 (1953). There, a defendant partner had surreptitiously purchased the building which housed the partnership's business and was collecting rents from the partnership for his own profit. What plaintiff is alleging in the instant case, however, concerns failure to reveal information regarding changes in the internal structure of the firm. No court has recognized a fiduciary duty to disclose this type of information, the concealment of which does not produce any profit for the offending partners nor any financial loss for the partnership as a whole. Not only was there no financial gain for defendants, but the remaining partners did not acquire any more power within the firm as the result of the alleged withholding of information from plaintiff. They were already members of the executive committee and as such had wide-ranging authority with regard to firm management. Thus plaintiff's claim of breach of fiduciary duty must fail.

What this Court perceives from Mr. Day's pleadings and affidavits is that he may be suffering from a bruised ego but that the facts fail to establish a legal cause of action. As an able and experienced attorney, it should have been clear that the differences and misunderstandings which developed with his former partners were business risks of the sort which cannot be resolved by judicial proceedings. Mr. Day, a knowledgeable, sophisticated and experienced businessman and a responsible member of a large law firm, bound himself to a well-defined contractual arrangement when he executed the 1970 Partnership Agreement. The contract clearly provided for management authority in the executive committee and for majority approval of the merger with the Liebman firm. Even if plaintiff had voted against the merger, he could not have stopped it. Furthermore, the partnership agreement, to which he freely consented denies the existence of a contractual right to any particular status within the firm for plaintiff. If plaintiff's partners did indeed combine against him, it is clear that their alleged activities did not amount to illegality, and that any personal humiliation or injury was a risk that he assumed when he joined with others in the partnership.

Accordingly it is this 29th of May, 1975

Ordered that defendants' motion for summary judgment is granted and the complaint in this proceeding is dismissed with prejudice.

NOTE

Suppose a law partnership consists of 200 partners and that one of them retires. Obviously, the remaining 199 partners will continue to practice law without any noticeable change. Technically, however, under UPA (1914) §§ 29 and 31, the old partnership is dissolved by the retirement of any partner and when the remaining partners continue their practice a new partnership is formed. The partners may have a written partnership agreement that specifies what happens when a partner retires—most particularly, how that partner is paid off for her or his interest in the partnership. The agreement may also contain a provision specifying that the remaining partners will continue as partners under the existing agreement. That provision is a "continuation" agreement—that is, an agreement obligating the remaining partners to continue to associate with one another as partners under the existing agreement (or, perhaps, some variation of it). Thus, when Sidley & Austin and the Liebman firm merged, technically, the two firms dissolved (legally, they ceased to exist) and a new firm was formed. But the Sidley & Austin partnership agreement obligated all of its partners to become partners in the new firm. Any partner who objected to the merger could, before the merger, withdraw from the Sidley & Austin partnership, subject to the provisions of the Sidley & Austin agreement relating to withdrawal.

Under UPA (1996), if a partner retires (and in various other situations), there is a "dissociation" (§ 601) rather than a "dissolution" (§ 801). Where there has been a dissociation, the partnership continues as to the remaining partners and the dissociated partner is entitled, in the absence of an agreement to the contrary, to be paid an amount determined as if "on the date of dissociation, the assets of the partnership were sold at a price equal to the greater of the liquidation value or the value based on a sale of the entire business as a going concern without the dissociated partner," plus interest from the date of dissociation. § 701(a) and (b).

What is probably most important about Day v. Sidley & Austin is its illustration of the rule of partnership law that partners are free to make any agreement that suits them, without concern about niceties of partnership theory, and its illustration of the principle of contract law, "You made your bed, now you must lie in it."

ANALYSIS

1. Before the merger, to what extent did Mr. Day have a legal right to share in control? Was there any difference in his legal right to share in control after the merger?

2. Does the Sidley & Austin system for control seem to you to be a sensible one? Why?

3. What should Mr. Day have done, at the time he was about to join Sidley & Austin as manager of its Washington office, to protect himself from the mistreatment he claims he suffered?

4. Presumably the Sidley & Austin partnership agreement contained a provision allowing the firm to oust a partner and specifying a formula for determining the amount the ousted partner was to be paid for his or her share in partnership receivables, work in progress, office equipment, etc. Assuming that Mr. Day was correct in his assertion that he was forced out, in what circumstances, if any, should he be entitled to more than the amount so specified?

Section 8.   Partners at Loggerheads: The Dissolution Solution

A.   The Right to Dissolve

Owen v. Cohen

19 Cal.2d 147, 119 P.2d 713 (1941).

This is an action in equity brought for the dissolution of a partnership and for the sale of the partnership assets in connection with the settlement of its affairs.

On or about January 2, 1940, plaintiff and defendant entered into an oral agreement whereby they contracted to become partners in the operation of a bowling-alley business in Burbank, California.   The parties did not expressly fix any definite period of time for the duration of this undertaking.   For the purpose of securing necessary equipment, plaintiff advanced the sum of $6,986.63 to the partnership, with the understanding that the amount so contributed was to be considered a loan to the partnership and was to be repaid to the plaintiff out of the prospective profits of the business as soon as it could reasonably do so.   . . .

Plaintiff and defendant opened their partnership bowling-alley on March 15, 1940.   From the day of its beginning until the institution of the present action on June 28, 1940—a period of approximately three and one-half months—the business was operated at a profit.   During this time the partners paid off a part of the capital indebtedness and each took a salary of $50 per week.   However, shortly after the business was begun differences arose between the partners with regard to the management of the partnership affairs and their respective rights and duties under their agreement.   This continuing lack of harmonious relationship between the partners had its effect on the monthly gross receipts, which, though still substantial, were steadily declining, and at the date of the filing of this action much of the partnership indebtedness, including the aforementioned loan made by plaintiff, remained unpaid.   On July 5, 1940, in response to plaintiff's complaint and upon order to show cause, the court appointed a receiver to take charge of the partnership business, which ever since has been under his control and management.

As the result of the trial of this action the court found . . . that the parties disagreed "on practically all matters essential to the operation of the partnership business and upon matters of policy in connection therewith"; that the defendant had "committed breaches of the partnership agreement" and had "so conducted himself in affairs relating to the business" that it was "not reasonably practicable to carry on the partnership business with him".   From this finding it was concluded that the

159

partnership was dissoluble by court decree in accordance with the provisions of section 2426 of the Civil Code.

Pursuant to these findings of fact and conclusions of law, the trial court rendered a decree adjudging the partnership dissolved and ordering the assets sold by the receiver. It was further decreed that the proceeds of such sale and of the receiver's operation of the business on hand upon the consummation of such sale be applied, after allowance for the receiver's fees and expenses, to payment of the partnership debts, including the amount of $6,986.63 loaned by plaintiff to the business; that one-half of the remainder of the proceeds be paid to plaintiff, together with the additional sum of $100.17 for his costs; and that defendant be given what was left. . . .

The principal question presented for consideration is whether or not the evidence warrants a decree of dissolution of the partnership. . . .

It is not necessary to enter into a detailed statement of the quarrel between the partners. Whether the disharmony was the result of a difference in disposition or other causes, the effect is the same. Most of the acts of which complaint is made are individually trivial, but from the aggregate the court found, and the record so indicates, that the breach between the partners was due in large measure to defendant's persistent endeavors to become the dominating figure of the enterprise and to humiliate plaintiff before the employees and customers of the bowling-alley. In this connection plaintiff testified that defendant declined to do any substantial amount of the work required for the successful operation of the business; that defendant informed him that he (defendant) "had not worked yet in 47 years and did not intend to start now"; and that he (plaintiff) "should do whatever manual work he could do on the premises, but that he (defendant) would act as manager and wear the dignity." The record also discloses that during the preparation and before the opening of the bowling-alley establishment, defendant told a mutual acquaintance that plaintiff would not be there very long. Corroborative of this evidence is plaintiff's testimony that a few weeks prior to the filing of this action, when he had concluded that he and defendant could not reconcile their differences, he asked defendant to make an offer either to buy out his (plaintiff's) interest in the business or to sell to him (plaintiff); that defendant replied, in effect, that when he was ready to sell to plaintiff, he would set the price himself and it would cost plaintiff plenty to get rid of him. In addition, there is considerable evidence demonstrating that the partners disagreed on matters of policy relating to the operation of the business. One cause of dispute in this connection was defendant's desire to open a gambling room on the second floor of the bowling-alley property and plaintiff's opposition to such move. Another was defendant's dissatisfaction with the agreed salary of $50 per week fixed for each partner to take from the business and his desire to withdraw additional amounts therefrom. This constant dissension over money affairs culminated in defendant's appropriation of small sums from the partnership's funds to his own use without plaintiff's knowledge, approval or consent. In justification of his conduct defendant claimed that on each occasion he set aside a like amount for plaintiff. This extenuating circumstance, however, does not serve to eliminate from the record the fact that monetary matters were a continual source of argument between the partners.

Defendant urges that the evidence shows only petty discord between the partners, and he advances, as applicable here, the general rule that trifling and minor differences and grievances which involve no permanent mischief will not authorize a court to decree a dissolution of a partnership. 20 R.C.L. 958, par. 182. However, as indicated by the same section in Ruling Case Law and previous sections, courts of equity may order the dissolution of a partnership where there are quarrels and disagreements of such a nature and to such extent that all confidence and cooperation between the parties has been destroyed or where one of the parties by his misbehavior materially hinders a proper conduct of the partnership business. It is not only large affairs which produce trouble. The continuance of overbearing and vexatious petty treatment of one partner by another frequently is more serious in its disruptive character than would be larger differences which would be discussed and settled. For the purpose of demonstrating his own preeminence in the business one partner cannot constantly minimize and deprecate the importance of the other without undermining the basic status upon which a successful partnership rests. In our opinion the court in the instant case was warranted in finding from the evidence that there was very bitter, antagonistic feeling between the parties; that under the arrangement made by the parties for the handling of the partnership business, the duties of these parties required cooperation, coordination and harmony; and that under the existent conditions the parties were incapable of carrying on the business to their mutual advantage. As the court concluded, plaintiff has made out a cause for judicial dissolution of the partnership under section 2426 of the Civil Code [U.P.A. § 32]:

"(1) On application by or for a partner the court shall decree a dissolution whenever: . . . .

"(c) A partner has been guilty of such conduct as tends to affect prejudicially the carrying on of the business,

"(d) A partner wilfully or persistently commits a breach of the partnership agreement, or otherwise so conducts himself in matters relating to the partnership business that it is not reasonably practicable to carry on the business in partnership with him, ...

"(f) Other circumstances render a dissolution equitable."

Defendant next questions the propriety of that portion of the decree which provides for the payment of plaintiff's loan to the business, to-wit, the sum of $6,986.63, from the proceeds realized upon the sale of the partnership assets. It is his contention that since the partners agreed that the amount so contributed was to be repaid from the profits of the business, which the evidence established to be a profitable enterprise, the court's order directing the discharge of this partnership obligation in a manner violative of the express understanding of the parties is unjustifiable. . . . That a party to a contract may absolutely limit his right to receive a sum of money from a specified source is indisputable. . . . But defendant's argument based upon this settled precept is of no avail here, for his above-described conduct, creative of a condition of disharmony in derogation of the best interests of the partnership, constituted ground for the court's decree of dissolution and its order directing the sale of the assets for the purpose of forwarding the settlement of the partnership affairs. Defendant, whose persistence in the commission of acts provocative of dissension and disagreement between the partners made it impossible for them to carry on the partnership business, is in no position now to insist on its continued operation. These circumstances not only render the assailed provision of the decree invulnerable to defendant's objection, but also establish its complete accord with established principles of equity jurisprudence.

. . .

The judgment is affirmed.

LEGAL ANALYSIS

1. Why do you suppose the plaintiff filed a lawsuit seeking dissolution rather than simply giving notice of dissolution and demanding a winding up?

2. What is the legal effect of the order for dissolution? What is the likely practical effect?

NOTE AND QUESTION

Under Uniform Partnership Act (UPA) (1996) § 801(5) a partnership is dissolved "on application by a partner, [by] a judicial decree that: (i) the economic purpose of the partnership is likely to be reasonably frustrated; (ii) another partner has engaged in conduct relating to the partnership business that makes it not reasonably practicable to carry on the business in partnership with that partner; or (iii) it is not otherwise reasonably practicable to carry on the partnership business in conformity with the partnership agreement." Do you think this is a change in the right direction?

Collins v. Lewis

283 S.W.2d 258 (Texas Court of Civil Appeals, 1955).

This suit was instituted in the District Court of Harris County by the appellants, who, as the owners of a fifty per cent (50%) interest in a partnership known as the L–C Cafeteria, sought a receivership of the partnership business, a judicial dissolution of the partnership, and foreclosure of a mortgage upon appellees' interest in the partnership assets. Appellees denied appellants' right to the relief sought, and filed a cross-action for damages for breach of contract in the event dissolution should be decreed. Appellants' petition for receivership having been denied after a hearing before the court, trial of the issues of dissolution and foreclosure, and of appellees' cross-action, proceeded before the court and a jury. At the conclusion of such trial, the jury, in response to special issues submitted, returned a verdict upon which the trial court entered judgment denying all relief sought by appellants.

The facts are substantially as follows:

In the latter part of 1948 appellee John L. Lewis obtained a commitment conditioned upon adequate financial backing from the Brown–Bellows–Smith Corporation for a lease on the basement space under the then projected San Jacinto Building for the purpose of constructing and operating a large cafeteria therein. Lewis contacted appellant Carr P. Collins, a resident of Dallas, proposing that he (Lewis) would furnish the lease, the experience and management ability for the operation of a cafeteria, and Collins would furnish the money; that all revenue of the business, except for an agreed salary to Lewis, would be applied to the repayment of such money, and that thereafter all profits would be divided equally between Lewis and Collins. These negotiations failed to materialize because of the inability of Lewis to conclude satisfactory terms with the building owners. Thereafter, in 1949, negotiations along substantially the same terms were reopened, and culminated in the execution between the building owners, as lessors, and Lewis and Collins, as lessees, of a lease upon such basement space for a term of 30 years. Thereafter Lewis and Collins entered into a partnership agreement to endure throughout the term of the lease contract. This agreement is in part evidenced by a formal contract between the parties, but both litigants concede that the complete agreement is ascertainable only from the verbal understandings and exchanges of letters between the principals. . . . The substance of the agreement was that Collins was to furnish all of the funds necessary to build, equip, and open the cafeteria for business. Lewis was to plan and supervise such construction, and, after opening for business, to manage the operation of the cafeteria. As a part of his undertaking, he guaranteed that moneys advanced by Collins would be repaid at the rate of at least $30,000, plus interest, in the first year of operation, and $60,000 per year, plus interest, thereafter, upon default of which Lewis would surrender his interest to Collins. In addition Lewis guaranteed Collins against loss to the extent of $100,000. In the partnership agreement fifty per cent interest therein is reflected to be owned by Collins and certain members of his family, in stated proportions, and the other fifty per cent is reflected to be owned by Lewis and members of his family. However, in their conduct of the business of the partnership, it is conceded by all litigants that Lewis and Collins completely controlled the respective equal fifty per cent interests in the business to the same extent as if the actual ownership were so vested. For the purpose of this opinion, they are treated as if that were in fact the case.

Immediately after the lease agreement had been executed Lewis began
the preparation of detailed plans and specifications for the cafeteria.
Initially Lewis had estimated, and had represented to Collins, that the cost
of completing the cafeteria ready for operation would be approximately
$300,000. Due to delays on the part of the building owners in completing
the building, and delays in procuring the equipment deemed necessary to
opening the cafeteria for business, the actual opening did not occur until
September 18, 1952, some 2½ years after the lease had been executed. The
innumerable problems which arose during that period are in part reflected
in the exchange of correspondence between the partners. Such evidence
reflects that as to the solution of most of such problems the partners were
in entire agreement. It further reflects that such disagreements as did
arise were satisfactorily resolved. It likewise appears that the actual costs
incurred during that period greatly exceeded the amount previously estimated by Lewis to be necessary. The cause of such increase is disputed by
the litigants. Appellants contend that it was brought about largely by the
extravagance and mismanagement of appellee Lewis. Appellees contend
that it resulted from inflation, increased labor and material costs, caused by
the Korean War, and unanticipated but necessary expenses. Whatever
may have been the reason, it clearly appears that Collins, while expressing
concern over the increasing cost, and urging the employment of every
possible economy, continued to advance funds and pay expenses, which, by
the date of opening for business, had exceeded $600,000.

Collins' concern over the mounting costs of the cafeteria appears to
have been considerably augmented by the fact that after opening for
business the cafeteria showed expenses considerably in excess of receipts.
Upon being informed, shortly after the cafeteria had opened for business,
that there existed incurred but unpaid items of cost over and above those
theretofore paid, Collins made demand upon Lewis that the cafeteria be
placed immediately upon a profitable basis, failing which he (Collins) would
advance no more funds for any purpose. There followed an exchange of
recriminatory correspondence between the parties, Collins on the one hand
charging Lewis with extravagant mismanagement, and Lewis on the other
hand charging Collins with unauthorized interference with the management of the business. Futile attempts were made by Lewis to obtain
financial backing to buy Collins' interest in the business. Numerous
threats were made by Collins to cause Lewis to lose his interest in the
business entirely. This suit was filed by Collins in January of 1953.

The involved factual background of this litigation was presented to the
jury in a trial which extended over five weeks, and is reflected in a record
consisting of a transcript of 370 pages, a statement of facts of 1,400 pages,
and 163 original exhibits. At the conclusion of the evidence 23 special
issues of fact were submitted to the jury. The controlling issues of fact, as
to which a dispute existed, were resolved by the jury in their answers to
Issues 1 to 5, inclusive, in which they found that Lewis was competent to
manage the business of the L–C Cafeteria; that there is not a reasonable
expectation of profit under the continued management of Lewis; that but
for the conduct of Collins there would be a reasonable expectation of profit

under the continued management of Lewis; that such conduct on the part
of Collins was not that of a reasonably prudent person acting under the
same or similar circumstances; and that such conduct on the part of
Collins materially decreased the earnings of the cafeteria during the first
year of its operation.   .   .   .

We agree with appellants' premise that there is no such thing as an
indissoluble partnership only in the sense that there always exists the
power, as opposed to the right, of dissolution.   But legal right to dissolution
rests in equity, as does the right to relief from the provisions of any legal
contract.   The jury finding that there is not a reasonable expectation of
profit from the L–C Cafeteria under the continued management of Lewis,
must be read in connection with their findings that Lewis is competent to
manage the business of L–C Cafeteria, and that but for the conduct of
Collins there would be a reasonable expectation of profit therefrom.   In our
view those are the controlling findings upon the issue of dissolution.   It
was Collins' obligation to furnish the money;   Lewis' to furnish the management, guaranteeing a stated minimum repayment of the money.   The
jury has found that he was competent, and could reasonably have performed his obligation but for the conduct of Collins.   We know of no rule
which grants Collins, under such circumstances, the right to dissolution of
the partnership.   .   .   .

The basic agreement between Lewis and Collins provided that Collins
would furnish money in an amount sufficient to defray the cost of building,
equipping and opening the L–C Cafeteria for operation.   As a part of the
agreement between Lewis and Collins, Lewis executed, and delivered to
Collins, a mortgage upon Lewis' interest in the partnership "until the
indebtedness incurred by the said Carr P. Collins .   .   . has been paid in
full out of income derived from the said L–C Cafeteria, Houston, Texas."

The evidence shows that a substantial portion of the money used to
build, equip and open the cafeteria was borrowed by Collins from the First
National Bank in Dallas.   The bank credit was admittedly extended upon
Collins' financial responsibility.   In the mechanics of arranging for such
credit, however, Collins prepared and requested Lewis and his family to
execute notes in the total sum of $175,000 payable to the First National
Bank in Dallas on demand.   Lewis expressed concern at creating an
obligation payable on terms which he felt unable to meet, whereupon
Collins addressed a signed letter to Lewis, containing language as follows:
" .   .   . If you are apprehensive because of the fear that there might be a
foreclosure of these notes or a failure to renew these notes for a sufficient
period of time to liquidate them at a rate of not more than $2,500 per
month the first year and $5,000 per month the second year, I can assure
you that the notes will be renewed as often as is necessary to protect you
on that point.   .   .   ."

.   .   .

At about the time this suit was instituted, the First National Bank in
Dallas made demand upon Lewis for payment of the notes described, thus

maturing the liability of Collins upon his endorsement of the notes.   The failure of Lewis to pay such notes on demand constitutes the default, by reason of which Collins seeks foreclosure of his mortgage on Lewis' interest in the partnership.   We are unable to agree with appellants in this contention, and must overrule their points presenting it.   Regardless of the legal relationship between Lewis and the First National Bank in Dallas, created by the notes described, Lewis' obligation to Collins is limited to repaying money advanced by Collins at the minimum rate of $30,000 the first year and $60,000 per year thereafter.   Only upon default of that obligation does the right of foreclosure ripen.   There is testimony in the record to the effect that Collins, as a director and stockholder in the Dallas Bank had induced the bank to make demand for payment in order to effect foreclosure.   That proof appears to us to be entirely immaterial to the determination of the rights of these litigants.   The proof is undisputed that the bank, after maturing the notes, took no further steps to effect collection.   Aside from that, however, as we construe the partnership agreement, it was Collins' obligation to furnish all money needed to build, equip and open the cafeteria for business.   With particular reference to the notes, it was Collins' obligation to protect Lewis against any demand for payment so long as Lewis met his obligation of repaying money advanced by Collins at the rate agreed upon.   Failure on Collins' part to protect Lewis on his obligation to the bank would constitute a breach of contract by Collins.

Collins' right to foreclose, therefore, depends upon whether or not Lewis has met his basic obligation of repayment at the rate agreed upon. Appellees contend, we think correctly, that he has, in the following manner: the evidence shows that Collins advanced a total of $636,720 for the purpose of building, equipping and opening the cafeteria for business.   The proof also shows that Lewis contended that the actual cost exceeded that amount by over $30,000.   The litigants differed in regard to such excess, it being Collins' contention that it represented operating expense rather than cost of building, equipping and opening the cafeteria.   The jury heard the conflicting proof relative to these contentions, and resolved the question by their answer to Special Issue 20, whereby they found that the minimum cost of building, equipping and opening the cafeteria for operation amounted to $697,603.36.   Under the basic agreement of the partners, therefore, this excess was properly Collins' obligation.   Upon the refusal of Collins to pay it, Lewis paid it out of earnings of the business during the first year of its operation.   Thus it clearly appears that Lewis met his obligation, and the trial court properly denied foreclosure of the mortgage.

In their brief, appellants repeatedly complain that they should not be forced to endure a continuing partnership wherein there is no reasonable expectation of profit, which they say is the effect of the trial court's judgment.   The proper and equitable solution of the differences which arise between partners is never an easy problem, especially where the relationship is as involved as this present one.   We do not think it can properly be said, however, that the judgment of the trial court denying appellants the dissolution which they seek forces them to endure a partnership wherein there is no reasonable expectation of profit.   We have already pointed out the ever present inherent power, as opposed to the legal right, of any partner to terminate the relationship. Pursuit of that course presents the problem of possible liability for such damages as flow from the breach of contract. The alternative course available to appellants seems clearly legible in the verdict of the jury, whose services in that connection were invoked by appellants.

Judgment affirmed.

NOTE

This case arose before Texas adopted its version of the UPA (1914) or, later, UPA (1996). These rules of these acts are essentially the same as those applied by the court in Collins v. Lewis.

ANALYSIS

1. What did Collins hope to gain by obtaining a decree of dissolution?

2. Where does the court's refusal to order dissolution leave Collins? What is likely to happen next?

PLANNING

What protection should Collins have had in the partnership agreement? If he had sought such protection, is it likely that Lewis would have objected?

The next case, Page v. Page, is an action for a declaratory judgment in which the plaintiff sought a declaration that the partnership was not for any definite term and therefore could be dissolved at the will of either partner. The California Supreme Court's discussion of implied agreements creating partnerships for a definite term is interesting and valuable. For present purposes, however, our focus is on the court's dictum about the process of dissolution. The business of the partnership was linen supply. After a long period of losses, it appeared that the business might finally be able to earn a profit. So why was the plaintiff anxious to have a declaratory judgment that the partnership was subject to dissolution at will?

Page v. Page

55 Cal.2d 192, 10 Cal.Rptr. 643, 359 P.2d 41 (1961).

■ TRAYNOR, JUSTICE.

Plaintiff and defendant are partners in a linen supply business in Santa Maria, California. Plaintiff appeals from a judgment declaring the partnership to be for a term rather than at will.

The partners entered into an oral partnership agreement in 1949. Within the first two years each partner contributed approximately $43,000 for the purchase of land, machinery, and linen needed to begin the business. From 1949 to 1957 the enterprise was unprofitable, losing approximately $62,000. The partnership's major creditor is a corporation, wholly owned by plaintiff, that supplies the linen and machinery necessary for the day-to-day operation of the business. This corporation holds a $47,000 demand note of the partnership. The partnership operations began to improve in 1958. The partnership earned $3,824.41 in that year and $2,282.30 in the first three months of 1959. Despite this improvement plaintiff wishes to terminate the partnership.

The Uniform Partnership Act provides that a partnership may be dissolved "By the express will of any partner when no definite term or particular undertaking is specified." Corp.Code, § 15031, subd. (1)(b). The trial court found that the partnership is for a term, namely, "such reasonable time as is necessary to enable said partnership to repay from partnership profits, indebtedness incurred for the purchase of land, buildings, laundry and delivery equipment and linen for the operation of such business. . . ." Plaintiff correctly contends that this finding is without support in the evidence.

Defendant testified that the terms of the partnership were to be similar to former partnerships of plaintiff and defendant, and that the understanding of these partnerships was that "we went into partnership to start the business and let the business operation pay for itself,—put in so much money, and let the business pay itself out." There was also testimony that one of the former partnership agreements provided in writing that the profits were to be retained until all obligations were paid.

Upon cross-examination defendant admitted that the former partnership in which the earnings were to be retained until the obligations were repaid was substantially different from the present partnership. The former partnership was a limited partnership and provided for a definite term of five years and a partnership at will thereafter. Defendant insists, however, that the method of operation of the former partnership showed an understanding that all obligations were to be repaid from profits. He nevertheless concedes that there was no understanding as to the term of the present partnership in the event of losses. He was asked: "[W]as there any discussion with reference to the continuation of the business in the event of losses?" He replied, "Not that I can remember." He was then asked, "Did you have any understanding with Mr. Page, your brother, the plaintiff in this action, as to how the obligations were to be paid if there were losses?" He replied, "Not that I can remember. I can't remember discussing that at all. We never figured on losing, I guess."

Viewing this evidence most favorably for defendant, it proves only that the partners expected to meet current expenses from current income and to recoup their investment if the business were successful.

Defendant contends that such an expectation is sufficient to create a partnership for a term under the rule of Owen v. Cohen, 19 Cal.2d 147, 150, 119 P.2d 713. In that case we held that when a partner advances a sum of money to a partnership with the understanding that the amount contributed was to be a loan to the partnership and was to be repaid as soon as feasible from the prospective profits of the business, the partnership is for the term reasonably required to repay the loan. It is true that Owen v. Cohen, supra, and other cases hold that partners may impliedly agree to continue in business until a certain sum of money is earned . . ., or one or more partners recoup their investments . . ., or until certain debts are paid . . ., or until certain property could be disposed of on favorable terms. . . . In each of these cases, however, the implied agreement found support in the evidence.

. . .

In the instant case, however, defendant failed to prove any facts from which an agreement to continue the partnership for a term may be implied. The understanding to which defendant testified was no more than a common hope that the partnership earnings would pay for all the necessary expenses. Such a hope does not establish even by implication a "definite term or particular undertaking" as required by section 15031, subdivision (1)(b) of the Corporations Code. All partnerships are ordinarily entered into with the hope that they will be profitable, but that alone does not make them all partnerships for a term and obligate the partners to continue in the partnerships until all of the losses over a period of many years have been recovered.

Defendant contends that plaintiff is acting in bad faith and is attempting to use his superior financial position to appropriate the now profitable business of the partnership. Defendant has invested $43,000 in the firm, and owing to the long period of losses his interest in the partnership assets is very small. The fact that plaintiff's wholly-owned corporation holds a $47,000 demand note of the partnership may make it difficult to sell the business as a going concern. Defendant fears that upon dissolution he will receive very little and that plaintiff, who is the managing partner and knows how to conduct the operations of the partnership, will receive a business that has become very profitable because of the establishment of Vandenberg Air Force Base in its vicinity. Defendant charges that plaintiff has been content to share the losses but now that the business has become profitable he wishes to keep all the gains.

There is no showing in the record of bad faith or that the improved profit situation is more than temporary. In any event these contentions are irrelevant to the issue whether the partnership is for a term or at will. Since, however, this action is for a declaratory judgment and will be the basis for future action by the parties, it is appropriate to point out that defendant is amply protected by the fiduciary duties of co-partners.

Even though the Uniform Partnership Act provides that a partnership at will may be dissolved by the express will of any partner (Corp.Code, § 15031, subd. (1)(b)), this power, like any other power held by a fiduciary, must be exercised in good faith.

. . .

A partner at will is not bound to remain in a partnership, regardless of whether the business is profitable or unprofitable. A partner may not, however, by use of adverse pressure "freeze out" a co-partner and appropriate the business to his own use. A partner may not dissolve a partnership to gain the benefits of the business for himself, unless he fully compensates his co-partner for his share of the prospective business opportunity. . . .

[I]n the instant case, plaintiff has the power to dissolve the partnership by express notice to defendant. If, however, it is proved that plaintiff acted in bad faith and violated his fiduciary duties by attempting to appropriate to his own use the new prosperity of the partnership without adequate compensation to his co-partner, the dissolution would be wrongful and the plaintiff would be liable as provided by subdivision (2)(a) of Corporations Code, § 15038 (rights of partners upon wrongful dissolution) for violation of the implied agreement not to exclude defendant wrongfully from the partnership business opportunity.

The judgment is reversed.

■ GIBSON, C.J., McCOMB, PETERS, WHITE, and DOOLING, JJ., and WOOD, J. pro tem., concur.

PROBLEMS

1. Suppose the plaintiff wishes to buy the assets of the partnership and continue its business with a new partner (who will take over as manager and will have a 25 percent share). How should he proceed?

2. Suppose the plaintiff intends to liquidate the business (that is, shut it down and sell off its physical assets) and pick up its better accounts through his corporation. What advice would you give?

B. THE CONSEQUENCES OF DISSOLUTION

Prentiss v. Sheffel

20 Ariz.App. 411, 513 P.2d 949 (1973).

OPINION

The question presented by this appeal is whether two majority partners in a three-man partnership-at-will, who have excluded the third partner from partnership management and affairs, should be allowed to purchase the partnership assets at a judicially supervised dissolution sale. We hold that on the facts of this case, such a purchase is proper, and affirm the judgment entered by the trial court.

Suit was originally brought by plaintiffs-appellees seeking dissolution of a partnership they had formed with defendant-appellant. The partnership was created for the purpose of acquiring and operating the West Plaza

Shopping Center located at Bethany Home Road and 35th Avenue in Phoenix, Arizona. (Hereinafter referred to as the Center).

As grounds for dissolution the plaintiffs contended that the defendant had in general been derelict in his partnership duties, and in particular that he had failed to contribute the balance of his proportionate share ($6,000) of the operating losses incurred by the Center. The plaintiffs also sought the trial court's permission to continue the partnership business both during the pendency of the suit and thereafter, and requested that a value be fixed on the defendant's interest in the partnership.

Defendant filed a counterclaim seeking a winding up of the partnership and the appointment of a receiver. He contended that his rights as a partner had been violated in that he had been wrongfully excluded from the partnership.

After an extended evidentiary hearing, the trial court made certain pertinent findings of fact which are here summarized:

1. That each of the plaintiffs owned a 42½% interest in the partnership, with an aggregate interest of 85%, while the defendant was the owner of a 15% interest.

2. That no detailed partnership agreement as to how the business would be supervised, how management decisions would be made, or the term of the partnership's existence, was ever made or entered into at any time between the parties, although there were frequent attempts to arrive at such an agreement.

3. That numerous unresolved disputes arose between the parties, most notably as to how title to the partnership property was to be held, and how management decisions should be made.

4. That as a result of these disputes the relationship between the parties deteriorated, culminating with plaintiffs notifying defendant that any further dealings between them should be through their attorney.

5. That defendant had never been denied physical access to the Center; that he visited there from time to time; and that he also engaged in conversations with the resident manager of the Center.

6. That because of his poor financial condition, defendant had not made payments of all of his pro-rata share of the deficits incurred by the Center when called upon to do so.

7. That since its acquisition, the Center's losses from operations had been materially reduced, and certain more advantageous lease provisions had been secured; that there had been no showing of waste nor detriment to the Center as a result of management operations.

8. That there was a freeze-out or exclusion of the defendant from partnership management and affairs.

Based upon these and other findings of fact the trial court concluded that a partnership-at-will existed between the plaintiffs and the defendant which was dissolved as a result of a freeze-out or exclusion of the defendant from the management and affairs of the partnership. A receiver was appointed by the court until the partnership property could be sold and a partition and distribution of assets could be made. The trial court expressly refused the defendant's request that an order be entered forbidding the plaintiffs from bidding at the contemplated judicial sale.

The receiver and the trial court proceeded with the liquidation and sale of the Center. The plaintiffs were the high bidders at the sale which was held in open court. Subsequently, the court entered an order confirming the sale of the Center to them. It is from this order that the defendant appeals.

The principal contention urged by the defendant is that he was *wrongfully* excluded from the management of the partnership, and therefore, because he would in some way be disadvantaged, the plaintiffs should not be allowed to purchase the partnership assets at a judicial sale. The record, however, does not support the defendant's position on two particulars. While the trial court did find that the defendant was excluded from the management of the partnership, there was no indication that such exclusion was done for the wrongful purpose of obtaining the partnership assets in bad faith rather than being merely the result of the inability of the partners to harmoniously function in a partnership relationship.

Moreover, the defendant has failed to demonstrate how he was injured by the participation of the plaintiffs in the judicial sale. To the contrary, from all the evidence it appears that if the plaintiffs had not participated, the sales price would have been considerably lower. Absent the plaintiffs' bid, there would have been only two qualified initial bids, which were $2,076,000 and $2,040,000 respectively. However, with the participation of plaintiffs, whose initial bid was $2,100,000, the final sales price was bid to $2,250,000. Thus it appears that defendant's 15% interest in the partnership was considerably *enhanced* by the plaintiffs' participation.

. . . The defendant characterizes the sale to plaintiffs as a forced sale of his partnership interest. However, defendant was not forced to sell his interest to the plaintiffs. He had the same right to purchase the partnership assets as they did, by submitting the highest bid at the judicial sale. His argument that the plaintiffs were bidding "paper" dollars due to their 85% partnership interest is without force. He too could have bid "paper" dollars to the extent of his 15% interest. Moreover, the fact that the plaintiffs could bid "paper" dollars made it possible, as defendant recognizes in his brief, for them to bid higher than outsiders. As a consequence of this ability to enter a higher bid, the value of the defendant's 15% interest in the sale proceeds increased proportionately.

. . .

The defendant has cited no cases, nor has this court found any, which have prohibited a partner from bidding at a judicial sale of the partnership assets. . . .

It must be emphasized that on this appeal the defendant does not attack the fact that the trial court ordered a sale of the assets. The only area of attack is that plaintiffs have been allowed to participate and bid in that sale. . . .

The judgment of the superior court is affirmed.

ANALYSIS AND PLANNING

1.   Prentiss v. Sheffel involves a partnership for the ownership and operation of a shopping center. Among the decisions that must be made for such a venture are the terms of rental agreements (amount of rent, duration of lease, etc.), selection and compensation of a manager, and the budget for advertising, repairs, and maintenance, and amounts to be spent on improvements. Suppose the two plaintiffs have found that the defendant is difficult to work with and generally uninformed and unhelpful. Their inclination is simply to avoid discussing partnership business with him at all, since they invariably outvote him whenever there is disagreement and they do not want to waste any more of their time trying to work with him. They come to you, asking what problems might be created for them if they proceed in accordance with this inclination and what suggestions you might have. What is your response?

2.   (a) Property may be worth more to its current owners than to outsiders. One reason for this may be that the outsiders may fear that the owners are aware of some defect that the outsiders cannot observe. It may be that there are no such defects, but the owners may not be able to convince outsiders of that reality. Costs of transfer of ownership and management also may explain why property may be worth more to its current owners than to potential buyers.

(b) Suppose Amy, Bob, and Carol are equal partners in a firm that owns a shopping center. The partnership is terminable at will. Amy and Bob work together well. Their relationship with Carol is unpleasant and unproductive. They would like to buy Carol's one-third interest and would be willing to pay up to $700,000 for it, but they would prefer to pay less. They believe that the most an outsider would be willing to pay for the shopping center would be $1,800,000 ($600,000 for each partner). Consider two possible rules of law. Under Rule A (the rule of Prentiss v. Sheffel), Amy and Bob can dissolve the partnership, can insist on an auction, and can bid for the property themselves, using their interest in the partnership as partial payment. Under Rule B, Amy and Bob can dissolve the partnership, which will result in an auction of the property, but they will not be permitted to bid on the property. Suppose that Amy and Bob offer Carol $610,000 for her interest in the partnership. If Rule A is the law, how is Carol likely to respond? What if Rule B is the law? What do your answers to these questions tell you about which rule you would propose for a partnership agreement if you were advising the parties at the outset, at a time when all the partners anticipate cordial and productive relationships with one another? What are the results under each rule if the parties have different beliefs about what price an outsider would bid at an auction? For example, what if Amy and Bob think an outsider would bid at most $1,800,000, while Carol thinks an outsider would bid $2,400,000? What if these expectations are reversed?

Monin v. Monin

785 S.W.2d 499 (Ky.App.1989).
Discretionary Review Denied by Supreme Court 1990.

■ McDONALD, JUDGE. This is a partnership case. The parties, Charles Monin and Joseph Monin (a/k/a Sonny), are brothers who formed a partnership in 1967 for the purpose of hauling milk. In 1984 the relationship between Charles and Sonny deteriorated such that Sonny no longer desired to continue the partnership. Some efforts were made to resolve their affairs, to no avail. In July, 1984, Sonny notified Charles of his intention to dissolve the partnership, and the next day wrote to Dairymen Incorporated (DI) to notify them that he was canceling the partnership's contract with DI effective October 16, 1984, the annual renewal date of the hauling contract. Sonny also informed DI he wanted to apply for the right to haul milk for DI after the expiration of the partnership's contract. On September 24, 1984, Charles and Sonny executed an agreement to resolve their business arrangement. The document entitled "Partnership Sales Agreement" provided that they would hold a private auction between themselves for all the assets of the partnership "including equipment, and milk routes." As the contract with DI required approval of any sale or transfer of the milk hauling agreement, the sales agreement provided that such approval from DI would be sought and the sales agreement would be "null and void" if approval from DI was not forthcoming. The agreement also contained a covenant not to compete. Charles was the successful bidder at the auction, having bid $86,000.

On the same day as the auction, September 27, 1984, DI called a producers meeting at which time those present voted not to approve Charles as their hauler. Instead they voted to have Sonny haul their milk. Sonny accepted the offer and has since hauled milk for DI as Sonny Monin, Inc. As a result Sonny ended up with the major asset of the partnership, the milk hauling contract, at no cost to him.

On February 11, 1985, Charles commenced this action in the Nelson Circuit Court alleging that Sonny violated his fiduciary duty to the partnership and that he had tortiously interfered with the partnership's contractual relation with clients and customers.* A bench trial was conducted in December, 1986. In its judgment for Sonny the trial court reasoned as follows:

---

* [Editors.—It would seem that Charles was entitled under the terms of the Sales Agreement to declare it "null and void" and recover the amount he paid for the partnership assets. Presumably he thought he could recover more by suing for damages for tortious breach of fiduciary duty.]

When Charles was the high bidder at $86,000, the value of the partnership assets, including milk routes, was established as far as Charles was concerned. Sonny had no further say in establishing a value for such assets. When the producers and D.I. rejected Charles as a milk hauler, the value of the partnership assets became adjusted from $86,000 to $22,000 (the value of the milk hauling equipment).

When the producers voted for Sonny to haul their milk, they were not voting on a partnership matter. They were voting on Sonny's individual application. Furthermore, they were privileged to vote for some third person to haul their milk.

In summary, the affairs of the Monin Brothers partnership were finally settled on September 27, 1984. As a result of the actions of that date, the assets of the partnership were finally valued at $22,000. When Charles was rejected as the D.I.'s milk hauler on that date, the partnership had no interest in the milk routes and neither partner had any claim to same as part of their partnership interests.

We conclude the trial court's reasoning is flawed in that it ignores Sonny's duties to the partnership with respect to the most valuable asset of that entity, the milk hauling contract. As stated in Van Hooser v. Keenon, Ky., 271 S.W.2d 270, 273 (1954), "[T]here is no relation of trust or confidence known to the law that requires of the parties a higher degree of good faith than that of a partnership. *Nothing less than absolute fairness will suffice.*" (Emphasis added.) Importantly, that decision holds that a partner's fiduciary duties extend beyond the partnership "to persons who have dissolved the partnership, and have not completely wound up and settled the partnership affairs." Sonny's continuing duty was especially applicable here as he agreed to sell his interest to Charles so Charles could continue the partnership business. . . . Nothing in the Uniform Partnership Act (KRS Chapter 362) changes the high degree of good faith partners must maintain in their relations with one another. . . .

Thus, when Sonny failed to withdraw his application with D.I. for the milk routes after agreeing to allow Charles to buy his interest in those routes and continue the partnership business, Sonny obviously breached his duties to the partnership. As the court found, the value of the partnership assets dropped from $86,000 to $22,000 when Sonny was awarded the contract by D.I. While it is possible D.I. would not have awarded the contract to Charles even if Sonny had withdrawn his name from contention, there is no evidence that any other person or entity was available or willing to take over the route. The law is clear that one partner cannot benefit at the expense of the partnership. . . . Sonny, by agreeing to sell his share of the assets to Charles and by actively pursuing those same assets from D.I., positioned himself such that whatever D.I. did, he could not lose. Understandably, Charles believes he was abused by the obvious conflict of interest. Thus, the trial court's dismissal of Charles's breach of fiduciary duty claim is reversed and remanded for entry of judgment in favor of Charles. We do not believe a new trial on damages is required; nor do we believe Charles is entitled to an accounting from Sonny for profits made since 1984. The value of the asset at issue was determined by the parties at or very near the time of Sonny's breach of duty to the partnership ($86,000 minus $22,000, or $64,000), and that should form the measure of damages to which Charles is entitled.

Finally, the trial court's findings concerning the tortious interference with contractual relations are supported by substantial evidence and will not be disturbed. CR 52.01. The evidence of Sonny's behind-the-back efforts to convince producers not to work with or accept Charles as their hauler was conflicting, and the trial court, as fact finder, could believe Sonny's version of the facts on that claim.

Accordingly, the judgment of the Nelson Circuit Court is reversed and remanded for entry of a new judgment consistent with this opinion.

■ HOWARD, JUDGE, concurs.

■ EMBERTON, JUDGE, dissenting. I respectfully dissent.

I cannot agree with the majority that Sonny's actions constitute a breach of his fiduciary obligation to Charles. Evidence indicates that numerous efforts toward resolution of the problem—which efforts appeared to be made in good faith by Sonny—were summarily rebuffed by Charles. There is no evidence but that both parties were genuinely bidding at the September 27 private auction. Both understood that the successful bidder won equipment, the routes and the other assets only if DI approved the new contract.

Upon polling the affected producers, only 1 out of 12 indicated a preference for Charles. In fact, evidence was strong that most of the producers would not allow Charles to haul their milk; that the DI field representative stated DI could not work with Charles; and, that drivers stated they would quit before driving for Charles. The trial court, having heard the evidence, found that none of such positions taken by DI, or by the producers, were the result of actions taken (or statements made) by Sonny. DI, having such information, made a decision in its own best interest—not as a result of influence from Sonny.

I find nothing in the record to support a reversal of the trial court's decision. I would affirm.

ANALYSIS

1. How do you suppose the majority in *Monin* would have resolved the dispute in *Page*? What about the dissenter?

2. Is *Monin* just a case of bad lawyering? If the issue presented by the case had been addressed by the Monin brothers at the time they were drafting the "Partnership Sales Agreement," what do you suppose they would have agreed to?

3. Do we really need the concept of fiduciary obligation to decide a case like *Monin*? Is the case properly viewed as a partnership-duty case rather than as a contract case?

Pav–Saver Corporation v. Vasso Corporation

143 Ill.App.3d 1013, 97 Ill.Dec. 760, 493 N.E.2d 423 (1986).

The matter before us arises out of the dissolution of the parties' partnership, the Pav–Saver Manufacturing Company. The facts are not in dispute, and only those needed to explain our disposition on the issues on appeal will be stated.

Plaintiff, Pav–Saver Corporation ("PSC") is the owner of the Pav–Saver trademark and certain patents for the design and marketing of concrete paving machines. Harry Dale is the inventor of the Pav–Saver "slip-form" paver and the majority shareholder of PSC, located in Moline, Illinois. H. Moss Meersman is an attorney who is also the owner and sole shareholder of Vasso Corporation. In 1974 Dale, individually, together with PSC and Meersman formed Pav–Saver Manufacturing Company for the manufacture and sale of Pav–Saver machines. Dale agreed to contribute his services, PSC contributed the patents and trademark necessary to the proposed operation, and Meersman agreed to obtain financing for it. The partnership agreement was drafted by Meersman and approved by Attorney Charles Peart, president of PSC. The agreement contained two paragraphs which lie at the heart of the appeal and cross-appeal before us:

"3. The duties, obligations and functions of the respective partners shall be:

A. Meersman shall provide whatever financing is necessary for the joint venture, as required.

B. (1) PAV–SAVER shall grant to the partnership without charge the exclusive right to use on all machines manufactured and sold, its trademark 'PAV–SAVER' during the term of this Agreement. In order to preserve and maintain the good will and other values of the trademark PAV–SAVER, it is agreed between the parties that PAV–SAVER Corporation shall have the right to inspect from time to time the quality of machines upon which the licensed trademark PAV–SAVER is used . . . . Any significant changes in structure, materials or components shall be disclosed in writing or by drawings to PAV–SAVER Corporation.

(2) PAV–SAVER grants to the partnership exclusive license without charge for its patent rights in and to its Patent # 3,377,933 for the term of this agreement and exclusive license to use its specifications and drawings for the Slip-form paving machine known as Model MX 6–33, plus any specifications and drawings for any extensions, additions and attachments for said machine for said term. It [is] understood and agreed that same shall remain the property of PAV–SAVER and all copies shall be returned to PAV–SAVER at the expiration of this

partnership. Further, PAV–SAVER, so long as this agreement is honored and is in force, grants a license under any patents of PAV–SAVER granted in the United States and/or other countries applicable to the Slip–Form paving machine.

. . .

"11.   It is contemplated that this joint venture partnership shall be permanent, and same shall not be terminated or dissolved by either party except upon mutual approval of both parties. If, however, either party shall terminate or dissolve said relationship, the terminating party shall pay to the other party, as liquidated damages, a sum equal to four (4) times the gross royalties received by PAV–SAVER Corporation in the fiscal year ending July 31, 1973, as shown by their corporate financial statement. Said liquidated damages to be paid over a ten (10) year period next immediately following the termination, payable in equal installments."

In 1976, upon mutual consent, the PSC/Dale/Meersman partnership was dissolved and replaced with an identical one between PSC and Vasso, so as to eliminate the individual partners.

It appears that the Pav–Saver Manufacturing Company operated and thrived according to the parties' expectations until around 1981, when the economy slumped, sales of the heavy machines dropped off significantly, and the principals could not agree on the direction that the partnership should take to survive. On March 17, 1983, Attorney Charles Peart, on behalf of PSC, wrote a letter to Meersman terminating the partnership and invoking the provisions of paragraph 11 of the parties' agreement.

In response, Meersman moved into an office on the business premises of the Pav–Saver Manufacturing Company, physically ousted Dale, and assumed a position as the day-to-day manager of the business. PSC then sued in the circuit court of Rock Island County for a court-ordered dissolution of the partnership, return of its patents and trademark, and an accounting. Vasso counterclaimed for declaratory judgment that PSC had wrongfully terminated the partnership and that Vasso was entitled to continue the partnership business, and other relief pursuant to the Illinois Uniform Partnership Act. . . . After protracted litigation, the trial court ruled that PSC had wrongfully terminated the partnership; that Vasso was entitled to continue the partnership business and to possess the partnership assets, including PSC's trademark and patents; that PSC's interest in the partnership was $165,000, based on a $330,000 valuation for the business; and that Vasso was entitled to liquidated damages in the amount of $384,612, payable pursuant to paragraph 11 of the partnership agreement. Judgment was entered accordingly.

Both parties appealed. PSC takes issue with the trial court's failure to order the return of its patents and trademark or, in the alternative, to assign a value to them in determining the value of the partnership assets. Further, neither party agrees with the trial court's enforcement of their agreement for liquidated damages. In its cross-appeal, PSC argues that the amount determined by the formula in paragraph 11 is a penalty. Vasso, on the other hand, contends in its appeal that the amount is unobjectionable, but the installment method of pay-out should not be enforced.

In addition to the afore-cited paragraphs of the parties' partnership agreement, the resolution of this case is controlled by the dissolution provision of the Uniform Partnership Act [§ 38] (Ill.Rev.Stat.1983, ch. 106½, pars. 29–43). The Act provides:

"(2). When dissolution is caused in contravention of the partnership agreement the rights of the partners shall be as follows:

(a) Each partner who has not caused dissolution wrongfully shall have

. . .

II.   The right, as against each partner who has caused the dissolution wrongfully, to damage for breach of the agreement.

(b) The partners who have not caused the dissolution wrongfully, if they all desire to continue the business in the same name, either by themselves or jointly with others, may do so, during the agreed term for the partnership and for that purpose may possess the partnership property, provided they secure the payment by bond approved by the court, or pay to any partner who has caused the dissolution wrongfully, the value of his interest in the partnership at the dissolution, less any damages recoverable under clause (2a II) of this section, and in like manner indemnify him against all present or future partnership liabilities.

(c) A partner who has caused the dissolution wrongfully shall have:

. . .

II.   If the business is continued under paragraph (2b) of this section the right as against his co-partners and all claiming through them in respect of their interests in the partnership, to have the value of his interest in the partnership, less any damages caused to his co-partners by the dissolution, ascertained and paid to him in cash, or the payment secured by bond approved by the court and to be released from all existing liabilities of the partnership; but in ascertaining the value of the partner's interest the value of the good will of the business shall not be considered." Ill.Rev.Stat.1983, ch. 106½, par. 38(2).

Initially we must reject PSC's argument that the trial court erred in refusing to return Pav–Saver's patents and trademark pursuant to paragraph 3 of the partnership agreement, or in the alternative that the court erred in refusing to assign a value to PSC's property in valuing the partnership assets. The partnership agreement on its face contemplated a "permanent" partnership, terminable only upon mutual approval of the parties (paragraph 11). It is undisputed that PSC's unilateral termination was in contravention of the agreement. The wrongful termination necessarily invokes the provisions of the Uniform Partnership Act so far as they concern the rights of the partners. Upon PSC's notice terminating the partnership, Vasso elected to continue the business pursuant to section 38(2)(b) of the Uniform Partnership Act. As correctly noted by Vasso, the statute was enacted "to cover comprehensively the problem of dissolution . . . [and] to stabilize business." (Kurtzon v. Kurtzon (1st Dist. 1950), 339 Ill.App. 431, 437, 90 N.E.2d 245, 248.) Ergo, despite the parties' contractual direction that PSC's patents would be returned to it upon the mutually approved expiration of the partnership (paragraph 3), the right to possess the partnership property and continue in business upon a wrongful termination must be derived from and is controlled by the statute. Evidence at trial clearly established that the Pav–Saver machines being manufactured by the partnership could not be produced or marketed without PSC's patents and trademark. Thus, to continue in business pursuant to the statutorily-granted right of the party not causing the wrongful dissolution, it is essential that paragraph 3 of the parties' agreement—the return to PSC of its patents—not be honored.

Similarly, we find no merit in PSC's argument that the trial court erred in not assigning a value to the patents and trademark. The only evidence adduced at trial to show the value of this property was testimony relating to good will. It was unrefuted that the name Pav–Saver enjoys a good reputation for a good product and reliable service. However, inasmuch as the Uniform Partnership Act specifically states that "the value of the good will of the business shall not be considered" (Ill.Rev.Stat.1983, ch. 106½, par. 38(2)(c)(II)), we find that the trial court properly rejected PSC's good will evidence of the value of its patents and trademark in valuing its interest in the partnership business.

[In the portion of the opinion omitted here the court rejects PSC's argument that the liquidated damages amount was an unenforceable "penalty." Among other observations, the court notes that the amount, $384,-612, was payable in equal installments over a period of 10 years, which means that the present value, or current lump-sum equivalent, was substantially less.]

. . .

Affirmed.

■ JUSTICE STOUDER concurring in part—dissenting in part.

I generally agree with the result of the majority. I cannot, however, accept the majority's conclusion the defendant is entitled to retention of the patents.

. . .

The plaintiff (PSC) brought this action at law seeking dissolution of the partnership before expiration of the agreed term of its existence. Under the Uniform Partnership Act where dissolution is caused by an act in violation of the partnership agreement, the other partner(s) are accorded certain rights. The partnership agreement is a contract, and even though a partner may have the power to dissolve, he does not necessarily have the right to do so. Therefore, if the dissolution he causes is a violation of the agreement, he is liable for any damages sustained by the innocent partner(s) as a result thereof. The innocent partner(s) also have the option to continue the business in the firm name provided they pay the partner causing the dissolution the value of his interest in the partnership. (Ill. Rev.Stat.1983, ch. 106½, par. 38(1), (2).)

The duties and obligations of partners arising from a partnership relation are regulated by the express contract as far as they are covered thereby. A written agreement is not necessary but where it does exist it constitutes the measure of the partners' rights and obligations. While the rights and duties of the partners in relation to the partnership are governed by the Uniform Partnership Act, the uniform act also provides that such rules are subject to any agreement between the parties. . . .

The partnership agreement entered into by PSC and Vasso in pertinent part provides:

"3.B.(2) [PSC] grants to the partnership exclusive license without charge for its patent rights . . . for the term of this agreement. . . . [I]t being understood and agreed that same shall remain the property of [PSC] . . . and shall be returned to [PSC] at the expiration of this partnership . . . ."

The majority holds this provision in the contract is unenforceable. The only apparent reason for such holding is that its enforcement would affect defendant's option to continue the business. No authority is cited to support such a rule.

The partnership agreement further provides:

"11. . . . If either party shall terminate or dissolve said [partnership], the terminating party shall pay to the other party as liquidated damages . . . [$384,612]."

This provision becomes operative at the same time as the provision relating to the return of the patents.

. . .

Here, [because] express terms of the partnership agreement deal with the status of the patents and measure of damages, the question is settled thereby. I think it clear the parties agreed the partnership only be allowed the use of the patents during the term of the agreement. The agreement having been terminated, the right to use the patents is terminated. The provisions in the contract do not conflict with the statutory option to continue the business and even if there were a conflict the provisions of the contract should prevail. The option to continue the business does not carry with it any guarantee or assurance of success and it may often well be that liquidation rather than continuation would be the better option for a partner not at fault.

As additional support for my conclusion, it appears the liquidated damages clause was insisted upon by the defendant because of earlier conduct of the plaintiff withdrawing from a former partnership. Thus, the existence of the liquidated damages clause recognizes the right of plaintiff to withdraw the use of his patents in accordance with the specific terms of the partnership agreement. Since liquidated damages depends on return of the patents, I would vacate that part of the judgment providing defendant is entitled to continue use of the patents and provide that use shall remain with plaintiff.

ANALYSIS AND PLANNING

1. Under the decision of the court, what happens next? Is PSC ever entitled to a cash distribution for its interest in the partnership?

2. This case provides a good illustration of a common problem in drafting agreements: the failure to think through and specify how the terms of the agreement are to be carried out. Here the agreement provided for termination, and liquidated damages, but failed to specify, step by step, precisely what would happen following a notice of termination. If you had been called upon to draft the agreement, what questions of implementation, following termination, would you have raised with the parties? What possibilities for resolving those questions would you have been prepared to offer?

NOTE

Under § 701 of the Uniform Partnership Act (1996), if a partner withdraws from a partnership in contravention of the partnership agreement, the partnership does not necessarily dissolve. If it does not, the partnership must buy out the withdrawing ("dissociated") partner for an amount equal to his or her share of the value of the assets of the partnership if "sold at a price equal to the greater of the liquidation value or the value based on a sale of the entire business as a going concern without the dissociated partner." This amount is reduced by any damages for wrongful withdrawal. Contrary to UPA (1914) § 38(2)(c)(II), however, there is no reduction for the value of goodwill.

C. THE SHARING OF LOSSES

Kovacik v. Reed

49 Cal.2d 166, 315 P.2d 314 (Cal. 1957).

[Early in November 1952, Kovacik told Reed that he (Kovacik) had a chance to remodel some kitchens in San Francisco, and asked Reed to become his job superintendent and estimator. Kovacik explained that he had about $10,000.00 to invest and that, if Reed would superintend and estimate the jobs, he would share profits on a 50–50 basis. Kovacik did not ask Reed to share any losses that might result, and Reed did not offer to do so. Indeed, the two did not discuss possible losses at all. Reed accepted Kovacik's proposal and began work on the venture immediately. Through their venture, the two were able to obtain several remodeling jobs. Reed worked on all of the jobs as job superintendent, but contributed no funds. Instead, Kovacik provided the financing. In August, 1953, Kovacik (who kept all of the financial records) told Reed that the venture had lost money. He then demanded that Reed contribute to the amounts that he (Kovacik) had advanced beyond the income he received. Reed claimed that he never agreed to be liable for losses, and refused to pay.*]

Kovacik thereafter instituted this proceeding, seeking an accounting of the affairs of the venture and to recover from Reed one half of the losses. Despite the evidence above set forth from the statement of the oral proceedings, showing that at no time had defendant agreed to be liable for any of the losses, the trial court "found"—more accurately, we think, concluded as a matter of law—that "plaintiff and defendant were to share equally all their joint venture profits and losses between them," and that defendant "agreed to share equally in the profits and losses of said joint venture." Following an accounting taken by a referee appointed by the court, judgment was rendered awarding plaintiff recovery against defendant of some $4,340, as one half the monetary losses[1] found by the referee to have been sustained by the joint venture.

It is the general rule that in the absence of an agreement to the contrary the law presumes that partners and joint adventurers intended to participate equally in the profits and losses of the common enterprise, irrespective of any inequality in the amounts each contributed to the capital employed in the venture, with the losses being shared by them in the same proportions as they share the profits. . . .

However, it appears that in the cases in which the above stated general rule has been applied, each of the parties had contributed capital consisting of either money or land or other tangible property, or else was to receive compensation for services rendered to the common undertaking which was to be paid before computation of the profits or losses.

Where, however, as in the present case, one partner or joint adventurer contributes the money capital as against the other's skill and labor, all the

---

* [Eds. The statement of facts is taken from a stipulated version relied upon by the court.]

1. The record is silent as to the factors taken into account by the referee in determining the "loss" suffered by the venture. However, there is no contention that defendant's services were ascribed any value whatsoever. It may also be noted that the trial court "found" that "neither plaintiff nor defendant was to receive compensation for their services rendered to said joint venture, but plaintiff and defendant were to share equally all their joint venture profits and losses between them." Neither party suggests that plaintiff actually rendered services to the venture in the same sense that defendant did. And, as is clear from the settled statement, plaintiff's proposition to defendant was that plaintiff would provide the money as against defendant's contribution of services as estimator and superintendent.

cases cited, and which our research has discovered, hold that neither party is liable to the other for contribution for any loss sustained. Thus, upon loss of the money the party who contributed it is not entitled to recover any part of it from the party who contributed only services.

The rationale of this rule . . . is that where one party contributes money and the other contributes services, then in the event of a loss each would lose his own capital—the one his money and the other his labor. Another view would be that in such a situation the parties have, by their agreement to share equally in profits, agreed that the values of their contributions—the money on the one hand and the labor on the other— were likewise equal; it would follow that upon the loss, as here, of both money and labor, the parties have shared equally in the losses. Actually, of course, plaintiff here lost only some $8,680—or somewhat less than the $10,000 which he originally proposed and agreed to invest. . . .

The judgment is reversed.

NOTES AND QUESTIONS

1. The relevant statutory provisions are UPA (1914) §§ 18(a) and 40. The former provides, in pertinent part:

The rights and duties of the partners in relation to the partnership shall be determined, subject to any agreement between them, by the following rules:

(a) Each partner shall be repaid his contributions, whether by way of capital or advances to the partnership property and share equally in the profits and surplus remaining after all liabilities, including those to partners, are satisfied; and must contribute towards the losses, whether of capital or otherwise sustained by the partnership according to his share in the profits.

Section 40(b) provides that, subject to any contrary agreement, upon dissolution, liabilities of the partnership shall be paid in the following order:

I. Those owing to creditors other than partners,

II. Those owing to partners other than for capital and profits,

III. Those owing to partners in respect of capital,

IV. Those owing to partners in respect of profits.

Subsection 40(d) further provides, in pertinent part: "The partners shall contribute, as provided by section 18(a) the amount necessary to satisfy the liabilities [set forth in § 40(b)]."

Is the holding in *Kovacik* consistent with the plain meaning, if any, of these provisions? The drafters of the revised Uniform Partnership Act (1996) apparently did not believe so. Section 401(b) readopts the loss sharing rule of UPA section 18(a): "Each partner is entitled to an equal share of the partnership profits and is chargeable with a share of partnership losses in proportion to the partner's share of the profits." Even more to the point, the official comment thereto expressly rejects *Kovacik*.

> Subsection (b) establishes the default rules for the sharing of partnership profits and losses. The UPA § 18(a) rules that profits are shared equally and that losses, whether capital or operating, are shared in proportion to each partner's share of the profits are continued. . . . The default rules apply, as does UPA § 18(a), where one or more of the partners contribute no capital, although there is case law to the contrary [citing, inter alia, *Kovacik*].

2. What result if Reed had made even a nominal monetary contribution to the partnership's capital or had received some compensation for his services? What result if Kovacik had done as much work on the partnership's jobs as had Reed? What if Kovacik had done about half—or one quarter—as much work as Reed?

3. Were Kovacik and Reed free to adopt any rule they wanted for sharing of losses? If so, why do you suppose they failed to do so?

4. Is it likely in this case that Kovacik was more wealthy than Reed? Is it more likely in most cases that the contributor of capital will be more wealthy than the contributor of services? If so, how should that affect the outcome of the case?

5. Should the outcome in a case like *Kovacik* turn on which of the partners originated the project or business? If so, should the legal rule turn on the how this issue is resolved in each case or on how it is likely to turn out in most cases?

6. Under the *Kovacik* rule, the services-only partner does not share in loss of the amount initially invested by the capital-only partner. What concern might the capital-only partner have about the effect of this rule on the job performance or the decisionmaking by the services-only partner? How might that concern affect the bargain over loss sharing?

7. It appears that Kovacik and Reed had not bargained over, or even discussed, the question of allocating losses in the event the partnership failed. If they had bargained, what rule do you suppose they would have adopted? Would they have agreed that Reed had no obligation to contribute to partnership losses? Does your answer to that question inform your analysis of the merits of the rule announced in *Kovacik*?

D. BUYOUT AGREEMENTS

A buy-out, or buy-sell, agreement is an agreement that allows a partner to end her or his relationship with the other partners and receive a cash payment, or series of payments, or some assets of the firm, in return for her or his interest in the firm. There are many possible approaches. A good buy-out agreement must be tailored to the needs and circumstances of each firm. Here is a brief outline of some of the issues and alternatives:

I. "Trigger" events
  A. Death
  B. Disability
  C. Will of any partner
II. Obligation to buy versus option
  A. Firm
  B. Other investors
  C. Consequences of refusal to buy
    i. If there is an obligation
    ii. If there is no obligation
III. Price
  A. Book value
  B. Appraisal
  C. Formula (e.g., five times earnings)
  D. Set price each year
  E. Relation to duration (e.g., lower price in first five years)
IV. Method of payment
  A. Cash
  B. Installments (with interest?)
V. Protection against debts of partnership
VI. Procedure for offering either to buy or sell
  A. First mover sets price to buy or sell
  B. First mover forces others to set price

What terms would you propose for a buy-out agreement in the situations described in each of the cases presented in the preceding section?

G & S Investments v. Belman

145 Ariz. 258, 700 P.2d 1358 (Ct. App., Div. 2, 1984).

This case involves a partnership dispute arising out of the misconduct and subsequent death of Thomas N. Nordale. There are two principal issues in this case: whether the surviving general partner, G & S Investments, is entitled to continue the partnership after the death of Nordale, and how the value of Nordale's interest in partnership property is to be computed. The trial court, after making findings of fact and conclusions of law, entered judgment in favor of G & S Investments, finding that it had the right to continue the partnership and that the estate was owed $4,867.57. . . .

Century Park, Ltd., is a limited partnership which was formed to receive ownership of a 62–unit apartment complex in Tucson. In 1982 the general partners were G & S Investments (51 per cent) and Nordale (25.5

per cent). The remaining partnership interest was owned by the limited partners, Jones and Chapin.

In 1979 Nordale began using cocaine, which caused a personality change. He became suspicious of his partners and other people, and he could not communicate with other people. He stopped going to work and stopped keeping normal business hours. He stopped returning phone calls and became hyperactive, agitated and angry toward people for no reason. Commencing in 1980 he made threats to some of the other partners, stating that he was going to get them and fix them.

Nordale lived in the apartment complex. This led to several problems. He sexually solicited an underage female tenant of the complex. Despite repeated demands, he refused to give up possession or pay rent on an apartment that the partnership had allowed him to use temporarily during his divorce. His lifestyle in the apartment complex created a great deal of tension and disturbance and frightened the tenants. At least one tenant was lost because of the disturbances.

Fundamental business and management disputes also arose. Nordale irrationally insisted upon converting the apartment complex into condominiums despite adverse tax consequences and mortgage interest rates that were at an all-time high. He also insisted on raising the rents despite the fact that recent attempts to do so had resulted in mass vacancies which had a devastating economic effect on the partnership enterprise.

By 1981 Gary Gibson and Steven Smith (G & S Investments) had come to the conclusion that Nordale was incapable of making rational business decisions and that they should seek a dissolution of the partnership which would allow them to carry on the business and buy out Nordale's interest.

The original complaint, filed on September 11, 1981, sought a judicial dissolution and the right to carry on the business and buy out Nordale's interest as permitted by [UPA (1914) § 38].

. . .

After the filing of the complaint, on February 16, 1982, Nordale died. On June 28, 1982, appellees filed a supplemental complaint invoking their right to continue the partnership and acquire Nordale's interest under article 19 of the partnership's Articles of Limited Partnership. The key provisions of article 19 are as follows:

"(a) In the interest of a continuity of the partnership it is agreed that upon the death, retirement, insanity or resignation of one of the general partners . . . *the surviving or remaining general partners may continue the partnership business.* . . .

. . .

(e) Rules as to resignation or retirement [which under Article 19(d) includes death].

. . .

(2) In the event the surviving or remaining general partner shall desire to continue the partnership business, *he shall purchase the interest of the retiring or resigning general partner. . . ."* (Emphasis added)

. . .

THE FILING OF THE ORIGINAL COMPLAINT

Appellant contends that the mere filing of the complaint acted as a dissolution of the partnership, requiring the liquidation of the assets and distribution of the net proceeds to the partners. He takes this position because he believes the estate will receive more money under this theory than if the other partners are allowed to carry on the business upon payment of the amount which was due to Nordale under the partnership agreement. Appellees contend that the filing of the complaint did not cause a dissolution but that the wrongful conduct of Nordale, in contravention of the partnership agreement, gave the court the power to dissolve the partnership and allow them to carry on the business by themselves. See [UPA (1914) § 38.] We agree with appellees.

Contrary to appellant's contention, Nordale's conduct was in contravention of the partnership agreement. Nordale's conduct affected the carrying on of the business and made it impracticable to continue in partnership with him. His conduct was wrongful and was in contravention of the partnership agreement, thus allowing the court to permit appellees to carry on the business. . . . [UPA (1914) § 32] authorizes the court to dissolve a partnership when:

" . . .

(2) A partner becomes in any other way incapable of performing his part of the partnership contract.

(3) A partner has been guilty of such conduct as tends to affect prejudicially the carrying on of the business.

(4) A partner willfully or persistently commits a breach of the partnership agreement, or otherwise so conducts himself in matters relating to the partnership business that it is not reasonably practicable to carry on the business in partnership with him. . . ."

In the case of Cooper v. Isaacs, 448 F.2d 1202 (D.C.Cir.1971) the court was met with the same contention made here, to-wit, that the mere filing of the complaint acted as a dissolution. The court rejected this contention. To paraphrase the reasoning of the court in Cooper v. Isaacs, supra, because the Uniform Partnership Act provides for dissolution for cause by decree of court and appellees have alleged facts which would entitle them to a dissolution on this ground if proven, their filing of the complaint cannot be said to effect a dissolution, wrongful or otherwise, under the act; dissolution would occur only when decreed by the court or when brought about by other acts.

ARTICLE 19 OF THE ARTICLES OF PARTNERSHIP

Article 19 of the Articles of Partnership provides that upon the death, retirement, insanity or resignation of one of the general partners the surviving or remaining general partners may continue the partnership business. It further provides that should the surviving or remaining general partners desire to continue the partnership business, they must purchase the interest of the retiring or resigning general partner.   .   .   .

THE BUY–OUT FORMULA

Article 19(e)(2)(i) contains the following buy-out provision:

"The amount shall be calculated as follows:

By the addition of the sums of the amount of the resigning or retiring general partner's *capital account* plus an amount equal to the average of the prior three years' profits and gains actually paid to the general partner, or as agreed upon by the general partners, provided said agreed sum does not exceed the calculated sum in dollars." (Emphasis added)

Appellant claims that the term "capital account" in article 19(e)(2)(i) is ambiguous. The estate relies on the testimony of an accountant, Jon Young, that the term "capital account" is ambiguous merely because there is no definition of the term in the articles. He claimed that it was not clear whether the cost basis or the fair market value of the partnership's assets should be used in determining the capital account. Even on direct examination, however, Young admitted that read literally the buy-out formula takes the capital account of the deceased partner and adds to that amount the average of the prior three years' earnings. On cross-examination he admitted that generally accepted accounting principles require the partnership capital accounts be maintained on a cost basis and that he has never seen a partnership in which the capital accounts in the books and records were based on the fair market value.   .   .   .

In contrast, Gibson and Smith testified that the parties actually intended and understood "capital account" to mean exactly what it literally says, the account which shows a partner's capital contribution to the partnership plus profits minus losses.* Smith, an accountant, further testified that while there is a relationship between the capital accounts and valuation of the partnership assets, the valuation of the assets does not affect the actual entries made on the capital account.

---

* [Eds.—The capital account is also reduced by the amount of any distributions. To illustrate, suppose the total cash amount initially contributed by the partners was $400,000; that Nordale contributed $100,000 (25 percent), which is his initial capital account; that there were no further contributions; that the partnership had net profits of $40,000 in each of its first three years (a total of $120,000). Nordale's share of the profit would be $30,000, which would increase his capital account to $130,000. If there had been a total distribution of $40,000 to the partners, Nordale would have received $10,-000 and that would have reduced his capital account to $120,000. If there had been total losses of $500,000 in the first three years, and no distributions, Nordale's share of the losses would have been $125,000 and his capital account would have been a negative $25,000. Any change in the value of the partnerships real estate investment is ignored. Suppose, for example, that there had been total losses of $500,000, financed by borrowing against the security of the real estate, which had increased in fair market value by $1.3 million. The fair market value of Nor-

There was no dispute that Nordale's capital account showed a negative balance of $44,510.09, . . . [while] the fair market value of his interest in the partnership . . . would have amounted to the sum of $76,714.24.

. . .

The words "capital account" are not ambiguous and clearly mean the partner's capital account as it appears on the books of the partnership. Our conclusion is further buttressed by the entire language of article 19(e)(2)(i) which requires, for a buy-out, the payment of the amount of the partner's capital account plus other sums. This is "capital account" language and not "fair market value" language.

. . .

Because partnerships result from contract, the rights and liabilities of the partners among themselves are subject to such agreements as they may make. . . .

Partnership buy-out agreements are valid and binding although the purchase price agreed upon is less or more than the actual value of the interest at the time of death. . . .

We do not have the power to rewrite article 19 based upon subjective notions of fairness arising long after the agreement was made or because the agreement did not turn out to be an advantageous one. Modern business practice mandates that the parties be bound by the contract they enter into, absent fraud or duress. . . . It is not the province of this court to act as a post-transaction guardian for either party.

PLANNING

1. What, if any, are the virtues of the buyout agreement in this case?

2. What alternative valuation formula would you suggest? What other terms would you want to discuss if you were representing the parties?

3. Might your advice vary depending on whether you represented Nordale or G & S Investments?

E. LAW PARTNERSHIP DISSOLUTIONS

Jewel v. Boxer

156 Cal.App.3d 171, 203 Cal.Rptr. 13 (1984).

In this case we hold that in the absence of a partnership agreement, the Uniform Partnership Act requires that attorneys' fees received on cases

dale's interest would have increased by $200,000 (25 percent of the $1.3 million increase in fair market value less 25 percent of the $500,000 loan). But his capital account would still be a negative $25,000. The court in the present case observes that "capital account" and "book value," though not "synonymous," are "functional equivalents."]

in progress upon dissolution of a law partnership are to be shared by the former partners according to their right to fees in the former partnership, regardless of which former partner provides legal services in the case after the dissolution. The fact that the client substitutes one of the former partners as attorney of record in place of the former partnership does not affect this result.

Howard H. Jewel and Brian O. Leary appeal from a judgment, after dissolution of the former law partnership of Jewel, Boxer and Elkind, allocating postdissolution fees on a quantum meruit basis. We reverse the judgment and remand the cause for allocation based upon the respective interests in the former partnership.

On December 2, 1977, the law firm of Jewel, Boxer and Elkind was dissolved by mutual agreement of its four partners—Howard H. Jewel, Stewart N. Boxer, Peter F. Elkind, and Brian O. Leary. The partners formed two new firms: Jewel and Leary, and Boxer and Elkind. Three associates employed by the old firm were employed by Boxer and Elkind. The partners in the old firm not only lacked an agreement about the allocation of fees from active cases upon a dissolution of the partnership but, contrary to the sound legal advice they undoubtedly always gave their partnership clients, they had no written partnership agreement. The absence of a written partnership agreement was an invitation to litigation upon a dissolution of the partnership.

On the date of dissolution the former partnership had numerous active cases. Boxer, Elkind, and the three associates had handled most of the active personal injury and workers' compensation cases; the rest, as well as other kinds of cases, had been handled by Jewel and Leary. Shortly after dissolution, each former partner sent a letter to each client whose case he had handled for the old firm, announcing the dissolution. Enclosed in the letter was a substitution of attorney form, which was executed and returned by each client retaining the attorney who had handled the case for the old firm.[1] The new firms represented the clients under fee agreements entered into between the client and the old firm.

At issue here is the proper allocation of attorneys' fees received from these cases, some of which were still active at trial. Jewel and Leary filed a complaint for an accounting of these fees, contending they were assets of the dissolved partnership.

In a nonjury trial the court first determined that the partnership interests in income of the old firm were 30 percent for Jewel, 27 percent each for Boxer and Elkind and 16 percent for Leary. The court then allocated the disputed fees among the old and new firms by considering three factors: the time spent by each firm in the handling of each case, the source of each case (always the old firm), and, in the personal injury contingency fee cases, the result achieved by the new firm. The court assigned a value of 25 percent to the source factor, and thus allocated 25

---

1. Neither party challenged at trial or on appeal the authority of a former partner to execute a substitution of attorney on behalf of the dissolved partnership.

percent of the total fees to the old firm for this factor. In the personal
injury cases the court assigned values of 20 percent, 30 percent, and 40
percent for the result factor, depending on when the cases were settled or if
they were tried. Remaining percentages (35 percent to 55 percent in the
personal injury cases and 75 percent in the other cases) were allocated in
accordance with the amount of attorney time expended upon the case
before and after dissolution. Under this formula, Jewel and Leary was
determined to owe $115,041.16 to the old firm, and Boxer and Elkind was
determined to owe $291,718.60 to the old firm. The court rendered
judgment in these amounts, plus interest at the legal rate from the date of
receipt of each fee on the amount due the old firm. Although we reverse
the judgment, we cannot do so without expressing admiration for the
laudable efforts of the learned trial judge who masterfully developed a
formula geared to achieving a just and equitable result for each party.

Under the Uniform Partnership Act (Corp.Code, § 15001 et seq.), a
dissolved partnership continues until the winding up of unfinished partnership business. (Corp.Code, § 15030.) No partner (except a surviving
partner) is entitled to extra compensation for services rendered in completing unfinished business.[2] (Corp.Code, § 15018, subd. (f).) Thus, absent a
contrary agreement, any income generated through the winding up of
unfinished business is allocated to the former partners according to their
respective interests in the partnership.

The trial court in the present case recognized these principles, but
followed a Texas decision which cited no supporting authority but held that
the rule precluding extra compensation for postdissolution services should
not apply to a law partnership, because fees are generated by a former
partner's postdissolution time, skill and labor. (Cofer v. Hearne (Tex.Civ.
App.1970) 459 S.W.2d 877, 879.) The trial court also cited Fracasse v.
Brent (1972) 6 Cal.3d 784 [100 Cal.Rptr. 385, 494 P.2d 9], which held that
a client has an absolute right to discharge an attorney employed under a
contingent fee contract and the attorney is entitled only to the reasonable
value of the services rendered before discharge.

Jewel and Leary contend that the court erred in failing to adhere to
the rule precluding extra compensation, and should have allocated all
postdissolution fees from the old firm's unfinished cases to the four former
partners according to their respective percentage interests in the old firm.
Boxer and Elkind argue that the substitutions of attorneys transformed the
old firm's unfinished business into new firm business and removed that
business from the purview of the Uniform Partnership Act, with the old
firm thereafter, under Fracasse v. Brent, supra, 6 Cal.3d 784, limited to a
quantum meruit recovery for services rendered before discharge.

The decision in Cofer v. Hearne, supra, 459 S.W.2d 877, was plainly
wrong. The Uniform Partnership Act unequivocally prohibits extra com-

2. As used in this opinion extra compensation means receipt by a former partner
of the dissolved partnership of an amount of
compensation which is greater than would
have been received as the former partner's
share of the dissolved partnership.

pensation for postdissolution services, with a single exception for surviving partners. (Corp.Code, § 15018, subd. (f).) The definition of "business" in the Uniform Partnership Act as including "every trade, occupation, or profession" (Corp.Code, § 15002) precludes an exception for law partnerships. (Resnick v. Kaplan (1981) 49 Md.App. 499 [434 A.2d 582, 588].)

Accordingly, several courts in other states have held that after dissolution of a law partnership, income received by the former partners from cases unfinished at the time of dissolution is to be allocated on the basis of the partners' respective interests in the dissolved partnership, not on a quantum meruit basis. . . .

The decision in Resnick v. Kaplan, supra, 434 A.2d 582, is closely analogous to the present case. Resnick, a former partner in a dissolved law partnership, opened his own office and continued to represent clients of the former firm in cases for which he had been responsible before dissolution. The other partners continued to represent other clients of the old firm. (Id., at pp. 584–585.) In an ensuing action for an accounting, the trial court allocated all fees collected in these cases among the former partners according to their percentage interests in the former partnership. The appellate court affirmed, stating that the Uniform Partnership Act "conferred no right upon either side to compensation for services rendered in this winding up process, [citation] and, in the absence of any provision in the partnership document, it was correctly held that the aggregate of the fees collected should be allocated according to the percentages specified in the agreement for the distribution of profits and losses." (Id., at p. 587.) . . .

The court in *Resnick* also rejected an argument made by Boxer and Elkind in the present case (and asserted by the court below in citing Fracasse v. Brent), that clients have an absolute right to the attorney of their choice. The *Resnick* court recognized this right of clients, but said, "it does not mean, as appellant contends, that the fees thereafter earned by the partner chosen by the client are not subject to division in accordance with the partnership agreement." (Id., at p. 588.) . . .

There are sound policy reasons for applying the rule against extra compensation to law partnerships. The rule prevents partners from competing for the most remunerative cases during the life of the partnership in anticipation that they might retain those cases should the partnership dissolve. It also discourages former partners from scrambling to take physical possession of files and seeking personal gain by soliciting a firm's existing clients upon dissolution. Boxer and Elkind argue that application of the rule in the present context will discourage continued representation of clients by the attorney of their choice, as former partners will not want to perform all of the postdissolution work on a particular case while receiving only a portion of the income generated by such work. Of course, this is all the former partners would have received had the partnership not dissolved. Additionally, the former partners will receive, in addition to their partnership portion of such income, their partnership share of income generated by the work of the other former partners, without performing any postdissolution work in those cases. On balance, the allocation of fees according to each partner's interest in the former partnership should not work an undue hardship as to any partner where each partner completes work on the partnership's cases which are active upon its dissolution.

As previously indicated, the trial court's attempt to achieve an equitable result was laudable. At first glance, strict application of the rule against extra compensation might appear to have unjust results (e.g., where a former partner obtains a highly remunerative case just before dissolution, and nearly all work is performed after dissolution). But undue hardship should be prevented by two basic fiduciary duties owed between the former partners. First, each former partner has a duty to wind up and complete the unfinished business of the dissolved partnership. This would prevent a partner from refusing to furnish any work and imposing this obligation totally on the other partners, thus unfairly benefiting from their efforts while putting forth none of his or her own. Second, no former partner may take any action with respect to unfinished business which leads to purely personal gain. . . . Thus, the former partners are obligated to ensure that a disproportionate burden of completing unfinished business does not fall on one former partner or one group of former partners, unless the former partners agree otherwise. It is unlikely that the partners, in discharging their mutual fiduciary duties, will be able to achieve a distribution of the burdens of completing unfinished business that corresponds precisely to their respective interests in the partnership. But partners are free to include in a written partnership agreement provisions for completion of unfinished business that ensure a degree of exactness and certainty unattainable by rules of general application. If there is any disproportionate burden of completing unfinished business here, it results from the parties' failure to have entered into a partnership agreement which could have assured such a result would not occur. The former partners must bear the consequences of their failure to provide for dissolution in a partnership agreement.

In short, the trial court's allocation of postdissolution income to the old and new firms on a quantum meruit basis constituted error. The appropriate remedy is to remand the cause for posttrial proceedings to allocate such income to the former partners of the old firm in accordance with their respective percentage interests in the former partnership. This will also allow the trial court to allocate fees received since the trial.

Under the provisions of the Uniform Partnership Act, the former partners will be entitled to reimbursement for reasonable overhead expenses (excluding partners' salaries) attributable to the production of postdissolution partnership income; in other words, it is net postdissolution income, not gross income, that is to be allocated to the former partners. . . . A reimbursement of reasonable and necessary overhead expenses attributable to the winding up of partnership business is certainly an equitable result. When partners fail to have a partnership agreement which determines how and to what extent such reimbursement should take place, they have no cause to complain about the law supplying an equitable resolution of the issue.   .   .   .

The judgment is reversed and the cause is remanded for further proceedings consistent with this opinion.

PROBLEM

Suppose a law partnership has five equal partners, Bill, Jennifer, Matthew, Renée, and Sean.   The firm engages in a general business practice, including some litigation.   Recently, the firm took on, on a contingent-fee basis, a complex antitrust case, on which Bill has spent 200 hours.   It will probably be at least five years before the case is resolved and Bill expects to spend about half his time on it.   There is a good chance of victory and a large fee but also a good chance of defeat and no fee at all. Virtually all the other matters pending in the firm are ones that can be wound up within six months.   Bill is a litigator and comes to you for business advice.   He has been having trouble getting along with the other partners and would like to strike out on his own.   He wonders what will happen to the antitrust case if that happens and asks for your suggestions about what he should do.   What do you say to him?

QUESTIONS

1.   The court in Jewel v. Boxer says that its rule promotes public policy because it "prevents partners from competing for the most remunerative cases during the life of the partnership in anticipation that they might retain those cases should the partnership dissolve."   In what way, if at all, does the competition to which the court refers violate public policy? Might such competition promote public policy?

2.   In law firms engaged mainly in planning for business clients, rather than in litigating cases, is there likely to be competition for clients? How can firms try to keep this competition from becoming unhealthy?

3.   The court defends its rule on grounds of public policy.   Nonetheless, it says that partners are free to adopt a different rule.   Suppose you are about to enter into a partnership to engage in general civil litigation, with two other people.   One of them is especially good at developing new business and the other at handling the litigation.   You are reasonably good at both aspects of the practice.   What rule would you propose to your intended partners for dividing cases and fees following a dissolution?

Meehan v. Shaughnessy

404 Mass. 419, 535 N.E.2d 1255 (1989).

[The fiduciary-obligation aspects of this case were presented earlier in this Chapter, at page 105, where the statement of facts appears.   Briefly, the court found that Meehan and Boyle, who had been partners in the law firm of Parker Coulter and left to form their own firm, had violated their fiduciary obligations to Parker Coulter by using impermissible methods to line up clients for their new firm before they left Parker Coulter. In the portion of the opinion presented here, the court addresses the legal rights of the Parker Coulter partners in case of dissolution. The court's analysis begins with a review of the provisions of the UPA (1914) (as embodied in Massachusetts law) bearing on dissolution—provisions considered in earlier cases in this Section of the casebook—and then turns to the effect of the Parker Coulter express agreement.]

The Parker Coulter partnership agreement provided for rights on a dissolution caused by the will of a partner which are different from those [the UPA] provides. Because going concerns are typically destroyed in the dissolution process of liquidation and windup, . . . the agreement minimizes the impact of this process. The agreement provides for an allocation to the departing partner of a share of the firm's current net income, and a return of his or her capital contributions. In addition, the agreement also recognizes that a major asset of a law firm is the expected fees it will receive from unfinished business currently being transacted. Instead of assigning a value to the departing partner's interest in this unfinished business, or waiting for the unfinished business to be "wound up" and liquidated, which is the method of division [the UPA] provides, the agreement gives the partner the right to remove any case which came to the firm "through the personal effort or connection" of the partner, if the partner compensates the dissolved partnership "for the services to and expenditures for the client." [8] Once the partner has removed a case, the agreement provides that the partner is entitled to retain all future fees in the case, with the exception of the "fair charge" owed to the dissolved firm.[9]

Although the provision in the partnership agreement which divides the dissolved firm's unfinished business does not expressly apply to the removal of cases which did not come to Parker Coulter through the efforts of the departing partner, we believe that the parties intended this provision to apply to these cases also. We interpret this provision to cover these additional cases for two reasons. First, according to the Canons of Ethics and Disciplinary Rules Regulating the Practice of Law (S.J.C. Rule 3:07, Canon 2, as amended through 398 Mass. 1108 [1986]), a lawyer may not participate in an agreement which restricts the right of a lawyer to practice law after the termination of a relationship created by the agreement. One

---

8. The agreement expressly protects a client's right to choose his or her attorney, by providing that the right to remove a case is "subject to the right of the client to direct that the matter be retained by the continuing firm of remaining partners."

9. The agreement provides that this "fair charge" is a "receivable account of the earlier partnership . . . and [is] divided between the remaining partners and the retiring partner on the basis of which they share in the profits of the firm at the time of the withdrawal." This fair charge is thus treated as an asset of the former partnership. Because the partnership, upon the receipt of the fair charge, gives up all future rights to income from the removed case, the partnership's collective interest in the case is effectively "wound up." The fair charge, therefore, is a method of valuing the partnership's unfinished business as it relates to the removed case.

reason for this rule is to protect the public. . . . The strong public interest in allowing clients to retain counsel of their choice outweighs any professional benefits derived from a restrictive covenant. Thus, the Parker Coulter partners could not restrict a departing partner's right to remove any clients who freely choose to retain him or her as their legal counsel. Second, we believe the agreement's carefully drawn provisions governing dissolution and the division of assets indicate the partners' strong intent not to allow the provisions of [the UPA (1914)] concerning liquidation and windup to govern any portion of the dissolved firm's unfinished business. Therefore, based on the partners' intent, and on the prohibition against restrictive covenants between attorneys, we interpret the agreement to provide that, upon the payment of a fair charge, any case may be removed regardless of whether the case came to the firm through the personal efforts of the departing partner. This privilege to remove, as is shown in our later discussion, is of course dependent upon the partner's compliance with fiduciary obligations.

Under the agreement, therefore, a partner who separates his or her practice from that of the firm receives (1) the right to his or her capital contribution,* (2) the right to a share of the net income to which the dissolved partnership is currently entitled, and (3) the right to a portion of the firm's unfinished business, and in exchange gives up all other rights in the dissolved firm's remaining assets. As to (3) above, "unfinished business," the partner gives up all right to proceeds from any unfinished business of the dissolved firm which the new, surviving firm retains. Under the agreement, the old firm's unfinished business is, in effect, "wound up" immediately; the departing partner takes certain of the unfinished business of the old, dissolved Parker Coulter on the payment of a "fair charge," and the new, surviving Parker Coulter takes the remainder of the old partnership's unfinished business.[11] The two entities surviving

---

* [Editors.—By "capital contribution" apparently the court means "capital account." A partner's capital account is an accounting concept that reflects the partner's initial investment of cash or property, increased by any later such contributions, increased by profits over the years, decreased by losses, and decreased by amounts withdrawn (the "draw"). For example, suppose three equal partners each contribute $50,000 in cash upon the formation of the partnership, to get the firm started. In the first year of operation the firm earns $330,000, allocated $110,000 to each partner (since they are equal partners). Also, during the first year each partner draws (that is, receives from the partnership checking account) $90,000 for personal living expenses. The capital account of each partner at the end of the year would be $70,000: the initial $50,000 plus the $110,000 profit less the $90,000 draw.]

11. A more equitable provision would require that the new, surviving partnership also pay a "fair charge" on the cases it takes from the dissolved partnership. This "fair charge" from the new firm, as is the "fair charge" from the departing partner, would be an asset of the dissolved partnership, in which the departing partner has an interest.

[Editors.—To illustrate the Parker Coulter formula, imagine the following facts: The firm consists of three partners, Ann, Betty, and Carlos, and three cases, X, Y, and Z. The partners have devoted 10 hours to each case and have agreed that the hourly rate for work done is $150. (It does not matter whose time was spent on each case; before dissolution it is all partnership time.) Carlos decides to leave the firm and is entitled to, and does, take with him Case Z. Under the Parker Coulter formula, Carlos would be required to pay $1,500 (10 hours at $150 per

after the dissolution possess "new business," unconnected with that of the old firm, and the former partners no longer have a continuing fiduciary obligation to windup for the benefit of each other the business they shared in their former partnership.

In sum, the statute gives a partner the power to dissolve a partnership at any time. Under the statute, the assets of the dissolved partnership are divided among the former partners through the process of liquidation and windup. The statute, however, allows partners to design their own methods of dividing assets and, provided the dissolution is not premature, expressly states that the partners' method controls. Here, the partners have fashioned a division method which immediately winds up unfinished business, allows for a quick separation of the surviving practices, and minimizes the disruptive impact of a dissolution.

[The court next considers the damages owed by Meehan and Boyle to Parker Coulter for the violation of fiduciary obligation. The gist of the court's conclusion is that the defendants, Meehan and Boyle, have the burden of proving that clients who were improperly taken by them would have consented to the removal in the absence of the fiduciary breach. As to the nature of the proof, the court states:]

Circumstantial factors relevant to whether a client freely exercised his or her right to choose include the following: (1) who was responsible for initially attracting the client to the firm; (2) who managed the case at the firm; (3) how sophisticated the client was and whether the client made the decision with full knowledge; and (4) what was the reputation and skill of the removing attorneys.

[The court proceeds to specify the rule for determining damages:]

In those cases, if any, where the judge concludes, in accordance with the above analysis, that Meehan and Boyle have met their burden, we resolve the parties' dispute over fees solely under the partnership agreement. . . .

We [next] address the correct remedy in those cases, if any, which the judge determines Meehan and Boyle unfairly removed. In light of a conclusion that Meehan and Boyle have failed to prove that certain clients would not have preferred to stay with Parker Coulter, granting Parker Coulter merely a fair charge on these cases pursuant to the partnership agreement would not make it whole. We turn, therefore, to [UPA (1914) § 21]: "Every partner must account to the partnership for any benefit, and hold as trustee for it any profits derived by him without the consent of the other partners from any transaction connected with the formation, conduct or liquidation of the partnership. . . ." We have consistently applied

hour) to the "new, surviving" Ann/Betty firm for the work completed on Case Z; but Ann and Betty would not be required to pay Carlos anything for the work done on the other two cases. Of the $1,500 paid to the Ann/Betty firm, Carlos would be entitled to his one-third share, or $500. Thus, even though the cases are alike financially, and are split equally, the dissolution will cost Carlos $1,000, and Ann and Betty will each gain $500.]

this statute, and held that a partner must account for any profits which flow from a breach of fiduciary duty. . . .

Meehan and Boyle breached the duty they owed to Parker Coulter. If the judge determines that, as a result of this breach, certain clients left the firm, Meehan and Boyle must account to the partnership for any profits they receive on these cases pursuant to [the UPA (1914)], in addition to paying the partnership a fair charge on these cases pursuant to the agreement. The "profit" on a particular case is the amount by which the fee received from the case exceeds the sum of (1) any reasonable overhead expenses MBC [the firm formed by Meehan and Boyle, with Cohen also a partner] incurs in resolving the case, see Jewel v. Boxer, 156 Cal.App.3d 171, 180 (1984) . . ., and (2) the fair charge it owes under the partnership agreement. We emphasize that reasonable overhead expenses on a particular case are not the equivalent of the amount represented by the hours MBC attorneys have expended on the case multiplied by their hourly billing rate. Reasonable overhead expenses are to include only MBC's costs in generating the fee, and are not to include any profit margin for MBC. We treat this profit on a particular case as if it had been earned in the usual course of business of the partnership which included Meehan and Boyle as partners. . . . Failing to treat this profit as if it had been earned by Meehan or Boyle while at their former partnership would exclude Meehan and Boyle from participating in the fruits of their labors and, more importantly, would provide Parker Coulter with an unjustified windfall. Parker Coulter would receive a windfall because there is no guarantee that the profit would have been generated had the case not been handled at MBC. Meehan's and Boyle's former partners are thus entitled to their portion of the fair charge on each of the unfairly removed cases (89.2%), and to that amount of profit from an unfairly removed case which they would have enjoyed had the MBC attorneys handled the case at Parker Coulter (89.2%).

The MBC attorneys argue that any remedy which grants Parker Coulter a recovery in excess of a fair charge on cases removed impermissibly infringes on an attorney's relationship with clients and reduces his or her incentive to use best efforts on their behalf. We agree that punitive measures may infringe on a client's right to adequate representation, and to counsel of his or her own choosing. Cf. *Jewel*, supra at 178 (how fee distributed among former partners of no concern to client); . . . .

We believe, however, that the remedy we impose does not suffer from the MBC attorneys' claimed defects. Under the constructive trust we impose, Meehan and Boyle will receive a share of the fruits of their efforts in the unfairly removed cases which is the same as that which they would have enjoyed at Parker Coulter. We note, moreover, that incentives other than profit motivate attorneys. These incentives include an attorney's ethical obligations to the client and the profession, and a concern for his or her reputation. . . .

Furthermore, the MBC attorneys' argument would provide us with no mechanism to enforce the partners' fiduciary duties. Imposition of a narrowly tailored constructive trust will enforce the obligations resulting from a breach of duty and will not harm the innocent clients. We conclude, therefore, that Meehan and Boyle hold in a constructive trust for the benefit of the former partnership the profits they have derived or may derive from any cases which they unfairly removed.

ANALYSIS

1.   How much worse off are Meehan and Boyle by virtue of their breach of fiduciary duty than they would have been if Parker Coulter had had no agreement, there had been no such breach, and the rule of Jewel v. Boxer had been applied?

2.   The court in Meehan v. Shaughnessy does not consider whether Meehan and Boyle violated their fiduciary obligation to their Parker Coulter partners when, while still acting as partners of Parker Coulter, they talked Cohen (a junior partner at Parker Coulter) and Schafer (an associate) into joining their new firm. Assuming that this conduct was a violation of fiduciary obligation, what are the damages?

SECTION 9. LIMITED PARTNERSHIPS

Holzman v. De Escamilla

86 Cal.App.2d 858, 195 P.2d 833 (1948).

This is an appeal by James L. Russell and H.W. Andrews from a judgment decreeing they were general partners in Hacienda Farms, Limited, a limited partnership, from February 27, to December 1, 1943, and as such were liable as general partners to the creditors of the partnership.

Early in 1943, Hacienda Farms, Limited, was organized as a limited partnership (Secs. 2477 et seq., Civil Code) with Ricardo de Escamilla as the general partner and James L. Russell and H.W. Andrews as limited partners.

The partnership went into bankruptcy in December, 1943, and Lawrence Holzman was appointed and qualified as trustee of the estate of the bankrupt. On November 13, 1944, he brought this action for the purpose of determining that Russell and Andrews, by taking part in the control of the partnership business, had become liable as general partners to the creditors of the partnership. The trial court found in favor of the plaintiff on this issue and rendered judgment to the effect that the three defendants were liable as general partners.

The findings supporting the judgment are so fully supported by the testimony of certain witnesses, although contradicted by Russell and Andrews, that we need mention but a small part of it. We will not mention conflicting evidence as conflicts in the evidence are settled in the trial court and not here.

De Escamilla was raising beans on farm lands near Escondido at the time the partnership was formed. The partnership continued raising vegetable and truck crops which were marketed principally through a produce concern controlled by Andrews.

The record shows the following testimony of de Escamilla:

"A. We put in some tomatoes.

"Q. Did you have a conversation or conversations with Mr. Andrews or Mr. Russell before planting the tomatoes? A. We always conferred and agreed as to what crops we would put in. . . .

"Q. Who determined that it was advisable to plant watermelons? A. Mr. Andrews. . . .

"Q. Who determined that string beans should be planted? A. All of us. There was never any planting done—except the first crop that was put into the partnership as an asset by myself, there was never any crop that

201

was planted or contemplated in planting that wasn't thoroughly discussed and agreed upon by the three of us; particularly Andrews and myself."

De Escamilla further testified that Russell and Andrews came to the farms about twice a week and consulted about the crops to be planted. He did not want to plant peppers or egg plant because, as he said, "I don't like that country for peppers or egg plant; no, sir," but he was overruled and those crops were planted. The same is true of the watermelons.

Shortly before October 15, 1943, Andrews and Russell requested de Escamilla to resign as manager, which he did, and Harry Miller was appointed in his place.

Hacienda Farms, Limited, maintained two bank accounts, one in a San Diego bank and another in an Escondido bank. It was provided that checks could be drawn on the signatures of any two of the three partners. It is stated in plaintiff's brief, without any contradiction (the checks are not before us) that money was withdrawn on twenty checks signed by Russell and Andrews and that all other checks except three bore the signatures of de Escamilla, the general partner, and one of the other defendants. The general partner had no power to withdraw money without the signature of one of the limited partners.

Section 2483 of the Civil Code provides as follows:

"A limited partner shall not become liable as a general partner, unless, in addition to the exercise of his rights and powers as a limited partner, he takes part in the control of the business."

The foregoing illustrations sufficiently show that Russell and Andrews both took "part in the control of the business." The manner of withdrawing money from the bank accounts is particularly illuminating. The two men had absolute power to withdraw all the partnership funds in the banks without the knowledge or consent of the general partner. Either Russell or Andrews could take control of the business from de Escamilla by refusing to sign checks for bills contracted by him and thus limit his activities in the management of the business. They required him to resign as manager and selected his successor. They were active in dictating the crops to be planted, some of them against the wish of Escamilla. This clearly shows they took part in the control of the business of the partnership and thus became liable as general partners.   .   .   .

Judgment affirmed.

QUESTION

The Revised Uniform Limited Partnership Act (RULPA) now provides that a limited partner who participates in control is liable "only to persons who transact business with the limited partnership reasonably believing, based upon the limited partner's conduct, that the limited partner is a general partner." § 303(a). The RULPA also provides that "a limited partner does not participate in control . . . solely by . . . (2) consulting with and advising a general partner with respect to the business of the limited partnership.'' § 303(b). In Mt. Vernon Sav. and Loan v. Partridge Associates, 679 F.Supp. 522 (D.Md.1987), the court stated:

> [A] limited partner who disregards the limited partnership form to such an extent that he becomes substantially the same as a general partner has unlimited liability regardless of a plaintiff's knowledge of his role. At the same time, a limited partner may have unlimited liability for exercising less than a general partner's power if the fact that he acted as more than a limited partner was actually known to the plaintiff.

Under these rules, suppose that a creditor of Hacienda Farms, who had delivered fertilizer to the farm on de Escamilla's order, saw and heard Andrews and Russell engaging in the conversations about which de Escamilla testified. Would Andrews and Russell be liable to the creditor? What if, in addition, the creditor had in the past received payment by checks that bore the signatures of Andrews and of Russell?

CHAPTER 3

THE NATURE OF THE CORPORATION

SECTION 1. PROMOTERS AND THE CORPORATE ENTITY

We begin with two issues relating to corporations and their promoters. In the corporate context, the word "promoter" is a term of art referring to a person who identifies a business opportunity and puts together a deal, forming a corporation as the vehicle for investment by other people. First we will examine the fiduciary obligations of promoters to the corporation and then the obligations of promoters to third persons for pre-incorporation commitments. The objective is in part to consider certain legal doctrine and planning issues, but also to begin to develop a sense of what is meant by the concept of the corporation as a separate entity and how that concept affects the relationships among individuals involved in the corporate enterprise.

HYPOTHETICAL CASES: FIDUCIARY OBLIGATIONS

The following set of hypotheticals is derived from a famous pair of cases involving the Old Dominion Copper Company. Old Dominion Copper Mining & Smelting Co. v. Lewisohn, 210 U.S. 206, 28 S.Ct. 634, 52 L.Ed. 1025 (1908); Old Dominion Copper Mining & Smelting Co. v. Bigelow, 203 Mass. 159, 89 N.E. 193 (1909), affirmed, 225 U.S. 111, 32 S.Ct. 641, 56 L.Ed. 1009 (1912).

Case 1. Ann buys land for $125,000 and shortly thereafter sells it to a total stranger, Sean, for $200,000. Ann makes no misrepresentations. Sean does not ask what Ann paid for the property, or when she bought it, and Ann does not say. Thus, there is no basis for a common-law action for fraud or deceit. There is no fiduciary obligation of Ann to Sean and no duty to disclose the purchase price. Ann is entitled to keep her $75,000 profit. Of course, if Ann lies to Sean, she may be liable to him for damages. What if he asks her what she paid for the land? If she is reluctant to reveal her purchase price but wants to avoid liability, how might she respond? Suppose Sean says, "I heard that you bought the land for $125,000 only a month ago. Is that true?" Assuming that Ann in fact bought the land two months ago, for $125,000, how might she respond?

Case 2. Art has recently bought land for $125,000. Shortly thereafter he meets Paula, an individual for whom he has in the past served as agent in the acquisition of land. Paula expresses an interest in the land that Art has just bought but does not know that Art is the owner and Art does nothing to inform her. Paula asks Art to represent her in seeking to acquire the land. Art agrees to do so. Art then sells the land to Paula for

$200,000, without revealing his interest in the transaction. Assume that the land is in fact worth $200,000 (and that Art had in fact been offered $195,000 for it). Can Paula recover the $75,000 profit that Art has made? The relevant legal doctrine is stated as follows in Section 388 of the Restatement of Agency (Second): "Unless otherwise agreed, an agent who makes a profit in connection with transactions conducted by him on behalf of the principal is under a duty to give such profit to the principal." Does that seem to you to be a good rule? Why?

Case 3. With the basic principles reflected in the first two cases in mind, we can turn to the question of how the results are affected by the interposition of a corporation. Suppose the facts are the same as in Case 2, except that the buyer is a corporation, P Corp., instead of an individual, and that the corporation is owned by Paula (that is, she owns all the shares of its stock). Suppose further that Paula is the president of the corporation and she conducts the negotiations with Art by virtue of which he agrees to act for the corporation. Art would become an agent of the corporation and its legal position would be the same as that of Paula in Case 2. Paula herself would not be allowed to proceed as an individual against Art, either in her role as shareholder or in her role as president of the corporation.

Case 4. Suppose that Art has just bought land for $125,000 and contemplates selling it to Paula for use in a residential development. Art has developed a plan that contemplates that the development will be conducted by a corporation called Art Corp., in which he will have no interest. He considers three approaches to selling his land to Paula. Under the first approach he causes a corporation to be formed. The corporation then sells all the shares of its stock in the corporation to Paula for $200,000 cash. Paula, her husband Peter, and her daughter Peggy become the directors of the corporation and Paula becomes its president. Art then sells the land to the corporation for $200,000; the transaction is approved by the corporation's board of directors. In this scenario, the relevant general rule of corporate law is that Art, as a promoter, owes a fiduciary obligation to the corporation. His obligation is like that of an agent to a principal (as in Case 2). If he does not reveal his interest in the land, and his profit, and adequately secure the approval of directors of the corporation (or, possibly, the approval of Paula as sole shareholder), can the corporation recover the $75,000 profit? In other words, can Art deal with the corporation at arm's length? Is there any good reason why he should not be allowed to do so? That is, is there any good reason why the result here should be different from the result in Case 1?

Under a second approach, Art sells the land to Paula for $200,000. Paula then forms the corporation and contributes the land to it in exchange for all of its shares of common stock. If this approach is followed, under what legal theories, if any, might Paula or the corporation recover Art's $75,000 profit? Can you think of any good reason why the result should be different under this approach than it would be under the first approach?

Under the third approach, Art forms a corporation and contributes $200,000 cash to it in return for all of its shares of common stock. He elects himself, his wife Alice, and his son Abe as directors and the directors appoint him president. He sells the land to the corporation for $200,000; the transaction is approved by the board of directors. Five days later, according to a preconceived plan, Art sells all his shares to Paula for $200,000. Art, Alice, and Abe are immediately replaced as directors of the corporation by Paula, Peter, and Peggy, and Paula replaces Art as president. Assume that Paula has no cause of action on a theory of common law fraud (which requires misrepresentation and reliance) or under any state or federal laws affecting the sale of securities. Should the corporation be allowed to recover the $75,000 secret profit, without proof of unfairness? (Don't leap to conclusions. The U.S. Supreme Court and the Massachusetts Supreme Judicial Court reached opposite conclusions on a question much like this one in the *Old Dominion* cases referred to above.) If you conclude that the corporation should be allowed to recover the $75,000, suppose Paula had held the shares for six months, during which time she had done nothing to develop or use the land, and then had sold the shares for $250,000 to a shrewd real estate investor who had thoroughly inspected the land, and that thereafter it is discovered for the first time that Art made the $75,000 profit. Should the corporation still be allowed to recover the profit? What if the amount contributed to the corporation by Art and used by the corporation to buy the property was $125,000 instead of $200,000, but Art nonetheless sold the shares to Paula for $200,000?

Southern–Gulf Marine Co. No. 9, Inc. v. Camcraft, Inc.

410 So.2d 1181 (La.App.1982).

Plaintiff, a corporation chartered under the laws of Cayman, British West Indies, filed suit alleging breach of a contract to furnish a ship. Defendant responded with a peremptory exception of no cause of action based upon the plaintiff's lack of corporate existence at the time of entering into the contract, and the plaintiff's subsequent incorporation under the laws of a sovereign different than that represented in the contract. The motion was sustained and plaintiff appeals. We reverse.

On December 6, 1978 a "Letter of Agreement" was entered into, which by its terms obligated "Southern–Gulf Marine Co. No. 9, Inc., a company to be formed, to purchase one 156 foot supply vessel from Camcraft, Inc. for a price of $1,350,000.00." The agreement further provided for an anticipated delivery date, authority for Camcraft to begin purchasing components, and stated that a definite set of specifications and a Vessel Construction Contract would be written in the near future. The agreement was signed by Mr. Dudley Bowman, as President of Camcraft, Inc., and by Mr. D.W. Barrett, both individually and as President of Southern–Gulf Marine Co. No. 9, Inc.

Thereafter, on May 30, 1979, the Vessel Construction Contract was executed between Camcraft and Southern–Gulf Marine Co. No. 9, Inc., the latter of which was listed in the preamble as a corporation organized by virtue of the laws of Texas, appearing through D.W. Barrett, its President. The contract, prepared on a form supplied by Camcraft, recited that both parties acknowledge receipt of valuable consideration, then went on to list the mutual promises of Builder (Camcraft) and Owner (Southern–Gulf). Among the conditions which followed on the form contract was one entitled "Shipping Act of 1916," whereby the owner warranted that it was a citizen of the United States within the meaning of the Shipping Act of 1916, as amended (46 U.S.C. § 835) and that provisions of said act restricting transfer of ownership are applicable. The agreement further listed causes for default and the effect thereof. Another provision afforded Builder the right to assign its interest provided such would not violate any law of the United States.

Subsequently Mr. D.W. Barrett, President of Southern–Gulf Marine Co. No. 9, Inc., wrote to Mr. Bowman in a letter dated February 21, 1980, informing him that his organization was incorporated in the Cayman Islands of British West Indies on February 15, 1980. Mr. Barrett explained that such incorporation was done to make the vessel's use in foreign commerce more economical. As President and Managing Director, he further informed Camcraft of the Board of Directors' resolution to ratify, confirm, and adopt the aforesaid agreements. The letter was signed by Mr. Barrett individually and as President. Mr. Bowman signed a written acceptance and agreement to the letter on February 22, 1980.[1]

Defendant subsequently defaulted on its obligation and this suit followed, wherein plaintiff sought to sequester the vessel involved and demanded specific performance and damages occasioned by defendant's failure to timely deliver the vessel. The defendant then sought to escape liability via a peremptory exception of no cause of action based upon the legal status of plaintiff.

The trial judge, in his Reasons for Judgment, reasoned that a contract requires two parties, and as plaintiff was not incorporated as of the date of the Vessel Construction Contract, there was no contract. He further reasoned that the purported ratification by Southern–Gulf Marine Co. No. 9, Inc., as evidenced by the letter of February 21, 1980, was ineffective because Southern–Gulf Marine Co. No. 9, Inc. never appeared as a Texas corporation and approved of any substitution of parties or assignment. The trial judge also rejected plaintiff's claim that D.W. Barrett could enforce the contract individually.

On appeal, the plaintiff assigns as error the following trial court actions: 1) Finding that the defendant had not agreed with the plaintiff to be bound to the May 30, 1979 Vessel Construction Contract, by virtue of

---

1. The last paragraph in the body of the letter of February 21, 1980, requested Mr. Bowman to acknowledge the terms therein by signing the below form and returning a duplicate thereof to plaintiff.

"ACCEPTED AND AGREED THIS _____ DAY OF FEBRUARY, 1980.

CAMCRAFT, INC.

BY: _____

Dudley E. Bowman, President"

the letter dated February 21, 1980; 2) Finding that the May 30, 1979 Vessel Construction Contract was no contract at all; 3) Failure to hold the defendant estopped to deny the corporate existence of Southern–Gulf Marine Co. No. 9, Inc., a Texas corporation; and 4) Failure to consider the February 21, 1980 letter as evidence of a valid assignment if the trial court was correct in stating that defendant did not consent to the terms set out in the letter. Although we find merit in the argument that D.W. Barrett could enforce the contract individually, this was not urged on appeal, and thus is considered abandoned.

We address ourselves first to whether the defendant should be estopped from asserting the plaintiff's lack of corporate capacity at the time the Vessel Construction Contract was executed after dealing with the plaintiff as a corporation. We believe the defendant, having given its promise to construct the vessel, should not be permitted to escape performance by raising an issue as to the character of the organization to which it is obligated, unless its substantial rights might thereby be affected. As was stated in Latiolais v. Citizens' Bank, 33 La.Ann. 1444 (1881), overruled on other grounds in General Motors Acceptance Corp. v. Anzelmo, 222 La. 1019, 64 So.2d 417, 418–419 (1953):

> "It is settled, by an overwhelming array of indisputable precedents, that, as a rule, one who contracts with what he acknowledges to be and treats as a corporation, incurring obligations in its favor, is estopped from denying its corporate existence, particularly when the obligations are sought to be enforced. It is right that it should be so. If a party have no other objection to oppose to the enforcement of the contract than that the obligee is incompetent to sue, for reasons anterior to his contract, or last acknowledgement, he should not be permitted to escape liability. The case would be different where the incompetency is the result of something happening subsequent to the contract, or last acknowledgement of existence and capacity. It is a familiar principle that one cannot be permitted to play fast and loose, so as to take advantage of his own unfair vacillations."

The above rule has been repeatedly applied in this and other jurisdictions. . . .

The rule was stated in Casey v. Galli, 94 U.S. 673, 680, 24 L.Ed. 168 (1877) as follows:

> "Where a party has contracted with a corporation, and is sued upon the contract, neither is permitted to deny the existence, or the legal validity of such corporation. To hold otherwise would be contrary to the plainest principles of reason and of good faith, and involve a mockery of justice."

The record discloses nothing indicating that the substantial rights of defendant were affected by the plaintiff's de facto status. The plaintiff relied upon the contract and secured financing. The defendant likewise relied on the contract and began construction of the vessel. We have no doubts that defendant would assert that plaintiff and D.W. Barrett were liable on the contract had they defaulted and enforcement was advantageous, but defendants refuse to recognize any rights they may have therein. In all likelihood, the true state of affairs is as represented by plaintiff's counsel: the vessel appreciated in value above the contract price between the time of the contract and the agreed delivery date. We hold the defendant estopped to deny the corporate existence of plaintiff in this regard. Such a result is in accord with construction of contracts so as to give them effect, . . . and the rule of construction which adapts an interpretation in accordance with justice and fair dealing with doubts resolved against the seller. . . .

The question remains whether defendant should be able to inject into the case the fact that plaintiff subsequently did incorporate in the Cayman Islands rather than in Texas, as originally represented. Paragraph 25 of the contract provides that an assignment or transfer shall not violate the Shipping Act of 1916 which prohibits transfer in the event of war or national emergency. Defendant apparently had no objections to the plaintiff's altered status, as a Cayman rather than de facto corporation, at the time the letter of February 21, 1980 was accepted and agreed to. And we all know that no war or national emergency existed. Thus the evidence indicates that the plaintiff's legal status is not germane to any cause for the contract and as such should not be grounds for avoidance of the contract. However, as the trial judge did not reach this consideration, we reserve unto defendant, upon remand, the right to raise the issue of the relevance of Cayman incorporation rather than Texan. It should be noted that defendant has not questioned plaintiff's right to do business within Louisiana, ...

The judgment appealed from is reversed and remanded to the trial court for further consideration consistent with the views herein. All costs taxed to appellee.

REVERSED AND REMANDED.

ANALYSIS

1. Why did Barrett on May 30, 1979, sign a contract on behalf of Southern–Gulf Marine Co. No. 9, when the corporation had not yet been formed?

2. Suppose the corporation was never formed and Barrett tried to enforce the contract individually. Should he be allowed to succeed?

3. Suppose the corporation was never formed and Camcraft sued Barrett as an individual to enforce the contract. On what theories might it rely and what proof would be required for each?

PLANNING

Suppose you represent Camcraft. Bowman, its president, calls you and says that he has shaken hands with Barrett on an agreement for the purchase and sale of a ship to be built by Camcraft. Bowman tells you that Barrett represents a group of investors who intend to form a corporation that is to become liable on the contract. Bowman is about to board a plane and has no time to talk, but wants you to meet him the next day at his office with a proposal for a contract to be signed by him and Barrett. You know that Bowman and Barrett are the kind of men who tend to focus on important business issues and to ignore the niceties of legal obligation. You also know that both like to think of themselves as reasonable, fair people and that they are anxious to pin down the deal as quickly and as pleasantly as possible and, therefore, want to avoid proposing unreasonable terms. What terms would you propose to take account of the fact that Barrett's corporation has not yet been formed? Suppose you represent Barrett and receive a similar hurried call from him seeking similar advice. Again, what terms would you propose to take account of the fact that the corporation has not yet been formed?

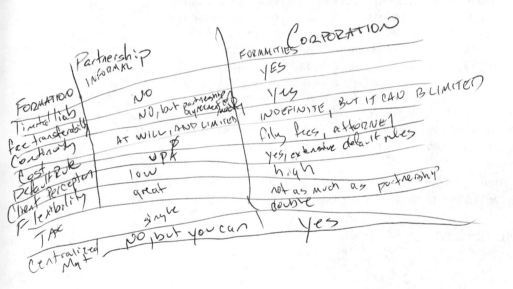

SECTION 2. THE CORPORATE ENTITY AND LIMITED LIABILITY

Walkovszky v. Carlton

18 N.Y.2d 414, 276 N.Y.S.2d 585, 223 N.E.2d 6 (1966).

■ FULD, JUDGE.

This case involves what appears to be a rather common practice in the taxicab industry of vesting the ownership of a taxi fleet in many corporations, each owning only one or two cabs.

The complaint alleges that the plaintiff was severely injured four years ago in New York City when he was run down by a taxicab owned by the defendant Seon Cab Corporation and negligently operated at the time by the defendant Marchese. The individual defendant, Carlton, is claimed to be a stockholder of 10 corporations, including Seon, each of which has but two cabs registered in its name, and it is implied that only the minimum automobile liability insurance required by law (in the amount of $10,000) is carried on any one cab. Although seemingly independent of one another, these corporations are alleged to be "operated . . . as a single entity, unit and enterprise" with regard to financing, supplies, repairs, employees and garaging, and all are named as defendants.[1] The plaintiff asserts that he is also entitled to hold their stockholders personally liable for the damages sought because the multiple corporate structure constitutes an unlawful attempt "to defraud members of the general public" who might be injured by the cabs.

The defendant Carlton has moved, pursuant to CPLR 3211(a)7, to dismiss the complaint on the ground that as to him it "fails to state a cause of action." The court at Special Term granted the motion but the Appellate Division, by a divided vote, reversed, holding that a valid cause of action was sufficiently stated. The defendant Carlton appeals to us, from the nonfinal order, by leave of the Appellate Division on a certified question.

The law permits the incorporation of a business for the very purpose of enabling its proprietors to escape personal liability . . . but, manifestly, the privilege is not without its limits. Broadly speaking, the courts will disregard the corporate form, or, to use accepted terminology, "pierce the corporate veil", whenever necessary "to prevent fraud or to achieve equity." International Aircraft Trading Co. v. Manufacturers Trust Co., 297 N.Y. 285, 292, 79 N.E.2d 249, 252. In determining whether liability should be extended to reach assets beyond those belonging to the corporation, we are guided, as Judge Cardozo noted, by "general rules of agency." Berkey v. Third Ave. Ry. Co., 144 N.Y. 84, 95, 155 N.E. 58, 61, 50 A.L.R. 599. In

---

1. The corporate owner of a garage is   also included as a defendant.

other words, whenever anyone uses control of the corporation to further his own rather than the corporation's business, he will be liable for the corporation's acts "upon the principle of *respondeat superior* applicable even where the agent is a natural person." Rapid Tr. Subway Constr. Co. v. City of New York, 259 N.Y. 472, 488, 182 N.E. 145, 150. Such liability, moreover, extends not only to the corporation's commercial dealings . . . but to its negligent acts as well.

. . .

In the case before us, the plaintiff has explicitly alleged that none of the corporations "had a separate existence of their own" and, as indicated above, all are named as defendants. However, it is one thing to assert that a corporation is a fragment of a larger corporate combine which actually conducts the business. . . . It is quite another to claim that the corporation is a "dummy" for its individual stockholders who are in reality carrying on the business in their personal capacities for purely personal rather than corporate ends. . . . Either circumstance would justify treating the corporation as an agent and piercing the corporate veil to reach the principal but a different result would follow in each case. In the first, only a larger *corporate* entity would be held financially responsible . . . while, in the other the stockholder would be personally liable. . . . Either the stockholder is conducting the business in his individual capacity or he is not. If he is, he will be liable; if he is not, then, it does not matter—insofar as his personal liability is concerned—that the enterprise is actually being carried on by a larger "enterprise entity."

At this stage in the present litigation, we are concerned only with the pleadings and, since CPLR 3014 permits causes of action to be stated "alternatively or hypothetically," it is possible for the plaintiff to allege both theories as the basis for his demand for judgment. . . . Reading the complaint in this case most favorably and liberally, we do not believe that there can be gathered from its averments the allegations required to spell out a valid cause of action against the defendant Carlton.

The individual defendant is charged with having "organized, managed, dominated and controlled" a fragmented corporate entity but there are no allegations that he was conducting business in his individual capacity. Had the taxicab fleet been owned by a single corporation, it would be readily apparent that the plaintiff would face formidable barriers in attempting to establish personal liability on the part of the corporation's stockholders. The fact that the fleet ownership has been deliberately split up among many corporations does not ease the plaintiff's burden in that respect. The corporate form may not be disregarded merely because the assets of the corporation, together with the mandatory insurance coverage of the vehicle which struck the plaintiff, are insufficient to assure him the recovery sought. If Carlton were to be held individually liable on those facts alone, the decision would apply equally to the thousands of cabs which are owned by their individual drivers who conduct their businesses through corporations organized pursuant to section 401 of the Business Corporation Law, Consol.Laws, c. 4 and carry the minimum insurance required by subdivision 1 (par. [a]) of section 370 of the Vehicle and Traffic Law, Consol.Laws, c. 71.   These taxi owner-operators are entitled to form such corporations . . . and we agree with the court at Special Term that, if the insurance coverage required by statute "is inadequate for the protection of the public, the remedy lies not with the courts but with the Legislature." It may very well be sound policy to require that certain corporations must take out liability insurance which will afford adequate compensation to their potential tort victims.   However, the responsibility for imposing conditions on the privilege of incorporation has been committed by the Constitution to the Legislature (N.Y. Const. art. X, § 1) and it may not be fairly implied, from any statute, that the Legislature intended, without the slightest discussion or debate, to require of taxi corporations that they carry automobile liability insurance over and above that mandated by the Vehicle and Traffic Law.

This is not to say that it is impossible for the plaintiff to state a valid cause of action against the defendant Carlton.   However, the simple fact is that the plaintiff has just not done so here.   While the complaint alleges that the separate corporations were undercapitalized and that their assets have been intermingled, it is barren of any "sufficiently particular[ized] statements" (CPLR 3013) . . . that the defendant Carlton and his associates are actually doing business in their individual capacities, shuttling their personal funds in and out of the corporations "without regard to formality and to suit their immediate convenience."   Weisser v. Mursam Shoe Corp., 2d Cir., 127 F.2d 344, 345, 145 A.L.R. 467, supra.   Nothing of the sort has in fact been charged, and it cannot reasonably or logically be inferred from the happenstance that the business of Seon Cab Corporation may actually be carried on by a larger corporate entity composed of many corporations which, under general principles of agency, would be liable to each other's creditors in contract and in tort.

In point of fact, the principle relied upon in the complaint to sustain the imposition of personal liability is not agency but fraud.   Such a cause of action cannot withstand analysis.   If it is not fraudulent for the owner-operator of a single cab corporation to take out only the minimum required liability insurance, the enterprise does not become either illicit or fraudulent merely because it consists of many such corporations.   The plaintiff's injuries are the same regardless of whether the cab which strikes him is owned by a single corporation or part of a fleet with ownership fragmented among many corporations.   Whatever rights he may be able to assert against parties other than the registered owner of the vehicle come into being not because he has been defrauded but because, under the principle of *respondeat superior,* he is entitled to hold the whole enterprise responsible for the acts of its agents.

In sum, then, the complaint falls short of adequately stating a cause of action against the defendant Carlton in his individual capacity.

The order of the Appellate Division should be reversed, with costs in this court and in the Appellate Division, the certified question answered in the negative and the order of the Supreme Court, Richmond County, reinstated, with leave to serve an amended complaint.

■ KEATING, JUDGE (dissenting).

The defendant Carlton, the shareholder here sought to be held for the negligence of the driver of a taxicab, was a principal shareholder and organizer of the defendant corporation which owned the taxicab. The corporation was one of 10 organized by the defendant, each containing two cabs and each cab having the "minimum liability" insurance coverage mandated by section 370 of the Vehicle and Traffic Law. The sole assets of these operating corporations are the vehicles themselves and they are apparently subject to mortgages.*

From their inception these corporations were intentionally undercapitalized for the purpose of avoiding responsibility for acts which were bound to arise as a result of the operation of a large taxi fleet having cars out on the street 24 hours a day and engaged in public transportation. And during the course of the corporations' existence all income was continually drained out of the corporations for the same purpose.

The issue presented by this action is whether the policy of this State, which affords those desiring to engage in a business enterprise the privilege of limited liability through the use of the corporate device, is so strong that it will permit that privilege to continue no matter how much it is abused, no matter how irresponsibly the corporation is operated, no matter what the cost to the public. I do not believe that it is.

Under the circumstances of this case the shareholders should all be held individually liable to this plaintiff for the injuries he suffered. . . .

The policy of this State has always been to provide and facilitate recovery for those injured through the negligence of others. The automobile, by its very nature, is capable of causing severe and costly injuries when not operated in a proper manner. The great increase in the number of automobile accidents combined with the frequent financial irresponsibility of the individual driving the car led to the adoption of section 388 of the Vehicle and Traffic Law which had the effect of imposing upon the owner of the vehicle the responsibility for its negligent operation. It is upon this very statute that the cause of action against both the corporation and the individual defendant is predicated.

In addition the Legislature, still concerned with the financial irresponsibility of those who owned and operated motor vehicles, enacted a statute requiring minimum liability coverage for all owners of automobiles. The important public policy represented by both these statutes is outlined in section 310 of the Vehicle and Traffic Law. That section provides that: "The legislature is concerned over the rising toll of motor vehicle accidents and the suffering and loss thereby inflicted. The legislature determines that it is a matter of grave concern that motorists shall be financially able

* It appears that the medallions, which are of considerable value, are judgment proof.   (Administrative Code of City of New York, § 436–2.0.)

to respond in damages for their negligent acts, so that innocent victims of motor vehicle accidents may be recompensed for the injury and financial loss inflicted upon them."

The defendant Carlton claims that, because the minimum amount of insurance required by the statute was obtained, the corporate veil cannot and should not be pierced despite the fact that the assets of the corporation which owned the cab were "trifling compared with the business to be done and the risks of loss" which were certain to be encountered. I do not agree.

The Legislature in requiring minimum liability insurance of $10,000, no doubt, intended to provide at least some small fund for recovery against those individuals and corporations who just did not have and were not able to raise or accumulate assets sufficient to satisfy the claims of those who were injured as a result of their negligence. It certainly could not have intended to shield those individuals who organized corporations, with the specific intent of avoiding responsibility to the public, where the operation of the corporate enterprise yielded profits sufficient to purchase additional insurance. Moreover, it is reasonable to assume that the Legislature believed that those individuals and corporations having substantial assets would take out insurance far in excess of the minimum in order to protect those assets from depletion. Given the costs of hospital care and treatment and the nature of injuries sustained in auto collisions, it would be unreasonable to assume that the Legislature believed that the minimum provided in the statute would in and of itself be sufficient to recompense "innocent victims of motor vehicle accidents . . . for the injury and financial loss inflicted upon them".

The defendant, however, argues that the failure of the Legislature to increase the minimum insurance requirements indicates legislative acquiescence in this scheme to avoid liability and responsibility to the public. In the absence of a clear legislative statement, approval of a scheme having such serious consequences is not to be so lightly inferred.

. . .

The defendant contends that a decision holding him personally liable would discourage people from engaging in corporate enterprise.

What I would merely hold is that a participating shareholder of a corporation vested with a public interest, organized with capital insufficient to meet liabilities which are certain to arise in the ordinary course of the corporation's business, may be held personally responsible for such liabilities. Where corporate income is not sufficient to cover the cost of insurance premiums above the statutory minimum or where initially adequate finances dwindle under the pressure of competition, bad times or extraordinary and unexpected liability, obviously the shareholder will not be held liable . . . .

The only types of corporate enterprises that will be discouraged as a result of a decision allowing the individual shareholder to be sued will be those such as the one in question, designed solely to abuse the corporate privilege at the expense of the public interest.

For these reasons I would vote to affirm the order of the Appellate Division.

■ DESMOND, C.J., and VAN VOORHIS, BURKE and SCILEPPI, JJ., concur with FULD, J.

■ KEATING, J., dissents and votes to affirm in an opinion in which BERGAN, J., concurs.

Order reversed, etc.

ANALYSIS

There are three separate legal doctrines that the plaintiff might invoke in a case like Walkovszky v. Carlton: (a) enterprise liability; (b) respondeat superior (agency); and (c) disregard of the corporate entity ("piercing the corporate veil"). Assume that the shares of each of the ten corporations in *Walkovszky* were owned 75 percent by Carlton, who ran the business and served as president of each corporation, as well as being a director; 10 percent each by two investors who were also directors but were otherwise inactive; and 5 percent by an investor who had inherited his shares, and had no role in the management of the business and only a vague idea of how it operated.

1. Articulate more fully each of the three legal doctrines and distinguish it from the others.

2. What facts would the plaintiff hope to find and seek to prove in support of each theory?

3. What persons are liable under each theory?

PLANNING AND POLICY

1. Assume that the law is correctly stated and applied by Judge Fuld in the majority opinion in *Walkovszky*. If you had acted as lawyer for Carlton and the other investors at the inception of the business, what advice would you have given them about what they must do to achieve their goals of insulating themselves from personal liability and insulating each corporation from the obligations of the others? How would your answer change if you had advised an individual who owned only two cabs and drove one of them himself?

2. Assume that the law is correctly stated and applied by Judge Keating in the dissenting opinion. How would your advice to Carlton and the other investors have changed? What about your advice to the individual with only two cabs?

3. What, if anything, do your answers to the preceding questions add to the policy debate between Judge Fuld and Judge Keating?

Sea-Land Services, Inc. v. Pepper Source

941 F.2d 519 (7th Cir.1991).

■ BAUER, CHIEF JUDGE.

This spicy case finds its origin in several shipments of Jamaican sweet peppers. Appellee Sea–Land Services, Inc. ("Sea–Land"), an ocean carrier, shipped the peppers on behalf of The Pepper Source ("PS"), one of the appellants here. PS then stiffed Sea–Land on the freight bill, which was rather substantial. Sea–Land filed a federal diversity action for the money it was owed. On December 2, 1987, the district court entered a default judgment in favor of Sea–Land and against PS in the amount of $86,767.70. But PS was nowhere to be found; it had been "dissolved" in mid–1987 for failure to pay the annual state franchise tax. Worse yet for Sea–Land, even had it not been dissolved, PS apparently had no assets. With the well empty, Sea–Land could not recover its judgment against PS. Hence the instant lawsuit.

In June 1988, Sea–Land brought this action against Gerald J. Marchese and five business entities he owns: PS, Caribe Crown, Inc., Jamar Corp., [and] Salescaster Distributors, Inc., ... Sea–Land sought by this suit to pierce PS's corporate veil and render Marchese personally liable for the judgment owed to Sea–Land, and then "reverse pierce" Marchese's other corporations so that they, too, would be on the hook for the $87,000. Thus, Sea–Land alleged in its complaint that all of these corporations "are alter egos of each other and hide behind the veils of alleged separate corporate existence for the purpose of defrauding plaintiff and other creditors." Not only are the corporations alter egos of each other, alleged Sea–Land, but also they are alter egos of Marchese, who should be held individually liable for the judgment because he created and manipulated these corporations and their assets for his own personal uses. Count III, paras. 9–10. (Hot on the heels of the filing of Sea–Land's complaint, PS took the necessary steps to be reinstated as a corporation in Illinois.)

In early 1989, Sea–Land filed an amended complaint adding Tie–Net International, Inc., as a defendant. Unlike the other corporate defendants, Tie–Net is not owned solely by Marchese: he holds half of the stock, and an individual named George Andre owns the other half. Sea–Land alleged that, despite this shared ownership, Tie–Net is but another alter ego of Marchese and the other corporate defendants, and thus it also should be held liable for the judgment against PS.

Through 1989, Sea–Land pursued discovery in this case, including taking a two-day deposition from Marchese. In December 1989, Sea–Land moved for summary judgment. In that motion—which, with the brief in support and the appendices, was about three inches thick—Sea–Land argued that it was "entitled to judgment as a matter of law, since the evidence including deposition testimony and exhibits in the appendix will show that piercing the corporate veil and finding the status of an alter ego is merited in this case." Marchese and the other defendants filed brief responses.

In an order dated June 22, 1990, the court granted Sea–Land's motion. The court discussed and applied the test for corporate veil-piercing explicated in Van Dorn Co. v. Future Chemical and Oil Corp., 753 F.2d 565 (7th Cir.1985). Analyzing Illinois law, we held in *Van Dorn* :

> [A] corporate entity will be disregarded and the veil of limited liability pierced when two requirements are met: First, there must be such unity of interest and ownership that the separate personalities of the corporation and the individual [or other corporation] no longer exist; and second, circumstances must be such that adherence to the fiction of separate corporate existence would sanction a fraud or promote injustice.

753 F.2d at 569–70 (quoting Macaluso v. Jenkins, 95 Ill.App.3d 461, 420 N.E.2d 251, 255 (1981)) (other citations omitted). . . . As for determining whether a corporation is so controlled by another to justify disregarding their separate identities, the Illinois cases . . . focus on four factors: "(1) the failure to maintain adequate corporate records or to comply with corporate formalities, (2) the commingling of funds or assets, (3) undercapitalization, and (4) one corporation treating the assets of another corporation as its own."   753 F.2d at 570 (citations omitted). . . .

Following the lead of the parties, the district court in the instant case laid the template of *Van Dorn* over the facts of this case. The court concluded that both halves and all features of the test had been satisfied, and, therefore, entered judgment in favor of Sea–Land and against PS, Caribe Crown, Jamar, Sales-caster, Tie–Net, and Marchese individually. These defendants were held jointly liable for Sea–Land's $87,000 judgment, as well as for post-judgment interest under Illinois law. From that judgment Marchese and the other defendants brought a timely appeal.

Because this is an appeal from a grant of summary judgment, our review is de novo. . . .

The first and most striking feature that emerges from our examination of the record is that these corporate defendants are, indeed, little but Marchese's playthings. Marchese is the sole shareholder of PS, Caribe Crown, Jamar, and Salescaster. He is one of the two shareholders of Tie–Net. Except for Tie–Net, none of the corporations ever held a single corporate meeting. (At the handful of Tie–Net meetings held by Marchese and Andre, no minutes were taken.) During his deposition, Marchese did not remember any of these corporations ever passing articles of incorporation, bylaws, or other agreements. As for physical facilities, Marchese runs all of these corporations (including Tie–Net) out of the same, single office, with the same phone line, the same expense accounts, and the like. And how he does "run" the expense accounts! When he fancies to, Marchese "borrows" substantial sums of money from these corporations— interest free, of course. The corporations also "borrow" money from each other when need be, which left at least PS completely out of capital when the Sea–Land bills came due. What's more, Marchese has used the bank accounts of these corporations to pay all kinds of personal expenses, including alimony and child support payments to his ex-wife, education expenses for his children, maintenance of his personal automobiles, health care for his pet—the list goes on and on. Marchese did not even have a personal bank account! (With "corporate" accounts like these, who needs one?) And Tie–Net is just as much a part of this as the other corporations. On appeal, Marchese makes much of the fact that he shares ownership of Tie–Net, and that Sea–Land has not been able to find an example of funds flowing from PS to Tie–Net to the detriment of Sea–Land and PS's other creditors. So what? The record reveals that, in all material senses, Marchese treated Tie–Net like his other corporations: he "borrowed" over $30,000 from Tie–Net; money and "loans" flowed freely between Tie–Net and the other corporations; and Marchese charged up various personal expenses (including $460 for a picture of himself with President Bush) on Tie–Net's credit card. Marchese was not deterred by the fact that he did not hold all of the stock of Tie–Net; why should his creditors be?

In sum, we agree with the district court that there can be no doubt that the "shared control/unity of interest and ownership" part of the *Van Dorn* test is met in this case: corporate records and formalities have not been maintained; funds and assets have been commingled with abandon; PS, the offending corporation, and perhaps others have been undercapitalized; and corporate assets have been moved and tapped and "borrowed" without regard to their source. Indeed, Marchese basically punted this part of the inquiry before the district court by coming forward with little or no evidence in response to Sea–Land's extensively supported argument on these points. That fact alone was enough to do him in; opponents to summary judgment motions cannot simply rest on their laurels, but must come forward with specific facts showing that there is a genuine issue for trial. . . . Regarding the elements that make up the first half of the *Van Dorn* test, Marchese and the other defendants have not done so. Thus, Sea–Land is entitled to judgment on these points.

The second part of the *Van Dorn* test is more problematic, however. "Unity of interest and ownership" is not enough; Sea–Land also must show that honoring the separate corporate existences of the defendants "would sanction a fraud or promote injustice." *Van Dorn*, 753 F.2d at 570. This last phrase truly is disjunctive:

> Although an intent to defraud creditors would surely play a part if established, the Illinois test does not require proof of such intent. Once the first element of the test is established, *either* the sanctioning of a fraud (intentional wrongdoing) or the promotion of injustice, will satisfy the second element.

Id. (emphasis in original). Seizing on this, Sea–Land has abandoned the language in its two complaints that make repeated references to "fraud" by Marchese, and has chosen not to attempt to prove that PS and Marchese intended to defraud it—which would be quite difficult on summary judgment. Instead, Sea–Land has argued that honoring the defendants' separate identities would "promote injustice."

But what, exactly, does "promote injustice" mean, and how does one establish it on summary judgment? These are the critical, troublesome questions in this case. To start with, as the above passage from *Van Dorn* makes clear, "promote injustice" means something less than an affirmative showing of fraud—but how much less? In its one-sentence treatment of this point, the district court held that it was enough that "Sea–Land would be denied a judicially-imposed recovery." Sea–Land defends this reasoning on appeal, arguing that "permitting the appellants to hide behind the shield of limited liability would clearly serve as an injustice against appellee" because it would "impermissibly deny appellee satisfaction." Appellee's Brief at 14–15. But that cannot be what is meant by "promote injustice." The prospect of an unsatisfied judgment looms in every veil-piercing action; why else would a plaintiff bring such an action? Thus, if an unsatisfied judgment is enough for the "promote injustice" feature of the test, then every plaintiff will pass on that score, and *Van Dorn* collapses into a one-step "unity of interest and ownership" test.

Because we cannot abide such a result, we will undertake our own review of Illinois cases to determine how the "promote injustice" feature of the veil-piercing inquiry has been interpreted. In Pederson [v. Paragon Enterprises, 214 Ill.App.3d 815, 158 Ill.Dec. 371, 373, 574 N.E.2d 165, 167 (1st Dist.1991)], . . . the court offered the following summary: "Some element of unfairness, something akin to fraud or deception or the existence of a compelling public interest must be present in order to disregard the corporate fiction." 214 Ill.App.3d at 821, 158 Ill.Dec. at 375, 574 N.E.2d at 169. (The court ultimately refused to pierce the corporate veil in *Pederson*, at least in part because "nothing in these facts provides evidence of scheming on the part of defendant to commit a fraud on potential creditors [of the two defendant corporations]." 214 Ill.App.3d at 823, 158 Ill.Dec. at 376, 574 N.E.2d at 169.)

The light shed on this point by other Illinois cases can be seen only if we examine the cases on their facts. Perivoliotis v. Pierson, 167 Ill.App.3d 259, 521 N.E.2d 254 (1988), was a complicated adverse possession case that addresses briefly the meaning of the "injustice" requirement. The issue in the case was whether an individual (Woulfe) could possess a strip of land adversely to a corporation (TomDon) that held title to the land, when Woulfe was the president and one of only two shareholders (the other, his wife) of TomDon. The court held that, because TomDon was merely Woulfe's alter ego, Woulfe could not possess the land "adversely." In so holding, the court stated that "the running of the prescriptive period against a corporation's property during a period when the corporation's principal owner and president mistakenly possessed the encroachment area in his individual capacity defies common sense and is the type of 'injustice' that would justify piercing the corporate veil." Id. at 256.

Gromer, Wittenstrom & Meyer, P.C. v. Strom, 140 Ill.App.3d 349, 489 N.E.2d 370 (1986), was another unfortunately complicated case in which our issue was addressed. Basically, three individuals, W, M, and S, were partners. All three signed a note agreeing to be jointly and severally liable for a debt owed to a bank. S left the partnership and it dissolved. W & M then formed a new corporation, W & M Co., of which they were the sole shareholders. W & M Co. paid off the bank and became the assignee of the note, and then promptly sued S for collection on the note. Putting to one side the rather abstruse procedural posture of the case, suffice it to say that W & M Co. won at the trial level and appealed [sic]. On appeal, S claimed that the court should pierce the corporate veil and recognize W & M Co. for what it really was—his former partners and cosigners on the note; the reason being that cosigners cannot payoff [sic] a note and then take judgment on the note against another cosigner. The appellate court agreed and vacated the judgment:

> We believe that these facts and arguments sufficiently indicate that to recognize [W & M Co.] as an entity separate from its shareholders would be to sanction an injustice. Where such an injustice would result and there is such unity of interest between the corporation and the individual shareholders that the separate personalities no longer exist, the corporate veil must be pierced.

Id. at 374 (citations omitted).

In B. Kreisman & Co. v. First Arlington Nat'l Bank of Arlington Heights, 91 Ill.App.3d 847, 415 N.E.2d 1070 (1980), the appellate court reversed the trial court's refusal to pierce the veil. Defendant corporation stiffed plaintiff for the bill on some restaurant equipment, so plaintiff sued for a mechanics lien. Plaintiff won at trial, but the trial court would not pierce the defendant corporation's veil and also hold liable the individual who was the "dominant force" controlling the defendant corporation. Noting that the equipment, though never paid for, was used by the defendant corporation for several years, the appellate court stated, "Under these circumstances we believe the corporate veil should be pierced to require [the 'dominant individual'] to be personally liable; to say otherwise would promote an injustice and permit her to be unjustly enriched at plaintiff's expense." Id. at 1073 (citations omitted).

. . .

Generalizing from these cases, we see that the courts that properly have pierced corporate veils to avoid "promoting injustice" have found that, unless it did so, some "wrong" beyond a creditor's inability to collect would result: the common sense rules of adverse possession would be undermined; former partners would be permitted to skirt the legal rules concerning monetary obligations; a party would be unjustly enriched; a parent corporation that caused a sub's liabilities and its inability to pay for them would escape those liabilities; or an intentional scheme to squirrel assets into a liability-free corporations while heaping liabilities upon an asset-free corporation would be successful. Sea–Land, although it alleged in its complaint the kind of intentional asset- and liability-shifting found in Van Dorn, has yet to come forward with evidence akin to the "wrongs" found in these cases. Apparently, it believed, as did the district court, that its unsatisfied judgment was enough. That belief was in error, and the entry of summary judgment premature. We, therefore, reverse the judgment and remand the case to the district court.

On remand, the court should require that Sea–Land produce, if it desires summary judgment, evidence and argument that would establish the kind of additional "wrong" present in the above cases. For example, perhaps Sea–Land could establish that Marchese, like Roth in *Van Dorn*, used these corporate facades to avoid its responsibilities to creditors; or that PS, Marchese, or one of the other corporations will be "unjustly enriched" unless liability is shared by all. Of course, Sea–Land is not required fully to prove intent to defraud, which it probably could not do on summary judgment anyway. But it is required to show the kind of injustice to merit the evocation of the court's essentially equitable power to prevent "injustice." It may well be that, after more of such evidence is adduced, no genuine issue of fact exists to prevent Sea–Land from reaching Marchese's other pet corporations for PS's debt. Or it may be that only a finder of fact will be able to determine whether fraud or "injustice" is involved here. In any event, the record as it currently stands is insufficient to uphold the entry of summary judgment.

REVERSED and REMANDED with instructions.

NOTE

On remand of *Sea–Land*, the district court found in favor of Sea–Land and entered a judgment against Marchese for $86,768 plus post-judgment interest of $31,365. In concluding that protecting Marchese would "sanction a fraud or promote injustice," the court relied on the fact that Marchese had engaged in blatant tax fraud by treating his personal expenses as deductible corporate business expenses, and had used corporate funds for his own benefit while avoiding corporate debts. The court also found that Marchese had assured a Sea–Land representative in a telephone conversation that the freight bill would be paid, even though he knew at the time that he would "manipulate" the corporate funds "to insure there would not be funds to pay" the Sea–Land bills. This, said the court, constituted "fraud." Sea–Land Services, Inc. v. Pepper Source, 1992 WL 168537 (N.D.Ill.1992). The district court judgment was affirmed on appeal, Sea–Land Services, Inc. v. Pepper Source, 993 F.2d 1309 (7th Cir. 1993), with the observation that there was more than the mere fact that Marchese's corporations did not pay their debts: he had received "countless benefits at the expense of" Sea–Land and other creditors, including loans and salaries paid in such a way as to "insur[e] that his corporations had insufficient funds with which to pay their debts."

QUESTIONS

1. Once the plaintiff had pierced PS's corporate veil to impose personal liability on Marchese, it could have levied on the stock he owned in the

other affiliated firms. What would it gain by having the court "reverse pierce" the other corporate veils?

2. Why is not the owner of a corporation that has escaped personal liability for its debts necessarily unjustly enriched?

Kinney Shoe Corporation v. Polan

939 F.2d 209 (4th Cir.1991).

Plaintiff-appellant Kinney Shoe Corporation ("Kinney") brought this action against . . . Lincoln M. Polan ("Polan") seeking to recover money owed on a sublease between Kinney and Industrial Realty Company ("Industrial"). Polan is the sole shareholder of Industrial. The district court found that Polan was not personally liable on the lease between Kinney and Industrial. Kinney appeals asserting that the corporate veil should be pierced, and we agree.

I.

. . . In 1984 Polan formed two corporations, Industrial and Polan Industries, Inc., for the purpose of re-establishing an industrial manufacturing business. . . . Polan was the owner of both corporations. Although certificates of incorporation were issued, no organizational meetings were held, and no officers were elected.

In November 1984 Polan and Kinney began negotiating the sublease of a building in which Kinney held a leasehold interest. . . . Under the terms of the lease, Kinney was legally obligated to make payments on the bonds on a semi-annual basis through January 1, 1993, at which time it had the right to purchase the property. . . .

The term of the sublease from Kinney to Industrial commenced in December 1984, even though the written lease was not signed by the parties until April 5, 1985. On April 15, 1985, Industrial subleased part of the building to Polan Industries for fifty percent of the rental amount due Kinney. Polan signed both subleases on behalf of the respective companies.

Other than the sublease with Kinney, Industrial had no assets, no income and no bank account. Industrial issued no stock certificates because nothing was ever paid in to this corporation. Industrial's only income was from its sublease to Polan Industries, Inc. The first rental payment to Kinney was made out of Polan's personal funds, and no further payments were made by Polan or by Polan Industries, Inc. to either Industrial or to Kinney.

Kinney filed suit against Industrial for unpaid rent and obtained a judgment in the amount of $166,400.00 on June 19, 1987. . . . Since the amount to which Kinney is entitled is undisputed, the only issue is whether Kinney can pierce the corporate veil and hold Polan personally liable.

The district court held that Kinney had assumed the risk of Industrial's undercapitalization and was not entitled to pierce the corporate veil. Kinney appeals, and we reverse.

II.

We have long recognized that a corporation is an entity, separate and distinct from its officers and stockholders, and the individual stockholders are not responsible for the debts of the corporation. . . . This concept, however, is a fiction of the law " 'and it is now well settled, as a general principle, that the fiction should be disregarded when it is urged with an intent not within its reason and purpose, and in such a way that its retention would produce injustices or inequitable consequences.' " Laya v. Erin Homes, Inc., 352 S.E.2d 93, 97–98 (W.Va.1986) (quoting Sanders v. Roselawn Memorial Gardens, Inc., 152 W.Va. 91, 159 S.E.2d 784, 786 (1968)). Piercing the corporate veil is an equitable remedy, and the burden rests with the party asserting such claim. A totality of the circumstances test is used in determining whether to pierce the corporate veil, and each case must be decided on its own facts. . . .

Kinney seeks to pierce the corporate veil of Industrial so as to hold Polan personally liable on the sublease debt. The Supreme Court of Appeals of West Virginia has set forth a two prong test to be used in determining whether to pierce a corporate veil in a breach of contract case. This test raises two issues: first, is the unity of interest and ownership such that the separate personalities of the corporation and the individual shareholder no longer exist; and second, would an equitable result occur if the acts are treated as those of the corporation alone. Laya, 352 S.E.2d at 99. Numerous factors have been identified as relevant in making this determination.

The district court found that the two prong test of Laya had been satisfied. The court concluded that Polan's failure to carry out the corporate formalities with respect to Industrial, coupled with Industrial's gross undercapitalization, resulted in damage to Kinney. We agree.

It is undisputed that Industrial was not adequately capitalized. Actually, it had no paid-in capital. Polan had put nothing into this corporation, and it did not observe any corporate formalities. As the West Virginia court stated in Laya, " 'individuals who wish to enjoy limited personal liability for business activities under a corporate umbrella should be expected to adhere to the relatively simple formalities of creating and maintaining a corporate entity.' " Laya, 352 S.E.2d at 100 n.6 (quoting Labadie Coal Co. v. Black, 217 App. D.C. 239, 672 F.2d 92, 96–97 (D.C.Cir. 1982)). This, the court stated, is " 'a relatively small price to pay for limited liability.' " Id. Another important factor is adequate capitalization. "Grossly inadequate capitalization combined with disregard of corporate formalities, causing basic unfairness, are sufficient to pierce the corporate veil in order to hold the shareholder(s) actively participating in the operation of the business personally liable for a breach of contract to the party who entered into the contract with the corporation." Laya, 352 S.E.2d at

101–02. In this case, Polan bought no stock, made no capital contribution, kept no minutes, and elected no officers for Industrial. In addition, Polan attempted to protect his assets by placing them in Polan Industries, Inc. and interposing Industrial between Polan Industries, Inc. and Kinney so as to prevent Kinney from going against the corporation with assets. . . . These facts present the classic scenario for an action to pierce the corporate veil so as to reach the responsible party and produce an equitable result. Accordingly, we hold that the district court correctly found that the two prong test in *Laya* had been satisfied.

In *Laya*, the court also noted that when determining whether to pierce a corporate veil a third prong may apply in certain cases. The court stated:

> When, under the circumstances, it would be reasonable for that particular type of a party [those contract creditors capable of protecting themselves] entering into a contract with the corporation, for example, a bank or other lending institution, to conduct an investigation of the credit of the corporation prior to entering into the contract, such party will be charged with the knowledge that a reasonable credit investigation would disclose. If such an investigation would disclose that the corporation is grossly undercapitalized, based upon the nature and the magnitude of the corporate undertaking, such party will be deemed to have assumed the risk of the gross undercapitalization and will not be permitted to pierce the corporate veil.

Laya, 352 S.E.2d at 100. The district court applied this third prong and concluded that Kinney "assumed the risk of Industrial's defaulting" and that "the application of the doctrine of 'piercing the corporate veil' ought not and does not [apply]." While we agree that the two prong test of *Laya* was satisfied, we hold that the district court's conclusion that Kinney had assumed the risk is clearly erroneous.

Without deciding whether the third prong should be extended beyond the context of the financial institution lender mentioned in *Laya*, we hold that, even if it applies to creditors such as Kinney, it does not prevent Kinney from piercing the corporate veil in this case. The third prong is permissive and not mandatory. This is not a factual situation that calls for the third prong, if we are to seek an equitable result. Polan set up Industrial to limit his liability and the liability of Polan Industries, Inc. in their dealings with Kinney. A stockholder's liability is limited to the amount he has invested in the corporation, but Polan invested nothing in Industrial. This corporation was no more than a shell—a transparent shell. When nothing is invested in the corporation, the corporation provides no protection to its owner; nothing in, nothing out, no protection. . . .

REVERSED AND REMANDED WITH INSTRUCTIONS.

ANALYSIS

1. Why do you suppose Kinney subleased to Industrial without a personal guarantee by Polan?

2. What actions might Polan have taken that would have been least onerous to him while allowing him to avoid personal liability? In what way, if any, would any such actions have protected the interests of Kinney and other creditors?

3. It would seem that Polan Industries owes Industrial for unpaid rent. Should Kinney be allowed to go after Polan Industries as well as Polan?

4. What would the outcome of this case have been under the law of Illinois as described in *Sea–Land*?

5. In Victoria Elevator Company of Minneapolis v. Meriden Grain Co., Inc., 283 N.W.2d 509, 513 (Minn.1979), the court concluded, "Since defendant did not treat the corporation as a separate legal entity, he should not be entitled to its protection against personal liability." Is this statement consistent with the statements of the law in *Sea–Land* and in *Kinney Shoe*? Does it help explain the results in those cases?

Perpetual Real Estate Services, Inc. v. Michaelson Properties, Inc.

974 F.2d 545 (4th Cir.1992).

. . .

I.

In August 1981, defendant Aaron Michaelson formed Michaelson Properties, Inc., for the purpose of entering into joint real estate ventures. MPI was incorporated under the laws of the state of Illinois with initial paid-in capital of $1,000. Michaelson was the president and sole shareholder.

MPI subsequently entered into two joint ventures with Perpetual Real Estate Services, Inc. (PRES), the plaintiff in this case, involving the conversion of apartment buildings into condominiums. The first was formed in October 1981, and was known as Bethesda Apartment Associates (BAA). Under the BAA partnership agreement, each partner was to contribute $100,000 to a working capital fund, and MPI was to put up a $1 million letter of credit. Michaelson and his wife, Barbara, agreed to personally indemnify PRES against any loss on MPI's letter of credit. The BAA partnership sold the last condominium unit in 1983, and distributed about $600,000 in profits to each partner in 1985.

The second partnership, known as Arlington Apartment Associates (AAA), was formed in November 1983. Under the AAA partnership agreement, both PRES and MPI contributed $50,000 in capital, and each agreed to share pro rata in satisfying any liabilities of the partnership. The partnership also borrowed $24 million from Perpetual Savings Bank, PRES's parent corporation, but only after Aaron and Barbara Michaelson agreed to personally guarantee repayment of $750,000 of the loan. When an additional $2.1 million was needed to complete the project, MPI could not come up with the money so PRES loaned MPI $1.05 million, again after PRES secured a personal guarantee of repayment from the Michaelsons.

During 1985 and 1986, the AAA partnership made various distributions of the profits from the condominium units. . . . Three distributions were made to PRES and MPI, totalling approximately $456,000 to each partner. MPI then authorized distributions of its profits to its sole shareholder, Aaron Michaelson.

In 1987, more than a year after the last of these distributions, several condominium purchasers filed suit against AAA, asserting breach of warranty claims in the amount of $5.5 million. . . . The case was ultimately settled for $950,000. PRES paid the full amount on behalf of the partnership; MPI made no contribution toward the settlement since its profits had been distributed years earlier.

PRES then filed this diversity action against Michaelson and MPI. The complaint sought indemnity from MPI pursuant to the AAA partnership agreement. . . . PRES also asserted two theories for holding Michaelson personally responsible for MPI's debt: (1) that Michaelson had made an oral promise during settlement negotiations to answer for MPI's debt; and (2) that MPI was Michaelson's "alter ego or mere instrumentality" and that MPI's corporate veil should be pierced. . . .

The jury subsequently returned a verdict in favor of PRES on the veil piercing count, but decided in Michaelson's favor on the oral promise count. Michaelson filed a motion for jnov, which was rejected by the district court. . . . Michaelson appeals.

II.

. . .

A.

Virginia courts have long recognized the basic proposition that a corporation is a legal entity separate and distinct from its shareholders. . . . A fundamental purpose of incorporation is to "enable a group of persons to limit their liability in a joint venture to the extent of their contributions to the capital stock." Beale [v. Kappa Alpha Order], 64 S.E.2d [789] at 796 [(Va.1951)]. This concept of limited liability "supports a vital economic policy," Cheatle [v. Rudd's Swimming Pool Supply Co.], 360 S.E.2d [828] at 831 [(Va.1987)], a policy on which "large undertakings are rested, vast enterprises are launched, and huge sums of capital attracted." Anderson v. Abbott, 321 U.S. 349, 362, 64 S.Ct. 531, 537, 88 L.Ed. 793 (1944).

Virginia courts have assiduously defended this "vital economic policy," lifting the veil of immunity only in "extraordinary" cases. . . . Under Virginia law, plaintiff bears the burden of convincing the court to disregard the corporate form, and must first establish that "the corporate entity was the alter ego, alias, stooge, or dummy of the individuals sought to be charged personally." *Cheatle*, 360 S.E.2d at 831. This element may be established by evidence that the defendant exercised "undue domination and control" over the corporation, *Beale,* 64 S.E.2d at 797, and the jury instruction in this case fairly described this aspect of the test. Under this element of the test, the court properly permitted the jury to consider such factors as whether Michaelson "observe[d] corporate formalities," whether he kept "corporate records," whether he paid dividends, and whether there were "other officers and directors."

The Supreme Court of Virginia has specifically held, however, that proof that some person "may dominate or control" the corporation, or "may treat it as a mere department, instrumentality, agency, etc." is not enough to pierce the veil. *Beale,* 64 S.E.2d at 798. In Virginia, "something more is required to induce the court to disregard the entity of a corporation." *Id.* at 797. Hence, plaintiff must also establish "that the corporation was a device or sham used to disguise wrongs, obscure fraud, or conceal crime." *Cheatle,* 360 S.E.2d at 831.   . . .

B.

. . . Under the correct standard of Virginia law, . . . we think for the reasons that follow that PRES is unable to raise a triable issue with respect to piercing the corporate veil in this case.

The district court pointed to several factors established by the evidence that purportedly justify such action. The district court noted that there was evidence from which a jury could find that Michaelson was the sole shareholder of MPI, that he was the sole director of MPI, that corporate formalities were not observed, that corporate capitalization was not adequate, and that corporate records did not indicate payment of any dividends. . . .

Michaelson has offered his own version of the evidence on these issues, and has suggested that the court's findings were clearly erroneous. We shall not reach this question, however, since the findings of the district court focus primarily on the first part of the test announced in *Cheatle,* and ignore the second half of that test. Even if we assume that MPI was Michaelson's "alter ego, alias, stooge, or dummy," *Cheatle,* 360 S.E.2d at 831, or that Michaelson exercised "undue domination and control" over MPI, *Beale,* 64 S.E.2d at 797, PRES's attempt to pierce the corporate veil must fail unless Michaelson used MPI to "disguise wrongs, obscure fraud, or conceal crime." *Cheatle,* 360 S.E.2d at 831. The district court found— and PRES appears to concede—that there was no evidence that Michaelson used the corporation to "obscure fraud" or "conceal crime." The only question, then, is whether a reasonable jury could have found that Michaelson somehow used MPI to "disguise wrongs."

PRES has simply failed to show that Michaelson used the corporate form to "disguise wrongs." PRES and MPI had entered into a longstanding contractual relationship, and PRES had full knowledge of the nature of its corporate partner, including its ownership structure and capitalization. PRES even participated in the decisions to distribute money to itself and to MPI after determining that the AAA partnership had sufficient assets to cover its anticipated expenses, and PRES apparently sought no limitations on what MPI did with those funds. PRES has sought on appeal to attack MPI's distributions to Michaelson by labelling them an unfair "siphoning" of funds. It was entirely foreseeable to PRES, however, that MPI would distribute those funds to Michaelson, its sole shareholder. When MPI did distribute the funds, it did so well before any claims were filed against the partnership and in a manner that PRES has not shown would violate Virginia law.

PRES points out, however, that in a number of contexts PRES did negotiate personal guarantees from Michaelson, and insists that such guarantees weaken MPI's corporate veil. We think, to the contrary, that they fortify it. Courts have been extraordinarily reluctant to lift the veil in contract cases, such as this one, where the "creditor has willingly transacted business" with the corporation. United States v. Jon–T Chemicals, Inc., 768 F.2d 686, 693 (5th Cir.1985). In other words,

> courts usually apply more stringent standards to piercing the corporate veil in a contract case than they do in tort cases. This is because the party seeking relief in a contract case is presumed to have voluntarily and knowingly entered into an agreement with a corporate entity, and is expected to suffer the consequences of the limited liability associated with the corporate business form, while this is not the situation in tort cases.

1 William M. Fletcher, Fletcher Cyclopedia of the Law of Private Corporations ¶ 41.85 at 712 (1990 ed.). Thus, in contract cases, . . . courts have required proof of some form of misrepresentation to the creditor:

> Unless the [corporation] misrepresents its financial condition to the creditor, the creditor should be bound by its decision to deal with the [corporation]; it should not be able to complain later that the [corporation] is unsound.

Jon–T Chemicals, 768 F.2d at 693. . . . Here PRES and MPI were joint venturers in real estate, each familiar with the other. PRES has failed to point to anything that suggests that Michaelson misled PRES as to its financial condition—there is simply no indication that Michaelson used MPI to "disguise" anything. . . .

Absent some evidence of misrepresentation, "courts should not rewrite contracts or disturb the allocation of risk the parties have themselves established." Fletcher, supra, ¶ 41.85 at 713. Parties to a commercial transaction must be free to negotiate questions of limited liability and to enforce their agreements by recourse to the law of contracts. PRES surely understood that principle, and thus went to the trouble of securing Michaelson's personal guarantees on several matters. . . . Significantly, the AAA joint venture agreement included no personal guarantees by Michaelson, and the jury, as noted, found that Michaelson had made no oral promises to answer for MPI's debt. As a matter of contract, then, Michaelson was entitled to insulation from personal liability on the claims from the AAA partners, and it is not our place to restructure the parties' agreement. . . .

ANALYSIS

1. How would the *Kinney* court have decided this case? The *Sea-Land* court?

2. Should PRES have demanded that Michaelson form MPI as a partnership rather than a corporation? Why did it not do so?

INTRODUCTORY NOTE

In the following case a corporation owns all the shares of common stock of another corporation. The first corporation is generally referred to as a "parent" corporation and the second as a "subsidiary." Why would the parent choose this form of organization rather than simply run all its activities out of a single corporation (with "divisions" for separate activities)? There are a number of reasons, but one important one is that generally the parent, like any other shareholder, is not liable for the debts of the subsidiary, so the parent can undertake an activity without putting at risk its own assets, beyond those it decides to commit to the subsidiary. Like an individual shareholder, however, a corporate shareholder must be aware of the danger that if it is not careful, the creditors of the subsidiary may be able to pierce the corporate veil of the subsidiary. The parent must also be careful not to become directly liable by virtue of its participation in the activities of the subsidiary.

In re Silicone Gel Breast Implants Products Liability Litigation

887 F.Supp. 1447 (N.D.Ala.1995).

■ POINTER, CHIEF JUDGE.

Under submission after appropriate discovery, extensive briefing, and oral argument is the motion for summary judgment filed by defendant Bristol–Myers Squibb Co. Bristol is the sole shareholder of Medical Engineering Corporation, a major supplier of breast implants, but has never itself manufactured or distributed breast implants. Bristol asserts that the evidence is insufficient for the plaintiffs' claims to proceed against it, whether through piercing the corporate veil or under a theory of direct liability. The parties agree that, with discovery substantially complete, this motion is ripe for decision. For the reasons stated below, the court concludes that Bristol is not entitled to summary judgment.

. . .

II. CHOICE OF LAW

In federal multidistrict proceedings, the transferee court applies the substantive law of the transferor courts. . . . The transferor courts in diversity cases would be bound to apply the law of the forum state, including its choice of law rules. . . .

This MDL proceeding involves diversity-jurisdiction cases filed in, or removed to, federal courts in 90 of the 94 districts, located in virtually every state, the District of Columbia, Puerto Rico, and the Virgin Islands. This court must therefore look to the laws of the several states to determine whether Bristol's motion should be granted. Many states would call for this court, when addressing "alter ego" and other "veil piercing" issues, to apply the law of Delaware, where Bristol and MEC are incorporated. But, under choice-of-law rules in other jurisdictions, this court may be obliged to apply the laws of many different states. Because of variations in applicable state law, summary judgment could be proper in some cases while not warranted in others.

III. FACTS

For purposes of Bristol's summary judgment motion, the court treats the following facts as established, either because they are not in genuine dispute or because they are supported by evidence viewed in the light most favorable to the plaintiffs.

MEC was incorporated in Wisconsin in 1969, with its principal place of business in Racine. It was an independent, privately-held corporation manufacturing a variety of medical and plastic surgery devices, including breast implants. In 1982, after an extensive due diligence review that included information regarding capsular contracture, rupture, and gel bleed, Bristol, a Delaware corporation, purchased MEC's stock for $28 million through a series of mergers and corporate reorganizations. [After a series of formalistic transactions, MEC became, in 1982, a Delaware corporation, wholly owned by Bristol.]

In 1988 Bristol expanded its breast implant business by purchasing from the Cooper Companies two other breast-implant manufacturers, Natural Y Surgical Specialties, Inc. and Aesthetech Corporation. Though executed in the name of MEC and the Cooper Companies, the purchase was negotiated between Bristol and the Cooper Companies, and the purchase price of $8.7 million was paid from a Bristol account (though charged to MEC). The due diligence review, which indicated potential hazards and possible liability relating to polyurethane-coated breast implants, was conducted jointly by MEC and Bristol.

Documents reflect that MEC has had, at least in form, a board of three directors, generally consisting of the Bristol Vice President then serving as President of Bristol's Health Care Group, another Bristol executive, and MEC's president. Bristol's Health Care Group President, who reported to Bristol's president or chairman, could not be outvoted by the other two MEC board members. Several of the former MEC presidents did not recall that MEC had a board, let alone that they were members; and one of these stated that he did not attend, call, or receive notice of board meetings in his five years of service because he had a designated Bristol officer to contact.

The few resolutions that were adopted by MEC's board were apparently prepared by Bristol officials.

MEC prepared "significant event" reports for Bristol's Corporate Policy Committee. These reports included information on breast implant production, such as publicity, testing, expenses, lawsuit settlements, and backorders caused by sterilization difficulties. Neither Bristol managers nor MEC Presidents recall any orders or recommendations being issued by Bristol as a result of these reviews. Bristol also required MEC to prepare and submit a five-year plan for its review.

MEC submitted budgets for approval by Bristol's senior management. For this submission, MEC filled out a series of standard Bristol forms that included information on projected sales, profits and losses, cash flow, balance sheets, and capital requirements. Bristol had the authority to modify this budget, though it rarely, if ever, actually did so. Cash received by MEC was transferred to an account maintained by Bristol. This money was credited to MEC, but the interest earned was credited to Bristol. Bristol was MEC's banker, providing such loans as it determined MEC needed. Bristol required MEC to obtain its approval for capital appropriations,[1] though most, if not all, of these requests were approved.

Bristol set the employment policies and wage scales that applied to MEC's employees. Before hiring a top executive or negotiating the salary, MEC was required to seek Bristol's approval. Before hiring a vice president of MEC, MEC's president and his superior at Bristol interviewed the candidate. Key executive employees were rated on the Bristol schedule. Bristol set a target for salary increases below the key executive level and approved those for employees above that level. Key executives of MEC received stock options for Bristol stock. MEC employees could participate in Bristol's pension and savings plans.

Bristol provided various services to MEC. Zimmer International, another Bristol subsidiary, distributed MEC breast implants but did not receive any benefit for doing so. Bristol's corporate development group assisted MEC in seeking out new product lines. Bristol's scientific experts researched the hazards of breast implants and polyurethane foam. Bristol provided funds for MEC to conduct sales contests. Bristol funded tests on breast implants. Another Bristol subsidiary, ConvaTec, assisted MEC in developing its premarket approval application (PMAA) regarding breast implants for the FDA. In addition to this assistance, Bristol hired an outside laboratory to verify ConvaTec's analysis. Bristol also conducted post-market surveillance at the request of the FDA. Some of Bristol's in-house counsel acted as MEC attorneys. These attorneys advised MEC on virtually every aspect of its business including budgets, price increases, new product development, package inserts, liability, compliance with FDA regulations, and negotiated settlements with individuals claiming damages from

---

1. The evidence reflects, for example, that MEC sought this approval before purchasing a laboratory sink costing $4,600.

breast implants. They also developed the system for handling complaints about MEC products. They reviewed all breast implant promotional materials and responses to allegations of harm and liability.

Bristol's Technical Evaluation and Service Department ("TESD") performed auditing and review functions for MEC once or twice a year. They performed all Good Manufacturing Practices (GMP) audits at MEC. These audits were designed to ensure consistent quality of MEC's products. Bristol expected MEC to comply with any manufacturing deficiencies TESD found. A number of the conditions listed as needing corrective action regarded breast implants. TESD also audited MEC's sterilization and lab companies.

Bristol's public relations department issued statements regarding the allegations of TDA production and cancer in rats implanted with polyurethane implants. Bristol's corporate communication department prepared question and answer scripts for MEC employees for use in responding to questions about breast implant safety. Bristol's public affairs department developed a strategic plan to address concerns about the MEME implant and to respond to questions and concerns about the safety of breast implants in general. Bristol's press releases consistently represented that Bristol was researching breast implant safety. For example, in a release dated July 9, 1991, Bristol stated that tests underway would "confirm the well-established safety profile of polyurethane coated breast implants" and that Bristol completed testing which showed that earlier findings concerning the production of TDA from the breakdown of polyurethane were the result of inappropriate testing conditions. In a statement dated July 24, 1991, Bristol represented that numerous other studies were being undertaken to assure the public and the FDA of the safety of polyurethane coated breast implants.

Bristol's name and logo were contained in the package inserts and promotional products regarding breast implants, apparently as a marketing tool to increase confidence in the product. Bristol's name was used in all sales and promotional communications with physicians.

MEC posted a profit every year between 1983 and 1990. Total sales increased from approximately $14 million in 1983 to $65 million in 1990. Bristol never received dividends from MEC. Bristol prepared consolidated federal income tax returns but MEC prepared its own Wisconsin tax forms. Bristol also purchased insurance for MEC under its policy. This insurance has a face value of over $2 billion.

Bristol's executive vice president suspended MEC's sales of polyurethane coated breast implants on April 17, 1991, and determined not to submit a PMAA for the implants to the FDA. MEC ceased its breast implant business in 1991 and later that year MEC ceased all operations by selling its urology division. This sale could not have occurred without Bristol's approval, and proceeds from the sale were turned over to Bristol, which then executed a low-interest demand note for $57,518,888 payable to MEC. MEC's only assets at this time are this demand note and its indemnity insurance.

IV. Analysis

The various theories of recovery made by plaintiffs against Bristol can be generally divided between those involving "corporate control" and those asserting direct liability. The corporate control claims deal with piercing the corporate veil to abrogate limited liability and hold Bristol responsible for actions of MEC. The direct liability theories include strict products liability, negligence, negligent failure to warn, negligence per se for not complying with FDA regulations, misrepresentation, fraud, and participation.

A. "Corporate Control" Claims

The potential for abuse of the corporate form is greatest when, as here, the corporation is owned by a single shareholder. The evaluation of corporate control claims cannot, however, disregard the fact that, no different from other stockholders, a parent corporation is expected—indeed, required—to exert some control over its subsidiary. Limited liability is the rule, not the exception. . . . However, when a corporation is so controlled as to be the alter ego or mere instrumentality of its stockholder, the corporate form may be disregarded in the interests of justice. So far as this court has been able to determine, some variation of this theory of liability is recognized in all jurisdictions.

An initial question is whether veil-piercing may ever be resolved by summary judgment. Ordinarily the fact-intensive nature of the issue will require that it be resolved only through a trial. Summary judgment, however, can be proper if, as occurred earlier in this litigation with respect to claims against Dow Chemical and Corning, the evidence presented could lead to but one result. Because the court concludes that a jury (or in some jurisdictions, the judge acting in equity) could—and, under the laws of many states, probably should—find that MEC was but the alter ego of Bristol, summary judgment must be denied.

The totality of circumstances must be evaluated in determining whether a subsidiary may be found to be the alter ego or mere instrumentality of the parent corporation. Although the standards are not identical in each state, all jurisdictions require a showing of substantial domination. Among the factors to be considered are whether:

- the parent and the subsidiary have common directors or officers

- the parent and the subsidiary have common business departments

- the parent and the subsidiary file consolidated financial statements and tax returns

- the parent finances the subsidiary

- the parent caused the incorporation of the subsidiary

- the subsidiary operates with grossly inadequate capital

- the parent pays the salaries and other expenses of the subsidiary

- the subsidiary receives no business except that given to it by the parent
- the parent uses the subsidiary's property as its own
- the daily operations of the two corporations are not kept separate
- the subsidiary does not observe the basic corporate formalities, such as keeping separate books and records and holding shareholder and board meetings.

. . .

The fact-finder at a trial could find that the evidence supports the conclusion that many of these factors have been proven: two of MEC's three directors were Bristol directors; MEC was part of Bristol's Health Care group and used Bristol's legal, auditing, and communications departments; MEC and Bristol filed consolidated federal tax returns and Bristol prepared consolidated financial reports; Bristol operated as MEC's finance company, providing loans for the purchase of Aesthetech and Natural Y, receiving interest on MEC's funds, and requiring MEC to make requests for capital appropriations; Bristol effectively used MEC's resources as its own by obtaining interest on MEC's money and requiring MEC to make requests for capital appropriations to obtain its own funds; some members of MEC's board were not aware that MEC had a board of directors, let alone that they were members; and the senior Bristol member of MEC's board could not be out-voted by the other two directors. These facts, even apart from evidence that might establish some of the other factors listed above, would provide significant support for a finding at trial that MEC is Bristol's alter ego.

Bristol contends that a finding of fraud or like misconduct is necessary to pierce the corporate veil. Despite Bristol's contentions to the contrary, Delaware courts—to which Bristol would have this court look—do not necessarily require a showing of fraud if a subsidiary is found to be the mere instrumentality or alter ego of its sole stockholder. . . . In addition, many jurisdictions that require a showing of fraud, injustice, or inequity in a contract case do not in a tort situation. . . . A rational distinction can be drawn between tort and contract cases. In actions based on contract, "the creditor has willingly transacted business with the subsidiary" although it could have insisted on assurances that would make the parent also responsible. [United States v. Jon–T Chemicals, Inc., 768 F.2d 686, 693 (5th Cir.1985), cert. denied, 475 U.S. 1014, 106 S.Ct. 1194, 89 L.Ed.2d 309 (1986).] In a tort situation, however, the injured party had no such choice; the limitations on corporate liability were, from its standpoint, fortuitous and non-consensual.

There is, however, evidence precluding summary judgment even in jurisdictions that require a finding of fraud, inequity, or injustice. This conclusion is not based merely on the evidence that, even accepting Bristol's contentions regarding the amount of insurance available to MEC, MEC may have insufficient funds to satisfy the potential risks of responding to, and defending against, the numerous existing and potential claims of the plaintiffs. Equally significant is the fact that Bristol permitted its name to appear on breast implant advertisements, packages, and product inserts to improve sales by giving the product additional credibility. Combined with the evidence of potentially insufficient assets, this fact would support a finding that it would be inequitable and unjust to allow Bristol now to avoid liability to those induced to believe Bristol was vouching for this product.

Because the evidence available at a trial could support—if not, under some state laws, perhaps mandate—a finding that the corporate veil should be pierced, Bristol is not entitled through summary judgment to dismissal of the claims against it.

B.   Direct Liability Claims

There is an additional reason why Bristol is not entitled to summary judgment. Under the law in most jurisdictions, it may also be subject to liability under at least one of the direct liability claims made by plaintiffs; namely, the theory of negligent undertaking pursuant to Restatement (Second) of Torts § 324A. That section provides:

> One who undertakes, gratuitously or for consideration, to render services to another which he should recognize as necessary for the protection of a third person or his things, is subject to liability to the third person for physical harm resulting from his failure to exercise reasonable care to [perform] his undertakings, if
>
>> (a) his failure to exercise reasonable care increases the risk of harm, or
>>
>> (b) he has undertaken to perform a duty owed by the other to the third person, or
>>
>> (c) the harm is suffered because of a reliance of the other or the third person upon the undertaking.

Under this theory, frequently applied in connection with safety inspections by insurers or with third-party repairs to equipment or premises, a duty that would not otherwise have existed can arise when an individual or company nevertheless undertakes to perform some action. . . .   The potential liability for failure to use reasonable care in such circumstances extends to persons who may reasonably be expected to suffer harm from that negligence. Doctrinally, a cause of action under § 324A does not involve an assertion of derivative liability but one of direct liability, since it is based on the actions of defendant itself. The existence of a parent-subsidiary relationship, while not required, is obviously no defense to such a claim.

. . .

By allowing its name to be placed on breast implant packages and product inserts, Bristol held itself out as supporting the product, apparently to increase confidence in the product and to increase sales. Bristol also issued press releases stating that polyurethane-coated breast implants were safe. Having engaged in this type of marketing, it cannot now deny its potential responsibility under § 324A.

. . .

Plaintiffs have asserted various other direct liability claims against Bristol in addition to those under § 324A. Having concluded that, because of genuine disputes relating to corporate control issues and relating to potential liability under § 324A, Bristol is not entitled to summary judgment, the court declines to address such alternative causes of action.

V. Conclusion

By separate order, Bristol's motion for summary judgment will be denied. As with other orders denying summary judgment, this decision is interlocutory and does not constitute a holding that Bristol is liable to the plaintiffs.

. . .

QUESTIONS

1. Which of the various "factors to be considered" are most important and which, if any, seem irrelevant, and why?

2. What is the relevance of the use of Bristol's name on "advertisements, packages, and product inserts" under a theory of (a) piercing the corporate veil or (b) direct liability under Restatement (Second) of Torts § 324A?

3. Is there any other theory under which the use of Bristol's name would be relevant?

4. If you had been Bristol's lawyer, what advice would you have given (if asked) about how to avoid liability for the debts of MEC? Bear in mind the importance of the need of Bristol to exercise control over MEC in a practical manner and the distaste of people in business for pettifogging lawyers.

INTRODUCTORY NOTE

Beginning in the 1960s, limited partnerships came into widespread use for "tax shelter" investments. Tax shelter investments are ones that show losses for tax purposes even though they may be successful economically. Such investments were of considerable economic importance (particularly in certain sectors, such as real estate and oil and gas) until the tax benefits were substantially curtailed in the 1980s, particularly in 1986. The tax advantage of the use of the limited partnership form of organization was that the investors were able to claim their pro rata share of the (economically artificial) losses of the partnership on their individual tax returns, which is not possible for tax-shelter-type investments if the corporate form is used. While the basic partnership form bestowed this tax benefit—the so called "pass-through" of losses—the use of the *limited* partnership form gave the (mostly passive) investors the corporate advantage of limited liability. Beginning in the late 1960s, lawyers for the promoters of tax shelter investments developed a variation on the basic limited partnership: a limited partnership with a corporation as the sole general partner. With the use of this form, no individual was liable for the debts of the partnership. Initially some observers thought that that was too good to be true, but eventually it became accepted as a standard form of tax shelter organization. As the preceding material in this section suggests, however, it is often easier for a lawyer to form a corporation (or a limited partnership with a corporate general partner) than for the clients to respect the form and thereby make it effective.

Frigidaire Sales Corporation v. Union Properties, Inc.

88 Wash. 2d 400, 562 P.2d 244 (1977).

Petitioner, Frigidaire Sales Corporation, sought review of a Court of Appeals decision which held that limited partners do not incur general liability for the limited partnership's obligations simply because they are officers, directors, or shareholders of the corporate general partner. . . . We granted review, and now affirm the decision of the Court of Appeals.

. . . Petitioner entered into a contract with Commercial Investors (Commercial), a limited partnership. Respondents, Leonard Mannon and Raleigh Baxter, were limited partners of Commercial. Respondents were also officers, directors, and shareholders of Union Properties, Inc., the only general partner of Commercial. Respondents controlled Union Properties, and through their control of Union Properties they exercised the day-to-day control and management of Commercial. Commercial breached the contract, and petitioner brought suit against Union Properties and respondents. The trial court concluded that respondents did not incur general liability for Commercial's obligations by reason of their control of Commercial, and the Court of Appeals affirmed.

We first note that petitioner does not contend that respondents acted improperly by setting up the limited partnership with a corporation as the sole general partner. Limited partnerships are a statutory form of business organization, and parties creating a limited partnership must follow the statutory requirements. In Washington, parties may form a limited partnership with a corporation as the sole general partner. . . .

Petitioner's sole contention is that respondents should incur general liability for the limited partnership's obligations [under the Uniform Limited Partnership Act provision that removes the limitation of liability of a limited partner who "takes part in the control of the business"], because they exercised the day-to-day control and management of Commercial. Respondents, on the other hand, argue that Commercial was controlled by Union Properties, a separate legal entity, and not by respondents in their individual capacities.

[The court distinguishes Delaney v. Fidelity Lease Ltd., 526 S.W.2d 543 (Tex.1975), in which, among other things, the Texas Supreme Court expressed concern about the use of corporate general partners with "minimum capitalization and therefore minimum liability."]

However, we agree with our Court of Appeals analysis that this concern with minimum capitalization is not peculiar to limited partnerships with corporate general partners, but may arise anytime a creditor deals with a corporation. . . . Because our limited partnership statutes permit parties to form a limited partnership with a corporation as the sole general partner, this concern about minimal capitalization, standing by itself, does not justify a finding that the limited partners incur general liability for their control of the corporate general partner. . . . If a corporate general partner is inadequately capitalized, the rights of a creditor are adequately protected under the "piercing-the-corporate-veil" doctrine of corporation law. . . .

Furthermore, petitioner was never led to believe that respondents were acting in any capacity other than in their corporate capacities. The parties stipulated at the trial that respondents never acted in any direct, personal capacity. When the shareholders of a corporation, who are also the corporation's officers and directors, conscientiously keep the affairs of the corporation separate from their personal affairs, and no fraud or manifest injustice is perpetrated upon third persons who deal with the corporation, the corporation's separate entity should be respected. . . .

For us to find that respondents incurred general liability for the limited partnership's obligations . . . would require us to . . . totally ignore the corporate entity of Union Properties, when petitioner knew it was dealing with that corporate entity. There can be no doubt that respondents, in fact, controlled the corporation. However, they did so only in their capacities as agents for their principal, the corporate general partner. Although the corporation was a separate entity, it could act only through its board of directors, officers, and agents. . . . Petitioner entered into the contract with Commercial. Respondents signed the contract in their capacities as president and secretary-treasurer of Union Properties, the general partner of Commercial. In the eyes of the law it was Union Properties, as a separate corporate entity, which entered into the contract with petitioner and controlled the limited partnership.

Further, because respondents scrupulously separated their actions on behalf of the corporation from their personal actions, petitioner never mistakenly assumed that respondents were general partners with general liability. . . . Petitioner knew Union Properties was the sole general partner and did not rely on respondents' control by assuming that they were also general partners. If petitioner had not wished to rely on the solvency of Union Properties as the only general partner, it could have insisted that respondents personally guarantee contractual performance. Because petitioner entered into the contract knowing that Union Properties was the only party with general liability, and because in the eyes of the law it was Union Properties, a separate entity, which controlled the limited partnership, there is no reason for us to find that respondents incurred general liability for their acts done as officers of the corporate general partner.

The decision of the Court of Appeals is affirmed.

ANALYSIS

In *Frigidaire* the individual defendants were limited partners of Commercial Investors as well as officers, directors and shareholders of Union Properties, Inc., the general partner. If they had not been limited partners might they still have been personally liable (if they had not been so scrupulous about respecting the corporate form)? On what theory or theories? How would the proof differ, depending on whether they were or were not limited partners?

NOTE ON LIMITED LIABILITY COMPANIES

In general, the law on piercing the corporate veil probably applies to LLCs as well. In some states, the LLC statute makes the point explicit. The Minnesota statute, for example, provides: "The case law that states the conditions and circumstances under which the corporate veil of a corporation may be pierced under Minnesota law also applies to limited liability companies." Minn.Stat. § 322B.303(2).

Section 3. Shareholder Derivative Actions

A. Introduction

Cohen v. Beneficial Industrial Loan Corp.

337 U.S. 541, 69 S.Ct. 1221, 93 L.Ed. 1528 (1949).

■ MR. JUSTICE JACKSON delivered the opinion of the Court.

The ultimate question here is whether a federal court, having jurisdiction of a stockholder's derivative action only because the parties are of diverse citizenship, must apply a statute of the forum state which makes the plaintiff, if unsuccessful, liable for the reasonable expenses, including attorney's fees, of the defense and entitles the corporation to require security for their payment.

Petitioners' decedent, as plaintiff, brought in the United States District Court for New Jersey an action in the right of the Beneficial Industrial Loan Corporation, a Delaware corporation doing business in New Jersey. The defendants were the corporation and certain of its managers and directors. The complaint alleged generally that since 1929 the individual defendants engaged in a continuing and successful conspiracy to enrich themselves at the expense of the corporation. Specific charges of mismanagement and fraud extended over a period of eighteen years and the assets allegedly wasted or diverted thereby were said to exceed $100,000,000. The stockholder had demanded that the corporation institute proceedings for its recovery but, by their control of the corporation, the individual defendants prevented it from doing so. This stockholder, therefore, sought to assert the right of the corporation. One of 16,000 stockholders, he owned 100 of its more than two million shares, so that his holdings, together with 150 shares held by the intervenor, approximated 0.0125% of the outstanding stock and had a market value that had never exceeded $9,000.

The action was brought in 1943, and various proceedings had been taken therein when, in 1945, New Jersey enacted the statute which is here involved.[1] Its general effect is to make a plaintiff having so small an

1. Chapter 131, New Jersey Laws of 1945, provides in pertinent part as follows:

"1. In any action instituted or maintained in the right of any domestic or foreign corporation by the holder or holders of shares, or of voting trust certificates representing shares, of such corporation having a total par value or stated capital value of less than five per centum (5%) of the aggregate par value or stated capital value of all the outstanding shares of such corporation's stock of every class . . . unless the shares or voting trust certificates held by such holder or holders have a market value in excess of fifty thousand dollars ($50,000.00), the corporation in whose right such action is brought shall be entitled, at any stage of the proceeding before final judgment, to require the com-

241

interest liable for the reasonable expenses and attorney's fees of the defense if he fails to make good his complaint and to entitle the corporation to indemnity before the case can be prosecuted. These conditions are made applicable to pending actions. The corporate defendant therefore moved to require security, pointed to its by-laws by which it might be required to indemnify the individual defendants, and averred that a bond of $125,000 would be appropriate.

Constitutionality.

Petitioners deny the validity of the statute under the Federal Constitution.   . . .

The background of stockholder litigation with which this statute deals requires no more than general notice. As business enterprise increasingly sought the advantages of incorporation, management became vested with almost uncontrolled discretion in handling other people's money. The vast aggregate of funds committed to corporate control came to be drawn to a considerable extent from numerous and scattered holders of small interests. The director was not subject to an effective accountability. That created strong temptation for managers to profit personally at expense of their trust. The business code became all too tolerant of such practices. Corporate laws were lax and were not self-enforcing, and stockholders, in face of gravest abuses, were singularly impotent in obtaining redress of abuses of trust.

Equity came to the relief of the stockholder, who had no standing to bring civil action at law against faithless directors and managers. Equity, however, allowed him to step into the corporation's shoes and to seek in its right the restitution he could not demand in his own. It required him first to demand that the corporation vindicate its own rights, but when, as was usual, those who perpetrated the wrongs also were able to obstruct any remedy, equity would hear and adjudge the corporation's cause through its stockholder with the corporation as a defendant, albeit a rather nominal one. This remedy, born of stockholder helplessness, was long the chief regulator of corporate management and has afforded no small incentive to avoid at least grosser forms of betrayal of stockholders' interests. It is

plainant or complainants to give security for the reasonable expenses, including counsel fees, which may be incurred by it in connection with such action and by the other parties defendant in connection therewith for which it may become subject pursuant to law, its certificate of incorporation, its by-laws or under equitable principles, to which the corporation shall have recourse in such amount as the court having jurisdiction shall determine upon the termination of such action. . . .

"2. In any action, suit or proceeding brought or maintained in the right of a domestic or foreign corporation by the holder or holders of shares, or of voting trust certificates representing shares, of such corporation, it must be made to appear that the complainant was a shareholder or the holder of a voting trust certificate at the time of the transaction of which he complains or that his share or voting trust certificate thereafter devolved upon him by operation of law.

"3. This act shall take effect immediately and shall apply to all such actions, suits or proceedings now pending in which no final judgment has been entered, and to all future actions, suits and proceedings."

argued, and not without reason, that without it there would be little practical check on such abuses.

Unfortunately, the remedy itself provided opportunity for abuse, which was not neglected. Suits sometimes were brought not to redress real wrongs, but to realize upon their nuisance value. They were bought off by secret settlements in which any wrongs to the general body of share owners were compounded by the suing stockholder, who was mollified by payments from corporate assets.* These litigations were aptly characterized in professional slang as "strike suits." And it was said that these suits were more commonly brought by small and irresponsible than by large stockholders, because the former put less to risk and a small interest was more often within the capacity and readiness of management to compromise than a large one.

We need not determine the measure of these abuses or the evils they produced on the one hand or prevented and redressed on the other. The Legislature of New Jersey, like that of other states, considered them sufficient to warrant some remedial measures.

[A] stockholder who brings suit on a cause of action derived from the corporation assumes a position, not technically as a trustee perhaps, but one of a fiduciary character. He sues, not for himself alone, but as representative of a class comprising all who are similarly situated. The interests of all in the redress of the wrongs are taken into his hands, dependent upon his diligence, wisdom and integrity. And while the stockholders have chosen the corporate director or manager, they have no such election as to a plaintiff who steps forward to represent them. He is a self-chosen representative and a volunteer champion. The Federal Constitution does not oblige the state to place its litigating and adjudicating processes at the disposal of such a representative, at least without imposing standards of responsibility, liability and accountability which it considers will protect the interests he elects himself to represent. . . . We conclude that the state has plenary power over this type of litigation.

. . . .

In considering whether the statute offends the Due Process Clause we can judge it only by its own terms, for it has had no interpretation or application as yet. It imposes liability and requires security for "the *reasonable* expenses, including counsel fees, which may be incurred" (emphasis supplied) by the corporation and by other parties defendant. The amount of security is subject to increase if the progress of the litigation reveals that it is inadequate, or to decrease if it is proved to be excessive. A state may set the terms on which it will permit litigations in its courts. No type of litigation is more susceptible of regulation than that of a fiduciary nature. And it cannot seriously be said that a state makes such

* [Eds.—Generally it was not the shareholder who was "mollified by payments from corporate assets," but the shareholder's lawyer, who received a generous legal fee. To this day, the principal effective incentive that generates derivative actions is legal fees, not shareholder dissatisfaction.]

unreasonable use of its power as to violate the Constitution when it provides liability and security for payment of *reasonable* expenses if a litigation of this character is adjudged to be unsustainable.   . . .

The contention that the statute denies equal protection of the laws is based upon the fact that it enables a stockholder who owns 5% of a corporation's outstanding shares, or $50,000 in market value, to proceed without either security or liability and imposes both upon those who elect to proceed with a smaller interest. We do not think the state is forbidden to use the amount of one's financial interest, which measures his individual injury from the misconduct to be redressed, as some measure of the good faith and responsibility of one who seeks at his own election to act as custodian of the interests of all stockholders, and as an indication that he volunteers for the large burdens of the litigation from a real sense of grievance and is not putting forward a claim to capitalize personally on its harassment value. These may not be the best ways of precluding "strike lawsuits," but we are unable to say that a classification for these purposes, based upon the percentage or market value of the stock alleged to be injured by the wrongs, is an unconstitutional one.

Applicability in Federal Court.

The Rules of Decision Act, in effect since the First Congress of the United States and now found at 28 U.S.C. § 1652, provides: "The laws of the several states, except where the Constitution or treaties of the United States or Acts of Congress otherwise require or provide, shall be regarded as rules of decision in civil actions in the courts of the United States, in cases where they apply." This Court in Erie R. Co. v. Tompkins, 304 U.S. 64, held that judicial decisions are laws of the states within its meaning. But *Erie R. Co. v. Tompkins* and its progeny have wrought a more far-reaching change in the relation of state and federal courts and the application of state law in the latter whereby in diversity cases the federal court administers the state system of law in all except details related to its own conduct of business. . . . The only substantial argument that this New Jersey statute is not applicable here is that its provisions are mere rules of procedure rather than rules of substantive law.

Even if we were to agree that the New Jersey statute is procedural, it would not determine that it is not applicable. Rules which lawyers call procedural do not always exhaust their effect by regulating procedure. But this statute is not merely a regulation of procedure. With it or without it the main action takes the same course. However, it creates a new liability where none existed before, for it makes a stockholder who institutes a derivative action liable for the expense to which he puts the corporation and other defendants, if he does not make good his claims. Such liability is not usual and it goes beyond payment of what we know as "costs." If all the Act did was to create this liability, it would clearly be substantive. But this new liability would be without meaning and value in many cases if it resulted in nothing but a judgment for expenses at or after the end of the case. Therefore, a procedure is prescribed by which the liability is insured by entitling the corporate defendant to a bond of indemnity before the outlay is incurred. We do not think a statute which so conditions the stockholder's action can be disregarded by the federal court as a mere procedural device.

We hold that the New Jersey statute applies in federal courts and that the District Court erred in declining to fix the amount of indemnity reasonably to be exacted as a condition of further prosecution of the suit.

The judgment of the Court of Appeals is

Affirmed.

■ [Eds.—The dissenting opinions of JUSTICE DOUGLAS (joined by JUSTICE FRANKFURTER) and JUSTICE RUTLEDGE are omitted.]

ANALYSIS

1. Think about the role of the shareholder in the legal structure of the corporation. Why is the derivative action one in equity rather than at law?

2. Is there anything unique about derivative actions that has led New Jersey and other states to reject the normal rule of American law that each party bears her or his own legal expenses, regardless of who prevails?

Eisenberg v. Flying Tiger Line, Inc.

451 F.2d 267 (2d Cir.1971).

■ IRVING R. KAUFMAN, CIRCUIT JUDGE:

Max Eisenberg, a resident of New York, "as stockholder of The Flying Tiger Line, Inc. [Flying Tiger], on behalf of himself and all other stockholders of said corporation similarly situated" commenced this action in the Supreme Court of the State of New York to enjoin the effectuation of a plan of reorganization and merger.* Flying Tiger, a Delaware corporation with its principal place of business in California, removed the action to the District Court for the Eastern District of New York.

Flying Tiger pleaded several affirmative defenses and moved for an order to require Eisenberg to comply with New York Business Corporation Law § 627 (McKinney's Consol.Laws, c. 4 1963), which requires a plaintiff suing derivatively on behalf of a corporation to post security for the corporation's costs. Judge Travia granted the motion without opinion and afforded Eisenberg thirty days to post security in the sum of $35,000. Eisenberg did not comply, his action was dismissed and he appeals. We find Eisenberg's cause of action to be personal and not derivative within the meaning of § 627. We therefore reverse the dismissal.

* [Eds.—Eisenberg represented himself.]

In this action, Eisenberg is seeking to overturn a reorganization and merger which Flying Tiger effected in 1969. He charges that a series of corporate maneuvers were intended to dilute his voting rights. In order to achieve this end, he alleges, Flying Tiger in July 1969 organized a wholly owned Delaware subsidiary, the Flying Tiger Corporation ("FTC"). In August, FTC in turn organized a wholly owned subsidiary, FTL Air Freight Corporation ("FTL"). The three Delaware corporations then entered into a plan of reorganization, subject to stockholder approval, by which Flying Tiger merged into FTL and only FTL survived. A proxy statement dated August 11 was sent to stockholders, who approved the plan by the necessary two-thirds vote at the stockholders' meeting held on September 15.

Upon consummation of this merger Flying Tiger ceased as the operating company, FTL took over operations and Flying Tiger shares were converted into an identical number of FTC shares. Thereafter, FTL changed its name to "Flying Tiger Line, Inc.," for the obvious purpose of continuing without disruption the business previously conducted by Flying Tiger. The approximately 4,500,000 shares of the company traded on the New York and Pacific Coast stock exchanges are now those of the holding company, FTC, rather than those of the operating company, Flying Tiger. The effect of the merger is that business operations are now confined to a wholly owned subsidiary of a holding company whose stockholders are the former stockholders of Flying Tiger.

It is of passing interest that Eisenberg contends that the end result of this complex plan was to deprive minority stockholders of any vote or any influence over the affairs of the newly spawned company. Flying Tiger insists the plan was devised to bring about diversification without interference from the Civil Aeronautics Board, which closely regulates air carriers, and to better use available tax benefits. Even if any of these motives prove to be relevant, the alleged illegality is not relevant to the questions before this court. We are called on to decide, assuming Eisenberg's complaint is sufficient on its face, only whether he should have been required to post security for costs as a condition to prosecuting his action.

To resolve this question we look first to Cohen v. Beneficial Industrial Loan Corp., 337 U.S. 541 (1949), which instructs that a federal court with diversity jurisdiction must apply a state statute providing security for costs if the state court would require the security in similar circumstances. . . . [T]his Court still must determine whether to apply the New York costs security statute, Business Corporation Law § 627, or, as Eisenberg contends, Delaware law, which has no such requirement. New York clearly has indicated that § 627 will be applied in its courts whether or not New York substantive law controls the merits of the case. . . . Since New York courts would invoke its own law on security for costs rather than Delaware's, we are required to do the same. . . .

Eisenberg argues, however, that New York courts would refuse to invoke § 627 in the instant case because the section applies exclusively to derivative actions . . . . He urges that his class action is representative and not derivative.

We are told that if the gravamen of the complaint is injury to the corporation the suit is derivative, but "if the injury is one to the plaintiff as a stockholder and to him individually and not to the corporation," the suit is individual in nature and may take the form of a representative class action. 13 Fletcher, Private Corporation § 5911 (1970 Rev.Vol.). This generalization is of little use in our case which is one of those "borderline cases which are more or less troublesome to classify." Id. The essence of Eisenberg's claimed injury is that the reorganization has deprived him and fellow stockholders of their right to vote on the operating company affairs and that this right in no sense ever belonged to Flying Tiger itself. This right, he says, belonged to the stockholders *per se.* Flying Tiger notes, however, that the stockholders were harmed, if at all, only because their company was dissolved, and their vote can be restored only if that company is revived. It insists, therefore, that stockholders are affected only secondarily or derivatively because we must first breathe life back into their dissolved corporation before the stockholders can be helped.

Despite a leading New York case which would seem at first glance to support Flying Tiger's position, we find that its contention misses the mark by a wide margin in its failure to distinguish between derivative and non-derivative class actions. In Gordon v. Elliman, 306 N.Y. 456, 119 N.E.2d 331 (1954), by a vote of 4 to 3, the Court of Appeals took an expansive view of the coverage of § 627's predecessor, General Corporation Law § 61–b. The majority held that an action to compel the payment of a dividend was derivative in nature and security for costs could be required. The test formulated by the majority was "whether the object of the lawsuit is to recover upon a chose in action belonging directly to the stockholders, or whether it is to compel the performance of corporate acts which good faith requires the directors to take in order to perform a duty which they owe to the corporation, and through it, to its stockholders." 306 N.Y. at 459, 119 N.E.2d at 334. Pursuant to this test it is argued that, if Flying Tiger's directors had a duty not to merge the corporation, that duty was owed to the corporation and only derivatively to its stockholders. Both the 4–1 Appellate Division and the 4–3 Court of Appeals opinions evoked the quick and unanimous condemnation of commentators. Moreover, this test, "which appears to sweep away the distinction between a representative and a derivative action," in effect classifying all stockholder class actions as derivative, has been limited strictly to its facts by lower New York courts. Lazar v. Knolls Cooperative Section No. 2, Inc., 205 Misc. 748, 130 N.Y.S.2d 407, 410 (Sup.Ct.1954). . . . In *Lazar,* a stockholder sought to force directors to call a stockholders' meeting. The court stated security for costs could not be required where a plaintiff

> "does not challenge acts of the management on behalf of the corporation. He challenges the right of the present management to exclude him and other stockholders from proper participation in the affairs of the corporation. He claims that the defendants are interfering with the plaintiff's rights and privileges as stockholders."

130 N.Y.S. at 410, 205 Misc. at 752.   In substance, this is similar to what Eisenberg challenges here.

The legislature also was concerned with the sweeping breadth of *Gordon*.   In the recodification of corporate statutes completed in 1963, it added three words to the definition of derivative suits contained in § 626.   Suits are now derivative only if brought in the right of a corporation to procure a judgment "in its favor."   This was to "forestall any such pronouncement in the future as that made by the Court of Appeals in Gordon v. Elliman."   Hornstein, "Analysis of Business Corporation Law," 6 McKinney's Consolidated Laws of New York Ann. 483 (1963).

. . .

Eisenberg's position is even stronger than it would be in the ordinary merger case.   In routine merger circumstances the stockholders retain a voice in the operation of the company, albeit a corporation other than their original choice.   Here, however, the reorganization deprived him and other minority stockholders of any voice in the affairs of their previously existing operating company.

It is thus clear to us that *Gordon* is factually distinguishable from the instant case.   Moreover, a close analysis of other New York cases, the amendment to § 626 and the major treatises, lead us to conclude that *Gordon* has lost its viability as stating a broad principle of law.

Perhaps the strongest string in Eisenberg's bow is one he helped to fashion when he made an investment some forty years ago in Central Zone Property Corp.   In 1952 that New York corporation obtained stockholder approval to transfer its assets to a new Delaware corporation in return for the new company's stock.   The stock was to be held by trustees in a voting trust, and the former stockholders received voting trust certificates.   Eisenberg complained that this effectively deprived him of a voice in the operation of his company which would be run in the future by the trustees of the voting trust.   The Court of Appeals agreed that New York law did not permit such a reorganization.   Eisenberg v. Central Zone Property Corp., 203 Misc. 59, 116 N.Y.S.2d 154, aff'd, 306 N.Y. 58, 115 N.E.2d 652 (1953).   Although we have emphasized that we do not reach the merits of Eisenberg's present complaint, it is of some interest that security for costs was neither sought nor was it discussed in the *Central Zone* opinions, even though Eisenberg did not own five percent of the shares of the corporation. It was clear to all that the allegations of the complaint, quite similar in character to the instant one, stated a representative cause of action. . . .   We believe Eisenberg's actions should not have been dismissed for failure to post security pursuant to § 627.

Reversed.

ANALYSIS

1.   How, if at all, was Eisenberg deprived of voting rights by the Flying Tiger reorganization?

2. Would the result in the case have been different if Eisenberg had alleged that the directors of Flying Tiger Line, Inc., had violated their duty of loyalty to the corporation and had sought damages in the amount of the legal and other costs of effecting the reorganization?

NOTE ON SETTLEMENTS AND ATTORNEY FEES

If a derivative action is settled before judgment, the corporation can pay the legal fees of the plaintiff and of the defendants. If, on the other hand, a judgment for money damages is imposed on the defendants, except to the extent that they are covered by insurance, they will be required to pay those damages and may be required to bear the cost of their defense as well. See Del.Gen.Corp.Law § 145(b) (The corporation may pay the defendants' expenses only if the court determines that "despite the adjudication of liability but in view of all the circumstances of the case, [the defendant] is fairly entitled to indemnity."); Cal.Corp.Code § 317(c) (to the same effect). On the plaintiff's side the real party in interest in a derivative action often is the attorney. Putting these rules and observations together, corporate managers who have harmed the corporation generally will be relieved of risk of personal losses if the corporation pays large fees to the plaintiff's attorneys in return for their willingness to accept a settlement, especially one with a form of relief other than money damages. The plaintiff's attorneys may be willing to accept such a settlement in order to avoid the risks of litigation or simply because they are well paid to do so. The court in which the derivative suit is filed must approve any settlement, but a busy judge is not likely to challenge a settlement that is supported by both the parties.

In re General Tire and Rubber Company Securities Litigation, 726 F.2d 1075 (6th Cir.1984), provides a nice illustration of a non-monetary settlement with seemingly generous attorney fees. In that case, General Tire, and its subsidiary, RKO General, had engaged in "ubiquitous corporate improprieties and apparent illegalities." The Securities and Exchange Commission (SEC) brought an action that resulted in recommendations for administrative changes such as expanded review by independent accountants. Derivative actions were also filed, complaining, in part, about dishonest reports by RKO General that led to the loss of a TV license worth over $100 million. The derivative actions were settled, with judicial approval, with the payment of $500,000 as fees to the plaintiffs' attorney. The settlement agreement "acknowledge[d] the plaintiffs' role in implementing remedial action to prevent future improprieties," but in light of the SEC role in the matter, this language seems to be a smokescreen. The only substantive relief was an agreement by General Tire that it would for three years appoint to the RKO board two members who were neither officers nor employees of General Tire or RKO. As the dissenting judge pointed out this relief provided "no real benefit in view of the absolute control of RKO by General Tire."

NOTE AND QUESTION ON INDIVIDUAL RECOVERY IN A DERIVATIVE ACTION

Sometimes a court awards an individual recovery in a derivative action. For example, in Lynch v. Patterson, 701 P.2d 1126 (Wyo.1985), Pat Patterson, Birl Lynch, and R.C. Lynch had carried on an oil-field consulting business in corporate form. Patterson owned 30 percent of the common stock and Birl Lynch and R.C. Lynch each owned 35 percent. Patterson quit working for the corporation and set up his own consulting business. Thereafter, Birl Lynch and R.C. Lynch increased their own pay and ultimately, it was found, paid themselves $266,000 in excess compensation. Patterson filed a derivative action to recover the excess salaries of $266,000 from the Lynches. The trial court awarded him damages as an individual in the amount of 30 percent of the $266,000, or $79,800. The Wyoming Supreme Court upheld this judgment, noting that "corporate recovery would simply return the funds to the control of the wrongdoers." Suppose Patterson's legal fees were $21,000. Should he have been entitled to recover part or all of this outlay? If so, how much? (There is no mention of this issue in the opinion.)

B.   THE REQUIREMENT OF DEMAND ON THE DIRECTORS

Grimes v. Donald

673 A.2d 1207 (Del.Sup.Ct.1996).

In this appeal we address the following issues: (1) the distinction between a direct claim of a stockholder and a derivative claim; (2) a direct claim of alleged abdication by a board of directors of its statutory duty; (3) when a pre-suit demand in a derivative suit is required or excused; and (4) the consequences of demand by a stockholder and the refusal by the board to act on such a demand.

.   .   .

We hold as follows: First, an abdication claim can be stated by a stockholder as a direct claim, as distinct from a derivative claim, but here the complaint fails to state a claim upon which relief can be granted. Second, when a stockholder demands that the board of directors take action on a claim allegedly belonging to the corporation and demand is refused, the stockholder may not thereafter assert that demand is excused with respect to other legal theories in support of the same claim, although the stockholder may have a remedy for wrongful refusal or may submit further demands which are not repetitious.

Accordingly, on the state of this record, we AFFIRM the dismissal of this action by the Court of Chancery.

I.   The Facts

C.L. Grimes ("Grimes"), plaintiff below-appellant, appeals from the dismissal, for failure to state a claim, of his complaint against James L.

Donald ("Donald") (the CEO) and the Board of Directors (the "Board") of DSC Communications Corporation ("DSC" or the "Company"). Grimes seeks a declaration of the invalidity of the Agreements between Donald and the Company. He also seeks an award of damages against Donald and other members of the Board. He alleges that the Board has breached its fiduciary duties by abdicating its authority, failing to exercise due care and committing waste.

The following facts have been drawn from the face of the complaint. The Company is a Delaware corporation headquartered in Plano, Texas, a suburb of Dallas. The Company, whose shares are traded on the Nasdaq National Market System, designs, manufactures, markets and services telecommunication systems.

The Agreements, executed during 1990, are the focus of the complaint. The Employment Agreement provides that Donald "shall be responsible for the general management of the affairs of the company . . .," and that Donald "shall report to the Board." The Employment Agreement runs until the earlier of Donald's 75th birthday or his termination (1) by reason of death or disability; (2) for cause; or (3) without cause. Under the Employment Agreement, Donald can declare a "Constructive Termination Without Cause" by the Company of his employment as a result of, inter alia, "unreasonable interference, in the good-faith judgment of . . . [Donald], by the Board or a substantial stockholder of the Company, in [Donald's] carrying out his duties and responsibilities under the [Employment] Agreement." A Constructive Termination Without Cause takes effect after delivery of notice by Donald and the failure by the Board to remedy such interference.

In the event of a Termination Without Cause, constructive or otherwise, Donald is entitled to the following:

1. Continued payment of his "Base Salary" at the level in effect immediately prior to termination for the remainder of his "Term of Employment," which, as stated, will be 6 1/2 years unless Donald dies or turns 75 first. In 1992, Donald's Base Salary exceeded $650,000.

2. Annual incentive awards for the remainder of the Term of Employment equal to the average of the three highest annual bonuses awarded to Donald during his last ten years as CEO. In 1992, such award allegedly equaled $300,000.

3. Medical benefits for Donald and his wife for life, as well as his children until the age of 23.

4. Continued participation in all employee benefit plans in which Donald is participating on the date of termination until the earlier of the expiration of the Term of Employment or the date on which he receives equivalent benefits from a subsequent employer.

5. Other (unidentified) benefits in accordance with DSC's plans and programs.

Grimes v. Donald, Del. Ch., 20 Del.J.Corp.L. 757, 765, 1995 WL 54441 (1995).

The Income Continuation Plan provides, inter alia, that after Base Salary payments cease under the Employment Agreement, Donald is entitled to receive, for the remainder of his life, annual payments equal to the average of the sum of his Base Salary plus bonuses in the three highest years, multiplied by 3%, multiplied by his years of service. Donald has also been awarded 200,000 "units" under the Long Term Incentive Plan. In the event of a Change of Control, as defined in the Incentive Plan, Donald will have the right to cash payments for his units, which Grimes alleges could total $60,000,000 at the stock price in effect at the time the complaint was filed.

As required by Court of Chancery Rule 23.1, Grimes alleges in his complaint that he wrote to the Board on September 23, 1993 and demanded that the Board abrogate the Agreements. . . .

The Board refused the demand in a letter dated November 8, 1993, which states in part:

The Compensation Committee of our Board of Directors, as well as the entire Board, have seriously considered the issues set forth in your letter of September 29. To assist in the review, the Board obtained reports analyzing the relevant issues from the Company's outside benefits consultant, Hirschfeld, Stern, Moyer & Ross, Inc. and from the Company's outside legal counsel, Jones, Day, Reavis & Pogue. The Compensation Committee and the full Board of Directors believe that a thorough analysis of the applicable provisions of Delaware law necessarily leads to a conclusion that Mr. Donald's duties as described in the Employment Agreement do not constitute an impermissible delegation of the duties of the Board of Directors. . . .

II. Grimes Has Not Stated a Claim for Abdication of Directorial Duty

. . . The due care, waste and excessive compensation claims asserted here are derivative and will be considered as such. Kramer v. Western Pacific Indus., Inc., Del.Supr., 546 A.2d 348, 353 (1988). The abdication claim, however, is a direct claim. In order to reach this conclusion, we believe a further exploration of the distinction between direct and derivative claims is appropriate.

A. Distinction Between Direct and Derivative Claims, Generally

As the Court of Chancery has noted: "Although the tests have been articulated many times, it is often difficult to distinguish between a derivative and an individual action." In re Rexene Corp. Shareholders Litig., Del.Ch., 17 Del.J.Corp.L. 342, 348, 1991 WL 77529 (1991); . . . The distinction depends upon " 'the nature of the wrong alleged' and the relief, if any, which could result if plaintiff were to prevail." Kramer v. Western Pacific, 546 A.2d at 352 (quoting Elster v. American Airlines, Inc., Del.Ch., 100 A.2d 219, 221–223 (1953)). To pursue a direct action, the stockholder-plaintiff "must allege more than an injury resulting from a wrong to the corporation." Id. at 351. The plaintiff must state a claim for " 'an injury which is separate and distinct from that suffered by other shareholders,' . . . or a wrong involving a contractual right of a shareholder . . . which exists independently of any right of the corporation." Moran v. Household Int'l, Inc., Del.Ch., 490 A.2d 1059, 1070, aff'd, Del. Supr., 500 A.2d 1346 (1985) (quoting 12B FLETCHER CYCLOPEDIA CORPS., § 5291 (Perm.Ed.1984)).

. . .

With respect to the abdication claim, Grimes seeks only a declaration of the invalidity of the Agreements. Monetary recovery will not accrue to the corporation as a result. Chancellor Seitz illustrated this distinction in Bennett [v. Breuil Petroleum Corp., Del.Ch., 99 A.2d 236 (1953)]. The Court of Chancery there allowed the plaintiff-stockholder to proceed individually on his claim that stock was issued for an improper purpose and entrenchment; he proceeded derivatively on his claim that the stock was issued for an insufficient price. 99 A.2d at 241.

. . .

C. Analysis of Grimes' Abdication Claim

In the case before us, the abdication claim fails as a matter of law. Grimes claims that the potentially severe financial penalties which the Company would incur in the event that the Board attempts to interfere in Donald's management of the Company will inhibit and deter the Board from exercising its duties under Section 141(a). The Court of Chancery assumed that, if a contract could have the practical effect of preventing a board from exercising its duties, it would amount to a de facto abdication of directorial authority. The Chancellor concluded, however, that Grimes has not set forth well-pleaded allegations which would establish such a situation. We agree.

. . .

Directors may not delegate duties which lie "at the heart of the management of the corporation." Chapin v. Benwood, Del.Ch., 402 A.2d 1205, 1210 (1979), aff'd sub nom. Harrison v. Chapin, Del.Supr., 415 A.2d 1068 (1980). A court "cannot give legal sanction to agreements which have the effect of removing from directors in a very substantial way their duty to use their own best judgment on management matters." Abercrombie v. Davies, Del.Ch., 123 A.2d 893, 899 (1956), rev'd on other grounds, Del. Supr., 130 A.2d 338 (1957). Distinguishing these cases, however, the Court of Chancery stated: "[U]nlike the agreements considered in Abercrombie and Chapin, the Donald Agreements do not formally preclude the DSC board from exercising its statutory powers and fulfilling its fiduciary duty." Grimes, 20 Del.J.Corp.L. at 774–775. Compare Rosenblatt v. Getty Oil Co., Del.Supr., 493 A.2d 929, 943–44 (1985) (delegation to independent appraiser of responsibility to value oil and gas reserves as part of a merger agreement was proper exercise of business judgment).

With certain exceptions, "an informed decision to delegate a task is as much an exercise of business judgment as any other." Rosenblatt, 493 A.2d at 943. Likewise, business decisions are not an abdication of directorial authority merely because they limit a board's freedom of future action. A board which has decided to manufacture bricks has less freedom to decide to make bottles. In a world of scarcity, a decision to do one thing will commit a board to a certain course of action and make it costly and difficult (indeed, sometimes impossible) to change course and do another. This is an inevitable fact of life and is not an abdication of directorial duty.

If the market for senior management, in the business judgment of a board, demands significant severance packages, boards will inevitably limit their future range of action by entering into employment agreements. Large severance payments will deter boards, to some extent, from dismissing senior officers. If an independent and informed board, acting in good faith, determines that the services of a particular individual warrant large amounts of money, whether in the form of current salary or severance provisions, the board has made a business judgment. That judgment normally will receive the protection of the business judgment rule unless the facts show that such amounts, compared with the services to be received in exchange, constitute waste or could not otherwise be the product of a valid exercise of business judgment. . . .

The Board of DSC retains the ultimate freedom to direct the strategy and affairs of the Company. If Donald disagrees with the Board, the Company may or may not (depending on the circumstances) be required to pay him a substantial sum of money in order to pursue its chosen course of action. So far, we have only a rather unusual contract, but not a case of abdication.[4] The Chancellor correctly dismissed the abdication claim.

III. Grimes' Demand on The Board With Respect to The Derivative Claim Conceded That Demand Was Required

The complaint alleges that Grimes made a pre-suit demand on the Board in the [letter referred to] above. In summary, the letter described the relevant provisions of the Donald Agreements and demanded that the Board "take immediate steps to abrogate" the cited sections of the Agreements. The Court of Chancery held that, by "making demand upon the board, plaintiff has in effect conceded that the board was in a position to consider and act upon his demand." *Grimes*, 20 Del.J.Corp.L. at 772 (citing

---

4. The unfortunate choice of language in the Employment Agreement should not obscure the fact that, in many cases, large severance payments do not necessarily preclude a formerly passive board from asserting its power over a CEO. The Court of Chancery, in dismissing the claim, nonetheless disparaged as "foolish" and "ill-conceived" the language of the agreement introducing the concept of the Board committing "unreasonable interference" in the discharge of Donald's duties, "in the good faith judgment of the Executive. . ." 20 Del.J.Corp.L. at 777. We agree that, on the surface, this unfortunate choice of words is "badly flawed" in terms of traditional concepts of corporate governance. Id. When the Employment Agreement is read as a whole, however, the initial perception of unlawful delegation gives way to the reality that the Agreement is not—on its face—a wrongful delegation. . . .

Spiegel v. Buntrock, Del.Supr., 571 A.2d 767, 775 (1990)). Contending that demand was excused, Grimes later filed suit alleging waste, excessive compensation and due care claims arising out of the Agreements. But the Chancellor held that Grimes waived his right to argue that demand was excused with respect to these claims because he had already made demand that the agreements be abrogated as unlawful. Id. We agree.

A.   The Demand Requirement in Perspective

.   .   .

If a claim belongs to the corporation, it is the corporation, acting through its board of directors, which must make the decision whether or not to assert the claim.   .   .   .   "[T]he derivative action impinges on the managerial freedom of directors." Pogostin v. Rice, Del. Supr., 480 A.2d 619, 624 (1984). "[T]he demand requirement is a recognition of the fundamental precept that directors manage the business and affairs of the corporation." Aronson v. Lewis, Del.Supr., 473 A.2d 805, 812 (1984).

A stockholder filing a derivative suit must allege either that the board rejected his pre-suit demand that the board assert the corporation's claim or allege with particularity why the stockholder was justified in not having made the effort to obtain board action. One ground for alleging with particularity that demand would be futile is that a "reasonable doubt" exists that the board is capable of making an independent decision to assert the claim if demand were made. The basis for claiming excusal would normally be that: (1) a majority of the board has a material financial or familial interest; (2) a majority of the board is incapable of acting independently for some other reason such as domination or control;[6] or (3) the underlying transaction is not the product of a valid exercise of business judgment. If the stockholder cannot plead such assertions consistent with Chancery Rule 11, after using the "tools at hand"[7] to obtain the necessary

---

6. Rales v. Blasband, Del.Supr., 634 A.2d 927, 936 (1993). Demand is not excused simply because plaintiff has chosen to sue all directors. Id. Likewise, a plaintiff cannot necessarily disqualify all directors simply by attacking a transaction in which all participated. Pogostin v. Rice, 480 A.2d at 627.

7. In *Rales* we undertook to describe some of those "tools at hand":

> Although derivative plaintiffs may believe it is difficult to meet the particularization requirement of Aronson because they are not entitled to discovery to assist their compliance with Rule 23.1, see Levine, 591 A.2d [194], 208–10 [(Del. 1991)], they have many avenues available to obtain information bearing on the subject of their claims. For example, there is a variety of public sources from which the details of a corporate act may

be discovered, including the media and governmental agencies such as the Securities and Exchange Commission. In addition, a stockholder who has met the procedural requirements and has shown a specific proper purpose may use the summary procedure embodied in 8 Del.C. § 220 [shareholder right to inspect books and records] to investigate the possibility of corporate wrongdoing. Compaq Computer Corp. v. Horton, Del.Supr., 631 A.2d 1 (1993).   .   .   .   Surprisingly, little use has been made of section 220 as an information-gathering tool in the derivative context. Perhaps the problem arises in some cases out of an unseemly race to the court house, chiefly generated by the "first to file" custom seemingly permitting the winner of the race to be named lead counsel. The result has been

information before filing a derivative action, then the stockholder must make a pre-suit demand on the board.

The demand requirement serves a salutary purpose. First, by requiring exhaustion of intracorporate remedies, the demand requirement invokes a species of alternative dispute resolution procedure which might avoid litigation altogether. Second, if litigation is beneficial, the corporation can control the proceedings. Third, if demand is excused or wrongfully refused, the stockholder will normally control the proceedings.[8]

The jurisprudence of *Aronson* and its progeny is designed to create a balanced environment which will: (1) on the one hand, deter costly, baseless suits by creating a screening mechanism to eliminate claims where there is only a suspicion expressed solely in conclusory terms; and (2) on the other hand, permit suit by a stockholder who is able to articulate particularized facts showing that there is a reasonable doubt either that (a) a majority of the board is independent for purposes of responding to the demand, or (b) the underlying transaction is protected by the business judgment rule.

Aronson introduced the term "reasonable doubt" into corporate derivative jurisprudence. Some courts and commentators have questioned why a concept normally present in criminal prosecution would find its way into derivative litigation. Yet the term is apt and achieves the proper balance. Reasonable doubt can be said to mean that there is a reason to doubt.[9] This concept is sufficiently flexible and workable to provide the stockholder with "the keys to the courthouse" in an appropriate case where the claim is not based on mere suspicions or stated solely in conclusory terms.

B. Wrongful Refusal Distinguished from Excusal

Demand has been excused in many cases in Delaware under the *Aronson* test. The law regarding wrongful refusal is not as well developed, however. Although Delaware law does not require demand in every case[10]

---

a plethora of superficial complaints that could not be sustained. Nothing requires the Court of Chancery, or any other court having appropriate jurisdiction, to countenance this process by penalizing diligent counsel who has employed these methods, including section 220, in a deliberate and thorough manner in preparing a complaint that meets the demand excused test of Aronson.

634 A.2d at 934–935 n. 10.

8. This Court has held that in demand-excused cases the board of directors may sometimes reassert its authority over a derivative claim in certain instances through the device of the Special Litigation Committee ("SLC"). Zapata Corp. v. Maldonado, Del. Supr., 430 A.2d 779 (1981). The use of a committee of the board formed to respond to a demand or to advise the board on its duty in responding to a demand is not the same as the SLC process contemplated by *Zapata*, however. It is important that these discrete and quite different processes not be confused.

9. Stated obversely, the concept of reasonable doubt is akin to the concept that the stockholder has a "reasonable belief" that the board lacks independence or that the transaction was not protected by the business judgment rule. . . .

10. The ALI [American Law Institute] Principles [of Corporate Governance: Analysis and Recommendations (1992)] and the American Bar Association's Model Business Corporation Act § 7.42(1), both are premised upon the concept of universal demand—that

because Delaware does have the mechanism of demand excusal, it is important that the demand process be meaningful. Therefore, a stockholder who makes a demand is entitled to know promptly what action the board has taken in response to the demand. A stockholder who makes a serious demand and receives only a peremptory refusal has the right to use the "tools at hand" to obtain the relevant corporate records, such as reports or minutes, reflecting the corporate action and related information in order to determine whether or not there is a basis to assert that demand was wrongfully refused. . . .

If a demand is made, the stockholder has spent one—but only one—"arrow" in the "quiver." The spent "arrow" is the right to claim that demand is excused. The stockholder does not, by making demand, waive the right to claim that demand has been wrongfully refused.

Simply because the composition of the board provides no basis ex ante for the stockholder to claim with particularity and consistently with Rule 11 that it is reasonable to doubt that a majority of the board is either interested or not independent, it does not necessarily follow ex post that the board in fact acted independently, disinterestedly or with due care in response to the demand. . . . If a demand is made and rejected, the board rejecting the demand is entitled to the presumption of the business judgment rule unless the stockholder can allege facts with particularity creating a reasonable doubt that the board is entitled to the benefit of the presumption. If there is reason to doubt that the board acted independently or with due care in responding to the demand, the stockholder may have the basis ex post to claim wrongful refusal. The stockholder then has the right to bring the underlying action with the same standing which the stockholder would have had, ex ante, if demand had been excused as futile. . . .

C. Application to This Case

In the case before the Court, plaintiff made a pre-suit demand. Later, however, plaintiff contended that demand was excused. Under the doctrine articulated by this Court in Spiegel v. Buntrock, [571 A.2d 767 (Del.1990)] plaintiff, by making a demand, waived his right to contest the independence of the board. As the Court of Chancery properly held, plaintiff may not bifurcate his theories relating to the same claim. Thus, demand having been made as to the propriety of the Agreements, it cannot be excused as to

is, a requirement that demand must be made in every case. The Principles and the Model Act then go in directions which are different from Delaware law and different from each other in determining the manner in which derivative litigation is to be conducted or terminated after demand has been made. In reversing the decision of the United States Court of Appeals for the Seventh Circuit, which had adopted the universal demand rule in a derivative suit under the Investment Company Act of 1940, the Supreme Court of the United States held that state law applied and analyzed the implications of the universal demand rule compared with the traditional rule exemplified by Delaware law. Kamen v. Kemper Fin. Svcs., Inc., 500 U.S. 90, 101–08 (1991).

the claim that the Agreements constituted waste, excessive compensation or was the product of a lack of due care.

. . .

In *Spiegel*, this Court held that "[a] shareholder who makes a demand can no longer argue that demand is excused." 571 A.2d at 775. Permitting a stockholder to demand action involving only one theory or remedy and to argue later that demand is excused as to other legal theories or remedies arising out of the same set of circumstances as set forth in the demand letter would create an undue risk of harassment.

In this case, the Board of DSC considered and rejected the demand. After investing the time and resources to consider and decide whether or not to take action in response to the demand, the Board is entitled to have its decision analyzed under the business judgment rule unless the presumption of that rule can be rebutted. . . . Grimes cannot avoid this result by holding back or bifurcating legal theories based on precisely the same set of facts alleged in the demand.

Since Grimes made a pre-suit demand with respect to all claims arising out of the Agreements, he was required by Chancery Rule 23.1 to plead with particularity why the Board's refusal to act on the derivative claims was wrongful. . . . The complaint recites the Board's rejection of Grimes' demand and proceeds to assert why Grimes disagrees with the Board's conclusion. The complaint generally asserts that the refusal could not have been the result of an adequate, good faith investigation since the Board decided not to act on the demand. Such conclusory, ipse dixit, assertions are inconsistent with the requirements of Chancery Rule 23.1. . . . The complaint fails to include particularized allegations which would raise a reasonable doubt that the Board's decision to reject the demand was the product of a valid business judgment.

ANALYSIS

1. Under Delaware law, what is the legal effect and likely consequence of a shareholder demand that the board pursue a corporate cause of action?

2. Under Delaware law, when is demand excused? What must a shareholder allege in her or his complaint to establish that demand is excused? How does the plaintiff find the necessary facts?

3. In a derivative suit in which the plaintiff seeks money damages from corporate officers, and in which the plaintiff is required to post a bond to pay the defendant's legal expenses if the defendant prevails, what justification is there for allowing the board to dismiss the suit? What does the corporation have to lose?

4. Is it not true that a derivative suit is always a challenge to the wisdom, judgment, or competence of the board? Suppose you have been a member of the board of a corporation for ten years and a suit is filed

naming other long-time members of the board as defendants. Do you think you could be fair and unbiased in deciding whether the suit should be dismissed? If not, what would you do?

5. Suppose a plaintiff in a derivative suit seeks recovery of funds embezzled by one of the corporation's officers and alleges with particularity the facts of the embezzlement and the failure of the board to seek recovery. Under the Delaware rule, is demand required? Should it be?

Marx v. Akers

644 N.Y.S.2d 121, 666 N.E.2d 1034 (1996).

Plaintiff commenced this shareholder derivative action against International Business Machines Corporation (IBM) and IBM's board of directors without first demanding that the board initiate a lawsuit. The amended complaint (complaint) alleges that the board wasted corporate assets by awarding excessive compensation to IBM's executives and outside directors. The issues raised on this appeal are whether the Appellate Division abused its discretion by dismissing plaintiff's complaint for failure to make a demand and whether plaintiff's complaint fails to state a cause of action. . . .

Facts and Procedural History

The complaint alleges that during a period of declining profitability at IBM the director defendants engaged in self-dealing by awarding excessive compensation to the 15 outside directors on the 18–member board. Although the complaint identifies only one of the three inside directors as an IBM executive (defendant Akers is identified as a former chief executive officer of IBM), plaintiff also appears to allege that the director defendants violated their fiduciary duties to IBM by voting for unreasonably high compensation for IBM executives.

. . .

Background

. . .

[New York] Business Corporation Law § 626(c) provides that in any shareholders' derivative action, "the complaint shall set forth with particularity the efforts of the plaintiff to secure the initiation of such action by the board or the reasons for not making such effort." Enacted in 1961 (L.1961, ch. 855), § 626(c) codified a rule of equity developed in early shareholder derivative actions requiring plaintiffs to demand that the corporation initiate an action, unless such demand was futile, before commencing an action on the corporation's behalf (Barr v. Wackman, 36 N.Y.2d 371, 377, 368 N.Y.S.2d 497, 329 N.E.2d 180). The purposes of the demand requirement are to (1) relieve courts from deciding matters of internal corporate governance by providing corporate directors with opportunities to correct alleged abuses, (2) provide corporate boards with reasonable protection from harassment by litigation on matters clearly within the discretion of directors, and (3) discourage "strike suits" commenced by shareholders for personal gain rather than for the benefit of the corporation. . . . By their very nature, shareholder derivative actions infringe upon the managerial discretion of corporate boards. . . . Consequently, we have historically been reluctant to permit shareholder derivative suits, noting that the power of courts to direct the management of a corporation's affairs should be "exercised with restraint" (Gordon v. Elliman, 306 N.Y. 456, 462, 119 N.E.2d 331).

In permitting a shareholder derivative action to proceed because a demand on the corporation's directors would be futile,

> "the object is for the court to chart the course for the corporation which the directors should have selected, and which it is presumed that they would have chosen if they had not been actuated by fraud or bad faith. Due to their misconduct, the court substitutes its judgment ad hoc for that of the directors in the conduct of its business" (id., at 462, 119 N.E.2d 331).

Achieving a balance between preserving the discretion of directors to manage a corporation without undue interference, through the demand requirement, and permitting shareholders to bring claims on behalf of the corporation when it is evident that directors will wrongfully refuse to bring such claims, through the demand futility exception, has been accomplished by various jurisdictions in different ways. One widely cited approach to demand futility which attempts to balance these competing concerns has been developed by Delaware courts and applies a two-pronged test to each case to determine whether a failure to serve a demand is justified. At the other end of the spectrum is a universal demand requirement which would abandon particularized determinations in favor of requiring a demand in every case before a shareholder derivative suit may be filed.

The Delaware Approach

[The court summarizes Delaware law, which is described in *Grimes*, supra.]

The two branches of the [Delaware] test are disjunctive. . . . Once director interest has been established, the business judgment rule becomes inapplicable and the demand excused without further inquiry. . . . Whether a board has validly exercised its business judgment must be evaluated by determining whether the directors exercised procedural (informed decision) and substantive (terms of the transaction) due care.

. . .

Universal Demand

A universal demand requirement would dispense with the necessity of making case-specific determinations and impose an easily applied bright line rule. The Business Law Section of the American Bar Association has proposed requiring a demand in all cases, without exception, and permits the commencement of a derivative proceeding within 90 days of the demand unless the demand is rejected earlier. . . . However, plaintiffs may file suit before the expiration of 90 days, even if their demand has not

by a self-interested director. (2) Demand is excused because of futility when a complaint alleges with particularity that the board of directors did not fully inform themselves about the challenged transaction to the extent reasonably appropriate under the circumstances. . . . (3) Demand is excused because of futility when a complaint alleges with particularity that the challenged transaction was so egregious on its face that it could not have been the product of sound business judgment of the directors.

The Current Appeal

. . .

As in *Barr*, we look to the complaint here to determine whether the allegations are sufficient and establish with particularity that demand would have been futile.* Here, the plaintiff alleges that the compensation awarded to IBM's outside directors . . . was excessive.

Defendants' motion to dismiss for failure to make a demand as to the allegations concerning the compensation paid to IBM's executive officers was properly granted. A board is not interested "in voting compensation for one of its members as an executive or in some other nondirectorial capacity, such as a consultant to the corporation," although "so-called 'back-scratching' arrangements, pursuant to which all directors vote to approve each other's compensation as officers or employees, do not constitute disinterested directors' action" (1 ALI, [Principles of Corporate Governance], § 5.03, Comment g, at 250 [1992]). Since only three directors are alleged to have received the benefit of the executive compensation scheme, plaintiff has failed to allege that a majority of the board was interested in setting executive compensation. . . . The complaint does not allege particular facts in contending that the board failed to deliberate or exercise its business judgment in setting those levels. Consequently, the failure to make a demand regarding the fixing of executive compensation was fatal to that portion of the complaint challenging that transaction.

However, a review of the complaint indicates that plaintiff also alleged that a majority of the board was self-interested in setting the compensation of outside directors because the outside directors comprised a majority of the board.

Directors are self-interested in a challenged transaction where they will receive a direct financial benefit from the transaction which is different

---

* [Eds: The court reproduced and focused on the following language from the complaint:

Plaintiff has made no demand upon the directors of IBM to institute this lawsuit because such demand would be futile. As set forth above, each of the directors authorized, approved, participated and/or acquiesced in the acts and transactions complained of herein and are liable therefor. Further, each of the Non–Employee [outside] Directors has received and retained the benefit of his excessive compensation and each of the other directors has received and retained the benefit of the incentive compensation described above. The defendants cannot be expected to vote to prosecute an action against themselves. Demand upon the company to bring action [sic] to redress the wrongs herein is therefore unnecessary.]

from the benefit to shareholders generally. . . . A director who votes for a raise in directors' compensation is always "interested" because that person will receive a personal financial benefit from the transaction not shared in by stockholders. . . . Consequently, a demand was excused as to plaintiff's allegations that the compensation set for outside directors was excessive.

Corporate Waste

Our conclusion that demand should have been excused as to the part of the complaint challenging the fixing of directors' compensation does not end our inquiry. We must also determine whether plaintiff has stated a cause of action regarding director compensation, i.e., some wrong to the corporation. We conclude that plaintiff has not, and thus dismiss the complaint in its entirety.

. . . [A] complaint challenging the excessiveness of director compensation must—to survive a dismissal motion—allege compensation rates excessive on their face or other facts which call into question whether the compensation was fair to the corporation when approved, the good faith of the directors setting those rates, or that the decision to set the compensation could not have been a product of valid business judgment.

Applying the foregoing principles to plaintiff's complaint, it is clear that it must be dismissed. The complaint alleges that the directors increased their compensation rates from a base of $20,000 plus $500 for each meeting attended to a retainer of $55,000 plus 100 shares of IBM stock over a five-year period. . . .

These conclusory allegations do not state a cause of action. There are no factually based allegations of wrongdoing or waste which would, if true, sustain a verdict in plaintiff's favor.

ANALYSIS

1. How do you suppose this case would have been decided under Delaware law as described by the court in this case and by the *Grimes* court?

2. The court lists three "purposes" for the demand requirement. How well does the requirement serve each of these purposes?

3. What is the function of demand under a requirement of universal demand? Is the court correct in stating that a requirement of universal demand "would dispense with the necessity of making case-specific determinations"?

4. In *Marx*, the court determined that demand should be excused but that plaintiff had failed to state a cause of action. Accordingly, plaintiff's complaint was dismissed on the merits. What would have happened if the court had made the opposite determination; i.e., that demand was required, but that the complaint stated a cause of action?

PROBLEMS

Agricorp Corp. is an agribusiness: it owns and operates many large farms. It has five directors, including Alice Adams, who is the Chairman of the Board and Chief Executive Officer. Adams learns of an opportunity to purchase a large farm in Indiana.

1. Adams and two of the other directors decide to buy the Indiana farm for themselves. Assume that this constitutes self-dealing in violation of the duty of loyalty. A shareholder wants to sue. Is this a direct or derivative lawsuit?

2. Assuming the lawsuit is derivative in nature, is demand required or excused under New York and/or Delaware law?

3. Suppose only Adams is going to buy the land. She discloses the opportunity to the other directors. The other directors vote to have the corporation reject the opportunity and to approve Adams's personal purchase of the land. A derivative suit is to be brought. Is demand required or excused under New York and/or Delaware law?

4. Suppose that the other directors had not voted on Adams's purchase, but had merely acquiesced in it. Is demand required or excused under New York and/or Delaware law?

C. THE ROLE OF SPECIAL COMMITTEES

Auerbach v. Bennett

47 N.Y.2d 619, 419 N.Y.S.2d 920, 393 N.E.2d 994 (1979).

■ JONES, JUDGE.

. . .

In the summer of 1975 the management of General Telephone & Electronics Corporation, in response to reports that numerous other multinational companies had made questionable payments to public officials or political parties in foreign countries, directed that an internal preliminary investigation be made to ascertain whether that corporation had engaged in similar transactions. On the basis of the report of this survey, received in October, 1975, management brought the issue to the attention of the corporation's board of directors. At a meeting held on November 6 of that year the board referred the matter to the board's audit committee. The audit committee retained as its special counsel the Washington, D.C., law firm of Wilmer, Cutler & Pickering, which had not previously acted as counsel to the corporation. With the assistance of such special counsel and Arthur Andersen & Co., the corporation's outside auditors, the audit committee engaged in an investigation into the corporation's world-wide operations, focusing on whether, in the period January 1, 1971 to December 31, 1975, corporate funds had been (1) paid directly or indirectly to any political party or person or to any officer, employee, shareholder or director of any governmental or private customer, or (2) used to reimburse any officer of the corporation or other person for such payments.

On March 4, 1976 the audit committee released its report which was filed with the Securities and Exchange Commission and disclosed to the corporation's shareholders in a proxy statement prior to the annual meeting of shareholders held in April, 1976. The audit committee reported that it had found evidence that in the period from 1971 to 1975 the corporation or its subsidiaries had made payments abroad and in the United States constituting bribes and kickbacks in amounts perhaps totaling more than 11 million dollars and that some of the individual defendant directors had been personally involved in certain of the transactions.

Almost immediately Auerbach, a shareholder in the corporation, instituted the present shareholders' derivative action on behalf of the corporation against the corporation's directors, Arthur Andersen & Co. and the corporation. The complaint alleged that in connection with the transactions reported by the audit committee defendants, present and former members of the corporation's board of directors, and Arthur Andersen & Co., are liable to the corporation for breach of their duties to the corporation and should be made to account for payments made in those transactions.

On April 21, 1976 the board of directors of the corporation adopted a resolution creating a special litigation committee "for the purpose of establishing a point of contract [sic] between the Board of Directors and the Corporation's General Counsel concerning the position to be taken by the Corporation in certain litigation involving shareholder derivative claims on behalf of the Corporation against certain of its directors and officers" and authorizing that committee "to take such steps from time to time as it deems necessary to pursue its objectives including the retention of special outside counsel." The special committee comprised three disinterested directors who had joined the board after the challenged transactions had occurred. The board subsequently additionally vested in the committee "all of the authority of the Board of Directors to determine, on behalf of the Board, the position that the Corporation shall take with respect to the derivative claims alleged on its behalf" in the present and similar shareholder derivative actions.

The special litigation committee reported under date of November 22, 1976. It found that defendant Arthur Andersen & Co. had conducted its examination of the corporation's affairs in accordance with generally accepted auditing standards and in good faith and concluded that no proper interest of the corporation or its shareholders would be served by the continued assertion of a claim against it. The committee also concluded that none of the individual defendants had violated the New York State statutory standard of care, that none had profited personally or gained in any way, that the claims asserted in the present action are without merit, that if the action were allowed to proceed the time and talents of the corporation's senior management would be wasted on lengthy pretrial and trial proceedings, that litigation costs would be inordinately high in view of the unlikelihood of success, and that the continuing publicity could be damaging to the corporation's business. The committee determined that it would not be in the best interests of the corporation for the present derivative action to proceed, and, exercising the authority delegated to it, directed the corporation's general counsel to take that position in the present litigation as well as in pending comparable shareholders' derivative actions.

[The original plaintiff, Auerbach, decided not to appeal, and Stanley Wallenstein was substituted as plaintiff.]

As all parties and both courts below recognize, the disposition of this case on the merits turns on the proper application of the business judgment doctrine, in particular to the decision of a specially appointed committee of disinterested directors acting on behalf of the board to terminate a shareholders' derivative action.   .   .   .

In this instance our inquiry, to the limited extent to which it may be pursued, has a two-tiered aspect. The complaint initially asserted liability on the part of defendants based on the payments made to foreign governmental customers and privately owned customers, some unspecified portions of which were allegedly passed on to officials of the customers, i.e., the focus was on first-tier bribes and kickbacks. Then subsequent to the service of the complaint there came the report of a special litigation committee, particularly appointed by the corporation's board of directors to consider the merits of the present and similar shareholders' derivative actions, and its determination that it would not be in the best interests of the corporation to press claims against defendants based on their possible first-tier liability. The motions for summary judgment were predicated principally on the report and determination of the special litigation committee and on the contention that this second-tier corporate action insulated the first-tier transactions from judicial inquiry and was itself subject to the shelter of the business judgment doctrine.

.   .   .

We [conclude] that the determination of the special litigation committee forecloses further judicial inquiry in this case.

It appears to us that the business judgment doctrine, at least in part, is grounded in the prudent recognition that courts are ill equipped and infrequently called on to evaluate what are and must be essentially business judgments.   .   .   .

In the present case we confront a special instance of the application of the business judgment rule and inquire whether it applies in its full vigor to shield from judicial scrutiny the decision of a three-person minority committee of the board acting on behalf of the full board not to prosecute a shareholder's derivative action. The record in this case reveals that the board is a 15–member board, and that the derivative suit was brought against four of the directors. Nothing suggests that any of the other directors participated in any of the challenged first-tier transactions. Indeed the report of the audit committee on which the complaint is based specifically found that no other directors had any prior knowledge of or were in any way involved in any of these transactions. Other directors had, however, been members of the board in the period during which the transactions occurred. Each of the three director members of the special litigation committee joined the board thereafter.

The business judgment rule does not foreclose inquiry by the courts into the disinterested independence of those members of the board chosen by it to make the corporate decision on its behalf—here the members of the special litigation committee. Indeed the rule shields the deliberations and conclusions of the chosen representatives of the board only if they possess a disinterested independence and do not stand in a dual relation which prevents an unprejudicial exercise of judgment. . . .

We examine then the proof submitted by defendants. It is not disputed that the members of the special litigation committee were not members of the corporation's board of directors at the time of the first-tier transactions in question. . . . Notwithstanding the vigorous and imaginative hypothesizing and innuendo of counsel there is nothing in this record to raise a triable issue of fact as to the independence and disinterested status of these three directors.

The contention of Wallenstein that any committee authorized by the board of which defendant directors were members must be held to be legally infirm and may not be delegated power to terminate a derivative action must be rejected. In the very nature of the corporate organization it was only the existing board of directors which had authority on behalf of the corporation to direct the investigation and to assure the cooperation of corporate employees, and it is only that same board by its own action—or as here pursuant to authority duly delegated by it—which had authority to decide whether to prosecute the claims against defendant directors. The board in this instance, with slight adaptation, followed prudent practice in observing the general policy that when individual members of a board of directors prove to have personal interests which may conflict with the interests of the corporation, such interested directors must be excluded while the remaining members of the board proceed to consideration and action. . . .

Courts have consistently held that the business judgment rule applies where some directors are charged with wrongdoing, so long as the remaining directors making the decision are disinterested and independent. . . .

To accept the assertions of the intervenor and to disqualify the entire board would be to render the corporation powerless to make an effective business judgment with respect to prosecution of the derivative action. The possible risk of hesitancy on the part of the members of any committee, even if composed of outside, independent, disinterested directors, to investigate the activities of fellow members of the board where personal liability is at stake is an inherent, inescapable, given aspect of the corporation's predicament. . . .

We turn then to the action of the special litigation committee itself, which comprised two components. First, there was the selection of procedures appropriate to the pursuit of its charge, and second, there was the ultimate substantive decision, predicated on the procedures chosen and the data produced thereby, not to pursue the claims advanced in the shareholders' derivative actions. The latter, substantive decision falls squarely within the embrace of the business judgment doctrine, involving as it did the weighing and balancing of legal, ethical, commercial, promotional, public relations, fiscal and other factors familiar to the resolution of many if not most corporate problems. To this extent the conclusion reached by the special litigation committee is outside the scope of our review. . . .

As to the other component of the committee's activities, however, the situation is different . . . . As to the methodologies and procedures best suited to the conduct of an investigation of facts and the determination of legal liability, the courts are well equipped by long and continuing experience and practice to make determinations. . . .

While the court may properly inquire as to the adequacy and appropriateness of the committee's investigative procedures and methodologies, it may not under the guise of consideration of such factors trespass in the domain of business judgment. At the same time those responsible for the procedures by which the business judgment is reached may reasonably be required to show that they have pursued their chosen investigative methods in good faith. What evidentiary proof may be required to this end will, of course, depend on the nature of the particular investigation, and the proper reach of disclosure at the instance of the shareholders will in turn relate inversely to the showing made by the corporate representatives themselves. The latter may be expected to show that the areas and subjects to be examined are reasonably complete and that there has been a good-faith pursuit of inquiry into such areas and subjects. What has been uncovered and the relative weight accorded in evaluating and balancing the several factors and considerations are beyond the scope of judicial concern. Proof, however, that the investigation has been so restricted in scope, so shallow in execution, or otherwise so *pro forma* or halfhearted as to constitute a pretext or sham, consistent with the principles underlying the application of the business judgment doctrine, would raise questions of good faith or conceivably fraud which would never be shielded by that doctrine.

In addition to the issue of the disinterested independence of the special litigation committee, addressed above, the disposition of the present appeal turns, then, on whether on defendants' motions for summary judgment predicated on the investigation and determination of the special litigation committee, Wallenstein by tender of evidentiary proof in admissible form has shown facts sufficient to require a trial of any material issue of fact as to the adequacy or appropriateness of the *modus operandi* of that committee or has demonstrated acceptable excuse for failure to make such tender. . . . We conclude that the requisite showing has not been made on this record.

On the submissions made by defendants in support of their motions, we do not find either insufficiency or infirmity as to the procedures and methodologies chosen and pursued by the special litigation committee. That committee promptly engaged eminent special counsel to guide its deliberations and to advise it. The committee reviewed the prior work of the audit committee, testing its completeness, accuracy and thoroughness by interviewing representatives of Wilmer, Cutler & Pickering, reviewing transcripts of the testimony of 10 corporate officers and employees before the Securities and Exchange Commission, and studying documents collected by and work papers of the Washington law firm. Individual interviews were conducted with the directors found to have participated in any way in the questioned payments, and with representatives of Arthur Andersen & Co. Questionnaires were sent to and answered by each of the corporation's nonmanagement directors. At the conclusion of its investigation the special litigation committee sought and obtained pertinent legal advice from its special counsel. The selection of appropriate investigative methods must always turn on the nature and characteristics of the particular subject being investigated, but we find nothing in this record that requires a trial of any material issue of fact concerning the sufficiency or appropriateness of the procedures chosen by this special litigation committee. Nor is there anything in this record to raise a triable issue of fact as to the good-faith pursuit of its examination by that committee.

■ COOKE, CHIEF JUDGE (dissenting).

. . .

Since the continuation of the suit is dependent, in large measure, upon the motives and actions of the defendants and the special litigation committee, and since knowledge of these matters "is peculiarly in the possession of the defendants themselves", summary judgment should not be granted prior to disclosure proceedings . . . .

ANALYSIS

1. By way of review, note that in Auerbach v. Bennett there is no mention of the demand issue. Presumably the parties assumed that demand was excused. Were they right about that?

2. In the Auerbach v. Bennett situation, how do you suppose the three new, independent members of the board were selected? Who do you suppose identified them as likely prospects? What other methods of selection might be sensible?

Zapata Corp. v. Maldonado

430 A.2d 779 (Del.1981).

■ QUILLEN, JUSTICE: . . .

In June, 1975, William Maldonado, a stockholder of Zapata, instituted a derivative action in the Court of Chancery on behalf of Zapata against ten officers and/or directors of Zapata, alleging, essentially, breaches of fiduciary duty. Maldonado did not first demand that the board bring this action, stating instead such demand's futility because all directors were named as defendants and allegedly participated in the acts specified.[1] . . .

By June, 1979, four of the defendant-directors were no longer on the board, and the remaining directors appointed two new outside directors to the board. The board then created an "Independent Investigation Committee" (Committee), composed solely of the two new directors, to investigate Maldonado's actions, as well as a similar derivative action then pending in Texas, and to determine whether the corporation should continue any or all of the litigation. The Committee's determination was stated to be "final, . . . not . . . subject to review by the Board of Directors and . . . in all respects . . . binding upon the Corporation."

Following an investigation, the Committee concluded, in September, 1979, that each action should "be dismissed forthwith as their continued maintenance is inimical to the Company's best interests. . . ." Consequently, Zapata moved for dismissal or summary judgment. . . .

We limit our review in this interlocutory appeal to whether the Committee has the power to cause the present action to be dismissed.

We begin with an examination of the carefully considered opinion of the Vice Chancellor which states, in part, that the "business judgment" rule does not confer power "to a corporate board of directors to terminate a derivative suit," [Maldonado v. Flynn, 413 A.2d 1251, 1257 (Del.Ch.1980)]. His conclusion is particularly pertinent because several federal courts, applying Delaware law, have held that the business judgment rule enables boards (or their committees) to terminate derivative suits, decisions now in conflict with the holding below.

As the term is most commonly used, and given the disposition below, we can understand the Vice Chancellor's comment that "the business judgment rule is irrelevant to the question of whether the Committee has the authority to compel the dismissal of this suit." 413 A.2d at 1257. Corporations, existing because of legislative grace, possess authority as granted by the legislature. Directors of Delaware corporations derive their managerial decision making power, which encompasses decisions whether to initiate, or refrain from entering, litigation, from 8 Del.C. § 141(a).[6]

---

1. Court of Chancery Rule 23.1 states in part:

"The complaint shall also allege with particularity the efforts, if any, made by the plaintiff to obtain the action he desires from the directors or comparable authority and the reasons for his failure to obtain the action or for not making the effort."

6. 8 Del.C. § 141(a) states:

"The business and affairs of every corporation organized under this chapter shall be managed by or under the direction of a board of directors, except as may be otherwise provided in this chapter or in its certificate of incorporation. If any such provision is made in the certificate of incorporation, the powers and duties conferred or imposed upon the board of directors by this chapter shall be exercised or performed to such extent and by such person or persons as shall be provided in the certificate of incorporation."

This statute is the fount of directorial powers. The "business judgment" rule is a judicial creation that presumes propriety, under certain circumstances, in a board's decision. Viewed defensively, it does not create authority. In this sense the "business judgment" rule is not relevant in corporate decision making until after a decision is made. It is generally used as a defense to an attack on the decision's soundness. The board's managerial decision making power, however, comes from § 141(a). The judicial creation and legislative grant are related because the "business judgment" rule evolved to give recognition and deference to directors' business expertise when exercising their managerial power under § 141(a).

In the case before us, although the corporation's decision to move to dismiss or for summary judgment was, literally, a decision resulting from an exercise of the directors' (as delegated to the Committee) business judgment, the question of "business judgment," in a defensive sense, would not become relevant until and unless the decision to seek termination of the derivative lawsuit was attacked as improper. . . . This question was not reached by the Vice Chancellor because he determined that the stockholder had an individual right to maintain this derivative action. . . .

Thus, the focus in this case is on the power to speak for the corporation as to whether the lawsuit should be continued or terminated. As we see it, this issue in the current appellate posture of this case has three aspects: the conclusions of the Court below concerning the continuing right of a stockholder to maintain a derivative action; the corporate power under Delaware law of an authorized board committee to cause dismissal of litigation instituted for the benefit of the corporation; and the role of the Court of Chancery in resolving conflicts between the stockholder and the committee.

Accordingly, we turn first to the Court of Chancery's conclusions concerning the right of a plaintiff stockholder in a derivative action. We find that its determination that a stockholder, once demand is made and refused, possesses an independent, individual right to continue a derivative suit for breaches of fiduciary duty over objection by the corporation, . . . as an absolute rule, is erroneous. The Court of Chancery relied principally upon Sohland v. Baker, Del.Supr., 141 A. 277 (1927), for this statement of the Delaware rule. . . . Sohland is sound law. But Sohland cannot be fairly read as supporting the broad proposition which evolved in the opinion below.

In Sohland, the complaining stockholder was allowed to file the derivative action in equity after making demand and after the board refused to bring the lawsuit. But the question before us relates to the power of the corporation by motion to terminate a lawsuit properly commenced by a stockholder without prior demand. No Delaware statute or case cited to us directly determines this new question and we do not think that Sohland addresses it by implication.

The language in Sohland relied on by the Vice Chancellor negates the contention that the case stands for the broad rule of stockholder right which evolved below. This Court therein stated that "a stockholder *may sue* in his own name for the purpose of enforcing corporate rights . . . in a proper case if the corporation on the demand of the stockholder refuses to bring suit."   141 A. at 281 (emphasis added). The Court also stated that "whether ['[t]he right of a stockholder *to file a bill* to litigate corporate rights'] exists necessarily depends on the facts of each particular case." 141 A. at 282 (emphasis added). Thus, the precise language only supports the stockholder's right to initiate the lawsuit. It does not support an absolute right to continue to control it.

Additionally, the issue and context in *Sohland* are simply different from this case. Baker, a stockholder, suing on behalf of Bankers' Mortgage Co., sought cancellation of stock issued to Sohland, a director of Bankers', in a transaction participated in by a "great majority" of Bankers' board. Before instituting his suit, Baker requested the board to assert the cause of action. The board refused. Interestingly, though, on the same day the board refused, it authorized payment of Baker's attorneys fees so that he could pursue the claim; one director actually escorted Baker to the attorneys suggested by the board. At this chronological point, Sohland had resigned from the board, and it was he, not the board, who was protesting Baker's ability to bring suit. In sum, despite the board's refusal to bring suit, it is clear that the board supported Baker in his efforts. It is not surprising then that he was allowed to proceed as the corporation's representative "for the prevention of injustice," because "the corporation itself refused to litigate an apparent corporate right." 141 A. at 282.

Moreover, McKee v. Rogers, Del.Ch., 156 A. 191 (1931), stated "as a general rule" that "a stockholder cannot be permitted . . . to invade the discretionary field committed to the judgment of the directors and sue in the corporation's behalf when the managing body refuses. This rule is a well settled one." 156 A. at 193.

The *McKee* rule, of course, should not be read so broadly that the board's refusal will be determinative in every instance. Board members, owing a well-established fiduciary duty to the corporation, will not be allowed to cause a derivative suit to be dismissed when it would be a breach of their fiduciary duty. Generally disputes pertaining to control of the suit arise in two contexts.

Consistent with the purpose of requiring a demand, a board decision to cause a derivative suit to be dismissed as detrimental to the company, after demand has been made and refused, will be respected unless it was wrongful.[10] . . . . A claim of a wrongful decision not to sue is thus the first exception and the first context of dispute. Absent a wrongful refusal,

---

10. In other words, when stockholders, after making demand and having their suit rejected, attack the board's decision as improper, the board's decision falls under the "business judgment" rule and will be respected if the requirements of the rule are met.   . . . That situation should be distinguished from the instant case, where demand was not made, and the *power* of the board to seek a dismissal, due to disqualification, presents a threshold issue.   . . .

the stockholder in such a situation simply lacks legal managerial power. . . .

But it cannot be implied that, absent a wrongful board refusal, a stockholder can never have an individual right to initiate an action. For, as is stated in *McKee,* a "well settled" exception exists to the general rule.

> "[A] stockholder may sue in equity in his derivative right to assert a cause of action in behalf of the corporation, *without prior demand* upon the directors to sue, when it is apparent that a demand would be futile, that the officers are under an influence that sterilizes discretion and could not be proper persons to conduct the litigation."

156 A. at 193 (emphasis added). This exception, the second context for dispute, is consistent with the Court of Chancery's statement below, that "[t]he stockholders' individual right to bring the action does not ripen, however, . . . unless he can show a demand to be futile." *Maldonado,* 413 A.2d at 1262.

These comments in *McKee* and in the opinion below make obvious sense. A demand, when required and refused (if not wrongful), terminates a stockholder's legal ability to initiate a derivative action. But where demand is properly excused, the stockholder does possess the ability to initiate the action on his corporation's behalf.

These conclusions, however, do not determine the question before us. Rather, they merely bring us to the question to be decided. It is here that we part company with the Court below. Derivative suits enforce corporate rights and any recovery obtained goes to the corporation. . . . "The right of a stockholder to file a bill to litigate corporate rights is, therefore, solely for the purpose of preventing injustice where it is apparent that material corporate rights would not otherwise be protected." *Sohland,* 141 A. at 282. We see no inherent reason why the "two phases" of a derivative suit, the stockholder's suit to compel the corporation to sue and the corporation's suit (see 413 A.2d at 1261–62), should automatically result in the placement in the hands of the litigating stockholder sole control of the corporate right throughout the litigation. To the contrary, it seems to us that such an inflexible rule would recognize the interest of one person or group to the exclusion of all others within the corporate entity. Thus, we reject the view of the Vice Chancellor as to the first aspect of the issue on appeal.

The question to be decided becomes: When, if at all, should an authorized board committee be permitted to cause litigation, properly initiated by a derivative stockholder in his own right, to be dismissed? As noted above, a board has the power to choose not to pursue litigation when demand is made upon it, so long as the decision is not wrongful. If the board determines that a suit would be detrimental to the company, the board's determination prevails. Even when demand is excusable, circumstances may arise when continuation of the litigation would not be in the corporation's best interests. Our inquiry is whether, under such circumstances, there is a permissible procedure under § 141(a) by which a corporation can rid itself of detrimental litigation. If there is not, a single stockholder in an extreme case might control the destiny of the entire corporation. This concern was bluntly expressed by the Ninth Circuit in Lewis v. Anderson, 9th Cir., 615 F.2d 778, 783 (1979), cert. denied, ___ U.S. ___, 101 S.Ct. 206, 66 L.Ed.2d 89 (1980): "To allow one shareholder to incapacitate an entire board of directors merely by leveling charges against them gives too much leverage to dissident shareholders." But, when examining the means, including the committee mechanism examined in this case, potentials for abuse must be recognized. This takes us to the second and third aspects of the issue on appeal.

Before we pass to equitable considerations as to the mechanism at issue here, it must be clear that an independent committee possesses the corporate power to seek the termination of a derivative suit. Section 141(c) allows a board to delegate all of its authority to a committee.[13] Accordingly, a committee with properly delegated authority would have the power to move for dismissal or summary judgment if the entire board did.

Even though demand was not made in this case and the initial decision of whether to litigate was not placed before the board, Zapata's board, it seems to us, retained all of its corporate power concerning litigation decisions. If Maldonado had made demand on the board in this case, it could have refused to bring suit. Maldonado could then have asserted that the decision not to sue was wrongful and, if correct, would have been allowed to maintain the suit. The board, however, never would have lost its statutory managerial authority. The demand requirement itself evidences that the managerial power is retained by the board. When a derivative plaintiff is allowed to bring suit after a wrongful refusal, the board's authority to choose whether to pursue the litigation is not chal-

---

13. 8 Del.C. § 141(c) states:

"The board of directors may, by resolution passed by a majority of the whole board, designate 1 or more committees, each committee to consist of 1 or more of the directors of the corporation. The board may designate 1 or more directors as alternative members of any committee, who may replace any absent or disqualified member at any meeting of the committee. The bylaws may provide that in the absence or disqualification of a member of a committee, the member or members present at any meeting and not disqualified from voting, whether or not he or they constitute a quorum, may unanimously appoint another member of the board of directors to act at the meeting in the place of any such absent or disqualified member. Any such committee, to the extent provided in the resolution of the board of directors, or in the bylaws of the corporation, shall have and may exercise all the powers and authority of the board of directors in the management of the business and affairs of the corporation, and may authorize the seal of the corporation to be affixed to all papers which may require it; but no such committee shall have the power or authority in reference to amending the certificate of incorporation, adopting an agreement of merger or consolidation, recommending to the stockholders the sale, lease or exchange of all or substantially all of the corporation's property and assets, recommending to the stockholders a dissolution of the corporation or a revocation of a dissolution, or amending the bylaws of the corporation; and, unless the resolution, bylaws, or certificate of incorporation expressly so provide, no such committee shall have the power or authority to declare a dividend or to authorize the issuance of stock."

lenged although its conclusion—reached through the exercise of that authority—is not respected since it is wrongful. . . .

The corporate power inquiry then focuses on whether the board, tainted by the self-interest of a majority of its members, can legally delegate its authority to a committee of two disinterested directors. We find our statute clearly requires an affirmative answer to this question. As has been noted, under an express provision of the statute, § 141(c), a committee can exercise all of the authority of the board to the extent provided in the resolution of the board. Moreover, at least by analogy to our statutory section on interested directors, 8 Del.C. § 141, it seems clear that the Delaware statute is designed to permit disinterested directors to act for the board.[14] . . .

We do not think that the interest taint of the board majority is per se a legal bar to the delegation of the board's power to an independent committee composed of disinterested board members. The committee can properly act for the corporation to move to dismiss derivative litigation that is believed to be detrimental to the corporation's best interest.

Our focus now switches to the Court of Chancery which is faced with a stockholder assertion that a derivative suit, properly instituted, should continue for the benefit of the corporation and a corporate assertion, properly made by a board committee acting with board authority, that the same derivative suit should be dismissed as inimical to the best interests of the corporation.

At the risk of stating the obvious, the problem is relatively simple. If, on the one hand, corporations can consistently wrest bona fide derivative actions away from well-meaning derivative plaintiffs through the use of the

---

14. 8 Del.C. § 144 states:

"§ 144. Interested directors; quorum.

(a) No contract or transaction between a corporation and 1 or more of its directors or officers, or between a corporation and any other corporation, partnership, association, or other organization in which 1 or more of its directors or officers are directors or officers, or have a financial interest, shall be void or voidable solely for this reason, or solely because the director or officer is present at or participates in the meeting of the board or committee which authorizes the contract or transaction, or solely because his or their votes are counted for such purpose, if:

(1) The material facts as to his relationship or interest and as to the contract or transaction are disclosed or are known to the board of directors or the committee, and the board or committee in good faith authorizes the contract or transaction by the affirmative votes of a majority of the disinterested directors, even though the disinterested directors be less than a quorum; or

(2) The material facts as to his relationship or interest and as to the contract or transaction are disclosed or are known to the shareholders entitled to vote thereon, and the contract or transaction is specifically approved in good faith by vote of the shareholders; or

(3) The contract or transaction is fair to the corporation as of the time it is authorized, approved or ratified, by the board of directors, a committee, or the shareholders.

(b) Common or interested directors may be counted in determining the presence of a quorum at a meeting of the board of directors or of a committee which authorizes the contract or transaction."

committee mechanism, the derivative suit will lose much, if not all, of its generally-recognized effectiveness as an intra-corporate means of policing boards of directors. . . . If, on the other hand, corporations are unable to rid themselves of meritless or harmful litigation and strike suits, the derivative action, created to benefit the corporation, will produce the opposite, unintended result. . . . It thus appears desirable to us to find a balancing point where bona fide stockholder power to bring corporate causes of action cannot be unfairly trampled on by the board of directors, but the corporation can rid itself of detrimental litigation.

As we noted, the question has been treated by other courts as one of the "business judgment" of the board committee. If a "committee, composed of independent and disinterested directors, conducted a proper review of the matters before it, considered a variety of factors and reached, in good faith, a business judgment that [the] action was not in the best interest of [the corporation]," the action must be dismissed. See, e.g., Maldonado v. Flynn, [485 F.Supp. 274, 282, 286 (S.D.N.Y.1980)]. The issues become solely independence, good faith, and reasonable investigation. The ultimate conclusion of the committee, under that view, is not subject to judicial review.

We are not satisfied, however, that acceptance of the "business judgment" rationale at this stage of derivative litigation is a proper balancing point. While we admit an analogy with a normal case respecting board judgment, it seems to us that there is sufficient risk in the realities of a situation like the one presented in this case to justify caution beyond adherence to the theory of business judgment.

The context here is a suit against directors where demand on the board is excused. We think some tribute must be paid to the fact that the lawsuit was properly initiated. It is not a board refusal case. Moreover, this complaint was filed in June of 1975 and, while the parties undoubtedly would take differing views on the degree of litigation activity, we have to be concerned about the creation of an "Independent Investigation Committee" four years later, after the election of two new outside directors. Situations could develop where such motions could be filed after years of vigorous litigation for reasons unconnected with the merits of the lawsuit.

Moreover, notwithstanding our conviction that Delaware law entrusts the corporate power to a properly authorized committee, we must be mindful that directors are passing judgment on fellow directors in the same corporation and fellow directors, in this instance, who designated them to serve both as directors and committee members. The question naturally arises whether a "there but for the grace of God go I" empathy might not play a role. And the further question arises whether inquiry as to independence, good faith and reasonable investigation is sufficient safeguard against abuse, perhaps subconscious abuse. . . .

Whether the Court of Chancery will be persuaded by the exercise of a committee power resulting in a summary motion for dismissal of a derivative action, where a demand has not been initially made, should rest, in our judgment, in the independent discretion of the Court of Chancery. We thus steer a middle course between those cases which yield to the independent business judgment of a board committee and this case as determined below which would yield to unbridled plaintiff stockholder control. In pursuit of the course, we recognize that "[t]he final substantive judgment whether a particular lawsuit should be maintained requires a balance of many factors—ethical, commercial, promotional, public relations, employee relations, fiscal as well as legal." Maldonado v. Flynn, supra, 485 F.Supp. at 285. But we are content that such factors are not "beyond the judicial reach" of the Court of Chancery which regularly and competently deals with fiduciary relationships, disposition of trust property, approval of settlements and scores of similar problems. We recognize the danger of judicial overreaching but the alternatives seem to us to be outweighed by the fresh view of a judicial outsider. Moreover, if we failed to balance all the interests involved, we would in the name of practicality and judicial economy foreclose a judicial decision on the merits. At this point, we are not convinced that is necessary or desirable.

After an objective and thorough investigation of a derivative suit, an independent committee may cause its corporation to file a pretrial motion to dismiss in the Court of Chancery. The basis of the motion is the best interests of the corporation, as determined by the committee. The motion should include a thorough written record of the investigation and its findings and recommendations. Under appropriate Court supervision, akin to proceedings on summary judgment, each side should have an opportunity to make a record on the motion. As to the limited issues presented by the motion noted below, the moving party should be prepared to meet the normal burden under Rule 56 that there is no genuine issue as to any material fact and that the moving party is entitled to dismiss as a matter of law. The Court should apply a two-step test to the motion.

First, the Court should inquire into the independence and good faith of the committee and the bases supporting its conclusions. Limited discovery may be ordered to facilitate such inquiries. The corporation should have the burden of proving independence, good faith and a reasonable investigation, rather than presuming independence, good faith and reasonableness. If the Court determines either that the committee is not independent or has not shown reasonable bases for its conclusions, or, if the Court is not satisfied for other reasons relating to the process, including but not limited to the good faith of the committee, the Court shall deny the corporation's motion. If, however, the Court is satisfied under Rule 56 standards that the committee was independent and showed reasonable bases for good faith findings and recommendations, the Court may proceed, in its discretion, to the next step.

The second step provides, we believe, the essential key in striking the balance between legitimate corporate claims as expressed in a derivative stockholder suit and a corporation's best interests as expressed by an independent investigating committee. The Court should determine, applying its own independent business judgment, whether the motion should be granted. This means, of course, that instances could arise where a committee can establish its independence and sound bases for its good faith decisions and still have the corporation's motion denied. The second step is intended to thwart instances where corporate actions meet the criteria of step one, but the result does not appear to satisfy its spirit, or where corporate actions would simply prematurely terminate a stockholder grievance deserving of further consideration in the corporation's interest. The Court of Chancery of course must carefully consider and weigh how compelling the corporate interest in dismissal is when faced with a non-frivolous lawsuit. The Court of Chancery should, when appropriate, give special consideration to matters of law and public policy in addition to the corporation's best interests.

If the Court's independent business judgment is satisfied, the Court may proceed to grant the motion, subject, of course, to any equitable terms or conditions the Court finds necessary or desirable.

The interlocutory order of the Court of Chancery is reversed and the cause is remanded for further proceedings consistent with this opinion.

ANALYSIS

1. Why does the *Zapata* court distinguish between cases where the independent litigation committee investigates whether to sue after a derivative plaintiff has made demand on the firm, and cases where the plaintiff's demand on the firm has been excused? Should the *Zapata* court's two-step review of the litigation committee's decision also apply to cases where a plaintiff demands of the board that it litigate the alleged corporate claim and the board refuses to do so?

2. What is the likely difference in practical effect of the various rules relating to special committees? Suppose you are counsel to a special litigation committee of a Delaware corporation, appointed to decide whether to seek dismissal of a derivative suit. What advice would you give as to how the committee should proceed? How, if at all, would your advice be different in the case of a New York corporation?

Section 4.   The Role and Purposes of Corporations

A.P. Smith Mfg. Co. v. Barlow

13 N.J. 145, 98 A.2d 581, appeal dismissed, 346 U.S. 861 (1953).

The Chancery Division, in a well-reasoned opinion by Judge Stein, determined that a donation by the plaintiff The A.P. Smith Manufacturing Company to Princeton University was *intra vires.*   .   .   .

The company was incorporated in 1896 and is engaged in the manufacture and sale of valves, fire hydrants and special equipment, mainly for water and gas industries.   Its plant is located in East Orange and Bloomfield and it has approximately 300 employees.   Over the years the company has contributed regularly to the local community chest and on occasions to Upsala College in East Orange and Newark University, now part of Rutgers, the State University.   On July 24, 1951 the board of directors adopted a resolution which set forth that it was in the corporation's best interests to join with others in the 1951 Annual Giving to Princeton University, and appropriated the sum of $1,500 to be transferred by the corporation's treasurer to the university as a contribution towards its maintenance.   When this action was questioned by stockholders the corporation instituted a declaratory judgment action in the Chancery Division and trial was had in due course.

Mr. Hubert F. O'Brien, the president of the company, testified that he considered the contribution to be a sound investment, that the public expects corporations to aid philanthropic and benevolent institutions, that they obtain good will in the community by so doing, and that their charitable donations create favorable environment for their business operations.   In addition, he expressed the thought that in contributing to liberal arts institutions, corporations were furthering their self-interest in assuring the free flow of properly trained personnel for administrative and other corporate employment.   .   .   .   Mr. Irving S. Olds, former chairman of the board of the United States Steel Corporation, pointed out that corporations have a self-interest in the maintenance of liberal education as the bulwark of good government.   He stated that "Capitalism and free enterprise owe their survival in no small degree to the existence of our private, independent universities" and that if American business does not aid in their maintenance it is not "properly protecting the long-range interest of its stockholders, its employees and its customers."   Similarly, Dr. Harold W. Dodds, President of Princeton University, suggested that if private institutions of higher learning were replaced by governmental institutions our society would be vastly different and private enterprise in other fields would fade out rather promptly.   Further on he stated that "democratic society will not long endure if it does not nourish within itself strong centers of non-governmental fountains of knowledge, opinions of all sorts not governmentally or politically originated. If the time comes when all these centers are absorbed into government, then freedom as we know it, I submit, is at an end."

The objecting stockholders have not disputed any of the foregoing testimony nor the showing of great need by Princeton and other private institutions of higher learning and the important public service being rendered by them for democratic government and industry alike. Similarly, they have acknowledged that for over two decades there has been state legislation on our books which expresses a strong public policy in favor of corporate contributions such as that being questioned by them. Nevertheless, they have taken the position that (1) the plaintiff's certificate of incorporation does not expressly authorize the contribution and under common-law principles the company does not possess any implied or incidental power to make it, and (2) the New Jersey statutes which expressly authorize the contribution may not constitutionally be applied to the plaintiff, a corporation created long before their enactment. . . .

In his discussion of the early history of business corporations Professor Williston refers to a 1702 publication where the author stated flatly that "The general intent and end of all civil incorporations is for better government." And he points out that the early corporate charters, particularly their recitals, furnish additional support for the notion that the corporate object was the public one of managing and ordering the trade as well as the private one of profit for the members. . . . However, with later economic and social developments and the free availability of the corporate device for all trades, the end of private profit became generally accepted as the controlling one in all businesses other than those classed broadly as public utilities. . . . As a concomitant the common-law rule developed that those who managed the corporation could not disburse any corporate funds for philanthropic or other worthy public cause unless the expenditure would benefit the corporation. . . . During the 19th Century when corporations were relatively few and small and did not dominate the country's wealth, the common-law rule did not significantly interfere with the public interest. But the 20th Century has presented a different climate. . . . Control of economic wealth has passed largely from individual entrepreneurs to dominating corporations, and calls upon the corporations for reasonable philanthropic donations have come to be made with increased public support. In many instances such contributions have been sustained by the courts within the common-law doctrine upon liberal findings that the donations tended reasonably to promote the corporate objectives. . . .

When the wealth of the nation was primarily in the hands of individuals they discharged their responsibilities as citizens by donating freely for charitable purposes. With the transfer of most of the wealth to corporate hands and the imposition of heavy burdens of individual taxation, they have been unable to keep pace with increased philanthropic needs. They have therefore, with justification, turned to corporations to assume the modern obligations of good citizenship in the same manner as humans do. . . . In actual practice corporate giving has correspondingly increased. Thus, it is estimated that annual corporate contributions throughout the nation aggregate over 300 million dollars, with over 60 million dollars thereof going to universities and other educational institutions. . . .

During the first world war corporations loaned their personnel and contributed substantial corporate funds in order to insure survival; during the depression of the '30s they made contributions to alleviate the desperate hardships of the millions of unemployed; and during the second world war they again contributed to insure survival. They now recognize that we are faced with other, though nonetheless vicious, threats from abroad which must be withstood without impairing the vigor of our democratic institutions at home and that otherwise victory will be pyrrhic indeed. More and more they have come to recognize that their salvation rests upon sound economic and social environment which in turn rests in no insignificant part upon free and vigorous nongovernmental institutions of learning. It seems to us that just as the conditions prevailing when corporations were originally created required that they serve public as well as private interests, modern conditions require that corporations acknowledge and discharge social as well as private responsibilities as members of the communities within which they operate. . . .

In 1930 a statute was enacted in our State which expressly provided that any corporation could cooperate with other corporations and natural persons in the creation and maintenance of community funds and charitable, philanthropic or benevolent instrumentalities conducive to public welfare, and could for such purposes expend such corporate sums as the directors "deem expedient and as in their judgment will contribute to the protection of the corporate interests." L.1930, c. 105; L.1931, c. 290; R.S. 14:3–13, N.J.S.A. See 53 N.J.L.J. 335 (1930). Under the terms of the statute donations in excess of 1% of the capital stock required 10 days' notice to stockholders and approval at a stockholders' meeting if written objections were made by the holders of more than 25% of the stock; in 1949 the statute was amended to increase the limitation to 1% of capital and surplus. See L.1949, c. 171. In 1950 a more comprehensive statute was enacted. L.1950, c. 220; N.J.S.A. 14:3–13.1 et seq. . . .

The appellants contend that the foregoing New Jersey statutes may not be applied to corporations created before their passage. Fifty years before the incorporation of The A.P. Smith Manufacturing Company our Legislature provided that every corporate charter thereafter granted "shall be subject to alteration, suspension and repeal, in the discretion of the legislature." L.1846, p. 16; R.S. 14:2–9, N.J.S.A. A similar reserved power was placed into our State Constitution in 1875 (Art. IV, Sec. VII, par. 11), and is found in our present Constitution. Art. IV, Sec. VII, par. 9. In the early case of Zabriskie v. Hackensack & New York Railroad Company, 18 N.J.Eq. 178 (Ch.1867), the court was called upon to determine whether a railroad could extend its line, above objection by a stockholder, under a legislative enactment passed under the reserve power after the incorporation of the railroad. Notwithstanding the breadth of the statutory language and persuasive authority elsewhere . . . it was held that the proposed extension of the company's line constituted a vital change of its corporate object which could not be accomplished without unanimous consent. . . . The court announced the now familiar New Jersey doctrine that although the reserved power permits alterations in the public interest of the contract between the state and the corporation, it has no effect on the contractual rights between the corporation and its stockholders and between stockholders *inter se*. Unfortunately, the court did not consider whether it was not contrary to the public interest to permit the single minority stockholder before it to restrain the railroad's normal corporate growth and development as authorized by the Legislature and approved, reasonably and in good faith, by the corporation's managing directors and majority stockholders. Although the later cases in New Jersey have not disavowed the doctrine of the Zabriskie case, it is noteworthy that they have repeatedly recognized that where justified by the advancement of the public interest the reserved power may be invoked to sustain later charter alterations even though they affect contractual rights between the corporation and its stockholders and between stockholders *inter se*. . . .

State legislation adopted in the public interest and applied to preexisting corporations under the reserved power has repeatedly been sustained by the United States Supreme Court above the contention that it impairs the rights of stockholders and violates constitutional guarantees under the Federal Constitution. . . .

It seems clear to us that the public policy supporting the statutory enactments under consideration is far greater and the alteration of preexisting rights of stockholders much lesser than in the cited cases sustaining various exercises of the reserve power. In encouraging and expressly authorizing reasonable charitable contributions by corporations, our State has not only joined with other states in advancing the national interest but has also specially furthered the interests of its own people who must bear the burdens of taxation resulting from increased state and federal aid upon default in voluntary giving. . . .

In the light of all of the foregoing we have no hesitancy in sustaining the validity of the donation by the plaintiff. There is no suggestion that it was made indiscriminately or to a pet charity of the corporate directors in furtherance of personal rather than corporate ends. On the contrary, it was made to a preeminent institution of higher learning, was modest in amount and well within the limitations imposed by the statutory enactments, and was voluntarily made in the reasonable belief that it would aid the public welfare and advance the interests of the plaintiff as a private corporation and as part of the community in which it operates. We find that it was a lawful exercise of the corporation's implied and incidental powers under common-law principles and that it came within the express authority of the pertinent state legislation. . . .

The judgment entered in the Chancery Division is in all respects Affirmed.

ANALYSIS

1.   What is the holding of this case?

2.   What is its likely effect on shareholders and on contributions to charities? What charities are likely to benefit the most? In this connection consider the following comment (made as part of a panel discussion) by Warren Buffet, who is one of the most successful and respected investors in recent decades:

> I have a friend who is the chief fundraiser for a philanthropy. Been that for about five years. And he calls on corporate officers and he has a very simple technique when he calls. All he wants is to take some other big shot with him who will sort of nod affirmatively while he meets with the CEO [chief executive officer]. He has found that what many big shots love is what I call elephant bumping. I mean they like to go to the places where other elephants are, because it reaffirms the fact that when they look around the room and they see all these other elephants that they must be an elephant too, or why would they be there? .   .   . So my friend always takes an elephant with him when he goes to call on another elephant. And the soliciting elephant, as my friend goes through his little pitch, nods and the receiving elephant listens attentively, and as long as the visiting elephant is appropriately large, my friend gets his money. And it's rather interesting, in the last five years he's raised 8 million dollars. He's raised it from 60 corporations. It almost never fails if he has the right elephant. And in the process of raising this 8 million dollars from 60 corporations from people who nod and say it's a marvelous idea, its prosocial, etc., not one CEO has reached in his pocket and pulled out 10 bucks of his own to give to this marvelous charity. They've given 8 million dollars collectively of other people's money. And so far he's yet to get his first 10–dollar bill. So far, the Salvation Army has done better at Christmas than essentially he's done with all these well-reasoned arguments that lead people to spend other people's money.

From J. Coffee, L. Lowenstein, and S. Rose–Ackerman, Knights, Raiders, and Targets: The Impact of the Hostile Takeover 14 (1988).

NOTE

The Delaware General Corporation Law, § 122, provides, "Every corporation created under this chapter shall have the power to .   .   . (9) Make donation for the public welfare or for charitable, scientific or educational purposes, and in time of war or other national emergency in aid thereof. .   .   ." Note, however, that this is one of the powers that a corporation has. Other listed powers include the power to "sue and be sued" and the power to "make contracts, including contracts of guaranty and suretyship." Thus, § 122(9) can be read merely as an authorization to make charitable contributions that serve the basic purpose of business corporations, which is to maximize profit. The courts have been extremely tolerant, however, in accepting the business judgment of the officers and directors of corporations, including their business judgment about whether a charitable donation will be good for the corporation in the long run. One of the rare exceptions to the judicial deference to the business judgment of a board of directors is found in the next case to be considered, Dodge v. Ford Motor Company.

The California Corporations Code, § 207(e), gives corporations the power to "make donations, regardless of *specific* corporate benefit, for the public welfare or for community fund, hospital, charitable, educational, scientific, civic or similar purposes." (Emphasis supplied.)

The New York Business Corporations Law, § 202(a)(12) (McKinney, 1986), includes in the general powers of corporations, the power "to make donations, irrespective of corporate benefit, for the public welfare or for community fund, hospital, charitable, educational, scientific, civic or similar purposes, and in time of war or other national emergency in aid thereof."

A Pennsylvania provision, enacted in 1990, provides, as part of its rules on duties of directors, that directors "may, in considering the best interests of the corporation," consider the effects of their actions on "any or all groups affected by such actions, including shareholders, employees, suppliers, customers and creditors of the corporation, and upon communities in which offices or other establishments of the corporation are located." Penn.Consol. Statutes, Title 15, § 102(d). This provision then goes further by providing that the directors "shall not be required, in considering the best interests of the corporation or the effects of any action, to regard any corporate interest or the interests of any particular group affected by such action as a dominant or controlling interest or factor." This language was part of a package of provisions intended primarily to allow Pennsylvania corporations to fend off hostile takeovers (considered further at page 819), but is not limited to such situations. The basic rule of corporate choice of law in all states is that the law of the state of incorporation controls on issues relating to a corporation's "internal affairs," which includes responsibilities of directors to shareholders. Thus, under the Pennsylvania statute, if a corporation is incorporated in Pennsylvania, its directors can take account of the effects of their actions on people in other states. But the actions of directors of a corporation that has its headquarters in Pennsylvania and does most of its business in that state, but is incorporated in, say, Delaware, are controlled by Delaware law.

Under the federal income tax law (Int.Rev.Code of 1986, § 170(b)(2)), the deduction for charitable contributions by corporations is limited to 10 percent of taxable income. The deduction is not dependent on the existence of a business purpose for the contribution.

PROBLEM

Suppose you are outside counsel to a public corporation engaged in the manufacture and sale of automobile replacement parts. The CEO calls you for advice about having the corporation make a gift of $100,000 to a charitable organization in which a good friend of his is involved. The organization operates a private school for poor minority children and has had considerable success over a number of years in motivating and educating children who might otherwise not have had much of a chance to succeed academically. The before-tax earnings of the corporation for the current year will be about $20 million. The CEO says that he is beseiged by requests for charitable donations and, to avoid creating ill will with people seeking funds for other causes (some of whom are important customers), wants the corporation's gift to the school to be anonymous. He asks if there is any problem with doing so. Assume the corporation is incorporated in Delaware. What is your advice? What if the state of incorporation were California? New York? Pennsylvania?

PLANNING

It is possible for corporations to adopt charter provisions expressly limiting or prohibiting charitable contributions. Such provisions are unheard of. Suppose you are about to invest, as a 20 percent shareholder, in a new corporation; that two other individuals will each own 40 percent of the shares; and that, while you admire the business acumen of the other two, you are deeply at odds with them on political and social issues. Would you want to include in the charter a provision limiting the power of the corporation to make charitable contributions? If so, what language would you propose?

Dodge v. Ford Motor Co.

204 Mich. 459, 170 N.W. 668 (1919).

[Ford Motor Co. was incorporated in 1903 with an investment of $150,000. Henry Ford was the majority shareholder and the brothers Horace E. Dodge and John F. Dodge were among the other shareholders. In 1908 the amount invested was increased to $2 million. The company grew rapidly. The car it made sold initially for $900, but by 1916, despite improvements, the price had been lowered to $440, and in August of that year was lowered to $360. Profits soared. For the three fiscal years ending July 31, 1916, the total number of cars sold was 472,350 and the total profit was almost $60 million. Beginning in 1911, regular yearly dividends were $1.2 million, or 60 percent of the amount initially invested. In addition, the following special dividends were paid:

1911	$ 1,000,000
1912	4,000,000
1913	10,000,000
1914	11,000,000
1915	10,000,000

The company's profits were far in excess of the amount of these dividends—a cumulative total at the end of the 1916 fiscal year of almost $174 million. At that time the company had more than $50 million cash on hand.[1]

In 1916 Henry Ford, who owned 58 percent of the common shares, announced that in the future no special dividends would be paid. Profits would be reinvested in the business—for example, to expand the existing plant and to build an iron ore smelting plant so as to permit the company to make its own metal parts. In addition, the price of the company's cars would be reduced.

The Dodge brothers owned 10 percent of the common shares; they were not members of the board of directors and were not employed by the company. In 1915 their share of the regular dividend was $120,000 and their share of the special dividend was $1 million, with a prospect of even greater dividends in the future. Under Henry Ford's announced policy they could expect to receive only $120,000 per year for the indefinite future. In 1913 they had formed an auto company of their own, which competed with Ford. In 1916, after the announcement of the new dividend policy, John Dodge met with Henry Ford, complained of the new dividend policy, and offered to sell his and his brother's shares to Ford for $35 million. Ford expressed no interest in buying at any price. The Dodge brothers then sued, attacking both the dividend policy and Ford's proposed plans to expand the company's manufacturing facilities. They prevailed in the lower court, which enjoined the building of the new smelting plant and ordered the payment of a dividend of $19.3 million out of what amounted to spare cash.]

[T]he case for plaintiffs must rest upon the claim, and the proof in support of it, that the proposed expansion of the business of the corporation, involving the further use of profits as capital, ought to be enjoined because inimical to the best interests of the company and its shareholders, and upon the further claim that in any event the withholding of the special dividend asked for by plaintiffs is arbitrary action of the directors requiring judicial interference.

The rule which will govern courts in deciding these questions is not in dispute. . . .   This court, in Hunter v. Roberts, Throp & Co., 83 Mich. 63, 71, 47 N.W. 131, 134, recognized the rule in the following language:

---

1. The facts are taken from the opinion and from P. Collier and D. Horowitz, The Fords: An American Epic 80–81 (1987). In 1913, upon the urging of one of his top employees, Ford raised the wages of the company's workers overnight from $2.50 per day to $5.00 per day. Other automakers accused him of being a "traitor to his class," but Ford apparently believed that the new wage would be good for the image of the company, would help sell cars, and, presumably, would enable him to hire more productive workers. Ford also hired social workers to improve the workers' "sobriety and industry." Id. at 66–67.

"It is a well-recognized principle of law that the directors of a corporation, and they alone, have the power to declare a dividend of the earnings of the corporation, and to determine its amount. 5 Amer. & Eng.Enc.Law, 725. Courts of equity will not interfere in the management of the directors unless it is clearly made to appear that they are guilty of fraud or misappropriation of the corporate funds, or refuse to declare a dividend when the corporation has a surplus of net profits which it can, without detriment to its business, divide among its stockholders, and when a refusal to do so would amount to such an abuse of discretion as would constitute a fraud, or breach of that good faith which they are bound to exercise towards the stockholders."

. . .

When plaintiffs made their complaint and demand for further dividends, the Ford Motor Company had concluded its most prosperous year of business. The demand for its cars at the price of the preceding year continued. It could make and could market in the year beginning August 1, 1916, more than 500,000 cars. Sales of parts and repairs would necessarily increase. The cost of materials was likely to advance, and perhaps the price of labor; but it reasonably might have expected a profit for the year of upwards of $60,000,000. It had assets of more than $132,000,000, a surplus of almost $112,000,000, and its cash on hand and municipal bonds were nearly $54,000,000. Its total liabilities, including capital stock, was a little over $20,000,000. It had declared no special dividend during the business year except the October, 1915, dividend. It had been the practice, under similar circumstances, to declare larger dividends. Considering only these facts, a refusal to declare and pay further dividends appears to be not an exercise of discretion on the part of the directors, but an arbitrary refusal to do what the circumstances required to be done. These facts and others call upon the directors to justify their action, or failure or refusal to act. In justification, the defendants have offered testimony tending to prove, and which does prove, the following facts: It had been the policy of the corporation for a considerable time to annually reduce the selling price of cars, while keeping up, or improving, their quality. As early as in June, 1915, a general plan for the expansion of the productive capacity of the concern by a practical duplication of its plant had been talked over by the executive officers and directors and agreed upon; not all of the details having been settled, and no formal action of directors having been taken. The erection of a smelter was considered, and engineering and other data in connection therewith secured. In consequence, it was determined not to reduce the selling price of cars for the year beginning August 1, 1915, but to maintain the price and to accumulate a large surplus to pay for the proposed expansion of plant and equipment, and perhaps to build a plant for smelting ore. It is hoped, by Mr. Ford, that eventually 1,000,000 cars will be annually produced. The contemplated changes will permit the increased output.

The plan, as affecting the profits of the business for the year beginning August 1, 1916, and thereafter, calls for a reduction in the selling price of the cars. It is true that this price might be at any time increased, but the plan called for the reduction in price of $80 a car. The capacity of the plant, without the additions thereto voted to be made (without a part of them at least), would produce more than 600,000 cars annually. This number, and more, could have been sold for $440 instead of $360, a difference in the return for capital, labor, and materials employed of at least $48,000,000. In short, the plan does not call for and is not intended to produce immediately a more profitable business, but a less profitable one; not only less profitable than formerly, but less profitable than it is admitted it might be made. The apparent immediate effect will be to diminish the value of shares and the returns to shareholders.

It is the contention of plaintiffs that the apparent effect of the plan is intended to be the continued and continuing effect of it, and that it is deliberately proposed, not of record and not by official corporate declaration, but nevertheless proposed, to continue the corporation henceforth as a semi-eleemosynary institution and not as a business institution. In support of this contention, they point to the attitude and to the expressions of Mr. Henry Ford.

Mr. Henry Ford is the dominant force in the business of the Ford Motor Company. No plan of operations could be adopted unless he consented, and no board of directors can be elected whom he does not favor. One of the directors of the company has no stock. One share was assigned to him to qualify him for the position, but it is not claimed that he owns it. A business, one of the largest in the world, and one of the most profitable, has been built up. It employs many men, at good pay.

"My ambition," said Mr. Ford, "is to employ still more men, to spread the benefits of this industrial system to the greatest possible number, to help them build up their lives and their homes. To do this we are putting the greatest share of our profits back in the business."

With regard to dividends, the company paid sixty per cent. on its capitalization of two million dollars, or $1,200,000, leaving $58,000,000 to reinvest for the growth of the company. This is Mr. Ford's policy at present, and it is understood that the other stockholders cheerfully accede to this plan.

He had made up his mind in the summer of 1916 that no dividends other than the regular dividends should be paid, "for the present."

"Q. For how long? Had you fixed in your mind any time in the future, when you were going to pay—A. No.

"Q. That was indefinite in the future? A. That was indefinite; yes, sir."

The record, and especially the testimony of Mr. Ford, convinces that he has to some extent the attitude towards shareholders of one who has dispensed and distributed to them large gains and that they should be content to take what he chooses to give. His testimony creates the impression, also, that he thinks the Ford Motor Company has made too much money, has had too large profits, and that, although large profits might be still earned, a sharing of them with the public, by reducing the price of the output of the company, ought to be undertaken. We have no doubt that certain sentiments, philanthropic and altruistic, creditable to Mr. Ford, had large influence in determining the policy to be pursued by the Ford Motor Company—the policy which has been herein referred to.

It is said by his counsel that—

"Although a manufacturing corporation cannot engage in humanitarian works as its principal business, the fact that it is organized for profit does not prevent the existence of implied powers to carry on with humanitarian motives such charitable works as are incidental to the main business of the corporation."

.   .   .

In discussing this proposition, counsel have referred to decisions such as Hawes v. Oakland, 104 U.S. 450, 26 L.Ed. 827 .   .   .   . These cases, after all, like all others in which the subject is treated, turn finally upon the point, the question, whether it appears that the directors were not acting for the best interests of the corporation. We do not draw in question, nor do counsel for the plaintiffs do so, the validity of the general proposition stated by counsel nor the soundness of the opinions delivered in the cases cited. The case presented here is not like any of them. The difference between an incidental humanitarian expenditure of corporate funds for the benefit of the employés, like the building of a hospital for their use and the employment of agencies for the betterment of their condition, and a general purpose and plan to benefit mankind at the expense of others, is obvious. There should be no confusion (of which there is evidence) of the duties which Mr. Ford conceives that he and the stockholders owe to the general public and the duties which in law he and his codirectors owe to protesting, minority stockholders. A business corporation is organized and carried on primarily for the profit of the stockholders. The powers of the directors are to be employed for that end. The discretion of directors is to be exercised in the choice of means to attain that end, and does not extend to a change in the end itself, to the reduction of profits, or to the nondistribution of profits among stockholders in order to devote them to other purposes.

.   .   .

It is said by appellants that the motives of the board members are not material and will not be inquired into by the court so long as their acts are within their lawful powers. As we have pointed out, and the proposition does not require argument to sustain it, it is not within the lawful powers of a board of directors to shape and conduct the affairs of a corporation for the merely incidental benefit of shareholders and for the primary purpose of benefiting others, and no one will contend that, if the avowed purpose of the defendant directors was to sacrifice the interests of shareholders, it would not be the duty of the courts to interfere.

We are not, however, persuaded that we should interfere with the proposed expansion of the business of the Ford Motor Company. In view of the fact that the selling price of products may be increased at any time, the ultimate results of the larger business cannot be certainly estimated. The judges are not business experts. It is recognized that plans must often be made for a long future, for expected competition, for a continuing as well as an immediately profitable venture. The experience of the Ford Motor Company is evidence of capable management of its affairs. . . .

Defendants say, and it is true, that a considerable cash balance must be at all times carried by such a concern. But, as has been stated, there was a large daily, weekly, monthly, receipt of cash. The output was practically continuous and was continuously, and within a few days, turned into cash. Moreover, the contemplated expenditures were not to be immediately made. The large sum appropriated for the smelter plant was payable over a considerable period of time. So that, without going further, it would appear that, accepting and approving the plan of the directors, it was their duty to distribute on or near the 1st of August, 1916, a very large sum of money to stockholders.

. . .

[The Court reversed the portion of the decree of the lower court enjoining the building of the smelting plant, but upheld the portion of that decree ordering the payment of a dividend of $19.3 million.]

Shlensky v. Wrigley

95 Ill.App.2d 173, 237 N.E.2d 776 (1968).

This is an appeal from a dismissal of plaintiff's amended complaint on motion of the defendants. The action was a stockholders' derivative suit against the directors for negligence and mismanagement. The corporation was also made a defendant. Plaintiff sought damages and an order that defendants cause the installation of lights in Wrigley Field and the scheduling of night baseball games.

Plaintiff is a minority stockholder of defendant corporation, Chicago National League Ball Club (Inc.), a Delaware corporation with its principal place of business in Chicago, Illinois. Defendant corporation owns and operates the major league professional baseball team known as the Chicago Cubs. The corporation also engages in the operation of Wrigley Field, the Cubs' home park, the concessionaire sales during Cubs' home games, television and radio broadcasts of Cubs' home games, the leasing of the field for football games and other events and receives its share, as visiting team, of admission moneys from games played in other National League stadia. The individual defendants are directors of the Cubs and have served for varying periods of years. Defendant Philip K. Wrigley is also president of the corporation and owner of approximately 80% of the stock therein.

Plaintiff alleges that since night baseball was first played in 1935 nineteen of the twenty major league teams have scheduled night games. In 1966, out of a total of 1620 games in the major leagues, 932 were played at night. Plaintiff alleges that every member of the major leagues, other than the Cubs, scheduled substantially all of its home games in 1966 at night, exclusive of opening days, Saturdays, Sundays, holidays and days prohibited by league rules. Allegedly this has been done for the specific purpose of maximizing attendance and thereby maximizing revenue and income.

The Cubs, in the years 1961–65, sustained operating losses from its direct baseball operations. Plaintiff attributes those losses to inadequate attendance at Cubs' home games. He concludes that if the directors continue to refuse to install lights at Wrigley Field and schedule night baseball games, the Cubs will continue to sustain comparable losses and its financial condition will continue to deteriorate.

Plaintiff alleges that, except for the year 1963, attendance at Cubs' home games has been substantially below that at their road games, many of which were played at night.

Plaintiff compares attendance at Cubs' games with that of the Chicago White Sox, an American League club, whose weekday games were generally played at night. The weekend attendance figures for the two teams were similar; however, the White Sox week-night games drew many more patrons than did the Cubs' weekday games.

Plaintiff alleges that the funds for the installation of lights can be readily obtained through financing and the cost of installation would be far more than offset and recaptured by increased revenues and incomes resulting from the increased attendance.

Plaintiff further alleges that defendant Wrigley has refused to install lights, not because of interest in the welfare of the corporation but because of his personal opinions "that baseball is a 'daytime sport' and that the installation of lights and night baseball games will have a deteriorating effect upon the surrounding neighborhood." It is alleged that he has admitted that he is not interested in whether the Cubs would benefit financially from such action because of his concern for the neighborhood, and that he would be willing for the team to play night games if a new stadium were built in Chicago.

Plaintiff alleges that the other defendant directors, with full knowledge of the foregoing matters, have acquiesced in the policy laid down by Wrigley and have permitted him to dominate the board of directors in matters involving the installation of lights and scheduling of night games, even though they knew he was not motivated by a good faith concern as to the best interests of defendant corporation, but solely by his personal views set forth above. It is charged that the directors are acting for a reason or reasons contrary and wholly unrelated to the business interests of the corporation; that such arbitrary and capricious acts constitute mismanagement and waste of corporate assets, and that the directors have been negligent in failing to exercise reasonable care and prudence in the management of the corporate affairs.

The question on appeal is whether plaintiff's amended complaint states a cause of action. It is plaintiff's position that fraud, illegality and conflict of interest are not the only bases for a stockholder's derivative action against the directors. Contrariwise, defendants argue that the courts will not step in and interfere with honest business judgment of the directors unless there is a showing of fraud, illegality or conflict of interest.

The cases in this area are numerous and each differs from the others on a factual basis. However, the courts have pronounced certain ground rules which appear in all cases and which are then applied to the given factual situation. . . .

. . . . In Davis v. Louisville Gas & Electric Co., 16 Del.Ch. 157, 142 A. 654, a minority shareholder sought to have the directors enjoined from amending the certificate of incorporation. The court said on page 659:

"We have then a conflict in view between the responsible managers of a corporation and an overwhelming majority of its stockholders on the one hand and a dissenting minority on the other—a conflict touching matters of business policy, such as has occasioned innumerable applications to courts to intervene and determine which of the two conflicting views should prevail. The response which courts make to such applications is that it is not their function to resolve for corporations questions of policy and business management. The directors are chosen to pass upon such questions and their judgment *unless shown to be tainted with fraud* is accepted as final. The judgment of the directors of corporations enjoys the benefit of a presumption that it was formed in good faith and was designed to promote the best interests of the corporation they serve." (Emphasis supplied)

Similarly, the court in Toebelman v. Missouri–Kansas Pipe Line Co., D.C., 41 F.Supp. 334, said at page 339:

"The general legal principle involved is familiar. Citation of authorities is of limited value because the facts of each case differ so widely. Reference may be made to the statement of the rule in Helfman v. American Light & Traction Company, 121 N.J.Eq. 1, 187 A. 540, 550, in which the Court stated the law as follows: 'In a purely business corporation . . . the authority of the directors in the conduct of the business of the corporation must be regarded as absolute when they act within the law, and the court is without authority to substitute its judgment for that of the directors.'"

Plaintiff argues that the allegations of his amended complaint are sufficient to set forth a cause of action under the principles set out in Dodge v. Ford Motor Co., 204 Mich. 459, 170 N.W. 668. In that case plaintiff, owner of about 10% of the outstanding stock, brought suit against the directors seeking payment of additional dividends and the enjoining of further business expansion. In ruling on the request for dividends the court indicated that the motives of Ford in keeping so much money in the corporation for expansion and security were to benefit the public generally and spread the profits out by means of more jobs, etc. The court felt that these were not only far from related to the good of the stockholders, but amounted to a change in the ends of the corporation and that this was not a purpose contemplated or allowed by the corporate charter. . . .

[Nonetheless] it is clear that the [*Dodge*] court felt that there must be fraud or a breach of that good faith which directors are bound to exercise toward the stockholders in order to justify the courts entering into the internal affairs of corporations. This is made clear when the court refused to interfere with the directors' decision to expand the business. . . .

Plaintiff in the instant case argues that the directors are acting for reasons unrelated to the financial interest and welfare of the Cubs. However, we are not satisfied that the motives assigned to Philip K. Wrigley, and through him to the other directors, are contrary to the best interests of the corporation and the stockholders. For example, it appears to us that the effect on the surrounding neighborhood might well be considered by a director who was considering the patrons who would or would not attend the games if the park were in a poor neighborhood. Furthermore, the long run interest of the corporation in its property value at Wrigley Field might demand all efforts to keep the neighborhood from deteriorating. By these thoughts we do not mean to say that we have decided that the decision of the directors was a correct one. That is beyond our jurisdiction and ability. We are merely saying that the decision is one properly before directors and the motives alleged in the amended complaint showed no fraud, illegality or conflict of interest in their making of that decision.

While all the courts do not insist that one or more of the three elements must be present for a stockholder's derivative action to lie, nevertheless we feel that unless the conduct of the defendants at least borders on one of the elements, the courts should not interfere. The trial court in the instant case acted properly in dismissing plaintiff's amended complaint.

We feel that plaintiff's amended complaint was also defective in failing to allege damage to the corporation. . . .

There is no allegation that the night games played by the other nineteen teams enhanced their financial position or that the profits, if any, of those teams were directly related to the number of night games scheduled. There is an allegation that the installation of lights and scheduling of night games in Wrigley Field would have resulted in large amounts of additional revenues and incomes from increased attendance and related sources of income. Further, the cost of installation of lights, funds for which are allegedly readily available by financing, would be more than offset and recaptured by increased revenues. However, no allegation is made that there will be a net benefit to the corporation from such action, considering all increased costs.

Plaintiff claims that the losses of defendant corporation are due to poor attendance at home games. However, it appears from the amended complaint, taken as a whole, that factors other than attendance affect the net earnings or losses. For example, in 1962, attendance at home and road games decreased appreciably as compared with 1961, and yet the loss from direct baseball operation and of the whole corporation was considerably less.

The record shows that plaintiff did not feel he could allege that the increased revenues would be sufficient to cure the corporate deficit. The only cost plaintiff was at all concerned with was that of installation of lights. No mention was made of operation and maintenance of the lights or other possible increases in operating costs of night games and we cannot speculate as to what other factors might influence the increase or decrease of profits if the Cubs were to play night home games.

. . . [P]laintiff's allegation that the minority stockholders and the corporation have been seriously and irreparably damaged by the wrongful conduct of the defendant directors is a mere conclusion and not based on well pleaded facts in the amended complaint.

Finally, we do not agree with plaintiff's contention that failure to follow the example of the other major league clubs in scheduling night games constituted negligence. Plaintiff made no allegation that these teams' night schedules were profitable or that the purpose for which night baseball had been undertaken was fulfilled. Furthermore, it cannot be said that directors, even those of corporations that are losing money, must follow the lead of the other corporations in the field. Directors are elected for their business capabilities and judgment and the courts cannot require them to forego their judgment because of the decisions of directors of other companies. Courts may not decide these questions in the absence of a clear showing of dereliction of duty on the part of the specific directors and mere failure to "follow the crowd" is not such a dereliction.

For the foregoing reasons the order of dismissal entered by the trial court is affirmed.

Affirmed.

ANALYSIS

1. If Shlensky was unhappy with the way Wrigley wanted to operate, why did he not just sell his shares?

2. Does the decision in the case leave open the possibility that Shlensky might have prevailed?

3. Suppose you represent Shlensky, that the case is being tried, and that you have called Wrigley as a hostile witness. What strategy would you adopt in your questioning of him?

NOTE

The American Law Institute took the following approach in its Principles of Corporate Governance: Analysis and Recommendations (1994)*:

§ 2.01. The Objective and Conduct of the Corporation.

(a) Subject to the provisions of Subsection (b) and § 6.02 (Action of Directors That Has the Foreseeable Effect of Blocking Unsolicited Tender Offers), a corporation should have as its objective the conduct of business activities with a view to enhancing corporate profit and shareholder gain.

(b) Even if corporate profit and shareholder gain are not thereby enhanced, the corporation, in the conduct of its business:

(1) Is obliged, to the same extent as a natural person, to act within the boundaries set by law;

(2) May take into account ethical considerations that are reasonably regarded as appropriate to the responsible conduct of business; and

(3) May devote a reasonable amount of resources to public welfare, humanitarian, educational, and philanthropic purposes.

PROBLEMS

1. Ann and Bill long ago established a salami making business, with a factory, machinery, etc. For many years they made high-quality salami. Ann died several years ago and left her share of the business to her daughter Carol. Carol is an expert in marketing and thinks the salami can be made at lower cost by using cheaper meat and more nitrate and that this will have no adverse effect on sales. She has strong evidence to support her position. Bill does not disagree with her facts but says that he and Ann always believed in making a high-quality product because that way they slept better. Moreover, if the method of making salami were changed, there would no longer be jobs for some of the long-time employees, and Bill feels an obligation to them. If the business is in corporate form and Bill owns 60 percent, is President, and controls the board of directors, what chance does Carol have in succeeding by litigation in forcing Bill to abandon his old-style methods of making salami and adopting her proposals?

2. The basic facts about Bill and Carol and the salami factory are the same as in the preceding problem. Bill has a heart attack, following which he becomes well informed about the role of animal fat in coronary artery disease. Carol's income consists entirely of her dividends from the corporation. Bill has substantial income from other sources. Bill decides that salami is bad for one's health; it substantially increases the risk of heart attacks. He wants to produce low-fat salami. He says that he must do this

---

* © 1994 by The American Institute. Reprinted with permission.

as a matter of social responsibility. He admits that this will reduce, and possibly even eliminate, profits. Since he is wealthy he doesn't care about profits. If Bill proceeds with his plan for producing low-fat salami, does Carol have a good cause of action? Should she have? If she does, what is the proper remedy? What if Bill had claimed that it would be possible to make big profits from low-fat salami?

CHAPTER 4

THE DUTIES OF OFFICERS, DIRECTORS, AND OTHER INSIDERS

SECTION 1.   THE OBLIGATIONS OF CONTROL: DUTY OF CARE

Kamin v. American Express Company

86 Misc.2d 809, 383 N.Y.S.2d 807, affirmed, 54 A.D.2d 654, 387 N.Y.S.2d 993 (1st Dept.1976).

In this stockholders' derivative action, the individual defendants, who are the directors of the American Express Company, move for an order dismissing the complaint for failure to state a cause of action pursuant to CPLR 3211(a)(7), and alternatively, for summary judgment pursuant to CPLR 3211(c).

The complaint is brought derivatively by two minority stockholders of the American Express Company, asking for a declaration that a certain dividend in kind is a waste of corporate assets, directing the defendants not to proceed with the distribution, or, in the alternative, for monetary damages. The motion to dismiss the complaint requires the Court to presuppose the truth of the allegations. It is the defendants' contention that, conceding everything in the complaint, no viable cause of action is made out.

After establishing the identity of the parties, the complaint alleges that in 1972 American Express acquired for investment 1,954,418 shares of common stock of Donaldson, Lufken and Jenrette, Inc. (hereafter DLJ), a publicly traded corporation, at a cost of $29.9 million. It is further alleged that the current market value of those shares is approximately $4.0 million. On July 28, 1975, it is alleged, the Board of Directors of American Express declared a special dividend to all stockholders of record pursuant to which the shares of DLJ would be distributed in kind. Plaintiffs contend further that if American Express were to sell the DLJ shares on the market, it would sustain a capital loss of $25 million, which could be offset against taxable capital gains on other investments. Such a sale, they allege, would result in tax savings to the company of approximately $8 million, which would not be available in the case of the distribution of DLJ shares to stockholders. It is alleged that on October 8, 1975 and October 16, 1975, plaintiffs demanded that the directors rescind the previously declared dividend in DLJ shares and take steps to preserve the capital loss which would result from selling the shares. This demand was rejected by the Board of Directors on October 17, 1975.

It is apparent that all the previously-mentioned allegations of the complaint go to the question of the exercise by the Board of Directors of business judgment in deciding how to deal with the DLJ shares. The crucial allegation which must be scrutinized to determine the legal sufficiency of the complaint is paragraph 19, which alleges:

"19. All of the defendant Directors engaged in or acquiesced in or negligently permitted the declaration and payment of the Dividend in violation of the fiduciary duty owed by them to Amex to care for and preserve Amex's assets in the same manner as a man of average prudence would care for his own property."

Plaintiffs never moved for temporary injunctive relief, and did nothing to bar the actual distribution of the DLJ shares. The dividend was in fact paid on October 31, 1975. Accordingly, that portion of the complaint seeking a direction not to distribute the shares is deemed to be moot, and the Court will deal only with the request for declaratory judgment or for damages.

Examination of the complaint reveals that there is no claim of fraud or self-dealing, and no contention that there was any bad faith or oppressive conduct. The law is quite clear as to what is necessary to ground a claim for actionable wrongdoing.

"In actions by stockholders, which assail the acts of their directors or trustees, courts will not interfere unless the powers have been illegally or unconscientiously executed; or unless it be made to appear that the acts were fraudulent or collusive, and destructive of the rights of the stockholders. Mere errors of judgment are not sufficient as grounds for equity interference, for the powers of those entrusted with corporate management are largely discretionary." Leslie v. Lorillard, 110 N.Y. 519, 532, 18 N.E. 363, 365. . . .

More specifically, the question of whether or not a dividend is to be declared or a distribution of some kind should be made is exclusively a matter of business judgment for the Board of Directors.

". . . Courts will not interfere with such discretion unless it be first made to appear that the directors have acted or are about to act in bad faith and for a dishonest purpose. It is for the directors to say, acting in good faith of course, when and to what extent dividends shall be declared. . . . The statute confers upon the directors this power, and the minority stockholders are not in a position to question this right, so long as the directors are acting in good faith. . . ." Liebman v. Auto Strop Co., 241 N.Y. 427, 433–4, 150 N.E. 505, 506.

. . .

Thus, a complaint must be dismissed if all that is presented is a decision to pay dividends rather than pursuing some other course of conduct. . . . A complaint which alleges merely that some course of action other than that pursued by the Board of Directors would have been more advantageous gives rise to no cognizable cause of action. Courts have more than enough to do in adjudicating legal rights and devising remedies for wrongs. The directors' room rather than the courtroom is the appropriate forum for thrashing out purely business questions which will have an impact on profits, market prices, competitive situations, or tax advantages. . . .

It is not enough to allege, as plaintiffs do here, that the directors made an imprudent decision, which did not capitalize on the possibility of using a potential capital loss to offset capital gains. More than imprudence or mistaken judgment must be shown.

. . . Section 720(a)(1)(A) of the Business Corporation Law permits an action against directors for "the neglect of, or failure to perform, or other violation of his duties in the management and disposition of corporate assets committed to his charge." This does not mean that a director is chargeable with ordinary negligence for having made an improper decision, or having acted imprudently. The "neglect" referred to in the statute is neglect of duties (i.e., malfeasance or nonfeasance) and not misjudgment. To allege that a director "negligently permitted the declaration and payment" of a dividend without alleging fraud, dishonesty or nonfeasance, is to state merely that a decision was taken with which one disagrees.

Nor does this appear to be a case in which a potentially valid cause of action is inartfully stated. The defendants have moved alternatively for summary judgment and have submitted affidavits under CPLR 3211(c), and plaintiffs likewise have submitted papers enlarging upon the allegations of the complaint. The affidavits of the defendants and the exhibits annexed thereto demonstrate that the objections raised by the plaintiffs to the proposed dividend action were carefully considered and unanimously rejected by the Board at a special meeting called precisely for that purpose at the plaintiffs' request. The minutes of the special meeting indicate that the defendants were fully aware that a sale rather than a distribution of the DLJ shares might result in the realization of a substantial income tax saving. Nevertheless, they concluded that there were countervailing considerations primarily with respect to the adverse effect such a sale, realizing a loss of $25 million, would have on the net income figures in the American Express financial statement. Such a reduction of net income would have a serious effect on the market value of the publicly traded American Express stock. This was not a situation in which the defendant directors totally overlooked facts called to their attention. They gave them consideration, and attempted to view the total picture in arriving at their decision. While plaintiffs contend that according to their accounting consultants the loss on the DLJ stock would still have to be charged against current earnings even if the stock were distributed, the defendants' accounting experts assert that the loss would be a charge against earnings only in the event of a sale, whereas in the event of distribution of the stock as a dividend, the proper accounting treatment would be to charge the loss only against surplus. While the chief accountant for the SEC raised some question as to the appropriate accounting treatment of this transaction, there was no basis for any action to be taken by the SEC with respect to the American Express financial statement.

The only hint of self-interest which is raised, not in the complaint but in the papers on the motion, is that four of the twenty directors were officers and employees of American Express and members of its Executive Incentive Compensation Plan. Hence, it is suggested, by virtue of the action taken earnings may have been overstated and their compensation affected thereby. Such a claim is highly speculative and standing alone can hardly be regarded as sufficient to support an inference of self-dealing. There is no claim or showing that the four company directors dominated and controlled the sixteen outside members of the Board. Certainly, every action taken by the Board has some impact on earnings and may therefore affect the compensation of those whose earnings are keyed to profits. That does not disqualify the inside directors, nor does it put every policy adopted by the Board in question. All directors have an obligation, using sound business judgment, to maximize income for the benefit of all persons having a stake in the welfare of the corporate entity.   .   .   . What we have here as revealed both by the complaint and by the affidavits and exhibits, is that a disagreement exists between two minority stockholders and a unanimous Board of Directors as to the best way to handle a loss already incurred on an investment. The directors are entitled to exercise their honest business judgment on the information before them, and to act within their corporate powers. That they may be mistaken, that other courses of action might have differing consequences, or that their action might benefit some shareholders more than others presents no basis for the superimposition of judicial judgment, so long as it appears that the directors have been acting in good faith. The question of to what extent a dividend shall be declared and the manner in which it shall be paid is ordinarily subject only to the qualification that the dividend be paid out of surplus (Business Corporation Law Section 510, subd. b). The Court will not interfere unless a clear case is made out of fraud, oppression, arbitrary action, or breach of trust.

.   .   .

In this case it clearly appears that the plaintiffs have failed as a matter of law to make out an actionable claim. Accordingly, the motion by the defendants for summary judgment and dismissal of the complaint is granted.

Joy v. North

692 F.2d 880 (2d Cir.1982), cert. denied, 460 U.S. 1051 (1983).

[This is a derivative action against officers and directors of a Connecticut bank, Citytrust Bancorp, Inc. (Citytrust). The gist of the action is that the defendants violated their duty of care in allowing Citytrust to make a series of loans to a real estate development company, Katz Corporation (Katz), "a respected developer," for the construction of an office building.

Citytrust was dominated by its CEO, Nelson North.   The court divided the defendants into two groups, one consisting of 23 individuals, mostly directors, referred to as the "outside" defendants, and the other, "inside" defendants, consisting of seven senior officers of Citytrust involved in approving the Katz loans.

After the derivative action was brought, the board appointed a special litigation committee to make a recommendation whether the action should be dismissed.   The committee was composed of two directors who became members of the board after the events complained of and who were not defendants.   The special committee recommended that the suit be discontinued as to the outside defendants and that settlement be sought as to the inside defendants.   The trial judge, having allowed discovery, granted a motion for summary judgment and dismissed the suit as to the outside defendants.   In doing so, the judge applied a standard limiting judicial review of the recommendation of a special committee to its good faith, independence, and thoroughness.   The majority opinion of the court of appeals concludes that the standard of review should be broader, with the trial court required to find that "in its independent business judgment as to the corporation's best interests, the action should be dismissed."   For our present purposes, it is the following portions of the opinion, per Ralph K. Winter, Circuit Judge, covering the standard for duty of care that is relevant.]

While it is often stated that corporate directors and officers will be liable for negligence in carrying out their corporate duties, all seem agreed that such a statement is misleading. . . .   Whereas an automobile driver who makes a mistake in judgment as to speed or distance injuring a pedestrian will likely be called upon to respond in damages, a corporate officer who makes a mistake in judgment as to economic conditions, consumer tastes or production line efficiency will rarely, if ever, be found liable for damages suffered by the corporation. . . . Whatever the terminology, the fact is that liability is rarely imposed upon corporate directors or officers simply for bad judgment and this reluctance to impose liability for unsuccessful business decisions has been doctrinally labelled the business judgment rule.   Although the rule has suffered under academic criticism, . . . it is not without rational basis.

First, shareholders to a very real degree voluntarily undertake the risk of bad business judgment. . . .

Second, courts recognize that after-the-fact litigation is a most imperfect device to evaluate corporate business decisions.   The circumstances surrounding a corporate decision are not easily reconstructed in a courtroom years later, since business imperatives often call for quick decisions, inevitably based on less than perfect information.   The entrepreneur's function is to encounter risks and to confront uncertainty, and a reasoned decision at the time made may seem a wild hunch viewed years later against a background of perfect knowledge.

Third, because potential profit often corresponds to the potential risk, it is very much in the interest of shareholders that the law not create incentives for overly cautious corporate decisions. Some opportunities offer great profits at the risk of very substantial losses, while the alternatives offer less risk of loss but also less potential profit. Shareholders can reduce the . . . risk by diversifying their holdings. In the case of the diversified shareholder, the seemingly more risky alternatives may well be the best choice since great losses in some stocks will over time be offset by even greater gains in others.[6] Given mutual funds and similar forms of diversified investment, courts need not bend over backwards to give special protection to shareholders who refuse to reduce the . . . risk by not diversifying. A rule which penalizes the choice of seemingly riskier alternatives thus may not be in the interest of shareholders generally.

Whatever its merit, however, the business judgment rule extends only as far as the reasons which justify its existence. Thus, it does not apply in cases, *e.g.,* in which the corporate decision lacks a business purpose, . . . is tainted by a conflict of interest, . . . is so egregious as to amount to a no-win decision, . . . or results from an obvious and prolonged failure to exercise oversight or supervision, ... Other examples may occur.

B. Shareholder Derivative Actions

Whereas ordinary lenders may and will sue directly to enforce their rights and debentureholders look to indenture trustees to enforce obligations to them, direct actions by individual shareholders for injuries to the value of their investment would be an inefficient and wasteful method of enforcing management obligations. The stake of each shareholder in the likely return is usually too small to justify bringing a lawsuit and a multiplicity of such actions would result in corporate and judicial waste. Moreover, the costs of organizing a large number of geographically diverse shareholders to bring an action are usually prohibitively high. If an alternative remedy were not available, therefore, the fiduciary obligations of corporate management, however limited, might well be unenforceable. . . .

6. Consider the choice between two investments . . . . :

INVESTMENT A			INVESTMENT B		
Estimated Probability of Outcome	Outcome Profit or Loss	Value	Estimated Probability of Outcome	Outcome Profit or Loss	Value
.4	+15	6.0	.4	+6	2.4
.4	+1	.4	.4	+2	.8
.2	−13	−2.6	.2	+1	.2
1.0		3.8	1.0		3.4

Although A is clearly "worth" more than B, it is riskier because it is more volatile. Diversification lessens the volatility by allowing investors to invest in 20 or 200 A's which will tend to guarantee a total result near the [expected 3.8] value. Shareholders are thus better off with the various firms selecting A over B, although after the fact they will complain in each case of the 2.6 loss. If the courts did not abide by the business judgment rule, they might well penalize the choice of A in each such case and thereby unknowingly injure shareholders generally by creating incentives for management always to choose B.

The derivative action is the common law's inventive solution to the problem of actions to protect shareholder interests. In its classic form, a derivative suit involves two actions brought by an individual shareholder: (i) an action against the corporation for failing to bring a specified suit and (ii) an action on behalf of the corporation for harm to it identical to the one which the corporation failed to bring. . . . Moreover, the shareholder plaintiffs are quite often little more than a formality for purposes of the caption rather than parties with a real interest in the outcome. Since any judgment runs to the corporation, shareholder plaintiffs at best realize an appreciation in the value of their shares. The real incentive to bring derivative actions is usually not the hope of return to the corporation but the hope of handsome fees to be recovered by plaintiffs' counsel.

However, there is a danger in authorizing lawyers to bring actions on behalf of unconsulted groups. Derivative suits may be brought for their nuisance value, the threat of protracted discovery and litigation forcing settlement and payment of fees even where the underlying suit has modest merit. Such suits may be harmful to shareholders because the costs offset the recovery. Thus, a continuing debate surrounding derivative actions has been over restricting their use to situations where the corporation has a reasonable chance for benefit.

C. Termination of Derivative Suits by Special Litigation Committees

In the normal course of events a decision whether to bring a lawsuit is a corporate economic decision subject to the business judgment rule. . . . Thus, shareholders upset at a corporate failure to bring actions for, say, non-payment of a debt for goods sold and delivered, may not initiate a derivative suit without first making a demand upon the directors to bring the action. Where the directors refuse, and the derivative action challenges that refusal, courts apply the business judgment rule to the action of the directors. In a demand-required case, therefore, the directors' decision will be conclusive unless bad faith is proven.

Different rules apply, however, in the cases which primarily concern us here. When there is a conflict of interest in the directors' decision not to sue because the directors themselves have profited from the transaction underlying the litigation or are named defendants, no demand need be made and shareholders can proceed directly with a derivative suit. . . . It is in demand-not-required cases that the special litigation committee plays its role.

Appellees argue that, because special litigation committees are composed of "independent" directors—usually newly-elected directors who are not defendants—courts should treat their recommendations as the equivalent of a board refusal to bring an action in demand-required cases. If that proposition were accepted, the business judgment rule would apply in full force to the recommendation, and judicial scrutiny would be limited to the good faith, independence and thoroughness of the committee, as it is in the case of everyday business decisions. Appellant argues, on the other hand, that such committees are transparent devices enabling implicated directors to avoid liability and that derivative actions in demand-not-required cases are immune from termination whatever the recommendation of special litigation committees. We disagree with both parties. We believe Connecticut would not adopt appellees' contention that the business judgment rule should play a major role where a special litigation committee recommends termination of an action in a demand-not-required case, such as the one before us. As a practical matter, new board members are selected by incumbents. The reality is, therefore, that special litigation committees created to evaluate the merits of certain litigation are appointed by the defendants to that litigation. It is not cynical to expect that such committees will tend to view derivative actions against the other directors with skepticism. Indeed, if the involved directors expected any result other than a recommendation of termination at least as to them, they would probably never establish the committee. The conflict of interest which renders the business judgment rule inapplicable in the case of directors who are defendants is hardly eliminated by the creation of a special litigation committee.

It is here that we part company with Judge Cardamone. While he recognizes that the business judgment rule has never applied to corporate decisions tainted by a conflict of interest, he argues that the conflict in the defendants' creation of a committee to determine whether this action should be terminated is wholly cured by a judicial finding that the committee acted independently and in good faith. . . . To be sure, Judge Cardamone is correct in anticipating difficulties in judicial review of the recommendations of special litigation committees. These difficulties are not new, however, but have confronted every court which has scrutinized the fairness of corporate transactions involving a conflict of interest.

Moreover, the difficulties courts face in evaluation of business decisions are considerably less in the case of recommendations of special litigation committees. The relevant decision—whether to continue litigation—is at hand and the danger of deceptive hindsight simply does not exist. Moreover, it can hardly be argued that terminating a lawsuit is an area in which courts have no special aptitude. . . . The rule we predict Connecticut would establish emphasizes matters such as probable liability and extent of recovery. For these reasons we hold that the wide discretion afforded directors under the business judgment rule does not apply when a special litigation committee recommends dismissal of a suit.

We think Connecticut would reject appellees' argument for a second reason. Limiting judicial scrutiny in cases such as the one before us to the good faith, thoroughness and independence of the special litigation committee would effectively eliminate the fiduciary obligation of directors and officers. As adumbrated further below, the present action involves classic allegations and substantial evidence of mismanagement and perhaps deliberate wrongdoing resulting in a loss exceeding 10% of the shareholders' capital and equity. The traditional fiduciary obligations of directors and officers under Connecticut law can hardly be said to exist if the sole enforcement method can be eliminated on a recommendation of the defendants' appointees. . . .

We are aware that Auerbach v. Bennett, 47 N.Y.2d 619, 419 N.Y.S.2d 920, 393 N.E.2d 994 (1979), held that the business judgment rule limits judicial scrutiny of the recommendations of special litigation committees to their good faith, thoroughness and independence. Because we believe that test would work a major transformation of Connecticut corporate law, we predict that Connecticut would not adopt it. . . .

. . .

We turn now to the contents of the Special Litigation Committee's Report. We emphasize that this recitation is the Committee's version of the facts. The record suggests that a trial might reveal sharply differing versions of the same events from various witnesses as well as sharply differing inferences drawn from that testimony.

According to the Report, Nelson L. North was Citytrust's Chief Executive Officer and Norman Schaff, Jr. was its Chief Lending Officer during the period in question. The management of Citytrust was completely dominated by North. Bank officers who did not temper themselves to his regime had a short tenure at the bank. North also exercised strong control over the activities of the Board of Directors. Board members were given neither materials nor agendas prior to meetings and requests for long range planning documents were left unanswered. North's control is illustrated by the fact that contrary to the recommendation of Citytrust's outside auditors, the bank's Audit Committee was not composed solely of outside directors but instead counted among its members Mr. North and one other officer. Minutes of the Audit Committee between 1971 and 1974 are largely incomplete.

Mr. North apparently brought the initial proposal for the Katz loan to Citytrust. From 1971 to 1976, North's son was employed by Katz, and he apparently deemed this a sufficient conflict of interest to preclude his voting on the Katz transactions in Executive Committee meetings. This fastidiousness appears to have been limited to the formality of voting, for the Report strongly suggests that North was deeply involved in the Katz transactions, although the full degree of his involvement is left uncertain. The Report also adds that Mr. North has destroyed his records.

Katz appears to have been experiencing financial difficulties as early as 1971. Chase Manhattan [initially the principal lender] in fact opposed financing the Katz building in part because of a $1.6 million shortfall between the building cost and available lending; it was North who persuaded Chase to make the initial mortgage loan. By 1972, Katz was falling behind in its loans and by December of that year owed Citytrust $990,000 with respect to the building. The Report concludes that by then Citytrust was effectively a joint venturer with Katz in the building, sharing the risk of loss but entitled at best only to interest and principal if things went well. There is also some indication that a portion of the unsecured advance made by Citytrust was being applied to the Chase mortgage.

Notwithstanding the increasingly evident peril in Citytrust's transactions with Katz, no appraisals of the buildings were undertaken until 1976, and no rentability study until 1974. Although Katz had suggested that a public offering would alleviate the situation, no professional review of the preliminary prospectus was undertaken. From 1972 through 1973, only one meeting of the Board of Directors or Executive Committee considered the Katz loans. The Senior Loan Committee did meet on the Katz matter late in 1972 and may have adopted a very cautious attitude toward further credit extension. Despite this, and despite the absence of Executive Committee and Board support, senior management extended almost a million dollars in loans to Katz between 1972 and 1973.

From 1973 through 1974, the number of Board meetings at which the Katz loans were considered increased to five. This is roughly contemporaneous with the recommendation of the outside auditors that a 50% special fund be set up for the Katz loans and the National Bank Examiners' classification of the total outstanding Katz indebtedness as substandard. It is, as the Report notes, "unsettling" that neither Schaff nor Citytrust's Comptroller recall being advised of the recommendation as to the special reserve. Moreover, it is not established that the Directors were advised of this recommendation.

By late 1974, the Katz loans were so clearly a problem that they were extensively considered by the Board and the Executive Committee. In fact, the Report notes that these loans were discussed at a minimum of 25 Board and Executive Committee meetings. Nevertheless, when, on August 18, 1976, the Board was presented with the request to go over the 10% limit,* there was no prior mention of the issue on the agenda nor was opinion of counsel presented to the Board or even sought. Indeed, copies of the Comptroller's letter suggesting that Directors might wish to consult their personal counsel were not distributed to the Board.

The Report estimates a loss of $5.1 million to Citytrust. As stated earlier, there is an indication in the record that since the Report was issued, the new owner has defaulted and Citytrust again owns the building. If so, $5.1 million may be considerably less than the actual loss. In any event, a loss exceeding 10% of shareholder equity seems quite likely.

The Report contains the opinion of two experts. One concluded that the impact on morale of bank personnel, on the image of Citytrust among the banking public, upon persons who might be asked to become directors and upon potential new customers would offset even a recovery of $5.5 million.[12] The other reached a different conclusion, stating that a recovery of even $2 million would be worth pursuing notwithstanding speculation about the public impact. It stated that this opinion would stand whether or not the outside directors continue as defendants, "as long as the

---

* [Editors.—A federal statute limited individual loans to ten percent of the bank's capital and surplus—that is, to ten percent of the book value of shareholder equity.]

12. This opinion was not substantiated by verifiable historical evidence or other factual material. As such, we believe it is entitled to no weight in the determination whether a suit such as this should be dismissed.

insurance carrier is obligated through the 'D and O policy'." This last phrase might have given the Committee some pause since the letter requesting the opinion indicated that the insurance carrier had raised a question as to its liability.

. . .

As to the claims of breach of fiduciary duty, the Committee recommended that the suit be discontinued as to the outside defendants because there is "no reasonable possibility" that they might be found liable. As to the others, it concluded merely that

> there is a possibility that a finding of negligence could be rendered against any one or more of the senior loan officers who participated in the Katz Corporation loans. Although it is emphasized that there is no evidence whatsoever of any self-dealing or of any deliberate impropriety, there is some indication that the most prudent lending principles were not adhered to during the evolution of those loans.

Applying the standard of review set out above to the Committee's recommendation, we look first to potential liability generally without regard to which defendants are responsible. As to that liability, we find that plaintiff's chances of success are rather high. The loss to Citytrust resulted from decisions which put the bank in a classic "no win" situation. The Katz venture was risky and increasingly so. By continuing extensions of substantial amounts of credit the bank subjected the principal to those risks although its potential gain was no more than the interest it could have earned in less risky, more diversified loans. In a real sense, there was a low ceiling on profits but only a distant floor for losses. It is so similar to the classic case of Litwin v. Allen, [25 N.Y.S.2d 667 (N.Y.Co.Sup.Ct.1940)] (bank purchase of bonds with an option in the seller to repurchase at the original price, the bank thus bearing the entire risk of a drop in price with no hope of gain beyond the stipulated interest) that we cannot agree with the Committee's conclusion that only a "possibility of a finding of negligence" exists.

The issue as to which defendants are responsible is less clear. The Committee concluded that there is "no reasonable possibility" of the outside defendants being found liable because they had neither information nor reasonable notice of the problems raised by the Katz transactions. We note first that members of the inside defendants may contradict that version and, if so, a possibility of liability in the outside group exists. Moreover, lack of knowledge is not necessarily a defense, if it is the result of an abdication of directional responsibility. . . . Directors who willingly allow others to make major decisions affecting the future of the corporation wholly without supervision or oversight may not defend on their lack of knowledge, for that ignorance itself is a breach of fiduciary duty. The issue turns in large part upon how and why these defendants were left in the dark. See Graham v. Allis–Chalmers Mfg. Co., 41 Del.Ch. 78, 188 A.2d 125 (1963). An individual analysis of each outside defendant's role may show that some are blameless or even that they all were justified in not acting before they did, but neither is an inexorable conclusion on the basis of the present record.

The Report concluded as to the inside defendants that there was a "possibility" of liability. This conclusion is a considerable understatement and not entirely consistent with the Report's finding as to the outside defendants. The outsiders' best defense may well be that the inside group actively concealed the Katz problem. Given the fact that exoneration of the outside defendants may show culpability of the insiders and our conclusion that the probability of liability somewhere is high, we think the exposure of the inside group is considerably more than a "possibility." Nor do we agree that "there is no evidence whatsoever" of deliberate impropriety. Not only is there the problem of North's apparently inconsistent behavior with respect to the appropriateness of his participation in the considerations of Katz transactions, but his failure to keep the Board of Directors informed may well entail more than a negligent omission.

A precise estimate of potential damages is not possible since the trier must determine at what point liability begins. We think, however, that on the present record, a trier might easily find liability extending back to early 1972 or before (assuming no statute of limitations problem), resulting in a return of several million dollars to Citytrust, or perhaps 10% or more of the shareholder equity. This far exceeds the potential cost of the litigation to the corporation.

Conclusion

Applying the analysis described above, we conclude that the probability of a substantial net return to the corporation is high. We reject, therefore, the recommendation of the Special Litigation Committee. The grant of summary judgment is reversed, the protective order is vacated, and the case is remanded.   .   .   .

ANALYSIS

1.   In *Kamin,* what standard does the court adopt for the duty of care of directors? What must a plaintiff prove?

2.   In *Kamin,* the directors of American Express had two possible courses of action. They could have sold the shares of DLJ and distributed the proceeds to the shareholders of American Express. The alternative, which they adopted, was to distribute the DLJ shares in kind to the American Express shareholders. According to the facts pleaded by the plaintiff, the cost to American Express of the second course of action was $8 million in lost tax benefits. What was the offsetting benefit? What was the likelihood that the value to the shareholders of that benefit would be greater than the cost?

3.   The court in *Kamin* says that the decision not to sell the DLJ shares might have benefited four of the defendants who were employees of American Express, because of the operation of the corporation's incentive

compensation plan (under which, presumably, bonuses or other benefits were based on reported profits). What does this suggest to you about how incentive compensation provisions of employment contracts should be drafted?

4. How do you suppose the court that decided Joy v. North would have decided *Kamin*?

Francis v. United Jersey Bank

87 N.J. 15, 432 A.2d 814 (1981).

[Pritchard & Baird Intermediaries Corp. (Pritchard & Baird) was in the business of acting as a reinsurance broker. Reinsurance is the process by which an insurance company that has agreed to insure a risk (the ceding company) assigns all or a portion of that risk to another company (the reinsurer), along with a share of the premium. The broker acts as intermediary. In doing so, it receives funds from ceding companies and is obligated to pay these funds over to the reinsurers. Lillian Pritchard had inherited a 48 percent interest in Pritchard & Baird from her husband, Charles Pritchard, Sr. She was the largest single shareholder and a director. The remaining shares of the corporation were owned by her sons, Charles, Jr. and William, who also served as directors. Charles, Jr. dominated the management of the corporation after the death of his father. Charles, Jr. and William over a period of several years withdrew large sums of money from the corporation in the form of "loans." By the time the corporation finally became bankrupt, the total of the loans was over $12 million. In effect, the loans came from money that the corporation was supposed to have been holding in trust for its clients. In effect, the purported loans were simply misappropriations by the two sons. After the discovery of the misappropriations and the consequent insolvency of the corporation, Mrs. Pritchard died. The present suit is by the trustee in bankruptcy (representing the interests of the various creditors) against Mrs. Pritchard's estate to recover the misappropriated amounts.]

Mrs. Pritchard was not active in the business of Pritchard & Baird and knew virtually nothing of its corporate affairs. She briefly visited the corporate offices in Morristown on only one occasion, and she never read or obtained the annual financial statements. She was unfamiliar with the rudiments of reinsurance and made no effort to assure that the policies and practices of the corporation, particularly pertaining to the withdrawal of funds, complied with industry custom or relevant law. Although her husband had warned her that Charles, Jr. would "take the shirt off my back," Mrs. Pritchard did not pay any attention to her duties as a director or to the affairs of the corporation.

After her husband died in December 1973, Mrs. Pritchard became incapacitated and was bedridden for a six-month period. She became listless at this time and started to drink rather heavily. Her physical condition deteriorated, and in 1978 she died. The trial court rejected testimony seeking to exonerate her because she "was old, was grief-stricken at the loss of her husband, sometimes consumed too much alcohol and was psychologically overborne by her sons." 162 N.J.Super. at 371, 392 A.2d 1233. That court found that she was competent to act and that the reason Mrs. Pritchard never knew what her sons "were doing was because she never made the slightest effort to discharge any of her responsibilities as a director of Pritchard & Baird." 162 N.J.Super. at 372, 392 A.2d 1233.

. . . Individual liability of a corporate director for acts of the corporation is a prickly problem. Generally directors are accorded broad immunity and are not insurers of corporate activities. The problem is particularly nettlesome when a third party asserts that a director, because of nonfeasance, is liable for losses caused by acts of insiders, who in this case were officers, directors and shareholders. Determination of the liability of Mrs. Pritchard requires findings that she had a duty to the clients of Pritchard & Baird, that she breached that duty and that her breach was a proximate cause of their losses.

The New Jersey Business Corporation Act, which took effect on January 1, 1969, was a comprehensive revision of the statutes relating to business corporations. One section, N.J.S.A. 14A:6–14, concerning a director's general obligation had no counterpart in the old Act. That section makes it incumbent upon directors to

> discharge their duties in good faith and with that degree of diligence, care and skill which ordinarily prudent men would exercise under similar circumstances in like positions. [N.J.S.A. 14A:6–14]

. .

Because N.J.S.A. 14A:6–14 is modeled in part upon section 717 of the New York statute, N.Y.Bus.Corp. Law § 717 (McKinney), we consider also the law of New York in interpreting the New Jersey statute. . . .

Prior to the enactment of section 717, the New York courts, like those of New Jersey, had espoused the principle that directors owed that degree of care that a businessman of ordinary prudence would exercise in the management of his own affairs. . . . In addition to requiring that directors act honestly and in good faith, the New York courts recognized that the nature and extent of reasonable care depended upon the type of corporation, its size and financial resources. Thus, a bank director was held to stricter accountability than the director of an ordinary business.[1]

. . .

As a general rule, a director should acquire at least a rudimentary understanding of the business of the corporation. Accordingly, a director

---

1. The obligations of directors of banks involve some additional consideration because of their relationship to the public generally and depositors in particular. Statutes impose certain requirements on bank directors. For example, directors of national banks must take an oath that they will diligently and honestly administer the affairs of the bank and will not permit violation of the banking laws. Moreover, they must satisfy certain requirements such as residence, citizenship, stockholdings and not serving as an investment banker. . . .

should become familiar with the fundamentals of the business in which the corporation is engaged. . . . Because directors are bound to exercise ordinary care, they cannot set up as a defense lack of the knowledge needed to exercise the requisite degree of care. If one "feels that he has not had sufficient business experience to qualify him to perform the duties of a director, he should either acquire the knowledge by inquiry, or refuse to act." Ibid.

Directors are under a continuing obligation to keep informed about the activities of the corporation. . . .

Directors may not shut their eyes to corporate misconduct and then claim that because they did not see the misconduct, they did not have a duty to look. The sentinel asleep at his post contributes nothing to the enterprise he is charged to protect. . . .

Directorial management does not require a detailed inspection of day-to-day activities, but rather a general monitoring of corporate affairs and policies. . . .

While directors are not required to audit corporate books, they should maintain familiarity with the financial status of the corporation by a regular review of financial statements. . . .

Of some relevance in this case is the circumstance that the financial records disclose the "shareholders' loans." Generally directors are immune from liability if, in good faith,

> they rely upon the opinion of counsel for the corporation or upon written reports setting forth financial data concerning the corporation and prepared by an independent public accountant or certified public accountant or firm of such accountants or upon financial statements, books of account or reports of the corporation represented to them to be correct by the president, the officer of the corporation having charge of its books of account, or the person presiding at a meeting of the board. [N.J.S.A. 14A:6–14]

The review of financial statements, however, may give rise to a duty to inquire further into matters revealed by those statements. . . . Upon discovery of an illegal course of action, a director has a duty to object and, if the corporation does not correct the conduct, to resign. . . .

In certain circumstances, the fulfillment of the duty of a director may call for more than mere objection and resignation. Sometimes a director may be required to seek the advice of counsel. . . . A director may have a duty to take reasonable means to prevent illegal conduct by co-directors; in any appropriate case, this may include threat of suit. . . .

A director's duty of care does not exist in the abstract, but must be considered in relation to specific obligees. In general, the relationship of a corporate director to the corporation and its stockholders is that of a fiduciary. . . . Shareholders have a right to expect that directors will exercise reasonable supervision and control over the policies and practices of a corporation. The institutional integrity of a corporation depends upon the proper discharge by directors of those duties.

While directors may owe a fiduciary duty to creditors also, that obligation generally has not been recognized in the absence of insolvency. . . . With certain corporations, however, directors are deemed to owe a duty to creditors and other third parties even when the corporation is solvent. Although depositors of a bank are considered in some respects to be creditors, courts have recognized that directors may owe them a fiduciary duty. . . . Directors of nonbanking corporations may owe a similar duty when the corporation holds funds of others in trust. . . .

The most striking circumstances affecting Mrs. Pritchard's duty as a director are the character of the reinsurance industry, the nature of the misappropriated funds and the financial condition of Pritchard & Baird. The hallmark of the reinsurance industry has been the unqualified trust and confidence reposed by ceding companies and reinsurers in reinsurance brokers. Those companies entrust money to reinsurance intermediaries with the justifiable expectation that the funds will be transmitted to the appropriate parties. Consequently, the companies could have assumed rightfully that Mrs. Pritchard, as a director of a reinsurance brokerage corporation, would not sanction the comingling and the conversion of loss and premium funds for the personal use of the principals of Pritchard & Baird.

As a reinsurance broker, Pritchard & Baird received annually as a fiduciary millions of dollars of clients' money which it was under a duty to segregate. To this extent, it resembled a bank rather than a small family business. Accordingly, Mrs. Pritchard's relationship to the clientele of Pritchard & Baird was akin to that of a director of a bank to its depositors. All parties agree that Pritchard & Baird held the misappropriated funds in an implied trust. That trust relationship gave rise to a fiduciary duty to guard the funds with fidelity and good faith. . . .

As a director of a substantial reinsurance brokerage corporation, she should have known that it received annually millions of dollars of loss and premium funds which it held in trust for ceding and reinsurance companies. Mrs. Pritchard should have obtained and read the annual statements of financial condition of Pritchard & Baird. Although she had a right to rely upon financial statements prepared in accordance with N.J.S.A. 14A:6–14, such reliance would not excuse her conduct. The reason is that those statements disclosed on their face the misappropriation of trust funds.

From those statements, she should have realized that, as of January 31, 1970, her sons were withdrawing substantial trust funds under the guise of "Shareholders' Loans." The financial statements for each fiscal year commencing with that of January 31, 1970, disclosed that the working capital deficits and the "loans" were escalating in tandem. Detecting a misappropriation of funds would not have required special expertise or extraordinary diligence; a cursory reading of the financial statements would have revealed the pillage. Thus, if Mrs. Pritchard had read the financial statements, she would have known that her sons were converting trust funds. When financial statements demonstrate that insiders are bleeding a corporation to death, a director should notice and try to stanch the flow of blood.

In summary, Mrs. Pritchard was charged with the obligation of basic knowledge and supervision of the business of Pritchard & Baird. Under the circumstances, this obligation included reading and understanding financial statements, and making reasonable attempts at detection and prevention of the illegal conduct of other officers and directors. She had a duty to protect the clients of Pritchard & Baird against policies and practices that would result in the misappropriation of money they had entrusted to the corporation. She breached that duty.

IV

Nonetheless, the negligence of Mrs. Pritchard does not result in liability unless it is a proximate cause of the loss. . . .

Usually a director can absolve himself from liability by informing the other directors of the impropriety and voting for a proper course of action. . . . Conversely, a director who votes for or concurs in certain actions may be "liable to the corporation for the benefit of its creditors or shareholders, to the extent of any injuries suffered by such persons, respectively, as a result of any such action." N.J.S.A. 14A:6–12 (Supp. 1981–1982). A director who is present at a board meeting is presumed to concur in corporate action taken at the meeting unless his dissent is entered in the minutes of the meeting or filed promptly after adjournment. N.J.S.A. 14A:6–13. In many, if not most, instances an objecting director whose dissent is noted in accordance with N.J.S.A. 14A:6–13 would be absolved after attempting to persuade fellow directors to follow a different course of action. Cf. *McGlynn* [*v. Schultz,* 90 N.J. Super. 505, 520–521, 218 A.2d 408 (Ch.Div.1966), aff'd 95 N.J.Super. 412, 231 A.2d 386 (App.Div.), cert. den. 50 N.J. 409, 235 A.2d 901 (1967)] (receiver had no case against director who advised president that certain funds should be escrowed, wrote to executive committee to that effect, and objected at special meeting of board of directors); *Selheimer v. Manganese Corp.,* 423 Pa. 563, 572, 584, 224 A.2d 634, 640, 646 (Sup.Ct.1966) (dissenting minority director in publicly held corporation absolved because he did all he could to divert majority directors from their course of conduct by complaining to management, threatening to institute suit and organizing a stockholders' committee).

Even accepting the hypothesis that Mrs. Pritchard might not be liable if she had objected and resigned, there are two significant reasons for holding her liable. First, she did not resign until just before the bankruptcy. Consequently, there is no factual basis for the speculation that the losses would have occurred even if she had objected and resigned. Indeed, the trial court reached the opposite conclusion: "The actions of the sons were so blatantly wrongful that it is hard to see how they could have resisted any moderately firm objection to what they were doing." 162 N.J.Super. at 372, 392 A.2d 1233. Second, the nature of the reinsurance business distinguishes it from most other commercial activities in that reinsurance brokers are encumbered by fiduciary duties owed to third parties. In other corporations, a director's duty normally does not extend beyond the shareholders to third parties.

In this case, the scope of Mrs. Pritchard's duties was determined by the precarious financial condition of Pritchard & Baird, its fiduciary relationship to its clients and the implied trust in which it held their funds. Thus viewed, the scope of her duties encompassed all reasonable action to stop the continuing conversion. Her duties extended beyond mere objection and resignation to reasonable attempts to prevent the misappropriation of the trust funds. . . .

Within Pritchard & Baird, several factors contributed to the loss of the funds: comingling of corporate and client monies, conversion of funds by Charles, Jr. and William and dereliction of her duties by Mrs. Pritchard. The wrongdoing of her sons, although the immediate cause of the loss, should not excuse Mrs. Pritchard from her negligence which also was a substantial factor contributing to the loss. . . . Her sons knew that she, the only other director, was not reviewing their conduct; they spawned their fraud in the backwater of her neglect. Her neglect of duty contributed to the climate of corruption; her failure to act contributed to the continuation of that corruption. Consequently, her conduct was a substantial factor contributing to the loss.

. . .

The judgment of the Appellate Division is affirmed.

PROBLEM

Assume you are a member of the board of directors of a corporation that operates a chain of "health spas." Business has not been good and rents and salaries are high. The corporation is deeply in debt to landlords, suppliers, utilities, and employees. The corporation's method of operation is to require customers to pay a membership fee of $500 for one year, in advance. All the money collected this way within the past year has been spent, except for $5,000 collected within the past week or so. At a regular meeting of the board, the CEO reviews the financial status of the corporation and says that he intends to spend the $5,000 on an advertising campaign that he hopes will turn the business around. If that does not work, there will be no alternative but to close the doors and go out of business, in which case there will be no assets available for creditors or to pay wages owed to employees. A member of the board whose business judgment you respect says that in her opinion the chance of success of the advertising campaign is about 5 percent. In the meantime, you know that the corporation is continuing to sign up new customers (at $500 each) and to hire new employees. Some of the shareholders of the corporation are people of modest means who are your friends and who invested on the basis of your recommendation. Consider both the ethical and legal implications of your actions. As a director, what would you do? Assume, initially, that you have ruled out resignation.

On the possibility of resignation, assume that the corporation is incorporated in Delaware. Del.Gen.Corp.L. § 141(a) provides: "Each director shall hold office until his successor is elected or until his earlier resignation or removal." What would you think about the possibility of resigning?

Smith v. Van Gorkom

488 A.2d 858 (Del.Sup.Ct.1985)

■ HORSEY, JUSTICE (for the majority):

This appeal from the Court of Chancery involves a class action brought by shareholders of the defendant Trans Union Corporation . . . against the defendant members of the Board of Directors . . . .

Following trial, the former Chancellor granted judgment for the defendant directors . . .

Speaking for the majority of the Court, we . . . reverse and direct that judgment be entered in favor of the plaintiffs and against the defendant directors for the fair value of the plaintiffs' stockholdings in Trans Union, in accordance with Weinberger v. UOP, Inc., Del.Supr., 457 A.2d 701 (1983).

We hold: (1) that the Board's decision, reached September 20, 1980, to approve the proposed cash-out merger was not the product of an informed business judgment; (2) that the Board's subsequent efforts to amend the Merger Agreement and take other curative action were ineffectual, both legally and factually; and (3) that the Board did not deal with complete candor with the stockholders by failing to disclose all material facts, which they knew or should have known, before securing the stockholders' approval of the merger.

I.

. . .

Trans Union was a publicly-traded, diversified holding company, the principal earnings of which were generated by its railcar leasing business. During the period here involved, the Company had a cash flow of hundreds of millions of dollars annually. However, the Company had difficulty in generating sufficient taxable income [to be able to make use of certain federal income tax benefits called] investment tax credits (ITCs). . . .

On August 27, 1980, [Trans Union CEO Jerome] Van Gorkom met with Senior Management of Trans Union. . . . Various alternatives were suggested and discussed preliminarily, including the sale of Trans Union to a company with a large amount of taxable income.

Donald Romans, Chief Financial Officer of Trans Union, stated that his department had done a "very brief bit of work on the possibility of a leveraged buy-out." * . . . The work consisted of a "preliminary study" of the cash which could be generated by the Company if it participated in a leveraged buy-out. . . .

On September 5, at another Senior Management meeting which Van Gorkom attended, Romans again brought up the idea of a leveraged buy-out . . . Romans and Bruce S. Chelberg, President and Chief Operating Officer of Trans Union, had been working on the matter in preparation for the meeting. According to Romans: They did not "come up" with a price for the Company. They merely "ran the numbers" at $50 a share and at $60 a share with the "rough form" of their cash figures at the time. Their "figures indicated that $50 would be very easy to do but $60 would be very difficult to do under those figures." . . .

At this meeting, Van Gorkom stated that he would be willing to take $55 per share for his own 75,000 shares. He vetoed the suggestion of a leveraged buy-out by Management, however, as involving a potential conflict of interest for Management. Van Gorkom, a certified public accountant and lawyer, had been an officer of Trans Union for 24 years, its Chief Executive Officer for more than 17 years, and Chairman of its Board for 2 years. It is noteworthy in this connection that he was then approaching 65 years of age and mandatory retirement.

. . .

Van Gorkom decided to meet with Jay A. Pritzker, a well-known corporate takeover specialist and a social acquaintance. However, rather than approaching Pritzker simply to determine his interest in acquiring Trans Union, Van Gorkom assembled a proposed per share price for sale of the Company and a financing structure by which to accomplish the sale. Van Gorkom did so without consulting either his Board or any members of Senior Management except one: Carl Peterson, Trans Union's Controller. Telling Peterson that he wanted no other person on his staff to know what he was doing, but without telling him why, Van Gorkom directed Peterson to calculate the feasibility of a leveraged buy-out at an assumed price per share of $55. Apart from the Company's historic stock market price [in the $30 to $40 price range] and Van Gorkom's long association with Trans Union, the record is devoid of any competent evidence that $55 represented the per share intrinsic value of the Company.

Having thus chosen the $55 figure, based solely on the availability of a leveraged buy-out, Van Gorkom multiplied the price per share by the number of shares outstanding to reach a total value of the Company of $690 million. Van Gorkom told Peterson to use this $690 million figure and to assume a $200 million equity contribution by the buyer. Based on these assumptions, Van Gorkom directed Peterson to determine whether

* [Eds.—A leveraged buyout (LBO) is simply a purchase of a company financed by a relatively small amount of equity (common stock) and a large amount of debt (which provides the leverage). Often assets of the company are sold to pay off part of the debt.]

the debt portion of the purchase price could be paid off in five years or less if financed by Trans Union's cash flow as projected in the Five Year Forecast, and by the sale of certain weaker divisions identified in a study done for Trans Union by the Boston Consulting Group ("BCG study"). Peterson reported that, of the purchase price, approximately $50–80 million would remain outstanding after five years. Van Gorkom was disappointed, but decided to meet with Pritzker nevertheless.

Van Gorkom arranged a meeting with Pritzker at the latter's home on Saturday, September 13, 1980. Van Gorkom prefaced his presentation by stating to Pritzker: "Now as far as you are concerned, I can, I think, show how you can pay a substantial premium over the present stock price and pay off most of the loan in the first five years. . . ."

Van Gorkom then reviewed with Pritzker his calculations based upon his proposed price of $55 per share. Although Pritzker mentioned $50 as a more attractive figure, no other price was mentioned. However, Van Gorkom stated that to be sure that $55 was the best price obtainable, Trans Union should be free to accept any better offer. Pritzker demurred, stating that his organization would serve as a "stalking horse" for an "auction contest" only if Trans Union would permit Pritzker to buy 1,750,000 shares of Trans Union stock at market price which Pritzker could then sell to any higher bidder. . . .

On Monday, September 15, Pritzker advised Van Gorkom that he was interested in the $55 cash-out merger proposal and requested more information on Trans Union. . . . Van Gorkom was "astounded that events were moving with such amazing rapidity."

On Thursday, September 18, Van Gorkom met again with Pritzker. At that time, Van Gorkom knew that Pritzker intended to make a cash-out merger offer at Van Gorkom's proposed $55 per share. Pritzker instructed his attorney, a merger and acquisition specialist, to begin drafting merger documents. There was no further discussion of the $55 price. However, the number of shares to be offered [by the company] to Pritzker was negotiated down to one million shares; the price was set at $38—75 cents above the per share price at the close of the market on September 19. At this point, Pritzker insisted that the Trans Union Board act on his merger proposal within the next three days, stating to Van Gorkom: "We have to have a decision by no later than Sunday [evening, September 21] before the opening of the English stock exchange on Monday morning." . . .

On Friday, September 19, Van Gorkom, Chelberg, and Pritzker consulted with Trans Union's lead bank regarding the financing of Pritzker's purchase of Trans Union. The bank indicated that it could form a syndicate of banks that would finance the transaction. . . .

On Friday, September 19, Van Gorkom called a special meeting of the Trans Union Board for noon the following day. He also called a meeting of the Company's Senior Management to convene at 11:00 a.m., prior to the meeting of the Board. . . .

Of those present at the Senior Management meeting on September 20, only Chelberg and Peterson had prior knowledge of Pritzker's offer. Van Gorkom disclosed the offer and described its terms, but he furnished no copies of the proposed Merger Agreement. . . .

Senior Management's reaction to the Pritzker proposal was completely negative. No member of Management, except Chelberg and Peterson, supported the proposal. Romans objected to the price as being too low; he was critical of the timing and suggested that consideration should be given to the adverse tax consequences of an all-cash deal for low-basis shareholders; and he took the position that the agreement to sell Pritzker one million newly-issued shares at market price would inhibit other offers, as would the prohibitions against soliciting bids and furnishing inside information to other bidders. . . . Nevertheless, Van Gorkom proceeded to the Board meeting as scheduled without further delay. . . .

Van Gorkom began the Special Meeting of the Board with a twenty-minute oral presentation. Copies of the proposed Merger Agreement were delivered too late for study before or during the meeting. He reviewed the Company's ITC and depreciation problems and the efforts theretofore made to solve them. He discussed his initial meeting with Pritzker and his motivation in arranging that meeting. Van Gorkom did not disclose to the Board, however, the methodology by which he alone had arrived at the $55 figure, or the fact that he first proposed the $55 price in his negotiations with Pritzker.

Van Gorkom outlined the terms of the Pritzker offer as follows: Pritzker would pay $55 in cash for all outstanding shares of Trans Union stock upon completion of which Trans Union would be merged into New T Company, a subsidiary wholly-owned by Pritzker and formed to implement the merger; for a period of 90 days, Trans Union could receive, but could not actively solicit, competing offers; the offer had to be acted on by the next evening, Sunday, September 21; Trans Union could only furnish to competing bidders published information, and not proprietary information; the offer was subject to Pritzker obtaining the necessary financing by October 10, 1980; if the financing contingency were met or waived by Pritzker, Trans Union was required to sell to Pritzker one million newly-issued shares of Trans Union at $38 per share.

Van Gorkom took the position that putting Trans Union "up for auction" through a 90–day market test would validate a decision by the Board that $55 was a fair price. He told the Board that the "free market will have an opportunity to judge whether $55 is a fair price." Van Gorkom framed the decision before the Board not as whether $55 per share was the highest price that could be obtained, but as whether the $55 price was a fair price that the stockholders should be given the opportunity to accept or reject.

Attorney Brennan advised the members of the Board that they might be sued if they failed to accept the offer and that a fairness opinion was not required as a matter of law.

Romans attended the meeting as chief financial officer of the Company. . . . Romans testified:

> I told the Board that the study ran the numbers at 50 and 60, and then the subsequent study at 55 and 65, and that was not the same thing as saying that I have a valuation of the company at X dollars. But it was a way—a first step towards reaching that conclusion.

Romans told the Board that, in his opinion, $55 was "in the range of a fair price," but "at the beginning of the range."

Chelberg, Trans Union's President, supported Van Gorkom's presentation and representations. . . .

The Board meeting of September 20 lasted about two hours. Based solely upon Van Gorkom's oral presentation, Chelberg's supporting representations, Romans' oral statement, Brennan's legal advice, and their knowledge of the market history of the Company's stock,[9] the directors approved the proposed Merger Agreement. However, the Board later claimed to have attached two conditions to its acceptance: (1) that Trans Union reserved the right to accept any better offer that was made during the market test period; and (2) that Trans Union could share its proprietary information with any other potential bidders. While the Board now claims to have reserved the right to accept any better offer received after the announcement of the Pritzker agreement (even though the minutes of the meeting do not reflect this), it is undisputed that the Board did not reserve the right to actively solicit alternate offers.

The Merger Agreement was executed by Van Gorkom during the evening of September 20 at a formal social event that he hosted for the opening of the Chicago Lyric Opera. Neither he nor any other director read the agreement prior to its signing and delivery to Pritzker.

. . .

On Monday, September 22, the Company issued a press release announcing that Trans Union had entered into a "definitive" Merger Agreement with an affiliate of the Marmon Group, Inc., a Pritzker holding company. Within 10 days of the public announcement, dissent among Senior Management over the merger had become widespread. Faced with threatened resignations of key officers, Van Gorkom met with Pritzker who agreed to several modifications of the Agreement. Pritzker was willing to do so provided that Van Gorkom could persuade the dissidents to remain on the Company payroll for at least six months after consummation of the merger.

9. The Trial Court stated the premium relationship of the $55 price to the market history of the Company's stock as follows:

. . . the merger price offered to the stockholders of Trans Union represented a premium of 62% over the average of the high and low prices at which Trans Union stock had traded in 1980, a premium of 48% over the last closing price, and a premium of 39% over the highest price at which the stock of Trans Union had traded any time during the prior six years.

Van Gorkom reconvened the Board on October 8 and secured the directors' approval of the proposed amendments [to the merger agreement]—sight unseen. The Board also authorized the employment of Salomon Brothers, its investment banker, to solicit other offers for Trans Union during the proposed "market test" period.

. . .

It was not until the following day, October 10, that the actual amendments to the Merger Agreement were prepared by Pritzker and delivered to Van Gorkom for execution. As will be seen, the amendments were considerably at variance with Van Gorkom's representations of the amendments to the Board on October 8; and the amendments placed serious constraints on Trans Union's ability to negotiate a better deal and withdraw from the Pritzker agreement. Nevertheless, Van Gorkom proceeded to execute what became the October 10 amendments to the Merger Agreement without conferring further with the Board members and apparently without comprehending the actual implications of the amendments.

. . .

Salomon Brothers' efforts over a three-month period from October 21 to January 21 produced only one serious suitor for Trans Union—General Electric Credit Corporation ("GE Credit"), a subsidiary of the General Electric Company. However, GE Credit was unwilling to make an offer for Trans Union unless Trans Union first rescinded its Merger Agreement with Pritzker. When Pritzker refused, GE Credit terminated further discussions with Trans Union in early January.

In the meantime, in early December, the investment firm of Kohlberg, Kravis, Roberts & Co. ("KKR"), the only other concern to make a firm offer for Trans Union, withdrew its offer under circumstances hereinafter detailed.

On December 19, this litigation was commenced and, within four weeks, the plaintiffs had deposed eight of the ten directors of Trans Union, including Van Gorkom, Chelberg and Romans, its Chief Financial Officer. On January 21, Management's Proxy Statement for the February 10 shareholder meeting was mailed to Trans Union's stockholders. On January 26, Trans Union's Board met and, after a lengthy meeting, voted to proceed with the Pritzker merger. The Board also approved for mailing, "on or about January 27," a Supplement purportedly setting forth all information relevant to the Pritzker Merger Agreement, which had not been divulged in the first Proxy Statement.

. . .

On February 10, the stockholders of Trans Union approved the Pritzker merger proposal. Of the outstanding shares, 69.9% were voted in favor of the merger; 7.25% were voted against the merger; and 22.85% were not voted.

II.

We turn to the issue of the application of the business judgment rule to the September 20 meeting of the Board.

The Court of Chancery concluded from the evidence that the Board of Directors' approval of the Pritzker merger proposal fell within the protection of the business judgment rule. . . . The Court ruled:

> . . . that given the market value of Trans Union's stock, the business acumen of the members of the board of Trans Union, the substantial premium over market offered by the Pritzkers and the ultimate effect on the merger price provided by the prospect of other bids for the stock in question, . . . the board of directors of Trans Union did not act recklessly or improvidently in determining on a course of action which they believed to be in the best interest of the stockholders of Trans Union.

. . . The Court's explicit finding was that Trans Union's Board was "free to turn down the Pritzker proposal" not only on September 20 but also on October 8, 1980 and on January 26, 1981. The Court's implied, subordinate findings were: (1) that no legally binding agreement was reached by the parties until January 26; and (2) that if a higher offer were to be forthcoming, the market test would have produced it, and Trans Union would have been contractually free to accept such higher offer. . . .

Under Delaware law, the business judgment rule is the offspring of the fundamental principle, codified in 8 Del.C. § 141(a), that the business and affairs of a Delaware corporation are managed by or under its board of directors. . . . The rule itself "is a presumption that in making a business decision, the directors of a corporation acted on an informed basis, in good faith and in the honest belief that the action taken was in the best interests of the company." [Aronson v. Lewis, 473 A.2d 805, 812 (Del. 1984).] . . . Thus, the party attacking a board decision as uninformed must rebut the presumption that its business judgment was an informed one.

The determination of whether a business judgment is an informed one turns on whether the directors have informed themselves "prior to making a business decision, of all material information reasonably available to them." Id.

Under the business judgment rule there is no protection for directors who have made "an unintelligent or unadvised judgment." Mitchell v. Highland–Western Glass, Del.Ch., 167 A. 831, 833 (1933). . . . [As we have held in other contexts, however,] we think the concept of gross negligence is the proper standard for determining whether a business judgment reached by a board of directors was an informed one.

In the specific context of a proposed merger of domestic corporations, a director has a duty under 8 Del.C. 251(b), along with his fellow directors, to act in an informed and deliberate manner in determining whether to approve an agreement of merger before submitting the proposal to the stockholders. Certainly in the merger context, a director may not abdicate that duty by leaving to the shareholders alone the decision to approve or disapprove the agreement. . . .

III.

. . . [T]he question of whether the directors reached an informed business judgment in agreeing to sell the Company, pursuant to the terms of the September 20 Agreement presents, in reality, two questions: (A) whether the directors reached an informed business judgment on September 20, 1980; and (B) if they did not, whether the directors' actions taken subsequent to September 20 were adequate to cure any infirmity in their action taken on September 20. . . .

–A–

On the record before us, we must conclude that the Board of Directors did not reach an informed business judgment on September 20, 1980 in voting to "sell" the Company for $55 per share pursuant to the Pritzker cash-out merger proposal. . . .

The directors (1) did not adequately inform themselves as to Van Gorkom's role in forcing the "sale" of the Company and in establishing the per share purchase price; (2) were uninformed as to the intrinsic value of the Company; and (3) given these circumstances, at a minimum, were grossly negligent in approving the "sale" of the Company upon two hours' consideration, without prior notice, and without the exigency of a crisis or emergency.

As has been noted, the Board based its September 20 decision to approve the cash-out merger primarily on Van Gorkom's representations. None of the directors, other than Van Gorkom and Chelberg, had any prior knowledge that the purpose of the meeting was to propose a cash-out merger of Trans Union. No members of Senior Management were present, other than Chelberg, Romans and Peterson; and the latter two had only learned of the proposed sale an hour earlier. . . .

Without any documents before them concerning the proposed transaction, the members of the Board were required to rely entirely upon Van Gorkom's 20–minute oral presentation of the proposal. No written summary of the terms of the merger was presented; the directors were given no documentation to support the adequacy of $55 price per share for sale of the Company; and the Board had before it nothing more than Van Gorkom's statement of his understanding of the substance of an agreement which he admittedly had never read, nor which any member of the Board had ever seen.

Under 8 Del.C. § 141(e), "directors are fully protected in relying in good faith on reports made by officers." Michelson v. Duncan, Del.Ch., 386 A.2d 1144, 1156 (1978); aff'd in part and rev'd in part on other grounds, Del.Supr., 407 A.2d 211 (1979). . . . The term "report" has been liberally construed to include reports of informal personal investigations by corporate officers. . . . However, there is no evidence that any "report," as defined under § 141(e), concerning the Pritzker proposal, was presented to the Board on September 20. Van Gorkom's oral presentation of his understanding of the terms of the proposed Merger Agreement, which he had not seen, and Romans' brief oral statement of his preliminary study regarding the feasibility of a leveraged buy-out of Trans Union do not qualify as § 141(e) "reports" for these reasons: The former lacked substance because Van Gorkom was basically uninformed as to the essential provisions of the very document about which he was talking. Romans' statement was irrelevant to the issues before the Board since it did not purport to be a valuation study. At a minimum for a report to enjoy the status conferred by § 141(e), it must be pertinent to the subject matter upon which a board is called to act, and otherwise be entitled to good faith, not blind, reliance. . . .

The defendants rely on the following factors to sustain the Trial Court's finding that the Board's decision was an informed one: (1) the magnitude of the premium or spread between the $55 Pritzker offering price and Trans Union's current market price of $38 per share; (2) the amendment of the Agreement as submitted on September 20 to permit the Board to accept any better offer during the "market test" period; (3) the collective experience and expertise of the Board's "inside" and "outside" directors; and (4) their reliance on Brennan's legal advice that the directors might be sued if they rejected the Pritzker proposal. . . .

(1)

A substantial premium may provide one reason to recommend a merger, but in the absence of other sound valuation information, the fact of a premium alone does not provide an adequate basis upon which to assess the fairness of an offering price. . . .

The record is clear that before September 20, Van Gorkom and other members of Trans Union's Board knew that the market had consistently undervalued the worth of Trans Union's stock, despite steady increases in the Company's operating income in the seven years preceding the merger. The Board related this occurrence in large part to Trans Union's inability to use its ITCs as previously noted. . . .

The parties do not dispute that a publicly-traded stock price is solely a measure of the value of a minority position and, thus, market price represents only the value of a single share. Nevertheless, on September 20, the Board assessed the adequacy of the premium over market, offered by Pritzker, solely by comparing it with Trans Union's current and historical stock price.

Indeed, as of September 20, the Board had no other information on which to base a determination of the intrinsic value of Trans Union as a going concern. As of September 20, the Board had made no evaluation of the Company designed to value the entire enterprise, nor had the Board ever previously considered selling the Company or consenting to a buy-out merger. . . .

The record also establishes that the Board accepted without scrutiny Van Gorkom's representation as to the fairness of the $55 price per share for sale of the Company—a subject that the Board had never previously considered. The Board thereby failed to discover that Van Gorkom had suggested the $55 price to Pritzker and, most crucially, that Van Gorkom had arrived at the $55 figure based on calculations designed solely to determine the feasibility of a leveraged buy-out. No questions were raised either as to the tax implications of a cash-out merger or how the price for the one million share option granted Pritzker was calculated.

. . .

None of the directors, Management or outside, were investment bankers or financial analysts. . . .

(2)

This brings us to the post-September 20 "market test" upon which the defendants ultimately rely to confirm the reasonableness of their September 20 decision to accept the Pritzker proposal. In this connection, the directors present a two-part argument: (a) that by making a "market test" of Pritzker's $55 per share offer a condition of their September 20 decision to accept his offer, they cannot be found to have acted impulsively or in an uninformed manner on September 20; and (b) that the adequacy of the $17 premium for sale of the Company was conclusively established over the following 90 to 120 days by the most reliable evidence available—the marketplace. . . .

Again, the facts of record do not support the defendants' argument. There is no evidence: (a) that the Merger Agreement was effectively amended to give the Board freedom to put Trans Union up for auction sale to the highest bidder; or (b) that a public auction was in fact permitted to occur. . . .

Van Gorkom states that the Agreement as submitted incorporated the ingredients for a market test by authorizing Trans Union to receive competing offers over the next 90–day period. However, he concedes that the Agreement barred Trans Union from actively soliciting such offers and from furnishing to interested parties any information about the Company other than that already in the public domain. . . .

. . . The only clause in the Agreement as finally executed to which the defendants can point as "keeping the door open" is the following underlined statement found in subparagraph (a) of section 2.03 of the Merger Agreement as executed:

> The Board of Directors shall recommend to the stockholders of Trans Union that they approve and adopt the Merger Agreement ("the stockholders' approval") and to use its best efforts to obtain the requisite votes therefor. *GL acknowledges that Trans Union directors may have a competing fiduciary obligation to the shareholders under certain circumstances.*

Clearly, this language on its face cannot be construed as incorporating either . . . the right to accept a better offer or the right to distribute proprietary information to third parties.

. . .

(3)

The directors' unfounded reliance on both the premium and the market test as the basis for accepting the Pritzker proposal undermines the defendants' remaining contention that the Board's collective experience and sophistication was a sufficient basis for finding that it reached its September 20 decision with informed, reasonable deliberation. . . .

–B–

We now examine the Board's post-September 20 conduct for the purpose of determining first, whether it was informed and not grossly negligent; and second, if informed, whether it was sufficient to legally rectify and cure the Board's derelictions of September 20.[23]

(1)

. . .

Van Gorkom . . . called a special meeting of Trans Union's Board for October 8. . . . [T]he primary purpose of the October 8 Board meeting was to amend the Merger Agreement, in a manner agreeable to Pritzker, to permit Trans Union to conduct a "market test." Van Gorkom understood that the proposed amendments were intended to give the Company an unfettered "right to openly solicit offers down through January 31." Van Gorkom presumably so represented the amendments to Trans Union's Board members on October 8. In a brief session, the directors approved Van Gorkom's oral presentation of the substance of the proposed amendments, the terms of which were not reduced to writing until October 10. But rather than waiting to review the amendments, the Board again approved them sight unseen and adjourned, giving Van Gorkom authority to execute the papers when he received them.

. . .

The next day, October 9, and before the Agreement was amended, Pritzker moved swiftly to off-set the proposed market test amendment. First, Pritzker informed Trans Union that he had completed arrangements for financing its acquisition and that the parties were thereby mutually bound to a firm purchase and sale arrangement. Second, Pritzker announced the exercise of his option to purchase one million shares of Trans Union's treasury stock at $38 per share—75 cents above the current market price. . . .

The next day, October 10, Pritzker delivered to Trans Union the proposed amendments to the September 20 Merger Agreement. Van

23. As will be seen, we do not reach the second question.

Gorkom promptly proceeded to countersign all the instruments on behalf of Trans Union without reviewing the instruments to determine if they were consistent with the authority previously granted him by the Board. . . .

The October 10 amendments to the Merger Agreement did authorize Trans Union to solicit competing offers, but the amendments had more far-reaching effects. The most significant change was in the definition of the third-party "offer" available to Trans Union as a possible basis for withdrawal from its Merger Agreement with Pritzker. Under the October 10 amendments, a better *offer* was no longer sufficient to permit Trans Union's withdrawal. Trans Union was now permitted to terminate the Pritzker Agreement and abandon the merger only if, prior to February 10, 1981, Trans Union had either consummated a merger (or sale of assets) with a third party or had entered into a "definitive" merger agreement more favorable than Pritzker's and for a greater consideration—subject only to stockholder approval. Further, the "extension" of the market test period to February 10, 1981 was circumscribed by other amendments which required Trans Union to file its preliminary proxy statement on the Pritzker merger proposal by December 5, 1980 and use its best efforts to mail the statement to its shareholders by January 5, 1981. Thus, the market test period was effectively reduced, not extended. . . .

In our view, the record compels the conclusion that the directors' conduct on October 8 exhibited the same deficiencies as did their conduct on September 20. The Board permitted its Merger Agreement with Pritzker to be amended in a manner it had neither authorized nor intended. . . .

(2)

Next, as to the "curative" effects of the Board's post-September 20 conduct, we review in more detail the reaction of Van Gorkom to the KKR proposal and the results of the Board-sponsored "market test."

The KKR proposal was the first and only offer received subsequent to the Pritzker Merger Agreement. The offer resulted primarily from the efforts of Romans and other senior officers to propose an alternative to Pritzker's acquisition of Trans Union. . . . By early October, Henry R. Kravis of KKR gave Romans written notice of KKR's "interest in making an offer to purchase 100%" of Trans Union's common stock.

Thereafter, and until early December, Romans' group worked with KKR to develop a proposal. It did so with Van Gorkom's knowledge and apparently grudging consent. On December 2, Kravis and Romans hand-delivered to Van Gorkom a formal letter-offer to purchase all of Trans Union's assets and to assume all of its liabilities for an aggregate cash consideration equivalent to $60 per share. The offer was contingent upon completing equity and bank financing of $650 million, which Kravis represented as 80% complete. The KKR letter made reference to discussions with major banks regarding the loan portion of the buy-out cost and stated that KKR was "confident that commitments for the bank financing . . . can be obtained within two or three weeks." . . . Kravis stated that they were willing to enter into a "definitive agreement" under terms and conditions "substantially the same" as those contained in Trans Union's agreement with Pritzker. . . .

Van Gorkom's reaction to the KKR proposal was completely negative; he did not view the offer as being firm because of its financing condition. It was pointed out, to no avail, that Pritzker's offer had not only been similarly conditioned, but accepted on an expedited basis. . . .

Within a matter of hours . . . Kravis withdrew his letter-offer. He gave as his reason a sudden decision by the Chief Officer of Trans Union's rail car leasing operation to withdraw from the KKR purchasing group. Van Gorkom had spoken to that officer about his participation in the KKR proposal immediately after his meeting with Romans and Kravis. However, Van Gorkom denied any responsibility for the officer's change of mind.

. . .

GE Credit Corporation's interest in Trans Union did not develop until November; and it made no written proposal until mid-January. Even then, its proposal was not in the form of an offer. Had there been time to do so, GE Credit was prepared to offer between $2 and $5 per share above the $55 per share price which Pritzker offered. But GE Credit needed an additional 60 to 90 days; and it was unwilling to make a formal offer without a concession from Pritzker extending the February 10 "deadline" for Trans Union's stockholder meeting. As previously stated, Pritzker refused to grant such extension; and on January 21, GE Credit terminated further negotiations with Trans Union. . . .

. . . Our review of the record compels a finding that confirmation of the appropriateness of the Pritzker offer by an unfettered or free market test was virtually meaningless in the face of the terms and time limitations of Trans Union's Merger Agreement with Pritzker as amended October 10, 1980.

. . .

V.

The defendants ultimately rely on the stockholder vote of February 10 for exoneration. . . .

. . .

The parties tacitly agree that a discovered failure of the Board to reach an informed business judgment in approving the merger constitutes a voidable, rather than a void, act. Hence, the merger can be sustained, notwithstanding the infirmity of the Board's action, if its approval by majority vote of the shareholders is found to have been based on an informed electorate. . . .

. . . The question of whether shareholders have been fully informed such that their vote can be said to ratify director action, "turns on the fairness and completeness of the proxy materials submitted by the management to the . . . shareholders." Michelson v. Duncan, [407 A.2d 211, 220 (Del.1979)]. . . .

Applying this standard to the record before us, we find that Trans Union's stockholders were not fully informed of all facts material to their vote on the Pritzker Merger and that the Trial Court's ruling to the contrary is clearly erroneous. We list the material deficiencies in the proxy materials:

(1) The fact that the Board had no reasonably adequate information indicative of the intrinsic value of the Company, other than a concededly depressed market price, was without question material to the shareholders voting on the merger. . . .

(2) We find false and misleading the Board's characterization of the Romans report in the Supplemental Proxy Statement. The Supplemental Proxy stated:

At the September 20, 1980 meeting of the Board of Directors of Trans Union, Mr. Romans indicated that while he could not say that $55.00 per share was an unfair price, he had prepared a preliminary report which reflected that the value of the Company was in the range of $55.00 to $65.00 per share.

Nowhere does the Board disclose that Romans stated to the Board that his calculations were made in a "search for ways to justify a price in connection with" a leveraged buy-out transaction, "rather than to say what the shares are worth," . . . .

. . .

(3) We find misleading the Board's references to the "substantial" premium offered, [for] the Board did not disclose its failure to assess the premium offered in terms of other relevant valuation techniques, thereby rendering questionable its determination as to the substantiality of the premium over an admittedly depressed stock market price.

. . .

VI.

To summarize: we hold that the directors of Trans Union breached their fiduciary duty to their stockholders (1) by their failure to inform themselves of all information reasonably available to them and relevant to their decision to recommend the Pritzker merger; and (2) by their failure to disclose all material information such as a reasonable stockholder would consider important in deciding whether to approve the Pritzker offer.

. . .

On remand, the Court of Chancery shall conduct an evidentiary hearing to determine the fair value of the shares represented by the plaintiffs' class, based on the intrinsic value of Trans Union on September

20, 1980. . . . Thereafter, an award of damages may be entered to the extent that the fair value of Trans Union exceeds $55 per share.

. . .

REVERSED and REMANDED for proceedings consistent herewith.

■ McNEILLY, JUSTICE, dissenting:

The majority opinion reads like an advocate's closing address to a hostile jury. And I say that not lightly. Throughout the opinion great emphasis is directed only to the negative, with nothing more than lip service granted the positive aspects of this case. . . .

The majority has spoken and has effectively said that Trans Union's Directors have been the victims of a "fast shuffle" by Van Gorkom and Pritzker. That is the beginning of the majority's comedy of errors. The first and most important error made is the majority's assessment of the directors' knowledge of the affairs of Trans Union and their combined ability to act in this situation under the protection of the business judgment rule.

Trans Union's Board of Directors consisted of ten men, five of whom were "inside" directors and five of whom were "outside" directors. The "inside" directors were Van Gorkom, Chelberg, Bonser, William B. Browder, Senior Vice–President–Law, and Thomas P. O'Boyle, Senior Vice–President–Administration. At the time the merger was proposed the inside five directors had collectively been employed by the Company for 116 years and had 68 years of combined experience as directors. The "outside" directors were A.W. Wallis, William B. Johnson, Joseph B. Lanterman, Graham J. Morgan and Robert W. Reneker. With the exception of Wallis, these were all chief executive officers of Chicago based corporations that were at least as large as Trans Union. The five "outside" directors had 78 years of combined experience as chief executive officers, and 53 years cumulative service as Trans Union directors.

The inside directors wear their badge of expertise in the corporate affairs of Trans Union on their sleeves. But what about the outsiders? Dr. Wallis is or was an economist and math statistician, a professor of economics at Yale University, dean of the graduate school of business at the University of Chicago, and Chancellor of the University of Rochester. Dr. Wallis had been on the Board of Trans Union since 1962. He also was on the Board of Bausch & Lomb, Kodak, Metropolitan Life Insurance Company, Standard Oil and others.

William B. Johnson is a University of Pennsylvania law graduate, President of Railway Express until 1966, Chairman and Chief Executive of I.C. Industries Holding Company, and member of Trans Union's Board since 1968.

[The opinion then details the comparable backgrounds of three other outside directors.]

Directors of this caliber are not ordinarily taken in by a "fast shuffle." I submit they were not taken into this multi-million dollar corporate transaction without being fully informed and aware of the state of the art as it pertained to the entire corporate panorama of Trans Union. . . . I do not believe that to be the case here. These men knew Trans Union like the back of their hands and were more than well qualified to make on the spot informed business judgments concerning the affairs of Trans Union including a 100% sale of the corporation. Lest we forget, the corporate world of then and now operates on what is so aptly referred to as "the fast track." These men were at the time an integral part of that world, all professional business men, not intellectual figureheads.

. . .

Following the October 8 board meeting of Trans Union, the investment banking firm of Salomon Brothers was retained by the corporation to search for better offers . . . In undertaking such project, it was agreed that Salomon Brothers would be paid the amount of $500,000 to cover its expenses as well as a fee equal to ⅜ths of 1% of the aggregate fair market value of the consideration to be received by the company in the case of a merger or the like, which meant that in the event Salomon Brothers should find a buyer willing to pay a price of $56.00 a share instead of $55.00, such firm would receive a fee of roughly $2,650,000 plus disbursements.

. . . Salomon Brothers . . . prepared a list of over 150 companies which it believed might be suitable merger partners, and while four of such companies, namely, General Electric, Borg–Warner, Bendix, and Genstar, Ltd. showed some interest in such a merger, none made a firm proposal to Trans Union and only General Electric showed a sustained interest. . . .

[The] directors were acutely aware of the historical problems facing Trans Union which were caused by the tax laws. They had discussed these problems ad nauseam. In fact, within two months of the September meeting the board had reviewed and discussed an outside study of the company done by The Boston Consulting Group and an internal five year forecast prepared by management. . . .

The majority finds that . . . the directors breached their fiduciary duty of complete candor to the stockholders . . . in that the proxy materials were deficient in five areas.

. . . [W]hat did the proxy materials disclose? The proxy material informed the shareholders that projections were furnished to potential purchasers and such projections indicated that Trans Union's net income might increase to approximately $153 million in 1985. That projection, which is almost three times the net income of $58,248,000 reported by Trans Union as its net income for December 31, 1979 confirmed the statement in the proxy materials that the "Board of Directors believes that, assuming reasonably favorable economic and financial conditions, the Company's prospects for future earnings growth are excellent." This material was certainly sufficient to place the Company's stockholders on notice that there was a reasonable basis to believe that the prospects for future earnings growth were excellent, and that the value of their stock was more than the stock market value of their shares reflected.

. . .

AFTERMATH

Following remand, the case was settled, with the approval of the trial court, for $23 million. Of this, $10 million came from insurance covering the directors and almost $11 million came from the Pritzkers. The rest was paid by the directors, but Van Gorkom paid "substantially more" than the five outside directors. See Chicago Tribune, Feb. 8, 1987, § 7, p. 9, col. 4, and Feb. 15, 1987, § C, p. 2.

Van Gorkom claimed after the decision that the board had not intended to take the position that $55 per share was a "fair" price. Instead, he said, "We decided that $55 was too good a price to take away from shareholders without giving them the opportunity to vote and decide for themselves whether or not they wanted to take the offer." Not too long after sale to the Pritzkers, there developed a glut of rail cars. Rates plummeted and two of Trans Union's competitors filed for bankruptcy. Id.

NOTE ON CINERAMA, INC. v. TECHNICOLOR, INC.

Smith v. Van Gorkom was decided in 1985. In 1983, Ronald Perelman, operating through MacAndrews and Forbes Group, Inc., of which he was the chairman and controlling shareholder, acquired Technicolor, Inc. at a price of $23 per share. The pre-offer price was $11 per share. The acquisition proved to be highly profitable for Perelman, who later acquired Revlon, Inc. (see Chapter 6, Section 2(B)) and became one of the richest men in America.

Cinerama, Inc. was a Technicolor shareholder. It opposed the acquisition; it voted against the merger of Technicolor into a MacAndrews & Forbes subsidiary and perfected its appraisal rights. While pursuing its appraisal remedy, Cinerama discovered facts that led it to file an action in the Delaware Chancery Court opposing the merger and claiming the nonappraisal remedy of rescission (which would have resulted in a substantial recovery because of a post-merger increase in the value of Technicolor). Cinerama was allowed to proceed with both actions (see Cede & Co. v. Technicolor, Inc., 542 A.2d 1182 (1988) (Cede I)) and ultimately abandoned the appraisal action after the Chancery Court found that the fair price for appraisal purposes was $21.60 per share.

In the action for rescission (or other remedies) the Chancery Court found that the Technicolor board had violated its duty of care. The story was similar to that in Smith v. Van Gorkom in that the CEO had in effect made the deal with Perelman and then presented it to the board, which approved it quickly, without adequate information and adequate deliberation and without conducting a "market check." The case was more favorable to the defendants in that the CEO had done a thorough job of investigation, had bargained hard (raising the price from an initial offer of $15 per share and from a later, more serious, offer of $20 per share), and had hired experts who had done a thorough job in support of the fairness of the deal for Technicolor. This, however, did not relieve the board of its own obligations.

Despite the defect in the process of approval, the Chancery Court rejected Cinerama's action on the theory that the price was fair, so there was no harm and, therefore, no cause of action. In short, as Chick Hearn (Los Angeles Lakers broadcaster) would put it, "no harm, no foul." This ruling was reversed on appeal and the case was remanded. Cede & Co. v. Technicolor, Inc., 634 A.2d 345 (1993), modified upon motion for reargument 636 A.2d 956 (1994) (Cede II).

On remand, the Chancery Court found that the defendant had met its burden of proving entire fairness and dismissed the action. On appeal the Delaware Supreme Court affirmed. Cinerama, Inc. v. Technicolor, Inc., 663 A.2d 1156 (1995). The Supreme Court opinion begins with the following statement of basic legal principles:

> . . . A combination of the fiduciary duties of care and loyalty gives rise to the requirement that "a director disclose to shareholders all material facts bearing upon a merger vote. . . ." Zirn v. VLI Corp., Del.Supr., 621 A.2d 773, 778 (1993). Moreover, in Delaware, "existing law and policy have evolved into a virtual per se rule of [awarding] damages for breach of the fiduciary duty of disclosure." In re Tri–Star Pictures, Inc. Litig., 634 A.2d at 333.

The court then distinguishes *Van Gorkom*:

> In *Van Gorkom*, this Court concluded that the board of directors' failure to inform itself before recommending a merger to the stockholders constituted a breach of the fiduciary duty of care and rebutted the presumptive protection of the business judgment rule. Smith v. Van Gorkom, 488 A.2d at 893. In *Van Gorkom*, this Court also concluded that the directors had violated the duty of disclosure. This Court then held that the directors were liable for damages, since the record after trial reflected that the compound breaches of the duties of care and disclosure could not withstand an entire fairness analysis. Consequently, . . . the only issue to remand was the amount of damages the Court of Chancery should assess. . . .

The court then proceeds to discuss various factors that must be considered in a analysis of the entire fairness of a transaction: the timing, initiation, negotiation, and structure of the transaction, the disclosure to and approval by the directors, and the disclosure to and approval by the shareholders. The court upholds the Chancery Court decision for the defendants after quoting the following portion of that court's summary description of the important facts:

(1) CEO Kamerman consistently sought the highest price that Perelman would pay; (2) Kamerman was better informed about the strengths and weaknesses of Technicolor as a business than anyone else; . . . (3) Kamerman and later the board were advised by firms who were among the best in the country; (4) the negotiations led to a price that was very high when compared to the prior market price of the stock (about a 100% premium over unaffected market price) or when compared to premiums paid in more or less comparable transactions during the period; (5) while the company was not shopped, there is no indication in the record that more money was possible from Mr. Perelman or likely from anyone else; management declined to do an MBO transaction at a higher price and while I did conclude that the deal was "probably locked up," if the value of the company at that time was or appeared to be remotely close to the value Cinerama claimed at trial, any "lock-up" arrangement present would not have created an insuperable financial or legal obstacle to an alternative buyer. Indeed the conclusion that the transaction was probably locked up was logically and actually premised upon the belief that the $23 price was high.

ANALYSIS

1. The *Van Gorkom* court refers to the board's views about the "intrinsic" value of the shares of stock of Trans Union. In the case of a publicly held corporation what is the difference, if any, between the "intrinsic" value and the market price?

2. If $55 per share was good enough for Van Gorkom, who held 75,000 shares, why was it not good enough for the rest of the shareholders? Did Van Gorkom's interests or goals differ from those of a typical shareholder?

3. Is it the assumption of the court in *Van Gorkom* that the duty of the directors was to obtain the highest possible price for the company or was the assumption that the duty was simply to obtain a "fair" price, whatever that may mean? What duty should directors be charged with? Note that in a situation like that facing the directors of Trans Union, a decision to seek a higher price creates a risk that the favorable deal at hand may fall through, with the shareholders left with shares trading at their old price. How serious, in fact, do you suppose that risk was? Do you suppose that when Pritzker put a short time limit on his offer he was bluffing?

4. One way in which directors faced with the opportunity to sell the company can protect themselves is to hire an investment banking firm to issue an opinion as to the fairness of the price that has been offered. Should directors be encouraged to ask for such "second opinions"? What might an investment banker have known that the outside directors of Trans Union did not know? Is it likely that there was any information about Trans Union known by its employees that would not be known by investors in general and that would be important to them? Who should

pay for the investment banker's fairness opinion? What is the relevance, if any, of time constraints imposed on an existing offer?

5. After the decision in Smith v. Van Gorkom, is a board of directors permitted to accept an offer for the company without shopping for a better offer? Should it be? Was it wrong for the directors to approve the sale of the one million shares to Pritzker for $38 per share?

6. What is the likely effect of this decision on the behavior of directors? On the welfare of shareholders? On the welfare of lawyers and investment bankers?

NOTE AND QUESTIONS ON THE ROLE OF THE CEO AND OF THE DIRECTORS

In the legal model, the CEO and other officers of a corporation are supposed to be subservient to the will of the board of directors. It is the board that has the legal power and the responsibility to manage, or at least supervise the management of, the corporation. While the CEO and other members of the management team must and do have authority to make routine operating decisions, and develop corporate plans and strategies, major decisions require board approval. For the board to be effective in its supervisory role, it must be well informed and, to a considerable extent, must participate in the formulation of plans and strategies. One good rule of thumb to describe a CEO's obligation to the board is, "no faits accomplis and no surprises."

One of the largest of U.S. corporations is RJR Nabisco, which, until 1989, was publicly held. In 1986, the members of the RJR Nabisco board learned, by accident, that its CEO had for the past five years supported a major project for the development of a smokeless cigarette. The total investment in that project had been $68 million, which far exceeded the amount the CEO was authorized to spend without board approval, but he had spent the money in small increments to avoid having to seek such approval. When the board members learned of the project, most of them were upset that they had not been advised or consulted. One member of the board was Juanita Kreps, who, among other accomplishments, had been Secretary of Commerce of the United States. When she asked why the board had not been told sooner about the project, the CEO said that he considered it important to keep the project a secret. Kreps pointed out that hundreds of other people, who had been working on the project, had, by necessity, been aware of it, yet the board members had been kept in the dark. She concluded, "I, for one, absolutely resent that." The CEO shortly thereafter was fired.[1]

1. This account is taken from B. Burrough and J. Helyar, Barbarians at the Gate 73–75 (1990). The book is a fascinating and valuable account of the history of RJR Nabisco and its takeover in 1989, in an LBO engineered by the firm of Kohlberg, Kravis, and Roberts (KKR). (KKR, you will recall, was a potential bidder for Trans Union.) In the case of the RJR Nabisco sale, a management-supported group initially offered $75 per share for the company, at a time when the shares had been trading at about $55 per

1. If Juanita Kreps had been a member of the Trans Union board, what do you suppose her reaction would have been when Van Gorkom showed up and announced that he had made a deal to sell the company to Pritzker and wanted the board's approval?

2. Would it be a good idea for the board of directors of a large publicly held corporation to adopt a resolution specifying the obligation of the CEO to keep the board informed of plans and programs? If you were representing the directors in negotiations for the employment of a CEO, what, if anything, would you seek to include in the employment contract to permit discharge for cause (that is, without damages) for failure of communication and trust of the sort resented by Ms. Kreps?

NOTE AND QUESTION ON LEGISLATIVE RESPONSE

The decision in Smith v. Van Gorkom caused considerable consternation and anxiety among corporate directors. To relieve the anxiety, many states adopted provisions designed to afford directors protection from liability. The Delaware legislation is found in Del.Gen.Corp.Law § 102(b)(7), which allows any corporation to include in its certificate of incorporation:

> A provision eliminating or limiting the personal liability of a director to the corporation or its stockholders for monetary damages for breach of fiduciary duty as a director, provided that such provision shall not eliminate or limit the liability of a director: (i) For any breach of the director's duty of loyalty to the corporation or its stockholders; (ii) for acts or omissions not in good faith or which involve intentional misconduct or a knowing violation of law; (iii) under § 174 of this title [relating to payment of dividends]; or (iv) for any transaction from which the director derived an improper personal benefit. . . .

There has been widespread adoption, with shareholder approval, of amendments to corporate certificates of incorporation to provide the protection contemplated by this provision (and provisions in other states with similar objectives [2]). Note that a provision of the sort contemplated by

share. The board responded to the offer by actively encouraging competing bids, with KKR ultimately prevailing at a price of about $109 per share. The aggressiveness of the RJR Nabisco board in seeking the best possible price for the company is in stark contrast with the passivity of the Trans Union board. One factor that accounts in part for the difference in behavior between the two boards is that the RJR Nabisco board members had developed some antagonism toward the corporation's CEO, who was a leader of the management-supported group that had initially offered $75 per share. Another factor may simply have been the decision in Smith v. Van Gorkom.

2. The legislation in other states has taken various forms. For example, the rule in Florida applies to all corporations incorporated in that state (as opposed to the Delaware rule, which applies only to those corporations that elect, with shareholder approval, to be covered). Fla.Stat.Ann. § 607.1645 (Supp.1990). Under the Florida rule, a director is liable in a suit by the corporation if the misconduct involved a "conscious disregard for the best interests of the corporation, or willful misconduct." In suits by someone other than the corporation or a shareholder the standard is "recklessness," "bad faith," "malicious purpose," or "exhibiting wanton and willful disregard of human rights, safety

§ 102(b)(7) would foreclose liability of the directors for damages in a case like Smith v. Van Gorkom, but would not foreclose injunctive relief.

In Francis v. United Jersey Bank, supra, if the case had arisen after the adoption of § 102(b)(7) and the corporation had adopted a provision of the sort contemplated by that section, would Mrs. Pritchard have avoided liability? Did she derive an "improper personal benefit"? Could the creditors have successfully framed a suit that did not depend on liability to the corporation?

NOTE AND QUESTION ON LOCKUPS

The agreement by Trans Union allowing Pritzker to buy 1 million shares at $38 per shares is sometimes called a "lockup option" or, simply, a "lockup." Assuming that Trans Union would be sold to someone for at least $55 per share, the lockup granted to Pritzker was worth $17 per share or a total of $17 million. In essence, when Trans Union granted the lockup, Pritzker was assured a profit of at least $17 million, assuming that the ultimate sale of Trans Union for at least $55 per share was a certainty. At the same time the lockup granted to Pritzker reduced the value to other potential bidders by $17 million, since they would be stuck with the obligation to sell to Pritzker for $38 a million shares worth $55 per share. Consider the effect on Pritzker and on other potential bidders:

At $55 per share, according to the facts stated by the court, the total price for all the shares was $690 million. Suppose that Pritzker figured that the total value to him was $700 million, and that in the absence of the lockup he would have been willing to pay up to that amount but no more. $700 million is his "indifference point." At a purchase price of $690 million, Pritzker would have a gain or "profit" of $10 million. Now suppose that the lockup has been granted to Pritzker and another bidder comes along that values Trans Union at a total of $710 million, less the $17 million lockup obligation to Pritzker, or $693 million, and offers to pay $691 million. If Pritzker raises the bid to $692 million and prevails, he winds up owning a company he values at $700 million and realizes a gain of $8 million. On the other hand, if he drops out of the bidding and the other

or property," with a narrow definition of "recklessness."

The Virginia law applies to officers as well as directors and limits liability to the lesser of an amount specified in the articles or, if approved by the shareholders, in the bylaws, the "greater of (i) $100,000 or (ii) the amount of cash compensation received by the officer or director from the corporation during the twelve months immediately preceding the act or omission for which liability was imposed."   Va.Code Ann. § 13.1–692.1 (1989). The limitation does not apply, however, where the officer or director was guilty of "willful misconduct or a knowing violation

of the criminal law or of any state or federal securities law."

Federal Deposit Insurance Corporation v. McSweeney, 976 F.2d 532 (9th Cir.1992), cert. denied, 508 U.S. 950 (1993), holds that the Financial Institutions Reform, Recovery, and Enforcement Act of 1989 (FIRREA), allows recoveries from directors of federally insured savings institution for gross negligence, despite state laws generally establishing a more protective standard (e.g., willful misconduct or recklessness), while at the same time preserving the right to recover under state rules imposing a lesser standard (e.g., simple negligence).

bidder acquires Trans Union, Pritzker winds up with a gain from the lockup of slightly more than $17 million (slightly more because the price has been raised slightly above $55 per share). Assuming that Pritzker is a rational person (what else would he be?), he will drop out of the bidding and Trans Union will be sold for $692 million. In the absence of a lockup, however, Pritzker might have remained in the bidding until he had forced the other bidder up to around $700 million. Thus, it seems that the lockup should not change the identity of the ultimate purchaser—whoever values Trans Union highest should wind up owning it—but the effect of the lockup will be that the total paid is reduced.

If you had been a member of the board of Trans Union might you still have voted in favor of granting the lockup? Why? What important element of reality has been left out of the facts as stated in this Note?

In re Caremark International Inc. Derivative Litigation

698 A.2d 959 (Del.Ch.1996).

MEMORANDUM OPINION

■ ALLEN, CHANCELLOR.

Pending is a motion . . . to approve as fair and reasonable a proposed settlement of a consolidated derivative action on behalf of Caremark International, Inc. ("Caremark"). The suit involves claims that the members of Caremark's board of directors (the "Board") breached their fiduciary duty of care to Caremark in connection with alleged violations by Caremark employees of federal and state laws and regulations applicable to health care providers. As a result of the alleged violations, . . . Caremark was charged in an indictment with multiple felonies. It thereafter entered into a number of agreements with the Department of Justice and others. Those agreements included a plea agreement in which Caremark pleaded guilty to a single felony of mail fraud and agreed to pay civil and criminal fines. Subsequently, Caremark agreed to make reimbursements to various private and public parties. In all, the payments that Caremark has been required to make total approximately $250 million.

This suit was filed in 1994, purporting to seek on behalf of the company recovery of these losses from the individual defendants who constitute the board of directors of Caremark. The parties now propose that it be settled and, after notice to Caremark shareholders, a hearing on the fairness of the proposal was held on August 16, 1996.

A motion of this type requires the court to assess the strengths and weaknesses of the claims asserted in light of the discovery record and to evaluate the fairness and adequacy of the consideration offered to the corporation in exchange for the release of all claims made or arising from the facts alleged. The ultimate issue then is whether the proposed settlement appears to be fair to the corporation and its absent shareholders. . . .

Legally, evaluation of the central claim made entails consideration of the legal standard governing a board of directors' obligation to supervise or monitor corporate performance. For the reasons set forth below I conclude, in light of the discovery record, that there is a very low probability that it would be determined that the directors of Caremark breached any duty to appropriately monitor and supervise the enterprise.   .   .   .

I. BACKGROUND

.   .   . Caremark, a Delaware corporation with its headquarters in Northbrook, Illinois, .   .   . was involved in two main health care business segments, providing patient care and managed care services.   .   .   .

A. Events Prior to the Government Investigation

A substantial part of the revenues generated by Caremark's businesses is derived from third party payments, insurers, and Medicare and Medicaid reimbursement programs. The latter source of payments are subject to the terms of the Anti–Referral Payments Law ("ARPL"), which prohibits health care providers from paying any form of remuneration to induce the referral of Medicare or Medicaid patients. From its inception, Caremark entered into a variety of agreements with hospitals, physicians, and health care providers for advice and services, as well as distribution agreements with drug manufacturers, as had its predecessor prior to 1992. Specifically, Caremark did have a practice of entering into contracts for services (e.g., consultation agreements and research grants) with physicians at least some of whom prescribed or recommended services or products that Caremark provided to Medicare recipients and other patients. Such contracts were not prohibited by the ARPL but they obviously raised a possibility of unlawful "kickbacks."

As early as 1989, Caremark's predecessor issued an internal "Guide to Contractual Relationships" ("Guide") to govern its employees in entering into contracts with physicians and hospitals. The Guide tended to be reviewed annually by lawyers and updated. Each version of the Guide stated as Caremark's and its predecessor's policy that no payments would be made in exchange for or to induce patient referrals. But what one might deem a prohibited quid pro quo was not always clear.   .   .   .

To clarify the scope of the ARPL, the United States Department of Health and Human Services ("HHS") issued "safe harbor" regulations in July 1991 stating conditions under which financial relationships between health care service providers and patient referral sources, such as physicians, would not violate the ARPL. Caremark contends that the narrowly drawn regulations gave limited guidance as to the legality of many of the agreements used by Caremark that did not fall within the safe-harbor. Caremark's predecessor, however, amended many of its standard forms of agreement with health care providers and revised the Guide in an apparent attempt to comply with the new regulations.

B.   Government Investigation and Related Litigation

In August 1991, the HHS Office of the Inspector General ("OIG") initiated an investigation of Caremark's predecessor. Caremark's predecessor was served with a subpoena requiring the production of documents, including contracts between Caremark's predecessor and physicians (Quality Service Agreements ("QSAs")). Under the QSAs, Caremark's predecessor appears to have paid physicians fees for monitoring patients under Caremark's predecessor's care, including Medicare and Medicaid recipients. Sometimes apparently those monitoring patients were referring physicians, which raised ARPL concerns.

In March 1992, the Department of Justice ("DOJ") joined the OIG investigation and separate investigations were commenced by several additional federal and state agencies.

C.   Caremark's Response to the Investigation

During the relevant period, Caremark had approximately 7,000 employees and ninety branch operations. It had a decentralized management structure.   .   .   . The first action taken by management, as a result of the initiation of the OIG investigation, was an announcement that as of October 1, 1991, Caremark's predecessor would no longer pay management fees to physicians for services to Medicare and Medicaid patients. Despite this decision, Caremark asserts that its management, pursuant to advice, did not believe that such payments were illegal under the existing laws and regulations.

During this period, Caremark's Board took several additional steps consistent with an effort to assure compliance with company policies concerning the ARPL and the contractual forms in the Guide.   .   .   .

Although there is evidence that inside and outside counsel had advised Caremark's directors that their contracts were in accord with the law, Caremark recognized that some uncertainty respecting the correct interpretation of the law existed. In its 1992 annual report, Caremark disclosed the ongoing government investigations, acknowledged that if penalties were imposed on the company they could have a material adverse effect on Caremark's business, and stated that no assurance could be given that its interpretation of the ARPL would prevail if challenged.

Throughout the period of the government investigations, Caremark had an internal audit plan designed to assure compliance with business and ethics policies. In addition, Caremark employed Price Waterhouse as its outside auditor. On February 8, 1993, the Ethics Committee of Caremark's Board received and reviewed an outside auditors report by Price Waterhouse which concluded that there were no material weaknesses in Caremark's control structure. Despite the positive findings of Price Waterhouse, however, on April 20, 1993, the Audit & Ethics Committee adopted a new internal audit charter requiring a comprehensive review of compliance policies and the compilation of an employee ethics handbook concerning such policies.

The Board appears to have been informed about this project and other efforts to assure compliance with the law. . . . On July 27, 1993, the new ethics manual, expressly prohibiting payments in exchange for referrals and requiring employees to report all illegal conduct to a toll free confidential ethics hotline, was approved and allegedly disseminated. The record suggests that Caremark continued these policies in subsequent years, causing employees to be given revised versions of the ethics manual and requiring them to participate in training sessions concerning compliance with the law.

During 1993, Caremark took several additional steps which appear to have been aimed at increasing management supervision. These steps included new policies requiring local branch managers to secure home office approval for all disbursements under agreements with health care providers and to certify compliance with the ethics program. In addition, the chief financial officer was appointed to serve as Caremark's compliance officer. In 1994, a fifth revised Guide was published.

D. Federal Indictments Against Caremark and Officers

On August 4, 1994, a federal grand jury in Minnesota issued a 47 page indictment charging Caremark, two of its officers (not the firm's chief officer), an individual who had been a sales employee of Genentech, Inc., and David R. Brown, a physician practicing in Minneapolis, with violating the ARPL over a lengthy period. According to the indictment, over $1.1 million had been paid to Brown to induce him to distribute Protropin, a human growth hormone drug marketed by Caremark. The substantial payments involved started, according to the allegations of the indictment, in 1986 and continued through 1993. Some payments were "in the guise of research grants," and others were "consulting agreements." The indictment charged, for example, that Dr. Brown performed virtually none of the consulting functions described in his 1991 agreement with Caremark, but was nevertheless neither required to return the money he had received nor precluded from receiving future funding from Caremark. In addition the indictment charged that Brown received from Caremark payments of staff and office expenses, including telephone answering services and fax rental expenses.

In reaction to the Minnesota Indictment and the subsequent filing of this and other derivative actions in 1994, the Board met and was informed by management that the investigation had resulted in an indictment; Caremark denied any wrongdoing relating to the indictment and believed that the OIG investigation would have a favorable outcome. Management reiterated the grounds for its view that the contracts were in compliance with law.

Subsequently, five stockholder derivative actions were filed in this court and consolidated into this action. The original complaint, dated August 5, 1994, alleged, in relevant part, that Caremark's directors breached their duty of care by failing adequately to supervise the conduct of

Caremark employees, or institute corrective measures, thereby exposing Caremark to fines and liability.

. . .

According to defendants, if a settlement had not been reached in this action, the case would have been dismissed on two grounds. First, they contend that the complaints fail to allege particularized facts sufficient to excuse the demand requirement under Delaware Chancery Court Rule 23.1. Second, defendants assert that plaintiffs had failed to state a cause of action due to the fact that Caremark's charter eliminates directors' personal liability for money damages, to the extent permitted by law.

E.   Settlement Negotiations

In September, ... Caremark publicly announced that as of January 1, 1995, it would terminate all remaining financial relationships with physicians in its home infusion, hemophilia, and growth hormone lines of business. In addition, Caremark asserts that it extended its restrictive policies to all of its contractual relationships with physicians, rather than just those involving Medicare and Medicaid patients, and terminated its research grant program which had always involved some recipients who referred patients to Caremark.

Caremark began settlement negotiations with federal and state government entities in May 1995. In return for a guilty plea to a single count of mail fraud by the corporation, the payment of a criminal fine, the payment of substantial civil damages, and cooperation with further federal investigations on matters relating to the OIG investigation, the government entities agreed to negotiate a settlement that would permit Caremark to continue participating in Medicare and Medicaid programs. On June 15, 1995, the Board approved a settlement ("Government Settlement Agreement") with the DOJ, OIG, U.S. Veterans Administration, U.S. Federal Employee Health Benefits Program, federal Civilian Health and Medical Program of the Uniformed Services, and related state agencies in all fifty states and the District of Columbia. No senior officers or directors were charged with wrongdoing in the Government Settlement Agreement or in any of the prior indictments. In fact, as part of the sentencing in the Ohio action on June 19, 1995, the United States stipulated that no senior executive of Caremark participated in, condoned, or was willfully ignorant of wrongdoing in connection with the home infusion business practices. . . .

Settlement negotiations between the parties in this action commenced in May 1995 as well, based upon a letter proposal of the plaintiffs, dated May 16, 1995. These negotiations resulted in a memorandum of understanding ("MOU"), dated June 7, 1995, and the execution of the Stipulation and Agreement of Compromise and Settlement on June 28, 1995, which is the subject of this action.[16] The MOU, approved by the Board on

16. Plaintiffs' initial proposal had both a monetary component, requiring Caremark's director-officers to relinquish stock options, and a remedial component, requiring man-

June 15, 1995, required the Board to adopt several resolutions, discussed below, and to create a new compliance committee. The Compliance and Ethics Committee has been reporting to the Board in accord with its newly specified duties.

. . .

F.   The Proposed Settlement of this Litigation

In relevant part the terms upon which these claims asserted are proposed to be settled are as follows:

1.   That Caremark, undertakes that it and its employees, and agents not pay any form of compensation to a third party in exchange for the referral of a patient to a Caremark facility or service or the prescription of drugs marketed or distributed by Caremark for which reimbursement may be sought from Medicare, Medicaid, or a similar state reimbursement program;

2.   That Caremark, undertakes for itself and its employees, and agents not to pay to or split fees with physicians . . . in exchange for the referral of a patient to a Caremark facility or service or the prescription of drugs marketed or distributed by Caremark for which reimbursement may be sought from Medicare, Medicaid, or a similar state reimbursement program;

3.   That the full Board shall discuss all relevant material changes in government health care regulations and their effect on relationships with health care providers on a semi-annual basis;

4.   That Caremark's officers will remove all personnel from health care facilities or hospitals who have been placed in such facility for the purpose of providing remuneration in exchange for a patient referral for which reimbursement may be sought from Medicare, Medicaid, or a similar state reimbursement program;

5.   That every patient will receive written disclosure of any financial relationship between Caremark and the health care professional or provider who made the referral;

6.   That the Board will establish a Compliance and Ethics Committee of four directors, two of which will be non-management directors, to meet at least four times a year to effectuate these policies and monitor business segment compliance with the ARPL, and to report to the Board semi-annually concerning compliance by each business segment; and

7.   That corporate officers responsible for business segments shall serve as compliance officers who must report semi-annually to the Compliance and Ethics Committee and, with the assistance of outside

agement to adopt and implement several compliance related measures. The monetary   component was subsequently eliminated.

counsel, review existing contracts and get advanced approval of any new contract forms.

II.   LEGAL PRINCIPLES

A.   Principles Governing Settlements of Derivative Claims

As noted at the outset of this opinion, this Court is now required to exercise an informed judgment whether the proposed settlement is fair and reasonable in the light of all relevant factors.   .   .   . On an application of this kind, this Court attempts to protect the best interests of the corporation and its absent shareholders, all of whom will be barred from future litigation on these claims if the settlement is approved. The parties proposing the settlement bear the burden of persuading the court that it is in fact fair and reasonable.   .   .   .

B.   Directors' Duties To Monitor Corporate Operations

The complaint charges the director defendants with breach of their duty of attention or care in connection with the on-going operation of the corporation's business. The claim is that the directors allowed a situation to develop and continue which exposed the corporation to enormous legal liability and that in so doing they violated a duty to be active monitors of corporate performance.   .   .   .

1.   Potential liability for directorial decisions: Director liability for a breach of the duty to exercise appropriate attention may, in theory, arise in two distinct contexts. First, such liability may be said to follow from a board decision that results in a loss because that decision was ill advised or "negligent." Second, liability to the corporation for a loss may be said to arise from an unconsidered failure of the board to act in circumstances in which due attention would, arguably, have prevented the loss.   .   .   . The first class of cases will typically be subject to review under the director-protective business judgment rule, assuming the decision made was the product of a process that was either deliberately considered in good faith or was otherwise rational.   .   .   . What should be understood, but may not widely be understood by courts or commentators who are not often required to face such questions, is that compliance with a director's duty of care can never appropriately be judicially determined by reference to the content of the board decision that leads to a corporate loss, apart from consideration of the good faith or rationality of the process employed. That is, whether a judge or jury considering the matter after the fact, believes a decision substantively wrong, or degrees of wrong extending through "stupid" to "egregious" or "irrational," provides no ground for director liability, so long as the court determines that the process employed was either rational or employed in a good faith effort to advance corporate interests. To employ a different rule—one that permitted an "objective" evaluation of the decision—would expose directors to substantive second guessing by ill-equipped judges or juries, which would, in the long-run, be injurious to investor interests.[17] Thus, the business judgment rule is process oriented and informed by a deep respect for all good faith board decisions.

Indeed, one wonders on what moral basis might shareholders attack a good faith business decision of a director as "unreasonable" or "irrational." Where a director in fact exercises a good faith effort to be informed and to exercise appropriate judgment, he or she should be deemed to satisfy fully the duty of attention. If the shareholders thought themselves entitled to some other quality of judgment than such a director produces in the good faith exercise of the powers of office, then the shareholders should have elected other directors. . . .

2. *Liability for failure to monitor:* The second class of cases in which director liability for inattention is theoretically possible entail circumstances in which a loss eventuates not from a decision but from unconsidered inaction. Most of the decisions that a corporation, acting through its human agents, makes are, of course, not the subject of director attention. Legally, the board itself will be required only to authorize the most significant corporate acts or transactions: mergers, changes in capital structure, fundamental changes in business, appointment and compensation of the CEO, etc. As the facts of this case graphically demonstrate, ordinary business decisions that are made by officers and employees deeper in the interior of the organization can, however, vitally affect the welfare of the corporation and its ability to achieve its various strategic and financial goals. [Recent financial and organizational disasters at major corporations] raise the question, what is the board's responsibility with respect to the organization and monitoring of the enterprise to assure that the corporation functions within the law to achieve its purposes?

[In recent years] this question has been given special importance by an increasing tendency, especially under federal law, to employ the criminal law to assure corporate compliance with external legal requirements, including environmental, financial, employee and product safety as well as assorted other health and safety regulations. In 1991, pursuant to the Sentencing Reform Act of 1984, the United States Sentencing Commission adopted Organizational Sentencing Guidelines which impact importantly on the prospective effect these criminal sanctions might have on business corporations. The Guidelines set forth a uniform sentencing structure for

17. The vocabulary of negligence, while often employed, . . . is not well-suited to judicial review of board attentiveness, . . ., especially if one attempts to look to the substance of the decision as any evidence of possible "negligence." Where review of board functioning is involved, courts leave behind as a relevant point of reference the decisions of the hypothetical "reasonable person," who typically supplies the test for negligence liability. It is doubtful that we want business men and women to be encouraged to make decisions as hypothetical persons of ordinary judgment and prudence might. The corporate form gets its utility in large part from its ability to allow diversified investors to accept greater investment risk. If those in charge of the corporation are to be adjudged personally liable for losses on the basis of a substantive judgment based upon what persons of ordinary or average judgment and average risk assessment talent regard as "prudent," "sensible," or even "rational," such persons will have a strong incentive at the margin to authorize less risky investment projects.

organizations to be sentenced for violation of federal criminal statutes and provide for penalties that equal or often massively exceed those previously imposed on corporations. The Guidelines offer powerful incentives for corporations today to have in place compliance programs to detect violations of law, promptly to report violations to appropriate public officials when discovered, and to take prompt, voluntary remedial efforts.

In 1963, the Delaware Supreme Court in Graham v. Allis–Chalmers Mfg. Co.,[23] addressed the question of potential liability of board members for losses experienced by the corporation as a result of the corporation having violated the anti-trust laws of the United States. There was no claim in that case that the directors knew about the behavior of subordinate employees of the corporation that had resulted in the liability. Rather, as in this case, the claim asserted was that the directors ought to have known of it and if they had known they would have been under a duty to bring the corporation into compliance with the law and thus save the corporation from the loss. The Delaware Supreme Court concluded that, under the facts as they appeared, there was no basis to find that the directors had breached a duty to be informed of the ongoing operations of the firm. In notably colorful terms, the court stated that "absent cause for suspicion there is no duty upon the directors to install and operate a corporate system of espionage to ferret out wrongdoing which they have no reason to suspect exists." The Court found that there were no grounds for suspicion in that case and, thus, concluded that the directors were blamelessly unaware of the conduct leading to the corporate liability.

How does one generalize this holding today? Can it be said today that, absent some ground giving rise to suspicion of violation of law, corporate directors have no duty to assure that a corporate information gathering and reporting system exists which represents a good faith attempt to provide senior management and the Board with information respecting material acts, events or conditions within the corporation, including compliance with applicable statutes and regulations? I certainly do not believe so. I doubt that such a broad generalization of the *Graham* holding would have been accepted by the Supreme Court in 1963. The case can be more narrowly interpreted as standing for the proposition that, absent grounds to suspect deception, neither corporate boards nor senior officers can be charged with wrongdoing simply for assuming the integrity of employees and the honesty of their dealings on the company's behalf. . . .

A broader interpretation of Graham v. Allis Chalmers—that it means that a corporate board has no responsibility to assure that appropriate information and reporting systems are established by management—would not, in any event, be accepted by the Delaware Supreme Court in 1996, in my opinion. In stating the basis for this view, I start with the recognition that in recent years the Delaware Supreme Court has made clear—especially in its jurisprudence concerning takeovers, from Smith v. Van Gorkom through QVC v. Paramount Communications[26]—the seriousness

---

23. Del.Supr., 188 A.2d 125 (1963).

26. E.g., Smith v. Van Gorkom, Del. Supr., 488 A.2d 858 (1985); Paramount Com-

with which the corporation law views the role of the corporate board. Secondly, I note the elementary fact that relevant and timely information is an essential predicate for satisfaction of the board's supervisory and monitoring role under Section 141 of the Delaware General Corporation Law. Thirdly, I note the potential impact of the federal organizational sentencing guidelines on any business organization. Any rational person attempting in good faith to meet an organizational governance responsibility would be bound to take into account this development and the enhanced penalties and the opportunities for reduced sanctions that it offers.

.   .   .

Obviously the level of detail that is appropriate for [the requisite] information system is a question of business judgment. And obviously too, no rationally designed information and reporting system will remove the possibility that the corporation will violate laws or regulations, or that senior officers or directors may nevertheless sometimes be misled or otherwise fail reasonably to detect acts material to the corporation's compliance with the law. But it is important that the board exercise a good faith judgment that the corporation's information and reporting system is in concept and design adequate to assure the board that appropriate information will come to its attention in a timely manner as a matter of ordinary operations, so that it may satisfy its responsibility.

Thus, I am of the view that a director's obligation includes a duty to attempt in good faith to assure that a corporate information and reporting system, which the board concludes is adequate, exists, and that failure to do so under some circumstances may, in theory at least, render a director liable for losses caused by non-compliance with applicable legal standards.[27] I now turn to an analysis of the claims asserted with this concept of the directors duty of care, as a duty satisfied in part by assurance of adequate information flows to the board, in mind.

III.   ANALYSIS OF THIRD AMENDED COMPLAINT AND SETTLEMENT

A.   The Claims

On balance, after reviewing an extensive record in this case, including numerous documents and three depositions, I conclude that this settlement is fair and reasonable. In light of the fact that the Caremark Board already has a functioning committee charged with overseeing corporate compliance, the changes in corporate practice that are presented as consideration for the settlement do not impress one as very significant. Nonetheless, that consideration appears fully adequate to support dismissal of the derivative claims of director fault asserted, because those claims find no substantial

munications v. QVC Network, Del.Supr., 637 A.2d 34 (1993).

27. Any action seeking to recover for losses would logically entail a judicial determination of proximate cause, since, for reasons that I take to be obvious, it could never be assumed that an adequate information system would be a system that would prevent all losses.   .   .   .

evidentiary support in the record and quite likely were susceptible to a motion to dismiss in all events.

In order to show that the Caremark directors breached their duty of care by failing adequately to control Caremark's employees, plaintiffs would have to show either (1) that the directors knew or (2) should have known that violations of law were occurring and, in either event, (3) that the directors took no steps in a good faith effort to prevent or remedy that situation, and (4) that such failure proximately resulted in the losses complained of.   .   .   .

1.   Knowing violation of statute: Concerning the possibility that the Caremark directors knew of violations of law, none of the documents submitted for review, nor any of the deposition transcripts appear to provide evidence of it.   .   .   . [T]he Board appears to have been informed by experts that the company's practices while contestable, were lawful. There is no evidence that reliance on such reports was not reasonable.   .   .   .

2.   Failure to monitor: Since it does appears that the Board was to some extent unaware of the activities that led to liability, I turn to a consideration of the other potential avenue to director liability that the pleadings take: director inattention or "negligence." Generally where a claim of directorial liability for corporate loss is predicated upon ignorance of liability creating activities within the corporation, as in *Graham* or in this case, in my opinion only a sustained or systematic failure of the board to exercise oversight—such as an utter failure to attempt to assure a reasonable information and reporting system exits—will establish the lack of good faith that is a necessary condition to liability. Such a test of liability—lack of good faith as evidenced by sustained or systematic failure of a director to exercise reasonable oversight—is quite high. But, a demanding test of liability in the oversight context is probably beneficial to corporate shareholders as a class, as it is in the board decision context, since it makes board service by qualified persons more likely, while continuing to act as a stimulus to good faith performance of duty by such directors.

Here the record supplies essentially no evidence that the director defendants were guilty of a sustained failure to exercise their oversight function.   .   .   .

.   .   .

B.   The Consideration For Release of Claim

The proposed settlement provides very modest benefits. Under the settlement agreement, plaintiffs have been given express assurances that Caremark will have a more centralized, active supervisory system in the future.   .   .   . Nonetheless, given the weakness of the plaintiffs' claims the proposed settlement appears to be an adequate, reasonable, and beneficial outcome for all of the parties. Thus, the proposed settlement will be approved.

IV. ATTORNEYS' FEES

The various firms of lawyers involved for plaintiffs seek an award of $1,025,000 in attorneys' fees and reimbursable expenses. . . . I conclude that an award of a fee determined by reference to the time expended at normal hourly rates plus a premium of 15% of that amount to reflect the limited degree of real contingency in the undertaking, is fair. Thus I will award a fee of $816,000 plus $53,000 of expenses advanced by counsel.

ANALYSIS

1. Chancellor Allen states that, under the business judgment rule, directors are protected from liability if their "decision was the product of a process that was either deliberately considered in good faith or was otherwise rational," even if a judge or jury were to conclude that the decision was " 'stupid' " or " 'irrational'." How can a decision made by a rational process lead to an irrational result?

2. What is the relevance of the federal criminal law and its level of sanctions to the state-law duty of care that is the focus of this case?

3. Suppose a board of directors of a company like Caremark decides on the basis of a cost/benefit analysis to adopt a minimal compliance program and that the board recognizes there will be some significant probability of violation of law, with costly results, but that the probability of detection is low. If a violation is detected and the corporation is required to pay substantial penalties and damages, are the directors personally liable?

4. Chancellor Allen concludes that there was a "very low probability" that Caremark's directors would be found to have breached their fiduciary duties if the case had gone to trial. Why then did the defendants settle? Conversely, Chancellor Allen also concluded that the "proposed settlement provides very modest benefits." Why then did the plaintiffs settle?

5. The court awarded the plaintiffs' attorneys $869,000 in fees and expenses. Caremark's fees and expenses were probably at least as much. If you had been a Caremark shareholder would you have felt that you got your money's worth?

PROBLEMS

1. Suppose you are a member of the board of directors of a trucking company that operates tank trucks carrying bulk liquids between Florida and New York. In all the states along the route between Florida and New York except Pennsylvania, trucks are permitted a maximum weight of up to 60,000 pounds (including the equipment), but in Pennsylvania the maximum weight is 45,000 pounds. The penalty for violation of the maximum weight law is a fine of $200. Under Pennsylvania law it is plain that the fine is "penal"; it is not regarded as a type of toll or use tax. The risk of being caught and fined on any one trip is about 20 percent. The practice of

your corporation and, as far as you are aware, of all your competitors, is to ignore the 45,000 maximum weight law and treat the fines as a cost of doing business. The alternative is either to comply with the 45,000 pound limit along the entire route or to reduce the load at the border of Pennsylvania, carry the excess to the other border in another truck, and then load the excess back onto the through-route truck. The cost of either alternative would make it impossible to compete with other trucking firms and with individual truckers and with other forms of transportation without losing money. Moreover, compliance with the 45,000 limit would require carrying less than a full load and would increase safety hazards. You have just learned of these facts. What do you do?

2.   Suppose the facts are the same as in the preceding paragraph, but you also learn that it is often possible to avoid the $200 fine by paying a bribe of $50 to the state official at the weight station whenever a violation is discovered and that your drivers have been instructed to do that whenever possible. Bribery of a public official is a felony punishable by a fine and a jail sentence, but there has been virtually no enforcement. What do you do? (Assume that the corporation is privately held and thus is not subject to the accounting rules imposed by the securities laws.)

3.   Suppose the facts are the same as in the preceding paragraph except that time has passed and you and the other directors have ordered the CEO to do what is required to prevent the payment of bribes by the company's drivers. The CEO has complied and the result has been an increase in costs such that the company no longer can operate at a profit. The CEO proposes that the company sell all its tractors (the part of the rig that contains the engine and cab) and hire independent tractor owners to haul the company's trailers. What is your reaction?

SECTION 2. DUTY OF LOYALTY

A. DIRECTORS AND MANAGERS

Bayer v. Beran
49 N.Y.S.2d 2 (Sup.Ct.1944).

.   .   .

To encourage freedom of action on the part of directors, or to put it another way, to discourage interference with the exercise of their free and independent judgment, there has grown up what is known as the "business judgment rule."   .   .   .   "Questions of policy of management, expediency of contracts or action, adequacy of consideration, lawful appropriation of corporate funds to advance corporate interests, are left solely to their honest and unselfish decision, for their powers therein are without limitation and free from restraint, and the exercise of them for the common and general interests of the corporation may not be questioned, although the results show that what they did was unwise or inexpedient."   Pollitz v. Wabash R. Co., 207 N.Y. 113, 124, 100 N.E. 721, 724.   Indeed, although the concept of "responsibility" is firmly fixed in the law, it is only in a most unusual and extraordinary case that directors are held liable for negligence in the absence of fraud, or improper motive, or personal interest.

The "business judgment rule," however, yields to the rule of undivided loyalty.   This great rule of law is designed "to avoid the possibility of fraud and to avoid the temptation of self-interest."   Conway, J., in Matter of Ryan's Will, 291 N.Y. 376, 406, 52 N.E.2d 909, 923.   It is "designed to obliterate all divided loyalties which may creep into a fiduciary relation .   .   .   ."   Thatcher, J., in City Bank Farmers Trust Co. v. Cannon, 291 N.Y. 125, 132, 51 N.E.2d 674, 676.   "Included within its scope is every situation in which a trustee chooses to deal with another in such close relation with the trustee that possible advantage to such other person might influence, consciously or unconsciously, the judgment of the trustee .   .   .   ."   Lehman, Ch. J., in Albright v. Jefferson County National Bank, 292 N.Y. 31, 39, 53 N.E.2d 753, 756. The dealings of a director with the corporation for which he is the fiduciary are therefore viewed "with jealousy by the courts."   Globe Woolen Co. v. Utica Gas & Electric Co., 224 N.Y. 483, 121 N.E. 378, 380. Such personal transactions of directors with their corporations, such transactions as may tend to produce a conflict between self-interest and fiduciary obligation, are, when challenged, examined with the most scrupulous care, and if there is any evidence of improvidence or oppression, any indication of unfairness or undue advantage, the transactions will be voided.   .   .   .   "Their dealings with the corporation are subjected to rigorous scrutiny and where any of their contracts or engagements with the corporation are challenged the burden is

351

on the director not only to prove the good faith of the transaction but also to show its inherent fairness from the viewpoint of the corporation and those interested therein." Pepper v. Litton, 308 U.S. 295, 306, 60 S.Ct. 238, 245, 84 L.Ed. 281.

The . . . "advertising" cause of action charges the directors with negligence, waste and improvidence in embarking the corporation [Celanese Corporation of America] upon a radio advertising program beginning in 1942 and costing about $1,000,000 a year. It is further charged that they were negligent in selecting the type of program and in renewing the radio contract for 1943. More serious than these allegations is the charge that the directors were motivated by a noncorporate purpose in causing the radio program to be undertaken and in expending large sums of money therefor. It is claimed that this radio advertising was for the benefit of Miss Jean Tennyson, one of the singers on the program, who in private life is Mrs. Camille Dreyfus, the wife of the president of the company and one of its directors; that it was undertaken to "further, foster and subsidize her career"; to "furnish a vehicle" for her talents.

Eliminating for the moment the part played by Miss Tennyson in the radio advertising campaign, it is clear that the character of the advertising, the amount to be expended therefor, and the manner in which it should be used, are all matters of business judgment and rest peculiarly within the discretion of the board of directors. Under the authorities previously cited, it is not, generally speaking, the function of a court of equity to review these matters or even to consider them. Had the wife of the president of the company not been involved, the advertising cause of action could have been disposed of summarily. Her connection with the program, however, makes it necessary to go into the facts in some detail.

Before 1942 the company had not resorted to radio advertising. While it had never maintained a fixed advertising budget, the company had, through its advertising department, spent substantial sums of money for advertising purposes. In 1941, for example, the advertising expense was $683,000, as against net sales for that year of $62,277,000 and net profits (before taxes) of $13,972,000. The advertising was at all times directed towards the creation of a consumer preference which would compel or induce the various trade elements linking the corporation to the consumer to label the corporation's products so that the consumer would know he was buying the material he wanted. The company had always claimed that its products, which it had called or labeled "Celanese," were different from rayon, chemically and physically; that its products had qualities, special and unique, which made them superior to rayon. The company had never called or designated its products as rayon.

As far back as ten years ago, a radio program was considered, but it did not seem attractive. In 1937, the Federal Trade Commission promulgated a rule, the effect of which was to require all celanese products to be designated and labeled rayon. The name "Celanese" could no longer be used alone. The products had to be called or labeled "rayon" or "celanese rayon." This gave the directors much concern. As one of them expressed it, "When we were compelled to put our product under the same umbrella with rayon rather than being left outside as a separate product, a thermoplastic such as nylon is, we believed we were being treated in an unfair manner and that it was up to us, however, to do the best we could to circumvent the situation in which we found ourselves. . . . All manner of things were considered but there seemed only one thing we could do. We could either multiply our current advertising and our method of advertising in the same mediums we had been using, or we could go into radio."

The directors, in considering the matter informally, but not collectively as a board, decided towards the end of 1941 to resort to the radio and to have the company go on the air with a dignified program of fine music, the kind of program which they felt would be in keeping with what they believed to be the beauty and superior quality of their products. The radio program was not adopted on the spur of the moment or at the whim of the directors. They acted after studies reported to them, made by the advertising department, beginning in 1939. A radio consultant was employed to advise as to time and station. An advertising agency of national repute was engaged to take charge of the formulation and production of the program. It was decided to expend about $1,000,000 a year, but the commitments were to be subject to cancellation every thirteen weeks, so that the maximum obligation of the company would be not more than $250,000.

So far, there is nothing on which to base any claim of breach of fiduciary duty. Some care, diligence and prudence were exercised by these directors before they committed the company to the radio program. It was for the directors to determine whether they would resort to radio advertising; it was for them to conclude how much to spend; it was for them to decide the kind of program they would use. It would be an unwarranted act of interference for any court to attempt to substitute its judgment on these points for that of the directors, honestly arrived at. The expenditure was not reckless or unconscionable. Indeed, it bore a fair relationship to the total amount of net sales and to the earnings of the company. . . . That a program of classical and semiclassical music was selected, rather than a variety program, or a news commentator program, furnishes no ground for legal complaint. True, variety programs have a wider popular appeal than do musicals, but it would be a very sad thing if the former were the only kind of radio programs to be used. Some of the largest industrial concerns in the country have recognized this and have maintained fine musical programs on the radio for many years.

Now we have to take up an unfortunate incident, one which cannot be viewed with the complacency displayed by some of the directors of the company. This is not a closely held family corporation. The Doctors Dreyfus and their families own about 135,000 shares of common stock, the other directors about 10,000 shares out of a total outstanding issue of 1,376,500 shares. Some of these other directors were originally employed by Dr. Camille Dreyfus, the president of the company. His wife, to whom he has been married for about twelve years, is known professionally as Miss Jean Tennyson and is a singer of wide experience.

Dr. Dreyfus, as was natural, consulted his wife about the proposed radio program; he also asked the advertising agency, that had been retained, to confer with her about it. She suggested the names of the artists, all stars of the Metropolitan Opera Company, and the name of the conductor, prominent in his field. She also offered her own services as a paid artist. All of her suggestions as to personnel were adopted by the advertising agency. While the record shows Miss Tennyson to be a competent singer, there is nothing to indicate that she was indispensable or essential to the success of the program. She received $500 an evening. It would be far-fetched to suggest that the directors caused the company to incur large expenditures for radio advertising to enable the president's wife to make $24,000 in 1942 and $20,500 in 1943.

Of course it is not improper to appoint relatives of officers or directors to responsible positions in a company. But where a close relative of the chief executive officer of a corporation, and one of its dominant directors, takes a position closely associated with a new and expensive field of activity, the motives of the directors are likely to be questioned. The board would be placed in a position where selfish, personal interests might be in conflict with the duty it owed to the corporation. That being so, the entire transaction, if challenged in the courts, must be subjected to the most rigorous scrutiny to determine whether the action of the directors was intended or calculated "to subserve some outside purpose, regardless of the consequences to the company, and in a manner inconsistent with its interests."

After such careful scrutiny I have concluded that, up to the present, there has been no breach of fiduciary duty on the part of the directors. The president undoubtedly knew that his wife might be one of the paid artists on the program. The other directors did not know this until they had approved the campaign of radio advertising and the general type of radio program. The evidence fails to show that the program was designed to foster or subsidize "the career of Miss Tennyson as an artist" or to "furnish a vehicle for her talents." That her participation in the program may have enhanced her prestige as a singer is no ground for subjecting the directors to liability, as long as the advertising served a legitimate and a useful corporate purpose and the company received the full benefit thereof.

The musical quality of "Celanese Hour" has not been challenged, nor does the record contain anything reflecting on Miss Tennyson's competence as an artist. There is nothing in the testimony to show that some other soprano would have enhanced the artistic quality of the program or its advertising appeal. There is no suggestion that the present program is inefficient or that its cost is disproportionate to what a program of that character reasonably entails. Miss Tennyson's contract with the advertising agency retained by the directors was on a standard form, negotiated through her professional agent. Her compensation, as well as that of the other artists, was in conformity with that paid for comparable work. She received less than any of the other artists on the program. Although she appeared with greater regularity than any other singer, she received no undue prominence, no special build-up. Indeed, all of the artists were subordinated to the advertisement of the company and of its products. The company was featured. It appears also that the popularity of the program has increased since it was inaugurated.

It is clear, therefore, that the directors have not been guilty of any breach of fiduciary duty, in embarking upon the program of radio advertising and in renewing it.   .   .   .

It is urged that the expenditures were illegal because the radio advertising program was not taken up at any formal meeting of the board of directors, and no resolution approving it was adopted by the board or by the executive committee. The general rule is that directors acting separately and not collectively as a board cannot bind the corporation. There are two reasons for this: first, that collective procedure is necessary in order that action may be deliberately taken after an opportunity for discussion and an interchange of views; and second, that directors are the agents of the stockholders and are given by law no power to act except as a board.   .   .   .   Liability may not, however, be imposed on directors because they failed to approve the radio program by resolution at a board meeting.

It is desirable to follow the regular procedure, prescribed by law, which is something more than what has, at times, thoughtlessly been termed red tape. Long experience has demonstrated the necessity for doing this in order to safeguard the interests of all concerned, particularly where, as here, the company has over 1,375,000 shares outstanding in the hands of the public, of which about 10% are held by the officers and directors.

But the failure to observe the formal requirements is by no means fatal.   .   .   .   The directorate of this company is composed largely of its executive officers. It is a close, working directorate. Its members are in daily association with one another and their full time is devoted to the business of the company with which they have been connected for many years. In this respect it differs from the boards of many corporations of comparable size, where the directorate is made up of men of varied interests who meet only at stated, and somewhat infrequent, intervals.

The same informal practice followed in this transaction had been the customary procedure of the directors in acting on corporate projects of equal and greater magnitude. All of the members of the executive committee were available for daily consultation and they discussed and approved the plan for radio advertising. While a greater degree of formality should undoubtedly be exercised in the future, it is only just and proper to point out that these directors, with all their loose procedure, have done very well for the corporation. Under their administration the company has thrived and prospered.   .   .   .

The expenditures for radio advertising, although made without resolution at a formal meeting of the board, were approved and authorized by the members individually, and may in no sense be considered to have been ultra vires. The resolution adopted by the board on July 6, 1943, with all of the directors present, except two who were resident in England, while expressly ratifying only the renewal of the broadcasting contract, may be deemed a ratification of all prior action taken in connection with the radio advertising. When this resolution was adopted, the Celanese Hour had been on the air to the knowledge of all the directors for eighteen months. Moreover, acceptance and retention of the benefits of the radio advertising, with full knowledge thereof, was as complete a ratification as would have resulted from any formal all-inclusive resolution. . . .

On the entire case, the directors acted in the free exercise of their honest business judgment and their conduct in the transactions challenged did not constitute negligence, waste or improvidence. The complaint is accordingly dismissed on the merits.

Lewis v. S.L. & E., Inc.

629 F.2d 764 (2d Cir.1980).

I

For many years Leon Lewis, Sr., the father of Donald and the defendant directors, was the principal shareholder of SLE and LGT. LGT, formed in 1933, operated a tire dealership in Rochester, New York. SLE, formed in 1943, owned the land and complex of buildings at 260 East Avenue in Rochester. This property was SLE's only significant asset. Prior to 1956 LGT occupied SLE's premises without benefit of a lease; the rent paid was initially $200 per month, and had increased over the years to $800 per month by 1956, when additional parcels were added. On February 28, 1956, SLE granted LGT a 10–year lease on the newly expanded property ("the Property"), for a rent of $1200 per month, or $14,400 per year. Under the terms of the lease, SLE was responsible for payment of real estate taxes on the Property, while all other current expenses were to be borne by the tenant, LGT.

In 1962, Leon Lewis, Sr., transferred his SLE stock, 90 shares in all, to his six children (defendants Richard, Alan and Leon, Jr., plaintiff Donald, and two daughters, Margaret and Carol), giving 15 shares to each. At that time Richard, Alan and Leon, Jr., were already shareholders, officers and directors of LGT. Contemporaneously with their receipt of SLE stock, all six of the children entered into a "shareholders' agreement" with LGT, under which each child who was not a shareholder of LGT on June 1, 1972 would be required to sell his or her SLE shares to LGT, within 30 days of that date, at a price equal to the book value of the SLE stock as of June 1, 1972.

LGT's lease on the SLE property expired on February 28, 1966. At that time the directors of SLE were Richard, Alan, Leon, Jr., Leon, Sr., and Henry Etsberger; these five were also the directors of LGT. In 1966 Alan owned 44% of LGT, Richard owned 30%, Leon, Jr., owned 19%, and Leon,

Sr., owned 7%. From 1967 to 1972 Richard owned 61% of LGT and Leon, Jr., owned the remaining 39%. When the lease expired in 1966, no new lease was entered into. LGT nonetheless continued to occupy the property and to pay SLE at the old rate, $14,400 per year. According to the defendants' testimony at trial, there was never any thought or discussion among the SLE directors of entering into a new lease or of increasing the rent. Richard testified: "We never gave consideration to a new lease." From all that appears, the defendant directors viewed SLE as existing purely for the benefit of LGT. Richard testified, for example, that although real estate taxes rose sharply during the period 1966–1971, from approximately $7,800 to more than $11,000, to be paid by SLE out of its constant $14,400 rental income, raising the rent was never mentioned. When this suit was commenced there had not been a formal meeting of either the shareholders or the directors of SLE since 1962. Richard, Alan and Leon, Jr., had largely ignored SLE's separate corporate existence and disregarded the fact that SLE had shareholders who were not shareholders of LGT and who therefore could not profit from actions that used SLE solely for the benefit of LGT.

Neither Donald nor his sisters ever owned LGT stock. As the June 1972 date approached for the required sale of their SLE stock to LGT, Donald apparently came to believe that SLE's book value was lower than it should have been. He sought SLE financial information from Richard, who had been president of SLE since 1967. Richard refused to provide information. Donald therefore refused to sell his SLE shares in 1972, and commenced this shareholders' derivative action in the district court in August 1973, basing jurisdiction on diversity of citizenship. The sole claim raised in the complaint was that the defendant directors had wasted the assets of SLE by "grossly undercharging" LGT for the latter's occupancy and use of the Property. . . .

There ensued an eight-day bench trial, at which plaintiff sought to prove, by the testimony of several expert witnesses, that the fair rental value of the Property was greater than the $14,400 per year that SLE had been paid by LGT. . . . The district court subsequently filed lengthy and detailed findings of fact and conclusions of law. . . . On this basis, the court held that Donald had failed to establish the rental value of the Property during the period at issue, and that defendants were therefore entitled to judgment on the derivative claims. Implicit in the district court's ruling, granting judgment for defendants upon plaintiff's failure to prove waste, was a determination that plaintiff bore the burden of proof on that issue. . . .

II

Turning first to the question of burden of proof, we conclude that the district court erred in placing upon plaintiff the burden of proving waste. Because the directors of SLE were also officers, directors and/or shareholders of LGT, the burden was on the defendant directors to demonstrate that the transactions between SLE and LGT were fair and reasonable. . . .

Under normal circumstances the directors of a corporation may determine, in the exercise of their business judgment, what contracts the corporation will enter into and what consideration is adequate, without review of the merits of their decisions by the courts. The business judgment rule places a heavy burden on shareholders who would attack corporate transactions. . . . But the business judgment rule presupposes that the directors have no conflict of interest. When a shareholder attacks a transaction in which the directors have an interest other than as directors of the corporation, the directors may not escape review of the merits of the transaction. At common law such a transaction was voidable unless shown by its proponent to be fair, and reasonable to the corporation. BCL § 713, in both its current and its prior versions, carries forward this common law principle, and provides special rules for scrutiny of a transaction between the corporation and an entity in which its directors are directors or officers or have a substantial financial interest.

The current version of § 713,[12] which became effective on September 1, 1971, and governs at least so much of the dealing between SLE and LGT as occurred after that date, expressly provides that a contract between a corporation and an entity in which its directors are interested may be set aside unless the proponent of the contract "shall establish affirmatively that the contract or transaction was fair and reasonable as to the corpora-

---

12. BCL § 713 (McKinney Supp.1979) provides in pertinent part:

(a) No contract or other transaction between a corporation and one or more of its directors, or between a corporation and any other corporation, firm, association or other entity in which one or more of its directors are directors or officers, or have a substantial financial interest, shall be either void or voidable for this reason alone or by reason alone that such director or directors are present at the meeting of the board, or of a committee thereof, which approves such contract or transaction, or that his or their votes are counted for such purpose:

(1) If the material facts as to such director's interest in such contract or transaction and as to any such common directorship, officership or financial interest are disclosed in good faith or known to the board or committee, and the board or committee approves such contract or transaction by a vote sufficient for such purpose without counting the vote of such interested director or,

(2) If the material facts as to such director's interest in such contract or transaction and as to any such common

directorship, officership or financial interest are disclosed in good faith or known to the shareholders entitled to vote thereon, and such contract or transaction is approved by vote of such shareholders.

(b) If such good faith disclosure of the material facts as to the director's interest in the contract or transaction and as to any such common directorship, officership or financial interest is made to the directors or shareholders, or known to the board or committee or shareholders approving such contract or transaction, as provided in paragraph (a), the contract or transaction may not be avoided by the corporation for the reasons set forth in paragraph (a). If there was no such disclosure or knowledge, or if the vote of such interested director was necessary for the approval of such contract or transaction at a meeting of the board or committee at which it was approved, the corporation may avoid the contract or transaction unless the party or parties thereto shall establish affirmatively that the contract or transaction was fair and reasonable as to the corporation at the time it was approved by the board, a committee or the shareholders.

tion at the time it was approved by the board. . . ." § 713(b). Thus when the transaction is challenged in a derivative action against the interested directors, they have the burden of proving that the transaction was fair and reasonable to the corporation. . . .

The same was true under the predecessor to § 713(b), former § 713(a)(3), which was in effect prior to September 1, 1971. . . .

During the entire period 1966–1972, Richard, Alan and Leon, Jr., were directors of both SLE and LGT; there were no SLE directors who were not also directors of LGT. Richard, Alan and Leon, Jr., were all shareholders of LGT in 1966, and from 1967 to 1972 Richard and Leon, Jr., were the sole shareholders of LGT. Under BCL § 713, therefore, Richard, Alan and Leon, Jr., had the burden of proving that $14,400 was a fair and reasonable annual rent for the SLE property for the period February 28, 1966 through June 1, 1972.

Our review of the record convinces us that defendants failed to carry their burden. . . .

Quite clearly Richard, Alan and Leon, Jr., had made no effort to determine contemporaneously what rental would be fair during the years 1966–1972. Their view was that the rent should simply cover expenses and that SLE existed for the benefit of LGT.

[At trial, the parties introduced extensive evidence on the fair rental value of the property. The court reviewed the evidence, and held:]

We conclude, therefore, that defendants failed to prove that the rental paid by LGT to SLE for the years 1966–1972 was fair and reasonable. Thus, Donald is not required to sell his SLE shares to LGT without such upward adjustment in the June 1, 1972, book value of SLE as may be necessary to reflect the amount by which the fair rental value of the Property exceeded $14,400 in any of the years 1966–1972. . . .

NOTES ON DUTY OF LOYALTY

1. Late-nineteenth-century courts generally held that a corporation could freely void any contract between it and one of its directors or officers. By the early twentieth century, courts hesitated to let firms void their contracts so easily. As a result, if a disinterested majority of directors had ratified a contract and if the complaining party could not prove it unfair, the courts generally held the contract valid. *Bayer* takes the rule one step further: because the contract is fair, it is valid even though disinterested directors have not formally ratified it.[3]

2. The *Bayer* court did not refer to a statute, but in most modern disputes courts will turn to the corporations code to determine when a firm

3. See generally Harold Marsh, Jr., Are   Corporate Morality, 22 Bus.Law. 35 (1966). Directors Trustees? Conflict of Interest and can void a contract between it and one of its directors or officers. *Lewis* gives an example of one such statute; in *Wheelabrator* we consider such statutes in more detail.

3. In Cinerama, Inc. v. Technicolor, Inc., summarized supra page 317, the Delaware Supreme Court held, inter alia:

> The Court of Chancery concluded that a material interest of "one or more directors less than a majority of those voting" would rebut the application of the business judgment rule if the plaintiff proved that "the interested director controls or dominates the board as a whole or [that] the interested director fail[ed] to disclose his interest in the transaction to the board and a reasonable board member would have regarded the existence of the material interest as a significant fact in the evaluation of the proposed transaction." We hold that the Court of Chancery's conclusion is correct, as a matter of law.

QUESTION ON COMPENSATION

Few issues are as inherently fraught with a conflict of interest as salaries. Given the potential for litigation over conflicts of interest, how should managers and directors go about setting appropriate pay scales for themselves?

PROBLEM

Susan Alexander is a "singer" who is trying to break into the big-time opera circuit. A few years ago, she took up with wealthy Charlie Kane, and has now married him. He would like to promote her career. Kane is CEO and majority shareholder in the Chicago *Inquirer*. The shares of the *Inquirer* are worth a total of $100 million.

1. Suppose that the *Inquirer*'s board of directors votes to make a $20 million donation to start a Chicago City Opera Co. (CCO). The Chicago community is eager to have this opera company, and the company thus stands to receive much goodwill in the area. If Alexander does not sing with the company, is there a problem?

2. Suppose that, out of appreciation for Kane, the music director of the CCO offers to star Alexander as the lead soprano in a new production of the opera "Rosebud." Is there a problem? Suppose that, when offered the lead, Alexander responds: "Thanks, you're so sweet. But Charlie is so rich, you know, and we really don't need more money. I'd love to sing the lead, but how would it be if I did it for free?"

3. Suppose that Kane owns 100% of the stock of the *Inquirer*. Do your answers to the questions above change?

4. Suppose that Alexander is a genuine star, and the CCO offers her the "Rosebud" lead after holding an audition at which the judges unanimously voted her the best lyric soprano.

B.   CORPORATE OPPORTUNITIES

Broz v. Cellular Information Systems, Inc.

673 A.2d 148 (Del.1996).

. . .

I.   THE CONTENTIONS OF THE PARTIES
AND THE DECISION BELOW

Robert F. Broz ("Broz") is the President and sole stockholder of RFB Cellular, Inc. ("RFBC"), a Delaware corporation engaged in the business of providing cellular telephone service in the Midwestern United States. At the time of the conduct at issue in this appeal, Broz was also a member of the board of directors of plaintiff below . . ., Cellular Information Systems, Inc. ("CIS"). CIS is a publicly held Delaware corporation and a competitor of RFBC.

The conduct before the Court involves the purchase by Broz of a cellular telephone service license for the benefit of RFBC. The license in question, known as the Michigan–2 Rural Service Area Cellular License ("Michigan–2"), is issued by the Federal Communications Commission ("FCC") and entitles its holder to provide cellular telephone service to a portion of northern Michigan. . . .

II.   FACTS

. . . RFBC owns and operates an FCC license area, known as the Michigan–4 Rural Service Area Cellular License ("Michigan–4"). The license entitles RFBC to provide cellular telephone service to a portion of rural Michigan. Although Broz' efforts have been devoted primarily to the business operations of RFBC, he also served as an outside director of CIS at the time of the events at issue in this case. . . .

In April of 1994, Mackinac Cellular Corp. ("Mackinac") sought to divest itself of Michigan–2, the license area immediately adjacent to Michigan–4. To this end, Mackinac contacted Daniels & Associates ("Daniels") and arranged for the brokerage firm to seek potential purchasers for Michigan–2. In compiling a list of prospects, Daniels included RFBC as a likely candidate. In May of 1994, David Rhodes, a representative of Daniels, contacted Broz and broached the subject of RFBC's possible acquisition of Michigan–2. . . .

Michigan–2 was not, however, offered to CIS. Apparently, Daniels did not consider CIS to be a viable purchaser for Michigan–2 in light of CIS' recent financial difficulties. The record shows that, at the time Michigan–2 was offered to Broz, CIS had recently emerged from lengthy and contentious [insolvency reorganization] . . . . .

During the period from early 1992 until the time of CIS' emergence from bankruptcy in 1994, CIS divested itself of some fifteen separate cellular license systems. CIS contracted to sell four additional license areas on May 27, 1994, leaving CIS with only five remaining license areas, all of which were outside of the Midwest.

On June 13, 1994, following a meeting of the CIS board, Broz spoke with CIS' Chief Executive Officer, Richard Treibick ("Treibick"), concerning his interest in acquiring Michigan–2. Treibick communicated to Broz that CIS was not interested in Michigan–2.[16] Treibick further stated that he had been made aware of the Michigan–2 opportunity prior to the conversation with Broz, and that any offer to acquire Michigan–2 was rejected. . . . [I]n August of 1994, Broz contacted another CIS director, Peter Schiff ("Schiff"), to discuss the possible acquisition of Michigan–2 by RFBC. Schiff, like Treibick, indicated that CIS had neither the wherewithal nor the inclination to purchase Michigan–2. In late September of 1994, Broz also contacted Stanley Bloch ("Bloch"), a director and counsel for CIS, to request that Bloch represent RFBC in its dealings with Mackinac. Bloch agreed to represent RFBC, and, like Schiff and Treibick, expressed his belief that CIS was not at all interested in the transaction. Ultimately, all the CIS directors testified at trial that, had Broz inquired at that time, they each would have expressed the opinion that CIS was not interested in Michigan–2.[17]

On June 28, 1994, following various overtures from PriCellular concerning an acquisition of CIS, six CIS directors entered into agreements with PriCellular to sell their shares in CIS at a price of $2.00 per share. These agreements were contingent upon, inter alia, the consummation of a PriCellular tender offer* for all CIS shares at the same price. . . .

. . . Financing difficulties ultimately caused PriCellular to delay the closing date of the tender offer from September 16, 1994 until October 14, 1994 and then again until November 9, 1994.

On August 6, September 6 and September 21, 1994, Broz submitted written offers to Mackinac for the purchase of Michigan–2. During this time period, PriCellular also began negotiations with Mackinac to arrange an option for the purchase of Michigan–2. PriCellular's interest in Michigan–2 was fully disclosed to CIS' chief executive, Treibick, who did not express any interest in Michigan–2, and was actually incredulous that PriCellular would want to acquire the license. . . .

---

16. In fact, during a deposition given in March of 1995, Treibick testified that he didn't "know who frankly was hawking [the Michigan–2 license] . . . at the time. . . . [W]e said forget it. It was not something we would have bought if they offered it to us for nothing."

17. We assume arguendo that informal contacts and individual opinions of board members are not a substitute for a formal process of presenting an opportunity to a board of directors. Nevertheless, in our view such a formal process was not necessary under the circumstances of this case in order for Broz to avoid liability. These contacts with individual board members do, however, tend to show that Broz was not acting surreptitiously or in bad faith.

* [Eds.—A "tender offer" is an offer to buy shares of stock from shareholders, who are invited to tender their shares to the offeror for purchase at a specified price within some specified period of time. Often the completion of the transaction is made contingent on the offeror receiving some specified number of shares, sufficient, for example, to give it control of the target corporation.]

In late September of 1994, PriCellular reached agreement with Mackinac on an option to purchase Michigan–2. The exercise price of the option agreement was set at $6.7 million, with the option remaining in force until December 15, 1994.   .   .   . The agreement further provided that Mackinac was free to sell Michigan–2 to any party who was willing to exceed the exercise price of the Mackinac–PriCellular option contract by at least $500,000. On November 14, 1994, Broz agreed to pay Mackinac $7.2 million for the Michigan–2 license, thereby meeting the terms of the option agreement. An asset purchase agreement was thereafter executed by Mackinac and RFBC.

Nine days later, on November 23, 1994, PriCellular completed its financing and closed its tender offer for CIS. Prior to that point, PriCellular owned no equity interest in CIS.   .   .   .

IV. APPLICATION OF THE CORPORATE OPPORTUNITY DOCTRINE

The doctrine of corporate opportunity represents but one species of the broad fiduciary duties assumed by a corporate director or officer. A corporate fiduciary agrees to place the interests of the corporation before his or her own in appropriate circumstances.   .   .   . The classic statement of the doctrine is derived from the venerable case of Guth v. Loft, Inc., [5 A.2d 503 (Del.1939)]. In *Guth*, this Court held that:

> if there is presented to a corporate officer or director a business opportunity which the corporation is financially able to undertake, is, from its nature, in the line of the corporation's business and is of practical advantage to it, is one in which the corporation has an interest or a reasonable expectancy, and, by embracing the opportunity, the self-interest of the officer or director will be brought into conflict with that of the corporation, the law will not permit him to seize the opportunity for himself.

Guth, 5 A.2d at 510–11.

.   .   .

We note at the outset that Broz became aware of the Michigan–2 opportunity in his individual and not his corporate capacity.   .   .   . In fact, it is clear from the record that Mackinac did not consider CIS a viable candidate for the acquisition of Michigan–2. Accordingly, Mackinac did not offer the property to CIS. In this factual posture, many of the fundamental concerns undergirding the law of corporate opportunity are not present (e.g., misappropriation of the corporation's proprietary information). The burden imposed upon Broz to show adherence to his fiduciary duties to CIS is thus lessened to some extent.   .   .   . Nevertheless, this fact is not dispositive.   .   .   .

We turn now to an analysis of the factors relied on by the trial court. First, we find that CIS was not financially capable of exploiting the Michigan–2 opportunity. Although the Court of Chancery concluded otherwise, we hold that this finding was not supported by the evidence. The record shows that CIS was in a precarious financial position at the time Mackinac presented the Michigan–2 opportunity to Broz.   .   .   .

.   .   .

[Moreover], while it may be said with some certainty that the Michigan–2 opportunity was within CIS' line of business, it is not equally clear that CIS had a cognizable interest or expectancy in the license.   .   .   . Despite the fact that the nature of the Michigan–2 opportunity was historically close to the core operations of CIS, changes were in process. At the time the opportunity was presented, CIS was actively engaged in the process of divesting its cellular license holdings. CIS' articulated business plan did not involve any new acquisitions. Further, as indicated by the testimony of the entire CIS board, the Michigan–2 license would not have been of interest to CIS even absent CIS' financial difficulties and CIS' then current desire to liquidate its cellular license holdings. Thus, CIS had no interest or expectancy in the Michigan–2 opportunity.   .   .   .

Finally, the corporate opportunity doctrine is implicated only in cases where the fiduciary's seizure of an opportunity results in a conflict between the fiduciary's duties to the corporation and the self-interest of the director as actualized by the exploitation of the opportunity. In the instant case, Broz' interest in acquiring and profiting from Michigan–2 created no duties that were inimical to his obligations to CIS.   .   .   . Broz   .   .   . comported himself in a manner that was wholly in accord with his obligations to CIS. Broz took care not to usurp any opportunity which CIS was willing and able to pursue. Broz sought only to compete with an outside entity, PriCellular, for acquisition of an opportunity which both sought to possess. Broz was not obligated to refrain from competition with PriCellular.   .   .   .

In concluding that Broz had usurped a corporate opportunity, the Court of Chancery placed great emphasis on the fact that Broz had not formally presented the matter to the CIS board.   .   .   . In so holding, the trial court erroneously grafted a new requirement onto the law of corporate opportunity, viz., the requirement of formal presentation under circumstances where the corporation does not have an interest, expectancy or financial ability.

The teaching of *Guth* and its progeny is that the director or officer must analyze the situation ex ante to determine whether the opportunity is one rightfully belonging to the corporation. If the director or officer believes, based on one of the factors articulated above, that the corporation is not entitled to the opportunity, then he may take it for himself. Of course, presenting the opportunity to the board creates a kind of "safe harbor" for the director, which removes the specter of a post hoc judicial determination that the director or officer has improperly usurped a corporate opportunity.   .   .   . It is not the law of Delaware that presentation to the board is a necessary prerequisite to a finding that a corporate opportunity has not been usurped.

.   .   .

In concluding that Broz usurped an opportunity properly belonging to CIS, the Court of Chancery held that "[f]or practical business reasons CIS' interests with respect to the Mackinac transaction came to merge with those of PriCellular, even before the closing of its tender offer for CIS stock." Based on this fact, the trial court concluded that Broz was required to consider PriCellular's prospective, post-acquisition plans for CIS in determining whether to forgo the opportunity or seize it for himself. Had Broz done this, the Court of Chancery determined that he would have concluded that CIS was entitled to the opportunity by virtue of the alignment of its interests with those of PriCellular.

We disagree. Broz was under no duty to consider . . . the contingent and uncertain plans of PriCellular in reaching his determination of how to proceed.

. . .

Broz, as an active participant in the cellular telephone industry, was entitled to proceed in his own economic interest in the absence of any countervailing duty. The right of a director or officer to engage in business affairs outside of his or her fiduciary capacity would be illusory if these individuals were required to consider every potential, future occurrence in determining whether a particular business strategy would implicate fiduciary duty concerns. . . .

V. CONCLUSION

. . . [W]e hold that Broz did not breach his fiduciary duties to CIS. . . .

ANALYSIS

1. Suppose that PriCellular had had no financial problems and could easily have invested enough money in CIS to buy Michigan–2. What would the result have been?

2. Suppose that RFBC had had shareholders other than Broz and that CIS had a potential interest in Michigan–2, unknown to Rhodes (the broker for the seller), and the ability to finance a purchase. What should Broz have done? Was he obligated only to inform CIS or, rather, to allow CIS to proceed without competition from RFBC?

3. Suppose Broz had been an officer (e.g., vice president for development) of CIS, in addition to his board membership at CIS and his RFBC positions. Assuming all the other facts remain the same, what result? Suppose we change one other fact as well: Rhodes, in bringing the opportunity to Broz, did not distinguish between Broz's role in CIS and his role in RFBC? What result?

4. Why did PriCellular not simply outbid Broz and buy Michigan–2 for itself?

5. Was the court fair in treating CIS's interest in Michigan–2 as separate from that of PriCellular?

6. The court suggests that a rule that would have required Broz to formally present the opportunity to the CIS board would generate uncertainty and economic inefficiency. How does the court know this to be true? Do you agree?

Energy Resources Corp., Inc. v. Porter

14 Mass.App.Ct. 296, 438 N.E.2d 391 (1982).

■ KASS, JUSTICE.

From 1976 to 1979, James H. Porter was vice-president and chief scientist of Energy Resources Corporation, Inc. (ERCO). On October 5, 1979, he resigned and organized Energy & Environmental Engineering, Inc. (EEE).   .   .   .

ERCO is a science and engineering company, located in Cambridge, which provides products and services in energy and environmental fields. Among its areas of investigation was staged fluidized bed combustion of coal. By that process, coal mixed with limestone could be burned so as to capture sulfur as a solid, rather than allowing it to escape into the atmosphere as a gas. To the end of developing a commercially efficient coal-fired furnace which harnessed that process, ERCO operated a fluidized bed combustor pilot plant and a full-scale fluid bed combustor test facility.

Porter had come to ERCO from the Massachusetts Institute of Technology, from which he held a doctoral degree and where he had been an associate professor in the department of chemical engineering. Fluidized bed combustion was a subject to which Porter had given attention at M.I.T. and about which he had written as early as 1963. At ERCO, research and development concerning application of the fluidized bed combustion process was under Porter's general direction. As to royalties earned by ERCO from his inventions, Porter, under his employment agreement, was to receive 18% in addition to his annual salary (which was $52,000 in 1979).

In December, 1977, Porter went to Washington, D.C., to deliver a paper on fluidized bed combustion at a fifth annual meeting on that subject sponsored by the United States Environmental Protection Agency and the Department of Energy (DOE). While in Washington Porter looked up two colleagues at Howard University, Professors Cannon and Jackson, with whom he had been earlier acquainted. Cannon is chairman of the department of chemical engineering at Howard and Jackson is director of its fossil fuel laboratory.

This encounter led in due course to a joint proposal to DOE by Howard and ERCO for a development grant involving staged fluidized bed combustion of coal. Jackson had told Porter that DOE would be favorably disposed to a proposal from a "minority institution." Howard, traditionally, has a black student body, and Cannon and Jackson are black. So is Porter. Howard was to be the primary applicant and ERCO would be the subcontractor. ERCO's participation was approved by other executives of ERCO. . . .

In early May, 1979, during the course of a ride from Washington National Airport to DOE, Jackson advised Porter of a change of heart about working with ERCO. Jackson had become apprehensive that ERCO would claim the entire enterprise as its idea and that because "we are just little black people at a black university everybody was going to believe them." Moreover, Jackson said, he didn't want to be a part of something that might be seen as "blacks serving as sort of fronts for white firms getting minority money." Finally, he thought that in the long run more money would flow from DOE if there were a minority subcontractor in the picture. Porter attempted to persuade Jackson to continue to work with ERCO.

During the conversation at DOE which followed, Jackson broached the subject of dealing with a subcontractor other than ERCO and was told by a DOE official that the key man was Porter, whether he was at ERCO or elsewhere. Cannon and Jackson came up to Cambridge a week later to see Porter at M.I.T. and suggested that if he were to form his own company, they would be pleased to substitute it for ERCO in the proposal to DOE. Porter agreed to do so. Cannon and Jackson deleted references to ERCO and substituted EEE, a corporation to be formed by Porter. Thereafter, although he continued to work at ERCO, Porter cut himself off from the Howard submission to DOE. "I knew I was in a ticklish position, sought advice of counsel and decided it best I just not do anything on that proposal."

About three weeks later, Richard H. Rosen, the president of ERCO, Robert S. Davis, an executive vice-president, and Porter met for a routine review of pending ERCO projects. At that meeting Rosen asked Porter, "How about the Howard proposal?" Porter responded, "We're not going to get that." Rosen and Davis made no further inquiry and went on to the next item of business. Davis asked Porter about the Howard proposal on a later occasion and, once again, was told, without further elaboration, that ERCO wasn't going to get a subcontract from Howard.

Toward the end of September or the beginning of October, 1979, DOE awarded a grant to Howard and on or about October 5, 1979, Porter resigned his offices at ERCO on one day's notice. He told Davis and Rosen that his reason for leaving was to organize a corporation which would work in the area of computerized cars. Rosen, still unaware of Porter's participation in the Howard project, hired Porter as an independent consultant to ERCO for a period of sixty days.

1. *The corporate opportunity.* None of the parties debates that exploitation of the fluidized bed combustion process was squarely within ERCO's corporate activity and that, without more, an officer of ERCO had a fiduciary duty not to divert that opportunity for his own benefit. . . . Indeed, Porter used his time as an employee of ERCO and the time of other employees of ERCO, as well as certain graphics, in preparing a draft of the submission to DOE which ultimately reeled in a grant. . . .

Porter's defense is that the staged fluidized bed combustion project with Howard ceased being a corporate opportunity for ERCO when Jackson refused to deal with ERCO. When a corporation is unable to avail itself of an opportunity, its employee, officer or director is free to exploit it. . . . It was a defense which the trial judge thought convincing: "[N]o amount of persuasion," he wrote, "could alter Dr. Jackson's resolve that the subcontractor be a minority concern." Porter was not to be asked for "performance of fiduciary duty even to the point of futility." The difficulty with the judge's reasoning is that the unalterability of Jackson's resolve can by no means be certain so long as Porter, by keeping Jackson's position and his reasons for it a secret, never afforded ERCO a chance to test it. Had Porter told ERCO about Howard University's desire (as manifested by Jackson) to deal with a subcontractor controlled by persons who were black, the matter might have taken a variety of turns. Other officers of ERCO might have persuaded Jackson and Cannon—or others at Howard— that the status of Porter with ERCO was such that their unease about ERCO was not warranted. It might have been possible to organize a corporation in which Porter had a majority position and ERCO had a minority position. These are but two of many possibilities.

For the reason that the firmness of a refusal to deal cannot be adequately tested by the corporate executive alone, it has not been favored as a defense unless the refusal has first been disclosed to the corporation. Without full disclosure it is too difficult to verify the unwillingness to deal and too easy for the executive to induce the unwillingness. . . .

Although the defense of a refusal to deal has not been squarely confronted in Massachusetts cases, similar defenses of corporate inability to exploit an opportunity have had a cool reception. In Durfee v. Durfee & Canning, Inc., [323 Mass. 187, 200–202, 80 N.E.2d 522 (1948)], the credit weakness of the corporation did not permit Canning, who was a director and principal officer, to turn to his own account the purchase of gasoline which would have been advantageous to the corporation. Production Mach. Co. v. Howe, 327 Mass. 372, 375–378, 99 N.E.2d 32 (1951), required disclosure of the availability of a line of business that, although new to the corporation, was within its manufacturing capacity. "Breach of the duty [to protect the interests of the corporation] could be found although no corruption, dishonesty, or bad faith was involved." Id. at 378, 99 N.E.2d 32. In Cain v. Cain, 3 Mass.App. 467, 476–477, 334 N.E.2d 650 (1975), we required the defendant to inform the corporation of which he was a director and treasurer that the loss of certain business was imminent.

. . . We conclude that before a person invokes refusal to deal as a reason for diverting a corporate opportunity he must unambiguously disclose that refusal to the corporation to which he owes a duty, together with a fair statement of the reasons for that refusal. Porter's statement, "We're not going to get that," fell far short of that standard. Indeed, Porter went beyond nondisclosure. He acted secretively and even on the occasion of his departure from ERCO masked his true reason for leaving. . . .

The judgment is reversed and the case is remanded to the Superior Court for assessment of damages based on a computation of EEE's net profits from the DOE grant. The court should disallow as deductions from EEE's gross profits fees and expenses incident to the DOE project which ERCO would not have had to incur, and distributions to Porter in excess of $52,000 per year.

. . .

■ BROWN, JUSTICE (concurring).

I continue to be amazed at the role often played by counsel in circumstances such as here presented. It appears that the advice given was either unwise or of questionable competence, or both, especially if one has in mind that the client has stated on the record that "I knew I was in a ticklish position, [and] sought advice of counsel." When lawyers have the opportunity to keep their clients at least at the moral level of the market place, they have a public duty to avail themselves of it. After a great deal of court time and massive legal fees, this court has now stated what should have been obvious at the outset: a fiduciary's silence is equivalent to a stranger's lie.

NOTE ON THE FINANCIAL CAPACITY DEFENSE

Much of the litigation over corporate opportunities has involved cases where the director or officer who used the opportunity argued that the corporation lacked the money to exploit it effectively. The argument has surface appeal—why, after all, should an executive bother presenting a business opportunity to his or her corporation if it lacks the funds to make use of it? Despite this logic, courts generally reject the argument unless the executive has explicitly offered the opportunity to the corporation. At root, the argument is simply too convenient. The defendant who exploited the corporate opportunity is often a senior executive at the firm, and thus is often someone who would have been involved in raising any funds the firm needed. Hence, if a court allows a generous lack-of-funds defense, it creates an incentive for executives to fail to use their best efforts to help the firm raise the necessary funds.

NOTE ON ALI § 5.05

The American Law Institute (ALI) took the following approach in its Principles of Corporate Governance: Analysis and Recommendations (1994):*

§ 5.05. Taking of Corporate Opportunities by Directors or Senior Executives.

(a) General Rule. A director or senior executive may not take advantage of a corporate opportunity unless:

(1) The director or senior executive first offers the corporate opportunity to the corporation and makes disclosure concerning the conflict of interest and the corporate opportunity.

(2) The corporate opportunity is rejected by the corporation; and

(3) Either:

(A) The rejection of the opportunity is fair to the corporation;

(B) The opportunity is rejected in advance, following such disclosure, by disinterested directors, or, in the case of a senior executive who is not a director, by a disinterested superior, in a manner that satisfies the standards of the business judgment rule; or

(C) The rejection is authorized in advance or ratified, following such disclosure, by disinterested shareholders, and the rejection is not equivalent to a waste of corporate assets.

(b) Definition of a Corporate Opportunity. For purposes of this Section, a corporate opportunity means:

(1) Any opportunity to engage in a business activity of which a director or senior executive becomes aware, either:

(A) In connection with the performance of functions as a director or senior executive, or under circumstances that should reasonably lead the director or senior executive to believe that the person offering the opportunity expects it to be offered to the corporation; or

(B) Through the use of corporation information or property, if the resulting opportunity is one that the director or senior executive should reasonably be expected to believe would be of interest to the corporation; or

(2) Any opportunity to engage in a business activity of which a senior executive becomes aware and knows is closely related to a business in which the corporation is engaged or expects to engage.

(c) Burden of Proof. A party who challenges the taking of a corporate opportunity has the burden of proof, except that if such party establishes that the requirements of Subsection (a)(3)(B) or (C) are not met, the director or the senior executive has the burden of proving that the rejection and the taking of the opportunity were fair to the corporation.

(d) Ratification of Defective Disclosure. A good faith but defective disclosure of the facts concerning the corporate opportunity may be cured if at any time (but no later than a reasonable time after suit is filed challenging the taking of the corporate opportunity) the original rejection of the corporate opportunity is ratified, following the required disclosure, by the board, the shareholders, or the corporate decisionmaker who initially approved the rejection of the corporate opportunity, or such decisionmaker's successor.

(e) Special Rule Concerning Delayed Offering of Corporate Opportunities. Relief based solely on failure to first offer an opportunity to the corporation under Subsection (a)(1) is not available if: (1) such failure resulted from a good faith belief that the business activity did not constitute a corporate opportunity, and (2) not later than a reasonable time after suit is filed challenging the taking of the corporate opportunity, the corporate opportunity is to the extent possible offered to the corporation and rejected in a manner that satisfies the standards of Subsection (a).

PROBLEMS

George is Vice–President for Marketing of Zapco Enterprises, Inc., a manufacturer of video game software used in arcades and home systems (such as the Ninetendo system). One of George's duties is to test competitor models. One day George leaves work and travels to a near-by video arcade to test a new game put out by Zapco's principal competitor. While visiting the arcade, George meets two young computer software engineers who have developed a new word processing program for personal computers. After further meetings with the engineers, George decides the program has promise and offers to help market it. The two engineers set up a new corporation called "Wordco, Inc.," and hire George as a marketing consultant. George receives 10 percent of Wordco's common stock and also becomes entitled to a commission of $10 for every copy of the program sold by Wordco. Zapco sues George for violating the corporate opportunity doctrine.

1. Assuming Zapco is incorporated in Delaware, has George violated the corporate opportunity doctrine?

2. Assuming Zapco is incorporated in a state following ALI § 5.05, has George violated the corporate opportunity doctrine?

3. What if the engineers had approached George at Zapco's booth at a computer trade fair?

4. Would it be relevant to the outcome in either Delaware or under the ALI that the two engineers refused to work with Zapco, because they refused to work with a mere game company?

5. Assume that after meeting with the engineers, but before signing the contract with Wordco, George approached Zapco's Chief Executive Officer and told him about this project. The CEO said Zapco had no interest in the project and no objection to George working for Wordco as long as it did not interfere with his Zapco duties. Result in Delaware? Result under ALI § 5.05? Would the result change if George had been a director of Zapco, as well as an officer?

6. Suppose the transaction was a corporate opportunity. In perfect good faith, George takes it for himself. He then mentions to the firm's lawyer that he (George) is working on this word-processing project on the side. The lawyer sees that this is a corporate opportunity, which should

have been offered to the company. Based on the lawyer's advice, George tells the board of directors and asks them to ratify his taking the opportunity. The board does so. If the ALI rules apply, is George insulated from liability?

C.   DOMINANT SHAREHOLDERS

Sinclair Oil Corp. v. Levien

280 A.2d 717 (Del.1971).

This is an appeal by the defendant, Sinclair Oil Corporation (hereafter Sinclair), from an order of the Court of Chancery, 261 A.2d 911, in a derivative action requiring Sinclair to account for damages sustained by its subsidiary, Sinclair Venezuelan Oil Company (hereafter Sinven), organized by Sinclair for the purpose of operating in Venezuela, as a result of dividends paid by Sinven, the denial to Sinven of industrial development, and a breach of contract between Sinclair's wholly owned subsidiary, Sinclair International Oil Company, and Sinven.

Sinclair, operating primarily as a holding company, is in the business of exploring for oil and of producing and marketing crude oil and oil products.   At all times relevant to this litigation, it owned about 97% of Sinven's stock.   The plaintiff owns about 3000 of 120,000 publicly held shares of Sinven.   Sinven, incorporated in 1922, has been engaged in petroleum operations primarily in Venezuela and since 1959 has operated exclusively in Venezuela.

Sinclair nominates all members of Sinven's board of directors.   The Chancellor found as a fact that the directors were not independent of Sinclair.   Almost without exception, they were officers, directors, or employees of corporations in the Sinclair complex.   By reason of Sinclair's domination, it is clear that Sinclair owed Sinven a fiduciary duty.   . . .

The Chancellor held that because of Sinclair's fiduciary duty and its control over Sinven, its relationship with Sinven must meet the test of intrinsic fairness.   The standard of intrinsic fairness involves both a high degree of fairness and a shift in the burden of proof.   Under this standard the burden is on Sinclair to prove, subject to careful judicial scrutiny, that its transactions with Sinven were objectively fair.   . . .

Sinclair argues that the transactions between it and Sinven should be tested, not by the test of intrinsic fairness with the accompanying shift of the burden of proof, but by the business judgment rule under which a court will not interfere with the judgment of a board of directors unless there is a showing of gross and palpable overreaching.   . . .

A board of directors enjoys a presumption of sound business judgment, and its decisions will not be disturbed if they can be attributed to any rational business purpose.   A court under such circumstances will not substitute its own notions of what is or is not sound business judgment.

We think, however, that Sinclair's argument in this respect is misconceived. When the situation involves a parent and a subsidiary, with the parent controlling the transaction and fixing the terms, the test of intrinsic fairness, with its resulting shifting of the burden of proof, is applied. . . . The basic situation for the application of the rule is the one in which the parent has received a benefit to the exclusion and at the expense of the subsidiary. . . .

A parent does indeed owe a fiduciary duty to its subsidiary when there are parent-subsidiary dealings. However, this alone will not evoke the intrinsic fairness standard. This standard will be applied only when the fiduciary duty is accompanied by self-dealing—the situation when a parent is on both sides of a transaction with its subsidiary. Self-dealing occurs when the parent, by virtue of its domination of the subsidiary, causes the subsidiary to act in such a way that the parent receives something from the subsidiary to the exclusion of, and detriment to, the minority stockholders of the subsidiary.

We turn now to the facts. The plaintiff argues that, from 1960 through 1966, Sinclair caused Sinven to pay out such excessive dividends that the industrial development of Sinven was effectively prevented, and it became in reality a corporation in dissolution.

From 1960 through 1966, Sinven paid out $108,000,000 in dividends ($38,000,000 in excess of Sinven's earnings during the same period). The Chancellor held that Sinclair caused these dividends to be paid during a period when it had a need for large amounts of cash. Although the dividends paid exceeded earnings, the plaintiff concedes that the payments were made in compliance with 8 Del.C. § 170, authorizing payment of dividends out of surplus or net profits. However, the plaintiff attacks these dividends on the ground that they resulted from an improper motive— Sinclair's need for cash. The Chancellor, applying the intrinsic fairness standard, held that Sinclair did not sustain its burden of proving that these dividends were intrinsically fair to the minority stockholders of Sinven. . . .

We do not accept the argument that the intrinsic fairness test can never be applied to a dividend declaration by a dominated board, although a dividend declaration by a dominated board will not inevitably demand the application of the intrinsic fairness standard. . . .

If such a dividend is in essence self-dealing by the parent, then the intrinsic fairness standard is the proper standard. For example, suppose a parent dominates a subsidiary and its board of directors. The subsidiary has outstanding two classes of stock, X and Y. Class X is owned by the parent and Class Y is owned by minority stockholders of the subsidiary. If the subsidiary, at the direction of the parent, declares a dividend on its Class X stock only, this might well be self-dealing by the parent. It would be receiving something from the subsidiary to the exclusion of and detrimental to its minority stockholders. This self-dealing, coupled with the parent's fiduciary duty, would make intrinsic fairness the proper standard by which to evaluate the dividend payments.

Consequently it must be determined whether the dividend payments by Sinven were, in essence, self-dealing by Sinclair. The dividends resulted in great sums of money being transferred from Sinven to Sinclair. However, a proportionate share of this money was received by the minority shareholders of Sinven. Sinclair received nothing from Sinven to the exclusion of its minority stockholders. As such, these dividends were not self-dealing. We hold therefore that the Chancellor erred in applying the intrinsic fairness test as to these dividend payments. The business judgment standard should have been applied.

We conclude that the facts demonstrate that the dividend payments complied with the business judgment standard and with 8 Del.C. § 170. The motives for causing the declaration of dividends are immaterial unless the plaintiff can show that the dividend payments resulted from improper motives and amounted to waste. The plaintiff contends only that the dividend payments drained Sinven of cash to such an extent that it was prevented from expanding.

The plaintiff proved no business opportunities which came to Sinven independently and which Sinclair either took to itself or denied to Sinven. As a matter of fact, with two minor exceptions which resulted in losses, all of Sinven's operations have been conducted in Venezuela, and Sinclair had a policy of exploiting its oil properties located in different countries by subsidiaries located in the particular countries.

From 1960 to 1966 Sinclair purchased or developed oil fields in Alaska, Canada, Paraguay, and other places around the world. The plaintiff contends that these were all opportunities which could have been taken by Sinven.   .   .   .

However, the plaintiff could point to no opportunities which came to Sinven. Therefore, Sinclair usurped no business opportunity belonging to Sinven. Since Sinclair received nothing from Sinven to the exclusion of and detrimental to Sinven's minority stockholders, there was no self-dealing. Therefore, business judgment is the proper standard by which to evaluate Sinclair's expansion policies.

Since there is no proof of self-dealing on the part of Sinclair, it follows that the expansion policy of Sinclair and the methods used to achieve the desired result must, as far as Sinclair's treatment of Sinven is concerned, be tested by the standards of the business judgment rule. Accordingly, Sinclair's decision, absent fraud or gross overreaching, to achieve expansion through the medium of its subsidiaries, other than Sinven, must be upheld.

Even if Sinclair was wrong in developing these opportunities as it did, the question arises, with which subsidiaries should these opportunities have been shared? No evidence indicates a unique need or ability of Sinven to develop these opportunities. The decision of which subsidiaries would be used to implement Sinclair's expansion policy was one of business judgment with which a court will not interfere absent a showing of gross and palpable overreaching.   .   .   .   No such showing has been made here.

Next, Sinclair argues that the Chancellor committed error when he held it liable to Sinven for breach of contract.

In 1961 Sinclair created Sinclair International Oil Company (hereafter International), a wholly owned subsidiary used for the purpose of coordinating all of Sinclair's foreign operations. All crude purchases by Sinclair were made thereafter through International.

On September 28, 1961, Sinclair caused Sinven to contract with International whereby Sinven agreed to sell all of its crude oil and refined products to International at specified prices. The contract provided for minimum and maximum quantities and prices. The plaintiff contends that Sinclair caused this contract to be breached in two respects. Although the contract called for payment on receipt, International's payments lagged as much as 30 days after receipt. Also, the contract required International to purchase at least a fixed minimum amount of crude and refined products from Sinven. International did not comply with this requirement.

Clearly, Sinclair's act of contracting with its dominated subsidiary was self-dealing. Under the contract Sinclair received the products produced by Sinven, and of course the minority shareholders of Sinven were not able to share in the receipt of these products. If the contract was breached, then Sinclair received these products to the detriment of Sinven's minority shareholders. We agree with the Chancellor's finding that the contract was breached by Sinclair, both as to the time of payments and the amounts purchased.

Although a parent need not bind itself by a contract with its dominated subsidiary, Sinclair chose to operate in this manner. As Sinclair has received the benefits of this contract, so must it comply with the contractual duties.

Under the intrinsic fairness standard, Sinclair must prove that its causing Sinven not to enforce the contract was intrinsically fair to the minority shareholders of Sinven. Sinclair has failed to meet this burden. Late payments were clearly breaches for which Sinven should have sought and received adequate damages. As to the quantities purchased, Sinclair argues that it purchased all the products produced by Sinven. This, however, does not satisfy the standard of intrinsic fairness. Sinclair has failed to prove that Sinven could not possibly have produced or in some way have obtained the contract minimums. As such, Sinclair must account on this claim. . . .

We will therefore reverse that part of the Chancellor's order that requires Sinclair to account to Sinven for damages sustained as a result of dividends paid between 1960 and 1966, and by reason of the denial to Sinven of expansion during that period. We will affirm the remaining portion of that order and remand the cause for further proceedings.

ANALYSIS

1. Perhaps the most well known statement of corporate fiduciary duties appears in the Supreme Court bankruptcy case of Pepper v. Litton, 308 U.S. 295, 306 (1939):

> A director is a fiduciary. . . . So is a dominant or controlling stockholder or group of stockholders. . . . Their powers are in trust. . . . Their dealings with the corporation are subjected to rigorous scrutiny and where any of their contracts or engagements with the corporation is challenged the burden is on the director or shareholder not only to prove the good faith of the transaction but also to show its inherent fairness from the viewpoint of the corporation and those interested therein.

2. Was the shareholder duty-of-loyalty analysis necessary to decide *Sinclair.* How might one have resolved the case using only the law regarding the duty of loyalty of directors?

3. When corporation P owns a large percentage of the stock of corporation S, P almost inevitably dominates S. However hard P tries to insulate S from P's influence, S managers will know that P can decide whether to fire them or promote them. Given that fact, how might P try to deal with the risk that the minority shareholders in S may file fiduciary duty suits against it? We shall revisit this issue in our discussion of mergers and acquisitions in Chapter 6, Section 1.

Zahn v. Transamerica Corporation

162 F.2d 36 (3d Cir.1947).

Zahn, a holder of Class A common stock of Axton–Fisher Tobacco Company, a corporation of Kentucky, sued Transamerica Corporation, a Delaware company, on his own behalf and on behalf of all stockholders similarly situated, in the District Court of the United States for the District of Delaware. (His complaint as amended asserts that Transamerica caused Axton–Fisher to redeem its Class A stock at $80.80 per share on July 1, 1943, instead of permitting the Class A stockholders to participate in the assets on the liquidation of their company in June, 1944.) He alleges in brief that if the Class A stockholders had been allowed to participate in the assets on liquidation of Axton–Fisher and had received their respective shares of the assets, he and the other Class A stockholders would have received $240 per share instead of $80.80. . . .

Prior to April 30, 1943, Axton–Fisher had authorized and outstanding three classes of stock, designated respectively as preferred stock, Class A stock and Class B stock. Each share of preferred stock had a par value of $100 and was entitled to cumulative dividends at the rate of $6 per annum and possessed a liquidation value of $105 plus accrued dividends. The Class A stock, specifically described in the charter as a "common" stock, was entitled to an annual cumulative dividend of $3.20 per share. The Class B stock was next entitled to receive an annual dividend of $1.60 per share. If further funds were made available by action of the board of directors by way of dividends, the Class A stock and the Class B stock were entitled to share equally therein. Upon liquidation of the company and the payment of the sums required by the preferred stock, the Class A stock was entitled to share with the Class B stock in the distribution of the remaining assets, but the Class A stock was entitled to receive twice as much per share as the Class B stock.[2]

Each share of Class A stock was convertible at the option of the shareholder into one share of Class B stock. All or any of the shares of Class A stock were callable by the corporation at any quarterly dividend date upon sixty days' notice to the shareholders, at $60 per share with accrued dividends.[3] The voting rights were vested in the Class B stock but if there were four successive defaults in the payment of quarterly dividends, the class or classes of stock as to which such defaults occurred gained voting rights equal share for share with the Class B stock. By reason of this provision the Class A stock had possessed equal voting rights with the Class B stock since on or about January 1, 1937.

On or about May 16, 1941, Transamerica purchased 80,160 shares of Axton–Fisher's Class B common stock. This was about 71.5% of the outstanding Class B stock and about 46.7% of the total voting stocks of Axton–Fisher. By August 15, 1942, Transamerica owned 5,332 shares of Class A stock and 82,610 shares of Class B stock. By March 31, 1943, the amount of Class A stock of Axton–Fisher owned by Transamerica had grown to 30,168 shares or about 66⅔% of the total amount of this stock outstanding, and the amount of Class B stock owned by Transamerica had increased to 90,768 shares or about 80% of the total outstanding. . . .

---

2. The charter provides as follows:

   "In the event of the dissolution, liquidation, merger or consolidation of the corporation, or sale of substantially all its assets, whether voluntary or involuntary, there shall be paid to the holders of the preferred stock then outstanding $105 per share, together with all unpaid accrued dividends thereon, before any sum shall be paid to or any assets distributed among the holders of the Class A common stock and/or the holders of the Class B common stock. After such payment to the holders of the preferred stock, and all unpaid accrued dividends on the Class A common stock shall have been paid, then all remaining assets and funds of the corporation shall be divided among and paid to the holders of the Class A common stock and to the holders of the Class B common stock in the ratio of 2 to 1; that is to say, there shall be paid upon each share of Class A common stock twice the amount paid upon each

share of Class B common stock, in any such event."

3. The charter provides as follows:

   "The whole or any part of the Class A common stock of the corporation, at the option of the Board of Directors, may be redeemed on any quarterly dividend payment date by paying therefor in cash Sixty dollars ($60.00) per share and all unpaid and accrued dividends thereon at the date fixed for such redemption, upon sending by mail to the registered holders of the Class A common stock at least sixty (60) days' notice of the exercise of such option. If at any time the Board of Directors shall determine to redeem less than the whole amount of Class A common stock then outstanding, the particular stock to be so redeemed shall be determined in such manner as the Board of Directors shall prescribe; provided, however, that no holder of Class A common stock shall be preferred over any other holder of such stock."

Since May 16, 1941, Transamerica had control of and had dominated the management, directorate, financial policies, business and affairs of Axton–Fisher. Since the date last stated Transamerica had elected a majority of the board of directors of Axton–Fisher. These individuals are in large part officers or agents of Transamerica.

In the fall of 1942 and in the spring of 1943 Axton–Fisher possessed as its principal asset leaf tobacco which had cost it about $6,361,981. This asset was carried on Axton–Fisher's books in that amount. The value of leaf tobacco had risen sharply and, to quote the words of the complaint, "unbeknown to the public holders of . . . Class A common stock of Axton–Fisher, but known to Transamerica, the market value of . . . [the] tobacco had, in March and April of 1943, attained the huge sum of about $20,000,000."

The complaint then alleges the gist of the plaintiff's grievance, viz., that Transamerica, knowing of the great value of the tobacco which Axton–Fisher possessed, conceived a plan to appropriate the value of the tobacco to itself by redeeming the Class A stock at the price of $60 a share plus accrued dividends, the redemption being made to appear as if "incident to the continuance of the business of Axton–Fisher as a going concern," and thereafter, the redemption of the Class A stock being completed, to liquidate Axton–Fisher; that this would result, after the disbursal of the sum required to be paid to the preferred stock, in Transamerica gaining for itself most of the value of the warehouse tobacco. The complaint further alleges that in pursuit of this plan Transamerica, by a resolution of the Board of Directors of Axton–Fisher on April 30, 1943, called the Class A stock at $60 and, selling a large part of the tobacco to Phillip–Morris Company, Ltd., Inc., together with substantially all of the other assets of Axton–Fisher, thereafter liquidated Axton–Fisher, paid off the preferred stock and pocketed the balance of the proceeds of the sale. Warehouse receipts representing the remainder of the tobacco were distributed to the Class B stockholders.

Assuming as we must that the allegations of the complaint are true, it will be observed that agents or representatives of Transamerica constituted Axton–Fisher's board of directors at the times of the happening of the events complained of, and that Transamerica was Axton–Fisher's principal and controlling stockholder at such times. . . .

. . .

The circumstances of the case at bar are *sui generis* and we can find no Kentucky decision squarely in point. In our opinion, however, the law of Kentucky imposes upon the directors of a corporation or upon those who are in charge of its affairs by virtue of majority stock ownership or otherwise the same fiduciary relationship in respect to the corporation and to its stockholders as is imposed generally by the laws of Kentucky's sister States or which was imposed by federal law prior to Erie R. Co. v. Tompkins, 304 U.S. 64.

The tenor of the federal decisions in respect to the general fiduciary duty of those in control of a corporation is unmistakable. The Supreme Court in Southern Pacific Co. v. Bogert, 250 U.S. 483, 487, 488, said: ["The rule of corporation law and of equity invoked is well settled and has been often applied. The majority has the right to control; but when it does so, it occupies a fiduciary relation toward the minority, as much so as the corporation itself or its officers and directors." .] . .

It is appropriate to emphasize at this point that the right to call the Class A stock for redemption was confided by the charter of Axton–Fisher to the directors and not to the stockholders of that corporation. We must also emphasize . . . that there is a radical difference when a stockholder is voting strictly as a stockholder and when voting as a director; that when voting as a stockholder he may have the legal right to vote with a view of his own benefits and to represent himself only; but that when he votes as a director he represents all the stockholders in the capacity of a trustee for them and cannot use his office as a director for his personal benefit at the expense of the stockholders.

Two theories are presented on one of which the case at bar must be decided: One, vigorously asserted by Transamerica and based on its interpretation of the decision in the Taylor case, is that the board of directors of Axton–Fisher, whether or not dominated by Transamerica, the principal Class B stockholder, at any time and for any purpose, might call the Class A stock for redemption; the other, asserted with equal vigor by Zahn, is that the board of directors of Axton–Fisher as fiduciaries were not entitled to favor Transamerica, the Class B stockholder, by employing the redemption provisions of the charter for its benefit.

We must of course treat the decision of the Court of Appeals of Kentucky [in another case arising from the same transactions] as evidence of what is the law of Kentucky. The Court took the position on that record that the directors at any time might call the Class A stock for redemption and that the redemption provision of the charter was written as much for the benefit of the Class B stock as for the Class A stock. It is argued by Transamerica very persuasively that what the Court of Appeals of Kentucky held was that when the Class A stock received its allocation of $60 a share plus accrued dividends it received its full due and that the directors had the right at any time to eliminate Class A stock from the corporate setup for the benefit of the Class B stock. It does not appear from the opinion of the Court of Appeals of Kentucky whether or not the subsequent liquidation of Axton–Fisher was brought to the attention of the Court. But it is clear from the pleading that the subsequent liquidation was not an issue in the case. . . . We think that it is the settled law of Kentucky that directors may not declare or withhold the declaration of dividends for the purpose of personal profit or, by analogy, take any corporate action for such a purpose.

The difficulty in accepting Transamerica's contentions in the case at bar is that the directors of Axton–Fisher, if the allegations of the complaint be accepted as true, were the instruments of Transamerica, were directors voting in favor of their special interest, that of Transamerica, could not and did not exercise an independent judgment in calling the Class A stock, but made the call for the purpose of profiting their true principal, Transamerica.   In short a puppet-puppeteer relationship existed between the directors of Axton–Fisher and Transamerica.

The act of the board of directors in calling the Class A stock, an act which could have been legally consummated by a disinterested board of directors, was here effected at the direction of the principal Class B stockholder in order to profit it.   Such a call is voidable in equity at the instance of a stockholder injured thereby.   It must be pointed out that under the allegations of the complaint there was no reason for the redemption of the Class A stock to be followed by the liquidation of Axton–Fisher except to enable the Class B stock to profit at the expense of the Class A stock.   As has been hereinbefore stated the function of the call was confided to the board of directors by the charter and was not vested by the charter in the stockholders of any class.   It was the intention of the the framers of Axton–Fisher's charter to require the board of directors to act disinterestedly if that body called the Class A stock, and to make the call with a due regard for its fiduciary obligations.   If the allegations of the complaint be proved, it follows that the directors of Axton–Fisher, the instruments of Transamerica, have been derelict in that duty.   Liability which flows from the dereliction must be imposed upon Transamerica which, under the allegations of the complaint, constituted the board of Axton–Fisher and controlled it.

.   .   .

.   .   .   In our opinion, if the allegations of the complaint be proved, Zahn may maintain his cause of action to recover from Transamerica the value of the stock retained by him as that shall be represented by its aliquot share of the proceeds of Axton–Fisher on dissolution. .   .   .

The judgment will be reversed.

AFTERMATH

The case was returned to the district court for a determination of the amount of damages.   The district court ruling, on *Zahn* and related cases, was reviewed by the court of appeals in Speed v. Transamerica Corporation, 235 F.2d 369 (3d Cir.1956), with the following result:

In the Zahn and Friedman actions the district court found that Transamerica had exercised its position as controlling stockholder to cause the board of directors of Axton–Fisher to call the Class A stock for redemption and that although Transamerica at that time knew that the board was doing so on the assumption that it was for the purpose of improving the capital structure of the company as a going concern, the real purpose of Transamerica in causing the call to be made was by liquidation, merger, consolidation or sale of Axton–Fisher's assets to gain for itself the appreciation in the value of those assets. Accordingly the district court held Transamerica accountable to the Class A stockholders, both those who had redeemed their stock pursuant to the call and those who had not done so. . . . The court found that a disinterested board of directors of Axton–Fisher would undoubtedly have exercised its powers to call the Class A stock before liquidation, disclosing the intention to liquidate together with full information as to the appreciated value of Axton–Fisher's tobacco inventory, and that the Class A stockholders would thereupon have exercised their privilege to convert their stock, share for share, into Class B stock and would thus have participated equally with the Class B stockholders in the proceeds of the liquidation. Applying this rule in the Friedman and Zahn cases, after deducting the sum of $80.80 per share received by the Class A stockholders or set aside for them on the redemption call of April 30, 1943, the court found those stockholders entitled to $21.02 per share. . . .

As we have indicated, the district court concluded that Transamerica was liable both in tort for fraud and deceit and because of its violation of Rule X–10B–5 of the Securities and Exchange Commission. These conclusions were based upon its finding of Transamerica's deceptive concealment of the great appreciation in value of Axton–Fisher's tobacco inventory and of its secret intention to capture that appreciation for itself to the exclusion of the public stockholders. . . .

The Court of Appeals of Kentucky has held that the Axton–Fisher Class A stock, although designated as a common stock was in the nature of a junior preferred stock, and that the provision of the charter for the redemption of the Class A stock was a continuing option allowed to the holders of the Class B common stock which the board of directors could exercise in their favor.[6] This construction of the Axton–Fisher charter by the highest court of the state of its incorporation was, of course, binding on the district court. We agree with the district court that the provisions of the Axton–Fisher charter with respect to liquidation must be read realistically with the provisions for redemption of the Class A stock and its conversion into Class B stock. When so read it becomes apparent that a disinterested board of directors discharging its responsibility to the Class B stockholders in case of liquidation would call the Class A stock for redemption at $60 per share if it appeared that the distribution in liquidation to that stock would exceed that figure on a two-to-one basis. Since the board would have the right to do this and the Class B stockholders would be entitled to such action, the failure to do so would be an arbitrary act which would confer a windfall to which they were not entitled under the charter upon the Class A stockholders at the direct expense of the

---

6. Taylor v. Axton–Fisher Tobacco Co., 1943, 295 Ky. 226, 229–231, 173 S.W.2d 377, 379–380, 148 A.L.R. 834, 837–838.

holders of the Class B stock. The district court was therefore quite right in determining that the damages to be awarded to the Class A stockholders should be measured by what they would have received if they had converted their shares into Class B stock prior to the liquidation.   .   .   .

ANALYSIS

1.   What purpose was served by having the two classes of stock that were the focus of attention in this case? In the situation that gave rise to the case, the Class A shareholders should have converted their A shares to B shares, and would have done so if they had had full information. What, then, is the function of the provision in the corporate charter for redemption of the Class A shares at $60 per share? What about the provision for a 2:1 division of assets, in favor of the Class A shares, in the event of liquidation?

2.   What is the relevance, if any, of the *Zahn* court's discussion of the duty of controlling shareholders to minority shareholders?

D.   RATIFICATION

Fliegler v. Lawrence

361 A.2d 218 (Del. 1976).

In this shareholder derivative action brought on behalf of Agau Mines, Inc., a Delaware corporation, (Agau) against its officers and directors and United States Antimony Corporation, a Montana corporation (USAC), we are asked to decide whether the individual defendants, in their capacity as directors and officers of both corporations, wrongfully usurped a corporate opportunity belonging to Agau, and whether all defendants wrongfully profited by causing Agau to exercise an option to purchase that opportunity.   .   .   .

I

In November, 1969, defendant, John C. Lawrence (then president of Agau, a publicly held corporation engaged in a dual-phased gold and silver exploratory venture) in his individual capacity, acquired certain antimony properties under a lease-option for $60,000. Lawrence offered to transfer the properties, which were then 'a raw prospect', to Agau, but after consulting with other members of Agau's board of directors, he and they agreed that the corporation's legal and financial position would not permit acquisition and development of the properties at that time. Thus, it was decided to transfer the properties to USAC, (a closely held corporation formed just for this purpose and a majority of whose stock was owned by the individual defendants) where capital necessary for development of the properties could be raised without risk to Agau through the sale of USAC stock; it was also decided to grant Agau a long-term option to acquire USAC if the properties proved to be of commercial value.

In January, 1970, the option agreement was executed by Agau and USAC. Upon its exercise and approval by Agau shareholders, Agau was to deliver 800,000 shares of its restricted investment stock for all authorized and issued shares of USAC. The exchange was calculated on the basis of reimbursement to USAC and its shareholders for their costs in developing the properties to a point where it could be ascertained if they had commercial value.

. . .

In July, 1970, the Agau board resolved to exercise the option, an action which was approved by majority vote of the shareholders in October, 1970. Subsequently, plaintiff instituted this suit on behalf of Agau to recover the 800,000 shares and for an accounting. . . .

III

A.

Preliminarily, defendants argue that they have been relieved of the burden of proving fairness by reason of shareholder ratification of the Board's decision to exercise the option. They rely on 8 Del.C. § 144(a)(2) and Gottlieb v. Heyden Chemical Corp., Del.Supr., 33 Del.Ch. 177, 91 A.2d 57 (1952).

In *Gottlieb*, this Court stated that shareholder ratification of an "interested transaction", although less than unanimous, shifts the burden of proof to an objecting shareholder to demonstrate that the terms are so unequal as to amount to a gift or waste of corporate assets. . . . The Court explained:

> "[T]he entire atmosphere is freshened and a new set of rules invoked where formal approval has been given by a majority of independent, fully informed [share]holders." 91 A.2d at 59.

The purported ratification by the Agau shareholders would not affect the burden of proof in this case because the majority of shares voted in favor of exercising the option were cast by defendants in their capacity as Agau shareholders. Only about one-third of the "disinterested" shareholders voted, and we cannot assume that such non-voting shareholders either approved or disapproved. Under these circumstances, we cannot say that "the entire atmosphere has been freshened" and that departure from the objective fairness test is permissible. . . . In short, defendants have not established factually a basis for applying *Gottlieb*.

Nor do we believe the Legislature intended a contrary policy and rule to prevail by enacting 8 Del.C. § 144, which provides, in part:

> (a) No contract or transaction between a corporation and 1 or more of its directors or officers, or between a corporation and any other corporation, partnership, association, or other organization in which 1 or more of its directors or officers, are directors or officers, or

have a financial interest, shall be void or voidable solely for this reason, or solely because the director or officer is present at or participates in the meeting of the board or committee which authorizes the contract or transaction, or solely because his or their votes are counted for such purpose, if:

(1) The material facts as to his relationship or interest and as to the contract or transaction are disclosed or are known to the board of directors or the committee, and the board of committee in good faith authorizes the contract or transaction by the affirmative votes of a majority of the disinterested directors, even though the disinterested directors be less than a quorum; or

(2) The material facts as his relationship or interest and as to the contract or transaction are disclosed or are known to the shareholders entitled to vote thereon, and the contract or transaction is specifically approved in good faith by vote of the shareholders; or

(3) The contract or transaction is fair as to the corporation as of the time it is authorized, approved or ratified, by the board of directors, a committee, or the shareholders.

Defendants argue that the transaction here in question is protected by § 144(a)(2) which, they contend, does not require that ratifying shareholders be "disinterested" or "independent"; nor, they argue, is there warrant for reading such a requirement into the statute.   .   .   .

We do not read the statute as providing the broad immunity for which defendants contend. It merely removes an "interested director" cloud when its terms are met and provides against invalidation of an agreement "solely" because such a director or officer is involved. Nothing in the statute sanctions unfairness to Agau or removes the transaction from judicial scrutiny.

[After an elaborate inquiry into the economics of the transaction, the court held:]

Considering all of the above factors, we conclude that defendants have proven the intrinsic fairness of the transaction. Agau received properties which by themselves were clearly of substantial value. But more importantly, it received a promising, potentially self-financing and profit generating enterprise with proven markets and commercial capability which could well be expected to provide Agau at the very least with the cash it sorely needed to undertake further exploration and development of its own properties if not to stay in existence. For those reasons, we believe that the interest given to the USAC shareholders was a fair price to pay. Accordingly, we have no doubt but that this transaction was one which at that time would have commended itself to an independent corporation in Agau's position.

Affirmed.

ANALYSIS

1. Section 144 of the Delaware statute provides that a properly ratified contract between a corporation and one of its directors is not necessarily "void or voidable" because of the conflict of interest. What does this mean? Is a *non*ratified contract between a corporation and one of its directors necessarily void or voidable? If not, then what difference could ratification make?

2. Section 144 provides that a ratified contract is not void or voidable "solely" because of the conflict. What purpose does the "solely" serve? Does it mean the fact that a ratified contract involves an interested director will continue to be a factor that contributes to the contract's voidability? What other reasons might there be?

3. Consider again New York Bus. Corp. Law § 713, quoted in footnote 12 of Lewis v. S.L. & E., Inc. Does that statute lead to different results than the Delaware statute?

4. Suppose you had represented the corporation in the negotiations with Jean Tennyson over the Celanese Hour. What procedures would you have followed if the statute quoted in *Fliegler* had governed?

In re Wheelabrator Technologies, Inc. Shareholders Litigation

663 A.2d 1194 (Del.Ch.1995).

Opinion

■ JACOBS, VICE CHANCELLOR.

[Waste Management, Inc. (Waste) and Wheelabrator Technologies, Inc. (WTI) were both in the "waste management" industry. In 1988, Waste bought 22 percent of WTI stock and elected four of its own directors to serve on WTI's eleven-member board. In 1990, for reasons never made clear by the court, Waste and WTI negotiated a "merger" agreement in which (i) Waste would acquire another 33 percent of WTI stock, and (ii) WTI shareholders would receive .574 WTI shares and .469 Waste shares for each WTI share they held.

To consider this agreement, WTI's board held a special meeting. All members other than the Waste designees attended. They reviewed copies of the agreement and materials furnished by the investment bankers involved (Lazard Freres and Salomon Brothers). They also listened to presentations from both these investment bankers and WTI's attorneys. All of the speakers declared that the transaction was fair.

The seven non-Waste directors of WTI then unanimously approved the merger agreement. Upon the completion of that vote, the four Waste directors joined the meeting and the full board unanimously approved it as well. The two firms then distributed a proxy statement explaining the transaction to WTI shareholders. At a special shareholders meeting, a majority of WTI shareholders (not counting Waste) approved the agreement.]

. . . .

IV.   THE DISCLOSURE CLAIM

Delaware law imposes upon a board of directors the fiduciary duty to disclose fully and fairly all material facts within its control that would have a significant effect upon a stockholder vote. . . . The plaintiffs argue that the defendants breached their duty of disclosure because the proxy statement issued in connection with the merger was materially misleading in several respects. . . .

[T]he plaintiffs contend that the proxy disclosure that the WTI Board had "carefully considered the financial, business and tax aspects" of the merger was materially misleading. In fact, plaintiffs argue, the WTI board had deliberated for only three hours before voting to approve and recommend the merger to WTI shareholders.

This argument also lacks evidentiary support. The assertion that the WTI board could not have considered the merger proposal carefully rests upon an unsupported inference from one fact: the three hour length of the March 30, 1990 board meeting. Given the other undisputed facts of record, that inference is unreasonable and does not create a triable fact issue. First, the board meeting was attended by WTI's investment bankers and outside counsel who made presentations and thereafter answered the board members' questions. Second, the proxy statement describes in detail the various factors that the board considered in deciding whether to approve and recommend the merger. . . . The plaintiffs offer no evidence that that description was in any way inaccurate. Third, Waste and WTI had had a close business relationship for over two years before the merger, during which time many discussions concerning the future of that relationship had taken place. It is reasonable to (and I do) infer that WTI's directors already had, and were able to draw upon, a substantial working knowledge of Waste during the March 30, 1990 meeting.

. . . .

For the foregoing reasons, summary judgment will be granted dismissing the remaining duty of disclosure claim.

V.   THE FIDUCIARY DUTY CLAIMS

In rejecting the disclosure claim, the Court necessarily has determined that the merger was approved by a fully informed vote of a majority of WTI's disinterested stockholders. . . .

A.   The Duty of Care Claim.

As noted, the plaintiffs concede that if the WTI shareholder vote was fully informed, the effect of that informed vote would be to extinguish the claim that the WTI board failed to exercise due care in negotiating and approving the merger. Given the ratification holding of Smith v. Van

Gorkom, Del.Supr., 488 A.2d 858, 889–90 (1985), that concession is not surprising. In *Van Gorkom,* the defendant directors argued that the shareholder vote approving a challenged merger agreement "had the legal effect of curing any failure of the board to reach an informed business judgment in its approval of the merger." Id. at 889. Accepting that legal principle (but not its application to the facts before it[1]), the Supreme Court stated:

> The parties tacitly agree that a discovered failure of the Board to reach an informed business judgment constitutes a voidable, rather than a void, act. Hence, the merger can be sustained, notwithstanding the infirmity of the Board's actions, if its approval by majority vote of the shareholders is found to have been based on an informed electorate.

Id. at 889.

Accordingly, summary judgment dismissing the plaintiffs' due care claim will be granted. . . .

B. The Duty of Loyalty Claim.

. . .

The [Delaware] ratification decisions that involve duty of loyalty claims are of two kinds: (a) "interested" transaction cases between a corporation and its directors (or between the corporation and an entity in which the corporation's directors are also directors or have a financial interest), and (b) cases involving a transaction between the corporation and its controlling shareholder.

Regarding the first category, 8 Del.C. § 144(a)(2) pertinently provides that an "interested" transaction of this kind will not be voidable if it is approved in good faith by a majority of disinterested stockholders. Approval by fully informed, disinterested shareholders pursuant to § 144(a)(2) invokes "the business judgment rule and limits judicial review to issues of gift or waste with the burden of proof upon the party attacking the transaction." Marciano v. Nakash, 535 A.2d 400, 405 n. 3 (Del.Supr.1987). The result is the same in "interested" transaction cases not decided under § 144:

> Where there has been independent shareholder ratification of interested director actions, the objecting stockholder has the burden of showing that no person of ordinary sound business judgment would say that the consideration received for the options was a fair exchange for the options granted.

Michelson, 407 A.2d at 224 (quoting Kaufman v. Shoenberg, Del.Ch., 91 A.2d 786, 791 (1952), at 791); . . . .

The second category concerns duty of loyalty cases arising out of transactions between the corporation and its controlling stockholder.

1. [Eds. Recall that in *Van Gorkom* the court held that the directors had not fully disclosed and that therefore the shareholder vote was not fully informed.]

Those cases involve primarily parent-subsidiary mergers that were conditioned upon receiving "majority of the minority" stockholder approval. In a parent-subsidiary merger, the standard of review is ordinarily entire fairness, with the directors having the burden of proving that the merger was entirely fair. Weinberger v. UOP, Inc., 457 A.2d 701, 703. But where the merger is conditioned upon approval by a "majority of the minority" stockholder vote, and such approval is granted, the standard of review remains entire fairness, but the burden of demonstrating that the merger was unfair shifts to the plaintiff. . . . That burden-shifting effect of ratification has also been held applicable in cases involving mergers with a de facto controlling stockholder, and in a case involving a transaction other than a merger.

. . .

C.   The Appropriate Review Standard and Burden of Proof.

Having determined what effect shareholder ratification does not have, the Court must now determine what effect it does have. The plaintiffs argue that their duty of loyalty claim is governed by the entire fairness standard, with ratification operating only to shift the burden on the fairness issue to the plaintiffs. That is incorrect, because this merger did not involve an interested and controlling stockholder.

[T]he [Delaware] Supreme Court determined that the effect of a fully informed shareholder vote was to shift the burden of proof within the *entire fairness* standard of review. [Emphasis added.] . . . Critical to the result in those cases was that the transaction involved a de facto . . . or de jure . . . controlling stockholder. That circumstance brought those cases within the purview of the ratification doctrine articulated in [cases] involving mergers between a corporation and its majority stockholder-parent. The participation of the controlling interested stockholder is critical to the application of the entire fairness standard because . . . the potential for process manipulation by the controlling stockholder, and the concern that the controlling stockholder's continued presence might influence even a fully informed shareholder vote, justify the need for the exacting judicial scrutiny and procedural protection afforded by the entire fairness form of review.

In this case, there is no contention or evidence that Waste, a 22% stockholder of WTI, exercised de jure or de facto control over WTI. . . . Accordingly, the review standard applicable to this merger is business judgment, with the plaintiffs having the burden of proof.

The final question concerns the proper application of that review standard to the facts at bar. Because no party has yet been heard on that subject, that issue cannot be determined on this motion. Its resolution must await further proceedings, which counsel may present (if they so choose) on a supplemental motion for summary judgment.

. . .

ANALYSIS

1. Why should the effect of a fully informed shareholder vote on the standard of review be different for duty of care cases than for duty of loyalty cases not involving de jure or de facto control?

2. What must the plaintiff in *Wheelabrator* be prepared to prove at trial or to resist a renewed motion for summary judgment? What do you suppose is the likelihood of success?

3. In Smith v. Van Gorkom, why was the shareholder action in approving the merger, by an overwhelming majority, not a complete defense to the action against the directors?

PROBLEMS

DreamTeam, Inc. (DTI), which is incorporated in Delaware, is a Hollywood studio owned in equal parts by Mouse, Duck, and Flintstone. The three also constitute the board. DTI has recently signed a contract with director Olivia Stone for a new movie, *Fillmore*. Stone has based the film on (what she considers) the scandalous presidency of Millard Fillmore. In the movie, Stone will star Flintstone as the diabolical mastermind behind (what Stone claims is) the newly discovered CIA plot to assassinate Fillmore. For directing this movie, Stone will receive $25 million; for playing the villain, Flintstone will receive $5 million.

1. The Stone contract was approved by a 2–1 vote among the board of directors, with Mouse objecting. Mouse now brings a derivative suit to enjoin the contract. What result?

2. The Flintstone contract was approved by a 2–1 vote among the board of directors, with Mouse objecting. Mouse similarly sues to enjoin the contract. What result?

3. Stone will use the movie to push her distinctive fringe-left political philosophy. Mouse shares this philosophy; Duck does not share it, but does not care as long as the movie makes money; Flintstone objects to the philosophy. Can Flintstone block the use of a DTI movie for political ends?

4. Suppose Mouse had been absent when the Flintstone contract was considered by the board. The contract was approved by a vote of 2–0, both Duck and Flintstone voting in the affirmative. Mouse objects (a) that the action was invalid for lack of a quorum and (b) that the contract should be enjoined as unfair and unauthorized. What result?

SECTION 3. DISCLOSURE AND FAIRNESS

Trading in corporate securities, such as stocks or bonds, takes place on two basic types of markets: (1) the primary market, in which the issuer of the securities—i.e., the company that created the securities—sells them to investors; and (2) the secondary market, in which investors trade securities among themselves without any significant participation by the original issuer. An initial public offering by a corporation, for example, takes place in the primary market. In contrast, trading between investors on the floor of the New York Stock Exchange is a highly organized and regulated example of a secondary market.

Regulation of the primary market in this country began with the passage of the first state "blue sky law" by Kansas in 1911.[24] These statutes had a limited jurisdictional reach, they contained many special interest exemptions, and the states had limited enforcement resources. In the aftermath of the Great Crash of 1929 and subsequent Great Depression, there was general agreement that the time had come for federal regulation of the securities markets. Between 1933 and 1940 Congress passed 7 statutes regulating various aspects of the industry. Of these, the most important for our purposes are the Securities Act of 1933 and the Securities Exchange Act of 1934.

The Securities Act is principally concerned with the primary market. In drafting it, Congress rejected proposals for federal merit review of securities. Instead, Congress concentrated on two goals: mandating disclosure of material information to investors and prevention of fraud. As to disclosure, the Securities Act follows a transactional disclosure model—i.e. mandating disclosures by issuers in connection with primary market transactions.

The Securities Exchange Act ("Exchange Act") is principally concerned with secondary market transactions. A whole host of issues fall within its purview, including a number that figure prominently in this course: insider trading and other forms of securities fraud, short-swing profits by corporate insiders, regulation of shareholder voting via proxy solicitations, and

---

24. All states still have so-called "blue-sky" laws. The name comes from the claim that such statutes protect investors from "speculative schemes which have no more basis than so many feet of 'blue sky.'" Hall v. Geiger–Jones Co., 242 U.S. 539, 550 (1917). Some of these statutes are much more restrictive than the Securities Act. They may, for example, allow the state administrator to deny registration if he or she considers the securities too speculative or otherwise unsat- isfactory. When Apple Computer Inc. "went public" in 1980, Massachusetts banned the sale of its stock for just that reason. From time to time, the SEC and various scholars and regulators have tried to reduce the costs that overlapping and inconsistent state and federal securities laws impose. They have had modest (if incomplete) success. The Uniform Securities Act, adopted (in modified form) by a majority of the states, does reduce some of those costs.

regulation of tender offers. Another important element of the Exchange Act is its requirement of periodic disclosures by publicly held corporations.

The Exchange Act is also important because it created the Securities and Exchange Commission as the primary federal agency charged with administering the various securities laws. There are five Commissioners, who must be confirmed by the Senate and no more than three of whom can belong to the same political party. Most of the work, of course, is done not by the Commissioners but by the professional staff. The staff is mainly comprised of lawyers, although there are a fair number of accountants and other specialists, and is organized into Divisions and Offices having various responsibilities. The staff has three primary functions: it provides interpretative guidance to private parties raising questions about the application of the securities laws to a particular transaction; it advises the Commission as to new rules or revisions of existing rules; and it investigates and prosecutes violations of the securities laws. Those of you who ultimately decide to practice in this area will spend most of your careers dealing with the staff; only very rarely will you actually have occasion to deal with the Commissioners.

A. DEFINITION OF A SECURITY

It is perhaps a cheap way of getting your attention, but it is nevertheless worth pointing out that securities regulation issues reportedly are the single most common source of legal malpractice claims against business lawyers. Why? Put bluntly, because there are so many ways the lawyer can go awry. One of the easiest mistakes a lawyer can make is to fail to recognize that he or she is dealing with a security. This typically has adverse consequences for the client, which often turns out to have adverse consequences for the lawyer.

Knowing whether or not a particular type of instrument or investment will be deemed to be a security is important for at least two reasons. First, it tells you whether the registration requirements of the Securities Act apply to the transaction. One need only go through the registration process if the thing your client is selling is a security. If the SEC or a private plaintiff sues your client for failing to register securities, your first response thus might be that what you sold is not a security. If that doesn't work, you will next argue that one of the exemptions from registration is available. And if that doesn't work, you'll try to settle the case on the best terms you can get.

The other reason the definition of a security is important relates to the antifraud provisions of the Acts. In general, plaintiffs have a much easier time when they bring suit under the securities laws than they would if they had to bring suit under state common law fraud rules. For one thing, the elements of federal securities fraud are less demanding and thus easier to prove. For another thing, there are certain procedural advantages, such as liberal venue and service of process provisions. As a result, plaintiffs defrauded in what looks like a garden variety fraud often allege that a security is present in the scheme so as to bring their claims under the federal securities laws. Such attempts not infrequently succeed, because the securities laws apply to lots of things that don't look very much like securities at first glance. For example, investments in worm farms. Smith v. Gross, 604 F.2d 639 (9th Cir.1979).

The statutory definition of a security in § 2(1) of the Securities Act is divided into two broad categories. (The Exchange Act definitional section is substantially identical and the two are usually interpreted as in pari materia.) First, a list of rather specific instruments, including "stock," "notes," and "bonds." Second, a list of general, catch-all phrases, such as "evidence of indebtedness," "investment contracts" and, in perhaps the most general description of them all, "any instrument commonly known as a 'security.'" The situation is further complicated by the first sentence of § 2, which provides that the terms used in the Act shall be defined in accordance with the various provisions of § 2, "unless the context otherwise requires." This "context" clause is an escape hatch. Courts have sometimes used it to hold that although an instrument appears to fall within one of the listed types of securities, the instrument shall not be held to constitute a security for purposes of the securities laws if "the context otherwise requires." In other words, the "context" clause can be used to say: yes, this thing looks like a security, but given the nature of the transaction we're going to hold that it does not come within the Securities Act. And vice-versa.

Most of the litigation involving atypical instruments claimed to be securities turns on whether the instrument in question falls within one of the catch-all phrases in § 2, especially the term "investment contract." The following case provides a good example of the issues business lawyers often face in this context.

Koch v. Hankins

928 F.2d 1471 (9th Cir.1991).

The plaintiff-investors ("investors") appeal from the district court's summary judgment that the investments did not constitute securities within the meaning of the Securities Exchange Act of 1934. . . .

The investors are primarily doctors [and] dentists . . . who invested between $23,000 and $500,000 each in general partnerships formed to purchase land for the production of jojoba.* [Defendants included a number of plaintiffs' accountants and lawyers who promoted the partnerships.] The investments were undertaken in part for tax purposes and allegedly were promoted to the [investors] on that basis.

The overall investment scheme involved thirty-five different general partnerships, each of which purchased eighty acres of land from "selling corporations" owned by the promoters, which in turn purchased land from a common seller. In all, approximately 2700 acres and 160 investors were

---

* [Eds. Jojoba is a shrub whose seeds produce a commercially valuable wax.]

involved in the various general partnerships. Although the promoters present the general partnerships as independent entities, the investors assert that the promoters told them at the outset that it was not economically feasible to farm jojoba in eighty-acre parcels; that they never regarded their general partnerships as separate eighty-acre farms but rather as part of a 2700–acre plantation; and indeed that the promoters themselves did not view the general partnerships as separate farms with the capability of operating independently. . . . [T]he thirty-five general partnerships all specified identically that the general partners would initially employ Franklin W. Rogers as foreman to carry out the onsite farming cultural practices . . .; that [each] partnership would execute an irrigation lease for a term of five years for an annual rental of $2,800; and that [each] partnership would purchase from the promoters by bill of sale a supply of jojoba seeds, fertilizer, weed control and other materials at a cost of $300 per acre. In addition, the thirty-five partnerships shared a common field office financed by an administrative fund to which all the partnerships contributed. At a minimum, therefore, whether the eighty-acre partnerships could or were intended to operate independently from the 2700–acre Great Western Jojoba plantation is a disputed question of fact.

Each general partnership was comprised of one operating general partner and a number of general partners. The thirty-five partnership agreements detail identically the rights and responsibilities of the partners. The operating general partners have responsibility for executing the general partners' decisions about the management and control of partnership business. Within each partnership, the general partners have full and exclusive control of the business of the partnership and can take action in that regard only upon a majority vote. Within each partnership, the general partners have the ability to remove any person from a management position by majority vote and have access to the partnership's books and records.

The degree of actual participation by the general partners and operating general partners and its significance to the endeavor is a matter of considerable dispute. The promoters point out that some investors have voted on such partnership business decisions as whether to pay additional assessments to meet operating budgets, a proposed sale of partnership assets in response to an offer by a third party, whether to interplant alfalfa between rows of jojoba, whether to join a marketing cooperative, whether to amend the partnership agreement, water district elections, and whether to stop farming their parcel or section. In addition, some investors have visited the property their partnerships purchased and tested the soil. There are also letters and memoranda in the record from operating general partners and general partners which suggest that the operating general partners paid careful attention to the status of their particular farms and kept the general partners informed in some detail as to the status of particular plots.

The investors argue, on the other hand, that their role was essentially passive. It is undisputed that none of them had any experience in jojoba farming. It appears that even those investors who nominally held the role of operating general partner usually acted as conduits for materials created by the promoters. The investors assert that the operating general partners did not even generate the pro rata assessments for operating expenses for each general partner. Those figures were determined by the promoters. Finally, the investors assert that any voting they did was largely pro forma in light of their lack of expertise, their inability to devote time to direct participation in the project, and their ability at best to shape decisionmaking only for the eighty acres owned by their particular general partnership. It is even disputed in the record whether, had investors actively exercised decisionmaking regarding the farming of their particular parcels of land, their decisions would have been implemented.

As one might guess from the fact that the parties are now in court, the investments proved less than successful.   .   .   .

.   .   . Both § 2 of the Securities Act of 1933, and § 3 of the Securities Exchange Act of 1934, define the term "security" to include, inter alia, any "investment contract." Since the investments involved in this case do not constitute any of the other types of securities protected by the Acts, the critical threshold inquiry is whether the general partnerships constitute "investment contracts" within the meaning of the Acts.

The term "investment contract" has been interpreted by the Supreme Court broadly to reach "novel, uncommon, or irregular devices, whatever they appear to be .   .   ." SEC v. C.M. Joiner Leasing Corp., 320 U.S. 344, 351, 88 L. Ed. 88, 64 S. Ct. 120 (1943). "It embodies a flexible rather than a static principle, one that is capable of adaptation to meet the countless and variable schemes devised by those who seek the use of the money of others on the promise of profits." SEC v. W.J. Howey Co., 328 U.S. 293, 299, 90 L. Ed. 1244, 66 S. Ct. 1100 (1946) (holding that a combined sale of units of a citrus grove development coupled with a contract for cultivating, marketing and remitting the net proceeds to the investor was an "investment contract").   .   .   . Thus, the fact that the investments here are structured as "general partnerships" is not determinative of their status as securities; rather, we must examine the economic realities of the transactions to determine whether they are, in fact, investment contracts.

The Supreme Court in *Howey* set out the classic three-part definition of an investment contract: "An investment contract for purposes of the Securities Act means a contract, transaction or scheme whereby a person [1] invests his money in [2] a common enterprise and is led to [3] expect profits solely from the efforts of the promoter or a third party." 328 U.S. at 298–99. The Ninth Circuit has held that "the word 'solely' should not be read as a strict or literal limitation on the definition of an investment contract." SEC v. Glenn W. Turner Enters., Inc., 474 F.2d 476, 482 (9th Cir.), cert. denied, 414 U.S. 821, 38 L. Ed. 2d 53, 94 S. Ct. 117 (1973). Instead, this circuit looks to whether "the efforts made by those other than the investor are the undeniably significant ones, those essential managerial efforts which affect the failure or success of the enterprise." Id. Here, as in most cases dealing with the *Howey* test, the inquiry revolves around the third, "control," element of the test—whether the investors had an expectation of profits which would be produced in essential part through the efforts of others.

. . .

The Fifth Circuit held in [Williamson v. Tucker, 645 F.2d 404, 424 (5th Cir.1981)] that:

> A general partnership or joint venture interest can be designated a security if the investor can establish, for example, that (1) an agreement among the parties leaves so little power in the hands of the partner or venturer that the arrangement in fact distributes power as would a limited partnership; or (2) the partner or venturer is so inexperienced and unknowledgeable in business affairs that he is incapable of intelligently exercising his partnership or venture powers; or (3) the partner or venturer is so dependent on some unique entrepreneurial or managerial ability of the promoter or manager that he cannot replace the manager of the enterprise or otherwise exercise meaningful partnership or venture powers.

According to *Williamson* the critical determination is whether, although "on the face of a partnership agreement, the investor retains substantial control over his investment and an ability to protect himself from the managing partner or hired manager . . ., [the investor can demonstrate that] he was so dependent on the promoter or on a third party that he was in fact unable to exercise meaningful partnership powers." Id. The *Williamson* opinion made clear that the three factors are not exclusive and that "other factors could . . . also give rise to such a dependence." Id. at 424, n.15. *Williamson* likewise specified that the inquiry is not directed to what actually transpires after the investment is made, i.e., whether the investor later decides to be passive or to delegate all powers and duties to a promoter or managing partner; rather, "one would have to show that the reliance on the manager which forms the basis of the partner's expectations was an understanding in the original transaction." Id. at 424, n. 14. [The court next held that Ninth Circuit's en banc opinion in Hocking v. Dubois, 885 F.2d 1449 (9th Cir.1989) (en banc),* had adopted *Williamson* as a controlling precedent.]

In determining whether the investors relied on the efforts of others, we look not only to the partnership agreement itself, but also to other documents structuring the investment, to promotional materials, to oral representations made by the promoters at the time of the investment, and

* [Eds. In *Hocking*, the plaintiff purchased a condominium in a resort community. The purchaser hoped to generate rental income rather than to acquire a place to live. Plaintiff also entered into a rental agreement pursuant to which an agent recommended by the promoter handled all aspects of renting the condo to vacationers. Rents generated by the condo were not paid directly to the purchaser, but were pooled with the rentals generated by all condos in the facility and then shared out among their owners on a pro rata basis. The *Hocking* court held that the condo purchase and its associated rent pooling agreements constituted a security. 885 F.2d 1449 (9th Cir.1989).]

to the practical possibility of the investors exercising the powers they possessed pursuant to the partnership agreements. . . .

Assuming the disputed facts in favor of the nonmoving party (the investors), . . . none of the investors knew anything about jojoba farming and, taking their allegations as true, none of them intended to engage actively in the business of jojoba farming. Rather, they relied substantially on the knowledge of the promoters and experts, and on the services to be provided by the on-site manager. . . .

The investors argue that all three *Williamson* factors tilt in favor of a finding that the investments here were securities. Because of the reliance of the individual partnerships on participation in the larger plantation, the investors contend that the power of the partnership is distributed as is the power in a limited partnership, thus implicating the first *Williamson* factor. The investors, however, are jumping ahead to the third factor and ignoring the crux of the first. It is clear from both *Williamson* itself and from *Hocking* that the first factor is addressed to the legal powers afforded the investor by the formal documents without regard to the practical impossibility of the investors invoking them. Here, the partnership agreement clearly affords the partners significant legal powers.

As a legal matter, the partners have the responsibility and authority to control every aspect of the jojoba cultivation process. Additional assessments of capital must be approved by 75 percent of the partnership units; a majority of the partnership units can remove any person from a management position; decisions regarding the management and control of the business must be made by a majority vote.[12] . . . Like the condominium purchaser in *Hocking*, who was free to terminate the rental pooling agreement, occupy the unit himself, rent the unit out on his own, or sell the unit, the investors here could—theoretically, at least—vote to cease farming, replace the operating general partner, terminate services by the on-site manager, vote to interplant rows of alfalfa, etc. Compare *Howey*, 328 U.S. 293 (orange grove investment gave the management company a leasehold interest and full and complete possession of the acreage, along with full discretion and authority over the cultivation, harvest and marketing of the crops such that investors had no right of entry to market the crop without the consent of the company). Under these facts, as in *Hocking*, the investors have not demonstrated that their partnership agreements leave them "with so little power as to place [them] in a position analogous to a limited partner." 885 F.2d at 1461. It therefore appears that the first *Williamson* factor tilts in favor of the promoters.

---

12. Although an investor participating in a general partnership obviously relinquishes some control since decisions must be made by majority vote, this type of diminution in control by itself would not satisfy the third prong of *Howey* unless the numbers of partners became so large "that a partnership vote would be more like a corporate vote, each partner's role having been diluted to the level of a single shareholder." *Williamson*, 645 F.2d at 423. Such is not the case here. Even though each investor's absolute control is reduced by the voting structure, the general partners as a legal matter "do have the sort of influence [within the partnership] which generally provides them with access to important information and protection against a dependence on others." Id. at 422.

Under the second *Williamson* factor we consider the investors' sophistication and expertise. . . . Under *Williamson*, the relevant inquiry is whether "the partner or venturer is so inexperienced and unknowledgeable in business affairs that he is incapable of intelligently exercising his partnership or venture powers." 645 F.2d at 424. Here, while the investors were doctors and dentists as opposed to business people, all of them had at least $23,000 to invest in the venture and some had considerably more. The record indicates that some of the investors had prior experience in pistachio ventures and other tax shelters at the time of their investment. However, since the district court focused exclusively on the investors' formal status, the record is not fully developed on this issue and we simply have no basis for evaluating the sophistication of many of the investors. The question of the investors' expertise or lack thereof and its effect on their ability to exercise their powers intelligently is a question of fact which should be resolved in the first instance by the trial court. Since the record is insufficiently developed on this issue, we remand to the district court to determine whether the investors have raised a genuine issue of fact as to whether their lack of expertise prevented them from exercising meaningful control over their investment.

We turn finally to the third *Williamson* factor, which involves whether "the partner or venturer is so dependent on some unique entrepreneurial or managerial ability of the promoter or manager that he cannot replace the manager of the enterprise or otherwise exercise meaningful partnership or venture powers." 645 F.2d at 424. In this case, the investors' reliance on participation in the larger, 2700–acre jojoba plantation is analogous to, and arguably more extreme than, Hocking's reliance on the rental pooling agreement. In *Hocking*, the en banc panel noted that while the investor enjoyed complete legal control over his particular condominium unit, he had made the investment in anticipation of receiving income from the rental pooling agreement, and in order for him to replace the management of that agreement he would have had to gain the votes of 75 percent of participating investors. The court in *Hocking* held that "[those] facts alone create[d] a real question of whether Hocking was stuck with HCP as a rental manager." 885 F.2d at 1461. Because the rental pooling agreement resulted in the condominiums being managed as a resort hotel, and "the commercial viability of a one-room hotel [did] not strongly argue for separate management," the court found that "the individual investor may have [had] no choice but to place his condominium in the rental pool, if he [were] to receive significant rental income." Id. It thus reversed the district court's summary judgment that the investment was not a security.

Here, as in *Hocking*, there is a question of fact as to whether the investors could, as a practical matter, pull out of the larger enterprise and still receive the income they had contemplated when they made the investment. The promoters focus on the significant management powers and access to information afforded the general partners by the partnership agreements. The partnership agreement, however, only provides for the exercise of general partner control and decisionmaking within each partnership, and as to the land controlled by each partnership, not as to issues concerning the entire plantation. Likewise, the access to information provisions of the partnership agreement apply only to information related to the partnership and available to the partnership or the operating general partner. . . .

As in *Hocking*, while the investors here could readily order the on-site manager to cease cultivating their particular plot, it would be difficult if not impossible for an investor to affect the management of the plantation as a whole. There is not even a formalized mechanism in the partnership agreements for attempting to effect change on behalf of all thirty-five partnerships. Therefore, to replace the on-site manager for the entire plantation, an investor would have to catalyze a vote in each of the thirty-five partnerships (an endeavor which would be rendered difficult if not impossible by the fact that many of the investors did not even know the names of their own partners, much less have such information regarding the other thirty-four partnerships) and obtain the approval of a significant enough bloc of the partnerships to make it impracticable for the on-site manager to continue farming the remaining sections. In addition, the ready availability of alternative jojoba farm managers is more questionable than the availability of alternative realtors to manage a rental pool agreement in Hawaii, the situation presented in *Hocking*.

The fact that some investors were provided with detailed information about the status of their eighty acres and that some investors visited the land and even offered evaluations and suggestions to the on-site managers is not dispositive. . . . In this case, even if a general partner vigorously exercised his or her rights under the partnership agreement, he or she arguably could have no impact on the investment (other than to ensure its failure by withdrawing from the larger plantation).

Thus, the investors here have at least raised an issue of fact as to the necessity of participating in the 2700–acre plantation in order to produce income from the general partnership acreage, and as to their ability to affect decisionmaking regarding that larger plantation. They have not, as did the plaintiff-investors in *Williamson*, made only vague statements that they relied and were dependent upon the efforts of the promoters. Having raised a genuine question as to the third *Williamson* factor, they likewise have created a genuine question for the trier of fact as to whether at the time of their investment they expected any profit to arise essentially through the efforts of others. The district court's grant of summary judgment in favor of the promoters must therefore be reversed.

. . . .

B.   THE REGISTRATION PROCESS

The Securities Act prohibits the sale of securities unless the company issuing the securities (the issuer) has "registered" them with the SEC. More specifically, § 5 of the Act imposes three basic rules: (1) a security may not be offered for sale through the mails or by use of other means of interstate commerce unless a registration statement has been filed with the

SEC; (2) securities may not be sold until the registration statement has become effective; and (3) the prospectus (a disclosure document) must be delivered to the purchaser before a sale.

To register securities, the issuer must give the Commission extensive information about its finances and business. A large company about to sell stock to the public for the first time will need to file a registration statement that can easily exceed a hundred pages. In the process, it will involve its general counsel and outside accountants. The lawyers' fees alone can exceed $100,000, and the investment banking firm that underwrites the issue (i.e., attempts to find buyers for the stock) will charge a fee several times that amount.

When the SEC reviews a registration statement, it does not ask whether the security would be a good investment. Instead, it asks whether the registration statement contains the disclosures required by the statute and the SEC rules thereunder and whether that information appears to be accurate. The core of the registration statement thus is the "prospectus," the principal disclosure document issuers are required by the Securities Act to give prospective buyers. Until the SEC has approved the disclosures made in the prospectus, companies cannot sell the new securities.[25]

Because of the cost and delay associated with the registration process, many issuers work hard to find ways to sell securities without registering them. The Securities Act includes two types of exemptions to the registration requirement: it exempts some securities entirely and exempts some transactions in securities not otherwise exempt. In general, an exempt security need never be registered, either when initially sold by the issuer or in any subsequent transaction. Exempt transactions, in contrast, are one-time exemptions. If A sells a non-exempt security to B in an exempt transaction, B is not automatically free to resell that security. B must either register it or utilize another exempt transaction. Because exempt securities tend to be highly specialized, business lawyers are far more likely to encounter transactional exemptions, such as the statutory private placement exemption discussed in the following case.

Doran v. Petroleum Management Corp.

545 F.2d 893 (5th Cir.1977).

In this case a sophisticated investor who purchased a limited partnership interest in an oil drilling venture seeks to rescind. The question raised

---

25. To be sure, the Securities Act technically allows the issuer to sell securities twenty days after it files a registration statement with the SEC (unless the SEC issues an order halting the process). Hence, issuers could simply file the statement, wait twenty days, and then sell. In practice, however, the scheme would not work: the proposed price of a security is part of the registration statement, and issuers seldom know the price they should charge twenty days in advance. Accordingly, issuers wait until the SEC finds the registration statement satisfactory. They then price the security, amend the registration statement to incorporate that price, and ask the SEC to make the amendment effective immediately. As the SEC is satisfied with the issuer's disclosure, it agrees.

is whether the sale was part of a private offering exempted by § 4(2) of the Securities Act of 1933, from the registration requirements of that Act.[1] . . .

We hold that in the absence of findings of fact that each offeree had been furnished information about the issuer that a registration statement would have disclosed or that each offeree had effective access to such information, the district court erred in concluding that the offering was a private placement. Accordingly, we reverse and remand.

I. Facts

Prior to July 1970, Petroleum Management Corporation (PMC) organized a California limited partnership for the purpose of drilling and operating four wells in Wyoming. . . . As found by the district court, PMC contacted only four other persons with respect to possible participation in the partnership. All but the plaintiff declined.

During the late summer of 1970, plaintiff William H. Doran, Jr., received a telephone call from a California securities broker previously known to him. The broker, Phillip Kendrick, advised Doran of the opportunity to become a "special participant" in the partnership. PMC then sent Doran the drilling logs and technical maps of the proposed drilling area. PMC informed Doran that two of the proposed four wells had already been completed. Doran agreed to become a "special participant" in the Wyoming drilling program. In consideration for his partnership share, Doran agreed to contribute $125,000 toward the partnership. Doran was to discharge this obligation by paying PMC $25,000 down and in addition assuming responsibility for the payment of a $113,643 note owed by PMC to Mid–Continent Supply Co. Doran's share in the production payments* from the wells was to be used to make the installment payments on the Mid–Continent note. . . .

During 1970 and 1971, PMC periodically sent Doran production information on the completed wells of the limited partnership. Throughout this period, however, the wells were deliberately overproduced in violation of the production allowances established by the Wyoming Oil and Gas Conservation Commission. As a consequence, on November 16, 1971, the Commission ordered the partnership's wells sealed for a period of 338 days. On May 1, 1972, the Commission notified PMC that production from the wells could resume on August 9, 1972. After August 9, the wells yielded a production income level below that obtained prior to the Commission's order.

Following the cessation of production payments between November 1971 and August 1972 and the decreased yields thereafter, the Mid–Continent note upon which Doran was primarily liable went into default. Mid–Continent subsequently obtained a state court judgment against Do-

---

1. Section 4. The provisions of section 5 shall not apply to—

(1) transactions by any person other than an issuer, underwriter, or dealer.

(2) transactions by an issuer not involving any public offering.

* [Eds.—A production payment is a portion of the earnings from the well.]

ran, PMC, and the two signatory officers of PMC for $50,815.50 plus interest and attorney's fees.

On October 16, 1972, Doran filed this suit in federal district court seeking damages for breach of contract, rescission of the contract based on violations of the Securities Acts of 1933 and 1934, and a judgment declaring the defendants liable for payment of the state judgment obtained by Mid–Continent.

The court below found that the offer and sale of the "special participant" interest was a private offering because Doran was a sophisticated investor who did not need the protection of the Securities Acts. The court also found that there was no evidence that PMC, its officers, or Kendrick made any misrepresentation or omissions of material facts to Doran. Finally, the court found that the overproduction of the wells was not a breach of the partnership agreement, but in any event there was no evidence that Doran suffered any losses as a result of the overproduction. The court concluded that all relief requested by Doran should be denied. Doran filed this appeal.

II. The Private Offering Exemption

No registration statement was filed with any federal or state regulatory body in connection with the defendants' offering of securities.[4] Along with two other factors that we may take as established—that the defendants sold or offered to sell these securities, and that the defendants used interstate transportation or communication in connection with the sale or offer of sale—the plaintiff thus states a prima facie case for a violation of the federal securities laws. . . .[5]

The defendants do not contest the existence of the elements of plaintiff's prima facie case but raise an affirmative defense that the relevant transactions came within the exemption from registration found in § 4(2), 15 U.S.C. § 77d(2). Specifically, they contend that the offering of securities

4. The district court correctly concluded that the limited partnership interest was a "security" as that term is defined by the Securities Act of 1933 and the Securities and Exchange Act of 1934. . . .

5. Section 5. (a) Unless a registration statement is in effect as to a security, it shall be unlawful for any person, directly or indirectly—

(1) to make use of any means or instruments of transportation or communication in interstate commerce or of the mails to sell such security through the use or medium of any prospectus or otherwise . . .

(b) It shall be unlawful for any person, directly or indirectly—

(1) to make use of any means or instruments of transportation or communication in interstate commerce or of the mails to carry or transmit any prospectus relating to any security with respect to which a registration statement has been filed under this title, unless such prospectus meets the requirements of section 10 [specifying the required contents of a prospectus] . . .

(c) It shall be unlawful for any person, directly or indirectly, to make use of any means or instruments of transportation or communication in interstate commerce or of the mails to offer to sell or offer to buy through the use or medium of any prospectus or otherwise any security, unless a registration statement has been filed as to such security, . . .

was not a public offering. The defendants, who of course bear the burden of proving this affirmative defense, must therefore show that the offering was private. . . .

This court has in the past identified four factors relevant to whether an offering qualifies for the exemption. The consideration of these factors, along with the policies embodied in the 1933 Act, structure the inquiry. . . . The relevant factors include the number of offerees and their relationship to each other and the issuer, the number of units offered, the size of the offering, and the manner of the offering. . . .

The term, "private offering," is not defined in the Securities Act of 1933. The scope of the § 4(2) private offering exemption must therefore be determined by reference to the legislative purposes of the Act. In SEC v. Ralston Purina Co., [346 U.S. 119 (1953)], the SEC had sought to enjoin a corporation's offer of unregistered stock to its employees, and the Court grappled with the corporation's defense that the offering came within the private placement exemption. The Court began by looking to the statutory purpose:

> Since exempt transactions are those as to which "there is no practical need for . . . [the bill's] application," the applicability of [§ 4(2)] should turn on whether the particular class of persons affected need the protection of the Act. An offering to those who are shown to be able to fend for themselves is a transaction "not involving any public offering."

346 U.S. at 124, 73 S.Ct. at 984. According to the Court, the purpose of the Act was "to protect investors by promoting full disclosure of information thought necessary to informed investment decisions." Id. at 124, 73 S.Ct. at 984. It therefore followed that "the exemption question turns on the knowledge of the offerees." Id. at 126–27, 73 S.Ct. at 985. That formulation remains the touchstone of the inquiry into the scope of the private offering exemption. It is most nearly reflected in the first of the four factors: the number of offerees and their relationship to each other and to the issuer.

In the case at bar, the defendants may have demonstrated the presence of the latter three factors. A small number of units offered, relatively modest financial stakes, and an offering characterized by personal contact between the issuer and offerees free of public advertising or intermediaries such as investment bankers or securities exchanges—these aspects of the instant transaction aid the defendants' search for a § 4(2) exemption.

Nevertheless, with respect to the first, most critical, and conceptually most problematic factor, the record does not permit us to agree that the defendants have proved that they are entitled to the limited sanctuary afforded by § 4(2). We must examine more closely the importance of demonstrating both the number of offerees and their relationship to the issuer in order to see why the defendants have not yet gained the § 4(2) exemption.

A. *The Number of Offerees*

Establishing the number of persons involved in an offering is important both in order to ascertain the magnitude of the offering and in order to determine the characteristics and knowledge of the persons thus identified.

The number of offerees, not the number of purchasers, is the relevant figure in considering the number of persons involved in an offering. . . . A private placement claimant's failure to adduce any evidence regarding the number of offerees will be fatal to the claim. . . . The number of offerees is not itself a decisive factor in determining the availability of the private offering exemption. Just as an offering to few may be public, so an offering to many may be private. . . . Nevertheless, "the more offerees, the more likelihood that the offering is public." . . . In the case at bar, the record indicates that eight investors were offered limited partnership shares in the drilling program—a total that would be entirely consistent with a finding that the offering was private. . . .

In considering the number of offerees solely as indicative of the magnitude or scope of an offering, the difference between one and eight offerees is relatively unimportant. Rejecting the argument that Doran was the sole offeree is significant, however, because it means that in considering the need of the offerees for the protection that registration would have afforded we must look beyond Doran's interests to those of all his fellow offerees. Even the offeree-plaintiff's 20–20 vision with respect to the facts underlying the security would not save the exemption if any one of his fellow offerees was blind.

B. *The Offerees' Relationship to the Issuer*

Since SEC v. Ralston, supra, courts have sought to determine the need of offerees for the protections afforded by registration by focusing on the relationship between offerees and issuer and more particularly on the information available to the offerees by virtue of that relationship. Id., 346 U.S. at 126–27, 73 S.Ct. at 985. Once the offerees have been identified, it is possible to investigate their relationship to the issuer.

1. *The role of investment sophistication*

The lower court's finding that Doran was a sophisticated investor is amply supported by the record, as is the sophistication of the other offerees. Doran holds a petroleum engineering degree from Texas A & M University. His net worth is in excess of $1,000,000. His holdings of approximately twenty-six oil and gas properties are valued at $850,000.

Nevertheless, evidence of a high degree of business or legal sophistication on the part of all offerees does not suffice to bring the offering within the private placement exemption. We clearly established that proposition in Hill York Corp. v. American International Franchises, Inc., [448 F.2d 680, 690 (5th Cir.1971)]. We reasoned that "if the plaintiffs did not possess the information requisite for a registration statement, they could not bring their sophisticated knowledge of business affairs to bear in deciding whether or not to invest.   .   .   ." Sophistication is not a substitute for access to the information that registration would disclose. As we said in *Hill York,* although the evidence of the offerees' expertise "is certainly favorable to the defendants, the level of sophistication will not carry the point. In this context, the relationship between the promoters and the purchasers and the 'access to the kind of information which registration would disclose' become highly relevant factors." .   .   .

In short, there must be sufficient basis of accurate information upon which the sophisticated investor may exercise his skills. Just as a scientist cannot be without his specimens, so the shrewdest investor's acuity will be blunted without specifications about the issuer. For an investor to be invested with exemptive status he must have the required data for judgment.

2.   *The requirement of available information*

More specifically, we shall require on remand that the defendants demonstrate that all offerees, whatever their expertise, had available the information a registration statement would have afforded a prospective investor in a public offering. Such a showing is not independently sufficient to establish that the offering qualified for the private placement exemption, but it is necessary to gain the exemption and is to be weighed along with the sophistication and number of the offerees, the number of units offered, and the size and manner of the offering.   .   .   .

Because in this case these latter factors weigh heavily in favor of the private offering exemption, satisfaction of the necessary condition regarding the availability of relevant information to the offerees would compel the conclusion that this offering fell within the exemption.   .   .   .

C.   *On Remand: The Issuer–Offeree Relationship*

In determining on remand the extent of the information available to the offerees, the district court must keep in mind that the "availability" of information means either disclosure of or effective access to the relevant information. The relationship between issuer and offeree is most critical when the issuer relies on the latter route.

To begin with, if the defendants could prove that all offerees were actually furnished the information a registration statement would have provided, whether the offerees occupied a position of access pre-existing such disclosure would not be dispositive of the status of the offering.   .   .   .

Alternatively it might be shown that the offeree had access to the files and record of the company that contained the relevant information. Such access might be afforded merely by the position of the offeree or by the issuer's promise to open appropriate files and records to the offeree as well as to answer inquiries regarding material information.   .   .   .

IV. Conclusion

An examination of the record and the district court's opinion in this case leaves unanswered the central question in all cases that turn on the availability of the § 4(2) exemption. Did the offerees know or have a realistic opportunity to learn facts essential to an investment judgment? We remand so that the trial court can answer that question.

This opinion focuses on facts because the Securities Act focuses on facts—facts disclosed, facts known, or access to facts. "Insider" or "outsider" labels are not determinative. Traditional forms are not determinative. In adjusting the generalities of § 4(2) to the realities of the contemporary market, we have seized on the availability to all offerees of pertinent facts. We have conditioned the private offering exemption on either actual disclosure of the information registration would provide or the offerees' effective access to such information. If the issuer has not disclosed but instead relies on the offerees' access, the privileged status of the offerees relative to the issuer must be shown. . . .

We must reverse in part the judgment of the district court and remand for proceedings not inconsistent with this opinion.

NOTE ON OTHER EXEMPTIONS

Most of the transactions exempted from the Securities Act appear in § 4. These include the "private placements" under § 4(2) discussed in *Doran,* and "transactions by any person other than an issuer, underwriter, or dealer" (§ 4(1)). Private placements are common—and becoming ever more so. As the § 4(2) exemption is notably imprecise, however, most issuers who hope to rely on it will turn to the SEC's Regulation D (rules 501–506).[26]

Regulation D provides a series of safe-harbors that issuers can use to come within the private-placement exemption and avoid (or reduce) their required disclosure. For example, if an issuer raises no more than $1 million through the securities, it generally may sell them to an unlimited number of buyers without registering the securities. (Rule 504.) If it raises no more than $5 million, it may sell the securities to 35 buyers but no more. (Rule 505.) And if it raises more than $5 million, it may sell to no more than 35 buyers, and each buyer must pass various tests of financial sophistication. (Rule 506.) In most cases, the issuer cannot widely advertise the security, and in all cases must file with the SEC a notice of the sale shortly after it issues the securities. The limits on the number of buyers do not apply to "accredited investors"—in general, banks, brokers, and other financial institutions and wealthy buyers. In most cases, the issuer must

---

26. Issuers could also make offerings of under $5 million under another set of safe harbor rules—"Regulation A"—and take advantage of Regulation A's reduced disclosure requirements. The attractiveness of Regulation D, however, has reduced the number of firms using Regulation A.

give buyers some information about the company—but the extent of the information required varies with the amount of money at stake in the issue.

Regulation D (and § 4(2)) generally exempts only the initial sale. As a result, most buyers can resell the securities only if they find another exemption. If the buyer is not "an issuer, underwriter, or dealer," he or she will be able to rely on § 4(1). But this exclusion may be misleading. Suppose Mary buys stock because she sees it as a good deal, and plans to resell it quickly at a higher price. Because § 2(11) defines an underwriter as someone who buys the security "with a view to" reselling it, Mary may be an underwriter. If so, § 4(1) will not exempt her sale. Worse, should she resell her shares to a large number of people, a court could integrate her resale into the initial offering and invalidate the issuer's exemption for the entire issue.

To deal with these resale problems, Regulation D provides that issuers can protect the exemption by using "reasonable care" to make sure the buyers are planning to hold the stock themselves. To show that care, they should exercise "reasonable inquiry" into the buyer's plans, disclose to the buyers that the stock is unregistered and subject to various resale restrictions, and print those restrictions directly on the stock. In addition, many lawyers will rely on yet another safe-harbor rule—rule 144. Subject to various qualifications, the rule allows buyers to resell stock they acquire in a Regulation D offering if they first hold it for two years and then resell it in limited volumes.

QUESTIONS

Two sisters and their husbands form a corporation. The new firm will develop word-processing software to help lawyers rewrite plain English into prose appropriate for SEC (and IRS) filings. The elder sister, Emiko, invests $1,400,000 and receives 70 percent of the stock. Each of the others invests $200,000 for 10 percent of the stock. After one year, the younger sister, Yoshiko, decides to sell her stock to three cousins.

1.   What exemptions might apply to the initial issue of stock?

2.   What exemptions might apply to Yoshiko's sale? Does your answer depend on why Yoshiko initially bought the stock? What if she asked her broker to find buyers for her stock?

3.   Suppose our four initial investors had formed a partnership rather than a corporation. How would your analysis change? Suppose they had formed a limited partnership, with Emiko as the general partner and the other three as limited partners, and that only Emiko planned to work at the company.

NOTE ON SECURITIES ACT CIVIL LIABILITIES

Before the adoption of Securities Act of 1933, securities fraud was solely a matter for state law. At common law, plaintiff had to prove that the

defendant had misrepresented a material fact. Plaintiff also had to prove all of the other elements of common law fraud: reliance, causation, scienter and injury. Plaintiff's recovery was limited to the amount of loss: the difference between what he or she paid and what the security was worth. The common law of misrepresentation thus was almost incapable of dealing with securities fraud. Consider the reliance element. Many securities cases involve omissions: failures to speak. But how do you rely on silence? Even if the fraud involved a misrepresentation, what happens if only some investors received the misrepresentations? The causation element also caused problems. It is always hard to prove what portion of one's loss was caused by the fraud and what portion of the loss was caused by other factors, such as general market conditions.

If the Securities Act had left it to the common law, civil liability to private party plaintiffs would not have played an important enforcement role.[27] However, Congress considered civil liability to private parties to be an important deterrent and therefore enacted various express private rights of action for private parties injured by securities law violations. In addition, the courts have implied private rights of action under several other provisions of the Acts. The most important of these is under Exchange Act § 10(b), which is discussed in the following section.

Securities Act § 11 is the principal express cause of action directed at fraud committed in connection with the sale of securities through the use of a registration statement. Because the material misrepresentation or omission must be in the registration statement, § 11 may not be used in connection with an exempt offering. Neither reliance nor causation generally are an element of the plaintiff's prima facie case. To the contrary, in a curious twist, it is the defendant who has the burden of proving that its misconduct did not cause plaintiff's damages. Pursuant to § 11(e), a defendant may reduce the amount of damages if it is able to prove that the reduction in value was caused by some other factor.

Because § 11 does not contain any privity requirement, the list of potential defendants is quite expansive. It includes: everyone who signed the registration statement, which by statute must at a minimum include the issuer, its principal executive officers, and a majority of its board of directors; every director of the issuer at the time the registration statement

---

27. Section 20(a) of the Securities Act gives the SEC broad power to investigate violations of the Act or the SEC rules adopted under the Act. Section 20(b) gives the SEC the power to bring a civil action in US District Court seeking an injunction against on-going or future violations. A number of other sanctions are potentially available under other statutes. For example, the SEC can suspend or bar a professional underwriter, broker or dealer from working in the securities industry. The SEC may also impose a variety of administrative penalties on violators.

Section 20(b) also authorizes the SEC to refer violations to the Attorney General who may then institute criminal proceedings against the violator. Section 24 provides the criminal penalties associated with securities violations: each violation subjects the perpetrator to a potential penalty of a fine of up to $10,000 and/or a prison term of up to five years. The penalties for violating the 1934 Act are even more severe, because they were recently raised to create greater deterrents against illegal insider trading. Section 32 of that Act no provides for fines of up to $2.5 million and a jail term of up to 10 years.

became effective, including directors who did not sign the registration statement; every person named in the registration statement as someone about to become a director is a defendant; every "expert" named as having prepared or certified any part of the statement, or as having prepared any report or valuation used in connection with the statement; and every underwriter involved in the distribution.

Securities Act § 12(a)(1) imposes strict liability on sellers of securities for offers or sales made in violation of § 5. Section 12(a)(1) liability thus arises, for example, where the seller improperly fails to register the securities. Section 12(a)(1) is also available if the seller registers but fails to deliver a statutory prospectus, violates the gun-jumping rules, or commits any other violation of § 5. Under § 12(a)(1) the main remedy is rescission: the buyer can recover the consideration paid, plus interest, less income received on the security. If the buyer is no longer the owner of the securities he or she can recover damages comparable to those which would be provided by rescission.

Section 12(a)(2) is the Securities Act's general civil liability provision for fraud and misrepresentation. As such, it overlaps somewhat with § 11, but it is a somewhat broader remedy. Section 12(a)(2) liability may be imposed for material misrepresentations or omissions in a registration statement. But § 12(a)(2) liability may also be imposed where the defendant made oral statements containing a material misrepresentation or omission. Section 12(a)(2) liability may also be imposed where the defendant used written selling materials containing a material misrepresentation or omission. Finally, § 12(a)(2) liability may also be imposed in exempt offerings where the defendant made material misrepresentations or omissions. As with § 12(a)(1), liability is limited to the seller of a security.

For a plaintiff's lawyer, these provisions are like an artist's palette: you have an array of options, each having unique advantages and disadvantages. Exchange Act § 10(b) requires the plaintiff to prove that the defendant acted with scienter, for example, while § 11 does not require plaintiff to prove anything about defendant's state of mind. Similar disparities could be cited about each of the sections. The lawyer's task thus is to identify the remedy best suited to the facts at bar.

For a transactional lawyer representing an issuer or other participant in the offering process, due diligence is the principal fallout of these provisions. At common law, plaintiff had to prove scienter—i.e., that defendant acted with the intent to commit fraud. In a § 11 case, by contrast, as to the issuer, plaintiff need not prove anything with respect to the defendant's state of mind. Once plaintiff makes out his prima facie case, the issuer is strictly liable. The issuer can be held liable even if the misrepresentation or omission was an inadvertent mistake. As to defendants other than the issuer, the degree of fault required is essentially a negligence standard. The burden of proof, however, is on the defendants to prove that they were not negligent in connection with the preparation of the registration statement. Similarly, under § 12(a)(2), defendants who conduct a reasonable investigation cannot be held liable. Taken together, these defenses gave rise to the due diligence process.

Due diligence is not an affirmative obligation; if the client does not want to perform it, the client is not required to do so. All rational participants in a registered offering perform due diligence, however, because it is usually the only viable defense to a § 11 claim. In practice, due diligence review is delegated to lawyers. The issuer's officers and directors delegate their due diligence obligations to the firm's lawyers. The underwriters will delegate their due diligence the lead underwriter's counsel. If the lawyers fail to carry out an adequate due diligence review, any defendants who delegated their due diligence tasks to that counsel will lose the defense. On the other hand, such defendants have a claim for legal malpractice against the lawyers who failed to do a proper due diligence review, which is why the following case is at least as scary for lawyers as it is for clients.

Escott v. BarChris Construction Corp.

283 F.Supp. 643 (S.D.N.Y.1968).

This is an action by purchasers of 5½ per cent convertible subordinated fifteen year debentures of BarChris Construction Corporation (BarChris). Plaintiffs purport to sue on their own behalf and "on behalf of all other . . . present and former holders" of the debentures. . . .

The action is brought under § 11 of the Securities Act of 1933 (15 U.S.C. § 77k). Plaintiffs allege that the registration statement with respect to these debentures filed with the Securities and Exchange Commission, which became effective on May 16, 1961, contained material false statements and material omissions.

Defendants fall into three categories: (1) the persons who signed the registration statement; (2) the underwriters, consisting of eight investment banking firms, led by Drexel & Co. (Drexel); and (3) BarChris's auditors, Peat, Marwick, Mitchell & Co. (Peat, Marwick).

The signers, in addition to BarChris itself, were the nine directors of BarChris, plus its controller, defendant Trilling, who was not a director. Of the nine directors, five were officers of BarChris, i.e., defendants Vitolo, president; Russo, executive vice president; Pugliese, vice president; Kircher, treasurer; and Birnbaum, secretary. Of the remaining four, defendant Grant was a member of the firm of Perkins, Daniels, McCormack & Collins, BarChris's attorneys. He became a director in October 1960. Defendant Coleman, a partner in Drexel, became a director on April 17, 1961, as did the other two, Auslander and Rose, who were not otherwise connected with BarChris. . . .

. . . On the main issue of liability, the questions to be decided are (1) did the registration statement contain false statements of fact, or did it omit to state facts which should have been stated in order to prevent it from being misleading; (2) if so, were the facts which were falsely stated or omitted "material" within the meaning of the Act; (3) if so, have defendants established their affirmative defenses?

Before discussing these questions, some background facts should be mentioned. At the time relevant here, BarChris was engaged primarily in the construction of bowling alleys, somewhat euphemistically referred to as "bowling centers." These were rather elaborate affairs. They contained not only a number of alleys or "lanes," but also, in most cases, bar and restaurant facilities.   . . .

The introduction of automatic pin setting machines in 1952 gave a marked stimulus to bowling. It rapidly became a popular sport, with the result that "bowling centers" began to appear throughout the country in rapidly increasing numbers. BarChris benefited from this increased interest in bowling. Its construction operations expanded rapidly. It is estimated that in 1960 BarChris installed approximately three per cent of all lanes built in the United States.   . . .

BarChris's sales increased dramatically from 1956 to 1960. According to the prospectus, net sales, in round figures, in 1956 were some $800,000, in 1957 $1,300,000, in 1958 $1,700,000. In 1959 they increased to over $3,300,000, and by 1960 they had leaped to over $9,165,000.   . . .

BarChris was compelled to expend considerable sums in defraying the cost of construction before it received reimbursement. As a consequence, BarChris was in constant need of cash to finance its operations, a need which grew more pressing as operations expanded.

In December 1959, BarChris sold 560,000 shares of common stock to the public at $3.00 per share. This issue was underwritten by Peter Morgan & Company, one of the present defendants.

By early 1961, BarChris needed additional working capital. The proceeds of the sale of the debentures involved in this action were to be devoted, in part at least, to fill that need.

The registration statement of the debentures, in preliminary form, was filed with the Securities and Exchange Commission on March 30, 1961. A first amendment was filed on May 11 and a second on May 16. The registration statement became effective on May 16. The closing of the financing took place on May 24. On that day BarChris received the net proceeds of the financing.

By that time BarChris was experiencing difficulties in collecting amounts due from some of its customers. Some of them were in arrears in payments due to factors on their discounted notes. As time went on those difficulties increased. Although BarChris continued to build alleys in 1961 and 1962, it became increasingly apparent that the industry was overbuilt. Operators of alleys, often inadequately financed, began to fail. Precisely when the tide turned is a matter of dispute, but at any rate, it was painfully apparent in 1962.

In May of that year BarChris made an abortive attempt to raise more money by the sale of common stock. It filed with the Securities and

Exchange Commission a registration statement for the stock issue which it later withdrew. In October 1962 BarChris came to the end of the road. On October 29, 1962, it filed in this court a petition for an arrangement under Chapter XI of the Bankruptcy Act. BarChris defaulted in the payment of the interest due on November 1, 1962 on the debentures.

[The court then undertook a lengthy analysis of the accuracy of BarChris's documents.]

Summary

For convenience, the various falsities and omissions which I have discussed in the preceding pages are recapitulated here. They were as follows:

1. 1960 Earnings
   (a) Sales

As per prospectus	$9,165,320
Correct figure	$8,511,420
Overstatement	$ 653,900

   (b) Net Operating Income

As per prospectus	$1,742,801
Correct figure	$1,496,196
Overstatement	$ 246,605

   (c) Earnings per Share

As per prospectus	$ .75
Correct figure	$ .65
Overstatement	$ .10

2. 1960 Balance Sheet
   Current Assets

As per prospectus	$4,524,021
Correct figure	$3,914,332
Overstatement	$ 609,689

3. Contingent Liabilities as of December 31, 1960 on Alternative Method of Financing

As per prospectus	$ 750,000
Correct figure	$1,125,795
Understatement	$ 375,795
Capitol Lanes should have been shown as a direct liability	$ 325,000

4. Contingent Liabilities as of April 30, 1961

As per prospectus	$ 825,000
Correct figure	$1,443,853
Understatement	$ 618,853
Capitol Lanes should have been shown as a direct liability	$ 314,166

5. Earnings Figures for Quarter ending March 31, 1961
   (a) Sales

As per prospectus	$2,138,455

	Correct figure	$1,618,645
	Overstatement	$ 519,810
(b)	Gross Profit	
	As per prospectus	$ 483,121
	Correct figure	$ 252,366
	Overstatement	$ 230,755
6.	Backlog as of March 31, 1961	
	As per prospectus	$6,905,000
	Correct figure	$2,415,000
	Overstatement	$4,490,000
7.	Failure to Disclose Officers' Loans Outstanding and Unpaid on May 16, 1961	$ 386,615
8.	Failure to Disclose Use of Proceeds in Manner not Revealed in Prospectus	
	Approximately	$1,160,000
9.	Failure to Disclose Customers' Delinquencies in May 1961 and BarChris's Potential Liability with Respect Thereto	
		Over $1,350,000

Materiality

It is a prerequisite to liability under § 11 of the Act that the fact which is falsely stated in a registration statement, or the fact that is omitted when it should have been stated to avoid misleading, be "material." The regulations of the Securities and Exchange Commission pertaining to the registration of securities define the word as follows. . . .

"The term 'material', when used to qualify a requirement for the furnishing of information as to any subject, limits the information required to those matters as to which an average prudent investor ought reasonably to be informed before purchasing the security registered."

What are "matters as to which an average prudent investor ought reasonably to be informed"? It seems obvious that they are matters which such an investor needs to know before he can make an intelligent, informed decision whether or not to buy the security. . . .

The average prudent investor is not concerned with minor inaccuracies or with errors as to matters which are of no interest to him. The facts which tend to deter him from purchasing a security are facts which have an important bearing upon the nature or condition of the issuing corporation or its business.

Judged by this test, there is no doubt that many of the misstatements and omissions in this prospectus were material. This is true of all of them which relate to the state of affairs in 1961, i.e., the overstatement of sales and gross profit for the first quarter, the understatement of contingent liabilities as of April 30, the overstatement of orders on hand and the failure to disclose the true facts with respect to officers' loans, customers' delinquencies, application of proceeds and the prospective operation of several alleys.

The misstatements and omissions pertaining to BarChris's status as of December 31, 1960, however, present a much closer question. The 1960 earnings figures, the 1960 balance sheet and the contingent liabilities as of December 31, 1960 were not nearly as erroneous as plaintiffs have claimed. But they were wrong to some extent, as we have seen. Would it have deterred the average prudent investor from purchasing these debentures if he had been informed that the 1960 sales were $8,511,420 rather than $9,165,320, that the net operating income was $1,496,196 rather than $1,742,801 and that the earnings per share in 1960 were approximately 65¢ rather than 75¢? According to the unchallenged figures, sales in 1959 were $3,320,121, net operating income was $441,103, and earnings per share were 33?. Would it have made a difference to an average prudent investor if he had known that in 1960 sales were only 256 per cent of 1959 sales, not 276 per cent; that net operating income was up by only $1,055,093, not by $1,301,698, and that earnings per share, while still approximately twice those of 1959, were not something more than twice?

These debentures were rated "B" by the investment rating services. They were thus characterized as speculative, as any prudent investor must have realized. It would seem that anyone interested in buying these convertible debentures would have been attracted primarily by the conversion feature, by the growth potential of the stock. The growth which the company enjoyed in 1960 over prior years was striking, even on the correct figures. It is hard to see how a prospective purchaser of this type of investment would have been deterred from buying if he had been advised of these comparatively minor errors in reporting 1960 sales and earnings.

Since no one knows what moves or does not move the mythical "average prudent investor," it comes down to a question of judgment, to be exercised by the trier of the fact as best he can in the light of all the circumstances. It is my best judgment that the average prudent investor would not have cared about these errors in the 1960 sales and earnings figures, regrettable though they may be. I therefore find that they were not material within the meaning of § 11. . . .

This leaves for consideration the errors in the 1960 balance sheet figures which have previously been discussed in detail. Current assets were overstated by approximately $600,000. Liabilities were understated by approximately $325,000 by the failure to treat the liability on Capitol Lanes as a direct liability of BarChris on a consolidated basis. Of this $325,000 approximately $65,000, the amount payable on Capitol within one year, should have been treated as a current liability.

As per balance sheet, cash was $285,482. In fact, $145,000 of this had been borrowed temporarily from Talcott [with whom BarChris had a financing arrangement] and was to be returned by January 16, 1961 so that realistically, cash was only $140,482. Trade accounts receivable were overstated by $150,000 by including Howard Lanes Annex, an alley which was not sold to an outside buyer.

As per balance sheet, total current assets were $4,524,021, and total current liabilities were $2,413,867, a ratio of approximately 1.9 to 1. This was bad enough, but on the true facts, the ratio was worse. As corrected, current assets, as near as one can tell, were approximately $3,924,000, and current liabilities approximately $2,478,000, a ratio of approximately 1.6 to 1.

Would it have made any difference if a prospective purchaser of these debentures had been advised of these facts? There must be some point at which errors in disclosing a company's balance sheet position become material, even to a growth-oriented investor. On all the evidence I find that these balance sheet errors were material within the meaning of § 11.

Since there was an abundance of material misstatements pertaining to 1961 affairs, whether or not the errors in the 1960 figures were material does not affect the outcome of this case except to the extent that it bears upon the liability of Peat, Marwick. That subject will be discussed hereinafter.

The "Due Diligence" Defenses

Section 11 . . . of the Act provides that:

[§ 11. (a) In case any part of the registration statement, when such part became effective, contained an untrue statement of a material fact or omitted to state a material fact required to be stated therein or necessary to make the statements therein not misleading, any person acquiring such security (unless it is proved that at the time of such acquisition he knew of such untruth or omission) may, . . . sue—

(1) every person who signed the registration statement;

(2) every person who was a director of . . . the issuer . . .; . . .

(4) every accountant, engineer, or appraiser, or any person whose profession gives authority to a statement made by him, who has with his consent been named as having prepared or certified any part of the registration statement, with respect to the statement in such registration statement, . . . which purports to have been prepared or certified by him;

(5) every underwriter with respect to such security. . . .

(b) Notwithstanding the provisions of subsection (a) no person, other than the issuer, shall be liable as provided therein who shall sustain the burden of proof . . .

(3) that (A) as regards any part of the registration statement not purporting to be made on the authority of an expert, . . . he had, after reasonable investigation, reasonable ground to believe and did believe, at the time such part of the registration statement became effective, that the statements therein were true and that there was no omission to state a material fact required to be stated therein or necessary to make the statements therein not mislead-

ing; and (B) as regards any part of the registration statement purporting to be made upon his authority as an expert . . . (i) he had, after reasonable investigation, reasonable ground to believe and did believe, at the time such part of the registration statement became effective, that the statements therein were true and that there was no omission to state a material fact required to be stated therein or necessary to make the statements therein not mislead- ing, or (ii) such part of the registration statement did not fairly represent his statement as an expert or was not a fair copy of or extract from his report or valuation as an expert; and (C) as regards any part of the registration statement purporting to be made on the authority of an expert (other than himself) . . . he had no reasonable ground to believe and did not believe, at the time such part of the registration statement became effective, that the statements therein were untrue or that there was an omission to state a material fact required to be stated therein or necessary to make the statements therein not misleading, or that such part of the registration statement did not fairly represent the state- ment of the expert or was not a fair copy of or extract from the report or valuation of the expert;. . . .]

Section 11(c) defines "reasonable investigation" as follows:

"In determining, for the purpose of paragraph (3) of subsection (b) of this section, what constitutes reasonable investigation and reasonable ground for belief, the standard of reasonableness shall be that required of a prudent man in the management of his own property."

Every defendant, except BarChris itself, to whom, as the issuer, these defenses are not available, . . . has pleaded these affirmative defens- es. . . .

Before considering the evidence, a preliminary matter should be dis- posed of. The defendants do not agree among themselves as to who the "experts" were or as to the parts of the registration statement which were expertised. Some defendants say that Peat, Marwick was the expert, others say that BarChris's attorneys, Perkins, Daniels, McCormack & Collins, and the underwriters' attorneys, Drinker, Biddle & Reath, were also the ex- perts. On the first view, only those portions of the registration statement purporting to be made on Peat, Marwick's authority were expertised portions. On the other view, everything in the registration statement was within this category, because the two law firms were responsible for the entire document.

The first view is the correct one. To say that the entire registration statement is expertised because some lawyer prepared it would be an unreasonable construction of the statute. Neither the lawyer for the compa- ny nor the lawyer for the underwriters is an expert within the meaning of § 11. The only expert, in the statutory sense, was Peat, Marwick, and the only parts of the registration statement which purported to be made upon the authority of an expert were the portions which purported to be made on Peat, Marwick's authority.

The parties also disagree as to what those portions were. Some defendants say that it was only the 1960 figures (and the figures for prior years, which are not in controversy here). Others say in substance that it was every figure in the prospectus. The plaintiffs take a somewhat intermediate view. They do not claim that Peat, Marwick expertised every figure, but they do maintain that Peat, Marwick is responsible for a portion of the text of the prospectus, i.e., that pertaining to "Methods of Operation," because a reference to it was made in footnote 9 to the balance sheet.

Here again, the more narrow view is the correct one. The registration statement contains a report of Peat, Marwick as independent public accountants dated February 23, 1961. This relates only to the consolidated balance sheet of BarChris and consolidated subsidiaries as of December 31, 1960, and the related statement of earnings and retained earnings for the five years then ended. This is all that Peat, Marwick purported to certify. It is perfectly clear that it did not purport to certify the 1961 figures, some of which are expressly stated in the prospectus to have been unaudited. . . .

Vitolo and Pugliese

They were the founders of the business who stuck with it to the end. Vitolo was president and Pugliese was vice president. Despite their titles, their field of responsibility in the administration of BarChris's affairs during the period in question seems to have been less all-embracing than Russo's. Pugliese in particular appears to have limited his activities to supervising the actual construction work.

Vitolo and Pugliese are each men of limited education. It is not hard to believe that for them the prospectus was difficult reading, if indeed they read it at all.

But whether it was or not is irrelevant. The liability of a director who signs a registration statement does not depend upon whether or not he read it or, if he did, whether or not he understood what he was reading.

And in any case, Vitolo and Pugliese were not as naive as they claim to be. They were members of BarChris's executive committee. At meetings of that committee BarChris's affairs were discussed at length. They must have known what was going on. Certainly they knew of the inadequacy of cash in 1961. They knew of their own large advances to the company which remained unpaid. They knew that they had agreed not to deposit their checks until the financing proceeds were received. They knew and intended that part of the proceeds were to be used to pay their own loans.

All in all, . . . Vitolo and Pugliese . . . could not have believed that the registration statement was wholly true and that no material facts had been omitted. And in any case, there is nothing to show that they made any investigation of anything which they may not have known about or understood. They have not proved their due diligence defenses.

Kircher

Kircher was treasurer of BarChris and its chief financial officer. He is a certified public accountant and an intelligent man. He was thoroughly familiar with BarChris's financial affairs. . . . He knew of the customers' delinquency problem. . . .

Kircher worked on the preparation of the registration statement. He conferred with Grant and on occasion with Ballard [the underwriters' counsel]. He supplied information to them about the company's business. He read the prospectus and understood it. He knew what it said and what it did not say.

Kircher's contention is that he had never before dealt with a registration statement, that he did not know what it should contain, and that he relied wholly on Grant, Ballard and Peat, Marwick to guide him. He claims that it was their fault, not his, if there was anything wrong with it. He says that all the facts were recorded in BarChris's books where these "experts" could have seen them if they had looked. He says that he truthfully answered all their questions. In effect, he says that if they did not know enough to ask the right questions and to give him the proper instructions, that is not his responsibility.

There is an issue of credibility here. In fact, Kircher was not frank in dealing with Grant and Ballard. He withheld information from them. But even if he had told them all the facts, this would not have constituted the due diligence contemplated by the statute. Knowing the facts, Kircher had reason to believe that the expertised portion of the prospectus, i.e., the 1960 figures, was in part incorrect. He could not shut his eyes to the facts and rely on Peat, Marwick for that portion. . . .

Kircher has not proved his due diligence defenses.

Birnbaum

Birnbaum was a young lawyer, admitted to the bar in 1957, who, after brief periods of employment by two different law firms and an equally brief period of practicing in his own firm, was employed by BarChris as house counsel and assistant secretary in October 1960. Unfortunately for him, he became secretary and a director of BarChris on April 17, 1961, after the first version of the registration statement had been filed with the Securities and Exchange Commission. He signed the later amendments, thereby becoming responsible for the accuracy of the prospectus in its final form.

Although the prospectus, in its description of "management," lists Birnbaum among the "executive officers" and devotes several sentences to a recital of his career, the fact seems to be that he was not an executive officer in any real sense. He did not participate in the management of the company. As house counsel, he attended to legal matters of a routine nature. Among other things, he incorporated subsidiaries, with which BarChris was plentifully supplied. . . .

Birnbaum examined contracts. In that connection he advised BarChris that the T–Bowl contracts were not legally enforceable. He was thus aware of that fact.   .   .   .

It seems probable that Birnbaum did not know of many of the inaccuracies in the prospectus. He must, however, have appreciated some of them. In any case, he made no investigation and relied on the others to get it right.   .   .   . As a lawyer, he should have known his obligations under the statute. He should have known that he was required to make a reasonable investigation of the truth of all the statements in the unexpertised portion of the document which he signed. Having failed to make such an investigation, he did not have reasonable ground to believe that all these statements were true. Birnbaum has not established his due diligence defenses except as to the audited 1960 figures.

Auslander

Auslander was an "outside" director, i.e., one who was not an officer of BarChris. He was chairman of the board of Valley Stream National Bank in Valley Stream, Long Island. In February 1961 Vitolo asked him to become a director of BarChris. Vitolo gave him an enthusiastic account of BarChris's progress and prospects. As an inducement, Vitolo said that when BarChris received the proceeds of a forthcoming issue of securities, it would deposit $1,000,000 in Auslander's bank.

In February and early March 1961, before accepting Vitolo's invitation, Auslander made some investigation of BarChris. He obtained Dun & Bradstreet reports which contained sales and earnings figures for periods earlier than December 31, 1960. He caused inquiry to be made of certain of BarChris's banks and was advised that they regarded BarChris favorably.   .   .   .

On March 3, 1961, Auslander indicated his willingness to accept a place on the board. Shortly thereafter, on March 14, Kircher sent him a copy of BarChris's annual report for 1960. Auslander observed that BarChris's auditors were Peat, Marwick. They were also the auditors for the Valley Stream National Bank. He thought well of them.

Auslander was elected a director on April 17, 1961. The registration statement in its original form had already been filed, of course without his signature. On May 10, 1961, he signed a signature page for the first amendment to the registration statement which was filed on May 11, 1961. This was a separate sheet without any document attached. Auslander did not know that it was a signature page for a registration statement. He vaguely understood that it was something "for the SEC."

Auslander attended a meeting of BarChris's directors on May 15, 1961. At that meeting he, along with the other directors, signed the signature sheet for the second amendment which constituted the registration statement in its final form. Again, this was only a separate sheet without any document attached. Auslander never saw a copy of the registration statement in its final form.

At the May 15 directors' meeting, however, Auslander did realize that what he was signing was a signature sheet to a registration statement. This was the first time that he had appreciated that fact. A copy of the registration statement in its earlier form as amended on May 11, 1961 was passed around at the meeting. Auslander glanced at it briefly. He did not read it thoroughly.   .   .   .

In considering Auslander's due diligence defenses, a distinction is to be drawn between the expertised and non-expertised portions of the prospectus. As to the former, Auslander knew that Peat, Marwick had audited the 1960 figures. He believed them to be correct because he had confidence in Peat, Marwick. He had no reasonable ground to believe otherwise.

As to the non-expertised portions, however, Auslander is in a different position. He seems to have been under the impression that Peat, Marwick was responsible for all the figures. This impression was not correct, as he would have realized if he had read the prospectus carefully. Auslander made no investigation of the accuracy of the prospectus. He relied on the assurance of Vitolo and Russo, and upon the information he had received in answer to his inquiries back in February and early March. These inquiries were general ones, in the nature of a credit check. The information which he received in answer to them was also general, without specific reference to the statements in the prospectus, which was not prepared until some time thereafter.

It is true that Auslander became a director on the eve of the financing. He had little opportunity to familiarize himself with the company's affairs. The question is whether, under such circumstances, Auslander did enough to establish his due diligence defense with respect to the non-expertised portions of the prospectus.   .   .   .

Section 11 imposes liability in the first instance upon a director, no matter how new he is. He is presumed to know his responsibility when he becomes a director. He can escape liability only by using that reasonable care to investigate the facts which a prudent man would employ in the management of his own property. In my opinion, a prudent man would not act in an important matter without any knowledge of the relevant facts, in sole reliance upon representations of persons who are comparative strangers and upon general information which does not purport to cover the particular case. To say that such minimal conduct measures up to the statutory standard would, to all intents and purposes, absolve new directors from responsibility merely because they are new. This is not a sensible construction of § 11, when one bears in mind its fundamental purpose of requiring full and truthful disclosure for the protection of investors.

I find and conclude that Auslander has not established his due diligence defense with respect to the misstatements and omissions in those portions of the prospectus other than the audited 1960 figures.   .   .   .

Grant

Grant became a director of BarChris in October 1960. His law firm was counsel to BarChris in matters pertaining to the registration of securities.

Grant drafted the registration statement for the stock issue in 1959 and for the warrants in January 1961. He also drafted the registration statement for the debentures. In the preliminary division of work between him and Ballard, the underwriters' counsel, Grant took initial responsibility for preparing the registration statement, while Ballard devoted his efforts in the first instance to preparing the indenture.

Grant is sued as a director and as a signer of the registration statement. This is not an action against him for malpractice in his capacity as a lawyer. Nevertheless, in considering Grant's due diligence defenses, the unique position which he occupied cannot be disregarded. As the director most directly concerned with writing the registration statement and assuring its accuracy, more was required of him in the way of reasonable investigation than could fairly be expected of a director who had no connection with this work.

There is no valid basis for plaintiffs' accusation that Grant knew that the prospectus was false in some respects and incomplete and misleading in others. Having seen him testify at length, I am satisfied as to his integrity. I find that Grant honestly believed that the registration statement was true and that no material facts had been omitted from it.

In this belief he was mistaken, and the fact is that for all his work, he never discovered any of the errors or omissions which have been recounted at length in this opinion, with the single exception of Capitol Lanes. He knew that BarChris had not sold this alley and intended to operate it, but he appears to have been under the erroneous impression that Peat, Marwick had knowingly sanctioned its inclusion in sales because of the allegedly temporary nature of the operation.

Grant contends that a finding that he did not make a reasonable investigation would be equivalent to a holding that a lawyer for an issuing company, in order to show due diligence, must make an independent audit of the figures supplied to him by his client. I do not consider this to be a realistic statement of the issue. There were errors and omissions here which could have been detected without an audit. The question is whether, despite his failure to detect them, Grant made a reasonable effort to that end.

Much of this registration statement is a scissors and paste-pot job. Grant lifted large portions from the earlier prospectuses, modifying them in some instances to the extent that he considered necessary. But BarChris's affairs had changed for the worse by May 1961. Statements that were accurate in January were no longer accurate in May. Grant never discovered this. He accepted the assurances of Kircher and Russo that any change which might have occurred had been for the better, rather than the contrary.

It is claimed that a lawyer is entitled to rely on the statements of his client and that to require him to verify their accuracy would set an unreasonably high standard. This is too broad a generalization. It is all a matter of degree. To require an audit would obviously be unreasonable. On the other hand, to require a check of matters easily verifiable is not unreasonable. Even honest clients can make mistakes. The statute imposes liability for untrue statements regardless of whether they are intentionally untrue. The way to prevent mistakes is to test oral information by examining the original written record.

There were things which Grant could readily have checked which he did not check. For example, he was unaware of the provisions of the agreements between BarChris and Talcott. He never read them. Thus, he did not know, although he readily could have ascertained, that BarChris's contingent liability on Type B leaseback arrangements was 100 per cent, not 25 per cent. He did not appreciate that if BarChris defaulted in repurchasing delinquent customers' notes upon Talcott's demand, Talcott could accelerate all the customer paper in its hands, which amounted to over $3,000,000. . . .

Grant was unaware of the fact that BarChris was about to operate Bridge and Yonkers. He did not read the minutes of those subsidiaries which would have revealed that fact to him. On the subject of minutes, Grant knew that minutes of certain meetings of the BarChris executive committee held in 1961 had not been written up. Kircher, who had acted as secretary at those meetings, had complete notes of them. Kircher told Grant that there was no point in writing up the minutes because the matters discussed at those meetings were purely routine. Grant did not insist that the minutes be written up, nor did he look at Kircher's notes. If he had, he would have learned that on February 27, 1961 there was an extended discussion in the executive committee meeting about customers' delinquencies, that on March 8, 1961 the committee had discussed the pros and cons of alley operation by BarChris, that on March 18, 1961 the committee was informed that BarChris was constructing or about to begin constructing twelve alleys for which it had no contracts, and that on May 13, 1961 Dreyfuss, one of the worst delinquents, had filed a petition in Chapter X. . . .

Grant was entitled to rely on Peat, Marwick for the 1960 figures. He had no reasonable ground to believe them to be inaccurate. But the matters which I have mentioned were not within the expertised portion of the prospectus. As to this, Grant, was obliged to make a reasonable investigation. I am forced to find that he did not make one. After making all due allowances for the fact that Bar Chris's officers misled him, there are too many instances in which Grant failed to make an inquiry which he could easily have made which, if pursued, would have put him on his guard. In my opinion, this finding on the evidence in this case does not establish an unreasonably high standard in other cases for company counsel who are also directors. Each case must rest on its own facts. I conclude that Grant has not established his due diligence defenses except as to the audited 1960 figures. . . .

Peat, Marwick

The part of the registration statement purporting to be made upon the authority of Peat, Marwick as an expert was, as we have seen, the 1960 figures. But because the statute requires the court to determine Peat, Marwick's belief, and the grounds thereof, "at the time such part of the registration statement became effective," for the purposes of this affirmative defense, the matter must be viewed as of May 16, 1961, and the question is whether at that time Peat, Marwick, after reasonable investigation, had reasonable ground to believe and did believe that the 1960 figures were true and that no material fact had been omitted from the registration statement which should have been included in order to make the 1960 figures not misleading.   .   .   .

Peat, Marwick's work was in general charge of a member of the firm, Cummings, and more immediately in charge of Peat, Marwick's manager, Logan. Most of the actual work was performed by a senior accountant, Berardi.   .   .   .

Berardi was then about thirty years old. He was not yet a C.P.A. He had had no previous experience with the bowling industry. This was his first job as a senior accountant. He could hardly have been given a more difficult assignment.

After obtaining a little background information on BarChris by talking to Logan and reviewing Peat, Marwick's work papers on its 1959 audit, Berardi examined the results of test checks of BarChris's accounting procedures which one of the junior accountants had made, and he prepared an "internal control questionnaire" and an "audit program." Thereafter, for a few days subsequent to December 30, 1960, he inspected BarChris's inventories and examined certain alley construction. Finally, on January 13, 1961, he began his auditing work which he carried on substantially continuously until it was completed on February 24, 1961. Toward the close of the work, Logan reviewed it and made various comments and suggestions to Berardi.

It is unnecessary to recount everything that Berardi did in the course of the audit. We are concerned only with the evidence relating to what Berardi did or did not do with respect to those items which I have found to have been incorrectly reported in the 1960 figures in the prospectus. More narrowly, we are directly concerned only with such of those items as I have found to be material.   .   .   .

First and foremost is Berardi's failure to discover that Capitol Lanes had not been sold. This error affected both the sales figure and the liability side of the balance sheet.   .   .   .

Berardi knew from various BarChris records that Capitol Lanes, Inc. was paying rentals to Talcott. Also, a Peat, Marwick work paper bearing Kennedy's initials recorded that Capitol Lanes, Inc. held certain insurance policies, including a fire insurance policy on "contents," a workmen's compensation and a public liability policy.   .   .   .

Berardi testified that he inquired of Russo about Capitol Lanes and that Russo told him that Capitol Lanes, Inc. was going to operate an alley some day but as yet it had no alley. Berardi testified that he understood that the alley had not been built and that he believed that the rental payments were on vacant land.

I am not satisfied with this testimony. If Berardi did hold this belief, he should not have held it. The entries as to insurance and as to "operation of alley" should have alerted him to the fact that an alley existed. He should have made further inquiry on the subject. It is apparent that Berardi did not understand this transaction.

[The court continued with a discussion of other mistakes by Berardi.]

In substance, what Berardi did is similar to what Grant and Ballard did. He asked questions, he got answers which he considered satisfactory, and he did nothing to verify them. . . .

Accountants should not be held to a standard higher than that recognized in their profession. I do not do so here. Berardi's review did not come up to that standard. He did not take some of the steps which Peat, Marwick's written program prescribed. He did not spend an adequate amount of time on a task of this magnitude. Most important of all, he was too easily satisfied with glib answers to his inquiries.

. . . . .

Defendants' motions to dismiss this action, upon which decision was reserved at the trial, are denied. . . .

QUESTIONS

1. How does Peat Marwick's potential liability differ from that of the directors? Why should it differ?

2. Is BarChris itself liable under the statute? Why?

3. Should a director who also serves as general counsel to the issuer be held to a different standard than the other directors?

4. How should a law firm respond to a request from a client that a partner serve on its board of directors?

5. Who was harmed by the defendants' misconduct? Did anyone benefit from it?

PROBLEM

US Way is a marketing firm. Sales agents for the firm sell microwave ovens door-to-door, keep a 6 percent commission on any sales they make, and forward the remainder to their supervising manager. Those managers (who recruit the sales agents) keep a 6 percent commission for themselves and forward the rest to USW. USW then pays the wholesalers and the firm's salaried officers. Neither the sales staff nor the managers earn any other compensation.

Sales staff may become managers if they recruit other sales agents to work under them. If, however, total commissions would otherwise exceed 15 percent of the sales price (as would happen if a manager recruited a sales agent who in turn recruited another sales agent and all three collected 6 percent) the managers and sales staff in the chain divide the 15 percent equally.

1. Suppose the USW president owns all the stock of USW. Would USW need to register with the SEC?

2. Suppose the stock of USW is traded on the New York Stock Exchange. Suppose further that in March scientists discover that microwave ovens present a non-negligible risk of causing brain cancer, particularly among small children. In April, USW issues additional stock to the public for $50 per share.

(a) Suppose that the market for microwave ovens collapses in May and USW becomes insolvent. A buyer of one of the April USW shares sues the directors personally, on the ground that the registration statement inadequately disclosed the cancer-risk problem. If a court finds the registration statement materially misleading, can the buyer recover? Must the buyer have seen the registration statement before buying the stock? What would be the buyer's damages?

(b) Suppose again the facts as stated in 2(a). Is the buyer likely to be successful in a suit against the accounting firm that audited the registration statement?

NOTE ON INTEGRATED DISCLOSURE AND EXCHANGE ACT DISCLOSURES

The Securities Act and the Exchange Act originally established two separate disclosure systems. The former requires disclosures with respect to particular transactions, such as new issues of stocks or bonds to the public, while the latter imposes a system of periodic disclosures on certain companies—most importantly, the obligation to file annual and quarterly reports.

For publicly traded companies that must file periodic disclosure reports under the Exchange Act, there was a substantial amount of overlap and duplication between those reports and the Securities Act registration statement disclosures it was obliged to make when selling securities to the public. In response to the substantial regulatory burden this overlap created, the SEC adopted the modern integrated disclosure system.

Integrated disclosure starts with the reports that must be filed under the Exchange Act. We therefore begin with the question—who must file? A full answer to that question is complicated, involving a convoluted review of multiple sections of the Exchange Act. For our purposes, it suffices to say that effectively all publicly traded companies, as well as some large close corporations, are required to file Exchange Act reports.

Covered corporations must register with the SEC by filing an initial Form 10. This form only needs to be filed once with respect to a particular class of securities—the first time the issuer registers that class of securities under the Act. It contains exhaustive disclosures similar to those required in a Securities Act registration statement.[28] The corporation thereafter must annually file a Form 10–K, which contains audited financial statements and management's report of the previous year's activities and usually also incorporates the annual report sent to shareholders. The company also must file a Form 10–Q for each of first three quarters of the year. It will contain unaudited financial statements and management's report on material recent developments. Finally, the corporation must file a Form 8–K within 15 days after certain important events affecting the company's operations or financial condition. In other words, if a major event happens, the company must report it immediately instead of waiting for the next quarterly or annual report. The Form specifies events that are considered sufficiently important to require filing, such as sales or purchases of significant assets or a change in control of the company.

In addition to the periodic disclosure obligations, registering a class of securities under the Exchange Act triggers a variety of other requirements. For example, the issuer becomes subject to the proxy rules under § 14, the tender offer rules under sections 13 and 14, and certain of the anti-fraud provisions of the Act.

Before the integrated disclosure system came into being, a reporting company that wished to sell securities in a registered public offering was obliged to prepare a registration statement containing most of the information that had already been disclosed in its Exchange Act periodic disclosure reports. Worse yet, the Securities Act and Exchange Act forms differed somewhat both as to style and content. As a result, the disclosure process was enormously expensive for reporting firms.

To economists all of this duplication of effort required by the two Acts was not only expensive, but was also unnecessary. The efficient capital markets hypothesis posits that all publicly available information is more or less instantaneously incorporated into the market price of its securities. Because the theory is reasonably well-accepted for this purpose, we may assume that all of the information released in the firm's regular Exchange Act disclosure statements will be digested by securities analysts and reflected in the firm's market price. Because virtually all securities offerings

28. Be careful to distinguish registration of a class of securities under the Exchange Act from registration of an offering of securities under the Securities Act—a company that has registered a class of securities under the Exchange Act will still have to register a particular offering of securities of that class under the Securities Act. For example, suppose ABC Corporation has registered its common stock under the Exchange Act. ABC now wants to sell an additional 1 million shares of common stock in a new public offering. Unless an exemption is available, the shares to be sold in the offering must still be registered under the Securities Act, even though the class itself is registered under the Exchange Act. Although it is slightly inaccurate, it might be helpful if you think about the difference as follows: the Exchange Act registers companies; the Securities Act registers offerings.

by established companies are made either at the current market price of its securities or at a slight discount from market price, there is no need to reiterate all of the Exchange Act information in a Securities Act filing. The market has already gotten the information and accounted for it.

The SEC eventually saw the efficient capital markets hypothesis as providing a way out of the box—a way of eliminating the complex and expensive dual disclosure system. It therefore adopted the so-called "Integrated Disclosure System," one of the truly major changes in its history. Under the integrated disclosure system, an issuer planning a registered offering first looks to the various registration statement forms to determine which form it is eligible to use. The forms then direct the drafter to Regulation S–K for the substantive disclosure requirements. Regulation S–K adopted uniform disclosure standards for both Acts, so that virtually all filings are now prepared under identical instructions. As a result, the style and content of disclosure documents under both Acts are now essentially identical. Thus, for example, the annual 10–K report contains information that can be directly transferred into a registration statement.

Each of the main registration statement forms requires disclosure of two basic types of information: information about the transaction and information about the issuer (a/k/a registrant). Form S–1, the basic registration statement form, requires detailed disclosure about both categories. But Form S–3 only requires disclosure of information about the transaction. Information about the issuer is incorporated by reference from the last 10–K and other Exchange Act disclosure documents. In order to use Form S–3, an issuer must meet two basic requirements—it must be large and seasoned. It must have a substantial number of shares outstanding and must have been a reporting company for several years. The basic idea is that an issuer eligible to use Form S–3 will be one that is regularly providing disclosure to the market about itself and whose securities are traded in an efficient market that impounds the disclosed information into price quickly. Given these criteria, the SEC posited that registrant-related information would be unnecessarily duplicative.

C.   RULE 10b–5

Where Congress is silent as to whether or not a private right of action exists under a particular statute, courts have sometimes implied a private right of action. In securities law, the most important of these undoubtedly is the private right of action under Exchange Act § 10(b) and Rule 10b–5 thereunder. Section 10(b) provides:

> It shall be unlawful for any person, directly or indirectly, by the use of any means or instrumentality of interstate commerce or of the mails, or of any facility of any national securities exchange.   .   .   .
>
> > (b) To use or employ, in connection with the purchase or sale of any security registered on a national securities exchange or any security not so registered, any manipulative or deceptive device or contrivance in contravention of such rules and regulations as the

Commission may prescribe as necessary or appropriate in the public interest or for the protection of investors.

Notice that § 10(b) applies to any security, including securities of closely held corporations that generally are not subject to the Exchange Act and to transactions in government securities. Notice also that § 10(b) is not self-executing—it did not prohibit anything until the SEC adopted rules implementing it.

Our attention therefore turns to Rule 10b–5—easily the most famous, and arguably the most important, of all the SEC's many rules:

It shall be unlawful for any person, directly or indirectly, by the use of any means or instrumentality of interstate commerce, or of the mails or of any facility of any national securities exchange,

(a) To employ any device, scheme, or artifice to defraud,

(b) To make any untrue statement of a material fact or to omit to state a material fact necessary in order to make the statements made, in the light of the circumstances under which they were made, not misleading, or

(c) To engage in any act, practice, or course of business which operates or would operate as a fraud or deceit upon any person,

in connection with the purchase or sale of any security.

The central theme of the rule's history is one of repeated judicial glosses on this relatively innocuous—and vague—text. As Justice Rehnquist has observed, Rule 10b–5 is now "a judicial oak which has grown from little more than a legislative acorn." Blue Chip Stamps v. Manor Drug Stores, 421 U.S. 723 (1975). In a very real sense, Rule 10b–5 jurisprudence is a species of federal common law only loosely tied to the statutory text.

Basic Inc. v. Levinson

485 U.S. 224, 108 S.Ct. 978, 99 L.Ed.2d 194 (1988).

.   .   .

I

Prior to December 20, 1978, Basic Incorporated was a publicly traded company primarily engaged in the business of manufacturing chemical refractories for the steel industry. As early as 1965 or 1966, Combustion Engineering, Inc., a company producing mostly alumina-based refractories, expressed some interest in acquiring Basic, but was deterred from pursuing this inclination seriously because of antitrust concerns it then entertained. In 1976, however, regulatory action opened the way to a renewal of Combustion's interest. The "Strategic Plan," dated October 25, 1976, for Combustion's Industrial Products Group included the objective: "Acquire Basic Inc. $30 million."

Beginning in September 1976, Combustion representatives had meetings and telephone conversations with Basic officers and directors, including petitioners here, concerning the possibility of a merger. During 1977 and 1978, Basic made three public statements denying that it was engaged in merger negotiations.[4] On December 18, 1978, Basic asked the New York Stock Exchange to suspend trading in its shares and issued a release stating that it had been "approached" by another company concerning a merger. On December 19, Basic's board endorsed Combustion's offer of $46 per share for its common stock, and on the following day publicly announced its approval of Combustion's tender offer for all outstanding shares.

Respondents are former Basic shareholders who sold their stock after Basic's first public statement of October 21, 1977, and before the suspension of trading in December 1978. Respondents brought a class action against Basic and its directors, asserting that the defendants issued three false or misleading public statements and thereby were in violation of § 10(b) of the 1934 Act and of Rule 10b–5. Respondents alleged that they were injured by selling Basic shares at artificially depressed prices in a market affected by petitioners' misleading statements and in reliance thereon.

The District Court adopted a presumption of reliance by members of the plaintiff class upon petitioners' public statements that enabled the court to conclude that common questions of fact or law predominated over particular questions pertaining to individual plaintiffs. See Fed. Rule Civ. Proc. 23(b)(3). The District Court therefore certified respondents' class. On the merits, however, the District Court granted summary judgment for the defendants. It held that, as a matter of law, any misstatements were immaterial: there were no negotiations ongoing at the time of the first statement, and although negotiations were taking place when the second and third statements were issued, those negotiations were not "destined, with reasonable certainty, to become a merger agreement in principle."

The United States Court of Appeals for the Sixth Circuit affirmed the class certification, but reversed the District Court's summary judgment, and remanded the case. 786 F.2d 741 (1986). The court reasoned that while

---

4. On October 21, 1977, after heavy trading and a new high in Basic stock, the following news item appeared in the Cleveland Plain Dealer:

> "[Basic] President Max Muller said the company knew no reason for the stock's activity and that no negotiations were under way with any company for a merger. He said Flintkote recently denied Wall Street rumors that it would make a tender offer of $25 a share for control of the Cleveland-based maker of refractories for the steel industry."

On September 25, 1978, in reply to an inquiry from the New York Stock Exchange, Basic issued a release concerning increased activity in its stock and stated that

> "management is unaware of any present or pending company development that would result in the abnormally heavy trading activity and price fluctuation in company shares that have been experienced in the past few days."

On November 6, 1978, Basic issued to its shareholders a "Nine Months Report 1978." This Report stated:

> "With regard to the stock market activity in the Company's shares we remain unaware of any present or pending developments which would account for the high volume of trading and price fluctuations in recent months."

petitioners were under no general duty to disclose their discussions with
Combustion, any statement the company voluntarily released could not be
" 'so incomplete as to mislead.' " Id., at 746, quoting SEC v. Texas Gulf
Sulphur Co., 401 F.2d 833, 862 (C.A.2 1968) (en banc), cert. denied sub
nom. Coates v. SEC, 394 U.S. 976 (1969). In the Court of Appeals' view,
Basic's statements that no negotiations were taking place, and that it knew
of no corporate developments to account for the heavy trading activity,
were misleading. With respect to materiality, the court rejected the argument that preliminary merger discussions are immaterial as a matter of
law, and held that "once a statement is made denying the existence of any
discussions, even discussions that might not have been material in absence
of the denial are material because they make the statement made untrue."
786 F.2d, at 749.

The Court of Appeals joined a number of other Circuits in accepting
the "fraud-on-the-market theory" to create a rebuttable presumption that
respondents relied on petitioners' material misrepresentations, noting that
without the presumption it would be impractical to certify a class under
Federal rule of Civil Procedure 23(b)(3). See 786 F.2d, at 750–751.

We granted certiorari, 479 U.S. 1083 (1987), to resolve the split, see
Part III, infra, among the Courts of Appeals as to the standard of materiality applicable to preliminary merger discussions, and to determine whether
the courts below properly applied a presumption of reliance in certifying
the class, rather than requiring each class member to show direct reliance
on Basic's statements.

II

. . . . Judicial interpretation and application, legislative acquiescence,
and the passage of time have removed any doubt that a private cause of
action exists for a violation of § 10(b) and rule 10b–5, and constitutes an
essential tool for enforcement of the 1934 Act's requirements. . . .

The Court previously has addressed various positive and common-law
requirements for a violation of § 10(b) or of rule 10b–5. See, e.g., Santa Fe
Industries, Inc. v. Green, [430 U.S. 462 (1977)] ("manipulative or deceptive" requirement of the statute); Blue Chip Stamps v. Manor Drug Stores,
[421 U.S. 723 (1975)] ("in connection with the purchase or sale" requirement of the rule); Dirks v. SEC, 463 U.S. 646 (1983) (duty to disclose);
Chiarella v. United States, 445 U.S. 222 (1980) (same); Ernst & Ernst v.
Hochfelder, [425 U.S. 185 (1976)] (scienter). See also Carpenter v. United
States, 484 U.S. 19 (1987) (confidentiality). The Court also explicitly has
defined a standard of materiality under the securities laws, see TSC
Industries, Inc. v. Northway, Inc., 426 U.S. 438 (1976), concluding in the
proxy-solicitation context that "[a]n omitted fact is material if there is a
substantial likelihood that a reasonable shareholder would consider it
important in deciding how to vote." Id., at 449. Acknowledging that certain
information concerning corporate developments could well be of "dubious
significance," id., at 448, the Court was careful not to set too low a
standard of materiality; it was concerned that a minimal standard might

bring an overabundance of information within its reach, and lead management "simply to bury the shareholders in an avalanche of trivial information—a result that is hardly conducive to informed decisionmaking." Id., at 448–449. It further explained that to fulfill the materiality requirement "there must be a substantial likelihood that the disclosure of the omitted fact would have been viewed by the reasonable investor as having significantly altered the 'total mix' of information made available." Id., at 449. We now expressly adopt the *TSC Industries* standard of materiality for the § 10(b) and rule 10b–5 context.

III

The application of this materiality standard to preliminary merger discussions is not self-evident. Where the impact of the corporate development on the target's fortune is certain and clear, the *TSC Industries* materiality definition admits straightforward application. Where, on the other hand, the event is contingent or speculative in nature, it is difficult to ascertain whether the "reasonable investor" would have considered the omitted information significant at the time. Merger negotiations, because of the ever-present possibility that the contemplated transaction will not be effectuated, fall into the latter category.

A

Petitioners urge upon us a Third Circuit test for resolving this difficulty. Under this approach, preliminary merger discussions do not become material until "agreement-in-principle" as to the price and structure of the transaction has been reached between the would-be merger partners. See Greenfield v. Heublein, Inc., 742 F.2d 751, 757 (C.A.3 1984), cert. denied, 469 U.S. 1215 (1985). By definition, then, information concerning any negotiations not yet at the agreement-in-principle stage could be withheld or even misrepresented without a violation of rule 10b–5.

Three rationales have been offered in support of the "agreement-in-principle" test. The first derives from the concern expressed in *TSC Industries* that an investor not be overwhelmed by excessively detailed and trivial information, and focuses on the substantial risk that preliminary merger discussions may collapse: because such discussions are inherently tentative, disclosure of their existence itself could mislead investors and foster false optimism.   .   .   . The other two justifications for the agreement-in-principle standard are based on management concerns: because the requirement of "agreement-in-principle" limits the scope of disclosure obligations, it helps preserve the confidentiality of merger discussions where earlier disclosure might prejudice the negotiations; and the test also provides a usable, brightline rule for determining when disclosure must be made.

None of these policy-based rationales, however, purports to explain why drawing the line at agreement-in-principle reflects the significance of the information upon the investor's decision. The first rationale, and the only one connected to the concerns expressed in *TSC Industries*, stands soundly rejected, even by a Court of Appeals that otherwise has accepted the wisdom of the agreement-in-principle test. "It assumes that investors are nitwits, unable to appreciate—even when told—that mergers are risky propositions up until the closing." Flamm v. Eberstadt, 814 F.2d 1169, 1175 (CA7), cert. denied, 484 U.S. 853 (1987). Disclosure, and not paternalistic withholding of accurate information, is the policy chosen and expressed by Congress. We have recognized time and again, a "fundamental purpose" of the various Securities Acts, "was to substitute a philosophy of full disclosure for the philosophy of *caveat emptor* and thus to achieve a high standard of business ethics in the securities industry." SEC v. Capital Gains Research Bureau, Inc., [375 U.S. 180, 186 (1963)]. . . . The role of the materiality requirement is not to "attribute to investors a child-like simplicity, an inability to grasp the probabilistic significance of negotiations," Flamm v. Eberstadt, 814 F.2d, at 1175, but to filter out essentially useless information that a reasonable investor would not consider significant, even as part of a larger "mix" of factors to consider in making his investment decision. TSC Industries, Inc. v. Northway, Inc., 426 U.S., at 448–449.

The second rationale, the importance of secrecy during the early stages of merger discussions, also seems irrelevant to an assessment whether their existence is significant to the trading decision of a reasonable investor. To avoid a "bidding war" over its target, an acquiring firm often will insist that negotiations remain confidential, . . . and at least one Court of Appeals has stated that "silence pending settlement of the price and structure of a deal is beneficial to most investors, most of the time." Flamm v. Eberstadt, 814 F.2d, at 1177.

We need not ascertain, however, whether secrecy necessarily maximizes shareholder wealth—although we note that the proposition is at least disputed as a matter of theory and empirical research—for this case does not concern the *timing* of a disclosure; it concerns only its accuracy and completeness. We face here the narrow question whether information concerning the existence and status of preliminary merger discussions is significant to the reasonable investor's trading decision. Arguments based on the premise that some disclosure would be "premature" in a sense are more properly considered under the rubric of an issuer's duty to disclose. The "secrecy" rationale is simply inapposite to the definition of materiality.

The final justification offered in support of the agreement-in-principle test seems to be directed solely at the comfort of corporate managers. A bright-line rule indeed is easier to follow than a standard that requires the exercise of judgment in the light of all the circumstances. But ease of application alone is not an excuse for ignoring the purposes of the Securities Acts and Congress' policy decisions. . . .

We therefore find no valid justification for artificially excluding from the definition of materiality information concerning merger discussions, which would otherwise be considered significant to the trading decision of a reasonable investor, merely because agreement-in-principle as to price and structure has not yet been reached by the parties or their representatives.

C

Even before this Court's decision in *TSC Industries*, the Second Circuit had explained the role of the materiality requirement of rule 10b–5, with respect to contingent or speculative information or events, in a manner that gave that term meaning that is independent of the other provisions of the rule. Under such circumstances, materiality "will depend at any given time upon a balancing of both the indicated probability that the event will occur and the anticipated magnitude of the event in light of the totality of the company activity." SEC v. Texas Gulf Sulphur Co., 401 F.2d, at 849. . . .

In a subsequent decision, the late Judge Friendly, writing for a Second Circuit panel, applied the *Texas Gulf Sulphur* probability/magnitude approach in the specific context of preliminary merger negotiations. After acknowledging that materiality is something to be determined on the basis of the particular facts of each case, he stated:

> "Since a merger in which it is bought out is the most important event that can occur in a small corporation's life, to wit, its death, we think that inside information, as regards a merger of this sort, can become material at an earlier stage than would be the case as regards lesser transactions—and this even though the mortality rate of mergers in such formative stages is doubtless high." SEC v. Geon Industries, Inc., 531 F.2d 39, 47–48 (1976).

We agree with that analysis.

Whether merger discussions in any particular case are material therefore depends on the facts. Generally, in order to assess the probability that the event will occur, a factfinder will need to look to indicia of interest in the transaction at the highest corporate levels. Without attempting to catalog all such possible factors, we note by way of example that board resolutions, instructions to investment bankers, and actual negotiations between principals or their intermediaries may serve as indicia of interest. To assess the magnitude of the transaction to the issuer of the securities allegedly manipulated, a factfinder will need to consider such facts as the size of the two corporate entities and of the potential premiums over market value. No particular event or factor short of closing the transaction need be either necessary or sufficient by itself to render merger discussions material.[17]

---

17. To be actionable, of course, a statement must also be misleading. Silence, absent a duty to disclose, is not misleading under rule 10b–5. "No comment" statements are generally the functional equivalent of silence. . . .

It has been suggested that given current market practices, a "no comment" statement is tantamount to an admission that merger discussions are underway. . . . That may well hold true to the extent that issuers adopt a policy of truthfully denying merger rumors when no discussions are underway, and of issuing "no comment" statements when they are in the midst of negotiations. There are, of course, other statement policies firms could adopt; we need not now advise issuers as to what kind of practice to follow, within the range permitted by law. Perhaps more importantly, we think that creating an exception to a regulatory scheme founded on a prodisclosure legislative philosophy, be-

As we clarify today, materiality depends on the significance the reasonable investor would place on the withheld or misrepresented information. . . . Because the standard of materiality we have adopted differs from that used by both courts below, we remand the case for reconsideration of the question whether a grant of summary judgment is appropriate on this record.

IV

A

We turn to the question of reliance and the fraud-on-the-market theory. Succinctly put:

> "The fraud on the market theory is based on the hypothesis that, in an open and developed securities market, the price of a company's stock is determined by the available material information regarding the company and its business. . . . Misleading statements will therefore defraud purchasers of stock even if the purchasers do not directly rely on the misstatements. . . . The causal connection between the defendants' fraud and the plaintiffs' purchase of stock in such a case is no less significant than in a case of direct reliance on misrepresentations."
> Peil v. Speiser, 806 F.2d 1154, 1160–1161 (C.A.3 1986).

Our task, of course, is not to assess the general validity of the theory, but to consider whether it was proper for the courts below to apply a rebuttable presumption of reliance, supported in part by the fraud-on-the-market theory. . . .

This case required resolution of several common questions of law and fact concerning the falsity or misleading nature of the three public statements made by Basic, the presence or absence of scienter, and the materiality of the misrepresentations, if any. In their amended complaint, the named plaintiffs alleged that in reliance on Basic's statements they sold their shares of Basic stock in the depressed market created by petitioners. . . . Requiring proof of individualized reliance from each member of the proposed plaintiff class effectively would have prevented respondents from proceeding with a class action, since individual issues then would have overwhelmed the common ones. . . .

Petitioners and their *amici* complain that the fraud-on-the-market theory effectively eliminates the requirement that a plaintiff asserting a claim under rule 10b–5 prove reliance. They note that reliance is and long has been an element of common-law fraud, . . . and argue that because the analogous express right of action includes a reliance requirement, . . . so too must an action implied under § 10(b).

We agree that reliance is an element of a rule 10b–5 cause of action. . . . Reliance provides the requisite causal connection between a

cause complying with the regulation might be "bad for business," is a role for Congress, not   this Court. . . .

defendant's misrepresentation and a plaintiff's injury. . . . There is, however, more than one way to demonstrate the causal connection. Indeed, we previously have dispensed with a requirement of positive proof of reliance, where a duty to disclose material information had been breached, concluding that the necessary nexus between the plaintiffs' injury and the defendant's wrongful conduct had been established. . . .

The modern securities markets, literally involving millions of shares changing hands daily, differ from the face-to-face transactions contemplated by early fraud cases, and our understanding of rule 10b–5's reliance requirement must encompass these differences.

"In face-to-face transactions, the inquiry into an investor's reliance upon information is into the subjective pricing of that information by that investor. With the presence of a market, the market is interposed between seller and buyer and, ideally, transmits information to the investor in the processed form of a market price. Thus the market is performing a substantial part of the valuation process performed by the investor in a face-to-face transaction. The market is acting as the unpaid agent of the investor, informing him that given all the information available to it, the value of the stock is worth the market price." In re LTV Securities Litigation, 88 F.R.D. 134, 143 (N.D.Tex.1980).

B

Presumptions typically serve to assist courts in managing circumstances in which direct proof, for one reason or another, is rendered difficult. . . . The courts below accepted a presumption, created by the fraud-on-the-market theory and subject to rebuttal by petitioners, that persons who had traded Basic shares had done so in reliance on the integrity of the price set by the market, but because of petitioners' material misrepresentations that price had been fraudulently depressed. Requiring a plaintiff to show a speculative state of facts, *i.e.,* how he would have acted if omitted material information had been disclosed, . . . or if the misrepresentation had not been made, . . . would place an unnecessarily unrealistic evidentiary burden on the rule 10b–5 plaintiff who has traded on an impersonal market. . . .

The presumption is also supported by common sense and probability. Recent empirical studies have tended to confirm Congress' premise that the market price of shares traded on well-developed markets reflects all publicly available information, and, hence, any material misrepresentations.[24] It has been noted that "it is hard to imagine that there ever is a buyer or seller who does not rely on market integrity. Who would knowingly roll the dice in a crooked crap game?" Schlanger v. Four–Phase Systems Inc., 555 F. Supp. 535, 538 (S.D.N.Y.1982). Indeed, nearly every court that has

24. . . . We need not determine by adjudication what economists and social scientists have debated through the use of sophisticated statistical analysis and the application of economic theory. For purposes of accepting the presumption of reliance in this case, we need only believe that market professionals generally consider most publicly announced material statements about companies, thereby affecting stock market prices.

considered the proposition has concluded that where materially misleading statements have been disseminated into an impersonal, well-developed market for securities, the reliance of individual plaintiffs on the integrity of the market price may be presumed. Commentators generally have applauded the adoption of one variation or another of the fraud-on-the-market theory. An investor who buys or sells stock at the price set by the market does so in reliance on the integrity of that price. Because most publicly available information is reflected in market price, an investor's reliance on any public material misrepresentations, therefore, may be presumed for purposes of a rule 10b–5 action.

C

The Court of Appeals found that petitioners "made public, material misrepresentations and [respondents] sold Basic stock in an impersonal, efficient market. Thus the class, as defined by the district court, has established the threshold facts for proving their loss." 786 F.2d, at 751. The court acknowledged that petitioners may rebut proof of the elements giving rise to the presumption, or show that the misrepresentation in fact did not lead to a distortion of price or that an individual plaintiff traded or would have traded despite his knowing the statement was false.

Any showing that severs the link between the alleged misrepresentation and either the price received (or paid) by the plaintiff, or his decision to trade at a fair market price, will be sufficient to rebut the presumption of reliance. For example, if petitioners could show that the "market makers" were privy to the truth about the merger discussions here with Combustion, and thus that the market price would not have been affected by their misrepresentations, the causal connection could be broken: the basis for finding that the fraud had been transmitted through market price would be gone. Similarly, if, despite petitioners' allegedly fraudulent attempt to manipulate market price, news of the merger discussions credibly entered the market and dissipated the effects of the misstatements, those who traded Basic shares after the corrective statements would have no direct or indirect connection with the fraud. Petitioners also could rebut the presumption of reliance as to plaintiffs who would have divested themselves of their Basic shares without relying on the integrity of the market. For example, a plaintiff who believed that Basic's statements were false and that Basic was indeed engaged in merger discussions, and who consequently believed that Basic stock was artificially underpriced, but sold his shares nevertheless because of other unrelated concerns, e.g., potential antitrust problems, or political pressures to divest from shares of certain businesses, could not be said to have relied on the integrity of a price he knew had been manipulated.

V

. . .

The judgment of the Court of Appeals is vacated, and the case is remanded to that court for further proceedings consistent with this opinion.

It is so ordered.

■ THE CHIEF JUSTICE, JUSTICE SCALIA, and JUSTICE KENNEDY took no part in the consideration or decision of this case.

■ JUSTICE WHITE, with whom JUSTICE O'CONNOR joins, concurring in part and dissenting in part.

I join Parts I–III of the Court's opinion, as I agree that the standard of materiality we set forth in *TSC Industries, Inc. v. Northway, Inc.,* 426 U.S. 438, 449 (1976), should be applied to actions under § 10(b) and rule 10b–5. But I dissent from the remainder of the Court's holding because I do not agree that the "fraud-on-the-market" theory should be applied in this case.

I

A

At the outset, I note that there are portions of the Court's fraud-on-the-market holding with which I am in agreement.   .   .   .

I agree with the Court that if rule 10b–5's reliance requirement is to be left with any content at all, the fraud-on-the-market presumption must be capable of being rebutted by a showing that a plaintiff did not "rely" on the market price. For example, a plaintiff who decides, months in advance of an alleged misrepresentation, to purchase a stock; one who buys or sells a stock for reasons unrelated to its price; one who actually sells a stock "short" days before the misrepresentation is made—surely none of these people can state a valid claim under rule 10b–5. Yet, some federal courts have allowed such claims to stand under one variety or another of the fraud-on-the-market theory.

B

But even as the Court attempts to limit the fraud-on-the-market theory it endorses today, the pitfalls in its approach are revealed by previous uses by the lower courts of the broader versions of the theory. Confusion and contradiction in court rulings are inevitable when traditional legal analysis is replaced with economic theorization by the federal courts.

In general, the case law developed in this Court with respect to § 10(b) and rule 10b–5 has been based on doctrines with which we, as judges, are familiar: common-law doctrines of fraud and deceit.   .   .   . The federal courts have proved adept at developing an evolving jurisprudence of rule 10b–5 in such a manner. But with no staff economists, no experts schooled in the "efficient-capital-market hypothesis," no ability to test the validity of empirical market studies, we are not well equipped to embrace novel constructions of a statute based on contemporary microeconomic theory.

For while the economists' theories which underpin the fraud-on-the-market presumption may have the appeal of mathematical exactitude and scientific certainty, they are—in the end—nothing more than theories which may or may not prove accurate upon further consideration. Even the most earnest advocates of economic analysis of the law recognize this.

. . .

Consequently, I cannot join the Court in its effort to reconfigure the securities laws, based on recent economic theories, to better fit what it perceives to be the new realities of financial markets. I would leave this task to others more equipped for the job than we.

C

At the bottom of the Court's conclusion that the fraud-on-the-market theory sustains a presumption of reliance is the assumption that individuals rely "on the integrity of the market price" when buying or selling stock in "impersonal, well-developed market[s] for securities." Even if I was prepared to accept (as a matter of common sense or general understanding) the assumption that most persons buying or selling stock do so in response to the market price, the fraud-on-the-market theory goes further. For in adopting a "presumption of reliance," the Court *also* assumes that buyers and sellers rely—not just on the market price—but on the *"integrity"* of that price. It is this aspect of the fraud-on-the-market hypothesis which most mystifies me.

To define the term "integrity of the market price," the majority quotes approvingly from cases which suggest that investors are entitled to " 'rely on the price of a stock as a reflection of its value.' " .   . But the meaning of this phrase eludes me, for it implicitly suggests that stocks have some "true value" that is measurable by a standard other than their market price. While the Scholastics of Medieval times professed a means to make such a valuation of a commodity's "worth," I doubt that the federal courts of our day are similarly equipped.

Even if securities had some "value"—knowable and distinct from the market price of a stock—investors do not always share the Court's presumption that a stock's price is a "reflection of [this] value." Indeed, "many investors purchase or sell stock because they believe the price *inaccurately* reflects the corporation's worth." See Black, Fraud on the Market: A Criticism of Dispensing with Reliance Requirements in Open Market Transactions, 62 N.C.L.Rev. 435, 455 (1984) (emphasis added).

I do not propose that the law retreat from the many protections that § 10(b) and rule 10b–5, as interpreted in our prior cases, provide to investors. But any extension of these laws, to approach something closer to an investor insurance scheme, should come from Congress, and not from the courts.

III

Finally, the particular facts of this case make it an exceedingly poor candidate for the Court's fraud-on-the-market theory, and illustrate the illogic achieved by that theory's application in many cases.

Respondents here are a class of sellers who sold Basic stock between October 1977 and December 1978, a 14–month period. At the time the class period began, Basic's stock was trading at $20 a share (at the time, an all-time high); the last members of the class to sell their Basic stock got a price of just over $30 a share. It is indisputable that virtually every member of the class made money from his or her sale of Basic stock.

The oddities of applying the fraud-on-the-market theory in this case are manifest. First, there are the facts that the plaintiffs are sellers and the class period is so lengthy—both are virtually without precedent in prior fraud-on-the-market cases. . . . I think these two facts render this case less apt to application of the fraud-on-the-market hypothesis.

Second, there is the fact that in this case, there is no evidence that petitioner Basic's officials made the troublesome misstatements for the purpose of manipulating stock prices, or with any intent to engage in underhanded trading of Basic stock. Indeed, during the class period, petitioners do not appear to have purchased or sold *any* Basic stock whatsoever. . . .

And it is difficult to square liability in this case with § 10(b)'s express provision that it prohibits fraud "*in connection with* the purchase or sale of any security." . . .

Third, there are the peculiarities of what kinds of investors will be able to recover in this case. As I read the District Court's class certification order, . . . there are potentially many persons who did not purchase Basic stock until *after* the first false statement (October 1977), but who nonetheless *will* be able to recover under the Court's fraud-on-the-market theory. Thus, it is possible that a person who heard the first corporate misstatement and *disbelieved* it—*i.e.*, someone who purchased Basic stock thinking that petitioners' statement was false—may still be included in the plaintiff-class on remand. How a person who undertook such a speculative stock-investing strategy—and made $10 a share doing so (if he bought on October 22, 1977, and sold on December 15, 1978)—can say that he was "defrauded" by virtue of his reliance on the "integrity" of the market price is beyond me. And such speculators may not be uncommon, at least in this case.

Indeed, the facts of this case lead a casual observer to the almost inescapable conclusion that many of those who bought or sold Basic stock during the period in question flatly disbelieved the statements which are alleged to have been "materially misleading." Despite three statements denying that merger negotiations were underway, Basic stock hit record-high after record-high during the 14–month class period. It seems quite possible that, like Casca's knowing disbelief of Caesar's "thrice refusal" of the Crown, clever investors were skeptical of petitioners' three denials that merger talks were going on. Yet such investors, the saviest of the savvy, will be able to recover under the Court's opinion, as long as they now claim that they believed in the "integrity of the market price" when they sold their stock (between September and December 1978). Thus, persons who bought after hearing and relying on the *falsity* of petitioners' statements may be able to prevail and recover money damages on remand.

And who will pay the judgments won in such actions? I suspect that all too often the majority's rule will "lead to large judgments, payable in the last analysis by innocent investors, for the benefit of speculators and their lawyers." Cf. SEC v. Texas Gulf Sulphur Co., 401 F.2d 833, 867 (C.A.2 1968) (en banc) (Friendly, J., concurring), cert. denied, 394 U.S. 976 (1969). . . .

IV

In sum, I think the Court's embracement of the fraud-on-the-market theory represents a departure in securities law that we are ill-suited to commence—and even less equipped to control as it proceeds. As a result, I must respectfully dissent.

QUESTIONS

1. Were the statements issued by Basic, Inc., calculated to mislead? Does it follow that people were in fact misled? Suppose that the price of the shares of Basic, Inc. was $20 per share when negotiations began, rose gradually as the negotiations continued to $35 per share one day before the announcement, and rose to $42 per share when the merger agreement (providing for a price of $43 per share, but subject to shareholder approval) was announced. Note that the price on announcement day ($42), would not be the proper price for measuring the damages of a person who sold during the period of concealed negotiations, since at any time during those negotiations there would be uncertainty over whether those negotiations would result in a merger agreement. Would the fact that the price rose during the period of negotiations negate any claim to reliance on allegedly misleading statements, or would that fact be relevant only to damages?

2. If a false statement is intentionally made but it is not material, is there a violation of § 10(b) and Rule 10b–5? Should anyone care?

3. What is the "fraud on the market" theory? How is the plaintiff in a suit based on this theory defrauded? Suppose an individual was aware of the statements issued in Basic Inc. v. Levinson, but did not believe them, and sold shares at the market price because she needed money to pay medical bills. Does such an individual have a cause of action? Has she been damaged?

4. Is it Justice White's view, in his dissent in *Basic Inc.,* that Basic's statements about the merger negotiations did not affect the price?

5. If you rely on the "integrity" of the market price, does it follow that you think that that price is the "true value" of your shares?

6. On the remand of *Basic Inc.,* what must the plaintiff prove to satisfy the scienter requirement?

7.   What general advice would you give to officers of a public corporation on the divulgence of information about merger negotiations?

8.   What is the class of individuals who will recover damages in *Basic Inc.*, if a violation of § 10(b) and Rule 10b–5 is established? What individuals will bear the burden of those damages?

PROBLEMS

1.   Suppose that 30 percent of the shares of Tanaka Corp. are owned by the Tanaka family. The head of the family, and founder of the corporation, is Ken Tanaka, who has effective control and serves on the board (but is not an officer or otherwise employed), and has decided to sell out to Big Blue Corp. Negotiations have taken place between representatives of Big Blue and Ken Tanaka, as a result of which a tentative agreement has been reached that Big Blue will buy all of the Tanaka family shares for $30 per share and will offer to buy all the remaining, publicly held shares for the same price. A number of nonprice terms of the agreement, including Ken Tanaka's role in the merged firm, have not yet been resolved.

The Big Blue representatives have told Ken Tanaka that they are not willing to get into a bidding war and that if news of their interest in buying is disclosed prematurely they may withdraw their offer. There have been rumors, some published in the Wall Street Journal, of the possibility of a sale, and the price of the Tanaka Corp. shares trading on the NYSE has risen over the past two weeks from $20 per share to $23 per share.

A financial reporter calls the public relations officer of Tanaka Corp., Abe Ahnust, and asks if there is any truth to the rumors and whether there is any other explanation for the rise in the price of the shares. Abe, who is fully informed about the negotiations between Ken Tanaka and representatives of Big Blue, makes the following statement: "I am aware of no corporate development that would explain the recent rise in the price of the shares." Following the issuance of this statement, the price of the Tanaka Corp. shares falls to $22 per share. (a) Has Abe, or Tanaka Corp., violated § 10(b) and rule 10b–5? (b) If your answer to the preceding question is yes, would it change if Abe had not been informed of the negotiations between Ken Tanaka and Big Blue's representatives? (c) Suppose Abe's statement was not authorized by Ken but that Ken reads it the following day in the Wall Street Journal. Does Ken have any duty to make a further announcement or tell Abe to do so?

2.   Suppose you are outside counsel to a major bank, whose shares are traded on the New York Stock Exchange. The CEO of the bank calls you and says that the bank has made many loans for real estate developments and some of the biggest of these have turned out badly. The next quarterly report of the bank will be published in two weeks and it will lay out the bad news about these loans. The loss on the loans will eliminate the profits for the quarter, but the bank will remain solvent. There has been much speculation among stock analysts and other financial people about the bank's bad loans and this speculation seems to have resulted in some

decline in the price of its shares. For this reason it is not clear that the issuance of the quarterly report will result in any further decline in price.

Over the years, with the encouragement of the board of directors and consistently with the practice of other CEOs, the bank's CEO has tried to remain on good terms with leading stock market analysts and certain major mutual fund managers. One of the mutual fund managers, whose fund holds a substantial block of the bank's shares, called the CEO five minutes ago and asked what there is in the rumors about the bank's bad loans. The CEO said he was tied up in a conference but would call back within an hour. He now calls you and asks what he can say. He asks you to bear in mind his strong urge to maintain the goodwill of the mutual fund manager. What is your advice? If the CEO confirms the bad news, and the mutual fund sells its shares (or holds the shares but buys puts), what is its liability, and that of the bank, if any, under rule 10b–5?

Pommer v. Medtest Corporation

961 F.2d 620 (7th Cir.1992).

■ EASTERBROOK, CIRCUIT JUDGE. Medtest Corporation has a single asset: the intellectual property in a self-administered cervico-vaginal cytology testing process. Patrick Manning devised the process and together with Donald West, a lawyer, formed Medtest in December 1981 to obtain a patent and undertake development to make the process commercially attractive. Manning held 31% of the stock, West 26%, and the remainder was scattered among friends and relatives. In 1982 Manning sold some of his stock in Medtest to Robert and Anna Lisa Pommer: 250 shares in September for $25,000, and later another 2,750 shares for $175,000. The Pommers thus acquired 3% of Medtest's outstanding stock, which is valuable only to the extent the firm pays dividends, goes public, or is acquired by a third party.

None of these things has happened, and the Pommers believe that they are the victims of fraud. A jury agreed in this action under § 10(b) of the Securities Exchange Act of 1934 and the SEC's rule 10b–5. It awarded the Pommers more than $300,000 in damages, representing the purchase price of the stock plus interest. A magistrate judge, presiding by consent under 28 U.S.C. § 636(c), set aside the verdict and entered judgment for the defendants. She concluded that none of the representations made to the Pommers was materially false.

I

Given the verdict, we must take all of the evidence in the light most favorable to the Pommers. A jury could have concluded that West told the Pommers, while they were negotiating to buy the stock, that Medtest had a U.S. patent on the process and that a sale of Medtest to Abbott Laboratories, at a price between $50 million and $100 million, was imminent ("almost a finished deal"). A 3% interest in Medtest would have been worth between $1.5 million and $3 million had such a sale been consummated. In fact Medtest did not have a patent at the time. Counsel informed

West in December 1981 that the process was patentable; the firm filed an application on September 30, 1982, and the patent issued on August 14, 1984. Medtest was not in the last stage of negotiation with Abbott Laboratories; it raised the subject with Abbott, and Abbott's employees mentioned a price in the $50 to $100 million range, but no details had been discussed, no hands had been shaken—and on October 28, 1982, Abbott sent Medtest a letter stating that it was not interested in acquiring Medtest. Since then Medtest has been developing the process on its own.

The magistrate judge concluded that the representations about the existence of a patent were not material—and therefore did not support relief under the securities laws—because counsel had told West that the process was patentable, and Medtest obtained a patent in due course. The judge continued: "It is true that Pommer testified that he would not have purchased his shares had he known the patent had not actually issued, but he never explained this self-serving conclusion or suggested any reason why it would make a difference to him." As for the sale to Abbott, the judge wrote: "Pommer's own testimony demonstrated that he knew that the time of sale and its terms were indefinite. . . . Any person of Mr. Pommer's intelligence and sophistication [knows that nothing under negotiation is] absolutely certain. . . . Negotiations involving a price range of between 50 and 100 million dollars indisputably indicate that a lot remains to be negotiated and decided."

Considerations of this kind show that a verdict in defendants' favor could not be disturbed. They do not, however, show that no reasonable juror could think the statements material. A statement is material when there is "a substantial likelihood that the disclosure of the omitted fact would have been viewed by the reasonable investor as having significantly altered the 'total mix' of information made available." TSC Industries, Inc. v. Northway, Inc., 426 U.S. 438, 449 (1976), applied to § 10(b) actions by Basic Inc. v. Levinson, 485 U.S. 224, 231–32 (1988). West told the Pommers that Medtest had a patent, doubtless recognizing that in selling stock as in other endeavors a bird in the hand is worth two in the bush. Counsel's belief that the process is patentable is a fair distance from a patent. . . . And it does not matter that Medtest obtained the patent two years later. The securities laws approach matters from an ex ante perspective: just as a statement true when made does not become fraudulent because things unexpectedly go wrong, so a statement materially false when made does not become acceptable because it happens to come true. . . . Good fortune may affect damages, but it does not make the falsehood any the less material.

So too with the negotiations to sell Medtest to Abbott Laboratories. Until the last minute a deal may collapse, but some deals are more likely to close than others. Probabilities determine the value of stock. At a 90% chance of a buyout for $50 million, the Pommers' stock was worth $1.35 million; at a 10% chance it was worth $150,000. A jury could determine that West conveyed to the Pommers a substantially higher probability than the facts supported—that although West represented that the parties were just about to sign on the dotted line, actually there had been no more than superficial discussions, and Abbott had no serious interest in acquiring Medtest. There is "a substantial likelihood" that the Pommers (and any other "reasonable investor") would have viewed the truth about the negotiations with Abbott as "significantly altering the 'total mix' of information made available."

One could recast the magistrate judge's conclusion about the sale to Abbott as a finding that the Pommers knew enough of the truth that West's lies did not significantly affect their appreciation of the situation. An issuer that utters a mixture of truth and falsehood may have furnished the information necessary for an accurate appreciation of the securities' value—especially when the truth is written and the lie is oral. . . .

The Pommers must have been aware that a deal with Abbott was not just around the corner. A substantial range of price implied that hard negotiations lay ahead. West told them that Medtest needed to secure foreign patents, and that with these in hand it would be an attractive acquisition candidate. As the magistrate judge remarked, foreign patents cannot be obtained in a flash. The Pommers waited more than a year before beefing; would they have sat quietly so long if they really thought they had been promised a bonanza in a few weeks? The price of the securities also implies that a sale was a long shot: Why would Manning sell 3% of Medtest to the Pommers for $200,000 if the stock soon would be worth $1.5 million and up? Even if Manning desperately needed to raise capital, better terms must have been available. Robert Pommer said at one point that he viewed the investment in Medtest as his chance to hit the Lotto—yet he persuaded the jury that the defendants sold him a sure thing.

Whether these things would be enough to neutralize the representations about Abbott we need not say. The falsehood about the patent remains. . . . It is not enough that the other party must have recognized a risk. Risks are ubiquitous. Disclosures assist investors in determining the magnitude of risks. Even savvy investors may recover when a bald lie understates the gravity of a known risk. . . . Although [the defendants] direct us to an agreement between Manning and the Pommers, that two-page document contains no information beyond a boilerplate warning that Medtest's process "has only speculative value at the present time and may prove to be totally worthless, in which event the Shares purchased by Buyer pursuant hereto may also become worthless." Such generic warnings do not enlighten investors about the status of patent applications, negotiations to sell the business, and the like; they do nothing to disabuse an Investor influenced by false oral statements purporting to describe the status of the firm's affairs. . . .

III

Several other issues may come up on remand, and we comment briefly on them to speed this litigation along.

1. Manning sold the stock, yet Medtest and West are the defendants. West may be liable for his own misstatements, if made "in connection

with'' Manning's sale of stock. In addition to the "connection" language of both statute and rule, see Blue Chip Stamps [v. Manor Drugs, 421 U.S. 723 (1975) (described at casebook page 445)]. Whether West knew that Manning was dealing with the Pommers is an important issue that the trier of fact should resolve.

2. If West was ignorant of Manning's dealings or stood to gain nothing from them, then his own statements to the Pommers look more like boasting over the coffee table (they were social friends). Scienter, another element of liability under § 10(b) and Rule 10b–5, would be hard to establish. . . .

3. Vicarious liability remains a possibility. . . .

[W]hat makes Medtest liable? . . . It takes common law vicarious liability to reach Medtest, and such liability would depend on a finding that Manning or West acted as Medtest's agents, and within the scope of their authority. Manning sold for his own account, not for Medtest's. Investors, acting as investors, are not agents of the corporation. . . . The magistrate judge thought it sufficient that "West and Manning had apparent authority to act on behalf of Medtest and to sell stock", but she did not mention the fact that Manning was not selling "on behalf of" Medtest. He sold his own shares, a fact conspicuously disclosed to the Pommers. The subject bears a fresh look on remand.

5. The jury awarded as damages the full price of the stock, plus interest. This is a rescissionary measure, and although §§ 11 and 12 of the '33 Act use such a starting point, those sections also allow the defendant to reduce the award by demonstrating that the misstatement did not cause the decline in value. Damages under § 10(b), by contrast, usually are the difference between the price of the stock and its value on the date of the transaction if the full truth were known. . . . Sometimes this principle comes under the name "loss causation": the plaintiff must establish that the misstatement caused him to incur the loss of which he complains; it is not enough to establish that the misrepresentation caused him to buy or sell the securities. . . .

A rescissionary measure of damages implies that the Medtest stock was worthless in late 1982. Yet the corporation is still in business, apparently close to putting its process on the market (or selling it to a larger firm). Although a patent application is worth (materially) less than a patent, it is worth something, and some patent applications are worth a great deal. Apparently neither the Pommers nor defendants attempted to enlighten the jury about the value of Medtest's stock in 1982. They might believe it prudent to do so if there is a second trial.

REVERSED AND REMANDED

ANALYSIS

1. Why do you suppose West told the Pommers that the patent had been issued when in fact it had not? Was it most likely a lie, wishful thinking, or faulty understanding?

2. The court states, "Good fortune may affect damages, but it does not make the falsehood any the less material." Why so? Do you agree that the falsehood was material?

3. Would a "no comment" or "just the facts" policy work in a situation such as the one presented in this case? What advice would you give to clients like West and Manning?

4. Since it was Manning who sold shares to the Pommers, how can Medtest and West be liable? What must the plaintiffs prove on remand to establish the liability of Medtest and West?

5. Do the Pommers, as a matter of law, bear responsibility for failing to ask tough questions about the deal with Abbott Laboratories? As a matter of fairness, economic order, or common sense?

NOTE ON JUDICIAL LIMITATIONS ON ACTIONS UNDER RULE 10b–5

Standing: In Blue Chip Stamps v. Manor Drug Stores, 421 U.S. 723 (1975), the Court put some bite in the rule that the protections of Rule 10b–5 extend only to purchasers and sellers of a corporation's securities. In that case the defendant corporation had been required by an antitrust action to offer its common stock to some of its customers, including the plaintiff. The plaintiff claimed that it had been misled by the defendant's prospectus, which the plaintiff argued was unduly pessimistic. Because it relied on that prospectus, explained the plaintiff, it had not exercised its right to buy shares on which it would have made a profit. The Court held that the plaintiff had no cause of action under Rule 10b–5 because it had neither bought nor sold shares.

Scienter: In Ernst & Ernst v. Hochfelder, 425 U.S. 185 (1976), the Court held that liability for issuance of a false or misleading statement required proof of a state of mind referred to as "scienter"; that is, the person making the false statement must have made it with an "intent to deceive, manipulate, or defraud." The Court reserved judgment on the question whether recklessness would be sufficient, but later decisions have answered that question affirmatively.

Secondary Liability and Scope of Interpretation: Until quite recently, Rule 10b–5 was regarded as an example of interstitial lawmaking in which the courts used common-law adjudicatory methods to flesh out the text's bare bones. In Central Bank of Denver v. First Interstate Bank, 511 U.S. 164 (1994), however, the Supreme Court held that there was no implied private right of action against those who aid and abet violations of Rule 10b–5. *Central Bank* thus substantially limited the scope of secondary liability under the rule, at least insofar as private party causes of action are concerned. For our purposes, however, the case is more significant for its methodology than its holding. The court held that the scope of conduct prohibited by § 10(b) (and thus Rule 10b–5) is controlled by the text of the statute. Where the plain text does not resolve some aspect of the Rule 10b–5 cause of action, courts must "infer 'how the 1934 Congress would have addressed the issue had the 10b–5 action been included as an express provision of the 1934 Act.' " Id. at 178 (quoting Musick, Peeler & Garrett v. Employers Ins., 508 U.S. 286 , 294 (1993)). The court admits this is an "awkward task." Lampf, Pleva, Lipkind, Prupis & Petigrow v. Gilbertson, 501 U.S. 350, 357 (1991). Justice Scalia put it more colorfully: "We are imagining here." Id. at 360. *Central Bank* constrained this imaginative process by requiring courts to "use the express causes of action in the securities acts as the primary model for the § 10(b) action." *Central Bank*, 511 U.S. at 178.

Santa Fe Industries, Inc. v. Green

430 U.S. 462, 97 S.Ct. 1292, 51 L.Ed.2d 480 (1977).

. . .

I

In 1936, petitioner Santa Fe Industries, Inc. (Santa Fe), acquired control of 60% of the stock of Kirby Lumber Corp. (Kirby), a Delaware corporation. Through a series of purchases over the succeeding years, Santa Fe increased its control of Kirby's stock to 95%; the purchase prices during the period 1968–1973 ranged from $65 to $92.50 per share. In 1974, wishing to acquire 100% ownership of Kirby, Santa Fe availed itself of § 253 of the Delaware Corporation Law, known as the "short-form merger" statute. Section 253 permits a parent corporation owning at least 90% of the stock of a subsidiary to merge with that subsidiary, upon approval by the parent's board of directors, and to make payment in cash for the shares of the minority stockholders. The statute does not require the consent of, or advance notice to, the minority stockholders. However, notice of the merger must be given within 10 days after its effective date, and any stockholder who is dissatisfied with the terms of the merger may petition the Delaware Court of Chancery for a decree ordering the surviving corporation to pay him the fair value of his shares, as determined by a court-appointed appraiser subject to review by the court. . . .

Santa Fe obtained independent appraisals of the physical assets of Kirby—land, timber, buildings, and machinery—and of Kirby's oil, gas, and mineral interests. These appraisals, together with other financial information, were submitted to Morgan Stanley & Co. (Morgan Stanley), an investment banking firm retained to appraise the fair market value of Kirby stock. Kirby's physical assets were appraised at $320 million (amounting to $640 for each of the 500,000 shares); Kirby's stock was valued by Morgan Stanley at $125 per share. Under the terms of the merger, minority stockholders were offered $150 per share.

The provisions of the short-form merger statute were fully complied with. The minority stockholders of Kirby were notified the day after the merger became effective and were advised of their right to obtain an appraisal in Delaware court if dissatisfied with the offer of $150 per share. They also received an information statement containing, in addition to the relevant financial data about Kirby, the appraisals of the value of Kirby's assets and the Morgan Stanley appraisal concluding that the fair market value of the stock was $125 per share.

Respondents, minority stockholders of Kirby, objected to the terms of the merger, but did not pursue their appraisal remedy in the Delaware Court of Chancery. Instead, they brought this action in federal court on behalf of the corporation and other minority stockholders, seeking to set aside the merger or to recover what they claimed to be the fair value of their shares. The amended complaint asserted that, based on the fair market value of Kirby's physical assets as revealed by the appraisal included in the information statement sent to minority shareholders, Kirby's stock was worth at least $772 per share. The complaint alleged further that the merger took place without prior notice to minority stock-holders; that the purpose of the merger was to appropriate the difference between the "conceded pro rata value of the physical assets," App. 103a, and the offer of $150 per share—to "freez[e] out the minority stockholders at a wholly inadequate price," id., at 100a; and that Santa Fe, knowing the appraised value of the physical assets, obtained a "fraudulent appraisal" of the stock from Morgan Stanley and offered $25 above that appraisal "in order to lull the minority stockholders into erroneously believing that [Santa Fe was] generous." Id., at 103a. This course of conduct was alleged to be "a violation of Rule 10b–5 because defendants employed a 'device, scheme, or artifice to defraud' and engaged in an 'act, practice or course of business which operates or would operate as a fraud or deceit upon any person, in connection with the purchase or sale of any security.' " Ibid.

. . .

The District Court dismissed the complaint for failure to state a claim upon which relief could be granted. As the District Court understood the complaint, respondents' case rested on two distinct grounds. First, federal law was assertedly violated because the merger was for the sole purpose of eliminating the minority from the company, therefore lacking any justifi-able business purpose, and because the merger was undertaken without prior notice to the minority shareholders. Second, the low valuation placed on the shares in the cash-exchange offer was itself said to be a fraud actionable under Rule 10b–5. In rejecting the first ground for recovery, the District Court reasoned that Delaware law required neither a business purpose for a short-form merger nor prior notice to the minority sharehold-ers who the statute contemplated would be removed from the company, and that Rule 10b–5 did not override these provisions of state corporate law by independently placing a duty on the majority not to merge without prior notice and without a justifiable business purpose.

As for the claim that actionable fraud inhered in the allegedly gross undervaluation of the minority shares, the District Court . . . thought that if "full and fair disclosure is made, transactions eliminating minority interests are beyond the purview of Rule 10b–5," and concluded that the "complaint fail[ed] to allege an omission, misstatement or fraudulent course of conduct that would have impeded a shareholder's judgment of the value of the offer." [391 F. Supp. 849, 854 (S.D.N.Y.1975).] The complaint therefore failed to state a claim and was dismissed.

A divided Court of Appeals for the Second Circuit reversed. . . . As to the first aspect of the case, the Court of Appeals did not disturb the District Court's conclusion that the complaint did not allege a material misrepresentation or nondisclosure with respect to the value of the stock; and the court declined to rule that a claim of gross undervaluation itself would suffice to make out a rule 10b–5 case. With respect to the second aspect of the case, however, the court fundamentally disagreed with the District Court as to the reach and coverage of rule 10b–5. The Court of Appeals' view was that, although the rule plainly reached material misrepresentations and nondisclosures in connection with the purchase or sale of securities, neither misrepresentation nor nondisclosure was a necessary element of a rule 10b–5 action; the rule reached "breaches of fiduciary duty by a majority against minority shareholders without any charge of misrepresentation or lack of disclosure." [533 F.2d 1283, 1287 (2d Cir. 1976).] . . .

II

Section 10(b) of the 1934 Act makes it "unlawful for any person . . . to use or employ . . . any manipulative or deceptive device or contrivance in contravention of [SEC rules]"; rule 10b–5, promulgated by the SEC under § 10(b), prohibits, in addition to nondisclosure and misrepresentation, any "artifice to defraud" or any act "which operates or would operate as a fraud or deceit." . . .

[Ernst & Ernst v. Hochfelder, 425 U.S. 185 (1976)] makes clear that in deciding whether a complaint states a cause of action for "fraud" under rule 10b–5, "we turn first to the language of § 10(b), for '[t]he starting point in every case involving construction of a statute is the language itself.' " Id., at 197, quoting Blue Chip Stamps v. Manor Drug Stores, 421 U.S. 723, 756 (1975) (Powell, J., concurring). . . .

The language of § 10(b) gives no indication that Congress meant to prohibit any conduct not involving manipulation or deception. Nor have we been cited to any evidence in the legislative history that would support a departure from the language of the statute. "When a statute speaks so specifically in terms of manipulation and deception, . . . and when its history reflects no more expansive intent, we are quite unwilling to extend the scope of the statute. . . ." Id., at 214. Thus the claim of fraud and fiduciary breach in this complaint states a cause of action under any part of rule 10b–5 only if the conduct alleged can be fairly viewed as "manipulative or deceptive" within the meaning of the statute.

III

It is our judgment that the transaction, if carried out as alleged in the complaint, was neither deceptive nor manipulative and therefore did not violate either § 10(b) of the Act or rule 10b–5.

As we have indicated, the case comes to us on the premise that the complaint failed to allege a material misrepresentation or material failure to disclose. The finding of the District Court, undisturbed by the Court of Appeals, was that there was no "omission" or "misstatement" in the information statement accompanying the notice of merger. On the basis of the information provided, minority shareholders could either accept the price offered or reject it and seek an appraisal in the Delaware Court of Chancery. Their choice was fairly presented, and they were furnished with all relevant information on which to base their decision.

We therefore find inapposite the cases relied upon by respondents and the court below, in which the breaches of fiduciary duty held violative of rule 10b–5 included some element of deception. Those cases forcefully reflect the principle that "[§] 10(b) must be read flexibly, not technically and restrictively" and that the statute provides a cause of action for any plaintiff who "suffer[s] an injury as a result of deceptive practices touching its sale [or purchase] of securities. . . ." Superintendent of Insurance v. Bankers Life & Cas. Co., 404 U.S. 6, 12–13 (1971). But the cases do not support the proposition, adopted by the Court of Appeals below and urged by respondents here, that a breach of fiduciary duty by majority stockholders, without any deception, misrepresentation, or nondisclosure, violates the statute and the rule.

It is also readily apparent that the conduct alleged in the complaint was not "manipulative" within the meaning of the statute. "Manipulation" is "virtually a term of art when used in connection with securities markets." *Ernst & Ernst,* 425 U.S., at 199. The term refers generally to practices, such as wash sales, matched orders, or rigged prices, that are intended to mislead investors by artificially affecting market activity. . . . Section 10(b)'s general prohibition of practices deemed by the SEC to be "manipulative"—in this technical sense of artificially affecting market activity in order to mislead investors—is fully consistent with the fundamental purpose of the 1934 Act " 'to substitute a philosophy of full disclosure for the philosophy of *caveat emptor.* . . .' " Affiliated Ute Citizens v. United States, 406 U.S. 128, 151 (1972), quoting SEC v. Capital Gains Research Bureau, 375 U.S. 180, 186 (1963). Indeed, nondisclosure is usually essential to the success of a manipulative scheme. No doubt Congress meant to prohibit the full range of ingenious devices that might be used to manipulate securities prices. But we do not think it would have chosen this "term of art" if it had meant to bring within the scope of § 10(b) instances of corporate mismanagement such as this, in which the essence of the complaint is that shareholders were treated unfairly by a fiduciary.

IV

The language of the statute is, we think, "sufficiently clear in its context" to be dispositive here, *Ernst & Ernst,* supra, at 201; but even if it were not, there are additional considerations that weigh heavily against permitting a cause of action under rule 10b–5 for the breach of corporate fiduciary duty alleged in this complaint. Congress did not expressly provide a private cause of action for violations of § 10(b). Although we have recognized an implied cause of action under that section in some circumstances, . . . we have also recognized that a private cause of action under the antifraud provisions of the Securities Exchange Act should not be implied where it is "unnecessary to ensure the fulfillment of Congress' purposes" in adopting the Act. Piper v. Chris–Craft Industries, [430 U.S. 1, 41 (1977)]. . . . As we noted earlier, the Court repeatedly has described the "fundamental purpose" of the Act as implementing a "philosophy of full disclosure"; once full and fair disclosure has occurred, the fairness of the terms of the transaction is at most a tangential concern of the statute. . . . As in Cort v. Ash, 422 U.S. 66, 80 (1975), we are reluctant to recognize a cause of action here to serve what is "at best a subsidiary purpose" of the federal legislation.

A second factor in determining whether Congress intended to create a federal cause of action in these circumstances is "whether 'the cause of action [is] one traditionally relegated to state law. . . .' " Piper v. Chris–Craft Industries, Inc., ante, at 40, quoting Cort v. Ash, supra, at 78. The Delaware Legislature has supplied minority shareholders with a cause of action in the Delaware Court of Chancery to recover the fair value of shares allegedly undervalued in a short-form merger. . . . Of course, the existence of a particular state-law remedy is not dispositive of the question whether Congress meant to provide a similar federal remedy, but as in *Cort* and *Piper,* we conclude that "it is entirely appropriate in this instance to relegate respondent and others in his situation to whatever remedy is created by state law." 422 U.S., at 84; ante, at 41.

The reasoning behind a holding that the complaint in this case alleged fraud under rule 10b–5 could not be easily contained. It is difficult to imagine how a court could distinguish, for purposes of rule 10b–5 fraud, between a majority stockholder's use of a short-form merger to eliminate the minority at an unfair price and the use of some other device, such as a long-form merger, tender offer, or liquidation, to achieve the same result; or indeed how a court could distinguish the alleged abuses in these going private transactions from other types of fiduciary self-dealing involving transactions in securities. The result would be to bring within the rule a wide variety of corporate conduct traditionally left to state regulation. In addition to posing a "danger of vexatious litigation which could result from a widely expanded class of plaintiffs under rule 10b–5," Blue Chip Stamps v. Manor Drug Stores, [421 U.S. 723, 740 (1975)], this extension of the federal securities laws would overlap and quite possibly interfere with state corporate law. Federal courts applying a "federal fiduciary principle" under rule 10b–5 could be expected to depart from state fiduciary standards at least to the extent necessary to ensure uniformity within the federal system. Absent a clear indication of congressional intent, we are reluctant to federalize the substantial portion of the law of corporations that deals with transactions in securities, particularly where established state policies of corporate regulation would be overridden. As the Court stated in *Cort v. Ash,* supra: "Corporations are creatures of state law, and investors commit their funds to corporate directors on the understanding that, except where federal law *expressly* requires certain responsibilities of directors with respect to stockholders, state law will govern the internal affairs of the corporation." 422 U.S., at 84 (emphasis added).

We thus adhere to the position that "Congress by § 10(b) did not seek to regulate transactions which constitute no more than internal corporate mismanagement." Superintendent of Insurance v. Bankers Life & Cas. Co., 404 U.S., at 12. There may well be a need for uniform federal fiduciary standards to govern mergers such as that challenged in this complaint. But those standards should not be supplied by judicial extension of § 10(b) and rule 10b–5 to "cover the corporate universe."

The judgment of the Court of Appeals is reversed, and the case is remanded for further proceedings consistent with this opinion.

NOTE

The holders of about 5,000 shares of Kirby Lumber dissented from the merger and demanded appraisal. After litigation, it was determined that they were entitled to $254.40 per share, representing the value of the corporation as a going concern. See Bell v. Kirby Lumber Corp., 413 A.2d 137 (Del.1980). In upholding this appraisal amount, the Delaware Supreme Court observed that, based on one appraisal, Santa Fe "could have liquidated Kirby and realized $670 per share for each stockholder." The court concluded, however, that since Santa Fe, as 95 percent owner, "had the power [right?] to do with Kirby what it chose," the liquidation value was essentially irrelevant.

ANALYSIS

1. Many states have short-form merger statutes similar to the one used in *Santa Fe*. Suppose that the Supreme Court had affirmed the Court of Appeals. What would have been the practical effect on these statutes?

2. Suppose that the defendants in *Santa Fe* had used the short-form merger, but had issued a misleading notice to the minority shareholders in connection with the merger. What would the Court have likely held?

Deutschman v. Beneficial Corp.

841 F.2d 502 (3d Cir.1988).

Robert M. Deutschman appeals from a Fed.R.Civ.P. 12(b)(6) dismissal of his amended class action complaint against Beneficial Corporation (Beneficial), Finn M.W. Caspersen, Beneficial's Chairman and Chief Executive Officer, and Andrew C. Halvorsen, its Chief Financial Officer. The . . . complaint alleges that the defendants violated § 10(b) . . . of the Securities Exchange Act of 1934. . . .

. . . . Deutschman alleges that in 1986 and part of 1987 Beneficial's insurance division suffered severe losses which had an adverse impact on Beneficial's financial condition; that Caspersen and Halvorsen held stock and stock options in Beneficial which would be adversely affected by a decline in the market price of that stock; that disclosures were made about the losses in Beneficial's insurance division which caused declines in that market price; that in order to prevent further declines Caspersen and Halvorsen, on Beneficial's behalf, issued statements about the problems in the insurance division, which they knew to be false and misleading, to the effect that those problems were behind it and were covered by sufficient reserves; that these misleading statements placed an artificial floor under the market price of Beneficial stock; that purchasers of Beneficial stock and purchasers of call options in Beneficial stock made purchases at prices which were artificially inflated by the market's reliance on defendants' misstatements, and that both purchasers of Beneficial stock and purchasers of Beneficial call options suffered losses as a consequence. Beneficial stock is traded on the New York Stock Exchange and on other national stock exchanges. Options on Beneficial stock are traded on the Pacific Stock Exchange. The complaint does not allege that Beneficial, Caspersen, or Halvorsen, during the time period complained of, traded in Beneficial stock or in put or call options on Beneficial stock. It alleges that Deutschman suffered losses when, upon disclosure of the facts, call options on Beneficial's stock that he had purchased in reliance on the market price created by defendants' misstatements, became worthless. It does not allege that Deutschman purchased Beneficial stock.

The district court held that option traders who suffered losses as a result of intentional misstatements by the management of a corporation, the stock of which is the subject of those options, lack standing to assert a cause of action for damages under § 10(b) of the 1934 Act and rule 10b–5 of the Securities and Exchange Commission. The court reasoned that in the absence of an allegation that Deutschman bought or sold Beneficial stock, or of an allegation that the defendants bought or sold options, there was no duty owed to him to refrain even from affirmative misstatements which would affect the market price of Beneficial stock.

Put and call options have been a feature of the national financial markets since 1790. Under these contracts a seller agrees to sell or a purchaser agrees to buy a security at a fixed price on or before a fixed date in the future. Such contracts permit investors to hedge against future movements in the market price of securities. Prior to the early 1970s the utility of put and call options was limited because of high transaction costs, and because of the absence of a secondary market for the option contracts. In 1973, the Chicago Board Options Exchange became the first registered exchange for trading in option contracts. Within a short time that exchange had been joined by the American, Philadelphia, Pacific, and Midwest exchanges. By 1985, those exchanges were trading options on over 400 stocks, and the volume of contracts traded exceeded 118.6 million. . . . .

The option contract gives its owner the right to buy (call) or sell (put) a fixed number of shares of a specified underlying stock at a given price (the striking price) on or before the expiration date of the contract. For this option a premium is paid, and the contract is worth more or less than the premium depending upon the direction of the market price of the underlying stock relative to the striking price. The market price for options is directly responsive, therefore, to changes in the market price of the underlying stock, and to information affecting that price. . . .

Because the market value of an option contract is responsive to changes in the market price of the underlying stock, holders of option contracts are susceptible to two separate types of deceptive practices: insider trading and affirmative misrepresentation. Insiders trading on undisclosed material information can injure option holders either by market activity which causes the price of the underlying stock to move, or by market activity directly in the options market. Insiders or others who do not trade in either market can injure option holders by misstating material facts to the public, thereby causing a distortion in the market price of the underlying security, and in the necessarily related market price of the option contract. Only the second type of harm is pleaded by Deutschman: affirmative misrepresentation by corporate managers having the effect of artificially supporting the market price of the underlying stock, and concomitantly the market price of the option contract for that stock.

Section 10(b) prohibits the use "in connection with the purchase or sale of any security . . . [of] any manipulative or deceptive device or contrivance in contravention of such rules and regulations as the [SEC] may prescribe." . . . The defendants do not deny that the affirmative misrepresentations pleaded by Deutschman would, if proved, amount to untrue statements of material fact which would operate to deceive a purchaser of Beneficial stock. The complaint alleges that the misrepresentations were made intentionally or with reckless disregard of the truth. It, therefore, satisfies the § 10(b) scienter requirement. . . . Thus defendants do not dispute that even though they did not trade in Beneficial stock they could, if Deutschman's allegations are proved, be held liable in a suit by a purchaser of such stock. . . . Finally, defendants do not dispute that Deutschman is a purchaser of a security. Congress placed that question beyond debate when . . . it amended the Securities and Exchange Act of 1934 and other federal statutes so as explicitly to include option contracts. . . .

The only standing limitation recognized by the Supreme Court with respect to § 10(b) damage actions is the requirement that the plaintiff be a purchaser or seller of a security. See Blue Chip Stamps v. Manor Drug Stores, 421 U.S. 723, 95 S.Ct. 1917, 44 L.Ed.2d 539 (1975); Birnbaum v. Newport Steel Corp., 193 F.2d 461 (2d Cir.), cert. denied, 343 U.S. 956, 72 S.Ct. 1051, 96 L.Ed. 1356 (1952). When in *Manor Drug Stores* the Supreme Court adopted the *Birnbaum* requirement that a § 10(b) plaintiff be a purchaser or seller of a security, however, it expressly recognized that such plaintiffs need not be in any relationship of privity with the defendant charged with misrepresentation. The underlying purpose of the 1934 Act was the protection of actual participants in the securities markets, and the *Birnbaum* rule was consistent with that purpose because it limited "the class of plaintiffs to those who have at least dealt in the security to which the prospectus, representation, or omission relates."

Deutschman's complaint appears, therefore, to satisfy every requirement for a § 10(b) damage action imposed by the Supreme Court when dealing with affirmative misrepresentations which may affect the market price of a security. The district court nevertheless dismissed it. The court acted in reliance on Chiarella v. United States, 445 U.S. 222, 100 S.Ct. 1108, 63 L.Ed.2d 348 (1980), and Dirks v. Securities & Exchange Comm., 463 U.S. 646, 103 S.Ct. 3255, 77 L.Ed.2d 911 (1983), construing those cases as limiting exposure to liability for damages under § 10(b) to persons in some special relationship of trust or confidence toward the § 10(b) plaintiff.

The district court's reliance on *Chiarella* and *Dirks* is entirely misplaced. Those cases dealt not with injury caused by affirmative misrepresentations which affected the market price of securities, but with the analytically distinct problem of trading on undisclosed information; a theory of recovery which Deutschman does not plead. The "disclose or abstain from trading" rule laid down in the insider trading cases imposes on insiders a duty to disclose information which need not otherwise be disclosed before they act on that information in any uninformed marketplace. . . . *Chiarella* and *Dirks* involve only the question of when outsiders and nonfiduciaries will be treated as insiders or fiduciaries for purposes of the affirmative duty to disclose or refrain from trading. The court in those cases declined to extend the duty to disclose or abstain to mere tippees who came into possession of otherwise undisclosed information. Nothing in those opinions, however, can be construed to require the existence of a fiduciary relationship between a § 10(b) defendant and the victim of that defendant's affirmative misrepresentation. Except to the extent that other federal statutes may have imposed a disclosure obligation (none are relied on by Deutschman), Beneficial and its officers were free to keep quiet about its business affairs so long as they stayed out of the market. According to Deutschman, however, they chose to speak, and in speaking they were not free to lie.

Another policy argument advanced by the defendants is that although purchasers of option contracts do purchase securities they are entitled to less protection under the 1934 Act because option trading, like blackjack or craps, is "gambling." By characterizing option traders as "gamblers" the defendants hope that we will draw the conclusion that they are fair game for affirmative misrepresentation, while stock traders are not. We are not persuaded that the difference between trading in the two types of securities should lead to different treatment. Since the price of option contracts is closely dependent upon the price of the underlying stocks, the degree of risk involved in trading in one over the other is not self-evidently greater. The time element of a put or call option does increase exposure to price movements, but the ability to buy or sell such options in the interim does not. Moreover, the availability of option contracts permits traders in common stocks to engage in hedging transactions, which are often used as a means of reducing exposure to market fluctuations and are thus risk reducing. This method of risk reduction, formerly available only through put and call options in an over-the-counter market, has since 1973 been available at lower cost. Finally, it is not our role as a court to pass judgment on the soundness of the legislative policy judgments which led to the creation of exchanges for option contracts, and their treatment as securities. Congress, the Securities and Exchange Commission, the Board of Governors of the Federal Reserve System, and the Commodity Futures Trading Commission all have had a role in the evolution of the market for these securities, and the policy judgment was their responsibility, not ours.

We hold that Deutschman has standing as a purchaser of an option contract to seek damages under § 10(b) for the affirmative misrepresentations he alleges were made by the defendants, Beneficial, Caspersen, and Halvorsen. The judgment dismissing Deutschman's § 10(b) claim must therefore be reversed.   .   .   .

PROBLEMS

1.   Monarch Mining Corporation is a publicly held corporation in the business of exploring for, developing, and mining various ores. At a quarterly meeting of its board of directors, the CEO announces that she has received good reports about a major exploration project. The reports are preliminary, however. It may turn out that the project will turn into a major discovery, but it is still possible that it will turn out to be worthless. The present price of a share of Monarch's common stock is $69. The board members are aware that certain publicly traded call options on some of its shares have an exercise price of $72 per share and will expire in three days. It is reasonable to suppose that if the good news is released, the price of the shares will rise to $75. The CEO proposes that the news not be released, because her experience leads her to believe that shareholders and analysts become disgruntled when favorable prospects are reported and it later turns out that the prospects come to nothing. If the board decides to hold off on the release of the news, is there any liability under § 10(b) and rule 10b–5 or under common-law rules of fiduciary obligation? What if there is no basis for concern about adverse reaction to favorable announcements that do not pan out?

2.   Cashrich Corporation is a publicly held corporation that recently sold one of its divisions and is holding the cash from the sale. Cashrich has no debts. Its common shares are currently selling for $69 per share. Certain options on some of the shares have an exercise price of $70 and will expire in two months. At the quarterly board meeting the CEO presents two alternatives for use of the cash on hand. Alternative A is to use it to pay a dividend of $20 per share one month hence. It is reasonable to suppose that after payment of the dividend, the price of the shares will fall by $20 per share. Alternative B is to invest the cash in a project that the staff has

studied. This is a risky project and it is unclear how investors might react to it. The best guess of the more sophisticated members of the board is that there is a 50 percent chance that the Cashrich shares will rise to $73 and a 50 percent chance that they will fall to $65. If the directors decide to adopt Alternative A (payment of a dividend), might they be liable to the option holders?

SECTION 4. INSIDE INFORMATION

Goodwin v. Agassiz

283 Mass. 358, 186 N.E. 659 (1933).

A stockholder in a corporation seeks in this suit relief for losses suffered by him in selling shares of stock in Cliff Mining Company by way of accounting, rescission of sales, or redelivery of shares. The named defendants are MacNaughton, a resident of Michigan not served or appearing, and Agassiz, a resident of this commonwealth, the active party defendant. . . .

. . . The defendants, in May, 1926, purchased through brokers on the Boston stock exchange seven hundred shares of stock of the Cliff Mining Company which up to that time the plaintiff had owned. Agassiz was president and director and MacNaughton a director and general manager of the company. They had certain knowledge, material as to the value of the stock, which the plaintiff did not have. The plaintiff contends that such purchase in all the circumstances without disclosure to him of that knowledge was a wrong against him. That knowledge was that an experienced geologist had formulated in writing in March, 1926, a theory as to the possible existence of copper deposits under conditions prevailing in the region where the property of the company was located. That region was known as the mineral belt in Northern Michigan, where are located mines of several copper mining companies. Another such company, of which the defendants were officers, had made extensive geological surveys of its lands. In consequence of recommendations resulting from that survey, exploration was started on property of the Cliff Mining Company in 1925. That exploration was ended in May, 1926, because completed unsuccessfully, and the equipment was removed. The defendants discussed the geologist's theory shortly after it was formulated. Both felt that the theory had value and should be tested, but they agreed that, before starting to test it, options should be obtained by another copper company of which they were officers on land adjacent to or nearby in the copper belt, that if the geologist's theory were known to the owners of such other land there might be difficulty in securing options, and that that theory should not be communicated to any one unless it became absolutely necessary. Thereafter, options were secured which, if taken up, would involve a large expenditure by the other company. The defendants both thought, also that, if there was any merit in the geologist's theory, the price of Cliff Mining Company stock in the market would go up. Its stock was quoted and bought and sold on the Boston Stock Exchange. Pursuant to agreement, they bought many shares of that stock through agents on joint account. The plaintiff first learned of the closing of exploratory operations on property of the Cliff Mining Company from an article in a paper on May 15,

1926, and immediately sold his shares of stock through brokers. It does not appear that the defendants were in any way responsible for the publication of that article. The plaintiff did not know that the purchase was made for the defendants and they did not know that his stock was being bought for them. There was no communication between them touching the subject. The plaintiff would not have sold his stock if he had known of the geologist's theory. The finding is express that the defendants were not guilty of fraud, that they committed no breach of duty owed by them to the Cliff Mining Company, and that that company was not harmed by the nondisclosure of the geologist's theory, or by their purchases of its stock, or by shutting down the exploratory operations.

The contention of the plaintiff is that the purchase of his stock in the company by the defendants without disclosing to him as a stockholder their knowledge of the geologist's theory, their belief that the theory was true, . . ., the keeping secret the existence of the theory, discontinuance by the defendants of exploratory operations begun in 1925 on property of the Cliff Mining Company and their plan ultimately to test the value of the theory, constitute actionable wrong for which he as stockholder can recover. . . .

The directors of a commercial corporation stand in a relation of trust to the corporation and are bound to exercise the strictest good faith in respect to its property and business. . . . The contention that directors also occupy the position of trustee toward individual stockholders in the corporation is plainly contrary to repeated decisions of this court and cannot be supported. . . .

The principle thus established is supported by an imposing weight of authority in other jurisdictions. . . .

While the general principle is as stated, circumstances may exist requiring that transactions between a director and a stockholder as to stock in the corporation be set aside. The knowledge naturally in the possession of a director as to the condition of a corporation places upon him a peculiar obligation to observe every requirement of fair dealing when directly buying or selling its stock. Mere silence does not usually amount to a breach of duty, but parties may stand in such relation to each other that an equitable responsibility arises to communicate facts. . . . Purchases and sales of stock dealt in on the stock exchange are commonly impersonal affairs. An honest director would be in a difficult situation if he could neither buy nor sell on the stock exchange shares of stock in his corporation without first seeking out the other actual ultimate party to the transaction and disclosing to him everything which a court or jury might later find that he then knew affecting the real or speculative value of such shares. Business of that nature is a matter to be governed by practical rules. Fiduciary obligations of directors ought not to be made so onerous that men of experience and ability will be deterred from accepting such office. Law in its sanctions is not coextensive with morality. It cannot undertake to put all parties to every contract on an equality as to knowledge, experience, skill and shrewdness. It cannot undertake to relieve

against hard bargains made between competent parties without fraud.   On
the other hand, directors cannot rightly be allowed to indulge with impunity in practices which do violence to prevailing standards of upright business
men.   Therefore, where a director personally seeks a stockholder for the
purpose of buying his shares without making disclosure of material facts
within his peculiar knowledge and not within reach of the stockholder, the
transaction will be closely scrutinized and relief may be granted in appropriate instances.   .   .   .

The precise question to be decided in the case at bar is whether on the
facts found the defendants as directors had a right to buy stock of the
plaintiff, a stockholder.   Every element of actual fraud or misdoing by the
defendants is negatived by the findings.   Fraud cannot be presumed; it
must be proved.   .   .   .   The facts found afford no ground for inferring
fraud or conspiracy.   The only knowledge possessed by the defendants not
open to the plaintiff was the existence of a theory formulated in a thesis by
a geologist as to the possible existence of copper deposits where certain
geological conditions existed common to the property of the Cliff Mining
Company and that of other mining companies in its neighborhood.   This
thesis did not express an opinion that copper deposits would be found at
any particular spot or on property of any specified owner.   Whether that
theory was sound or fallacious, no one knew, and so far as appears has
never been demonstrated.   The defendants made no representations to
anybody about the theory.   No facts found placed upon them any obligation
to disclose the theory.   A few days after the thesis expounding the theory
was brought to the attention of the defendants, the annual report by the
directors of the Cliff Mining Company for the calendar year 1925, signed by
Agassiz for the directors, was issued.   It did not cover the time when the
theory was formulated.   The report described the status of the operations
under the exploration which had been begun in 1925.   At the annual
meeting of the stockholders of the company held early in April, 1926, no
reference was made to the theory.   It was then at most a hope, possibly an
expectation.   It had not passed the nebulous stage.   No disclosure was
made of it.   The Cliff Mining Company was not harmed by the nondisclosure.   There would have been no advantage to it, so far as appears, from a
disclosure.   The disclosure would have been detrimental to the interests of
another mining corporation in which the defendants were directors.   In the
circumstances there was no duty on the part of the defendants to set forth
to the stockholders at the annual meeting their faith, aspirations and plans
for the future.   Events as they developed might render advisable radical
changes in such views.   Disclosure of the theory, if it ultimately was proved
to be erroneous or without foundation in fact, might involve the defendants
in litigation with those who might act on the hypothesis that it was correct.
The stock of the Cliff Mining Company was bought and sold on the stock
exchange.   The identity of buyers and seller of the stock in question in fact
was not known to the parties and perhaps could not readily have been
ascertained.   The defendants caused the shares to be bought through
brokers on the stock exchange.   They said nothing to anybody as to the
reasons actuating them.   The plaintiff was no novice.   He was a member of

the Boston Stock Exchange and had kept a record of sales of Cliff Mining Company stock. He acted upon his own judgment in selling his stock. He made no inquiries of the defendants or of other officers of the company. The result is that the plaintiff cannot prevail.

Securities and Exchange Commission v. Texas Gulf Sulphur Co.

401 F.2d 833 (2d Cir.), cert. denied sub nom. Coates v. S.E.C., 394 U.S. 976 (1969).

[In the late 1950s, the mining firm Texas Gulf Sulphur (TGS) began exploratory drilling in eastern Canada. Defendant TGS Vice President Richard D. Mollison, a mining engineer, supervised the project. Defendant Richard H. Clayton, an electrical engineer, was also on the site. On October 29 and 30, 1963, TGS located a segment of land that looked especially promising. It drilled an exploratory hole (K–55–1) on it in early November and found extraordinarily high mineral content. By November 12 it decided that it should buy the land in the area.

To preserve the opportunity for the company to buy the land without driving up prices, defendant TGS President Claude O. Stephens ordered company employees to keep drilling results secret. By March 27, 1964, the company had bought enough of the land that it could safely resume drilling. The on-site officials began to send daily reports to Stephens and defendant Vice President Charles F. Fogarty.

From November 12, 1963 to March 31, 1964, several TGS employees and their "tippees" bought TGS stock and calls (options) on stock. Where in November they had owned 1135 shares of TGS and no calls, by the end of March they owned 8,235 shares and 12,300 calls. Other defendants discussed below include TGS director Frances G. Coates and TGS Secretary David M. Crawford.]

Meanwhile, rumors that a major ore strike was in the making had been circulating throughout Canada. On the morning of Saturday, April 11, Stephens at his home in Greenwich, Conn., read in the New York Herald Tribune and in the New York Times unauthorized reports of the TGS drilling which seemed to infer a rich strike from the fact that the drill cores had been flown to the United States for chemical assay. Stephens immediately contacted Fogarty at his home in Rye, N.Y., who in turn telephoned and later that day visited Mollison at Mollison's home in Greenwich to obtain a current report and evaluation of the drilling progress. The following morning, Sunday, Fogarty again telephoned Mollison, inquiring whether Mollison had any further information and told him to return to Timmins with Holyk, the TGS Chief Geologist, as soon as possible "to move things along." With the aid of one Carroll, a public relations consultant, Fogarty drafted a press release designed to quell the rumors, which release, after having been channeled through Stephens and Hunting-ton, a TGS attorney, was issued at 3:00 P.M. on Sunday, April 12, and which appeared in the morning newspapers of general circulation on Monday, April 13. It read in pertinent part as follows:

NEW YORK, April 12—The following statement was made today by Dr. Charles F. Fogarty, executive vice president of Texas Gulf Sulphur Company, in regard to the company's drilling operations near Timmins, Ontario, Canada. Dr. Fogarty said:

"During the past few days, the exploration activities of Texas Gulf Sulphur in the area of Timmins, Ontario, have been widely reported in the press, coupled with rumors of a substantial copper discovery there. These reports exaggerate the scale of operations, and mention plans and statistics of size and grade of ore that are without factual basis and have evidently originated by speculation of people not connected with TGS.

"The facts are as follows. TGS has been exploring in the Timmins area for six years as part of its overall search in Canada and elsewhere for various minerals—lead, copper, zinc, etc. During the course of this work, in Timmins as well as in Eastern Canada, TGS has conducted exploration entirely on its own, without the participation by others. Numerous prospects have been investigated by geophysical means and a large number of selected ones have been core-drilled. These cores are sent to the United States for assay and detailed examination as a matter of routine and on advice of expert Canadian legal counsel. No inferences as to grade can be drawn from this procedure.

"Most of the areas drilled in Eastern Canada have revealed either barren pyrite or graphite without value; a few have resulted in discoveries of small or marginal sulphide ore bodies.

"Recent drilling on one property near Timmins has led to preliminary indications that more drilling would be required for proper evaluation of this prospect. The drilling done to date has not been conclusive, but the statements made by many outside quarters are unreliable and include information and figures that are not available to TGS.

"The work done to date has not been sufficient to reach definite conclusions and any statement as to size and grade of ore would be premature and possibly misleading. When we have progressed to the point where reasonable and logical conclusions can be made, TGS will issue a definite statement to its stockholders and to the public in order to clarify the Timmins project."

*   *   *   *   *   *

The release purported to give the Timmins drilling results as of the release date, April 12. From Mollison, Fogarty had been told of the developments through 7:00 P.M. on April 10, and of the remarkable discoveries made up to that time, detailed supra, which discoveries, according to the calculations of the experts who testified for the SEC at the hearing, demonstrated that TGS had already discovered 6.2 to 8.3 million tons of proven ore having gross assay values from $26 to $29 per ton. TGS experts, on the other hand, denied at the hearing that proven or probable ore could have been calculated on April 11 or 12 because there was then no assurance of continuity in the mineralized zone.

The evidence as to the effect of this release on the investing public was equivocal and less than abundant. On April 13 the New York Herald Tribune in an article head-noted "Copper Rumor Deflated" quoted from the TGS release of April 12 and backtracked from its original April 11 report of a major strike but nevertheless inferred from the TGS release that "recent mineral exploratory activity near Timmins, Ontario, has provided preliminary favorable results, sufficient at least to require a step-up in drilling operations." Some witnesses who testified at the hearing stated that they found the release encouraging. On the other hand, a Canadian mining security specialist, Roche, stated that "earlier in the week [before April 16] we had a Dow Jones saying that they [TGS] didn't have anything basically" and a TGS stock specialist for the Midwest Stock Exchange became concerned about his long position in the stock after reading the release. The trial court stated only that "While, in retrospect, the press release may appear gloomy or incomplete, this does not make it misleading or deceptive on the basis of the facts then known." . . .

While drilling activity ensued to completion, TGS officials were taking steps toward ultimate disclosure of the discovery. On April 13, a previously-invited reporter for The Northern Miner, a Canadian mining industry journal, visited the drillsite, interviewed Mollison, Holyk and Darke, and prepared an article which confirmed a 10 million ton ore strike. This report, after having been submitted to Mollison and returned to the reporter unamended on April 15, was published in the April 16 issue. A statement relative to the extent of the discovery, in substantial part drafted by Mollison, was given to the Ontario Minister of Mines for release to the Canadian media. Mollison and Holyk expected it to be released over the airways at 11 P.M. on April 15th, but, for undisclosed reasons, it was not released until 9:40 A.M. on the 16th. An official detailed statement, announcing a strike of at least 25 million tons of ore, based on the drilling data set forth above, was read to representatives of American financial media from 10:00 A.M. to 10:10 or 10:15 A.M. on April 16, and appeared over Merrill Lynch's private wire at 10:29 A.M. and, somewhat later than expected, over the Dow Jones ticker tape at 10:54 A.M.

Between the time the first press release was issued on April 12 and the dissemination of the TGS official announcement on the morning of April 16, the only defendants before us on appeal who engaged in market activity were Clayton and Crawford and TGS director Coates. Clayton ordered 200 shares of TGS stock through his Canadian broker on April 15 and the order was executed that day over the Midwest Stock Exchange. Crawford ordered 300 shares at midnight on the 15th and another 300 shares at 8:30 A.M. the next day, and these orders were executed over the Midwest Exchange in Chicago at its opening on April 16. Coates left the TGS press conference and called his broker son-in-law Haemisegger shortly before 10:20 A.M. on the 16th and ordered 2,000 shares of TGS for family trust accounts of which Coates was a trustee but not a beneficiary; Haemisegger executed this order over the New York and Midwest Exchanges, and he and his customers purchased 1500 additional shares.

During the period of drilling in Timmins, the market price of TGS stock fluctuated but steadily gained overall. On Friday, November 8, when the drilling began, the stock closed at 17⅜; on Friday, November 15, after K–55–1 had been completed, it closed at 18. After a slight decline to 16⅜ by Friday, November 22, the price rose to 20⅞ by December 13, when the chemical assay results of K–55–1 were received, and closed at a high of 24⅛ on February 21, the day after the stock options had been issued. It had reached a price of 26 by March 31, after the land acquisition program had been completed and drilling had been resumed, and continued to ascend to 30⅛ by the close of trading on April 10, at which time the drilling progress up to then was evaluated for the April 12th press release. On April 13, the day on which the April 12 release was disseminated, TGS opened at 30⅛, rose immediately to a high of 32 and gradually tapered off to close at 30⅞. It closed at 30¼ the next day, and at 29⅜ on April 15. On April 16, the day of the official announcement of the Timmins discovery, the price climbed to a high of 37 and closed at 36⅜. By May 15, TGS stock was selling at 58¼.*

I. The Individual Defendants

A. *Introductory*

Rule 10b–5, 17 CFR 240.10b–5, on which this action is predicated, provides:

> It shall be unlawful for any person, directly or indirectly, by the use of any means or instrumentality of interstate commerce, or of the mails, or of any facility of any national securities exchange,
>
> (1) to employ any device, scheme, or artifice to defraud,
>
> (2) to make any untrue statement of a material fact or to omit to state a material fact necessary in order to make the statements made, in the light of the circumstances under which they were made, not misleading, or
>
> (3) to engage in any act, practice, or course of business which operates or would operate as a fraud or deceit upon any person,
>
> in connection with the purchase or sale of any security.

Rule 10b–5 was promulgated pursuant to the grant of authority given the SEC by Congress in Section 10(b) of the Securities Exchange Act of 1934 (15 U.S.C. § 78j(b)).[8] By that Act Congress purposed to prevent

---

* [Eds.—The Dow–Jones Industrial Average, a widely used index of general stock market performance, was 755 on October 30, 815 on March 30, and 820 on May 28.]

8. 15 U.S.C. § 78j reads in pertinent part as follows:

§ 78j. Manipulative and deceptive devices

It shall be unlawful for any person, directly or indirectly, by the use of any means or instrumentality of interstate commerce or of the mails, or of any facility of any national securities exchange—

inequitable and unfair practices and to insure fairness in securities transactions generally, whether conducted face-to-face, over the counter, or on exchanges. . . . [T]he Rule is based in policy on the justifiable expectation of the securities marketplace that all investors trading on impersonal exchanges have relatively equal access to material information. . . .

The essence of the Rule is that anyone who, trading for his own account in the securities of a corporation, has "access, directly or indirectly, to information intended to be available only for a corporate purpose and not for the personal benefit of anyone" may not take "advantage of such information knowing it is unavailable to those with whom he is dealing," i.e., the investing public. Matter of Cady, Roberts & Co., 40 SEC 907, 912 (1961). Insiders, as directors or management officers are, of course, by this Rule, precluded from so unfairly dealing, but the Rule is also applicable to one possessing the information who may not be strictly termed an "insider" within the meaning of Sec. 16(b) of the Act. Cady, Roberts, supra. Thus, anyone in possession of material inside information must either disclose it to the investing public, or, if he is disabled from disclosing it in order to protect a corporate confidence, or he chooses not to do so, must abstain from trading in or recommending the securities concerned while such inside information remains undisclosed. So, it is here no justification for insider activity that disclosure was forbidden by the legitimate corporate objective of acquiring options to purchase the land surrounding the exploration site; if the information was, as the SEC contends, material,[9] its possessors should have kept out of the market until disclosure was accomplished. Cady, Roberts, supra at 911.

B. *Material Inside Information*

An insider is not, of course, always foreclosed from investing in his own company merely because he may be more familiar with company operations than are outside investors. An insider's duty to disclose information or his duty to abstain from dealing in his company's securities arises only in "those situations which are essentially extraordinary in nature and which are reasonably certain to have a substantial effect on the market price of the security if [the extraordinary situation is] disclosed." Fleischer, Securities Trading and Corporate Information Practices: The Implications of the Texas Gulf Sulphur Proceeding, 51 Va.L.Rev. 1271, 1289.

Nor is an insider obligated to confer upon outside investors the benefit of his superior financial or other expert analysis by disclosing his educated guesses or predictions.

. . .

(b) To use or employ, in connection with the purchase or sale of any security registered on a national securities exchange or any security not so registered, any manipulative or deceptive device or contrivance in contravention of such rules and regulations as the Commission may prescribe as necessary or appropriate in the public interest or for the protection of investors.

9. Congress intended by the Exchange Act to eliminate the idea that the use of inside information for personal advantage was a normal emolument of corporate office. . . .

This is not to suggest, however, as did the trial court, that "the test of materiality must necessarily be a conservative one, particularly since many actions under Section 10(b) are brought on the basis of hindsight," 258 F.Supp. 262 at 280, in the sense that the materiality of facts is to be assessed solely by measuring the effect the knowledge of the facts would have upon prudent or conservative investors. As we stated in List v. Fashion Park, Inc., 340 F.2d 457, 462, "The basic test of materiality . . . is whether a *reasonable* man would attach importance . . . in determining his choice of action in the transaction in question. Restatement, Torts § 538(2)(a); accord Prosser, Torts 554–55; I Harper & James, Torts 565–66." (Emphasis supplied.) This, of course, encompasses any fact " . . . which in reasonable and objective contemplation *might* affect the value of the corporation's stock or securities. . . ." List v. Fashion Park, Inc., supra at 462, quoting from Kohler v. Kohler Co., 319 F.2d 634, 642 (7 Cir.1963). (Emphasis supplied.) Such a fact is a material fact and must be effectively disclosed to the investing public prior to the commencement of insider trading in the corporation's securities. The speculators and chartists of Wall and Bay Streets are also "reasonable" investors entitled to the same legal protection afforded conservative traders. Thus, material facts include not only information disclosing the earnings and distributions of a company but also those facts which affect the probable future of the company and those which may affect the desire of investors to buy, sell, or hold the company's securities.

In each case, then, whether facts are material within Rule 10b–5 when the facts relate to a particular event and are undisclosed by those persons who are knowledgeable thereof will depend at any given time upon a balancing of both the indicated probability that the event will occur and the anticipated magnitude of the event in light of the totality of the company activity. Here, notwithstanding the trial court's conclusion that the results of the first drill core, K–55–1, were "too 'remote' . . . to have had any significant impact on the market, i.e., to be deemed material," 258 F.Supp. at 283, knowledge of the possibility, which surely was more than marginal, of the existence of a mine of the vast magnitude indicated by the remarkably rich drill core located rather close to the surface (suggesting mineability by the less expensive open-pit method) within the confines of a large anomaly (suggesting an extensive region of mineralization) might well have affected the price of TGS stock and would certainly have been an important fact to a reasonable, if speculative, investor in deciding whether he should buy, sell, or hold. After all, this first drill core was "unusually good and . . . excited the interest and speculation of those who knew about it." 258 F.Supp. at 282.

. . . Our survey of the facts found below conclusively establishes that knowledge of the results of the discovery hole, K–55–1, would have been important to a reasonable investor and might have affected the price of the stock.[12] On April 16, The Northern Miner, a trade publication in

---

12. We do not suggest that material facts must be disclosed immediately; the tim- ing of disclosure is a matter for the business judgment of the corporate officers entrusted

wide circulation among mining stock specialists, called K–55–1, the discovery hole, "one of the most impressive drill holes completed in modern times."

Finally, a major factor in determining whether the K–55–1 discovery was a material fact is the importance attached to the drilling results by those who knew about it. In view of other unrelated recent developments favorably affecting TGS, participation by an informed person in a regular stock-purchase program, or even sporadic trading by an informed person, might lend only nominal support to the inference of the materiality of the K–55–1 discovery; nevertheless, the timing by those who knew of it of their stock purchases and their purchases of *short-term* calls—purchases in some cases by individuals who had never before purchased calls or even TGS stock—virtually compels the inference that the insiders were influenced by the drilling results. . . .

Our decision to expand the limited protection afforded outside investors by the trial court's narrow definition of materiality is not at all shaken by fears that the elimination of insider trading benefits will deplete the ranks of capable corporate managers by taking away an incentive to accept such employment. Such benefits, in essence, are forms of secret corporate compensation, . . . derived at the expense of the uninformed investing public and not at the expense of the corporation which receives the sole benefit from insider incentives. Moreover, adequate incentives for corporate officers may be provided by properly administered stock options and employee purchase plans of which there are many in existence. In any event, the normal motivation induced by stock ownership, i.e., the identification of an individual with corporate progress, is ill-promoted by condoning the sort of speculative insider activity which occurred here; for example, some of the corporation's stock was sold at market in order to purchase short-term calls upon that stock, calls which would never be exercised to increase a stockholder equity in TGS unless the market price of that stock rose sharply.

The core of Rule 10b–5 is the implementation of the Congressional purpose that all investors should have equal access to the rewards of participation in securities transactions. It was the intent of Congress that all members of the investing public should be subject to identical market risks—which market risks include, of course the risk that one's evaluative capacity or one's capital available to put at risk may exceed another's capacity or capital. The insiders here were not trading on an equal footing with the outside investors. . . .

with the management of the corporation within the affirmative disclosure requirements promulgated by the exchanges and by the SEC. Here, a valuable corporate purpose was served by delaying the publication of the K–55–1 discovery. We do intend to convey, however, that where a corporate purpose is thus served by withholding the news of a material fact, those persons who are thus quite properly true to their corporate trust must not during the period of non-disclosure deal personally in the corporation's securities or give to outsiders confidential information not generally available to all the corporations' stockholders and to the public at large.

We hold, therefore, that all transactions in TGS stock or calls by individuals apprised of the drilling results of K–55–1 were made in violation of Rule 10b–5. Inasmuch as the visual evaluation of that drill core (a generally reliable estimate though less accurate than a chemical assay) constituted material information, those advised of the results of the visual evaluation as well as those informed of the chemical assay traded in violation of law. The geologist Darke possessed undisclosed material information and traded in TGS securities. Therefore we reverse the dismissal of the action as to him and his personal transaction. . . .

Coates was absolved by the court below because his telephone order was placed shortly before 10:20 A.M. on April 16, which was after the announcement had been made even though the news could not be considered already a matter of public information. . . . This result seems to have been predicated upon a misinterpretation of dicta in *Cady, Roberts,* where the SEC instructed insiders to "keep out of the market until the established procedures for public release of the information are *carried out* instead of hastening to execute transactions in advance of, and in frustration of, the objectives of the release," 40 SEC at 915 (emphasis supplied). The reading of a news release, which prompted Coates into action, is merely the first step in the process of dissemination required for compliance with the regulatory objective of providing all investors with an equal opportunity to make informed investment judgments. Assuming that the contents of the official release could instantaneously be acted upon,[18] at the minimum Coates should have waited until the news could reasonably have been expected to appear over the media of widest circulation, the Dow Jones broad tape, rather than hastening to insure an advantage to himself and his broker son-in-law.

. . .

II. The Corporate Defendant

A. *Introductory*

At 3:00 P.M. on April 12, 1964, evidently believing it desirable to comment upon the rumors concerning the Timmins project, TGS issued the press release quoted in pertinent part in the text at [above]. The SEC argued below and maintains on this appeal that this release painted a misleading and deceptive picture of the drilling progress at the time of its issuance, and hence violated Rule 10b–5(2). TGS relies on the holding of the court below that "The issuance of the release produced no unusual

---

18. Although the only insider who acted after the news appeared over the Dow Jones broad tape is not an appellant and therefore we need not discuss the necessity of considering the advisability of a "reasonable waiting period" during which outsiders may absorb and evaluate disclosures, we note in passing that, where the news is of a sort which is not readily translatable into investment action, insiders may not take advantage of their advance opportunity to evaluate the information by acting immediately upon dissemination. In any event, the permissible timing of insider transactions after disclosures of various sorts is one of the many areas of expertise for appropriate exercise of the SEC's rule-making power, which we hope will be utilized in the future to provide some predictability and certainty for the business community.

market action" and "In the absence of a showing that the purpose of the April 12 press release was to affect the market price of TGS stock to the advantage of TGS or its insiders, the issuance of the press release did not constitute a violation of Section 10(b) or Rule 10b–5 since it was not issued 'in connection with the purchase or sale of any security'" and, alternatively, "even if it had been established that the April 12 release was issued in connection with the purchase or sale of any security, the Commission has failed to demonstrate that it was false, misleading or deceptive." 258 F.Supp. at 294.

. . .

B. *The "In Connection With . . ." Requirement*

In adjudicating upon the relationship of this phrase to the case before us it would appear that the court below used a standard that does not reflect the congressional purpose that prompted the passage of the Securities Exchange Act of 1934.

The dominant congressional purposes underlying the Securities Exchange Act of 1934 were to promote free and open public securities markets and to protect the investing public from suffering inequities in trading, including, specifically, inequities that follow from trading that has been stimulated by the publication of false or misleading corporate information releases.

. . .

[I]t seems clear from the legislative purpose Congress expressed in the Act, and the legislative history of Section 10(b) that Congress when it used the phrase "in connection with the purchase or sale of any security" intended only that the device employed, whatever it might be, be of a sort that would cause reasonable investors to rely thereon, and, in connection therewith, so relying, cause them to purchase or sell a corporation's securities. There is no indication that Congress intended that the corporations or persons responsible for the issuance of a misleading statement would not violate the section unless they engaged in related securities transactions or otherwise acted with wrongful motives; indeed, the obvious purposes of the Act to protect the investing public and to secure fair dealing in the securities markets would be seriously undermined by applying such a gloss onto the legislative language. . . .

C. *Did the Issuance of the April 12 Release Violate Rule 10b–5?*

Turning first to the question of whether the release was misleading, i.e., whether it conveyed to the public a false impression of the drilling situation at the time of its issuance, we note initially that the trial court did not actually decide this question. Its conclusion that "the Commission has failed to demonstrate that it was false, misleading or deceptive," 258 F.Supp. at 294, seems to have derived from its views that "The defendants are to be judged *on the facts known to them* when the April 12 release was issued," 258 F.Supp. at 295 (emphasis supplied), that the draftsmen "exercised reasonable business judgment under the circumstances," 258 F.Supp. at 296, and that the release was not "misleading or deceptive *on the basis of the facts then known*," 258 F.Supp. at 296 (emphasis supplied) rather than from an appropriate primary inquiry into the meaning of the statement to the reasonable investor and its relationship to truth. While we certainly agree with the trial court that "in retrospect, the press release may appear gloomy or incomplete," 258 F.Supp. at 296, we cannot, from the present record, by applying the standard Congress intended, definitively conclude that it was deceptive or misleading to the reasonable investor, or that he would have been misled by it. Certain newspaper accounts of the release viewed the release as confirming the existence of preliminary favorable developments, and this optimistic view was held by some brokers, so it could be that the reasonable investor would have read between the lines of what appears to us to be an inconclusive and negative statement and would have envisioned the actual situation at the Kidd segment on April 12. On the other hand, in view of the decline of the market price of TGS stock from a high of 32 on the morning of April 13 when the release was disseminated to 29⅜ by the close of trading on April 15, and the reaction to the release by other brokers, it is far from certain that the release was generally interpreted as a highly encouraging report or even encouraging at all. Accordingly, we remand this issue to the district court that took testimony and heard and saw the witnesses for a determination of the character of the release in the light of the facts existing at the time of the release, by applying the standard of whether the reasonable investor, in the exercise of due care, would have been misled by it.

. . .

PROBLEMS

1. Martha, a successful lawyer in Boston, inherited a tract of ranch land in Oklahoma several years ago. She leased out the land through a local Oklahoma real estate agent, Rose, who found the lessee, took care of all the details, and sent checks to Martha for the net amount after deducting her commission and expenses. A month ago Martha was in Oklahoma on business and drove to the town nearest to the ranch. She made some inquiries that caused her to think there might be oil on the land, whereupon she hired a geologist to advise her. The geologist was optimistic about finding oil. Martha also spoke briefly with Rose and Rose mentioned in passing that Martha's distant cousin, George, whom Martha had not seen for twenty years, had inherited the adjacent ranch and had been leasing it through Rose. Rose also told Martha that George was a stock broker in San Francisco.

Martha then returned to Boston and called George. After some friendly conversation about their family ties, Martha steered the conversation to their ranches and offered to buy George's ranch for a price reflecting its value as ranch land with little prospect of producing oil.

George accepted the offer. Before doing so, he called Rose and was told that the price offered by Martha was a fair price for ranch land. Rose was unaware that Martha had inspected the land and was unaware of any of the information that led Martha to hire the geologist. Shortly after she bought George's land, Martha sold the land to a Texas oil speculator for a price that gave her a substantial profit on the land that she had just bought. (a) Is George legally entitled to recover this profit from Martha? (b) Should he be? (c) Suppose that when Martha called him, George had asked, "Do you know anything about the land, such as evidence that there might be oil under it, that might give it value beyond its value simply as ranch land?" Martha had responded, "How would I know anything more than what you know?"—which George, not knowing of Martha's trip to Oklahoma, took to mean "No."

Suppose that Rose had hired the geologist and, after receiving the report suggesting that there was oil under George's ranch, bought George's ranch from him without revealing to him this information. Would George be legally entitled to recover from Rose any profit she made on the sale of the ranch?

2. Juan and Betty were partners in a cattle ranch in Oklahoma. The land on which the ranch was operated was owned as partnership property. It is located in an area in which there has never been any significant discovery of oil. One night in a bar Juan met a young geologist who had some new theories about how oil is deposited and had convincing evidence of a high probability of finding oil under the Juan/Betty ranch. Juan, knowing that Betty wanted to retire from cattle ranching and go to law school, offered to buy her out. He did not tell her what he knew about the possibility of finding oil under the land. Betty accepted Juan's offer. Shortly thereafter Juan sold the ranch to a Texas oil speculator for a handsome profit. Is Betty legally entitled to recover this profit from Juan?

3. Eve is a shareholder in Maximine Corp., a mining company with claims in Wyoming. Maximine Corp. shares are traded on the New York Stock Exchange. While traveling in Wyoming on vacation, Eve overheard a conversation in a bar between two of Maximine Corp.'s geologists and concluded that the corporation's crews had discovered a valuable ore deposit. She spent more time hanging around, listening, and asking questions, and confirmed her conclusion. She then approached Bob, an acquaintance back home in Chicago who, she knew, owned shares of Maximine Corp. stock. She bought Bob's shares without telling him what she knew about the ore discovery. Shortly thereafter the information about the ore discovery was disclosed in a press release by Maximine Corp. and Eve sold the shares she bought from Bob at a substantial profit. (a) Is Bob legally entitled to recover the profit from Eve? (b) Should he be?

4. The facts about Maximine Corp. are the same as in the preceding paragraph. Carlos is the CEO of Maximine Corp. and learned of the ore discovery because of his position in the firm.

(a) Carlos called his broker and told the broker to buy 1,000 shares of Maximine Corp. stock for him at the market price of $10 per share. A week later the news of the ore discovery was released and the price of u02 the shares started to rise. Two weeks later Carlos sold the 1,000 shares at $18 per share. At common law, has Carlos incurred any legal liability?

(b) Suppose the shares of Maximine Corp. are not publicly traded. There are 50 shareholders and only two or three purchases and sales each year. Carlos knew that Wilma, the widow of a former executive of the company, owned 1,000 shares of stock of Maximine Corp. and that she needed money. He went to her home, asked how she was doing, and offered to buy her shares for $10 per share. Based on her knowledge of a few previous sales and of the earnings and dividends of Maximine Corp., Wilma decided that this was a fair price and accepted the offer. A week later the news of the ore discovery was published. Does Wilma have a common-law cause of action against Carlos?

NOTES AND QUESTIONS

1. There has been considerable academic debate over the years about whether insider trading should be prohibited. Part of the argument for elimination of the prohibition rests on the fact that most insider trading escapes detection. If the existence of the legal prohibition conveys to the public the impression that stock market trading is an unrigged game that anyone can play, that impression may be misleading. Another line of analysis questions whether there are any victims deserving of protection. Here there are two issues, (a) whether a person suffers a loss and (b) whether that person should be owed any duty by the insider. In the TGS context, consider four possible market participants, all of whom bought or sold 100 shares of TGS common stock on January 30, 1964, at the market price of $23 per share.

   i. Grace bought 100 shares on the basis of her broker's advice and her own study of financial data.

   ii. Isabel sold 100 shares that she had held for five years. She sold because she needed the money for the downpayment on a house.

   iii. Christine sold 100 shares that she had bought six months earlier for $17 per share. She sold because she concluded, based on the information available to her, that the shares were worth no more than $20 per share.

   iv. Alison never owned any TGS shares. On January 30, 1964, she considered buying 100 shares but concluded that the price at that time ($23 per share) was too high. If the price had been $22 or less she would have bought.

2. Part of the debate over whether insider trading should be prohibited is based on judgments about whether allowing insider trading would be a good way of compensating employees. Suppose that federal law allowed insider trading by officers, directors, or other employees, or by the corporation, if such trading is permitted in the corporation's articles of incorporation; that you are a member of the board of directors of a corporation

whose articles authorize the board to permit individuals whom it identifies to trade on inside information; and that the corporation's business is similar to that of TGS.

(a) Whom would you authorize to take advantage of the opportunity to engage in trading on nonpublic information, when would you do so, and what limits, if any, would you impose?

(b) How would you react to a proposal that the corporation itself buy or sell shares based on nonpublic information?

(c) Suppose you are an investor with a large portfolio of stocks and you are considering the purchase of shares of stock of two different corporations that seem to you to be equally attractive in all other respects, except that the articles of one authorize insider trading and the articles of the other do not. Which would you buy?

3. *Texas Gulf Sulphur* was an SEC enforcement action. It had previously been established that § 10(b) gave rise to a private cause of action for damages, though the question of who can sue whom for what amounts has given rise to considerable litigation and is still largely unsettled. In a private action for damages the plaintiff must prove (1) the materiality of the concealed or misstated fact, (2) reliance, (3) scienter, and (4) causation. These elements are examined in Basic Inc. v. Levinson, supra Chapter 4, Sec. 3.

In 1984, Congress amended § 21(d) of the '34 Act to allow the SEC to seek a civil penalty up to three times the insider's profits. In the Insider Trading and Securities Fraud Enforcement Act of 1988, Congress added § 20A to the '34 Act. This provision gives an express cause of action for damages to contemporaneous traders against inside traders and tippers. "Contemporaneous" is not defined. The amount that can be recovered is limited to the amount of the insider's profit reduced by any amount disgorged in an SEC enforcement action. Section 20A(d) preserves but does not clarify existing law relating to implied causes of action under § 10(b) and Rule 10b–5. The Act provides expressly for derivative liability of employers for the actions of their employees (for example, the actions of employees of brokerage firms), but (contrary to the general rule for vicarious tort liability) not if the employer is able to prove good faith and noninducement.

INTRODUCTORY NOTE ON CURRENT LAW

Chiarella v. United States, 445 U.S. 222 (1980), involved a criminal prosecution. The defendant had been a "markup man" in the composing room of a financial printing company. The printing company had been retained by the acquiring corporation in a tender offer for the shares of another corporation. The acquiring corporation made every reasonable effort to keep the identity of the tender offer target a secret, even from the employees of the printer. Chiarella, by virtue of his job and ingenuity, correctly identified the target and bought shares of its stock through a broker. When the tender offer was announced, the target shares rose in value and Chiarella sold his shares at a profit. When his conduct was brought to light he was fired and he agreed to give up ("disgorge," in the current parlance) his profit. In addition, he was indicted for violating § 10(b) and Rule 10b–5.

The Supreme Court, reversing the court of appeals, held that Chiarella's conduct was not a violation because he was not an "insider" of the corporation whose shares he had traded (that is, the target corporation). Starting with the observation that the "case concerns the legal effect of [Chiarella's] silence," and the basic proposition that, under § 10(b) and Rule 10b–5, "a corporate insider must abstain from trading in the shares of his corporation unless he has first disclosed all material inside information known to him," the Court concluded that the duty to abstain arises from the relationship of trust between a corporation's shareholders and its employees. Since there was no relationship of trust between Chiarella and the shareholders of the corporations whose shares he traded, he had no duty to "disclose or abstain." Citing *Santa Fe Industries, Inc.,* supra, Chapter 4, Sec. 3, the Court stated, "not every instance of financial unfairness constitutes fraudulent activity under § 10(b)." As an alternative theory to support Chiarella's conviction, the government argued that he had violated a duty to the acquiring corporation; the theory is that Chiarella "misappropriated" information. The Court declined to consider this alternative theory because it was not submitted to the jury.

Chief Justice Burger dissented on the basis of the "misappropriation" theory. This theory was presented to the Court later in United States v. O'Hagan, infra page 481.

Dirks v. Securities & Exchange Commission

463 U.S. 646, 103 S.Ct. 3255, 77 L.Ed.2d 911 (1983).

■ JUSTICE POWELL delivered the opinion of the Court.

Petitioner Raymond Dirks received material nonpublic information from "insiders" of a corporation with which he had no connection. He disclosed this information to investors who relied on it in trading in the shares of the corporation. The question is whether Dirks violated the antifraud provisions of the federal securities laws by this disclosure.

I

In 1973, Dirks was an officer of a New York broker-dealer firm who specialized in providing investment analysis of insurance company securities to institutional investors. On March 6, Dirks received information from Ronald Secrist, a former officer of Equity Funding of America. Secrist alleged that the assets of Equity Funding, a diversified corporation primarily engaged in selling life insurance and mutual funds, were vastly overstated as the result of fraudulent corporate practices. Secrist also stated that various regulatory agencies had failed to act on similar charges made by Equity Funding employees. He urged Dirks to verify the fraud and disclose it publicly.

Dirks decided to investigate the allegations. He visited Equity Funding's headquarters in Los Angeles and interviewed several officers and employees of the corporation. The senior management denied any wrongdoing, but certain corporation employees corroborated the charges of fraud. Neither Dirks nor his firm owned or traded any Equity Funding stock, but throughout his investigation he openly discussed the information he had obtained with a number of clients and investors. Some of these persons sold their holdings of Equity Funding securities, including five investment advisers who liquidated holdings of more than $16 million.[2]

While Dirks was in Los Angeles, he was in touch regularly with William Blundell, the Wall Street Journal's Los Angeles bureau chief. Dirks urged Blundell to write a story on the fraud allegations. Blundell did not believe, however, that such a massive fraud could go undetected and declined to write the story. He feared that publishing such damaging hearsay might be libelous.

During the 2–week period in which Dirks pursued his investigation and spread word of Secrist's charges, the price of Equity Funding stock fell from $26 per share to less than $15 per share. This led the New York Stock Exchange to halt trading on March 27. Shortly thereafter California insurance authorities impounded Equity Funding's records and uncovered evidence of the fraud. Only then did the Securities and Exchange Commission (SEC) file a complaint against Equity Funding and only then, on April 2, did the Wall Street Journal publish a front-page story based largely on information assembled by Dirks. Equity Funding immediately went into receivership.

The SEC began an investigation into Dirks' role in the exposure of the fraud. After a hearing by an Administrative Law Judge, the SEC found that Dirks had aided and abetted violations of § 17(a) of the Securities Act of 1933,* 48 Stat. 84, as amended, 15 U.S.C. § 77q(a), § 10(b) of the Securities Exchange Act of 1934, 48 Stat. 891, 15 U.S.C. § 78j(b), and SEC Rule 10b–5, 17 CFR § 240.10b–5 (1983), by repeating the allegations of fraud to members of the investment community who later sold their Equity Funding stock. The SEC concluded: "Where 'tippees'—regardless of their motivation or occupation—come into possession of material 'corporate information that they know is confidential and know or should know came from a corporate insider,' they must either publicly disclose that information or refrain from trading." 21 S.E.C. Docket 1401, 1407 (1981) (foot-

---

2. Dirks received from his firm a salary plus a commission for securities transactions above a certain amount that his clients directed through his firm. . . . But "[i]t is not clear how many of those with whom Dirks spoke promised to direct some brokerage business through [Dirks' firm] to compensate Dirks, or how many actually did so." 220 U.S.App.D.C., at 316, 681 F.2d, at 831. The Boston Company Institutional Investors, Inc., promised Dirks about $25,000 in commissions, but it is unclear whether Boston actually generated any brokerage business for his firm. . .

* [Eds.—Section 17(a) uses language similar to that of § 10(b) of the '34 Act.]

note omitted) (quoting Chiarella v. United States, 445 U.S. 222, 230, n. 12 (1980)). Recognizing, however, that Dirks "played an important role in bringing [Equity Funding's] massive fraud to light," 21 S.E.C. Docket, at 1412, the SEC only censured him.

II

In the seminal case of In re Cady, Roberts & Co., 40 S.E.C. 907 (1961), the SEC recognized that the common law in some jurisdictions imposes on "corporate 'insiders,' particularly officers, directors, or controlling stockholders" an "affirmative duty of disclosure . . . when dealing in securities." Id., at 911, and n. 13. The SEC found that not only did breach of this common-law duty also establish the elements of a Rule 10b–5 violation, but that individuals other than corporate insiders could be obligated either to disclose material nonpublic information before trading or to abstain from trading altogether. Id., at 912. In *Chiarella,* we accepted the two elements set out in *Cady, Roberts* for establishing a Rule 10b–5 violation: "(i) the existence of a relationship affording access to inside information intended to be available only for a corporate purpose, and (ii) the unfairness of allowing a corporate insider to take advantage of that information by trading without disclosure." 445 U.S., at 227. In examining whether Chiarella had an obligation to disclose or abstain, the Court found that there is no general duty to disclose before trading on material nonpublic information, and held that "a duty to disclose under § 10(b) does not arise from the mere possession of nonpublic market information." Such a duty arises rather from the existence of a fiduciary relationship.

Not "all breaches of fiduciary duty in connection with a securities transaction," however, come within the ambit of Rule 10b–5. Santa Fe Industries, Inc. v. Green, 430 U.S. 462, 472 (1977). There must also be "manipulation or deception." Id., at 473. In an inside-trading case this fraud derives from the "inherent unfairness involved where one takes advantage" of "information intended to be available only for a corporate purpose and not for the personal benefit of anyone." In re Merrill Lynch, Pierce, Fenner & Smith, Inc., 43 S.E.C. 933, 936 (1968). Thus, an insider will be liable under Rule 10b–5 for inside trading only where he fails to disclose material nonpublic information before trading on it and thus makes "secret profits." *Cady, Roberts,* supra, at 916, n. 31.

III

We were explicit in *Chiarella* in saying that there can be no duty to disclose where the person who has traded on inside information "was not [the corporation's] agent, . . . was not a fiduciary, [or] was not a person in whom the sellers [of the securities] had placed their trust and confidence." 445 U.S., at 232. Not to require such a fiduciary relationship, we recognized, would "depar[t] radically from the established doctrine that duty arises from a specific relationship between two parties" and would amount to "recognizing a general duty between all participants in market transactions to forgo actions based on material, nonpublic information." Id., at 232, 233. This requirement of a specific relationship between the shareholders and the individual trading on inside information has created analytical difficulties for the SEC and courts in policing tippees who trade on inside information. Unlike insiders who have independent fiduciary duties to both the corporation and its shareholders, the typical tippee has no such relationships.[14] In view of this absence, it has been unclear how a tippee acquires the *Cady, Roberts* duty to refrain from trading on inside information.

A

The SEC's position, as stated in its opinion in this case, is that a tippee "inherits" the *Cady, Roberts* obligation to shareholders whenever he receives inside information from an insider:

> "In tipping potential traders, Dirks breached a duty which he had assumed as a result of knowingly receiving confidential information from [Equity Funding] insiders. Tippees such as Dirks who receive non-public, material information from insiders become 'subject to the same duty as [the] insiders.' *Shapiro v. Merrill Lynch, Pierce, Fenner & Smith, Inc.* [495 F.2d 228, 237 (C.A.2 1974) (quoting *Ross v. Licht*, 263 F.Supp. 395, 410 (S.D.N.Y.1967))]. Such a tippee breaches the fiduciary duty which he assumes from the insider when the tippee knowingly transmits the information to someone who will probably trade on the basis thereof. . . . Presumably, Dirks' informants were entitled to disclose the [Equity Funding] fraud in order to bring it to light and its perpetrators to justice. However, Dirks—standing in their shoes—committed a breach of the fiduciary duty which he had assumed in dealing with them, when he passed the information on to traders." 21 S.E.C. Docket, at 1410, n. 42.

This view differs little from the view that we rejected as inconsistent with congressional intent in *Chiarella*. In that case, the Court of Appeals agreed with the SEC and affirmed Chiarella's conviction, holding that "*[a]nyone*—corporate insider or not—who regularly receives material non-public information may not use that information to trade in securities without incurring an affirmative duty to disclose." *United States v. Chiarella*, 588 F.2d 1358, 1365 (C.A.2 1978) (emphasis in original). Here, the SEC maintains that anyone who knowingly receives nonpublic material information from an insider has a fiduciary duty to disclose before trading.[15]

---

14. Under certain circumstances, such as where corporate information is revealed legitimately to an underwriter, accountant, lawyer, or consultant working for the corporation, these outsiders may become fiduciaries of the shareholders. The basis for recognizing this fiduciary duty is not simply that such persons acquired nonpublic corporate information, but rather that they have entered into a special confidential relationship in the conduct of the business of the enterprise and are given access to information solely for corporate purposes. . . .

For such a duty to be imposed, however, the corporation must expect the outsider to keep the disclosed nonpublic information confidential, and the relationship at least must imply such a duty.

15. Apparently, the SEC believes this case differs from *Chiarella* in that Dirks' receipt of inside information from Secrist, an

In effect, the SEC's theory of tippee liability in both cases appears rooted in the idea that the antifraud provisions require equal information among all traders. This conflicts with the principle set forth in *Chiarella* that only some persons, under some circumstances, will be barred from trading while in possession of material nonpublic information.

Imposing a duty to disclose or abstain solely because a person knowingly receives material nonpublic information from an insider and trades on it could have an inhibiting influence on the role of market analysts, which the SEC itself recognizes is necessary to the preservation of a healthy market.[17] It is commonplace for analysts to "ferret out and analyze information," 21 S.E.C. Docket, at 1406,[18] and this often is done by meeting with and questioning corporate officers and others who are insiders. And information that the analysts obtain normally may be the basis for judgments as to the market worth of a corporation's securities. The analyst's judgment in this respect is made available in market letters or otherwise to clients of the firm. It is the nature of this type of information, and indeed of the

insider, carried Secrist's duties with it, while Chiarella received the information without the direct involvement of an insider and thus inherited no duty to disclose or abstain. The SEC fails to explain, however, why the receipt of nonpublic information from an insider automatically carries with it the fiduciary duty of the insider. As we emphasized in *Chiarella,* mere possession of nonpublic information does not give rise to a duty to disclose or abstain; only a specific relationship does that. And we do not believe that the mere receipt of information from an insider creates such a special relationship between the tippee and the corporation's shareholders.

Apparently recognizing the weakness of its argument in light of *Chiarella,* the SEC attempts to distinguish that case factually as involving not "inside" information, but rather "market" information, *i.e.,* "information originating outside the company and usually about the supply and demand for the company's securities." Brief for Respondent 22. This Court drew no such distinction in *Chiarella* and, as THE CHIEF JUSTICE noted, "[i]t is clear that § 10(b) and Rule 10b–5 by their terms and by their history make no such distinction." . . .

17. The SEC expressly recognized that "[t]he value to the entire market of [analysts'] efforts cannot be gainsaid; market efficiency in pricing is significantly enhanced by [their] initiatives to ferret out and analyze information, and thus the analyst's work redounds to the benefit of all investors." 21 S.E.C. Docket, at 1406. The SEC asserts

that analysts remain free to obtain from management corporate information for purposes of "filling in the 'interstices in analysis'. . . ." Brief for Respondent 42 (quoting *Investors Management Co.,* 44 S.E.C., at 646). But this rule is inherently imprecise, and imprecision prevents parties from ordering their actions in accord with legal requirements.

18. On its facts, this case is the unusual one. Dirks is an analyst in a broker-dealer firm, and he did interview management in the course of his investigation. He uncovered, however, startling information that required no analysis or exercise of judgment as to its market relevance. Nonetheless, the principle at issue here extends beyond these facts. The SEC's rule—applicable without regard to any breach by an insider—could have serious ramifications on reporting by analysts of investment views.

Despite the unusualness of Dirks' "find," the central role that he played in uncovering the fraud at Equity Funding, and that analysts in general can play in revealing information that corporations may have reason to withhold from the public, is an important one. Dirks' careful investigation brought to light a massive fraud at the corporation. And until the Equity Funding fraud was exposed, the information in the trading market was grossly inaccurate. But for Dirks' efforts, the fraud might well have gone undetected longer.

markets themselves, that such information cannot be made simultaneously available to all of the corporation's stockholders or the public generally.

B

The conclusion that recipients of inside information do not invariably acquire a duty to disclose or abstain does not mean that such tippees always are free to trade on the information. The need for a ban on some tippee trading is clear. Not only are insiders forbidden by their fiduciary relationship from personally using undisclosed corporate information to their advantage, but they also may not give such information to an outsider for the same improper purpose of exploiting the information for their personal gain. . . .

Similarly, the transactions of those who knowingly participate with the fiduciary in such a breach are "as forbidden" as transactions "on behalf of the trustee himself." Mosser v. Darrow, 341 U.S. 267, 272 (1951). . . . Thus, the tippee's duty to disclose or abstain is derivative from that of the insider's duty. . . . As we noted in *Chiarella,* "[t]he tippee's obligation has been viewed as arising from his role as a participant after the fact in the insider's breach of a fiduciary duty."

Thus, some tippees must assume an insider's duty to the shareholders not because they receive inside information, but rather because it has been made available to them *improperly.* And for Rule 10b–5 purposes, the insider's disclosure is improper only where it would violate his *Cady, Roberts* duty. Thus, a tippee assumes a fiduciary duty to the shareholders of a corporation not to trade on material nonpublic information only when the insider has breached his fiduciary duty to the shareholders by disclosing the information to the tippee and the tippee knows or should know that there has been a breach.

C

In determining whether a tippee is under an obligation to disclose or abstain, it thus is necessary to determine whether the insider's "tip" constituted a breach of the insider's fiduciary duty. All disclosures of confidential corporate information are not inconsistent with the duty insiders owe to shareholders. In contrast to the extraordinary facts of this case, the more typical situation in which there will be a question whether disclosure violates the insider's *Cady, Roberts* duty is when insiders disclose information to analysts. In some situations, the insider will act consistently with his fiduciary duty to shareholders, and yet release of the information may affect the market. For example, it may not be clear—either to the corporate insider or to the recipient analyst—whether the information will be viewed as material nonpublic information. Corporate officials may mistakenly think the information already has been disclosed or that it is not material enough to affect the market. Whether disclosure is a breach of duty therefore depends in large part on the purpose of the disclosure. This standard was identified by the SEC itself in *Cady, Roberts:* a purpose of the securities laws was to eliminate "use of inside information for personal advantage." 40 S.E.C., at 912, n. 15. . . . Thus, the test is whether the insider personally will benefit, directly or indirectly, from his disclosure. Absent some personal gain, there has been no breach of duty to stockholders. And absent a breach by the insider, there is no derivative breach.[22] . . .

Determining whether an insider personally benefits from a particular disclosure, a question of fact, will not always be easy for courts. But it is essential, we think to have a guiding principle for those whose daily activities must be limited and instructed by the SEC's inside-trading rules, and we believe that there must be a breach of the insider's fiduciary duty before the tippee inherits the duty to disclose or abstain. In contrast, the rule adopted by the SEC in this case would have no limiting principle.

IV

Under the inside-trading and tipping rules set forth above, we find that there was no actionable violation by Dirks. It is undisputed that Dirks himself was a stranger to Equity Funding, with no pre-existing fiduciary duty to its shareholders. He took no action, directly or indirectly, that induced the shareholders or officers of Equity Funding to repose trust or confidence in him. There was no expectation by Dirks' sources that he would keep their information in confidence. Nor did Dirks misappropriate or illegally obtain the information about Equity Funding. Unless the insiders breached their *Cady, Roberts* duty to shareholders in disclosing the nonpublic information to Dirks, he breached no duty when he passed it on to investors as well as to the Wall Street Journal.

It is clear that neither Secrist nor the other Equity Funding employees violated their *Cady, Roberts* duty to the corporation's shareholders by providing information to Dirks. The tippers received no monetary or personal benefit for revealing Equity Funding's secrets, nor was their purpose to make a gift of valuable information to Dirks. As the facts of this case clearly indicate, the tippers were motivated by a desire to expose the fraud. . . . In the absence of a breach of duty to shareholders by the insiders, there was no derivative breach by Dirks. . . . Dirks therefore could not have been "a participant after the fact in [an] insider's breach of a fiduciary duty." *Chiarella,* 445 U.S., at 230, n. 12.

---

22. An example of a case turning on the court's determination that the disclosure did not impose any fiduciary duties on the recipient of the inside information is Walton v. Morgan Stanley & Co., 623 F.2d 796 (C.A.2 1980). There, the defendant investment banking firm, representing one of its own corporate clients, investigated another corporation that was a possible target of a takeover bid by its client. In the course of negotiations the investment banking firm was given, on a confidential basis, unpublished material information. Subsequently, after the proposed takeover was abandoned, the firm was charged with relying on the information when it traded in the target corporation's stock. For purposes of the decision, it was assumed that the firm knew the information was confidential, but that it had been received in arm's-length negotiations. See id., at 798. In the absence of any fiduciary relationship, the Court of Appeals found no basis for imposing tippee liability on the investment firm. See id., at 799.

V

We conclude that Dirks, in the circumstances of this case, had no duty to abstain from use of the inside information that he obtained. The judgment of the Court of Appeals therefore is

Reversed.

■ JUSTICE BLACKMUN, with whom JUSTICE BRENNAN and JUSTICE MARSHALL join, dissenting.

The Court today takes still another step to limit the protections provided investors by § 10(b) of the Securities Exchange Act of 1934. See Chiarella v. United States, 445 U.S. 222, 246 (1980) (dissenting opinion). The device employed in this case engrafts a special motivational requirement on the fiduciary duty doctrine. This innovation excuses a knowing and intentional violation of an insider's duty to shareholders if the insider does not act from a motive of personal gain. Even on the extraordinary facts of this case, such an innovation is not justified.

. . .

ANALYSIS

1.   Why did the Court absolve Secrist of wrongdoing?

2.   What is the scope of the Court's doctrine on breaches of fiduciary duties? What if Dirks and Secrist had routinely exchanged stock tips? What if Secrist had disclosed the Equity Funding fraud in part because he had been fired over an unrelated matter? What if Dirks merely overheard Secrist describing the fraud in a public elevator?

3.   Suppose Secrist had disclosed inside information (not involving fraud) to Dirks because of a bribe from Dirks. Dirks then advised his clients to sell their Equity Funding stock. Dirks, of course, would have violated Rule 10b–5. Would his clients also have violated the rule?

4.   Stock analysts such as Dirks earn their livelihoods in part by supplying investors with analysis of public information. To this extent the activities of stock analysts seem unobjectionable. But analysts also spend time trying to obtain information that is not clearly public. They spend time talking with executives of the corporations in which they have an interest. It seems clear that the executives, the analysts, and the investors who pay for the services of the analysts all think that the analysts are able to obtain valuable information from their communications with the executives. The objective of the corporate executives is generally to paint a favorable picture of their corporations. The analysts seek an informational advantage for their investors over other investors.[5] They do not receive

5. A nice bit of evidence of this reality is found in a report that Household International, Inc. retaliated against an analyst who issued an unfavorable report about it by denying him telephone access to its executives and by refusing to send him its press releas-

discrete, material items of information of the sort described in the cases we have examined in this section. Rather, what they tend to get are details and analysis. They get answers to perceptive, sophisticated questions. The activities of stock analysts are widespread and their propriety seems generally to be regarded as beyond question. Is that as it should be? Should corporate insiders be prohibited from providing private briefings to analysts (or anyone else)? Suppose you are a major shareholder of a public corporation. Is there anything wrong with the CEO spending a couple of hours once or twice a year with you, answering your questions about the corporation's business?

United States v. O'Hagan

521 U.S. 642, 117 S.Ct. 2199, 138 L.Ed.2d 724 (1997).

This case concerns the interpretation and enforcement of § 10(b) and § 14(e) of the Securities Exchange Act of 1934, and rules made by the Securities and Exchange Commission pursuant to these provisions, Rule 10b–5 and Rule 14e–3(a). Two prime questions are presented. . . . (1) Is a person who trades in securities for personal profit, using confidential information misappropriated in breach of a fiduciary duty to the source of the information, guilty of violating § 10(b) and Rule 10b–5? (2) Did the Commission exceed its rulemaking authority by adopting Rule 14e–3(a), which proscribes trading on undisclosed information in the tender offer setting, even in the absence of a duty to disclose? Our answer to the first question is yes, and to the second question, viewed in the context of this case, no.

I

Respondent James Herman O'Hagan was a partner in the law firm of Dorsey & Whitney in Minneapolis, Minnesota. In July 1988, Grand Metropolitan PLC (Grand Met), a company based in London, England, retained Dorsey & Whitney as local counsel to represent Grand Met regarding a potential tender offer for the common stock of the Pillsbury Company, headquartered in Minneapolis. Both Grand Met and Dorsey & Whitney took precautions to protect the confidentiality of Grand Met's tender offer plans. . . . [O]n October 4, 1988, Grand Met publicly announced its tender offer for Pillsbury stock.

On August 18, 1988, while Dorsey & Whitney was still representing Grand Met, O'Hagan began purchasing call options for Pillsbury stock. Each option gave him the right to purchase 100 shares of Pillsbury stock by a specified date in September 1988. . . . By the end of September, he owned 2,500 unexpired Pillsbury options, apparently more than any other individual investor. O'Hagan also purchased, in September 1988, some 5,000 shares of Pillsbury common stock, at a price just under $39 per share.

es. Berg, Risks for Analysts Who Dare to
Say Sell, N.Y. Times, May 15, 1990, D1, col.
4.

When Grand Met announced its tender offer in October, the price of Pillsbury stock rose to nearly $60 per share. O'Hagan then sold his Pillsbury call options and common stock, making a profit of more than $4.3 million.

The Securities and Exchange Commission (SEC or Commission) initiated an investigation into O'Hagan's transactions, culminating in a 57–count indictment. The indictment alleged that O'Hagan defrauded his law firm and its client, Grand Met, by using for his own trading purposes material, nonpublic information regarding Grand Met's planned tender offer. According to the indictment, O'Hagan used the profits he gained through this trading to conceal his previous embezzlement and conversion of unrelated client trust funds.[2] . . . O'Hagan was charged with 20 counts of mail fraud; 17 counts of securities fraud, in violation of § 10(b) of the Securities Exchange Act of 1934 (Exchange Act), and SEC Rule 10b–5; 17 counts of fraudulent trading in connection with a tender offer, in violation of § 14(e) of the Exchange Act, and SEC Rule 14e–3(a); and 3 counts of violating federal money laundering statutes. A jury convicted O'Hagan on all 57 counts, and he was sentenced to a 41–month term of imprisonment.

A divided panel of the Court of Appeals for the Eighth Circuit reversed all of O'Hagan's convictions. Liability under § 10(b) and Rule 10b–5, the Eighth Circuit held, may not be grounded on the "misappropriation theory" of securities fraud on which the prosecution relied. The Court of Appeals also held that Rule 14e–3(a)—which prohibits trading while in possession of material, nonpublic information relating to a tender offer—exceeds the SEC's § 14(e) rulemaking authority because the rule contains no breach of fiduciary duty requirement. The Eighth Circuit further concluded that O'Hagan's mail fraud and money laundering convictions rested on violations of the securities laws, and therefore could not stand once the securities fraud convictions were reversed. . . .

Decisions of the Courts of Appeals are in conflict on the propriety of the misappropriation theory under § 10(b) and Rule 10b–5, and on the legitimacy of Rule 14e–3(a) under § 14(e). We granted certiorari, and now reverse the Eighth Circuit's judgment.

II

. . .

A

. . .

Under the "traditional" or "classical theory" of insider trading liability, § 10(b) and Rule 10b–5 are violated when a corporate insider trades in the securities of his corporation on the basis of material, nonpublic infor-

---

2. O'Hagan was convicted of theft in state court, sentenced to 30 months' imprisonment, and fined. . . . The Supreme Court of Minnesota disbarred O'Hagan from the practice of law. . . .

mation. Trading on such information qualifies as a "deceptive device" under § 10(b), we have affirmed, because "a relationship of trust and confidence [exists] between the shareholders of a corporation and those insiders who have obtained confidential information by reason of their position with that corporation." Chiarella v. United States, 445 U.S. 222, 228 (1980). That relationship, we recognized, "gives rise to a duty to disclose [or to abstain from trading] because of the 'necessity of preventing a corporate insider from . . . taking unfair advantage of . . . uninformed . . . stockholders.' " Id., at 228–229 (citation omitted). The classical theory applies not only to officers, directors, and other permanent insiders of a corporation, but also to attorneys, accountants, consultants, and others who temporarily become fiduciaries of a corporation. See Dirks v. SEC, 463 U.S. 646, 655, n. 14 (1983).

The "misappropriation theory" holds that a person commits fraud "in connection with" a securities transaction, and thereby violates § 10(b) and Rule 10b–5, when he misappropriates confidential information for securities trading purposes, in breach of a duty owed to the source of the information. Under this theory, a fiduciary's undisclosed, self-serving use of a principal's information to purchase or sell securities, in breach of a duty of loyalty and confidentiality, defrauds the principal of the exclusive use of that information. In lieu of premising liability on a fiduciary relationship between company insider and purchaser or seller of the company's stock, the misappropriation theory premises liability on a fiduciary-turned-trader's deception of those who entrusted him with access to confidential information.

The two theories are complementary, each addressing efforts to capitalize on nonpublic information through the purchase or sale of securities. The classical theory targets a corporate insider's breach of duty to shareholders with whom the insider transacts; the misappropriation theory outlaws trading on the basis of nonpublic information by a corporate "outsider" in breach of a duty owed not to a trading party, but to the source of the information. The misappropriation theory is thus designed to "protect the integrity of the securities markets against abuses by 'outsiders' to a corporation who have access to confidential information that will affect the corporation's security price when revealed, but who owe no fiduciary or other duty to that corporation's shareholders." [Brief for United States 14.]

In this case, the indictment alleged that O'Hagan, in breach of a duty of trust and confidence he owed to his law firm, Dorsey & Whitney, and to its client, Grand Met, traded on the basis of nonpublic information regarding Grand Met's planned tender offer for Pillsbury common stock. This conduct, the Government charged, constituted a fraudulent device in connection with the purchase and sale of securities.[5]

5. The Government could not have prosecuted O'Hagan under the classical theory, for O'Hagan was not an "insider" of Pillsbury, the corporation in whose stock he traded.

B

We agree with the Government that misappropriation, as just defined, satisfies § 10(b)'s requirement that chargeable conduct involve a "deceptive device or contrivance" used "in connection with" the purchase or sale of securities. We observe, first, that misappropriators, as the Government describes them, deal in deception. A fiduciary who "[pretends] loyalty to the principal while secretly converting the principal's information for personal gain," Brief for United States 17, "dupes" or defrauds the principal.

.   .   .

.   .   . Deception through nondisclosure is central to the theory of liability for which the Government seeks recognition. As counsel for the Government stated in explanation of the theory at oral argument: "To satisfy the common law rule that a trustee may not use the property that [has] been entrusted [to] him, there would have to be consent. To satisfy the requirement of the Securities Act that there be no deception, there would only have to be disclosure."[6]

The misappropriation theory advanced by the Government is consistent with Santa Fe Industries, Inc. v. Green, 430 U.S. 462 (1977), a decision underscoring that § 10(b) is not an all-purpose breach of fiduciary duty ban; rather, it trains on conduct involving manipulation or deception. .   .   . In contrast to the Government's allegations in this case, in *Santa Fe Industries*, all pertinent facts were disclosed by the persons charged with violating § 10(b) and Rule 10b–5 .   .   .; therefore, there was no deception through nondisclosure to which liability under those provisions could attach. .   .   . Similarly, full disclosure forecloses liability under the misappropriation theory: Because the deception essential to the misappropriation theory involves feigning fidelity to the source of information, if the fiduciary discloses to the source that he plans to trade on the nonpublic information, there is no "deceptive device" and thus no § 10(b) violation—although the fiduciary-turned-trader may remain liable under state law for breach of a duty of loyalty.[7]

We turn next to the § 10(b) requirement that the misappropriator's deceptive use of information be "in connection with the purchase or sale of [a] security." This element is satisfied because the fiduciary's fraud is consummated, not when the fiduciary gains the confidential information, but when, without disclosure to his principal, he uses the information to

6. Under the misappropriation theory urged in this case, the disclosure obligation runs to the source of the information, here, Dorsey & Whitney and Grand Met. Chief Justice Burger, dissenting in *Chiarella*, advanced a broader reading of § 10(b) and Rule 10b–5; the disclosure obligation, as he envisioned it, ran to those with whom the misappropriator trades. .   .   . The Government does not propose that we adopt a misappropriation theory of that breadth.

7. Where, however, a person trading on the basis of material, nonpublic information owes a duty of loyalty and confidentiality to two entities or persons—for example, a law firm and its client—but makes disclosure to only one, the trader may still be liable under the misappropriation theory.

purchase or sell securities. The securities transaction and the breach of duty thus coincide. This is so even though the person or entity defrauded is not the other party to the trade, but is, instead, the source of the nonpublic information. . . . A misappropriator who trades on the basis of material, nonpublic information, in short, gains his advantageous market position through deception; he deceives the source of the information and simultaneously harms members of the investing public. . . .

The misappropriation theory comports with § 10(b)'s language, which requires deception "in connection with the purchase or sale of any security," not deception of an identifiable purchaser or seller. The theory is also well-tuned to an animating purpose of the Exchange Act: to insure honest securities markets and thereby promote investor confidence. . . . Although informational disparity is inevitable in the securities markets, investors likely would hesitate to venture their capital in a market where trading based on misappropriated nonpublic information is unchecked by law. An investor's informational disadvantage vis-a-vis a misappropriator with material, nonpublic information stems from contrivance, not luck; it is a disadvantage that cannot be overcome with research or skill. . . .

In sum, considering the inhibiting impact on market participation of trading on misappropriated information, and the congressional purposes underlying § 10(b), it makes scant sense to hold a lawyer like O'Hagan a § 10(b) violator if he works for a law firm representing the target of a tender offer, but not if he works for a law firm representing the bidder. The text of the statute requires no such result.[9] The misappropriation at issue here was properly made the subject of a § 10(b) charge because it meets the statutory requirement that there be "deceptive" conduct "in connection with" securities transactions. . . .

III

We consider next the ground on which the Court of Appeals reversed O'Hagan's convictions for fraudulent trading in connection with a tender offer, in violation of § 14(e) of the Exchange Act and SEC Rule 14e–3(a). A sole question is before us as to these convictions: Did the Commission, as the Court of Appeals held, exceed its rulemaking authority under § 14(e) when it adopted Rule 14e–3(a) without requiring a showing that the trading at issue entailed a breach of fiduciary duty? We hold that the Commission, in this regard and to the extent relevant to this case, did not exceed its authority.

9. As noted earlier, however, the textual requirement of deception precludes § 10(b) liability when a person trading on the basis of nonpublic information has disclosed his trading plans to, or obtained authorization from, the principal—even though such conduct may affect the securities markets in the same manner as the conduct reached by the misappropriation theory. . . . [O]nce a disloyal agent discloses his imminent breach of duty, his principal may seek appropriate equitable relief under state law. Furthermore, in the context of a tender offer, the principal who authorizes an agent's trading on confidential information may, in the Commission's view, incur liability for an Exchange Act violation under Rule 14e–3(a).

The governing statutory provision, § 14(e) of the Exchange Act, reads in relevant part:

"It shall be unlawful for any person . . . to engage in any fraudulent, deceptive, or manipulative acts or practices, in connection with any tender offer. . . . The [SEC] shall, for the purposes of this subsection, by rules and regulations define, and prescribe means reasonably designed to prevent, such acts and practices as are fraudulent, deceptive, or manipulative."

. . .

Relying on § 14(e)'s rulemaking authorization, the Commission, in 1980, promulgated Rule 14e–3(a). That measure provides:

"(a) If any person has taken a substantial step or steps to commence, or has commenced, a tender offer (the 'offering person'), it shall constitute a fraudulent, deceptive or manipulative act or practice within the meaning of section 14(e) of the [Exchange] Act for any other person who is in possession of material information relating to such tender offer which information he knows or has reason to know is nonpublic and which he knows or has reason to know has been acquired directly or indirectly from:

"(1) The offering person,

"(2) The issuer of the securities sought or to be sought by such tender offer, or

"(3) Any officer, director, partner or employee or any other person acting on behalf of the offering person or such issuer,

"to purchase or sell or cause to be purchased or sold any of such securities or any securities convertible into or exchangeable for any such securities or any option or right to obtain or to dispose of any of the foregoing securities, unless within a reasonable time prior to any purchase or sale such information and its source are publicly disclosed by press release or otherwise."

. . .

In the Eighth Circuit's view, because Rule 14e–3(a) applies whether or not the trading in question breaches a fiduciary duty, the regulation exceeds the SEC's § 14(e) rulemaking authority. . . .

We need not resolve in this case whether the Commission's authority under § 14(e) to "define . . . such acts and practices as are fraudulent" is broader than the Commission's fraud-defining authority under § 10(b), [as the Government contended,] for we agree with the United States that Rule 14e–3(a), as applied to cases of this genre, qualifies under § 14(e) as a "means reasonably designed to prevent" fraudulent trading on material, nonpublic information in the tender offer context.[17] A prophylactic mea-

17. We leave for another day, when the issue requires decision, the legitimacy of Rule 14e–3(a) as applied to "warehousing," which the Government describes as "the practice by

sure, because its mission is to prevent, typically encompasses more than the core activity prohibited. . . .

Because Congress has authorized the Commission, in § 14(e), to prescribe legislative rules, we owe the Commission's judgment "more than mere deference or weight." Batterton v. Francis, 432 U.S. 416, 424–426 (1977). Therefore, in determining whether Rule 14e–3(a)'s "disclose or abstain from trading" requirement is reasonably designed to prevent fraudulent acts, we must accord the Commission's assessment "controlling weight unless [it is] arbitrary, capricious, or manifestly contrary to the statute." Chevron U.S.A. Inc. v. Natural Resources Defense Council, Inc., 467 U.S. 837, 844 (1984). In this case, we conclude, the Commission's assessment is none of these. . . .

[I]t is a fair assumption that trading on the basis of material, nonpublic information will often involve a breach of a duty of confidentiality to the bidder or target company or their representatives. The SEC, cognizant of the proof problem that could enable sophisticated traders to escape responsibility, placed in Rule 14e–3(a) a "disclose or abstain from trading" command that does not require specific proof of a breach of fiduciary duty. That prescription, we are satisfied, applied to this case, is a "means reasonably designed to prevent" fraudulent trading on material, nonpublic information in the tender offer context. . . .

NOTES AND QUESTIONS

1. The Supreme Court previously considered the misappropriation theory in Carpenter v. United States, 484 U.S. 19 (1987). R. Foster Winans wrote the widely read "Heard on the Street" column for the Wall Street Journal, which provides investing information and advice. Because that column apparently had a short-lived effect on the price of the stocks it covered, someone who knew the column's contents in advance could profit by trading in the affected stocks. Although Wall Street Journal policy stated that prior to their publication the contents of columns were the Journal's confidential property, Winans, before publication, disclosed the contents of his columns to several friends who then traded in the affected stocks. Winans and his friends were convicted of securities fraud and mail and wire fraud. The Supreme Court affirmed on all counts, but affirmed the securities fraud convictions (as opposed to the mail and wire fraud counts) only by an evenly divided Court (4–4) with respect to the misappropriation theory. By long-standing tradition, a decision by an evenly-divided court affirms the lower court result but has no precedential or stare decisis effect, leaving the validity of the misappropriation theory uncertain until *O'Hagan*. Would Winans' conviction stand under *O'Hagan*? Suppose the Wall Street Journal had a policy permitting employees to trade on the basis

which bidders leak advance information of a tender offer to allies and encourage them to purchase the target company's stock before the bid is announced." . . . .

of information about forthcoming articles. What result after *O'Hagan*? Could the Wall Street Journal itself trade on the basis of information about forthcoming articles?

2.   In United States v. Chestman, 947 F.2d 551 (2d Cir.1991), cert. denied 503 U.S. 1004 (1992), Ira Waldbaum was the president and controlling shareholder of Waldbaum, Inc., a publicly-traded supermarket chain. Ira decided to sell Waldbaum to A & P at $50 per share, a 100% premium over the prevailing market price. Ira informed his sister Shirley of the forthcoming transaction. Shirley told her daughter Susan Loeb, who in turn told her husband Keith Loeb. Each person in the chain told the next to keep the information confidential. Keith passed an edited version of the information to his stock broker, one Robert Chestman, who then bought Waldbaum stock for his own account and the accounts of other clients. Chestman was accused of violating Rule 10b–5. According to the Government's theory of the case, Keith Loeb misappropriated information from his wife Susan, which he then tipped to Chestman. The Second Circuit held that "a person violates Rule 10b–5 when he misappropriates material nonpublic information in breach of a fiduciary duty or similar relationship of trust and confidence and uses that information in a securities transaction." Id. at 566. The Court further held that in the absence of any evidence that Keith regularly participated in confidential business discussions, the familial relationship standing alone did not create a fiduciary relationship between Keith and Susan or any members of her family. Accordingly, Loeb's actions did not give rise to the requisite breach of fiduciary duty. Would *O'Hagan* change the Second Circuit's analysis in any material respect?

3.   Does a duty to disclose to the source of the information arise before trading in all fiduciary relationships? Consider ABA Model Rule of Professional Conduct 1.8(b), which states: "A lawyer shall not use information relating to representation of a client to the disadvantage of the client unless the client consents after consultation. . . ." Does a lawyer's use of confidential client information for insider trading purposes always operate to the client's disadvantage? If not, and assuming the Model Rule accurately states the lawyer's fiduciary obligation, does trading by a lawyer on the basis of confidential client information nevertheless always violate § 10(b) in the absence of disclosure by the lawyer to the client?

4.   According to the Court, liability under § 10(b) could not have been imposed if O'Hagan had disclosed "to the source of the information" that he planned to trade on the nonpublic information. Recall that O'Hagan was a partner in the Dorsey & Whitney law partnership. To whom should O'Hagan have made the requisite disclosure?

5.   Suppose O'Hagan had informed Dorsey & Whitney of his intentions to buy Pillsbury stock and the firm had approved. What result?

6.   Suppose O'Hagan had informed both Dorsey & Whitney and Grand Met of his intentions to buy Pillsbury stock for his own benefit, at least one of them had objected, but O'Hagan bought anyway. What result?

7. The Court states that "investors likely would hesitate to venture their capital in a market where trading based on misappropriated nonpublic information is unchecked." On what facts, if any, is the court's intuition premised? Do you agree with the Court?

8. Is *O'Hagan* premised mainly on an economic analysis of how capital markets function or on a moral intuition that insider trading is wrong? Is there an economic justification for prohibiting insider trading? Is there a moral justification for prohibiting insider trading? Is either economics or morality relevant to a case like *O'Hagan*, which after all purports to involve interpreting a statute?

9. Assuming arguendo that insider trading ought to be regulated, is it necessary to make a federal case out of it? As the fiduciary duty-based rationale for regulating insider trading suggests, the real concern in this area goes to the duty of loyalty rather than disclosure. It is the theft of information by an agent from his principal that is being punished here, not his failure to disclose information to those with whom he trades. Given that all other fiduciary duty issues have been left to state law, why is insider trading governed by federal law?

PROBLEMS

1. Taimie is the CEO of Target Co., whose shares are traded on the New York Stock Exchange. On April 1, Taimie receives a call from Beula, the CEO of Buyer Co., whose shares are also traded on the NYSE. Beula informs Taimie that Buyer Co. has just acquired 120,000 of the shares of Target Co., giving Buyer Co. 8 percent of the total shares outstanding, and that it is considering a tender offer for the rest of Target's shares at $9 per share. Beula also says that Buyer Co. has not yet announced its purchase, but will do so soon. Beula further says that she hopes that any acquisition can be friendly and that she is calling as a courtesy so that Taimie would not be caught by surprise by a public announcement. Target's shares are currently trading at $5 per share.

Taimie calls her personal lawyer, Larry, tells Larry about Beula's call, and asks Larry if she can buy Target shares. Larry tells her not to do so. That night, at dinner at home, Taimie tells her husband, John, about the events of the day. Their son, Sam, happens to be in the kitchen drinking a beer and overhears the part about the expected Buyer Co. tender offer. That same evening, John is chatting with one of his golfing pals, Harvey, and tells Harvey what Beula had said to Taimie. The next morning, April 2, Larry, Sam, and Harvey each buy 1,000 shares of Target stock at $5.50 per share. The following day, April 3, Target and Buyer each issue press releases describing the Buyer purchase and the prospect that Buyer will make a tender offer at $9 per share. On April 7, Larry, Sam, and Harvey each sell their 1,000 Target shares for $8.50 per share. What are the liabilities, if any, of (a) Beula, (b) Taimie, (c) Larry, (d) John, (e) Sam, and (f) Harvey, under Rule 10b–5 or the mail and wire fraud statutes?

2. Ten years ago Amy, Bob, and Carole formed the ABC Corp., which invests in local business ventures. Amy, Bob, and Carole each take part to

a modest degree in the strategic planning and supervision of ABC. Each of them is also a member of the board of directors. The general management of the firm, however, has been entrusted to Ernie, who screens all proposals. ABC shares are publicly, though thinly, traded.

One of the firms in which ABC Corp. has invested is Xanadu Corp. It has done well and its shares are now publicly traded. One day, while Amy is at the ABC Corp. offices studying some reports, Susan, the CEO of Xanadu Corp., enters the office. She starts talking to Amy, whom she knows to be a shareholder of ABC Corp., a member of its board of directors, and involved in its operation. Ernie is out of town at the time. Susan says that she came to talk to Ernie about the possibility of borrowing some money, short term. She says that Xanadu Corp. needs the money to finish work on a product that has been under development, secretly, for a couple of years. She describes the product and its state of development and Amy recognizes that it is a major breakthrough that will, if it turns out to be what Susan claims (and Amy has confidence in Susan's honesty and competence), substantially enhance Xanadu Corp.'s value.

(a) Suppose Amy tells Susan (truthfully) that ABC would not be willing to lend money in this situation except with the possibility of converting the loan to equity. Susan says that she is not willing to give up any equity and leaves. Amy immediately calls her broker, Barry, and tells Barry to buy Xanadu Corp. stock for her, which he does. Barry, who has followed Xanadu Corp. closely and owns some of its shares, surmises that Amy must know something important and buys additional shares for himself. Amy does not tell anyone else of the conversation with Susan or of her purchase of Xanadu Corp. shares. After the news of the new Xanadu Corp. product has been publicly disclosed, Amy and Barry sell their Xanadu Corp. shares for a profit. Is Amy subject to any penalties or liabilities as a result of the transaction? How about Barry?

(b) Suppose Susan tells her broker, Bob, to buy more Xanadu stock for her. Bob surmises, correctly, that Susan must be acting on important information and buys shares for himself. Has Bob violated § 10 and Rule 10b–5?

SECTION 5. SHORT-SWING PROFITS

In addition to banning insider trading through the judicial interpretation of § 10(b) (discussed in Section 4, supra), the 1934 Securities Exchange Act contains a prophylactic rule against it in § 16(b): officers, directors, and 10 percent shareholders must pay to the corporation any profits they make, within a six-month period, from buying and selling the firm's stock. As with most prophylactic rules, the section is both over- and under-inclusive. It both penalizes insiders for trades unrelated to non-public information and misses many trades based squarely on such information. But as with other prophylactic rules, it does draw sharp distinctions. The following cases, *Reliance Electric, Foremost–McKesson,* and *Kern County*, and the accompanying notes, trace the more prominent of those distinctions; the problems at the end of this section illustrate how they apply.

Reliance Electric Co. v. Emerson Electric Co.

404 U.S. 418, 92 S.Ct. 596, 30 L.Ed.2d 575, rehearing denied, 405 U.S. 969 (1972).

Section 16(b) of the Securities Exchange Act of 1934, 48 Stat. 896, 15 U.S.C. § 78p(b), provides, among other things, that a corporation may recover for itself the profits realized by an owner of more than 10% of its shares from a purchase and sale of its stock within any six-month period, provided that the owner held more than 10% "both at the time of the purchase and sale." [1] In this case, the respondent, the owner of 13.2% of a corporation's shares, disposed of its entire holdings in two sales, both of them within six months of purchase. The first sale reduced the respondent's holdings to 9.96%, and the second disposed of the remainder. The question presented is whether the profits derived from the second sale are recoverable by the Corporation under § 16(b). We hold that they are not.

---

1. Section 16(b) provides:

"For the purpose of preventing the unfair use of information which may have been obtained by such beneficial owner, director, or officer by reason of his relationship to the issuer, any profit realized by him from any purchase and sale, or any sale and purchase, of any equity security of such issuer (other than an exempted security) within any period of less than six months . . . shall inure to and be recoverable by the issuer, irrespective of any intention on the part of such beneficial owner, director, or officer in entering into such transaction of holding the security purchased or of not repurchasing the security sold for a period exceeding six months.

. . . This subsection shall not be construed to cover any transaction where such beneficial owner was not such both at the time of the purchase and sale, or the sale and purchase, of the security involved, or any transaction or transactions which the Commission by rules and regulations may exempt as not comprehended within the purpose of this subsection." 15 U.S.C. § 78p(b).

The term "such beneficial owner" refers to one who owns "more than 10 per centum of any class of any equity security (other than an exempted security) which is registered pursuant to section 12 of this title." Securities Exchange Act of 1934, § 16(a), 15 U.S.C. § 78p(a).

491

I

On June 16, 1967, the respondent, Emerson Electric Co., acquired 13.2% of the outstanding common stock of Dodge Manufacturing Co., pursuant to a tender offer made in an unsuccessful attempt to take over Dodge. The purchase price for this stock was $63 per share. Shortly thereafter, the shareholders of Dodge approved a merger with the petitioner, Reliance Electric Co. Faced with the certain failure of any further attempt to take over Dodge, and with the prospect of being forced to exchange its Dodge shares for stock in the merged corporation in the near future, Emerson, following a plan outlined by its general counsel, decided to dispose of enough shares to bring its holdings below 10%, in order to immunize the disposal of the remainder of its shares from liability under § 16(b). Pursuant to counsel's recommendation, Emerson on August 28 sold 37,000 shares of Dodge common stock to a brokerage house at $68 per share. This sale reduced Emerson's holdings in Dodge to 9.96% of the outstanding common stock. The remaining shares were then sold to Dodge at $69 per share on September 11.

After a demand on it by Reliance for the profits realized on both sales, Emerson filed this action seeking a declaratory judgment as to its liability under § 16(b). Emerson first claimed that it was not liable at all, because it was not a 10% owner at the time of the *purchase* of the Dodge shares. The District Court disagreed, holding that a purchase of stock falls within § 16(b) where the purchaser becomes a 10% owner by virtue of the purchase. The Court of Appeals affirmed this holding, and Emerson did not cross-petition for certiorari. Thus that question is not before us.

Emerson alternatively argued to the District Court that, assuming it was a 10% stockholder at the time of the purchase, it was liable only for the profits on the August 28 sale of 37,000 shares, because after that time it was no longer a 10% owner within the meaning of § 16(b). After trial on the issue of liability alone, the District Court held Emerson liable for the entire amount of its profits. The court found that Emerson's sales of Dodge stock were "effected pursuant to a single predetermined plan of disposition with the overall intent and purpose of avoiding Section 16(b) liability," and construed the term "time of . . . sale" to include "the entire period during which a series of related transactions take place pursuant to a plan by which a 10% beneficial owner disposes of his stock holdings" 306 F.Supp. 588, 592.

On an interlocutory appeal under 28 U.S.C. § 1292(b), the Court of Appeals upheld the finding that Emerson "split" its sale of Dodge stock simply in order to avoid most of its potential liability under § 16(b), but it held this fact irrelevant under the statute so long as the two sales are "not legally tied to each other and [are] made at different times to different buyers. . . ." 434 F.2d 918, 926. Accordingly, the Court of Appeals reversed the District Court's judgment as to Emerson's liability for its profits on the September 11 sale, and remanded for a determination of the amount of Emerson's liability on the August 28 sale. Reliance filed a petition for certiorari, which we granted in order to consider an unresolved question under an important federal statute. 401 U.S. 1008.

II

The history and purpose of § 16(b) have been exhaustively reviewed by federal courts on several occasions since its enactment in 1934. . . .

Those courts have recognized that the only method Congress deemed effective to curb the evils of insider trading was a flat rule taking the profits out of a class of transactions in which the possibility of abuse was believed to be intolerably great. As one court observed:

> "In order to achieve its goals, Congress chose a relatively arbitrary rule capable of easy administration. The objective standard of Section 16(b) imposes strict liability upon substantially all transactions occurring within the statutory time period, regardless of the intent of the insider or the existence of actual speculation. This approach maximized the ability of the rule to eradicate speculative abuses by reducing difficulties in proof. Such arbitrary and sweeping coverage was deemed necessary to insure the optimum prophylactic effect." Bershad v. McDonough, 428 F.2d 693, 696.

Thus Congress did not reach every transaction in which an investor actually relies on inside information. A person avoids liability if he does not meet the statutory definition of an "insider," or if he sells more than six months after purchase. . . .

Among the "objective standards" contained in § 16(b) is the requirement that a 10% owner be such "both at the time of the purchase and sale . . . of the security involved." Read literally, this language clearly contemplates that a statutory insider might sell enough shares to bring his holdings below 10%, and later—but still within six months—sell additional shares free from liability under the statute. Indeed, commentators on the securities laws have recommended this exact procedure for a 10% owner who, like Emerson, wishes to dispose of his holdings within six months of their purchase.

Under the approach urged by Reliance, and adopted by the District Court, the apparent immunity of profits derived from Emerson's second sale is lost where the two sales, though independent in every other respect, are "interrelated parts of a single plan." 306 F.Supp., at 592. But a "plan" to sell that is conceived within six months of purchase clearly would not fall within § 16(b) if the sale were made after the six months had expired, and we see no basis in the statute for a different result where the 10% requirement is involved rather than the six-month limitation. . . .

The judgment is

Affirmed.

Foremost–McKesson, Inc. v. Provident Securities Company

423 U.S. 232, 96 S.Ct. 508, 46 L.Ed.2d 464 (1976).

This case presents an unresolved issue under § 16(b) of the Securities Exchange Act of 1934 (Act). That section of the Act was designed to prevent a corporate director or officer or "the beneficial owner of more than 10 per centum" of a corporation from profiteering through short-swing securities transactions on the basis of inside information. It provides that a corporation may capture for itself the profits realized on a purchase and sale, or sale and purchase, of its securities within six months by a director, officer, or beneficial owner. Section 16(b)'s last sentence, however, provides that it "shall not be construed to cover any transaction where such beneficial owner was not such both at the time of the purchase and sale, or the sale and purchase, of the security involved. . . ." The question presented here is whether a person purchasing securities that put his holdings above the 10% Level is a beneficial owner "at the time of the purchase" so that he must account for profits realized on a sale of those securities within six months. The United States Court of Appeals for the Ninth Circuit answered this question in the negative. 506 F.2d 601 (1974). We affirm. . . . Respondent, Provident Securities Co., was a personal holding company.* In 1968 Provident decided tentatively to liquidate and dissolve, and it engaged an agent to find a purchaser for its assets. Petitioner, Foremost–McKesson, Inc., emerged as a potential purchaser, but extensive negotiations were required to resolve a disagreement over the nature of the consideration Foremost would pay. Provident wanted cash in order to facilitate its dissolution, while Foremost wanted to pay with its own securities.

Eventually a compromise was reached, and Provident and Foremost executed a purchase agreement embodying their deal on September 25, 1969. The agreement provided that Foremost would buy two-thirds of Provident's assets for $4.25 million in cash and $49.75 million in Foremost convertible subordinated debentures. The agreement further provided that Foremost would register under the Securities Act of 1933 $25 million in principal amount of the debentures and would participate in an underwriting agreement by which those debentures would be sold to the public. At the closing on October 15, 1969, Foremost delivered to Provident the cash and a $40 million debenture which was subsequently exchanged for two debentures in the principal amounts of $25 million and $15 million. Foremost also delivered a $2.5 million debenture to an escrow agent on the closing date. On October 20 Foremost delivered to Provident a $7.25 million debenture representing the balance of the purchase price. These debentures were immediately convertible into more than 10% of Foremost's outstanding common stock.

On October 21 Provident, Foremost, and a group of underwriters executed an underwriting agreement to be closed on October 28. The agreement provided for sale to the underwriters of the $25 million debenture. On October 24 Provident distributed the $15 million and $7.25 million debentures to its stockholders, reducing the amount of Foremost common into which the company's holdings were convertible to less than

* [Eds.—This is an investment vehicle largely earning passive income, such as interest, dividends, royalties, or rents.]

10%. On October 28 the closing under the underwriting agreement was accomplished. Provident thereafter distributed the cash proceeds of the debenture sale to its stockholders and dissolved.

Provident's holdings in Foremost debentures as of October 20 were large enough to make it a beneficial owner of Foremost within the meaning of § 16. Having acquired and disposed of these securities within six months, Provident faced the prospect of a suit by Foremost to recover any profits realized on the sale of the debenture to the underwriters. Provident therefore sued for a declaration that it was not liable to Foremost under s 16(b). The District Court granted summary judgment for Provident, and the Court of Appeals affirmed.

. . .

The meaning of the exemptive provision has been disputed since § 16(b) was first enacted. The discussion has focused on the application of the provision to a purchase-sale sequence, the principal disagreement being whether "at the time of the purchase" means "before the purchase" or "immediately after the purchase." The difference in construction is determinative of a beneficial owner's liability in cases such as Provident's where such owner sells within six months of purchase the securities the acquisition of which made him a beneficial owner. The commentators divided immediately over which construction Congress intended, and they remain divided. The Courts of Appeals also are in disagreement over the issue. . . .

The exemptive provision, which applies only to beneficial owners and not to other statutory insiders, must have been included in § 16(b) for a purpose. Although the extensive legislative history of the Act is bereft of any explicit explanation of Congress' intent, the evolution of § 16(b) from its initial proposal through passage does shed significant light on the purpose of the exemptive provision. . . .

The legislative record . . . reveals that the drafters focused directly on the fact that [the original draft of the bill that became § 16(b)] covered a short-term purchase-sale sequence by a beneficial owner only if his status existed before the purchase, and no concern was expressed about the wisdom of this requirement. But the explicit requirement was omitted from the operative language of the section when it was restructured to cover sale-repurchase sequences. In the same draft, however, the exemptive provision was added to the section. On this record we are persuaded that the exemptive provision was intended to preserve the requirement of beneficial ownership before the purchase. . . . We hold that, in a purchase-sale sequence, a beneficial owner must account for profits only if he was a beneficial owner "before the purchase." . . .

Our construction of § 16(b) also is supported by the distinction Congress recognized between short-term trading by mere stockholders and such trading by directors and officers. The legislative discourse revealed that Congress thought that all short-swing trading by directors and officers was vulnerable to abuse because of their intimate involvement in corporate affairs. But trading by mere stockholders was viewed as being subject to abuse only when the size of their holdings afforded the potential for access to corporate information. These different perceptions simply reflect the realities of corporate life.

It would not be consistent with this perceived distinction to impose liability on the basis of a purchase made when the percentage of stock ownership requisite to insider status had not been acquired. . . . While this reasoning might not compel our construction of the exemptive provision, it explains why Congress may have seen fit to draw the line it did.

Kern County Land Co. v. Occidental Petroleum Corp.

411 U.S. 582, 93 S.Ct. 1736, 36 L.Ed.2d 503 (1973).

Section 16(b) of the Securities Exchange Act of 1934 . . . provides that officers, directors, and holders of more than 10% of the listed stock of any company shall be liable to the company for any profits realized from any purchase and sale or sale and purchase of such stock occurring within a period of six months. Unquestionably, one or more statutory purchases occur when one company, seeking to gain control of another, acquires more than 10% of the stock of the latter through a tender offer made to its shareholders. But is it a § 16(b) "sale" when the target of the tender offer defends itself by merging into a third company and the tender offeror then exchanges his stock for the stock of the surviving company and also grants an option to purchase the latter stock that is not exercisable within the statutory six-month period? This is the question before us in this case.

I

On May 8, 1967, after unsuccessfully seeking to merge with Kern County Land Co. (Old Kern), Occidental Petroleum Corp. (Occidental) announced an offer, to expire on June 8, 1967, to purchase on a first-come, first-served basis 500,000 shares of Old Kern common stock at a price of $83.50 per share plus a brokerage commission of $1.50 per share. By May 10, 1967, 500,000 shares, more than 10% of the outstanding shares of Old Kern, had been tendered. On May 11, Occidental extended its offer to encompass an additional 500,000 shares. At the close of the tender offer, on June 8, 1967, Occidental owned 887,549 shares of Old Kern.

Immediately upon the announcement of Occidental's tender offer, the Old Kern management undertook to frustrate Occidental's takeover attempt. A management letter to all stockholders cautioned against tender and indicated that Occidental's offer might not be the best available, since the management was engaged in merger discussions with several companies. When Occidental extended its tender offer, the president of Old Kern sent a telegram to all stockholders again advising against tender. In addition, Old Kern undertook merger discussions with Tenneco, Inc. (Tenneco), and, on May 19, 1967, the Board of Directors of Old Kern announced that it had approved a merger proposal advanced by Tenneco.[9]   Under the terms of the merger, Tenneco would acquire the assets, property, and goodwill of Old Kern, subject to its liabilities, through "Kern County Land Co." (New Kern), a new corporation to be formed by Tenneco to receive the assets and carry on the business of Old Kern.   The shareholders of Old Kern would receive a share of Tenneco cumulative convertible preference stock in exchange for each share of Old Kern common stock which they owned.   On the same day, May 19, Occidental, in a quarterly report to stockholders, appraised the value of the new Tenneco stock at $105 per share.

Occidental, seeing its tender offer and takeover attempt being blocked by the Old Kern–Tenneco "defensive" merger, countered on May 25 and 31 with two mandamus actions in the California courts seeking to obtain extensive inspection of Old Kern books and records.   Realizing that, if the Old Kern–Tenneco merger were approved and successfully closed, Occidental would have to exchange its Old Kern shares for Tenneco stock and would be locked into a minority position in Tenneco, Occidental took other steps to protect itself.   Between May 30 and June 2, it negotiated an arrangement with Tenneco whereby Occidental granted Tenneco Corp., a subsidiary of Tenneco, an option to purchase at $105 per share all of the Tenneco preference stock to which Occidental would be entitled in exchange for its Old Kern stock when and if the Old Kern–Tenneco merger was closed.[13]   The premium to secure the option, at $10 per share, totaled $8,866,230 and was to be paid immediately upon the signing of the option agreement.   If the option were exercised, the premium was to be applied to the purchase price.   By the terms of the option agreement, the option could not be exercised prior to December 9, 1967, a date six months and one day after expiration of Occidental's tender offer.   On June 2, 1967, within six months of the acquisition by Occidental of more than 10% ownership of Old Kern, Occidental and Tenneco Corp. executed the option.   Soon thereafter, Occidental announced that it would not oppose the Old Kern–Tenneco merger and dismissed its state court suits against Old Kern.

The Old Kern–Tenneco merger plan was presented to and approved by Old Kern shareholders at their meeting on July 17, 1967.   Occidental refrained from voting its Old Kern shares, but in a letter read at the meeting Occidental stated that it had determined prior to June 2 not to oppose the merger and that it did not consider the plan unfair or inequitable.   Indeed, Occidental indicated that, had it been voting, it would have voted in favor of the merger.

.   .   .

9. Although technically a sale of assets, the corporate combination has been consistently referred to by the parties as a "merger" and will be similarly denominated in this opinion.   .   .   .

13. The agreement covered 886,623 shares.   This figure is 926 shares less than the number of Old Kern shares ultimately owned by Occidental.   This discrepancy apparently results from uncertainty as to the number of shares tendered.

The Old Kern–Tenneco merger transaction was closed on August 30. Old Kern shareholders thereupon became irrevocably entitled to receive Tenneco preference stock, share for share in exchange for their Old Kern stock. Old Kern was dissolved and all of its assets, including "all claims, demands, rights and choses in action accrued or to accrue under and by virtue of the Securities Exchange Act of 1934 . . .," were transferred to New Kern.

The option granted by Occidental on June 2, 1967, was exercised on December 11, 1967. Occidental, not having previously availed itself of its right, exchanged certificates representing 887,549 shares of Old Kern stock for a certificate representing a like number of shares of Tenneco preference stock. The certificate was then endorsed over to the optionee-purchaser, and in return $84,229,185 was credited to Occidental's accounts at various banks. Adding to this amount the $8,886,230 premium paid in June, Occidental received $93,905,415 for its Old Kern stock (including the 1,900 shares acquired prior to issuance of its tender offer). In addition, Occidental received dividends totaling $1,793,439.22. Occidental's total profit was $19,506,419.22 on the shares obtained through its tender offer.

On October 17, 1967, New Kern instituted a suit under § 16(b) against Occidental to recover the profits which Occidental had realized as a result of its dealings in Old Kern stock. The complaint alleged that the execution of the Occidental–Tenneco option on June 2, 1967, and the exchange of Old Kern shares for shares of Tenneco to which Occidental became entitled pursuant to the merger closed on August 30, 1967, were both "sales" within the coverage of § 16(b). Since both acts took place within six months of the date on which Occidental became the owner of more than 10% of the stock of Old Kern, New Kern asserted that § 16(b) required surrender of the profits realized by Occidental. New Kern eventually moved for summary judgment, and, on December 27, 1970, the District Court granted summary judgment in favor of New Kern. . . .

On appeal, the Court of Appeals reversed and ordered summary judgment entered in favor of Occidental. . . . The Court held that neither the option nor the exchange constituted a "sale" within the purview of § 16(b). We granted certiorari. . . . We affirm.

II

Section 16(b) provides, *inter alia,* that a statutory insider must surrender to the issuing corporation "any profit realized by him from any purchase and sale, or any sale and purchase, of any equity security of such issuer . . . within any period of less than six months." As specified in its introductory clause, § 16(b) was enacted "[f]or the purpose of preventing the unfair use of information which may have been obtained by [a statutory insider] . . . by reason of his relationship to the issuer." Congress recognized that short-swing speculation by stockholders with advance, inside information would threaten the goal of the Securities Exchange Act to "insure the maintenance of fair and honest markets." 15 U.S.C. § 78b. Insiders could exploit information not generally available to others to secure quick profits. As we have noted, "the only method Congress deemed effective to curb the evils of insider trading was a flat rule taking the profits out of a class of transactions in which the possibility of abuse was believed to be intolerably great." Reliance Electric Co. v. Emerson Electric Co., 404 U.S. 418, 422 (1972). As stated in the report of the Senate Committee, the bill aimed at protecting the public "by preventing directors, officers, and principal stockholders of a corporation . . . from speculating in the stock on the basis of information not available to others." S.Rep. No. 792, 73d Cong., 2d Sess., 9 (1934).

Although traditional cash-for-stock transactions that result in a purchase and sale or a sale and purchase within the six-month, statutory period are clearly within the purview of § 16(b), the courts have wrestled with the question of inclusion or exclusion of certain "unorthodox" transactions. The statutory definitions of "purchase" and "sale" are broad and, at least arguably, reach many transactions not ordinarily deemed a sale or purchase. In deciding whether borderline transactions are within the reach of the statute, the courts have come to inquire whether the transaction may serve as a vehicle for the evil which Congress sought to prevent—the realization of short-swing profits based upon access to inside information—thereby endeavoring to implement congressional objectives without extending the reach of the statute beyond its intended limits. The statute requires the inside, short-swing trader to disgorge all profits realized on all "purchases" and "sales" within the specified time period, without proof of actual abuse of insider information, and without proof of intent to profit on the basis of such information. Under these strict terms, the prevailing view is to apply the statute only when its application would serve its goals. . . . Thus, "[i]n interpreting the terms 'purchase' and 'sale,' courts have properly asked whether the particular type of transaction involved is one that gives rise to speculative abuse." Reliance Electric Co. v. Emerson Electric Co., supra, at 424 n. 4.

In the present case, it is undisputed that Occidental became a "beneficial owner" within the terms of § 16(b) when, pursuant to its tender offer, it "purchased" more than 10% of the outstanding shares of Old Kern. We must decide, however, whether a "sale" within the ambit of the statute took place either when Occidental became irrevocably bound to exchange its shares of Old Kern for shares of Tenneco pursuant to the terms of the merger agreement between Old Kern and Tenneco or when Occidental gave an option to Tenneco to purchase from Occidental the Tenneco shares so acquired.

III

On August 30, 1967, the Old Kern–Tenneco merger agreement was signed, and Occidental became irrevocably entitled to exchange its shares of Old Kern stock for shares of Tenneco preference stock. Concededly, the transaction must be viewed as though Occidental had made the exchange on that day. But, even so, did the exchange involve a "sale" of Old Kern shares within the meaning of § 16(b)? We agree with the Court of Appeals that it did not, for we think it totally unrealistic to assume or infer from the facts before us that Occidental either had or was likely to have access to inside information, by reason of its ownership of more than 10% of the outstanding shares of Old Kern, so as to afford it an opportunity to reap speculative, short-swing profits from its disposition within six months of its tender-offer purchases.

It cannot be contended that Occidental was an insider when, on May 8, 1967, it made an irrevocable offer to purchase 500,000 shares of Old Kern stock at a price substantially above market. At that time, it owned only 1,900 shares of Old Kern stock, far fewer than the 432,000 shares needed to constitute the 10% ownership required by the statute. There is no basis for finding that, at the time the tender offer was commenced, Occidental enjoyed an insider's opportunity to acquire information about Old Kern's affairs. . . .

By May 10, 1967, Occidental had acquired more than 10% of the outstanding shares of Old Kern. It was thus a statutory insider when, on May 11, it extended its tender offer to include another 500,000 shares. We are quite unconvinced, however, that the situation had changed materially with respect to the possibilities of speculative abuse of inside information by Occidental. Perhaps Occidental anticipated that extending its offer would increase the likelihood of the ultimate success of its takeover attempt or the occurrence of a defensive merger. But, again, the expectation of such benefits was unrelated to the use of information unavailable to other stockholders or members of the public with sufficient funds and the intention to make the purchases Occidental had offered to make before June 8, 1967.

The possibility that Occidental had, or had the opportunity to have, any confidential information about Old Kern before or after May 11, 1967, seems extremely remote. Occidental was, after all, a tender offeror, threatening to seize control of Old Kern, displace its management, and use the company for its own ends. The Old Kern management vigorously and immediately opposed Occidental's efforts. Twice it communicated with its stockholders, advising against acceptance of Occidental's offer and indicating prior to May 11 and prior to Occidental's extension of its offer, that there was a possibility of an imminent merger and a more profitable exchange. Old Kern's management refused to discuss with Occidental officials the subject of an Old Kern–Occidental merger. Instead, it undertook negotiations with Tenneco and forthwith concluded an agreement, announcing the merger terms on May 19. Requests by Occidental for inspection of Old Kern records were sufficiently frustrated by Old Kern's management to force Occidental to litigate to secure the information it desired.

There is, therefore, nothing in connection with Occidental's acquisition of Old Kern stock pursuant to its tender offer to indicate either the possibility of inside information being available to Occidental by virtue of its stock ownership or the potential for speculative abuse of such inside information by Occidental. Much the same can be said of the events leading to the exchange of Occidental's Old Kern stock for Tenneco preferred, which is one of the transactions that is sought to be classified a "sale" under § 16(b). The critical fact is that the exchange took place and was required pursuant to a merger between Old Kern and Tenneco. That merger was not engineered by Occidental but was sought by Old Kern to frustrate the attempts of Occidental to gain control of Old Kern. Occidental obviously did not participate in or control the negotiations or the agreement between Old Kern and Tenneco. . . .

We do not suggest that an exchange of stock pursuant to a merger may never result in § 16(b) liability. But the involuntary nature of Occidental's exchange, when coupled with the absence of the possibility of speculative abuse of inside information, convinces us that § 16(b) should not apply to transactions such as this one.

IV

Petitioner also claims that the Occidental–Tenneco option agreement should itself be considered a sale, either because it was the kind of transaction the statute was designed to prevent or because the agreement was an option in form but a sale in fact. But the mere execution of an option to sell is not generally regarded as a "sale." . . . And we do not find in the execution of the Occidental–Tenneco option agreement a sufficient possibility for the speculative abuse of inside information with respect to Old Kern's affairs to warrant holding that the option agreement was itself a "sale" within the meaning of § 16(b). The mutual advantages of the arrangement appear quite clear. As the District Court found, Occidental wanted to avoid the position of a minority stockholder with a huge investment in a company over which it had no control and in which it had not chosen to invest. On the other hand, Tenneco did not want a potentially troublesome minority stockholder that had just been vanquished in a fight for the control of Old Kern. Motivations like these do not smack of insider trading; and it is not clear to us, as it was not to the Court of Appeals, how the negotiation and execution of the option agreement gave Occidental any possible opportunity to trade on inside information it might have obtained from its position as a major stockholder of Old Kern. . . .

Nor can we agree that we must reverse the Court of Appeals on the ground that the option agreement was in fact a sale because the premium paid was so large as to make the exercise of the option almost inevitable, particularly when coupled with Tenneco's desire to rid itself of a potentially troublesome stockholder. The argument has force, but resolution of the question is very much a matter of judgment, economic and otherwise, and the Court of Appeals rejected the argument. That court emphasized that the premium paid was what experts had said the option was worth, the possibility that the market might drop sufficiently in the six months following execution of the option to make exercise unlikely, and the fact that here, unlike the situation in Bershad v. McDonough, 428 F.2d 693 (C.A.7 1970), the optionor did not surrender practically all emoluments of ownership by executing the option. Nor did any other special circumstances indicate that the parties understood and intended that the option was in fact a sale. We see no satisfactory basis or reason for disagreeing with the judgment of the Court of Appeals in this respect.

NOTES ON § 16(b)

1. *Issuers:* Section 16(b) applies only to companies that register their stock under the 1934 Act. These include companies with stock traded on a national exchange, and companies with assets of at least $5 million and 500 or more shareholders. See Securities Exchange Act § 12(g); Rule 12g–1.

2. *Officers:* In addition to trades by 10 percent owners, § 16(b) applies to trades by directors and officers. Rule 16a–1(f) provides, "The term 'officer' shall mean an issuer's president, principal financial officer, principal accounting officer (or, if there is no such accounting officer, the controller), any vice-president of the issuer in charge of a principal business unit, division or function (such as sales, administration or finance), and other officer who performs a policy-making function, or any other person who performs similar policy-making functions for the issuer." Officers and directors are subject to § 16(b) if they occupy that position *either* at the time of purchase *or* at the time of sale.[7]

3. *Deputization:* If a firm's employee serves as a director of another firm, § 16(b) may apply to the first firm's trades in the stock of the second. Suppose X Corp. asks one of its officers to serve on the board of directors of Y Corp. If X profits on Y stock within a six-month period, X may be liable under § 16(b) on the theory that it "deputized" the officer.[8]

4. *Stock classes and convertible debentures:* To determine stock percentages under § 16(b), courts consider classes of stock separately. Thus, a shareholder who owns 10 percent of one class of stock is subject to § 16(b), even if he or she does not own 10 percent of another class, or 10 percent of the company's total stock. That shareholder will be liable for the short-swing profits that he or she makes on *any* class of stock.

Section 16(b) applies only to "equity securities." The term covers convertible debt, but not other bonds or debentures. Suppose Alice holds a convertible bond. To decide what percentage of the equity security she holds, courts calculate the percentage of stock that she would own if she converted the bond into stock.[9]

5. *The politics of § 16(b):* Although recovery under § 16(b) accrues to the corporation, shareholders may enforce it derivatively. As a result, the American bar includes a cadre of lawyers who make their living finding

7. See Arrow Distributing Corp. v. Baumgartner, 783 F.2d 1274, 1279 (5th Cir. 1986); Feder v. Martin Marietta Corp., 406 F.2d 260, 266 (2d Cir.1969), cert. denied, 396 U.S. 1036 (1970); Adler v. Klawans, 267 F.2d 840, 843–44 (2d Cir.1959).

8. See Blau v. Lehman, 368 U.S. 403, 408–10, 82 S.Ct. 451, 454–55, 7 L.Ed.2d 403 (1962); Feder v. Martin Marietta Corp., supra note 7, 406 F.2d at 263.

9. See Chemical Fund, Inc. v. Xerox Corp., 377 F.2d 107 (2d Cir.1967).

§ 16(b) claims, filing derivative suits, and then claiming attorneys' fees.[10] They generally obtain the information about the inside trades by scrutinizing the stock transaction reports that the insiders must file with the SEC. In most cases, they settle the suits out of court.

6. *Matching stock:* To calculate a company's recovery under § 16(b), a court must match a defendant's purchases with her or his sales. Because shareholders may buy and sell a company's stock at a wide variety of prices within any given six-month period, this is no easy task. The solution that the courts have adopted, however, is for many observers the harshest principle of all in § 16(b) jurisprudence. Simply put, the courts match stock sales and purchases in whatever way (within the confines of the rules above) maximizes the amount the company can recover. They do not use any of the standard accounting tools (e.g., FIFO: first-in, first-out). Much less do they let shareholders identify specific shares of stock (e.g., "In November I sold the share I bought in January, not the share I bought in October.") Instead, they match the lowest priced purchases and the highest priced sales. (See Smolowe v. Delendo Corp., 136 F.2d 231 (2d Cir.), cert. denied, 320 U.S. 751 (1943).)

Consider an example. Brown is president of Techniflex, Inc., a successful software company. On January 1, he bought 800 shares of Techniflex at $30 per share. In February, during a temporary slowdown in production, he bought 200 shares at $10. In March, he sold 300 shares for $50. Brown owes Techniflex $10,000. Whichever shares Brown actually sold in March, he is treated as though he sold the 200 shares he bought at the lower price ($10), plus another 100 shares he bought at the higher price ($30). Thus, he owes (200)($50–$10) + (100)($50–$30) = $10,000. He owes this amount even if he sold the remaining shares in June for $1 per share, and thus generated a net loss on all transactions over the six-month period.

PROBLEMS

1. Bill is chief executive officer of SCLaw, Inc. (SCLI), a chain of proprietary law schools in southern California. SCLI stock is registered under the 1934 Act, and 1,000,000 shares are outstanding. On January 1, Bill purchased 200,000 shares of SCLI common stock for $10 per share. Determine his liability, if any, under § 16(b):

(a) If he sells all 200,000 shares on May 1 for $50 per share.

(b) If he sells 110,000 shares on May 1 for $50 per share, and the remainder on May 2 at the same price.

(c) If he sells 110,000 shares on May 1 for $50 per share, resigns from SCLI, and sells the remainder on May 2 at the same price.

---

10. See Gilson v. Chock Full O'Nuts Corp., 326 F.2d 246 (2d Cir.1964); Smolowe v. Delendo Corp., 136 F.2d 231, 241 (2d Cir. 1943), cert. denied, 320 U.S. 751 (1943).

2.   Renée is a shrewd investor with 200,000 shares of SCLI stock that she has held for several years. She is not an officer or director of the company. Determine her liability, if any, under § 16(b):

(a) If she sells her entire holding of SCLI shares (200,000 shares) on January 1 at $50 per share, buys 50,000 shares on May 1 for $10 per share, and buys 110,000 more shares on May 2 at the same price.

(b) If she sells her entire portfolio of SCLI shares (200,000 shares) on January 1 at $50 per share, buys 110,000 shares on May 1 for $10 per share, and 50,000 more shares on May 2 at the same price.

(c) If she sells 110,000 shares on January 1 at $50 per share, sells the remainder of her shares (90,000 shares) on January 2 at the same price, and buys 300,000 shares on May 1 for $10 per share.

3.   Bill, still the SCLI CEO, buys 100,000 shares on March 1 at $10 per share, 700,000 shares on April 1 at $90 per share, and sells all his shares on May 1 at $30 per share. Did he make any money? For what amount, if any, is he liable under § 16(b)?

4.   Suppose Renée owns none of the 1,000,000 shares of SCLI stock, but has owned, for several years, 5,000 convertible debentures, with a face amount of $1,000 each, for which she paid $1,000 each or $5,000,000 total. Each of the debentures is convertible into 100 shares of common stock. Suppose that Renée buys 100 additional debentures on March 1 at $800 each. Without converting any debentures, she then sells 100 debentures on April 1 at $900 each. Is she liable under § 16(b)? If so, for how much?

5.   Suppose there are 1,000,000 shares of class A SCLI stock, and 1,000,000 shares of class B SCLI stock. On March 1, Mary (not an officer or director) buys 110,000 shares of Class A at $10 per share. On March 2, she buys 50,000 shares of Class B at $10 per share. On April 1, she sells all her stock for $50 per share. What is the amount, if any, of her liability?

SECTION 6. INDEMNIFICATION AND INSURANCE

Most states have detailed statutory provisions covering the authority or obligation of a corporation to indemnify officers and directors for any damages they might incur in connection with their corporate activities, and for the expenses of defending themselves. In considering these statutes, several points should be kept in mind. First, there are several different situations that might give rise to liability. One situation involves claims by third persons—for example, where an officer or director is driving a company car on company business and negligently injures someone. Another situation involves injury to the corporation or its shareholders, as in the cases we have examined in this Chapter. Many of the suits in which officers and directors become defendants, along with the corporation, are brought by employees (for wrongful discharge or for violation of anti-discrimination laws), customers (for example, for harmful drugs sold by a pharmaceutical company), competitors (for violation of the anti-trust or unfair-competition laws), or government agencies. One may think of the corporation as being the principal defendant in these cases, but officers and directors cannot ignore their potential personal liability. Note that Delaware's protective provision, § 102(b)(7), applies only to "liability of a director to the corporation or its stockholders for monetary damages for breach of fiduciary duty as a director."

Second, the risk of liability may be remote, but the amount of the damages can be large in relation to the individual wealth of the officers and directors and there may be forms of relief other than money damages (for example, an injunction in the context of a takeover attempt). Even if no money damages are awarded, the expenses of defense can be substantial. Individual defendants will want to be assured not only of reimbursement of expenses, but also of advancement of expenses or assumption by the corporation of the obligation to provide a defense. (Bear in mind, it may be necessary for the corporation and the individual defendants to have separate counsel and for various individuals to have separate counsel.)

Third, corporations may be able to buy insurance to cover damages and expenses of defense (see discussion in the next note), but if they are allowed to do that, the question arises, why not allow them to become self-insurers? That is, is there any good reason for prohibiting a corporation from indemnifying an officer or director from liability when it would be permitted to provide insurance to cover that liability?

Fourth, officers and directors need to be concerned about the possibility that the corporation will be taken over by people hostile to them. That possibility affects the value of a right to reimbursement that is within the discretion of the board. Officers and directors also must be concerned in many cases about the risk that the corporation will become insolvent and that no funds will be available to reimburse them for judgments against them or (probably more important to conscientious directors) for their legal fees in defending themselves.

Statutory rules for indemnification are found in the corporate laws of the various states. The law of Delaware, reflected in the two cases in this section, is typical. You will note that it begins, in § 145(a), with a provision relating to suits by third parties, which allows indemnification in certain circumstances for "expenses . . ., judgments, fines, and amounts paid in settlement." The next paragraph, § 145(b), covers indemnification for suits "by or in the right of the corporation"—that is, derivative suits; it allows indemnification only for expenses and, if the person seeking indemnification has been found liable to the corporation, only with judicial approval. Under § 145(c) expenses must be reimbursed if the defendant was successful. Advancement of expenses, which may be of the utmost importance, is specifically addressed by § 145(e). Insurance is authorized by § 145(g).

Perhaps of most interest to officers, directors, and other employees is § 145(f), which expressly contemplates agreements that provide greater protection than does the statute by itself. The scope of this paragraph is not as clear as one might hope: Does "other rights" contemplate only those rights not of the same type as those covered by the statute? Can a corporation agree to indemnify against judgments payable to the corporation? Would such an agreement be nullified as a violation of "public policy"? These are interesting and important questions, but of greater importance for our purposes is the attention this provision draws to written indemnification agreements.

Waltuch v. Conticommodity Services, Inc.

88 F.3d 87 (2d Cir.1996).

Famed silver trader Norton Waltuch spent $2.2 million in unreimbursed legal fees to defend himself against numerous civil lawsuits and an enforcement proceeding brought by the Commodity Futures Trading Commission (CFTC). In this action under Delaware law, Waltuch seeks indemnification of his legal expenses from his former employer. The district court denied any indemnity, and Waltuch appeals.

As vice-president and chief metals trader for Conticommodity Services, Inc., Waltuch traded silver for the firm's clients, as well as for his own account. In late 1979 and early 1980, the silver price spiked upward as the then-billionaire Hunt brothers and several of Waltuch's foreign clients bought huge quantities of silver futures contracts. Just as rapidly, the price fell until (on a day remembered in trading circles as "Silver Thursday") the silver market crashed. Between 1981 and 1985, angry silver speculators filed numerous lawsuits against Waltuch and Conticommodity, alleging fraud, market manipulation, and antitrust violations. All of the suits eventually settled and were dismissed with prejudice, pursuant to settlements in which Conticommodity paid over $35 million to the various suitors. Waltuch himself was dismissed from the suits with no settlement contribution. His unreimbursed legal expenses in these actions total approximately $1.2 million. Waltuch was also the subject of an enforcement proceeding brought by the CFTC, charging him with fraud and market manipulation. The proceeding was settled, with Waltuch agreeing to a penalty that included a $100,000 fine and a six-month ban on buying or selling futures contracts from any exchange floor. Waltuch spent $1 million in unreimbursed legal fees in the CFTC proceeding.

Waltuch brought suit in the United States District Court for the Southern District of New York (Lasker, J.) against Conticommodity and its parent company, Continental Grain Co. (together "Conti"), for indemnification of his unreimbursed expenses. Only two of Waltuch's claims reach us on appeal.

Waltuch first claims that Article Ninth of Conticommodity's articles of incorporation requires Conti to indemnify him for his expenses in both the private and CFTC actions. Conti responds that this claim is barred by subsection (a) of § 145 of Delaware's General Corporation Law, which permits indemnification only if the corporate officer acted "in good faith," something that Waltuch has not established. Waltuch counters that subsection (f) of the same statute permits a corporation to grant indemnification rights outside the limits of subsection (a), and that Conticommodity did so with Article Ninth (which has no stated good-faith limitation). The district court held that, notwithstanding § 145(f), Waltuch could recover under Article Ninth only if Waltuch met the "good faith" requirement of § 145(a). On the factual issue of whether Waltuch had acted "in good faith," the court denied Conti's summary judgment motion and cleared the way for trial. The parties then stipulated that they would forgo trial on the issue of Waltuch's "good faith," agree to an entry of final judgment against Waltuch on his claim under Article Ninth and § 145(f), and allow Waltuch to take an immediate appeal of the judgment to this Court. Thus, as to Waltuch's first claim, the only question left is how to interpret §§ 145(a) and 145(f), assuming Waltuch acted with less than "good faith." As we explain in part I below, we affirm the district court's judgment as to this claim and hold that § 145(f) does not permit a corporation to bypass the "good faith" requirement of § 145(a).

Waltuch's second claim is that subsection (c) of § 145 requires Conti to indemnify him because he was "successful on the merits or otherwise" in the private lawsuits. The district court ruled for Conti on this claim as well. The court explained that, even though all the suits against Waltuch were dismissed without his making any payment, he was not "successful on the merits or otherwise," because Conti's settlement payments to the plaintiffs were partially on Waltuch's behalf. For the reasons stated in part II below, we reverse this portion of the district court's ruling, and hold that Conti must indemnify Waltuch under § 145(c) for the $1.2 million in unreimbursed legal fees he spent in defending the private lawsuits.

I

Article Ninth, on which Waltuch bases his first claim, is categorical and contains no requirement of "good faith":

> The Corporation shall indemnify and hold harmless each of its incumbent or former directors, officers, employees and agents . . . against expenses actually and necessarily incurred by him in connection with the defense of any action, suit or proceeding threatened, pending or completed, in which he is made a party, by reason of his serving in or having held such position or capacity, except in relation to matters as to which he shall be adjudged in such action, suit or proceeding to be liable for negligence or misconduct in the performance of duty.

Conti argues that § 145(a) of Delaware's General Corporation Law, which does contain a "good faith" requirement, fixes the outer limits of a corporation's power to indemnify; Article Ninth is thus invalid under Delaware law, says Conti, to the extent that it requires indemnification of officers who have acted in bad faith. The affirmative grant of power in § 145(a) is as follows:

> *A corporation shall have power to indemnify* any person who was or is a party . . . to any threatened, pending or completed action . . ., whether civil, criminal, administrative or investigative (other than an action by or in the right of the corporation) by reason of the fact that he is or was a director, officer, employee or agent of the corporation, . . . against expenses (including attorneys' fees), judgments, fines and amounts paid in settlement actually and reasonably incurred by him in connection with such action, . . . *if he acted in good faith and in a manner he reasonably believed to be in or not opposed to the best interests of the corporation,* and, with respect to any criminal action or proceeding, had no reasonable cause to believe his conduct was unlawful.

(Emphasis added.)

In order to escape the "good faith" clause of § 145(a), Waltuch argues that § 145(a) is not an exclusive grant of indemnification power, because § 145(f) expressly allows corporations to indemnify officers in a manner broader than that set out in § 145(a). The "nonexclusivity" language of § 145(f) provides:

> The indemnification and advancement of expenses provided by, or granted pursuant to, the other subsections of this section *shall not be deemed exclusive of any other rights* to which those seeking indemnification or advancement of expenses may be entitled under any bylaw, agreement, vote of stockholders or disinterested directors or otherwise, both as to action in his official capacity and as to action in another capacity while holding such office.

(Emphasis added.)

Waltuch contends that the "nonexclusivity" language in § 145(f) is a separate grant of indemnification power, not limited by the good faith clause that governs the power granted in § 145(a). Conti on the other hand contends that § 145(f) must be limited by "public policies," one of which is that a corporation may indemnify its officers only if they act in "good faith."

A. *Delaware Cases*

No Delaware court has decided the very issue presented here; but the applicable cases tend to support the proposition that a corporation's grant of indemnification rights cannot be *inconsistent* with the substantive statutory provisions of § 145, notwithstanding § 145(f). We draw this rule of "consistency" primarily from our reading of the Delaware Supreme Court's opinion in Hibbert v. Hollywood Park, Inc., 457 A.2d 339 (Del.1983). In that case, Hibbert and certain other directors sued the corporation and the remaining directors, and then demanded indemnification for their expenses and fees related to the litigation. The company refused indemnification on the ground that directors were entitled to indemnification only as defendants in legal proceedings. The court reversed the trial court and held that Hibbert was entitled to indemnification under the plain terms of a company bylaw that did not draw an express distinction between plaintiff directors and defendant directors. Id. at 343. The court then proceeded to test the bylaw for consistency with § 145(a):

> Furthermore, *indemnification here is consistent with current Delaware law*. Under 8 Del.C. § 145(a) . . ., "a corporation may indemnify any person who was or is a party or is threatened to be made a party to any threatened, pending or completed" derivative or third-party action. By this language, indemnity is *not limited* to only those who stand as a defendant in the main action. The corporation can also grant indemnification rights beyond those provided by statute.

Id. at 344 (emphasis added and citations omitted). . . . This passage contains two complementary propositions. Under § 145(f), a corporation may provide indemnification rights that go "beyond" the rights provided by § 145(a) and the other substantive subsections of § 145. At the same time, any such indemnification rights provided by a corporation must be "consistent with" the substantive provisions of § 145, including § 145(a). In *Hibbert*, the corporate bylaw was "consistent with" § 145(a), because this subsection was "not limited to" suits in which directors were defendants. *Hibbert* 's holding may support an inverse corollary that illuminates our case: if § 145(a) had been expressly limited to directors who were named as defendants, the bylaw could not have stood, regardless of § 145(f), because the bylaw would not have been "consistent with" the substantive statutory provision.

A more recent opinion of the Delaware Supreme Court, analyzing a different provision of § 145, also supports the view that the express limits in § 145's substantive provisions are not subordinated to § 145(f). In Citadel Holding Corp. v. Roven, 603 A.2d 818, 823 (Del.1992), a corporation's bylaws provided indemnification "to the full extent permitted by the General Corporation Law of Delaware." The corporation entered into an indemnification agreement with one of its directors, reciting the parties' intent to afford enhanced protection in some unspecified way. The director contended that the agreement was intended to afford mandatory advancement of expenses, and that this feature (when compared with the merely permissive advancement provision of § 145(e)) was the enhancement intended by the parties.* The corporation, seeking to avoid advancement of expenses, argued instead that the agreement enhanced the director's protection only in the sense that the pre-contract indemnification rights were subject to statute, whereas his rights under the contract could not be diminished without his consent. Id.

In rejecting that argument, the court explained that indemnification rights provided by contract could not exceed the "scope" of a corporation's indemnification powers as set out by the statute:

> If the General Assembly were to amend Delaware's director indemnification statute with the effect of curtailing the scope of indemnification a corporation may grant a director, the fact that [the director's] rights were also secured by contract would be of little use to him. Private parties may not circumvent the legislative will simply by agreeing to do so.

Id. *Citadel* thus confirms the dual propositions stated in *Hibbert*: indemnification rights may be broader than those set out in the statute, but they cannot be inconsistent with the "scope" of the corporation's power to indemnify, as delineated in the statute's substantive provisions. . . .

B. *Statutory Reading.*

The "consistency" rule suggested by these Delaware cases is reinforced by our reading of § 145 as a whole. Subsections (a) (indemnification for third-party actions) and (b) (similar indemnification for derivative suits) expressly grant a corporation the power to indemnify directors, officers, and others, if they "acted in good faith and in a manner reasonably believed to be in or not opposed to the best interest of the corporation."** These provisions thus limit the scope of the power that they confer. They are permissive in the sense that a corporation may exercise less than its full

---

* [Eds. § 145(e) provides:

(e) Expenses (including attorneys' fees) incurred by an officer or director in defending any civil, criminal, administrative or investigative action, suit or proceeding may be paid by the corporation in advance of the final disposition of such action, suit or proceeding upon receipt of an undertaking by or on behalf of such director or officer to repay such amount if it shall ultimately be determined that such person is not entitled to be indemnified by the corporation as authorized in this section. . . .]

** [Eds. Section 145(b) provides:

(b) A corporation shall have power to indemnify any person who was or is a party . . . to any threatened, pending or completed action . . . by or in the right of the corporation to procure a judgment in its favor by reason of the fact that the person is or was a director, officer, employee or agent of the corporation, . . . against expenses (including attorneys' fees) actually and reasonably incurred by the person in connection with the defense or settlement of such action or suit if the person acted in good faith and in a manner the person reasonably believed to be in or not opposed to the best interests of the corporation and except that no indemnification shall be made in respect of any claim, issue or matter as to which such person shall have been adjudged to be liable to the corporation unless and only to the extent that the Court of Chancery or the court in which such action or suit was brought shall determine upon application that, despite the adjudication of liability but in view of all the circumstances of the case, such person is fairly and reasonably entitled to indemnity for such expenses which the Court of Chancery or such other court shall deem proper.]

power to grant the indemnification rights set out in these provisions. . . . By the same token, subsection (f) permits the corporation to grant additional rights: the rights provided in the rest of § 145 "shall not be deemed exclusive of any other rights to which those seeking indemnification may be entitled." But crucially, subsection (f) merely acknowledges that one seeking indemnification may be entitled to "other rights" (of indemnification or otherwise); it does not speak in terms of corporate power, and therefore cannot be read to free a corporation from the "good faith" limit explicitly imposed in subsections (a) and (b).

. . .

When the Legislature intended a subsection of § 145 to augment the powers limited in subsection (a), it set out the additional powers expressly. Thus subsection (g) explicitly allows a corporation to circumvent the "good faith" clause of subsection (a) by purchasing a directors and officers liability insurance policy. Significantly, that subsection is framed as a grant of corporate power:

> A corporation shall have power to purchase and maintain insurance on behalf of any person who is or was a director, officer, employee or agent of the corporation . . . against any liability asserted against him and incurred by him in any such capacity, or arising out of his status as such, *whether or not the corporation would have the power to indemnify him against such liability under this section.*

(Emphasis added.) The italicized passage reflects the principle that corporations have the power under § 145 to indemnify in some situations and not in others. Since § 145(f) is neither a grant of corporate power nor a limitation on such power, subsection (g) must be referring to the limitations set out in § 145(a) and the other provisions of § 145 that describe corporate power. If § 145 (through subsection (f) or another part of the statute) gave corporations unlimited power to indemnify directors and officers, then the final clause of subsection (g) would be unnecessary: that is, its grant of "power to purchase and maintain insurance" (exercisable regardless of whether the corporation itself would have the power to indemnify the loss directly) is meaningful only because, in some insurable situations, the corporation simply lacks the power to indemnify its directors and officers directly.

. . .

[W]e hold that Conti's Article Ninth, which would require indemnification of Waltuch even if he acted in bad faith, is inconsistent with § 145(a) and thus exceeds the scope of a Delaware corporation's power to indemnify. Since Waltuch has agreed to forgo his opportunity to prove at trial that he acted in good faith, he is not entitled to indemnification under Article Ninth for the $2.2 million he spent in connection with the private lawsuits and the CFTC proceeding. We therefore affirm the district court on this issue.

II

Unlike § 145(a), which grants a discretionary indemnification power, § 145(c) affirmatively requires corporations to indemnify its officers and directors for the "successful" defense of certain claims:

> To the extent that a director, officer, employee or agent of a corporation has been successful on the merits or otherwise in defense of any action, suit or proceeding referred to in subsections (a) and (b) of this section, or in defense of any claim, issue or matter therein, he shall be indemnified against expenses (including attorneys' fees) actually and reasonably incurred by him in connection therewith.

Waltuch argues that he was "successful on the merits or otherwise" in the private lawsuits, because they were dismissed with prejudice without any payment or assumption of liability by him. Conti argues that the claims against Waltuch were dismissed only because of Conti's $35 million settlement payments, and that this payment was contributed, in part, "on behalf of Waltuch."

The district court agreed with Conti that "the successful settlements cannot be credited to Waltuch but are attributable solely to Conti's settlement payments. It was not Waltuch who was successful, but Conti who was successful for him." 833 F.Supp. at 311. The district court held that § 145(c) mandates indemnification when the director or officer "is vindicated," but that there was no vindication here:

> Vindication is also ordinarily associated with a dismissal with prejudice without any payment. However, a director or officer is not vindicated when the reason he did not have to make a settlement payment is because someone else assumed that liability. Being bailed out is not the same thing as being vindicated.

Id. We believe that this understanding and application of the "vindication" concept is overly broad and is inconsistent with a proper interpretation of § 145(c).

No Delaware court has applied § 145(c) in the context of indemnification stemming from the settlement of civil litigation. One lower court, however, has applied that subsection to an analogous case in the criminal context, and has illuminated the link between "vindication" and the statutory phrase, "successful on the merits or otherwise." In Merritt–Chapman & Scott Corp. v. Wolfson, 321 A.2d 138 (Del.Super.Ct.1974), the corporation's agents were charged with several counts of criminal conduct. A jury found them guilty on some counts, but deadlocked on the others. The agents entered into a "settlement" with the prosecutor's office by pleading nolo contendere to one of the counts in exchange for the dropping of the rest. Id. at 140. The agents claimed entitlement to mandatory indemnification under § 145(c) as to the counts that were dismissed. In opposition, the corporation raised an argument similar to the argument raised by Conti:

> [The corporation] argues that the statute and sound public policy require indemnification only where there has been vindication by a

finding or concession of innocence. *It contends that the charges against [the agents] were dropped for practical reasons*, not because of their innocence. . . .

The statute requires indemnification to the extent that the claimant "has been successful on the merits or otherwise." *Success is vindication.* In a criminal action, any result other than conviction must be considered success. *Going behind the result*, as [the corporation] attempts, is neither authorized by subsection (c) nor consistent with the presumption of innocence.

Id. at 141 (emphasis added).

Although the underlying proceeding in *Merritt* was criminal, the court's analysis is instructive here. The agents in *Merritt* rendered consideration—their guilty plea on one count—to achieve the dismissal of the other counts. The court considered these dismissals both "success" and (therefore) "vindication," and refused to "go[ ] behind the result" or to appraise the reason for the success. In equating "success" with "vindication," the court thus rejected the more expansive view of vindication urged by the corporation. Under *Merritt*'s holding, then, vindication, when used as a synonym for "success" under § 145(c), does not mean moral exoneration. Escape from an adverse judgment or other detriment, for whatever reason, is determinative. According to *Merritt*, the only question a court may ask is what the result was, not why it was.

Conti's contention that, because of its $35 million settlement payments, Waltuch's settlement without payment should not really count as settlement without payment, is inconsistent with the rule in *Merritt*. Here, Waltuch was sued, and the suit was dismissed without his having paid a settlement. Under the approach taken in *Merritt*, it is not our business to ask why this result was reached. Once Waltuch achieved his settlement gratis, he achieved success "on the merits or otherwise." And, as we know from *Merritt*, success is sufficient to constitute vindication (at least for the purposes of § 145(c)). Waltuch's settlement thus vindicated him.

The concept of "vindication" pressed by Conti is also inconsistent with the fact that a director or officer who is able to defeat an adversary's claim by asserting a technical defense is entitled to indemnification under § 145(c). . . . In such cases, the indemnitee has been "successful" in the palpable sense that he has won, and the suit has been dismissed, whether or not the victory is deserved in merits terms. If a technical defense is deemed "vindication" under Delaware law, it cannot matter why Waltuch emerged unscathed, or whether Conti "bailed [him] out", or whether his success was deserved. Under § 145(c), mere success is vindication enough.

. . .

ANALYSIS

1.   First consider only the $1.2 million of expenses Waltuch incurred in the private actions. Generally, private indemnification provisions such as Article Ninth of Conticommodity's articles of incorporation are intended to expand the right to reimbursement allowed or required by statute. Why did Waltuch lose his argument for reimbursement under Article Ninth and win under § 145(c)? Why is there a good faith requirement in § 145(a) but not in § 145(c)?

2.   Turning to the expenses in the CFTC action, disregarding § 145(a), does the language of Article Ninth require reimbursement?

3.   Suppose that Conticommodity, pursuant to a unanimous vote of its board of directors, had in fact reimbursed all of Waltuch's expenses and a shareholder files a derivative action to recover the amount of the reimbursement from the directors. What result?

4.   Why would a state legislature want to limit the power of a corporation to indemnify to those situations in which the officer or director acted in good faith? What if the directors and a majority (or all) of the shareholders were informed of the conduct in question (such as Waltuch's manipulation of silver prices) and approved because it was likely to enhance profits?

5.   In light of the court's analysis, is section 145(f) mere surplusage? Describe an indemnification provision that is "consistent" with section 145(a) but which requires section 145(f) in order to be valid.

Citadel Holding Corporation v. Roven

603 A.2d 818 (Del.1992).

This is an appeal from a decision of the Superior Court awarding damages in an action brought by a former director against Citadel Holding Corporation ("Citadel") under an indemnification agreement. The court ruled that the director, Alfred Roven ("Roven"), was entitled to reimbursement for sums paid or incurred by him to defray litigation expenses in a federal court action brought against him by Citadel. .   .   . We affirm the Superior Court's ruling on the merits of the contractual dispute. .   .   .

I

Citadel, a savings and loan holding company, is a Delaware corporation having its principal place of business in Glendale, California. Roven was a director of Citadel from July, 1985 to July, 1988. During most of that time, he beneficially owned 9.8 percent of Citadel's common stock.

In May of 1987, Citadel and Roven entered into an Indemnity Agreement ("the Agreement"). The stated purpose of the Agreement was to provide Roven with protection greater than already provided him by Citadel's Certificate of Incorporation, Bylaws and insurance.

.   .   .

The body of the Agreement consists of twelve numbered paragraphs, only a few of which are relevant here. Paragraph 1 contains Citadel's general obligation to indemnify Roven. That section provides, in part:

1. The Corporation shall indemnify the Agent against any expense or liability incurred in connection with any threatened, pending or completed action, suit or proceeding, whether civil or criminal, administrative or investigative, to which he is a party or is threatened to be made a party by reason of his service as a director. . . .

This general undertaking to indemnify for "any expense or liability" is limited later in the Agreement, however, by specific exceptions to the obligation. The exception which has pertinence to the present dispute is contained in paragraph 5(e):

5. The Corporation shall not be obligated under this Agreement to make payment in regard to any liability or expense of the Agent:

(e) for an accounting of profits made from the purchase or sale by the Agent of securities of the Corporation within the meaning of Section 16(b) of the Securities Exchange Act of 1934 and amendments thereto or similar provisions of any state statutory law or common law; . . .

Under Paragraph 7 of the agreement Roven is entitled to require Citadel to advance the costs of defending certain lawsuits. This paragraph was invoked by Roven as the basis for his Superior Court breach of contract action. It states:

7. Costs and expenses (including attorneys' fees) incurred by the Agent in defending or investigating any action, suit, proceeding or investigation shall be paid by the Corporation in advance of the final disposition of such matter, if the Agent shall undertake in writing to repay any such advances in the event that it is ultimately determined that the Agent is not entitled to indemnification under the terms of this Agreement.

Roven's claim for indemnification and reimbursement was prompted by a suit brought by Citadel against him in the United States District Court for the Central District of California ("the federal action"). In that proceeding, which is ongoing, Citadel alleged that Roven violated Section 16(b) of the Securities and Exchange Act of 1934 [see supra Chapter 4, Sec. 5] by purchasing certain options to buy Citadel stock while he was a director. Roven is contesting the claim that his option purchases violated Section 16(b) and contends that the federal action is but one chapter in a continuing fight for control of Citadel between Roven and another director of Citadel, James J. Cotter. . . .

II

. . .

Initially, Citadel argues that paragraph 7, the advancement provision of the Agreement, was never intended to cover the federal action in any event.   To support this proposition, it points to language of the advancement provision which requires Roven to secure any advance by a written promise to repay the advances "in the event that it is ultimately determined that [Roven] is not entitled to indemnification under the terms of this Agreement."   It further argues that the expense of defending the federal action is not subject to indemnification because the Section 16(b) claim does not arise "by reason of his service as a director" as required by the indemnification provision found in Paragraph 1.   Rather, it arises by reason of the fact that he is a director.   Furthermore, Citadel argues, a suit under Section 16(b) is specifically excluded from indemnification by Paragraph 5(e) which limits the scope of Paragraph 1.   Because Roven has no right to indemnification, the argument goes, he has no right to advances.   .   .   . This was a suit to enforce the advancement provision of the Agreement, not the indemnity provision.   The language of Paragraph 7 is therefore critical to any analysis of the obligations of the parties.

The language found in that paragraph in no way renders the right to advances dependent upon the right to indemnity.   The phrase "under the terms of this Agreement," relied upon by Citadel, refers only to the ultimate determination that the Agent is not entitled to indemnification. It describes, and thus conditions, the breadth of the written promise Roven is required to make to secure Citadel's advances.   It does not limit Roven's right to those advances initially.   Citadel's arguments regarding the exception in Paragraph 5(e) and the phrase "by reason of his service as a director" in Paragraph 1 are therefore irrelevant to the scope of Roven's rights under Paragraph 7.   Those provisions speak to Roven's right to indemnification, not advances.   It is clear, therefore, that nothing in Paragraph 1 or Paragraph 5(e) compels the conclusion that Roven is not entitled to advances for the costs of defending the federal action.

.   .   .

The General Corporation Law of Delaware expressly allows a corporation to advance the costs of defending a suit to a director.   8 Del. C. § 145(e).*   The authority conferred is permissive.   The corporation "may" pay an officer or director's expenses in advance.   The Agreement, on the other hand, renders the corporation's duty mandatory in providing that expenses shall be paid in advance.   Under the Agreement, Citadel is required to advance to Roven the costs of defending suits, rather than merely permitting it to make such advances as provided in the statute. The use of the word "shall" therefore simply reflects the parties' intention to provide Roven expanded protection.

Under both the statute and the Agreement, the corporation's obligation to pay expenses is subject to a reasonableness requirement.   We can assume that under the statute alone Citadel would never choose to advance unreasonable expenses, although it has the option to make reasonable advances.   As the Superior Court correctly determined, under the Agreement, Citadel is not required to advance unreasonable expenses but is

---

* [Editors: § 145(e) is quoted at page 510 supra.]

required to advance reasonable ones. Thus, although Citadel need not write Roven a blank check, Roven still achieves far greater protection by reason of his agreement as long as his expenses are deemed reasonable. This interpretation of the disputed provision advances the intent of the parties without producing an absurd result. . . .

This interpretation also clears up the ambiguity of the phrase "any action." For example, a demand for advances of costs incurred during a legal proceeding the subject of which was totally unrelated to the business of Citadel would clearly be unreasonable. We think it clear that the advancement provision of the agreement was never intended to cover unrelated legal proceedings.

. . .

V

In conclusion, we hold that the Agreement requires Citadel to advance to Roven all reasonable costs incurred in defending the federal action. . . .   Finally, we note again that our decision here concerns Roven's right to advances under the Agreement, not his right to indemnification. At the appropriate time in the future, if necessary, the parties may litigate their rights under the indemnification provision of the Agreement.

AFTERMATH

As to the substance of Citadel's claim against Roven under § 16(b), the trial court's grant of Roven's motion for summary judgment was affirmed in Citadel Holding Corp. v. Roven, 26 F.3d 960 (9th Cir.1994). The options at issue had been bought by Roven in privately negotiated transactions with two brokerage firms and were subject to substantial restrictions. In upholding the judgment in favor of Roven, the appellate court relied on the fact that the options had not been immediately exercisable. This being a sufficient basis for the result, it did not reach the alternative grounds on which the lower court had relied—namely, that there had been no purchase and sale within six months and no profits had been "realized" within six months. The appellate court decided the case under § 16(b) rules relating to the treatment of options that were in force at the time the case arose rather than the new rules that were adopted in 1991 and are now in force.

ANALYSIS

Would, and should, the result have been different if Roven had not claimed that "the federal action is but one chapter in a continuing fight for control of Citadel between Roven and another director of Citadel, James J. Cotter"?

PLANNING

1. How would you rewrite paragraph 7 of the agreement between Citadel and Roven to achieve a reasonable result and minimize the risk of litigation?

2.   How would you define the types of expenses that would be reimbursed? Is it reasonable to cover expenses associated with actions arising under § 16(b)?

NOTE ON INSURANCE

According to a 1992 survey by the Wyatt Company, of 1,342 companies surveyed, 1,090 (81 percent) carried director and officer ("D & O") liability insurance, with the percentage of coverage lower for small corporations and higher for larger ones. There have been reports of individuals refusing to serve as directors without such insurance. In recent years such insurance has become expensive and, in some instances, impossible to obtain. The policies typically have deductibles and worrisome maximum coverages, and some of them have important exclusions (e.g., for violation of anti-pollution laws, for conduct in connection with resistance to a takeover, for actions by regulatory agencies, and for certain violations of the securities laws).

Some corporations have combined to form their own "captive" insurance companies for writing D & O coverage. Others have established trust funds to pay damages or expenses, or both.

CHAPTER 5

PROBLEMS OF CONTROL

SECTION 1. PROXY FIGHTS

INTRODUCTION

Corporations hold annual meetings of shareholders for election of directors and, where necessary, for voting on other matters. Corporations may also call special meetings—for example, for shareholder approval or disapproval of a merger. Despite the potential importance of actions taken at shareholder meetings, few shareholders of public corporations actually attend them. Few shareholders own enough shares to make any difference at the meeting—even institutional shareholders such as pension funds and mutual funds (though the role of such shareholders, despite various legal and other obstacles, seems to be moving toward greater involvement in corporate governance). Even if individuals own shares worth tens of thousands of dollars, their stake will generally be too small to affect the outcome. As a result, such shareholders seldom find it cost-effective to become well informed about corporate disputes, much less to attend any meeting in person.

Thus, most annual shareholder meetings are uneventful, quiet affairs, where directors are reelected without opposition and certain other routine matters are attended to. The events preceding such meetings can become contentious, however, if insurgents seek to take control of the firm by electing themselves and their allies to the board. Contention can also arise when issues that require shareholder approval are scheduled for determination at the annual meeting, or at a special meeting called to decide certain issues basic to the corporation. Such issues include whether to amend the articles of incorporation (for example, to limit director liability), to liquidate the firm, to sell all or substantially all of the assets, or to engage in a merger.

With small firms, by contrast, shareholders may appear at the meeting and help decide the firm's business strategy. Shareholders of such firms may find it worthwhile to attend shareholder meetings because they own enough shares to affect the outcome of any vote.

Because few shareholders of public corporations attend the annual meeting, the outcome will generally depend on which group has collected the most "proxies." (Proxy voting is also available, but less common, for small corporations.) Under corporate law, shareholders may appoint an agent to attend the meeting and vote on their behalf. That agent is the shareholder's "proxyholder," sometimes simply called the shareholder's "proxy"; the document by which the shareholder appoints the agent is also called the "proxy" (or "proxy card"). Because the outcome of the meeting

519

depends on the number of votes cast, the person with the most proxies usually wins.

Generally, the incumbent managers of a large firm will solicit proxies from shareholders directly. Shortly before the annual meeting, they will write to the "shareholders of record" and ask them to sign and return the enclosed proxy card. By doing so, the shareholders authorize the management representative to vote on their behalf. If the stock is held in "street name," the broker or bank will forward the material to the "beneficial owner." [1]

"Proxy fights" result when an insurgent group tries to oust incumbent managers by soliciting proxy cards and electing its own representatives to the board. Such fights were relatively common in the 1950s, but fell out of favor when insurgent investors turned to tender offers as a more efficient way to gain corporate control. Recently, however, many states have passed statutes that increase the difficulty and reduce the cost-effectiveness of tender offers (see Chapter 6, Sec. 2). Accordingly, insurgent shareholders may once again be turning to proxy fights, but now sometimes to proxy fights that they coordinate with a tender offer campaign. An insurgent group may initiate a tender offer, for example, but combine it with a proxy fight to put added pressure on the incumbents. It may try to replace the existing board through the proxy fight, or use the proxies to fight any defensive measures that the management hopes to implement.

Like tender offers, proxy fights are subject both to the 1934 Securities Exchange Act and to state corporate statutes. In this section, we first examine some of the strategic aspects of proxy fights (*Levin* and *Rosenfeld*). We then turn to restrictions on "fraudulent" proxy solicitations under the 1934 Act and to restrictions on the opportunity to sue for violations (*Virginia Bankshares* and *Stahl*). Next we examine three cases involving shareholder proposals (*Lovenheim*, *Dole*, and *Austin*). Finally, we consider the ways in which one can gain access to the list of a firm's shareholders (*Crane*, *Pillsbury*, and *Sadler*).

A. STRATEGIC USE OF PROXIES

Levin v. Metro–Goldwyn–Mayer, Inc.

264 F.Supp. 797 (S.D.N.Y.1967).

■ RYAN, DISTRICT JUDGE.

This action was filed by six stockholders of Metro–Goldwyn–Mayer, Inc. (MGM), a Delaware corporation with its principal place of business in

---

1. Traditionally, an investor who bought stock notified the company and recorded the stock in his or her own name. Before the annual meeting, the board of directors would announce a given date as the "record date" for the meeting (or the by-laws would specify a date). People listed on the corporation's stock ledger as owning the stock on that date were called the "shareholders of record" and, even if they thereaf- ter sold the stock before the meeting, were the people entitled to vote at the meeting. In part to facilitate trades, however, many shareholders no longer bother to notify the company when they purchase. Instead, they simply leave the stock in the name of their broker (or depository trust company). Such stock is said to be held "in street name," and the investor is known as the "beneficial own- er."

New York.* The defendants named are MGM and five of the thirteen members of its Board of Directors. They are part of present MGM corporate management; all of them serve as officers or as members of the Executive Committee.

Plaintiff, Philip Levin, is and has been a director of MGM since February, 1965 and all of the plaintiffs hold substantial blocks of MGM common stock.[3]

The present action flows from a conflict for corporate control between present management—called "the O'Brien group" and "the Levin group." Each group intends to nominate a slate of directors at the MGM stockholder annual meeting which is to be held on February 23, 1967; each has been actively soliciting proxies for this meeting. . . .

Plaintiffs complain of the manner, method and means employed by defendants in the solicitation of proxies for the coming annual meeting of MGM stockholders. Specifically, plaintiffs charged that the defendants, in connection with the proxy solicitation contest, have wrongfully committed MGM to pay for the services of specially retained attorneys, a public relations firm and proxy soliciting organizations, and, in addition, have improperly used the offices and employees of MGM in proxy solicitation and the good-will and business contacts of MGM to secure support for the present management. Plaintiffs, in their complaint, pray for temporary and permanent injunctive relief against defendants' continuing this method of solicitation of proxies and against defendants' voting the proxies so obtained at the annual meeting. They also seek money damages of $2,500,000 on behalf of MGM from the individual defendants. . . .

Plaintiffs maintain the injunctive relief sought is required to prevent (1) the unlawful use of the corporate organization—its employees, good-will and offices and of corporate funds in the solicitation of proxies, (2) the retention of "the four top proxy-soliciting concerns and the passing of their bill for their services to the corporation rather than to the individuals" and (3) the employment at corporate expense of special counsel "for the sole and exclusive and no other purpose than the waging of a proxy contest on behalf of the individual defendants who have every right to pay for his valuable services" with their own private funds, particularly in view of the fact that regularly employed attorneys are available to represent the corporate interests of MGM.

Because of the nature of plaintiffs' allegations, we weigh the merits of this application for injunctive relief against the financial and business

---

* [Editors.—Jurisdiction was based both on diversity and on a federal cause of action arising out of alleged SEC proxy rule violations.]

3. Plaintiffs own 552,705 shares of MGM common stock, approximately 11% of the total outstanding shares, with a market value of nearly $20,000,000. Levin, one of the plaintiffs, also states by affidavit that he has other stockholders associated with him in the proxy contest who hold 127,150 shares of MGM common, with a market value of approximately $4,323,100.

background of MGM. As of August 31, 1966, MGM had total assets of $251,132,000 and a gross income for its 1966 fiscal year of approximately $185,000,000. It is one of the major producers and distributors of motion pictures in the world and markets to exhibitors films produced by others as well as its own films. . . . MGM is one of the "giants" in the entertainment industry.

. . . Defendants point with unabashed pride to the results they have achieved in their direction of the affairs of MGM. We do not question that the successful operation of MGM has been accomplished in no small measure by diligent and intelligent application to corporate affairs and by the exercise of sound and informed business judgment. The decision as to the continuance of the present management, however, rests entirely with the stockholders. A court may not override or dictate on a matter of this nature to stockholders.

. . . It is the concern of the law and of the Court that they be fully and truthfully informed as to the merits of the contentions of those soliciting their proxy. It is equally important that the Court should not unnecessarily exercise its injunctive power in such matters lest such judicial action operate to unduly influence a stockholder's decision as to which faction should receive his proxy.

It is quite plain that the differences between "the O'Brien group" and "the Levin group" are much more than mere personality conflicts. These might readily be resolved by reasoning and hard-headed, profit-minded business men. There are definite business policies advocated by each group, so divergent that reconciliation does not seem possible. They appear so evident from the papers before us that detailed analysis would be a waste of time.[7] However, in such a situation the right of an independent stockholder to be fully informed is of supreme importance. The controlling question presented on this application is whether illegal or unfair means of communication, such as demand judicial intervention, are being employed by the present management. We find that they are not and conclude that the injunctive relief now sought should be denied.

The proxy statement filed by MGM under date of January 6, 1967, opens with the statement that "MGM will bear all cost in connection with the management solicitation of proxies." . . . It discloses the employ-

---

7. The fundamental policy differences between the contesting groups concern, among other matters:

a. The annual number of feature pictures MGM should produce; management policy would limit them to approximately 25 top productions (with cost per picture from $5,000,000 to $8,000,000) and the balance costing down to approximately $500,000; "the Levin group" policy advocates up to 50 top productions a year.

b. "The Levin" policy would provide for a slow release of pictures to TV showing; management would license to TV pictures of more recent release date.
. . .

d. Levin policy would build up cash funds available for productions by reducing dividends, and thus reduce necessity for financing; present management policy is different.

ment of Georgeson & Co. at $15,000 and Kissel–Blake Organization, Inc. at $5,000 for services and estimated out-of-pocket expenses. . . .

It advises that "Proxies may also be solicited in newspapers or other publications" and that the total amount which it is estimated will be spent in the management solicitation is $125,000 "exclusive of amounts normally expended for a solicitation for an election of directors and costs represented by salaries and wages of regular employees and officers."

We do not find the amounts recited to be paid excessive, or the method of operation disclosed by MGM management to be unfair or illegal. It contravenes no federal statute or S.E.C. rule or regulation. . . .

Motion denied.

PROBLEM

Suppose you own 25 percent of the stock of True Love, Inc., a publisher of gothic romance novels. On the supposition that the novel market is shrinking, True Love has decided to start a new division, Amore Comics, to produce gothic romance comic books. You believe that the Amore Comics venture is doomed, and launch a proxy fight to install yourself and your literati friends on the board. Incumbent managers fight back by using corporate funds to hire a public relations firm that will mastermind their tactics.

You file a derivative suit challenging that use of the corporate treasury. What result? How would your answer change if you establish that 80 percent of the stock of the public relations firm is held by the older brother of the True Love CEO? What if you could also establish that three of the eleven True Love directors are personal friends of Lady Lucy Duff Gordon, the illustrator retained to draw the Amore Comics?

B.   REIMBURSEMENT OF COSTS

Rosenfeld v. Fairchild Engine & Airplane Corp.

309 N.Y. 168, 128 N.E.2d 291 (1955).

■ FROESSEL, JUDGE.

In a stockholder's derivative action brought by plaintiff, an attorney, who owns 25 out of the company's over 2,300,000 shares, seeks to compel the return of $261,522, paid out of the corporate treasury to reimburse both sides in a proxy contest for their expenses. The Appellate Division, . . . has unanimously affirmed a judgment of an Official Referee, . . . dismissing plaintiff's complaint on the merits, and we agree.

. . . .

Of the amount in controversy $106,000 was spent out of corporate funds by the old board of directors while still in office in defense of their position in said contest; $28,000 was paid to the old board by the new board after the change of management following the proxy contest, to compensate the former directors for such of the remaining expenses of their unsuccessful defense as the new board found was fair and reasonable; payment of $127,000, representing reimbursement of expenses to members of the prevailing group, was expressly ratified by a 16 to 1 majority vote of the stockholders.

. . . The Appellate Division found that the difference between plaintiff's group and the old board "went deep into the policies of the company", and that among these Ward's contract was one of the "main points of contention."

By way of contrast with the findings here, in Lawyers' Advertising Co. v. Consolidated Ry., Lighting & Refrigerating Co., 187 N.Y. 395, . . . which was an action to recover for the cost of publishing newspaper notices not authorized by the board of directors, it was expressly found that the proxy contest there involved was "by one faction in its contest with another for the control of the corporation . . . a contest for the perpetuation of their offices and control." We there said by way of *dicta* that under *such* circumstances the publication of certain notices on behalf of the management faction was not a corporate expenditure which the directors had the power to authorize.

Other jurisdictions and our own lower courts have held that management may look to the corporate treasury for the reasonable expenses of soliciting proxies to defend its position in a bona fide policy contest. . . .

It should be noted that plaintiff does not argue that the aforementioned sums were fraudulently extracted from the corporation; indeed, his counsel conceded that "the charges were fair and reasonable," but denied "they were legal charges which may be reimbursed for." . . .

If directors of a corporation may not in good faith incur reasonable and proper expenses in soliciting proxies in these days of giant corporations with vast numbers of stockholders, the corporate business might be seriously interfered with because of stockholder indifference and the difficulty of procuring a quorum, where there is no contest. In the event of a proxy contest, if the directors may not freely answer the challenges of outside groups and in good faith defend their actions with respect to corporate policy for the information of the stockholders, they and the corporation may be at the mercy of persons seeking to wrest control for their own purposes, so long as such persons have ample funds to conduct a proxy contest. The test is clear. When the directors act in good faith in a contest over policy, they have the right to incur reasonable and proper expenses for solicitation of proxies and in defense of their corporate policies, and are not obliged to sit idly by. . . .

It is also our view that the members of the so-called new group could be reimbursed by the corporation for their expenditures in this contest by affirmative vote of the stockholders. . . .

The rule then which we adopt is simply this: In a contest over policy, as compared to a purely personal power contest, corporate directors have the right to make reasonable and proper expenditures, subject to the scrutiny of the courts when duly challenged, from the corporate treasury for the purpose of persuading the stockholders of the correctness of their position and soliciting their support for policies which the directors believe, in all good faith, are in the best interests of the corporation. The stockholders, moreover, have the right to reimburse successful contestants for the reasonable and bona fide expenses incurred by them in any such policy contest, subject to like court scrutiny. That is not to say, however, that corporate directors can, under any circumstances, disport themselves in a proxy contest with the corporation's moneys to an unlimited extent. Where it is established that such moneys have been spent for personal power, individual gain or private advantage, and not in the belief that such expenditures are in the best interests of the stockholders and the corporation, or where the fairness and reasonableness of the amounts allegedly expended are duly and successfully challenged, the courts will not hesitate to disallow them.

The judgment of the Appellate Division should be affirmed, without costs.

■ VAN VOORHIS, JUDGE (dissenting).

.   .   .

No resolution was passed by the stockholders approving payment to the management group. It has been recognized that not all of the $133,966 in obligations paid or incurred by the management group was designed merely for information of stockholders. This outlay included payment for all of the activities of a strenuous campaign to persuade and cajole in a hard-fought contest for control of this corporation. It included, for example, expenses for entertainment, chartered airplanes and limousines, public relations counsel and proxy solicitors. However legitimate such measures may be on behalf of stockholders themselves in such a controversy, most of them do not pertain to a corporate function but are part of the familiar apparatus of aggressive factions in corporate contests.   .   .   .

The Appellate Division acknowledged in the instant case that "It is obvious that the management group here incurred a substantial amount of needless expense which was charged to the corporation," but this conclusion should have led to a direction that those defendants who were incumbent directors should be required to come forward with an explanation of their expenditures under the familiar rule that where it has been established that directors have expended corporate money for their own purposes, the burden of going forward with evidence of the propriety and reasonableness of specific items rests upon the directors.   .   .   .

The second ground assigned by the Appellate Division for dismissing the complaint against incumbent directors is stockholder ratification of reimbursement to the insurgent group. Whatever effect or lack of it this resolution had upon expenditures by the insurgent group, clearly the stockholders who voted to pay the insurgents entertained no intention of reimbursing the management group for their expenditures. . . . Upon the contrary, they were removing the incumbents from control mainly for the reason that they were charged with having mulcted the corporation by a long-term salary and pension contract to one of their number, J. Carlton Ward, Jr. . . .

There is no doubt that the management was entitled and under a duty to take reasonable steps to acquaint the stockholders with essential facts concerning the management of the corporation, and it may well be that the existence of a contest warranted them in circularizing the stockholders with more than ordinarily detailed information. . . .

What expenses of the incumbent group should be allowed and what should be disallowed should be remitted to the trial court to ascertain, after taking evidence, in accordance with the rule that the incumbent directors were required to assume the burden of going forward in the first instance with evidence explaining and justifying their expenditures. Only such as were reasonably related to informing the stockholders fully and fairly concerning the corporate affairs should be allowed. The concession by plaintiff that such expenditures as were made were reasonable in amount does not decide this question. By way of illustration, the costs of entertainment for stockholders may have been, and it is stipulated that they were, at the going rates for providing similar entertainment. That does not signify that entertaining stockholders is reasonably related to the purposes of the corporation. . . .

Regarding the $127,556 paid by the new management to the insurgent group for their campaign expenditures, the question immediately arises whether that was for a corporate purpose. The Appellate Division has recognized that upon no theory could such expenditures be reimbursed except by approval of the stockholders and, as has been said, it is the insurgents' expenditures alone to which the stockholders' resolution of ratification was addressed. If *unanimous* stockholder approval had been obtained and no rights of creditors or of the public intervened, it would make no practical difference whether the purpose were *ultra vires* —i.e., not a corporate purpose. . . . Upon the other hand, an act which is *ultra vires* cannot be ratified merely by a majority of the stockholders of a corporation.

The . . . cases which are cited consist of Hall v. Trans–Lux Daylight Picture Screen Corp., 20 Del.Ch. 78, 171 A. 226, . . . and the Federal cases applying Delaware law, Hand v. Missouri–Kansas Pipe Line Co., D.C., 54 F.Supp. 649, and Steinberg v. Adams, [90 F.Supp. 604]. . . .

The case most frequently cited and principally relied upon from among these Delaware decisions is Hall v. Trans–Lux Daylight Picture Screen Corp., supra. There the English case was followed of Peel v. London & North Western Ry. Co., [1 Ch. 5 (1907)], which distinguished between expenses merely for the purpose of maintaining control, and contests over policy questions of the corporation. In the *Hall* case the issues concerned a proposed merger, and a proposed sale of stock of a subsidiary corporation.

These were held to be policy questions, and payment of the management campaign expenses was upheld.

In our view, the impracticability of such a distinction is illustrated by the statement in the Hall case, . . . that "It is impossible in many cases of intracorporate contests over directors, to sever questions of policy from those of persons." This circumstance is stressed in Judge Rifkind's opinion in the Steinberg case . . .:

"The simple fact, of course, is that generally policy and personnel do not exist in separate compartments. A change in personnel is sometimes indispensable to a change of policy. A new board may be the symbol of the shift in policy as well as the means of obtaining it."

That may be all very well, but the upshot of this reasoning is that inasmuch as it is generally impossible to distinguish whether "policy" or "personnel" is the dominant factor, any averments must be accepted at their face value that questions of policy are dominant. Nowhere do these opinions mention that the converse is equally true and more pervasive, that neither the "ins" nor the "outs" ever say that they have no program to offer to the shareholders, but just want to acquire or to retain control, as the case may be. In common experience, this distinction is unreal. . . .

The main question of "policy" in the instant corporate election, as is stated in the opinions below and frankly admitted, concerns the long-term contract with pension rights of a former officer and director, Mr. J. Carlton Ward, Jr. The insurgents' chief claim of benefit to the corporation from their victory consists in the termination of that agreement, resulting in an alleged actuarial saving of $350,000 to $825,000 to the corporation, and the reduction of other salaries and rent by more than $300,000 per year. The insurgents had contended in the proxy contest that these payments should be substantially reduced so that members of the incumbent group would not continue to profit personally at the expense of the corporation. If these charges were true, which appear to have been believed by a majority of the shareholders, then the disbursements by the management group in the proxy contest fall under the condemnation of the English and the Delaware rule.

These circumstances are mentioned primarily to illustrate how impossible it is to distinguish between "policy" and "personnel," as Judge Rifkind expressed it, but they also indicate that personal factors are deeply rooted in this contest. That is certainly true insofar as the former management group is concerned. It would be hard to find a case to which the careful reservation made by the English Judge in the Peel case, supra, was more directly applicable.

NOTES ON THE REGULATION OF PROXY FIGHTS

1. *The Regulatory Scheme.* Section 14(a) of the 1934 Act prohibits people from soliciting proxies in violation of SEC rules. Consider the scope

of this statement. First, courts construe the concept of "solicitation" broadly. In Studebaker Corp. v. Gittlin, 360 F.2d 692 (2d Cir.1966), for example, an insurgent shareholder planned to solicit proxies from the other shareholders, and for that purpose wanted access to the list of the firm's shareholders. Because he held insufficient shares to demand the list under state law, he asked some other shareholders to join him in his effort. The court held that these preliminary requests constituted a proxy solicitation—he solicited proxies when he asked selected shareholders to join him in demanding the shareholder list, even though his purpose in getting the list was *then* to ask the shareholders for their proxies for the annual meeting.[1]

Second, the rules (Rules 14a–3, 14a–4, 14a–5, and 14a–11) require people who solicit proxies to furnish each shareholder with a "proxy statement." In it, they must disclose information that may be relevant to the decision the shareholder must make. Generally, for example, the management must include an annual report, and anyone soliciting the proxies must disclose conflicts of interest and any major issues he or she expects to raise at the shareholder meeting. In the case of proxies for contested meetings, the rules require particularly extensive disclosure. Under Rule 14a–6, the parties soliciting the proxies must file copies of this material with the SEC.

Third, when an insurgent group wants to contest management and solicit proxies, Rule 14a–7 gives management a choice: it can either mail the insurgent group's material to the shareholders directly and charge the group for the cost, or it can give the group a copy of the shareholder list and let it distribute its own material. Because the management often prefers to keep the list confidential, it generally opts for the former. Naturally, if the insurgent has a right to the shareholders list under state law (as discussed in several cases below), Rule 14a–7 does not circumscribe that right.[2]

2. *The economics of proxy fights.* Proxy fights fell out of favor in corporate control contests for simple economic reasons: if an insurgent group organized a proxy fight and lost, it bore the entire cost of soliciting the proxies; if it won and made the firm more profitable, it gained only a fraction of that increased profitability. To see the point, suppose you own 10 percent of a firm worth $8 million ($800,000), but believe it to be badly managed. You conclude that by firing the managers, you could raise the value of the firm by 20 percent (or $1.6 million). Your lawyer tells you that you could replace the managers in two ways: (a) you could organize a tender offer, buy up all the stock, and then replace the directors, or (b) you

---

1. In 1992, the SEC amended Rule 14a–2 to specify that a shareholder does not (subject to several qualifications) fall under the general SEC filing requirements if it does not solicit proxies for itself. A pension fund that submits a shareholder proposal, for example, may not be subject to the requirements since, even if it campaigns on behalf of its proposal, it is not asking shareholders to give it proxies.

2. See Wood, Walker & Co. v. Evans, 300 F.Supp. 171 (D.Colo.1969), affirmed, 461 F.2d 852 (10th Cir.1972); Kerkorian v. Western Air Lines, Inc., 253 A.2d 221, 225 (Del. Ch.1969), affirmed, 254 A.2d 240 (Del.1969).

could solicit proxies from the existing shareholders and elect new directors. Of these two, the tender offer will almost always require a larger outlay. Because you will buy the stock itself, you will need at least $7.2 million (for 90 percent of the stock of an $8 million company). If you do so, however, you will capture all of the gains from any improvement you make to the company.[3]

By contrast, suppose you organize a proxy fight. If you succeed, your stock will rise by only $160,000 (20% of your $800,000 investment). True, if you succeed, the firm may reimburse you for your proxy expenses. If you fail, though, you bear the entire cost of the proxy fight. As a result, you bear large risks, but stand to earn only a small portion of any gains you create. More generally, the point is this: investors who expect to incur large financial risks in rehabilitating a badly managed firm will prefer to keep for themselves any increased value they create. With a tender offer, they can buy all the corporate stock and do so. With a proxy fight, they must share that value with the other shareholders.

QUESTIONS

1. In order to find an inefficiently managed firm, a potential insurgent group will need to investigate many firms. Under *Rosenfeld,* it may be compensated for the cost of a proxy fight if it wins. Yet it will not be compensated either for the cost of investigating firms that it discovers are properly managed, or for the cost of proxy fights it loses. How does this affect the incentive to renovate inefficiently managed firms?

2. As a matter of policy, should a successful insurgent group receive a multiple of its expenses to compensate it for the proxy fights it loses? For the cost of investigating firms that it discovers are properly managed? Should it be compensated directly for proxy fights it loses?

3. If insurgent groups are reimbursed only when they win, should incumbents be reimbursed when they lose?

PROBLEM

Kane is a rich man who likes to run newspapers. He is the editor-in-chief of the New York *Inquirer* and CEO and 33 percent owner of the Inquirer Corp., the parent firm. Geddes owns 10 percent of the Inquirer Corp. and thinks he himself would make a better CEO and editor. He decides to launch a proxy fight.

Kane throws a lavish party at Xanadu, his country estate, for the lead shareholders (assorted managers of pension funds and mutual funds). He gives a short lecture about why the status quo should continue, and then invites everyone to party until dawn. Can Kane charge his expenses to the company?

3. You could, of course, simply buy another 41 percent of the stock and gain majority control. You would then, however, capture only half of any increased profitability you generate.

Geddes throws a lean-and-mean party aboard his yacht, the *Geddes Princess,* at which he harangues the same lead shareholders about Kane's mismanagement and about his own ability to run a newspaper. Can Geddes obtain reimbursement from the Inquirer Corp. if he wins? If he loses?

C.   PRIVATE ACTIONS FOR PROXY-RULE VIOLATIONS

Virginia Bankshares, Inc. v. Sandberg

501 U.S. 1083, 111 S.Ct. 2749, 115 L.Ed.2d 929 (1991).

■ JUSTICE SOUTER delivered the opinion of the Court.

Section 14(a) of the Securities Exchange Act of 1934 authorizes the Securities and Exchange Commission to adopt rules for the solicitation of proxies, and prohibits their violation.[1] In J. I. Case Co. v. Borak, 377 U.S. 426 (1964), we first recognized an implied private right of action for the breach of § 14(a) as implemented by SEC Rule 14a–9, which prohibits the solicitation of proxies by means of materially false or misleading statements.[2]

[First American Bankshares, Inc. (FABI) owned 100 percent of the stock of Virginia Bankshares, Inc. (VBI), and VBI owned 85 percent of the First American Bank of Virginia (Bank). In December 1986, FABI accomplished a "freeze-out" merger of Bank into VBI—that is, one in which Bank is absorbed by VBI and disappears and the minority shareholders of Bank receive cash for their shares (and are thus "frozen out"). As part of the merger procedure FABI asked the investment banking firm of Keefe, Bruyett & Woods (KBW) to issue an opinion on the appropriate price for the 15 percent of Bank that it would need to buy. KBW recommended $42 per share and Bank's executive committee approved the merger at that price.

Virginia law governed the merger of VBI and Bank and required only a 2/3 vote of shareholders to approve. As VBI already owned 85 percent, it

---

1.   Section 14(a) provides in full that:

It shall be unlawful for any person, by the use of the mails or by any means or instrumentality of interstate commerce or of any facility of a national securities exchange or otherwise, in contravention of such rules and regulations as the Commission may prescribe as necessary or appropriate in the public interest or for the protection of investors, to solicit or to permit the use of his name to solicit any proxy or consent or authorization in respect of any security (other than an exempted security) registered pursuant to section 78l of this title.

15 U.S.C. § 78n(a).

2.   This Rule provides in relevant part that:

No solicitation subject to this regulation shall be made by means of any proxy statement . . . containing any statement which, at the time and in the light of the circumstances under which it is made, is false or misleading with respect to any material fact, or which omits to state any material fact necessary in order to make the statements therein not false or misleading. . . .

17 CFR § 240.14a–9 (1990).

could readily "force through" the merger. Under Virginia law it nonetheless did need to hold a shareholders' meeting (and give advance notice of the merger), but it did not need to solicit proxies.

Notwithstanding, Bank directors solicited proxies for the shareholders meeting. In their solicitation, they urged shareholders to adopt the merger proposal, and stated that they had approved it because it gave minority shareholders a "high" value, a "fair" price: "The Plan of Merger has been approved by the Board of Directors because it provides an opportunity for the Bank's public shareholders to achieve a high value for their shares." Most minority shareholders gave the directors the proxies the directors wanted.

A shareholder, Sandberg, not only refused to give the directors a proxy, but sued for damages. She argued that they had violated Rule 14a–9. Among other things, she claimed that they had not actually believed that the merger price was high or fair and had approved the merger only because they thought they would be removed as directors if they did anything else. The jury below valued Sandberg's shares at $60 at the time of the merger and awarded her the $18 difference. The Court of Appeals affirmed.

On appeal, the Supreme Court faced two questions: (a) whether a statement about the directors' reasons for recommending corporate actions can be materially misleading under Rule 14a–9 and (b) whether a shareholder whose vote is not necessary for a merger can nonetheless show causation in a damage suit.]

II

. . .

A

We consider first the actionability per se of statements of reasons, opinion or belief. Because such a statement by definition purports to express what is consciously on the speaker's mind, we interpret the jury verdict as finding that the directors' statements of belief and opinion were made with knowledge that the directors did not hold the beliefs or opinions expressed. . . .[5] That such statements may be materially significant raises no serious question. The meaning of the materiality requirement for liability under § 14(a) was discussed at some length in TSC Industries, Inc. v. Northway, Inc., 426 U.S. 438 (1976), where we held a fact to be material "if there is a substantial likelihood that a reasonable shareholder would consider it important in deciding how to vote." Id., at 449. . . .

B

1

But, assuming materiality, the question remains whether statements of reasons, opinions, or beliefs are statements "with respect to . . . material

---

5. In TSC Industries, Inc. v. Northway, Inc., 426 U.S. 438, 444, n. 7 (1976), we reserved the question whether scienter was necessary for liability generally under § 14(a). We reserve it still.

facts" so as to fall within the strictures of the Rule. Petitioners argue that we would invite wasteful litigation of amorphous issues outside the readily provable realm of fact if we were to recognize liability here on proof that the directors did not recommend the merger for the stated reason. . . .

Reasons for directors' recommendations or statements of belief are . . . characteristically matters of corporate record subject to documentation, to be supported or attacked by evidence of historical fact outside a plaintiff's control. Such evidence would include not only corporate minutes and other statements of the directors themselves, but circumstantial evidence bearing on the facts that would reasonably underlie the reasons claimed and the honesty of any statement that those reasons are the basis for a recommendation or other action, a point that becomes especially clear when the reasons or beliefs go to valuations in dollars and cents.

. . .

Respondents adduced evidence for just such facts in proving that the statement was misleading about its subject matter and a false expression of the directors' reasons. Whereas the proxy statement described the $42 price as offering a premium above both book value and market price, the evidence indicated that a calculation of the book figure based on the appreciated value of the Bank's real estate holdings eliminated any such premium. The evidence on the significance of market price showed that KBW had conceded that the market was closed, thin and dominated by FABI, facts omitted from the statement. There was, indeed, evidence of a "going concern" value for the Bank in excess of $60 per share of common stock, another fact never disclosed. However conclusory the directors' statement may have been, then, it was open to attack by garden-variety evidence, subject neither to a plaintiff's control nor ready manufacture, and there was no undue risk of open-ended liability or uncontrollable litigation in allowing respondents the opportunity for recovery on the allegation that it was misleading to call $42 "high."

. . .

2

Under § 14(a), then, a plaintiff is permitted to prove a specific statement of reason knowingly false or misleadingly incomplete, even when stated in conclusory terms. In reaching this conclusion we have considered statements of reasons of the sort exemplified here, which misstate the speaker's reasons and also mislead about the stated subject matter (e.g., the value of the shares). A statement of belief may be open to objection only in the former respect, however, solely as a misstatement of the psychological fact of the speaker's belief in what he says. In this case, for example, the Court of Appeals alluded to just such limited falsity in observing that "the jury was certainly justified in believing that the directors did not believe a merger at $42 per share was in the minority stockholders' interest but, rather, that they voted as they did for other reasons, e.g., retaining their seats on the board." 891 F.2d, at 1121.

The question arises, then, whether disbelief, or undisclosed belief or motivation, standing alone, should be a sufficient basis to sustain an action under § 14(a), absent proof by the sort of objective evidence described above that the statement also expressly or impliedly asserted something false or misleading about its subject matter. We think that proof of mere disbelief or belief undisclosed should not suffice for liability under § 14(a). . . .

[T]o recognize liability on mere disbelief or undisclosed motive without any demonstration that the proxy statement was false or misleading about its subject would authorize § 14(a) litigation confined solely to what one skeptical court spoke of as the "impurities" of a director's "unclean heart." Stedman v. Storer, 308 F.Supp. 881, 887 (S.D.N.Y.1969) (dealing with § 10(b)). This, we think, would cross the line that [we have] sought to draw. . . .

. . .

III

The second issue before us, left open in Mills v. Electric Auto–Lite Co., 396 U.S. [375], 385, n. 7 [(1970)], is whether causation of damages compensable through the implied private right of action under § 14(a) can be demonstrated by a member of a class of minority shareholders whose votes are not required by law or corporate bylaw to authorize the transaction giving rise to the claim. J. I. Case Co. v. Borak, 377 U.S. 426 (1964), did not itself address the requisites of causation, as such, or define the class of plaintiffs eligible to sue under § 14(a). But its general holding, that a private cause of action was available to some shareholder class, acquired greater clarity with a more definite concept of causation in *Mills*, where we addressed the sufficiency of proof that misstatements in a proxy solicitation were responsible for damages claimed from the merger subject to complaint.

Although a majority stockholder in *Mills* controlled just over half the corporation's shares, a two-thirds vote was needed to approve the merger proposal. After proxies had been obtained, and the merger had carried, minority shareholders brought a *Borak* action. 396 U.S., at 379. The question arose whether the plaintiffs' burden to demonstrate causation of their damages traceable to the § 14(a) violation required proof that the defect in the proxy solicitation had had "a decisive effect on the voting." Id., at 385. The *Mills* Court avoided the evidentiary morass that would have followed from requiring individualized proof that enough minority shareholders had relied upon the misstatements to swing the vote. Instead, it held that causation of damages by a material proxy misstatement could be established by showing that minority proxies necessary and sufficient to authorize the corporate acts had been given in accordance with the tenor of the solicitation, and the Court described such a causal relationship by calling the proxy solicitation an "essential link in the accomplishment of the transaction." Ibid. In the case before it, the Court found the solicitation essential, as contrasted with one addressed to a class of minority shareholders without votes required by law or by-law to authorize the action proposed, and left it for another day to decide whether such a minority shareholder could demonstrate causation. Id., at 385, n. 7.

In this case, respondents address *Mills'* open question by proffering two theories that the proxy solicitation addressed to them was an "essential link" under the *Mills* causation test. They argue, first, that a link existed and was essential simply because VBI and FABI would have been unwilling to proceed with the merger without the approval manifested by the minority shareholders' proxies, which would not have been obtained without the solicitation's express misstatements and misleading omissions. On this reasoning, the causal connection would depend on a desire to avoid bad shareholder or public relations, and the essential character of the causal link would stem not from the enforceable terms of the parties' corporate relationship, but from one party's apprehension of the ill will of the other.

In the alternative, respondents argue that the proxy statement was an essential link between the directors' proposal and the merger because it was the means to satisfy a state statutory requirement of minority shareholder approval, as a condition for saving the merger from voidability resulting from a conflict of interest on the part of one of the Bank's directors, Jack Beddow, who voted in favor of the merger while also serving as a director of FABI. . . .   Under the terms of Va. Code § 13.1–691(A) (1989), minority approval after disclosure of the material facts about the transaction and the director's interest was one of three avenues to insulate the merger from later attack for conflict, the two others being ratification by the Bank's directors after like disclosure, and proof that the merger was fair to the corporation. On this theory, causation would depend on the use of the proxy statement for the purpose of obtaining votes sufficient to bar a minority shareholder from commencing proceedings to declare the merger void.

Although respondents have proffered each of these theories as establishing a chain of causal connection in which the proxy statement is claimed to have been an "essential link," neither theory presents the proxy solicitation as essential in the sense of *Mills'* causal sequence, in which the solicitation links a directors' proposal with the votes legally required to authorize the action proposed. As a consequence, each theory would, if adopted, extend the scope of *Borak* actions beyond the ambit of *Mills*, and expand the class of plaintiffs entitled to bring *Borak* actions to include shareholders whose initial authorization of the transaction prompting the proxy solicitation is unnecessary.

.   .   .

[W]e can find no manifestation of [Congressional] intent to recognize a cause of action (or class of plaintiffs) as broad as respondents' theory of causation would entail. . . .

A

. . .

[T]hreats of speculative claims and procedural intractability are inherent in respondents' theory of causation linked through the directors' desire for a cosmetic vote. Causation would turn on inferences about what the corporate directors would have thought and done without the minority shareholder approval unneeded to authorize action. A subsequently dissatisfied minority shareholder would have virtual license to allege that managerial timidity would have doomed corporate action but for the ostensible approval induced by a misleading statement, and opposing claims of hypothetical diffidence and hypothetical boldness on the part of directors would probably provide enough depositions in the usual case to preclude any judicial resolution short of the credibility judgments that can only come after trial. Reliable evidence would seldom exist. . . . The issues would be hazy, their litigation protracted, and their resolution unreliable. Given a choice, we would reject any theory of causation that raised such prospects, and we reject this one.

B

The theory of causal necessity derived from the requirements of Virginia law dealing with postmerger ratification seeks to identify the essential character of the proxy solicitation from its function in obtaining the minority approval that would preclude a minority suit attacking the merger. Since the link is said to be a step in the process of barring a class of shareholders from resort to a state remedy otherwise available, this theory of causation rests upon the proposition of policy that § 14(a) should provide a federal remedy whenever a false or misleading proxy statement results in the loss under state law of a shareholder plaintiff's state remedy for the enforcement of a state right. . . .

This case does not, however, require us to decide whether § 14(a) provides a cause of action for lost state remedies, since there is no indication in the law or facts before us that the proxy solicitation resulted in any such loss. The contrary appears to be the case. Assuming the soundness of respondents' characterization of the proxy statement as materially misleading, the very terms of the Virginia statute indicate that a favorable minority vote induced by the solicitation would not suffice to render the merger invulnerable to later attack on the ground of the conflict. The statute bars a shareholder from seeking to avoid a transaction tainted by a director's conflict if, inter alia, the minority shareholders ratified the transaction following disclosure of the material facts of the transaction and the conflict. Va. Code § 13.1–691(A)(2) (1989). Assuming that the material facts about the merger and Beddow's interests were not accurately disclosed, the minority votes were inadequate to ratify the merger under state law, and there was no loss of state remedy to connect the proxy solicitation with harm to minority shareholders irredressable under state law. . . .

IV

The judgment of the Court of Appeals is reversed.

It is so ordered.

■ JUSTICE SCALIA, concurring in part and concurring in the judgment.

I

As I understand the Court's opinion, the statement "In the opinion of the Directors, this is a high value for the shares" would produce liability if in fact it was not a high value and the Directors knew that. It would not produce liability if in fact it was not a high value but the Directors honestly believed otherwise. The statement "The Directors voted to accept the proposal because they believe it offers a high value" would not produce liability if in fact the Directors' genuine motive was quite different—except that it would produce liability if the proposal in fact did not offer a high value and the Directors knew that.

I agree with all of this. However, not every sentence that has the word "opinion" in it, or that refers to motivation for Directors' actions, leads us into this psychic thicket. Sometimes such a sentence actually represents facts as facts rather than opinions—and in that event no more need be done than apply the normal rules for § 14(a) liability. I think that is the situation here. In my view, the statement at issue in this case is most fairly read as affirming separately both the fact of the Directors' opinion and the accuracy of the facts upon which the opinion was assertedly based. It reads as follows: "The Plan of Merger has been approved by the Board of Directors because it provides an opportunity for the Bank's public shareholders to achieve a high value for their shares." Had it read "because in their estimation it provides an opportunity, etc." it would have set forth nothing but an opinion. As written, however, it asserts both that the Board of Directors acted for a particular reason and that that reason is correct. . . .

If the present case were to proceed, therefore, I think the normal § 14(a) principles governing misrepresentation of fact would apply.

[The opinion of Justice Stevens, with whom Justice Marshall joins, concurring in part and dissenting in part, is omitted.—Eds.]

■ JUSTICE KENNEDY, with whom JUSTICE MARSHALL, JUSTICE BLACKMUN, and JUSTICE STEVENS join, concurring in part and dissenting in part.

. . . . With respect, I dissent from Part III of the Court's opinion.

. . .

II

. . .

B

The Court seems to assume, based upon the footnote in *Mills* reserving the question, that Sandberg bears a special burden to demonstrate causation because the public shareholders held only 15 percent of the Bank's stock. . . . Here, First American Bankshares, Inc. (FABI) and Virginia Bankshares, Inc. (VBI) retained the option to back out of the transaction if dissatisfied with the reaction of the minority shareholders, or if concerned that the merger would result in liability for violation of duties to the minority shareholders. The merger agreement was conditioned upon approval by two-thirds of the shareholders and VBI could have voted its shares against the merger if it so decided. . . .

The Court's distinction presumes that a majority shareholder will vote in favor of management's proposal even if proxy disclosure suggests that the transaction is unfair to minority shareholders or that the board of directors or majority shareholder are in breach of fiduciary duties to the minority. If the majority shareholder votes against the transaction in order to comply with its state law duties, or out of fear of liability, or upon concluding that the transaction will injure the reputation of the business, this ought not to be characterized as nonvoting causation. Of course, when the majority shareholder dominates the voting process, as was the case here, it may prefer to avoid the embarrassment of voting against its own proposal and so may cancel the meeting of shareholders at which the vote was to have been taken. For practical purposes, the result is the same: because of full disclosure the transaction does not go forward and the resulting injury to minority shareholders is avoided. . . .

. . .

Stahl v. Gibraltar Financial Corporation

967 F.2d 335 (9th Cir.1992).

■ KOZINSKI, CIRCUIT JUDGE.

We consider whether a shareholder who receives false or misleading proxy statements must actually have cast his vote in reliance on them as a condition for bringing suit under section 14(a) of the Securities Exchange Act of 1934 and SEC Rule 14a–9.

Facts

Myron Stahl owned stock in Gibraltar Financial Corporation; he received an invitation to the company's 1987 annual meeting together with a proxy statement soliciting votes on several proposals for those shareholders unable to attend. One of these was a proposed amendment to the company's certificate of incorporation, purportedly in response to recent changes in Delaware law, that would insulate Gibraltar's directors from monetary liability. In connection with this proposal, the board of directors represented that it was "not aware of any pending or threatened litigation which would be affected by the approval of [the indemnity amendment]." Joint Proxy Statement/Prospectus at 26.

Stahl sued the corporation in an attempt to forestall the vote at the annual meeting. He alleged that the proxy statement "fails to disclose the existence of certain facts known by management to be relevant to the advisability of [the indemnity amendment]." In particular, Stahl alleged that a business of which he was a principal was involved in an ongoing legal dispute with Gibraltar, that Gibraltar's directors knew of this dispute and thus that the quoted representation was false or misleading. The district court denied the request for a preliminary injunction and Stahl did not appeal.

The annual meeting took place as scheduled; Stahl showed up in person and voted against the adoption of the indemnity amendment, but the effort was futile: The proposal was adopted by vote of a majority of the shareholders. Stahl's case was still pending in the district court, and several months later Stahl filed an amended complaint seeking to have the corporate action undone. The district court granted Gibraltar's motion for judgment on the pleadings, holding that because Stahl had not voted his proxy in reliance on the alleged misstatements he had no standing to sue as an individual. Stahl appeals.[6]

Discussion

. . .

In Gaines v. Haughton, 645 F.2d 761, 774 (9th Cir.1981), cert. denied, 454 U.S. 1145 (1982), we held that "shareholders who do not rely on allegedly misleading or deceptive proxy solicitations lack standing to assert direct (as opposed to derivative) equitable actions under § 14(a)." We derived this bright-line rule from Klaus v. Hi–Shear Corp., 528 F.2d 225 (9th Cir.1975). The *Klaus* analysis merits setting forth at length:

> In enacting section 14(a), Congress intended to guarantee the integrity of the processes of corporate democracy. Section 14(a) is intended to insure that a shareholder entitled to vote on corporate decisions knows how his vote will be cast before he grants his proxy to management or others. The harm to be averted is only indirectly that to the individual shareholder. Mills v. Electric Auto–Lite Co., 396 U.S. 375 (1970); J.I. Case Co. v. Borak, 377 U.S. 426, 432 (1964). Although a demonstration that proxies were obtained by materially misleading solicitation establishes a violation of section 14(a), the relief available to a plaintiff who did not himself grant a proxy depends on equitable considerations based on "the best interests of the shareholders as a whole." *Mills*, 396 U.S. at 388. Klaus did not himself grant a proxy. . . . [He] has not demonstrated equitable reasons that would justify rescinding, in effect, the proxies which may or may not have been illegally solicited.

Id. at 232.

The *Klaus–Gaines* rule is subject to criticism on several grounds. Section 14(a) states that "it *shall* be unlawful" for any person to solicit

---

6. Since this litigation was commenced, Gibraltar has filed for bankruptcy. This action continues by virtue of a bankruptcy court release of the automatic stay. 11 U.S.C. § 362.

proxies in contravention of SEC rules (emphasis added), while rule 14a–9 prohibits all proxy solicitations which are "false or misleading with respect to any material fact." As the Supreme Court noted in *Mills*, "use of a solicitation that is materially misleading *is itself* a violation of law." 396 U.S. at 383 (emphasis added). . . . As materiality is an objective standard, it should not matter whether any particular shareholder was actually misled by the challenged misrepresentations.

Moreover, it is somewhat incongruous to deny standing to those shareholders who ferret out the misstatements but grant it to those who were beguiled. Because "the purpose of § 14(a) is to prevent management or others from obtaining authorization for corporate action by means of deceptive or inadequate disclosure in proxy solicitation," *Borak*, 377 U.S. at 431, those shareholders who recognize the deception should be able to sue. The *Klaus–Gaines* rule means that shareholders who see through the deception can never sue to remedy it, because they will not have relied on the misstatements. Catch–22.

. . .

Perhaps recognizing its shortcomings, we have sharply circumscribed the *Klaus–Gaines* rule. In Western District Council v. Louisiana Pacific Corp., 892 F.2d 1412, 1414 n. 1 (9th Cir.1989), we noted that "we are bound by our decision in *Gaines*, and decline to reconsider it." Nevertheless, we held that a plaintiff could bring suit before the proxy vote:

> If *Gaines* bars Western's suit, then a shareholder who learns of a material omission in a proxy statement before an election could never sue directly, because a shareholder aware of the omission will not rely on the proxy statement when voting. Further, no shareholder could sue before the election, because those shareholders satisfying *Gaines'* requirement that they have relied on the statements would be precisely those who were ignorant of the information necessary to sue until after they voted. Direct action would be available only after the election and only to those shareholders who voted in reliance on the proxy statements. We decline so to limit shareholders' options.

Id. at 1415–16;. . . .

The rule in this circuit is thus that a shareholder such as Stahl, who did not rely on the alleged misrepresentations, has standing to bring a direct suit before the vote but not after. . . .

Although the distinctions between *Western* and the *Klaus–Gaines* rule may be somewhat arbitrary, we would be required to decide whether this case is closer to one than the other were it not for the Supreme Court's most recent section 14(a) case, Virginia Bankshares, Inc. v. Sandberg, __ U.S. __, 111 S.Ct. 2749 (1991). The Court noted: "Although most minority shareholders gave the proxies requested, respondent Sandberg *did not*, and *after* approval of the merger she sought damages in the United States District Court." 111 S.Ct. at 2756 (emphasis added). Because standing is a threshold question, without which a court is powerless to proceed, Sandberg presumably had standing to bring suit under section

14(a). . . . Because standing to sue is jurisdictional and was considered by the court below, we take the Supreme Court's consideration of Sandberg's section 14(a) action to mean that a plaintiff may bring a direct action after the complained-of proxy vote even where he has not himself relied on the challenged misstatements. As the Supreme Court's implicit holding in *Virginia Bankshares* is contrary to our opinions in *Klaus* and *Gaines*, we conclude that they have been overruled. Under *Virginia Bankshares*, shareholders such as Stahl who do not vote their proxies in reliance on the alleged misstatements have standing to sue under section 14(a)—both before and after the vote is taken.

Conclusion

Stahl has standing to sue. Accordingly, we REVERSE the judgment of the district court and REMAND for further proceedings consistent with this opinion.

NOTE

Under the corporate law of many states shareholders who object to a merger may sue for the appraised cash value of their shares. (This "appraisal right" is examined more fully in Chapter 6, Section 1.) If the proxy solicitation in *Virginia Bankshares* had induced Sandberg to give Bank directors a proxy, and if that proxy had caused her to lose her appraisal rights, would she have been able to show sufficient causation to sue for damages? In Wilson v. Great American Industries, Inc., 979 F.2d 924 (2d Cir.1992), the court held that she would indeed. "The deceptive proxy," it explained, "plainly constitutes an 'essential link' in accomplishing the forfeiture of this state right." Id. at 931.

ANALYSIS

1. In *Virginia Bankshares*, suppose the statement offered by the corporation had been, "The Board of Directors hired KBW to provide an objective opinion on whether the price of $42 per share is fair. KBW concluded that it is. The Board therefore recommends acceptance." Would Sandberg still have had a legitimate basis for complaint? What if the same language had been used except for excision of the word "therefore"? What if, after the second sentence within the quotation marks, the following sentence had been inserted, "On the basis of an appraisal of the value of the properties owned by the corporation, a higher book value might be found and a higher share value might also be regarded as fair."

2. Suppose that George Ramrod owns 60 percent of Parent Corporation and is CEO and Chair of the Board. Parent owns 55 percent of Childe Corp. and Ramrod owns 20 percent. Childe is merged into Parent in a transaction that required approval of two-thirds of the Childe shareholders. The merger is approved with the affirmative votes of Parent, Ramrod, and more than half of the remaining shareholders. Malcom Tent owns one

percent of the Childe shares and seeks to upset the merger on the basis of what he alleges to be a misleading proxy statement. Parent moves for summary judgment. What result?

3. In the *Virginia Bankshares* setting, if there was indeed a violation of the proxy rules, even though none of the minority shareholders had a right of action under the federal securities laws, the SEC could have brought some sort of enforcement action. (Generally the SEC may seek an injunction or some other equitable remedy or, if the violation was "willful," criminal penalties.) What do you suppose is the likelihood that it would do so? In J.I. Case Co. v. Borak, 377 U.S. 426 (1964), the Court offered the following explanation of its conclusion that there is an implied private right of action for violation of the proxy rules:

> Private enforcement of the proxy rules provides a necessary supplement to Commission action. . . . The Commission advises that it examines over 2,000 proxy statements annually and each of them must necessarily be expedited. Time does not permit an independent examination of the facts set out in the proxy material and this results in the Commission's acceptance of the representations contained therein at their face value, unless contrary to other material on file with it. Indeed, on the allegations of respondent's complaint, the proxy material failed to disclose alleged unlawful market manipulation . . . and this unlawful manipulation would not have been apparent to the Commission until after the merger.

How, if at all, can you reconcile this explanation of the need for a private right of action with the refusal by the majority in *Virginia Bankshares* to allow such an action?

4. In *Stahl*, the court noted (footnote 6) that Gibraltar had filed for bankruptcy. A bankruptcy filing automatically stays various types of actions, including Stahl's, but the bankruptcy judge had "released" the stay, which means that the judge decided that the action could proceed (and that Gibraltar could pay the lawyers presenting its case). Why should Gibraltar have continued to resist Stahl's lawsuit? If Gibraltar was plainly insolvent, was Stahl a proper plaintiff? What interest did he have in the outcome of the litigation? Was there any state-law remedy for the wrongful conduct of which Stahl complained?

PROBLEM

Cypress Club, Inc. (CC) owns an upscale and overpriced restaurant in the foothills of Topanga Canyon, northwest of Los Angeles. Because of the glut of upscale overpriced restaurants in the area, CC is losing money. Its stock is publicly traded on the over-the-counter market. Issued for $50 per share just five years ago, it now trades at $3.00. An elderly financier named General Guy Sternwood owns 65 percent of the stock.

1. Suppose that CC directors propose a merger with Sternwood Investments, Inc. (SII). Through the merger, CC shareholders will receive for each CC share SII shares worth $3.30. For the merger to take place, it

must be approved by a majority of the CC shares. Suppose further, however, that the proxy materials explaining the terms of the merger do not disclose (i) that Sternwood and one Eddie Mars each own 30 percent of SII and (ii) that Mars and Sternwood are about to be indicted in Tokyo for their role in a stock-manipulation scheme on the Tokyo Stock Exchange.

You, as a CC shareholder, discover the TSE connection and sue to block the vote. Will you win? Suppose you discover the TSE connection when the indictments are issued after the vote has taken place. Can you recover damages? What would they be? Does it matter whether SII stock is publicly traded?

2. Suppose that CC directors propose a merger with West Publishing Company. Through the merger, CC shareholders will receive for each CC share West shares worth $2.70. Suppose further that the management disclosed all the details of the merger, but few CC shareholders bothered to read the proxy material. Accordingly, 95 percent of the shareholders approved the merger. You sue for damages. What result?

D. SHAREHOLDER PROPOSALS

Lovenheim v. Iroquois Brands, Ltd.

618 F.Supp. 554 (D.D.C.1985).

I. BACKGROUND

Plaintiff Peter C. Lovenheim, owner of two hundred shares of common stock in Iroquois Brands, Ltd. (hereinafter "Iroquois/Delaware"), seeks to bar Iroquois/Delaware from excluding from the proxy materials being sent to all shareholders in preparation for an upcoming shareholder meeting information concerning a proposed resolution he intends to offer at the meeting. Mr. Lovenheim's proposed resolution relates to the procedure used to force-feed geese for production of pâté de foie gras in France,[2] a type of pâté imported by Iroquois/Delaware. Specifically, his resolution calls upon the Directors of Iroquois/Delaware to:

2. Pâté de foie gras is made from the liver of geese. According to Mr. Lovenheim's affidavit, force-feeding is frequently used in order to expand the liver and thereby produce a larger quantity of pate. Mr. Lovenheim's affidavit also contains a description of the force-feeding process:

Force-feeding usually begins when the geese are four months old. On some farms where feeding is mechanized, the bird's body and wings are placed in a metal brace and its neck is stretched. Through a funnel inserted 10–12 inches down the throat of the goose, a machine pumps up to 400 grams of corn-based mash into its stomach. An elastic band around the goose's throat prevents regurgitation. When feeding is manual, a handler uses a funnel and stick to force the mash down.

Affidavit of Peter C. Lovenheim at para. 7. Plaintiff contends that such force-feeding is a form of cruelty to animals. Id.

Plaintiff has offered no evidence that force-feeding is used by Iroquois/Delaware's supplier in producing the pâté imported by Iroquois/Delaware. However his proposal calls upon the committee he seeks to create to investigate this question.

form a committee to study the methods by which its French supplier produces pâté de foie gras, and report to the shareholders its findings and opinions, based on expert consultation, on whether this production method causes undue distress, pain or suffering to the animals involved and, if so, whether further distribution of this product should be discontinued until a more humane production method is developed.

Attachment to Affidavit of Peter C. Lovenheim.

Mr. Lovenheim's right to compel Iroquois/Delaware to insert information concerning his proposal in the proxy materials turns on the applicability of § 14(a) of the Securities Exchange Act of 1934 . . . . ("the Exchange Act"), and the shareholder proposal rule promulgated by the Securities and Exchange Commission ("SEC"), Rule 14a–8. That rule states in pertinent part:

> If any security holder of an issuer notifies the issuer of his intention to present a proposal for action at a forthcoming meeting of the issuer's security holders, the issuer shall set forth the proposal in its proxy statement and identify it in its form of proxy and provide means by which security holders [presenting a proposal may present in the proxy statement a statement of not more than [500] words in support of the proposal].

Iroquois/Delaware has refused to allow information concerning Mr. Lovenheim's proposal to be included in proxy materials being sent in connection with the next annual shareholders meeting. In doing so, Iroquois/Delaware relies on an exception to the general requirement of Rule 14a–8, Rule 14a–8([i])(5). That exception provides that an issuer of securities "may omit a proposal and any statement in support thereof" from its proxy statement and form of proxy:

> if the proposal relates to operations which account for less than 5 percent of the issuer's total assets at the end of its most recent fiscal year, and for less than 5 percent of its net earnings and gross sales for its most recent fiscal year, and is not otherwise significantly related to the issuer's business. . . .

II. LIKELIHOOD OF PLAINTIFF PREVAILING ON MERITS

. . .

C. Applicability of Rule 14a–8([i])(5) Exception

[T]he likelihood of plaintiff's prevailing in this litigation turns primarily on the applicability to plaintiff's proposal of the exception to the shareholder proposal rule contained in Rule 14a–8([i])(5).

Iroquois/Delaware's reliance on the argument that this exception applies is based on the following information contained in the affidavit of its president: Iroquois/Delaware has annual revenues of $141 million with $6 million in annual profits and $78 million in assets. In contrast, its pâté de foie gras sales were just $79,000 last year, representing a net loss on pâté sales of $3,121. Iroquois/Delaware has only $34,000 in assets related to pate. Thus none of the company's net earnings and less than .05 percent of its assets are implicated by plaintiff's proposal. These levels are obviously far below the five percent threshold set forth in the first portion of the exception claimed by Iroquois/Delaware.

Plaintiff does not contest that his proposed resolution relates to a matter of little economic significance to Iroquois/Delaware. Nevertheless he contends that the Rule 14a–8([i])(5) exception is not applicable as it cannot be said that his proposal "is not otherwise significantly related to the issuer's business" as is required by the final portion of that exception. In other words, plaintiff's argument that Rule 14a–8 does not permit omission of his proposal rests on the assertion that the rule and statute on which it is based do not permit omission merely because a proposal is not economically significant where a proposal has "ethical or social significance."[3]

. . .

The Court would note that the applicability of the Rule 14a–8([i])(5) exception to Mr. Lovenheim's proposal represents a close question given the lack of clarity in the exception itself. In effect, plaintiff relies on the word "otherwise," suggesting that it indicates the drafters of the rule intended that other noneconomic tests of significance be used. Iroquois/Delaware relies on the fact that the rule examines other significance in relation to the issuer's business. Because of the apparent ambiguity of the rule, the Court considers the history of the shareholder proposal rule in determining the proper interpretation of the most recent version of that rule.

Prior to 1983, paragraph 14a–8([i])(5) excluded proposals "not significantly related to the issuer's business" but did not contain an objective economic significance test such as the five percent of sales, assets, and earnings specified in the first part of the current version. Although a series of SEC decisions through 1976 allowing issuers to exclude proposals challenging compliance with the Arab economic boycott of Israel allowed exclusion if the issuer did less than one percent of their business with Arab countries or Israel, the Commission stated later in 1976 that it did "not believe that subparagraph ([i])(5) should be hinged solely on the economic relativity of a proposal." Securities Exchange Act Release No. 12,999, 41 Fed. Reg. 52,994, 52,997 (1976). Thus the Commission required inclusion "in many situations in which the related business comprised less than one

3. The assertion that the proposal is significant in an ethical and social sense relies on plaintiff's argument that "the very availability of a market for products that may be obtained through the inhumane force-feeding of geese cannot help but contribute to the continuation of such treatment." Plaintiff's brief characterizes the humane treatment of animals as among the foundations of western culture and cites in support of this view the Seven Laws of Noah, an animal protection statute enacted by the Massachu-setts Bay Colony in 1641, numerous federal statutes enacted since 1877, and animal protection laws existing in all fifty states and the District of Columbia. An additional indication of the significance of plaintiff's proposal is the support of such leading organizations in the field of animal care as the American Society for the Prevention of Cruelty to Animals and The Humane Society of the United States for measures aimed at discontinuing use of force-feeding.

percent" of the company's revenues, profits or assets "where the proposal has raised policy questions important enough to be considered 'significantly related' to the issuer's business."

As indicated above, the 1983 revision adopted the five percent test of economic significance in an effort to create a more objective standard. Nevertheless, in adopting this standard, the Commission stated that proposals will be includable notwithstanding their "failure to reach the specified economic thresholds if a significant relationship to the issuer's business is demonstrated on the face of the resolution or supporting statement." Securities Exchange Act Release No. 19,135, 47 Fed. Reg. 47,420, 47,428 (1982). Thus it seems clear based on the history of the rule that "the meaning of 'significantly related' is not limited to economic significance." . . .

This Court need not consider . . . whether a rule allowing exclusion of all proposals not meeting specified levels of economic significance violates the scope of § 14(a) of the Exchange Act. . . . Whether or not the Securities and Exchange Commission could properly adopt such a rule, the Court cannot ignore the history of the rule, which reveals no decision by the Commission to limit the determination to the economic criteria relied on by Iroquois/Delaware. The Court therefore holds that in light of the ethical and social significance of plaintiff's proposal and the fact that it implicates significant levels of sales, plaintiff has shown a likelihood of prevailing on the merits with regard to the issue of whether his proposal is "otherwise significantly related" to Iroquois/Delaware's business.[4]

III. OTHER FACTORS BEARING ON INJUNCTIVE RELIEF

In addition to considering the likelihood of plaintiff's prevailing on the merits, consideration of plaintiff's motion for preliminary injunction requires a determination as to whether plaintiff will suffer irreparable injury without such relief, whether issuance of the requested relief will substantially harm other parties, and the public interest. . . .

A. Irreparable Injury

In bringing this action, plaintiff sought to include his proposal in Iroquois/Delaware's 1985 proxy statement. Counsel for Iroquois/Delaware represents that the proxy statement is to be mailed on or immediately after April 6, 1985. Thus plaintiff contends that absent preliminary relief, the relief sought in his action will be moot.

In response, Iroquois/Delaware asserts there is no possibility of irreparable injury as plaintiff has conceded his resolution is likely to fail and even if the resolution passes, it would only require appointment of a study committee. This argument misstates the significance of the shareholder proposal rule, which is aimed at guaranteeing that shareholders have access

---

4. The result would, of course, be different if plaintiff's proposal was ethically significant in the abstract but had no meaningful relationship to the business of Iroquois/Delaware as Iroquois/Delaware was not engaged in the business of importing pâté de foie gras.

to proxy statements whether or not their proposals are likely to pass and regardless of the immediate force of the resolution if enacted. Absent a preliminary injunction, plaintiff will suffer irreparable harm by losing the opportunity to communicate his concern with those shareholders not attending the upcoming shareholder meeting.

B.   Injury to Iroquois/Delaware

Plaintiff asserts that requiring Iroquois/Delaware to include the Lovenheim proposal in its proxy statement would not cause undue harm to the company. Indeed, Iroquois/Delaware included the proposal in its 1983 proxy materials and has not claimed any resulting harm.

Iroquois/Delaware asserts that granting the injunction plaintiff seeks could have a distinctly adverse impact on the company. This contention is based on the affidavit of Iroquois/Delaware's president which reports that investors tend to react negatively to the institution of litigation and to the issuance of injunctions against a company. McCaffrey Affidavit para. 9. The affidavit also raises the possibility that investors may conclude that Iroquois/Delaware is involved in the mistreatment of animals. Id. at paras. 10–11. However, these contentions would appear to be largely speculative.

C.   Public Interest

Plaintiff contends that the public interest represented in the Exchange Act is served by granting injunctive relief and allowing all shareholders to make an informed vote on the proposal. In contrast, Iroquois/Delaware submits that an injunction would be contrary to the "public interest in permitting businesses to function free from harassment, and in preventing proxy statements from becoming cluttered." Given the "overriding" public interest embodied in § 14(a) and the shareholder proposal rule in assuring shareholders the right to control the important decisions which affect corporations . . ., the Court finds that granting the preliminary injunction would be consistent with the public interest.

IV.   CONCLUSION

For the reasons discussed above, the Court concludes that plaintiff's motion for preliminary injunction should be granted.

NOTE

The SEC reluctantly referees the shareholder proposal process. If the subject corporation's management believes the proposal can be excluded from the proxy statement, it files a notice with the SEC that the firm intends to exclude the proposal. If the SEC staff agrees that the proposal can be excluded, it will issue a so-called no-action letter, which simply states that the staff will not recommend that the Commission bring an enforcement proceeding against the issuer if the proposal is excluded. On the other hand, if the staff determines that the proposal should be included in management's proxy statement, the staff will notify the issuer that the SEC may bring an enforcement action if the proposal is excluded. The SEC staff can also take an intermediate position; in effect, it says to the proponent: "As your proposal or your supporting statement are presently drafted, they can be excluded under Rule 14a–8. However, if you revise them as follows, we believe that management must include the proposal." Whichever side loses at the staff level in theory can ask the actual Commissioners to review the staff's decision. After review by the Commissioners, the losing party can in theory seek judicial review by the United States Circuit Court of Appeals for the District of Columbia. These reviews are very rare; more typically, if management is the losing party it will simply acquiesce in the staff's decision. If the shareholder proponent loses, he or she may seek an injunction in federal district court, as did the plaintiff in the *Lovenheim* case.

ANALYSIS

1.   Why did Lovenheim merely ask Iroquois Brands' board to form a study committee? Put another way, why didn't Lovenheim offer a proposal prohibiting the company from selling pate?

2.   Think about your favorite social or political cause. Suppose you wanted to get a shareholder proposal relating on that cause on a corporate proxy statement. Assume that the proposal would not meet the 5 percent economic significance test of Rule 14a–8(i)(5). On what basis would you show that the proposal has sufficient ethical or social significance to justify its inclusion in the proxy statement under Lovenheim?

3.   Although Iroquois Brands contended that Lovenheim's proposal might cause investors to conclude that the company was involved in cruelty to animals, the court dismissed that concern as "largely speculative." Was the court correct in giving such short shrift to this possibility?

The New York City Employees' Retirement System v. Dole Food Company, Inc.

795 F.Supp. 95 (S.D.N.Y.), appeal dismissed as moot and order vacated, 969 F.2d 1430 (2d Cir.1992).

. . .

I. *Background*

   NYCERS is a public pension fund that owns approximately 164,841 shares of common stock in Dole Food Company, Inc. ("Dole"). . . .   On December 12, 1991, New York City Comptroller Elizabeth Holtzman, in her capacity as the custodian of NYCERS' assets, wrote to the executive vice president of Dole, requesting Dole to include the following proposal ("the NYCERS proposal") in its proxy statement prior to its annual meeting:

NEW YORK CITY EMPLOYEE'S [*sic.*]
RETIREMENT SYSTEM
SHAREHOLDER RESOLUTION
ON HEALTH CARE
TO DOLE FOOD COMPANY, INC.

WHEREAS: The Dole Food Company is concerned with remaining competitive in the domestic and world marketplace, acknowledging the positive relationship between the health and well being of its employees and productivity, and the resulting effect on corporate growth and financial stability; and

WHEREAS: Sustained double-digit increases in health care costs have put severe financial pressure on a company attempting to continue to provide adequate health care for its employees and their dependents; and

WHEREAS: The company has a societal obligation to conduct its affairs in a way which promotes the health and well being of all;

BE IT THEREFORE RESOLVED: That the shareholders request the Board of Directors to establish a committee of the Board consisting of outside and independent directors for the purpose of evaluating the impact of a representative cross section of the various health care reform proposals being considered by national policy makers on the company and their [*sic.*] competitive standing in domestic and international markets. These various proposals can be grouped in three generic categories; the single payor model (as in the Canadian plan), the limited payor (as in the Pepper Commission Report) and the employer mandated (as in the Kennedy–Waxman legislation).

Further, the aforementioned committee should be directed to prepare a report of its findings. The report should be prepared in a reasonable time, at a reasonable cost and should be made available to any shareholder upon written request.

SUPPORTING STATEMENT

Our nation is now at a crossroads on health care. Because of cutbacks in public programs, jobs that offer no benefits and efforts by employers to shift health care costs to workers, 50 million Americans have health care coverage that is inadequate to meet their needs and another 37 million have no protection at all.

The United States spends $2 billion a day, or eleven percent of its gross national product, on health care.

As insurance premiums increase 18 to 30 percent a year, basic health care has moved well beyond the reach of a growing number of working families. This increase also places heavy pressure on employer labor costs. There is no end in sight to this trend.

As a result and because of the significant social and public policy issues attendant to operations involving health care, we urge shareholders to SUPPORT the resolution.

On January 16, 1992, J. Brett Tibbitts, deputy general counsel of Dole Food Company, Inc., wrote to the office of chief counsel of the Securities & Exchange Commission's ("SEC") division of corporation finance and stated Dole's position that Dole could exclude the NYCERS proposal from its proxy statement because the proposal concerned employee benefits, an assertedly "ordinary business operation". . . .

On February 10, 1992, John Brousseau, special counsel to the SEC's division of corporation finance, responded to Tibbitts' letter with the following written statement:

> The proposal relates to the preparation of a report by a Committee of the Company's Board of Directors to evaluate various health-care proposals being considered by national policy makers.

> There appears to be some basis for your view that the proposal may be excluded pursuant to rule 14a–8(c)(7) because the proposal is directed at involving the Company in the political or legislative process relating to an aspect of the Company's operations. Accordingly, we will not recommend enforcement action to the Commission if the proposal is omitted from the Company's proxy materials. In reaching a position, the staff has not found it necessary to address the alternative basis for omission on which the Company relies.

On March 19, 1992, Brousseau reported to NYCERS that the SEC had denied NYCERS' request for the SEC to review the SEC staff determination on the NYCERS proposal. Holtzman Afft., Exhibit E. On April 9, 1992, NYCERS brought the instant action. In conjunction with NYCERS' request for an order to show cause, NYCERS submitted an affidavit of Theodore R. Marmor, a professor of political science and public policy at Yale University. In his affidavit, Professor Marmor averred, inter alia, that (1) at least 37 million Americans have no health insurance; (2) the United States spends more on health per capita than any other developed nation; (3) health care expenditures in 1989 represented 56 percent of pre-tax company profits in 1989, as compared to 8 percent in 1985; and (4) the national average cost for health care per employee is $3,200, and some large companies pay $5,000 or more per employee. . . .

II. *Discussion*

. . .

A. Substantial Likelihood of Success on the Merits

The federal securities regulation that governs proposals of securities holders is 17 C.F.R. § 14a–8 ("Rule 14a–8"). Rule 14a–8(a) states in pertinent part:

> If any security holder of a registrant notifies the registrant of his intention to present a proposal for action at a forthcoming meeting of the registrant's security holders, the registrant shall set forth the proposal in its proxy statement. . . .

However, Rule 14a–8[i] allows a corporation to omit a shareholder proposal from its proxy statement because of certain enumerated circumstances. In substance, Dole argues that the instant matter fits within the "ordinary business operations," "insignificant relation," and "beyond power to effectuate" exceptions enumerated in Rule 14a–8[i].

The corporation has the burden to show that a proposal fits within an exception to Rule 14a–8[i].   .   .   .

1. *Rule 14a–8[i](7): "Ordinary Business Operations"*

Rule 14a–8[i](7) states that a corporation may exclude a shareholder proposal from a proxy statement

> if the proposal deals with a matter relating to the conduct of the ordinary business operations of the registrant.[2]

.   .   . The SEC's commentary on the current version of the "ordinary business operations" exception states, "Where proposals involve business matters that are mundane in nature and do not involve any substantial policy or other considerations, the sub-paragraph may be relied upon to omit them." Adoption of Amendments Relating to Proposals by Security Holders, 41 Fed.Reg. 52,994, 52,998 (1976) (emphasis added). This commentary indicates that even if the proposal touches on the way daily business matters are conducted, the statement may not be excluded if it involves a significant strategic decision as to those daily business matters, i.e., one that will significantly affect the manner in which a company does business.   .   .   .

While we give due deference to the SEC staff opinion letter in this case and other similar cases, we find that NYCERS has shown that the proposal does not relate to "ordinary business operations." If one aspect of "ordinary business operations" is certain, it is that the outcome of close cases such as the instant one are largely fact-dependent. Nevertheless, Dole has not provided the Court with any information on (1) whether Dole has a health insurance program; (2) if such a program exists at Dole, how it operates; and (3) the amount of corporate financial resources that Dole devotes to health insurance. Instead, Dole argues, "To the extent [the NYCERS proposal] relates to Dole's business at all, it relates to its employee relations and health care benefits, a matter traditionally within the 'ordinary business' category."   .   .   .

.   .   . The question of which plan, if any, that Dole should support, and how Dole would choose to function under the plans (e.g., "pay or play") could have large financial consequences on Dole.   .   .   .

2. In 1983, the SEC stated that although the SEC had previously deemed requests for the corporation to prepare reports on specific aspects of their business to be not excludable under Rule 14a–8[i](7), "henceforth, the staff will consider whether the subject matter of the special report or the committee involves a matter of ordinary business; where it does, the proposal will be excludable under Rule 14a–8[i](7)." Exchange Act Release No. 20091 (August 13, 1983).

The proposed report primarily relates to Dole's policy making on an issue of social significance that, while not relating to a specific health care policy at Dole, nevertheless relates to a distinct type of operations that Dole has undoubtedly grappled with in the past. . . . Accordingly, we do not find that the instant proposal relates to "ordinary business operations."

2. *Rule 14a–8[i](5): "Insignificant Relationship"*

Exception

Rule 14a–8[i](5) states that a corporation may exclude a shareholder proposal from a proxy statement

> [i]f the proposal relates to operations which account for less than 5 percent of the registrant's total assets at the end of its most recent fiscal year, and for less than 5 percent of its net earnings and gross sales for its most recent fiscal year, *and* is not otherwise significantly related to the registrant's business. (Emphasis supplied.)

Dole does not dispute that the clear language of the NYCERS proposal in large part relates to national health insurance's impact on Dole. Without specific reference to Rule 14a–8[i](5), Dole argues that the NYCERS proposal lacked a discrete nexus to Dole's distinct line of business, presumably the manufacture of food products. Dole's argument is essentially the same as the exception referred to in the last phrase of Rule 14a–8[i](5), i.e., that the proposal is "not otherwise significantly related to the registrant's business." . . .

We need not address Dole's "nexus" argument because we find the activity addressed by the NYCERS proposal relates to activities that likely occupy in outlays more than five percent of Dole's income. It is substantially likely that Dole's health insurance outlays constitute more than five percent of its income.

3. *Rule 14a–8[i](6): "Beyond Power to Effectuate"*

Exception

Rule 14a–8[i](6) states that a corporation need not include a shareholder proposal on a proxy statement

> if the proposal deals with a matter beyond the registrant's power to effectuate. . . .

Dole argues, "The NYCERS proposal requests the analysis of, and implicitly suggests that Dole should attempt to influence the selection of, national health care reform proposals." Dole Supplemental Memo at 8. However, Dole does not point to any language that suggests that a necessary consequence of the proposal is political lobbying. While couched in language that clearly supports a national solution to the problems of growing health insurance costs, the NYCERS proposal merely calls for the commission of a research report on national health insurance proposals and their impact on Dole's competitive standing. Moreover, we fail to see why such a study necessarily "deals with a matter beyond the registrant's power to effectuate." . . .

Having found that the required showing has been met, this Court directs Dole to include in its proxy materials for its June 4, 1992 annual meeting NYCERS' shareholder proposal submitted to Dole by letter dated December 12, 1991.

SO ORDERED.

AFTERMATH

Of the shares voted at the meeting at which the proposal in the above case was considered, 5.4 percent voted in favor, 83.6 percent opposed, and 11 percent abstained.

Austin v. Consolidated Edison Company of New York, Inc.

788 F.Supp. 192 (S.D.N.Y.1992).

The three plaintiffs are stockholders of defendant; in addition, plaintiff Stewart Austin is a business agent and plaintiffs Daniel J. Daly and Leonard Hoffman are shop stewards of Local 1–2, Utility Workers Union (the "Union"), which represents defendant's employees. They sue as shareholders only. Defendant supplies gas, electricity and steam to customers in the New York metropolitan area.

Plaintiffs would compel defendant to include in its proxy materials for the upcoming annual shareholders meeting a non-binding resolution endorsing the idea that defendant's employees should be allowed to retire after 30 years of service, regardless of age. . . . Defendant has moved for summary judgment dismissing the complaint. For the reasons set forth below, plaintiffs' motion for a preliminary injunction is denied, defendant's motion is granted, and the complaint is dismissed.

I.

The few relevant facts are uncontested. On December 30, 1991, plaintiffs' counsel presented to defendant for inclusion in its proxy materials a proposed corporate resolution endorsing various changes in the pension rights of defendant's employees, most significant of which is one that would permit employees to retire with no actuarial reduction of their pension rights after 30 years of service, regardless of age. Under the current plan, the normal retirement age is 65, but employees may retire at or after age 60 if they meet the requirements of the so-called "rule of 75"— i.e., if their age plus years of service equal or exceed 75. The pension plan changes outlined in the proposed resolution have been announced by the Union to be a goal in its upcoming contract negotiations with Con Edison. . . .

On January 16, 1992, defendant wrote to the Securities and Exchange Commission stating its belief that the proposed resolution need not be included in the proxy materials, because the proposed resolution dealt merely with the company's day-to-day operations and because it was designed in essence to confer a benefit on and further a personal interest of its proponents that was not common to shareholders generally. Defendant sought assurance in a form referred to as a "no-action letter" that the SEC staff would not recommend that that agency sue to compel defendant to include the proposed resolution in the proxy materials. . . . On February 13, 1992 the SEC staff issued the requested no-action letter. . . .

. . .

II.

. . . Con Edison cites two [grounds for refusing to include the plaintiff's proposal]. One permits the issuing company to refuse to include a proposal in its proxy materials "if the proposal deals with a matter relating to the conduct of the ordinary business operations of the registrant." [Rule] 14a–8[i](7). The other permits the same result "if the proposal relates to the redress of a personal claim or grievance against the registrant or any other person, or if it is designed to result in a benefit to the proponent, or to further a personal interest, which benefit or interest is not shared with the other security holders at large." [Rule] 14a–8[i](4).

. . .

III.

. . .

Plaintiffs employ a variety of approaches to propel their resolution beyond the mundane. Thus, they cite the SEC's refusal to grant no-action letters in cases dealing with resolutions to employ an ombudsman who would review the fairness of public affairs programming, . . . to increase corporate charitable contributions by 400%, . . . and to limit the availability of "golden parachute" compensation packages. . . . They refer also to the agency's increasing willingness to require companies to submit to shareholder vote issues of executive compensation that go beyond "golden parachutes" to include the amount of executive salaries. . . .

. . .

Lost in this miasma of analogy and hyperbole is the SEC's long record of no-action letters on the precise subject at issue here: companies seeking to exclude pension proposals from their proxy materials. More than 50 such letters covering approximately a ten-year period are cited in an appendix to defendant's memorandum in opposition to plaintiffs' preliminary injunction motion. . . .

It is also relevant that plaintiffs have available to them the forum of collective bargaining, where they have announced their intention to raise the issue they now press. That is not to say that a subject that can be raised in collective bargaining always must be treated as "ordinary business operations." However, the availability of collective bargaining to resolve the issue does make it apparent that the issue is not so extraordinary that a shareholder vote is the only forum or the most effective forum in which it can be raised. In addition, the pension proposal in question relates to virtually the entire work force, not simply to senior management or any other particular group. It is thus not extraordinary in that sense either.

Further, however plaintiffs may perceive their own cause of enhanced pension rights, it has not yet captured public attention and concern as has the issue of senior executive compensation. Nor can plaintiffs reasonably liken their proposed resolution to the one pressed by plaintiffs in Medical Comm. for Human Rights [v. SEC, 432 F.2d 659 (D.C.Cir.), vacated as moot 404 U.S. 403 (1972)], who sought during the Viet Nam war to require a vote by Dow Chemical Company shareholders on whether that company would continue to manufacture napalm. The comparison is an uncomfortable one at best. Rather, plaintiffs' resolution shows that even an "audacious" proposal on a mundane topic is still mundane.

. . .

Because Con Edison has shown that the proffered resolution comes within the exception for "ordinary business operations," there is no need to deal also with whether it is designed simply to confer a benefit on and further a personal interest of its proponents. [Rule] 14a–8[i](4).

. . .

Because it appears that no further relief can or should be granted in this case, defendant's motion for summary judgment is granted, and the complaint is dismissed.

ANALYSIS

1. Do any of the proposals in the preceding three cases seem disingenuous? If so, so what?

2. If you had been a shareholder of any of the three corporations, what would your reaction have been to the question whether the corporation should include the proposal in its proxy materials? What if you had been a director? The CEO? Suppose a neo-Nazi group decided to use the proxy machinery to promote its positions. Would your reaction be the same?

3. In each case, why do you suppose the corporation opposed the inclusion of the proposal? What does it have to lose? What do you suppose is the likelihood that any of the proposals would attract substantial shareholder support?

NOTE ON SOCIAL ISSUE PROPOSALS AND THE ORDINARY BUSINESS EXCEPTION

The SEC's policy on shareholder proposals concerned mainly with social—rather than economic—issues has fluctuated over the years. The

SEC long handled such proposals on a case-by-case basis. In 1992, however, it departed from that practice and adopted a bright-line position that for the first time effectively excluded an entire category of social issue proposals. Cracker Barrel Old Country Stores, Inc., received and attempted to exclude a shareholder proposal calling on the board of directors to include sexual orientation in its anti-discrimination policy. In a no-action letter issued by the SEC's Division of Corporation Finance, the Commission took the position that all employment-related shareholder proposals raising social policy issues could be excluded under the "ordinary business" exclusion. The most significant effect of the *Cracker Barrel* decision was that companies were permitted to exclude shareholder proposals relating to affirmative action issues.

Subsequent litigation developed two issues. First, if a shareholder proponent sued a company whose management relied on *Cracker Barrel* to justify excluding an employment-related proposal from the proxy statement, should the reviewing court defer to the SEC's position? In Amalgamated Clothing and Textile Workers Union v. Wal–Mart Stores, Inc., 821 F.Supp. 877 (S.D.N.Y.), the court held that deference was not required and, moreover, that proposals relating to a company's affirmative action policies were not per se excludible as ordinary business under Rule 14a–8(i)(7). In a later case, the same district court judge ruled that the SEC's *Cracker Barrel* position was itself invalid because the SEC had failed to comply with federal administrative procedures in promulgating the position. The Second Circuit reversed, but in doing so concurred with the trial court's view that *Cracker Barrel* was not binding on courts. New York City Employees' Retirement System v. SEC, 45 F.3d 7 (2d Cir. 1995).

In 1998, the SEC adopted amendments to Rule 14a–8 that, among other things, reversed its *Cracker Barrel* position. In promulgating this change, the SEC explained:

. . . We believe that reversal of the Division's *Cracker Barrel* no-action letter, which the Commission had subsequently affirmed, is warranted. Since 1992, the relative importance of certain social issues relating to employment matters has reemerged as a consistent topic of widespread public debate. In addition, as a result of the extensive policy discussion that the *Cracker Barrel* position engendered, and through the rulemaking notice and comment process, we have gained a better understanding of the depth of interest among shareholders in having an opportunity to express their views to company management on employment-related proposals that raise sufficiently significant social policy issues.

Reversal of the *Cracker Barrel* no-action position will result in a return to a case-by-case analytical approach. In making distinctions in this area, the Division and the Commission will continue to apply the applicable standard for determining when a proposal relates to "ordinary business." The standard, originally articulated in the Commission's 1976 release, provided an exception for certain proposals that raise significant social policy issues. . . .

Going forward, companies and shareholders should bear in mind that the *Cracker Barrel* position relates only to employment-related proposals raising certain social policy issues. Reversal of the position does not affect the Division's analysis of any other category of proposals under the exclusion, such as proposals on general business operations.

Finally, we believe that it would be useful to summarize the principal considerations in the Division's application, under the Commission's oversight, of the "ordinary business" exclusion. The general underlying policy of this exclusion is consistent with the policy of most state corporate laws: to confine the resolution of ordinary business problems to management and the board of directors, since it is impracticable for shareholders to decide how to solve such problems at an annual shareholders meeting.

The policy underlying the ordinary business exclusion rests on two central considerations. The first relates to the subject matter of the proposal. Certain tasks are so fundamental to management's ability to run a company on a day-to-day basis that they could not, as a practical matter, be subject to direct shareholder oversight. Examples include the management of the workforce, such as the hiring, promotion, and termination of employees, decisions on production quality and quantity, and the retention of suppliers. However, proposals relating to such matters but focusing on sufficiently significant social policy issues (e.g., significant discrimination matters) generally would not be considered to be excludable, because the proposals would transcend the day-to-day business matters and raise policy issues so significant that it would be appropriate for a shareholder vote.

The second consideration relates to the degree to which the proposal seeks to "micro-manage" the company by probing too deeply into matters of a complex nature upon which shareholders, as a group, would not be in a position to make an informed judgment. This consideration may come into play in a number of circumstances, such as where the proposal involves intricate detail, or seeks to impose specific time-frames or methods for implementing complex policies. . . .

Amendments To Rules On Shareholder Proposals, Release No. 34–40018, 1998 SEC LEXIS 1001 (May 21, 1998).

PROBLEMS

1. Firm X makes three models of cars. Two of the models are four-door luxury sedans with V–12 engines and a slightly sporty image. Both are popular among the doctor-lawyer set, and highly profitable. The third model, the "X–Testosterosso," is a street-legal racing car with leather seats and mahogany trim added. It sells for $180,000, and loses money. X continues to make the X–Testosterosso solely because the managers believe that it increases the firm's luxury sedan sales by consolidating the firm's image as a producer of exciting cars.

X has received several shareholder proposals for this year's annual meeting. You are the firm's in-house lawyer. Your boss asks you whether she can exclude them. X is incorporated in Delaware.

Proposal A: "Resolved, that the Company shall discontinue the X–Testosterosso."

Proposal B: "Resolved, that the shareholders recommend that the Company discontinue the X–Testosterosso."

Proposal C: "Resolved, that the by-laws of X are hereby amended to include the following Section 12.2:

"12.2 The Company shall produce only four-door luxury sedans."

The proponents of A, B, and C argue simply that the company loses so much money on the X–Testosterosso that it should stop producing it. Section 109(a) of the Delaware General Corporation Law provides that by-laws may be adopted, amended, or repealed by the stockholders and, in addition, by the directors if the certificate of incorporation so provides. Section 109(b) provides:

The by-laws may contain any provision, not inconsistent with law or with the certificate of incorporation, relating to the business of the corporation, the conduct of its affairs, and its rights or powers or the rights or powers of its stockholders, directors, officers or employees.

2. Your law firm is approached by a group of high-tech entrepreneurs about to form a corporation. They think investors dislike the present proxy system, and that they could more easily raise money if they could make the proxy card into a genuine ballot for the board-of-director candidates. Accordingly, they propose to include in the firm's articles of incorporation a provision that would require the firm to include on its proxy (at no charge to the proponent) any rival slate of candidates proposed by a shareholder (or group of shareholders) owning at least 5 percent of the firm's stock. Would that be a good idea?

3. Your law firm is approached by another group of entrepreneurs about to form a corporation. They think investors are tired of the shareholder proposal system, and would like to contract out of it. Accordingly, they would like to include in the firm's articles of incorporation a provision that would allow management to refuse to include in its proxy solicitation material any proposal submitted by any shareholder. How should you respond? Who would lose if the firm adopted such a provision and it were enforceable?

E. SHAREHOLDER INSPECTION RIGHTS

INTRODUCTORY NOTE

Suppose you own shares of a firm you believe is badly managed. Suppose further that you want to communicate with the firm's other shareholders about that mismanagement. Under the federal proxy rules, you may, as we have seen, be able to force the incumbent board to include a proposal you draft in its proxy solicitation materials. But suppose you want to elect your own slate of directors and thereby gain control of the corporation. You cannot require the corporation to include your slate in its solicitation materials, so you will need to do your own proxy solicitation. If you pay the costs you may be able to require the corporation to mail your solicitation materials.[1] But that is not likely to satisfy you. In a real battle for control, information about shareholder identity may be crucial, for in such a battle you will not consider all shareholders alike. Instead, you will want to identify the holders of large blocks of stock and to spend most of your efforts trying to convince those major shareholders to support you. You will want the "shareholder list." Precisely because information about shareholder identity is valuable to you, incumbent managers are likely to resist your efforts to obtain it. There is nothing in the federal proxy rules requiring the corporation to give you the shareholder list, but the federal rules do not impair any rights you may have under state law. Thus, battles for the shareholder list are fought under state laws, as the cases in this section illustrate.

Crane Co. v. Anaconda Co.
39 N.Y.2d 14, 382 N.Y.S.2d 707, 346 N.E.2d 507 (1976).

In August, 1975, respondent Crane Company, an Illinois corporation, publicly announced a proposed offer to exchange up to 100 million dollars in subordinated debentures for as many as 5 million shares of common stock of the appellant Anaconda Company, a Montana corporation. This offer was vigorously opposed by Anaconda's management which sent four letters to shareholders asserting, *inter alia,* that the exchange offer was not in the best interests of Anaconda. Before the exchange offer could proceed Crane was obligated to file with the Securities and Exchange Commission a registration statement detailing the material facts of the offer in a prospectus. . . .

On November 19, 1975, Crane's registration statement became effective and Crane proceeded to distribute its prospectus to numerous brokers, dealers, commercial banks and trust companies for use in soliciting Anaconda stockholders. The next day Crane requested a copy of Anaconda's list of shareholders claiming that Anaconda had a fiduciary duty to its shareholders to present them with all the information pertinent to the pending tender offer. Crane owned no Anaconda stock at this time and Anaconda refused contending that there was no basis for Crane's request. However, as of December 11, 1975, approximately 2,350,000 Anaconda shares had been tendered to Crane, making Crane Anaconda's largest stockholder. The following day, a formal written demand to produce its stock book for inspection was made by Crane on Anaconda. This demand, accompanied by an affidavit stating that the inspection was "not desired

---

1. More precisely, under Rule 14a-7, the firm can choose either to mail your material and bill you for the costs or to give you the shareholder list instead. Most incumbent managements choose to mail the material themselves and keep the list confidential.

for a purpose which is in the interest of a business or object other than the business of Anaconda," was made pursuant to section 1315 of the Business Corporation Law * and the common-law right to inspect corporate records. Anaconda rejected the demand but offered to mail Crane's prospectus to its shareholders at Crane's expense. . . .

In its petition Crane stated that it held in excess of 11% of Anaconda's common stock and that its request conformed to the requirements of the Business Corporation Law in that the inspection was not required for a purpose other than the business of Anaconda and that Crane had not participated in the sale of any stockholder list within the last five years. . . . Crane also stated in substance that it desired to communicate directly with its fellow stockholders to inform them of the terms of . . . its tender offer . . ., to reply to misleading statements issued and distributed by Anaconda to its stockholders, and thereby to dispel any misconceptions and facilitate the further tender of Crane debentures. Anaconda answered by asserting that Crane's alleged reasons for inspection were not purposes relating to the business of Anaconda within the meaning of section 1315 of the Business Corporation Law.

Special Term found that neither Crane's overriding purpose to further its tender offer nor its ancillary purposes were proper in this context and dismissed the petition. The Appellate Division reversed, with two Justices dissenting. The majority concluded that the matter was proper being one of general interest to Anaconda's shareholders by virtue of their common interest in the corporation as shareholders. We agree with this determination.

Succinctly put, the issue here is whether a qualified stockholder may inspect the corporation's stock register to ascertain the identity of fellow stockholders for the avowed purpose of informing them directly of its

* [Editors.—The New York statute provided:

(a) Any resident of this state who shall have been a shareholder of record, for at least six months immediately preceding his demand, of a foreign corporation doing business in this state, or any resident of this state holding, or thereunto authorized in writing by the holders of, at least five percent of any class of the outstanding shares, upon at least five days' written demand may require such foreign corporation to produce a record of its shareholders setting forth the names and addresses of all shareholders, the number and class of shares held by each and the dates when they respectively became the owners of record thereof and shall have the right to examine . . . the record of shareholders or an exact copy thereof certified as correct by the corporate officer or agent responsible for keeping or producing such record and to make extracts therefrom. . . .

(b) An examination authorized by paragraph (a) may be denied to such shareholder or other person upon his refusal to furnish to the foreign corporation . . . an affidavit that such inspection is not desired for a purpose which is in the interest of a business or object other than the business of the foreign corporation and that such shareholder or other person has not within five years sold or offered for sale any list of shareholders of any corporation of any type or kind, whether or not formed under the laws of this state, or aided or abetted any person in procuring any such record of shareholders for any such purpose.

exchange offer and soliciting tenders of stock. In our view this question should be answered in the affirmative. A shareholder desiring to discuss relevant aspects of a tender offer should be granted access to the shareholder list unless it is sought for a purpose inimical to the corporation or its stockholders—and the manner of communication selected should be within the judgment of the shareholder.

The significance of this appeal is evident in view of the fact that this right is the one most frequently litigated by stockholders . . . and the fact that the tender offer is the primary method of corporate acquisition. . . . The conceptual basis for this right is derived from the shareholder's beneficial ownership of corporate assets and the concomitant right to protect his investment. . . .

The present statute (Business Corporation Law, §§ 1315, 624) was enacted in 1961 and provid[es] that access [must] be permitted to qualified shareholders on written demand, subject to denial if the petitioner refused to furnish an affidavit that the "inspection is not desired for a purpose . . . other than the business" of the corporation and that the petitioner has not been involved in the sale of stock lists within the last five years (Business Corporation Law, § 1315, subd. [b]; § 624, subd. [c]). . . .

In attempting to sustain its burden of proof, appellant contends that inspection should not be compelled where the stockholder desires to obtain the identity of other stockholders to convince them to sell their stock, since this does not involve the business of the corporation. . . . We read this authority to compel the opposite conclusion.

Although everything affecting the shareholders will not affect the corporation, the converse is not true. Whenever the corporation faces a situation having potential substantial effect on its wellbeing or value, the shareholders qua shareholders are necessarily affected and the business of the corporation is involved within the purview of section 1315 of the Business Corporation Law. This statute should be liberally construed in favor of the stockholder whose welfare as a stockholder or the corporation's welfare may be affected. To say, as Anaconda would, that a pending tender offer involving over one fifth of the corporation's common stock is a purpose other than the business of the corporation is myopic. Since the pendency of such an exchange offer may well affect not only the future direction of the corporation but the continued vitality of the shareholders' investment, inspection of the stock book should be allowed so that qualified shareholders may have the means to independently evaluate the situation. Nor do we consider it significant that the petitioning shareholder precipitated that which may affect the corporation or shareholders; the right adheres as one of property in the shareholder and one for the protection of that interest. . . .

Early in the proceedings Anaconda offered to have the corporation's transfer agent transmit the tender offer prospectus to all the stockholders. This was declined by Crane as much too expensive and not a productive way of soliciting tenders. . . . Obviously then, Crane was and is

interested in pursuing a selective and direct approach by other means to
stockholders. This is not by itself improper and is due to the pragmatics of
soliciting tenders from likely prospects who hold sufficient shares. . . .
Accordingly, since it appears that Anaconda has failed to sustain its burden
of proving an improper purpose and it cannot be said that the court below
abused its discretion, we conclude that inspection should be compelled.

State Ex Rel. Pillsbury v. Honeywell, Inc.

291 Minn. 322, 191 N.W.2d 406 (1971).

Petitioner appeals from an order and judgment of the district court
denying all relief prayed for in a petition for writs of mandamus to compel
respondent, Honeywell, Inc., (Honeywell) to produce its original shareholder ledger, current shareholder ledger, and all corporate records dealing with
weapons and munitions manufacture. We must affirm. . . .

Petitioner attended a meeting on July 3, 1969, of a group involved in
what was known as the "Honeywell Project." Participants in the project
believed that American involvement in Vietnam was wrong, that a substantial portion of Honeywell's production consisted of munitions used in that
war, and that Honeywell should stop this production of munitions. Petitioner had long opposed the Vietnam war, but it was at the July 3rd
meeting that he first learned of Honeywell's involvement. He was shocked
at the knowledge that Honeywell had a large government contract to
produce anti-personnel fragmentation bombs. Upset because of knowledge
that such bombs were produced in his own community by a company which
he had known and respected, petitioner determined to stop Honeywell's
munitions production.

On July 14, 1969, petitioner ordered his fiscal agent to purchase 100
shares of Honeywell. He admits that the sole purpose of the purchase was
to give himself a voice in Honeywell's affairs so he could persuade Honeywell to cease producing munitions. . . . In his deposition testimony
petitioner made clear the reason for his purchase of Honeywell's shares:

"Q . . . [D]o I understand that you requested Mr. Lacey to
buy these 100 shares of Honeywell in order to follow up on the desire
you had to bring to Honeywell management and to stockholders these
theses that you have told us about here today?

"A Yes. That was my motivation."

The "theses" referred to are petitioner's beliefs concerning the propriety of
producing munitions for the Vietnam war. . . .

Prior to the instigation of this suit, petitioner submitted two formal
demands to Honeywell requesting that it produce its original shareholder
ledger, current shareholder ledger, and all corporate records dealing with
weapons and munitions manufacture. Honeywell refused. . . .

In the deposition petitioner outlined his beliefs concerning the Vietnam
war and his purpose for his involvement with Honeywell. He expressed his

desire to communicate with other shareholders in the hope of altering Honeywell's board of directors and thereby changing its policy. To this end, he testified, business records are necessary to insure accuracy.

A hearing was held on January 8, 1970, during which Honeywell introduced the deposition, conceded all material facts stated therein, and argued that petitioner was not entitled to any relief as a matter of law. Petitioner asked that alternative writs of mandamus issue for all the relief requested in his petition. On April 8, 1970, the trial court dismissed the petition, holding that the relief requested was for an improper and indefinite purpose. Petitioner contends in this appeal that the dismissal was in error.

1. Honeywell is a Delaware corporation doing business in Minnesota. Both petitioner and Honeywell spent considerable effort in arguing whether Delaware or Minnesota law applies. The trial court, applying Delaware law, determined that the outcome of the case rested upon whether or not petitioner has a proper purpose germane to his interest as a shareholder. Del.Code Ann. tit. 8, § 220 (Supp.1968). This test is derived from the common law and is applicable in Minnesota.

. . .

Under the Delaware statute the shareholder must prove a proper purpose to inspect corporate records other than shareholder lists. Del. Code Ann. tit. 8, § 220. . . .*

2. The trial court ordered judgment for Honeywell, ruling that petitioner had not demonstrated a proper purpose germane to his interest as a stockholder. Petitioner contends that a stockholder who disagrees with management has an absolute right to inspect corporate records for pur-

---

* [Eds.—(b) Any stockholder . . . shall, upon written demand under oath stating the purpose thereof, have the right during the usual hours for business to inspect for any proper purpose the corporation's stock ledger, a list of its stockholders, and its other books and records, and to make copies or extracts therefrom. A proper purpose shall mean a purpose reasonably related to such person's interest as a stockholder. . . .

(c) If the corporation . . . refuses to permit an inspection sought by a stockholder . . . pursuant to sub-section (b) or does not reply to the demand within five business days after the demand has been made, the stockholder may apply to the Court of Chancery for an order to compel such inspection. . . . The Court may summarily order the corporation to permit the stockholder to inspect the corporation's stock ledger, an existing list of stockholders, and its other books and records, and to make copies or extracts therefrom; or the Court may order the corporation to furnish to the stockholder a list of its stockholders as of a specific date on condition that the stockholder first pay to the corporation the reasonable cost of obtaining and furnishing such list and on such other conditions as the Court deems appropriate. Where the stockholder seeks to inspect the corporation's books and records, other than its stock ledger or list of stockholders, he shall first establish (1) that he has complied with the provisions of this section respecting the form and manner of making demand for inspection of such document; and (2) that the inspection he seeks is for a proper purpose. Where the stockholder seeks to inspect the corporation's stock ledger or list of stockholders and he has complied with the provisions of this section respecting the form and manner of making demand for inspection of such documents, the burden of proof shall be upon the corporation to establish that the inspection he seeks is for an improper purpose.]

poses of soliciting proxies. He would have this court rule that such solicitation is per se a "proper purpose." Honeywell argues that a "proper purpose" contemplates concern with investment return. We agree with Honeywell. . . .

The act of inspecting a corporation's shareholder ledger and business records must be viewed in its proper perspective. In terms of the corporate norm, inspection is merely the act of the concerned owner checking on what is in part his property. In the context of the large firm, inspection can be more akin to a weapon in corporate warfare. The effectiveness of the weapon is considerable:

> "Considering the huge size of many modern corporations and the necessarily complicated nature of their bookkeeping, it is plain that to permit their thousands of stockholders to roam at will through their records would render impossible not only any attempt to keep their records efficiently, but the proper carrying on of their businesses."

. . . Because the power to inspect may be the power to destroy, it is important that only those with a bona fide interest in the corporation enjoy that power. . . .

Petitioner had utterly no interest in the affairs of Honeywell before he learned of Honeywell's production of fragmentation bombs. Immediately after obtaining this knowledge, he purchased stock in Honeywell for the sole purpose of asserting ownership privileges in an effort to force Honeywell to cease such production. We agree with the court in Chas. A. Day & Co. v. Booth, 123 Maine 443, 447, 123 A. 557, 558 (1924) that "where it is shown that such stockholding is only colorable, or solely for the purpose of maintaining proceedings of this kind, [we] fail to see how the petitioner can be said to be a 'person interested,' entitled as of right to inspect. . . ." But for his opposition to Honeywell's policy, petitioner probably would not have bought Honeywell stock, would not be interested in Honeywell's profits and would not desire to communicate with Honeywell's shareholders. His avowed purpose in buying Honeywell stock was to place himself in a position to try to impress his opinions favoring a reordering of priorities upon Honeywell management and its other shareholders. Such a motivation can hardly be deemed a proper purpose germane to his economic interest as a shareholder. . . .

We do not mean to imply that a shareholder with a bona fide investment interest could not bring this suit if motivated by concern with the long- or short-term economic effects on Honeywell resulting from the production of war munitions. Similarly, this suit might be appropriate when a shareholder has a bona fide concern about the adverse effects of abstention from profitable war contracts on his investment in Honeywell.

In the instant case, however, the trial court, in effect, has found from all the facts that petitioner was not interested in even the long-term well-being of Honeywell or the enhancement of the value of his shares. His sole purpose was to persuade the company to adopt his social and political concerns, irrespective of any economic benefit to himself or Honeywell.

This purpose on the part of one buying into the corporation does not entitle the petitioner to inspect Honeywell's books and records. . . .

The order of the trial court denying the writ of mandamus is affirmed.

QUESTIONS

1. Should companies be able to limit access to shareholder lists? Should u07 shareholder lists be treated differently from the firm's financial records? From its other business documents? What costs might firms incur if forced to give unrestricted access to the shareholder lists?

2. Should a firm be able to expand or contract the shareholder inspection right?

3. If a shareholder has a "proper purpose" in demanding the shareholder list, should it matter that he or she may have other purposes? Suppose, for example, that the shareholder making the demand is a broker trying to open a mail-order investment consulting service.

4. In light of *Pillsbury*, how might you coach a client who wants access to corporate records for a political cause?

Sadler v. NCR Corporation

928 F.2d 48 (2d Cir.1991).

This appeal concerns a limited but potentially important tactic in proxy contests—a stockholder's demand for a list of record shareholders and a list of beneficial owners of shares who do not object to disclosure of their names ("NOBO list"). The appeal raises issues under New York state law and the United States Constitution as to the power of New York to require an out-of-state corporation, doing business within New York, to provide resident shareholders with the list of record stockholders and to compile and produce the NOBO list, under circumstances where the requesting shareholders could not obtain such lists under the law of the state of incorporation. The lists are sought in connection with a tender offer and the solicitation of proxy votes in an effort to replace directors. . . .

We conclude that New York law authorizes production of the shareholder and NOBO lists in the circumstances of this case and that application of New York law does not violate the Commerce Clause of the Constitution. . . .

Background

NCR, a large computer company, is incorporated in Maryland and has its principal place of business in Dayton, Ohio. It is undisputed that NCR maintains at least eight offices in New York and conducts substantial business there. NCR has 75,000 shareholders. AT & T, the well-known telecommunications company, is a New York corporation with its principal executive offices in New York City. AT & T became a beneficial owner of

100 shares of NCR stock on November 21, 1990. The Sadlers are New York residents who own more than 6,000 shares of NCR stock and have been record holders of NCR stock for more than six months prior to this lawsuit.

On December 6, 1990, AT & T began a tender offer for the shares of NCR, offering to purchase all of the common stock of NCR for $90 a share.* In compliance with Rule 14d–5 of the Securities and Exchange Commission, 17 C.F.R. § 240.14d–5 (1990), NCR mailed the offer to purchase to all NCR stockholders. The NCR board rejected the tender offer and declined to redeem a "poison pill" shareholders' rights plan, which presented and continues to present an obstacle to a hostile tender offer.** AT & T responded to this opposition by soliciting NCR shareholders to convene a special meeting of stockholders to replace a majority of the NCR directors so that the barriers to the tender offer could be removed. Maryland law permits a special meeting of stockholders to be called upon the request of stockholders entitled to cast 25 percent of the votes at the meeting. Md. Corps. & Ass'ns Code Ann. § 2–502 (1985 & Supp. 1990). NCR's corporate charter permits directors to be replaced at a special meeting of stockholders upon the affirmative vote of 80 percent of all outstanding shares. Soon after soliciting calls for a special meeting, AT & T submitted to NCR requests for a special meeting from holders of more than half of NCR stock. NCR subsequently scheduled a special meeting for March 28, 1991, the date selected for its annual meeting.

Beginning in early January 1991, AT & T and the Sadlers, acting at AT & T's request, sought from NCR its stockholder list and related materials to facilitate communication with owners of NCR shares. In addition to the list of record owners, AT & T sought a magnetic computer tape of the list and daily transfer sheets showing changes in shareholders from the date of demand to the date of the annual meeting. AT & T also sought two other lists, a "CEDE list" and a "NOBO list." A "CEDE list" identifies the brokerage firms and other record owners who bought shares in a street name for their customers and who have placed those shares in the custody of depository firms such as Depository Trust Co.; these shares are reflected in the corporation's records only under the names of nominees used by such depository firms. Depository Trust Co. uses "Cede & Co." as the name of the nominee for shares it holds for brokerage firms, and such lists, regardless of the nominee names adopted by other depository firms, are known as "CEDE lists." . . . A "NOBO list" (non-objecting beneficial owners) contains the names of those owning beneficial interests in shares of a corporation who have given consent to the disclosure of their identities. The Securities and Exchange Commission requires brokers and other record holders of stock in street name to compile a NOBO list at a corporation's request. . . .

Upon NCR's refusal to produce the requested materials, the Sadlers and AT & T brought this suit in the Southern District, relying on section

---

* [Tender offers are discussed at Chapter 6, Section 2.—Eds.]   ** [Poison pills are discussed at Chapter 6, Section 2(B).—Eds.]

1315 of the New York Business Corporation Law, N.Y. Bus. Corp. Law § 1315 (McKinney 1986). Section 1315, which we consider in detail below, enables New York residents owning shares of a foreign corporation to obtain a list of the corporation's shareholders. On January 28, 1991, the District Court ruled that the Sadlers qualified under section 1315 to obtain NCR's stockholder list and that the statute could constitutionally be applied to require NCR to comply with their request, notwithstanding NCR's Commerce Clause objections. Later that day, [the district court judge] issued a supplemental ruling rejecting NCR's contention that the NOBO list was not producible under section 1315 because it was not then in existence but required compilation. He entered an order requiring NCR to produce all the materials sought by the Sadlers and AT & T.

Discussion

I. Application of section 1315

Section 1315(a) permits any New York resident who for six months has been a stockholder of record of a foreign corporation doing business in New York, or who holds or acts for those who hold five percent of any class of outstanding shares to require the corporation, on five days' written notice, to produce "a record of its shareholders setting forth the names and addresses of all shareholders, the number and class of shares held by each and the dates when they respectively became the owners of record." N.Y. Bus. Corp. Law (McKinney 1986). Such a resident is also entitled "to examine in person or by agent . . . the record of shareholders" at specified locations. Id. The corporation may require the requesting shareholder to furnish an affidavit assuring that "inspection is not desired for a purpose . . . other than the business of" the corporation and that the shareholder has not engaged in the sale of stockholder lists within the past five years. Id. § 1315(b). A substantially similar provision of New York law applies to stockholder lists of New York corporations. N.Y. Bus. Corp. Law § 624 (McKinney 1986). See Crane Co. v. Anaconda Co., 39 N.Y.2d 14, 18–20, 346 N.E.2d 507, 510–11, 382 N.Y.S.2d 707, 710–11 (1976) (outlining origin of the New York statutory right to inspect stockholder lists).

A. Eligibility of the Sadlers.

The Sadlers qualify under section 1315 as persons entitled to obtain a "record" of NCR's shareholders. The Sadlers are residents of New York and have owned NCR stock for six months prior to their demand. The corporation whose stockholder list they seek does business in New York.

Nevertheless, NCR challenges the Sadlers' right to invoke section 1315 because of the arrangement between the Sadlers and AT & T under which the Sadlers initiated their request. Since AT & T had not held its NCR stock for more than six months, it sought out a New York resident who qualified under section 1315. AT & T's agreement with the Sadlers provides that the Sadlers will demand the NCR stockholder list, that AT & T will reimburse the Sadlers for any expenses and indemnify them for any losses arising out of the demand, and that the Sadlers will not settle any claim or lawsuit concerning the demand without the consent of AT & T, which will not be unreasonably withheld. Pursuant to this agreement, the Sadlers requested that NCR produce the stockholder records to AT & T, which it characterized as "our agent," and informed NCR that AT & T would reimburse NCR for any expenses incurred in complying with the demand. NCR contends that AT & T is not the agent of the Sadlers, but in reality is the principal, using the Sadlers as its agent for a demand that AT & T itself is not entitled to make.

We agree with [the district court judge] that the agreement between the Sadlers and AT & T does not disqualify the Sadlers from invoking section 1315. Though section 1315 permits an "agent" to act for the qualifying New York resident in inspecting the shareholder record, it does not inevitably apply all the technical aspects of the law of agency to the permissible relationship between the requesting shareholder and another entity with whom the shareholder chooses to act. Section 1315 "should be liberally construed in favor of the stockholder," *Crane Co.*, 39 N.Y.2d at 20–21, 346 N.E.2d at 512, 382 N.Y.S.2d at 712. Once the resident shareholder alleges compliance with the statute, "the bona fides of the shareholder will be assumed . . . and it becomes incumbent on the corporation to justify its refusal by showing an improper purpose or bad faith." Id. at 20, 346 N.E.2d at 511, 382 N.Y.S.2d at 711 (citations omitted).

We see no reason to believe that New York would deny the Sadlers the right to invoke section 1315 because of the arrangement they have made with AT & T. . . .

B. The demand for the NOBO list.

Whether New York law entitles the Sadlers to require NCR to assemble a NOBO list presents a more substantial question. The parties agree that section 1315 applies to NOBO lists in a corporation's possession, but it is undisputed that at the time of the demand, NCR did not have a NOBO list in its possession. It is also undisputed that a corporation can obtain a NOBO list, normally within ten days, by requesting compilation of the list by firms that offer data processing services for this task. NCR reads section 1315 as limited to production of lists in existence, as distinguished from those readily capable of being compiled. . . .

The text of section 1315 does not resolve the dispute, although a narrow reading of its terms might favor NCR. The statute could be read to be limited to production or examination of lists already in existence and could also be limited to lists reflecting the names and addresses of owners of record. But New York courts have made clear that the statute is to be "liberally construed," *Crane Co.*, 39 N.Y.2d at 20–21, 346 N.E.2d at 512, 382 N.Y.S.2d at 712, to "facilitate communication among shareholders on issues respecting corporate affairs," *Bohrer* [v. International Banknote Co.], 150 A.D.2d 196, 540 N.Y.S.2d 445, 446 [(1st Dep't 1989)]. . . . A narrow reading of section 1315 would therefore not accord with New York law.

The precise issue of whether New York requires a corporation to obtain a NOBO list at the request of a shareholder qualified to demand stockholder records under section 1315 has not previously been decided. . . .

Other courts, however, construing statutes similar to section 1315, have expressly declined to order compilation of NOBO lists. RB Associates [v. The Gillette Co., C.A. No. 9711, 1988 WL 27731 (Del.Ch., Mar.22, 1988)]; Cenergy Corp. v. Bryson Oil & Gas P.L.C., 662 F.Supp. 1144, 1148 (D.Nev.1987). The matter was given extended consideration by Chancellor Allen in *RB Associates*. In declining to order compilation of a NOBO list, he distinguished it in two respect from CEDE lists, which Delaware and New York require a corporation to compile upon request of a qualified shareholder. . . . CEDE lists, he pointed out, can be generated rapidly by a computer, whereas a NOBO list takes up to ten days to compile. Second, he expressed the view that it would be extremely inefficient without a CEDE list to attempt to distribute proxy materials to persons for whom a depository company holds shares, whereas a NOBO list "plays no central role in a proxy contest." *RB Associates*, supra.

We do not find either distinction compelling. Since compilation of a NOBO list is a relatively simple mechanical task, the fact that compilation takes longer than for a CEDE list is an insubstantial basis for distinction. As to both sets of information, the underlying data exist in discrete records readily available to be compiled into an aggregate list. Nor are the functions of the lists significantly dissimilar. Both facilitate direct communication with stockholders, in the case of a NOBO list, at least with those beneficial owners who have indicated no objection to disclosure of their names and addresses.

Though Delaware chooses to construe the reach of its requirements on stockholder list disclosure narrowly in this respect, we think New York would construe section 1315 more generously. Once the Securities and Exchange Commission has acted to enable a corporation to obtain from brokers and other record owners a list of beneficial owners of its shares who do not object to such disclosure, we think New York would apply section 1315 to permit a qualifying shareholder to require the compilation and production of such a list.

Even if the statute might not require compilation of NOBO lists routinely, . . . compilation was properly ordered in this case. The effect of NCR's 80 percent rule is to count as a "no" vote on the replacement of directors every share that is not voted at the special meeting. Thus, the shares of non-voting beneficial owners who might oppose management if solicited by management opponents armed with a NOBO list are counted in favor of management. Denying such opponents an opportunity to contact the NOBOs is inconsistent with the statute's objective of seeking "to the extent possible, to place shareholders on an equal footing with management in obtaining access to shareholders." *Bohrer*, 150 A.D.2d at 196–97, 540 N.Y.S.2d at 446. In effect, NCR already has the votes of those NOBOs who, for lack of solicitation, decline to vote. As to them, NCR has all the access it needs.

II.   Commerce Clause Objection

NCR contends that application of section 1315 to require it to comply with demands for stockholder records that NCR is not required to honor under the law of the state of incorporation violates the Commerce Clause. The argument seeks to enlist the "dormant" Commerce Clause power, see CTS Corp. v. Dynamics Corp. of America, 481 U.S. 69, 87, 95 L.Ed.2d 67, 107 S.Ct. 1637 (1987) [infra Chapter 6, Section 2(C)], the implied prohibition upon certain types of state regulation arising from the available but unexercised power of Congress over interstate commerce. The prohibition has as its "principal objects" state regulations that "discriminate against interstate commerce," id. at 87, and also extends to those that "adversely affect interstate commerce by subjecting activities to inconsistent regulations," id. at 88, or that impose burdens on interstate commerce that outweigh local benefits, see Pike v. Bruce Church, Inc., 397 U.S. 137, 142, 25 L.Ed.2d 174, 90 S.Ct. 844 (1970). NCR relies primarily on the "inconsistent regulation" branch of the dormant Commerce Clause doctrine.

Maryland law requires Maryland corporations to disclose stockholder lists to one or more shareholders who have held for at least six months at least five percent of the outstanding stock of any class. Md. Corps.   & Ass'ns Code Ann. § 2–513(a) (1985). Neither AT & T nor the Sadlers meet the Maryland criteria. NCR contends that production of stockholder records pursuant to New York law subjects NCR to inconsistent regulation. We disagree.

Plainly there is no inconsistency in the sense of a direct conflict. Maryland law does not forbid NCR from disclosing its stockholder records to those who qualify under New York law. But, argues NCR, there is at least an indirect conflict in the sense that Maryland law permits NCR to refuse the Sadlers' request and New York law, as we construe it, forbids such refusal. That argument presses the "inconsistent regulation" branch of the dormant Commerce Clause theory too far. States are not prohibited from enacting regulations simply because they require more of an entity that is already subject to some less demanding regulation elsewhere.

However, NCR has a more plausible argument in pointing out that the Maryland disclosure obligations are not merely less generous than New York's, they are part of a balanced plan to regulate relations between a corporation and its shareholders. Maryland limits the shareholders who may demand inspection of stockholder records but at the same time extends shareholders a right to call a special meeting upon the request of those owning 25 percent of the shares. Md. Corps. & Ass'ns Code Ann. § 2–502 (1985 & Supp. 1990). New York does not provide shareholders with any statutory right to call a special meeting. Thus, NCR's "conflict" argument is that New York law accords the Sadlers rights not only greater than those accorded by Maryland law, but rights that it is reasonable to assume the Maryland legislature implicitly wished to deny them in the course of adjusting the competing claims of management and shareholders.

This implied conflict argument requires consideration of the issue of whether regulation of the right of shareholders to inspect stockholder lists is confided to the exclusive authority of the state of regulation, or, more precisely, whether the dormant Commerce Clause power itself creates such an exclusive sphere of regulation. On these issues, the parties both seek to enlist the Supreme Court's decision in *CTS*, supra. As NCR reminds us, the Court there observed,

> No principle of corporation law and practice is more firmly established than a State's authority to regulate domestic corporations, including the authority to define the voting rights of shareholders. See Restatement (Second) of Conflict of Laws § 304 (1971) (concluding that the law of the incorporating State generally should "determine the right of a shareholder to participate in the administration of the affairs of the corporation").

CTS, 481 U.S. at 89. AT & T counters that the very section of the Restatement cited by the Court in support of the so-called "internal affairs" doctrine expressly excludes access to stockholder lists from the doctrine. As AT & T points out, Comment d to section 304 states:

> The right of a shareholder to inspect the books of a corporation poses special problems. This is an issue which can practically be determined differently in different states. This is also an issue which, if decided differently in different states, will not seriously undermine the policy favoring uniform treatment for all shareholders of a corporation. For these reasons, a court will apply to a foreign corporation doing substantial business in the state a local statute providing for the inspection of books by a shareholder if in the court's opinion the statute embodies an important policy.

Restatement (Second) of Conflict of Laws § 304, comment d (1971) (hereafter "Restatement"). . . .

Though Comment d is relevant to the issue we confront, we do not think that this commentary, much less any aspect of the parties' conflicting exegeses on it, can be attributed to the Supreme Court by virtue of the citation to Section 304 in *CTS*. . . .

Though not necessarily endorsed by the Supreme Court in *CTS*, Comment d nevertheless substantially undermines NCR's claim that section 1315 subjects it to inconsistent regulation of a sort that the dormant Commerce Clause power prohibits. As the ALI and the case law have recognized, see Annot., 19 A.L.R.3d 869, 889–91 (1968), states have traditionally exercised authority to require disclosure of stockholder lists of foreign corporations doing business within their borders. Moreover, such authority will not normally create, and does not create in this case, the sort of irreconcilable conflict that would arise if a state purported to regulate voting rights or other aspects of the internal affairs of a foreign corporation that "admit only of one uniform system, or plan of regulation," Cooley v.

Board of Wardens, 53 U.S. (12 How.) 299, 319 (1851). ·Access to stockholder lists is a recognized exception to the internal affairs doctrine as a matter of corporate law and conflicts of law, and it should take a substantial threat of conflict adversely affecting interstate commerce before a court invalidates a state's assertion of this traditional authority. Though Maryland may well have balanced limited shareholder access to stockholder lists with generous authority for calling special meetings, it did so against the background of traditional foreign state regulation of such access, and it cannot expect courts to provide constitutional insulation for the particular arrangements it adopted. If the traditional role of states concerning access to stockholder lists of foreign corporations is to be circumscribed, that alteration will have to be undertaken by Congress.

NCR's remaining Commerce Clause contentions require little discussion. Section 1315 creates no discrimination against interstate commerce. . . . [I]t applies (for all practical purposes) equally to foreign and domestic corporations. . . .

Equally unavailing is the claim that section 1315 imposes unjustified burdens on interstate commerce. . . .

PROBLEMS

McWindsor, Inc., which is incorporated in New York, is a maker of upscale British-style fashions. To date, it has specialized in $1,000 all-cotton pea-green trench coats and $100 all-cotton umbrellas. Both sport the distinctive McWindsor plaid fabric, said to have been designed for the kilts of an obscure Scottish regiment in 1656. McWindsor stock trades at about $1,000 per share. Some shareholders have asked the company to perform a 10–for–1 stock split (each shareholder would tender his or her stock to the company, and receive 10 new shares of stock for each old share of stock). By doing so, the company would reduce the price of a share of McWindsor stock to about $100. The shareholders explain that these lower share prices would let them more easily fit McWindsor shares into diversified stock portfolios. The company has refused. Far better, CEO Prince George McWindsor announces, for stock to trade at the price of a rain coat than for it to trade at the price of an umbrella.

1. Suppose X (the manufacturer of the X–Testosterosso described on page 525) buys several shares of McWindsor stock and requests a shareholders list. Must McWindsor give X the list? What kind of list? Suppose X announces a sale: it will give one X–Testosterosso (generally selling at $180,000) to every McWindsor shareholder who tenders 150 shares of McWindsor stock. If it again asks for the shareholder list, must McWindsor give it the list?

2. Suppose an investor holding three McWindsor shares asks for the shareholder list. He explains that he wants to contact other shareholders and ask them to join him in demanding that the company effect a stock split. Must McWindsor provide the list?

3.   Suppose an investment bank holding 300 McWindsor shares asks for the list.   It explains that its stock analysts have developed a new formula for fitting McWindsor shares into diversified stock portfolios.   It thus wants to offer their services to McWindsor shareholders.   Must McWindsor provide the list?   Suppose instead that the investment bank forms a mutual fund called Diversified McWindsor, Inc. [DWI].   In exchange for several thousand shares of DWI stock, it has contributed several thousand shares of 20 companies that, together with McWindsor, form a well-diversified stock portfolio.   DWI now announces a tender offer for McWindsor stock: in exchange for every McWindsor share tendered, it will provide 10 shares (each worth $100) of DWI.   In order to publicize the tender offer, DWI asks for the shareholders list.   Must McWindsor provide the list?

4.   Suppose a group of shareholders ask for all records relating to the employment practices of McWindsor's supplier in Northern Ireland.   The shareholders explain that they have heard rumors that McWindsor's supplier discriminates against Catholic workers, and want to ascertain whether the rumors are true.   Must McWindsor provide the records?

Stroh v. Blackhawk Holding Corp.

48 Ill.2d 471, 272 N.E.2d 1 (1971).

The only issue before this court is the validity of the 500,000 shares of Class B stock, which by the articles of incorporation of Blackhawk were limited in their rights by the provision "none of the shares of Class B stock shall be entitled to dividends either upon voluntary or involuntary liquidation or otherwise." It is the plaintiffs' contention that because of the foregoing limitation—depriving the Class B shares of the "economic" incidents of shares of stock, or of the proportionate interest in the corporate assets—the Class B shares do not in fact constitute shares of stock.

Blackhawk Holding Corporation was organized under the Illinois Business Corporation Act in November of 1963. Its articles of incorporation authorized the issuance of 3,000,000 shares of Class A stock with a par value of $1, and 500,000 shares of Class B stock without par value. . . . Pursuant to the preorganization subscription agreements, 21 promoters purchased 87,868 shares of the Class A stock at the price of $3.40 per share ($298,751.20), and the 500,000 shares of Class B stock at ¼¢ per share ($1,250). Thereafter, the corporation registered the Class A shares with the securities division of the office of the Secretary of State of Illinois for the sale of 500,000 shares thereof to the general public at a price of $4 per share. The prospectus for the registration described the Class A and Class B stock, and quoted from the articles of incorporation relative to their respective rights and preferences. The prospectus explained that every share of each class of stock would be entitled to one vote on all general matters submitted to a vote of the shareholders. . . .

The prospectus also explained that no Class B stock was being offered for sale in that all of such stock has been previously issued. Under the heading "Organization and Development," the prospectus also stated: "Subscriptions for a total of $300,001.20 were sold to twenty-one persons, representing 87,868 class A shares, the class now being offered, at the price of $3.40 per share ($298,751.20) and 500,000 class B shares, at a price of one-fourth of a cent per share ($1,250.00); thus said subscribers by virtue of a $300,001.20 investment, have control of the corporation having an initial capitalization of $2,000,000.00 after this offering."

In August of 1964, there was a 2 for 1 split of the Class A stock, increasing the shares outstanding from 587,863 to 1,175,736 shares. The corporation sold additional Class A stock to the public in 1965 for $4 a share. As of June 1968, there were 1,237,681 Class A shares and 500,000

Class B shares outstanding, the latter representing 28.78% of the total voting shares of the company.

        .   .   .

Under the Illinois constitution of 1870, a stockholder in an Illinois corporation is guaranteed the right to vote based upon the number of shares owned by him. (Ill.Const. art. XI, sec. 3, S.H.A.) Section 14 of the Business Corporation Act (Ill.Rev.Stat.1969, ch. 32, par. 157.14) provides that shares of stock in an Illinois corporation may be divided into classes,

> "with such designations, preferences, qualifications, limitations, restrictions and such special or relative rights as shall be stated in the articles of incorporation. The articles of incorporation shall not limit or deny the voting power of the shares of any class.

> Without limiting the authority herein contained, a corporation when so provided in its articles of incorporation, may issue shares of preferred or special classes:

>   .   .   .

> (c) Having preference over any other class or classes of shares as to the payment of dividends.

> (d) Having preference as to the assets of the corporation over any other class or classes of shares upon the voluntary or involuntary liquidation of the corporation."

        .   .   .

Section 2.6 of the Act, in defining "shares" states, " 'Shares' means the units into which the proprietary interests in a corporation are divided." (Ill.Rev.Stat.1969, ch. 32, par. 157.2–6.) This was formerly section 2(f) of the Act (Ill.Rev.Stat.1955, ch. 32, par. 157.2(f)) which defined shares as "units into which shareholders' rights to participate in the control of a corporation, in its surplus or profits, or in the distribution of its assets, are divided." . . .

To the plaintiffs, "proprietary," as used in the definition of shares, means a property right, and shares must then represent some economic interest, or interest in the property or assets of the corporation. However, the word "proprietary" does not necessarily denote economic or asset rights, although it has been defined as synonymous with ownership or to denote legal title . . . and "proprietary rights" have been defined as those conferred by virtue of ownership of a thing. . . .

We agree with the defendants' construction. We interpret this statutory definition to mean that the proprietary rights conferred by the ownership of stock may consist of one or more of the rights to participate "in the control of the corporation, in its surplus or profits, *or* in the distribution of its assets." The use of the disjunctive conjunction "*or*" indicates that one or more of the three named rights may inure to a stockholder by virtue of his stock ownership. . . .

We must here decide the extent to which economic attributes of shares of stock may be eliminated.   .   .   .

Section 14 of the Act clearly expresses the intent of the legislature to be that parties to a corporate entity may create whatever restrictions and limitations they may want with regard to their corporate stock by expressing such restrictions and limitations in the articles of incorporation. These rights and powers granted by the legislature to the corporation to make the terms of its contract with its shareholders are limited only by the proviso that the articles may not limit or deny the voting power of any share. This section of the Act expressly confers the right to prefer a class of shares over another with regard to dividends and assets. Section 2.6 defines shares as "The units into which the proprietary interests in a corporation are divided."

In seeking the intent of the legislature, a statute should be construed as a whole and its separate parts considered together. Our present constitution requires only that a shareholder not be deprived of his voice in management. It does not require that a shareholder, in addition to the management aspect of ownership, must also have an economic interest.

Thus, section 14, like the constitution, limits the power of a corporation only as to the voting aspect of ownership.   .   .   .

When the relevant sections of the Act are read together with the constitution, it seems apparent that it was the intent of the legislature that the proprietary interests represented by the shares of stock consist of management or control rights, rights to earnings, and rights to assets. There are other rights which are incidental to these. Under our laws, the rights to earnings and the rights to assets—the "economic" rights—may be removed and eliminated from the other attributes of a share of stock. Only the management incident of ownership may not be removed.

.   .   .

The constitution requires only that the right to vote be proportionate to the number of shares owned, not to the investment made in a corporation. It has long been the common practice in Illinois to classify shares of stock such that one may invest less than another in a corporation, and yet have control. One .   .   . shareholder may purchase ten shares of a class of stock issued at its par value of $1,000 per share, and his business partner may purchase 100 shares of another class of the corporate stock issued at its par value of $10 per share. The parties, for varying reasons, may be very willing that the party investing the $1,000 have control of the management of the corporation, as opposed to the party having the investment of $10,000.   .   .   .

If there is overreaching or fraud in establishing the different relative voting rights of shares, that is another matter and there is a remedy available. We are aware that the classification of shares, so as to enable one class to obtain greater voting rights with the same or lesser investment in a corporation than another class, may carry with it the possibility for wrongdoing. However, it also often serves a valid purpose and there is nothing inherently wrong in such a scheme. The fact that a corporation makes a public offering of stock does not render the procedure outlined above less valid. The securities division of the Secretary of State's office has its particular guidelines to protect the public in such an offering.

In this case the parties went one step further than is customary. The stock which could be bought cheaper, and yet carry the same voting power per share, was not permitted to share at all in the dividends or assets of the corporation. This additional step did not invalidate the stock.

We find nothing in the declared public policy of this State to condemn stock of this nature.   .   .   .

Affirmed and remanded, with directions.

■ SCHAEFER, JUSTICE (dissenting).

.   .   .

"Under our laws," say the majority, "the rights to earnings and the rights to assets—the 'economic' rights—may be removed and eliminated from the other attributes of a share of stock. Only the management incident of ownership may not be removed." This seems to me to be saying that the ownership incidents of ownership may be eliminated. What remains, then, is a disembodied right to manage the assets of a corporation, divorced from any financial interest in those assets except such as may accrue from the power to manage them. In my opinion, what is left after the economic rights are "removed and eliminated" is not a share of corporate stock under the law of Illinois.

.   .   .

ANALYSIS

1. What might be the public policy underlying a prohibition of non-voting shares? Would that policy also be offended by shares with unequal voting power?

2. The opinion of the lower appellate court in *Stroh* reveals that in 1967 the Class A shares were selling for substantially less than the $4 per share initial offering price. At the same time, the Class B shares were selling for "about 20 times the original price." 253 N.E.2d 692, at 694. Does this tend to show that the initial investors in Class A shares were treated unfairly? Why would the Class B shares have any value at all? How would you determine what the value is?

3. At the time this case arose, the Illinois constitution contained provisions that in effect required all common shares to have equal voting rights. In a 1970 constitutional revision, these requirements were dropped. The Illinois Business Corporation Act of 1983, § 7.40(b), now provides that corporations, in their articles, "may limit or deny voting rights or may provide special voting rights as to any class or classes or series of shares." Under this law, how might the original 21 investors in

Blackhawk Holding Corp. have accomplished their apparent purpose (voting control disproportionate to profit claim) without using the peculiar Class B shares?

4. The original 21 investors in Blackhawk Holding Corp. obviously wanted to protect their control. One reason why people want control is that they (or their relations or friends) are, or expect to be, employed by the corporation and they want to protect their salaries and perquisites. To that extent, their interests may diverge from the interests of other shareholders. Are there reasons for wanting control that do not involve such blatant conflict of interest?

5. Suppose you have money to invest and are offered shares in a corporation with a control structure like that of Blackhawk Holding Corp. Suppose you believe that the people who will hold disproportionately large voting control will use their control to provide themselves and their children with jobs at salaries above the market rate and that there is no reasonable prospect that there will be anything you can do about it. Might you still be willing to buy shares in the corporation?

NOTE AND QUESTIONS

In Providence and Worcester Co. v. Baker, 378 A.2d 121 (Del.1977), the plaintiff owned 28 percent of the single class of voting shares of the Providence and Worcester Company (P & W). The corporation's articles of incorporation provided that "each shareholder shall be entitled to one vote for every share of the common stock of said company owned by him not exceeding fifty shares, and one vote for every twenty shares more than fifty owned by him; provided, that no stockholder shall be entitled to vote upon more than one fourth part of the whole number of shares issued and outstanding. . . ." The result of this provision was that the plaintiff, with 28 percent of the shares, had only 3 percent of the votes. The plaintiff argued that the corporation's voting rule violated § 151(a) of the Delaware corporation law, which provides that corporations may issue various classes or series of stock, "which classes or series may have such voting powers, full or limited, or no voting powers . . . as shall be stated and expressed in the certificate of incorporation." The plaintiff argued that this section of the Delaware law allows differences in voting power between classes of stock but not within a single class of stock and that, consequently, the P & W voting rule was impermissible. The Delaware Supreme Court rejected this argument and upheld the P & W rule.

Assume that at the time of its formation, P & W issued 35,000 shares and no shareholder held more than 200 shares. What legitimate purpose might be served by a voting rule like that of P & W? As a potential original investor in 100 of the P & W shares, what potential harm to your interests might you be concerned about as a result of the rule?

PROBLEM

Suppose a corporation is formed with 1 million Class A common shares, which are sold at $4 per share. No other shares are outstanding.

Two years later the shares are selling on the market for $6 per share. The managers of the corporation own 300,000 shares and control the board of directors. The board adopts the following plan: For each share of Class A stock that a shareholder owns, he or she will be entitled to buy either (i) one additional share of Class A Stock at $5.00 per share or (ii) five shares of a new Class B stock at 1 cent per share. The Class B shares will carry one vote per share but will be entitled to no dividends (current or liquidating). All the members of the management group will buy Class B shares. They will therefore wind up with their original Class A shares (300,000 votes) plus 1,500,000 Class B shares (1,500,000 votes). Suppose you own 1,000 of the original shares (now called Class A). You believe that there is a group of outside investors that would be willing to buy the entire corporation for $9 million ($9 per share for the existing shares). In fact, you believe that the reason for the board's plan to offer the new shares is its concern about the outside group taking over. The time has come when you must decide whether to buy new A shares or B shares, or neither. (a) What do you do? (b) Do you think the board should be allowed to put you to this choice? (c) Suppose you had been entitled to vote on whether the new Class B shares should have been authorized. How would you have voted?

SECTION 3.   CONTROL IN CLOSELY HELD CORPORATIONS

Ringling Bros.–Barnum & Bailey Combined Shows v. Ringling

29 Del.Ch. 610, 53 A.2d 441 (Del.Sup.Ct.1947).

The Court of Chancery was called upon to review an attempted election of directors at the 1946 annual stockholders meeting of the corporate defendant.   The pivotal questions concern an agreement between two of the three present stockholders, and particularly the effect of this agreement with relation to the exercise of voting rights by these two stockholders.   At the time of the meeting, the corporation had outstanding 1000 shares of capital stock held as follows: 315 by petitioner Edith Conway Ringling;   315 by defendant Aubrey B. Ringling Haley (individually or as executrix and legatee of a deceased husband);   and 370 by defendant John Ringling North.   The purpose of the meeting was to elect the entire board of seven directors.   The shares could be voted cumulatively.   Mrs. Ringling asserts that by virtue of the operation of an agreement between her and Mrs. Haley, the latter was bound to vote her shares for an adjournment of the meeting, or in the alternative, for a certain slate of directors.   Mrs. Haley contends that she was not so bound for reason that the agreement was invalid, or at least revocable.

The two ladies entered into the agreement in 1941.   It makes like provisions concerning stock of the corporate defendant and of another corporation, but in this case, we are concerned solely with the agreement as it affects the voting of stock of the corporate defendant.   The agreement recites that each party was the owner "subject only to possible claims of creditors of the estates of Charles Ringling and Richard Ringling, respectively" (deceased husbands of the parties), of 300 shares of the capital stock of the defendant corporation;   that in 1938 these shares had been deposited under a voting trust agreement which would terminate in 1947, or earlier, upon the elimination of certain liability of the corporation;   that each party also owned 15 shares individually;   that the parties had "entered into an agreement in April 1934 providing for joint action by them in matters affecting their ownership of stock and interest in" the corporate defendant;   that the parties desired "to continue to act jointly in all matters relating to their stock ownership or interest in" the corporate defendant (and the other corporation).   The agreement then provides as follows:

"Now, Therefore, in consideration of the mutual covenants and agreements hereinafter contained the parties hereto agree as follows:

. . .

579

"2. In exercising any voting rights to which either party may be entitled by virtue of ownership of stock or voting trust certificates held by them in either of said corporations, each party will consult and confer with the other and the parties will act jointly in exercising such voting rights in accordance with such agreement as they may reach with respect to any matter calling for the exercise of such voting rights.

"3. In the event the parties fail to agree with respect to any matter covered by paragraph 2 above, the question in disagreement shall be submitted for arbitration to Karl D. Loos, of Washington, D.C. as arbitrator and his decision thereon shall be binding upon the parties hereto. Such arbitration shall be exercised to the end of assuring for the respective corporations good management and such participation therein by the members of the Ringling family as the experience, capacity and ability of each may warrant. The parties may at any time by written agreement designate any other individual to act as arbitrator in lieu of said Loos.

. . .

"5. This agreement shall be in effect from the date hereof and shall continue in effect for a period of ten years unless sooner terminated by mutual agreement in writing by the parties hereto.

". . ."

The Mr. Loos mentioned in the agreement is an attorney and has represented both parties since 1937, and, before and after the voting trust was terminated in late 1942, advised them with respect to the exercise of their voting rights. At the annual meetings in 1943 and the two following years, the parties voted their shares in accordance with mutual understandings arrived at as a result of discussions. In each of these years, they elected five of the seven directors. Mrs. Ringling and Mrs. Haley each had sufficient votes, independently of the other, to elect two of the seven directors. By both voting for an additional candidate, they could be sure of his election regardless of how Mr. North, the remaining stockholder, might vote.[1]

Some weeks before the 1946 meeting, they discussed with Mr. Loos the matter of voting for directors. They were in accord that Mrs. Ringling should cast sufficient votes to elect herself and her son; and that Mrs. Haley should elect herself and her husband; but they did not agree upon a fifth director. The day before the meeting, the discussions were continued, Mrs. Haley being represented by her husband since she could not be present because of illness. In a conversation with Mr. Loos, Mr. Haley

---

1. Each lady was entitled to cast 2205 votes (since each had the cumulative voting rights of 315 shares, and there were 7 vacancies in the directorate). The sum of the votes of both is 4410, which is sufficient to allow 882 votes for each of 5 persons. Mr. North, holding 370 shares, was entitled to cast 2590 votes, which obviously cannot be divided so as to give to more than two candidates as many as 882 votes each. It will be observed that in order for Mrs. Ringling and Mrs. Haley to be sure to elect five directors (regardless of how Mr. North might vote) they must act together in the sense that their combined votes must be divided among five different candidates and at least one of the five must be voted for by both Mrs. Ringling and Mrs. Haley.

indicated that he would make a motion for an adjournment of the meeting for sixty days, in order to give the ladies additional time to come to an agreement about their voting. On the morning of the meeting, however, he stated that because of something Mrs. Ringling had done, he would not consent to a postponement. Mrs. Ringling then made a demand upon Mr. Loos to act under the third paragraph of the agreement "to arbitrate the disagreement" between her and Mrs. Haley in connection with the manner in which the stock of the two ladies should be voted. At the opening of the meeting, Mr. Loos read the written demand and stated that he determined and directed that the stock of both ladies be voted for an adjournment of sixty days. Mrs. Ringling then made a motion for adjournment and voted for it. Mr. Haley, as proxy for his wife, and Mr. North voted against the motion. Mrs. Ringling (herself or through her attorney, it is immaterial which) objected to the voting of Mrs. Haley's stock in any manner other than in accordance with Mr. Loos' direction. The chairman ruled that the stock could not be voted contrary to such direction, and declared the motion for adjournment had carried. Nevertheless, the meeting proceeded to the election of directors. Mrs. Ringling stated that she would continue in the meeting "but without prejudice to her position with respect to the voting of the stock and the fact that adjournment had not been taken." Mr. Loos directed Mrs. Ringling to cast her votes

882 for Mrs. Ringling,

882 for her son, Robert, and

441 for a Mr. Dunn,

who had been a member of the board for several years. She complied. Mr. Loos directed that Mrs. Haley's votes be cast

882 for Mrs. Haley,

882 for Mr. Haley, and

441 for Mr. Dunn.

Instead of complying, Mr. Haley attempted to vote his wife's shares

1103 for Mrs. Haley, and

1102 for Mr. Haley.

Mr. North voted his shares

864 for a Mr. Woods,

863 for a Mr. Griffin, and

863 for Mr. North.

The chairman ruled that the five candidates proposed by Mr. Loos, together with Messrs. Woods and North, were elected. The Haley–North group disputed this ruling insofar as it declared the election of Mr. Dunn; and insisted that Mr. Griffin, instead, had been elected. A directors' meeting followed in which Mrs. Ringling participated after stating that she would do so "without prejudice to her position that the stockholders' meeting had been adjourned and that the directors' meeting was not properly held."

Mr. Dunn and Mr. Griffin, although each was challenged by an opposing faction, attempted to join in voting as directors for different slates of officers. Soon after the meeting, Mrs. Ringling instituted this proceeding.

The Vice Chancellor determined that the agreement to vote in accordance with the direction of Mr. Loos was valid as a "stock pooling agreement" with lawful objects and purposes, and that it was not in violation of any public policy of this state. He held that where the arbitrator acts under the agreement and one party refuses to comply with his direction, "the Agreement constitutes the willing party . . . an implied agent possessing the irrevocable proxy of the recalcitrant party for the purpose of casting the particular vote." It was ordered that a new election be held before a master, with the direction that the master should recognize and give effect to the agreement if its terms were properly invoked.

Before taking up defendants' objections to the agreement, let us analyze particularly what it attempts to provide with respect to voting, including what functions and powers it attempts to repose in Mr. Loos, the "arbitrator." The agreement recites that the parties desired "to continue to act jointly in all matters relating to their stock ownership or interest in" the corporation. The parties agreed to consult and confer with each other in exercising their voting rights and to act jointly—that is, concertedly; unitedly; towards unified courses of action—in accordance with such agreement as they might reach. Thus, so long as the parties agree for whom or for what their shares shall be voted, the agreement provides no function for the arbitrator. His role is limited to situations where the parties fail to agree upon a course of action. In such cases, the agreement directs that "the question in disagreement shall be submitted for arbitration" to Mr. Loos "as arbitrator and his decision thereon shall be binding upon the parties." These provisions are designed to operate in aid of what appears to be a primary purpose of the parties, "to act jointly" in exercising their voting rights, by providing a means for fixing a course of action whenever they themselves might reach a stalemate.

Should the agreement be interpreted as attempting to empower the arbitrator to carry his directions into effect? Certainly there is no express delegation or grant of power to do so, either by authorizing him to vote the shares or to compel either party to vote them in accordance with his directions. The agreement expresses no other function of the arbitrator than that of deciding questions in disagreement which prevent the effectuation of the purpose "to act jointly." The power to enforce a decision does not seem a necessary or usual incident of such a function. Mr. Loos is not a party to the agreement. It does not contemplate the transfer of any shares or interest in shares to him, or that he should undertake any duties which the parties might compel him to perform. They provided that they might designate any other individual to act instead of Mr. Loos. The agreement does not attempt to make the arbitrator a trustee of an express trust. What the arbitrator is to do is for the benefit of the parties, not for his own benefit. Whether the parties accept or reject his decision is no concern of his, so far as the agreement or the surrounding circumstances reveal. We think the parties sought to bind each other, but to be bound only to each other, and not to empower the arbitrator to enforce decisions he might make.

From this conclusion, it follows necessarily that no decision of the arbitrator could ever be enforced if both parties to the agreement were unwilling that it be enforced, for the obvious reason that there would be no one to enforce it. Under the agreement, something more is required after the arbitrator has given his decision in order that it should become compulsory: at least one of the parties must determine that such decision shall be carried into effect. Thus, any "control" of the voting of the shares, which is reposed in the arbitrator, is substantially limited in action under the agreement in that it is subject to the overriding power of the parties themselves.

The agreement does not describe the undertaking of each party with respect to a decision of the arbitrator other than to provide that it "shall be binding upon the parties." It seems to us that this language, considered with relation to its context and the situations to which it is applicable, means that each party promised the other to exercise her own voting rights in accordance with the arbitrator's decision. The agreement is silent about any exercise of the voting rights of one party by the other. The language with reference to situations where the parties arrive at an understanding as to voting plainly suggests "action" by each, and "exercising" voting rights by each, rather than by one for the other. There is no intimation that this method should be different where the arbitrator's decision is to be carried into effect. Assuming that a power in each party to exercise the voting rights of the other might be a relatively more effective or convenient means of enforcing a decision of the arbitrator than would be available without the power, this would not justify implying a delegation of the power in the absence of some indication that the parties bargained for that means. The method of voting actually employed by the parties tends to show that they did not construe the agreement as creating powers to vote each other's shares; for at meetings prior to 1946 each party apparently exercised her own voting rights, and at the 1946 meeting, Mrs. Ringling, who wished to enforce the agreement, did not attempt to cast a ballot in exercise of any voting rights of Mrs. Haley. We do not find enough in the agreement or in the circumstances to justify a construction that either party was empowered to exercise voting rights of the other.

Having examined what the parties sought to provide by the agreement, we come now to defendants' contention that the voting provisions are illegal and revocable. They say that the courts of this state have definitely established the doctrine "that there can be no agreement, or any device whatsoever, by which the voting power of stock of a Delaware corporation may be irrevocably separated from the ownership of the stock, except by an agreement which complies with Section 18" of the Corporation Law, Rev.Code 1935, § 2050, and except by a proxy coupled with an interest. . . . The statute reads, in part, as follows:

"Sec. 18. Fiduciary Stockholders; Voting Power of; Voting Trusts:— Persons holding stock in a fiduciary capacity shall be entitled to vote the shares so held, and persons whose stock is pledged shall be entitled to vote, unless in the transfer by the pledgor on the books of the corporation he shall have expressly empowered the pledgee to vote thereon, in which case only the pledgee, or his proxy may represent said stock and vote thereon.

"One or more stockholders may by agreement in writing deposit capital stock of an original issue with or transfer capital stock to any person or persons, or corporation or corporations authorized to act as trustee, for the purpose of vesting in said person or persons, corporation or corporations, who may be designated Voting Trustee or Voting Trustees, the right to vote thereon for any period of time determined by such agreement, not exceeding ten years, upon the terms and conditions stated in such agreement. Such agreement may contain any other lawful provisions not inconsistent with said purpose.   .   .   .   Said Voting Trustees may vote upon the stock so issued or transferred during the period in such agreement specified; stock standing in the names of such Voting Trustees may be voted either in person or by proxy, and in voting said stock, such Voting Trustees shall incur no responsibility as stockholder, trustee or otherwise, except for their own individual malfeasance." [2]

In our view, neither the cases nor the statute sustain the rule for which the defendants contend. Their sweeping formulation would impugn well-recognized means by which a shareholder may effectively confer his voting rights upon others while retaining various other rights. For example, defendants' rule would apparently not permit holders of voting stock to confer upon stockholders of another class, by the device of an amendment of the certificate of incorporation, the exclusive right to vote during periods when dividends are not paid on stock of the latter class. The broad prohibitory meaning which defendants find in Section 18 seems inconsistent with their concession that proxies coupled with an interest may be irrevocable, for the statute contains nothing about such proxies. The statute authorizes, among other things, the deposit or transfer of stock in trust for a specified purpose, namely, "vesting" in the transferee "the right to vote thereon" for a limited period; and prescribes numerous requirements in this connection. Accordingly, it seems reasonable to infer that to establish the relationship and accomplish the purpose which the statute authorizes, its requirements must be complied with. But the statute does not purport to deal with agreements whereby shareholders attempt to bind each other as to how they shall vote their shares. Various forms of such pooling agreements, as they are sometimes called, have been held valid and have been distinguished from voting trusts.   .   .   .   We think the particular agreement before us does not violate Section 18 or constitute an

2. Omitted portions of the section provide requirements for the filing of a copy of the agreement in the principal Delaware office of the corporation for the issuance of certificates of stock to the voting trustees, for the voting of stock where there are more than one voting trustee, and for the extension of the agreement for additional periods, not exceeding ten years each.

attempted evasion of its requirements, and is not illegal for any other reason. Generally speaking, a shareholder may exercise wide liberality of judgment in the matter of voting, and it is not objectionable that his motives may be for personal profit, or determined by whims or caprice, so long as he violates no duty owed his fellow shareholders. . . . The ownership of voting stock imposes no legal duty to vote at all. A group of shareholders may, without impropriety, vote their respective shares so as to obtain advantages of concerted action. They may lawfully contract with each other to vote in the future in such way as they, or a majority of their group, from time to time determine. . . . Reasonable provisions for cases of failure of the group to reach a determination because of an even division in their ranks seem unobjectionable. The provision here for submission to the arbitrator is plainly designed as a deadlock-breaking measure, and the arbitrator's decision cannot be enforced unless at least one of the parties (entitled to cast one-half of their combined votes) is willing that it be enforced. We find the provision reasonable. It does not appear that the agreement enables the parties to take any unlawful advantage of the outside shareholder, or of any other person. It offends no rule of law or public policy of this state of which we are aware.

Legal consideration for the promises of each party is supplied by the mutual promises of the other party. The undertaking to vote in accordance with the arbitrator's decision is a valid contract. The good faith of the arbitrator's action has not been challenged and, indeed, the record indicates that no such challenge could be supported. Accordingly, the failure of Mrs. Haley to exercise her voting rights in accordance with his decision was a breach of her contract. It is no extenuation of the breach that her votes were cast for two of the three candidates directed by the arbitrator. His directions to her were part of a single plan or course of action for the voting of the shares of both parties to the agreement, calculated to utilize an advantage of joint action by them which would bring about the election of an additional director. The actual voting of Mrs. Haley's shares frustrates that plan to such an extent that it should not be treated as a partial performance of her contract.

Throughout their argument, defendants make much of the fact that all votes cast at the meeting were by the registered shareholders. The Court of Chancery may, in a review of an election, reject votes of a registered shareholder where his voting of them is found to be in violation of rights of another person. . . . It seems to us that upon the application of Mrs. Ringling, the injured party, the votes representing Mrs. Haley's shares should not be counted. Since no infirmity in Mr. North's voting has been demonstrated, his right to recognition of what he did at the meeting should be considered in granting any relief to Mrs. Ringling; for her rights arose under a contract to which Mr. North was not a party. With this in mind, we have concluded that the election should not be declared invalid, but that effect should be given to a rejection of the votes representing Mrs. Haley's shares. No other relief seems appropriate in this proceeding. Mr. North's vote against the motion for adjournment was sufficient to defeat it. With respect to the election of directors, the return of the inspectors should be corrected to show a rejection of Mrs. Haley's votes, and to declare the election of the six persons for whom Mr. North and Mrs. Ringling voted.

This leaves one vacancy in the directorate. The question of what to do about such a vacancy was not considered by the court below and has not been argued here. For this reason, and because an election of directors at the 1947 annual meeting (which presumably will be held in the near future) may make a determination of the question unimportant, we shall not decide it on this appeal. If a decision of the point appears important to the parties, any of them may apply to raise it in the Court of Chancery, after the mandate of this court is received there.

An order should be entered directing a modification of the order of the Court of Chancery in accordance with this opinion.

ANALYSIS

1. If you had been in the position of Loos, attorney for several years for Mrs. Ringling and Mrs. Haley, what would you have said when they asked you to act as arbitrator under their agreement?

2. Did Mrs. Haley win or lose?

3. Note that Mrs. Ringling did not seek specific performance. The suit she filed was to review an election. What would the result have been if she had sought specific performance?

4. How should the agreement have been drafted to make a lawsuit unnecessary?

McQuade v. Stoneham

263 N.Y. 323, 189 N.E. 234 (1934).

■ POUND, CHIEF JUDGE.

The action is brought to compel specific performance of an agreement between the parties, entered into to secure the control of National Exhibition Company, also called the Baseball Club (New York Nationals or "Giants"). This was one of Stoneham's enterprises which used the New York polo grounds for its home games. McGraw was manager of the Giants. McQuade was at the time the contract was entered into a city magistrate. He resigned December 8, 1930.

Defendant Stoneham became the owner of 1,306 shares, or a majority of the stock of National Exhibition Company. Plaintiff and defendant McGraw each purchased 70 shares of his stock. Plaintiff paid Stoneham $50,338.10 for the stock he purchased. As a part of the transaction, the agreement in question was entered into. It was dated May 21, 1919. Some of its pertinent provisions are

"VIII. The parties hereto will use their best endeavors for the purpose of continuing as directors of said Company and as officers thereof the following:

> "Directors:
>> "Charles A. Stoneham,
>> "John J. McGraw,
>> "Francis X. McQuade

"—with the right to the party of the first part [Stoneham] to name all additional directors as he sees fit:
> "Officers:
>> "Charles A. Stoneham, President,
>> "John J. McGraw, Vice–President,
>> "Francis X. McQuade, Treasurer.

"IX. No salaries are to be paid to any of the above officers or directors, except as follows:

> "President $45,000
> "Vice–President 7,500
> "Treasurer.................. 7,500

"X. There shall be no change in said salaries, no change in the amount of capital, or the number of shares, no change or amendment of the by-laws of the corporation or any matters regarding the policy of the business of the corporation or any matters which may in anywise affect, endanger or interfere with the rights of minority stockholders, excepting upon the mutual and unanimous consent of all of the parties hereto. . . .

"XIV. This agreement shall continue and remain in force so long as the parties or any of them or the representative of any, own the stock referred to in this agreement, to wit, the party of the first part, 1,166 shares, the party of the second part 70 shares and the party of the third part 70 shares, except as may otherwise appear by this agreement. . . ."

In pursuance of this contract Stoneham became president and McGraw vice president of the corporation. McQuade became treasurer. In June, 1925, his salary was increased to $10,000 a year. He continued to act until May 2, 1928, when Leo J. Bondy was elected to succeed him. The board of directors consisted of seven men. The four outside of the parties hereto were selected by Stoneham and he had complete control over them. At the meeting of May 2, 1928, Stoneham and McGraw refrained from voting, McQuade voted for himself, and the other four voted for Bondy. Defendants did not keep their agreement with McQuade to use their best efforts to continue him as treasurer. On the contrary, he was dropped with their entire acquiescence. At the next stockholders' meeting he was dropped as a director although they might have elected him.

The courts below have refused to order the reinstatement of McQuade, but have given him damages for wrongful discharge, with a right to sue for future damages.

The cause for dropping McQuade was due to the falling out of friends. McQuade and Stoneham had disagreed. The trial court has found in substance that their numerous quarrels and disputes did not affect the orderly and efficient administration of the business of the corporation; that plaintiff was removed because he had antagonized the dominant Stoneham by persisting in challenging his power over the corporate treasury and for no misconduct on his part. The court also finds that plaintiff was removed by Stoneham for protecting the corporation and its minority stockholders. We will assume that Stoneham put him out when he might have retained him, merely in order to get rid of him.

Defendants say that the contract in suit was void because the directors held their office charged with the duty to act for the corporation according to their best judgment and that any contract which compels a director to vote to keep any particular person in office and at a stated salary is illegal. Directors are the exclusive executive representatives of the corporation, charged with administration of its internal affairs and the management and use of its assets. They manage the business of the corporation. (General Corporation Law, Consol. Laws, c. 23, § 27.) "An agreement to continue a man as president is dependent upon his continued loyalty to the interests of the corporation." Fells v. Katz, 256 N.Y. 67, 72, 175 N.E. 516, 517. So much is undisputed.

Plaintiff contends that the converse of this proposition is true and that an agreement among directors to continue a man as an officer of a corporation is not to be broken so long as such officer is loyal to the interests of the corporation and that, as plaintiff has been found loyal to the corporation, the agreement of defendants is enforceable.

Although it has been held that an agreement among stockholders whereby it is attempted to divest the directors of their power to discharge an unfaithful employee of the corporation is illegal as against public policy (Fells v. Katz, supra), it must be equally true that the stockholders may not, by agreement among themselves, control the directors in the exercise of the judgment vested in them by virtue of their office to elect officers and fix salaries. Their motives may not be questioned so long as their acts are legal. The bad faith or the improper motives of the parties does not change the rule. . . . Directors may not by agreements entered into as stockholders abrogate their independent judgment. . . .

Stockholders may, of course, combine to elect directors. That rule is well settled. As Holmes, C.J., pointedly said (Brightman v. Bates, 175 Mass. 105, 111, 55 N.E. 809, 811): "If stockholders want to make their power felt, they must unite. There is no reason why a majority should not agree to keep together." The power to unite is, however, limited to the election of directors and is not extended to contracts whereby limitations are placed on the power of directors to manage the business of the corporation by the selection of agents at defined salaries.

The minority shareholders whose interests McQuade says he has been punished for protecting, are not, aside from himself, complaining about his discharge. He is not acting for the corporation or for them in this action.

It is impossible to see how the corporation has been injured by the substitution of Bondy as treasurer in place of McQuade. As McQuade represents himself in this action and seeks redress for his own wrongs, "we prefer to listen to [the corporation and the minority stockholders] before any decision as to their wrongs." Faulds v. Yates, 57 Ill. 416, 417, 11 Am.Rep. 24.

It is urged that we should pay heed to the morals and manners of the market place to sustain this agreement and that we should hold that its violation gives rise to a cause of action for damages rather than base our decision on any outworn notions of public policy. Public policy is a dangerous guide in determining the validity of a contract and courts should not interfere lightly with the freedom of competent parties to make their own contracts. We do not close our eyes to the fact that such agreements, tacitly or openly arrived at, are not uncommon, especially in close corporations where the stockholders are doing business for convenience under a corporate organization. We know that majority stockholders, united in voting trusts, effectively manage the business of a corporation by choosing trustworthy directors to reflect their policies in the corporate management. Nor are we unmindful that McQuade has, so the court has found, been shabbily treated as a purchaser of stock from Stoneham. We have said: "A trustee is held to something stricter than the morals of the market place" (Meinhard v. Salmon, 249 N.Y. 458, 464, 164 N.E. 545, 546), but Stoneham and McGraw were not trustees for McQuade as an individual. Their duty was to the corporation and its stockholders, to be exercised according to their unrestricted lawful judgment. They were under no legal obligation to deal righteously with McQuade if it was against public policy to do so.

The courts do not enforce mere moral obligations, nor legal ones either, unless someone seeks to establish rights which may be waived by custom and for convenience. We are constrained by authority to hold that a contract is illegal and void so far as it precludes the board of directors, at the risk of incurring legal liability, from changing officers, salaries, or policies or retaining individuals in office, except by consent of the contracting parties. On the whole, such a holding is probably preferable to one which would open the courts to pass on the motives of directors in the lawful exercise of their trust.

A further reason for reversal exists. At the time the contract was made the plaintiff was a city magistrate. . . .

The Inferior Criminal Courts Act (Laws of 1910, c. 659, as amended) provides that no "city magistrate shall engage in any other business, profession or hold any other public office or shall serve as the representative of any political party for any assembly, aldermanic, senatorial or congressional district in the executive committee or other governing body of any political party organization or political party association. No city magistrate shall engage in any other business or profession or act as referee, or receiver, but each of said justices and magistrates shall devote his whole time and capacity, so far as the public interest demands, to the duties of his office. . . ." (Section 161, Laws 1933, c. 746, formerly section 102, as amended, Laws 1915, c. 531.) The contract contemplated that the plaintiff should hold an executive office at a stipulated and substantial salary. . . .

Until the date when the defendant repudiated the agreement, its performance constituted a violation of the statute. . . .

■ LEHMAN, JUDGE.

I concur in the decision of the court on the second ground stated in the opinion. I desire to state the reasons why I do not accept the first ground.

. . .

We have said: "An ordinary agreement, among a minority in number, but a majority in shares, for the purpose of obtaining control of the corporation by the election of particular persons as directors is not illegal." Manson v. Curtis, 223 N.Y. 313, 319, 119 N.E. 559, 561, Ann.Cas. 1918E, 247. We are agreed that, if the contract had provided only for the election of directors, it would not have been illegal. Its vice, if any, is inherent in the provisions intended to give assurance that the directors so elected would act according to the prearranged design of the stockholders in apportioning the corporate offices and emoluments of such offices among the majority stockholders.

. . .

There can, I think, be no doubt that shareholders owning a majority of the corporate stock may combine to obtain and exercise any control which a single owner of such stock could exercise. What may lawfully be done by an individual may ordinarily be lawfully done by a combination, but no combination is legal if formed to accomplish an illegal object. No such combination or agreement may "contravene any express charter or statutory provision or contemplate any fraud, oppression or wrong against other stockholders or other illegal object." Manson v. Curtis, supra.

In that case we held invalid, on that ground, an agreement for the selection "of directors who should remain passive or mechanical to the will and word" of one of the parties to the agreement. Now it is said that, for the same reason, this agreement must be held unenforceable, though here the agreement contemplated no restriction upon the powers of the board of directors, and no dictation or interference by stockholders except in so far as concerns the election and remuneration of officers and the adhesion by the corporation to established policies.

It seems difficult to reconcile such a decision with the statements in the opinion in Manson v. Curtis that "it is not illegal or against public policy for two or more stockholders owning the majority of the shares of stock to unite upon a course of corporate policy or action, or upon the officers whom they will elect," and that "shareholders have the right to combine their interests and voting powers to secure such control of the corporation and the adoption of and adhesion by it to a specific policy and course of business." Obviously, a combination intended to effect the election of certain officers and to obtain control of the corporation and adhesion by it to a specific policy and course of business can accomplish its ends only to the extent that directors will bow to the will of those who united to elect them. The directors have the power and the duty to act in accordance with their own best judgment so long as they remain directors. The majority stockholders can compel no action by the directors, but at the expiration of the term of office of the directors the stockholders have the power to replace them with others whose actions coincide with the judgment or desires of the holders of a majority of the stock. The theory that directors exercise in all matters an independent judgment in practice often yields to the fact that the choice of directors lies with the majority stockholders and thus gives the stockholders a very effective control of the action by the board of directors. In truth the board of directors may check the arbitrary will of those who would otherwise completely control the corporation, but cannot indefinitely thwart their will.

A contract which destroys this check contravenes "express charter or statutory provisions" and is, therefore, illegal. A contract which merely provides that stockholders shall in combination use their power to achieve a legitimate purpose is not illegal. They may join in the election of directors who, in their opinion, will be in sympathy with the policies of the majority stockholders and who, in the choice of executive officers, will be influenced by the wishes of the majority stockholders. The directors so chosen may not act in disregard of the best interests of the corporation and its minority stockholders, but with that limitation they may and, in practice, usually are swayed by the wishes of the majority. Otherwise there would be no continuity of corporate policy and no continuity in management of corporate affairs.

The contract now under consideration provides, in a narrow field, for corporate action within these limitations. ... A contract which merely provides for the election of fit officers and adhesion to particular policy determined in advance constitutes an agreement by which men in combination exercise a power which could be lawfully exercised if lodged in a single man. It is legal, if designed to protect legitimate interests without wrong to others. Public policy should be governed by facts, not abstractions. The contract is, in my opinion, valid. It is unenforceable only because it resulted in an employment which was itself illegal.

■ CRANE, KELLOGG, O'BRIEN, and HUBBS, JJ., concur with POUND, C.J.

■ LEHMAN, J., concurs in result in opinion in which CROUCH, J., concurs.

Judgments reversed, etc.

Clark v. Dodge

269 N.Y. 410, 199 N.E. 641 (1936).

■ CROUCH, JUDGE.

· · ·

The two corporate defendants are New Jersey corporations manufacturing medicinal preparations by secret formulae. The main office, factory, and assets of both corporations are located in the state of New York.   In 1921, and at all times since, Clark owned 25 per cent. and Dodge 75 per cent. of the stock of each corporation.   Dodge took no active part in the business, although he was a director, and through ownership of their qualifying shares, controlled the other directors of both corporations.   He was the president of Bell & Co., Inc., and nominally general manager of Hollings–Smith Company, Inc.   The plaintiff, Clark, was a director and held the offices of treasurer and general manager of Bell & Co., Inc., and also had charge of the major portion of the business of Hollings–Smith Company, Inc.   The formulae and methods of manufacture of the medicinal preparations were known to him alone.   Under date of February 15, 1921, Dodge and Clark, the sole owners of the stock of both corporations, entered into a written agreement under seal, which after reciting the stock ownership of both parties, the desire of Dodge that Clark should continue in the efficient management and control of the business of Bell & Co., Inc., so long as he should "remain faithful, efficient and competent to so manage and control the said business"; and his further desire that Clark should not be the sole custodian of a specified formula, but should share his knowledge thereof and of the method of manufacture with a son of Dodge, provided, in substance, as follows: That Dodge during his lifetime and, after his death, a trustee to be appointed by his will, would so vote his stock and so vote as a director that the plaintiff (a) should continue to be a director of Bell & Co., Inc.; and (b) should continue as its general manager so long as he should be "faithful, efficient and competent"; (c) should during his life receive one-fourth of the net income of the corporations either by way of salary or dividends; and (d) that no unreasonable or incommensurate salaries should be paid to other officers or agents which would so reduce the net income as materially to affect Clark's profits.   Clark on his part agreed to disclose the specified formula to the son and to instruct him in the details and methods of manufacture; and, further, at the end of his life to bequeath his stock—if no issue survived him—to the wife and children of Dodge.

It was further provided that the provisions in regard to the division of net profits and the regulation of salaries should also apply to the Hollings–Smith Company.

The complaint alleges due performance of the contract by Clark and breach thereof by Dodge in that he has failed to use his stock control to continue Clark as a director and as general manager, and has prevented Clark from receiving his proportion of the income, while taking his own, by causing the employment of incompetent persons at excessive salaries, and otherwise.

The relief sought is reinstatement as director and general manager and an accounting by Dodge and by the corporations for waste and for the proportion of net income due plaintiff, with an injunction against further violations.

The only question which need be discussed is whether the contract is illegal as against public policy within the decision in McQuade v. Stoneham, 263 N.Y. 323, 189 N.E. 234, upon the authority of which the complaint was dismissed by the Appellate Division.

"The business of a corporation shall be managed by its board of directors." General Corporation Law (Consol.Laws, c. 23) § 27. That is the statutory norm. Are we committed by the McQuade Case to the doctrine that there may be no variation, however slight or innocuous, from that norm, where salaries or policies or the retention of individuals in office are concerned? There is ample authority supporting that doctrine, . . . and something may be said for it, since it furnishes a simple, if arbitrary, test. Apart from its practical administrative convenience, the reasons upon which it is said to rest are more or less nebulous. Public policy, the intention of the Legislature, detriment to the corporation, are phrases which in this connection mean little. Possible harm to bona fide purchasers of stock or to creditors or to stockholding minorities have more substance; but such harms are absent in many instances. If the enforcement of a particular contract damages nobody—not even, in any perceptible degree, the public—one sees no reason for holding it illegal, even though it impinges slightly upon the broad provision of section 27. Damage suffered or threatened is a logical and practical test, and has come to be the one generally adopted by the courts. . . . Where the directors are the sole stockholders, there seems to be no objection to enforcing an agreement among them to vote for certain people as officers. There is no direct decision to that effect in this court, yet there are strong indications that such a rule has long been recognized. The opinion in Manson v. Curtis, 223 N.Y. 313, 325, 119 N.E. 559, 562, Ann.Cas. 1918E, 247, closed its discussion by saying: "The rule that all the stockholders by their universal consent may do as they choose with the corporate concerns and assets, provided the interests of creditors are not affected, because they are the complete owners of the corporation, cannot be invoked here." That was because all the stockholders were not parties to the agreement there in question. So, where the public was not affected, "the parties in interest, might, by their original agreement of incorporation, limit their respective rights and powers," even where there was a conflicting statutory standard. Ripin v. United States Woven Label Co., 205 N.Y. 442, 448, 98 N.E. 855, 857. . . .

Except for the broad dicta in the McQuade opinion, we think there can be no doubt that the agreement here in question was legal and that the complaint states a cause of action. There was no attempt to sterilize the board of directors, as in the Manson and McQuade Cases. The only restrictions on Dodge were (a) that as a stockholder he should vote for Clark as a director—a perfectly legal contract; (b) that as director he should continue Clark as general manager, so long as he proved faithful, efficient, and competent—an agreement which could harm nobody; (c) that Clark should always receive as salary or dividends one-fourth of the "net income." For the purposes of this motion, it is only just to construe that phrase as meaning whatever was left for distribution after the directors had in good faith set aside whatever they deemed wise; (d) that no salaries to other officers should be paid, unreasonable in amount or incommensurate with services rendered—a beneficial and not a harmful agreement.

If there was any invasion of the powers of the directorate under that agreement, it is so slight as to be negligible; and certainly there is no damage suffered by or threatened to anybody. The broad statements in the McQuade opinion, applicable to the facts there, should be confined to those facts.

The judgment of the Appellate Division should be reversed and the order of the Special Term affirmed, with costs in this court and in the Appellate Division.

■ CRANE, C.J., and LEHMAN, O'BRIEN, HUBBS, LOUGHRAN, and FINCH, JJ., concur.

Judgment accordingly.

ANALYSIS AND PLANNING

1. In McQuade v. Stoneham, the court says that it is a matter of "public policy" that "stockholders may not, by agreement among themselves, control the directors in the exercise of the judgment vested in them by virtue of their office to elect officers and fix salaries." What, if any, are the goals or criteria of good government that underlie that public policy?

2. Was McQuade assured of representation on the board of directors? What legal devices are available to provide assurance of a seat on the board?

3. If McQuade had been assured of representation on the board of directors, how might he have been assured of continuation in his role as treasurer of the corporation?

4. Subsequent to the decisions in these cases, the New York Business Corporation Law was changed. It now provides, in § 620:

(a) An agreement between two or more shareholders, if in writing and signed by the parties thereto, may provide that in exercising any voting rights, the shares held by them shall be voted as therein provided, or as they may agree, or as determined in accordance with a procedure agreed upon by them.

(b) A provision in the certificate of incorporation otherwise prohibited by law because it improperly restricts the board in its management of the business of the corporation, or improperly transfers to one or more shareholders or to one of more persons or corporations to be selected by him or them, all or any part of such management otherwise within the authority of the board under this chapter, shall nevertheless be valid: (1) If all the incorporators or holders of record of all outstanding shares, whether or not having voting power, have authorized such provision in the certificate of incorporation or an amendment thereof; and (2) If, subsequent to the adoption of such provision, shares are transferred or issued only to persons who had knowledge or notice thereof or consented in writing to such provision.

. . .

Under this provision, how might you have protected McQuade's interests?

5. Section 141(a) of the Delaware General Corporation Law provides:

(a) The business and affairs of every corporation organized under this chapter shall be managed by or under the direction of a board of directors, except as may be otherwise provided in this chapter or in its certificate of incorporation. If any such provision is made in the certificate of incorporation, the powers and duties conferred or imposed upon the board of directors by this chapter shall be exercised or performed to such extent and by such person or persons as shall be provided in the certificate of incorporation.

Section 142(b) provides, in part:

(b) Officers shall be chosen in such manner and shall hold their offices for such terms as are prescribed by the by-laws or determined by the board of directors or other governing body.

With these provisions to rely upon, how might you have protected McQuade's interests? [6]

6. In Clark v. Dodge the court in effect granted specific performance of the agreement. Do you agree that this is the appropriate remedy?

7. Dodge and Clark agreed, according to the court, that Clark "should continue as [the corporation's] general manager so long as he should be 'faithful, efficient and competent.'" What do you think about the wisdom and efficacy of this agreement?

CORPORATE PLANNING BY USE OF EMPLOYMENT CONTRACTS

One way to give McQuade, in McQuade v. Stoneham, or Clark, in Clark v. Dodge, what he seemed to have wanted might have been to have the corporation enter into an employment contract with him. Here, in outline form, is a list of some issues that are presented by employment contracts.

I. Duration

    A. Number of years. Then what?

    B. Termination for cause

        1. By whom?

        2. What is "cause"?

6. Compare New York Business Corporation Law, § 715(b) ("The certificate of incorporation may provide that all officers or that specified officers shall be elected by the shareholders instead of by the board."); California Corporations Code, § 312(b) ("Except as otherwise provided by the articles or by-laws, officers shall be chosen by the board and serve at the pleasure of the board, . . .").

    C. Effect of illness, incapacity, etc.

II. Compensation

    A. Salary

    B. Adjustments (e.g., for inflation)

    C. Bonuses, stock options, etc.

    D. Benefits

    E. Travel and other expenses

    F. Perquisites

III. Duties and status

    A. Job description

    B. Other duties

    C. Amount of time; vacation

    D. Outside activities

IV. Competition and Trade Secrets

V. Consequences of termination

    A. Liquidated damages

    B. Duty to mitigate

VI. Parties

    A. Mergers, etc.

    B. Guarantee by majority shareholder

Assume that you represent McQuade, except that the time is now, and that he is about to invest a substantial amount of money in a major league baseball team and become its treasurer and chief financial officer. He wants to sit down with you and have you explain to him what the issues are and what he might reasonably seek in an employment contract and in any related agreements that you think important. What would you be prepared to ask him and tell him?

What if it were Clark, rather than McQuade, whom you were about to advise?

Do you think that the interests of the parties in the two cases would have been better served by the use of employment contracts than by the use of voting agreements? What other legal device should have been recommended?

NOTE ON SHAREHOLDER AGREEMENTS, VOTING TRUSTS, STATUTORY CLOSE CORPORATIONS, AND INVOLUNTARY DISSOLUTION

Shareholder agreements (sometimes called "pooling" agreements), designed to achieve objectives such as those reflected in McQuade v. Stoneham and in Clark v. Dodge, have often been used. Agreements by which the shareholders simply commit to electing themselves, or their representatives, as directors, are generally considered unobjectionable, and are now expressly validated in many jurisdictions (see, e.g., New York Bus. Corp. Law, § 620(a), validating shareholder voting agreements with other objectives as well). They do not interfere with the obligations of the directors to exercise their sound judgment in managing the affairs of the corporation.

The courts have had more difficulty with shareholder agreements requiring the appointment of particular individuals as officers or employees of the corporation, since such agreements do deprive the directors of one of their most important functions. The modern view, reflected in the next case (Galler v. Galler) and in the Note following it (summarizing Zion v. Kurtz), is that such agreements are enforceable, at least for closely held corporations, as long as they are signed by all shareholders (and, perhaps, in situations in which any nonsigning minority shareholders cannot or do not object).

Another device that can be used for control is the voting trust, a device specifically authorized by the corporation laws of most states. With a voting trust, shareholders who wish to act in concert turn their shares over to a trustee. The trustee then votes all the shares, in accordance with instructions in the document establishing the trust. Voting trusts are often used to maintain control of a corporation by a family or group, when there is a fear that some members of the family or group might form a coalition with minority shareholders to shift control. For example, suppose that five members of a family own 60 percent of the voting shares of the corporation. They can create a voting trust and instruct the trustee to vote all the shares for directors, and on other matters submitted to shareholder vote, in accordance with decisions reached by the five members by majority vote. Voting trusts generally must be made public. See Del.Gen.Corp. Law § 218.

Many states now have special statutory provisions for closely held corporations. These provisions vary widely from state to state. Generally they allow certain corporations to elect (it's voluntary) close corporation status (whereupon the corporation is said to be a statutory close corporation). For example, under the Delaware General Corporation Law close corporation status may be elected by corporations with not more than 30 shareholders. § 342(1). Under § 351, "The certificate of incorporation of a close corporation may provide that the business of the corporation shall be managed by the stockholders of the corporation rather than by a board of directors." Thus, one advantage of close corporation status is avoidance of any need to provide for certain corporate formalities (where otherwise the failure to do so might give rise to personal liability of shareholders for corporate debts). In many situations, however, electing close corporation status may be more trouble than it is worth. Most of what investors should have to protect their interests and ensure the effective control of their venture can be accomplished by adaptations of the articles of incorporation and bylaws, together with ancillary agreements such as voting agreements, employment agreements, and buy-sell agreements.

Of more current relevance is the recent innovation in small-business organization, the Limited Liability Company (LLC). With an LLC, issues of control are left largely to individual choice, reflected in a document, drafted by (or for) the investors (the "members") and called "regulations" or "operating agreement" or something of the sort. Broadly speaking, an LLC may be "member managed" (like a partnership) or "manager managed" (like a corporation), with virtually infinite variety available. Additional flexibility in organization and control is provided by the availability in most states of a Limited Liability Partnership (LLP) or Limited Liability Limited Partnership (LLLP).

A final aspect of corporate law affecting closely held corporations is the development of provisions in corporations codes allowing for involuntary dissolution by court order. These provisions can operate, in certain circumstances, as a bail-out remedy for shareholders who have failed to enter into effective control or buy-sell agreements. These agreements are examined in Section 5 of this Chapter.

Galler v. Galler

32 Ill.2d 16, 203 N.E.2d 577 (1964).

There is no substantial dispute as to the facts in this case. From 1919 to 1924, Benjamin and Isadore Galler, brothers, were equal partners in the Galler Drug Company, a wholesale drug concern. In 1924 the business was incorporated under the Illinois Business Corporation Act, each owning one half of the outstanding 220 shares of stock. In 1945 each contracted to sell 6 shares to an employee, Rosenberg, at a price of $10,500 for each block of 6 shares, payable within 10 years. . . . Rosenberg was not involved in this litigation either as a party or as a witness, and in July of 1961, prior to the time that the master in chancery hearings were concluded, defendants Isadore and Rose Galler purchased the 12 shares from Rosenberg. A supplemental complaint was filed by the plaintiff, Emma Galler, asserting an equitable right to have 6 of the 12 shares transferred to her and offering to pay the defendants one half of the amount that the defendants paid Rosenberg. The parties have stipulated that pending disposition of the instant case, these shares will not be voted or transferred. For approximately one year prior to the entry of the decree by the chancellor in July of 1962, there were no outstanding minority shareholder interests.

In March, 1954, Benjamin and Isadore, on the advice of their accountant, decided to enter into an agreement for the financial protection of their immediate families and to assure their families, after the death of either brother, equal control of the corporation. In June, 1954, while the agreement was in the process of preparation by an attorney-associate of the accountant, Benjamin suffered a heart attack. Although he resumed his business duties some months later, he was again stricken in February, 1955, and thereafter was unable to return to work. During his brother's illness, Isadore asked the accountant to have the shareholders' agreement put in final form in order to protect Benjamin's wife, and this was done by another attorney employed in the accountant's office. On a Saturday night in July, 1955, the accountant brought the agreement to Benjamin's home, and 6 copies of it were executed there by the two brothers and their wives. . . . Between the execution of the agreement in July, 1955, and Benjamin's death in December, 1957, the agreement was not modified. Benjamin suffered a stroke late in July, 1955. . . . Because of the state of Benjamin's health, nothing further was said to him by any of the parties concerning the agreement. It appears from the evidence that some months after the agreement was signed, the defendants Isadore and Rose Galler and their son, the defendant, Aaron Galler sought to have the agreements destroyed. The evidence is undisputed that defendants had decided prior to Benjamin's death they would not honor the agreement, but never disclosed their intention to plaintiff [Emma] or her husband [Benjamin].

On July 21, 1956, Benjamin executed an instrument creating a trust naming his wife as trustee. The trust covered, among other things, the 104 shares of Galler Drug Company stock and the stock certificates were endorsed by Benjamin and delivered to Emma. When Emma presented the certificates to defendants for transfer into her name as trustee, they sought to have Emma abandon the 1955 agreement or enter into some kind of a noninterference agreement as a price for the transfer of the shares. Finally, in September, 1956, after Emma had refused to abandon the shareholders' agreement, she did agree to permit defendant Aaron to become president for one year and agreed that she would not interfere with the business during that year. The stock was then reissued in her name as trustee. During the year 1957 while Benjamin was still alive, Emma tried many times to arrange a meeting with Isadore to discuss business matters but he refused to see her.

Shortly after Benjamin's death, Emma went to the office and demanded the terms of the 1955 agreement be carried out. Isadore told her that anything she had to say could be said to Aaron, who then told her that his father would not abide by the agreement. He offered a modification of the agreement by proposing the salary continuation payment but without her becoming a director. When Emma refused to modify the agreement and sought enforcement of its terms, defendants refused and this suit followed.

During the last few years of Benjamin's life both brothers drew an annual salary of $42,000. Aaron, whose salary was $15,000 as manager of the warehouse prior to September, 1956, has since the time that Emma agreed to his acting as president drawn an annual salary of $20,000. In 1957, 1958, and 1959 a $40,000 annual dividend was paid. Plaintiff has received her proportionate share of the dividend.

The July, 1955, agreement in question here, entered into between Benjamin, Emma, Isadore and Rose, recites that Benjamin and Isadore each own 47½% of the issued and outstanding shares of the Galler Drug Company, an Illinois corporation, and that Benjamin and Isadore desired to provide income for the support and maintenance of their immediate families. No reference is made to the shares then being purchased by Rosenberg. The essential features of the contested portions of the agreement are substantially as set forth in the opinion of the Appellate Court: (2) that the bylaws of the corporation will be amended to provide for a board of four directors; that the necessary quorum shall be three directors; and that no directors' meeting shall be held without giving ten days notice to all directors. (3) The shareholders will cast their votes for the above named persons (Isadore, Rose, Benjamin and Emma) as directors at said special meeting and at any other meeting held for the purpose of electing directors. (4, 5) In the event of the death of either brother his wife shall have the right to nominate a director in place of the decedent. (6) Certain annual dividends will be declared by the corporation. The dividend shall be $50,000 payable out of the accumulated earned surplus in excess of $500,-000. If 50% of the annual net profits after taxes exceeds the minimum $50,000, then the directors shall have discretion to declare a dividend up to 50% of the annual net profits. If the net profits are less than $50,000, nevertheless the minimum $50,000 annual dividend shall be declared, providing the $500,000 surplus is maintained. Earned surplus is defined. (9) The certificates evidencing the said shares of Benjamin Galler and Isadore Galler shall bear a legend that the shares are subject to the terms of this agreement. (10) A salary continuation agreement shall be entered into by the corporation which shall authorize the corporation upon the death of Benjamin Galler or Isadore Galler, or both, to pay a sum equal to twice the salary of such officer, payable monthly over a five-year period. Said sum shall be paid to the widow during her widowhood, but should be paid to such widow's children if the widow remarries within the five-year period. . . .

The Appellate Court found the 1955 agreement void because "the undue duration, stated purpose and substantial disregard of the provisions of the Corporation Act outweigh any considerations which might call for divisibility" and held that "the public policy of this state demands voiding this entire agreement."

While the conduct of defendants towards plaintiff was clearly inequitable, the basically controlling factor is the absence of an objecting minority interest, together with the absence of public detriment. Since the issues here presented must be resolved in accordance with the public policy of this State as exemplified in prior decisions or pertinent statutes, it will be helpful to review the applicable case law.

Faulds v. Yates, 57 Ill. 416, decided by this court in 1870, established the general rule that the owners of the majority of the stock of a corporation have the right to select the agents for the management of the corporation. . . .

In Kantzler v. Bensinger, 214 Ill. 589, p. 598, decided in 1905, the issue of statutory violation was raised, and this court again followed Faulds v. Yates, emphasizing and quoting the following:

"In Faulds v. Yates, 57 Ill. 416, it was objected that an agreement between certain persons, owning a majority of the stock of a corporation, that they would elect the directors and manage the business was against public policy. There were other stockholders, but they made no objection. The court upheld the agreement, and on page 420 of 57 Ill. said: 'There was no fraud in the agreement which has been so bitterly assailed in the argument. There was nothing unlawful in it. There was nothing which necessarily affected the rights and interests of the minority. Three persons, owning a majority of the stock, had the unquestioned right to combine, and thus secure the board of directors and the management of the property. Corporations are governed by the republican principle that the whole are bound by the acts of the majority, when the acts conform to the law of their creation. The co-operation, then, of these parties in the election of the officers of the company, and their agreement not to buy or sell stock except for their joint benefit, cannot properly be characterized as dishonest and violative of the rights of others, and in contravention of public policy." . . .

At this juncture it should be emphasized that we deal here with a so-called close corporation. Various attempts at definition of the close corporation have been made. For a collection of those most frequently proffered, see O'Neal, Close Corporations, § 1.02 (1958). For our purposes, a close corporation is one in which the stock is held in a few hands, or in a few families, and wherein it is not at all, or only rarely, dealt in by buying or selling. . . . Moreover, it should be recognized that shareholder agreements similar to that in question here are often, as a practical consideration, quite necessary for the protection of those financially interested in the close corporation. While the shareholder of a public-issue corporation may readily sell his shares on the open market should management fail to use, in his opinion, sound business judgment, his counterpart of the close corporation often has a large total of his entire capital invested in the business and has no ready market for his shares should he desire to sell. He feels, understandably, that he is more than a mere investor and that his voice should be heard concerning all corporate activity. Without a shareholder agreement, specifically enforceable by the courts, insuring him a modicum of control, a large minority shareholder might find himself at the mercy of an oppressive or unknowledgeable majority. Moreover, as in the case at bar, the shareholders of a close corporation are often also the directors and officers thereof. With substantial shareholding interests abiding in each member of the board of directors, it is often quite impossible to secure, as in the large public-issue corporation, independent board judgment free from personal motivations concerning corporate policy. For these and other reasons too voluminous to enumerate here, often the only sound basis for protection is afforded by a lengthy, detailed shareholder agreement securing the rights and obligations of all concerned.

As the preceding review of the applicable decisions of this court points out, there has been a definite, albeit inarticulate, trend toward eventual judicial treatment of the close corporation as *sui generis*. Several shareholder-director agreements that have technically "violated" the letter of the Business Corporation Act have nevertheless been upheld in the light of the existing practical circumstances, i.e., no apparent public injury, the absence of a complaining minority interest, and no apparent prejudice to creditors. However, we have thus far not attempted to limit these decisions as applicable only to close corporations and have seemingly implied that general considerations regarding judicial supervision of all corporate behavior apply.

. . .

Numerous helpful textual statements and law review articles dealing with the judicial treatment of the close corporation have been pointed out by counsel. One article concludes with the following: "New needs compel fresh formulation of corporate 'norms.' There is no reason why mature men should not be able to adapt the statutory form to the structure they want, so long as they do not endanger other stockholders, creditors, or the public, or violate a clearly mandatory provision of the corporation laws. In a typical close corporation the stockholders' agreement is usually the result of careful deliberation among all initial investors. In the large public-issue corporation, on the other hand, the 'agreement' represented by the corporate charter is not consciously agreed to by the investors; they have no voice in its formulation, and very few ever read the certificate of incorporation. Preservation of the corporate norms may there be necessary for the protection of the public investors." Hornstein, Stockholders' Agreements in the Closely Held Corporation, 59 Yale L. Journal, 1040, 1056.

This court has recognized, albeit *sub silentio,* the significant conceptual differences between the close corporation and its public-issue counterpart in, among other cases, Kantzler v. Benzinger, 214 Ill. 589, where an agreement quite similar to the one under attack here was upheld. Where, as in *Kantzler* and here, no complaining minority interest appears, no fraud or apparent injury to the public or creditors is present, and no clearly prohibitory statutory language is violated, we can see no valid reason for precluding the parties from reaching any arrangements concerning the management of the corporation which are agreeable to all.

. . .

We now, in the light of the foregoing, turn to specific provisions of the 1955 agreement.

The Appellate Court correctly found many of the contractual provisions free from serious objection, and we need not prolong this opinion with a discussion of them here. That court did, however, find difficulties in the stated purpose of the agreement as it relates to its duration, the election of certain persons to specific offices for a number of years, the requirement for the mandatory declaration of stated dividends (which the Appellate Court held invalid), and the salary continuation agreement.

Since the question as to the duration of the agreement is a principal source of controversy, we shall consider it first. The parties provided no specific termination date, and while the agreement concludes with a paragraph that its terms "shall be binding upon and shall inure to the benefits of" the legal representatives, heirs and assigns of the parties, this clause is, we believe, intended to be operative only as long as one of the parties is living. It further provides that it shall be so construed as to carry out its purposes, and we believe these must be determined from a consideration of the agreement as a whole. Thus viewed, a fair construction is that its purposes were accomplished at the death of the survivor of the parties. While these life spans are not precisely ascertainable, and the Appellate Court noted Emma Galler's life expectancy at her husband's death was 26.9 years, we are aware of no statutory or public policy provision against stockholder's agreements which would invalidate this agreement on that ground. (Thompson v. J.D. Thompson Carnation Co., 279 Ill. 54, 116 N.E. 648.) Vogel v. Melish, Ill., 203 N.E.2d 411, also involved a construction of a contract in a close corporation, but not the validity of the contract. While defendants argue that the public policy evinced by the legislative restrictions upon the duration of voting trust agreements (Ill.Rev.Stat. 1963, chap. 32, par. 157.30a) should be applied here, this agreement is not a voting trust, but as pointed out by the dissenting justice in the Appellate Court, is a straight contractual voting control agreement which does not divorce voting rights from stock ownership. That the policy against agreements in which stock ownership and voting rights are separated, indicated in Luthy v. Ream, 270 Ill. 170, is inapplicable to voting control agreements was emphasized in *Thompson* wherein a control agreement was upheld as not attempting to separate ownership and voting power. While limiting voting trusts in 1947 to a maximum duration of 10 years, the legislature has indicated no similar policy regarding straight voting agreements although these have been common since prior to 1870. In view of the history of decisions of this court generally upholding, in the absence of fraud or prejudice to minority interests or public policy, the right of stockholders to agree among themselves as to the manner in which their stock will be voted, we do not regard the period of time within which this agreement may remain effective as rendering the agreement unenforceable.

The clause that provides for the election of certain persons to specified offices for a period of years likewise does not require invalidation. In Kantzler v. Benzinger, 214 Ill. 589, this court upheld an agreement entered into by all the stockholders providing that certain parties would be elected to the offices of the corporation for a fixed period. In Faulds v. Yates, 57 Ill. 416, we upheld a similar agreement among the majority stockholders of a corporation, notwithstanding the existence of a minority which was not before the court complaining thereof. See also Hornstein, "Judicial Tolerance of the Incorporated Partnership," 18 Law and Contemporary Problems 435 at page 444.

We turn next to a consideration of the effect of the stated purpose of the agreement upon its validity. The pertinent provision is: "The said Benjamin A. Galler and Isadore A. Galler desire to provide income for the support and maintenance of their immediate families." Obviously, there is no evil inherent in a contract entered into for the reason that the persons originating the terms desired to so arrange their property as to provide post-death support for those dependent upon them. Nor does the fact that the subject property is corporate stock alter the situation so long as there exists no detriment to minority stock interests, creditors or other public injury. It is, however, contended by defendants that the methods provided by the agreement for implementation of the stated purpose are, as a whole, violative of the Business Corporation Act . . . to such an extent as to render it void *in toto*.

The terms of the dividend agreement require a minimum annual dividend of $50,000, but this duty is limited by the subsequent provision that it shall be operative only so long as an earned surplus of $500,000 is maintained. It may be noted that in 1958, the year prior to commencement of this litigation, the corporation's net earnings after taxes amounted to $202,759 while its earned surplus was $1,543,270, and this was increased in 1958 to $1,680,079 while earnings were $172,964. The minimum earned surplus requirement is designed for the protection of the corporation and its creditors, and we take no exception to the contractual dividend requirements as thus restricted. . . .

The salary continuation agreement is a common feature, in one form or another, of corporate executive employment. It requires that the widow should receive a total benefit, payable monthly over a five-year period, aggregating twice the amount paid her deceased husband in one year. This requirement was likewise limited for the protection of the corporation by being contingent upon the payments being income tax-deductible by the corporation. The charge made in those cases which have considered the validity of payments to the widow of an officer and shareholder in a corporation is that a gift of its property by a noncharitable corporation is in violation of the rights of its shareholders and *ultra vires*. Since there are no shareholders here other than the parties to the contract, this objection is not here applicable, and its effect, as limited, upon the corporation is not so prejudicial as to require its invalidation.

. . .

We hold defendants must account for all monies received by them from the corporation since September 25, 1956, in excess of that theretofore authorized.

Accordingly, the judgment of the Appellate Court is reversed except insofar as it relates to fees, and is, as to them affirmed. The cause is remanded to the circuit court of Cook County with directions to proceed in accordance herewith.

Affirmed in part and reversed in part, and remanded with directions.

ANALYSIS

1. In Galler v. Galler, as in Clark v. Dodge, the court in effect ordered specific performance. Is there a better remedy? If you think there is, what does that suggest about whether there was a better form of agreement available to the parties at the outset?

2. Under the court's order, what is the likelihood of a change in the salaries paid to Isadore and to Aaron as long as Emma lives?

3. Was there anything in the agreement about which Rosenberg might reasonably have complained? If he had complained, and had sided with the defendants in the litigation that resulted in the decision of the Illinois Supreme Court, what would the outcome have been?

4. The court in Galler v. Galler says, "Without a shareholder agreement, specifically enforceable by the courts, insuring him a modicum of control, a large minority shareholder might find himself at the mercy of an oppressive or unknowledgeable majority." Later the court says, "often the only sound basis for protection is afforded by a lengthy, detailed shareholder agreement securing the rights and obligations of all concerned." Does it follow that a lawyer who is asked to form a corporation for people about to embark on a business venture and who fails to urge the adoption of various protective agreements is guilty of malpractice?

5. At the time this case arose the use of the corporate form could produce some federal income tax advantages. Under the current tax regime those tax advantages have largely disappeared. Most closely held corporations are eligible to be treated for tax purposes as so-called S corporations, which are taxed much the same as partnerships. Moreover, closely held businesses can achieve desired tax outcomes by organizing as Limited Liability Companies, Limited Liability Partnerships, Limited Partnerships, or Limited Liability Limited Partnerships. Thus, tax considerations do not play an important role in crafting the substantive elements of a business organization. Do you think that in the Gallers' family business the partnership form would have been better than the corporate form? In answering this question think of the basic rules of partnership and corporate law relating to control, duration and termination, and share of profit and loss, and about how those rules need to be modified.

Ramos v. Estrada

8 Cal.App.4th 1070 10 Cal.Rptr.2d 833 (1992).

[Two groups of people separately sought from the Federal Communications Commission a permit to form a Spanish language television station in Ventura County. One group was called the Broadcast Group and included Leopoldo Ramos and his wife and Tila Estrada and her husband. The Ramoses owned 50 percent of the Broadcast Group and the Estradas and four other couples each owned 10 percent. The other group seeking the permit was called Ventura 41. Ultimately the two groups combined in a corporation called Television, Inc. and at some time in 1986 the shares of this corporation were issued to the individual members of each group. Initially, 5,000 shares of Television, Inc. were issued to the members of the Broadcast Group and 5,000 to the members of Ventura 41. The board of directors was to have eight members, four from each group. After the station was operated at full power for six months, however, two additional shares were to go to the Broadcast Group and the membership of the board of directors was to be increased to nine, of whom five would be elected by the Broadcast Group.

In June 1987, the members of Broadcast Group entered into an agreement to vote all their shares of Television, Inc. in a manner determined by a majority of them. The agreement also restricted transfer of the shares and provided that if any member of the group failed to abide by the voting provision, that member's shares would be sold to the other members at cost plus 8 percent per year.

The initial eight-member board of Television, Inc. elected Leopoldo Ramos as president. Tila Estrada was a member of the board. Thereafter, however, Estrada defected from the Broadcast Group, as described by the court below.]

At a special directors' meeting held on October 8, 1988, Tila Estrada voted with the Ventura 41 group block to remove Ramos as president and to replace him with Walter Ulloa, a member of Ventura 41. She also joined Ventura 41 in voting to remove Romualdo Ochoa, a Broadcast Group member, as secretary and to replace him with herself.

Under the June Broadcast Agreement and the Merger Agreement, each of the groups were required to vote for the directors upon whom a majority of each respective group had agreed. The terms of that agreement expressly state that failure to adhere to the agreement constitutes an election by the shareholder to sell his or her shares pursuant to buy/sell provisions of the agreement. The agreement also calls for specific enforcement of such buy/sell provisions.

On October 15, 1988, the Broadcast Group noticed another meeting to decide how its members would vote their shares for directors at the annual meeting. All members attended except the Estradas. The group agreed to nominate *another* slate of directors which did not include either of the Estradas. The Estradas were notified of the results of this meeting.

The Estradas unilaterally declared the June Broadcast Agreement null and void as of October 15, 1988, in a letter dictated for them by Paul Zevnik, the attorney for Ventura 41. Tila Estrada refused to recognize the October 15 vote of the majority of the Broadcast Group to replace her as a director of Television Inc. Ramos et al. sued the Estradas for breach of the June Broadcast Agreement, among other things.

The court ruled that the Estradas materially breached the valid June Broadcast Agreement, and it ordered their shares sold in accordance with the specific enforcement provisions of the June Broadcast Agreement. The court restrained the Estradas from voting their shares other than as provided in the June Broadcast Agreement.

Discussion

The Estradas contend that the June Broadcast Agreement is void because it constitutes an expired proxy which the Estradas validly revoked.

The interpretation of statutes and contracts is a matter of law subject to independent review by this court. . . .

Corporations Code [California] section 178 defines a proxy to be "a written authorization signed . . . by a shareholder . . . giving another person or persons power to vote with respect to the shares of such shareholder."

Section 7.1 of the June Broadcast Agreement details the voting arrangement among the shareholders. It states, in pertinent part: "The Stockholders agree that they shall consult with each other prior to voting their shares in the Company. They shall attempt in good faith to reach a consensus as to the outcome of any such vote. In the case of a vote for directors, they agree that no director shall be selected who is not acceptable to at least one member (i.e., spousal unit) of each of Group A and Group B. (See P 1.2(b)(1) above [which states that 'The Stockholders shall be divided into two groups, Group "A" being composed of Leopoldo Ramos and Cecilia Morris, and Group "B" being composed of all the other Stockholders'].) In the case of all *votes of Stockholders* they agree that, following consultation and compliance with the other provisions of this paragraph, *they will all vote their stock in the manner voted by a majority of the Stockholders.*" (Second emphasis in original.)

No proxies are created by this agreement. The agreement has the characteristics of a shareholders' voting agreement expressly authorized by section 706, subdivision (a) for close corporations. . . . Although the articles of incorporation do not contain the talismanic statement that "This corporation is a close corporation," the arrangements of this corporation, and in particular this voting agreement, are strikingly similar to ones authorized by the Code for close corporations.

Section 706, subdivision (a) states, in pertinent part: "an agreement between two or more shareholders of a close corporation, if in writing and signed by the parties thereto, may provide that in exercising any voting rights the shares held by them shall be voted as provided by the agreement, or as the parties may agree or as determined in accordance with a procedure agreed upon by them. . . ."

Here, the members of this corporation executed a written agreement providing that they shall try to reach a consensus on all votes and that they shall consult with one another and vote their own stock in accordance with the majority of the stockholders. They entered into this agreement because they "mutually desired" to limit the transferability of their stock to ensure "the Company does not pass into the control of persons whose interests might be incompatible with the interests of the Company and of the Stockholders, establishing their mutual rights and obligations in the event of death, and establishing a mechanism for determining how the Stockholders' voting rights in the Company shall be exercised. . . ."

Even though this corporation does not qualify as a close corporation, this agreement is valid and binding on the Estradas. Section 706, subdivision (d) states: "This section shall not invalidate any voting or other agreement among shareholders . . . which agreement . . . is not otherwise illegal."

The Legislative Committee comment regarding section 706, subdivision (d) states that "this subdivision is intended to preserve any agreements which would be upheld under court decisions *even though they do not comply with one or more of the requirements of this section, including voting agreements of corporations other than close corporations.*" (West's Ann. Corp. Code, § 706 (1990) p. 330, emphasis added.)

The California Practice Guide indicates that such "pooling" agreements are valid not only for close corporations, but also "among any number of shareholders of other corporations as well." (Friedman, Cal. Practice Guide Corporations (1992) § 3:159.2, p. 3–31.)

The Estradas cite Dulin v. Pacific Wood and Coal Co. (1894) 103 Cal. 357, and Smith v. S. F. & N. P. Ry. Co. (1897) 115 Cal. 584, as support for their argument that the agreement is an expired proxy which they revoked. Their reliance on these cases is misplaced.

. . . .

In *Smith*, supra, three individuals purchased a majority share of stock in a corporation. To keep control of the corporation, they entered into a written agreement to pool their votes so as to vote in a block for a five-year period. Although two of the three agreed on a slate for an election, the third attempted to repudiate the agreement. The two presented the vote of all the stock held by the trio in accordance with their agreement; the third attempted to vote his own stock in the manner he desired.

The court held that the express, written agreement validly called for the trio to vote their shares as a block. (Smith v. S. F. & N. P. Ry. Co., supra, 115 Cal. at p. 598.) The court viewed the agreement as a power (to vote) coupled with an interest (in purchasing stock) which was supported by consideration. (Id., at p. 600.) The court construed the agreement as an agency; a proxy which could not be repudiated. (Id., at pp. 598–599.)

There is dicta in *Smith* suggesting that the agreement in that case constituted an irrevocable proxy. . . .

The *Smith* court also held that "any plan of procedure they [stockholders] may agree upon implies a previous comparison of views, and there is nothing illegal in an agreement to be bound by the will of the majority as to the means by which the result shall be reached. If they are in accord as to the ultimate purpose, it is but reasonable that the will of the majority should prevail as to the mode by which it may be accomplished." (Smith v. S. F. & N. P. Ry. Co., supra, 115 Cal. at p. 601.)

In the instant case, the only difference from *Smith* is that the shareholders here chose to vote their stocks themselves, and not by proxy. What the *Smith* court held, however, is that voting agreements, like the one here, are valid. If the shareholders are unable to reach a consensus, then each shareholder must vote his or her shares according to the will of the majority.

The instant agreement is valid, enforceable and supported by consideration. It states, in pertinent part, that the stockholders entered into the agreement for the purposes of "limiting the transferability of . . . stock in the Company, ensuring that the Company does not pass into the control of persons whose interests might be incompatible with the interests of the Company and of the Stockholders, establishing their mutual rights and obligations in the event of death, and establishing a mechanism for determining how the Stockholders' voting rights . . . shall be exercised. . . ."

Section 7.2 of the agreement states that "the Stockholders understand and acknowledge that the purpose of the foregoing arrangement is to preserve their relative voting power in the Company. . . . Accordingly, in the event that a Stockholder fails to abide by this arrangement for whatever reason, that failure shall constitute on [sic] irrevocable election by the Stockholder to sell his stock in the Company, triggering the same rights of purchase provided in Article IV above."

The agreement calls for enforcement by specific performance of its terms because the stock is not readily marketable. [Corporations Code] Section 709, subdivision (c) expressly permits enforcement of shareholder voting agreements by such equitable remedies. It states, in pertinent part: "The court may determine the person entitled to the office of director or may order a new election to be held or appointment to be made, may determine the validity, effectiveness and construction of voting agreements . . . and the right of persons to vote and may direct such other relief as may be just and proper."

The Estradas contend that the forced sale provision is unconscionable and oppressive. They portray themselves as naive, small-town business people who were forced to sign an adhesion agreement without reviewing its contents.

Substantial evidence supports the findings that Tila Estrada has been a licensed real estate broker. She is an astute businesswoman experienced with contracts concerning real property. The consent and signatures of the Estradas to the agreement were not procured by fraud, duress or other wrongful conduct of Ramos. The Estradas read and discussed with other members of Broadcast Group, and with their own counsel, the voting, buy/sell and other provisions of the agreement and the January Broadcast Agreement, as well as various drafts of these documents, and they freely signed these agreements.

On direct examination, under Evidence Code section 776, Tila Estrada admitted she owns and operates a real estate brokerage business; she regularly reviews a broad variety of real estate documents; she and her husband own and manage investment property; and she has considered herself "to be an astute business woman" since 1985. Tila Estrada also has been a participant and owner in another application before the FCC, for an FM radio station, before the instant suit was filed.

Ms. Estrada stated she got copies "of all the drafts and all the Shareholders Agreements." She discussed these agreements with other members of Broadcast Group and with its counsel, Mr. Howard Weiss.

The June Broadcast Agreement, including its voting and buy/sell provisions, was unanimously executed after the Estradas had a full and fair opportunity to consider it in its entirety. As the trial court found, the buy-out provisions at issue here are valid, favored by courts and enforceable by specific performance. . . .

The Estradas breached the agreement by their written repudiation of it. Their breach constituted an election to sell their Television Inc. shares in accordance with the terms of the buy/sell provisions in the agreement. This election does not constitute a forfeiture—they violated the agreement voluntarily, aware of the consequences of their acts and they are provided full compensation, per their agreement.

The judgment is affirmed. Costs to Ramos.

ANALYSIS

1. If you had been consulted by Tila Estrada before she signed the June Broadcast Agreement, what advice would you have given her?

2. If Tila Estrada had consulted you after she formed the intent to defect from the Broadcast Group and vote with the Ventura 41 Group, what advice would you have given her (assuming you did not have the decision in the case as an authority on which to rely)?

NOTE ON THE LAW IN OTHER STATES

In Zion v. Kurtz, 50 N.Y.2d 92, 428 N.Y.S.2d 199, 405 N.E.2d 681 (1980), the Court of Appeals of New York, applying a basic choice-of-law rule, decided a shareholder-agreement case under Delaware law, but stated that the result would be the same under New York law. The facts in the case were complex and unusual. There were essentially two shareholders, with Kurtz holding the majority interest and Zion the minority. An agreement between them narrowly defined the intended activities of the corporation and provided that no other activities could be engaged in without the minority shareholder's consent.[7] In supporting its view that

---

7. Note that the shareholders' objective could have been achieved by use of a narrow statement of purposes in the articles of incorporation. Such a limitation might not have been enforceable as against a third party (see, e.g., Del.Gen.Corp.Law § 124), but the same would be true of the limitation in the contract in Zion v. Kurtz. A limitation in the articles might have created problems in selling shares to others, but again the problem also seems to arise with the use of a contract. Some shares were in fact sold to others, but subject to the terms of the agreement of the two original shareholders. Presumably the two could have abandoned their agreement without the consent of the new shareholders. Amendment of the articles of incorporation requires a vote of the shareholders, which might or might not have been a problem.

the agreement did not violate the public policy of Delaware, the court cited the Delaware provisions relating to statutory close corporations, although the corporation involved in the case was not a statutory close corporation and the restriction in the agreement was not made part of the articles of incorporation, as might be required in the case of a statutory close corporation (under Del.Gen.Corp.Law § 351). See also N.Y.Bus.Corp.Law § 620(b), set forth following Clark v. Dodge.

PROBLEM

Curlie, Moe, and Larry incorporate a restaurant. They each receive one-third of the stock.

1. If they agree to exercise their best efforts to ensure that each is elected to the board of directors, is the agreement enforceable? If they agree that they will, as directors, elect each other officers of the corporation, is the agreement enforceable?

2. Suppose Curlie and Moe (but not Larry) agree to exercise their best efforts to ensure that each is elected to the board and agree that they will, as directors, elect each other as officers. Is either agreement enforceable? Does the result change if they agree to elect each other as officers, "so long as each shall remain faithful, efficient and competent to manage and control the restaurant"?

NOTE AND QUESTIONS ON LIMITED LIABILITY COMPANIES

Under the Delaware Limited Liability Company Act, § 18–704(a),

An assignee of a limited liability company interest may become a member . . . upon:

(1) The approval of all of the members of the limited liability company . . .; or

(2) Compliance with any procedure provided for in the limited liability company agreement.

Notwithstanding the permissive language of (a)(2), do you think that most LLCs would be well advised to provide in their organizational documents for freely transferrable membership interests? What are the sensible alternatives?

SECTION 4. ABUSE OF CONTROL

Wilkes v. Springside Nursing Home, Inc.

370 Mass. 842, 353 N.E.2d 657 (1976).

In 1951 Wilkes acquired an option to purchase a building and lot located on the corner of Springside Avenue and North Street in Pittsfield, Massachusetts, the building having previously housed the Hillcrest Hospital. Though Wilkes was principally engaged in the roofing and siding business, he had gained a reputation locally for profitable dealings in real estate. Riche, an acquaintance of Wilkes, learned of the option, and interested Quinn (who was known to Wilkes through membership on the draft board in Pittsfield) and Pipkin (an acquaintance of both Wilkes and Riche) in joining Wilkes in his investment. The four men met and decided to participate jointly in the purchase of the building and lot as a real estate investment which, they believed, had good profit potential on resale or rental.

The parties later determined that the property would have its greatest potential for profit if it were operated by them as a nursing home. Wilkes consulted his attorney, who advised him that if the four men were to operate the contemplated nursing home as planned, they would be partners and would be liable for any debts incurred by the partnership and by each other. On the attorney's suggestion, and after consultation among themselves, ownership of the property was vested in Springside, a corporation organized under Massachusetts law.

Each of the four men invested $1,000 and subscribed to ten shares of $100 par value stock in Springside. At the time of incorporation it was understood by all of the parties that each would be a director of Springside and each would participate actively in the management and decision making involved in operating the corporation.[7] It was, further, the understanding and intention of all the parties that, corporate resources permitting, each would receive money from the corporation in equal amounts as long as each assumed an active and ongoing responsibility for carrying a portion of the burdens necessary to operate the business.

The work involved in establishing and operating a nursing home was roughly apportioned, and each of the four men undertook his respective

---

7. Wilkes testified before the master that, when the corporate officers were elected, all four men "were . . . guaranteed directorships." Riche's understanding of the parties' intentions was that they all wanted to play a part in the management of the corporation and wanted to have some "say" in the risks involved; that, to this end, they all would be directors; and that "unless you [were] a director and officer you could not participate in the decisions of [the] enterprise."

tasks.[8] Initially, Riche was elected president of Springside, Wilkes was elected treasurer, and Quinn was elected clerk.[9] Each of the four was listed in the articles of organization as a director of the corporation.

At some time in 1952, it became apparent that the operational income and cash flow from the business were sufficient to permit the four stockholders to draw money from the corporation on a regular basis. Each of the four original parties initially received $35 a week from the corporation. As time went on the weekly return to each was increased until, in 1955, it totalled $100.

In 1959, after a long illness, Pipkin sold his shares in the corporation to Connor, who was known to Wilkes, Riche and Quinn through past transactions with Springside in his capacity as president of the First Agricultural National Bank of Berkshire County. Connor received a weekly stipend from the corporation equal to that received by Wilkes, Riche and Quinn. He was elected a director of the corporation but never held any other office. He was assigned no specific area of responsibility in the operation of the nursing home but did participate in business discussions and decisions as a director and served additionally as financial adviser to the corporation.

In 1965 the stockholders decided to sell a portion of the corporate property to Quinn who, in addition to being a stockholder in Springside, possessed an interest in another corporation which desired to operate a rest home on the property. Wilkes was successful in prevailing on the other stockholders of Springside to procure a higher sale price for the property than Quinn apparently anticipated paying or desired to pay. After the sale was consummated, the relationship between Quinn and Wilkes began to deteriorate.

The bad blood between Quinn and Wilkes affected the attitudes of both Riche and Connor. As a consequence of the strained relations among the parties, Wilkes, in January of 1967, gave notice of his intention to sell his shares for an amount based on an appraisal of their value. In February of 1967 a directors' meeting was held and the board exercised its right to establish the salaries of its officers and employees.[10] A schedule of pay-

---

8. Wilkes took charge of the repair, upkeep and maintenance of the physical plant and grounds; Riche assumed supervision over the kitchen facilities and dietary and food aspects of the home; Pipkin was to make himself available if and when medical problems arose; and Quinn dealt with the personnel and administrative aspects of the nursing home, serving informally as a managing director. Quinn further coordinated the activities of the other parties and served as a communication link among them when matters had to be discussed and decisions had to be made without a formal meeting.

9. Riche held the office of president from 1951 to 1963; Quinn served as president from 1963 on, as clerk from 1951 to 1967, and as treasurer from 1967 on; Wilkes was treasurer from 1951 to 1967.

10. The by-laws of the corporation provided that the directors, subject to the approval of the stockholders, had the power to fix the salaries of all officers and employees. This power, however, up until February, 1967, had not been exercised formally; all payments made to the four participants in the venture had resulted from the informal but unanimous approval of all the parties concerned.

ments was established whereby Quinn was to receive a substantial weekly increase and Riche and Connor were to continue receiving $100 a week. Wilkes, however, was left off the list of those to whom a salary was to be paid. The directors also set the annual meeting of the stockholders for March, 1967.

At the annual meeting in March, Wilkes was not reelected as a director, nor was he reelected as an officer of the corporation. He was further informed that neither his services nor his presence at the nursing home was wanted by his associates.

The meetings of the directors and stockholders in early 1967, the master found, were used as a vehicle to force Wilkes out of active participation in the management and operation of the corporation and to cut off all corporate payments to him. Though the board of directors had the power to dismiss any officers or employees for misconduct or neglect of duties, there was no indication in the minutes of the board of directors' meeting of February, 1967, that the failure to establish a salary for Wilkes was based on either ground. The severance of Wilkes from the payroll resulted not from misconduct or neglect of duties, but because of the personal desire of Quinn, Riche and Connor to prevent him from continuing to receive money from the corporation. Despite a continuing deterioration in his personal relationship with his associates, Wilkes had consistently endeavored to carry on his responsibilities to the corporation in the same satisfactory manner and with the same degree of competence he had previously shown. Wilkes was at all times willing to carry on his responsibilities and participation if permitted so to do and provided that he receive his weekly stipend.

1. We turn to Wilkes's claim for damages based on a breach of the fiduciary duty owed to him by the other participants in this venture. In light of the theory underlying this claim, we do not consider it vital to our approach to this case whether the claim is governed by partnership law or the law applicable to business corporations. This is so because, as all the parties agree, Springside was at all times relevant to this action, a close corporation as we have recently defined such an entity in Donahue v. Rodd Electrotype Co. of New England, Inc., 367 Mass. 578, 585–586 (1975).

In *Donahue,* we held that "stockholders in the close corporation owe one another substantially the same fiduciary duty in the operation of the enterprise that partners owe to one another." Id. at 593 (footnotes omitted), 328 N.E.2d at 515. As determined in previous decisions of this court, the standard of duty owed by partners to one another is one of "utmost good faith and loyalty." Cardullo v. Landau, 329 Mass. 5, 8, 105 N.E.2d 843 (1952), and cases cited. . . .

Thus, we concluded in *Donahue,* with regard to "their actions relative to the operations of the enterprise and the effects of that operation on the rights and investments of other stockholders," "[s]tockholders in close corporations must discharge their management and stockholder responsibilities in conformity with this strict good faith standard. They may not act out of avarice, expediency or self-interest in derogation of their duty of loyalty to the other stockholders and to the corporation." 367 Mass. at 593, n. 18.

In the *Donahue* case we recognized that one peculiar aspect of close corporations was the opportunity afforded to majority stockholders to oppress, disadvantage or "freeze out" minority stockholders. In *Donahue* itself, for example, the majority refused the minority an equal opportunity to sell a ratable number of shares to the corporation at the same price available to the majority. The net result of this refusal, we said, was that the minority could be forced to "sell out at less than fair value," 367 Mass. at 593, since there is by definition no ready market for minority stock in a close corporation.

"Freeze outs," however, may be accomplished by the use of other devices. One such device which has proved to be particularly effective in accomplishing the purpose of the majority is to deprive minority stockholders of corporate offices and of employment with the corporation. . . . This "freeze-out" technique has been successful because courts fairly consistently have been disinclined to interfere in those facets of internal corporate operations, such as the selection and retention or dismissal of officers, directors and employees, which essentially involve management decisions subject to the principle of majority control. . . . As one authoritative source has said, "[M]any courts apparently feel that there is a legitimate sphere in which the controlling [directors or] shareholders can act in their own interest even if the minority suffers." F.H. O'Neal, ["Squeeze-Outs" of Minority Shareholders 59 (1975)] (footnote omitted). . . .

The denial of employment to the minority at the hands of the majority is especially pernicious in some instances. A guaranty of employment with the corporation may have been one of the "basic reason[s] why a minority owner has invested capital in the firm." Symposium—The Close Corporation, 52 Nw.U.L.Rev. 345, 392 (1957).

. . .

The minority stockholder typically depends on his salary as the principal return on his investment, since the "earnings of a close corporation . . . are distributed in major part in salaries, bonuses and retirement benefits." 1 F.H. O'Neal, Close Corporations § 1.07 (1971). Other noneconomic interests of the minority stockholder are likewise injuriously affected by barring him from corporate office. . . . Such action severely restricts his participation in the management of the enterprise, and he is relegated to enjoying those benefits incident to his status as a stockholder. . . . In sum, by terminating a minority stockholder's employment or by severing him from a position as an officer or director, the majority effectively frustrate the minority stockholder's purposes in entering on the corporate venture and also deny him an equal return on his investment.

The *Donahue* decision acknowledged, as a "natural outgrowth" of the case law of this Commonwealth, a strict obligation on the part of majority stockholders in a close corporation to deal with the minority with the utmost good faith and loyalty. On its face, this strict standard is applicable in the instant case. The distinction between the majority action in *Donahue* and the majority action in this case is more one of form than of substance. Nevertheless, we are concerned that untempered application of the strict good faith standard enunciated in *Donahue* to cases such as the one before us will result in the imposition of limitations on legitimate action by the controlling group in a close corporation which will unduly hamper its effectiveness in managing the corporation in the best interests of all concerned. The majority, concededly, have certain rights to what has been termed "selfish ownership" in the corporation which should be balanced against the concept of their fiduciary obligation to the minority. . . .

Therefore, when minority stockholders in a close corporation bring suit against the majority alleging a breach of the strict good faith duty owed to them by the majority, we must carefully analyze the action taken by the controlling stockholders in the individual case. It must be asked whether the controlling group can demonstrate a legitimate business purpose for its action. . . . In asking this question, we acknowledge the fact that the controlling group in a close corporation must have some room to maneuver in establishing the business policy of the corporation. It must have a large measure of discretion, for example, in declaring or withholding dividends, deciding whether to merge or consolidate, establishing the salaries of corporate officers, dismissing directors with or without cause, and hiring and firing corporate employees.

When an asserted business purpose for their action is advanced by the majority, however, we think it is open to minority stockholders to demonstrate that the same legitimate objective could have been achieved through an alternative course of action less harmful to the minority's interest. . . . If called on to settle a dispute, our courts must weigh the legitimate business purpose, if any, against the practicability of a less harmful alternative.

Applying this approach to the instant case it is apparent that the majority stockholders in Springside have not shown a legitimate business purpose for severing Wilkes from the payroll of the corporation or for refusing to reëlect him as a salaried officer and director. The master's subsidiary findings relating to the purpose of the meetings of the directors and stockholders in February and March, 1967, are supported by the evidence. There was no showing of misconduct on Wilkes's part as a director, officer or employee of the corporation which would lead us to approve the majority action as a legitimate response to the disruptive nature of an undesirable individual bent on injuring or destroying the corporation. On the contrary, it appears that Wilkes had always accomplished his assigned share of the duties competently, and that he had never indicated an unwillingness to continue to do so.

It is an inescapable conclusion from all the evidence that the action of the majority stockholders here was a designed "freeze out" for which no legitimate business purpose has been suggested. Furthermore, we may infer that a design to pressure Wilkes into selling his shares to the corporation at a price below their value well may have been at the heart of the majority's plan.[14]

In the context of this case, several factors bear directly on the duty owed to Wilkes by his associates. At a minimum, the duty of utmost good faith and loyalty would demand that the majority consider that their action was in disregard of a long-standing policy of the stockholders that each would be a director of the corporation and that employment with the corporation would go hand in hand with stock ownership; that Wilkes was one of the four originators of the nursing home venture; and that Wilkes, like the others, had invested his capital and time for more than fifteen years with the expectation that he would continue to participate in corporate decisions. Most important is the plain fact that the cutting off of Wilkes's salary, together with the fact that the corporation never declared a dividend . . . assured that Wilkes would receive no return at all from the corporation.

2. The question of Wilkes's damages at the hands of the majority has not been thoroughly explored on the record before us. Wilkes, in his original complaint, sought damages in the amount of the $100 a week he believed he was entitled to from the time his salary was terminated up until the time this action was commenced. However, the record shows that, after Wilkes was severed from the corporate payroll, the schedule of salaries and payments made to the other stockholders varied from time to time. In addition, the duties assumed by the other stockholders after Wilkes was deprived of his share of the corporate earnings appear to have changed in significant respects.[15] Any resolution of this question must take into account whether the corporation was dissolved during the pendency of this litigation.

Therefore our order is as follows: So much of the judgment as dismisses Wilkes's complaint and awards costs to the defendants is reversed. The case is remanded to the Probate Court for Berkshire County for further proceedings concerning the issue of damages. Thereafter a judgment shall be entered declaring that Quinn, Riche and Connor breached their fiduciary duty to Wilkes as a minority stockholder in Springside, and awarding money damages therefor. Wilkes shall be allowed to recover from Riche, the estate of T. Edward Quinn and the estate of Lawrence R. Connor, ratably, according to the inequitable enrichment of each, the salary he would have received had he remained an officer and director of Springside. In considering the issue of damages the judge on remand shall take

14. This inference arises from the fact that Connor, acting on behalf of the three controlling stockholders, offered to purchase Wilkes's shares for a price Connor admittedly would not have accepted for his own shares.

15. In fairness to Wilkes, who, as the master found, was at all times ready and willing to work for the corporation, it should be noted that neither the other stockholders nor their representatives may be heard to say that Wilkes's duties were performed by them and that Wilkes's damages should, for that reason, be diminished.

into account the extent to which any remaining corporate funds of Springside may be diverted to satisfy Wilkes's claim.

So ordered.

ANALYSIS

1.   According to normal, fundamental rules of corporate law, the board of directors appoints officers and sets their salaries.   The earlier cases in this section reveal the difficulties that courts generally have with deviations from the corporate norm of management by the board of directors.   In the present case, the parties did not, by written shareholder agreement, attempt to "sterilize" the board.   Why is it, then, that the plaintiff in this case, Wilkes, was not required to cast his argument in terms of abuse of discretion by the board?

2.   Suppose that the Springside Nursing Home board in 1967 had declared a dividend of $1,000 payable to each of Connor, Riche, and Quinn, with no dividend payable to Wilkes.   Would Wilkes have had a legal entitlement to object?   How would you frame the objection?   Does this line of inquiry suggest another approach to the actual case?

3.   Suppose there had been evidence in the case that the board had found another person to perform the duties that were being performed by Wilkes, but at a lower salary, and, after due deliberation, had fired Wilkes and hired the other person.   Would Wilkes still have prevailed?

4.   If the venture had been operated as a partnership, relying on the basic rules of the Uniform Partnership Act, what would Wilkes's position have been?   Could the other partners have fired him?   If they refused to pay him a salary, could they continue to pay themselves salaries?

5.   The court refers to a right of "selfish ownership" in a close corporation.   Suppose that Connor, Quinn, and Riche had decided on a substantial expansion of the nursing home; that this expansion would require suspension of the payment of salaries or dividends and would require considerable borrowing; and that there would, as a result, be a substantial risk of failure and loss of the entire investment.   Suppose that Connor, Quinn, and Riche were all wealthy and could afford the loss, but that Wilkes was a man of modest means and could not afford the loss. Would Wilkes have been legally entitled to block the action of the majority? Should he have been?   Would your answer be different if the majority had offered to buy out Wilkes's interest at a price about 40 percent below its existing market value?   How would your answers to these questions change, if at all, if the venture had been organized as a partnership?

6.   What is the appropriate remedy in this case?   If Wilkes is entitled to damages, what about the duty to mitigate?   Assuming that the corporation is to continue in existence, and that Connor, Quinn, and Riche are willing to forgo salary payments, must they pay dividends?

7. What planning techniques were available to the investors that would have allowed them to avoid litigation? If the lawyer who assisted in the formation of the corporation failed to discuss those planning techniques, is she or he guilty of malpractice? How does the decision in this case affect the obligations of lawyers in similar situations in the future?

8. Could the outcome in this case have been reached by applying ordinary principles of contract, rather than principles of fiduciary obligation? If so, would that have been a better approach? If you had been Wilkes's lawyer, which approach would you have emphasized?

Ingle v. Glamore Motor Sales, Inc.

73 N.Y.2d 183, 538 N.Y.S.2d 771, 535 N.E.2d 1311 (1989).

■ BELLACOSA, JUDGE.

.   .   .

In 1964, plaintiff-appellant Ingle sought to purchase an equity interest in respondent Glamore Motor Sales, Inc. from its then sole shareholder, respondent James Glamore. Ingle was not sold an interest in the corporation initially, but he was hired as sales manager. There was no express agreement between the parties establishing either the duration or conditions of employment.

In 1966, Glamore and Ingle entered into a written shareholders' agreement which provided that Ingle would purchase 22 of Glamore's 100 shares in the corporation, that Ingle would have a five-year option to purchase an additional 18 shares, and that Glamore would nominate and vote Ingle as a director and secretary of the corporation. The agreement also gave Glamore the right to repurchase all of Ingle's stock if "Ingle shall cease to be an employee of the Corporation *for any reason* " (emphasis added). Ingle later purchased the 18 additional shares and the parties executed a new shareholders' agreement, which updated some facets and eliminated outdated ones. The repurchase provision of the 1973 agreement tracked identically the 1966 version.

On January 1, 1982, the corporation issued 60 additional shares of stock. Glamore purchased 22 shares of the new issue and his two sons (respondents William and Robert Glamore) each purchased 19 shares. The three Glamores and Ingle, the only four shareholders, entered into a third agreement reflecting the corporate relationship. The repurchase provision pertinent to this litigation is: "(b) *Termination of employment.* In the event that any Stockholder shall *cease to be an employee of the Corporation for any reason*, Glamore shall have the option, for a period of 30 days after such termination of employment, to purchase all of the shares of stock then owned by such Stockholder" (emphasis supplied).

At a special meeting of the board of directors held on May 9, 1983, Ingle was voted out of his corporate posts and fired from his employment as operating manager of the business. The termination was effective May 31,

1983. On June 1, Glamore notified Ingle that he was exercising the repurchase-upon-termination-of-employment option and in due course paid Ingle $96,000 for his 40 shares in the corporation.

Plaintiff argues that as a minority shareholder of a closely held corporation, employed without the benefit of a contract containing a durational employment protection and without any limitation on the employer's right to discharge, he is nevertheless entitled by reason of his minority shareholder status to a fiduciary-rooted protection against being fired. His theory is that his employment status should not be governed by the employment at-will doctrine but, rather, that as a minority shareholder in a close corporation he should be treated as a co-owner, equivalent to a partner, whose employment rights flow from a special duty of loyalty and good faith. He next urges that an implicit covenant of good faith and fair dealing under the shareholders' agreement precluded his termination without cause, despite the express language and nature of the agreement in that regard. He concludes that even if he is an at-will employee, an action properly lies for the respondents' breach of fiduciary duties and for wrongful interference with his employment. Ingle started two separate actions seeking damages via seven causes of action alleging breach of fiduciary duty and of contract. Eventually all causes of action were dismissed—we believe correctly.

A minority shareholder in a close corporation, by that status alone, who contractually agrees to the repurchase of his shares upon termination of his employment for any reason, acquires no right from the corporation or majority shareholders against at-will discharge. There is nothing in law, in the agreement, or in the relationship of the parties to warrant such a contradictory and judicial alteration of the employment relationship or the express agreement. It is necessary in this case to appreciate and keep distinct the duty a corporation owes to a minority shareholder *as a shareholder* from any duty it might owe him as an employee.

Both lower courts agree, as do we, that Ingle did not sufficiently present facts raising a triable issue regarding the existence of either an oral or written employment contract fixing employment of a definite duration. . . . Under the established common-law rule—and without any reference to the shareholders' agreement—the corporation had the right to discharge plaintiff at will. . . .

The twist in this fact pattern is an asserted liability based on allegations that the corporate officers breached fiduciary duties of good faith and fair dealing arising from the shareholders' agreement and on tortious interference with Ingle's employment. The twist does not support a deviation from the governing principle in this case.

In Murphy v. American Home Prods. Corp., 58 N.Y.2d 293, 461 N.Y.S.2d 232, 448 N.E.2d 86, we concluded that there is no implied obligation of good faith and fair dealing in an employment at will, as that would be incongruous to the legally recognized jural relationship in that kind of employment relationship. . . .

Plaintiff confuses and tries to avoid the sequential relationship of his employment status to his shareholders' agreement by extracting an obligation from the agreement to manufacture a legally unrecognized employment security. Divestiture of his status as a shareholder, by operation of the repurchase provision, is a contractually agreed to consequence flowing directly from the firing, not vice versa. The dissent similarly confuses and inverts the Appellate Division's and our holding. . . .

As noted, Ingle argued that the corporation discharged him because James Glamore would then have a right to repurchase his shares under the terms of the shareholders' agreement. Notably, however, Ingle never asserted that the $2,400 per share paid to him upon termination was not fairly representative of his equity interest in the corporation. He does not contend that the corporation undervalued his shares, and he accepted payment from Glamore without reservation. Indeed, that, too, was fixed by the parties' buy-out agreement. . . .

Ingle's and the dissent's reliance on Fender v. Prescott, 101 A.D.2d 418, 422, 476 N.Y.S.2d 128, *expressly affirmed on grounds other than the corporate relationship discussion,* 64 N.Y.2d 1077, 1078–1079, 489 N.Y.S.2d 880, 479 N.E.2d 225, for an exception based on the close corporate form in which this employer and employee find themselves is unavailing. No duty of loyalty and good faith akin to that between partners, precluding termination except for cause, arises among those operating a business in the corporate form who "have only the rights, duties and obligations of stockholders" and not those of partners. . . .

Finally, the dissent essentially invokes an equity appeal. While we have no quarrel whatsoever with that magnificent juridical jewel applied in its proper setting, this lawsuit does not qualify. Here, fair principles of well-settled law, affecting employment and contractual relationships between private parties, govern and are entitled to respect and efficacy from this court. We cannot merely substitute our preferred notions for those of the parties themselves in such matters.

. . .

If there was no protection against discharge of an at-will employee in *Murphy* (supra) . . ., where there was no contractual arrangement at all, there surely can be none here where the related contract expressly confirms the unavailability of that protection. Moreover, to hold otherwise on the facts and pleadings of this case would confuse our recent holdings in an area of the law where certainty, predictability and reliability are highly prized common-law goals.

. . .

Accordingly, the order of the Appellate Division, 140 A.D.2d 493, 528 N.Y.S.2d 602, should be affirmed, with costs.

■ HANCOCK, JUDGE (dissenting).

This appeal presents a clear-cut legal question: whether plaintiff's status as an officer, director, substantial part owner and active participant in the affairs and management of Glamore Motor Sales, a close corporation, gives him equitable rights and remedies which are not subject to the ordinary legal rules of master and servant? The majority answers "no" and writes off the case as a routine application of New York's employment at-will rule. Because this produces a result which is egregiously unfair and one which, I am convinced, is not warranted under existing case law, I respectfully dissent.

By treating the essence of plaintiff's complaints as a claimed breach of a hiring contract by the employer rather than an unfair squeeze-out of a minority shareholder in a close corporation by the majority, the court simply concludes that plaintiff has no rights at all. . . .

The majority's decision summarily rejects, without discussion, plaintiff's underlying theory which is rooted in his equitable rights as a minority shareholder and principal in a close corporation and the fiduciary duty of fair dealing owed him by the majority shareholders—rights and duties which have been widely recognized in statutory and decisional law in this and other jurisdictions (*see, e.g.,* . . . .Wilkes v. Springside Nursing Home, 370 Mass. 842, 353 N.E.2d 657 [1976], . . .).

. . .

What is remarkable about the majority opinion is that it appears to treat the employment at-will rule as a sort of categorical imperative which necessarily dictates the result in this case. There can be no question about the harshness of the outcome—assuming plaintiff's allegations to be true: the controlling shareholders are permitted to have the corporation fire plaintiff arbitrarily and in bad faith solely for the purpose of getting rid of him as a 25% stock owner.[1] . . .

The Appellate Division, in dismissing plaintiff's complaints, and the majority of the court, in its affirmance, have adopted defendants' literal

---

1. The notion that plaintiff's loss must somehow be viewed as less onerous because he is not contesting the $2,400 per share cash-out price misses the point of the lawsuit. Plaintiff wants to *keep his stock*—not to sell it. The injury to plaintiff is that he is being involuntarily cashed out as a stockholder through the buy-back agreement and forced out of his investment and participation in Glamore Motor Sales, Inc. Obviously, if the buy-back agreement is held to be enforceable against plaintiff, he is precluded from complaining about the amount. He has agreed to it.

Moreover, it cannot seriously be suggested that plaintiff should be pleased with being repaid a total of $96,000 in 1983 for his $75,000 cash outlay made 17 to 15 years earlier, particularly in light of the high risk he assumed in guaranteeing the corporation's

loans up to $1,000,000. That he agreed to such buy-back figure, of course, supports his contention that he thought the buy-back agreement was intended to protect Glamore's control over plaintiff's stock by giving Glamore the right to repurchase the stock in the event that plaintiff died, wished to sell or transfer his shares, or voluntarily decided to quit; and that it was never in plaintiff's contemplation that the clause was to apply as the price for his shares in the event that he was involuntarily terminated. . . .

William Glamore and Robert Glamore, sons of James H. Glamore, were elected vice-president and secretary-treasurer, respectively; and . . ., thereafter, upon exercise of the purchase option in the shareholders' agreement, plaintiff was compelled to deliver his shares for the sum of $2,400 per share. About these facts there is no dispute.

interpretation of the phrase in paragraph 7(b) of the stockholders' agreement—"cease to be an employee of the Corporation for any reason"—as giving defendants the unfettered right to repurchase plaintiff's shares by firing him, even if arbitrarily or in bad faith.

The plain wording of the buy-back provision and its sense, when read in the context of the entire agreement and the circumstances surrounding its execution, by no means unequivocally support this interpretation. Plaintiff states that the purpose and intent of paragraph 7(b) was to protect James Glamore in case *plaintiff chose* to leave the business, not to give Glamore the right—at any time, for any reason or for no reason—to deprive plaintiff of all expectancies as coprincipal in the agency. He points to the other two contingencies giving Glamore the right to repurchase his shares: plaintiff's decision to sell his stock (para. 7[a]) and plaintiff's death (para. 7[c]); he argues that the purpose of paragraph 7(b) like that of the other provisions was solely to protect Glamore by giving him the right to repurchase upon the happening of a contingency beyond Glamore's control—i.e., in paragraph 7(b), plaintiff's voluntary decision to leave. The very choice of the wording to describe the contingency of plaintiff's leaving—i.e., "ceases to be an employee" rather than "is terminated"—tends to support plaintiff's argument. The word "ceases" suggests that it was action by plaintiff not by the employer in ending the relationship which was contemplated. Thus, in my opinion the repurchase option of 7(b) is not free from ambiguity. . . .

There is no employment agreement between plaintiff and the corporation. Nothing in the original stockholders' agreement between plaintiff and James Glamore or in the subsequent agreement between plaintiff and the additional members of the Glamore family as stockholders purports to set the terms of plaintiff's relationship with the corporation or to state when or under what circumstances it may be terminated. . . . Upholding the corporation's right to discharge plaintiff here, therefore, must rest squarely on the application of the employment at-will doctrine, "that where an employment is for an indefinite term it is presumed to be a hiring at will which may be freely terminated by either party at any time for any reason or even for no reason" (Murphy v. American Home Prods. Corp., 58 N.Y.2d [293,] 300, 461 N.Y.S.2d 232, 448 N.E.2d 86). Whether this rule may be properly and fairly applied in this case is the central issue on which we disagree.

II

New York, like many other States, unquestionably recognizes that the status of a minority shareholder in a close corporation requires special protection from the courts. . . .

Thus, for purposes of asserting rights as a minority shareholder under Business Corporation Law § 1104–a, we have held that a shareholder "who reasonably expected that ownership in the corporation would entitle him or her to a job, a share of corporate earnings, a place in corporate management, or some other form of security, would be oppressed in a very real sense when others in the corporation seek to defeat those expectations and there exists no effective means of salvaging the investment" (Matter of Kemp & Beatley [Gardstein], 64 N.Y.2d supra, at 72–73, 484 N.Y.S.2d 799, 473 N.E.2d 1173).

A person who, like plaintiff, buys a minority interest in a close corporation does so not only in the hope of enjoying an increase in value of his stake in the business but for the assurance of employment in the business in a managerial position.   .   .   .

Thus, the relationship of a minority shareholder to a close corporation, if fairly viewed, cannot possibly be equated with an ordinary hiring and, in the absence of a contract, regarded as nothing more than an employment at will.   But this is exactly how the majority of the court has treated plaintiff's association with Glamore Motor Sales. And it has done so by not addressing the multiple relationships and the expectancies and vulnerabilities peculiar to the status of a minority shareholder in plaintiff's position— those very considerations which call for the relief that only a court of equity can give.   .   .   .

III

Assuming for the moment that the case could properly be viewed merely as one at law for breach of a hiring contract, the application of the employment at-will rule in this context would still be particularly inappropriate and unfair. Nor is such application supported by our precedents.

There can be little question that the basis for the traditional employment at-will rule is in the contractual principle of mutuality of obligation, "that if the employee can quit his job at will, then so, too, must the employer have the right to terminate the relationship for any reason or no reason" (Blades, *Employment At Will vs. Individual Freedom on Limiting the Abusive Exercise of Employer Power,* 67 Colum.L.Rev. 1404, 1419; . . .).

To be sure, this court in recent years has shied away from the "mutuality" doctrine in favor of the doctrine of contractual consideration as the basis . . . .   Nevertheless, in adhering to the principle that "the law accords the employer an unfettered right to terminate the employment at any time" (see, Murphy v. American Home Prods. Corp., supra, at 304, 461 N.Y.S.2d 232, 448 N.E.2d 86), rejecting the tort of abusive discharge, and declining to read into an indefinite employment contract an implied obligation of fair dealing, the decisions have done so in recognition of the continued vitality of "the freedom of contract underpinnings of the [employment at-will] rule" (id., at 301, 461 N.Y.S.2d 232, 448 N.E.2d 86).   .   .   .

But whether it be lack of mutuality or lack of consideration, the rationale for the employment at-will rule does not fit the situation of the typical minority shareholder-participant in a close corporation. For such participant is *not truly free* to quit at any time; and *there is consideration* which would support an implied understanding that, at least, the majority owner will not discharge him arbitrarily or in bad faith and without some legitimate business reason. Unlike the employee of a large corporation, the minority shareholder in a close corporation has typically invested a large percentage of his financial wherewithal in the business. He has been willing to do so because of what he expects will be his long-term association with the business and his ability to protect his investment and, he hopes, to make it grow. The same features of the minority owner-participant's status which make him particularly vulnerable to action by the majority obviously work to compel him to stay on the job. He needs to do so to protect his investment and to share in any increase in its value.

. . . .

ORDER AFFIRMED, WITH COSTS.

NOTE

In affirming the trial court's dismissal of the complaint in this case, the lower appellate court stated, "plaintiff's claims of an oral agreement not to discharge him without cause are nebulous and without real substance." 140 A.D.2d 493, 528 N.Y.S.2d 602, 604.

ANALYSIS

1. Is it possible to reconcile the result in *Ingle* with the result in *Wilkes?*

2. What should Ingle have done to protect the rights he claimed he had? What should Glamore have done to make clear that Ingle had no such rights?

3. On what basis did the dissent conclude that the result was unfair to Ingle? What do you imagine is the story behind the termination of Ingle?

4. If Ingle had convinced the court of the correctness of his claim of unfair treatment, what would the appropriate remedy have been? Would Ingle have a job for life? What if the Glamores wanted to sell their interest in the corporation?

Sugarman v. Sugarman

797 F.2d 3 (1st Cir.1986).

Leonard Sugarman appeals from a judgment of the United States District Court for the District of Massachusetts, based on a finding that he breached his fiduciary duty to minority shareholders in a close corporation. We conclude that none of the various errors of fact or law alleged by appellant warrant reversal of the district court's judgment as to liability. . . .

I. *Factual Background*

In 1906, four brothers formed a partnership, Sugarman Brothers, for the purpose of selling paper products. By 1918, the partnership was owned in equal shares and managed by three of the four brothers: Joseph, Samuel and Myer Sugarman. Leonard Sugarman ("Leonard"), defendant-appellant, is the son of Myer, who died in 1983. Plaintiffs-appellees are the grandchildren of Samuel, who died in 1965.

In the 1930's, the principals in Sugarman Brothers organized Leonard Tissue Corporation, owned equally by Joseph, Myer and Samuel. Following World War II, Sugarman Brothers was incorporated, with its stock also owned equally by the three Sugarman branches. In 1964, Leonard Tissue changed its name to Statler Tissue and in 1969, Statler Tissue and Sugarman Brothers merged to create Statler Corporation. Statler's common stock was owned in approximately equal amounts by each of the three Sugarman branches. Leonard, his father Myer, and appellees' father, Hyman, were all officers and directors of the company.

The present difficulties arise from the fact that, after the original equal division which existed until 1974, one branch of the family has controlled a majority of the stock and all of the management. Defendant Leonard Sugarman, president of the company and chairman of the board, owns 61% of the stock; plaintiffs Jon Sugarman, James Sugarman, and Marjorie Sugarman Tyie, Hyman's children, own 21.78%. . . . Leonard effectively controlled the company. . . .

Members of the other branches of the family were employed by the company from time to time. The district court found that James Sugarman had never sought to be employed by the company, and that Marjorie Sugarman had sought to be employed, but was not. The court stated that Jon Sugarman was employed from 1974 until his discharge in 1978, but did not rule on whether that discharge was improper, as alleged by Jon.

In 1981, plaintiffs-appellees brought suit, alleging that Leonard had abused his fiduciary duty to Statler [the corporation] and to appellees. Count I of the complaint sought a derivative recovery against Leonard on behalf of Statler, alleging that Leonard had caused Statler to pay him excessive salary and bonuses and had engaged in other forms of prohibited self-dealing. Count II sought direct recovery for appellees against Leonard on the theory of "freeze-out" of minority shareholders. This theory was based on allegations that Leonard had deprived Jon and Marjorie Sugarman of desired employment with the company, had drained off the company's earnings in the form of excessive compensation to Leonard, and had refused to pay dividends.

The district court found that Leonard had given his father, Myer, salary and pension benefits that were not given equally to Hyman, appellees' father. In addition, it found that Leonard had offered to buy Jon and Marjorie's stock at a grossly inadequate price. The court also found that Leonard had received excessive compensation from Statler for the years 1978 to 1984 and that this overcompensation "was effected in bad faith, as part of an attempt to freeze out minority interests." The court concluded that this combination of factors was proof of Leonard's effort to improperly freeze appellees out of the company. Adding annual interest at twelve percent from the dates each of these payments were made, the court concluded that a total amount of $1,353,837 had been improperly paid to Leonard and Myer. The court further found that Leonard had improperly caused Statler to pay on his behalf an additional $82,201 in attorney's fees and $9,836 in expert witness fees in defending this action. The court then awarded damages directly to appellees in an amount equal to 21.78% of these improper payments, a percentage equivalent to the amount of stock owned by appellees. The court also awarded appellees their attorney's fees and costs in the amount of $115,720. The final amount awarded to appellees was $537,925.

II. *Freeze–Out*

We first examine the legal standard that must be met to establish a "freeze-out" of minority shareholders, and then analyze the evidence and findings of the district court. In Donahue v. Rodd Electrotype Co. of New England, 367 Mass. 578 (1975), the Massachusetts Supreme Judicial Court (SJC) held that shareholders in a close corporation owe one another a fiduciary duty of "'utmost good faith and loyalty'". 367 Mass. at 593 (quoting Cardullo v. Landau, 329 Mass. 5, 8 (1952)). According to the court, stockholders in a close corporation "may not act out of avarice, expediency or self-interest in derogation of their duty of loyalty to the other stockholders and to the corporation." Id.

The court's decision in *Donahue* was premised on the rationale that the corporate form of a close corporation "supplies an opportunity for the majority stockholders to oppress or disadvantage minority stockholders." Id., 367 Mass. at 588. . . .

In Wilkes v. Springside Nursing Home, Inc., 370 Mass. 842 (1976), the SJC held that three directors of a close corporation had improperly "frozen-out" Wilkes, a fourth director when they removed him from the payroll without any "legitimate business interest." 370 Mass. at 852. The court also stated that it could "infer that a design to pressure Wilkes into selling his shares to the corporation at a price below their value well may have been at the heart of the majority's plan." Id. This inference arose from the fact that "Connor [one of the stockholders], acting on behalf of the three controlling stockholders, offered to purchase Wilkes's shares for a price Connor admittedly would not have accepted for his own shares." Id. at 852, n. 14.

In these cases, the SJC has pioneered in developing an effective cause of action for minority shareholders who have been denied their fair share of benefits in close corporations. At the same time, it has carefully set out the contours of that cause of action. First, it is not sufficient for a minority shareholder to prove that the majority shareholder has taken excessive compensation or other payments from the corporation. See Bessette v. Bessette, 385 Mass. 806, 809–10 & n. 5 (1982) (right to recover overcompensation payments belongs to the corporation as a whole; suit must be brought as derivative action unless plaintiffs specifically allege that "defendant's conduct was an attempted 'freeze-out' of the minority stockholders by draining off 'the corporation's earnings in the form of exorbitant salaries and bonuses.' ") (quoting *Donahue,* 367 Mass. at 588–89). Here, appellees alleged a freeze-out attempt, and the district court found that Leonard's overcompensation was indeed "effected in bad faith, as part of an attempt to freeze out minority interests."

Second, it is not sufficient to allege that the majority shareholder has offered to buy the stock of a minority shareholder at an inadequate price. Majority shareholders have an independent duty to exercise complete candor with minority shareholders when they negotiate stock transactions; they must fully disclose all the material facts and circumstances surrounding or affecting a proposed transaction. . . . If a majority shareholder breaches this duty, and a minority shareholder sells stock at an inadequate price, the minority shareholder can seek damages based on the difference between the offered price and the fair value of the stock. . . .

In most cases, a stockholder must first sell his or her stock at an inadequate price before seeking damages. In a close corporation, however, a minority shareholder who merely receives an offer from a majority shareholder to sell stock at an inadequate price, but does not accept that offer, can still seek damages *if* the shareholder can prove that the offer was part of a plan to freeze the minority shareholder out of the corporation. That is, the minority shareholder must first establish that the majority shareholder employed various devices to ensure that the minority shareholder is frozen out of any financial benefits from the corporation through such means as the receipt of dividends or employment, and that the offer to buy stock at a low price is the "capstone of the majority plan" to freeze-out the minority. *Donahue,* 367 Mass. at 592.

The necessary ingredients of a freeze-out of minority shareholders are present in this case. The district court first had to find that Leonard Sugarman took actions to ensure that appellees would not receive any financial benefits from Statler. As noted, the court did find that Leonard's overcompensation was designed to freeze-out appellees from the company's benefits. The court also took note of the fact that dividends had never been paid by the company, although it concluded that dividends were only indirectly the issue in this case. The court also pointed out that Marjorie had sought and been denied employment with Statler and that Jon had alleged he was improperly discharged from employment at Statler. The court concluded, however, that it did not need to pass on this "doubtful proof" concerning employment in order to find freeze-out of the minority shareholders.

We agree that the district court was not required to find that every possible device for effectuating a freeze-out was employed by Leonard. Rather, the finding that was essential, and that was made by the district court, was that Leonard took some actions that were designed to freeze appellees out of the financial benefits they would ordinarily have received from Statler. Once the court made that finding, it could appropriately conclude that Leonard's offer to buy Jon and Marjorie's stock at an inadequate price was the capstone of a plan to freeze out appellees. . . .

III. *Payments to Myer*

As one of the factors establishing freeze-out, the district court found that Myer, Leonard's father, had received salary and pension benefits in excess of payments made to Hyman, appellees' father. Myer was one of the founding members of the company. From 1975–81, from ages 82–88, Myer received substantial salaries from Statler. In the last two years of his employment, 1980–81, Myer's salary approximately doubled, reaching $85,-000. On his retirement in 1982 at age 88, Myer was voted a pension of $75,000. Hyman, while employed by Statler, received a salary similar to Myer's pre–1980 salary. When Hyman's employment with Statler ended in 1980, however, he was not voted a similar pension payment.

Although the district court found that "soon after 1975 [Myer's] net value to the company declined from relatively little to zero," it went on to conclude that it did "not quarrel seriously with payments to Myer and Hyman, whether for working, or as a pension, as long as neither is favored." . . .

The judgment of the trial court is affirmed, except for that part relating to interest and attorney's fees, which is vacated and remanded.

ANALYSIS

1. What is the appropriate remedy in this case? Should Leonard be required to buy out the plaintiffs at a fair price? What would you expect to happen in the future under the court's order? Should the court order mediation? The appointment of an independent board? Psychological counseling?

2. What is the relevance of the offer by Leonard to buy the plaintiffs' shares for a low price? Would his case have been stronger if he had said he had no interest in buying their shares? If so, why?

3. How, if at all, are the plaintiffs injured by the corporate policy of not paying dividends? Is the injury one that is legally actionable?

4. Suppose you represent Leonard. What advice would you give him about setting his salary in the future?

Smith v. Atlantic Properties, Inc.

12 Mass.App.Ct. 201, 422 N.E.2d 798 (1981).

In December, 1951, Dr. Louis E. Wolfson agreed to purchase land in Norwood for $350,000, with an initial cash payment of $50,000 and a mortgage note of $300,000 payable in thirty-three months. Dr. Wolfson offered a quarter interest each in the land to Mr. Paul T. Smith, Mr.

Abraham Zimble, and William H. Burke. Each paid to Dr. Wolfson $12,500, one quarter of the initial payment. Mr. Smith, an attorney, organized the defendant corporation (Atlantic) in 1951 to operate the real estate. Each of the four subscribers received twenty-five shares of stock. Mr. Smith included, both in the corporation's articles of organization and in its by-laws, a provision reading, "No election, appointment or resolution by the Stockholders and no election, appointment, resolution, purchase, sale, lease, contract, contribution, compensation, proceeding or act by the Board of Directors or by any officer or officers shall be valid or binding upon the corporation until effected, passed, approved or ratified by an affirmative vote of eighty (80%) per cent of the capital stock issued outstanding and entitled to vote." This provision (hereafter referred to as the 80% provision) was included at Dr. Wolfson's request and had the effect of giving to any one of the four original shareholders a veto in corporate decisions.

Atlantic purchased the Norwood land. Some of the land and other assets were sold for about $220,000. Atlantic retained twenty-eight acres on which stood about twenty old brick or wood mill-type structures, which required expensive and constant repairs. After the first year, Atlantic became profitable and showed a profit every year prior to 1969, ranging from a low of $7,683 in 1953 to a high of $44,358 in 1954. The mortgage was paid by 1958 and Atlantic has incurred no long-term debt thereafter. Salaries of about $25,000 were paid only in 1959 and 1960. Dividends in the total amount of $10,000 each were paid in 1964 and 1970. By 1961, Atlantic had about $172,000 in retained earnings, more than half in cash.

For various reasons, which need not be stated in detail, disagreements and ill will soon arose between Dr. Wolfson, on the one hand, and the other stockholders as a group.[3] Dr. Wolfson wished to see Atlantic's earnings devoted to repairs and possibly some improvements in its existing buildings and adjacent facilities. The other stockholders desired the declaration of dividends. Dr. Wolfson fairly steadily refused to vote for any dividends. Although it was pointed out to him that failure to declare dividends might result in the imposition by the Internal Revenue Service of a penalty under the Internal Revenue Code, I.R.C. § 531 et seq. (relating to unreasonable accumulation of corporate earnings and profits), Dr. Wolfson persisted in his refusal to declare dividends. The other shareholders did agree over the years to making at least the most urgent repairs to Atlantic's buildings, but did not agree to make all repairs and improvements which were recommended in a 1962 report by an engineering firm retained by Atlantic to make a complete estimate of all repairs and improvements which might be beneficial.

The fears of an Internal Revenue Service assessment of a penalty tax were soon realized. Penalty assessments were made in 1962, 1963, and 1964. These were settled by Dr. Wolfson for $11,767.71 in taxes and

3. At least one cause of ill will on Dr. Wolfson's part may have been the refusal of the other shareholders to consent to his transferring his shares in Atlantic to the Louis E. Wolfson Foundation, a charitable foundation created by Dr. Wolfson.

interest. Despite this settlement, Dr. Wolfson continued his opposition to declaring dividends. The record does not indicate that he developed any specific and definitive schedule or plan for a series of necessary or desirable repairs and improvements to Atlantic's properties. At least none was proposed which would have had a reasonable chance of satisfying the Internal Revenue Service that expenditures for such repairs and improvements constituted "reasonable needs of the business," I.R.C. § 534(c), a term which includes (see I.R.C. § 537) "the reasonably anticipated needs of the business." Predictably, despite further warnings by Dr. Wolfson's shareholder colleagues, the Internal Revenue Service assessed further penalty taxes for the years 1965, 1966, 1967, and 1968. These taxes were upheld by the United States Tax Court in Atlantic Properties, Inc. v. Commissioner of Int. Rev., 62 T.C. 644 (1974), and on appeal in 519 F.2d 1233 (1st Cir.1975). . . .

An examination of these decisions makes it apparent that Atlantic has incurred substantial penalty taxes and legal expense largely because of Dr. Wolfson's refusal to vote for the declaration of sufficient dividends to avoid the penalty, a refusal which was (in the Tax Court and upon appeal) attributed in some measure to a tax avoidance purpose on Dr. Wolfson's part.

On January 30, 1967, the shareholders, other than Dr. Wolfson, initiated this proceeding in the Superior Court, later supplemented to reflect developments after the original complaint. The plaintiffs sought a court determination of the dividends to be paid by Atlantic, the removal of Dr. Wolfson as a director, and an order that Atlantic be reimbursed by him for the penalty taxes assessed against it and related expenses. . . .

The trial judge made findings (but in more detail) of essentially the facts outlined above and concluded that Dr. "Wolfson's obstinate refusal to vote in favor of . . . dividends was . . . caused more by his dislike for other stockholders and his desire to avoid additional tax payments than . . . by any genuine desire to undertake a program for improving . . . [Atlantic] property." She also determined that Dr. Wolfson was liable to Atlantic for taxes and interest amounting to "$11,767.11 plus interest from the commencement of this action, plus $35,646.14 plus interest from August 11, 1975," the date of the First Circuit decision affirming the second penalty tax assessment. The latter amount includes an attorney's fee of $7,500 in the Federal tax cases. She also ordered the directors of Atlantic to declare "a reasonable dividend at the earliest practical date and reasonable dividends annually thereafter consistent with good business practice." In addition, the trial judge directed that jurisdiction of the case be retained in the Superior Court "for a period of five years to [e]nsure compliance." Judgment was entered pursuant to the trial judge's order. . . .

After the entry of judgment, Dr. Wolfson and Atlantic filed a motion for a new trial and to amend the judge's findings. This motion, after hearing, was denied, and Dr. Wolfson and Atlantic claimed an appeal from the judgment and the former from the denial of the motion. The plaintiffs . . . requested payment of their attorneys' fees in this proceeding and filed supporting affidavits. The motion was denied, and the plaintiffs appealed.

1. The trial judge, in deciding that Dr. Wolfson had committed a breach of his fiduciary duty to other stockholders, relied greatly on broad language in Donahue v. Rodd Electrotype Co., 367 Mass. 578, 586–597 (1975), in which the Supreme Judicial Court afforded to a minority stockholder in a close corporation equality of treatment (with members of a controlling group of shareholders) in the matter of the redemption of shares. The court (at 592–593) relied on the resemblance of a close corporation to a partnership and held that "stockholders in the close corporation owe one another substantially the same fiduciary duty in the operation of the enterprise that partners owe to one another" (footnotes omitted). That standard of duty, the court said, was the "utmost good faith and loyalty." The court went on to say that such stockholders "may not act out of avarice, expediency or self-interest in derogation of their duty of loyalty to the other stockholders and to the corporation." Similar principles were stated in Wilkes v. Springside Nursing Home, Inc., 370 Mass. 842, 848–852, (1976), but with some modifications . . . of the sweeping language of the *Donahue* case. . . .

In the *Donahue* case, 367 Mass. at 593 n. 17, the court recognized that cases may arise in which, in a close corporation, majority stockholders may ask protection from a minority stockholder. Such an instance arises in the present case because Dr. Wolfson has been able to exercise a veto concerning corporate action on dividends by the 80% provision (in Atlantic's articles or organization and by-laws) already quoted. The 80% provision may have substantially the effect of reversing the usual roles of the majority and the minority shareholders. The minority, under that provision, becomes an ad hoc controlling interest.[6]

. . . In the present case, Dr. Wolfson testified that he requested the inclusion of the 80% provision "in case the people [the other shareholders] whom I knew, but not very well, ganged up on me." The possibilities of shareholder disagreement on policy made the provision seem a sensible precaution.[8] A question is presented, however, concerning the extent to

6. The majority shareholders, in the event of a deadlock, at least may seek dissolution of the corporation if forty percent of the voting power can be mustered, whereas a single stockholder with only twenty-five percent of the stock may not do so. See G.L. c. 156B, § 99(*b*), as amended by St.1969, c. 392, § 23.

8. . . . It was reasonably foreseeable that there might be differences of opinion between Dr. Wolfson, a man with substantial income likely to be in a high income tax bracket, and less affluent shareholders on such matters of policy as dividend declara-

tions, salaries, and investment in improvements in the property. The other shareholders, two of whom were attorneys, should have known that it was as open to Dr. Wolfson reasonably to exercise the veto provided to him by the 80% provision in favor of a policy of reinvestment of earnings in Atlantic's properties, which would probably avoid taxes and increase the value of the corporate assets, as it was for them (possessed of the same veto) to use reasonably their voting power in favor of a more generous dividend and salary policy.

which such a veto power possessed by a minority stockholder may be exercised as its holder may wish, without a violation of the "fiduciary duty" referred to in the *Donahue* case, 367 Mass. at 593, 328 N.E.2d 505, as modified in the *Wilkes* case.   . . .

2.   With respect to the past damage to Atlantic caused by Dr. Wolfson's refusal to vote in favor of any dividends, the trial judge was justified in finding that his conduct went beyond what was reasonable.   The other stockholders shared to some extent responsibility for what occurred by failing to accept Dr. Wolfson's proposals with much sympathy, but the inaction on dividends seems the principal cause of the tax penalties.   Dr. Wolfson had been warned of the dangers of an assessment under the Internal Revenue Code, I.R.C. § 531 et seq.   He had refused to vote dividends in any amount adequate to minimize that danger and had failed to bring forward, within the relevant taxable years, a convincing, definitive program of appropriate improvements which could withstand scrutiny by the Internal Revenue Service.   Whatever may have been the reason for Dr. Wolfson's refusal to declare dividends (and even if in any particular year he may have gained slight, if any, tax advantage from withholding dividends) we think that he recklessly ran serious and unjustified risks of precisely the penalty taxes eventually assessed, risks which were inconsistent with any reasonable interpretation of a duty of "utmost good faith and loyalty." The trial judge (despite the fact that the other shareholders helped to create the voting deadlock and despite the novelty of the situation) was justified in charging Dr. Wolfson with the out-of-pocket expenditure incurred by Atlantic for the penalty taxes and related counsel fees of the tax cases.[10]

3.   . . .

[T]he judgment should be revised to provide: (a) a direction that Atlantic's directors prepare promptly financial statements and copies of State and Federal income and excise tax returns for the five most recent calendar or fiscal years, and a balance sheet as of as current a date as is possible; (b) an instruction that they confer with one another with a view to stipulating a general dividend and capital improvements policy for the next ensuing three fiscal years; (c) an order that, if such a stipulation is not filed with the clerk of the Superior Court within sixty days after the receipt of the rescript in the Superior Court, a further hearing shall be held promptly (either before the court or before a special master with substantial experience in business affairs), at which there shall be received in evidence at least the financial statements and tax returns above mentioned, as well as other relevant evidence.   Thereafter, the court, after due consideration of the circumstances then existing, may direct the adoption (and carrying out), if it be then deemed appropriate, of a specific dividend

---

10. We do not now suggest that the standard of "utmost good faith and loyalty" may require some relaxation when applied to a minority ad hoc controlling interest, created by some device, similar to the 80% provision, designed in part to protect the selfish interests of a minority shareholder.   This seems to us a difficult area of the law best developed on a case by case basis.

and capital improvements policy adequate to minimize the risk of further penalty tax assessments for the then current fiscal year of Atlantic. The court also may reserve jurisdiction to take essentially the same action for each subsequent fiscal year until the parties are able to reach for themselves an agreed program.

.   .   .

ANALYSIS

1.   What is the logic of the case? Why is the problem Wolfson's fault?

2.   If you had been Wolfson's lawyer and he had told you he was adamant in his intention to use earnings for rehabilitation, what would you have advised him to do? What does your answer tell you about the legal doctrine of the decision and about the effect of that doctrine on behavior and on economic entitlements?

PLANNING

How could the problems encountered by the investors in this case have been avoided by adoption of appropriate provisions at the time of formation of the enterprise?

NOTE AND QUESTIONS

Nixon v. Blackwell, 626 A.2d 1366, 1379–81 (Del.1993) (en banc), the Delaware Supreme Court offered the following comments (which were not necessary to analysis of the legal issues raised by the case):

> The case at bar points up the basic dilemma of minority stockholders in receiving fair value for their stock as to which there is no market and no market valuation. It is not difficult to be sympathetic, in the abstract, to a stockholder who finds himself or herself in that position. A stockholder who bargains for stock in a closely held corporation .   .   . can make a business judgment whether to buy into such a minority position, and if so on what terms. One could bargain for definitive provisions of self-ordering permitted to a Delaware corporation through the certificate of incorporation or by-laws by reason of the provisions in 8 Del.C. §§ 102, 109, and 141(a). Moreover, in addition to such mechanisms, a stockholder intending to buy into a minority position in a Delaware corporation may enter into definitive stockholder agreements, and such agreements may provide for elaborate earnings tests, buy-out provisions, voting trusts, or other voting agreements.   .   .   .

> The tools of good corporate practice are designed to give a purchasing minority stockholder the opportunity to bargain for protection before parting with consideration. It would do violence to normal corporate practice and our corporation law to fashion an ad hoc ruling

which would result in a court-imposed stockholder buy-out for which the parties had not contracted. . . .

It would . . . be inappropriate judicial legislation for this Court to fashion a special judicially created rule for minority investors when . . . there are no negotiated special provisions in the certificate of incorporation, by-laws, or stockholder agreements.

1. How would *Wilkes* and *Sugarman* have been decided under Delaware law?

2. Which approach do you prefer—Delaware's (you made your bed and you must lie in it) or Massachusetts's (the Golden Rule)? Why? What are the likely consequences of each approach?

Jordan v. Duff and Phelps, Inc.

815 F.2d 429 (7th Cir.1987).
Cert. dismissed, 485 U.S. 901 (1988).

■ BEFORE CUDAHY, POSNER, and EASTERBROOK, CIRCUIT JUDGES.

■ EASTERBROOK, CIRCUIT JUDGE.

. . .

I

The case is here following a grant of summary judgment for the defendants [in an action founded on § 10(b) and Rule 10b–5, common law fraud, and breach of fiduciary duty].

Duff and Phelps, Inc., evaluates the risk and worth of firms and their securities. It sells credit ratings, investment research, and financial consulting services to both the firms under scrutiny and potential investors in them. Jordan started work at Duff & Phelps in May 1977 and was viewed as a successful securities analyst. In 1981 the firm offered Jordan the opportunity to buy some stock. By November 1983 Jordan had purchased 188 of the 20,100 shares outstanding. He was making installment payments on another 62 shares. Forty people other than Jordan held stock in Duff & Phelps.

Jordan purchased his stock at its "book value" (the accounting net worth of Duff & Phelps, divided by the number of shares outstanding). Before selling him any stock, Duff & Phelps required Jordan to sign a "Stock Restriction and Purchase Agreement" (the Agreement). This provided in part:

Upon the termination of any employment with the Corporation . . . for any reason, including resignation, discharge, death, disability or retirement, the individual whose employment is terminated or his estate shall sell to the Corporation, and the Corporation shall buy, all Shares of the Corporation then owned by such individual or his estate. The price to be paid for such Shares shall be equal to the adjusted book value (as hereinafter defined) of the Shares on the December 31 which coincides with, or immediately precedes, the date of termination of such individual's employment.

Duff & Phelps enforced this restriction with but a single exception. During 1983 the board of directors of Duff & Phelps adopted a resolution— of which Jordan did not learn until 1984—allowing employees fired by the firm to keep their stock for five years.   The resolution followed the discharge of Carol Franchik, with whom Claire Hansen, the (married) chairman of the board, had been having an affair.   When Franchik threatened suit, the board allowed her to keep her stock.

While Jordan was accumulating stock, Hansen, the chairman of the board, was exploring the possibility of selling the firm.   Between May and August 1983 Hansen and Francis Jeffries, another officer of Duff & Phelps, negotiated with Security Pacific Corp., a bank holding company.   The negotiators reached agreement on a merger, in which Duff & Phelps would be valued at $50 million, but a higher official within Security Pacific vetoed the deal on August 11, 1983.   As of that date, Duff & Phelps had no irons in the fire.

Jordan, however, was conducting a search of his own—for a new job. Jordan's family lived near Chicago, the headquarters of Duff & Phelps, and Jordan's wife did not get along with Jordan's mother.   The strain between the two occasionally left his wife in tears.   He asked Duff & Phelps about the possibility of a transfer to the firm's only branch office, in Cleveland, but the firm did not need Jordan's services there.   Concluding that it was time to choose between his job and his wife, Jordan chose his wife and started looking for employment far away from Chicago.   His search took him to Houston, where Underwood Neuhaus & Co., a broker-dealer in securities, offered him a job at a salary ($110,000 per year) substantially greater than his compensation ($67,000) at Duff & Phelps.   Jordan took the offer on the spot during an interview in Houston, but Underwood would have allowed Jordan to withdraw this oral acceptance.

On November 16, 1983, Jordan told Hansen that he was going to resign and accept employment with Underwood.   Jordan did not ask Hansen about potential mergers; Hansen did not volunteer anything. Jordan delivered a letter of resignation, which Duff & Phelps accepted the same day.   By mutual agreement, Jordan worked the rest of the year for Duff & Phelps even though his loyalties had shifted.   He did this so that he could receive the book value of the stock as of December 31, 1983—for under the Agreement a departure in November would have meant valuation as of December 31, 1982.   Jordan delivered his certificates on December 30, 1983, and the firm mailed him a check for $23,225, the book value (at $123.54 per share) of the 188 shares of stock.   Jordan surrendered, as worthless under the circumstances, the right to buy the remaining 62 shares.

Before Jordan cashed the check, however, he was startled by the announcement on January 10, 1984, of a merger between Duff & Phelps and a subsidiary of Security Pacific.   Under the terms of the merger Duff & Phelps would be valued at $50 million.   If Jordan had been an employee on

January 10, had quickly paid for the other 62 shares, and the merger had closed that day, he would have received $452,000 in cash and the opportunity to obtain as much as $194,000 more in "earn out" (a percentage of Duff & Phelps's profits to be paid to the former investors—an arrangement that keeps the employees' interest in the firm keen and reduces the buyer's risk if profits fall short). Jordan refused to cash the check and demanded his stock back; Duff & Phelps told him to get lost. He filed this suit in March 1984, asking for damages measured by the value his stock would have had under the terms of the acquisition.

The public announcement on January 10 explained that the boards of the two firms had reached an agreement in principle on January 6. The definitive agreement was signed on March 23. Because Security Pacific is a bank holding company, the acquisition required the approval of the Board of Governors of the Federal Reserve. The Fed granted approval, but with a condition so onerous that the firms abandoned the transaction. The Fed objected to Security Pacific's acquisition of Duff & Phelps's credit rating business. 71 Fed. Res. Bull. 118 (1985). The agreement was formally cancelled on January 9, 1985. Duff & Phelps quickly asked the district court to dismiss Jordan's suit, on the ground that he could not establish damages. Jordan responded by amending his complaint, with Judge Hart's permission, to ask for rescission rather than damages.

Throughout 1985 Duff & Phelps continued looking for a partner; finding none, it decided to dance with itself. The firm's management formed an "Employee Stock Ownership Trust", which was able to borrow $40 million against the security of the firm's assets and business. The Trust acquired Duff & Phelps through a new firm, Duff Research, Inc. This transaction occurred in December 1985. The employees at the time, together with Carol Franchik, received cash, notes, and beneficial interests in the Trust. Jordan asserts that the package was worth almost $2000 per share, or $497,000 if he had held 250 shares in December 1985.

. . .

II

Michaels [v. Michaels, 767 F.2d 1185, 1194–97 (7th Cir.1985)] holds that close corporations that purchase their own stock must disclose to the sellers all information that meets the standard of "materiality" set out in TSC Industries, Inc. v. Northway, Inc., 426 U.S. 438, 449, 48 L.Ed. 2d 757, 96 S.Ct. 2126 (1976).* . . . A jury would be free under *Michaels* to conclude that the board's decision of November 14 to seek a buyer for Duff & Phelps—coupled with the fact that at least one putative buyer thought Duff & Phelps worth $50 million, which casts an important light on the prospect of a profitable conclusion to the search—was "material" under the standard of TSC Industries. That is, there is a "substantial likelihood that, under all the circumstances, the omitted fact would have assumed actual significance in the deliberations of the reasonable shareholder" and

* [Editors.—A related issue raised in the case led to a "price and structure" rule later rejected by the Supreme Court in Basic, Inc. v. Levinson, Chapter 4, Sec. 3.]

"would have been viewed by the reasonable investor as having significantly altered the 'total mix' of information made available." 426 U.S. at 449 (footnote omitted.)

. . .

[T]his supposes that Duff & Phelps had a duty to disclose anything to Jordan. Most people are free to buy and sell stock on the basis of valuable private knowledge without informing their trading partners. Strangers transact in markets all the time using private information that might be called "material" and, unless one has a duty to disclose, both may keep their counsel. Dirks v. SEC, 463 U.S. 646, 653–64, 77 L.Ed. 2d 911, 103 S.Ct. 3255 (1983); Chiarella v. United States, 445 U.S. 222, 227–35, 63 L.Ed. 2d 348, 100 S.Ct. 1108 (1980); . . .. The ability to make profits from the possession of information is the principal spur to create the information, which the parties and the market as a whole may find valuable. The absence of a duty to disclose may not justify a lie about a material fact, but Duff & Phelps did not lie to Jordan. It simply remained silent when Jordan quit and tendered the stock, and it offered the payment required by the Agreement.

This argument is unavailing on the facts as we know them. The "duty" in question is the fiduciary duty of corporate law. Close corporations buying their own stock, like knowledgeable insiders of closely held firms buying from outsiders, have a fiduciary duty to disclose material facts. . . . The "special facts" doctrine developed by several courts at the turn of the century is based on the principle that insiders in closely held firms may not buy stock from outsiders in person-to-person transactions without informing them of new events that substantially affect the value of the stock. . . .

Because the fiduciary duty is a standby or off-the-rack guess about what parties would agree to if they dickered about the subject explicitly, parties may contract with greater specificity for other arrangements. It is a violation of duty to steal from the corporate treasury; it is not a violation to write oneself a check that the board has approved as a bonus. . . . The obligation to break silence is itself based on state law, . . . and so may be redefined to the extent state law permits. . . . But we need not decide how far contracts can redefine obligations to disclose. Jordan was an employee at will; he signed no contract.

The stock was designed to bind Duff & Phelps's employees loyally to the firm. The buy-sell agreement tied ownership to employment. Understandably Duff & Phelps did not want a viper in its nest, a disgruntled employee remaining only in the hope of appreciation of his stock. So there could have been reason to divorce the employment decision from the value of the stock. Perhaps it would have been rational for each employee to agree with Duff & Phelps to look to salary alone in deciding whether to stay. A contractual agreement that the firm had no duty to disclose would have uncoupled the investment decision from the employment decision, leaving whoever was in the firm on the day of a merger to receive a surprise appreciation. . . .

Yet an explicit agreement to make all employment decisions in ignorance of the value of the stock might not have been in the interests of the firm or its employees. Duff & Phelps was trying to purchase loyalty by offering stock to its principal employees. The package of compensation contained salary and the prospect of appreciation of the stock. Perhaps it paid a lower salary than, say, Underwood Neuhaus & Co., because its package contained a higher component of gain from anticipated appreciation in the stock. It is therefore unwarranted to say that the implicit understanding between Jordan and Duff & Phelps should be treated as if it had such a no-duty clause; we are not confident that this is the clause firms and their employees regularly would prefer. . . .

The course of dealing between Jordan and Duff & Phelps suggests that the firm did not demand that employees decide whether to stay or go without regard to the value of the stock. It apparently informed Jordan what the book value was expected to be on December 31, 1983, so that Jordan could decide whether to leave in November (receiving the value as of December 31, 1982) or stay for another six weeks. The firm did not demand that Jordan depart as soon as it learned he had switched loyalties; it allowed employees to time their departures to obtain the maximum advantage from their stock. The Agreement did not ensure that employees disregard the value of the stock when deciding what to do, and neither did the usual practice at Duff & Phelps. So the possibility that a firm could negotiate around the fiduciary duty does not assist Duff & Phelps; it did not obtain such an agreement, express or implied.

The closest Duff & Phelps came is the provision in the Agreement fixing the price of the stock at book value. Yet although the Agreement fixed the price to be paid those who quit, it did not establish the terms on which anyone would leave. Thus cases such as Toledo Trust [Co. v. Nye, 588 F.2d 202, 206 (6th Cir.1978)] and St. Louis Union Trust Co. v. Merrill Lynch, Pierce, Fenner & Smith, Inc., 562 F.2d 1040 (8th Cir.1977), do not assist Duff & Phelps. These cases dealt with agreements calling for valuation at a formula price on a fixed date. In *St. Louis Union Trust* the date was the death of the employee, the formula was book value. The court of appeals held that there was no need to pay the employee's estate a different price, just because a few weeks later Merrill Lynch went public at a higher price. The employee presumably did not take the possibility of a merger into account in deciding whether to die, and the formula price made "disclosure" irrelevant. *Toledo Trust*, too, discussed a buy back triggered by death. . . . Jordan, though, exercised choice about the date on which the formula would be triggered. He could have remained at Duff & Phelps; his decision to depart was affected by his wife's distress, his salary, his working conditions, the enjoyment he received from the job, and the value of his stock. The departure of such an employee is an investment decision as much as it is an employment decision. It is not fanciful to suppose that Mrs. Jordan would have found her mother in law a whole lot more tolerable if she had known that Jordan's stock might shortly be worth 20 times book value.

. . .

Our dissenting colleague concludes that all of this is beside the point because Hansen could have said, on receiving Jordan's letter on November 16: "In a few weeks we will pull off a merger that would have made your stock 20 times more valuable. It's a shame you so foolishly resigned. But even if you hadn't resigned, we would have fired you, the better to engross the profits of the merger for ourselves. So long, sucker." This would have been permissible, under our colleague's interpretation, because Jordan was an employee at will and therefore could have been fired at any time, even the day before the merger, for any reason—including the desire to deprive Jordan of a share of the profits. The ability to fire Jordan enabled the firm to "call" his shares, at book value, on whim. On this view, it is foolish to say that Duff & Phelps had a duty to disclose, because disclosure would have been no use to Jordan. (Perhaps this is really an argument about "causation" rather than "duty," but the terminology is unimportant.) But Duff & Phelps itself does not press this argument, and in civil litigation an appellate court ought not put words in a party's mouth and use them as the grounds on which to decide. . . . Perhaps Duff & Phelps does not want to establish a reputation for shoddy dealing; as our dissenting brother observes, a firm's desire to preserve its reputation is a powerful inducement to treat its contractual partners well. To attribute to a litigant an argument that it will take every possible advantage is to assume that the party wishes to dissipate its reputation, and the assumption is unwarranted.

More than that, a person's status as an employee "at will" does not imply that the employer may discharge him for every reason. Illinois, where Jordan was employed, has placed some limits on the discharge of at-will employees. . . . But employment at will is still a contractual relation, one in which a particular duration ("at will") is implied in the absence of a contrary expression. . . . One term implied in every unwritten contract and therefore, we suppose, every written one, is that neither party will try to take opportunistic advantage of the other. "[T]he fundamental function of contract law (and recognized as such at least since Hobbes's day) is to deter people from behaving opportunistically toward their contracting parties, in order to encourage the optimal timing of economic activity and to make costly self-protective measures unnecessary." Richard A. Posner, Economic Analysis of Law 81 (3d ed. 1986). . . .

Employment creates occasions for opportunism. . . . The difficulties of separating opportunistic conduct from honest differences of opinion about an employee's performance on the job may lead firms and their employees to transact on terms that keep such disputes out of court—which employment at will usually does. But no one . . . doubts that an avowedly opportunistic discharge is a breach of contract, although the employment is at-will. . . .

. . . We do not suppose for a second that if Jordan had not resigned on November 16, the firm could have fired him on January 9 with a little note saying: "Dear Mr. Jordan: There will be a lucrative merger tomorrow. You have been a wonderful employee, but in order to keep the proceeds of the merger for ourselves, we are letting you go, effective this instant. Here is the $23,000 for your shares." Had the firm fired Jordan for this stated reason, it would have broken an implied pledge to avoid opportunistic conduct. . . .

The timing of the sale and the materiality of the information Duff & Phelps withheld on November 16 are for the jury to determine. Our dissenting colleague stresses that businesses would be shocked to learn that they must disclose valuable corporate information to fickle employees. If disclosure is unthinkable, however, Jordan may have trouble establishing that Duff & Phelps acted with intent to defraud, a necessary element of a case under Rule 10b–5.

III

Jordan's complaint, as amended, asks for rescission of the sale of stock. . . . [District Court] Judge Leinenweber held that rescission is unavailable as a matter of law. Judge Leinenweber concluded that the sale cannot be rescinded because employment at Duff & Phelps is a condition of ownership of the stock, one not waived by the settlement with Franchik. Because of the Agreement, Jordan could not own the stock after December 31 and may not own it now. . . .

. . .

We need not say more . . . because Judge Leinenweber's reason is persuasive. Rescission entails the undoing of the deal, the return of the parties to the position they occupied before. Jordan quit on December 31, 1983, and moved to Houston. His employment was a quid pro quo for ownership of the stock. It is too late to restore his employment for 1984–86, and he has not offered to go back to work at Duff & Phelps if he wins the case. We therefore need not discuss whether a district court could force Duff & Phelps to take him back. Jordan is entitled only to damages, as his initial complaint requested. . . .

But what might the damages be? Judge Leinenweber held that there are none, as a matter of law, because the merger with Security Pacific fell through. Doubtless the news of the deal with Security Pacific was the reason Jordan filed this suit. Yet the rationale of finding a securities violation—if there was one, a qualification we will not repeat—is that Jordan sold his stock in ignorance of facts that would have established a higher value. The relevance of the fact does not depend on how things turn out. Just as a lie that overstates a firm's prospects is a violation even if, against all odds, every fantasy comes true, . . . so a failure to disclose an important beneficent event is a violation even if things later go sour. The news, here that some firm was willing to pay $50 million for Duff & Phelps in an arms' length transaction, allows investors to assess the worth of the stock. If one deal for $50 million falls through, another may be possible at a similar price. Investors will either hold the stock or demand a price that reflects the value of that information. The conclusion that because the first deal collapsed there are no damages must reflect a belief that if the firm was not worth $50 million, then it was worth only $2.5 million (its book value). That is implausible. Security Pacific was willing to pay $50 million because, it concluded, Duff & Phelps was worth that much. If it was worth that much to Security Pacific, it was worth that much to someone else. Some value may be produced by interactions unique to Security Pacific, but there is no reason to think that Security Pacific would pay the investors of Duff & Phelps for the elements of value Security Pacific brought to the deal. The price of an asset usually is what the second-highest bidder will pay. So if Security Pacific bid $50 million, it believed that someone else would pay that much too (or that Duff & Phelps would hold out as part of a risky gaming strategy); otherwise Security Pacific would have bid less. The end of Security Pacific's bid—for reasons unrelated to a reassessment of the value of Duff & Phelps—therefore does not show that Jordan was uninjured. And less than a year later Duff & Phelps sold the firm to a trust (which is to say, to the syndicate of banks that loaned the money to the trust) for about $40 million.

The sticky problem is not whether Jordan can show some damages in principle but whether he can establish causation. . . . Because of the Agreement, employment and ownership of the shares were tied. Jordan could sell his stock in two ways: by leaving the firm and receiving book value, or by holding the stock until a merger or LBO [that is, leveraged buyout, which is the type of transaction that was ultimately concluded] and receiving the offered price. Even if the stock was worth more than book value, Jordan could not receive that price without holding on. So it seems that to recover, Jordan must establish that on learning of the negotiations with Security Pacific he would have dropped plans to go to Houston, and that even after the disappointment of the Fed's action that scuttled the deal with Security Pacific Jordan would have stuck around until the end of 1985, finally receiving the payment from the LBO. Judge Hart denied defendants' motion for summary judgment, holding that causation is a question for the jury. We think that right. Because a reasonable investor would not conclude that the withdrawal of one bid implies that there will be no others—and because Jordan would have known of the board's decision to sell the firm—a jury would be entitled to conclude that Jordan would have stuck around. Difficulties with a mother-in-law are a strain, but families bear strains greater than that for the prospect of financial gain.

. . .

REVERSED AND REMANDED

[The short concurring opinion of Judge Cudahy is omitted.]

■ POSNER, CIRCUIT JUDGE, dissenting. A corporate employee at will quit, owning shares that he had agreed to sell back to the corporation at book value. The agreement was explicit that his status as a shareholder conferred no job rights on him. Nevertheless the court holds that the corporation had, as a matter of law, a duty, enforceable by proceedings under Rule 10b–5 of the Securities Exchange Act, to volunteer to the employee information about the corporation's prospects that might have led him to change his mind about quitting, although as an employee at will he had no right to change his mind. I disagree with this holding. The terms of the stockholder agreement show that there was no duty of disclosure, and since there was no duty there was no violation of Rule 10b–5

.   .   .

We should ask why liability for failing to disclose, as distinct from liability for outright misrepresentation, depends on proof of duty. The reason is that information is a valuable commodity, and its production is discouraged if the producer must share it with the whole world. Hence an investor is not required to blurt out his secrets, and a skilled investor is not required to disclose the results of his research and insights before he is able to profit from them. .   .   . But one who makes a contract, express or implied, to disclose information to another acts wrongfully if he then withholds the information. The question is whether Duff and Phelps made an undertaking, and therefore assumed a duty, to disclose to any stockholding employee who announced his resignation information regarding the prospects for a profitable sale of the company.

My brethren find such a duty implicit in the fiduciary relationship between a closely held corporation and its shareholders. By this approach, what should be the beginning of analysis becomes its end. .   .   . [T]he mere existence of a fiduciary relationship between a corporation and its shareholders does not require disclosure of material information to the shareholders. A further inquiry is necessary, and here must focus on the particulars of Jordan's relationship with Duff and Phelps.

.   .   . The contingent nature of Jordan's status as a shareholder [that is, he could remain a shareholder only if he also remained an employee] has a twofold significance. First, it raises a question about the applicability of the majority's rule requiring disclosure "in the course of negotiating to purchase stock." One may doubt whether there was any real negotiation in this case, for once Jordan resigned he was contractually obligated to sell back his stock at a predetermined price. Second, and more important, the contingent nature of Jordan's status as a shareholder negates the existence of a right to be informed and hence a duty to disclose. This point is central to my dissent and has now to be explained.

Jordan's deal with Duff and Phelps required him to surrender his stock at book value if he left the company. It didn't matter whether he quit or was fired, retired or died; the agreement is explicit on these matters. My brethren hypothesize "implicit parts of the relations between Duff & Phelps and its employees." But those relations are totally defined by (1) the absence of an employment contract, which made Jordan an employee at will; (2) the shareholder agreement, which has no "implicit parts" that bear on Duff and Phelps' duty to Jordan, and explicitly ties his rights as a shareholder to his status as an employee at will; (3) a provision in the stock purchase agreement between Jordan and Duff and Phelps (signed at the same time as the shareholder agreement) that "nothing herein contained shall confer on the Employee any right to be continued in the employment of the Corporation." There is no occasion to speculate about "the implicit understanding" between Jordan and Duff and Phelps. The parties left nothing to the judicial imagination. The effect of the shareholder and stock purchase agreements (which for simplicity I shall treat as a single "stockholder agreement"), against a background of employment at will, was to strip Jordan of any contractual protection against what happened to him, and indeed against worse that might have happened to him. Duff and Phelps points out that it would not have had to let Jordan withdraw his resignation had he gotten wind of the negotiations with Security Pacific and wanted to withdraw it. On November 14 Hansen could have said to Jordan, "I accept your resignation effective today; we hope to sell Duff and Phelps for $50 million but have no desire to see you participate in the resulting bonanza. You will receive the paltry book value of your shares as of December 31, 1982." The "nothing herein contained" provision in the stockholder agreement shows that this tactic is permitted. Equally, on November 14, at the board meeting before Hansen knew that Jordan wanted to quit, the board could have decided to fire Jordan in order to increase the value of the deal with Security Pacific to the remaining shareholders.

.   .   .

My brethren correctly observe that, "Because the fiduciary duty is a standby or off-the-rack guess about what parties would agree to if they dickered about the subject explicitly, parties may contract with greater specificity for other arrangements." But, they add, "we need not decide how far contracts can redefine obligations to disclose. Jordan was an employee at will; he signed no contract." It is true that he signed no contract of employment, but he signed a stockholder agreement that defined his rights as a shareholder "with greater specificity." The agreement entitled Duff and Phelps to terminate Jordan as shareholder, subject only to a duty to buy back his shares at book value. The arrangement that resulted (call it "shareholder at will") is incompatible with an inference that Duff and Phelps undertook to keep him abreast of developments affecting the value of the firm.

.   .   .

Since receipt of the information would have conferred no right on Jordan to benefit from the information, how can the parties be thought to have intended Duff and Phelps to have an enforceable duty to disclose the information to him? There is no duty to give shareholders information that they have no right to benefit from. .   .   . By signing the stockholder agreement Jordan gave Duff and Phelps in effect an option .   .   . to buy back his stock at any time at a fixed price. The grant of the option denied Jordan the right to profit from any information that the company might have about its prospects but prefer not to give him. If Hansen had known of the rule of law that my brethren adopt today, he could have avoided liability simply by telling Jordan that, come what may, December 30 would be Jordan's last day working for Duff and Phelps. Failure to disclose would be immaterial because Jordan could not act on the disclosure. Only because Hansen failed to make Jordan's resignation effective immediately (a generous gesture, which we have given Hansen cause to regret), as he could have done without violating any contractual obligation, is he held to have violated a duty of disclosure.

. . .

Was Jordan a fool to have become a shareholder of Duff and Phelps on such disadvantageous terms as I believe he agreed to? (If so, that might be a reason for doubting whether those were the real terms.) He was not. Few business executives in this country have contractual entitlements to earnings, bonuses, or even retention of their jobs. They would rather take their chances on their employer's good will and interest in reputation, and on their own bargaining power and value to the firm, than pay for contract rights that are difficult and costly to enforce. . . . If Jordan had had greater rights as a shareholder he would have had a lower salary; when he went to work for a new employer in Houston and received no stock rights he got a higher salary.

I go further: Jordan was protected by Duff and Phelps' own self-interest from being exploited. The principal asset of a service company such as Duff and Phelps is good will. It is a product largely of its employees' efforts and skills. If Jordan were a particularly valuable employee, so that the firm would be worth less without him, Hansen, desiring as he did to sell the firm for the highest possible price, would have told him about the prospects for selling the company. If Jordan was not a particularly valuable employee—if his departure would not reduce the value of the firm—there was no reason why he should participate in the profits from the sale of the firm, unless perhaps he had once been a particularly valuable employee but had ceased to be so. That possibility might, but did not, lead him to negotiate for an employment contract, or for stock rights that would outlast his employment. By the type of agreement that he made with Duff and Phelps, Jordan gambled that he was and would continue to be such a good employee that he would be encouraged to stay long enough to profit from the firm's growth. The relationship that the parties created aligned their respective self-interests better than the legal protections that the court devises today.

My brethren are well aware that Duff and Phelps faced market constraints against exploiting its employee shareholders, but seem to believe that this implies that the company also assumed contractual duties. Businessmen, however, are less enthusiastic about contractual duties than lawyers are, . . . so it is incorrect to infer from the existence of market constraints against exploitation that the parties also imposed a contractual duty against exploitation. Contractual obligation is a source of uncertainty and cost, and is therefore an expensive way of backstopping market forces. That is why employment at will is such a common form of employment relationship. It is strange to infer that firms invariably assume a legal obligation not to do what is not in their self-interest to do, and stranger to suppose—in the face of an explicit disclaimer—that by "allowing employees to time their departures to obtain the maximum advantage from their stock," Duff and Phelps obligated itself to allow them to do this.

Having earlier in its opinion tried to get mileage out of the fact that Jordan "signed no [employment] contract," the majority later tries to get additional mileage from the observation that employment at will is a "contractual relation." This is the kind of legal half-truth that should make us thankful that our opinions are not subject to Rule 10b–5. Employment at will is a voluntary relationship, and thus contractual in the sense in which the word contract is used in the expression "freedom of contract." And the relationship can provide a framework for contracting: if Duff and Phelps had not paid Jordan his agreed-on wage after he had earned it, he could have sued the company for breach of contract. But the only element of employment at will that is relevant to this case is that employment at will is terminable at will, meaning that the employer can fire the employee without worrying about legal sanctions and likewise the employee can quit without worrying about them. Freedom of contract includes freedom not to contract.

.   .   .

The inroads that the majority opinion makes on freedom of contract are not justified by its quotation from my academic writings concerning the purpose of contract law (which presupposes an agreement that the parties regard as legally enforceable) or by the possibility that corporations will exploit their junior executives, which may well be the least urgent problem facing our nation. The majority's statement that "one term implied in every written contract and therefore, we suppose, every unwritten one, is that neither party will try to take opportunistic advantage of the other" confuses the underlying rationale of contract law with the actual requirements of that law, and is anyway irrelevant since the parties decided not to subject the relevant parts of their relationship to the law of contracts and not to give Jordan any contractual protections against being fired. There was no "implied pledge to avoid opportunistic conduct" any more than there were "implicit parts of the relations" giving rise to contractual obligations.   .   .   .

.   .   .

ANALYSIS

1. What relationship should be the focus of attention in this case: employer and employee, corporation and shareholder, or majority share-

holder and minority shareholder? In other words, is this an employee-compensation case or a shareholder-oppression case? Or is it just an old-fashioned contract case, with the terms incompletely specified?

2. What is the relevance, if any, of fraud or fiduciary obligation? How do these questions bear on the question whether the plaintiff is entitled to relief under § 10(b) and Rule 10b–5? Is it possible to ignore all the linguistic frameworks, the legal "cubbyholes," and examine the case in some other, more fundamental way? One possibility is to describe the facts as objectively as possible and then to examine various possible outcomes in light of the goals or criteria of a good system of rules of law for such situations. What are those goals or criteria? What are the implicit criteria applied by Judge Easterbrook? By Judge Posner?

3. Judge Easterbrook asserts, "Duff & Phelps was trying to purchase loyalty by offering stock to its principal employees." Is that statement accurate? Helpful?

4. Suppose Jordan's contract with Duff & Phelps made clear that his employment could be terminated at any time, even if termination meant that he would lose out on an expected appreciation in the value of his shares, and that Duff & Phelps had no obligation to provide him with any information regarding the value of his shares. Or suppose that the contract had provided clearly that all that Jordan could ever expect was the book value of his shares; that he would never be entitled to the benefit of a sale of the entire corporation. Would Jordan have been foolish to accept employment on those terms? Would enforcement of such a term in the contract be "opportunistic"? A violation of Rule 10b–5?

5. How would Jordan have fared (without benefit of litigation) if his contract with Duff & Phelps had provided for a buyout at "fair market value" rather than book value? Why did the parties use book value?

SECTION 5. CONTROL, DURATION, AND STATUTORY DISSOLUTION

In this section, as in the preceding section, we examine situations in which minority shareholders of closely held corporations claim that they have been treated unfairly by the majority. In the cases in this section, however, the minority shareholders have invoked special statutory provisions allowing the courts to order dissolution in certain circumstances and the general equitable powers of the courts. We will now focus our attention on those statutory provisions and equitable powers, on the remedies available under them, and on the strategies both majority and minority shareholders should consider.

Alaska Plastics, Inc. v. Coppock

621 P.2d 270 (Alaska 1980).

The issue in this case involves the rights of a minority shareholder in a close corporation who allegedly has been deprived of benefits accorded other shareholders. The trial judge concluded that the corporation was obligated to buy the minority shareholder's stock at its fair value. We have concluded that this remedy is not available on the present record as a matter of law. Accordingly, we remand to the superior court to determine whether, based upon adequate findings of fact and conclusions of law, a remedy more appropriate to the alleged facts is available.

Those facts which the parties have stipulated to or which appear to be undisputed in the record are summarized below.

In 1961 the three individual appellants, Ralph Stefano, C. Harold Gillam, and Robert Crow formed a corporation known as Alaska Plastics and began to produce foam insulation at a building they bought in Fairbanks. Each of the three incorporators held 300 shares of stock. In 1970 Crow was divorced and, as part of a property settlement, gave his former wife, Patricia Muir, 150 shares or a one-sixth interest in the corporation.[1] From the time of incorporation until this lawsuit, Stefano, Gillam and Crow have been the only directors and officers of Alaska Plastics.

Stefano conceded at trial that the corporation forgot to notify Muir of annual shareholders meetings in 1971 and 1974. It was also undisputed that Muir was not notified of a shareholders meeting in 1972. According to Muir's testimony she was told of the 1973 shareholders meeting about three hours before the meeting was held.

---

1. At the time this action was filed Muir had remarried and assumed the name of Patricia Coppock. She has since that time resumed using her maiden name.

In 1971 and 1972, Stefano, Gillam and Crow held the shareholders meetings in Seattle. It appears from Stefano's testimony that he and Gillam also brought their wives to these meetings at company expense, but he conceded that there was no business purpose for doing so.

In 1971, Stefano, Gillam and Crow voted themselves each a $3,000 annual director's fee. Although director's fees were apparently paid from 1971 through 1974, the three directors have never authorized Alaska Plastics to pay dividends. In 1974 the three board members also authorized an annual salary of $30,000 a year for Gillam, who was then employed as general manager of Alaska Plastics. Muir testified that she has never received any money from the corporation.

At the 1974 board meeting Stefano, Gillam and Crow also decided to offer Muir $15,000 for her shares and on May 1, 1974, Stefano wrote Muir informing her of the corporation's offer. Thinking the firm's offer was too low, Muir retained a lawyer who wrote the corporation expressing her concern both regarding the offered price and regarding the corporation's failure to inform Muir of shareholders meetings. In July, 1974, Muir's lawyer made a further demand on the corporation to inspect the books and records of the corporation. Gillam apparently advised Muir where the firm kept its books and told her they could be made available. An accountant employed by Muir did investigate the company's books and estimated that the shares might have a value somewhere between $23,000 and $40,000. Muir also ordered an appraisal of Alaska Plastics' Fairbanks property.

Later that same year, at a special director's meeting in October, 1974, the three board members agreed to make a $50,000 offer for Broadwater Industries, a firm located near Palmer that made a type of plastic foam insulation similar to that produced by Alaska Plastics at their Fairbanks plant. The purchase was apparently accomplished at some time between October and the next shareholders meeting, which was held on April 25, 1975. Muir testified that she was never consulted about the purchase and first learned about it at the 1975 meeting. At that meeting, however, she did not dissent from a shareholder vote ratifying all the acts of the directors and officers for the previous year.

Broadwater Industries was subsequently renamed Valley Plastics and is now a wholly-owned subsidiary of Alaska Plastics. The directors and officers of Valley Plastics are Stefano, Gillam and Crow.

At the 1975 shareholders meeting, Muir offered her stock to the corporation for $40,000. In June, 1975, the board raised its offer to $20,000, which Muir again rejected.

Shortly after these negotiations failed, Alaska Plastics' Fairbanks plant, which was not insured, burned to the ground. The fire caused a total loss. Since the fire, Alaska Plastics has ceased production from Fairbanks and the corporation has not made an attempt to resume production in Fairbanks. All the remaining manufacturing and sales of Alaska Plastics are accomplished through its subsidiary, Valley Plastics. The fire, in effect, turned Alaska Plastics into a holding company for its affiliate.

About a year after the fire, in 1976, Stefano, acting as an individual, made a further offer of $20,000 to Muir, but the purchase never took place. Further attempts by the parties to negotiate a purchase or settlement failed and a lawsuit was filed in October 1976.

An amended complaint alleges ten separate causes of action, and prays for relief both in the name of the corporation and individually for Muir. After trial, . . . the trial judge issued a judgment which states in part:

> "[T]he continued retention by Plaintiff of one-sixth of the shares in Alaska Plastics, Inc. following the offer on April 1974 was oppressive to Plaintiff and . . . an appropriate remedy would be to direct the transfer of Plaintiff's shares to Alaska Plastics, Inc. in exchange for a fair and equitable value. . . ."

A total judgment was entered against the three individual appellants and Alaska Plastics for $52,314, which represented $32,000 for the value of the shares, $5,200 for attorney's fees, and $15,144 in interest and costs. Muir was in turn required to convey her shares to Alaska Plastics. Both sides subsequently filed appeals.

I.   SHAREHOLDER REMEDIES

In a corporation with publicly traded stock, dissatisfied shareholders can sell their stock on the market, recover their assets, and invest elsewhere. In a close corporation there is not likely to be a ready market for the corporation's shares. The corporation itself, or one of the other individual shareholders of the corporation, who are likely to provide the only market, may not be interested in buying out another shareholder. If they are interested, majority shareholders who control operating policy are in a unique position to "squeeze out" a minority shareholder at an unreasonably low price.

From a dissatisfied shareholder's point of view, the most successful remedy is likely to be a requirement that the corporation buy his or her shares at their fair value. Ordinarily, there are four ways in which this can occur. First, there may be a provision in the articles of incorporation or by-laws that provides for the purchase of shares by the corporation, contingent upon the occurrence of some event, such as the death of a shareholder or transfer of shares. Second, the shareholder may petition the court for involuntary dissolution of the corporation. Third, upon some significant change in corporate structure, such as a merger, the shareholder may demand a statutory right of appraisal. Finally, in some circumstances, a purchase may be justified as an equitable remedy upon a finding of a breach of a fiduciary duty between directors and shareholders and the corporation or other shareholders.

It does not appear from the record that there is any provision in the articles of incorporation or by-laws which would allow Muir to force Alaska Plastics to purchase her shares. Muir has not suggested that there is such provision, and we, therefore, do not consider the availability of this first method.

As to the second method, Alaska's corporation code provides in AS 10.05.540(2) that a shareholder may bring an action to liquidate the assets of a corporation upon a showing that "the acts of the directors or those in control of the corporation are illegal, oppressive or fraudulent. . . ." A shareholder may also seek liquidation when "corporate assets are being misapplied or wasted." AS 10.05.540(4). Upon a liquidation of assets all creditors and the cost of liquidation must be paid and the remainder distributed among all the shareholders "according to their respective rights and interests." AS 10.05.561. There is no indication whether Muir would have received more or less than the $32,000 price for her shares ordered by the court if Alaska Plastics had been liquidated.

Liquidation is an extreme remedy. In a sense, forced dissolution allows minority shareholders to exercise retaliatory oppression against the majority. Absent compelling circumstances, courts often are reluctant to order involuntary dissolution. . . . As a result, courts have recognized alternative remedies based upon their inherent equitable powers. Thus in Baker [v. Commercial Body Builders, Inc., 264 Or. 614, 507 P.2d 387, 395–97 (1973)], interpreting a statute substantially similar to AS 10.05.540, the court authorized numerous alternative remedies for oppressive or fraudulent conduct by the majority. Among those would be:

> "an order requiring the corporation or a majority of its stockholders to purchase the stock of the minority shareholders at a price to be determined according to a specified formula or at a price determined by the court to be a fair and reasonable price." (footnote omitted).

Baker, 507 P.2d at 396. . . .

We are persuaded by *Baker* and conclude that Muir's request in her amended complaint for liquidation, although not actively pursued, could justify the trial court's order as an equitable remedy less drastic than liquidation. To prevail on this basis, Muir must establish on remand that the acts of Stefano, Gillam and Crow were "illegal, oppressive or fraudulent," AS 10.05.540(2), or alternatively, constituted a waste or misapplication of corporate assets. AS 10.05.540(4). Because the trial court did not reach the issue, we express no opinion here on whether Muir has satisfied the statutory standards of AS 10.05.540.

The third method of forcing a corporation to purchase a minority shareholder's shares is a statutory appraisal remedy, which may be available under the Alaska Business Corporation Act in two circumstances where there is some fundamental corporate change. The remedy is available upon the merger or consolidation with another corporation, AS 10.05.417, or upon a sale of substantially all of the corporation's assets. AS 10.05.447. There is no suggestion that either statute is applicable in this case. In some circumstances, however, courts have found that a corporate transaction so fundamentally changes the nature of the business that there is a "de facto" merger which triggers the same statutory appraisal remedy.

[The court concludes that the "de facto" merger doctrine is not applicable in this case. That doctrine is examined later in this casebook. Chapter 6, Sec. 1.]

We turn, then, to the fourth possibility by which a minority shareholder may force a corporation to purchase his or her shares. Two leading cases have concluded that transactions by one group of shareholders that enable it to derive some special benefit not shared in common by all shareholders should be subject to close judicial scrutiny. The Massachusetts Supreme Judicial Court concluded that shareholders in closely held corporations owe one another a fiduciary duty:

> "Because of the fundamental resemblance of the close corporation to the partnership, the trust and confidence which are essential to this scale and manner of enterprise, and the inherent danger to minority interests in the close corporation, we hold that stockholders in the close corporation owe one another substantially the same fiduciary duty in the operation of the enterprise that partners owe to one another. In our previous decisions, we have defined the standard of duty owed by partners to one another as the 'utmost good faith and loyalty.'" (footnotes and citations omitted).

Donahue v. Rodd Electrotype Co., 367 Mass. 578, 328 N.E.2d 505, 515 (1975). The California Supreme Court concluded that a controlling group of shareholders owes a similar duty to minority shareholders. In Jones v. H.F. Ahmanson & Co., 1 Cal.3d 93, 81 Cal.Rptr. 592, 460 P.2d 464 (1969), the court held that a control block of stock could not be used to give the majority benefits that were not shared with the minority.

We believe that *Donahue* and *Ahmanson* correctly state the law applicable to the relationship between shareholders in closely held corporations, or between those holding a controlling block of stock, and minority shareholders. We do not believe, though, that the existence and breach of a fiduciary duty among corporate shareholders supports the appraisal remedy ordered by the trial court in this case.

The trial judge made no findings of fact or conclusions of law, but the basis for his decision is clear from extensive discussions that took place prior to instructing the jury and the form of the judge's final order. The court concluded that once the corporation made an offer to Muir it was under an obligation to purchase her stock at a "fair" price, regardless of what price the corporation had initially offered. Had Muir actually sold the stock at an unfairly low price, she might have brought an action to set the transaction aside. The existence of a fiduciary duty between shareholders would justify careful scrutiny and shifting the burden onto the defendants to show that the transaction was fair.   . . .   In this case, however, Muir rejected both of the corporation's offers. We are not aware of any authority which would allow a court to order specific performance on the basis of an unaccepted offer, particularly on terms totally different from those offered. Such a rule would place a court in the impossible position of making and enforcing contracts between unwilling parties.

Donahue and *Ahmanson* do suggest the appropriate form of a remedy in this case, however. In *Donahue,* one of the controlling shareholders caused the corporation to purchase forty-five of his shares, but then refused to buy an equal number of shares held by a minority shareholder. The court first noted the benefit that a shareholder in a close corporation gained by forcing the corporation to buy his shares.

"The benefits conferred by the purchase are twofold: (1) provision of a market for shares; (2) access to corporate assets for personal use. By definition, there is no ready market for shares of a close corporation. The purchase creates a market for shares which previously had been unmarketable. It transforms a previously illiquid investment into a liquid one."

328 N.E.2d at 518. The court then went on to conclude that where a controlling shareholder took advantage of such a special benefit, the fiduciary duty owed to other shareholders required that the corporation offer such a benefit equally:

"The rule of equal opportunity in stock purchases by close corporations provides equal access to these benefits for all stockholders."

Id. at 519.

In *Ahmanson,* the controlling group of shareholders transferred its control block of stock to a holding company which in turn offered its stock to the public. There were relatively few shares of stock in the active company in which the plaintiffs owned shares, and the price of each share was so high that they had little market appeal. The holding company, on the other hand, offered numerous shares at far lower prices. Because of the ready market for holding company shares, the controlling shareholders were able to sell part of their investment in the active company through the holding company at a huge profit. The court held that the majority shareholders had to offer this same opportunity to minority shareholders.

As we read Muir's complaint, the essence of her action is that Stefano, Gillam and Crow enjoyed benefits from the corporation which should have been shared equally with her. None of the other shareholders of Alaska Plastics have sold their stock to the corporation so it would not be appropriate to order the corporation to purchase Muir's stock. Unlike *Donahue,* this was not one of the benefits which the majority received and which they did not share with Muir. There was evidence, however, that the corporation paid Stefano, Gillam and Crow "director's fees." Gillam received a substantial salary. The corporation apparently paid some of the personal expenses of the directors' wives. Regardless of how the corporation labels these expenditures, if they were not made for the reasonable value of services rendered to the corporation, some portion of these payments might be characterized as constructive dividends.

We express no opinion as to whether Muir has shown that these payments were a distribution of dividends, whether she was deprived of other corporate benefits which she should have shared in equally with the other three shareholders, or whether the majority shareholders violated AS

10.05.540. The case must be remanded to the trial court to make appropriate findings of fact and conclusions of law based upon the present record.

II. THE DERIVATIVE CLAIM

At the conclusion of trial, the judge dismissed Muir's derivative suit. In her brief, Muir suggests that a number of acts taken by the corporation amounted to a breach of the director's duty of care toward the corporation. For example, the directors failed to insure the Fairbanks plant, they kept large reserves of cash in noninterest-bearing checking accounts, and they loaned an employee money at a rate below prevailing rates of interest. Viewing the plaintiff's evidence alone, which amounted to little more than the fact that these acts had taken place, we conclude that the evidence was insufficient to establish a breach of duty towards the corporation.

Judges are not business experts, Dodge v. Ford Motor Co., 204 Mich. 459, 170 N.W. 668, 684 (1919), a fact which has become expressed in the so-called "business judgment rule." The essence of that doctrine is that courts are reluctant to substitute their judgment for that of the board of directors unless the board's decisions are unreasonable. No *proof* was presented that the alleged acts were unreasonable in the sense that they would not have been taken by "an ordinarily prudent man . . . in the management of his own affairs of like magnitude and importance." Nanfito v. Tekseed Hybrid Co., 341 F.Supp. 240, 244 (D.Neb.1972). The proof offered was therefore insufficient to present a question for the trier of fact.

In Santarelli v. Katz, 270 F.2d 762 (7th Cir.1959), the evidence showed that one of the director's wives in a closely held corporation had been receiving thousands of dollars a year to attend three or four conventions. In a stockholders derivative suit, the court noted:

> "[I]f a stockholder is being unjustly deprived of dividends that should be his, a court of equity will not permit management to cloak itself in the immunity of the business judgment rule."

Id. at 768.

There is thus authority for concluding that an unfair distribution of corporate funds would be a proper subject for a derivative suit. Nevertheless, as we read the gravamen of Muir's complaint, it is that she was harmed as an individual by not receiving the same benefits as the other shareholders received, not that the corporation itself was harmed. Therefore, we believe that a derivative action would not be the appropriate form of action in this case, . . . Furthermore, Muir's rights are adequately protected by an individual action. The trial court thus properly dismissed this claim.

The case is REMANDED to the superior court for further proceedings in accordance with this opinion.

AFTERMATH

On remand, the trial court entered a judgment for Muir for $32,000 as the fair and reasonable value of her shares. On appeal, the Supreme Court upheld the trial court's "findings of oppressive or fraudulent conduct sufficient to warrant a remedy as 'drastic' as involuntary dissolution of the corporation or a forced buy-out of Muir's shares." Stefano v. Coppock, 705 P.2d 443 (Alaska 1985). The Supreme Court stated:

> It is clear that AS § 10.05.540(2) allows the superior court to liquidate a corporation when it is shown that the acts of those in control are oppressive or fraudulent. However, courts retain equitable authority to fashion a less drastic remedy to fit the parties' situation.

NOTE ON MEISELMAN v. MEISELMAN

In a leading case, Meiselman v. Meiselman, 309 N.C. 279, 307 S.E.2d 551 (1983), the corporation owned movie theaters and real estate, with a book value of over $11 million. The shareholders were brothers, Ira and Michael Meiselman, whose father had founded the business. Ira, the younger of the brothers, was the majority shareholder (by virtue of dispro-portionate gifts from the father) and ran the business. Michael had been excluded from management decision-making but had been employed in the business and had drawn a salary for many years. Over the years there had been personal antagonism between Ira and Michael. In 1979, Michael filed suit against Ira, complaining of the fact that Ira owned 100 percent of the shares of a company that provided management services to the jointly owned corporation. Shortly thereafter, Michael was fired and thereby lost his salary and fringe benefits. He did, however, receive dividends ($54,591 in 1979 and $61,845 in 1980). Michael then filed the suit that gave rise to the cited decision. Initially he sought dissolution but subsequently changed the claim for relief and sought to compel the corporation to buy his shares for a fair price.

Michael invoked N.C.G.S. § 55–125(a), which allows a court to order dissolution where such relief is "reasonably necessary for the protection of the rights and interests of the complaining shareholder." Under § 55–125.1, the court may, as an alternative to dissolution, order a buy-out of the complaining shareholder's shares. The trial court denied relief. The Supreme Court returned the case to the trial court, holding that, at least in cases involving close corporations, the complaining shareholder need not establish oppressive or fraudulent conduct by the controlling shareholder or shareholders. Instead, it said, "rights and interests," under the statute include "reasonable expectations," which include expectations that the minority shareholder "will participate in the management of the business or be employed by the company," but limited to "expectations embodied in understandings, express or implied, among the participants." In its lengthy opinion, the court referred to the statutes of seven states (Illinois, Maryland, Michigan, New Jersey, New York, South Carolina, and Virginia) in which dissolution may be granted for oppressive conduct, with some decisions under these statutes interpreting "oppressive" broadly; and statutes in three states (California, Michigan, and New Jersey) in which dissolution (or other relief) may be granted for "unfair" conduct. The court also relied on the writings of Professors O'Neal and Hetherington in support of the idea that it is often unrealistic to expect minority shareholders in close corporations to bargain for protection of their expectations and that, consequently, judicial intervention on their behalf is appropriate.

ANALYSIS AND PLANNING

1.   In Alaska Plastics, Inc. v. Coppock, did the trial court have authority to order dissolution? If it had ordered dissolution, what do you suppose would have happened?

2.   What was the legal theory for the remedy that the court ordered on remand? What was the virtue of that remedy? What other remedies might the court have ordered and what are the virtues and defects of each?

3.   Why was Muir not required to pursue her derivative action? Would a judgment on the derivative claim have given Muir all that to which she was entitled?

4.   Suppose that the individual defendants had caused the corporation to offer either to buy Muir's one-sixth interest in the corporation for $25,000 or to sell the other five-sixths of the corporation to her for the same pro rata price, $125,000, and she had refused either to sell or to buy. Would the trial court still have had authority to order that her shares be purchased for $32,000?

5.   Suppose the defendants had never offered to buy Muir's shares. Would Muir's case have been weaker or stronger?

6.   Suppose that before the case came to trial the individual defendants had each repaid to the corporation $2,500 of their annual directors' fees, plus the expenses for which they had been reimbursed for attending meetings of the board, plus interest. Could the trial court still have ordered the defendants to buy Muir's shares?

7.   Suppose you had represented Patricia Muir at the time of her divorce from Robert Crow and that Crow had no cash to buy out Muir's interest in the shares of stock of the corporation. What kind of deal would you have sought with respect to the shares?

8.   Suppose you had represented all three of the original investors at the time of the formation of the corporation and you had been aware that Crow's marriage was in difficulty. What would you have advised in anticipation of the possibility that Muir might claim a right to half of the shares of stock of the corporation that were to be issued to Crow?

NOTE AND QUESTION ON LIMITED LIABILITY COMPANIES

Under the Delaware Limited Liability Co. Act, § 18–604:

[U]pon resignation, any resigning member is entitled to receive any distribution to which he is entitled under a limited liability company agreement and, if not otherwise provided in a limited liability company agreement, he is entitled to receive, within a reasonable time after resignation, the fair value of his limited liability company interest as of the date of resignation based upon his right to share in distributions from the limited liability company.

This provision roughly parallels the partnership rules outlined in Chapter 2, Sections 1 and 8.

Consider the implications. If investors form a corporation, the default rule generally (note the occasional exception for close corporations discussed in the next case, Abrams v. Abrams–Rubaloff & Associates, Inc.) will be one of no right to dissolution or buyout. If investors want the right to "put" their stock to the firm, they must so provide in their charter or a shareholders' agreement. If they instead form an LLC, the default rule will grant them that right. Granted, LLC members can modify the default rule through their organizational documents. What modifications are likely to be desirable?

Abrams v. Abrams–Rubaloff & Associates, Inc.

114 Cal.App.3d 240, 170 Cal.Rptr. 656 (1980).

Abrams–Rubaloff & Associates, Inc. (the corporation) and Noel K. Rubaloff (Rubaloff) appeal a decree of the trial court confirming the majority appraisal valuation of Harry Abrams' shares of the corporation's stock, directing Rubaloff and the corporation to file a written election specifying which one of them is to be the purchasing party, and ordering the wind up and dissolution of the corporation unless payment for Abrams' shares is timely made. (Corp.Code, § 2000.) Harry Abrams (Abrams) appeals the portions of the decree valuing his shares at $355,000 and denying him interest from the date of valuation.

STATUTE

[Eds.—California Corporations Code § 1900(a) provides: "Any corporation may elect voluntarily to wind up and dissolve by the vote of shareholders holding shares representing 50 percent or more of the voting power."]

Corporations Code section 2000, effective January 1, 1977, provides in pertinent part: "(a) . . . [I]n any proceeding for voluntary dissolution initiated by the vote of shareholders representing only 50 percent of the voting power, the corporation or, if it does not elect to purchase, the holders of 50 percent or more of the voting power of the corporation (the 'purchasing parties') may avoid the dissolution of the corporation and the appointment of any receiver by purchasing for cash the shares owned . . . by the shareholders so initiating the proceeding (the 'moving parties') at their fair value. The fair value shall be determined on the basis of the liquidation value but taking into account the possibility, if any, of sale of the entire business as a going concern in a liquidation. In fixing the value, the amount of any damages resulting if the initiation of the dissolution is a breach by any moving party . . . of an agreement with the purchasing party . . . may be deducted from the amount payable to such moving party. . . .

"(b) If the purchasing parties (1) elect to purchase shares owned by the moving parties, and (2) are unable to agree with the moving parties upon the fair value of such shares, and (3) give bond with sufficient security to pay the estimated reasonable expenses (including attorneys' fees) of the moving parties if such expenses are recoverable under subdivision (c), the court upon application of the purchasing parties, either in the pending action or in a proceeding initiated . . . by the purchasing parties in the case of a voluntary election to wind up and dissolve, shall stay the winding up and dissolution proceeding and shall proceed to ascertain and fix the fair value of the shares owned by the moving parties.

"(c) The court shall appoint three disinterested appraisers to appraise the fair value of the shares owned by the moving parties, and shall make an order referring the matter to the appraisers so appointed for the purpose of ascertaining such value. The order shall prescribe the time and manner of producing evidence, if evidence is required. The award of the appraisers or a majority of them, when confirmed by the court shall be final and conclusive upon all parties. The court shall enter a decree which shall provide in the alternative for winding up and dissolution of the corporation unless payment is made for the shares within the time specified by the decree. If the purchasing parties do not make payment for the shares within the time specified, judgment shall be entered against them and the surety or sureties on the bond for the amount of the expenses (including attorneys' fees) of the moving parties. . . .

"(d) If the purchasing parties desire to prevent the winding up and dissolution, they shall pay to the moving parties the value of their shares ascertained and decreed within the time specified pursuant to this section, or, in the case of an appeal, as fixed on appeal. . . ."

FACTS

Abrams–Rubaloff & Associates, Inc., formed in December 1964, acts as an artists' manager (agent) for actors, directors, writers, and producers. Harry Abrams and Noel Rubaloff each own 50 percent of the corporation's outstanding shares. On January 25, 1977, Abrams filed with the Secretary of State a certificate of election to wind up and dissolve the corporation (Corp.Code, § 1900, subd. (a)), and thereafter he filed a petition with the superior court to invoke its supervision of the wind up and dissolution. (Corp.Code, § 1904.) On February 22, 1977, Rubaloff and the corporation terminated Abrams' employment with the corporation and delivered to Abrams an "election" to avoid dissolution by purchasing his shares pursuant to the provisions of Corporations Code section 2000. The "election," however, did not specify whether Rubaloff or the corporation (hereinafter referred to collectively as Rubaloff) would be the actual purchaser.

On April 12, 1977, the superior court assumed jurisdiction over the wind up and dissolution of the corporation, stayed the dissolution proceedings, set the amount of bond, specified the procedure for the appointment of three appraisers, and directed the appraisers, or a majority of them, to "determine the time and manner in which the parties may introduce evidence . . . bearing upon valuation." (Corp.Code, § 2000, subds. (b), (c).) Based upon the procedure set forth in the April 12 order, Abrams selected I.M. Zeman as an appraiser, Rubaloff selected Ronald Karno, and Zeman and Karno together then selected Larry Grant of Business Enterprise Appraisal Company as the third appraiser.

In May 1978 Grant transmitted to counsel for both sides his appraisal valuing Abrams' shares as of February 22, 1977, at $355,000. In early June Zeman sent his appraisal, agreeing with Grant's valuation, to the attorneys. On June 16, 1978, Abrams moved the superior court for an order confirming the valuation determined by the majority of the appraisers. Subsequently, Karno filed a report concluding that the liquidation value of Abrams' interest was $139,750.

In the interim Rubaloff filed a demand for a jury trial (which the court denied), and noticed a deposition of Grant (which the court quashed). On July 26, 1978, Rubaloff filed a cross-complaint and statement of offsets against Abrams for general damages and $150,000 punitive damages allegedly caused by Abrams' material breach of his employment contract and subsequent violation of a covenant not to compete with the corporation, allegations which had already been resolved in Abrams' favor in an arbitration award confirmed by the superior court and affirmed by this court. Abrams successfully moved to strike the cross-complaint and statement of offsets as untimely and unauthorized in a section 2000 proceeding.

On December 15, 1978, the trial court found and confirmed that the fair value of Abrams' shares, "determined on the basis of the liquidation value but taking into account the possibility, if any, of sale of the entire business as a going concern in a liquidation," (Corp.Code, § 2000, subd. (a)) was $355,000. Its decree ordered Rubaloff and the corporation to file an election indicating which of them would purchase Abrams' stock and to make payment by January 15, 1979, absent which the corporation would be wound up and dissolved.

Discussion

Appeal.

1. Rubaloff's first contention on appeal is that the procedure used by the appraisers and the trial court for valuing Abrams' shares was "fatally defective and prejudicial." Rubaloff complains he was not given an opportunity to examine witnesses interviewed by Grant, either during the interviews or at a full evidentiary hearing, and was not permitted to depose Grant. . . .

Corporations Code section 2000 established a special proceeding to enable a 50 percent shareholder to avoid dissolution of the corporation by purchasing the stock of the shareholder(s) seeking to dissolve the corporation.   . . .   Clearly, the section contemplates a summary proceeding, and with good reason, for if the party seeking the appraisal is dissatisfied with the valuation, he may then choose to proceed with dissolution. (Corp.Code, § 2000, subds. (a), (b).) At bench, the procedure used by the appraisers and the trial court complied with the provisions of this section, and it was not required to comply with the provisions of the Code of Civil Procedure. We therefore reject Rubaloff's first contention.

2.   Rubaloff next contends the evidence was insufficient to support the trial court's finding that the fair value of Abrams' shares was $355,000. Corporations Code section 2000, subdivision (a) provides that the "fair value shall be determined on the basis of the liquidation value but taking into account the possibility, if any, of sale of the entire business as a going concern." The value of the shares is to be assessed by three appraisers, whose majority appraisal becomes binding upon the parties when confirmed by the court.   . . .

At bench, Grant filed a 138–page report in which he concluded that the business could be sold as a going concern if Abrams and Rubaloff would agree not to compete with the business immediately after its sale. Grant opined that if, on the other hand, Abrams and Rubaloff intended to compete with the corporation after its sale, a prudent purchaser would not be likely to buy the business as a going concern. The corporation's contracts with its artists would have little or no value, and the corporation's tangible assets would probably be sold piecemeal at a lower market price than would be realizable if the business were sold as a going concern. In determining the value of the business if sold as a going concern under an agreement by Abrams and Rubaloff not to compete, he appraised the fair value of the business at $712,477, comprised of $462,477 of tangible assets and $250,000 of intangible assets, including artists' contracts and goodwill. Grant then concluded that the fair value of Abrams' 50 percent undivided interest was approximately $355,000. In valuing Abrams' interest in a forced liquidation, Grant reasoned that on liquidation of the business the shareholders would most likely divide the contracts between them, rather than sell them to a third party and start anew. Grant then determined that the net proceeds which the business would realize in a forced liquidation was approximately $700,000, resulting in a value of $355,000 [sic.] for Abrams' undivided half interest. Finally, although noting that section 2000 does not ask for a determination of this particular value, Grant calculated that the approximate going concern value of the corporation and its assets to Rubaloff and Abrams, rather than to a third-party purchaser, would be $965,000, or $482,500 for Abrams' half interest. Grant then concluded that the "fair value" of Abrams' share on February 22, 1977, as defined in section 2000, was $355,000. Zeman concurred in Grant's findings that the fair value of Abrams' undivided 50 percent interest in the corporation was $355,000, "whether the sale approach or the actual liquidation approach is used," and that under the going concern value to the parties, rather than on a sale to a third party, Abrams' share would be $482,500.

Rubaloff contends that Grant's and Zeman's appraisals are insufficient to support a trial court's finding that the fair value of Abrams' shares was $355,000, . . . because section 2000 does not allow for a computation based upon a hypothetical covenant not to compete.   . . .

Both Grant and Zeman determined that the fair value of Abrams' shares would be $355,000 in a forced liquidation, as well as in a sale of the business as a going concern. We think the appraisers properly considered a hypothetical covenant not to compete in evaluating a sale of the business as a going concern. Section 2000 states that the appraisers should consider the "possibility of a sale as a going concern in a liquidation." Under the statute, the appraisers are not only entitled, but are required, to consider the manner in which the parties to such a hypothetical sale are most likely to maximize their return. We conclude that the trial court's findings and confirmation were supported by substantial evidence. We note again that if Rubaloff is dissatisfied with this result he is entitled under section 2000 and under the trial court's decree, to dissolve the corporation instead of purchasing Abrams' shares.

The decree of the trial court staying the wind up and dissolution of Abrams–Rubaloff & Associates, Inc. is vacated, effective 10 days after this decision becomes final. At that time Abrams–Rubaloff & Associates, Inc. will be wound up and dissolved unless $355,000 together with interest from January 15, 1979, is paid to Harry Abrams on or before that date by Noel Rubaloff or Abrams–Rubaloff & Associates, Inc. In all other respects the decree of the trial court is affirmed. Costs on both appeals to be borne by Noel Rubaloff and Abrams–Rubaloff & Associates.

ANALYSIS

For purposes of discussion, suppose that Rubaloff considers the values of the assets of Abrams–Rubaloff & Associates, Inc. to be as follows:

Physical assets and accounts receivable	$450,000
Goodwill	
Abrams's clients	100,000
Rubaloff's clients	100,000
Firm's clients	50,000
Total	$700,000

Thus, if the firm is sold with covenants not to compete from Abrams and from Rubaloff, the amount received should be $700,000 for the firm, or $350,000 for each of the shareholders. If the firm is liquidated and each takes half of the physical assets and accounts receivable, plus half of the firm's clients, plus his own clients, each should wind up with assets worth $350,000.

Now suppose Abrams, as in the actual case, has invoked Cal.Corp.Code § 1900(a), and you represent Rubaloff, who asks you what to do. Suppose you think that appraisals are often unreliable and that there is a 50 percent probability that the appraisers will value the corporation at $600,000, a 25 percent probability of an appraisal at $400,000, and a 25 percent probability of an appraisal at $900,000. The expenses referred to in § 2000(c) will be $20,000 for each side. What is your advice?

Suppose you represent Abrams before he has invoked § 1900(a) and his view of the value of the firm is the same as Rubaloff's. Assuming you view the probabilities of the outcome of the appraisal, and the costs, as specified above, what is your advice to Abrams?

PLANNING ISSUE

How do the rules encountered in this section affect your judgment about the need for a buy-sell agreement in closely held corporations?

Pedro v. Pedro

489 N.W.2d 798 (Minn.App.1992).

After a request for dissolution of The Pedro Companies by respondent, Alfred Pedro, appellants, Carl and Eugene Pedro and The Pedro Companies, moved that the action proceed as a buyout pursuant to Minn. Stat. § 302A.751 (1990).*

After a jury awarded damages, this court determined the jury's verdict was merely advisory and remanded the case to the trial court to make findings. Pedro v. Pedro, 463 N.W.2d 285 (Minn.App.1990) (Pedro 1), pet. for rev. denied (Minn. Jan. 24, 1991). On remand, the trial court awarded damages for breach of fiduciary duty and for wrongful termination of lifetime employment. In addition to other issues, appellants challenge the propriety of the trial court's rulings on these matters.

Facts

Alfred, Carl, and Eugene Pedro are brothers who each owned a one-third interest in The Pedro Companies ("TPC"), a closely held Minnesota corporation, which manufactures and sells luggage and leather products. All three brothers worked in the business for all or most of their adult

---

* [Editors.—This section of the Minnesota Business Corporations law provides for judicial dissolution at the request of a shareholder on a finding of deadlock among directors or shareholders, or waste of assets, or if "those in control have acted fraudulently, illegally, or in a manner unfairly prejudicial toward one or more shareholders," etc. As a remedy, in the case of a "closely held corporation," the court may order a buy-out of the shares of either party, at "fair value," with the purchase price payable in installments, but with the purchaser required to post a bond for the purchase price. A "closely held corporation" is one with not more than 35 shareholders. Minn. Stat. § 302A.011, subd. 6a.

In its earlier opinion in this case, the court described this provision as follows:

> [I]t provides the courts with equitable authority to protect the rights and *reasonable expectations* of minority shareholders. . . . [T]he primary expectations of minority shareholders include *an active voice in management* of the corporation and *input as an employee.*

463 N.W.2d at 289 (emphasis supplied.)]

lives. TPC has annual sales of approximately $6 million. Carl has worked for TPC since 1940 and he is currently employed by the company. Eugene has worked for TPC since 1939 and is also currently employed by the company. Alfred worked for TPC for 45 years and was fired in 1987 at the age of 62. Each brother, as an equal shareholder, received the same benefit and compensation as the others. Each shareholder had an equal vote in the management of the company.

In 1968, all of the company's shareholders (the three brothers and their father) entered into a stock retirement agreement ("SRA") which was designed to facilitate the purchase of the shareholder's stock upon death, or when a living shareholder wished to sell his stock. In 1975, the father died and the company purchased his stock from his estate, pursuant to the terms of the SRA.

In 1979, the remaining shareholders (the three brothers) modified and re-executed the SRA, reducing the purchase price of the shares. The agreement provided in part:

> Until and unless changed the value of each share of stock shall be as follows: 75% of net book value at the end of the preceding calendar year. It is the intent of the parties that the value of a Stockholder's interest as herein determined does include good will.

The relationship between respondent and the other two shareholders deteriorated through 1987 and 1988, after Alfred discovered an apparent discrepancy of almost $330,000 between the internal accounting records and the TPC checking account. Approximately $40,000 was discovered in an emergency investigation, yet about $270,000 of the discrepancy remained unexplained.

Alfred was very concerned and insisted that an independent accountant be retained to locate the source of the discrepancy. In May 1987, Carl and Eugene agreed to retain an accountant to investigate the cash shortage. After a month with no results, TPC dismissed the accountant. Alfred testified that soon afterwards, the corporate accountant admitted in a meeting with all three brothers that there was a $140,000 to $147,000 discrepancy which was unexplainable.

Alfred testified that during this time, Eugene would interfere with his area of responsibility in the TPC plant and undermine his management authority. Alfred testified that he was told to cooperate, resign or be fired. He was told if he did not forget about the apparent discrepancy, his brothers would fire him. Alfred again repeated his demand that the corporation hire an independent accountant to investigate the situation.

In October 1987, a second independent accountant was hired to investigate the shortage. After concluding his investigation, the accountant issued a report identifying a $140,000 discrepancy which could not be reconciled. He testified that throughout his investigation, he was refused access to numerous documents. He also stated there were over 20 leads never followed up before he ended his investigation.

Alfred was placed on a mandatory leave of absence from TPC on October 27, 1987. In December 1987, Alfred received a written notice that he was fired and all of his pay and benefits were discontinued. Employees were informed that Alfred had a nervous breakdown.

Alfred commenced this action in February 1988. Upon remand from this court on the earlier appeal, the trial court made the following findings of fact and conclusions of law. The court awarded Alfred $766,582.33 as damages for his one-third ownership in TPC which was determined by the terms of the SRA.* Alfred was awarded $58,260.69 for prejudgment interest on this award.

The trial court also awarded Alfred $563,417.67 based on its finding that the individual defendants had breached their fiduciary duties to Alfred. The award represented the difference between the fair market value of Alfred Pedro's stock as determined by the trial court and the value provided by the SRA. In addition, the trial court awarded $68,690.05 for prejudgment interest on this award.

The trial court further found that Alfred had a contract of lifetime employment with TPC. The court found wrongful termination and awarded him $256,740 as compensation for lost wages. Because the contract was for lifetime employment, the award represented lost wages until he reached the age of 72. The court reduced this award by payments made to Alfred since December 1989. Moreover, the court awarded prejudgment interest in the sum of $31,750.37 on this award.

The trial court also awarded Alfred $200,000 for attorney fees and expenses incurred by him. This award was based on the trial court's finding that appellants had acted in a manner which was "arbitrary, vexatious and otherwise not in good faith . . . prior to and during this action." The court awarded Alfred an additional $6,063 for attorney fees for having to respond to appellants' motion to recuse the trial judge and for the preparation of Findings of Fact, Conclusions of Law and Order for Judgment.

Issues

1. Was the evidence sufficient to support the trial court's finding of breach of fiduciary duty?

2. Did the trial court properly determine Alfred Pedro had a reasonable expectation of lifetime employment, thereby awarding him damages for lost wages following the buyout until he reached age 72?

3. Did the trial court make proper determinations regarding joint and several liability, prejudgment interest, recusal of the trial judge, and attorney fees?

---

* [Editors—In its earlier (1990) opinion in the case, the court had held, "Inasmuch as appellants' breaches of fiduciary duty forced the buyout, they cannot benefit from wrong-ful treatment of their fellow shareholder and must disgorge any such gain." 463 N.W.2d at 288.]

Analysis

I.

. . .

The relationship among shareholders in closely held corporations is analogous to that of partners. . . . Shareholders in closely held corporations owe one another a fiduciary duty. . . . Owing a fiduciary duty includes dealing "openly, honestly and fairly with other shareholders." Evans [v. Blesi, 345 N.W.2d 775, 779 (Minn.App.1984)].

The court's findings of fact contain many examples where appellants did not act openly, honestly, and fairly with respondent Alfred Pedro. The trial court found that at no time since the action was commenced, did appellants ever implement payments admittedly due under the SRA. Appellants interfered with respondent's responsibilities in TPC and hired a private investigator to follow him when he was not in the office. The court found appellants fabricated accusations of neglect and malfeasance which were not substantiated during the trial.

Moreover, an employee testified that after respondent was terminated, employees were informed that he had a nervous breakdown. Also, respondent testified he was told if he did not forget about the discrepancies in the financial records, his brothers would fire him. Finally, appellants admitted in their motion requesting a buyout, that they were acting "in a manner unfairly prejudicial" toward respondent pursuant to Minn. Stat. § 302A.751, subd. 1(b)(2) (1990). This admission supports a finding of breach of fiduciary duty.

Appellants claim no breach of fiduciary duty can exist because there has been no diminution in the value of the corporation or the stock value of respondent's shares. In support of this assertion, appellants cite several cases where actions by an officer or director did reduce the value of the corporation, constituting a breach or fiduciary duty. . . .

However, an action depleting a corporation's value is not the exclusive method of breaching one's fiduciary duties. See *Evans*, 345 N.W.2d at 779–80 (majority shareholders breached fiduciary duty to minority shareholder by forcing his resignation). Moreover, loss in value of a shareholder's stock is not the only measure of damages. See Pavlidis v. New England Patriots Football Club, Inc., 675 F.Supp. 701, 703 (D.Mass.1987) (damages for corporate director's breach of fiduciary duty was either profits made by director or value of property at time of breach plus interest).

Moreover, the measure of damages for the buyout was proper. In *Pedro 1* [Pedro v. Pedro, 463 N.W.2d 285 (Minn.App.1990) (an earlier decision in this case)], this court stated:

> If the fair value of the shares is greater than the purchase price for the buyout as calculated from the formula in the SRA, the difference is the measure of respondent's damage resulting from having been forced to sell his shares in the company.

Pedro, 463 N.W.2d at 288. Here there was evidence in the record that the fair market value of respondent's shares equalled $1,330,000. After subtracting the undisputed purchase price set forth under the SRA of $766,-582.33, the trial court properly awarded damages for breach of fiduciary duty of $563,417.67.

II.

Appellants claim the evidence was insufficient for the court to find a contract for lifetime employment. They also assert damages for lost wages following the buyout were improper. Again, we are unable to set aside findings of fact unless they are clearly erroneous. . . . Based upon the unique facts in this case, we affirm the trial court's award of damages for lost wages.

Trial courts have broad equitable powers in fashioning relief for the buyout of shareholders in a closely held corporation. Minn. Stat. § 302A.751, subd. 3a provides:

> In determining whether to order equitable relief, dissolution, or a buyout, the court shall take into consideration the duty which all shareholders in a closely held corporation owe one another to act in an honest, fair and reasonable manner in the operation of the corporation and the reasonable expectations of the shareholders as they exist at the inception and develop during the course of the shareholders' relationship with the corporation and with each other.

This section allows courts to look to respondent's reasonable expectations when awarding damages. In addition to an ownership interest,

> the reasonable expectations of such a shareholder are a job, salary, a significant place in management, and economic security for his family.

Joseph E. Olson, A Statutory Elixir for the Oppression Malady, 36 Mercer L. Rev. 627, 629 (1985) (footnote omitted).

In Pine River State Bank v. Mettille, 333 N.W.2d 622 (Minn.1983), the supreme court explained that the court must ascertain the intent of the parties to the employment contract. Id. at 628. When ascertaining the intent, trial courts must consider the written and oral negotiations of the parties as well as the parties' situation, the type of employment and the particular circumstances of the case. Eklund v. Vincent Brass and Aluminum Co., 351 N.W.2d 371, 376 (Minn.App.1984), pet. for rev. denied (Minn. Nov. 1, 1984).

> In a closely held corporation the nature of the employment of a shareholder may create a reasonable expectation by the employee-owner that his employment is not terminable at will.

Pedro, 463 N.W.2d at 289.

The unique facts in the record support the trial court's finding of an agreement to provide lifetime employment to respondent. Carl Pedro, Sr. worked at the corporation until his death. Eugene Pedro, who worked for over 50 years at TPC, testified that he intended to always work for the company. Carl Pedro, Jr. worked at TPC for over 34 years. Alfred Pedro testified of his expectation of a lifetime job like his father. He had already been employed by TPC for 45 years. Even the corporate accountant testified regarding Carl's and Eugene's expectations that they would work for the corporation as long as they wanted. Based upon this evidence it was reasonable for the trial court to determine that the parties did in fact have a contract that was not terminable at will.

Appellants claim a grant of damages for both lost wages and breach of fiduciary duty under § 302A.751, subd. 3a allows respondent a double recovery. . . . Even appellants concede respondent has two separate interests, as owner and employee. Thus, allowing recovery for each interest is appropriate and will not be considered a double recovery.

Finally, appellants dispute the trial court's award of damages for lost wages following the buyout. They claim once respondent's ownership interest is severed, he has no right to damages for lost wages. We believe the trial court's award of future damages for lost wages is wholly consistent with the court's broad equitable powers found in § 302A.751, subd. 3a and is warranted based upon its finding of a contract for lifetime employment.

III.

. . .

[A]ppellants challenge the trial court's award of attorney fees. Under section 302A.751, subd. 4, if the court finds a party to a proceeding brought under this section has acted arbitrarily, vexatiously or otherwise not in good faith, it may, in its discretion, award reasonable expenses, including attorneys fees and disbursements to any of the other parties. Here, the trial court made specific findings that appellants both breached fiduciary duties and acted arbitrarily, vexatiously or otherwise not in good faith. Once this has been done, the trial court has discretion to award attorney fees. . . .

Decision

The facts of this case support the trial court's findings that appellants breached their fiduciary duties to respondent and wrongfully terminated his contract for lifetime employment.

Affirmed.

ANALYSIS

1. How would you have drafted the SRA?

2. Could the parties have avoided the court's result by drafting the contract differently? Would they have wanted to do so? Does the court interpret the SRA or does it impose mandatory contractual terms?

3. Does the Minnesota statute, with its interpretation in *Pedro,* reduce the need for buy/sell agreements in closely held corporations?

Eliminate them? Suppose you are about to invest in such a corporation. If you tell the other investors that you do not like the state's "default" rule and want to hammer out a control agreement, employment agreements, and a buy/sell agreement, what adverse message might you be conveying?

NOTE

The following case is not strictly related to the material on statutory dissolution that is covered in this section of the casebook. It does, however, present an important issue that arises in buy-outs of shareholders by corporations. Moreover, it illustrates some principles relating to limitations on corporate distributions to shareholders, limitations that are essentially the same for dividends as for distributions in liquidation or partial liquidation.

In Re Northwest Oxygen, Inc.

99 B.R. 703 (Bkrtcy.M.D.N.C.1989).

. . .

Findings of Fact

Northwest Oxygen, Inc. (hereinafter "Oxygen") is a corporation organized under the laws of the state of North Carolina. Oxygen had two principal shareholders, Frank H. Wright, Jr. and Richard D. Hancock, the movant herein. Each shareholder owned 500 shares of the capital stock of Oxygen, which shares represented 50 percent of the issued and outstanding shares of the corporation. These shares were issued to Wright and Hancock on June 12, 1974. . . .

After enjoying several years of successful operations, disagreement between the two principal shareholders resulted in Oxygen purchasing from Hancock his 500 shares of capital stock in the corporation. On or about August 31, 1984, Mr. Wright, Mr. Hancock, Mrs. Wright, Northwest Oxygen, Inc., and Cardio–Pulmonary Associates, Inc., a related entity, entered into an agreement for the purchase of the Hancock stock, ... This agreement culminated in the execution of a promissory note dated September 6, 1984, in the face amount of $1,440,085. . . . The evidence indicated the sales price was based on a multiple of annual pre-tax earnings and not asset value. This was represented to be an industry standard for distribution type companies. Pursuant to the terms of the promissory note Oxygen was to make monthly payments of $20,661 commencing October 6, 1984, for a period of ten years. Oxygen made such monthly payments from October 6, 1984 through February 6, 1988. . . .

The promissory note to Hancock was secured by all assets of Oxygen including equipment, inventory, vehicles, accounts receivable, contract rights, general intangibles, furniture, fixtures, all other personal property, and all replacements, additions, accessions or substitutions of the foregoing. The security interest is evidenced by a collateral security agreement and stock pledge agreement.   Hancock perfected the security interest as required by state law by notations of liens and filing financing statements in the proper locations.   Hancock further agreed to subordinate his security interest in accounts receivable, inventory and equipment to a lien in favor of NCNB, Oxygen's primary lending institution.

The promissory note dated December 6, 1984, was modified by a settlement agreement and release dated April 27, 1987.   The modifications consisted of a change in the minimum interest rate of the note and the term of the note, a requirement of Oxygen to retain pretax earnings of at least $200,000 for each fiscal year until the note is paid in full, and made a default by Oxygen on any loan to NCNB a default under the security agreement with Hancock.   Oxygen experienced difficulties during the latter part of 1987 which resulted in the filing of an involuntary petition under Chapter 11 of the United States Bankruptcy Code against Northwest Oxygen, Inc. on April 13, 1988.   Oxygen answered that petition on May 9, 1988, admitting the material allegations contained in the involuntary petition and showing debts of $8,167,513 against assets of $4,998,177.

. . .

Issues

The principal question at hand is whether a promissory note to a former shareholder in exchange for the redemption of his shares in the corporation is rendered unenforceable by the corporation's subsequent insolvency.   Second, if the Court determines the promissory note is unenforceable, it must then determine whether the underlying security interest would also be unenforceable thereby destroying any interest in cash collateral the movant might wish to protect.

[The case is decided under the law of North Carolina.]

Conclusions of Law

. . .

The debtor . . . has attacked the validity and extent of the security interest alleged by Hancock by questioning the validity and effect of the September 9, 1984 promissory note and security agreement.   Oxygen states that its promissory note to a former shareholder, made in partial payment for the purchase of its stock from the shareholder, is unenforceable after the corporation becomes insolvent.   The debtor goes on to state that once the underlying promissory note becomes unenforceable so does the security agreement creating an interest in the property of the debtor. . . .   In support of its position, the debtor offers N.C.Gen.Stat. section 55–52 as providing the relevant statutory law to render unenforceable the security interest of Hancock.

North Carolina Business Corp. Act, N.C.Gen.Stat. section 55–52.

The debtor provides evidence to the Court that N.C.Gen. Stat. section 55–52, entitled "Acquisition by a Corporation of Its Own Shares" prohibits a corporation from purchasing or paying for its stock in a transaction such as the one at bar from anything but surplus. N.C.Gen.Stat. section 55–52(b) provides the instances when a corporation may purchase and pay for its shares out of capital. N.C.Gen.Stat. section 55–52(c) provides the instances when a corporation may purchase and pay for its shares, but only out of surplus. Hancock argues that the correct subsection to be applied in the instant case is section 55–52(b)(4) which states that a corporation may purchase and pay for its shares regardless of any impairment to stated capital:

> (4) To perform its obligations or exercise its right to purchase shares of an employee or former employee under a written agreement relating to the employment, or to perform its obligation or exercise its right under a written agreement to purchase shares of a deceased or disabled shareholder upon death or disability, or *to perform its obligations or exercise its rights to purchase shares of a shareholder under any other written agreement to which all shareholders are parties* or if all shareholders are not parties then under such written agreement that has been approved by the majority of the outstanding shares, regardless of limitation on voting rights, other than shares owned by the shareholder who are parties to such agreement. (Emphasis added)

The debtor on the other hand argues that the transaction in question is governed by N.C.Gen.Stat. section 55–52(c)(3), and therefore, any payment made on a note in satisfaction of the stock purchase agreement must be paid out of surplus. Section 55–52(c)(3) provides for a corporation to purchase and pay for its shares, but only out of surplus:

> (3) From any shareholder of any class, if the board of directors shall have obtained authorization so to purchase, within a period of one year preceding the purchase, by vote of a majority of the shares of the corporation entitled to vote after full disclosure to the holders of all such shares of the specific purpose of the proposed purchase, together with a statement of the number and class of shares proposed to be purchased. Such vote shall not be required for each specific purchase, provided the total number of shares purchased from any class shall not exceed the maximum number of shares of that class authorized to be purchased.

This Court must agree with the debtor's analysis for two reasons. First, the agreement between Hancock and the debtor was executed in 1984. The provision which Hancock seeks to rely on in section 55–52(b)(4) was an amendment to the original provision of N.C.Gen.Statute section 55–52(b)(4), and became effective April 23, 1985. Therefore, at the time of the agreement N.C.Gen.Stat. section 55–52(c)(3) was the only statutory provision permitting Oxygen's purchase of its stock from Hancock, and that purchase was required by law to come from surplus. No other statutory authority existed for such stock purchase agreement.

Second, upon examination of the legislative history and purpose for the 1985 amendment to the statute authorizing acquisition by a corporation of its own shares, it is evident that the amendment to section 55–52(b)(4) was established to enable corporations to enter into written agreements with shareholders at the outset of the relationship for the issuance of stock redeemable at the shareholder's option. The statute was not designed to simply allow the corporation to enter into a written agreement with a shareholder to redeem stock out of and as an impairment to stated capital, which stock was already being held by the shareholder as common stock. Legislative History, Exhibit D, p. 9, "Supplemental Brief Supporting Debtor Response to the Motion of Richard D. Hancock for Order Prohibiting or Conditioning Debtor's Use of Cash Collateral" (hereinafter "Supplemental Brief"). The purpose was to provide a new method for North Carolina corporations to raise needed capital by readily available cash infusions from shareholders in exchange for stock redeemable at their request. Legislative History, Exhibit F, p.2, "Supplemental Brief." In this respect, the amendment to section 55–52(b)(4) permitting written agreements was an accommodation for the amendments to section 55–40(e) and section 55–43)(e) of the North Carolina Business Corporation Act. It was amended to ensure continuity among the statutes in the Business Corporation Act and to facilitate the amendments authorizing the issuance of shares subject to redemption at designated times or upon the happening of a certain event.

The case at bar in no way resembles a section 55–52(b)(4) transaction. Hancock was the owner of 500 shares of common stock in Oxygen. Hancock and the debtor entered into a written agreement some ten years after issuance of the shares for the sale of the common stock owned by Hancock. This was not a written agreement between the corporation and the shareholder for the issuance of stock redeemable at the shareholder's option pursuant to N.C.Gen.Stat. section 55–52(b)(4) as amended. Therefore, the transaction was authorized by law only under N.C.Gen.Stat. section 55–52(c)(3) and must only be paid out of surplus.

A further restriction on a corporation's ability to acquire its stock is found in subsection (e) of N.C.Gen.Stat. section 55–52. That subsection prohibits the acquisition, if at any time, or as a result of the acquisition there is reasonable ground for believing that the corporation would be unable to meet its obligations as they become due, or the liabilities of the corporation would exceed the fair present value of its assets. Reading N.C.Gen.Stat. section 55–52(c) and (e) together it is clear that in North Carolina a corporation may only purchase and pay for the acquisition of its shares in a transaction such as the one at bar out of surplus.

In light of the statutory requirement of N.C.Gen.Stat. section 55–52(c), that the stock may only be purchased and paid for out of surplus, the question now becomes "When is the solvency of the corporation measured in order to determine whether a sufficient surplus exists?" The overwhelming majority of courts addressing this issue have followed the leading case of In re Fechheimer Fishel Company, establishing that despite the good faith of the parties at the time the note was given, and the apparent solvency of the corporation at the time the note was given, such note will be rendered unenforceable as against other creditors of the corporation if the corporation was insolvent or lacked sufficient surplus to retire the installment at the time the payment was to be made out of the assets of the corporation. In re Fechheimer Fishel Company, 212 F. 357 (2d Cir.1914). [Supporting citations to numerous other decision omitted.]

Most of the above-mentioned courts relied on statutes similar to N.C.Gen.Stat. section 55–52(c), [but] even in those jurisdictions where corporate statutes do not expressly prevent payment for stock except out of surplus, the courts have nonetheless held that payments must be made out of surplus. . . . [The statutory] restriction is incorporated in and made a part of the stock purchase agreement between Oxygen and Hancock, by virtue of the fact that it is contained in the language of the only statutory authority existing at the time of the transaction which allowed such an acquisition of stock. This is a condition which the law attaches to the agreement in order for it to have full force and effect. . . .

The rationale behind such statutory language is the recognition of the paramount interest of creditors of the corporation as against the interest of a former shareholder who takes a note, a mere promise to pay, in exchange for his shares of stock in the corporation. The promissory note between Hancock and the corporation was executory in nature until paid for in cash. Therefore, although the note may have been valid when entered into, because there existed sufficient surplus under section 55–52(c)(3) and the stock agreement did not render the corporation insolvent under section 55–52(e), the note cannot be enforceable once insolvency occurs.

Rationale Based in Equity

There are several reasons why a stock purchase agreement should be treated differently than the issuance of a promissory note and the taking of a security interest by any other creditor. First, as stated above, is the fact that state law requires such transactions to be paid out of surplus, with that surplus being measured at the time payment is made out of the assets of the corporation. N.C.Gen.Stat. section 55–52(c). Second, shareholders have a special relationship with the corporation different from other creditors of the corporation. Thus, they assume the risk when agreeing to accept payment at a subsequent time for the exchange of their stock, that the corporation will remain solvent and enjoy future profitability from which their debt will be satisfied. This was aptly reasoned in the In re Fechheimer Fishel Company case wherein the court stated that a stockholder who accepts a note for the redemption of his stock "sells at his peril and assumes the risk of consummation of the transaction without encroachment upon the funds which belong to the corporation in trust for the payment of its creditors." In re Fechheimer Fishel Company, 212 F.2d at 363. This special relationship of the shareholder to the corporation was further addressed in the case of In re Salem Tool Company, 82 B.R. 52 (Bankr.N.D.Ohio 1988). Here the court stated that a shareholder may not change his relationship from that of a shareholder to that of a creditor in the face of insolvency of the corporation by entering a stock purchase agreement and taking a note from the corporation. In re Salem Tool Co., 82 B.R. at 54, citing, Squire v. Rafferty, 2 N.E.2d 255–59 (1936).

The third reason former shareholders are treated differently from other creditors regarding a stock purchase transaction is that a transfer of the shareholder's shares of stock back to the corporation as Treasury shares is really not a sale. This is true because the corporation does not acquire anything of value in exchange for the depletion of its assets each time a payment is made, while the stock is held by the corporation as Treasury stock. Rather, it is merely held by the corporation while distribution to the shareholder of corporate assets is made. . . . Upon the purchase of its stock, Oxygen held the 500 shares previously owned by Hancock as Treasury shares and those shares remain Treasury shares today.

Since the underlying promissory note is rendered unenforceable by the debtor's subsequent insolvency, so, too, is the security agreement. Thus, Hancock does not have an enforceable security interest from which the protection of cash collateral can be demanded by this motion. Hancock has no present interest in cash collateral of the debtor and, therefore, his motion to prohibit or condition the use of debtor's cash collateral is denied.

Conclusion

The holding of this Court may appear harsh at first blush. However, any hardship imposed upon Hancock by rendering the note and underlying security agreement unenforceable by reason of subsequent insolvency of the debtor does not outweigh the overwhelming majority of courts approving such result in the interest of intervening creditors. The debtor's intervening insolvency will prevent enforcement of the stock purchase agreement when it will be prejudicial to creditors. This Court must now look to the paramount interest of creditors of the estate and protect those interests. For the reasons mentioned above, this Court holds that the note and security agreement of Richard D. Hancock is unenforceable due to the debtor's subsequent insolvency and inability to make payment on the obligation out of sufficient surplus of corporate assets. Hancock assumed the risk when he took a note in exchange for his shares of stock in the corporation. Hancock had alternatives to accepting a note for payment at a subsequent time. He could have demanded cash payment of the fair value of the stock at the time of the transaction. Instead, he accepted a de minimis fraction of the purchase price in cash and a promise to pay in the future for the balance. By accepting that promise to pay Hancock committed himself to reliance on the future success and profitability of the corporation and bound the payment on his note to surplus earnings.

NOTES

1. Present North Carolina law (§ 55–6–40(e)(1)) rejects the rule applied in *Northwest Oxygen* and tests the permissibility of a distribution at the time the shareholder surrenders his or her shares and thereby stops being a shareholder.

H2. In Neimark v. Mel Kramer Sales, Inc., 102 Wis.2d 282, 306 N.W.2d 278 (App.1981), the shareholders of a closely held corporation, and the corporation, had entered into an agreement to redeem the stock of any deceased shareholder at a fixed price per share with installment payments over a period of several years. When the majority shareholder died, the redemption price under the agreement was somewhat lower than the market value (as reflected in an offer to purchase the entire corporation). The majority of directors (the widow of the deceased shareholder and two relatives of his) voted that the corporation should not redeem the shares of the decedent. They relied on the advice of counsel (who had drafted the redemption agreement) that the redemption was not permissible under the Wisconsin statutory limitation on such purchases. The minority shareholder sued for specific performance of the stock redemption agreement, lost at trial, but prevailed in the court of appeals.

The court of appeals considered two statutory tests: (1) whether the redemption would render the corporation "insolvent," and (2) whether the corporation had sufficient "earned surplus" to cover the redemption. As to the first issue, the court simply found sufficient evidence in the record to support the trial court's determination that the redemption would not render the corporation insolvent. It adopted the majority American rule that the insolvency test must be met both at the time of the agreement to purchase and at the time of each installment.

As to the second test, however, the court concluded that compliance should be required only at the time of the initial decision to purchase, but cited a number of decisions (which it criticized for failure to distinguish the two tests) inconsistent with its conclusion.

ANALYSIS

1. What arguments can be made in response to the court's "Rationale Based in Equity"?

2. What would the result have been if the corporation had somehow paid cash to Hancock for his shares and Hancock had then loaned a similar amount to the corporation? What if the corporation had transferred to Hancock title to equipment used in its business and Hancock had then leased the equipment back to the corporation?

3. In states that still apply the rule of *Northwest Oxygen*, how can a shareholder who contemplates a buyout by the corporation protect against the effect of that rule?

Frandsen v. Jensen–Sundquist Agency, Inc.

802 F.2d 941 (7th Cir.1986).

■ POSNER, CIRCUIT JUDGE.

The appeals in this diversity suit require us to consider issues of Wisconsin contract and tort law in the settling of a dispute over the rights of a minority shareholder in a closely held corporation. The facts are as follows. In 1975 Walter Jensen owned all the stock of Jensen–Sundquist Agency, Inc., a holding company whose principal asset was a majority of the stock of the First Bank of Grantsburg; Jensen–Sundquist also owned a small insurance company. That year Jensen sold 52 percent of his stock in the holding company to members of his family—the "majority bloc," as we shall call them and the interest they acquired; 8 percent to Dennis Frandsen, a substantial businessman who was not a member of Jensen's family and who paid Jensen $97,000 for the stock; and the rest, in smaller chunks, to other non-family members. By a stockholder agreement drafted by Jensen and a lawyer representing the bank and Jensen's family, the majority bloc agreed "that should they at any time offer to sell their stock in Jensen–Sundquist, Inc., . . . they will first offer their stock to [Frandsen and six other minority shareholders who had negotiated for this provision] at the same price as may be offered to [the majority bloc] . . . and . . . they will not sell their stock to any other person, firm, or organization without first offering said stock" to these minority shareholders "at the same price and upon the same terms." The majority bloc also agreed not to "sell any of their shares to anyone without at the same time offering to purchase all the shares of" these minority shareholders "at the same price." Thus if the majority bloc offered to sell its shares it had to give Frandsen a right to buy the shares at the offer price. If Frandsen declined, the second protective provision came into play: the majority bloc had to offer to buy his shares at the same price at which it sold its own shares.

In 1984 the president of Jensen–Sundquist began discussions with First Wisconsin Corporation, Wisconsin's largest bank holding company, looking to the acquisition by First Wisconsin of First Bank of Grantsburg, Jensen–Sundquist's principal property. A price of $88 per share of stock in the First Bank of Grantsburg was agreed to in principle. The acquisition was to be effected (we simplify slightly) by First Wisconsin's buying Jensen–Sundquist for cash, followed by a merger of First Bank of Grantsburg into a bank subsidiary of First Wisconsin. Each stockholder of Jensen–Sundquist would receive $62 per share, which would translate into $88 per share of the bank. (The reasons that the share values were not the same were that there were more holding company shares than bank shares and that the holding company had another asset besides the bank—the insurance company.) Jensen–Sundquist asked each of the minority shareholders to sign a waiver of any rights he "may have" in the transaction, rights arising from the stockholder agreement, but advised each shareholder that in counsel's opinion the shareholder had no rights other than to receive $62 per share.

Each of the minority shareholders except Frandsen signed or was expected to sign the waiver. Frandsen not only refused to sign but announced that he was exercising his right of first refusal and would buy the majority bloc's shares at $62 a share. (He also offered to buy out the other minority shareholders.) The majority did not want to sell its shares to him—Frandsen says because the president of Jensen–Sundquist, who was also the chairman of the board of First Bank of Grantsburg and a member of the majority bloc, was afraid he would lose his job if Frandsen took over. The deal was restructured. Jensen–Sundquist agreed to sell its shares in First Bank of Grantsburg to First Wisconsin at $88 a share and then liquidate, so that in the end all the stockholders would end up with cash plus the insurance company and First Wisconsin would end up with the bank, which was all it had ever wanted out of the deal. All this was done over Frandsen's protest. He then brought this suit against the majority bloc, charging breach of the stockholder agreement, and against First Wisconsin, charging tortious interference with his contract rights. The district judge granted summary judgment for the defendants and Frandsen appeals.

. . .

The case would be easy if the transaction had been structured from the start as a simple acquisition by First Wisconsin of First Bank of Grantsburg from Jensen–Sundquist. Nothing in the stockholder agreement suggests that any minority shareholder has the right to block the sale by Jensen–Sundquist of any of its assets, including its principal asset, a controlling interest in First Bank of Grantsburg. The right of first refusal is a right to buy the shares of the majority bloc in Jensen–Sundquist if they are offered for sale, and there would be no offer of sale if Jensen–Sundquist simply sold some or for that matter all of its assets and became an investment company instead of a bank holding company. Nor did the contract entitle Frandsen to insist that the deal be configured so as to trigger his right of first refusal. . . .

The case is a little harder because the transaction was originally configured as a purchase of the holding company rather than just of the bank, an asset of the holding company. . . . And Frandsen points out that under the stockholder agreement his right of first refusal was triggered by an *offer,* so that the fact the offer was later withdrawn would not affect his right of first refusal if he had already tried to exercise it—and he had tried, before the defendants reconfigured the transaction. But the point is academic, because we agree with the district judge that there never was an offer within the scope of the agreement. The part of the agreement that grants a right of first refusal refers to an offer to sell "their stock," and to a sale of "their stock," and the "their" refers to the majority shareholders. They never offered to sell their stock to First Wisconsin. First Wisconsin was not interested in becoming a majority shareholder of Jensen–Sundquist, in owning an insurance company, and in dealing with Frandsen and the other minority shareholders. It just wanted the bank.

What is more, a sale of stock was never contemplated, again for the reason that First Wisconsin was not interested in becoming a shareholder of Jensen–Sundquist. The transaction originally contemplated was a merger of Jensen–Sundquist into First Wisconsin. In a merger, as the word implies, the acquired firm disappears as a distinct legal entity. . . . In effect, the shareholders of the merged firm yield up all of the assets of the firm, receiving either cash or securities in exchange, and the firm dissolves. . . . In this case the shareholders would have received cash. Their shares would have disappeared but not by sale, for in a merger the shares of the acquired firm are not bought, they are extinguished. There would have been no Jensen–Sundquist after the merger, and no shareholders in Jensen–Sundquist.

The distinction between a sale of shares and a merger is such a familiar one in the business world that it is unbelievable that so experienced a businessman as Frandsen would have overlooked it. It is true that he was not represented by a lawyer in connection with the stockholder agreement, but when an experienced businessman deliberately eschews legal assistance in making a contract he cannot by doing so obtain a legal advantage over a represented party should a dispute arise.

Nor are we persuaded by Frandsen's argument that if interpreted literally the stockholder agreement gave him no right of first refusal worthy of the name. It is true that under that interpretation if as happened the majority bloc did not want to sell out to him, all it had to do was find a merger partner. But these alternatives are not identical in all but form, as he argues. The majority bloc was only 52 percent. If the majority wanted to sell its stock to someone who wanted a controlling interest in the company rather than the company itself or an asset of the company such as the First Bank of Grantsburg, it had to offer its shares to Frandsen first (and to the other six minority shareholders who had a right of first refusal—what would have happened if all had exercised their right we need not speculate about). If it wanted to bypass Frandsen it had to find someone willing to buy not just its shares, but the company.

Most important, Frandsen may have been concerned not with a sale of the company itself at a price agreeable to a majority and therefore likely to be attractive to him as well, but with a sale of the majority bloc that would leave him a minority shareholder in a company owned by strangers. The lot of a minority shareholder in a closely held company is not an enviable one, even in the best of circumstances. A majority coalition may gang up on him. And he may not have the usual recourse of a victimized minority shareholder—to sell out. For there may be no market for his shares, except the very people who have ganged up on him. . . . Frandsen may just have wanted to protect himself against being put at the mercy of a new and perhaps hostile majority bloc. The right of first refusal was one protection against this danger.

Against this Frandsen argues that the right of first refusal must have had an additional purpose, for otherwise it would merely have duplicated the second protective provision in the stockholder agreement, which guaranteed that the majority bloc if it sold its shares would offer to buy his shares at the same price. It is true that this provision protected Frandsen against finding himself a minority shareholder in a company controlled by persons other than the members of the original majority bloc, but it did so at the price of forcing him to leave the company. The right of first refusal enabled him to remain in the company by buying out the majority bloc at the same price that the bloc was willing to sell its shares to others. It thus gave him additional protection. It did not give him protection against a sale of the company itself but this does not make the agreement incoherent or unclear, for his only concern may have been with the possibility of finding himself confronted with a new majority bloc, and that is the only possibility he may have thought it important to negotiate with reference to.

We note in this connection that Frandsen himself had once taken over a bank by paying a premium to a majority of shareholders and then, after he acquired control in this way, buying out the minority shareholders at a lower price. Evidently he wanted to make sure that no one did this to him in Jensen–Sundquist by buying the majority bloc and then making life uncomfortable for him and the other minority shareholders so that they would sell their shares on the cheap. The stockholder agreement that he negotiated with Jensen was well designed to protect him against a maneuver that he had practiced himself. The defendants' efforts to get Frandsen to sign a waiver do not as he argues establish a practical construction of the stockholder agreement as entitling him to exercise his right of first refusal in the event of a proposed merger. A waiver is like a quitclaim deed: the signer waives whatever rights he may have, but does not warrant that he has any rights to waive.

Frandsen's principal argument is that the word "sell" is sufficiently ambiguous to embrace a disposition that has the same practical effect as a sale of the majority bloc's shares. This may be; Wilson v. Whinery, 37 Wash.App. 24, 28–29, 678 P.2d 354, 357 (1984), held that a transfer of all beneficial use of parcel B, "thereby granting [the transferee] substantial control over parcel B," was a sale of B for purposes of a right of first refusal triggered by such a sale. But our main point has been that a sale of the majority bloc's shares is not the same thing as a sale of either all or some of the holding company's assets. The sale of assets does not result in substituting a new majority bloc, and that is the possibility at which the protective provisions are aimed. This appears with sufficient clarity, moreover, to justify the district judge's refusal to go outside the text of the contract to find its meaning.

Any lingering doubts of the propriety of this course are dispelled by the rule that rights of first refusal are to be interpreted narrowly.   .   .   . This may seem to be one of those fusty "canons of construction" that invite ridicule because they have no basis and contradict each other and are advanced simply as rhetorical flourishes to embellish decisions reached on other, more practical grounds.   . . . But actually it makes some sense. The effect of a right of first refusal is to add a party to a transaction, for the right is triggered by an offer of sale, and the effect is therefore to inject the holder of the right into the sale transaction. Adding a party to a transaction increases the costs of transacting exponentially; the formula for the number of links required to connect up all the members of an n-member set is $n(n–1)/2$, meaning that, for example, increasing the number of parties to a transaction from three to four increases the number of required linkages from three to six. Certainly the claim of a right of first refusal complicated the transaction here! If all the costs of the more complicated transaction were borne by the parties, it would hardly be a matter of social concern. But some of the costs are borne by the taxpayers who support the court system, and the courts are not enthusiastic about this, and have decided not to be hospitable to such rights. The right is enforceable but only if the contract clearly confers it.

. . .

If as we believe no contractual right of Frandsen's was violated by the transaction, it is more than difficult to see how First Wisconsin could have been guilty of a tortious interference with his contractual rights. It is true that this tort has undergone a steady expansion and now embraces situations in which the interference is not with a contract right but merely with an expectation.   . . . But expansion is limited by the pressure of competing policies. One of the most firmly established principles of the common law is that competition is not a tort.   . . . Although competition literally is an intentional interference with competitors' prospective contractual relations, to conclude that it is therefore a tort would be as unsound legally as it would be disastrous economically. The courts have not drawn this conclusion; instead they have ruled that while competition is not a defense to a charge of interfering with an existing contract (for a firm should have no right to compete by inducing its competitors' customers to break valid contracts), it is a defense to a charge of interfering with prospective contractual relations, provided it is fair competition, consistent with antitrust law and other principles.   . . . Competition means little if it does not mean competing for a rival's existing customers (provided they are not tied to him by contract) as well as for customers new to the market. First Wisconsin and Frandsen were competitors to acquire the First Bank of Grantsburg. As long as First Wisconsin did not violate the antitrust laws or other relevant laws or induce First Bank's owner, Jensen–Sundquist, to break the stockholder agreement, First Wisconsin was entitled to compete for this prize without worrying that its rival, Frandsen, if he lost the competition, would turn around and sue in an effort to take away the prize.

. . .

The district judge correctly dismissed all of Frandsen's claims.

AFFIRMED.

Zetlin v. Hanson Holdings, Inc.

48 N.Y.2d 684, 421 N.Y.S.2d 877, 397 N.E.2d 387 (1979).

Opinion of the Court

Memorandum.

The order of the Appellate Division should be affirmed, with costs.

Plaintiff Zetlin owned approximately 2% of the outstanding shares of Gable Industries, Inc., with defendants Hanson Holdings, Inc., and Sylvestri together with members of the Sylvestri family, owning 44.4% of Gable's shares. The defendants sold their interests to Flintkote Co. for a premium price of $15 per share, at a time when Gable was selling on the open market for $7.38 per share. It is undisputed that the 44.4% acquired by Flintkote represented effective control of Gable.

Recognizing that those who invest the capital necessary to acquire a dominant position in the ownership of a corporation have the right of controlling that corporation, it has long been settled law that, absent looting of corporate assets, conversion of a corporate opportunity, fraud or other acts of bad faith, a controlling stockholder is free to sell, and a purchaser is free to buy, that controlling interest at a premium price.

. . . .

Certainly, minority shareholders are entitled to protection against such abuse by controlling shareholders. They are not entitled, however, to inhibit the legitimate interests of the other stockholders. It is for this reason that control shares usually command a premium price. The premium is the added amount an investor is willing to pay for the privilege of directly influencing the corporation's affairs.

In this action plaintiff Zetlin contends that minority stockholders are entitled to an opportunity to share equally in any premium paid for a controlling interest in the corporation. This rule would profoundly affect the manner in which controlling stock interests are now transferred. It would require, essentially, that a controlling interest be transferred only by means of an offer to all stockholders, i.e., a tender offer. This would be contrary to existing law and if so radical a change is to be effected it would best be done by the Legislature.

Order affirmed.

NOTE AND QUESTIONS ON CONTROL PREMIUMS

The underlying issue in sale-of-control cases can be reflected by two paradigms. For the *first paradigm*, suppose there is a business firm that produces earnings of $200,000 per year before any payment of salary to its manager and suppose that a reasonable salary for the manager is $50,000 per year, so the net earnings are $150,000 per year. Suppose further that the market value of the firm is a multiple of five times the net earnings, or $750,000; that the firm is incorporated, with 1,500 common shares outstanding; that 1,000 (or 2/3) of these shares are owned by C (the controlling shareholder) and 500 by M (the minority shareholder); and that C has been acting as manager and taking a salary of $50,000 per year. Thus, the financial picture looks like this:

Gross earnings	$200,000
Reasonable salary	$ 50,000
Net earnings	$150,000
Market value of firm (5 times net earnings)	$750,000
C's shares	1,000
M's shares	500
Earnings allocable to C	$100,000
Earnings allocable to M	$ 50,000
Market value of C's shares	$500,000
Market value of M's shares	$250,000

Now suppose C's shares are bought by B, who elects his representatives to the board of directors, and that the board installs B's son, S, as manager; that S, as a manager, is competent but has no special qualities that add value to the business; that the board sets S's salary at $110,000 per year; and that, given the traditional judicial deference to decisions of boards of directors, there is no realistic prospect that a legal attack on this salary would be successful. The financial picture now looks like this:

Gross earnings	$200,000
S's salary	$110,000
Net earnings	$ 90,000
B's shares	1,000
M's shares	500
Earnings allocable to B	$ 60,000
Additional value to B from S's excess salary (yearly)	$ 60,000
Total annual return to B	$120,000
Market value of B's shares	$600,000
Earnings allocable to M	$ 30,000
Market value of M's shares	$150,000

On these assumed facts, which are extreme but may fairly depict reality in some situations, B has been able to shift $100,000 of the value of the firm from M to himself.[8] Thus, B might have been willing to pay C a premium

---

8. A thoughtful reader may detect a problem with the assumed facts. If it is so easy to increase the salary of the controlling shareholder or his son, why would M's shares initially be worth $250,000? Why would there not be at least some discount to reflect the prospect that the controlling shareholder would extract benefits not shared with the minority shareholder? The answer is that the initially assumed facts may in fact be unrealistic to some degree, but the observations generated by the facts assumed are

(that is, an amount in excess of C's allocable share of the total fair market value of the firm) for his shares. If, for example, B had paid $550,000 for C's 1,000 shares, C and B each would profit by $50,000—at the expense of M. On this view of control premiums, the premium is paid for control because the buyer intends to milk, or (a more extreme version) loot, the corporation. In thinking about this view of reality, however, one must wonder why (returning to our hypothetical facts) C had been paying himself a salary of only $50,000. If C had been paying himself $110,000, then C's shares would have been worth more than M's, but the sale of those shares to B, at a price in excess of the value of M's shares, would not have harmed M. The question left by this paradigm is, why not, by some legal rule or device, provide that a buyer such as B, who is willing to pay a premium for a controlling number of shares, must buy pro rata from all shareholders?

For the *second paradigm,* assume that we begin with the same facts as in the first paradigm, with the firm earning net revenues of $150,000 (after the $50,000 salary to C), and with C owning 1,000 shares worth $500,000 and M owning 500 shares worth $250,000. Along comes E, a successful entrepreneur, who examines the firm's methods of operations and concludes that by making some changes and by replacing C, as manager, with her own person (who will be willing to accept the same $50,000 salary), she can increase the net earnings to $200,000.[9] If E is right, she can increase the value of the firm from $750,000 to $1,000,000. Suppose E buys C's shares for $600,000. Everyone has an increase in wealth. C has sold shares worth $500,000 for $600,000, for a gain of $100,000. E has paid $600,000 for shares that should now be worth $666,667 (2/3 of the $1,000,-000 total value). And M's shares should increase in value from $250,000 to $333,333 (1/3 of $1,000,000), a gain of $83,333. The total gain is $250,000, which, of course, is the total increase in the value of the firm. It is difficult to see any basis for objection to the sale from C to E. But is this a realistic paradigm? In challenging the realism, a person might ask why, since E expected to make a profit from the purchase of C's shares at a 20 percent premium,[10] was she not also willing to offer the same premium for M's shares? Does the failure to do so necessarily establish that E does not

---

nonetheless interesting and useful. The implications of the thoughtful reader's concern with the realism of the assumed facts might be explored by starting with the firm under B's ownership, with B's shares worth $600,-000 and M's shares worth $150,000, and asking how one's reactions to sale of control shares for a premium price change if it is now B, rather than C, who is selling the shares.

9. Again the thoughtful reader might wonder why the initial value of the shares was not at least slightly greater than $750,-000, to reflect the prospect that the earnings might be increased through better strategies and management, or to reflect the probability that C was gaining intangible benefits from managing the firm in his own relatively inefficient way. Changing the facts to reflect this possibility would add complexity without altering the important implications.

10. It was assumed that C's shares were initially worth $500,000. E paid $600,-000, which includes a premium of $100,000 over the initial worth. $100,000 is 20 percent of $500,000.

genuinely expect to increase the firm's earnings, but rather intends to exploit the firm for her own personal advantage, as in the first paradigm?

PLANNING PROBLEM

Planny Poblem

Recall that in the *Frandsen* case, a minority shareholder bargained for a "take-me-along" or "equal-opportunity" provision. It was described by the court as follows:

> [I]f the majority bloc offered to sell its shares it had to give Frandsen a right to buy the shares at the offer price. If Frandsen declined, the second protective provision came into play: the majority bloc had to offer to buy his shares at the same price at which it sold its own shares.

Suppose that you are practicing law and that three people come to you and ask you to advise and assist them in forming a business organization to manufacture and sell computer components. The three individuals are Ida, Sally, and Maria. Ida has the product ideas and technical competence and will supervise production. Sally will be in charge of sales and promotion. Maria will supply the money for the start-up phase; she will play no active role in the business. The three principals tell you that if all goes well they expect to become rich from this venture (or, in Maria's case, richer). What advice would you give them about adopting an equal-opportunity provision? Would your advice change if you knew that Ida and Sally were sisters and always acted together, as if they were one person? (By the way, do you have a problem with advising all three?)

Perlman v. Feldmann

219 F.2d 173 (2d Cir.1955).

■ CLARK, CHIEF JUDGE.

This is a derivative action brought by minority stockholders of Newport Steel Corporation to compel accounting for, and restitution of, allegedly illegal gains which accrued to defendants as a result of the sale in August, 1950, of their controlling interest in the corporation. The principal defendant, C. Russell Feldmann, who represented and acted for the others, members of his family,[1] was at that time not only the dominant stockholder, but also the chairman of the board of directors and the president of the corporation. Newport, an Indiana corporation, operated mills for the production of steel sheets for sale to manufacturers of steel products, first at Newport, Kentucky, and later also at other places in Kentucky and Ohio. The buyers, a syndicate organized as Wilport Company, a Delaware corporation, consisted of end-users of steel who were

---

1. The stock was not held personally by Feldmann in his own name, but was held by the members of his family and by personal corporations. The aggregate of stock thus had amounted to 33% of the outstanding Newport stock and gave working control to the holder. The actual sale included 55,552 additional shares held by friends and associates of Feldmann, so that a total of 37% of the Newport stock was transferred.

interested in securing a source of supply in a market becoming ever tighter in the Korean War. Plaintiffs contend that the consideration paid for the stock included compensation for the sale of a corporate asset, a power held in trust for the corporation by Feldmann as its fiduciary. This power was the ability to control the allocation of the corporate product in a time of short supply, through control of the board of directors; and it was effectively transferred in this sale by having Feldmann procure the resignation of his own board and the election of Wilport's nominees immediately upon consummation of the sale.

. . .

Newport was a relative newcomer in the steel industry with predominantly old installations which were in the process of being supplemented by more modern facilities. Except in times of extreme shortage Newport was not in a position to compete profitably with other steel mills for customers not in its immediate geographical area. Wilport, the purchasing syndicate, consisted of geographically remote end-users of steel who were interested in buying more steel from Newport than they had been able to obtain during recent periods of tight supply. The price of $20 per share was found by Judge Hincks to be a fair one for a control block of stock, although the over-the-counter market price had not exceeded $12 and the book value per share was $17.03. . . .

Both as director and as dominant stockholder, Feldmann stood in a fiduciary relationship to the corporation and to the minority stockholders as beneficiaries thereof. . . .

It is true, as defendants have been at pains to point out, that this is not the ordinary case of breach of fiduciary duty. We have here no fraud, no misuse of confidential information, no outright looting of a helpless corporation. But on the other hand, we do not find compliance with that high standard which we have just stated and which we and other courts have come to expect and demand of corporate fiduciaries. In the often-quoted words of Judge Cardozo: "Many forms of conduct permissible in a workaday world for those acting at arm's length, are forbidden to those bound by fiduciary ties. A trustee is held to something stricter than the morals of the market place. Not honesty alone, but the punctilio of an honor the most sensitive, is then the standard of behavior. As to this there has developed a tradition that is unbending and inveterate. Uncompromising rigidity has been the attitude of courts of equity when petitioned to undermine the rule of undivided loyalty by the 'disintegrating erosion' of particular exceptions." Meinhard v. Salmon, supra, 249 N.Y. 458, 464, 164 N.E. 545, 546. The actions of defendants in siphoning off for personal gain corporate advantages to be derived from a favorable market situation do not betoken the necessary undivided loyalty owed by the fiduciary to his principal.

The corporate opportunities of whose misappropriation the minority stockholders complain need not have been an absolute certainty in order to support this action against Feldmann. . . . [I]n Irving Trust Co. v.

Deutsch, 2 Cir., 73 F.2d 121, 124, an accounting was required of corporate directors who bought stock for themselves for corporate use, even though there was an affirmative showing that the corporation did not have the finances itself to acquire the stock. Judge Swan speaking for the court pointed out that "The defendants' argument, contrary to Wing v. Dillingham [5 Cir., 239 F. 54], that the equitable rule that fiduciaries should not be permitted to assume a position in which their individual interests might be in conflict with those of the corporation can have no application where the corporation is unable to undertake the venture, is not convincing. If directors are permitted to justify their conduct on such a theory, there will be a temptation to refrain from exerting their strongest efforts on behalf of the corporation since, if it does not meet the obligations, an opportunity of profit will be open to them personally."

This rationale is equally appropriate to a consideration of the benefits which Newport might have derived from the steel shortage. In the past Newport had used and profited by its market leverage by operation of what the industry had come to call the "Feldmann Plan." This consisted of securing interest-free advances from prospective purchasers of steel in return for firm commitments to them from future production. The funds thus acquired were used to finance improvements in existing plants and to acquire new installations. In the summer of 1950 Newport had been negotiating for cold-rolling facilities which it needed for a more fully integrated operation and a more marketable product, and Feldmann plan funds might well have been used toward this end.

Further, as plaintiffs alternatively suggest, Newport might have used the period of short supply to build up patronage in the geographical area in which it could compete profitably even when steel was more abundant. Either of these opportunities was Newport's, to be used to its advantage only. Only if defendants had been able to negate completely any possibility of gain by Newport could they have prevailed. . . .

Defendants seek to categorize the corporate opportunities which might have accrued to Newport as too unethical to warrant further consideration. It is true that reputable steel producers were not participating in the gray market brought about by the Korean War and were refraining from advancing their prices, although to do so would not have been illegal. But Feldmann plan transactions were not considered within this self-imposed interdiction; the trial court found that around the time of the Feldmann sale Jones & Laughlin Steel Corporation, Republic Steel Company, and Pittsburgh Steel Corporation were all participating in such arrangements. In any event, it ill becomes the defendants to disparage as unethical the market advantages from which they themselves reaped rich benefits.

We do not mean to suggest that a majority stockholder cannot dispose of his controlling block of stock to outsiders without having to account to his corporation for profits or even never do this with impunity when the buyer is an interested customer, actual or potential, for the corporation's product. But when the sale necessarily results in a sacrifice of this element of corporate good will and consequent unusual profit to the fiduciary who

has caused the sacrifice, he should account for his gains. So in a time of
market shortage, where a call on a corporation's product commands an
unusually large premium, in one form or another, we think it sound law
that a fiduciary may not appropriate to himself the value of this premium. . . .

Hence to the extent that the price received by Feldmann and his co-
defendants included such a bonus, he is accountable to the minority
stockholders who sue here.   . . . And plaintiffs, as they contend, are
entitled to a recovery in their own right, instead of in right of the
corporation (as in the usual derivative actions), since neither Wilport nor
their successors in interest should share in any judgment which may be
rendered.   . . .

■ SWAN, CIRCUIT JUDGE (dissenting).

With the general principles enunciated in the majority opinion as to
the duties of fiduciaries I am, of course, in thorough accord. But, as Mr.
Justice Frankfurter stated in Securities and Exchange Comm. v. Chenery
Corp., 318 U.S. 80, 85, "to say that a man is a fiduciary only begins
analysis; it gives direction to further inquiry. To whom is he a fiduciary?
What obligations does he owe as a fiduciary? In what respect has he failed
to discharge these obligations?" My brothers' opinion does not specify
precisely what fiduciary duty Feldmann is held to have violated or whether
it was a duty imposed upon him as the dominant stockholder or as a
director of Newport.   . . .

The power to control the management of a corporation, that is, to elect
directors to manage its affairs, is an inseparable incident to the ownership
of a majority of its stock, or sometimes, as in the present instance, to the
ownership of enough shares, less than a majority, to control an election.
Concededly a majority or dominant shareholder is ordinarily privileged to
sell his stock at the best price obtainable from the purchaser. In so doing
he acts on his own behalf, not as an agent of the corporation. If he knows
or has reason to believe that the purchaser intends to exercise to the
detriment of the corporation the power of management acquired by the
purchase, such knowledge or reasonable suspicion will terminate the dominant shareholder's privilege to sell and will create a duty not to transfer
the power of management to such purchaser. The duty seems to me to
resemble the obligation which everyone is under not to assist another to
commit a tort rather than the obligation of a fiduciary. But whatever the
nature of the duty, a violation of it will subject the violator to liability for
damages sustained by the corporation. Judge Hincks found that Feldmann
had no reason to think that Wilport would use the power of management it
would acquire by the purchase to injure Newport, and that there was no
proof that it ever was so used. Feldmann did know, it is true, that the
reason Wilport wanted the stock was to put in a board of directors who
would be likely to permit Wilport's members to purchase more of Newport's steel than they might otherwise be able to get. But there is nothing
illegal in a dominant shareholder purchasing from his own corporation at
the same prices it offers to other customers. That is what the members of

Wilport did, and there is no proof that Newport suffered any detriment therefrom.

My brothers say that "the consideration paid for the stock included compensation for the sale of a corporate asset," which they describe as "the ability to control the allocation of the corporate product in a time of short supply, through control of the board of directors; and it was effectively transferred in this sale by having Feldmann procure the resignation of his own board and the election of Wilport's nominees immediately upon consummation of the sale." The implications of this are not clear to me. If it means that when market conditions are such as to induce users of a corporation's product to wish to buy a controlling block of stock in order to be able to purchase part of the corporation's output at the same mill list prices as are offered to other customers, the dominant stockholder is under a fiduciary duty not to sell his stock, I cannot agree. For reasons already stated, in my opinion Feldmann was not proved to be under any fiduciary duty as a stockholder not to sell the stock he controlled.

Feldmann was also a director of Newport. Perhaps the quoted statement means that as a director he violated his fiduciary duty in voting to elect Wilport's nominees to fill the vacancies created by the resignations of the former directors of Newport. As a director Feldmann was under a fiduciary duty to use an honest judgment in acting on the corporation's behalf. A director is privileged to resign, but so long as he remains a director he must be faithful to his fiduciary duties and must not make a personal gain from performing them. Consequently, if the price paid for Feldmann's stock included a payment for voting to elect the new directors, he must account to the corporation for such payment, even though he honestly believed that the men he voted to elect were well qualified to serve as directors. He can not take pay for performing his fiduciary duty.

. . .

The final conclusion of my brothers is that the plaintiffs are entitled to recover in their own right instead of in the right of the corporation. This appears to be completely inconsistent with the theory advanced at the outset of the opinion, namely, that the price of the stock "included compensation for the sale of a corporate asset." If a corporate asset was sold, surely the corporation should recover the compensation received for it by the defendants.   . . .

ANALYSIS

1. What did Feldmann do wrong? In what capacity?

2. How were plaintiffs harmed by the defendants' sale of their shares?

3. Why is this a derivative action?

Jones v. H.F. Ahmanson & Company

1 Cal.3d 93, 81 Cal.Rptr. 592, 460 P.2d 464 (1969).

■ TRAYNOR, CHIEF JUSTICE.

June K. Jones, the owner of 25 shares of the capital stock of United Savings and Loan Association of California brings this action on behalf of herself individually and of all similarly situated minority stockholders of the Association. The defendants are United Financial Corporation of California, fifteen individuals, and four corporations, all of whom are present or former stockholders or officers of the Association. Plaintiff seeks damages and other relief for losses allegedly suffered by the minority stockholders of the Association because of claimed breaches of fiduciary responsibility by defendants in the creation and operation of United Financial, a Delaware holding company that owns 87 percent of the outstanding Association stock.

[Jones had been a depositor in a mutual savings and loan institution. That savings and loan, as a mutual, was "owned" by its depositors. Over the years of its existence it had built up substantial net worth. In 1956 it "went private." That is, it became an ordinary corporation, owned by shareholders. Its new name was United Savings and Loan Association of California (the Association). The process of conversion from mutual to stock form was accomplished by allowing depositors and some of the key employees of the mutual to buy shares of the new corporation, at what, at least in retrospect, was a bargain price. Jones bought shares. Many other depositors did not.

H.F. Ahmanson & Company, which had accumulated substantial wealth by investments in other savings and loan institutions, was able to acquire a controlling block of shares of the Association. By May, 1959, together with members of the Ahmanson family and associates, it held 85 percent of the shares.]

The Association has retained the major part of its earnings in tax-free reserves with the result that the book value of the outstanding shares has increased substantially. The shares were not actively traded. This inactivity is attributed to the high book value, the closely held nature of the Association, and the failure of the management to provide investment information and assistance to shareholders, brokers, or the public.   . . .

In 1958 investor interest in shares of savings and loan associations and holding companies increased.   . . . Defendants determined to create a mechanism by which they could participate in the profit taking by attracting investor interest in the Association. They did not, however, undertake to render the Association shares more readily marketable. Instead, the United Financial Corporation of California was incorporated in Delaware by all of the other defendants except defendant Thatcher on May 8, 1959. On May 14, 1959, pursuant to a prior agreement, certain Association stockholders who among them owned a majority of the Association stock exchanged their shares for those of United Financial, receiving a "derived block" of 250 United Financial shares for each Association share.

After the exchange, United Financial held 85 percent of the outstanding Association stock.   . . .   The former majority stockholders of the Association had become the majority shareholders of United Financial and continued to control the Association through the holding company.   They did not offer the minority stockholders of the Association an opportunity to exchange their shares.

[Shares of United Financial were sold to the public and a market for the shares developed.   After certain complex transactions, a holder of one share of Association stock who became a holder of United stock wound up with what the court calls a "derived block" of United stock and, in addition, received a cash distribution of $927.50.]

. . .

In 1959 and 1960 extra dividends of $75 and $57 per share had been paid by the Association, but in December 1960, after the foregoing offer had been made, defendants caused the Association's president to notify each minority stockholder by letter that no dividends other than the regular $4.00 per share annual dividend would be paid in the near future.   The Association president, defendant M.D. Jameson, was then a director of both the Association and United Financial.

Defendants then proposed an exchange of United Financial shares for Association stock.   Under this proposal each minority stockholder would have received approximately 51 United Financial shares of a total value of $2,400 for each Association share.   When the application for a permit was filed with the California Corporations Commissioner on August 28, 1961, the value of the derived blocks of United Financial shares received by defendants in the initial exchange had risen to approximately $8,800.[9]   The book value of the Association stock was in excess of $1,700 per share, and the shares were earning at an annual rate of $615 per share.   . . . Plaintiff and other minority stockholders objected to the proposed exchange, contending that the plan was not fair, just, and equitable.   Defendants then asked the Commissioner to abandon the application without ruling on it.

Plaintiff contends that in following this course of conduct defendants breached the fiduciary duty owed by majority or controlling shareholders to minority shareholders.   She alleges that they used their control of the Association for their own advantage to the detriment of the minority when they created United Financial, made a public market for its shares that rendered Association stock unmarketable except to United Financial, and then refused either to purchase plaintiff's Association stock at a fair price or exchange the stock on the same basis afforded to the majority.   . . .

[The trial court granted the defendants' demurrer.]

---

9. The derived block sold for as much as $13,127.41 during 1960–1961.   On January 30, 1962, the date upon which plaintiff commenced this action, the mean value was $9,116.08.

I

Plaintiff's Capacity to Sue

We are faced at the outset with defendants' contention that if a cause of action is stated, it is derivative in nature since any injury suffered is common to all minority stockholders of the Association. . . .

It is clear from the stipulated facts and plaintiff's allegations that she does not seek to recover on behalf of the corporation for injury done to the corporation by defendants. Although she does allege that the value of her stock has been diminished by defendants' actions, she does not contend that the diminished value reflects an injury to the corporation and resultant depreciation in the value of the stock. Thus the gravamen of her cause of action is injury to herself and the other minority stockholders.

. . .

II

Majority Shareholders' Fiduciary Responsibility

. . . The Courts of Appeal have often recognized that majority shareholders, either singly or acting in concert to accomplish a joint purpose, have a fiduciary responsibility to the minority and to the corporation to use their ability to control the corporation in a fair, just, and equitable manner. Majority shareholders may not use their power to control corporate activities to benefit themselves alone or in a manner detrimental to the minority. Any use to which they put the corporation or their power to control the corporation must benefit all shareholders proportionately and must not conflict with the proper conduct of the corporation's business. . . .

Defendants assert, however, that in the use of their own shares they owed no fiduciary duty to the minority stockholders of the Association. They maintain that they made full disclosure of the circumstances surrounding the formation of United Financial, that the creation of United Financial and its share offers in no way affected the control of the Association, that plaintiff's proportionate interest in the Association was not affected, that the Association was not harmed, and that the market for Association stock was not affected. Therefore, they conclude, they have breached no fiduciary duty to plaintiff and the other minority stockholders.

Defendants would have us retreat from a position demanding equitable treatment of all shareholders by those exercising control over a corporation to a philosophy much criticized by commentators and modified by courts in other jurisdictions as well as our own. In essence defendants suggest that we reaffirm the so-called "majority" rule reflected in our early decisions. This rule, exemplified by the decision in Ryder v. Bamberger, 172 Cal. 791, 158 P. 753 but since severely limited, recognized the "perfect right [of majority shareholders] to dispose of their stock . . . without the slightest regard to the wishes and desires or knowledge of the minority stockholders; . . ." (p. 806, 158 P. p. 759) and held that such fiduciary duty as did exist in officers and directors was to the corporation only. . . .

. . . The case before us, in which no sale or transfer of actual control is directly involved, demonstrates that . . . injury . . . can be inflicted with impunity under the traditional rules and supports our conclusion that the comprehensive rule of good faith and inherent fairness to the minority in any transaction where control of the corporation is material properly governs controlling shareholders in this state.

We turn now to defendants' conduct to ascertain whether this test is met.

III

Formation of United Financial and Marketing its Shares

Defendants created United Financial during a period of unusual investor interest in the stock of savings and loan associations. They then owned a majority of the outstanding stock of the Association. This stock was not readily marketable owing to a high book value, lack of investor information and facilities, and the closely held nature of the Association. The management of the Association had made no effort to create a market for the stock or to split the shares and reduce their market price to a more attractive level. Two courses were available to defendants in their effort to exploit the bull market in savings and loan stock. Both were made possible by defendants' status as controlling stockholders. The first was either to cause the Association to effect a stock split (Corp.Code, § 1507) and create a market for the Association stock or to create a holding company for Association shares and permit all stockholders to exchange their shares before offering holding company shares to the public. All stockholders would have benefited alike had this been done, but in realizing their gain on the sale of their stock the majority stockholders would of necessity have had to relinquish some of their control shares. Because a public market would have been created, however, the minority stockholders would have been able to extricate themselves without sacrificing their investment had they elected not to remain with the new management.

The second course was that taken by defendants. A new corporation was formed whose major asset was to be the control block of Association stock owned by defendants, but from which minority shareholders were to be excluded. The unmarketable Association stock held by the majority was transferred to the newly formed corporation at an exchange rate equivalent to a 250 for 1 stock split. The new corporation thereupon set out to create a market for its own shares. Association stock constituted 85 percent of the holding company's assets and produced an equivalent proportion of its income. The same individuals controlled both corporations. It appears therefrom that the market created by defendants for United Financial shares was a market that would have been available for Association stock had defendants taken the first course of action.

After United Financial shares became available to the public it became a virtual certainty that no equivalent market could or would be created for Association stock. United Financial had become the controlling stockholder and neither it nor the other defendants would benefit from public trading in Association stock in competition with United Financial shares. Investors afforded an opportunity to acquire United Financial shares would not be likely to choose the less marketable and expensive Association stock in preference. Thus defendants chose a course of action in which they used their control of the Association to obtain an advantage not made available to all stockholders. They did so without regard to the resulting detriment to the minority stockholders and in the absence of any compelling business purpose. Such conduct is not consistent with their duty of good faith and inherent fairness to the minority stockholders. Had defendants afforded the minority an opportunity to exchange their stock on the same basis or offered to purchase them at a price arrived at by independent appraisal, their burden of establishing good faith and inherent fairness would have been much less. At the trial they may present evidence tending to show such good faith or compelling business purpose that would render their action fair under the circumstances. On appeal from the judgment of dismissal after the defendants' demurrer was sustained we decide only that the complaint states a cause of action entitling plaintiff to relief.

.   .   .

ANALYSIS

1. What would the value of Jones's shares have been if she had been willing to hold them indefinitely?

2. If the Ahmanson group had not wanted a public market for its shares and had been content to simply hold their shares of United without creating a public market, would Jones have been entitled to any relief? What if, instead of creating United, they had simply sold their shares to an existing bank or bank holding company, but had made no effort to make it possible for Jones to sell her shares?

3. The Supreme Court remanded the case for trial. Suppose the defendants could have established on remand that if they had wanted to offer Mrs. Jones and the other shareholders like her a "take me along" or "equal opportunity" option they would have had to comply with the federal and state securities registration rules and that this would have been costly and time-consuming. Would that have been relevant? Would motive have been relevant? Whose motive? What other evidence might have been relevant?

4. What is the relevance of the allegation that the defendants offered to buy Mrs. Jones's shares at a price substantially lower than the value of the corresponding derived block? What if they had never offered to buy her shares? What if their offer had been made only in response to a request by her that they buy her shares?

Essex Universal Corporation v. Yates

305 F.2d 572 (2d Cir.1962).

■ BEFORE LUMBARD, CHIEF JUDGE, and CLARK and FRIENDLY, CIRCUIT JUDGES.

■ LUMBARD, CHIEF JUDGE.

.   .   .

The defendant Herbert J. Yates, a resident of California, was president and chairman of the board of directors of Republic Pictures Corporation, a New York corporation which at the time relevant to this suit had 2,004,190 shares of common stock outstanding. Republic's stock was listed and traded on the New York Stock Exchange. In August 1957, Essex Universal Corporation, a Delaware corporation owning stock in various diversified businesses, learned of the possibility of purchasing from Yates an interest in Republic. Negotiations proceeded rapidly, and on August 28 Yates and Joseph Harris, the president of Essex, signed a contract in which Essex agreed to buy, and Yates agreed "to sell or cause to be sold" at least 500,000 and not more than 600,000 shares of Republic stock. The price was set at eight dollars a share, roughly two dollars above the then market price on the Exchange.   .   .   .   In addition to other provisions not relevant to the present motion, the contract contained the following paragraph:

"6. Resignations.

Upon and as a condition to the closing of this transaction if requested by Buyer at least ten (10) days prior to the date of the closing:

(a) Seller will deliver to Buyer the resignations of the majority of the directors of Republic.

(b) Seller will cause a special meeting of the board of directors of Republic to be held, legally convened pursuant to law and the by-laws of Republic, and simultaneously with the acceptance of the directors' resignations set forth in paragraph 6(a) immediately preceding will cause nominees of Buyer to be elected directors of Republic in place of the resigned directors."

Before the date of the closing, as provided in the contract, Yates notified Essex that he would deliver 566,223 shares, or 28.3 per cent of the Republic stock then outstanding, and Essex formally requested Yates to arrange for the replacement of a majority of Republic's directors with Essex nominees pursuant to paragraph 6 of the contract. This was to be accomplished by having eight of the fourteen directors resign seriatim, each in turn being replaced by an Essex nominee elected by the others; such a procedure was in form permissible under the charter and by-laws of Republic, which empowered the board to choose the successor of any of its members who might resign.

On September 18, the parties met as arranged for the closing at Republic's office in New York City. Essex tendered bank drafts and cashier's checks totalling $1,698,690, which was the 37½ per cent of the total price of $4,529,784 due at this time. The drafts and checks were payable to one Benjamin C. Cohen, who was Essex' banker and had arranged for the borrowing of the necessary funds. Although Cohen was prepared to endorse these to Yates, Yates upon advice of his lawyer rejected the tender as "unsatisfactory" and said, according to his deposition testimony, "Well, there can be no deal. We can't close it."

Essex began this action in the New York Supreme Court, and it was removed to the district court on account of diversity of citizenship. Essex seeks damages of $2,700,000, claiming that at the time of the aborted closing the stock was in actuality worth more than $12.75 a share. Yates' answer raised a number of defenses, but the motion for summary judgment now before us was made and decided only on the theory that the provision in the contract for immediate transfer of control of the board of directors was illegal *per se* and tainted the entire contract. We have no doubt, and the parties agree, that New York law governs.

Appellant's contention that the provision for transfer of director control is separable from the rest of the contract can quickly be rejected. . . .

Up to this point my brethren and I are in agreement. The following analysis is my own, except insofar as the separate opinions of Judges Clark and Friendly may indicate agreement.

It is established beyond question under New York law that it is illegal to sell corporate office or management control by itself (that is, accompanied by no stock or insufficient stock to carry voting control). . . . The same rule apparently applies in all jurisdictions where the question has arisen. . . . The rationale of the rule is undisputable: persons enjoying management control hold it on behalf of the corporation's stockholders, and therefore may not regard it as their own personal property to dispose of as they wish. . . .

Essex was, however, contracting with Yates for the purchase of a very substantial percentage of Republic stock. If, by virtue of the voting power carried by this stock, it could have elected a majority of the board of directors, then the contract was not a simple agreement for the sale of office to one having no ownership interest in the corporation, and the question of its legality would require further analysis. Such stock voting control would incontestably belong to the owner of a majority of the voting stock, and it is commonly known that equivalent power usually accrues to the owner of 28.3% of the stock. For the purpose of this analysis, I shall assume that Essex was contracting to acquire a majority of the Republic stock, deferring consideration of the situation where, as here, only 28.3% is to be acquired.

Republic's board of directors at the time of the aborted closing had fourteen members divided into three classes, each class being "as nearly as may be" of the same size. Directors were elected for terms of three years, one class being elected at each annual shareholder meeting on the first

Tuesday in April. Thus, absent the immediate replacement of directors provided for in this contract, Essex as the hypothetical new majority shareholder of the corporation could not have obtained managing control in the form of a majority of the board in the normal course of events until April 1959, some eighteen months after the sale of the stock. . . .

There is no question of the right of a controlling shareholder under New York law normally to derive a premium from the sale of a controlling block of stock. In other words, there was no impropriety *per se* in the fact that Yates was to receive more per share than the generally prevailing market price for Republic stock. . . .

The next question is whether it is legal to give and receive payment for the immediate transfer of management control to one who has achieved majority share control but would not otherwise be able to convert that share control into operating control for some time. I think that it is.

. . .

The easy and immediate transfer of corporate control to new interests is ordinarily beneficial to the economy and it seems inevitable that such transactions would be discouraged if the purchaser of a majority stock interest were required to wait some period before his purchase of control could become effective. Conversely it would greatly hamper the efforts of any existing majority group to dispose of its interest if it could not assure the purchaser of immediate control over corporation operations. I can see no reason why a purchaser of majority control should not ordinarily be permitted to make his control effective from the moment of the transfer of stock.

Thus if Essex had been contracting to purchase a majority of the stock of Republic, it would have been entirely proper for the contract to contain the provision for immediate replacement of directors. Although in the case at bar only 28.3 per cent of the stock was involved, it is commonly known that a person or group owning so large a percentage of the voting stock of a corporation which, like Republic, has at least the 1,500 shareholders normally requisite to listing on the New York Stock Exchange, is almost certain to have share control as a practical matter. If Essex was contracting to acquire what in reality would be equivalent to ownership of a majority of stock, i.e., if it would as a practical certainty have been guaranteed of the stock voting power to choose a majority of the directors of Republic in due course, there is no reason why the contract should not similarly be legal. Whether Essex was thus to acquire the equivalent of majority stock control would, if the issue is properly raised by the defendants, be a factual issue to be determined by the district court on remand.

Because 28.3 per cent of the voting stock of a publicly owned corporation is usually tantamount to majority control, I would place the burden of proof on this issue on Yates as the party attacking the legality of the transaction. Thus, unless on remand Yates chooses to raise the question whether the block of stock in question carried the equivalent of majority control, it is my view that the trial court should regard the contract as legal and proceed to consider the other issues raised by the pleadings. If Yates chooses to raise the issue, it will, on my view, be necessary for him to prove the existence of circumstances which would have prevented Essex from electing a majority of the Republic board of directors in due course.

. . .

■ CLARK, CIRCUIT JUDGE (concurring in the result).

Since Barnes v. Brown, 80 N.Y. 527, teaches us that not all contracts like the one before us are necessarily illegal, summary judgment seems definitely improper and the action should be remanded for trial. But particularly in view of our lack of knowledge of corporate realities and the current standards of business morality, I should prefer to avoid too precise instructions to the district court in the hope that if the action again comes before us the record will be generally more instructive on this important issue than it now is. . . .

. . .

■ FRIENDLY, CIRCUIT JUDGE (concurring).

I have no doubt that many contracts, drawn by competent and responsible counsel, for the purchase of blocks of stock from interests thought to "control" a corporation although owning less than a majority, have contained provisions like paragraph 6 of the contract *sub judice*. However, developments over the past decades seem to me to show that such a clause violates basic principles of corporate democracy. To be sure, stockholders who have allowed a set of directors to be placed in office, whether by their vote or their failure to vote, must recognize that death, incapacity or other hazard may prevent a director from serving a full term, and that they will have no voice as to his immediate successor. But the stockholders are entitled to expect that, in that event, the remaining directors will fill the vacancy in the exercise of their fiduciary responsibility. A mass seriatim resignation directed by a selling stockholder, and the filling of vacancies by his henchmen at the dictation of a purchaser and without any consideration of the character of the latter's nominees, are beyond what the stockholders contemplated or should have been expected to contemplate. . . .

Hence, I am inclined to think that if I were sitting on the New York Court of Appeals, I would hold a provision like paragraph 6 violative of public policy save when it was entirely plain that a new election would be a mere formality—i.e., when the seller owned more than 50% of the stock. . . . Moreover, in view of the perhaps unexpected character of such a holding, I doubt that I would give it retrospective effect.

NOTE ON WHAT IS A CONTROL BLOCK OF SHARES

In Essex Universal Corporation v. Yates the selling shareholder, Yates, was the incumbent—that is, Yates had control of the board of directors and of the management of the corporation. Control gave him, among other things, access to the corporation's list of shareholders and its funds (for waging a campaign to line up the votes of other shareholders in a proxy fight), and the advantage of inertia. Since he already held 28.3 percent of the voting shares, a challenger to his control would have been required to buy shares from the holders of the remaining 71.7 percent. The incumbent had a sufficiently large stake in the corporation to have a strong incentive to resist challenge. Given the likelihood of resistance, a battle for control might leave little gain for the challenger, even if the challenger did gain control. In this setting, the 28.3 percent voting block provides effective control.

Where there is an incumbent management team and board of directors that does not have a significant percentage of the voting shares, an outsider who acquires a large, but less-than-majority block of voting shares may well be unable to exert any control over the corporation. Indeed, it is not uncommon that outsiders who acquire substantial minority positions are denied any representation whatever on the board of directors, even though the incumbent directors collectively own far fewer shares than the outsider.

ANALYSIS

1. Suppose all the facts of the *Yates* case are as stated by the court except that Mr. Yates held, and sold, only 3 percent of the voting shares. What would the result have been?

2. Suppose a shareholder other than Yates had objected to the contract between Yates and Essex Universal Corporation. How might such a shareholder have challenged the contract, or its consequences, and what would have been the likelihood of success?

3. In *Yates,* the board was said to have been "classified." (Often the word used to describe the type of board encountered in the case is "staggered." A "classified" board, by contrast, is one for which different classes of stock elect different sets of directors.) How did the constitution of the board affect the strategy for the sale of the controlling block? How would the strategy have changed if the board had not been classified (that is, staggered)? In answering this question, assume that the time is now and that the applicable law is that of New York. Here are the relevant provisions:

§ 602. Meetings of shareholders

. . .

(b) A meeting of shareholders shall be held annually for the election of directors and the transaction of other business on a date fixed by or under the by-laws.

(c) Special meetings of the shareholders may be called by the board and by such person or persons as may be so authorized by the certificate of incorporation or the by-laws. . . .

§ 702.   Number of directors

. . .

(b) The number of directors may be increased or decreased by amendment of the by-laws, or by action of the shareholders or of the board under specific provisions of a by-law adopted by the shareholders.   . . .

§ 703.   Election and term of directors

(a) At each annual meeting of shareholders, directors shall be elected to hold office until the next annual meeting except as authorized by § 704 (classification of directors). The certificate of incorporation may provide for the election of one or more directors by the holders of the shares of any class or series, . . . voting as a class.

(b) Each director shall hold office until the expiration of the term for which he is elected, and until his successor has been elected and qualified.

§ 704.   Classification of directors

(a) The certificate of incorporation or the specific provisions of a by-law adopted by the shareholders may provide that the directors be divided into two, three, or four classes. All classes shall be as nearly equal in number as possible, and no class shall include less than three directors. The terms of office of the directors initially classified shall be as follows: that of the first class shall expire at the next annual meeting of shareholders, the second class at the succeeding annual meeting, the third class, if any, at the third succeeding annual meeting, and the fourth class, if any, at the fourth succeeding annual meeting.

(b) At each annual meeting after such initial classification, directors to replace those whose terms expire at such annual meeting shall be elected to hold office until the second succeeding annual meeting if there are two classes, the third succeeding annual meeting if there are three classes, or the fourth succeeding annual meeting if there are four classes.

(c) If directors are classified and the number of directors is thereafter changed:

(1) Any newly created directorships or any decrease in directorships shall be so apportioned among the classes as to make all classes as nearly equal in number as possible.

(2) When the number of directors is increased by the board and any newly created directorships are filled by the board, there shall be no classification of the additional directors until the next annual meeting of shareholders.

§ 705.   Newly created directorships and vacancies

(a) Newly created directorships resulting from an increase in the number of directors and vacancies occurring in the board for any reason except the removal of directors without cause may be filled by vote of the board.   . . .   Nothing in this paragraph shall affect any provision of the certificate of incorporation or the by-laws which provides that such newly created directorships or vacancies shall be filled by vote of the shareholders.   . . .

(b) Unless the certificate of incorporation or the specific provisions of a by-law adopted by the shareholders provides that the board may fill vacancies occurring by reason of the removal of directors without cause, such vacancies may be filled only by vote of the shareholders.

. . .

§ 706.   Removal of directors

(a) Any or all of the directors may be removed for cause by vote of the shareholders.   The certificate of incorporation or the specific provisions of a by-law adopted by the shareholders may provide for such removal by action of the board.   . . .

(b) If the certificate of incorporation or the by-laws so provide, any or all of the directors may be removed without cause by vote of the shareholders.

(c) The removal of directors, with or without cause, as provided in paragraphs (a) and (b) is subject to the following:

(1) In the case of a corporation having cumulative voting, no director may be removed when the votes cast against his removal would be sufficient to elect him.   . . .

(2) When by the provisions of the certificate of incorporation the holders of the shares of any class or series . . . voting as a class, are entitled to elect one or more directors, any director so elected may be removed only by the applicable vote of the holders of that class or series, . . . voting as a class.

4. The Delaware General Corporation Law, § 141(k), provides that "any director or the entire board of directors may be removed, with or without cause, by the holders of a majority of the shares then entitled to vote at an election of directors," with exceptions protecting cumulative voting, and with an exception that "(i) unless the certificate of incorporation otherwise provides, in the case of a corporation whose board is classified as provided in subsection (d) of this section, shareholders may effect such removal only for cause."   Subsection (d) of § 141 permits the certificate or the by-laws to provide that the board may be "divided into one, two, or three classes" to achieve staggered terms and for classification of shares for the purpose of electing directors.   How, if at all, does the Delaware law differ from the New York law?

Amendment of the articles of incorporation of a corporation requires, first, the adoption by the board of a resolution incorporating the amendment and, second, approval by a vote of the shareholders. See Del.Gen. Corp.Law § 242(b); N.Y.Bus.Corp.Law § 803 (following the basic two-step pattern but allowing certain minor amendments by action of the board alone).

PROBLEMS

1. Suppose Basic Press, Inc. has 100,000 shares outstanding, and is publicly held. You own 30,000 shares. The shares trade at $5.00 per share, but you have negotiated to sell your shares to the giant East Publishing Co. at $8.00 per share. Is there any legal impediment to the sale?

2. Suppose, instead, that Basic Press, Inc. has only four shareholders. Three of the shareholders own 30,000 shares each, and the fourth owns 10,000 shares. There is no market for the stock, and the company has issued no dividends for ten years. Suppose that the three major shareholders negotiate a sale of their stock to the East Publishing Co. Is there any legal impediment to the sale? Any ethical impediment?

3. Suppose, once again, that Basic Press is publicly held, and that you own 30,000 shares. You have negotiated a sale of your stock to the East Publishing Co.

(a) As a condition for closing the sale, East insists that Basic first replace its directors with East nominees. Is the agreement legally permissible?

(b) As a condition for closing the sale, East insists that Basic replace *one* of its directors with an East nominee. Is the agreement legally permissible?

(c) As a condition for closing the sale, East insists that the Basic directors appoint Mr. Greensmith, the CEO of East, to be the CEO of Basic. Is the agreement legally enforceable?

(d) Suppose that Basic is a closely held corporation. Would East be able to insist that Basic appoint Greensmith to be CEO of Basic?

CHAPTER 6

MERGERS, ACQUISITIONS, AND TAKEOVERS

SECTION 1. MERGERS AND ACQUISITIONS

A. THE DE FACTO MERGER DOCTRINE

INTRODUCTORY NOTE

In the first case that follows, Farris v. Glen Alden Corporation, two corporations, List Industries Corporation and Glen Alden Corporation, sought to combine. List was worth about three times as much as Glen Alden, so the List shareholders would wind up with about three quarters, and the Glen Alden shareholders one quarter, of the shares of the surviving corporation. Normally one would describe the combination as an acquisition of Glen Alden by List. One simple and obvious way to accomplish the combination would have been by a statutory merger.

A statutory merger is a combination accomplished by using a procedure prescribed in the state corporations laws (most of which are essentially the same in this respect). Under a statutory merger the terms of merger are spelled out in a document called a merger agreement, drafted by the parties, which prescribes, among other things, the treatment of the shareholders of each corporation. Considerable flexibility is available. In Farris v. Glen Alden, it was contemplated that the shareholders of each corporation would wind up owning stock in the surviving corporation. Thus, if the statutory merger procedure had been used, the merger agreement would have specified how many shares would go to the shareholders of each of the two corporations. It would have been natural to use List as the surviving corporation. Upon the filing of the merger agreement with the appropriate state official, Glen Alden would have disappeared and all the property interests, rights, and obligations of Glen Alden would have passed by law (under the merger provision of the corporation law) to List.

If the statutory merger procedure had been used, approval by votes of the boards of directors and the shareholders of each of the two corporations would have been required.[1] In addition, shareholders of each corporation who voted against the merger would have been entitled to demand that

---

1. Under the current laws of some states, no vote of a corporation's shareholders is required if the acquisition does not substantially diminish their control. See, e.g., Del.Gen.Corp. Law 251(f) (no vote necessary if new voting rights are less than 20 percent of total).

they be paid in cash the fair value of their shares (determined by agreement or, failing agreement, by a judicial proceeding). This right to be paid off is called the "appraisal right."

There are other ways in which combinations or, if you will, acquisitions, can be accomplished. These alternative methods are sometimes called "practical" mergers because they do not use the statutory procedure. One such alternative method would be that List would offer its shares to the shareholders of Glen Alden in return for their Glen Alden shares. By this method, List would seek to acquire enough Glen Alden shares to gain control of Glen Alden (and the offer could be made contingent on that outcome). Since the transaction would be between List and the individual shareholders of Glen Alden, no votes of the Glen Alden directors or shareholders would be required. Neither would there be any appraisal rights. Once it gained sufficient control of Glen Alden (typically, 90 percent), List could use a special procedure called a "short-form merger" to merge Glen Alden into List. List might also acquire Glen Alden shares for cash. And it might use a subsidiary to accomplish the acquisition. The common element would be a sale by the individual Glen Alden shareholders of their shares, for shares of List or for cash.

Another method of combination or acquisition would have List buy all the assets of Glen Alden for List stock (or for cash). Here List would deal with Glen Alden rather than with its shareholders. One supposed advantage of an assets acquisition is that the acquiring corporation does not succeed to unforeseen liabilities of the acquired corporation as it would under a statutory merger. (Known liabilities will be satisfied by the seller or assumed by the buyer and taken into account in the purchase price.) There is authority, however, for holding an acquiring corporation in an assets acquisition liable for product liabilities of the acquired corporation that did not arise until years after the asset transfer. See, e.g., Knapp v. North American Rockwell Corp., 506 F.2d 361 (3d Cir.1974), cert. denied, 421 U.S. 965 (1975).

If the assets-acquisition method had been used, Glen Alden would have been left with nothing but shares of List. Ordinarily, it would then have liquidated and distributed these shares to its shareholders. Glen Alden would have ceased to exist.

State laws vary on the requirement of a shareholder vote and on the availability of an appraisal right where a combination is accomplished by an asset acquisition.*

* Appraisal is generally thought of as a statutory protection associated with mergers, but the right to receive cash equal to the fair value of one's shares has also been granted as an equitable, judicially framed remedy. For example, in Jones v. Ahmanson, supra, Chapter 5, Sec. 6, the plaintiff was a shareholder who had been frozen out of a transaction in which the controlling shareholders' shares had been made marketable while the plaintiff's shares had not. As to damages, the court referred by analogy to the appraisal remedy for shareholders in mergers, and stated that the plaintiff should be entitled to damages equal to an appraised value (or, at her option, to an amount equal to the value of the defendants' shares). Similarly, in Alaska Plastics, Inc. v. Coppock, supra, Chap-

In Farris v. Glen Alden the combination was accomplished by having Glen Alden, the smaller corporation, acquire the assets of List (the minnow swallows the whale). To pay for the List assets, Glen Alden issued new shares to List, which in turn distributed them to its shareholders. The number of these shares was such that the List shareholders wound up owning 76.5 percent of the total number of outstanding shares of the surviving corporation, Glen Alden, which changed its name to List Alden.

Glen Alden was incorporated in Pennsylvania and List in Delaware. Under Delaware law, the sale of substantially all of the assets of List required the approval of a majority of the List shareholders, but the List shareholders did not have appraisal rights. Under Pennsylvania law, if Glen Alden had sold its assets to List, approval by a majority of the Glen Alden shareholders would have been required and dissenting shareholders would have had appraisal rights. Since, formally, Glen Alden acquired the assets of List, its position was that its shareholders were not entitled to appraisal rights (though a vote was required to authorize the issuance of the additional Glen Alden shares needed as consideration for the List assets).

It seems that the objective of casting the merger in the form that it took was to avoid appraisal rights. According to footnote 5 in the opinion, appraisal rights might have resulted in a cash drain that List considered unacceptable. It is not entirely clear why this should be a problem. If List were required to acquire shares for cash, it could sell new shares to the public to replace that cash. The result would be simply a new set of shareholders (as if the dissenting shareholders had sold their shares in the stock market). But that is easier said than done. Because of state and federal securities laws, selling shares to the public is sometimes costly and time consuming. Moreover, if appraisal rights had been available List could not have been certain of the total price that it would ultimately pay for Glen Alden.

It is also unclear why any Glen Alden shareholders would want appraisal rights. A majority of the Glen Alden shareholders did approve the transaction (in connection with approval of the issuance of new shares). Apparently, those shareholders found the deal attractive, which means that they thought their shares would not decline in value. Shareholders who did not like the idea of the combination with List could have sold their shares. It is difficult to see why they should be entitled to anything more in an appraisal proceeding than what they could have realized by a sale in the public market. This line of thought may explain why Delaware did not provide for appraisal rights in the case of a sale of substantially all the assets of a corporation and why, under present Delaware law, appraisal is not available in a merger if the shares relinquished are "(i) listed in a national securities exchange or (ii) held of record by more than 2,000 stockholders," and if the shares received have similar characteristics (e.g., voting and dividend rights). Del.Gen.Corp. Law § 262(b)(1).

ter 5, Sec. 5, the equitable remedy for oppression of a minority shareholder of a closely held corporation was a judgment for the fair value of the minority shareholder's shares.

Farris v. Glen Alden Corporation

393 Pa. 427, 143 A.2d 25 (1958).

Glen Alden is a Pennsylvania corporation engaged principally in the mining of anthracite coal and lately in the manufacture of air conditioning units and fire-fighting equipment. In recent years the company's operating revenue has declined substantially, and in fact, its coal operations have resulted in tax loss carryovers of approximately $14,000,000. In October 1957, List [Industries Corporation], a Delaware holding company owning interests in motion picture theaters, textile companies and real estate, and to a lesser extent, in oil and gas operations, warehouses and aluminum piston manufacturing, purchased through a wholly owned subsidiary 38.5% of Glen Alden's outstanding stock. This acquisition enabled List to place three of its directors on the Glen Alden board.

On March 20, 1958, the two corporations entered into a "reorganization agreement," subject to stockholder approval, which contemplated the following actions:

1. Glen Alden is to acquire all of the assets of List, excepting a small amount of cash reserved for the payment of List's expenses in connection with the transaction. These assets include over $8,000,000 in cash held chiefly in the treasuries of List's wholly owned subsidiaries.

2. In consideration of the transfer, Glen Alden is to issue 3,621,703 shares of stock to List. List in turn is to distribute the stock to its shareholders.   .   .   .

3. Further, Glen Alden is to assume all of List's liabilities including a $5,000,000 note incurred by List in order to purchase Glen Alden stock in 1957, outstanding stock options, incentive stock options plans, and pension obligations.

4. Glen Alden is to change its corporate name from Glen Alden Corporation to List Alden Corporation.

5. The present directors of both corporations are to become directors of List Alden.

6. List is to be dissolved and List Alden is to then carry on the operations of both former corporations.

Two days after the agreement was executed notice of the annual meeting of Glen Alden to be held on April 11, 1958, was mailed to the shareholders together with a proxy statement analyzing the reorganization agreement and recommending its approval as well as approval of certain amendments to Glen Alden's articles of incorporation and bylaws necessary to implement the agreement. At this meeting the holders of a majority of the outstanding shares, (not including those owned by List), voted in favor of a resolution approving the reorganization agreement.

On the day of the shareholders' meeting, plaintiff, a shareholder of Glen Alden, filed a complaint in equity against the corporation and its

officers seeking to enjoin them temporarily until final hearing, and perpetually thereafter, from executing and carrying out the agreement.

The gravamen of the complaint was that the notice of the annual
shareholders' meeting did not conform to the requirements of the Business
Corporation Law, 15 P.S. § 2852–1 et seq., in three respects: (1) It did not
give notice to the shareholders that the true intent and purpose of the
meeting was to effect a merger or consolidation of Glen Alden and List; (2)
It failed to give notice to the shareholders of their right to dissent to the
plan of merger or consolidation and claim fair value for their shares, and
(3) It did not contain copies of the text of certain sections of the Business
Corporation Law as required.[3]

By reason of these omissions, plaintiff contended that the approval of
the reorganization agreement by the shareholders at the annual meeting
was invalid and unless the carrying out of the plan were enjoined, he would
suffer irreparable loss by being deprived of substantial property rights.

The defendants answered admitting the material allegations of fact in
the complaint but denying that they gave rise to a cause of action because
the transaction complained of was a purchase of corporate assets as to
which shareholders had no rights of dissent or appraisal. For these
reasons the defendants then moved for judgment on the pleadings.[5]

The court below concluded that the reorganization agreement entered
into between the two corporations was a plan for a *de facto* merger, and
that therefore the failure of the notice of the annual meeting to conform to
the pertinent requirements of the merger provisions of the Business
Corporation Law rendered the notice defective and all proceedings in
furtherance of the agreement void. Wherefore, the court entered a final
decree denying defendants' motion for judgment on the pleadings, entering
judgment upon plaintiff's complaint and granting the injunctive relief
therein sought. This appeal followed.

When use of the corporate form of business organization first became
widespread, it was relatively easy for courts to define a "merger" or a "sale
of assets" and to label a particular transaction as one or the other.   .   .   .
But prompted by the desire to avoid the impact of adverse, and to obtain
the benefits of favorable, government regulations, particularly federal tax
laws, new accounting and legal techniques were developed by lawyers and
accountants which interwove the elements characteristic of each, thereby
creating hybrid forms of corporate amalgamation. Thus, it is no longer

---

3. The proxy statement included the
following declaration: "Appraisal Rights. In
the opinion of counsel, the shareholders of
neither Glen Alden nor List Industries will
have any rights of appraisal or similar rights
of dissenters with respect to any matter to be
acted upon at their respective meetings."

5. Counsel for the defendants concedes
that if the corporation is required to pay the
dissenting shareholders the appraised fair
value of their shares, the resultant drain of
cash would prevent Glen Alden from carrying
out the agreement. On the other hand,
plaintiff contends that if the shareholders
had been told of their rights as dissenters,
rather than specifically advised that they had
no such rights, the resolution approving the
reorganization agreement would have been
defeated.

helpful to consider an individual transaction in the abstract and solely by reference to the various elements therein determine whether it is a "merger" or a "sale." Instead, to determine properly the nature of a corporate transaction, we must refer not only to all the provisions of the agreement, but also to the consequences of the transaction and to the purposes of the provisions of the corporation law said to be applicable. We shall apply this principle to the instant case.

Section 908, subd. A of the Pennsylvania Business Corporation Law provides: "If any shareholder of a domestic corporation which becomes a party to a plan of merger or consolidation shall object to such plan of merger or consolidation . . . such shareholder shall be entitled to . . . [the fair value of his shares upon surrender of the share certificate or certificates representing his shares]." Act of May 5, 1933, P.L. 364, as amended, 15 P.S. § 2852–908, subd. A.[6]

This provision had its origin in the early decision of this Court in Lauman v. Lebanon Valley R.R. Co., 1858, 30 Pa. 42. There a shareholder who objected to the consolidation of his company with another was held to have a right in the absence of statute to treat the consolidation as a dissolution of his company and to receive the value of his shares upon their surrender.

The rationale of the Lauman case, and of the present section of the Business Corporation Law based thereon, is that when a corporation combines with another so as to lose its essential nature and alter the original fundamental relationships of the shareholders among themselves and to the corporation, a shareholder who does not wish to continue his membership therein may treat his membership in the original corporation as terminated and have the value of his shares paid to him.   . . .

Does the combination outlined in the present "reorganization" agreement so fundamentally change the corporate character of Glen Alden and the interest of the plaintiff as a shareholder therein, that to refuse him the rights and remedies of a dissenting shareholder would in reality force him to give up his stock in one corporation and against his will accept shares in another? If so, the combination is a merger within the meaning of section 908, subd. A of the corporation law.   . . .

If the reorganization agreement were consummated plaintiff would find that the "List Alden" resulting from the amalgamation would be quite a different corporation than the "Glen Alden" in which he is now a shareholder. Instead of continuing primarily as a coal mining company, Glen Alden would be transformed, after amendment of its articles of incorporation, into a diversified holding company whose interests would

---

6. Furthermore, section 902, subd. B provides that notice of the proposed merger and of the right to dissent thereto must be given the shareholders. "There shall be included in, or enclosed with . . . notice [of meeting of shareholders to vote on plan of merger] a copy or a summary of the plan of merger or plan of consolidation, as the case may be, and . . . a copy of subsection A of section 908 and of subsections B, C and D of section 515 of this act." Act of May 5, 1933, P.L. 364, § 902, subd. B, as amended, 15 P.S. § 2852–902, subd. B.

range from motion picture theaters to textile companies. Plaintiff would find himself a member of a company with assets of $169,000,000 and a long-term debt of $38,000,000 in lieu of a company one-half that size and with but one-seventh the long-term debt.

While the administration of the operations and properties of Glen Alden as well as List would be in the hands of management common to both companies, since all executives of List would be retained in List Alden, the control of Glen Alden would pass to the directors of List; for List would hold eleven of the seventeen directorships on the new board of directors.

As an aftermath of the transaction plaintiff's proportionate interest in Glen Alden would have been reduced to only two-fifths of what it presently is because of the issuance of an additional 3,621,703 shares to List which would not be subject to preemptive rights. In fact, ownership of Glen Alden would pass to the stockholders of List who would hold 76.5% of the outstanding shares as compared with but 23.5% retained by the present Glen Alden shareholders.

Perhaps the most important consequence to the plaintiff, if he were denied the right to have his shares redeemed at their fair value, would be the serious financial loss suffered upon consummation of the agreement. While the present book value of his stock is $38 a share after combination it would be worth only $21 a share. In contrast, the shareholders of List who presently hold stock with a total book value of $33,000,000 or $7.50 a share, would receive stock with a book value of $76,000,000 or $21 a share.

Under these circumstances it may well be said that if the proposed combination is allowed to take place without right of dissent, plaintiff would have his stock in Glen Alden taken away from him and the stock of a new company thrust upon him in its place. He would be projected against his will into a new enterprise under terms not of his own choosing. It was to protect dissident shareholders against just such a result that this Court one hundred years ago in the Lauman case, and the legislature thereafter in section 908, subd. A, granted the right of dissent. And it is to accord that protection to the plaintiff that we conclude that the combination proposed in the case at hand is a merger within the intendment of section 908, subd. A.

Nevertheless, defendants contend that the 1957 amendments to sections 311 and 908 of the corporation law preclude us from reaching this result and require the entry of judgment in their favor. Subsection F of section 311 dealing with the voluntary transfer of corporate assets provides: "The shareholders of a business corporation which acquires by sale, lease or exchange all or substantially all of the property of another corporation by the issuance of stock, securities or otherwise shall not be entitled to the rights and remedies of dissenting shareholders. . . ." Act of July 11, 1957, P.L. 711, § 1, 15 P.S. § 2852–311, subd. F.

And the amendment to section 908 reads as follows: "The right of dissenting shareholders . . . shall not apply to the purchase by a corporation of assets whether or not the consideration therefor be money or property, real or personal, including shares or bonds or other evidences of indebtedness of such corporation. The shareholders of such corporation shall have no right to dissent from any such purchase." Act of July 11, 1957, P.L. 711, § 1, 15 P.S. § 2852–908, subd. C.

Defendants view these amendments as abridging the right of shareholders to dissent to a transaction between two corporations which involves a transfer of assets for a consideration even though the transfer has all the legal incidents of a merger. They claim that only if the merger is accomplished in accordance with the prescribed statutory procedure does the right of dissent accrue. In support of this position they cite to us the comment on the amendments by the Committee on Corporation Law of the Pennsylvania Bar Association, the committee which originally drafted these provisions. The comment states that the provisions were intended to overrule cases which granted shareholders the right to dissent to a sale of assets when accompanied by the legal incidents of a merger. See 61 Ann.Rep.Pa.Bar Ass'n 277, 284 (1957).[7] Whatever may have been the intent of the *committee,* there is no evidence to indicate that the *legislature* intended the 1957 amendments to have the effect contended for. But furthermore, the language of these two provisions does not support the opinion of the committee and is inapt to achieve any such purpose. The amendments of 1957 do not provide that a transaction between two corporations which has the effect of a merger but which includes a transfer of assets for consideration is to be exempt from the protective provisions of sections 908, subd. A and 515. They provide only that the shareholders of a corporation which acquires the property or purchases the assets of another corporation, *without more,* are not entitled to the right to dissent from the transaction. So, as in the present case, when as part of a transaction between two corporations, one corporation dissolves, its liabilities are assumed by the survivor, its executives and directors take over the management and control of the survivor, and, as consideration for the transfer, its stockholders acquire a majority of the shares of stock of the survivor, then the transaction is no longer simply a purchase of assets or acquisition of property to which sections 311, subd. F and 908, subd. C apply, but a merger governed by section 908, subd. A of the corporation

---

7. "The amendment to Section 311 expressly provides that a sale, lease or exchange of substantially all corporate assets in connection with its liquidation or dissolution is subject to the provisions of Article XI of the Act, and that no consent or authorization of shareholders other than what is required by Article XI is necessary. The recent decision in Marks v. Autocar Co., D.C.E.D.Pa., Civil Action No. 16075 [153 F.Supp. 768] is to the contrary. This amendment, together with the proposed amendment to Section 1104 expressly permitting the directors in liquidating the corporation to sell only such assets as may be required to pay its debts and distribute any assets remaining among shareholders (Section 1108, [subd.] B now so provides in the case of receivers) have the effect of overruling Marks v. Autocar Co., . . . which permits a shareholder dissenting from such a sale to obtain the fair value of his shares. The Marks case relies substantially on Bloch v. Baldwin Locomotive Works, 75 [Pa.] Dist. & Co. R. 24, also believed to be an undesirable decision. That case permitted a holder of stock in a corporation which *purchased* for stock all the assets of another corporation to obtain the fair value of his shares. That case is also in effect overruled by the new Sections 311 [subd.] F and 908 [subd.] C." 61 Ann. Rep.Pa.Bar Ass'n, 277, 284 (1957).

law. To divest shareholders of their right of dissent under such circumstances would require express language which is absent from the 1957 amendments.

Even were we to assume that the combination provided for in the reorganization agreement is a "sale of assets" to which section 908, subd. A does not apply, it would avail the defendants nothing; we will not blind our eyes to the realities of the transaction. Despite the designation of the parties and the form employed, Glen Alden does not in fact acquire List, rather, List acquires Glen Alden, . . . and under section 311, subd. D [8] the right of dissent would remain with the shareholders of Glen Alden.

We hold that the combination contemplated by the reorganization agreement, although consummated by contract rather than in accordance with the statutory procedure, is a merger within the protective purview of sections 908, subd. A and 515 of the corporation law. The shareholders of Glen Alden should have been notified accordingly and advised of their statutory rights of dissent and appraisal. The failure of the corporate officers to take these steps renders the stockholder approval of the agreement at the 1958 shareholders' meeting invalid. The lower court did not err in enjoining the officers and directors of Glen Alden from carrying out this agreement.

Decree affirmed at appellants' cost.

AFTERMATH

After the decision in Farris v. Glen Alden, the Pennsylvania legislature again modified its corporation law in an effort to defeat the de facto merger doctrine. The new law was tested in Terry v. Penn Central Corporation, 668 F.2d 188 (3d Cir.1981). Penn Central had embarked on a program of acquisitions. To accomplish these acquisitions it formed a wholly owned subsidiary. The subsidiary, rather than Penn Central, acquired the target corporations, through mergers. One of the questions presented in *Terry* was whether an acquisition by merger with a subsidiary should be treated as a de facto merger with the parent, Penn Central, thereby giving the parent shareholders voting and appraisal rights. The court held that it should not, relying on the modifications in the Pennsylvania law and on a statement in a preamble to the new law stating that the objective was to "abolish the doctrine of de facto mergers." [2]

8. "If any shareholder of a business corporation which sells, leases or exchanges all or substantially all of its property and assets otherwise than (1) in the usual and regular course of its business, (2) for the purpose of relocating its business, or (3) in connection with its dissolution and liquidation, shall object to such sale, lease or exchange and comply with the provisions of section 515 of this act, such shareholder shall be entitled to the rights and remedies of dissenting shareholders as therein provided." Act of July 11, 1957, P.L. 711, 15 P.S. § 2852–311, subd. D.

2. To confuse matters, however, the court in *Terry* added, "A different result might be reached if here, as in *Farris,* the acquiring corporation were significantly smaller than the acquired corporation such

ANALYSIS

1.   How should the language of the Pennsylvania corporate law applicable in Farris v. Glen Alden have been drafted to accomplish the apparent objective of the members of the Committee on Corporation Law of the Pennsylvania Bar Association?   What arguments would you offer in support of that objective?

2.   Why does the court hold that the transaction was de facto a merger rather than an asset acquisition by List?   Would it make any difference?

3.   Suppose Glen Alden had had a market value of $10,000,000 and 1 million shares outstanding and that it had sold 3 million new shares for $30,000,000 cash and used the cash to buy all the assets of List.   If the de facto merger doctrine were still the law (as it is in some other states [3]), would it apply to these facts?

Hariton v. Arco Electronics, Inc.

188 A.2d 123 (Del.1963).

This case involves a sale of assets under § 271 of the corporation law, 8 Del.C.   .   .   . [The issue] may be stated as follows:

A sale of assets is effected under § 271 in consideration of shares of stock of the purchasing corporation.   The agreement of sale embodies also a plan to dissolve the selling corporation and distribute the shares so received to the stockholders of the seller, so as to accomplish the same result as would be accomplished by a merger of the seller into the purchaser.   Is the sale legal?

The facts are these:

The defendant Arco and Loral Electronics Corporation, a New York corporation, are both engaged, in somewhat different forms, in the electronic equipment business.   In the summer of 1961 they negotiated for an amalgamation of the companies.   As of October 27, 1961, they entered into a "Reorganization Agreement and Plan."   The provisions of this Plan pertinent here are in substance as follows:

1.   Arco agrees to sell all its assets to Loral in consideration (inter alia) of the issuance to it of 283,000 shares of Loral.

2.   Arco agrees to call a stockholders meeting for the purpose of approving the Plan and the voluntary dissolution.

3.   Arco agrees to distribute to its stockholders all the Loral shares received by it as a part of the complete liquidation of Arco.

that the acquisition greatly transformed the nature of the successor corporation."   668 F.2d at 194, n. 7.

   3.   See Rath v. Rath Packing Co., 257 Iowa 1277, 136 N.W.2d 410 (1965); Apple-stein v. United Board & Carton Corp., 60 N.J.Super. 333, 159 A.2d 146, aff'd, 33 N.J. 72, 161 A.2d 474 (1960).

At the Arco meeting all the stockholders voting (about 80%) approved the Plan. It was thereafter consummated.

Plaintiff, a stockholder who did not vote at the meeting, sued to enjoin the consummation of the Plan on the grounds (1) that it was illegal, and (2) that it was unfair. The second ground was abandoned. Affidavits and documentary evidence were filed, and defendant moved for summary judgment and dismissal of the complaint. The Vice Chancellor granted the motion and plaintiff appeals.

The question before us we have stated above. Plaintiff's argument that the sale is illegal runs as follows:

The several steps taken here accomplish the same result as a merger of Arco into Loral. In a "true" sale of assets, the stockholder of the seller retains the right to elect whether the selling company shall continue as a holding company. Moreover, the stockholder of the selling company is forced to accept an investment in a new enterprise without the right of appraisal granted under the merger statute. § 271 cannot therefore be legally combined with a dissolution proceeding under § 275 and a consequent distribution of the purchaser's stock. Such a proceeding is a misuse of the power granted under § 271, and a *de facto* merger results.

Plaintiff's contention that this sale has achieved the same result as a merger is plainly correct. . . . Accepting it as correct, we noted that this result is made possible by the overlapping scope of the merger statute and section 271. . . .

We . . . hold that the reorganization here accomplished through § 271 and a mandatory plan of dissolution and distribution is legal. This is so because the sale-of-assets statute and the merger statute are independent of each other. They are, so to speak, of equal dignity, and the framers of a reorganization plan may resort to either type of corporate mechanics to achieve the desired end. This is not an anomalous result in our corporation law. As the Vice Chancellor pointed out, the elimination of accrued dividends, though forbidden under a charter amendment . . . may be accomplished by a merger. . . .

Plaintiff concedes, as we read his brief, that if the several steps taken in this case had been taken separately they would have been legal. That is, he concedes that a sale of assets, followed by a separate proceeding to dissolve and distribute, would be legal, even though the same result would follow. This concession exposes the weakness of his contention. To attempt to make any such distinction between sales under § 271 would be to create uncertainty in the law and invite litigation.

ANALYSIS

Is there any good reason why the Delaware legislature would allow shareholders to choose appraisal rights in a statutory merger but not in an asset sale that accomplishes the same result as a statutory merger?

PROBLEM

Suppose you represent Donna, who has just agreed with Eve and Fred to form a Delaware corporation to own and operate a furniture manufacturing business. They have hired a lawyer, who is in the process of creating a simple form-book corporation with no ancillary agreements. They contemplate that Donna will be responsible for marketing and sales, Eve for manufacturing and operations, and Fred for research, design, and development. Each will own one-third of the shares of common stock of the corporation. Donna tells you that in the furniture manufacturing business, mergers and acquisitions are commonplace. In fact, she and Eve and Fred all expect that once their company has established itself, their best prospects for further growth will probably require some sort of combination with one or more other firms. Donna also tells you that Eve and Fred have been friends for a few years and she is concerned that they might act together in ways that might be to her detriment (for example, by approving a merger that would result in a firm in which they would have lucrative jobs but she would not). On the other hand, Donna thinks that both Eve and Fred tend at times to be petulant and petty. Donna can easily imagine a falling out between Eve and Fred and an alliance of herself with one of them. She asks for your advice on what she might do to protect herself in the event of a merger. What is your response?

B.   FREEZE–OUT MERGERS

Weinberger v. UOP, Inc.

457 A.2d 701 (Del.Sup.1983) (en banc).

This post-trial appeal was reheard en banc from a decision of the Court of Chancery. It was brought by the class action plaintiff below, a former shareholder of UOP, Inc., who challenged the elimination of UOP's minority shareholders by a cash-out merger between UOP and its majority owner, The Signal Companies, Inc. Originally, the defendants in this action were Signal, UOP, certain officers and directors of those companies, and UOP's investment banker, Lehman Brothers Kuhn Loeb, Inc. The present Chancellor held that the terms of the merger were fair to the plaintiff and the other minority shareholders of UOP. Accordingly, he entered judgment in favor of the defendants.

Numerous points were raised by the parties, but we address only the following questions presented by the trial court's opinion:

1) The plaintiff's duty to plead sufficient facts demonstrating the unfairness of the challenged merger;

2) The burden of proof upon the parties where the merger has been approved by the purportedly informed vote of a majority of the minority shareholders;

3) The fairness of the merger in terms of adequacy of the defendants' disclosures to the minority shareholders;

4) The fairness of the merger in terms of adequacy of the price paid for the minority shares and the remedy appropriate to that issue; and

5) The continued force and effect of Singer v. Magnavox Co., Del.Supr., 380 A.2d 969, 980 (1977), and its progeny.

In ruling for the defendants, the Chancellor re-stated his earlier conclusion that the plaintiff in a suit challenging a cash-out merger must allege specific acts of fraud, misrepresentation, or other items of misconduct to demonstrate the unfairness of the merger terms to the minority. We approve this rule and affirm it.

The Chancellor also held that even though the ultimate burden of proof is on the majority shareholder to show by a preponderance of the evidence that the transaction is fair, it is first the burden of the plaintiff attacking the merger to demonstrate some basis for invoking the fairness obligation. We agree with that principle. However, where corporate action has been approved by an informed vote of a majority of the minority shareholders, we conclude that the burden entirely shifts to the plaintiff to show that the transaction was unfair to the minority.   . . .   But in all this, the burden clearly remains on those relying on the vote to show that they completely disclosed all material facts relevant to the transaction.

Here, the record does not support a conclusion that the minority stockholder vote was an informed one. Material information, necessary to acquaint those shareholders with the bargaining positions of Signal and UOP, was withheld under circumstances amounting to a breach of fiduciary duty. We therefore conclude that this merger does not meet the test of fairness, at least as we address that concept, and no burden thus shifted to the plaintiff by reason of the minority shareholder vote. Accordingly, we reverse and remand for further proceedings consistent herewith.

In considering the nature of the remedy available under our law to minority shareholders in a cash-out merger, we believe that it is, and hereafter should be, an appraisal under 8 Del.C. § 262 as hereinafter construed. . . .   But to give full effect to section 262 within the framework of the General Corporation Law we adopt a more liberal, less rigid and stylized, approach to the valuation process than has heretofore been permitted by our courts. While the present state of these proceedings does not admit the plaintiff to the appraisal remedy per se, the practical effect of the remedy we do grant him will be co-extensive with the liberalized valuation and appraisal methods we herein approve for cases coming after this decision.

Our treatment of these matters has necessarily led us to a reconsideration of the business purpose rule announced in the trilogy of *Singer v. Magnavox Co.*, supra; Tanzer v. International General Industries, Inc., Del.Supr., 379 A.2d 1121 (1977); and Roland International Corp. v. Najjar, Del.Supr., 407 A.2d 1032 (1979). For the reasons hereafter set forth we consider that the business purpose requirement of these cases is no longer the law of Delaware.

I.

. . .

Signal is a diversified, technically based company operating through various subsidiaries. Its stock is publicly traded on the New York, Philadelphia and Pacific Stock Exchanges. UOP, formerly known as Universal Oil Products Company, was a diversified industrial company engaged in various lines of business, including petroleum and petro-chemical services and related products, construction, fabricated metal products, transportation equipment products, chemicals and plastics, and other products and services including land development, lumber products and waste disposal. Its stock was publicly held and listed on the New York Stock Exchange.

In 1974 Signal sold one of its wholly-owned subsidiaries for $420,000,-000 in cash.   . . . While looking to invest this cash surplus, Signal became interested in UOP as a possible acquisition. Friendly negotiations ensued, and Signal proposed to acquire a controlling interest in UOP at a price of $19 per share. UOP's representatives sought $25 per share. In the arm's length bargaining that followed, an understanding was reached whereby Signal agreed to purchase from UOP 1,500,000 shares of UOP's authorized but unissued stock at $21 per share.

This purchase was contingent upon Signal making a successful cash tender offer for 4,300,000 publicly held shares of UOP, also at a price of $21 per share. This combined method of acquisition permitted Signal to acquire 5,800,000 shares of stock, representing 50.5% of UOP's outstanding shares. The UOP board of directors advised the company's shareholders that it had no objection to Signal's tender offer at that price. Immediately before the announcement of the tender offer, UOP's common stock had been trading on the New York Stock Exchange at a fraction under $14 per share.

The negotiations between Signal and UOP occurred during April 1975, and the resulting tender offer was greatly oversubscribed. However, Signal limited its total purchase of the tendered shares so that, when coupled with the stock bought from UOP, it had achieved its goal of becoming a 50.5% shareholder of UOP.

Although UOP's board consisted of thirteen directors, Signal nominated and elected only six. Of these, five were either directors or employees of Signal. The sixth, a partner in the banking firm of Lazard Freres & Co., had been one of Signal's representatives in the negotiations and bargaining with UOP concerning the tender offer and purchase price of the UOP shares.

However, the president and chief executive officer of UOP retired during 1975, and Signal caused him to be replaced by James V. Crawford, a long-time employee and senior executive vice president of one of Signal's wholly-owned subsidiaries. Crawford succeeded his predecessor on UOP's board of directors and also was made a director of Signal.

By the end of 1977 Signal basically was unsuccessful in finding other suitable investment candidates for its excess cash, and by February 1978 considered that it had no other realistic acquisitions available to it on a friendly basis. Once again its attention turned to UOP.

The trial court found that at the instigation of certain Signal management personnel, including William W. Walkup, its board chairman, and Forrest N. Shumway, its president, a feasibility study was made concerning the possible acquisition of the balance of UOP's outstanding shares. This study was performed by two Signal officers, Charles S. Arledge, vice president (director of planning), and Andrew J. Chitiea, senior vice president (chief financial officer). Messrs. Walkup, Shumway, Arledge and Chitiea were all directors of UOP in addition to their membership on the Signal board.

Arledge and Chitiea concluded that it would be a good investment for Signal to acquire the remaining 49.5% of UOP shares at any price up to $24 each. Their report was discussed between Walkup and Shumway who, along with Arledge, Chitiea and Brewster L. Arms, internal counsel for Signal, constituted Signal's senior management. In particular, they talked about the proper price to be paid if the acquisition was pursued, purportedly keeping in mind that as UOP's majority shareholder, Signal owed a fiduciary responsibility to both its own stockholders as well as to UOP's minority. It was ultimately agreed that a meeting of Signal's executive committee would be called to propose that Signal acquire the remaining outstanding stock of UOP through a cash-out merger in the range of $20 to $21 per share.

The executive committee meeting was set for February 28, 1978. As a courtesy, UOP's president, Crawford, was invited to attend, although he was not a member of Signal's executive committee. On his arrival, and prior to the meeting, Crawford was asked to meet privately with Walkup and Shumway. He was then told of Signal's plan to acquire full ownership of UOP and was asked for his reaction to the proposed price range of $20 to $21 per share. Crawford said he thought such a price would be "generous," and that it was certainly one which should be submitted to UOP's minority shareholders for their ultimate consideration. . . .

Thus, Crawford voiced no objection to the $20 to $21 price range, nor did he suggest that Signal should consider paying more than $21 per share for the minority interests. Later, at the executive committee meeting the same factors were discussed, with Crawford repeating the position he earlier took with Walkup and Shumway. Also considered was the 1975 tender offer and the fact that it had been greatly oversubscribed at $21 per share. . . .

Thus, it was the consensus that a price of $20 to $21 per share would be fair to both Signal and the minority shareholders of UOP. Signal's executive committee authorized its management "to negotiate" with UOP "for a cash acquisition of the minority ownership in UOP, Inc., with the intention of presenting a proposal to [Signal's] board of directors . . . on March 6, 1978." . . .

Between Tuesday, February 28, 1978 and Monday, March 6, 1978, a total of four business days, Crawford spoke by telephone with all of UOP's non-Signal, i.e., outside, directors. Also during that period, Crawford retained Lehman Brothers to render a fairness opinion as to the price offered the minority for its stock. He gave two reasons for this choice. First, the time schedule between the announcement and the board meetings was short (by then only three business days) and since Lehman Brothers had been acting as UOP's investment banker for many years, Crawford felt that it would be in the best position to respond on such brief notice. Second, James W. Glanville, a long-time director of UOP and a partner in Lehman Brothers, had acted as a financial advisor to UOP for many years. Crawford believed that Glanville's familiarity with UOP, as a member of its board, would also be of assistance in enabling Lehman Brothers to render a fairness opinion within the existing time constraints.

Crawford telephoned Glanville, who gave his assurance that Lehman Brothers had no conflicts that would prevent it from accepting the task. Glanville's immediate personal reaction was that a price of $20 to $21 would certainly be fair, since it represented almost a 50% premium over UOP's market price.   . . .

Glanville assembled a three-man Lehman Brothers team to do the work on the fairness opinion. These persons examined relevant documents and information concerning UOP, including its annual reports and its Securities and Exchange Commission filings from 1973 through 1976, as well as its audited financial statements for 1977, its interim reports to shareholders, and its recent and historical market prices and trading volumes. In addition, on Friday, March 3, 1978, two members of the Lehman Brothers team flew to UOP's headquarters in Des Plaines, Illinois, to perform a "due diligence" visit, during the course of which they interviewed Crawford as well as UOP's general counsel, its chief financial officer, and other key executives and personnel.

As a result, the Lehman Brothers team concluded that "the price of either $20 or $21 would be a fair price for the remaining shares of UOP." They telephoned this impression to Glanville, who was spending the weekend in Vermont.

. . .

On March 6, 1978, both the Signal and UOP boards were convened to consider the proposed merger.   . . .

First, Signal's board unanimously adopted a resolution authorizing Signal to propose to UOP a cash merger of $21 per share as outlined in a certain merger agreement and other supporting documents. This proposal required that the merger be approved by a majority of UOP's outstanding minority shares voting at the stockholders meeting at which the merger would be considered, and that the minority shares voting in favor of the merger, when coupled with Signal's 50.5% interest would have to comprise at least two-thirds of all UOP shares. Otherwise the proposed merger would be deemed disapproved.

UOP's board then considered the proposal. Copies of the agreement were delivered to the directors in attendance, and other copies had been forwarded earlier to the directors participating by telephone. They also had before them UOP financial data for 1974–1977, UOP's most recent financial statements, market price information, and budget projections for 1978. In addition they had Lehman Brothers' hurriedly prepared fairness opinion letter finding the price of $21 to be fair. Glanville, the Lehman Brothers partner, and UOP director, commented on the information that had gone into preparation of the letter.

. . .

. . . While Signal's men on UOP's board participated in various aspects of the meeting, they abstained from voting. However, the minutes show that each of them "if voting would have voted yes."

. . .

Despite the swift board action of the two companies, the merger was not submitted to UOP's shareholders until their annual meeting on May 26, 1978. . . .

As of the record date of UOP's annual meeting, there were 11,488,302 shares of UOP common stock outstanding, 5,688,302 of which were owned by the minority. At the meeting only 56%, or 3,208,652, of the minority shares were voted. Of these, 2,953,812, or 51.9% of the total minority, voted for the merger, and 254,840 voted against it. When Signal's stock was added to the minority shares voting in favor, a total of 76.2% of UOP's outstanding shares approved the merger while only 2.2% opposed it.

By its terms the merger became effective on May 26, 1978, and each share of UOP's stock held by the minority was automatically converted into a right to receive $21 cash.

II.

A.

A primary issue mandating reversal is the preparation by two UOP directors, Arledge and Chitiea, of their feasibility study for the exclusive use and benefit of Signal. This document was of obvious significance to both Signal and UOP. Using UOP data, it described the advantages to Signal of ousting the minority at a price range of $21–$24 per share.

. . .

Having written [their report] solely for the use of Signal, it is clear from the record that neither Arledge nor Chitiea shared this report with their fellow directors of UOP. We are satisfied that no one else did either. This conduct hardly meets the fiduciary standards applicable to such a transaction. . . .

The Arledge–Chitiea report speaks for itself in supporting the Chancellor's finding that a price of up to $24 was a "good investment" for Signal. It shows that a return on the investment at $21 would be 15.7% versus

15.5% at $24 per share. This was a difference of only two-tenths of one percent, while it meant over $17,000,000 to the minority. Under such circumstances, paying UOP's minority shareholders $24 would have had relatively little long-term effect on Signal, and the Chancellor's findings concerning the benefit to Signal, even at a price of $24, were obviously correct. . . .

Certainly, this was a matter of material significance to UOP and its shareholders. Since the study was prepared by two UOP directors, using UOP information for the exclusive benefit of Signal, and nothing whatever was done to disclose it to the outside UOP directors or the minority shareholders, a question of breach of fiduciary duty arises. This problem occurs because there were common Signal–UOP directors participating, at least to some extent, in the UOP board's decision-making processes without full disclosure of the conflicts they faced.[7]

B.

In assessing this situation, the Court of Chancery was required to:

examine what information defendants had and to measure it against what they gave to the minority stockholders, in a context in which "complete candor" is required. In other words, the limited function of the Court was to determine whether defendants had disclosed all information in their possession germane to the transaction in issue. And by "germane" we mean, for present purposes, information such as a reasonable shareholder would consider important in deciding whether to sell or retain stock.

* * * * * *

. . . Completeness, not adequacy, is both the norm and the mandate under present circumstances.

Lynch v. Vickers Energy Corp., Del.Supr., 383 A.2d 278, 281 (1977) (*Lynch I*). This is merely stating in another way the long-existing principle of Delaware law that these Signal designated directors on UOP's board still owed UOP and its shareholders an uncompromising duty of loyalty. . . .

Given the absence of any attempt to structure this transaction on an arm's length basis, Signal cannot escape the effects of the conflicts it faced, particularly when its designees on UOP's board did not totally abstain from participation in the matter. There is no "safe harbor" for such divided loyalties in Delaware. When directors of a Delaware corporation are on

7. Although perfection is not possible, or expected, the result here could have been entirely different if UOP had appointed an independent negotiating committee of its outside directors to deal with Signal at arm's length. . . . Since fairness in this context can be equated to conduct by a theoretical, wholly independent, board of directors acting upon the matter before them, it is unfortunate that this course apparently was neither considered nor pursued. . . . Particularly in a parent-subsidiary context, a showing that the action taken was as though each of the contending parties had in fact exerted its bargaining power against the other at arm's length is strong evidence that the transaction meets the test of fairness. . . .

both sides of a transaction, they are required to demonstrate their utmost good faith and the most scrupulous inherent fairness of the bargain. . . .

There is no dilution of this obligation where one holds dual or multiple directorships, as in a parent-subsidiary context. . . . Thus, individuals who act in a dual capacity as directors of two corporations, one of whom is parent and the other subsidiary, owe the same duty of good management to both corporations, and in the absence of an independent negotiating structure (see note 7, supra), or the directors' total abstention from any participation in the matter, this duty is to be exercised in light of what is best for both companies. . . . The record demonstrates that Signal has not met this obligation.

C.

The concept of fairness has two basic aspects: fair dealing and fair price. The former embraces questions of when the transaction was timed, how it was initiated, structured, negotiated, disclosed to the directors, and how the approvals of the directors and the stockholders were obtained. The latter aspect of fairness relates to the economic and financial considerations of the proposed merger, including all relevant factors: assets, market value, earnings, future prospects, and any other elements that affect the intrinsic or inherent value of a company's stock. . . . However, the test for fairness is not a bifurcated one as between fair dealing and price. All aspects of the issue must be examined as a whole since the question is one of entire fairness. However, in a non-fraudulent transaction we recognize that price may be the preponderant consideration outweighing other features of the merger. Here, we address the two basic aspects of fairness separately because we find reversible error as to both.

D.

Part of fair dealing is the obvious duty of candor required by *Lynch I, supra.* Moreover, one possessing superior knowledge may not mislead any stockholder by use of corporate information to which the latter is not privy. . . . Delaware has long imposed this duty even upon persons who are not corporate officers or directors, but who nonetheless are privy to matters of interest or significance to their company. . . . With the well-established Delaware law on the subject, and the Court of Chancery's findings of fact here, it is inevitable that the obvious conflicts posed by Arledge and Chitiea's preparation of their "feasibility study," derived from UOP information, for the sole use and benefit of Signal, cannot pass muster.

The Arledge–Chitiea report is but one aspect of the element of fair dealing. How did this merger evolve? It is clear that it was entirely initiated by Signal. The serious time constraints under which the principals acted were all set by Signal. It had not found a suitable outlet for its excess cash and considered UOP a desirable investment, particularly since it was now in a position to acquire the whole company for itself. For whatever reasons, and they were only Signal's, the entire transaction was presented to and approved by UOP's board within four business days. Standing alone, this is not necessarily indicative of any lack of fairness by a majority shareholder. It was what occurred, or more properly, what did not occur, during this brief period that makes the time constraints imposed by Signal relevant to the issue of fairness.

The structure of the transaction, again, was Signal's doing. So far as negotiations were concerned, it is clear that they were modest at best. Crawford, Signal's man at UOP, never really talked price with Signal, except to accede to its management's statements on the subject, and to convey to Signal the UOP outside directors' view that as between the $20–$21 range under consideration, it would have to be $21. The latter is not a surprising outcome, but hardly arm's length negotiations. Only the protection of benefits for UOP's key employees and the issue of Lehman Brothers' fee approached any concept of bargaining.

As we have noted, the matter of disclosure to the UOP directors was wholly flawed by the conflicts of interest raised by the Arledge–Chitiea report. All of those conflicts were resolved by Signal in its own favor without divulging any aspect of them to UOP.

This cannot but undermine a conclusion that this merger meets any reasonable test of fairness. The outside UOP directors lacked one material piece of information generated by two of their colleagues, but shared only with Signal. True, the UOP board had the Lehman Brothers' fairness opinion, but that firm has been blamed by the plaintiff for the hurried task it performed, when more properly the responsibility for this lies with Signal. There was no disclosure of the circumstances surrounding the rather cursory preparation of the Lehman Brothers' fairness opinion. Instead, the impression was given UOP's minority that a careful study had been made, when in fact speed was the hallmark, and Mr. Glanville, Lehman's partner in charge of the matter, and also a UOP director, having spent the weekend in Vermont, brought a draft of the "fairness opinion letter" to the UOP directors' meeting on March 6, 1978 with the price left blank. We can only conclude from the record that the rush imposed on Lehman Brothers by Signal's timetable contributed to the difficulties under which this investment banking firm attempted to perform its responsibilities. Yet, none of this was disclosed to UOP's minority.

Finally, the minority stockholders were denied the critical information that Signal considered a price of $24 to be a good investment. Since this would have meant over $17,000,000 more to the minority, we cannot conclude that the shareholder vote was an informed one. Under the circumstances, an approval by a majority of the minority was meaningless. . . .

Given these particulars and the Delaware law on the subject, the record does not establish that this transaction satisfies any reasonable concept of fair dealing, and the Chancellor's findings in that regard must be reversed.

E.

Turning to the matter of price, plaintiff also challenges its fairness. His evidence was that on the date the merger was approved the stock was worth at least $26 per share. In support, he offered the testimony of a chartered investment analyst who used two basic approaches to valuation: a comparative analysis of the premium paid over market in ten other tender offer-merger combinations, and a discounted cash flow analysis.

In this breach of fiduciary duty case, the Chancellor perceived that the approach to valuation was the same as that in an appraisal proceeding. Consistent with precedent, he rejected plaintiff's method of proof and accepted defendants' evidence of value as being in accord with practice under prior case law. This means that the so-called "Delaware block" or weighted average method was employed wherein the elements of value, i.e., assets, market price, earnings, etc., were assigned a particular weight and the resulting amounts added to determine the value per share.   . . . This procedure has been in use for decades. However, to the extent it excludes other generally accepted techniques used in the financial community and the courts, it is now clearly outmoded. It is time we recognize this in appraisal and other stock valuation proceedings and bring our law current on the subject.

While the Chancellor rejected plaintiff's discounted cash flow method of valuing UOP's stock, as not corresponding with "either logic or the existing law" (426 A.2d at 1360), it is significant that this was essentially the focus, i.e., earnings potential of UOP, of Messrs. Arledge and Chitiea in their evaluation of the merger. Accordingly, the standard "Delaware block" or weighted average method of valuation, formerly employed in appraisal and other stock valuation cases, shall no longer exclusively control such proceedings. We believe that a more liberal approach must include proof of value by any techniques or methods which are generally considered acceptable in the financial community and otherwise admissible in court, subject only to our interpretation of 8 Del.C. § 262(h), *in-fra*.   . . .

Fair price obviously requires consideration of all relevant factors involving the value of a company.   . . .

This is not only in accord with the realities of present day affairs, but it is thoroughly consonant with the purpose and intent of our statutory law. Under 8 Del.C. § 262(h), the Court of Chancery:

> shall appraise the shares, determining their *fair* value exclusive of any element of value arising from the accomplishment or expectation of the merger, together with a fair rate of interest, if any, to be paid upon the amount determined to be the *fair* value. In determining such *fair* value, the Court shall take into account *all relevant factors* . . . (Emphasis added) . . .

It is significant that section 262 now mandates the determination of "fair" value based upon "all relevant factors." Only the speculative elements of value that may arise from the "accomplishment or expectation" of the merger are excluded.   We take this to be a very narrow exception to the appraisal process, designed to eliminate use of *pro forma* data and projections of a speculative variety relating to the completion of a merger.   But elements of future value, including the nature of the enterprise, which are known or susceptible of proof as of the date of the merger and not the product of speculation, may be considered.   When the trial court deems it appropriate, fair value also includes any damages, resulting from the taking, which the stockholders sustain as a class.   .   .   .

Although the Chancellor received the plaintiff's evidence, his opinion indicates that the use of it was precluded because of past Delaware practice. While we do not suggest a monetary result one way or the other, we do think the plaintiff's evidence should be part of the factual mix and weighed as such.   Until the $21 price is measured on remand by the valuation standards mandated by Delaware law, there can be no finding at the present stage of these proceedings that the price is fair.   Given the lack of any candid disclosure of the material facts surrounding establishment of the $21 price, the majority of the minority vote, approving the merger, is meaningless.

.   .   .

While a plaintiff's monetary remedy ordinarily should be confined to the more liberalized appraisal proceeding herein established, we do not intend any limitation on the historic powers of the Chancellor to grant such other relief as the facts of a particular case may dictate.   The appraisal remedy we approve may not be adequate in certain cases, particularly where fraud, misrepresentation, self-dealing, deliberate waste of corporate assets, or gross and palpable overreaching are involved.   .   .   .   Under such circumstances, the Chancellor's powers are complete to fashion any form of equitable and monetary relief as may be appropriate, including rescissory damages.   Since it is apparent that this long completed transaction is too involved to undo, and in view of the Chancellor's discretion, the award, if any, should be in the form of monetary damages based upon entire fairness standards, i.e., fair dealing and fair price.

.   .   .

III.

Finally, we address the matter of business purpose.   The defendants contend that the purpose of this merger was not a proper subject of inquiry by the trial court.   The plaintiff says that no valid purpose existed—the entire transaction was a mere subterfuge designed to eliminate the minority.   The Chancellor ruled otherwise, but in so doing he clearly circumscribed the thrust and effect of *Singer*.   .   .   .   This has led to the thoroughly sound observation that the business purpose test "may be .   .   . virtually interpreted out of existence, as it was in *Weinberger*".[9]

---

9.   Weiss, *The Law of Take Out Merg-*   624, 671, n. 300 (1981).
ers: A Historical Perspective, 56 N.Y.U.L.Rev.

The requirement of a business purpose is new to our law of mergers and was a departure from prior case law.   .   .   .

In view of the fairness test which has long been applicable to parent-subsidiary mergers, .   .   . the expanded appraisal remedy now available to shareholders, and the broad discretion of the Chancellor to fashion such relief as the facts of a given case may dictate, we do not believe that any additional meaningful protection is afforded minority shareholders by the business purpose requirement.   .   .   .   Accordingly, such requirement shall no longer be of any force or effect.

The judgment of the Court of Chancery, finding both the circumstances of the merger and the price paid the minority shareholders to be fair, is reversed.   The matter is remanded for further proceedings consistent herewith.   Upon remand the plaintiff's post-trial motion to enlarge the class should be granted.

ANALYSIS

1.   If the Signal directors on the UOP board had fought for a price of $24 for the minority UOP shareholders, and in doing so had revealed the contents of the Arledge–Chitiea report, might they have subjected themselves to liability to the Signal shareholders?

2.   If you had been counsel to the Signal board before any steps had been taken, how would you have advised them (with the benefit of hindsight) on how to proceed in the acquisition of the UOP minority shares?

NOTE

Del. Gen. Corp. Law § 262(h) provides that shareholders who dissent from a merger and seek appraisal are entitled to receive a cash payment equal to the "fair value" of the shares "exclusive of any element of value arising from the accomplishment or expectation of the merger." For example, suppose that the pre-acquisition fair market value of Target Corp. is $10 per share and that Acquiring Corp. values Target, under its management, at $14 per share. Further, suppose that Acquisition offers $12 per share to Target shareholders and that the offer is accepted and the merger approved by a sufficient number of Target shareholders. Dissenting shareholders will be entitled to only $10 per share, so they will have a strong incentive not to dissent. But suppose that there is a controlling shareholder who owns 50 percent of the Target shares and that Acquisition must pay $15 to acquire those shares. If the remaining shares can be cashed out at $10 per share in a second-stage merger transaction, the average price will be $12.50 per share and the merger will still be attractive to Acquisition and will take place. This outcome is consistent with the rule allowing controlling shareholders to receive a premium for their shares without sharing that premium with the majority. Now suppose that the rule is that once Acquisition has bought the 50 percent controlling interest (the first stage) and has taken over Target and installed its management and plans, the minority shareholders are entitled, in an appraisal action, to the newly created value of the corporation, which is $14 per share. Suppose that in the second stage, Acquisition attempts a cash-out merger of the noncontrolling shares at $10 per share. If all noncontrolling shareholders seek appraisal, Acquisition will pay $14 for those shares and its average price for all the shares will be $14.50, which is more than it would be willing to pay. Yet the majority shareholder is entitled to hold out for the $15 per share— even if Acquisition has offered, say, $14 for all the shares (and even if the controlling shareholder has offered to buy all the noncontrolling shares for, say, only $13 per share). See Mendel v. Carroll, 651 A.2d 297 (Del.Ch.1994).

In Armstrong v. Marathon Oil Co., 513 N.E.2d 776 (Ohio 1987), Marathon merged with U.S. Steel on March 11, 1982. U.S. Steel had acquired a majority of Marathon's stock in a previous cash tender offer at $125 per share. In the merger, U.S. Steel paid $100 per share in the form of newly issued U.S. Steel bonds. In a subsequent appraisal proceeding, the Ohio Supreme Court held that the $125 paid in the cash tender offer was irrelevant to determining the fair value of the shares subject to the appraisal proceeding. Control premia were not deemed relevant to the value of shares by a stockholder who already had control of the company. The value of plaintiffs' shares was to be determined by their market value on March 10, 1982, which was about $75, adjusted *downward* to the extent that the market price anticipated the pending merger.

By contrast, in Cede & Co. v. Technicolor, Inc., 684 A.2d 289 (Del.Sup. 1996), the court held that in a two-step cash-out merger (like the one in *Weinberger*), value added by the acquiring corporation subsequent to its initial purchase of a controlling block of shares was considered part of going concern value, which dissenting shareholders who sought appraisal were entitled to share. In its opinion the Supreme Court acknowledged the Court of Chancery objection that this rule "would be tantamount to awarding [the dissenting shareholder] a proportionate share of a control premium, which the Court of Chancery deemed to be both economically undesirable and contrary" to precedent. Id. at 298. The Supreme Court disagreed as to the precedent and offered the formalistic and conclusory observation that "[t]he underlying assumption in an appraisal valuation is that the dissenting shareholders would [have been] willing to maintain their investment position had the merger not occurred." Id. In discussing the Court of Chancery's economic argument, the Supreme Court referred to an article by Professor John C. Coffee, Jr., Transfers of Control and the Quest for Efficiency: Can Delaware Law Encourage Efficient Transactions While Chilling Inefficient Ones? 21 Del. J. Corp. L. 356 (1996), which describes how similar results can, in some circumstances, be produced by the "best price" rule of the federal Williams Act, which requires that in a tender offer the highest price paid to any shareholder must be paid to all shareholders, and by the "entire fairness" standard of *Weinberger*.

The obvious effect of the rule of Cede & Co. v. Technicolor, Inc. is to discourage the use of two-step acquisitions, but often there will be no alternative. This effect is diminished to some degree by the reality that few shareholders in fact find it feasible to seek appraisal. The dissenting shareholder in the *Technicolor* case owned shares worth more than $4 million.

Coggins v. New England Patriots Football Club, Inc.

397 Mass. 525, 492 N.E.2d 1112 (1986).

On November 18, 1959, William H. Sullivan, Jr. (Sullivan), purchased an American Football League (AFL) franchise for a professional football team. The team was to be the last of the eight original teams set up to form the AFL (now the American Football Conference of the National Football League). For the franchise, Sullivan paid $25,000. Four months later, Sullivan organized a corporation, the American League Professional Football Team of Boston, Inc. Sullivan contributed his AFL franchise; nine other persons each contributed $25,000. In return, each of the ten investors received 10,000 shares of voting common stock in the corporation. Another four months later, in July, 1960, the corporation sold 120,000 shares of nonvoting common stock to the public at $5 a share.

Sullivan had effective control of the corporation from its inception until 1974. By April, 1974, Sullivan had increased his ownership of shares from 10,000 shares of voting stock to 23,718 shares, and also had acquired 5,499 shares of nonvoting stock. Nevertheless, in 1974 the other voting stockholders ousted him from the presidency and from operating control of the corporation. He then began the effort to regain control of the corporation—an effort which culminated in this and other law suits.

In November, 1975, Sullivan succeeded in obtaining ownership or control of all 100,000 of the voting shares, at a price of approximately $102 a share (adjusted cash value), of the corporation, by that time renamed the New England Patriots Football Club, Inc. (Old Patriots). Upon completion of the purchase, he immediately used his 100% control to vote out the hostile directors, elect a friendly board and arrange his resumption of the presidency and the complete control of the Patriots. In order to finance this coup, Sullivan borrowed approximately $5,348,000 from the Rhode Island Hospital National Bank and the LaSalle National Bank of Chicago. As a condition of these loans, Sullivan was to use his best efforts to reorganize the Patriots so that the income of the corporation could be devoted to the payment of these personal loans and the assets of the corporation pledged to secure them. At this point they were secured by all of the voting shares held by Sullivan. In order to accomplish in effect the assumption by the corporation of Sullivan's personal obligations, it was necessary, as a matter of corporate law, to eliminate the interest of the nonvoting shares.

On October 20, 1976, Sullivan organized a new corporation called the New Patriots Football Club, Inc. (New Patriots). The board of directors of the Old Patriots and the board of directors of the New Patriots [5] executed an agreement of merger of the two corporations providing that, after the merger, the voting stock of the Old Patriots would be extinguished, the nonvoting stock would be exchanged for cash at the rate of $15 a share, and the name of the New Patriots would be changed to the name formerly used by the Old Patriots.[6] As part of this plan, Sullivan gave the New Patriots his 100,000 voting shares of the Old Patriots in return for 100% of the New Patriots stock.

General Laws c. 156B, § 78(c)(1)(iii), as amended through St.1976, c. 327, required approval of the merger agreement by a majority vote of each class of affected stock. Approval by the voting class, entirely controlled by Sullivan, was assured. The merger was approved by the class of nonvoting stockholders at a special meeting on December 8, 1976. On January 31, 1977, the merger of the New Patriots and the Old Patriots was consummated.

David A. Coggins (Coggins) was the owner of ten shares of nonvoting stock in the Old Patriots. Coggins, a fan of the Patriots from the time of their formation, was serving in Vietnam in 1967 when he purchased the shares through his brother. Over the years, he followed the fortunes of the team, taking special pride in his status as an owner.[8] When he heard of the proposed merger, Coggins was upset that he could be forced to sell. Coggins voted against the merger and commenced this suit on behalf of those stockholders, who, like himself, believed the transaction to be unfair and illegal. A judge of the Superior Court certified the class as "stockholders of New England Patriots Football Club, Inc. who have voted against the merger . . . but who have neither turned in their shares nor perfected their appraisal rights . . . [and who] desire only to void the merger."

The trial judge found in favor of the Coggins class but determined that the merger should not be undone. Instead, he ruled that the plaintiffs are entitled to rescissory damages, and he ordered that further hearings be held to determine the amount of damages. . . .

---

5. The two boards were identical.

6. Additional findings as to the purpose of this merger made by the Federal judge, as adopted by the trial judge, are: "Purported reasons for the merger [were] stated in the [proxy materials]. Three reasons are given: (1) the policy of the [National Football League] to discourage public ownership of member football teams, (2) the difficulty in reconciling management's obligations to the NFL with its obligations to public stockholders, and (3) the cost and possible revelation of confidential information resulting from the obligations of publicly owned corporations to file reports with various public bodies. . . . I find, however, that while some of the stated reasons may have been useful by-products of the merger, the true reason for the merger was to enable Sullivan to satisfy his $5,348,000 personal obligation to the banks. The merger would not have occurred for the considerations stated as reasons in the Proxy Statement. . . . The Proxy Statement is an artful attempt to minimize the future profitability of the Patriots and to put a wash of corporate respectability over Sullivan's diversion of the corporation's income for his own purposes."

8. It was, in part, the goal of the Old Patriots, in offering stock to the public, to generate loyal fans.

We conclude that the trial judge was correct in ruling that the merger was illegal and that the plaintiffs have been wronged. Ordinarily, rescission of the merger would be the appropriate remedy. This merger, however, is now nearly ten years old, and, because an effective and orderly rescission of the merger now is not feasible, we remand the case for proceedings to determine the appropriate monetary damages to compensate the plaintiffs. . . .

Scope of Judicial Review. In deciding this case, we address an important corporate law question: What approach will a Massachusetts court reviewing a cash freeze-out merger employ? This question has been considered by courts in a number of other States. . . .

The parties have urged us to consider the views of a court with great experience in such matters, the Supreme Court of Delaware. We note that the Delaware court announced one test in 1977, but recently has changed to another. In Singer v. Magnavox Co., 380 A.2d 969, 980 (Del.1977), the Delaware court established the so-called "business-purpose" test, holding that controlling stockholders violate their fiduciary duties when they "cause a merger to be made for the sole purpose of eliminating a minority on a cash-out basis." Id. at 978. In 1983, Delaware jettisoned the business-purpose test, satisfied that the "fairness" test "long . . . applicable to parent-subsidiary mergers, . . . the expanded appraisal remedy now available to stockholders, and the broad discretion of the Chancellor to fashion such relief as the facts of a given case may dictate" provided sufficient protection to the frozen-out minority. Weinberger v. UOP, Inc., 457 A.2d 701, 715 (Del.1983).[11] "The requirement of fairness is unflinching in its demand that where one stands on both sides of a transaction, he has the burden of establishing its entire fairness, sufficient to pass the test of careful scrutiny by the courts." Id. at 710. "The concept of fairness has two basic aspects: fair dealing and fair price." Id. at 711. We note that the "fairness" test to which the Delaware court now has adhered is, as we later show, closely related to the views expressed in our decisions. Unlike the Delaware court, however, we believe that the "business-purpose" test is an additional useful means under our statutes and case law for examining a transaction in which a controlling stockholder eliminates the minority interest in a corporation. Cf. Wilkes v. Springside Nursing Home, Inc., 370 Mass. 842, 851, 353 N.E.2d 657 (1976). This concept of fair dealing is not limited to close corporations but applies to judicial review of cash freeze-out mergers. . . .

The dangers of self-dealing and abuse of fiduciary duty are greatest in freeze-out situations like the Patriots merger, where a controlling stockholder and corporate director chooses to eliminate public ownership. It is in these cases that a judge should examine with closest scrutiny the motives and the behavior of the controlling stockholder. A showing of compliance with statutory procedures is an insufficient substitute for the

11. . . . That the new Delaware approach is not without its difficulties is illustrated by the opinion in Rabkin v. Philip A. Hunt Chem. Corp., 498 A.2d 1099 (Del.1985).

inquiry of the courts when a minority stockholder claims that the corporate action "will be or is illegal or fraudulent as to him." G.L. c. 156B, § 98.

A controlling stockholder who is also a director standing on both sides of the transaction bears the burden of showing that the transaction does not violate fiduciary obligations. . . . Judicial inquiry into a freeze-out merger in technical compliance with the statute may be appropriate, and the dissenting stockholders are not limited to the statutory remedy of judicial appraisal where violations of fiduciary duties are found.

Factors in judicial review. The defendants concentrate their arguments on the finding of the Superior Court judge that the offered price for nonvoting shares was inadequate. They claim that his conclusion that rescissory damages are due these plaintiffs is based wholly on a finding of price inadequacy. The trial judge, however, considered the totality of circumstances, including the purpose of the merger, the accuracy and adequacy of disclosure in connection with the merger, and the fairness of the price. The trial judge correctly considered the totality of circumstances, even though he failed to attach adequate significance to each of these factors and to structure them correctly in his analysis.

Judicial scrutiny should begin with recognition of the basic principle that the duty of a corporate director must be to further the legitimate goals of the corporation. The result of a freeze-out merger is the elimination of public ownership in the corporation. The controlling faction increases its equity from a majority to 100%, using corporate processes and corporate assets. The corporate directors who benefit from this transfer of ownership must demonstrate how the legitimate goals of the corporation are furthered. A director of a corporation violates his fiduciary duty when he uses the corporation for his or his family's personal benefit in a manner detrimental to the corporation. . . . Because the danger of abuse of fiduciary duty is especially great in a freeze-out merger, the court must be satisfied that the freeze-out was for the advancement of a legitimate corporate purpose. If satisfied that elimination of public ownership is in furtherance of a business purpose, the court should then proceed to determine if the transaction was fair by examining the totality of the circumstances.

The plaintiffs here adequately alleged that the merger of the Old Patriots and New Patriots was a freeze-out merger undertaken for no legitimate business purpose, but merely for the personal benefit of Sullivan. While we have recognized the right to "selfish ownership" in a corporation, such a right must be balanced against the concept of the majority stockholder's fiduciary obligation to the minority stockholders. Wilkes v. Springside Nursing Home, Inc., 370 Mass. 842, 851, 353 N.E.2d 657 (1976). Consequently, the defendants bear the burden of proving, first, that the merger was for a legitimate business purpose, and, second, that, considering totality of circumstances, it was fair to the minority.

The decision of the Superior Court judge includes a finding that "the defendants have failed to demonstrate that the merger served any valid corporate objective unrelated to the personal interests of the majority shareholders. It thus appears that the sole reason for the merger was to effectuate a restructuring of the Patriots that would enable the repayment of the [personal] indebtedness incurred by Sullivan. . . .'' The trial judge considered the defendants' claims that the policy of the National Football League (NFL) requiring majority ownership by a single individual or family made it necessary to eliminate public ownership. He found that "the stock ownership of the Patriots as it existed just prior to the merger fully satisfied the rationale underlying the policy as expressed by NFL Commissioner Pete Rozelle. Having acquired 100% control of the voting common stock of the Patriots, Sullivan possessed unquestionable authority to act on behalf of the franchise at League meetings and effectively foreclosed the possible recurrence of the internal management disputes that had existed in 1974. Moreover, as the proxy statement itself notes, the Old Patriots were under no legal compulsion to eliminate public ownership." Likewise, the defendants did not succeed in showing a conflict between the interests of the league owners and the Old Patriots' stockholders. We perceive no error in these findings. They are fully supported by the evidence. Under the approach we set forth above, there is no need to consider further the elements of fairness of a transaction that is not related to a valid corporate purpose.

Remedy. The plaintiffs are entitled to relief. They argue that the appropriate relief is rescission of the merger and restoration of the parties to their positions of 1976. We agree that the normally appropriate remedy for an impermissible freeze-out merger is rescission. Because Massachusetts statutes do not bar a cash freeze-out, however, numerous third parties relied in good faith on the outcome of the merger. The trial judge concluded that the expectations of those parties should not be upset, and so chose to award damages rather than rescission.

. . . The passage of time has made the 1976 position of the parties difficult, if not impossible, to restore. A substantial number of former stockholders have chosen other courses and should not be forced back into the Patriots corporation. In these circumstances the interests of the corporation and of the plaintiffs will be furthered best by limiting the plaintiffs' remedy to an assessment of damages. . . . On remand, the judge is to take further evidence on the present value of the Old Patriots on the theory that the merger had not taken place. Each share of the Coggins class is to receive, as rescissory damages, its aliquot share of the present assets.

The trial judge dismissed the plaintiffs' claims against the individual defendants based on waste of corporate assets. The remedy we order is intended to give the plaintiffs what they would have if the merger were undone and the corporation were put back together again. The trial judge's finding that the sole purpose of the merger was the personal financial benefit of William H. Sullivan, Jr., and the use of corporate assets to accomplish this impermissible purpose, leads inescapably to the conclusion that part of what the plaintiffs otherwise would have benefitted by, was removed from the corporation by the individual defendants. We reverse the dismissal of the claim for waste of corporate assets and remand this question to the trial court. The present value of the Patriots, as determined on remand, should include the amount wrongfully removed or diverted from the corporate coffers by the individual defendants.

We do not think it appropriate, however, to award damages based on a 1976 appraisal value. To do so would make this suit a nullity, leaving the plaintiffs with no effective remedy except appraisal, a position we have already rejected. Rescissory damages must be determined based on the present value of the Patriots, that is, what the stockholders would have if the merger were rescinded.   . . .

Summary. The freeze-out merger accomplished by William H. Sullivan, Jr., was designed for his own personal benefit to eliminate the interests of the Patriots' minority stockholders. The merger did not further the interests of the corporation and therefore was a violation of Sullivan's fiduciary duty to the minority stockholders, and so was impermissible. In most cases we would turn to rescission as the appropriate remedy. In the circumstances of this case, however, rescission would be an inequitable solution. Therefore, we remand for a determination of the present value of the non-voting stock, as though the merger were rescinded. The claim for waste of corporate assets brought against the individual defendants is reinstated. Those stockholders who voted against the merger, who did not turn in their shares, who did not perfect their appraisal rights, but who are part of the *Coggins* class, are to receive damages in the amount their stock would be worth today, plus interest at the statutory rate.

.   .   .

NOTE

Sarrouf v. New England Patriots Football Club, Inc., 397 Mass. 542, 492 N.E.2d 1122 (1986), was the appeal from the appraisal proceeding for those shareholders who had rejected the offered price of $15 per share and had perfected their appraisal rights. The Supreme Judicial Court upheld the trial court finding that the value was $80 per share.

ANALYSIS

1. What is a legitimate business purpose? Suppose Sullivan wanted a winning team and was not much concerned about profit, while most of the nonvoting shareholders wanted to maximize profits. Would that difference in goals have provided a legitimate business purpose to justify the cash-out merger of the nonvoting shares? What if the objectives of Sullivan and the nonvoting shareholders as to profit maximization had been reversed and for years nonvoting shareholders had been confronting Sullivan, demanding that he spend money to create a better team?

2.   One benefit of going private is that the corporation saves various expenses of being a public corporation (annual reports to the SEC and the shareholders, legal fees, accounting fees, etc.).   Is the elimination of these expenses a legitimate business purpose?   If so, will it always be possible for a public corporation seeking to go private to satisfy the business purpose test?

3.   What was wrong about Sullivan's actual purpose?   Suppose he needed money for another business venture and had caused the Patriots corporation to borrow money and declare a large dividend payable to all shareholders.   Assume that this action did not threaten the corporation with insolvency or require any significant change in its operations.   Would a shareholder such as Coggins have been entitled to an injunction to prevent the payment of the dividend?

4.   What if Sullivan had had "good" motives as well as the "bad" one on which the court focused?   Suppose, for example, that Sullivan had been concerned about the expenses and the staff time associated with the fact that the Patriots corporation was public, that he had been vexed and distracted by confrontations with nonvoting shareholders over policies and strategies, and that he found it disadvantageous to be required, as a public company, to disclose financial data.   Suppose that because of these considerations he had been considering a cash-out merger of the nonvoting shareholders and that while the cash-out merger was under consideration his personal bankers had, in effect, insisted that he do it.   Would Coggins have been entitled to block the merger, or would appraisal have been his sole remedy?

5.   Apart from the unique facts of *Coggins,* can you think of any reason why a majority would want to buy out a minority at a fair price (presumably assured by the appraisal right) except for some business purpose?

6.   On the question of damages, the court states, "each share of the Coggins class is to receive .   .   . its aliquot share of the present assets." In the next paragraph the court says that the "present value .   .   . should include the amount wrongfully removed or diverted from the corporate coffers by the individual defendants."   What if the corporation had paid normal, legally permissible dividends?

Rabkin v. Philip A. Hunt Chemical Corporation

498 A.2d 1099 (Del.1985).

.   .   .

I.

.   .   .   On July 5, 1984, [Philip A. Hunt Chemical Corp. (Hunt)] merged into [Olin Corp. (Olin)] pursuant to a merger agreement that was recommended by the Hunt board of directors.   Hunt was a Delaware corporation, while Olin is incorporated in Virginia.   On March 1, 1983,

Olin bought 63.4% of the outstanding shares of Hunt's common stock from Turner and Newall Industries, Inc. (Turner & Newall) at $25 per share pursuant to a Stock Purchase Agreement (the agreement).

At Turner & Newall's insistence, the agreement also required Olin to pay $25 per share if Olin acquired the remaining Hunt stock within one year thereafter (the one year commitment).   .   .   .

When Olin acquired its 63.4% interest in Hunt, Olin stated in a press release that while it was "considering the acquisition of the remaining public shares of Hunt, it [had] no present intention to do so." Apparently, there were no discussions or negotiations between the boards of Hunt and Olin regarding any purchase of Hunt stock during the one year commitment period.

However, it is clear that Olin always anticipated owning 100% of Hunt. Several Olin interoffice memoranda referred to the eventual merger of the two companies.

.   .   .

The Court of Chancery found that it was "apparent that, from the outset, Olin anticipated that it would eventually acquire the minority interest in Hunt." Rabkin v. Philip A. Hunt Chemical Corp., Del.Ch., 480 A.2d 655, 657–58 (1984). This observation is consistent with the Olin board's authorization, a week before the one year commitment period expired, for its Finance Committee to acquire the rest of Hunt should the Committee conclude on the advice of management that such an acquisition would be appropriate.

On Friday, March 23, 1984, the senior management of Olin met with a representative of the investment banking firm of Morgan, Lewis, Githens & Ahn, Inc. (Morgan Lewis) to discuss the possible acquisition and valuation of the Hunt minority stock. Olin proposed to pay $20 per share and asked Morgan Lewis to render a fairness opinion on that price. Four days later, on Tuesday, March 27, Morgan Lewis delivered its opinion to Olin that $20 per share was fair to the minority.   .   .   . In reaching its conclusion Morgan Lewis evidently gave no consideration to Olin's obligation, including the bases thereof, to pay $25 per share if the stock had been acquired prior to March 1, 1984.

The same day, March 27, 1984, Olin's management presented the Morgan Lewis fairness opinion to the Olin Finance Committee with the recommendation that the remaining Hunt stock be acquired for $20 per share. At that meeting it was stated that management had determined the price based on the following factors: the Morgan Lewis analysis, Hunt's net worth, Hunt's earnings history, including current prospects for 1984, Hunt's failures to achieve the earnings projections set forth in its business plans, and the current and historical market value of Hunt stock from 1982 to 1983. The Finance Committee unanimously voted to acquire the remaining Hunt stock for $20 per share.   .   .   .

Later that day the Hunt Board appointed a Special Committee, consisting of the four Hunt outside directors, to review and determine the fairness of Olin's merger proposal. These directors met on April 4, 1984, and retained Merrill Lynch as their financial advisor and the law firm of Shea and Gould as legal counsel. This committee met again on three other occasions. At the May 10, 1984 meeting the Special Committee heard a presentation by the lawyers for several plaintiffs who had filed class actions on behalf of the minority shareholders to enjoin the proposed merger. A representative of Merrill Lynch advised the meeting that $20 per share was fair to the minority from a financial standpoint, but that the range of values for the common stock was probably $19 to $25 per share.

The outside directors subsequently notified the Hunt board that they had unanimously found $20 per share to be fair but not generous. They therefore recommended that Olin consider increasing the price above $20. The next day, May 11, 1984, Olin informed the Hunt Special Committee that it had considered its recommendation but declined to raise the price. The Hunt outside directors then met again on May 14, 1984, by teleconference call, and at a meeting of the Hunt board on May 15, also held by teleconference, the Special Committee announced that it had unanimously found the $20 per share price fair and recommended approval of the merger.

On June 7, 1984, Hunt issued its proxy statement favoring the merger. That document also made clear Olin's intention to vote its Hunt shares in favor of the proposal, thereby guaranteeing its passage. There was no requirement of approval by a majority of the minority stockholders.

The proxy statement also described in substantial detail most of the facts related above. Specifically, it disclosed the existence of the one year commitment, the Merrill Lynch conclusion that a fair range for the Hunt common stock was between $19 and $25, and the pendency of these class actions opposing the merger.

II.

Taken together, the plaintiffs' complaints challenge the proposed Olin–Hunt merger on the grounds that the price offered was grossly inadequate because Olin unfairly manipulated the timing of the merger to avoid the one year commitment, and that specific language in Olin's Schedule 13D, filed when it purchased the Hunt stock, constituted a price commitment by which Olin failed to abide, contrary to its fiduciary obligations.

The Vice Chancellor granted the defendants' motion to dismiss on the ground that the plaintiffs' complaints failed to state claims upon which relief could be granted. The court's rationale was that absent claims of fraud or deception a minority stockholder's rights in a cash-out merger were limited to an appraisal. . . .

A.

The issue we address is whether the trial court erred, as a matter of law, in dismissing these claims on the ground that absent deception the plaintiffs' sole remedy under *Weinberger* is an appraisal. The plaintiffs' position is that in cases of procedural unfairness the standard of entire fairness entitles them to relief that is broader than an appraisal. Indeed, the thrust of plaintiffs' contentions is that they eschew an appraisal, since they consider Olin's manipulative conduct a breach of its fiduciary duty to pay the $25 per share guaranteed by the one year commitment. Furthermore, plaintiffs contend that an appraisal is inadequate here because: (1) the alleged wrongdoers are not parties to an appraisal proceeding, and thus are not personally accountable for their actions; (2) if such misconduct is proven, then the corporation should not have to bear the financial burden which only falls upon it in an appraisal award; and (3) overreaching and unfair dealing are not addressed by an appraisal.

The defendants answer that the plaintiffs' claims were primarily directed to the issue of fair value, and that under *Weinberger,* appraisal is the only available remedy.

B.

.   .   .

In ordering the complaints dismissed the Vice Chancellor reasoned that:

> Where, .   .   . there are no allegations of non-disclosures or misrepresentations, *Weinberger* mandates that plaintiffs' entire fairness claims be determined in an appraisal proceeding.

> *Rabkin,* 480 A.2d at 660.

Id. We consider that an erroneous interpretation of *Weinberger,* because it fails to take account of the entire context of the holding.

The Court of Chancery seems to have limited its focus to our statement in *Weinberger* that:

> [T]he provisions of 8 Del.C. § 262, as herein construed, respecting the scope of an appraisal and the means for perfecting the same, shall govern the financial remedy available to minority shareholders in a cash-out merger.   .   .   .

However, *Weinberger* makes clear that appraisal is not necessarily a stockholder's sole remedy. We specifically noted that:

> [W]hile a plaintiff's monetary remedy ordinarily should be confined to the more liberalized appraisal proceeding herein established, we do not intend any limitation on the historic powers of the Chancellor to grant such other relief as the facts of a particular case may dictate. The appraisal remedy we approve may not be adequate in certain cases, particularly where fraud, misrepresentation, self-dealing, deliberate waste of corporate assets, or gross and palpable overreaching are involved.   .   .   .

Thus, the trial court's narrow interpretation of *Weinberger* would render meaningless our extensive discussion of fair dealing found in that opinion. In *Weinberger* we defined fair dealing as embracing "questions of when the transaction was timed, how it was initiated, structured, negotiated, disclosed to the directors, and how the approvals of the directors and the stockholders were obtained." 457 A.2d at 711. While this duty of fairness certainly incorporates the principle that a cash-out merger must be free of fraud or misrepresentation, *Weinberger*'s mandate of fair dealing does not turn solely on issues of deception. We particularly noted broader concerns respecting the matter of procedural fairness. . . . Thus, while "in a non-fraudulent transaction . . . price *may* be the preponderant consideration," . . . it is not necessarily so.

Although the Vice Chancellor correctly understood *Weinberger* as limiting collateral attacks on cash-out mergers, her analysis narrowed the procedural protections which we still intended *Weinberger* to guarantee. Here, plaintiffs are not arguing questions of valuation which are the traditional subjects of an appraisal. Rather, they seek to enforce a contractual right to receive $25 per share, which they claim was unfairly destroyed by Olin's manipulative conduct.

While a plaintiff's mere allegation of "unfair dealing", without more, cannot survive a motion to dismiss, averments containing "specific acts of fraud, misrepresentation, or other items of misconduct" must be carefully examined in accord with our views expressed both here and in *Weinberger*. . . .

III.

A.

Having outlined the facts and applicable principles, we turn to the details of the Hunt–Olin merger and the plaintiffs' complaints to determine whether the specific acts of misconduct alleged are sufficient to withstand a motion to dismiss.

The Court of Chancery stated that "[t]he gravamen of all the complaints appears to be that the cash-out price is unfair." . . . However, this conclusion, which seems to be more directed to issues of valuation, is neither supported by the pleadings themselves nor the extensive discussion of unfair dealing found in the trial court's opinion. There is no challenge to any method of valuation or to the components of value upon which Olin's $20 price was based. The plaintiffs want the $25 per share guaranteed by the one year commitment, which they claim was unfairly denied them by Olin's manipulations.

. . .

B.

In *Weinberger* we observed that the timing, structure, negotiation and disclosure of a cash-out merger all had a bearing on the issue of procedural fairness. 457 A.2d at 711. The plaintiffs contend *inter alia* that Olin breached its fiduciary duty of fair dealing by purposely timing the merger, and thereby unfairly manipulating it, to avoid the one year commitment.

In support of that contention plaintiffs have averred specific facts indicating that Olin knew it would eventually acquire Hunt, but delayed doing so to avoid paying $25 per share. Significantly, the trial court's opinion seems to accept that point. . . .

Consistent with this observation are the confidential Berardino memo to the three Olin and Hunt directors, Henske, Johnstone and Berry, about the disadvantages of paying a higher price during the one year commitment; the deposition testimony of Olin's chief executive officer, Mr. Henske, that the one year commitment "meant nothing"; and what could be considered a quick surrender by the Special Committee of Hunt directors in the face of Olin's proposal to squeeze out the minority at $20 per share.[7] While we do not pass on the merits of such questions, Olin's alleged attitude toward the minority, at least as it appears on the face of the complaints and their proposed amendments, coupled with the apparent absence of any meaningful negotiations as to price, all have an air reminiscent of the dealings between Signal and UOP in *Weinberger*. . . . Certainly the Berardino memorandum, although not unusual as an Olin planning document, raises unanswered questions about the recognition by three of its recipients, all Hunt directors, of their undiminished duty of loyalty to Hunt.

. . . As we said in *Weinberger:*

There is no "safe harbor" for such divided loyalties in Delaware. When directors of a Delaware corporation are on both sides of a transaction, they are required to demonstrate their utmost good faith and the most scrupulous inherent fairness of the bargain. . . .

These are issues which an appraisal cannot address, and at this juncture are matters that cannot be resolved by a motion to dismiss.

In our opinion the facts alleged by the plaintiffs regarding Olin's avoidance of the one year commitment support a claim of unfair dealing sufficient to defeat dismissal at this stage of the proceedings. The defendants answer that they had no legal obligation to effect the cash-out merger during the one year period. While that may be so, . . . inequitable conduct will not be protected merely because it is legal.

IV.

In conclusion we find that the trial court erred in dismissing the plaintiffs' actions for failure to state a claim upon which relief could be granted. As we read the complaints and the proposed amendments, they assert a conscious intent by Olin, as the majority shareholder of Hunt, to deprive the Hunt minority of the same bargain that Olin made with Hunt's

---

7. As we noted in *Weinberger,* the use of an independent negotiating committee of outside directors may have significant advantages to the majority stockholder in defending suits of this type. . . . However, we recognize that there can be serious practical problems in the use of such a committee . . . Thus, we do not announce any rule, even in the context of a motion to dismiss, that the absence of such a bargaining structure will preclude dismissal in cases bottomed on claims of unfair dealing.

former majority shareholder, Turner and Newall. But for Olin's allegedly unfair manipulation, the plaintiffs contend, this bargain also was due them. In short, the defendants are charged with bad faith which goes beyond issues of "mere inadequacy of price." Cole v. National Cash Credit Association, Del.Ch., 156 A. 183, 187–88 (1931). In *Weinberger* we specifically relied upon this aspect of *Cole* in acknowledging the imperfections of an appraisal where circumstances of this sort are present.

Necessarily, this will require the Court of Chancery to closely focus upon *Weinberger's* mandate of entire fairness based on a careful analysis of both the fair price and fair dealing aspects of a transaction. We recognize that this can present certain practical problems, since stockholders may invariably claim that the price being offered is the result of unfair dealings. However, we think that plaintiffs will be tempered in this approach by the prospect that an ultimate judgment in defendants' favor may have cost plaintiffs their unperfected appraisal rights. . . .

Accordingly, the decision of the Court of Chancery dismissing these consolidated class actions is REVERSED. The matter is REMANDED with directions that the plaintiffs be permitted to file their proposed amendments to the pleadings.

AFTERMATH

On remand, after trial, on the basis of a lengthy review of all the facts, the chancery court entered a judgment for the defendants. 1990 WL 47648 (Del.Ch.) affirmed, 586 A.2d 1202 (1990).

ANALYSIS

1. What was the court's view of the relevance of the agreement to pay $25 per share in any acquisition before March 1, 1984? Apparently that price was high enough that Olin never seriously considered buying before March 1, 1984. If so, what was the objective of Turner and Newall, and of Olin, in agreeing to the one-year equal treatment provision? What is the relevance to the minority shareholders of the fact that Olin paid $25 per share for the Turner and Newall controlling block?

2. What, if anything, do the plaintiffs gain by blocking the merger rather than perfecting their appraisal rights and seeking $25 per share (or more) in the appraisal proceeding?

3. Is there a substantial difference between the Delaware rule and the Massachusetts rule on cash-out mergers? If majority shareholders have no business purpose for a cash-out merger, if they act in response to purely personal objectives, what is the likelihood that they will satisfy the Delaware "entire fairness" test? If the New England Patriots Football Club, Inc. had been incorporated in Delaware, so that Delaware law applied to Coggins's class action, what is the likelihood that the result would have been different?

C. DE FACTO NON–MERGER

Rauch v. RCA Corporation
861 F.2d 29 (2d Cir.1988).

Background

This case arises from the acquisition of RCA Corporation ("RCA") by General Electric Company ("GE"). On or about December 11, 1985, RCA, GE and Gesub, Inc. ("Gesub"), a wholly owned Delaware subsidiary of GE, entered into an agreement of merger. Pursuant to the terms of the agreement, all common and preferred shares of RCA stock (with one exception) were converted to cash. . . . Specifically, the merger agreement provided (subject in each case to the exercise of appraisal rights) that each share of RCA common stock would be converted into $66.50 . . . and each share of $3.50 cumulative first preferred stock (the stock held by plaintiff and in issue here, hereinafter the "Preferred Stock") would be converted into $40.00. . . .

On February 27, 1986, plaintiff, a holder of 250 shares of Preferred Stock, commenced this diversity class action on behalf of a class consisting of the holders of Preferred Stock. It is undisputed that this action is governed by the law of Delaware, the state of incorporation of both RCA and Gesub. Plaintiff claimed that the merger constituted a "liquidation or dissolution or winding up of RCA and a redemption of the [Preferred Stock]," as a result of which holders of the Preferred Stock were entitled to $100 per share in accordance with the redemption provisions of RCA's certificate of incorporation,[2] that defendants were in violation of the rights of the holders of Preferred Stock as thus stated; and that defendants thereby wrongfully converted substantial sums of money to their own use. Plaintiff sought damages and injunctive relief.

Defendants moved to dismiss the complaint pursuant to Fed.R.Civ.P. 12(b)(6), and plaintiff cross-moved for summary judgment. The district court concluded that the transaction at issue was a bona fide merger carried out in accordance with the relevant provisions of the Delaware General Corporation Law. Accordingly, the district court held that plaintiff's action was precluded by Delaware's doctrine of independent legal significance, and dismissed the complaint.

Discussion

. . .

2. RCA's Restated Certificate of Incorporation, paragraph Fourth, Part I, provides in relevant part:
  (c) The First Preferred Stock at any time outstanding *may be redeemed by the Corporation,* in whole or in part, *at its election,* expressed by resolution of the Board of Directors, at any time or times upon not less than sixty (60) days' previous notice to the holders of record of the First Preferred Stock to be redeemed, given as hereinafter provided, at the price of one hundred dollars ($100) per share and all dividends accrued or in arrears. . . . (emphasis added).

According to RCA's Restated Certificate of Incorporation, the owners of the Preferred Stock were entitled to $100 per share, plus accrued dividends, upon the redemption of such stock at the election of the corporation. Plaintiff contends that the merger agreement, which compelled the holders of Preferred Stock to sell their shares to RCA for $40.00, effected a redemption whose nature is not changed by referring to it as a conversion of stock to cash pursuant to a merger. Plaintiff's argument, however, is not in accord with Delaware law.

It is clear that under the Delaware General Corporation Law, a conversion of shares to cash that is carried out in order to accomplish a merger is legally distinct from a redemption of shares by a corporation. Section 251 of the Delaware General Corporation Law allows two corporations to merge into a single corporation by adoption of an agreement that complies with that section. Del.Code Ann. tit. viii, § 251(c) (1983). The merger agreement in issue called for the conversion of the shares of the constituent corporations into cash. The statute specifically authorizes such a transaction:

> The agreement shall state . . . the manner of converting the shares of each of the constituent corporations into shares or other securities of the corporation surviving or resulting from the merger or consolidation and, if any shares of any of the constituent corporations are not to be converted solely into shares or other securities of the surviving or resulting corporations, *the cash* . . . *which the holders of such shares are to receive* in exchange for, or upon conversion of such shares . . ., *which cash* . . . *may be* in addition to or *in lieu of shares* or other securities of the surviving or resulting corporation. . . .

Id. § 251(b) (emphasis added). Thus, the RCA–GE merger agreement complied fully with the merger provision in question, and plaintiff does not argue to the contrary.

Redemption, on the other hand, is governed by sections 151(b) and 160(a) of the Delaware General Corporation Law. Section 151(b) provides that a corporation may subject its preferred stock to redemption "by the corporation at its option or at the option of the holders of such stock or upon the happening of a specified event." Del.Code Ann. tit. viii, § 151(b) (1983). In this instance, the Preferred Stock was subject to redemption by RCA *at its election*. See supra note 2. Nothing in RCA's certificate of incorporation indicated that the holders of Preferred Stock could initiate a redemption, nor was there provision for any specified event, such as the Gesub–RCA merger, to trigger a redemption.[3]

---

3. Plaintiff points, however, to Del. Code Ann. tit. viii, § 251(e) (1983), which provides that "[i]n the case of a merger, the certificate of incorporation of the surviving corporation shall automatically be amended to the extent, if any, that changes in the certificate of incorporation are set forth in the agreement of merger." Plaintiff contends that the agreement of merger "purports to alter or impair existing preferential rights," Brief for Plaintiff-Appellant at 14, thus requiring a class vote under other provisions of Delaware law. There are a number of problems with this contention, but the decisive threshold difficulty is that no "existing preferential rights" are altered or im-

Plaintiff's contention that the transaction was essentially a redemption rather than a merger must therefore fail. RCA chose to convert its stock to cash to accomplish the desired merger, and in the process chose not to redeem the Preferred Stock. It had every right to do so in accordance with Delaware law. As the district court aptly noted, to accept plaintiff's argument "would render nugatory the conversion provisions within Section 251 of the Delaware Code."

Delaware courts have long held that such a result is unacceptable. Indeed, it is well settled under Delaware law that "action taken under one section of [the Delaware General Corporation Law] is legally independent, and its validity is not dependent upon, nor to be tested by the requirements of other unrelated sections under which the same final result might be attained by different means." Rothschild Int'l Corp. v. Liggett Group, 474 A.2d 133, 136 (Del.1984) (quoting Orzeck v. Englehart, 41 Del.Ch. 361, 365, 195 A.2d 375, 378 (Del.1963)). The rationale of the doctrine is that the various provisions of the Delaware General Corporation Law are of equal dignity, and a corporation may resort to one section thereof without having to answer for the consequences that would have arisen from invocation of a different section. See Hariton v. Arco Electronics, Inc., 41 Del.Ch. 74, 77, 188 A.2d 123, 125 (Del.1963).   . . .

We note in this regard that plaintiff's complaint nowhere alleges that the $40.00 per share conversion rate for the Preferred Stock was unfair. Rather, "[p]laintiff is complaining of a breach of *contractual* rights, entirely divorced from the purported 'fairness' of the transaction." Brief for Plaintiff–Appellant at 23. Moreover, as the district court stated: "Delaware provides specific protection to shareholders who believe that they have received insufficient value for their stock as the result of a merger: they may obtain an appraisal under § 262 of the General Corporation Law." Plaintiff, however, explicitly disavows any appraisal theory or remedy, consistent with her position that fairness is not the issue.

. . .

ANALYSIS

In *Rauch,* the plaintiff urged adoption of, and the court rejected, what might be called a "de facto non-merger" doctrine. The transaction took the form of a merger but the plaintiff argued that it was in substance, or de facto, a sale of assets followed by a redemption. If the sale-of-assets route had been followed, then, in the absence of any change in the redemption price of the preferred shares, those shares would have been entitled to $100 per share, plus any previously unpaid dividends, before the common shares received anything. Under Delaware General Corporation Law § 242(b)(2),

paired in any way, since the holders of Preferred Stock never had any right to initiate a redemption.

however, the redemption price could have been altered by a majority vote of the preferred shares. A sale-of-assets transaction might have been made contingent on a prior vote of the preferred shares, approving amendment of the certificate of incorporation to lower the liquidation preference to $40 per share.[1]

Why might a majority of the preferred shareholders have voted to approve the reduction of their liquidation preference? What does your answer tell you about why the plaintiff in *Rauch* did not challenge the fairness of the transaction and did not pursue her appraisal remedy? What does your answer to both of these questions tell you about the possible limitations on the legal rule applied in *Rauch?*

PROBLEM

Buyer Corp. has proposed to buy all the assets of Seller Corp. for $150 million. Seller has 10 million shares of common stock outstanding. The most recent market price of the common is $10 per share, making the total market value of all the common $100 million. Seller also has 1 million shares of preferred stock outstanding. The preferred shares are entitled to an annual dividend of $3 per share, which has always been paid as due. The preferred shares are entitled on liquidation to receive $100 per share before the common shares receive anything. The recent price of the preferred shares is $30 per share, making the total market value of all the preferred shares $30 million. Seller has no debt. Thus, its capital is:

	Common	Preferred
Per share market price	$10	$30
Number of shares	10 mil.	1 mil.
Liquidation Preference	–	$100 mil.
Market Value	$100 mil.	$ 30 mil.

You are outside general counsel for Seller. Both Buyer and Seller are Delaware corporations. Buyer's representatives have said that they are indifferent about how the total $150 million consideration is divided between the common and the preferred so long as whatever division is

---

1. See Goldman v. Postal Telegraph, Inc., 52 F.Supp. 763 (D.Del.1943). In this case, arising under Delaware law, no dividends had been paid on Postal Telegraph's preferred shares for many years. The corporation was on the verge of insolvency and going downhill. If the corporation had been liquidated, the common shareholders would have received nothing; the liquidation preference of the preferred far exceeded the value of the corporate assets. But the preferred shareholders did not have the legal right to force liquidation. Western Union offered to acquire the Postal Telegraph assets for Western Union shares. About one-sixth of those shares were to go to the Postal Telegraph common shareholders and the rest to its preferred shareholders. This plan required, and was made contingent upon, voting approval of both the classes of Postal Telegraph shareholders. After such voting approval was obtained, a preferred shareholder objected and brought suit. The court upheld the plan, stating, "I can see no reason why a Delaware corporation cannot agree to sell its assets conditioned upon the seller amending its certificate of incorporation as a part of the transaction. . . . The reality of the situation called for some inducement to be offered to the common stockholders to secure their favorable vote for the plan."

adopted will sustain legal challenge. The board of directors of Seller has asked for your legal advice on how the total consideration should be divided. What is your response? What if the market value of the common is $10 million, the market value of the preferred is $40 million and the consideration to be paid is $60 million?

SECTION 2. TAKEOVERS

A. INTRODUCTION

Cheff v. Mathes

41 Del.Ch. 494, 199 A.2d 548 (1964).

This is an appeal from the decision of the Vice–Chancellor in a derivative suit holding certain directors of Holland Furnace Company liable for loss allegedly resulting from improper use of corporate funds to purchase shares of the company.   . . .

Holland Furnace Company, a corporation of the State of Delaware, manufactures warm air furnaces, air conditioning equipment, and other home heating equipment. At the time of the relevant transactions, the board of directors was composed of the seven individual defendants. Mr. Cheff had been Holland's Chief Executive Officer since 1933, received an annual salary of $77,400, and personally owned 6,000 shares of the company. He was also a director. Mrs. Cheff, the wife of Mr. Cheff, was a daughter of the founder of Holland and had served as a director since 1922. She personally owned 5,804 shares of Holland and owned 47.9 percent of Hazelbank United Interest, Inc. Hazelbank is an investment vehicle for Mrs. Cheff and members of the Cheff–Landwehr family group, which owned 164,950 shares of the 883,585 outstanding shares of Holland. As a director, Mrs. Cheff received a compensation of $200.00 for each monthly board meeting, whether or not she attended the meeting.

The third director, Edgar P. Landwehr, is the nephew of Mrs. Cheff and personally owned 24,010 shares of Holland and 8.6 percent of the outstanding shares of Hazelbank. He received no compensation from Holland other than the monthly director's fee.

Robert H. Trenkamp is an attorney who first represented Holland in 1946. In May 1953, he became a director of Holland and acted as general counsel for the company. During the period in question, he received no retainer from the company, but did receive substantial sums for legal services rendered the company. Apart from the above-described payments, he received no compensation from Holland other than the monthly director's fee. He owned 200 shares of Holland Furnace stock. Although he owned no shares of Hazelbank, at the time relevant to this controversy, he was serving as a director and counsel of Hazelbank.

John D. Ames was then a partner in the Chicago investment firm of Bacon, Whipple & Co. and joined the board at the request of Mr. Cheff. During the periods in question, his stock ownership varied between ownership of no shares to ownership of 300 shares. He was considered by the other members of the Holland board to be the financial advisor to the board. He received no compensation from Holland other than the normal director's fee.

[There were two other directors, Boalt and Spatta, who were not substantial shareholders and were not employees of the firm. Both were businessmen who had become directors at the request of Mr. Cheff.]

The board of directors of Hazelbank included the five principal shareholders: Mrs. Cheff; Leona Kolb, who was Mrs. Cheff's daughter; Mr. Landwehr; Mrs. Bowles, who was Mr. Landwehr's sister; Mrs. Putnam, who was also Mr. Landwehr's sister; Mr. Trenkamp; and Mr. William DeLong, an accountant.

Prior to the events in question, Holland employed approximately 8500 persons and maintained 400 branch sales offices located in 43 states. The volume of sales had declined from over $41,000,000 in 1948 to less than $32,000,000 in 1956. Defendants contend that the decline in earnings is attributable to the artificial post-war demand generated in the 1946–1948 period. In order to stabilize the condition of the company, the sales department apparently was reorganized and certain unprofitable branch offices were closed. By 1957 this reorganization had been completed and the management was convinced that the changes were manifesting beneficial results. The practice of the company was to directly employ the retail salesman, and the management considered that practice—unique in the furnace business—to be a vital factor in the company's success.

During the first five months of 1957, the monthly trading volume of Holland's stock on the New York Stock Exchange ranged between 10,300 shares to 24,200 shares. In the last week of June 1957, however, the trading increased to 37,800 shares, with a corresponding increase in the market price. In June of 1957, Mr. Cheff met with Mr. Arnold H. Maremont, who was President of Maremont Automotive Products, Inc. and Chairman of the boards of Motor Products Corporation and Allied Paper Corporation. Mr. Cheff testified, on deposition, that Maremont generally inquired about the feasibility of merger between Motor Products and Holland. Mr. Cheff testified that, in view of the difference in sales practices between the two companies, he informed Mr. Maremont that a merger did not seem feasible. In reply, Mr. Maremont stated that, in the light of Mr. Cheff's decision, he had no further interest in Holland nor did he wish to buy any of the stock of Holland.

None of the members of the board apparently connected the interest of Mr. Maremont with the increased activity of Holland stock. However, Mr. Trenkamp and Mr. Staal, the Treasurer of Holland, unsuccessfully made an informal investigation in order to ascertain the identity of the purchaser or purchasers. The mystery was resolved, however, when Maremont called Ames in July of 1957 to inform the latter that Maremont then owned 55,000 shares of Holland stock. At this juncture, no requests for change in corporate policy were made, and Maremont made no demand to be made a member of the board of Holland.

Ames reported the above information to the board at its July 30, 1957 meeting. Because of the position now occupied by Maremont, the board elected to investigate the financial and business history of Maremont and corporations controlled by him. Apart from the documentary evidence produced by this investigation, which will be considered infra, Staal testified, on deposition, that "leading bank officials" had indicated that Maremont "had been a participant, or had attempted to be, in the liquidation of a number of companies." Staal specifically mentioned only one individual giving such advice, the Vice President of the First National Bank of Chicago. Mr. Cheff testified, at trial, of Maremont's alleged participation in liquidation activities. Mr. Cheff testified that: "Throughout the whole of the Kalamazoo–Battle Creek area, and Detroit too, where I spent considerable time, he is well known and not highly regarded by any stretch." This information was communicated to the board.

On August 23, 1957, at the request of Maremont, a meeting was held between Mr. Maremont and Cheff. At this meeting, Cheff was informed that Motor Products then owned approximately 100,000 shares of Holland stock. Maremont then made a demand that he be named to the board of directors, but Cheff refused to consider it. Since considerable controversy has been generated by Maremont's alleged threat to liquidate the company or substantially alter the sales force of Holland, we believe it desirable to set forth the testimony of Cheff on this point: "Now we have 8500 men, direct employees, so the problem is entirely different. He indicated immediately that he had no interest in that type of distribution, that he didn't think it was modern, that he felt furnaces could be sold as he sold mufflers, through half a dozen salesmen in a wholesale way."

Testimony was introduced by the defendants tending to show that substantial unrest was present among the employees of Holland as a result of the threat of Maremont to seek control of Holland. Thus, Mr. Cheff testified that the field organization was considering leaving in large numbers because of a fear of the consequences of a Maremont acquisition; he further testified that approximately "25 of our key men" were lost as the result of the unrest engendered by the Maremont proposal. Staal, corroborating Cheff's version, stated that a number of branch managers approached him for reassurances that Maremont was not going to be allowed to successfully gain control. Moreover, at approximately this time, the company was furnished with a Dun and Bradstreet report, which indicated the practice of Maremont to achieve quick profits by sales or liquidations of companies acquired by him. The defendants were also supplied with an income statement of Motor Products, Inc., showing a loss of $336,121.00 for the period in 1957.

On August 30, 1957, the board was informed by Cheff of Maremont's demand to be placed upon the board and of Maremont's belief that the retail sales organization of Holland was obsolete. The board was also informed of the results of the investigation by Cheff and Staal. Predicated upon this information, the board authorized the purchase of company stock on the market with corporate funds, ostensibly for use in a stock option plan.

Subsequent to this meeting, substantial numbers of shares were purchased and, in addition, Mrs. Cheff made alternate personal purchases of Holland stock. As a result of purchases by Maremont, Holland and Mrs. Cheff, the market price rose. On September 13, 1957, Maremont wrote to each of the directors of Holland and requested a broad engineering survey to be made for the benefit of all stockholders. During September, Motor Products released its annual report, which indicated that the investment in Holland was a "special situation" as opposed to the normal policy of placing the funds of Motor Products into "an active company." On September 4th, Maremont proposed to sell his current holdings of Holland to the corporation for $14.00 a share. However, because of delay in responding to this offer, Maremont withdrew the offer. At this time, Mrs. Cheff was obviously quite concerned over the prospect of a Maremont acquisition, and had stated her willingness to expend her personal resources to prevent it.

On September 30, 1957, Motor Products Corporation, by letter to Mrs. Bowles, made a buy-sell offer to Hazelbank. At the Hazelbank meeting of October 3, 1957, Mrs. Bowles presented the letter to the board. The board took no action, but referred the proposal to its finance committee. Although Mrs. Bowles and Mrs. Putnam were opposed to any acquisition of Holland stock by Hazelbank, Mr. Landwehr conceded that a majority of the board were in favor of the purchase. Despite this fact, the finance committee elected to refer the offer to the Holland board on the grounds that it was the primary concern of Holland.

Thereafter, Mr. Trenkamp arranged for a meeting with Maremont, which occurred on October 14–15, 1957, in Chicago. Prior to this meeting, Trenkamp was aware of the intentions of Hazelbank and Mrs. Cheff to purchase all or portions of the stock then owned by Motor Products if Holland did not so act. As a result of the meeting, there was a tentative agreement on the part of Motor Products to sell its 155,000 shares at $14.40 per share. On October 23, 1957, at a special meeting of the Holland board, the purchase was considered. All directors, except Spatta, were present. The dangers allegedly posed by Maremont were again reviewed by the board. Trenkamp and Mrs. Cheff agree that the latter informed the board that either she or Hazelbank would purchase part or all of the block of Holland stock owned by Motor Products if the Holland board did not so act. The board was also informed that in order for the corporation to finance the purchase, substantial sums would have to be borrowed from commercial lending institutions. A resolution authorizing the purchase of 155,000 shares from Motor Products was adopted by the board. The price paid was in excess of the market price prevailing at the time, and the book value of the stock was approximately $20.00 as compared to approximately $14.00 for the net quick asset value. The transaction was subsequently consummated. The stock option plan mentioned in the minutes has never been implemented. In 1959, Holland stock reached a high of $15.25 a share.*

On February 6, 1958, plaintiffs, owners of 60 shares of Holland stock, filed a derivative suit in the court below naming all of the individual directors of Holland, Holland itself and Motor Products Corporation as defendants. The complaint alleged that all of the purchases of stock by Holland in 1957 were for the purpose of insuring the perpetuation of control by the incumbent directors. . . .

After trial, the Vice Chancellor found the following facts: (a) Holland directly sells to retail consumers by means of numerous branch offices. There were no intermediate dealers. (b) Immediately prior to the complained-of transactions, the sales and earnings of Holland had declined and its marketing practices were under investigation by the Federal Trade Commission. (c) Mr. Cheff and Trenkamp had received substantial sums as Chief Executive and attorney of the company, respectively. (d) Maremont, on August 23rd, 1957, demanded a place on the board. (e) At the October 14th meeting between Trenkamp, Staal and Maremont, Trenkamp and Staal were authorized to speak for Hazelbank and Mrs. Cheff as well as Holland. (f) Only Mr. Cheff, Mrs. Cheff, Mr. Landwehr, and Mr. Trenkamp clearly understood, prior to the October 23rd meeting, that either Hazelbank or Mrs. Cheff would have utilized their funds to purchase the Holland stock if Holland had not acted. (g) There was no real threat posed by Maremont and no substantial evidence of intention by Maremont to liquidate Holland. (h) Any employee unrest could have been caused by factors other than Maremont's intrusion and "only one important employee was shown to have left, and his motive for leaving is not clear." (i) The Court rejected the stock option plan as a meaningful rationale for the purchase from Maremont or the prior open market purchases.

The Court then found that the actual purpose behind the purchase was the desire to perpetuate control, but because of its finding that only the four above-named directors knew of the "alternative," the remaining directors were exonerated. No appeal was taken by plaintiffs from that decision.

. . .

Under the provisions of 8 Del.C. § 160, a corporation is granted statutory power to purchase and sell shares of its own stock. Such a right, as embodied in the statute, has long been recognized in this State. . . . The charge here is not one of violation of statute, but the allegation is that

---

* [Eds.—The following data reveals Maremont's profit and his advantage over other shareholders. The closing price of Holland shares on October 23 (when the Holland board resolved to buy out Maremont at $14 per share) was $11–1/8. Wall St. J., Oct. 24, 1957, p. 26, col. 3. The range of prices in the first five months of 1957, when Maremont (or his corporation) acquired his shares, was $9– 1/4 to $11–3/8. Wall St. J., June 3, 1957, p. 22, col. 3. The closing price on May 31 was $9–1/4. Id. If Maremont paid an average of $10.40 for his 155,000 shares, he made a profit of $4 per share or $620,000, on an investment of $1,612,000—in less than six months. Note, however, the court's statement that the share price rose to $15.25 in 1959.]

the true motives behind such purchases were improperly centered upon perpetuation of control. In an analogous field, courts have sustained the use of proxy funds to inform stockholders of management's views upon the policy questions inherent in an election to a board of directors, but have not sanctioned the use of corporate funds to advance the selfish desires of directors to perpetuate themselves in office. . . . Similarly, if the actions of the board were motivated by a sincere belief that the buying out of the dissident stockholder was necessary to maintain what the board believed to be proper business practices, the board will not be held liable for such decision, even though hindsight indicates the decision was not the wisest course. See Kors v. Carey, Del.Ch., 158 A.2d 136. On the other hand, if the board has acted solely or primarily because of the desire to perpetuate themselves in office, the use of corporate funds for such purposes is improper. See Bennett v. Propp, Del., 187 A.2d 405. . . .

Our first problem is the allocation of the burden of proof to show the presence or lack of good faith on the part of the board in authorizing the purchase of shares. Initially, the decision of the board of directors in authorizing a purchase was presumed to be in good faith and could be overturned only by a conclusive showing by plaintiffs of fraud or other misconduct. . . . In *Kors*, cited supra, the court merely indicated that the directors are presumed to act in good faith and the burden of proof to show to the contrary falls upon the plaintiff. However, in Bennett v. Propp, supra, we stated:

> "We must bear in mind the inherent danger in the purchase of shares with corporate funds to remove a threat to corporate policy when a threat to control is involved. The directors are of necessity confronted with a conflict of interest, and an objective decision is difficult. . . . Hence, in our opinion, the burden should be on the directors to justify such a purchase as one primarily in the corporate interest." (187 A.2d 409, at page 409).

. . .

To say that the burden of proof is upon the defendants is not to indicate, however, that the directors have the same "self-dealing interest" as is present, for example, when a director sells property to the corporation. The only clear pecuniary interest shown on the record was held by Mr. Cheff, as an executive of the corporation, and Trenkamp, as its attorney. The mere fact that some of the other directors were substantial shareholders does not create a personal pecuniary interest in the decisions made by the board of directors, since all shareholders would presumably share the benefit flowing to the substantial shareholder. . . . Accordingly, these directors other than Trenkamp and Cheff, while called upon to justify their actions, will not be held to the same standard of proof required of those directors having personal and pecuniary interest in the transaction.

As noted above, the Vice Chancellor found that the stock option plan, mentioned in the minutes as a justification for the purchases, was not a motivating reason for the purchases. This finding we accept, since there is evidence to support it; in fact, Trenkamp admitted that the stock option plan was not the motivating reason.

. . .

Plaintiffs urge that the sale price was unfair in view of the fact that the price was in excess of that prevailing on the open market. However, as conceded by all parties, a substantial block of stock will normally sell at a higher price than that prevailing on the open market, the increment being attributable to a "control premium." Plaintiffs argue that it is inappropriate to require the defendant corporation to pay a control premium, since control is meaningless to an acquisition by a corporation of its own shares. However, it is elementary that a holder of a substantial number of shares would expect to receive the control premium as part of his selling price, and if the corporation desired to obtain the stock, it is unreasonable to expect that the corporation could avoid paying what any other purchaser would be required to pay for the stock. In any event, the financial expert produced by defendant at trial indicated that the price paid was fair and there was no rebuttal. Ames, the financial man on the board, was strongly of the opinion that the purchase was a good deal for the corporation. The Vice Chancellor made no finding as to the fairness of the price other than to indicate the obvious fact that the market price was increasing as a result of open market purchases by Maremont, Mrs. Cheff and Holland.

The question then presented is whether or not defendants satisfied the burden of proof of showing reasonable grounds to believe a danger to corporate policy and effectiveness existed by the presence of the Maremont stock ownership. It is important to remember that the directors satisfy their burden by showing good faith and reasonable investigation; the directors will not be penalized for an honest mistake of judgment, if the judgment appeared reasonable at the time the decision was made. . . .

In holding that employee unrest could as well be attributed to a condition of Holland's business affairs as to the possibility of Maremont's intrusion, the Vice Chancellor must have had in mind one or both of two matters: (1) the pending proceedings before the Federal Trade Commission concerning certain sales practices of Holland; (2) the decrease in sales and profits during the preceding several years. Any other possible reason would be pure speculation. In the first place, the adverse decision of the F.T.C. was not announced until *after* the complained-of transaction. Secondly, the evidence clearly shows that the downward trend of sales and profits had reversed itself, presumably because of the reorganization which had then been completed. Thirdly, everyone who testified on the point said that the unrest was due to the possible threat presented by Maremont's purchases of stock. There was, in fact, no *testimony* whatever of any connection between the unrest and either the F.T.C. proceedings or the business picture.

The Vice Chancellor found that there was no substantial evidence of a liquidation posed by Maremont. This holding overlooks an important contention. The fear of the defendants, according to their testimony, was not limited to the possibility of liquidation; it included the alternate possibility of a material change in Holland's sales policies, which the board considered vital to its future success. The *unrebutted* testimony before the court indicated: (1) Maremont had deceived Cheff as to his original intentions, since his open market purchases were contemporaneous with his disclaimer of interest in Holland; (2) Maremont had given Cheff some reason to believe that he intended to eliminate the retail sales force of Holland; (3) Maremont demanded a place on the board; (4) Maremont substantially increased his purchases after having been refused a place on the board; (5) the directors had good reason to believe that unrest among key employees had been engendered by the Maremont threat; (6) the board had received advice from Dun and Bradstreet indicating the past liquidation or quick sale activities of Motor Products; (7) the board had received professional advice from the firm of Merrill Lynch, Fenner & Beane, who recommended that the purchase from Motor Products be carried out; (8) the board had received competent advice that the corporation was over-capitalized; (9) Staal and Cheff had made informal personal investigations from contacts in the business and financial community and had reported to the board of the alleged poor reputation of Maremont. The board was within its rights in relying upon that investigation, since 8 Del.C. § 141(f) allows the directors to reasonably rely upon a report provided by corporate officers.   .   .   .

Accordingly, we are of the opinion that the evidence presented in the court below leads inevitably to the conclusion that the board of directors, based upon direct investigation, receipt of professional advice, and personal observations of the contradictory action of Maremont and his explanation of corporate purpose, believed, with justification, that there was a reasonable threat to the continued existence of Holland, or at least existence in its present form, by the plan of Maremont to continue building up his stock holdings. We find no evidence in the record sufficient to justify a contrary conclusion. The opinion of the Vice Chancellor that employee unrest may have been engendered by other factors or that the board had no grounds to suspect Maremont is not supported in any manner by the evidence.

As noted above, the Vice–Chancellor found that the purpose of the acquisition was the improper desire to maintain control, but, at the same time, he exonerated those individual directors whom he believed to be unaware of the possibility of using non-corporate funds to accomplish this purpose. Such a decision is inconsistent with his finding that the motive was improper.   .   .   . If the actions were in fact improper because of a desire to maintain control, then the presence or absence of a non-corporate alternative is irrelevant, as corporate funds may not be used to advance an improper purpose even if there is no non-corporate alternative available. Conversely, if the actions were proper because of a decision by the board made in good faith that the corporate interest was served thereby, they are not rendered improper by the fact that some individual directors were willing to advance personal funds if the corporation did not. It is conceivable that the Vice Chancellor considered this feature of the case to be of significance because of his apparent belief that any excess corporate funds should have been used to finance a subsidiary corporation. That action would not have solved the problem of Holland's over-capitalization. In any event, this question was a matter of business judgment, which furnishes no justification for holding the directors personally responsible in this case.

Accordingly, the judgment of the court below is reversed and remanded with instruction to enter judgment for the defendants.

OTHER FACTS

As the court in Cheff v. Mathes suggests, at the time of the events giving rise to the case, the Federal Trade Commission had been investigating the sales practices of the Holland Furnace Company for more than a year. As a result of the investigation, it eventually ordered Holland to cease and desist from "unfair and deceptive" practices. The Court of Appeals for the Seventh Circuit, on appeal, upheld the order in 1961, in Holland Furnace Company v. Federal Trade Commission, 295 F.2d 302. Most of Holland's business was in replacement furnaces. The evidence showed that Holland salesmen had gone door to door posing as inspectors from the government or a utility company. They would then dismantle a furnace and refuse to reassemble it, claiming that the furnace was unsafe and that parts necessary to make it safe were unavailable.

In 1965, the court of appeals found that Holland and Mr. Cheff had violated its order and held both in contempt. It found that Cheff had "knowingly, willfully and intentionally violated" the order by continuing Holland's deceptive practices, while disguising them through various schemes. It fined Holland and sent Cheff to prison for six months. See In re Holland Furnace Company, 341 F.2d 548 (7th Cir.1965), affirmed sub nom. Cheff v. Schnackenberg, 384 U.S. 373 (1966).

The Delaware Supreme Court in *Cheff* states that at the time Maremont was bought out, in 1957, the "downward trend of sales and profits had reversed itself." The court fails to note that soon the downward trend resumed. In 1958, net income was $795,352 on sales of $31.3 million. In 1960, sales were $29.6 million and net income $76,745, and in 1961 sales were $24.2 million and there was a net loss of $1.2 million. From then on the company went rapidly downhill, with total losses over the next four years of $13.8 million. Sales in 1965 were $1.1 million, and the stock traded at a high of $1.63 and a low of 38 cents. See Moody's Industrial Manual, 1958–1965. By 1966 Holland apparently was out of business; it was not listed in Moody's in that year.

Arnold Maremont died in 1978 at the age of 74. According to his obituary in the New York Times (Nov. 9, 1978, at D19), he had been a "well-known art collector and civic leader," and "a governing life member of the Art Institute of Chicago and a former trustee of the Lyric Opera and the Ballet Theater." The obituary also states that "Mr. Maremont was the first Illinois industrialist to back a law ending discrimination against hiring Negroes and, as chairman of the Illinois Public Aid Commission in the early

60's, he campaigned for publicly supported birth control for welfare families."

NOTE: "GREENMAIL"

During the 1980's, the purchase by a corporation of a potential acquirer's stock, at a premium over the market price, came to be called "greenmail." Buying off one person, however, provides no protection against later pursuers, except possibly to the extent that the premium paid to the first pursuer depletes the corporate resources and makes it a less attractive target. Such reduction in corporate resources could, of course, be achieved by managers simply by paying a dividend to all shareholders or by buying the corporation's shares from all shareholders wanting to sell.

Section 5881 of the Internal Revenue Code, enacted in 1987, imposes a penalty tax of 50 percent on the gain from greenmail, which is defined as gain from the sale of stock that was held for less than two years and sold to the corporation pursuant to an offer that "was not made on the same terms to all shareholders."

ANALYSIS

1. The court in *Cheff* seems to view the case as one involving a difference in business strategy, with the board concluding that the value of the corporation would be maximized by continuing the existing strategy and Maremont concluding that a different strategy was required. Should the choice of strategies have been put to the shareholders? How?

2. According to the defendants, what was the threat posed by Maremont that justified their purchase of his shares? How else might they have responded to this threat?

3. The court in *Cheff* observes that corporate control struggles pose a potential conflict of interest between the shareholders and members of the board. The potential acquirer generally challenges the board's judgment and sometimes poses a threat to the incumbents' salaries or other substantial benefits (e.g., legal fees). In response to this conflict, the court shifts the burden of proof to the board members (to different degrees, depending on what they have at stake), but still applies the business judgment rule (requiring only good faith and reasonable investigation). Does this go far enough? What do you think is the proper test for determining whether a corporation should be permitted to buy out a dissident shareholder? Should the test be the same where the plaintiff seeks an injunction as where the plaintiff seeks money damages?

4. Should any of the events after 1957 have been treated as relevant to the decision?

5. What more might the board members have done to protect themselves against attack on their decision to buy Maremont's shares?

6. Suppose it was clear that Maremont intended to liquidate; that upon liquidation the shareholders would receive $20 per share; and that

the present market price was $13 per share. What possible grounds would the directors have had for the purchase of Maremont's shares? Suppose you are a shareholder and support Maremont's plan to liquidate and one of the directors says to you, "A year from now the shares will be worth $25, so it would be foolish to take $20 now." What is your response? Think of yourself as a litigator preparing to cross-examine the director on that statement. What questions might you pose?

PROBLEM

Five individuals form a corporation to manufacture maternity dresses. They have all had experience in the business and expect to be involved in various roles in its operation. They pooled their own resources and borrowed money to buy the plant and various other assets of a corporation that recently became bankrupt. They intend to sell shares to the public to raise operating funds. You represent one of the founders, who asks you for a list of the pros and cons on a provision in the articles of incorporation that would prohibit the corporation from buying its own shares except in stock market transactions or pursuant to an offer to all shareholders. What is your response?

B. DEVELOPMENT

INTRODUCTORY NOTE

In the next case, Unocal Corporation v. Mesa Petroleum Co., the court discusses, and criticizes, the "two-tier 'front loaded' cash tender offer." In stripped-down form, here is how the offer works, and why the court thought it "coercive." Suppose you own shares in Sloth Co. Sloth trades at $50 per share, and T. Boone Pickens has announced a standard one-tiered tender offer for Sloth Co. at $60 per share with no limit on the number of shares he is willing to take, but conditioned on his acquiring at least 51 percent of the shares. Shareholders who think this is the best offer they are likely to receive can tender; those who think another raider will raise the stakes further can refuse.

Suppose, however, that Pickens instead uses a "two-tiered front-end-loaded" tender offer. For example, he could offer to buy 51 percent of the stock at $65 (the front end), and announce that he will thereafter merge Sloth into his own firm in a transaction that pays $55 cash per share for the remaining 49 percent of the stock (the back end).[4] Suppose further that you believe that, if the Pickens bid fails, rival raiders will bid the price of Sloth stock up to $70.

Consider your options.

---

4. Hence the term "cash-out merger." See generally Section 1 of this chapter. The tender offer is "front-end loaded" because the front end offers a higher price ($65) than the back end ($55). A two-tiered offer can be "coercive" even if the front end is an any-and-all offer rather than an offer for 51 percent of the stock.

(a) You tender your stock and the deal goes through. You will receive $65 for at least 51 percent of your stock (a larger percentage if some shareholders fail to tender) and $55 for the rest.

(b) You do not tender and the deal goes through. You will receive $55 (the back-end price) for all your stock.

(c) The deal does not go through. You will sell your stock for $70 regardless of whether you tender.

Of these options, (a) is a better deal than (b), and (c) is better than (a). If you owned enough stock to affect the chance that Pickens's bid would succeed, you might refuse to tender. But if Sloth Co. is a large company and you own only a few shares, your decision to tender will not noticeably affect the probability of success of the offer. As a result, you will calculate that (i) if you tender, you will receive up to $65 if Pickens succeeds and $70 if he fails, and (ii) if you do not tender, you will receive $55 if Pickens succeeds and $70 if he fails. Notwithstanding that you hope Pickens fails, you probably will tender your shares, as will your fellow shareholders, and the bid is likely to succeed. Even though all shareholders would prefer to see the bid fail, most are likely to tender (because of the fear of being left with the back-end price ($55)) and the bid is likely to succeed. Each will think as follows: If the bid fails, I will wind up with $70 per share. If it succeeds, I will receive either $55 or $65 per share, depending on what I do. Since I own so few shares, my decision is not likely to affect the outcome. So I had better tender and pin down my right to $65 per share for at least 51 percent of my shares if the offer succeeds. Thus, the two-tiered front-end-loaded offer "coerces" each shareholder into tendering, and forecloses a more advantageous auction for the stock.

This may not be the whole story. Suppose again that Sloth stock trades at $50 and Pickens makes a one-tiered tender offer at $60. Why is Pickens offering so much? Pickens is no fool, and does not run a charity. Hence, you may well conclude that he is willing to offer $60 because he thinks he can (by revamping Sloth Co. management) increase the value of Sloth stock to more than $60. After all, if he cannot raise the price of the stock above $60, he will make no money from the deal—and Pickens always tries to make money. Suppose, therefore, that you conclude that Pickens will increase the value of Sloth stock to $70 per share.

Consider again your options:

(a) You *do* tender and the tender offer at $60 goes through. You will get $60.

(b) You do *not* tender and the tender offer goes through. You will get $70. In effect, you will "free-ride" on Pickens's efforts to turn the company around.

(c) The tender offer does not go through. You will be left with stock worth the same amount regardless of what you do.

Given these choices, you have a strong incentive not to tender, hoping the offer will succeed and your stock will be worth $70 per share. If many other shareholders make the same calculation, relatively few people will tender. As a result, shareholders may tender less than 51 percent of the stock, and the tender offer will fail. Even though Pickens could turn Sloth Co. into a more profitable company, shareholders will try to free-ride on his efforts, and his tender offer probably will fail. According to this scenario, the "two-tiered offer" is simply an ingenious and efficient solution to this free-riding problem.

At the time the *Unocal* case arose many major oil companies such as Unocal had vast oil reserves (that is, they owned oil in the ground). For some of these companies, the value of the reserves substantially exceeded the aggregate market price of the company's securities. Thus, as the saying went, it was cheaper to buy oil on Wall Street than to drill for it in the field. How could it be that the total value of the securities of a corporation could be substantially less than the readily determinable value of its assets? One plausible explanation was that incumbent managers were committed, for reasons having to do with their own egos and self interest, to maintaining exploration and development programs that had subnormal rates of return—basically, wasting the valuable assets of the corporation.[5]

Unocal Corporation v. Mesa Petroleum Co.

493 A.2d 946 (Del.1985).

We confront an issue of first impression in Delaware—the validity of a corporation's self-tender for its own shares which excludes from participation a stockholder making a hostile tender offer for the company's stock.

The Court of Chancery granted a preliminary injunction to the plaintiffs, Mesa Petroleum Co., Mesa Asset Co., Mesa Partners II, and Mesa Eastern, Inc. (collectively "Mesa")[1], enjoining an exchange offer of the defendant, Unocal Corporation (Unocal) for its own stock. The trial court concluded that a selective exchange offer, excluding Mesa, was legally impermissible. We cannot agree with such a blanket rule. The factual findings of the Vice Chancellor, fully supported by the record, establish that Unocal's board, consisting of a majority of independent directors, acted in good faith, and after reasonable investigation found that Mesa's tender offer was both inadequate and coercive. Under the circumstances the

---

5. For empirical support of this theory, see M. Jensen, The Takeover Controversy: Analysis and Evidence, in J. Coffee, L. Lowenstein, and S. Rose–Ackerman (eds.), Knights, Raiders, and Targets, at 320, 330. Jensen claims that the defeat of the Pickens offer resulted in a loss to the Unocal shareholders of $1.1 billion (the difference between the value of the Pickens offer and the value of what the shareholders were left with when it was defeated), even though the financial restructuring that Unocal was forced to adopt in response to Pickens's tender offer increased the value of the firm by $2.1 billion. Despite his "service" to the shareholders, says Jensen, Pickens was "vilified in the press . . .—obviously a perversion of incentives." Id. at 345.

1. T. Boone Pickens, Jr., is President and Chairman of the Board of Mesa Petroleum and President of Mesa Asset and controls the related Mesa entities.

board had both the power and duty to oppose a bid it perceived to be harmful to the corporate enterprise. On this record we are satisfied that the device Unocal adopted is reasonable in relation to the threat posed, and that the board acted in the proper exercise of sound business judgment. We will not substitute our views for those of the board if the latter's decision can be "attributed to any rational business purpose." Sinclair Oil Corp. v. Levien, Del.Supr., 280 A.2d 717, 720 (1971). Accordingly, we reverse the decision of the Court of Chancery and order the preliminary injunction vacated.

I.

The factual background of this matter bears a significant relationship to its ultimate outcome.

On April 8, 1985, Mesa, the owner of approximately 13% of Unocal's stock, commenced a two-tier "front loaded" cash tender offer for 64 million shares, or approximately 37%, of Unocal's outstanding stock at a price of $54 per share. The "back-end" was designed to eliminate the remaining publicly held shares by an exchange of securities purportedly worth $54 per share. However, pursuant to an order entered by the United States District Court for the Central District of California on April 26, 1985, Mesa issued a supplemental proxy statement to Unocal's stockholders disclosing that the securities offered in the second-step merger would be highly subordinated, and that Unocal's capitalization would differ significantly from its present structure. Unocal has rather aptly termed such securities "junk bonds."

Unocal's board consists of eight independent outside directors and six insiders. It met on April 13, 1985, to consider the Mesa tender offer. Thirteen directors were present, and the meeting lasted nine and one-half hours. The directors were given no agenda or written materials prior to the session. However, detailed presentations were made by legal counsel regarding the board's obligations under both Delaware corporate law and the federal securities laws. The board then received a presentation from Peter Sachs on behalf of Goldman Sachs & Co. (Goldman Sachs) and Dillon, Read & Co. (Dillon Read) discussing the bases for their opinions that the Mesa proposal was wholly inadequate. Mr. Sachs opined that the minimum cash value that could be expected from a sale or orderly liquidation for 100% of Unocal's stock was in excess of $60 per share. In making his presentation, Mr. Sachs showed slides outlining the valuation techniques used by the financial advisors, and others, depicting recent business combinations in the oil and gas industry. The Court of Chancery found that the Sachs presentation was designed to apprise the directors of the scope of the analyses performed rather than the facts and numbers used in reaching the conclusion that Mesa's tender offer price was inadequate.

Mr. Sachs also presented various defensive strategies available to the board if it concluded that Mesa's two-step tender offer was inadequate and should be opposed. One of the devices outlined was a self-tender by Unocal for its own stock with a reasonable price range of $70 to $75 per share. The cost of such a proposal would cause the company to incur $6.1—6.5 billion of additional debt, and a presentation was made informing the board of Unocal's ability to handle it. The directors were told that the primary effect of this obligation would be to reduce exploratory drilling, but that the company would nonetheless remain a viable entity.

The eight outside directors, comprising a clear majority of the thirteen members present, then met separately with Unocal's financial advisors and attorneys. Thereafter, they unanimously agreed to advise the board that it should reject Mesa's tender offer as inadequate, and that Unocal should pursue a self-tender to provide the stockholders with a fairly priced alternative to the Mesa proposal. The board then reconvened and unanimously adopted a resolution rejecting as grossly inadequate Mesa's tender offer. Despite the nine and one-half hour length of the meeting, no formal decision was made on the proposed defensive self-tender.

On April 15, the board met again with four of the directors present by telephone and one member still absent. This session lasted two hours. Unocal's Vice President of Finance and its Assistant General Counsel made a detailed presentation of the proposed terms of the exchange offer. A price range between $70 and $80 per share was considered, and ultimately the directors agreed upon $72. The board was also advised about the debt securities that would be issued, and the necessity of placing restrictive covenants upon certain corporate activities until the obligations were paid. The board's decisions were made in reliance on the advice of its investment bankers, including the terms and conditions upon which the securities were to be issued. Based upon this advice, and the board's own deliberations, the directors unanimously approved the exchange offer. Their resolution provided that if Mesa acquired 64 million shares of Unocal stock through its own offer (the Mesa Purchase Condition), Unocal would buy the remaining 49% outstanding for an exchange of debt securities having an aggregate par value of $72 per share. The board resolution also stated that the offer would be subject to other conditions that had been described to the board at the meeting, or which were deemed necessary by Unocal's officers, including the exclusion of Mesa from the proposal (the Mesa exclusion). Any such conditions were required to be in accordance with the "purport and intent" of the offer.

Unocal's exchange offer was commenced on April 17, 1985, and Mesa promptly challenged it by filing this suit in the Court of Chancery. On April 22, the Unocal board met again and was advised by Goldman Sachs and Dillon Read to waive the Mesa Purchase Condition as to 50 million shares. This recommendation was in response to a perceived concern of the shareholders that, if shares were tendered to Unocal, no shares would be purchased by either offeror. The directors were also advised that they should tender their own Unocal stock into the exchange offer as a mark of their confidence in it.

Another focus of the board was the Mesa exclusion. Legal counsel advised that under Delaware law Mesa could only be excluded for what the directors reasonably believed to be a valid corporate purpose. The directors' discussion centered on the objective of adequately compensating shareholders at the "back-end" of Mesa's proposal, which the latter would finance with "junk bonds." To include Mesa would defeat that goal, because under the proration aspect of the exchange offer (49%) every Mesa share accepted by Unocal would displace one held by another stockholder. Further, if Mesa were permitted to tender to Unocal, the latter would in effect be financing Mesa's own inadequate proposal.

On April 24, 1985 Unocal issued a supplement to the exchange offer describing the partial waiver of the Mesa Purchase Condition. On May 1, 1985, in another supplement, Unocal extended the withdrawal, proration and expiration dates of its exchange offer to May 17, 1985.

Meanwhile, on April 22, 1985, Mesa amended its complaint in this action to challenge the Mesa exclusion. A preliminary injunction hearing was scheduled for May 8, 1985. However, on April 23, 1985, Mesa moved for a temporary restraining order in response to Unocal's announcement that it was partially waiving the Mesa Purchase Condition. After expedited briefing, the Court of Chancery heard Mesa's motion on April 26.

On April 29, 1985, the Vice Chancellor temporarily restrained Unocal from proceeding with the exchange offer unless it included Mesa. The trial court recognized that directors could oppose, and attempt to defeat, a hostile takeover which they considered adverse to the best interests of the corporation. However, the Vice Chancellor decided that in a selective purchase of the company's stock, the corporation bears the burden of showing: (1) a valid corporate purpose, and (2) that the transaction was fair to all of the stockholders, including those excluded.

. . . .

II.

The issues we address involve these fundamental questions: Did the Unocal board have the power and duty to oppose a takeover threat it reasonably perceived to be harmful to the corporate enterprise, and if so, is its action here entitled to the protection of the business judgment rule?

Mesa contends that the discriminatory exchange offer violates the fiduciary duties Unocal owes it. Mesa argues that because of the Mesa exclusion the business judgment rule is inapplicable, because the directors by tendering their own shares will derive a financial benefit that is not available to *all* Unocal stockholders. Thus, it is Mesa's ultimate contention that Unocal cannot establish that the exchange offer is fair to *all* shareholders, and argues that the Court of Chancery was correct in concluding that Unocal was unable to meet this burden.

Unocal answers that it does not owe a duty of "fairness" to Mesa, given the facts here. Specifically, Unocal contends that its board of directors reasonably and in good faith concluded that Mesa's $54 two-tier tender offer was coercive and inadequate, and that Mesa sought selective treatment for itself. Furthermore, Unocal argues that the board's approval of the exchange offer was made in good faith, on an informed basis, and in the exercise of due care. Under these circumstances, Unocal contends that its directors properly employed this device to protect the company and its stockholders from Mesa's harmful tactics.

III.

We begin with the basic issue of the power of a board of directors of a Delaware corporation to adopt a defensive measure of this type. Absent such authority, all other questions are moot. Neither issues of fairness nor business judgment are pertinent without the basic underpinning of a board's legal power to act.

The board has a large reservoir of authority upon which to draw. Its duties and responsibilities proceed from the inherent powers conferred by 8 Del.C. § 141(a), respecting management of the corporation's "business and affairs."[6] Additionally, the powers here being exercised derive from 8 Del.C. § 160(a), conferring broad authority upon a corporation to deal in its own stock.[7] From this it is now well established that in the acquisition of its shares a Delaware corporation may deal selectively with its stockholders, provided the directors have not acted out of a sole or primary purpose to entrench themselves in office. Cheff v. Mathes, Del.Supr., 199 A.2d 548, 554 (1964); Bennett v. Propp, Del.Supr., 187 A.2d 405, 408 (1962); . . . .

Finally, the board's power to act derives from its fundamental duty and obligation to protect the corporate enterprise, which includes stockholders, from harm reasonably perceived, irrespective of its source. . . .

Thus, we are satisfied that in the broad context of corporate governance, including issues of fundamental corporate change, a board of directors is not a passive instrumentality.

Given the foregoing principles, we turn to the standards by which director action is to be measured. In Pogostin v. Rice, Del.Supr., 480 A.2d 619 (1984), we held that the business judgment rule, including the standards by which director conduct is judged, is applicable in the context of a takeover. Id. at 627. The business judgment rule is a "presumption that in making a business decision the directors of a corporation acted on an informed basis, in good faith and in the honest belief that the action taken was in the best interests of the company." Aronson v. Lewis, Del.Supr., 473 A.2d 805, 812 (1984) (citations omitted). A hallmark of the business

---

6. The general grant of power to a board of directors is conferred by 8 Del.C. § 141(a), which provides:

(a) The business *and affairs* of every corporation organized under this chapter shall be managed by or under the direction of a board of directors, except as may be otherwise provided in this chapter or in its certificate of incorporation. . . .

7. This power under 8 Del.C. § 160(a), with certain exceptions not pertinent here, is as follows:

(a) Every corporation may purchase, redeem, receive, take or otherwise acquire, own and hold, sell, lend, exchange, transfer or otherwise dispose of, pledge, use and otherwise deal in and with its own shares. . . .

judgment rule is that a court will not substitute its judgment for that of the board if the latter's decision can be "attributed to any rational business purpose." Sinclair Oil Corp. v. Levien, Del.Supr., 280 A.2d 717, 720 (1971).

When a board addresses a pending takeover bid it has an obligation to determine whether the offer is in the best interests of the corporation and its shareholders. In that respect a board's duty is no different from any other responsibility it shoulders, and its decisions should be no less entitled to the respect they otherwise would be accorded in the realm of business judgment. . . . There are, however, certain caveats to a proper exercise of this function. Because of the omnipresent specter that a board may be acting primarily in its own interests, rather than those of the corporation and its shareholders, there is an enhanced duty which calls for judicial examination at the threshold before the protections of the business judgment rule may be conferred.

This Court has long recognized that:

> We must bear in mind the inherent danger in the purchase of shares with corporate funds to remove a threat to corporate policy when a threat to control is involved. The directors are of necessity confronted with a conflict of interest, and an objective decision is difficult.

Bennett v. Propp, Del.Supr., 187 A.2d 405, 409 (1962). In the face of this inherent conflict directors must show that they had reasonable grounds for believing that a danger to corporate policy and effectiveness existed because of another person's stock ownership. Cheff v. Mathes, 199 A.2d at 554–55. However, they satisfy that burden "by showing good faith and reasonable investigation. . . ." Id. at 555. Furthermore, such proof is materially enhanced, as here, by the approval of a board comprised of a majority of outside independent directors who have acted in accordance with the foregoing standards. . . .

IV.

A.

In the board's exercise of corporate power to forestall a takeover bid our analysis begins with the basic principle that corporate directors have a fiduciary duty to act in the best interests of the corporation's stockholders. . . . As we have noted, their duty of care extends to protecting the corporation and its owners from perceived harm whether a threat originates from third parties or other shareholders.[10] But such powers are not absolute. A corporation does not have unbridled discretion to defeat any perceived threat by any Draconian means available.

The restriction placed upon a selective stock repurchase is that the directors may not have acted solely or primarily out of a desire to perpetu-

---

10. It has been suggested that a board's response to a takeover threat should be a passive one. . . . However, that clearly is not the law of Delaware, and as the propo-nents of this rule of passivity readily concede, it has not been adopted either by courts or state legislatures. . . .

ate themselves in office. See Cheff v. Mathes, 199 A.2d at 556. . . .
Of course, to this is added the further caveat that inequitable action may
not be taken under the guise of law. . . . The standard of proof
established in *Cheff v. Mathes* and discussed supra, is designed to ensure
that a defensive measure to thwart or impede a takeover is indeed motivated by a good faith concern for the welfare of the corporation and its
stockholders, which in all circumstances must be free of any fraud or other
misconduct. . . . However, this does not end the inquiry.

B.

A further aspect is the element of balance. If a defensive measure is to
come within the ambit of the business judgment rule, it must be reasonable
in relation to the threat posed. This entails an analysis by the directors of
the nature of the takeover bid and its effect on the corporate enterprise.
Examples of such concerns may include: inadequacy of the price offered,
nature and timing of the offer, questions of illegality, the impact on
"constituencies" other than shareholders (i.e., creditors, customers, employees, and perhaps even the community generally), the risk of noncon-
summation, and the quality of securities being offered in the exchange. . . . While not a controlling factor, it also seems to us that a
board may reasonably consider the basic stockholder interests at stake,
including those of short term speculators, whose actions may have fueled
the coercive aspect of the offer at the expense of the long term investor.[11]

---

11. There has been much debate respecting such stockholder interests. One
rather impressive study indicates that the
stock of over 50 percent of target companies,
who resisted hostile takeovers, later traded at
higher market prices than the rejected offer
price, or were acquired after the tender offer
was defeated by another company at a price
higher than the offer price. *See* Lipton,
[Takeover Bids in the Target's Boardroom],
35 Bus.Law. 101, 106–109, 132–133 (1979).
Moreover, an update by Kidder Peabody &
Company of this study, involving the stock
prices of target companies that have defeated
hostile tender offers during the period from
1973 to 1982 demonstrates that in a majority
of cases the target's shareholders benefited
from the defeat. The stock of 81% of the
targets studied has, since the tender offer,
sold at prices higher than the tender offer
price. When adjusted for the time value of
money, the figure is 64%. See Lipton &
Brownstein, [Takeover Responsibilities and
Directors' Responsibilities: An Update, ABA
Nat'l Inst. on the Dynamics of Corporate
Control, p. 10 (Dec. 8, 1983)]. The thesis
being that this strongly supports application
of the business judgment rule in response to
takeover threats. There is, however, a rather vehement contrary view. *See* Easterbrook
& Fischel, [Takeover Bids, Defensive Tactics,
and Shareholders' Welfare], 36 Bus.Law.
1733, 1739–1745 (1981).

[Eds.—Martin Lipton, author of two of
the studies cited by the court was, and remains, one of the best-known lawyers in the
takeover field. He was especially well known
for his ingenuity and effectiveness in resist-
ing takeovers. His studies were criticized by
scholars for methodological deficiencies. In
Amanda Acquisition Corp. v. Universal Foods
Corp., infra, Judge (formerly Professor) Easterbrook refers to later studies showing that
"if a firm fends off a bid, its profits decline,
and its stock price (adjusted for inflation and
market-wide changes) never tops the initial
bid, even if it is later acquired by another
firm." A hostile bid almost always results in
a substantial increase in share price and if
the bid is defeated, and no other bidders
come along, the price generally returns to its
previous level or less. Some ability to resist
a takeover bid may, however, allow a corporation to stimulate a bidding contest that increases the price ultimately received by
shareholders.]

Here, the threat posed was viewed by the Unocal board as a grossly inadequate two-tier coercive tender offer coupled with the threat of greenmail.

Specifically, the Unocal directors had concluded that the value of Unocal was substantially above the $54 per share offered in cash at the front end. Furthermore, they determined that the subordinated securities to be exchanged in Mesa's announced squeeze out of the remaining shareholders in the "back-end" merger were "junk bonds" worth far less than $54. It is now well recognized that such offers are a classic coercive measure designed to stampede shareholders into tendering at the first tier, even if the price is inadequate, out of fear of what they will receive at the back end of the transaction. Wholly beyond the coercive aspect of an inadequate two-tier tender offer, the threat was posed by a corporate raider with a national reputation as a "greenmailer."[13]

In adopting the selective exchange offer, the board stated that its objective was either to defeat the inadequate Mesa offer or, should the offer still succeed, provide the 49% of its stockholders, who would otherwise be forced to accept "junk bonds," with $72 worth of senior debt. We find that both purposes are valid.

However, such efforts would have been thwarted by Mesa's participation in the exchange offer. First, if Mesa could tender its shares, Unocal would effectively be subsidizing the former's continuing effort to buy Unocal stock at $54 per share. Second, Mesa could not, by definition, fit within the class of shareholders being protected from its own coercive and inadequate tender offer.

Thus, we are satisfied that the selective exchange offer is reasonably related to the threats posed. It is consistent with the principle that "the minority stockholder shall receive the substantial equivalent in value of what he had before." Sterling v. Mayflower Hotel Corp., Del.Supr., 93 A.2d 107, 114 (1952). . . .

This concept of fairness, while stated in the merger context, is also relevant in the area of tender offer law. Thus, the board's decision to offer what it determined to be the fair value of the corporation to the 49% of its shareholders, who would otherwise be forced to accept highly subordinated "junk bonds," is reasonable and consistent with the directors' duty to ensure that the minority stockholders receive equal value for their shares.

V.

Mesa contends that it is unlawful, and the trial court agreed, for a corporation to discriminate in this fashion against one shareholder. It

---

13. The term "greenmail" refers to the practice of buying out a takeover bidder's stock at a premium that is not available to other shareholders in order to prevent the takeover. The Chancery Court noted that "Mesa has made tremendous profits from its takeover activities although in the past few years it has not been successful in acquiring any of the target companies on an unfriendly basis." Moreover, the trial court specifically found that the actions of the Unocal board were taken in good faith to eliminate both the inadequacies of the tender offer and to forestall the payment of "greenmail."

argues correctly that no case has ever sanctioned a device that precludes a raider from sharing in a benefit available to all other stockholders. However, as we have noted earlier, the principle of selective stock repurchases by a Delaware corporation is neither unknown nor unauthorized. Cheff v. Mathes, 199 A.2d at 554; Bennett v. Propp, 187 A.2d [405, 408 (Del. 1962)]; Martin v. American Potash & Chemical Corporation, 92 A.2d [295, 302 (Del.1952)]; Kaplan v. Goldsamt, 380 A.2d at 568–569; Kors v. Carey, 158 A.2d [136, 140–141 (Del.Ch.1960)]; 8 Del.C. § 160. The only difference is that heretofore the approved transaction was the payment of "greenmail" to a raider or dissident posing a threat to the corporate enterprise. All other stockholders were denied such favored treatment, and given Mesa's past history of greenmail, its claims here are rather ironic.

However, our corporate law is not static. It must grow and develop in response to, indeed in anticipation of, evolving concepts and needs. Merely because the General Corporation Law is silent as to a specific matter does not mean that it is prohibited. . . . In the days when *Cheff, Bennett, Martin* and *Kors* were decided, the tender offer, while not an unknown device, was virtually unused, and little was known of such methods as two-tier "front-end" loaded offers with their coercive effects. Then, the favored attack of a raider was stock acquisition followed by a proxy contest. Various defensive tactics, which provided no benefit whatever to the raider, evolved. Thus, the use of corporate funds by management to counter a proxy battle was approved. . . . Litigation, supported by corporate funds, aimed at the raider has long been a popular device.

More recently, as the sophistication of both raiders and targets has developed, a host of other defensive measures to counter such ever mounting threats has evolved and received judicial sanction. These include defensive charter amendments and other devices bearing some rather exotic, but apt, names: Crown Jewel, White Knight, Pac Man, and Golden Parachute. Each has highly selective features, the object of which is to deter or defeat the raider.

Thus, while the exchange offer is a form of selective treatment, given the nature of the threat posed here the response is neither unlawful nor unreasonable. If the board of directors is disinterested, has acted in good faith and with due care, its decision in the absence of an abuse of discretion will be upheld as a proper exercise of business judgment.

To this Mesa responds that the board is not disinterested, because the directors are receiving a benefit from the tender of their own shares, which because of the Mesa exclusion, does not devolve upon *all* stockholders equally. . . . However, Mesa concedes that if the exclusion is valid, then the directors and all other stockholders share the same benefit. The answer of course is that the exclusion is valid, and the directors' participation in the exchange offer does not rise to the level of a disqualifying interest. . . .

VI.

In conclusion, there was directorial power to oppose the Mesa tender offer, and to undertake a selective stock exchange made in good faith and upon a reasonable investigation pursuant to a clear duty to protect the corporate enterprise. Further, the selective stock repurchase plan chosen by Unocal is reasonable in relation to the threat that the board rationally and reasonably believed was posed by Mesa's inadequate and coercive two-tier tender offer. Under those circumstances the board's action is entitled to be measured by the standards of the business judgment rule. Thus, unless it is shown by a preponderance of the evidence that the directors' decisions were primarily based on perpetuating themselves in office, or some other breach of fiduciary duty such as fraud, overreaching, lack of good faith, or being uninformed, a Court will not substitute its judgment for that of the board.

.   .   .

NOTE ON SEC REACTION AND POISON PILLS

After the *Unocal* decision, the SEC demonstrated its disapproval of discriminatory self-tenders by amending its rules to prohibit issuer tender offers other than those made to all shareholders. Rule 13e–4(f)(8). The SEC rule does not, however, prohibit "poison pills," which can have much the same effect. Poison pills are widely used, highly complex plans designed to provide varying degrees of protection against takeovers.

Pills take a wide variety of forms, but most are based on a form of security known as a "right." (Hence, the pill's official name, the Shareholder Rights Plan.) A traditional right, typically known as a warrant, grants the holder the option to purchase new shares of stock of the issuing corporation. Warrants are traded as separate securities, having value because they typically confer on the holder the right to buy issuer common stock at a discount from the prevailing market price. The poison pill variant of the right adds three additional elements not found in traditional rights: a "flip-in" element, a "flip-over" element, and a redemption provision.

The pill is typically adopted by the board of directors without any shareholder action. When adopted, the rights attach to the corporation's outstanding common stock, cannot be traded separately from the common stock, and are priced so that exercise of the option would be economically irrational. The rights become exercisable, and can be traded separately from the common stock, upon a so-called distribution event, which is typically defined as the acquisition of, or announcement of an intent to acquire, some specified percentage of the issuer's stock by a prospective acquirer. (Twenty percent is a commonly used trigger level.) Although the rights are now exercisable, and will remain so for the remainder of their specified life (typically ten years), they remain "out of the money."

The pill's flip-in element is triggered, typically, by the actual acquisition of some specified percentage of the issuer's common stock. (Again, 20 percent is a commonly used trigger.) If triggered, the flip-in pill entitles the holder of each right—except, and this is key, the acquirer and its affiliates or associates—to buy two shares of the target issuer's common stock or other securities at half price. In other words, the value of the stock received when the right is exercised is equal to two times the exercise price of the right. The deterrent effect of such a flip-in pill arises out of the massive dilution the pill causes to the value of the target stock owned by unwanted acquirer.

The pill's "flip-over" feature typically is triggered if, following the acquisition of a specified percentage of the target's common stock, the target is subsequently merged into the acquirer or one of its affiliates. In such an event, the holder of each right becomes entitled to purchase common stock of the acquiring company, again at half-price, thereby impairing the acquirer's capital structure and drastically diluting the interest of the acquirer's other stockholders.

Because the rights trade separately from the issuer's common stock, an acquirer remains subject to the pill's poisonous effects even if an overwhelming majority of the target's shareholders accept the bidder's tender offer. In the face of a pill, a prospective acquirer thus has a strong incentive to negotiate with the target's board. Most pills include a redemption provision pursuant to which the board may redeem the rights at a nominal price at any time prior to the right being exercised. (Some pills become non-redeemable after the triggering event.) Proponents of pills contend that these plans thus do not deter takeover bids, but rather simply give the target board leverage to negotiate the best possible deal for their shareholders.

In Moran v. Household International, Inc., 500 A.2d 1346 (Del.1985), the Delaware Supreme Court upheld a flip-over pill against a *Unocal*-based. The court claimed that the pill allowed the Household board to prevent coercive offers and to ensure that, if the company was to be sold, an auction or bidding process could be initiated so that the shareholders would obtain the highest possible price for their shares.

NOTE ON "JUNK" BONDS AS THE BACK–END CONSIDERATION

The court in *Unocal* wrote that one of the factors a board may consider in determining how to react to a takeover threat is "the quality of the securities being offered." Later it stated that but for the board's action the shareholders would have been "forced to accept highly subordinated 'junk bonds.' " Junk bonds are debt obligations of a corporation that are usually subordinate to other debt (they are comparable to a second or third mortgage on a personal residence) and bear a relatively high level of risk and high interest rate. It is by no means clear that shareholders should be concerned about the riskiness of such obligations, for at least two reasons. First, while a corporation's junk bonds are riskier than its investment-grade bonds, they are less risky than the common stock that the shareholder already owns. Second, a person who is reluctant to hold junk bonds received in an exchange can sell them. That being so, the only rational concern should be the value of such bonds. On the other hand, the value of junk bonds offered in an exchange such as the one proposed by Pickens in *Unocal* may be difficult to determine. One might well ask Pickens, "If the bonds you offer are worth what you say they are worth, why don't you just sell them to the public, or to institutions such as insurance companies or mutual funds or pension funds, and pay us in cash?" Nevertheless, what is important (assuming marketability) is value, not "quality." Asking which is more valuable, $100 worth of junk bonds or $100 worth of investment-grade bonds, assuming both are readily salable, is like asking which is heavier, a pound of lead or a pound of feathers.

ANALYSIS

1. If the trial court in a case involving a defense against a hostile takeover bid finds that independent members of the board acted in good faith and with reasonable investigation (as required by the business judgment rule), is the board's defensive action immune from judicial review?

2. What is the relevance, if any, of the fact that Pickens had a reputation as a "greenmailer"? As a greenmailer, what threat did he pose?

3. Suppose Pickens had had a reputation not as a greenmailer but as a liquidator. Suppose, for example, that it had been clear that it was Pickens's intent, if he was successful in his takeover attempt, to reduce substantially Unocal's exploration and drilling program and fire a substantial number of employees involved in that program. What relevance would that have had?

4. Suppose Pickens had offered $54 cash for any and all shares, with a commitment, if successful in acquiring control, to effect a cash-out merger of the remaining shares at the same price. Suppose, further, that there was no reason to believe that Pickens would liquidate assets or fire employees, other than a few of the top executives, who would receive generous severance compensation. Would the board still have been justified in resisting the takeover? In using a discriminatory self-tender?

Revlon, Inc. v. MacAndrews & Forbes Holdings, Inc.

506 A.2d 173 (Del.1985).

In this battle for corporate control of Revlon, Inc. (Revlon), the Court of Chancery enjoined certain transactions designed to thwart the efforts of Pantry Pride, Inc. (Pantry Pride) to acquire Revlon. The defendants are Revlon, its board of directors, and Forstmann Little & Co. and the latter's affiliated limited partnership (collectively, Forstmann). The injunction barred consummation of an option granted Forstmann to purchase certain Revlon assets (the lock-up option), a promise by Revlon to deal exclusively with Forstmann in the face of a takeover (the no-shop provision), and the payment of a $25 million cancellation fee to Forstmann if the transaction was aborted. The Court of Chancery found that the Revlon directors had breached their duty of care by entering into the foregoing transactions and effectively ending an active auction for the company. The trial court ruled that such arrangements are not illegal *per se* under Delaware law, but that their use under the circumstances here was impermissible. We agree.

. . .

Additionally, we address for the first time the extent to which a corporation may consider the impact of a takeover threat on constituencies other than shareholders. See Unocal Corp. v. Mesa Petroleum Co., Del. Supr., 493 A.2d 946, 955 (1985).

In our view, lock-ups and related agreements are permitted under Delaware law where their adoption is untainted by director interest or other breaches of fiduciary duty. The actions taken by the Revlon directors, however, did not meet this standard. Moreover, while concern for various corporate constituencies is proper when addressing a takeover threat, that principle is limited by the requirement that there be some rationally related benefit accruing to the stockholders. We find no such benefit here.

Thus, under all the circumstances we must agree with the Court of Chancery that the enjoined Revlon defensive measures were inconsistent with the directors' duties to the stockholders. Accordingly, we affirm.

I.

The somewhat complex maneuvers of the parties necessitate a rather detailed examination of the facts. The prelude to this controversy began in June 1985, when Ronald O. Perelman, chairman of the board and chief executive officer of Pantry Pride, met with his counterpart at Revlon, Michel C. Bergerac, to discuss a friendly acquisition of Revlon by Pantry Pride. Perelman suggested a price in the range of $40–50 per share, but the meeting ended with Bergerac dismissing those figures as considerably below Revlon's intrinsic value. All subsequent Pantry Pride overtures were rebuffed, perhaps in part based on Mr. Bergerac's strong personal antipathy to Mr. Perelman.

Thus, on August 14, Pantry Pride's board authorized Perelman to acquire Revlon, either through negotiation in the $42–$43 per share range, or by making a hostile tender offer at $45. Perelman then met with Bergerac and outlined Pantry Pride's alternate approaches. Bergerac remained adamantly opposed to such schemes and conditioned any further discussions of the matter on Pantry Pride executing a standstill agreement prohibiting it from acquiring Revlon without the latter's prior approval.

On August 19, the Revlon board met specially to consider the impending threat of a hostile bid by Pantry Pride.[3] At the meeting, Lazard

3. There were 14 directors on the Revlon board. Six of them held senior management positions with the company, and two others held significant blocks of its stock.

Freres, Revlon's investment banker, advised the directors that $45 per share was a grossly inadequate price for the company. Felix Rohatyn and William Loomis of Lazard Freres explained to the board that Pantry Pride's financial strategy for acquiring Revlon would be through "junk bond" financing followed by a break-up of Revlon and the disposition of its assets. With proper timing, according to the experts, such transactions could produce a return to Pantry Pride of $60 to $70 per share, while a sale of the company as a whole would be in the "mid 50" dollar range. Martin Lipton, special counsel for Revlon, recommended two defensive measures: first, that the company repurchase up to 5 million of its nearly 30 million outstanding shares; and second, that it adopt a Note Purchase Rights Plan. Under this plan, each Revlon shareholder would receive as a dividend one Note Purchase Right (the Rights) for each share of common stock, with the Rights entitling the holder to exchange one common share for a $65 principal Revlon note at 12% interest with a one-year maturity. The Rights would become effective whenever anyone acquired beneficial ownership of 20% or more of Revlon's shares, unless the purchaser acquired all the company's stock for cash at $65 or more per share. In addition, the Rights would not be available to the acquiror, and prior to the 20% triggering event the Revlon board could redeem the rights for 10 cents each. Both proposals were unanimously adopted.

Pantry Pride made its first hostile move on August 23 with a cash tender offer for any and all shares of Revlon at $47.50 per common share and $26.67 per preferred share, subject to (1) Pantry Pride's obtaining financing for the purchase, and (2) the Rights being redeemed, rescinded or voided.

The Revlon board met again on August 26. The directors advised the stockholders to reject the offer. Further defensive measures also were planned. On August 29, Revlon commenced its own offer for up to 10 million shares, exchanging for each share of common stock tendered one Senior Subordinated Note (the Notes) of $47.50 principal at 11.75% interest, due 1995, and one-tenth of a share of $9.00 Cumulative Convertible Exchangeable Preferred Stock valued at $100 per share. Lazard Freres opined that the notes would trade at their face value on a fully distributed basis.[4] Revlon stockholders tendered 87 percent of the outstanding shares (approximately 33 million), and the company accepted the full 10 million shares on a pro rata basis. The new Notes contained covenants which limited Revlon's ability to incur additional debt, sell assets, or pay divi-

Four of the remaining six directors were associated at some point with entities that had various business relationships with Revlon. On the basis of this limited record, however, we cannot conclude that this board is entitled to certain presumptions that generally attach to the decisions of a board whose majority consists of truly outside independent directors.

4. Like bonds, the Notes actually were issued in denominations of $1,000 and integral multiples thereof. A separate certificate was issued in a total principal amount equal to the remaining sum to which a stockholder was entitled. Likewise, in the esoteric parlance of bond dealers, a Note trading at par ($1,000) would be quoted on the market at 100.

dends unless otherwise approved by the "independent" (non-management) members of the board.

At this point, both the Rights and the Note covenants stymied Pantry Pride's attempted takeover. The next move came on September 16, when Pantry Pride announced a new tender offer at $42 per share, conditioned upon receiving at least 90% of the outstanding stock. Pantry Pride also indicated that it would consider buying less than 90%, and at an increased price, if Revlon removed the impeding Rights. While this offer was lower on its face than the earlier $47.50 proposal, Revlon's investment banker, Lazard Freres, described the two bids as essentially equal in view of the completed exchange offer.

The Revlon board held a regularly scheduled meeting on September 24. The directors rejected the latest Pantry Pride offer and authorized management to negotiate with other parties interested in acquiring Revlon. Pantry Pride remained determined in its efforts and continued to make cash bids for the company, offering $50 per share on September 27, and raising its bid to $53 on October 1, and then to $56.25 on October 7.

In the meantime, Revlon's negotiations with Forstmann and the investment group Adler & Shaykin had produced results. The Revlon directors met on October 3 to consider Pantry Pride's $53 bid and to examine possible alternatives to the offer. Both Forstmann and Adler & Shaykin made certain proposals to the board. As a result, the directors unanimously agreed to a leveraged buyout by Forstmann. The terms of this accord were as follows: each stockholder would get $56 cash per share; management would purchase stock in the new company by the exercise of their Revlon "golden parachutes";[5] Forstmann would assume Revlon's $475 million debt incurred by the issuance of the Notes; and Revlon would redeem the Rights and waive the Notes covenants for Forstmann or in connection with any other offer superior to Forstmann's. The board did not actually remove the covenants at the October 3 meeting, because Forstmann then lacked a firm commitment on its financing, but accepted the Forstmann capital structure, and indicated that the outside directors would waive the covenants in due course. Part of Forstmann's plan was to sell Revlon's Norcliff Thayer and Reheis divisions to American Home Products for $335 million. Before the merger, Revlon was to sell its cosmetics and fragrance division to Adler & Shaykin for $905 million. These transactions would facilitate the purchase by Forstmann or any other acquiror of Revlon.

When the merger, and thus the waiver of the Notes covenants, was announced, the market value of these securities began to fall. The Notes, which originally traded near par, around 100, dropped to 87.50 by October 8. One director later reported (at the October 12 meeting) a "deluge" of

5. In the takeover context "golden parachutes" generally are understood to be termination agreements providing substantial bonuses and other benefits for managers and certain directors upon a change in control of a company.

telephone calls from irate noteholders, and on October 10 the Wall Street Journal reported threats of litigation by these creditors.

Pantry Pride countered with a new proposal on October 7, raising its $53 offer to $56.25, subject to nullification of the Rights, a waiver of the Notes covenants, and the election of three Pantry Pride directors to the Revlon board. On October 9, representatives of Pantry Pride, Forstmann and Revlon conferred in an attempt to negotiate the fate of Revlon, but could not reach agreement. At this meeting Pantry Pride announced that it would engage in fractional bidding and top any Forstmann offer by a slightly higher one. It is also significant that Forstmann, to Pantry Pride's exclusion, had been made privy to certain Revlon financial data. Thus, the parties were not negotiating on equal terms.

Again privately armed with Revlon data, Forstmann met on October 11 with Revlon's special counsel and investment banker. On October 12, Forstmann made a new $57.25 per share offer, based on several conditions.[6] The principal demand was a lock-up option to purchase Revlon's Vision Care and National Health Laboratories divisions for $525 million, some $100–$175 million below the value ascribed to them by Lazard Freres, if another acquiror got 40% of Revlon's shares. Revlon also was required to accept a no-shop provision. The Rights and Notes covenants had to be removed as in the October 3 agreement. There would be a $25 million cancellation fee to be placed in escrow, and released to Forstmann if the new agreement terminated or if another acquiror got more than 19.9% of Revlon's stock. Finally, there would be no participation by Revlon management in the merger. In return, Forstmann agreed to support the par value of the Notes, which had faltered in the market, by an exchange of new notes. Forstmann also demanded immediate acceptance of its offer, or it would be withdrawn. The board unanimously approved Forstmann's proposal because: (1) it was for a higher price than the Pantry Pride bid, (2) it protected the noteholders, and (3) Forstmann's financing was firmly in place.[7] The board further agreed to redeem the rights and waive the covenants on the preferred stock in response to any offer above $57 cash per share. The covenants were waived, contingent upon receipt of an investment banking opinion that the Notes would trade near par value once the offer was consummated.

---

6. Forstmann's $57.25 offer ostensibly is worth $1 more than Pantry Pride's $56.25 bid. However, the Pantry Pride offer was immediate, while the Forstmann proposal must be discounted for the time value of money because of the delay in approving the merger and consummating the transaction. The exact difference between the two bids was an unsettled point of contention even at oral argument.

7. Actually, at this time about $400 million of Forstmann's funding was still sub-ject to two investment banks using their "best efforts" to organize a syndicate to provide the balance. Pantry Pride's entire financing was not firmly committed at this point either, although Pantry Pride represented in an October 11 letter to Lazard Freres that its investment banker, Drexel Burnham Lambert, was highly confident of its ability to raise the balance of $350 million. Drexel Burnham had a firm commitment for this sum by October 18.

Pantry Pride, which had initially sought injunctive relief from the Rights plan on August 22, filed an amended complaint on October 14 challenging the lock-up, the cancellation fee, and the exercise of the Rights and the Notes covenants. Pantry Pride also sought a temporary restraining order to prevent Revlon from placing any assets in escrow or transferring them to Forstmann. Moreover, on October 22, Pantry Pride again raised its bid, with a cash offer of $58 per share conditioned upon nullification of the Rights, waiver of the covenants, and an injunction of the Forstmann lock-up.

On October 15, the Court of Chancery prohibited the further transfer of assets, and eight days later enjoined the lock-up, no-shop, and cancellation fee provisions of the agreement. The trial court concluded that the Revlon directors had breached their duty of loyalty by making concessions to Forstmann, out of concern for their liability to the noteholders, rather than maximizing the sale price of the company for the stockholders' benefit. . . .

II.

. . .

A.

We turn first to Pantry Pride's probability of success on the merits. The ultimate responsibility for managing the business and affairs of a corporation falls on its board of directors. . . .

While the business judgment rule may be applicable to the actions of corporate directors responding to takeover threats, the principles upon which it is founded—care, loyalty and independence—must first be satisfied. . . .

If the business judgment rule applies, there is a "presumption that in making a business decision the directors of a corporation acted on an informed basis, in good faith and in the honest belief that the action taken was in the best interests of the company." Aronson v. Lewis, 473 A.2d [805, 812 (Del.1984)]. However, when a board implements anti-takeover measures there arises "the omnipresent specter that a board may be acting primarily in its own interests, rather than those of the corporation and its shareholders . . ." Unocal Corp. v. Mesa Petroleum Co., 493 A.2d at 954. This potential for conflict places upon the directors the burden of proving that they had reasonable grounds for believing there was a danger to corporate policy and effectiveness, a burden satisfied by a showing of good faith and reasonable investigation. Id. at 955. In addition, the directors must analyze the nature of the takeover and its effect on the corporation in order to ensure balance—that the responsive action taken is reasonable in relation to the threat posed. Id.

B.

The first relevant defensive measure adopted by the Revlon board was the Rights Plan, which would be considered a "poison pill" in the current language of corporate takeovers—a plan by which shareholders receive the right to be bought out by the corporation at a substantial premium on the occurrence of a stated triggering event. . . . [T]he board clearly had the power to adopt the measure. . . . Thus, the focus becomes one of reasonableness and purpose.

The Revlon board approved the Rights Plan in the face of an impending hostile takeover bid by Pantry Pride at $45 per share, a price which Revlon reasonably concluded was grossly inadequate. Lazard Freres had so advised the directors, and had also informed them that Pantry Pride was a small, highly leveraged company bent on a "bust-up" takeover by using "junk bond" financing to buy Revlon cheaply, sell the acquired assets to pay the debts incurred, and retain the profit for itself.[12] In adopting the Plan, the board protected the shareholders from a hostile takeover at a price below the company's intrinsic value, while retaining sufficient flexibility to address any proposal deemed to be in the stockholders' best interests.

To that extent the board acted in good faith and upon reasonable investigation. Under the circumstances it cannot be said that the Rights Plan as employed was unreasonable, considering the threat posed. Indeed, the Plan was a factor in causing Pantry Pride to raise its bids from a low of $42 to an eventual high of $58. At the time of its adoption the Rights Plan afforded a measure of protection consistent with the directors' fiduciary duty in facing a takeover threat perceived as detrimental to corporate interests. . . .

Far from being a "show-stopper," . . . the measure spurred the bidding to new heights, a proper result of its implementation. . . .

Although we consider adoption of the Plan to have been valid under the circumstances, its continued usefulness was rendered moot by the directors' actions on October 3 and October 12. At the October 3 meeting the board redeemed the Rights conditioned upon consummation of a merger with Forstmann, but further acknowledged that they would also be redeemed to facilitate any more favorable offer. On October 12, the board unanimously passed a resolution redeeming the Rights in connection with any cash proposal of $57.25 or more per share. Because all the pertinent offers eventually equalled or surpassed that amount, the Rights clearly were no longer any impediment in the contest for Revlon. This mooted any question of their propriety under *Moran* or *Unocal*.

C.

The second defensive measure adopted by Revlon to thwart a Pantry Pride takeover was the company's own exchange offer for 10 million of its shares. The directors' general broad powers to manage the business and affairs of the corporation are augmented by the specific authority conferred under 8 Del.C. § 160(a), permitting the company to deal in its own

---

12. [A] "bust-up" takeover generally refers to a situation in which one seeks to finance an acquisition by selling off pieces of the acquired company, presumably at a substantial profit.

stock.   . . . However, when exercising that power in an effort to
forestall a hostile takeover, the board's actions are strictly held to the
fiduciary standards outlined in *Unocal*.   These standards require the
directors to determine the best interests of the corporation and its stockholders, and impose an enhanced duty to abjure any action that is motivated by considerations other than a good faith concern for such interests.   . . .

The Revlon directors concluded that Pantry Pride's $47.50 offer was
grossly inadequate.   In that regard the board acted in good faith, and on an
informed basis, with reasonable grounds to believe that there existed a
harmful threat to the corporate enterprise.   The adoption of a defensive
measure, reasonable in relation to the threat posed, was proper and fully
accorded with the powers, duties, and responsibilities conferred upon
directors under our law.   . . .

D.

However, when Pantry Pride increased its offer to $50 per share, and
then to $53, it became apparent to all that the break-up of the company
was inevitable.   The Revlon board's authorization permitting management
to negotiate a merger or buyout with a third party was a recognition that
the company was for sale.   The duty of the board had thus changed from
the preservation of Revlon as a corporate entity to the maximization of the
company's value at a sale for the stockholders' benefit.   This significantly
altered the board's responsibilities under the *Unocal* standards.   It no
longer faced threats to corporate policy and effectiveness, or to the stockholders' interests, from a grossly inadequate bid.   The whole question of
defensive measures became moot.   The directors' role changed from defenders of the corporate bastion to auctioneers charged with getting the
best price for the stockholders at a sale of the company.

III.

This brings us to the lock-up with Forstmann and its emphasis on
shoring up the sagging market value of the Notes in the face of threatened
litigation by their holders.   Such a focus was inconsistent with the changed
concept of the directors' responsibilities at this stage of the developments.
The impending waiver of the Notes covenants had caused the value of the
Notes to fall, and the board was aware of the noteholders' ire as well as
their subsequent threats of suit.   The directors thus made support of the
Notes an integral part of the company's dealings with Forstmann, even
though their primary responsibility at this stage was to the equity owners.

The original threat posed by Pantry Pride—the break-up of the company—had become a reality which even the directors embraced.   Selective
dealing to fend off a hostile but determined bidder was no longer a proper
objective.   Instead, obtaining the highest price for the benefit of the
stockholders should have been the central theme guiding director action.
Thus, the Revlon board could not make the requisite showing of good faith
by preferring the noteholders and ignoring its duty of loyalty to the

shareholders. The rights of the former already were fixed by contract. . . . The noteholders required no further protection, and when the Revlon board entered into an auction-ending lock-up agreement with Forstmann on the basis of impermissible considerations at the expense of the shareholders, the directors breached their primary duty of loyalty.

The Revlon board argued that it acted in good faith in protecting the noteholders because *Unocal* permits consideration of other corporate constituencies. Although such considerations may be permissible, there are fundamental limitations upon that prerogative. A board may have regard for various constituencies in discharging its responsibilities, provided there are rationally related benefits accruing to the stockholders. However, such concern for non-stockholder interests is inappropriate when an auction among active bidders is in progress, and the object no longer is to protect or maintain the corporate enterprise but to sell it to the highest bidder.

Revlon also contended that it had contractual and good faith obligations to consider the noteholders. However, any such duties are limited to the principle that one may not interfere with contractual relationships by improper actions. Here, the rights of the noteholders were fixed by agreement, and there is nothing of substance to suggest that any of those terms were violated. The Notes covenants specifically contemplated a waiver to permit sale of the company at a fair price. The Notes were accepted by the holders on that basis, including the risk of an adverse market effect stemming from a waiver. Thus, nothing remained for Revlon to legitimately protect, and no rationally related benefit thereby accrued to the stockholders. Under such circumstances we must conclude that the merger agreement with Forstmann was unreasonable in relation to the threat posed.

A lock-up is not *per se* illegal under Delaware law. . . . Such options can entice other bidders to enter a contest for control of the corporation, creating an auction for the company and maximizing shareholder profit. Current economic conditions in the takeover market are such that a "white knight" like Forstmann might only enter the bidding for the target company if it receives some form of compensation to cover the risks and costs involved. . . .

However, while those lock-ups which draw bidders into the battle benefit shareholders, similar measures which end an active auction and foreclose further bidding operate to the shareholders' detriment. . . .

The Forstmann option had a . . . destructive effect on the auction process. Forstmann had already been drawn into the contest on a preferred basis, so the result of the lock-up was not to foster bidding, but to destroy it. The board's stated reasons for approving the transactions were: (1) better financing, (2) noteholder protection, and (3) higher price. As the Court of Chancery found, and we agree, any distinctions between the rival bidders' methods of financing the proposal were nominal at best, and such a consideration has little or no significance in a cash offer for any and all shares. The principal object, contrary to the board's duty of care, appears to have been protection of the noteholders over the shareholders' interests.

While Forstmann's $57.25 offer was objectively higher than Pantry Pride's $56.25 bid, the margin of superiority is less when the Forstmann price is adjusted for the time value of money. In reality, the Revlon board ended the auction in return for very little actual improvement in the final bid. The principal benefit went to the directors, who avoided personal liability to a class of creditors to whom the board owed no further duty under the circumstances. . . .

In addition to the lock-up option, the Court of Chancery enjoined the no-shop provision as part of the attempt to foreclose further bidding by Pantry Pride. . . . The no-shop provision, like the lock-up option, while not *per se* illegal, is impermissible under the *Unocal* standards when a board's primary duty becomes that of an auctioneer responsible for selling the company to the highest bidder. The agreement to negotiate only with Forstmann ended rather than intensified the board's involvement in the bidding contest.

It is ironic that the parties even considered a no-shop agreement when Revlon had dealt preferentially, and almost exclusively, with Forstmann throughout the contest. After the directors authorized management to negotiate with other parties, Forstmann was given every negotiating advantage that Pantry Pride had been denied: cooperation from management, access to financial data, and the exclusive opportunity to present merger proposals directly to the board of directors. Favoritism for a white knight to the total exclusion of a hostile bidder might be justifiable when the latter's offer adversely affects shareholder interests, but when bidders make relatively similar offers, or dissolution of the company becomes inevitable, the directors cannot fulfill their enhanced *Unocal* duties by playing favorites with the contending factions. Market forces must be allowed to operate freely to bring the target's shareholders the best price available for their equity. Thus, as the trial court ruled, the shareholders' interests necessitated that the board remain free to negotiate in the fulfillment of that duty.

The court below similarly enjoined the payment of the cancellation fee, pending a resolution of the merits, because the fee was part of the overall plan to thwart Pantry Pride's efforts. We find no abuse of discretion in that ruling.

. . .

V.

In conclusion, the Revlon board was confronted with a situation not uncommon in the current wave of corporate takeovers. A hostile and determined bidder sought the company at a price the board was convinced was inadequate. The initial defensive tactics worked to the benefit of the shareholders, and thus the board was able to sustain its *Unocal* burdens in justifying those measures. However, in granting an asset option lock-up to Forstmann, we must conclude that under all the circumstances the directors allowed considerations other than the maximization of shareholder profit to affect their judgment, and followed a course that ended the auction for Revlon, absent court intervention, to the ultimate detriment of its shareholders. No such defensive measure can be sustained when it represents a breach of the directors' fundamental duty of care. See Smith v. Van Gorkom, Del.Supr., 488 A.2d 858, 874 (1985). In that context the board's action is not entitled to the deference accorded it by the business judgment rule. The measures were properly enjoined. The decision of the Court of Chancery, therefore, is

AFFIRMED.

SIDELIGHTS

The clash between Perelman of Pantry Pride and Bergerac of Revlon involved personalities as well as money and power. In a fascinating account of Perelman's eventually successful takeover (which ultimately resulted in Perelman becoming one of the richest people in America), Bergerac is described as "a courtly, somewhat imperious, urbane, witty Frenchman," while Perelman is "crude, brusque, humorless, speaks in a staccato manner and perpetually puffs on a cigar." C. Bruck, The Predators' Ball 194 (1988) (the story of Michael Milken of Drexel Burnham Lambert, who provided the financing for Perelman). Thus, the Revlon takeover was "a class war, between the corporate America and Wall Street elite, and the Drexel arrivistes." Id. at 197. Perelman won that war, but Bergerac's defeat was softened with $35 million in severance pay (id. at 232)—the corporate world's version of the Marshall plan.

NOTE ON SUBSEQUENT DELAWARE DECISIONS

In Ivanhoe Partners v. Newmont Mining Corp., 535 A.2d 1334 (Del. 1987), Pickens, acting through Ivanhoe Partners, sought control of Newmont, again with a two-tier offer that the court found to be inadequate and coercive. Newmont responded by paying a large cash dividend. This was intended to, and did, provide the cash that allowed one shareholder, a firm called Gold Fields PLC, which had itself shown some interest in gaining control, to buy shares in the market (in a "street sweep") and increase its ownership interest from 26 percent to 49.7 percent. Before Newmont declared the dividend, it had entered into a "standstill" agreement with Gold Fields. Under that agreement, Gold Fields was limited to 40 percent of the representation on the Newmont board of directors. Thus, Gold Fields accepted a noncontrolling but significant position on the board. The combination of the Gold Fields shares and the management-controlled shares was such that no one else could acquire enough shares to gain control. Thus, Pickens's effort to gain control was stymied. The court upheld the Newmont defense, distinguishing *Revlon* on the ground that "Newmont never was for sale," nor was its breakup inevitable. That was true, to be sure, but what did happen was that management ensured its control and the shareholders were deprived of the opportunity to sell their shares for a premium—leaving them worse off than the Revlon shareholders would have been if the Revlon defensive sale to Forstmann had succeeded.

In Mills Acquisition Co. v. Macmillan, Inc., 559 A.2d 1261 (Del.1989), however, the Delaware court made clear the limited scope of its *Ivanhoe Partners* holding. In *Macmillan,* another well-known bidder, Robert Maxwell, sought control of Macmillan. Its board responded by attempting a buyout by a group led by management in conjunction with a leading takeover specialist, the firm of Kohlberg, Kravis, Roberts and Company (KKR). The board granted special treatment to the insider group, including a "tip" as to the amount of Maxwell's bid and a lock-up asset option. The independent members of the board were largely passive, allowing the CEO to run the show and, the court found, failing in their obligation of "oversight." The court observed that "judicial reluctance to assess the merits of a business decision ends in the face of illicit manipulation of a board's deliberative processes by self-interested corporate fiduciaries." The court distinguished *Ivanhoe Partners* on the basis of its "special facts and circumstances . . . specifically, Newmont's management faced two potentially coercive offers" (from Pickens and from Gold Fields). The court also indicated that the *Revlon* duty could be triggered by a restructuring that shifted control to management, even without a "sale" of the corporation or of any existing shares.[7]

ANALYSIS

1. The court states that Revlon had about 30 million shares outstanding. Thus, Perelman's offer of $56 (roughly) per share implied that he was willing to pay $1,680 mil. for the entire firm. Suppose that in fact he had decided that he would bid as high as $1,800 mil. and that raising his offer to this amount would not impose any additional legal, accounting, or other such costs on him. Suppose further that Forstmann had decided that he would be willing to bid as high as $1,700 mil., after taking account of legal and accounting costs of $10 mil. In the absence of a termination fee or other lockup, who prevails and at what price in a fair auction? Forstmann will be unwilling to bid, because he will be reasonably certain that Perelman will outbid him and that he will therefore waste his $10 mil. Suppose that the Revlon board offers Forstmann a termination fee of $12 mil. in return for a bid of $1,700 mil. Forstmann will be happy to accept the offer. He will bid $1,700. Perelman will bid, say, $1,701 mil. If the Revlon board accepts the $1,701 mil. Perelman bid, Revlon's shareholders will net $1,701 mil. The $12 mil. payable to Forstmann will come from the Revlon assets and will therefore be paid, in effect, by Perelman. The Revlon shareholders will have increased their total proceeds by $21 mil. (the $1,701 mil. final bid less the $1,680 prior bid). Forstmann will be ahead $2 mil. for his

---

7. Maxwell ultimately succeeded with his takeover bid. He proceeded to sell off a number of MacMillan's subsidiaries, including the legal-books publisher, Michie Company, which was sold to Mead Corporation (which owns Lexis) for about $226.5 million in December, 1988. See N.Y. Times, Dec. 12, 1988, p. C24, col. 3 (western ed.).

efforts. Perelman will have bought the company for $1,713 mil. (his bid of $1,701 mil. plus the termination fee of $12 mil.).

What if the Revlon board offers Forstmann a termination fee of $20 mil. in return for a bid of $1,750 mil.? This would be a tough one for Forstmann—unless he is certain that Perelman will outbid him. If Perelman does not do so, Forstmann winds up buying the company for $50 mil. more than it is worth to him, and, of course, there is no termination fee. In fact, if Perelman values the company at $1,800 mil., he will bid up to $1,780 mil. when the termination fee is $20 mil., but Forstmann may not be sure of that. Note that the termination fee does not fall from heaven. It comes from Revlon and reduces the amount the Perelman is willing to pay and that the Revlon shareholders will receive.

Finally, suppose the board offers a termination fee of $150 mil. in return for a bid of $1,700 mil. The termination fee reduces the value to Perelman to $1,650 mil., so he will not outbid Forstmann. Thus, the company goes to Forstmann for $1,700 mil. even though Perelman values it at $1,800 mil.

Return to the facts as originally stated, with a termination fee of $12 mil. In the end, everyone is better off, but there has been a waste of $10 in expenses incurred by Forstmann. Is there a better way to induce Perelman to increase his bid—a way that avoids the waste?

2.   In *Revlon,* precisely when was it that the duty of the board to step back and act as auctioneers arose?

3.   Does the board of directors of a Delaware corporation have "fiduciary" obligations to its creditors?   Should it have?

Paramount Communications, Inc. v. Time Incorporated

571 A.2d 1140 (Del.1989).

.   .   .

I

Time is a Delaware corporation with its principal offices in New York City.   Time's traditional business is publication of magazines and books; however, Time also provides pay television programming through its Home Box Office, Inc. and Cinemax subsidiaries.   In addition, Time owns and operates cable television franchises through its subsidiary, American Television and Communication Corporation.   During the relevant time period, Time's board consisted of sixteen directors.   Twelve of the directors were "outside," nonemployee directors.   Four of the directors were also officers of the company.   .   .   .

As early as 1983 and 1984, Time's executive board began considering expanding Time's operations into the entertainment industry.   In 1987, Time established a special committee of executives to consider and propose corporate strategies for the 1990s.   The consensus of the committee was that Time should move ahead in the area of ownership and creation of video programming.   . . .

In late spring of 1987, a meeting took place between Steve Ross, CEO of Warner Brothers, and N.J. Nicholas [President and a director] of Time. Ross and Nicholas discussed the possibility of a joint venture between the two companies through the creation of a jointly-owned cable company. Time would contribute its cable system and HBO. Warner would contribute its cable system and provide access to Warner Brothers Studio. The resulting venture would be a larger, more efficient cable network, able to produce and distribute its own movies on a world-wide basis. Ultimately the parties abandoned this plan, determining that it was impractical for several reasons, chief among them being tax considerations.

On August 11, 1987, Gerald M. Levin, Time's vice chairman and chief strategist, wrote J. Richard Munro [Time Chairman] a confidential memorandum in which he strongly recommended a strategic consolidation with Warner. In June 1988, Nicholas and Munro sent to each outside director a copy of the "comprehensive long-term planning document" prepared by the committee of Time executives that had been examining strategies for the 1990s. The memo included reference to and a description of Warner as a potential acquisition candidate.

.   . . On July 21, 1988, Time's board met, with all outside directors present. The meeting's purpose was to consider Time's expansion into the entertainment industry on a global scale.   . . .

Without any definitive decision on choice of a company, the board approved in principle a strategic plan for Time's expansion.   . . .

The board's consensus was that a merger of Time and Warner was feasible, but only if Time controlled the board of the resulting corporation and thereby preserved a management committed to Time's journalistic integrity. To accomplish this goal, the board stressed the importance of carefully defining in advance the corporate governance provisions that would control the resulting entity.   . . .

Of a wide range of companies considered by Time's board as possible merger candidates, Warner Brothers, Paramount, Columbia, M.C.A., Fox, MGM, Disney, and Orion, the board, in July 1988, concluded that Warner was the superior candidate for a consolidation.   . . .

From the outset, Time's board favored an all-cash or cash and securities acquisition of Warner as the basis for consolidation. Bruce Wasserstein, Time's financial advisor, also favored an outright purchase of Warner. However, Steve Ross, Warner's CEO, was adamant that a business combination was only practicable on a stock-for-stock basis.   . . .

Eventually Time acquiesced in Warner's insistence on a stock-for-stock deal, but talks broke down over corporate governance issues. Time wanted Ross' position as a co-CEO to be temporary and wanted Ross to retire in five years. Ross, however, refused to set a time for his retirement and viewed Time's proposal as indicating a lack of confidence in his leadership.   . . .

Warner and Time resumed negotiations in January 1989. The catalyst for the resumption of talks was a private dinner between Steve Ross and Time outside director, Michael Dingman. Dingman was able to convince Ross that the transitional nature of the proposed co-CEO arrangement did not reflect a lack of confidence in Ross. Ross agreed that this course was best for the company and a meeting between Ross and Munro resulted. Ross agreed to retire in five years and let Nicholas succeed him. . . .

Time insider directors Levin and Nicholas met with Warner's financial advisors to decide upon a stock exchange ratio. Time's board had recognized the potential need to pay a premium in the stock ratio in exchange for dictating the governing arrangement of the new Time–Warner. . . . Warner's financial advisors informed its board that any exchange rate over .400 was a fair deal and any exchange rate over .450 was "one hell of a deal." The parties ultimately agreed upon an exchange rate favoring Warner of .465. On that basis, Warner stockholders would have owned approximately 62% of the common stock of Time–Warner.

On March 3, 1989, Time's board, with all but one director in attendance, met and unanimously approved the stock-for-stock merger with Warner. Warner's board likewise approved the merger. . . .

At its March 3, 1989 meeting, Time's board adopted several defensive tactics. Time entered an automatic share exchange agreement with Warner. Time would receive 17,292,747 shares of Warner's outstanding common stock (9.4%) and Warner would receive 7,080,016 shares of Time's outstanding common stock (11.1%). Either party could trigger the exchange. Time sought out and paid for "confidence" letters from various banks with which it did business. In these letters, the banks promised not to finance any third-party attempt to acquire Time. Time argues these agreements served only to preserve the confidential relationship between itself and the banks. The Chancellor found these agreements to be inconsequential and futile attempts to "dry up" money for a hostile takeover. Time also agreed to a "no-shop" clause, preventing Time from considering any other consolidation proposal, thus relinquishing its power to consider other proposals, regardless of their merits. Time did so at Warner's insistence. Warner did not want to be left "on the auction block" for an unfriendly suitor, if Time were to withdraw from the deal.

Time's board simultaneously established a special committee of outside directors, Finkelstein, Kearns, and Opel, to oversee the merger. The committee's assignment was to resolve any impediments that might arise in the course of working out the details of the merger and its consummation.

Time representatives lauded the lack of debt to the United States Senate and to the President of the United States. Public reaction to the announcement of the merger was positive. Time–Warner would be a media colossus with international scope. The board scheduled the stockholder vote for June 23; and a May 1 record date was set. On May 24, 1989, Time sent out extensive proxy statements to the stockholders regarding the approval vote on the merger. In the meantime, with the merger proceeding without impediment, the special committee had concluded, shortly after its creation, that it was not necessary either to retain independent consultants, legal or financial, or even to meet. Time's board was unanimously in favor of the proposed merger with Warner; and, by the end of May, the Time–Warner merger appeared to be an accomplished fact.

On June 7, 1989, these wishful assumptions were shattered by Paramount's surprising announcement of its all-cash offer to purchase all outstanding shares of Time for $175 per share. The following day, June 8, the trading price of Time's stock rose from $126 to $170 per share. Paramount's offer was said to be "fully negotiable."

Time found Paramount's "fully negotiable" offer to be in fact subject to at least three conditions. First, Time had to terminate its merger agreement and stock exchange agreement with Warner, and remove certain other of its defensive devices, including the redemption of Time's shareholder rights. Second, Paramount had to obtain the required cable franchise transfers from Time in a fashion acceptable to Paramount in its sole discretion. Finally, the offer depended upon a judicial determination that section 203 of the General Corporate Law of Delaware (The Delaware Anti–Takeover Statute [discussed after the *CTS* case, below]) was inapplicable to any Time–Paramount merger. . . .

On June 8, 1989, Time formally responded to Paramount's offer. Time's chairman and CEO, J. Richard Munro, sent an aggressively worded letter to Paramount's CEO, Martin Davis. Munro's letter attacked Davis' personal integrity and called Paramount's offer "smoke and mirrors."

. . .

Over the following eight days, Time's board met three times to discuss Paramount's $175 offer. The board viewed Paramount's offer as inadequate and concluded that its proposed merger with Warner was the better course of action. Therefore, the board declined to open any negotiations with Paramount and held steady its course toward a merger with Warner.

[On] June 16, Time's board met to take up Paramount's offer. The board's prevailing belief was that Paramount's bid posed a threat to Time's control of its own destiny and retention of the "Time Culture." Even after Time's financial advisors made another presentation of Paramount and its business attributes, Time's board maintained its position that a combination with Warner offered greater potential for Time. . . .

At the same meeting, Time's board decided to recast its consolidation with Warner into an outright cash and securities acquisition of Warner by Time; and Time so informed Warner. Time accordingly restructured its proposal to acquire Warner as follows: Time would make an immediate all-cash offer for 51% of Warner's outstanding stock at $70 per share. The remaining 49% would be purchased at some later date for a mixture of cash and securities worth $70 per share. To provide the funds required for its outright acquisition of Warner, Time would assume 7–10 billion dollars worth of debt, thus eliminating one of the principal transaction-related benefits of the original merger agreement. Nine billion dollars of the total purchase price would be allocated to the purchase of Warner's goodwill.

. . .

On June 23, 1989, Paramount raised its all-cash offer to buy Time's outstanding stock to $200 per share. Paramount still professed that all aspects of the offer were negotiable. Time's board met on June 26, 1989 and formally rejected Paramount's $200 per share second offer. The board reiterated its belief that, despite the $25 increase, the offer was still inadequate. The Time board maintained that the Warner transaction offered a greater long-term value for the stockholders and, unlike Paramount's offer, did not pose a threat to Time's survival and its "culture." Paramount then filed this action in the Court of Chancery.*

II

The Shareholder Plaintiffs first assert a *Revlon* claim. They contend that the March 4 Time–Warner agreement effectively put Time up for sale, triggering *Revlon* duties, requiring Time's board to enhance short-term shareholder value and to treat all other interested acquirors on an equal basis. The Shareholder Plaintiffs base this argument on two facts: (i) the ultimate Time–Warner exchange ratio of .465 favoring Warner, resulting in Warner shareholders' receipt of 62% of the combined company; and (ii) the subjective intent of Time's directors as evidenced in their statements that the market might perceive the Time–Warner merger as putting Time up "for sale" and their adoption of various defensive measures.

The Shareholder Plaintiffs further contend that Time's directors, in structuring the original merger transaction to be "takeover-proof," triggered *Revlon* duties by foreclosing their shareholders from any prospect of obtaining a control premium. In short, plaintiffs argue that Time's board's decision to merge with Warner imposed a fiduciary duty to maximize immediate share value and not erect unreasonable barriers to further bids. Therefore, they argue, the Chancellor erred in finding: that Paramount's bid for Time did not place Time "for sale"; that Time's transaction with Warner did not result in any transfer of control; and that the combined Time–Warner was not so large as to preclude the possibility of the stockholders of Time–Warner receiving a future control premium.

Paramount asserts only a *Unocal* claim in which the shareholder plaintiffs join. Paramount contends that the Chancellor, in applying the first part of the *Unocal* test, erred in finding that Time's board had reasonable grounds to believe that Paramount posed both a legally cognizable threat to Time shareholders and a danger to Time's corporate policy and effectiveness. Paramount also contests the court's finding that Time's board made a reasonable and objective investigation of Paramount's offer so as to be informed before rejecting it. Paramount further claims that the

---

* [Editors—Suits filed subsequently on   consolidated with the Paramount action.] behalf of Time shareholders were ultimately

court erred in applying *Unocal's* second part in finding Time's response to be "reasonable." Paramount points primarily to the preclusive effect of the revised agreement which denied Time shareholders the opportunity both to vote on the agreement and to respond to Paramount's tender offer. Paramount argues that the underlying motivation of Time's board in adopting these defensive measures was management's desire to perpetuate itself in office.

. . .

A.

We first take up plaintiffs' principal *Revlon* argument, summarized above. In rejecting this argument, the Chancellor found the original Time–Warner merger agreement not to constitute a "change of control" and concluded that the transaction did not trigger *Revlon* duties. The Chancellor's conclusion is premised on a finding that "[b]efore the merger agreement was signed, control of the corporation existed in a fluid aggregation of unaffiliated shareholders representing a voting majority—in other words, in the market." The Chancellor's findings of fact are supported by the record and his conclusion is correct as a matter of law. However, we premise our rejection of plaintiffs' *Revlon* claim on different grounds, namely, the absence of any substantial evidence to conclude that Time's board, in negotiating with Warner, made the dissolution or break-up of the corporate entity inevitable, as was the case in *Revlon*.

Under Delaware law there are, generally speaking and without excluding other possibilities, two circumstances which may implicate *Revlon* duties. The first, and clearer one, is when a corporation initiates an active bidding process seeking to sell itself or to effect a business reorganization involving a clear break-up of the company. . . . However, *Revlon* duties may also be triggered where, in response to a bidder's offer, a target abandons its long-term strategy and seeks an alternative transaction involving the breakup of the company. Thus, in *Revlon,* when the board responded to Pantry Pride's offer by contemplating a "bust-up" sale of assets in a leveraged acquisition, we imposed upon the board a duty to maximize immediate shareholder value and an obligation to auction the company fairly. If, however, the board's reaction to a hostile tender offer is found to constitute only a defensive response and not an abandonment of the corporation's continued existence, *Revlon* duties are not triggered, though *Unocal* duties attach. . . .

The plaintiffs insist that even though the original Time–Warner agreement may not have worked "an objective change of control," the transaction made a "sale" of Time inevitable. Plaintiffs rely on the subjective intent of Time's board of directors and principally upon certain board members' expressions of concern that the Warner transaction *might* be viewed as effectively putting Time up for sale. Plaintiffs argue that the use of a lock-up agreement, a no-shop clause, and so-called "dry-up" agreements prevented shareholders from obtaining a control premium in the immediate future and thus violated *Revlon*.

We agree with the Chancellor that such evidence is entirely insufficient to invoke *Revlon* duties; and we decline to extend *Revlon's* application to corporate transactions simply because they might be construed as putting a corporation either "in play" or "up for sale." . . . The adoption of structural safety devices alone does not trigger *Revlon*. Rather, as the Chancellor stated, such devices are properly subject to a *Unocal* analysis.

. . .

B.

We turn now to plaintiffs' *Unocal* claim. We begin by noting, as did the Chancellor, that our decision does not require us to pass on the wisdom of the board's decision to enter into the original Time–Warner agreement. That is not a court's task. Our task is simply to review the record to determine whether there is sufficient evidence to support the Chancellor's conclusion that the initial Time–Warner agreement was the product of a proper exercise of business judgment. . . .

Time's decision in 1988 to combine with Warner was made only after what could be fairly characterized as an exhaustive appraisal of Time's future as a corporation. . . .

We find ample evidence in the record to support the Chancellor's conclusion that the Time board's decision to expand the business of the company through its March 3 merger with Warner was entitled to the protection of the business judgment rule. . . .

The Chancellor reached a different conclusion in addressing the Time–Warner transaction as revised three months later. He found that the revised agreement was defense-motivated and designed to avoid the potentially disruptive effect that Paramount's offer would have had on consummation of the proposed merger were it put to a shareholder vote. Thus, the court declined to apply the traditional business judgment rule to the revised transaction and instead analyzed the Time board's June 16 decision under *Unocal*. The court ruled that *Unocal* applied to all director actions taken, following receipt of Paramount's hostile tender offer, that were reasonably determined to be defensive. Clearly that was a correct ruling and no party disputes that ruling.

. . .

Unocal involved a two-tier, highly coercive tender offer. In such a case, the threat is obvious: shareholders may be compelled to tender to avoid being treated adversely in the second stage of the transaction. . . . In subsequent cases, the Court of Chancery has suggested that an all-cash, all-shares offer, falling within a range of values that a shareholder might reasonably prefer, cannot constitute a legally recognized "threat" to shareholder interests sufficient to withstand a *Unocal* analysis. . . . In those cases, the Court of Chancery determined that whatever threat existed related only to the shareholders and only to price and not to the corporation.

From those decisions by our Court of Chancery, Paramount and the individual plaintiffs extrapolate a rule of law that an all-cash, all-shares offer with values reasonably in the range of acceptable price cannot pose any objective threat to a corporation or its shareholders. Thus, Paramount would have us hold that only if the value of Paramount's offer were determined to be clearly inferior to the value created by management's plan to merge with Warner could the offer be viewed—objectively—as a threat.

Implicit in the plaintiffs' argument is the view that a hostile tender offer can pose only two types of threats: the threat of coercion that results from a two-tier offer promising unequal treatment for nontendering shareholders; and the threat of inadequate value from an all-shares, all-cash offer at a price below what a target board in good faith deems to be the present value of its shares.   .   .   . Since Paramount's offer was all-cash, the only conceivable "threat" plaintiffs argue, was inadequate value. We disapprove of such a narrow and rigid construction of *Unocal,* for the reasons which follow.

Plaintiffs' position represents a fundamental misconception of our standard of review under *Unocal* principally because it would involve the court in substituting its judgment as to what is a "better" deal for that of a corporation's board of directors. To the extent that the Court of Chancery has recently done so in certain of its opinions, we hereby reject such approach as not in keeping with a proper *Unocal* analysis.   .   .   .

In this case, the Time board reasonably determined that inadequate value was not the only legally cognizable threat that Paramount's all-cash, all-shares offer could present. Time's board concluded that Paramount's eleventh hour offer posed other threats. One concern was that Time shareholders might elect to tender into Paramount's cash offer in ignorance or a mistaken belief of the strategic benefit which a business combination with Warner might produce. Moreover, Time viewed the conditions attached to Paramount's offer as introducing a degree of uncertainty that skewed a comparative analysis. Further, the timing of Paramount's offer to follow issuance of Time's proxy notice was viewed as arguably designed to upset, if not confuse, the Time stockholders' vote. Given this record evidence, we cannot conclude that the Time board's decision of June 6 that Paramount's offer posed a threat to corporate policy and effectiveness was lacking in good faith or dominated by motives of either entrenchment or self-interest.

Paramount also contends that the Time board had not duly investigated Paramount's offer. Therefore, Paramount argues, Time was unable to make an informed decision that the offer posed a threat to Time's corporate policy. Although the Chancellor did not address this issue directly, his findings of fact do detail Time's exploration of the available entertainment companies, including Paramount, before determining that Warner provided the best strategic "fit." In addition, the court found that Time's board rejected Paramount's offer because Paramount did not serve Time's objectives or meet Time's needs. Thus, the record does, in our judgment, demonstrate that Time's board was adequately informed of the potential benefits of a transaction with Paramount.   .   .   .

We turn to the second part of the *Unocal* analysis.   The obvious requisite to determining the reasonableness of a defensive action is a clear identification of the nature of the threat.   As the Chancellor correctly noted, this "requires an evaluation of the importance of the corporate objective threatened; alternative methods of protecting that objective; impacts of the 'defensive' action, and other relevant factors."   .   .   .   It is not until both parts of the *Unocal* inquiry have been satisfied that the business judgment rule attaches to defensive actions of a board of directors. *Unocal,* 493 A.2d at 954.[18]   As applied to the facts of this case, the question is whether the record evidence supports the Court of Chancery's conclusion that the restructuring of the Time–Warner transaction, including the adoption of several preclusive defensive measures, was a *reasonable response* in relation to a perceived threat.

Paramount argues that, assuming its tender offer posed a threat, Time's response was unreasonable in precluding Time's shareholders from accepting the tender offer or receiving a control premium in the immediately foreseeable future.   Once again, the contention stems, we believe, from a fundamental misunderstanding of where the power of corporate governance lies.   Delaware law confers the management of the corporate enterprise to the stockholders' duly elected board representatives.   .   .   .   The fiduciary duty to manage a corporate enterprise includes the selection of a time frame for achievement of corporate goals.   That duty may not be delegated to the stockholders.   .   .   .   Directors are not obliged to abandon a deliberately conceived corporate plan for a short-term shareholder profit unless there is clearly no basis to sustain the corporate strategy.   .   .   .

.   .   .

Here, on the record facts, the Chancellor found that Time's responsive action to Paramount's tender offer was not aimed at "cramming down" on its shareholders a management-sponsored alternative, but rather had as its goal the carrying forward of a pre-existing transaction in an altered form.[19] Thus, the response was reasonably related to the threat.   The Chancellor noted that the revised agreement and its accompanying safety devices did

---

18.   Some commentators have criticized *Unocal* by arguing that once the board's deliberative process has been analyzed and found not to be wanting in objectivity, good faith or deliberateness, the so-called "enhanced" business judgment rule has been satisfied and no further inquiry is undertaken. *See generally* Johnson & Siegel, *Corporate Mergers: Redefining the Role of Target Directors,* 136 U.Pa.L.Rev. 315 (1987).   We reject such views.

19.   The Chancellor cited Shamrock Holdings, Inc. v. Polaroid Corp., Del.Ch., 559 A.2d 257 (1989), as a closely analogous case. In that case, the Court of Chancery upheld, in the face of a takeover bid, the establishment of an employee stock ownership plan that had a significant anti-takeover effect. The Court of Chancery upheld the board's action largely because the ESOP had been adopted *prior* to any contest for control and was reasonably determined to increase productivity and enhance profits.   The ESOP did not appear to be primarily a device to affect or secure corporate control.

not preclude Paramount from making an offer for the combined Time–Warner company or from changing the conditions of its offer so as not to make the offer dependent upon the nullification of the Time–Warner agreement. Thus, the response was proportionate. We affirm the Chancellor's rulings as clearly supported by the record. Finally, we note that although Time was required, as a result of Paramount's hostile offer, to incur a heavy debt to finance its acquisition of Warner, that fact alone does not render the board's decision unreasonable so long as the directors could reasonably perceive the debt load not to be so injurious to the corporation as to jeopardize its well being.

C.

Conclusion

Applying the test for grant or denial of preliminary injunctive relief, we find plaintiffs failed to establish a reasonable likelihood of ultimate success on the merits. Therefore, we affirm.

NOTE

As the opinion in this case indicates, Paramount, on June 23, 1989, offered the Time, Inc. shareholders $200 per share for their shares and shortly thereafter the Time board rejected this offer as "inadequate." The decision of the Delaware Supreme Court was announced on July 24, 1989. The closing price of Time, Inc. shares on the New York Stock Exchange on July 25, 1989 was $137.50. The closing price on July 25, 1990, was $93.00 (with about 64.1 million shares outstanding).

ANALYSIS

1. The decision in this case allowed the board of directors to deny the shareholders an opportunity to choose between the Paramount offer of $200 per share and the alternative involving the combination with Warner. Given that most of the shares were held by institutions (e.g., mutual funds and pension funds), run by savvy people, what is the justification for that?

2. Did the merger of Time and Warner deprive the Time shareholders of the opportunity in the future to realize a premium for sale of control? After the merger, could Paramount, or some other corporation, have mounted a new takeover bid for the combined corporations? Is that relevant?

3. Recall the facts in *Revlon*, supra. Suppose that before Perelman had shown an interest in Revlon, a group of Revlon managers, together with Forstmann Little & Co., had been in negotiations to buy the company for $53 per share, a price that a reputable investment banker had advised, after thorough investigation, was a good one. Assume that it was contemplated that none of the Revlon divisions would be sold off; the company would be kept intact. Suppose that then Perelman had made an offer of

$56 per share, all cash, no strings. Suppose all the members of the board strongly favored the sale to the management/Forstmann group and sought your advice on how to proceed. What would your response have been?

Paramount Communications Inc. v. QVC Network Inc.

637 A.2d 34 (Del.1994).

In this appeal we review an order of the Court of Chancery dated November 24, 1993 (the "November 24 Order"), preliminarily enjoining certain defensive measures designed to facilitate a so-called strategic alliance between Viacom Inc. ("Viacom") and Paramount Communications Inc. ("Paramount") approved by the board of directors of Paramount (the "Paramount Board" or the "Paramount directors") and to thwart an unsolicited, more valuable, tender offer by QVC Network Inc. ("QVC"). In affirming, we hold that the sale of control in this case, which is at the heart of the proposed strategic alliance, implicates enhanced judicial scrutiny of the conduct of the Paramount Board under Unocal Corp. v. Mesa Petroleum Co., Del.Supr. 493 A.2d 946 (1985), and Revlon, Inc. v. MacAndrews & Forbes Holdings, Inc., Del.Supr., 506 A.2d 173 (1985). We further hold that the conduct of the Paramount Board was not reasonable as to process or result.

. . . . This action arises out of a proposed acquisition of Paramount by Viacom through a tender offer followed by a second-step merger (the "Paramount–Viacom transaction"), and a competing unsolicited tender offer by QVC. The Court of Chancery granted a preliminary injunction. . . .

. . .

I. FACTS

. . .

Paramount is a Delaware corporation with its principal offices in New York City. Approximately 118 million shares of Paramount's common stock are outstanding and traded on the New York Stock Exchange. The majority of Paramount's stock is publicly held by numerous unaffiliated investors. Paramount owns and operates a diverse group of entertainment businesses, including motion picture and television studios, book publishers, professional sports teams and amusement parks.

There are 15 persons serving on the Paramount Board. Four directors are officer-employees of Paramount: Martin S. Davis ("Davis"), Paramount's Chairman and Chief Executive Officer since 1983; Donald Oresman ("Oresman"), Executive Vice–President, Chief Administrative Officer, and General Counsel; Stanley R. Jaffe, President and Chief Operating Officer; and Ronald L. Nelson, Executive Vice President and Chief Financial Officer. Paramount's 11 outside directors are distinguished and experienced business persons who are present or former senior executives of public corporations or financial institutions.

Viacom is a Delaware corporation with its headquarters in Massachusetts. Viacom is controlled by Sumner M. Redstone ("Redstone"), its Chairman and Chief Executive Officer, who owns indirectly approximately 85.2 percent of Viacom's voting Class A stock and approximately 69.2 percent of Viacom's nonvoting Class B stock through National Amusements, Inc. ("NAI"), an entity 91.7 percent owned by Redstone. Viacom has a wide range of entertainment operations, including a number of well-known cable television channels such as MTV, Nickelodeon, Showtime, and The Movie Channel. Viacom's equity co-investors in the Paramount–Viacom transaction include NYNEX Corporation and Blockbuster Entertainment Corporation.

QVC is a Delaware corporation with its headquarters in West Chester, Pennsylvania. QVC has several large stockholders, including Liberty Media Corporation, Comcast Corporation, Advance Publications, Inc., and Cox Enterprises Inc. Barry Diller ("Diller"), the Chairman and Chief Executive Officer of QVC, is also a substantial stockholder. QVC sells a variety of merchandise through a televised shopping channel. QVC has several equity co-investors in its proposed combination with Paramount including BellSouth Corporation and Comcast Corporation.

Beginning in the late 1980s, Paramount investigated the possibility of acquiring or merging with other companies in the entertainment, media, or communications industry. Paramount considered such transactions to be desirable, and perhaps necessary, in order to keep pace with competitors in the rapidly evolving field of entertainment and communications. Consistent with its goal of strategic expansion, Paramount made a tender offer for Time Inc. in 1989, but was ultimately unsuccessful. See Paramount Communications, Inc. v. Time Inc., Del.Supr., 571 A.2d 1140 (1989) ("Time–Warner").

Although Paramount had considered a possible combination of Paramount and Viacom as early as 1990, recent efforts to explore such a transaction began at a dinner meeting between Redstone and Davis on April 20, 1993. Robert Greenhill ("Greenhill"), Chairman of Smith Barney Shearson Inc. ("Smith Barney"), attended and helped facilitate this meeting. After several more meetings between Redstone and Davis, serious negotiations began taking place in early July.

It was tentatively agreed that Davis would be the chief executive officer and Redstone would be the controlling stockholder of the combined company, but the parties could not reach agreement on the merger price and the terms of a stock option to be granted to Viacom. With respect to price, Viacom offered a package of cash and stock (primarily Viacom Class B nonvoting stock) with a market value of approximately $61 per share, but Paramount wanted at least $70 per share.

Shortly after negotiations broke down in July 1993, two notable events occurred. First, Davis apparently learned of QVC's potential interest in Paramount, and told Diller over lunch on July 21, 1993, that Paramount was not for sale. Second, the market value of Viacom's Class B nonvoting stock increased from $46.875 on July 6 to $57.25 on August 20. QVC claims (and Viacom disputes) that this price increase was caused by open market purchases of such stock by Redstone or entities controlled by him.

On August 20, 1993, discussions between Paramount and Viacom resumed when Greenhill arranged another meeting between Davis and Redstone. After a short hiatus, the parties negotiated in earnest in early September, and performed due diligence with the assistance of their financial advisors, Lazard Freres & Co. ("Lazard") for Paramount and Smith Barney for Viacom. On September 9, 1993, the Paramount Board was informed about the status of the negotiations and was provided information by Lazard, including an analysis of the proposed transaction.

On September 12, 1993, the Paramount Board met again and unanimously approved the Original Merger Agreement whereby Paramount would merge with and into Viacom. The terms of the merger provided that each share of Paramount common stock would be converted into 0.10 shares of Viacom Class A voting stock, 0.90 shares of Viacom Class B nonvoting stock, and $9.10 in cash. In addition, the Paramount Board agreed to amend its "poison pill" Rights Agreement to exempt the proposed merger with Viacom. The Original Merger Agreement also contained several provisions designed to make it more difficult for a potential competing bid to succeed. We focus, as did the Court of Chancery, on three of these defensive provisions: a "no-shop" provision (the "No–Shop Provision"), the Termination Fee, and the Stock Option Agreement.

First, under the No–Shop Provision, the Paramount Board agreed that Paramount would not solicit, encourage, discuss, negotiate, or endorse any competing transaction unless: (a) a third party "makes an unsolicited written, bona fide proposal, which is not subject to any material contingencies relating to financing"; and (b) the Paramount Board determines that discussions or negotiations with the third party are necessary for the Paramount Board to comply with its fiduciary duties.

Second, under the Termination Fee provision, Viacom would receive a $100 million termination fee if: (a) Paramount terminated the Original Merger Agreement because of a competing transaction; (b) Paramount's stockholders did not approve the merger; or (c) the Paramount Board recommended a competing transaction.

The third and most significant deterrent device was the Stock Option Agreement, which granted to Viacom an option to purchase approximately 19.9 percent (23,699,000 shares) of Paramount's outstanding common stock at $69.14 per share if any of the triggering events for the Termination Fee occurred. In addition to the customary terms that are normally associated with a stock option, the Stock Option Agreement contained two provisions that were both unusual and highly beneficial to Viacom: (a) Viacom was permitted to pay for the shares with a senior subordinated note of questionable marketability instead of cash, thereby avoiding the need to raise the $1.6 billion purchase price (the "Note Feature"); and (b) Viacom could elect to require Paramount to pay Viacom in cash a sum equal to the difference between the purchase price and the market price of Paramount's stock (the "Put Feature"). Because the Stock Option Agreement was not "capped" to limit its maximum dollar value, it had the potential to reach (and in this case did reach) unreasonable levels.

After the execution of the Original Merger Agreement and the Stock Option Agreement on September 12, 1993, Paramount and Viacom announced their proposed merger. In a number of public statements, the parties indicated that the pending transaction was a virtual certainty. Redstone described it as a "marriage" that would "never be torn asunder" and stated that only a "nuclear attack" could break the deal. Redstone also called Diller and John Malone of Tele–Communications Inc., a major stockholder of QVC, to dissuade them from making a competing bid.

Despite these attempts to discourage a competing bid, Diller sent a letter to Davis on September 20, 1993, proposing a merger in which QVC would acquire Paramount for approximately $80 per share, consisting of 0.893 shares of QVC common stock and $30 in cash. QVC also expressed its eagerness to meet with Paramount to negotiate the details of a transaction. When the Paramount Board met on September 27, it was advised by Davis that the Original Merger Agreement prohibited Paramount from having discussions with QVC (or anyone else) unless certain conditions were satisfied. In particular, QVC had to supply evidence that its proposal was not subject to financing contingencies. The Paramount Board was also provided information from Lazard describing QVC and its proposal.

On October 5, 1993, QVC provided Paramount with evidence of QVC's financing. The Paramount Board then held another meeting on October 11, and decided to authorize management to meet with QVC. Davis also informed the Paramount Board that Booz–Allen & Hamilton ("Booz–Allen"), a management consulting firm, had been retained to assess, inter alia, the incremental earnings potential from a Paramount–Viacom merger and a Paramount–QVC merger. Discussions proceeded slowly, however, due to a delay in Paramount signing a confidentiality agreement. In response to Paramount's request for information, QVC provided two binders of documents to Paramount on October 20.

On October 21, 1993, QVC filed this action and publicly announced an $80 cash tender offer for 51 percent of Paramount's outstanding shares (the "QVC tender offer"). Each remaining share of Paramount common stock would be converted into 1.42857 shares of QVC common stock in a second-step merger. The tender offer was conditioned on, among other things, the invalidation of the Stock Option Agreement, which was worth over $200 million by that point.[5] QVC contends that it had to commence a tender offer because of the slow pace of the merger discussions and the need to begin seeking clearance under federal antitrust laws.

Confronted by QVC's hostile bid, which on its face offered over $10 per share more than the consideration provided by the Original Merger Agreement, Viacom realized that it would need to raise its bid in order to remain competitive. Within hours after QVC's tender offer was announced, Via-

---

5. By November 15, 1993, the value of the Stock Option Agreement had increased to nearly $500 million based on the $90 QVC bid. . . .

com entered into discussions with Paramount concerning a revised transaction. These discussions led to serious negotiations concerning a comprehensive amendment to the original Paramount–Viacom transaction. In effect, the opportunity for a "new deal" with Viacom was at hand for the Paramount Board. With the QVC hostile bid offering greater value to the Paramount stockholders, the Paramount Board had considerable leverage with Viacom.

At a special meeting on October 24, 1993, the Paramount Board approved the Amended Merger Agreement and an amendment to the Stock Option Agreement. The Amended Merger Agreement was, however, essentially the same as the Original Merger Agreement, except that it included a few new provisions. One provision related to an $80 per share cash tender offer by Viacom for 51 percent of Paramount's stock, and another changed the merger consideration so that each share of Paramount would be converted into 0.20408 shares of Viacom Class A voting stock, 1.08317 shares of Viacom Class B nonvoting stock, and 0.20408 shares of a new series of Viacom convertible preferred stock. The Amended Merger Agreement also added a provision giving Paramount the right not to amend its Rights Agreement to exempt Viacom if the Paramount Board determined that such an amendment would be inconsistent with its fiduciary duties because another offer constituted a "better alternative." Finally, the Paramount Board was given the power to terminate the Amended Merger Agreement if it withdrew its recommendation of the Viacom transaction or recommended a competing transaction.

Although the Amended Merger Agreement offered more consideration to the Paramount stockholders and somewhat more flexibility to the Paramount Board than did the Original Merger Agreement, the defensive measures designed to make a competing bid more difficult were not removed or modified. In particular, there is no evidence in the record that Paramount sought to use its newly-acquired leverage to eliminate or modify the No–Shop Provision, the Termination Fee, or the Stock Option Agreement when the subject of amending the Original Merger Agreement was on the table.

Viacom's tender offer commenced on October 25, 1993, and QVC's tender offer was formally launched on October 27, 1993. Diller sent a letter to the Paramount Board on October 28 requesting an opportunity to negotiate with Paramount, and Oresman responded the following day by agreeing to meet. The meeting, held on November 1, was not very fruitful, however, after QVC's proposed guidelines for a "fair bidding process" were rejected by Paramount on the ground that "auction procedures" were inappropriate and contrary to Paramount's contractual obligations to Viacom.

On November 6, 1993, Viacom unilaterally raised its tender offer price to $85 per share in cash and offered a comparable increase in the value of the securities being proposed in the second-step merger. At a telephonic meeting held later that day, the Paramount Board agreed to recommend Viacom's higher bid to Paramount's stockholders.

QVC responded to Viacom's higher bid on November 12 by increasing its tender offer to $90 per share and by increasing the securities for its second-step merger by a similar amount. In response to QVC's latest offer, the Paramount Board scheduled a meeting for November 15, 1993. Prior to the meeting, Oresman sent the members of the Paramount Board a document summarizing the "conditions and uncertainties" of QVC's offer. One director testified that this document gave him a very negative impression of the QVC bid.

At its meeting on November 15, 1993, the Paramount Board determined that the new QVC offer was not in the best interests of the stockholders. The purported basis for this conclusion was that QVC's bid was excessively conditional. The Paramount Board did not communicate with QVC regarding the status of the conditions because it believed that the No–Shop Provision prevented such communication in the absence of firm financing. Several Paramount directors also testified that they believed the Viacom transaction would be more advantageous to Paramount's future business prospects than a QVC transaction.[7] Although a number of materials were distributed to the Paramount Board describing the Viacom and QVC transactions, the only quantitative analysis of the consideration to be received by the stockholders under each proposal was based on then-current market prices of the securities involved, not on the anticipated value of such securities at the time when the stockholders would receive them.[8]

The preliminary injunction hearing in this case took place on November 16, 1993. On November 19, Diller wrote to the Paramount Board to inform it that QVC had obtained financing commitments for its tender offer and that there was no anti-trust obstacle to the offer. On November 24, 1993, the Court of Chancery issued its decision granting a preliminary injunction in favor of QVC and the plaintiff stockholders. This appeal followed.

II. APPLICABLE PRINCIPLES OF ESTABLISHED DELAWARE LAW

The General Corporation Law of the State of Delaware (the "General Corporation Law") and the decisions of this Court have repeatedly recognized the fundamental principle that the management of the business and affairs of a Delaware corporation is entrusted to its directors, who are the duly elected and authorized representatives of the stockholders. . . . Under normal circumstances, neither the courts nor the stockholders should interfere with the managerial decisions of the directors. The

7. This belief may have been based on a report prepared by Booz–Allen and distributed to the Paramount Board at its October 24 meeting. The report, which relied on public information regarding QVC, concluded that the synergies of a Paramount–Viacom merger were significantly superior to those of a Paramount–QVC merger. QVC has labelled the Booz–Allen report as a "joke."

8. The market prices of Viacom's and QVC's stock were poor measures of their actual values because such prices constantly fluctuated depending upon which company was perceived to be the more likely to acquire Paramount.

business judgment rule embodies the deference to which such decisions are entitled.

Nevertheless, there are rare situations which mandate that a court take a more direct and active role in overseeing the decisions made and actions taken by directors. In these situations, a court subjects the directors' conduct to enhanced scrutiny to ensure that it is reasonable.[9] The decisions of this Court have clearly established the circumstances where such enhanced scrutiny will be applied. E.g., *Unocal*, 493 A.2d 946; . . . *Revlon*, 506 A.2d 173; Mills Acquisition Co. v. Macmillan, Inc., Del.Supr., 559 A.2d 1261 (1989) . . . The case at bar implicates two such circumstances: (1) the approval of a transaction resulting in a sale of control, and (2) the adoption of defensive measures in response to a threat to corporate control.

A.   The Significance of a Sale or Change of Control

When a majority of a corporation's voting shares are acquired by a single person or entity, or by a cohesive group acting together, there is a significant diminution in the voting power of those who thereby become minority stockholders. Under the statutory framework of the General Corporation Law, many of the most fundamental corporate changes can be implemented only if they are approved by a majority vote of the stockholders. Such actions include elections of directors, amendments to the certificate of incorporation, mergers, consolidations, sales of all or substantially all of the assets of the corporation, and dissolution. Because of the overriding importance of voting rights, this Court and the Court of Chancery have consistently acted to protect stockholders from unwarranted interference with such rights.

In the absence of devices protecting the minority stockholders, stockholder votes are likely to become mere formalities where there is a majority stockholder. For example, minority stockholders can be deprived of a continuing equity interest in their corporation by means of a cash-out merger. . . . Absent effective protective provisions, minority stockholders must rely for protection solely on the fiduciary duties owed to them by the directors and the majority stockholder, since the minority stockholders have lost the power to influence corporate direction through the ballot. . . .

In the case before us, the public stockholders (in the aggregate) currently own a majority of Paramount's voting stock. Control of the corporation is not vested in a single person, entity, or group, but vested in the fluid aggregation of unaffiliated stockholders. In the event the Paramount–Viacom transaction is consummated, the public stockholders will receive cash and a minority equity voting position in the surviving corporation. Following such consummation, there will be a controlling stockholder who will have the voting power to: (a) elect directors; (b) cause a break-up

9. Where actual self-interest is present and affects a majority of the directors approving a transaction, a court will apply even more exacting scrutiny to determine whether the transaction is entirely fair to the stockholders.

of the corporation; (c) merge it with another company; (d) cash-out the public stockholders; (e) amend the certificate of incorporation; (f) sell all or substantially all of the corporate assets; or (g) otherwise alter materially the nature of the corporation and the public stockholders' interests. . . .

Because of the intended sale of control, the Paramount–Viacom transaction has economic consequences of considerable significance to the Paramount stockholders. Once control has shifted, the current Paramount stockholders will have no leverage in the future to demand another control premium. As a result, the Paramount stockholders are entitled to receive, and should receive, a control premium and/or protective devices of significant value. There being no such protective provisions in the Viacom–Paramount transaction, the Paramount directors had an obligation to take the maximum advantage of the current opportunity to realize for the stockholders the best value reasonably available.

B. The Obligations of Directors in a Sale or Change of Control Transaction

The consequences of a sale of control impose special obligations on the directors of a corporation. In particular, they have the obligation of acting reasonably to seek the transaction offering the best value reasonably available to the stockholders. The courts will apply enhanced scrutiny to ensure that the directors have acted reasonably.

In the sale of control context, the directors must focus on one primary objective—to secure the transaction offering the best value reasonably available for the stockholders—and they must exercise their fiduciary duties to further that end. . . .

[S]ome of the methods by which a board can fulfill its obligation . . . include conducting an auction, canvassing the market, etc. Delaware law recognizes that there is "no single blueprint" that directors must follow. . . .

In determining which alternative provides the best value for the stockholders, a board of directors is not limited to considering only the amount of cash involved, and is not required to ignore totally its view of the future value of a strategic alliance. . . . Instead, the directors should analyze the entire situation and evaluate in a disciplined manner the consideration being offered. Where stock or other non-cash consideration is involved, the board should try to quantify its value, if feasible, to achieve an objective comparison of the alternatives. In addition, the board may assess a variety of practical considerations relating to each alternative including:

> [an offer's] fairness and feasibility; the proposed or actual financing for the offer, and the consequences of that financing; questions of illegality; . . . the risk of non-consummation; . . . the bidder's identity, prior background and other business venture experiences;

and the bidder's business plans for the corporation and their effects on stockholder interests.

Macmillan, 559 A.2d at 1282 n. 29. These considerations are important because the selection of one alternative may permanently foreclose other opportunities. While the assessment of these factors may be complex, the board's goal is straight-forward: Having informed themselves of all material information reasonably available, the directors must decide which alternative is most likely to offer the best value reasonably available to the stockholders.

C. Enhanced Judicial Scrutiny of a Sale or Change of Control Transaction

Board action in the circumstances presented here is subject to enhanced scrutiny. Such scrutiny is mandated by: (a) the threatened diminution of the current stockholders' voting power; (b) the fact that an asset belonging to public stockholders (a control premium) is being sold and may never be available again: and (c) the traditional concern of Delaware courts for actions which impair or impede stockholder voting rights. . . .

The key features of an enhanced scrutiny test are: (a) a judicial determination regarding the adequacy of the decisionmaking process employed by the directors, including the information on which the directors based their decision; and (b) a judicial examination of the reasonableness of the directors' action in light of the circumstances then existing. The directors have the burden of proving that they were adequately informed and acted reasonably.

Although an enhanced scrutiny test involves a review of the reasonableness of the substantive merits of a board's actions, a court should not ignore the complexity of the directors' task in a sale of control. There are many business and financial considerations implicated in investigating and selecting the best value reasonably available. The board of directors is the corporate decisionmaking body best equipped to make these judgments. Accordingly, a court applying enhanced judicial scrutiny should be deciding whether the directors made a reasonable decision, not a perfect decision. If a board selected one of several reasonable alternatives, a court should not second-guess that choice even though it might have decided otherwise or subsequent events may have cast doubt on the board's determination. Thus, courts will not substitute their business judgment for that of the directors, but will determine if the directors' decision was, on balance, within a range of reasonableness.

D. *Revlon* and *Time–Warner* Distinguished

The Paramount defendants and Viacom assert that the fiduciary obligations and the enhanced judicial scrutiny discussed above are not implicated in this case in the absence of a "break-up" of the corporation, and that the order granting the preliminary injunction should be reversed. This argument is based on their erroneous interpretation of our decisions in *Revlon* and *Time–Warner*.

In *Revlon,* we reviewed the actions of the board of directors of Revlon, Inc. ("Revlon"), which had rebuffed the overtures of Pantry Pride, Inc. and had instead entered into an agreement with Forstmann Little & Co. ("Forstmann") providing for the acquisition of 100 percent of Revlon's outstanding stock by Forstmann and the subsequent break-up of Revlon. Based on the facts and circumstances present in *Revlon,* we held that "the directors' role changed from defenders of the corporate bastion to auctioneers charged with getting the best price for the stockholders at a sale of the company." 506 A.2d at 182. We further held that "when a board ends an intense bidding contest on an insubstantial basis, . . . [that] action cannot withstand the enhanced scrutiny which Unocal requires of director conduct." Id. at 184.

It is true that one of the circumstances bearing on these holdings was the fact that "the break-up of the company . . . had become a reality which even the directors embraced." Id. at 182. It does not follow, however, that a "break-up" must be present and "inevitable" before directors are subject to enhanced judicial scrutiny and are required to pursue a transaction that is calculated to produce the best value reasonably available to the stockholders. In fact, we stated in *Revlon* that "when bidders make relatively similar offers, or dissolution of the company becomes inevitable, the directors cannot fulfill their enhanced *Unocal* duties by playing favorites with the contending factions." Id. at 184 (emphasis added). *Revlon* thus does not hold that an inevitable dissolution or "break-up" is necessary.

The decisions of this Court following *Revlon* reinforced the applicability of enhanced scrutiny and the directors' obligation to seek the best value reasonably available for the stockholders where there is a pending sale of control, regardless of whether or not there is to be a break-up of the corporation. . . .

[Nonetheless], the Paramount defendants have interpreted our decision in *Time–Warner* as requiring a corporate break-up in order for that obligation to apply. The facts in *Time–Warner,* however, were quite different from the facts of this case, and refute Paramount's position here. In *Time–Warner,* the Chancellor held that there was no change of control in the original stock-for-stock merger between Time and Warner because Time would be owned by a fluid aggregation of unaffiliated stockholders both before and after the merger. . . . Moreover, the transaction actually consummated in *Time–Warner* was not a merger, as originally planned, but a sale of Warner's stock to Time.

In our affirmance of the Court of Chancery's well-reasoned decision, this Court held that "The Chancellor's findings of fact are supported by the record and his conclusion is correct as a matter of law." 571 A.2d at 1150 (emphasis added). Nevertheless, the Paramount defendants here have argued that a break-up is a requirement. . . .

The Paramount defendants have misread the holding of *Time–Warner.* . . .

[W]hen a corporation undertakes a transaction which will cause: (a) a change in corporate control; or (b) a break-up of the corporate entity, the directors' obligation is to seek the best value reasonably available to the stockholders. This obligation arises because the effect of the Viacom–Paramount transaction, if consummated, is to shift control of Paramount from the public stockholders to a controlling stockholder, Viacom. Neither *Time–Warner* nor any other decision of this Court holds that a "break-up" of the company is essential to give rise to this obligation where there is a sale of control.

III.   BREACH OF FIDUCIARY DUTIES BY PARAMOUNT BOARD

.   .   .

A.   The Specific Obligations of the Paramount Board

Under the facts of this case, the Paramount directors had the obligation: (a) to be diligent and vigilant in examining critically the Paramount–Viacom transaction and the QVC tender offers; (b) to act in good faith; (c) to obtain, and act with due care on, all material information reasonably available, including information necessary to compare the two offers to determine which of these transactions, or an alternative course of action, would provide the best value reasonably available to the stockholders; and (d) to negotiate actively and in good faith with both Viacom and QVC to that end.

Having decided to sell control of the corporation, the Paramount directors were required to evaluate critically whether or not all material aspects of the Paramount–Viacom transaction (separately and in the aggregate) were reasonable and in the best interests of the Paramount stockholders in light of current circumstances, including: the change of control premium, the Stock Option Agreement, the Termination Fee, the coercive nature of both the Viacom and QVC tender offers,[18] the No–Shop Provision, and the proposed disparate use of the Rights Agreement as to the Viacom and QVC tender offers, respectively.

These obligations necessarily implicated various issues, including the questions of whether or not those provisions and other aspects of the Paramount–Viacom transaction (separately and in the aggregate): (a) adversely affected the value provided to the Paramount stockholders; (b) inhibited or encouraged alternative bids; (c) were enforceable contractual obligations in light of the directors' fiduciary duties; and (d) in the end would advance or retard the Paramount directors' obligation to secure for the Paramount stockholders the best value reasonably available under the circumstances.

---

18. Both the Viacom and the QVC tender offers were for 51 percent cash and a "back-end" of various securities, the value of each of which depended on the fluctuating value of Viacom and QVC stock at any given time. Thus, both tender offers were two-tiered, front-end loaded, and coercive. Such coercive offers are inherently problematic and should be expected to receive particularly careful analysis by a target board. See *Unocal*, 493 A.2d at 956.

The Paramount defendants contend that they were precluded by certain contractual provisions, including the No–Shop Provision, from negotiating with QVC or seeking alternatives. Such provisions, whether or not they are presumptively valid in the abstract, may not validly define or limit the directors' fiduciary duties under Delaware law or prevent the Paramount directors from carrying out their fiduciary duties under Delaware law. To the extent such provisions are inconsistent with those duties, they are invalid and unenforceable. See *Revlon,* 506 A.2d at 184–85.

Since the Paramount directors had already decided to sell control, they had an obligation to continue their search for the best value reasonably available to the stockholders. This continuing obligation included the responsibility, at the October 24 board meeting and thereafter, to evaluate critically both the QVC tender offers and the Paramount–Viacom transaction to determine if: (a) the QVC tender offer was, or would continue to be, conditional; (b) the QVC tender offer could be improved; (c) the Viacom tender offer or other aspects of the Paramount–Viacom transaction could be improved; (d) each of the respective offers would be reasonably likely to come to closure, and under what circumstances; (e) other material information was reasonably available for consideration by the Paramount directors; (f) there were viable and realistic alternative courses of action; and (g) the timing constraints could be managed so the directors could consider these matters carefully and deliberately.

B.   The Breaches of Fiduciary Duty by the Paramount Board

The Paramount directors made the decision on September 12, 1993, that, in their judgment, a strategic merger with Viacom on the economic terms of the Original Merger Agreement was in the best interests of Paramount and its stockholders. Those terms provided a modest change of control premium to the stockholders. The directors also decided at that time that it was appropriate to agree to certain defensive measures (the Stock Option Agreement, the Termination Fee, and the No–Shop Provision) insisted upon by Viacom as part of that economic transaction. Those defensive measures, coupled with the sale of control and subsequent disparate treatment of competing bidders, implicated the judicial scrutiny of *Unocal, Revlon, Macmillan,* and their progeny. We conclude that the Paramount directors' process was not reasonable, and the result achieved for the stockholders was not reasonable under the circumstances.

When entering into the Original Merger Agreement, and thereafter, the Paramount Board clearly gave insufficient attention to the potential consequences of the defensive measures demanded by Viacom. The Stock Option Agreement had a number of unusual and potentially "draconian" provisions, including the Note Feature and the Put Feature. Furthermore, the Termination Fee, whether or not unreasonable by itself, clearly made Paramount less attractive to other bidders, when coupled with the Stock Option Agreement. Finally, the No–Shop Provision inhibited the Paramount Board's ability to negotiate with other potential bidders, particularly QVC which had already expressed an interest in Paramount.

Throughout the applicable time period, and especially from the first QVC merger proposal on September 20 through the Paramount Board meeting on November 15, QVC's interest in Paramount provided the opportunity for the Paramount Board to seek significantly higher value for the Paramount stockholders than that being offered by Viacom. QVC persistently demonstrated its intention to meet and exceed the Viacom offers, and frequently expressed its willingness to negotiate possible further increases.

The Paramount directors had the opportunity in the October 23–24 time frame, when the Original Merger Agreement was renegotiated, to take appropriate action to modify the improper defensive measures as well as to improve the economic terms of the Paramount–Viacom transaction. Under the circumstances existing at that time, it should have been clear to the Paramount Board that the Stock Option Agreement, coupled with the Termination Fee and the No–Shop Clause, were impeding the realization of the best value reasonably available to the Paramount stockholders. Nevertheless, the Paramount Board made no effort to eliminate or modify these counterproductive devices, and instead continued to cling to its vision of a strategic alliance with Viacom. Moreover, based on advice from the Paramount management, the Paramount directors considered the QVC offer to be "conditional" and asserted that they were precluded by the No–Shop Provision from seeking more information from, or negotiating with, QVC.

. . .

When the Paramount directors met on November 15 to consider QVC's increased tender offer, they remained prisoners of their own misconceptions and missed opportunities to eliminate the restrictions they had imposed on themselves. Yet, it was not "too late" to reconsider negotiating with QVC. The circumstances existing on November 15 made it clear that the defensive measures, taken as a whole, were problematic: (a) the No–Shop Provision could not define or limit their fiduciary duties; (b) the Stock Option Agreement had become "draconian"; and (c) the Termination Fee, in context with all the circumstances, was similarly deterring the realization of possibly higher bids. Nevertheless, the Paramount directors remained paralyzed by their uninformed belief that the QVC offer was "illusory." This final opportunity to negotiate on the stockholders' behalf and to fulfill their obligation to seek the best value reasonably available was thereby squandered.

IV. VIACOM'S CLAIM OF VESTED CONTRACT RIGHTS

Viacom argues that it had certain "vested" contract rights with respect to the No–Shop Provision and the Stock Option Agreement. In effect, Viacom's argument is that the Paramount directors could enter into an agreement in violation of their fiduciary duties and then render Paramount, and ultimately its stockholders, liable for failing to carry out an agreement in violation of those duties. Viacom's protestations about vested rights are without merit. This Court has found that those defensive measures were improperly designed to deter potential bidders, and that such measures do not meet the reasonableness test to which they must be subjected. They are consequently invalid and unenforceable under the facts of this case.

Viacom, a sophisticated party with experienced legal and financial advisors, knew of (and in fact demanded) the unreasonable features of the Stock Option Agreement. . . .

AFTERMATH

After the Delaware Supreme Court issued its order, the Paramount board adopted procedures to encourage Viacom and QVC to bid against one another so as to maximize the consideration to be paid to Paramount's shareholders. Ultimately, Viacom prevailed, with a combination of cash and securities worth a total of about $10 billion, compared with a value of about $8 billion for the cash and securities that had been approved by the Paramount board for thc friendly acquisition, before the offer by QVC.

ANALYSIS

1. What would the result have been if the Viacom bid had been such that Viacom would have wound up with only 49 percent of the voting shares of the surviving corporation?

2. If there is no conflict of interest on the part of the independent directors of Paramount, why should there be "enhanced scrutiny." Why not simply apply the business judgment rule?

3. Suppose a potential buyer of a public corporation suggests that it might make an offer at a significant premium but that it is not willing to be a "stalking horse," and therefore will make the offer only if it receives a no-shop clause and a termination fee. How should the board proceed?

4. The American Law Institute (ALI) took the following approach in its Principles of Corporate Governance: Analysis and Recommendations (1994):*

§ 6.02. Action of Directors That Has the Foreseeable Effect of Blocking Unsolicited Tender Offers.

(a) The board of directors may take an action that has the foreseeable effect of blocking an unsolicited tender offer, if the action is a reasonable response to the offer.

(b) In considering whether its action is a reasonable response to the offer:

(1) The board may take into account all factors relevant to the best interests of the corporation and shareholders, including, among other things, questions of legality and whether the offer, if

* © 1994 by The American Law Insti-   tute. Reprinted with permission.

successful, would threaten the corporation's essential economic prospects; and

(2) The board may, in addition to the analysis under § 6.02(b)(1), have regard for interests or groups (other than shareholders) with respect to which the corporation has a legitimate concern if to do so would not significantly disfavor the long-term interests of shareholders.

(c) A person who challenges an action of the board on the ground that it fails to satisfy the standards of Subsection (a) has the burden of proof that the board's action is an unreasonable response to the offer.

(d) An action that does not meet the standards of Subsection (a) may be enjoined or set aside, but directors who authorize such an action are not subject to liability for damages if their conduct meets the standard of the business judgment rule.

———

Would any of the cases in this section have come out differently under the ALI proposal than as they were decided under Delaware law? Is the ALI proposal preferable as a policy matter?

NOTE

In Unitrin v. American General Corp., 651 A.2d 1361 (Del.1995), the court approved a defensive repurchase of shares and in the process generated a couple of new phrases. A defensive measure approved by an independent board is permissible if it is not "draconian," which means that it is not "coercive or preclusive." In the case itself, the shareholders, according to the court, were not foreclosed from receiving a control premium in the future and a change of control by proxy battle was still possible. The court emphasized the discretion of the board to choose a defensive measure from among alternatives that are within the "range of reasonableness" (from *QVC*). If the measure adopted is within this range, the plaintiff will not be heard to argue that another measure might have been better.

Hilton Hotels Corp. v. ITT Corp.

978 F.Supp. 1342 (D.Nev.1997).

. . .

I. FACTS

On January 27, 1997, Hilton announced a $55.00 per share tender offer for the stock of ITT, and announced plans for a proxy contest at ITT's 1997 annual meeting. This litigation commenced on the same date with the filing of Hilton's Complaint for Injunctive and Declaratory Relief. . . .

On February 11, 1997, ITT formally rejected Hilton's tender offer. ITT proceeded to sell several of its non-core assets and opposed Hilton's takeover attempt before gaming regulatory bodies in Nevada, New Jersey and Mississippi.

When it became apparent that ITT would not conduct its annual meeting in May 1997, as it had customarily done in preceding years, Hilton filed a motion for a mandatory injunction to compel ITT to conduct the annual meeting in May. On April 21, 1997, this Court denied Hilton's Motion finding that Nevada law and ITT's by-laws did not require that ITT conduct its annual meeting within twelve months of the prior meeting, but rather that ITT had eighteen months within which to do so. . . .

On July 15, 1997, ITT announced a Comprehensive Plan which, among other things, proposed to split ITT into three new entities, the largest of which would become ITT Destinations. ITT Destinations would be comprised of the current ITT's hotel and gaming business[es] which account for approximately 93% of ITT's current assets. A second entity, ITT Educational Services, would consist of the current ITT's technical schools, and ITT's European Yellow Pages Division would remain with the current ITT as ITT World Directories.

Most significantly, under the Comprehensive Plan, the board of directors of the new ITT Destinations would be comprised of the members of ITT's current board with one important distinction. The new board would be a "classified" or "staggered" board divided into three classes with each class of directors serving for a term of three years, and with one class to be elected each year. Moreover, a shareholder vote of 80% would be required to remove directors without cause, and [an] 80% shareholder vote would also be required to repeal the classified board provision or the 80% requirement to remove directors without cause.*

* [Eds.—Nevada corporation code section 330 (Nev. Rev. Stat. § 78.330) provides, in pertinent part:

1. . . . [D]irectors of every corporation must be elected at the annual meeting of the stockholders by a plurality of the votes cast at the election. Unless otherwise provided in the bylaws, the board of directors have the authority to set the date, time and place for the annual meeting of the stockholders. If for any reason directors are not elected . . . at the annual meeting of the stockholders, they may be elected at any special meeting of the stockholders which is called and held for that purpose.

2. The articles of incorporation or the bylaws may provide for the classification of directors as to the duration of their respective terms of office or as to their election by one or more authorized classes or series of shares, but at least one-fourth in number of the directors of every corporation must be elected annually.

3. The articles of incorporation may provide that the voting power of individual directors or classes of directors may be greater than or less than that of any other individual directors or classes of directors, and the different voting powers may be stated in the articles of incorporation or may be dependent upon any fact or event that may be ascertained outside the articles of incorporation if the manner in which the fact or event may operate on those voting powers is stated in the articles of incorporation. If the articles of incorporation provide that any directors may have voting power greater than or less than other directors, every reference in this chapter

Additionally, the record fairly supports Hilton's contention that the Comprehensive Plan contains a "poison pill" resulting in a $1.4 billion tax liability which would be triggered if Hilton successfully acquired more than 50% of ITT Destinations and that Hilton would be liable for 90% of the tax bill.

Finally, and critical to this Court's analysis, ITT seeks to implement the Comprehensive Plan prior to ITT's 1997 annual meeting and without obtaining shareholder approval.

II. THE PARTIES' CONTENTIONS AND APPLICABLE LEGAL STANDARDS

.   .   .

Shortly after ITT's announcement of its Comprehensive Plan, Hilton announced an amended tender offer of $70.00 per share, which was rejected by ITT. On August 26, 1997, Hilton filed its Motion for Injunctive and Declaratory Relief (#29) seeking:

1. A preliminary and permanent injunction enjoining ITT from proceeding with its Comprehensive Plan;

2. Declaring that by adopting the Comprehensive Plan, ITT's directors had breached their fiduciary duties to ITT and its shareholders;

3. Declaring that ITT may not implement its Comprehensive Plan without obtaining a shareholder vote; and

4. Requiring ITT to conduct its 1997 annual meeting for the election of directors not later than November 14, 1997.

.   .   .

Where, as here, Hilton's Motion seeks mandatory injunctive relief in the sense that a trial on the merits could not practically reverse a preliminary decision enjoining implementation of ITT's Comprehensive Plan until after the 1997 annual meeting, the Motion is subject to heightened scrutiny and the injunction requested should not issue unless the facts and the law clearly favor the party requesting such relief. .   .   . Therefore, this Court will apply the standard for permanent injunctive relief with regard to Hilton's Motion.

[Hilton must show irreparable injury and] "must actually succeed on the merits of their claims." Coleman v. Wilson, 912 F.Supp. 1282, 1311 (E.D.Ca.1995) (citing Sierra Club v. Penfold, 857 F.2d 1307, 1318 (9th Cir.1988)).

.   .   .

to a majority or other proportion of directors shall be deemed to refer to a majority or other proportion of the voting power of all of the directors or classes of directors, as may be required by the articles of incorporation.]

III. DISCUSSION

This case involves consideration of the powers and duties of the board of directors of a Nevada corporation in responding to a hostile takeover attempt, and the importance of protecting the franchise of the shareholders of the corporation in the process. Many courts have grappled with legal issues presented by the strategies employed by hostile bidders, such as Hilton, and the concomitant anti-takeover defensive measures utilized by target companies, such as ITT. Coupling an unsolicited tender offer with a proxy contest to replace the incumbent board is a favored strategy of would-be acquirors. A variety of sophisticated defensive measures, including "poison pill" plans have also evolved to frustrate a host of takeover attempts. As a result, "replacing the incumbent directors of the target corporation is viewed as an efficient way to eliminate the target company's ability to utilize these anti-takeover defenses." Kidsco v. Dinsmore III, 674 A.2d 483, 490 (Del.Ch.1995). . . .

Nevada state case law is virtually silent on the subject. However, provisions of Chapter 78 of the Nevada Revised Statutes ("N.R.S.") speak to the respective rights and duties of directors and officers of corporations, and the rights of corporate stockholders. Nevada's statutory scheme does not, however, provide clear guidance in this case. While N.R.S. § 78.138 addresses several powers of a corporate board in undertaking defensive measures to resist a hostile takeover,* nothing in the Nevada statutes, or

* [Eds.—Nevada corporation code § 138 (Nev. Rev. Stat. § 78.138) provides, in pertinent part:

1. Directors and officers shall exercise their powers in good faith and with a view to the interests of the corporation. . . .

3. Directors and officers, in exercising their respective powers with a view to the interests of the corporation, may consider:

(a) The interests of the corporation's employees, suppliers, creditors and customers;

(b) The economy of the state and nation;

(c) The interests of the community and of society; and

(d) The long-term as well as short-term interests of the corporation and its stockholders, including the possibility that these interests may be best served by the continued independence of the corporation.

This subsection does not create or authorize any causes of action against the corporation or its directors or officers.

4. Directors may resist a change or potential change in control of the corporation if the directors by a majority vote of a quorum determine that the change or potential change is opposed to or not in the best interest of the corporation:

(a) Upon consideration of the interests of the corporation's stockholders and any of the matters set forth in subsection 3; or

(b) Because the amount or nature of the indebtedness and other obligations to which the corporation or any successor to the property of either may become subject in connection with the change or potential change in control provides reasonable grounds to believe that, within a reasonable time:

(1) The assets of the corporation or any successor would be or become less than its liabilities;

(2) The corporation or any successor would be or become insolvent; or

(3) Any voluntary or involuntary proceeding under the federal bankruptcy laws concerning the corporation

elsewhere in the law of Nevada, authorizes the incumbent board of a corporation to entrench itself by effectively removing the right of the corporation's shareholders to vote on who may serve on the board of the corporation in which they own a share. Whether a target corporation such as ITT can do so in the face of a hostile takeover attempt by Hilton is the dispositive issue presented in this case.

Where, as here, there is no Nevada statutory or case law on point for an issue of corporate law, this Court finds persuasive authority in Delaware case law,. . . .

A. Legal Framework for Board Action in Response to a Proxy Contest and Tender Offer.

As this case involves both a tender offer and a proxy contest by Hilton, the proper legal standard is a *Unocal/Blasius** analysis as articulated in Stroud v. Grace, 606 A.2d 75, 92 n. 3 (Del.1992), and Unitrin, [Inc. v. American Gen. Corp., 651 A.2d 1361], 1379 [(Del.1995)].

> In assessing a challenge to defensive actions by a target corporation's board of directors in a takeover context, this Court has held that the Court of Chancery should evaluate the board's overall response, including the justification for each contested defensive measure, and the results achieved thereby. Where all of the target board's defensive actions are *inextricably related*, the principles of *Unocal* require that such actions be scrutinized collectively as a unitary response to the perceived threat.

Unitrin, 651 A.2d at 1386–87 (emphasis supplied). . . .

> Where an acquiror launches both a proxy fight and a tender offer, it

> "necessarily invoke[s] both *Unocal* and *Blasius*" because "both [tests] recognize the inherent conflicts of interest that arise when shareholders are not permitted free exercise of their franchise. . . . [I]n certain circumstances, [the judiciary] must recognize the special import of protecting the shareholders' franchise within *Unocal*'s requirement that any defensive measure be proportionate and 'reasonable in relation to the threat posed.' "

or any successor would be commenced by any person.

Consider also Nevada Corporate Code § 120 (Nev. Rev. Stat. § 78.120), which provides in pertinent part:

> 1. Subject only to such limitations as may be provided by this chapter, or the articles of incorporation of the corporation, the board of directors has full control over the affairs of the corporation. . . .

> 3. The selection of a period for the achievement of corporate goals is the responsibility of the directors.]

* [Eds.—In Stroud v. Grace, 606 A.2d 75 (Del.1992), and Blasius Indus. v. Atlas Corp., 564 A.2d 651 (Del. Ch. 1988), the Delaware courts held that board action intended to thwart the free exercise of the shareholder franchise must satisfy the "heavy burden" of demonstrating a "compelling justification" for their action. In cases, such as *Hilton*, in which the board's action takes place in the context of an unsolicited tender offer, *Unocal* provides the basic standard of review for the board's actions, but in applying *Unocal*'s proportionality prong the courts will treat board action that purposefully disenfranchises the shareholders as "strongly suspect."]

Unitrin, 651 A.2d at 1379 (quoting *Stroud*, 606 A.2d at 92 n. 3).

> A board's unilateral decision to adopt a defensive measure touching "upon issues of control" that purposefully disenfranchises its shareholders is strongly suspect under *Unocal*, and cannot be sustained without a "compelling justification."

Stroud, 606 A.2d at 92 n. 3.

These cases have drawn a distinction between the exercise of two types of corporate power: 1) power over the assets of the corporation and 2) the power relationship between the board (management) and the shareholders. Actions involving the first type of power invoke the business judgment rule, or *Unocal* if an action is in response to a reasonably perceived threat to the corporation. Actions involving the second power invoke a *Blasius* analysis. The issues raised in this case require the Court to focus on the power relationship between ITT's board and ITT shareholders, not on the ITT board's actions relating to corporate assets.

Several amicus briefs have been filed on behalf of ITT shareholders, urging that they be allowed to vote on the Comprehensive Plan and the board of directors at the 1997 annual meeting. This Court has found no legal basis mandating a shareholder vote on the adoption of ITT's Comprehensive Plan in its entirety. However, as the Court finds that the Comprehensive Plan would violate the power relationship between ITT's board and ITT's shareholders by impermissibly infringing on the shareholders' right to vote on members of the board of directors, it must be enjoined.

ITT argues that Nevada does not follow Delaware case law since N.R.S. § 78.138 provides that a board, exercising its powers in good faith and with an view to the interests of the corporation can resist potential changes in control of a corporation based on the effect [on] constituencies other than the shareholders. However, the corporate rights provided under N.R.S. § 78.138 are not incompatible with the duties articulated in [the Delaware cases].

Delaware case law merely clarifies the basic duties established by the Nevada statutes. . . .

Thus, Delaware precedent establishes that a board has power over the management and assets of a corporation, but that power is not unbridled. That power is limited by the right of shareholders to vote for the members of the board. . . .

Unocal requires the Court to consider the following two questions: 1) Does ITT have reasonable grounds for believing a danger to corporate policy and effectiveness exists? 2) Is the response reasonable in relation to the threat? If it is a defensive measure touching on issues of control, the court must examine whether the board purposefully disenfranchised its shareholders, an action that cannot be sustained without a compelling justification. *Stroud*, 606 A.2d at 92 n. 3.

1. The Classified Board for ITT Destinations

The first defensive action this Court will analyze under the *Unocal* standard is the provision in the Comprehensive Plan for a classified board for ITT Destinations.

a. Reasonable Grounds for Believing a Threat to Corporate Policy and Effectiveness Exists.

Nine of ITT's eleven directors are outside directors. Under *Unocal*, such a majority materially enhances evidence that a hostile offer presents a threat warranting a defensive response. *Unitrin*, 651 A.2d at 1375.

ITT argues strenuously that the Comprehensive Plan is better than Hilton's offer. This is not for the Court to decide, and it is not determinative under its analysis. Under *Unocal*, a court must first determine if there is a threat to corporate policy and effectiveness. ITT has failed to demonstrate such a threat.

ITT has made no showing that Hilton will pursue a different corporate policy than ITT seeks to implement through its Comprehensive Plan. In fact, over the past few months, ITT has to a large extent adopted Hilton's proposed strategy of how it says it will govern ITT if its slate of directors is elected. There has also been no showing of Hilton's inability or ineffectiveness to run ITT if it does succeed in its takeover attempt. . . .

The ITT board has also failed to meet its burden of showing "good faith and reasonable investigation" of a threat to corporate policy or effectiveness which would meet the burden placed on the board under the first prong of the *Unocal* test. Since Hilton's tender offer was announced, the ITT board has not met with Hilton to discuss the offer. Moreover the overwhelming majority of ITT's evidence of good faith relates to its approval of the Comprehensive Plan, not to the inadequacy of Hilton's offer.

The sole "threat" ITT points to is that Hilton's offer of $70 a share is inadequate, primarily because this price does not contain a control premium. However, at the August 14, 1997, ITT board meeting, Goldman Sachs told the ITT board that the market valued ITT's plan at $62 to $64 dollars a share. This contradicts ITT's argument that there is no control premium over market price contained in Hilton's offer. That ITT itself was offering to buy back roughly 26% of its stock at $70 a share does not nullify this fact.

The only attempt ITT has made to satisfy the first prong of the *Unocal* analysis is to argue that Hilton's price is inadequate. However, while inadequacy of an offer is a legally cognizable threat, Paramount Communications, Inc. v. Time, Inc., 571 A.2d 1140, 1153 (Del.1989), ITT has shown no real harm to corporate policy or effectiveness. The facts in *Unocal* illustrate this point well. *Unocal* involved a tender offer with a back-end offer of junk bonds. Junk bond financing could reasonably harm the future policy and effectiveness of a company. As ITT itself is offering only $70 a share, and the Comprehensive Plan involves greatly increasing the leveraging of ITT, its claim that Hilton's offer of $70 a share is a threat to policy or effectiveness is unpersuasive. In light of these facts, the alleged inadequacy of Hilton's offer is not a severe threat to ITT. Under the proportionality requirement, the nature of Hilton's threat will set the parameters for the range of permissible defensive tactics under the second prong of the *Unocal* test.

    b. ITT's Response was Preclusive

Assuming Hilton's offer constitutes a cognizable threat under *Unocal*, ITT's response cannot be preclusive or coercive, and it must be within the range of reasonableness. As articulated in *Unitrin*, a board cannot "cram down" on shareholders a management sponsored alternative. The installation of a classified board for ITT Destinations, a company which will encompass 93% of the current ITT's assets and 87% of its revenues, is clearly preclusive and coercive under *Unitrin*. The classified board provision for ITT Destinations will preclude current ITT shareholders from exercising a right they currently possess—to determine the membership of the board of ITT. At the very minimum, ITT shareholders will have no choice but to accept the Comprehensive Plan and a majority of ITT's incumbent board members for another year. Therefore, the Comprehensive Plan is preclusive.

    c. The Primary Purpose of the Comprehensive Plan is to Interfere with Shareholder Franchise

ITT's response to Hilton's tender offer touches upon issues of control, and this Court must determine whether the response purposefully disenfranchises ITT's shareholders. If so, under the analysis of *Stroud* and *Unitrin*, it is not a reasonable response unless a "compelling justification" exists. It is important to note that in *Blasius*, the board did something that normally would be entirely permissible under Delaware law and its own by-laws: it expanded the board from seven to nine individuals. It did this in the face of a hostile takeover by a company financed through "junk bonds" and two individuals who sought to substantially "cash out" many of the target corporation's assets. Still, while the board in *Blasius* had a good faith reason to act as it did, and it acted with appropriate care, the board could not lawfully prevent the shareholders from electing a majority of new directors.

Blasius' factual scenario is strikingly similar to the circumstances surrounding ITT's actions. Normally, a corporation is free to adopt a classified board structure. In fact many companies, including Hilton, have classified boards. As long as the classified board is adopted in the proper manner, whether through charter amendment, changes in the by-laws of a company or through shareholder vote, it is permissible. However, *Blasius* illustrates that even if an action is normally permissible, and the board adopts it in good faith and with proper care, a board cannot undertake such action if the primary purpose is to disenfranchise the shareholders in light of a proxy contest. Thus, while ITT could normally adopt a classified board or issue a dividend of shares creating ITT Destinations, it cannot undertake these actions if the primary purpose is to disenfranchise ITT shareholders in light of Hilton's tender offer and proxy contest.

As a board would likely never concede that its primary purpose was to entrench itself, this Court must look to circumstantial evidence to determine the primary purpose of ITT's action touching upon issues of control. While none of the following factors are dispositive, collectively they eliminate all questions of material fact, and demonstrate that the primary purpose of ITT's Comprehensive Plan was to disenfranchise its shareholders.

i. Timing

The intent evidenced by the timing of the Comprehensive Plan is transparent. Although ITT claims that a spin-off or sale was contemplated before Hilton's tender offer, it makes no mention of when the board determined to move from an annually elected board to a classified board. Moreover, all aspects of ITT's Comprehensive Plan were formulated against the backdrop of Hilton's tender offer and proxy contest, and the Plan was not announced until well after Hilton's initial tender offer. Finally, this major restructuring of ITT was announced and to be implemented in a little over two months, and designed to take effect less than two months before the annual meeting was to be held at which shareholders would have the opportunity to vote on an annually elected rather than a classified board.

ii. Entrenchment

The ITT directors who are approving the Comprehensive Plan are the same directors who will fill the classified board positions of ITT Destinations. ITT and its advisors recognized from the outset that they were vulnerable because they did not have a staggered board of directors. The members of ITT's board are appointing themselves to new, more insulated positions, and at least seven of the eleven directors are avoiding the shareholder vote that would otherwise occur at ITT's 1997 annual meeting. While companies may convert from annual to classified boards, as *Blasius* illustrates, the rub is in the details. It is the manner of adopting the Comprehensive Plan with its provision for a new certified board comprised of incumbent ITT directors which supports the conclusion that ITT's Plan is primarily designed to entrench the incumbent board.

iii. ITT's Stated Purpose

ITT has offered no credible justification for not seeking shareholder approval of the Comprehensive Plan. ITT simply claims that it wants to "avoid market risks and other business problems." . . . . Such vague generalizations do not approach the required showing of a reasonable justification other than entrenchment for the board's action. Simply stating that its "advisors" suggested a rapid implementation of the Comprehensive Plan, without pointing to a specific risk or problem, is insufficient to meet ITT's burden.

iv. Benefits of Comprehensive Plan

ITT argues that there are economic benefits to the Comprehensive Plan, and general benefits of the classified board provision for ITT Destinations, That may be true, but the additional benefits of a plan infringing on shareholder voting rights do not remedy the fundamental flaw of board entrenchment.

v. Effect of Classified Board

The classified board provision for ITT Destinations under ITT's Comprehensive Plan ensures that ITT shareholders will be absolutely precluded from electing a majority of the directors nominated under Hilton's proxy contest at the 1997 annual meeting. Such a Plan, coupled with ITT's vehement opposition to Hilton's tender offer, is inconsistent with ITT's earlier argument that a delay of the 1997 annual meeting from May to November would afford shareholders additional time to inform themselves and more fully consider the implications of their vote for directors at the 1997 annual meeting.

ITT's position is particularly anomalous given the fact that when ITT previously split the company in 1995, it sought shareholder approval. While shareholder approval may not be absolutely required to split ITT now any more than it was in 1995, the fact that the ITT board decided to subject the 1995 split of the company to a shareholder vote is strong evidence that the primary purpose of its attempts to implement the Comprehensive Plan prior to the 1997 annual meeting is to entrench the incumbent ITT board.

vi. Failure to Obtain an IRS Opinion as to Effects of the Comprehensive Plan

ITT is not seeking an Internal Revenue Service opinion regarding the tax consequences of the three-way split of ITT under the Comprehensive Plan. It is doubtful that an Internal Revenue Service opinion on the matter could be obtained before ITT's 1997 annual meeting. Furthermore, there are serious questions as to the extent to which implementation of the Comprehensive Plan will constitute a taxable event to ITT and its shareholders, or the extent to which Hilton would incur adverse tax consequences if it attempted to take over ITT Destinations once the Comprehensive Plan is implemented. . . . While obtaining a tax opinion from the Internal Revenue Service may not be mandatory, ITT's failure to seriously consider obtaining such an opinion provides additional evidence that ITT's primary intention in implementing the Comprehensive Plan at this time was to impede the shareholder franchise.

2. Other Provisions of the Comprehensive Plan

This Court's analysis regarding the threat to ITT under the first prong of *Unocal* is equally applicable to the remaining elements of the Comprehensive Plan. Whether the other aspects of ITT's Comprehensive Plan violate the second step of the *Unocal* analysis, that is, whether they are preclusive or coercive, is problematic. Certainly the record before the Court supports Hilton's contention that the "tax poison pill" relating to its potential purchase of ITT Destinations is preclusive and coercive. . . .

. . . . This Court finds it unnecessary . . . to undertake an exhaustive analysis of the laundry list of issues presented by both parties. The different provisions of the Comprehensive Plan are inextricably related, and this Court has already concluded that the staggered board provision is preclusive and was enacted for the primary purpose of entrenching the current board. Therefore, the entire Comprehensive Plan must be enjoined.

3.   Duty to Maximize Value to Shareholders Under Revlon

Hilton further argues that injunctive relief is warranted based on an analysis of the Comprehensive Plan under the *Revlon* standard. The Court finds that Hilton has not extinguished all material facts as to whether the Comprehensive Plan involves: 1) an abandonment of the long-term strategy of ITT involving a breakup of the company or 2) a sale of control is contemplated in *Revlon* and Paramount v. QVC, 637 A.2d 34 (Del.1994). Therefore, permanent injunctive relief on this basis is not warranted.

IV.   CONCLUSION

. . .

Shareholders do not exercise day-to-day business judgments regarding the operation of a corporation—those are matters left to the reasonable discretion of directors, officers and the corporation's management team. Corporate boards have great latitude in exercising their business judgments as they should. As a result, shareholders generally have only two protections against perceived inadequate business performance. They may sell their stock or vote to replace incumbent board members. For this reason, interference with the shareholder franchise is especially serious. It is not to be left to the board's business judgment, precisely because it undercuts a primary justification for allowing directors to rely on their business judgment in almost every other context. . . .

ITT strongly argues that its Comprehensive Plan is superior to Hilton's alternative tender offer. This argument should be directed to ITT's shareholders, not this Court.

. . .

This Court concludes that the structure and timing of ITT's Comprehensive Plan with its classified board provision for ITT Destinations, is preclusive and leaves no doubt that the primary purpose for ITT's proposed implementation of the Comprehensive Plan before the 1997 annual meeting is to impermissibly impede the exercise of the shareholder franchise by depriving shareholders of the opportunity to vote to re-elect or to oust all or as many of the incumbent ITT directors as they may choose at the upcoming annual meeting. It has as its primary purpose the entrenchment of the incumbent ITT board. As a result, the Court concludes that Hilton has prevailed on the merits of its claim for permanent injunctive relief.

IT IS THEREFORE ORDERED that Hilton's Motion for Permanent Injunctive Relief is granted to the extent that ITT is hereby enjoined from implementing its Comprehensive Plan announced July 15, 1997.

IT IS FURTHER ORDERED that ITT's annual meeting shall be held no later than November 14, 1997.

. . .

AFTERMATH

In September 1997, Starwood Lodging, Inc. launched a competing bid for ITT. ITT's board announced its support for the Starwood offer. Hilton started a proxy fight to install its slate of directors for ITT, but at the November shareholder meeting the directors supported by ITT and Starwood were elected, whereupon Hilton withdrew its offer (which caused the market price of its shares to rise, a sign that people who followed the stock thought that Hilton had offered more for ITT than it was worth).

ANALYSIS

1. How persuasive is the court's finding that the classified board scheme was "preclusive"? Suppose ITT had been allowed to set up ITT Destinations, with a classified board. If Hilton had thereupon acquired a majority of ITT Destination's stock, would Hilton's efforts to obtain control of ITT in fact have been significantly impeded?

2. Why didn't ITT's board of directors simply adopt a by-law creating a classified board without going through the rigmarole of establishing three new corporations? Would your answer change under Delaware law?

3. The court appears to assume that Nevada courts would follow *Revlon*, as interpreted by *Time* and *QVC*. In light of Nev. Rev. Stat. §§ 78.120(3) and 78.138, does that conclusion appear plausible?

4. The court dismisses Hilton's *Revlon* claims on procedural grounds relating to the standard for granting injunctions. If the court had reached the merits of those claims, how should it have ruled?

5. Would the result in this case have changed if Hilton had not launched a proxy contest concurrently with its tender offer? Why did Hilton do so?

6. In view of the Delaware Supreme Court's holdings in Paramount Communications, Inc. v. Time Inc., was the *Hilton* court correct in holding that the only legally cognizable threat for purposes of *Unocal*'s first prong was price inadequacy? Did Hilton's bid raise any of the other threats validated by the Delaware Supreme Court in *Time*?

7. The court states, in connection with its discussion of *Unocal*, "Junk bond financing could . . . harm the future policy and effectiveness of the company." So what? Should the shareholders care? Suppose a corporation's board decides on a policy of expansion that is to be financed by junk bonds and a shareholder challenges that policy in a derivative action. What would the shareholder be required to prove in order to prevail?

NOTE ON RECENT DELAWARE DEVELOPMENTS

In Carmody v. Toll Brothers, Inc., 723 A.2d 1180 (Del.Ch.1998), the Delaware Chancery Court addressed the validity of a so-called "dead hand poison pill." In addition to fairly standard flip-in and flip-over features, the Toll Brothers pill provided that the pill could be redeemed only by those directors who had been in office when the shareholder rights constituting the pill had become exercisable (or their approved successors). This provision was intended to foreclose a loophole in standard poison pills. Most pills are subject to redemption at nominal cost by the target's board of directors. Such redemption provisions purportedly allow the target's board to use the pill as a negotiating device: The poison pill makes an acquisition of the target prohibitively expensive. If the prospective acquirer makes a sufficiently attractive offer, however, the board may redeem the pill and allow the offer to go forward unimpaired by the pill's dilutive effects. Although such redemption provisions gave the target's board considerable negotiating leverage, and were one of the justifications used to defend the whole idea of the poison pill, they also made the target vulnerable to a combined tender offer and proxy contest. The prospective acquirer could trigger the pill, conduct a proxy contest to elect a new board, which, if elected, would then redeem the pill to permit the tender offer to go forward. The dead hand pill was intended to close this loophole by depriving any such newly elected directors from redeeming the pill.

In denying Toll Brothers' motion to dismiss for failure to state a claim a shareholder suit challenging the validity of the dead hand pill, Vice Chancellor Jacobs indicated that the pill likely ran afoul of several aspects of Delaware law. First, it implicated the Delaware statutes governing the powers of directors: "Absent express language in the charter, nothing in Delaware law suggests that some directors of a public corporation may be created less equal than other directors, and certainly not by unilateral board action." Id. at 1191. Second, the dead hand pill effectively disenfranchised shareholders who wished to elect a board committed to redeeming the pill by deterring proxy contests by prospective acquirers. Accordingly, the challenge to the pill stated a claim under the Delaware Supreme Court's holding in Stroud v. Grace, 606 A.2d 75, 92 n. 3 (Del.1992), that defensive measures that disenfranchise shareholders are strongly suspect and cannot be sustained absent a compelling justification. *Toll Brothers*, 723 A.2d at 1193–94. Finally, the shareholder had also stated a "far from conclusory" claim under Unocal Corp. v. Mesa Petroleum Co., 493 A.2d 946 (Del.1985). Although standard pills had been upheld under the *Unocal* standard, the dead hand pill was both preclusive and coercive. It was coercive because the pill effectively forced shareholders to re-elect the incumbent directors if they wished to be represented by a board entitled to exercise its full statutory powers. The pill was preclusive because the added deterrent effect of the dead hand provision made a takeover prohibitively expensive and effectively impossible. *Toll Brothers*, 723 A.2d at 1195.

In Mentor Graphics Corp. v. Quickturn Design Systems, Inc., 728 A.2d 25 (Del.Ch.1998), Vice Chancellor Jacobs invalidated (after trial) a so-called "no hand" pill, which he distinguished from the Toll Brothers pill as follows:

> The "no hand" poison pill being challenged here is a variation of, and operates in a different manner from, the "dead hand" pill addressed in *Toll Brothers*. The pill in *Toll Brothers* created two classes of directors. One would have the power to redeem and the other would not. That limitation would last the entire lifetime of the pill. In contrast, the "no hand" pill in this case would create no classes. It would evenhandedly prevent all members of a newly elected target board, whose majority is nominated or supported by the hostile bidder, from redeeming the rights to facilitate an acquisition by the bidder. The duration of this "no hand" pill would be for six months after the new directors take office.

728 A.2d at 28. The target "board's stated rationale for adopting the [no hand pill] was to afford any newly elected board sufficient time to adequately inform itself about Quickturn, its business, and its true value, and also to allow stockholders sufficient time to consider alternatives, before the board decided to sell the company to any acquiror." 728 A.2d at 36. Jacobs concluded that the no hand pill violated the target board's *Unocal* duties and, accordingly, declined to address plaintiff's statutory and *Stroud*-based claims. As to the former, his analysis began with the Delaware Supreme Court's statement in Unitrin v. American General Corp., 651 A.2d 1361 (Del.1995), that Delaware law recognized three basic categories of threats to corporate policy and effectiveness for purposes of *Unocal*'s first prong:

> (i) opportunity loss . . . [where] a hostile offer might deprive target shareholders of the opportunity to select a superior alternative offered by target management [or, we would add, offered by another bidder]; (ii) structural coercion, . . . the risk that disparate treatment of non-tendering shareholders might distort shareholders' tender decisions; and . . . (iii) substantive coercion, . . . the risk that shareholders will mistakenly accept an underpriced offer because they disbelieve management's representations of intrinsic value.

Mentor Graphics, 728 A.2d at 45. Jacobs found that the board reasonably and in good faith believed that the prospective acquirer's offer was inadequate, hence invoking the substantive coercion threat. Id. at 47. Jacobs concluded, however, that the pill ran afoul of *Unocal*'s second prong. Although the board claimed the no hand provision was intended to give a new board time to learn about the target before deciding whether to sell the company, the pill in fact precluded only a sale to the initial bidder. Sales to other potential buyers were not foreclosed. In addition, the board failed to explain why the six-month delay on such a sale imposed by the no hand provision was reasonable. Accordingly, Jacobs held that the pill was disproportionate to the claimed substantive coercion threat. Id. at 47–51.

The Delaware Supreme Court recently affirmed, but on different grounds. Quickturn Design Systems, Inc. v. Mentor Graphics Corporation, 721 A.2d 1281 (Del.1998). The court explained:

> One of the most basic tenets of Delaware corporate law is that the board of directors has the ultimate responsibility for managing the business and affairs of a corporation. Section 141(a) requires that any limitation on the board's authority be set out in the certificate of incorporation. The Quickturn certificate of incorporation contains no provision purporting to limit the authority of the board in any way. The Delayed Redemption Provision, however, would prevent a newly elected board of directors from completely discharging its fundamental management duties to the corporation and its stockholders for six months. While the Delayed Redemption Provision limits the board of directors' authority in only one respect, the suspension of the Rights Plan, it nonetheless restricts the board's power in an area of fundamental importance to the shareholders—negotiating a possible sale of the corporation. Therefore, we hold that the Delayed Redemption Provision is invalid under Section 141(a), which confers upon any newly elected board of directors full power to manage and direct the business and affairs of a Delaware corporation.
>
> In discharging the statutory mandate of Section 141(a), the directors have a fiduciary duty to the corporation and its shareholders. . . .
>
> This Court has recently observed that "although the fiduciary duty of a Delaware director is unremitting, the exact course of conduct that must be charted to properly discharge that responsibility will change in the specific context of the action the director is taking with regard to either the corporation or its shareholders." This Court has held "to the extent that a contract, or a provision thereof, purports to require a board to act or not act in such a fashion as to limit the exercise of fiduciary duties, it is invalid and unenforceable." The Delayed Redemption Provision "tends to limit in a substantial way the freedom of [newly elected] directors' decisions on matters of management policy." Therefore, "it violates the duty of each [newly elected] director to exercise his own best judgment on matters coming before the board."

Id. at 1291–92.

C.   STATE AND FEDERAL LEGISLATION

CTS Corporation v. Dynamics Corporation of America
481 U.S. 69, 107 S.Ct. 1637, 95 L.Ed.2d 67 (1987).

■ JUSTICE POWELL delivered the opinion of the Court.

This case presents the questions whether the Control Share Acquisitions Chapter of the Indiana Business Corporation Law . . . is preempted by the Williams Act .   .   . or violates the Commerce Clause of the Federal Constitution, Art. I, § 8, cl. 3.

I

A

On March 4, 1986, the Governor of Indiana signed a revised Indiana Business Corporation Law, Ind.Code § 23–1–17–1 et seq. (Supp.1986). That law included the Control Share Acquisitions Chapter (Indiana Act or Act). Beginning on August 1, 1987, the Act will apply to any corporation incorporated in Indiana, § 23–1–17–3(a), unless the corporation amends its articles of incorporation or bylaws to opt out of the Act, § 23–1–42–5. Before that date, any Indiana corporation can opt into the Act by resolution of its board of directors. § 23–1–17–3(b). The Act applies only to "issuing public corporations." The term "corporation" includes only businesses incorporated in Indiana. See § 23–1–20–5. An "issuing public corporation" is defined as:

"a corporation that has:

"(1) one hundred (100) or more shareholders;

"(2) its principal place of business, its principal office, or substantial assets within Indiana; and

"(3) either:

"(A) more than ten percent (10%) of its shareholders resident in Indiana;

"(B) more than ten percent (10%) of its shares owned by Indiana residents; or

"(C) ten thousand (10,000) shareholders resident in Indiana." § 23–1–42–4(a).

The Act focuses on the acquisition of "control shares" in an issuing public corporation. Under the Act, an entity acquires "control shares" whenever it acquires shares that, but for the operation of the Act, would bring its voting power in the corporation to or above any of three thresholds: 20%, 33⅓%, or 50%. § 23–1–42–1. An entity that acquires control shares does not necessarily acquire voting rights. Rather, it gains those rights only "to the extent granted by resolution approved by the shareholders of the issuing public corporation." § 23–1–42–9(a). Section 9 requires a majority vote of all disinterested [2] shareholders holding each class of stock for passage of such a resolution. § 23–1–42–9(b). The practical effect of this requirement is to condition acquisition of control of a corporation on approval of a majority of the pre-existing disinterested shareholders.

The shareholders decide whether to confer rights on the control shares at the next regularly scheduled meeting of the shareholders, or at a

---

2. "Interested shares" are shares with respect to which the acquiror, an officer or an inside director of the corporation "may exer-cise or direct the exercise of the voting power of the corporation in the election of di-rectors." § 23–1–42–3. .   .   .

specially scheduled meeting. The acquiror can require management of the corporation to hold such a special meeting within 50 days if it files an "acquiring person statement," [4] requests the meeting, and agrees to pay the expenses of the meeting. See § 23–1–42–7. If the shareholders do not vote to restore voting rights to the shares, the corporation may redeem the control shares from the acquiror at fair market value, but it is not required to do so. § 23–1–42–10(b). Similarly, if the acquiror does not file an acquiring person statement with the corporation, the corporation may, if its bylaws or articles of incorporation so provide, redeem the shares at any time after 60 days after the acquiror's last acquisition. § 23–1–42–10(a).

B

On March 10, 1986, appellee Dynamics Corporation of America (Dynamics) owned 9.6% of the common stock of appellant CTS Corporation, an Indiana corporation. On that day, six days after the Act went into effect, Dynamics announced a tender offer for another million shares in CTS; purchase of those shares would have brought Dynamics' ownership interest in CTS to 27.5%. Also on March 10, Dynamics filed suit in the United States District Court for the Northern District of Illinois, alleging that CTS had violated the federal securities laws in a number of respects no longer relevant to these proceedings. On March 27, the Board of Directors of CTS, an Indiana corporation, elected to be governed by the provisions of the Act, see § 23–1–17–3.

Four days later, on March 31, Dynamics moved for leave to amend its complaint to allege that the Act is pre-empted by the Williams Act, 15 U.S.C. §§ 78m(d)–(e) and 78n(d)–(f) (1982 ed. and Supp. III), and violates the Commerce Clause, Art. I, § 8, cl. 3. Dynamics sought a temporary restraining order, a preliminary injunction, and declaratory relief against CTS's use of the Act. On April 9, the District Court ruled that the Williams Act pre-empts the Indiana Act and granted Dynamics' motion for declaratory relief. 637 F.Supp. 389 (N.D.Ill.1986). Relying on Justice WHITE's plurality opinion in Edgar v. MITE Corp., 457 U.S. 624 (1982), the court concluded that the Act "wholly frustrates the purpose and objective of Congress in striking a balance between the investor, management, and the takeover bidder in takeover contests." 637 F.Supp., at 399. A week later, on April 17, the District Court issued an opinion accepting Dynamics' claim that the Act violates the Commerce Clause. This holding rested on the court's conclusion that "the substantial interference with interstate commerce created by the [Act] outweighs the articulated local benefits so as to create an impermissible indirect burden on interstate commerce." Id., at 406. The District Court certified its decisions on the Williams Act and Commerce Clause claims as final under Fed.Rule Civ. Proc. 54(b). Ibid.

---

4. An "acquiring person statement" is an information statement describing, *inter alia,* the identity of the acquiring person and the terms and extent of the proposed acquisition. See § 23–1–42–6.

[The Court of Appeals, in an opinion by Judge Richard Posner, affirmed.]

After disposing of a variety of questions not relevant to this appeal, the Court of Appeals examined Dynamics' claim that the Williams Act pre-empts the Indiana Act. The court looked first to the plurality opinion in Edgar v. MITE Corp., supra, in which three Justices found that the Williams Act pre-empts state statutes that upset the balance between target management and a tender offeror. The court noted that some commentators had disputed this view of the Williams Act, concluding instead that the Williams Act was "an anti-takeover statute, expressing a view, however benighted, that hostile takeovers are bad." Id., at 262. It also noted:

> "[I]t is a big leap from saying that the Williams Act does not itself exhibit much hostility to tender offers to saying that it implicitly forbids states to adopt more hostile regulations. . . . But whatever doubts of the Williams' Act preemptive intent we might entertain as an original matter are stilled by the weight of precedent." Ibid.

Once the court had decided to apply the analysis of the *MITE* plurality, it found the case straightforward:

> "Very few tender offers could run the gauntlet that Indiana has set up. In any event, if the Williams Act is to be taken as a congressional determination that a month (roughly) is enough time to force a tender offer to be kept open, 50 days is too much; and 50 days is the minimum under the Indiana act if the target corporation so chooses." Id., at 263.

The court next addressed Dynamic's Commerce Clause challenge to the Act. Applying the balancing test articulated in Pike v. Bruce Church, Inc., 397 U.S. 137 (1970), the court found the Act unconstitutional:

> "Unlike a state's blue sky law the Indiana statute is calculated to impede transactions between residents of other states. For the sake of trivial or even negative benefits to its residents Indiana is depriving nonresidents of the valued opportunity to accept tender offers from other nonresidents.
>
> ". . . Even if a corporation's tangible assets are immovable, the efficiency with which they are employed and the proportions in which the earnings they generate are divided between management and shareholders depends on the market for corporate control—an interstate, indeed international, market that the State of Indiana is not authorized to opt out of, as in effect it has done in this statute." 794 F.2d, at 264.

Finally, the court addressed the "internal affairs" doctrine, a "principle of conflict of laws . . . designed to make sure that the law of only one state shall govern the internal affairs of a corporation or other association." Ibid. It stated:

"We may assume without having to decide that Indiana has a broad latitude in regulating those affairs, even when the consequence may be to make it harder to take over an Indiana corporation.   .   .   .   But in this case the effect on the interstate market in securities and corporate control is direct, intended, and substantial.   .   .   .   [T]hat the mode of regulation involves jiggering with voting rights cannot take it outside the scope of judicial review under the commerce clause."   Ibid.

Accordingly, the court affirmed the judgment of the District Court.

.   .   .

II

The first question in this case is whether the Williams Act pre-empts the Indiana Act. As we have stated frequently, absent an explicit indication by Congress of an intent to pre-empt state law, a state statute is pre-empted only

" 'where compliance with both federal and state regulations is a physical impossibility .   .   .,' *Florida Lime & Avocado Growers, Inc. v. Paul,* 373 U.S. 132, 142–143 (1963), or where the state 'law stands as an obstacle to the accomplishment and execution of the full purposes and objectives of Congress.' *Hines v. Davidowitz,* 312 U.S. 52, 67 [61 S.Ct. 399, 404, 85 L.Ed. 581] (1941).   .   .   ."   *Ray v. Atlantic Richfield Co.,* 435 U.S. 151 (1978).

Because it is entirely possible for entities to comply with both the Williams Act and the Indiana Act, the state statute can be pre-empted only if it frustrates the purposes of the federal law.

A

Our discussion begins with a brief summary of the structure and purposes of the Williams Act. Congress passed the Williams Act in 1968 in response to the increasing number of hostile tender offers. Before its passage, these transactions were not covered by the disclosure requirements of the federal securities laws.   .   .   .

The Williams Act, backed by regulations of the Securities and Exchange Commission (SEC), imposes requirements in two basic areas. First, it requires the offeror to file a statement disclosing information about the offer, including: the offeror's background and identity; the source and amount of the funds to be used in making the purchase; the purpose of the purchase, including any plans to liquidate the company or make major changes in its corporate structure; and the extent of the offeror's holdings in the target company.

Second, the Williams Act, and the regulations that accompany it, establish procedural rules to govern tender offers. For example, stockholders who tender their shares may withdraw them during the first 15 business days of the tender offer and, if the offeror has not purchased their shares, any time after 60 days from commencement of the offer.   .   .   .   The offer must remain open for at least 20 business days.   .   .   .   If more shares are tendered than the offeror sought to purchase, purchases must be made on a pro rata basis from each tendering shareholder.   .   .   .Finally, the offeror must pay the same price for all purchases; if the offering price is increased before the end of the offer, those who already have tendered must receive the benefit of the increased price.   .   .   .

B

The Indiana Act differs in major respects from the Illinois statute that the Court considered in Edgar v. MITE Corp., 457 U.S. 624 (1982). After reviewing the legislative history of the Williams Act, Justice WHITE, joined by Chief Justice Burger and Justice BLACKMUN (the plurality), concluded that the Williams Act struck a careful balance between the interests of offerors and target companies, and that any state statute that "upset" this balance was pre-empted. Id., at 632–634.

The plurality then identified three offending features of the Illinois statute. Justice WHITE's opinion first noted that the Illinois statute provided for a 20–day precommencement period. During this time, management could disseminate its views on the upcoming offer to shareholders, but offerors could not publish their offers. The plurality found that this provision gave management "a powerful tool to combat tender offers." Id., at 635. This contrasted dramatically with the Williams Act; Congress had deleted express precommencement notice provisions from the Williams Act. According to the plurality, Congress had determined that the potentially adverse consequences of such a provision on shareholders should be avoided. Thus, the plurality concluded that the Illinois provision "frustrate[d] the objectives of the Williams Act." Ibid. The second criticized feature of the Illinois statute was a provision for a hearing on a tender offer that, because it set no deadline, allowed management " 'to stymie indefinitely a takeover,' " id., at 637 (quoting MITE Corp. v. Dixon, 633 F.2d 486, 494 (C.A.7 1980)). The plurality noted that " 'delay can seriously impede a tender offer,' " 457 U.S., at 637, (quoting Great Western United Corp. v. Kidwell, 577 F.2d 1256, 1277 (C.A.5 1978) (per Wisdom, J.)), and that "Congress anticipated that investors and the takeover offeror would be free to go forward without unreasonable delay," 457 U.S., at 639. Accordingly, the plurality concluded that this provision conflicted with the Williams Act. The third troublesome feature of the Illinois statute was its requirement that the fairness of tender offers would be reviewed by the Illinois Secretary of State. Noting that "Congress intended for investors to be free to make their own decisions," the plurality concluded that " '[t]he state thus offers investor protection at the expense of investor autonomy—an approach quite in conflict with that adopted by Congress.' " Id., at 639–640 (quoting MITE Corp. v. Dixon, supra, at 494).

C

As the plurality opinion in *MITE* did not represent the views of a majority of the Court, we are not bound by its reasoning. We need not question that reasoning, however, because we believe the Indiana Act passes muster even under the broad interpretation of the Williams Act articulated by Justice WHITE in *MITE*. As is apparent from our summary of its reasoning, the overriding concern of the *MITE* plurality was that the Illinois statute considered in that case operated to favor management against offerors, to the detriment of shareholders. By contrast, the statute now before the Court protects the independent shareholder against both of the contending parties. Thus, the Act furthers a basic purpose of the Williams Act, " 'plac[ing] investors on an equal footing with the takeover bidder,' " Piper v. Chris–Craft Industries, [430 U.S. 1, 30 (1977)] (quoting the Senate Report accompanying the Williams Act, S.Rep. No. 550, 90th Cong., 1st Sess., 4 (1967)).

The Indiana Act operates on the assumption, implicit in the Williams Act, that independent shareholders faced with tender offers often are at a disadvantage. By allowing such shareholders to vote as a group, the Act protects them from the coercive aspects of some tender offers. If, for example, shareholders believe that a successful tender offer will be followed by a purchase of nontendering shares at a depressed price, individual shareholders may tender their shares—even if they doubt the tender offer is in the corporation's best interest—to protect themselves from being forced to sell their shares at a depressed price. . . .   In such a situation under the Indiana Act, the shareholders as a group, acting in the corporation's best interest, could reject the offer, although individual shareholders might be inclined to accept it. . . .

In implementing its goal, the Indiana Act avoids the problems the plurality discussed in *MITE*. Unlike the *MITE* statute, the Indiana Act does not give either management or the offeror an advantage in communicating with the shareholders about the impending offer. The Act also does not impose an indefinite delay on tender offers. Nothing in the Act prohibits an offeror from consummating an offer on the 20th business day, the earliest day permitted under applicable federal regulations, see 17 CFR § 240.14e–1(a) (1986). Nor does the Act allow the state government to interpose its views of fairness between willing buyers and sellers of shares of the target company. Rather, the Act allows *shareholders* to evaluate the fairness of the offer collectively.

D

The Court of Appeals based its finding of pre-emption on its view that the practical effect of the Indiana Act is to delay consummation of tender offers until 50 days after the commencement of the offer. 794 F.2d, at 263. As did the Court of Appeals, Dynamics reasons that no rational offeror will purchase shares until it gains assurance that those shares will carry voting rights. Because it is possible that voting rights will not be conferred until a shareholder meeting 50 days after commencement of the offer, Dynamics concludes that the Act imposes a 50–day delay. This, it argues, conflicts with the shorter 20–business–day period established by the SEC as the minimum period for which a tender offer may be held open. . . . We find the alleged conflict illusory.

The Act does not impose an absolute 50–day delay on tender offers, nor does it preclude an offeror from purchasing shares as soon as federal law permits. If the offeror fears an adverse shareholder vote under the Act, it can make a conditional tender offer, offering to accept shares on the condition that the shares receive voting rights within a certain period of time. The Williams Act permits tender offers to be conditioned on the offeror's subsequently obtaining regulatory approval. . . . There is no reason to doubt that this type of conditional tender offer would be legitimate as well.

Even assuming that the Indiana Act imposes some additional delay, nothing in *MITE* suggested that *any* delay imposed by state regulation, however short, would create a conflict with the Williams Act. The plurality argued only that the offeror should "be free to go forward without *unreasonable* delay." 457 U.S., at 639, 102 S.Ct., at 2639 (emphasis added). In that case, the Court was confronted with the potential for indefinite delay and presented with no persuasive reason why some deadline could not be established. By contrast, the Indiana Act provides that full voting rights will be vested—if this eventually is to occur—within 50 days after commencement of the offer. . . .

Finally, we note that the Williams Act would pre-empt a variety of state corporate laws of hitherto unquestioned validity if it were construed to pre-empt any state statute that may limit or delay the free exercise of power after a successful tender offer. State corporate laws commonly permit corporations to stagger the terms of their directors. . . .

By staggering the terms of directors, and thus having annual elections for only one class of directors each year, corporations may delay the time when a successful offeror gains control of the board of directors. Similarly, state corporation laws commonly provide for cumulative voting. . . . By enabling minority shareholders to assure themselves of representation in each class of directors, cumulative voting provisions can delay further the ability of offerors to gain untrammeled authority over the affairs of the target corporation. . . .

In our view, the possibility that the Indiana Act will delay some tender offers is insufficient to require a conclusion that the Williams Act pre-empts the Act. . . .

III

As an alternative basis for its decision, the Court of Appeals held that the Act violates the Commerce Clause of the Federal Constitution. We now address this holding. On its face, the Commerce Clause is nothing more than a grant to Congress of the power "[t]o regulate Commerce . . . among the several States . . .," Art. I, § 8, cl. 3. But it has been settled for more than a century that the Clause prohibits States from taking certain actions respecting interstate commerce even absent congressional action. . . .

A

The principal objects of dormant Commerce Clause scrutiny are statutes that discriminate against interstate commerce.   .   .   . The Indiana Act is not such a statute. It has the same effects on tender offers whether or not the offeror is a domiciliary or resident of Indiana.   .   .   .

Dynamics nevertheless contends that the statute is discriminatory because it will apply most often to out-of-state entities. This argument rests on the contention that, as a practical matter, most hostile tender offers are launched by offerors outside Indiana. But this argument avails Dynamics little. "The fact that the burden of a state regulation falls on some interstate companies does not, by itself, establish a claim of discrimination against interstate commerce." Exxon Corp. v. Governor of Maryland, 437 U.S. 117, 126, 98 S.Ct. 2207, 2214, 57 L.Ed.2d 91 (1978).   .   .   .

B

This Court's recent Commerce Clause cases also have invalidated statutes that adversely may affect interstate commerce by subjecting activities to inconsistent regulations.   .   .   . The Indiana Act poses no such problem. So long as each State regulates voting rights only in the corporations it has created, each corporation will be subject to the law of only one State. No principle of corporation law and practice is more firmly established than a State's authority to regulate domestic corporations, including the authority to define the voting rights of shareholders.   .   .   .

C

The Court of Appeals did not find the Act unconstitutional for either of these threshold reasons. Rather, its decision rested on its view of the Act's potential to hinder tender offers. We think the Court of Appeals failed to appreciate the significance for Commerce Clause analysis of the fact that state regulation of corporate governance is regulation of entities whose very existence and attributes are a product of state law.   .   .   .

Every State in this country has enacted laws regulating corporate governance. By prohibiting certain transactions, and regulating others, such laws necessarily affect certain aspects of interstate commerce. This necessarily is true with respect to corporations with shareholders in States other than the State of incorporation.   .   .   .

These regulatory laws may affect directly a variety of corporate transactions. Mergers are a typical example. In view of the substantial effect that a merger may have on the shareholders' interests in a corporation, many States require supermajority votes to approve mergers.   .   .   .

By requiring a greater vote for mergers than is required for other transactions, these laws make it more difficult for corporations to merge. State laws also may provide for "dissenters' rights" under which minority shareholders who disagree with corporate decisions to take particular actions are entitled to sell their shares to the corporation at fair market value.   .   .   . By requiring the corporation to purchase the shares of dissenting shareholders, these laws may inhibit a corporation from engaging in the specified transactions.

It thus is an accepted part of the business landscape in this country for States to create corporations, to prescribe their powers, and to define the rights that are acquired by purchasing their shares. A State has an interest in promoting stable relationships among parties involved in the corporations it charters, as well as in ensuring that investors in such corporations have an effective voice in corporate affairs.

There can be no doubt that the Act reflects these concerns. The primary purpose of the Act is to protect the shareholders of Indiana corporations. It does this by affording shareholders, when a takeover offer is made, an opportunity to decide collectively whether the resulting change in voting control of the corporation, as they perceive it, would be desirable. A change of management may have important effects on the shareholders' interests; it is well within the State's role as overseer of corporate governance to offer this opportunity. The autonomy provided by allowing shareholders collectively to determine whether the takeover is advantageous to their interests may be especially beneficial where a hostile tender offer may coerce shareholders into tendering their shares.

Appellee Dynamics responds to this concern by arguing that the prospect of coercive tender offers is illusory, and that tender offers generally should be favored because they reallocate corporate assets into the hands of management who can use them most effectively. . . . Indiana's concern with tender offers is not groundless. Indeed, the potentially coercive aspects of tender offers have been recognized by the Securities and Exchange Commission, . . . and by a number of scholarly commentators. . . . The Constitution does not require the States to subscribe to any particular economic theory. We are not inclined "to second-guess the empirical judgments of lawmakers concerning the utility of legislation," Kassel v. Consolidated Freightways Corp., [450 U.S., 662, 679 (1981)] (Brennan, J., concurring in judgment). In our view, the possibility of coercion in some takeover bids offers additional justification for Indiana's decision to promote the autonomy of independent shareholders.

Dynamics argues in any event that the State has " 'no legitimate interest in protecting the nonresident shareholders.' " Brief for Appellee Dynamics Corp. of America 21 (quoting Edgar v. MITE Corp., 457 U.S., at 644). Dynamics relies heavily on the statement by the *MITE* Court that "[i]nsofar as the . . . law burdens out-of-state transactions, there is nothing to be weighed in the balance to sustain the law." 457 U.S., at 644. But that comment was made in reference to an Illinois law that applied as well to out-of-state corporations as to in-state corporations. We agree that Indiana has no interest in protecting non-resident shareholders *of nonresident corporations*. But this Act applies only to corporations incorporated in Indiana. We reject the contention that Indiana has no interest in providing for the shareholders of its corporations the voting autonomy granted by the Act. . . .

IV

On its face, the Indiana Control Share Acquisitions Chapter evenhandedly determines the voting rights of shares of Indiana corporations. The Act does not conflict with the provisions or purposes of the Williams Act. To the limited extent that the Act affects interstate commerce, this is justified by the State's interests in defining the attributes of shares in its corporations and in protecting shareholders. . . . Accordingly, we reverse the judgment of the Court of Appeals.

It is so ordered.

■ JUSTICE SCALIA, concurring in part and concurring in the judgment.

. . .

One commentator has suggested that, at least much of the time, we do not in fact mean what we say when we declare that statutes which neither discriminate against commerce nor present a threat of multiple and inconsistent burdens might nonetheless be unconstitutional under a "balancing" test. See Regan, The Supreme Court and State Protectionism: Making Sense of the Dormant Commerce Clause, 84 Mich.L.Rev. 1091 (1986). If he is not correct, he ought to be. As long as a State's corporation law governs only its own corporations and does not discriminate against out-of-state interests, it should survive this Court's scrutiny under the Commerce Clause, whether it promotes shareholder welfare or industrial stagnation. Beyond that, it is for Congress to prescribe its invalidity.

. . .

I do not share the Court's apparent high estimation of the beneficence of the state statute at issue here. But a law can be both economic folly and constitutional. The Indiana Control Shares Acquisition Chapter is at least the latter. I therefore concur in the judgment of the Court.

■ JUSTICE WHITE, with whom JUSTICE BLACKMUN and JUSTICE STEVENS join as to Part II, dissenting.

The majority today upholds Indiana's Control Share Acquisitions Chapter, a statute which will predictably foreclose completely some tender offers for stock in Indiana corporations. I disagree with the conclusion that the Chapter is neither preempted by the Williams Act nor in conflict with the Commerce Clause. The Chapter undermines the policy of the Williams Act by effectively preventing minority shareholders, in some circumstances, from acting in their own best interests by selling their stock. In addition, the Chapter will substantially burden the interstate market in corporate ownership, particularly if other States follow Indiana's lead as many already have done. The Chapter, therefore, directly inhibits interstate commerce, the very economic consequences the Commerce Clause was intended to prevent. The opinion of the Court of Appeals is far more persuasive than that of the majority today, and the judgment of that court should be affirmed.

. . .

ANALYSIS

1. Underlying the decision in *CTS* is a nearly universal choice-of-law rule under which the law of the state of incorporation governs a corporation's "internal affairs" (which includes voting rights and other matters relating to the structure of ownership). Is this a sound rule? Why should it be, for example, that the law of Delaware governs the structure of about half of all major corporations in the United States? Does Congress have the power to impose a uniform federal law for the internal affairs of corporations?

2. Does the Indiana statute seem to you to be a justifiable response, as the Court suggests, to the need "to protect shareholders of Indiana corporations from [two-tier] coercive offer[s]"? If the objective was to protect shareholders from coercive bids, what aspect of the Indiana statute might seem incongruous? If the Supreme Court had found that the purpose of the Indiana statute was to protect local employees and business rather than shareholders, what relevance would, and should, that finding have had?

3. Think about how the Indiana law works. Suppose that on Day 1 a bidder announces a tender offer. At the same time it requests a special shareholder meeting to confer voting rights. Its offer is made contingent on a favorable vote on its voting rights. What is the timetable thereafter? How much disadvantage does the bidder suffer by virtue of the control share acquisition law?

NOTE ON OTHER STATE ANTI–TAKEOVER LEGISLATION

Several states had adopted anti-takeover statutes by the time of the Supreme Court's decision in *MITE* (discussed in *CTS*). After *MITE*, states adopted a second wave of statutes designed to block takeovers, but now designed them to fit within the strictures of *MITE*. After *CTS*, a third wave followed.

Particularly important is the 1988 Delaware anti-takeover statute. Del.Gen.Corp.Law § 203. Sometimes called a moratorium statute, the law kicks in if a bidder acquires at least 15 percent of a target's stock. Thereafter, the bidder may not engage in a "business combination" with the target for three years. The statute defines "business combination" broadly to include a merger between the bidder and the target, and a host of other transactions that accomplish much the same effect. Often, this inability to engage in a merger (particularly cash-out mergers to eliminate the minority shareholders) will chill any potential bidder's interest.

The Delaware statute has three important exceptions to the general ban. First, should a bidder acquire 85 percent or more of a target's stock, the ban will not apply. If the bidder buys a large enough stake, in other words, it may merge the target into itself.

Second, should a target board approve a tender offer or business combination *before* a bidder acquires 15 percent, the ban will not apply. If a bidder starts by cutting a deal with the target board, in short, the statute will let it later do a cash-out merger.

Last, the ban will not apply if a target board approves a merger after the bidder acquires its 15 percent threshold stake and ⅔ of the shares (other than shares held by the bidder) also approve the merger. Suppose, in other words, that the bidder acquires its stock and then replaces the board through a proxy fight. If it wants to cash-out the remaining target shareholders, it will need the approval of ⅔ of the other shares as well as the approval of the new board.

The Delaware statute allows corporations to opt out of the anti-takeover statute by so stating in their charter or by-laws. Note, however, that such an opt-out will not take effect for twelve months. Neither will it apply to any bidder who bought 15 percent before the amendment.

Although the Court in *CTS* ducks the issue, many states adopted their anti-takeover statutes straightforwardly to protect local managerial interests. Indiana adopted the statute in *CTS*, for example, to protect Arvin Industries. Headquartered in Columbus, Indiana (population 30,000), Arvin had made auto parts and employed about 2000 workers. It supported the local public schools and maintained good relations with the town. In December 1985, the Belzberg family (noted for greenmail attempts) threatened a takeover. Arvin responded by enlisting the aid of a friendly state legislator and had its lawyer write the first draft of what would become the Control Share Acquisition Chapter. The legislature adopted the bill and Arvin escaped the takeover.[21] Similarly, the Wisconsin legislature adopted the statute in *Amanda* (the next case) in 1987 to protect the G. Heileman Brewing Company. An Australian firm threatened to take over the firm, and Heileman's lawyers responded by drafting protective legislation.[22]

Amanda Acquisition Corporation v. Universal Foods Corporation

877 F.2d 496 (7th Cir.), cert. denied, 493 U.S. 955 (1989).

■ EASTERBROOK, CIRCUIT JUDGE.

I

Amanda Acquisition Corporation is a shell with a single purpose: to acquire Universal Foods Corporation, a diversified firm incorporated in Wisconsin and traded on the New York Stock Exchange. Universal is covered by Wisconsin's anti-takeover law. . . .

---

21. See Miller, Safe at Home: How Indiana Shielded a Firm and Changed the Takeover Business, Wall Street Journal, July 1, 1987, at 1, col. 6. In 1986, Arvin bought the Maremount Corporation, founded by Ar-

nold Maremount. See Moody's Indus. Man. 1989, p. 957.

22. See Davis, Epilogue: The Role of the Hostile Takeover and the Role of the States, 1988 Wis.L.Rev. 491, 493–97.

In mid-November 1988 Universal's stock was trading for about $25 per share. On December 1 Amanda commenced a tender offer at $30.50. . . . This all-cash, all-shares offer has been increased by stages to $38.00. Amanda's financing is contingent on a prompt merger with Universal if the offer succeeds, so the offer is conditional on a judicial declaration that the law is invalid. . . .

No firm incorporated in Wisconsin and having its headquarters, substantial operations, or 10% of its shares or shareholders there may "engage in a business combination with an interested stockholder . . . for 3 years after the interested stockholder's stock acquisition date unless the board of directors of the [Wisconsin] corporation has approved, before the interested stockholder's stock acquisition date, that business combination or the purchase of stock", Wis.Stat. § 180.726(2). An "interested stockholder" is one owning 10% of the voting stock, directly or through associates (anyone acting in concert with it), § 180.726(1)(j). A "business combination" is a merger with the bidder or any of its affiliates, sale of more than 5% of the assets to bidder or affiliate, liquidation of the target, or a transaction by which the target guarantees the bidder's or affiliate's debts or passes tax benefits to the bidder or affiliate, § 180.726(1)(e). The law, in other words, provides for almost hermetic separation of bidder and target for three years after the bidder obtains 10% of the stock—unless the target's board consented before then. No matter how popular the offer, the ban applies: obtaining 85% (even 100%) of the stock held by non-management shareholders won't allow the bidder to engage in a business combination, as it would under Delaware law. . . . Wisconsin firms cannot opt out of the law, as may corporations subject to almost all other state takeover statutes. In Wisconsin it is management's approval in advance, or wait three years. Even when the time is up, the bidder needs the approval of a majority of the remaining investors, without any provision disqualifying shares still held by the managers who resisted the transaction, § 180.726(3)(b). The district court found that this statute "effectively eliminates hostile leveraged buyouts." As a practical matter, Wisconsin prohibits any offer contingent on a merger between bidder and target, a condition attached to about 90% of contemporary tender offers.

Amanda filed this suit seeking a declaration that this law is preempted by the Williams Act and inconsistent with the Commerce Clause. . . .

A

If our views of the wisdom of state law mattered, Wisconsin's takeover statute would not survive. Like our colleagues who decided [Edgar v. MITE Corp., 457 U.S. 624 (1982)] and [CTS Corporation v. Dynamics Corporation of America, 481 U.S. 69 (1987)], we believe that anti-takeover legislation injures shareholders.[5] Managers frequently realize gains for

---

5. Because both the district court and the parties—like the Williams Act—examine tender offers from the perspective of equity investors, we employ the same approach. States could choose to protect "constituencies" other than stockholders. Creditors, managers, and workers invest human rather than financial capital. But the limitation of

investors via voluntary combinations (mergers). If gains are to be had, but managers balk, tender offers are investors' way to go over managers' heads. If managers are not maximizing the firm's value—perhaps because they have missed the possibility of a synergistic combination, perhaps because they are clinging to divisions that could be better run in other hands, perhaps because they are just not the best persons for the job—a bidder that believes it can realize more of the firm's value will make investors a higher offer. Investors tender; the bidder gets control and changes things.

. . . The prospect of monitoring by would-be bidders, and an occasional bid at a premium, induces managers to run corporations more efficiently and replaces them if they will not.

Premium bids reflect the benefits for investors. The price of a firm's stock represents investors' consensus estimate of the value of the shares under current and anticipated conditions. Stock is worth the present value of anticipated future returns—dividends and other distributions. Tender offers succeed when bidders offer more. Only when the bid exceeds the value of the stock (however investors compute value) will it succeed. A statute that precludes investors from receiving or accepting a premium offer makes them worse off. It makes the economy worse off too, because the higher bid reflects the better use to which the bidder can put the target's assets. (If the bidder can't improve the use of the assets, it injures itself by paying a premium.)

Universal, making an argument common among supporters of anti-takeover laws, contends that its investors do not appreciate the worth of its business plans, that its stock is trading for too little, and that if investors tender reflexively they injure themselves. If only they would wait, Universal submits, they would do better under current management. A variant of the argument has it that although smart investors know that the stock is underpriced, many investors are passive and will tender; even the smart investors then must tender to avoid doing worse on the "back end" of the deal. State laws giving management the power to block an offer enable the managers to protect the investors from themselves.

Both versions of this price-is-wrong argument imply: (a) that the stock of firms defeating offers later appreciates in price, topping the bid, thus revealing the wisdom of waiting till the market wises up; and (b) that investors in firms for which no offer is outstanding gain when they adopt devices so that managers may fend off unwanted offers (or states adopt laws with the same consequence). Efforts to verify these implications have failed. The best available data show that if a firm fends off a bid, its profits decline, and its stock price (adjusted for inflation and market-wide

our inquiry to equity investors does not affect the analysis, because no evidence of which we are aware suggests that bidders confiscate workers' and other participants' investments to any greater degree than do incumbents—who may (and frequently do) close or move plants to follow the prospect of profit. Jo-seph A. Grundfest, a Commissioner of the SEC, showed in *Job Loss and Takeovers*, address to University of Toledo College of Law, Mar. 11, 1988, that acquisitions have no logical (or demonstrable) effect on employment. . . .

changes) never tops the initial bid, even if it is later acquired by another firm.   .   .   . Stock of firms adopting poison pills falls in price, as does the stock of firms that adopt most kinds of anti-takeover amendments to their articles of incorporation.   .   .   . Studies of laws similar to Wisconsin's produce the same conclusion: share prices of firms incorporated in the state drop when the legislation is enacted.   .   .   .

Although a takeover-*proof* firm leaves investors at the mercy of incumbent managers (who may be mistaken about the wisdom of their business plan even when they act in the best of faith), a takeover-*resistant* firm may be able to assist its investors. An auction may run up the price, and delay may be essential to an auction. Auctions transfer money from bidders to targets, and diversified investors would not gain from them (their left pocket loses what the right pocket gains); diversified investors would lose from auctions if the lower returns to bidders discourage future bids. But from targets' perspectives, once a bid is on the table an auction may be the best strategy. The full effects of auctions are hard to unravel, sparking scholarly debate. Devices giving managers some ability to orchestrate investors' responses, in order to avoid panic tenders in response to front-end-loaded offers, also could be beneficial, as the Supreme Court emphasized in *CTS*, 481 U.S. at 92–93, 107 S.Ct. at 1651–52. ("Could be" is an important qualifier; even from a perspective limited to targets' shareholders given a bid on the table, it is important to know whether managers use this power to augment bids or to stifle them, and whether courts can tell the two apart.)

State anti-takeover laws do not serve these ends well, however. Investors who prefer to give managers the discretion to orchestrate responses to bids may do so through "fair-price" clauses in the articles of incorporation and other consensual devices.* Other firms may choose different strategies. A law such as Wisconsin's does not add options to firms that would like to give more discretion to their managers; instead it destroys the possibility of divergent choices. Wisconsin's law applies even when the investors prefer to leave their managers under the gun, to allow the market full sway. [A recent study] found that state anti-takeover laws have little or no effect on the price of shares if the firm already has poison pills (or related devices) in place, but strongly negative effects on price when firms have no such contractual devices. To put this differently, state laws have bite only when investors, given the choice, would deny managers the power to interfere with tender offers (maybe already *have* denied managers that power).   .   .   .

B

Skepticism about the wisdom of a state's law does not lead to the conclusion that the law is beyond the state's power, however. We have not

---

* [Eds.—A fair price clause in the articles (or in the state law) is designed to prevent the "coercion" in two-tiered tender offers. Broadly put, such a provision assures that the price paid in the second stage of a tender offer (generally, the cash-out merger) will be at least as high as the first-stage price.]

been elected custodians of investors' wealth. States need not treat investors' welfare as their summum bonum. Perhaps they choose to protect managers' welfare instead, or believe that the current economic literature reaches an incorrect conclusion and that despite appearances takeovers injure investors in the long run. Unless a federal statute or the Constitution bars the way, Wisconsin's choice must be respected.

. . .

Preemption has not won easy acceptance among the Justices for several reasons. First there is § 28(a) of the '34 Act, 15 U.S.C. § 78bb(a), which provides that "[n]othing in this chapter shall affect the jurisdiction of the securities commission . . . of any State over any security or any person insofar as it does not conflict with the provisions of this chapter or the rules and regulations thereunder." Although some of the SEC's regulations (particularly the one defining the commencement of an offer) conflict with some state takeover laws, the SEC has not drafted regulations concerning mergers with controlling shareholders, and the Act itself does not address the subject. States have used the leeway afforded by § 28(a) to carry out "merit regulation" of securities—"blue sky" laws that allow securities commissioners to forbid sales altogether, in contrast with the federal regimen emphasizing disclosure. So § 28(a) allows states to stop some transactions federal law would permit, in pursuit of an approach at odds with a system emphasizing disclosure and investors' choice. Then there is the traditional reluctance of federal courts to infer preemption of "state law in areas traditionally regulated by the States", California v. ARC America Corp., [490] U.S. [93] (1989). . . . States have regulated corporate affairs, including mergers and sales of assets, since before the beginning of the nation.

. . .

Nothing in the Williams Act says that the federal compromise among bidders, targets' managers, and investors is the only permissible one.
. . .

The Williams Act regulates the *process* of tender offers: timing, disclosure, proration if tenders exceed what the bidder is willing to buy, best-price rules. It slows things down, allowing investors to evaluate the offer and management's response. Best-price, proration, and short-tender rules ensure that investors who decide at the end of the offer get the same treatment as those who decide immediately, reducing pressure to leap before looking. After complying with the disclosure and delay requirements, the bidder is free to take the shares. *MITE* held invalid a state law that increased the delay and, by authorizing a regulator to nix the offer, created a distinct possibility that the bidder would be unable to buy the stock (and the holders to sell it) despite compliance with federal law. Illinois tried to regulate the process of tender offers, contradicting in some respects the federal rules. Indiana, by contrast, allowed the tender offer to take its course as the Williams Act specified but "sterilized" the acquired shares until the remaining investors restored their voting rights. Congress said nothing about the voting power of shares acquired in tender offers. Indiana's law reduced the benefits the bidder anticipated from the acquisition but left the process alone. So the Court . . . held that Indiana's rules do not conflict with the federal norms.

CTS observed that laws affecting the voting power of acquired shares do not differ in principle from many other rules governing the internal affairs of corporations. Laws requiring staggered or classified boards of directors delay the transfer of control to the bidder; laws requiring supermajority vote for a merger may make a transaction less attractive or impossible. 481 U.S. at 85–86, 107 S.Ct. at 1647–48. Yet these are not preempted by the Williams Act, any more than state laws concerning the *effect* of investors' votes are preempted by the portions of the Exchange Act, 15 U.S.C. § 78n(a)–(c), regulating the process of soliciting proxies. Federal securities laws frequently regulate process while state corporate law regulates substance. Federal proxy rules demand that firms disclose many things, in order to promote informed voting. Yet states may permit or compel a supermajority rule (even a unanimity rule) rendering it all but impossible for a particular side to prevail in the voting.   . . .

Any bidder complying with federal law is free to acquire shares of Wisconsin firms on schedule. Delay in completing a second-stage merger may make the target less attractive, and thus depress the price offered or even lead to an absence of bids; it does not, however, alter any of the procedures governed by federal regulation. Indeed Wisconsin's law does not depend in any way on how the acquiring firm came by its stock: open-market purchases, private acquisitions of blocs, and acquisitions via tender offers are treated identically. Wisconsin's law is no different in effect from one saying that for the three years after a person acquires 10% of a firm's stock, a unanimous vote is required to merge. Corporate law once had a generally-applicable unanimity rule in major transactions, a rule discarded because giving every investor the power to block every reorganization stopped many desirable changes. (Many investors could use their "hold-up" power to try to engross a larger portion of the gains, creating a complex bargaining problem that often could not be solved.) Wisconsin's more restrained version of unanimity also may block beneficial transactions, but not by tinkering with any of the procedures established in federal law.

. . .

C

The Commerce Clause, Art. I, § 8 cl. 3 of the Constitution, grants Congress the power "[t]o regulate Commerce . . . among the several States".   . . .

When state law discriminates against interstate commerce expressly—for example, when Wisconsin closes its border to butter from Minnesota—the negative Commerce Clause steps in. The law before us is not of this type: it is neutral between inter-state and intra-state commerce. Amanda therefore presses on us the broader, all-weather, be-reasonable vision of the

Constitution. Wisconsin has passed a law that unreasonably injures investors, most of whom live outside of Wisconsin, and therefore it *has* to be unconstitutional, as Amanda sees things. Although Pike v. Bruce Church, Inc., 397 U.S. 137 (1970), sometimes is understood to authorize such general-purpose balancing, a closer examination of the cases may support the conclusion that the Court has looked for discrimination rather than for baleful effects. . . .

Illinois's law, held invalid in *MITE,* regulated sales of stock elsewhere. Illinois tried to tell a Texas owner of stock in a Delaware corporation that he could not sell to a buyer in California. By contrast, Wisconsin's law, like the Indiana statute sustained by *CTS,* regulates the internal affairs of firms incorporated there. Investors may buy or sell stock as they please.

. . .

Buyers of stock in Wisconsin firms may exercise full rights as investors, taking immediate control. No interstate transaction is regulated or forbidden. True, Wisconsin's law makes a potential buyer less willing to buy (or depresses the bid), but this is equally true of Indiana's rule. Many other rules of corporate law—supermajority voting requirements, staggered and classified boards, and so on—have similar or greater effects on some persons' willingness to purchase stock. . . . States could ban mergers outright, with even more powerful consequences. . . . Wisconsin did not allow mergers among firms chartered there until 1947. We doubt that it was violating the Commerce Clause all those years. . . . Every rule of corporate law affects investors who live outside the state of incorporation, yet this has never been thought sufficient to authorize a form of cost-benefit inquiry through the medium of the Commerce Clause.

. . .

To say that states have the power to enact laws whose costs exceed their benefits is not to say that investors should kiss their wallets goodbye. States compete to offer corporate codes attractive to firms. Managers who want to raise money incorporate their firms in the states that offer the combination of rules investors prefer. . . . Laws that in the short run injure investors and protect managers will in the longer run make the state less attractive to firms that need to raise new capital. If the law is "protectionist", the protected class is the existing body of managers (and other workers), suppliers, and so on, which bears no necessary relation to state boundaries. States regulating the affairs of domestic corporations cannot in the long run injure anyone but themselves. . . . The long run takes time to arrive, and it is tempting to suppose that courts could contribute to investors' welfare by eliminating laws that impose costs in the short run. . . . The price of such warfare, however, is a reduction in the power of competition among states. Courts seeking to impose "good" rules on the states diminish the differences among corporate codes and dampen competitive forces. Too, courts may fail in their quest. How do judges know which rules are best? Often only the slow forces of competition reveal that information. Early economic studies may mislead, or judges (not trained as social scientists) may misinterpret the available data or act precipitously. Our Constitution allows the states to act as laboratories; slow migration (or national law on the authority of the Commerce Clause) grinds the failures under. No such process weeds out judicial errors, or decisions that, although astute when rendered, have become anachronistic in light of changes in the economy. Judges must hesitate for these practical reasons—and not only because of limits on their constitutional competence—before trying to "perfect" corporate codes.

The three district judges who have considered and sustained Delaware's law delaying mergers did so in large measure because they believed that the law left hostile offers "a meaningful opportunity for success". BNS, Inc. v. Koppers Co., [683 F.Supp. 458, 469 (D.Del.1988)]. . . . Delaware allows a merger to occur forthwith if the bidder obtains 85% of the shares other than those held by management and employee stock plans. If the bid is attractive to the bulk of the unaffiliated investors, it succeeds. Wisconsin offers no such opportunity, which Amanda believes is fatal.

Even in Wisconsin, though, options remain. . . . The cheapest is to lower the bid to reflect the costs of delay. Because every potential bidder labors under the same drawback, the firm placing the highest value on the target still should win. Or a bidder might take down the stock and pledge it (or its dividends) as security for any loans. That is, the bidder could operate the target as a subsidiary for three years. The corporate world is full of partially owned subsidiaries. If there is gain to be had from changing the debt-equity ratio of the target, that can be done consistent with Wisconsin law. The prospect of being locked into place as holders of illiquid minority positions would cause many persons to sell out, and the threat of being locked in would cause many managers to give assent in advance, as Wisconsin allows. (Or bidders might demand that directors waive the protections of state law, just as Amanda believes that the directors' fiduciary duties compel them to redeem the poison pill rights.) Many bidders would find lock-in unattractive because of the potential for litigation by minority investors, and the need to operate the firm as a subsidiary might foreclose savings or synergies from merger. So none of these options is a perfect substitute for immediate merger, but each is a crack in the defensive wall allowing some value-increasing bids to proceed.

At the end of the day, however, it does not matter whether these countermeasures are "enough". The Commerce Clause does not demand that states leave bidders a "meaningful opportunity for success". . . . Wisconsin's law may well be folly; we are confident that it is constitutional.

AFFIRMED.

ANALYSIS

1. How serious is the impediment to takeovers imposed by the Wisconsin statute? Is it a "show stopper"?

2. The court says that apart from its effects on shareholder wealth a statute like that of Wisconsin, by impeding takeovers, "makes the economy

worse off . . ., because the higher bid reflects the better use to which the bidder can put the target's assets." What is meant by "the economy"? Just who is harmed—consumers, suppliers? What about competitors and their shareholders? To make these questions more concrete, consider RJR Nabisco in the period just before its takeover in 1989. Among other extravagances, the corporation, at the behest of its CEO, Ross Johnson, maintained a large fleet of jet planes and retained, at lavish levels of compensation, a number of golf and other sports celebrities. The celebrities (Jack Nicklaus, O.J. Simpson, Don Meredith, and others) made occasional appearances on behalf of the corporation but were hired mostly, it seems, to make Johnson (an avid golfer and world-class bon vivant) happy.

The Nabisco part of the RJR Nabisco empire produced such well-known products as Oreo cookies, Planters peanuts, and Baby Ruth candy bars. The head of Nabisco at the time of the takeover is reported to have confided that he could have increased its profits by as much as 40 percent, but that he would have gotten "in trouble" if he did. As he put it, "our charter is to run the company on a steady basis," which apparently meant that there should be enough slack so that reported profits would never decline from one year to the next. He claimed that he wasted vast sums of money on product promotion and on uneconomical investments in manufacturing technology. See B. Burrough and J. Helyar, Barbarians at the Gate 370–371 (1990). This method of management helps explain why the shareholders realized a large gain in their wealth when the company was taken over. Apart from the waste of part of the profits, however, apparently the company was well run and its brands were enormously valuable.

In a case like this, does anyone else gain? Who loses? If the corporation had been able to immunize itself from takeovers and continue to do business as usual, who, other than the shareholders, would have been the losers?

3. The court in *Amanda Acquisition* seems to assume that the objective of the Wisconsin law was to promote the welfare not of the shareholders of Wisconsin public corporations (many, or most, of whom were presumably not residents of Wisconsin), but rather of managers, other employees, suppliers, and other people whose livelihoods depended on the financial well-being of such people. A troubling aspect of the Wisconsin approach is that its effects are not limited to Wisconsin. Suppose that Wisconsin had adopted a labor law providing that if a Wisconsin corporation wished to close a plant anywhere in the world, it would be required to give six-months' notice to all employees before they could be taken off the payroll. Would such a law be enforceable with respect to the closing of a plant in, say, New York? If so, what would be the likely effect in the long run? What if the plant-closing law applied to any corporation the majority of whose shareholders were residents of Wisconsin?

NOTE ON THE PENNSYLVANIA STATUTE

In 1990, Pennsylvania enacted a wide-ranging set of anti-takeover rules, more extreme than those of any other state. As later amended, the Pennsylvania law contains the following provisions:

First, directors are allowed to take account of the interests not only of shareholders but also of "employees, suppliers, customers and creditors of the corporation, and . . . communities in which offices or other establishments of the corporation are located." Penn.Consol.Stat. Title 15, §§ 515(a)(1), 1715(a)(1). Even more important, the directors are expressly relieved of any obligation to treat the interests of shareholders as "dominant or controlling." §§ 515(b), 1715(b). These rules expressly apply to decisions about redeeming rights under a poison pill plan and to other decisions relating to takeovers. § 1715(c)(1). Thus, even if a change in control is inevitable and even if the result of refusing to redeem a poison pill right will be that the price paid for shares will be less than what the shareholders might have received from a hostile bidder, the board is not obligated to redeem. These rules were initially subject to a limited opt-out provision: the board (not the shareholders) could elect to opt out within 90 days of the effective date of the new law (one year in case of non-publicly traded corporations). Corporations formed after the effective date must opt out at the time of formation or soon thereafter. § 1711(b). There is still a requirement that directors must act in "good faith," which provides the authority for a court to intervene in extreme cases, but lack of good faith must be proved by "clear and convincing evidence." § 1715(d).

Second, there are provisions on control-share acquisitions (again, subject to the limited opt-out). §§ 2561–2668. In part, they follow the pattern of the Indiana law described in *CTS*. If a bidder acquires a controlling interest (20, 33⅓, or 50 percent of the voting power), the bidder loses voting rights unless it gains approval of a majority of the "disinterested" shares and a majority of all shares (other than its own). Disinterested shares are those that have been held the later of (i) twelve months before the record date for voting or (ii) five days before the first disclosure of the takeover bid. The vote-stripping rule does not apply to a person who acquires less than a controlling interest and then acquires additional voting power by obtaining revocable proxies obtained without consideration. A bidder is entitled to a special meeting on restoration of voting rights within 50 days of a request for such a meeting.

Third, and perhaps most innovative, is a provision calling for disgorgement (that is, payment to the corporation) of any gain from the sale of a corporation's shares by a person within 18 months after that person has sought or expressed an intent to seek control (20 percent of the voting power). §§ 2571–2576. The expressed intention of this provision is to remove the profit from greenmail or from putting a corporation "in play." Exemptions may be granted with the approval of both the board and the shareholders. Proxy contests are not covered if the objective was not to put the corporation "in play." Jurisdiction is asserted over persons and transactions having no connection with Pennsylvania other than purchase and sale of shares of a Pennsylvania corporation. Actions to enforce the corporation's right of recovery may be brought by a shareholder if the corporation fails to act; the shareholder is entitled to costs and attorney fees.

Fourth, there is a "tin parachute"—a provision for severance pay for all employees. An employee who is fired as a result of a takeover is entitled to a week's pay for each year of prior employment (with a maximum of 26 weeks' pay). §§ 2581–2583. This right applies only to employment in Pennsylvania. A similar tin parachute provision in the Massachusetts law has been held preempted by the federal Employee Retirement Income Security Act (ERISA), which explicitly preempts "any and all State laws" that "relate to any employee benefit plan." Simas v. Quaker Fabric Corp. of Fall River, 6 F.3d 849 (1st Cir.1993).

Finally, the new law provides that after a takeover all labor contracts are to remain in force. §§ 2585–2588.

The various provisions are severable.

QUESTIONS

1. Are any parts of the new Pennsylvania law preempted by the Williams Act?

2. Do any parts of the Pennsylvania law violate the Commerce Clause?

3. What, if anything, should Congress do in response to the Pennsylvania law? Is there reason to suppose that Congress would be more likely than the states to favor shareholder interests over the interests of others?

4. How would the adoption of the Pennsylvania law affect your decision to invest in a corporation incorporated in Pennsylvania that did not opt out of the provisions that are optional?

5. Are there better ways than the Pennsylvania legislation to protect nonshareholder interests? Is corporate law ever a good device for protecting nonshareholder interests?

CHAPTER 7

CORPORATE DEBT

SECTION 1. INTRODUCTION

In this chapter we examine some aspects of corporate bonds and debentures. Debentures are long-term unsecured debt obligations, while bonds are long-term debt obligations secured by property of the debtor, but the word "bonds" is often used (and will be used here) in referring to debentures as well as bonds. Bonds and debentures are forms of debt owed by corporations, typically to individuals and to institutions such as pension funds, insurance companies, and mutual funds. The legal and economic issues presented in these debt instruments are much the same as those arising with bank debt (generally memorialized in a "loan agreement") and other financing. In financial parlance, corporations are said to "issue" bonds and debentures, but they "borrow" from banks; the financial relationship is essentially the same regardless of the lingo. Currently, most debt obligations to banks are secured but most other debt obligations are not. The aversion to secured debt in nonbank borrowing reflects the fact that a security interest in a corporation's property disadvantageously constrains business decisions; with a single lender, like a bank, it may be feasible to waive the constraint, while with debt held by many persons that may not be so. Moreover, the main function of a security interest is to give some creditors priority over others and there is an alternative method of doing that. The alternative is the subordination agreement, which allows debt to be issued in layers of priority. Thus, for example, a corporation might issue senior debentures and subordinated debentures, with the latter being entitled to payment only after the claims of the former have been fully satisfied.

The rights of bondholders are largely governed by private contract. Most of the contractual terms are contained in a document called an indenture, which includes, among other things, various covenants (promises). Bond indenture forms have evolved over the years and are often long and complex. Yet in the case of publicly issued bonds, the evolution is a slow process and the contractual language is highly standardized. Lenders are most concerned about the financial soundness of the borrower and the interest rate to be paid. Covenants and other terms are relatively less important and it is not practical to negotiate over these terms every time a new bond is issued. In addition to the cost of negotiation is the problem of explaining new terms to a large number of potential buyers of the bonds. This is true even though most bonds these days are sold to sophisticated institutional buyers. With sizable bank loans, however, the terms of the loan agreement may be the subject of considerable negotiation and some-times even some innovation—not to mention hair-splitting.

Generally a corporate trustee is appointed to enforce the terms of the indenture. Corporate indenture trustees are subject to certain conflicts of interest. For one thing, the corporate trustee is likely to be part of a bank, which may have loaned money to the corporation that issued the deben-ture, and occasions can arise when there will be a conflict between the interests of the bank, as lender, and the interests of the debenture holders. When this happens suspicions are aroused about the loyalties of the trustee to the debenture holders. A more subtle, but perhaps more important, influence arises from the trustee's need to attract new business and from the fact that trustees are selected by issuers (who are in turn advised by people called investment bankers). The effect of this reality was illustrated in Broad v. Rockwell International Corporation, 642 F.2d 929 (5th Cir.), cert. denied, 454 U.S. 965 (1981). The issuer of the debentures in that case was merged into another firm and a question arose as to the effect on a conversion privilege (that is, a right to convert the debentures into common stock). The trustee consulted its own lawyers, who took a position con-trary to that of the issuer and unfavorable to it. This gave rise to "heated disagreement" between the lawyers for the issuer and the lawyers for the trustee. There was "evidence in the record indicating that [the issuer] exerted considerable pressure on the [trustee] to change its position, threatening the withdrawal of certain other business from the [trustee] and possible litigation if the [trustee] blocked the merger by refusing to execute a supplemental indenture." 642 F.2d at 936. The upshot was that the trustee decided to "refuse to take a position as to the rights of the holders of the Debentures after the merger, relying on the provisions in the Indenture and in the supplemental indenture by which [the issuer] would indemnify the [trustee] in any lawsuits that might later be brought." Id.

Sharon Steel Corporation v. Chase Manhattan Bank, N.A.

691 F.2d 1039 (2d Cir.1982), cert. denied, 460 U.S. 1012 (1983).

[Several years before the events giving rise to this case, UV Industries (UV) had issued certain debentures. These debentures bore interest at rates lower than the prevailing market rates for newly issued obligations with similar characteristics. Because of the low interest rates, the debentures' market value was less than their face amount (that is, the amount payable on maturity).

Early in 1979, UV adopted a plan to liquidate by selling all its assets and distributing the proceeds to its shareholders. Under tax rules in effect at the time (but not now), it was important that the liquidation be accomplished within twelve months.

UV had three lines of business. One was carried on by a subsidiary called Federal Pacific Electric Company (Federal), which generated 60 percent of UV's operating revenue and 81 percent of its operating profits. The second line of business consisted of oil and gas properties that generated 2 percent of operating revenues and 6 percent of operating profits. The third line of business, involving metal mining and manufacturing, was carried on largely by a subsidiary called Mueller Brass Company, and accounted for 38 percent of operating revenues and 13 percent of operating profits. UV also held substantial cash and other liquid assets.

On March 29, 1979, UV sold Federal to Reliance Electric Company for $345 million in cash, part of which was distributed to the UV shareholders.

On October 2, UV sold the oil and gas properties to Tenneco Oil Company for $135 million in cash.

That left UV with Mueller Brass and some mining properties, plus cash of $322 million, subject to the claim of the debenture holders in a total face amount of $411 million. On November 26, Sharon Steel Corporation (Sharon) bought all of UV's remaining assets (including the cash). Sharon paid UV cash of $107 million and assumed UV's debenture obligations. The total face amount of the debentures was $411 million, but, as previously stated, their market value was lower because they had been issued at a time when interest rates were lower. Apparently it was not feasible for UV or Sharon to buy back the debentures in market transactions (presumably because, as bondholders became aware of efforts by UV or Sharon to purchase, they would hold out for a higher-than-market price). The question then arose whether, by virtue of the liquidation of UV, the

841

debentures became due and payable. If they did, then the debenture holders would be better off. They would receive the face amount of the debentures and could reinvest at current interest rates. Correspondingly, Sharon would need to borrow at a higher interest cost.[1]

The following provision, from one of the indentures at issue in the case, uses typical language relating to assumption of indebtedness in the event of merger, consolidation, or sale of all or substantially all of the assets of the debtor:

> *Company May Consolidate, etc., on Certain Terms.* Nothing contained in this Indenture or in any of the Notes shall prevent any consolidation or merger of the Company with or into any other corporation or corporations (whether or not affiliated with the Company), . . . or shall prevent any sale, conveyance or lease of all or substantially all of the property of the Company to any other corporation (whether or not affiliated with the Company) authorized to acquire and operate the same; *provided, however,* and the Company hereby covenants and agrees, that any such consolidation, merger, sale, conveyance or lease shall be upon the condition that (a) immediately after such consolidation, merger, sale, conveyance or lease the corporation (whether the Company or such other corporation) formed by or surviving any such consolidation or merger, or to which such sale, conveyance or lease shall have been made, shall not be in default in the performance or observance of any of the terms, covenants and conditions of this Indenture to be kept or performed by the Company; (b) the corporation (if other than the Company) formed by or surviving any such consolidation or merger, or to which such sale, conveyance or lease shall have been made, shall be a corporation organized under the laws of the United States of America or any State thereof; and (c) the due and punctual payment of the principal of and interest on all of the Notes, according to their tenor, and the due and punctual performance and observance of all of the covenants and conditions of this Indenture to be performed or observed by the Company, shall be expressly assumed, by supplemental indenture satisfactory in form to the Trustee, executed and delivered to the Trustee, by the corporation (if other than the Company) formed by such consolidation . . ., or by the corporation which shall have acquired or leased such property.

The opinion of the court, by Ralph K. Winter, Circuit Judge, follows.]

---

1. Suppose, for example, that the interest rate on the debentures was 7 percent. The total annual interest payment would then be 7 percent of $411 million, or $28.77 million. Suppose that the current interest rate was 10 percent. If Sharon were obligated to redeem the debentures for the face amount of $411 million, the holders could reinvest that amount and earn 10 percent, or $41 million, annually and Sharon's interest cost for replacing the funds would be the same amount. The total value to the debenture holders, and the total cost to Sharon, over time would depend on the number of years until the debentures would be paid off in any event—that is, the number of years to maturity.

Sharon Steel argues that [the trial judge] erred in not submitting to the jury issues going to the meaning of the successor obligor clauses. We disagree.

Successor obligor clauses are "boilerplate" or contractual provisions which are standard in a certain genre of contracts. Successor obligor clauses are thus found in virtually all indentures. Such boilerplate must be distinguished from contractual provisions which are peculiar to a particular indenture and [thus such boilerplate] must be given a consistent, uniform interpretation. As the American Bar Foundation *Commentaries on Indentures* (1971) ("*Commentaries*") state:

> Since there is seldom any difference in the intended meaning, [boiler-plate] provisions are susceptible of standardized expression. The use of standardized language can result in a better and quicker under-standing of those provisions and a substantial saving of time not only for the draftsman but also for the parties and all others who must comply with or refer to the indenture, including governmental bodies whose approval or authorization of the issuance of the securities is required by law.

Id.

Boilerplate provisions are thus not the consequence of the relationship of particular borrowers and lenders and do not depend upon particularized intentions of the parties to an indenture. There are no adjudicative facts relating to the parties to the litigation for a jury to find and the meaning of boilerplate provisions is, therefore, a matter of law rather than fact.

Moreover, uniformity in interpretation is important to the efficiency of capital markets. . . . Whereas participants in the capital market can adjust their affairs according to a uniform interpretation, whether it be correct or not as an initial proposition, the creation of enduring uncertain-ties as to the meaning of boilerplate provisions would decrease the value of all debenture issues and greatly impair the efficient working of capital markets. . . .

We turn now to the meaning of the successor obligor clauses. Inter-pretation of indenture provisions is a matter of basic contract law. As the *Commentaries* at 2 state:

> The second fundamental characteristic of long term debt financing is that the rights of holders of the debt securities are largely a matter of contract. There is no governing body of statutory or common law that protects the holder of unsecured debt securities against harmful acts by the debtor except in the most extreme situations . . . [T]he debt securityholder can do nothing to protect himself against actions of the borrower which jeopardize its ability to pay the debt unless he . . . establishes his rights through contractual provisions set forth in the . . . indenture.

Contract language is thus the starting point in the search for meaning and Sharon argues strenuously that the language of the successor obligor clauses clearly permits its assumption of UV's public debt. Sharon's argument is a masterpiece of simplicity: on November 26, 1979, it bought everything UV owned; therefore, the transaction was a "sale" of "all" UV's "assets." In Sharon's view, the contention of the Indenture Trustees and Debentureholders that proceeds from earlier sales in a predetermined plan of piecemeal liquidation may not be counted in determining whether a later sale involves "all assets" must be rejected because it imports a meaning not evident in the language.

Sharon's literalist approach simply proves too much. If proceeds from earlier piecemeal sales are "assets," then UV continued to own "all" its "assets" even after the Sharon transaction since the proceeds of that transaction, including the $107 million cash for cash "sale," went into the UV treasury. If the language is to be given the "literal" meaning attributed to it by Sharon, therefore, UV's "assets" were not "sold" on November 26 and the ensuing liquidation requires the redemption of the debentures by UV. Sharon's literal approach is thus self-defeating.

The words "all or substantially all" are used in a variety of statutory and contractual provisions relating to transfers of assets and have been given meaning in light of the particular context and evident purpose. . . . [A] literal reading of the words "all or substantially all" is not helpful apart from reference to the underlying purpose to be served. We turn, therefore, to that purpose.

Sharon argues that the sole purpose of successor obligor clauses is to leave the borrower free to merge, liquidate or to sell its assets in order to enter a wholly new business free of public debt and that they are not intended to offer any protection to lenders. On their face, however, they seem designed to protect lenders as well by assuring a degree of continuity of assets. Thus, a borrower which sells all its assets does not have an option to continue holding the debt. It must either assign the debt or pay it off.

Where contractual language seems designed to protect the interests of both parties and where conflicting interpretations are argued, the contract should be construed to sacrifice the principal interests of each party as little as possible. An interpretation which sacrifices a major interest of one of the parties while furthering only a marginal interest of the other should be rejected in favor of an interpretation which sacrifices marginal interests of both parties in order to protect their major concerns.

Of the contending positions, we believe that of the Indenture Trustees and Debentureholders best accommodates the principal interests of corporate borrowers and their lenders. Even if the UV/Sharon transaction is held not to be covered by the successor obligor clauses, borrowers are free to merge, consolidate or dispose of the operating assets of the business. Accepting Sharon's position, however, would severely impair the interests of lenders. Sharon's view would allow a borrowing corporation to engage in a piecemeal sale of assets, with concurrent liquidating dividends to that point at which the asset restrictions of an indenture prohibited further distribution. A sale of "all or substantially all" of the remaining assets could then be consummated, a new debtor substituted, and the liquidation of the borrower completed. The assignment of the public debt might thus be accomplished, even though the last sale might be nothing more than a cash for cash transaction in which the buyer purchases the public indebtedness. The UV/Sharon transaction is not so extreme, but the sale price paid by Sharon did include a cash for cash exchange of $107 million. Twenty-three percent of the sale price was, in fact, an exchange of dollars for dollars. Such a transaction diminishes the protection for lenders in order to facilitate deals with little functional significance other than substituting a new debtor in order to profit on a debenture's low interest rate. We hold, therefore, that boilerplate successor obligor clauses do not permit assignment of the public debt to another party in the course of a liquidation unless "all or substantially all" of the assets of the company at the time the plan of liquidation is determined upon are transferred to a single purchaser.

The application of this rule to the present case is not difficult. The plan of liquidation was approved by UV's shareholders on March 26, 1978. Since the Indenture Trustees make no claim as to an earlier time, e.g., the date of the Board recommendation, we accept March 26 as the appropriate reference date. The question then is whether "all or substantially all" of the assets held by UV on that date were transferred to Sharon. That is easily answered. The assets owned by UV on March 26 and later transferred to Sharon were Mueller Brass, certain metals mining property, and substantial amounts of cash and other liquid assets. . . . Mueller Brass and the metals mining properties were responsible for only 38% of UV's 1978 operating revenues and 13% of its operating profits. They constitute 41% of the book value of UV's operating properties. When the cash and other liquid assets are added, the transaction still involved only 51% of the book value of UV's total assets.

Since we do not regard the question in this case as even close, we need not determine how the substantiality of corporate assets is to be measured, what percentage meets the "all or substantially all" test or what role a jury might play in determining those issues. Even when the liquid assets (other than proceeds from the sale of Federal and the oil and gas properties) are aggregated with the operating properties, the transfer to Sharon accounted for only 51% of the total book value of UV's assets. In no sense, therefore, are they "all or substantially all" of those assets. The successor obligor clauses are, therefore, not applicable. UV is thus in default on the indentures and the debentures are due and payable.

. . .

CONCLUSION

We affirm [the trial judge's] dismissal of Sharon's amended complaint and award of judgment to the Indenture Trustees and Debentureholders on their claim that the debentures are due and payable. . . .

ANALYSIS

1.   If the decision had been in favor of Sharon, what, if any, meaning and effect would the "substantially all" language have had?

2.   UV was constrained by federal tax rules in effect at the time the case arose. Under those rules, in order to avoid corporate tax on the sale of its assets, UV needed to sell all its assets and distribute the proceeds within a twelve-month period following the adoption of the liquidation plan. Had it not been for this tax constraint, how would you have advised UV to proceed with its liquidation, given its goal of preserving the favorable loans.

3.   The court also says, "Accepting Sharon's position . . . would severely impair the interests of lenders." Do you agree? By comparison, suppose Jack buys a house, for use as a personal residence, for $100,000, using $20,000 of his own money and $80,000 from a nonrecourse 30–year loan. Two years later the amount that remains due on the loan is $79,000; the market value of the house has declined to $78,000, but interest rates have risen and the value of the loan has declined to $70,000. Jack then sells the house to Jill, who pays Jack $8,000 and assumes the mortgage, which is assignable and does not include a due-on-sale clause. Is the lender harmed by the transfer? Is this situation different from that in *Sharon Steel*?

PLANNING

Suppose you had represented UV at the time it prepared to issue the debentures and that you had anticipated the problem that gave rise to the *Sharon Steel* decision. Suppose further that the debentures were to be sold to a small number of large insurance companies represented by shrewd, tough-minded, but reasonable, lawyers. What language might you have sought to include in the indenture to allow UV to take full advantage of a favorable loan in the event of a liquidation subject to the tax constraint?

Metropolitan Life Insurance Company v. RJR Nabisco, Inc.

716 F.Supp. 1504 (S.D.N.Y.1989).

I.   Introduction

The corporate parties to this action are among the country's most sophisticated financial institutions, as familiar with the Wall Street investment community and the securities market as American consumers are with the Oreo cookies and Winston cigarettes made by defendant RJR Nabisco, Inc. (sometimes "the company" or "RJR Nabisco"). The present action traces its origins to October 20, 1988, when F. Ross Johnson, then the Chief Executive Officer of RJR Nabisco, proposed a $17 billion leveraged buy-out ("LBO") of the company's shareholders, at $75 per share. Within a few days, a bidding war developed among the investment group led by Johnson and the investment firm of Kohlberg Kravis Roberts & Co. ("KKR"), and others. On December 1, 1988, a special committee of RJR Nabisco directors, established by the company specifically to consider the competing proposals, recommended that the company accept the KKR proposal, a $24 billion LBO that called for the purchase of the company's outstanding stock at roughly $109 per share.

. . .

Plaintiffs . . . allege, in short, that RJR Nabisco's actions have drastically impaired the value of bonds previously issued to plaintiffs by, in effect, misappropriating the value of those bonds to help finance the LBO and to distribute an enormous windfall to the company's shareholders. As a result, plaintiffs argue, they have unfairly suffered a multimillion dollar loss in the value of their bonds.

. . .

Plaintiffs move for summary judgment pursuant to Fed.R.Civ.P. 56 against the company on Count I, which alleges a "Breach of Implied Covenant of Good Faith and Fair Dealing," and against both defendants on Count V, which is labeled simply "In Equity."

Although the numbers involved in this case are large, and the financing necessary to complete the LBO unprecedented, the legal principles nonetheless remain discrete and familiar. Yet while the instant motions thus primarily require the Court to evaluate and apply traditional rules of equity and contract interpretation, plaintiffs do raise issues of first impression in the context of an LBO. At the heart of the present motions lies plaintiffs' claim that RJR Nabisco violated a restrictive covenant—not an

847

explicit covenant found within the four corners of the relevant bond indentures, but rather an *implied* covenant of good faith and fair dealing— not to incur the debt necessary to facilitate the LBO and thereby betray what plaintiffs claim was the fundamental basis of their bargain with the company. The company, plaintiffs assert, consistently reassured its bond-holders that it had a "mandate" from its Board of Directors to maintain RJR Nabisco's preferred credit rating. Plaintiffs ask this Court first to imply a covenant of good faith and fair dealing that would prevent the recent transaction, then to hold that this covenant has been breached, and finally to require RJR Nabisco to redeem their bonds.

RJR Nabisco defends the LBO by pointing to express provisions in the bond indentures that, *inter alia,* permit mergers and the assumption of additional debt. These provisions, as well as others that could have been included but were not, were known to the market and to plaintiffs, sophisticated investors who freely bought the bonds and were equally free to sell them at any time. Any attempt by this Court to create contractual terms *post hoc,* defendants contend, not only finds no basis in the controlling law and undisputed facts of this case, but also would constitute an impermissible invasion into the free and open operation of the marketplace.

For the reasons set forth below, this Court agrees with defendants. There being no express covenant between the parties that would restrict the incurrence of new debt, and no perceived direction to that end from covenants that are express, this Court will not imply a covenant to prevent the recent LBO and thereby create an indenture term that, while bargained for in other contexts, was not bargained for here and was not even within the mutual contemplation of the parties.

II. Background

. . .

A. *The Parties:*

Metropolitan Life Insurance Co. ("MetLife"), incorporated in New York, is a life insurance company that provides pension benefits for 42 million individuals. According to its most recent annual report, MetLife's assets exceed $88 billion and its debt securities holdings exceed $49 billion. . . . MetLife alleges that it owns $340,542,000 in principal amount of six separate RJR Nabisco debt issues, bonds allegedly purchased between July 1975 and July 1988. Some bonds become due as early as this year; others will not become due until 2017. The bonds bear interest rates of anywhere from 8 to 10.25 percent. MetLife also owned 186,000 shares of RJR Nabisco common stock at the time this suit was filed.

Jefferson–Pilot Life Insurance Co. ("Jefferson–Pilot") is a North Carolina company that has more than $3 billion in total assets, $1.5 billion of which are invested in debt securities. Jefferson–Pilot alleges that it owns $9.34 million in principal amount of three separate RJR Nabisco debt issues, allegedly purchased between June 1978 and June 1988. Those bonds, bearing interest rates of anywhere from 8.45 to 10.75 percent, become due in 1993 and 1998.

RJR Nabisco, a Delaware corporation, is a consumer products holding company that owns some of the country's best known product lines, including LifeSavers candy, Oreo cookies, and Winston cigarettes. The company was formed in 1985, when R.J. Reynolds Industries, Inc. ("R.J. Reynolds") merged with Nabisco Brands, Inc. ("Nabisco Brands"). In 1979, and thus before the R.J. Reynolds–Nabisco Brands merger, R.J. Reynolds acquired the Del Monte Corporation ("Del Monte"), which distributes canned fruits and vegetables. From January 1987 until February 1989, co-defendant Johnson served as the company's CEO. KKR, a private investment firm, organizes funds through which investors provide pools of equity to finance LBOs.

B. The Indentures:

The bonds [9] implicated by this suit are governed by long, detailed indentures, which in turn are governed by New York contract law.[10] No one disputes that the holders of public bond issues, like plaintiffs here, often enter the market after the indentures have been negotiated and memorialized. Thus, those indentures are often not the product of face-to-face negotiations between the ultimate holders and the issuing company. What remains equally true, however, is that underwriters ordinarily negotiate the terms of the indentures with the issuers. Since the underwriters must then sell or place the bonds, they necessarily negotiate in part with the interests of the buyers in mind. Moreover, these indentures were not secret agreements foisted upon unwitting participants in the bond market. No successive holder is required to accept or to continue to hold the bonds, governed by their accompanying indentures; indeed, plaintiffs readily admit that they could have sold their bonds right up until the announcement of the LBO. Instead, sophisticated investors like plaintiffs are well aware of the indenture terms and, presumably, review them carefully before lending hundreds of millions of dollars to any company.

Indeed, the prospectuses for the indentures contain a statement relevant to this action:

> The Indenture contains no restrictions on the creation of unsecured short-term debt by [RJR Nabisco] or its subsidiaries, no restriction on the creation of unsecured Funded Debt by [RJR Nabisco] or its subsidiaries which are not Restricted Subsidiaries, and no restriction on the payment of dividends by [RJR Nabisco].

Further, as plaintiffs themselves note, the contracts at issue "[do] not impose debt limits, since debt is assumed to be used for productive purposes."

---

9. For the purposes of this Opinion, the terms "bonds," "debentures," and "notes" will be used interchangeably. Any distinctions among these terms are not relevant to the present motions.

10. Both sides agree that New York law controls this Court's interpretation of the indentures, which contain explicit designations to that effect. . . .

1. The relevant Articles:

A typical RJR Nabisco indenture contains thirteen Articles. At least four of them are relevant to the present motions and thus merit a brief review.

Article Three delineates the covenants of the issuer. Most important, it first provides for payment of principal and interest. It then addresses various mechanical provisions regarding such matters as payment terms and trustee vacancies. The Article also contains "negative pledge" and related provisions, which restrict mortgages or other liens on the assets of RJR Nabisco or its subsidiaries and seek to protect the bondholders from being subordinated to other debt.

Article Five describes various procedures to remedy defaults and the responsibilities of the Trustee. This Article includes the distinction in the indentures noted above . . . . In seven of the nine securities at issue, a provision in Article Five prohibits bondholders from suing for any remedy based on rights in the indentures unless 25 percent of the holders have requested in writing that the indenture trustee seek such relief, and, after 60 days, the trustee has not sued. Defendants argue that this provision precludes plaintiffs from suing on these seven securities. Given its holdings today, see infra, the Court need not address this issue.

. . .

Article Ten addresses a potential "Consolidation, Merger, Sale or Conveyance," and explicitly sets forth the conditions under which the company can consolidate or merge into or with any other corporation. It provides explicitly that RJR Nabisco "may consolidate with, or sell or convey, all or substantially all of its assets to, or merge into or with any other corporation," so long as the new entity is a United States corporation, and so long as it assumes RJR Nabisco's debt. The Article also requires that any such transaction not result in the company's default under any indenture provision.

2. The elimination of restrictive covenants:

In its Amended Complaint, MetLife lists the six debt issues on which it bases its claims. Indentures for two of those issues . . . once contained express covenants that, among other things, restricted the company's ability to incur precisely the sort of debt involved in the recent LBO. In order to eliminate those restrictions, the parties to this action renegotiated the terms of those indentures, first in 1983 and then again in 1985.

. . .

3. The recognition and effect of the LBO trend:

Other internal MetLife documents help frame the background to this action, for they accurately describe the changing securities markets and the responses those changes engendered from sophisticated market participants, such as MetLife and Jefferson–Pilot. At least as early as 1982, MetLife recognized an LBO's effect on bond values. In the spring of that year, MetLife participated in the financing of an LBO of a company called Reeves Brothers ("Reeves"). At the time of that LBO, MetLife also held bonds in that company. Subsequent to the LBO, as a MetLife memorandum explained, the "Debentures of Reeves were downgraded by Standard & Poor's from BBB to B and by Moody's from Baa1 to Ba3, thereby lowering the value of the Notes and Debentures held by [MetLife]." MetLife Memorandum, dated August 20, 1982.

MetLife further recognized its "inability to force any type of payout of the [Reeves'] Notes or the Debentures as a result of the buy-out [which] was somewhat disturbing at the time we considered a participation in the new financing. However," the memorandum continued,

> our concern was tempered since, as a stockholder in [the holding company used to facilitate the transaction], we would benefit from the increased net income attributable to the continued presence of the low coupon indebtedness. The recent downgrading of the Reeves Debentures and the consequent "loss" in value has again raised questions regarding our ability to have forced a payout. *Questions have also been raised about our ability to force payouts in similar future situations, particularly when we would not be participating in the buyout financing.*

Id. (emphasis added). In the memorandum, MetLife sought to answer those very "questions" about how it might force payouts in "similar future situations."

> *A method of closing this apparent "loophole," thereby forcing a payout of [MetLife's] holdings, would be through a covenant dealing with a change in ownership.* Such a covenant is fairly standard in financings with privately-held companies . . . It provides the lender with an option to end a particular borrowing relationship via some type of special redemption . . .

Id., at 2 (emphasis added).

A more comprehensive memorandum, prepared in late 1985, evaluated and explained several aspects of the corporate world's increasing use of mergers, takeovers and other debt-financed transactions. That memorandum first reviewed the available protection for lenders such as MetLife:

> Covenants are incorporated into loan documents to ensure that after a lender makes a loan, the creditworthiness of the borrower and the lender's ability to reach the borrower's assets do not deteriorate substantially. *Restrictions on the incurrence of debt,* sale of assets, mergers, dividends, restricted payments and loans and advances to affiliates *are some of the traditional negative covenants that can help protect lenders in the event their obligors become involved in undesirable merger/takeover situations.*

MetLife Northeastern Office Memorandum, dated November 27, 1985, (emphasis added). The memorandum then surveyed market realities:

Because almost any industrial company is apt to engineer a takeover or be taken over itself, *Business Week* says that investors are beginning to view debt securities of high grade industrial corporations as Wall Street's riskiest investments. In addition, *because public bondholders do not enjoy the protection of any restrictive covenants,* owners of high grade corporates face substantial losses from takeover situations, if not immediately, then when the bond market finally adjusts. . . . [T]here have been 10–15 merger/takeover/LBO situations where, *due to the lack of covenant protection, [MetLife] has had no choice but to remain a lender to a less creditworthy obligor. . . . The fact that the quality of our investment portfolio is greater than the other large insurance companies . . . may indicate that we have negotiated better covenant protection than other institutions, thus generally being able to require prepayment when situations become too risky . . . [However,] a problem exists. And* because the current merger craze is not likely to decelerate *and because there exist vehicles to circumvent traditional covenants, the problem will probably continue. Therefore,* perhaps it is time to institute appropriate language designed to protect Metropolitan from the negative implications of mergers and takeovers.

Id. at 2–4 (emphasis added).

Indeed, MetLife does not dispute that, as a member of a bondholders' association, it received and discussed a proposed model indenture, which included a "comprehensive covenant" entitled "Limitations on Shareholders' Payments."[16] As becomes clear from reading the proposed—but never adopted—provision, it was "intend[ed] to provide protection against all of the types of situations in which shareholders profit at the expense of bondholders." Id. The provision dictated that the "[c]orporation will not, and will not permit any [s]ubsidiary to, directly or indirectly, make any [s]hareholder [p]ayment unless . . . (1) the aggregate amount of all [s]hareholder payments during the period [at issue] . . . shall not exceed [figure left blank]." The term "shareholder payments" is defined to include "restructuring distributions, stock repurchases, debt incurred or guaranteed to finance merger payments to shareholders, etc."

Apparently, that provision—or provisions with similar intentions—never went beyond the discussion stage at MetLife. That fact is easily understood; indeed, MetLife's own documents articulate several reasonable, undisputed explanations:

While it would be possible to broaden the change in ownership covenant to cover any acquisition-oriented transaction, *we might well encounter significant resistance in implementation with larger public companies. . . .* With respect to implementation, we would be

---

16. See Bradley Resp.Aff.Exh.F. That exhibit is an August 5, 1988 letter from the New York law firm of Kaye, Scholer, Fierman, Hays & Handler. A partner at that firm sent the letter to "Indenture Group Members," including MetLife, who partici-pated in the Institutional Bondholders' Rights Association ("the IBRA"). The "Limitations on Shareholders' Payments" provision appears in a draft IBRA model indenture.

faced with the task of imposing a non-standard limitation on potential borrowers, *which could be a difficult task in today's highly competitive marketplace. Competitive pressures notwithstanding, it would seem that management of larger public companies would be particularly opposed to such a covenant since its effect would be to increase the cost of an acquisition* (due to an assumed debt repayment), a factor that could well lower the price of any tender offer (thereby impacting shareholders).

Bradley Reply Aff.Exh.D, at 3 (emphasis added). The November 1985 memorandum explained that

[o]bviously, our ability to implement methods of takeover protection will vary between the public and private market. In that public securities do not contain any meaningful covenants, it would be very difficult for [MetLife] to demand takeover protection in public bonds. Such a requirement would effectively take us out of the public industrial market. A recent *Business Week* article does suggest, however, that there is increasing talk among lending institutions about requiring blue chip companies to compensate them for the growing risk of downgradings. *This talk, regarding such protection as restrictions on future debt financings, is met with skepticism by the investment banking community which feels that CFO's [chief financial officers] are not about to give up the option of adding debt and do not really care if their companies' credit ratings drop a notch or two.*

The Court quotes these documents at such length not because they represent an "admission" or "waiver" from MetLife, or an "assumption of risk" in any tort sense, or its "consent" to any particular course of conduct—all terms discussed at even greater length in the parties' submissions. Rather, the documents set forth the background to the present action, and highlight the risks inherent in the market itself, for any investor. Investors as sophisticated as MetLife and Jefferson–Pilot would be hard-pressed to plead ignorance of these market risks. Indeed, MetLife has not disputed the facts asserted in its own internal documents. Nor has Jefferson–Pilot—presumably an institution no less sophisticated than Met-Life—offered any reason to believe that its understanding of the securities market differed in any material respect from the description and analysis set forth in the MetLife documents. Those documents, after all, were not born in a vacuum. They are descriptions of, and responses to, the market in which investors like MetLife and Jefferson–Pilot knowingly participated.

These documents must be read in conjunction with plaintiffs' Amended Complaint. That document asserts that the LBO "undermines the foundation of the investment grade debt market . . .,"; that, although "the indentures do not purport to limit dividends or debt . . . [s]uch covenants were believed unnecessary with blue chip companies . . ."; that "the transaction contradicts the premise of the investment grade market . . ."; and, finally, that "[t]his buy-out was not contemplated at the time the debt was issued, contradicts the premise of the investment grade ratings that RJR Nabisco actively solicited and received, and is inconsistent with the understandings of the market . . . which [p]laintiffs relied upon.''

Solely for the purposes of these motions, the Court accepts various factual assertions advanced by plaintiffs: first, that RJR Nabisco actively solicited "investment grade" ratings for its debt; second, that it relied on descriptions of its strong capital structure and earnings record which included prominent display of its ability to pay the interest obligations on its long-term debt several times over, Am.Comp. ¶ 14; and third, that the company made express or implied representations not contained in the relevant indentures concerning its future creditworthiness. Id. ¶ 15. In support of those allegations, plaintiffs have marshaled a number of speeches made by co-defendant Johnson and other executives of RJR Nabisco.[18]

. . .

III. Discussion

At the outset, the Court notes that nothing in its evaluation is substantively altered by the speeches given or remarks made by RJR Nabisco executives, or the opinions of various individuals—what, for instance, former RJR Nabisco Treasurer Dowdle personally did or did not "firmly believe" the indentures meant. The parol evidence rule bars plaintiffs from arguing that the speeches made by company executives prove defendants agreed or acquiesced to a term that does not appear in the indenture. . . .

The indentures at issue clearly address the eventuality of a merger. They impose certain related restrictions not at issue in this suit, but no restriction that would prevent the recent RJR Nabisco merger transaction. . . .

Under certain circumstances, however, courts will, as plaintiffs note, consider extrinsic evidence to evaluate the scope of an implied covenant of good faith. See Valley National Bank v. Babylon Chrysler–Plymouth, Inc., 53 Misc.2d 1029, 1031–32, 280 N.Y.S.2d 786, 788–89 (Sup.Ct.Nassau), aff'd, 28 A.D.2d 1092, 284 N.Y.S.2d 849 (2d Dep't 1967) (Relying on custom and usage because "[w]hen a contract fails to establish the time for performance, the law implies that the act shall be done within a reasonable time . . ."). However, the Second Circuit has established a different rule for customary, or boilerplate, provisions of detailed indentures used and relied upon throughout the securities market, such as those at issue. [See]

---

18. See, e.g., Address by F. Ross Johnson, November 12, 1987, P.Exh. 8, at 5 ("Our strong balance sheet is a cornerstone of our strategies. It gives us the resources to modernize facilities, develop new technologies, bring on new products, and support our leading brands around the world."); Remarks of Edward J. Robinson, Executive Vice President and Chief Financial Officer, February 15, 1988, P.Exh. 6, at 1 ("RJR Nabisco's financial strategy is . . . to enhance the strength of the balance sheet by reducing the level of debt as well as lowering the cost of existing debt."); Remarks by Dr. Robert J. Carbonell, Vice Chairman of RJR Nabisco, June 3, 1987, P.Exh. 10, at 5 ("We will not sacrifice our longer-term health for the sake of short term heroics.").

Sharon Steel Corporation v. Chase Manhattan Bank, N.A., [supra page 722]. . . . Ignoring these principles, plaintiffs would have this Court vary what they themselves have admitted is "indenture boilerplate" of "standard" agreements to comport with collateral representations and their subjective understandings.[20]

A.   *Plaintiffs' Case Against the RJR Nabisco LBO:*

   1.   Count One: The implied covenant:

In their first count, plaintiffs assert that [d]efendant RJR Nabisco owes a continuing duty of good faith and fair dealing in connection with the contract [i.e., the indentures] through which it borrowed money from MetLife, Jefferson–Pilot and other holders of its debt, including a duty not to frustrate the purpose of the contracts to the debtholders or to deprive the debtholders of the intended object of the contracts— purchase of investment-grade securities.

In the "buy-out," the [c]ompany breaches the duty [or implied covenant] of good faith and fair dealing by, *inter alia,* destroying the investment grade quality of the debt and transferring that value to the "buy-out" proponents and to the shareholders.

In effect, plaintiffs contend that express covenants were not necessary because an *implied* covenant would prevent what defendants have now done.

A plaintiff always can allege a violation of an express covenant. If there has been such a violation, of course, the court need not reach the question of whether or not an *implied* covenant has been violated.

In contracts like bond indentures, "an implied covenant . . . derives its substance directly from the language of the Indenture, and 'cannot give the holders of Debentures any rights inconsistent with those set out in the Indenture.' *[Where] plaintiffs' contractual rights [have not been] violated, there can have been no breach of an implied covenant.*" Gardner & Florence Call Cowles Foundation v. Empire Inc., 589 F.Supp. 669, 673 (S.D.N.Y.1984), vacated on procedural grounds, 754 F.2d 478 (2d Cir.1985) (quoting Broad v. Rockwell, 642 F.2d 929, 957 (5th Cir.) (en banc), cert. denied, 454 U.S. 965, 102 S.Ct. 506, 70 L.Ed.2d 380 (1981)) (emphasis added).

. . .

---

20. To a certain extent, this discussion is academic. Even if the Court did consider the extrinsic evidence offered by plaintiffs, its ultimate decision would be no different. Based on that extrinsic evidence, plaintiffs attempt to establish that an implied covenant of good faith is necessary to protect the benefits of their agreements. That inquiry necessarily asks the Court to determine whether the existing contractual terms should be construed to preclude defendants from engaging in an LBO along the lines of the recently completed transaction. However, even evaluating *all* facts—such as the public statements made by company executives—in the light most favorable to plaintiffs, these plaintiffs fail as a matter of law to establish that the purported "fundamental basis" of their bargain with defendants created a contractual obligation on the part of the defendants not to engage in an LBO. . . .

The appropriate analysis, then, is first to examine the indentures to determine "the fruits of the agreement" between the parties, and then to decide whether those "fruits" have been spoiled—which is to say, whether plaintiffs' contractual rights have been violated by defendants.

The American Bar Foundation's *Commentaries on Indentures* ("the *Commentaries*"), relied upon and respected by both plaintiffs and defendants, describes the rights and risks generally found in bond indentures like those at issue:

> The most obvious and important characteristic of long-term debt financing is that the holder ordinarily has not bargained for and does not expect any substantial gain in the value of the security to compensate for the risk of loss . . . [T]he significant fact, *which accounts in part for the detailed protective provisions of the typical long-term debt financing instrument,* is that *the lender (the purchaser of the debt security) can expect only interest at the prescribed rate plus the eventual return of the principal.* Except for possible increases in the market value of the debt security because of changes in interest rates, the debt security will seldom be worth more than the lender paid for it . . . It may, of course, become worth much less. Accordingly, the typical investor in a long-term debt security is primarily interested in every reasonable assurance that the principal and interest will be paid when due. . . . Short of bankruptcy, *the debt security holder can do nothing to protect himself against actions of the borrower which jeopardize its ability to pay the debt unless he . . . establishes his rights through contractual provisions set forth in the debt agreement or indenture.*

Id. at 1–2 (1971) (emphasis added).

A review of the parties' submissions and the indentures themselves satisfies the Court that the substantive "fruits" guaranteed by those contracts and relevant to the present motions include the periodic and regular payment of interest and the eventual repayment of principal. . . .

It is not necessary to decide that indentures like those at issue could never support a finding of additional benefits, under different circumstances with different parties. Rather, for present purposes, it is sufficient to conclude what obligation is *not* covered, either explicitly or implicitly, by these contracts held by these plaintiffs. Accordingly, this Court holds that the "fruits" of these indentures do not include an implied restrictive covenant that would prevent the incurrence of new debt to facilitate the recent LBO. To hold otherwise would permit these plaintiffs to straightjacket the company in order to guarantee their investment. These plaintiffs do not invoke an implied covenant of good faith to protect a legitimate, mutually contemplated benefit of the indentures; rather, they seek to have this Court create an additional benefit for which they did not bargain.

. . .

The sort of unbounded and one-sided elasticity urged by plaintiffs would interfere with and destabilize the market. And this Court, like the parties to these contracts, cannot ignore or disavow the marketplace in which the contract is performed. Nor can it ignore the expectations of that market—expectations, for instance, that the terms of an indenture will be upheld, and that a court will not, *sua sponte,* add new substantive terms to that indenture as it sees fit. The Court has no reason to believe that the market, in evaluating bonds such as those at issue here, did not discount for the possibility that any company, even one the size of RJR Nabisco, might engage in an LBO heavily financed by debt. That the bonds did not lose any of their value until the October 20, 1988 announcement of a possible RJR Nabisco LBO only suggests that the market had theretofore evaluated the risks of such a transaction as slight.

. . .

Ultimately, plaintiffs cannot escape the inherent illogic of their argument. On the one hand, it is undisputed that investors like plaintiffs recognized that companies like RJR Nabisco strenuously opposed additional restrictive covenants that might limit the incurrence of new debt or the company's ability to engage in a merger. Furthermore, plaintiffs argue that they had no choice other than to accept the indentures as written, without additional restrictive covenants, or to "abandon" the market.

Yet on the other hand, plaintiffs ask this Court to imply a covenant that would have just that restrictive effect because, they contend, it reflects precisely the fundamental assumption of the market and the fundamental basis of their bargain with defendants. If that truly were the case here, it is difficult to imagine why an insistence on that term would have forced the plaintiffs to abandon the market. The Second Circuit has offered a better explanation: "[a] promise by the defendant should be implied only if the court may rightfully assume that the parties would have included it in their written agreement had their attention been called to it . . . *Any such assumption in this case would be completely unwarranted.*" Neuman v. Pike, 591 F.2d 191, 195 (2d Cir.1979) (emphasis added, citations omitted).

In the final analysis, plaintiffs offer no objective or reasonable standard for a court to use in its effort to define the sort of actions their "implied covenant" would permit a corporation to take, and those it would not.[28]

. . .

2. Count Five: In Equity:

Count Five substantially restates and realleges the contract claims advanced in Count I. . . . For present purposes, it makes no difference how plaintiffs characterize their arguments. Their equity claims cannot survive defendants' motion for summary judgment.

---

28. Under plaintiffs' theory, bondholders might ask a court to prohibit a company like RJR Nabisco not only from engaging in an LBO, but also from entering a new line of business—with the attendant costs of building new physical plants and hiring new workers—or from acquiring new businesses such as RJR Nabisco did when it acquired Del Monte.

In their papers, plaintiffs variously attempt to justify Count V as being based on unjust enrichment, frustration of purpose, an alleged breach of something approaching a fiduciary duty, or a general claim of unconscionability. Each claim fails.

B. Defendant's Remaining Motions:

. . .

1. Rule 10b–5:

Defendants move to dismiss pursuant to Fed.R.Civ.P. 12(c) Count III, the Rule 10b–5 counts, as to those six debt issues purchased by plaintiffs prior to September 1987, which is when plaintiffs allege in their complaint that defendants first began to develop an LBO plan. Plaintiffs admit that Rule 10b–5 is limited to purchases or sales during the period of nondisclosure or misrepresentation. . . . The rule does not afford relief to those who forgo a purchase or sale and instead merely hold in reliance of a nondisclosure or misrepresentation. . . .

The first, second, third, fifth, seventh and eighth securities listed in the Amended Complaint fail to satisfy this requirement, at least on the facts as presently pleaded. Accordingly, the Court grants defendants' motion on Count III as to those issues. Plaintiffs correctly note, however, that the disclosure-related common law fraud claims are not restricted to purchases and sales. . . . Thus, the Court denies defendants' motion to dismiss Count II on this basis.

AFTERMATH

The decision of the district court in *MetLife* left various claims pending, including claims of fraud and fraudulent conveyance. In January 1991, the case was settled. A Wall Street Journal article stated that the settlement "restore[d] much of the value of the RJR bonds that was lost when RJR was taken private in 1989." Hylton, Metropolitan Life Settles Bond Rift With RJR Nabisco, Wall St.J., Jan. 25, 1991, at C1, col. 1. The settlement was only for the benefit of MetLife and Jefferson–Pilot, but MetLife said that it would be willing to buy the bonds of other investors "at par or near par." A MetLife representative was quoted as saying, " 'Our claim was to be paid in full right away, and we're not getting that but we're very satisfied.' " In the settlement, MetLife and Jefferson–Pilot became entitled to receive a combination of cash, new debt securities, common stock, and a shorter duration for some of the existing debt. In addition, RJR agreed to pay MetLife's and Jefferson–Pilot's legal fees and other expenses of about $15 million.

ANALYSIS

1. Given MetLife's awareness of the risks associated with the RJR Nabisco bonds that it held, why did it not simply sell those bonds and invest in U.S. Treasury obligations?

2.   In discussing the plaintiffs' argument based on a theory of implied covenant of good faith and fair dealing, the court says that it must "decide whether [the] 'fruits' of the agreement have been spoiled." It later says that the fruits "include the periodic and regular payment of interest and the eventual repayment of principal," and concludes that these fruits were not spoiled. Is this mode of analysis helpful? Why did the value of the RJR Nabisco debentures held by MetLife decline?

3.   When a bank lends money to an individual to finance the purchase of a personal residence or an automobile, what type of provision is included in the loan that protects against the dilution of the value of the bank's claim by the borrower incurring additional debt? Do you suppose that similar protection is found in some corporate debt obligations? What other type of protective provision might a lender demand to protect itself from such dilution? [2]

4.   Suppose that you are outside counsel to a major institutional investor such as an insurance company, a pension fund, or a mutual fund, and have been asked to devise new provisions to protect against the type of loss experienced by the plaintiffs in *MetLife*. A lawyer from another firm has proposed a covenant stating that the debtor "will take no action that will materially reduce the probability that it will pay interest and principal when it is due." What is your reaction?

5.   The court in *MetLife* quotes the American Bar Foundation's Commentaries on Indentures, which asserts, "Except for possible increases in the market value of the debt security because of changes in interest rates, the debt security will seldom be worth more than the lender paid for it." Consider the new debentures issued by RJR Nabisco to finance the LBO. These debentures paid a high rate of interest because of a significant risk of default on the obligation to pay interest and to repay principal. They were known as "high-yield" or "junk" bonds. Suppose that two years after the LBO, RJR Nabisco has been extremely successful and the value of its equity has risen substantially. What would be the effect of such success on the value of the debentures? How, if at all, is your answer to that question relevant to the legal doctrine on responsibilities of directors toward debenture holders?

6.   Do you agree with the outcome in the case? Compare Wilkes v. Springside Nursing Home, Inc., supra page 612. There the plaintiff was a shareholder in a closely held corporation who complained about being

2.   One possibility (there are others) is, ironically, found in one of the indentures issued by the newly formed corporation, RJR Holdings Capital Corp., that was used as the vehicle for effectuating the RJR Nabisco LBO. The indenture provides that if a "Change of Control" occurs, each debenture holder may require that the issuer redeem its debenture for 101 percent of the principal amount plus accrued interest. "Change of Control" is defined, in part, as "the owner-ship of KKR and its affiliates, directly or indirectly, of less than 40% of the total voting power . . . of the Company. . . ." The debentures were also protected by a covenant severely limiting the amount of additional debt that the company might incur. See Prospectus dated April 4, 1989, for $750,000,000 **% Subordinated Debentures due 2001 and $750,000,000 Subordinated Extendible Reset Debentures.

ousted from his job with the corporation. Despite the fact that he had no employment contract, the court granted relief, relying on the conclusory statement that the majority owed the plaintiff a fiduciary duty. How can *Wilkes* and *MetLife* be reconciled?

7. Generally mergers must be approved by a vote of the shareholders. Why is a vote of the debenture holders not also required? Approval by debenture holders could be required by contract by including in the indenture a prohibition on mergers, together with a general provision (common in indentures) allowing waiver of indenture obligations by vote of the debenture holders. Another possibility would be a federal law,[3] comparable to the rule found in typical state corporations codes for shareholders, requiring creditor approval of any merger. Assuming you think creditor approval is a good idea, which would be the better approach? If the federal-law approach were adopted, should the rule be one that the parties to a loan can reject?

NEGATIVE PLEDGE COVENANT AND CURE PERIOD

Another aspect of the litigation between MetLife and RJR Nabisco arose from a negative pledge covenant. A negative pledge covenant prohibits a debtor from mortgaging specified assets to any lender without providing "equal and ratable" mortgage protection to the obligations covered by the covenant. Violation of this covenant would be an act of default, which would, among other things, accelerate the repayment obligation. Some of the RJR Nabisco obligations included negative pledge clauses but provided a "cure period"—a period of 90 days following a notice of default, during which time RJR Nabisco could cure the default.

To finance the LBO, the new owners had agreed to a requirement that RJR Nabisco would sell $5.5 billion of its assets and use the proceeds to repay certain debts incurred in connection with the LBO. MetLife (and other debenture holders) claimed that this violated the negative pledge covenant. RJR Nabisco went to the federal district court in New York for a declaratory judgment that its agreement did not constitute a violation of the covenant. Since this litigation would take more than 90 days (the debenture holders claimed they needed at least four months for discovery),

3. The state law applicable to relationships among shareholders (or, if you will, between the shareholders and the abstraction called the corporation) is, as we have seen in earlier chapters, that of the state of incorporation. The rule for choice of state law for debt instruments is essentially the common-law conflicts-of-law rule relating to contracts, which allows the parties to specify the state whose law they wish to apply. This choice-of-law rule could, however, be overridden by a state regulatory provision intended to affect transactions within the state. It turns out that most publicly traded debt obligations are governed by New York law, because such obligations are issued through Wall Street investment bankers and it is customary to specify that New York law applies. The New York legislature might be reluctant to impose a rule that issuers of debt found onerous, for fear of driving business away from Wall Street, and doubts might arise about the scope of any state's authority to control the terms of transactions with strong connections with other states. There is no doubt, however, about the authority of Congress to control the terms of any transaction that has an adequate impact, which generally need be only minimal, on interstate commerce.

it sought an order tolling the cure period. The district court granted the request for that order (Metropolitan Life Insurance Company v. RJR Nabisco, Inc., 716 F.Supp. 1526 (S.D.N.Y.1989), but was reversed on appeal. 906 F.2d 884 (2d Cir.1990). The Second Circuit, in a 2–1 decision, adopted a strong strict constructionist position, stating that the "cure provisions at issue here are unambiguous" and include "no mention . . . of a period for adjudication of any notice of default . . . [or] of an automatic extension of the cure period in the event of litigation over the merits of the default notice." Having thus demonstrated its support for the principle "you made your bed, now you must lie in it," the majority went on, however, to hold that in order to expedite the proceeding, the trial court could limit discovery and could "in order to protect both the right of the lender to obtain admissible evidence of default and the right of the borrower to use the full cure period to secure an adjudication, stay the running of the cure period for such time as the lender needs for discovery."

SECTION 4. EXCHANGE OFFERS

BACKGROUND NOTE

Most indentures include a provision permitting amendment by a vote of the bondholders, but for publicly issued debt, the federal Trust Indenture Act of 1939 prohibits the alteration of "core" terms—including interest payment, principal amount, and duration—without unanimous consent of the holders. This prohibition does not apply, however, to important protective covenants such as those limiting the payment of dividends and those requiring the maintenance of a specified ratio of equity to debt. The procedure for altering or eliminating such covenants is specified in the indenture; it is a matter of private law. Many indentures allow alteration or elimination of non-core covenants with the approval of a majority or, often, some higher percentage (e.g., two-thirds) of the debenture holders, with voting power based on face amounts of the debentures. Where such voting is permitted, however, the typical indenture will prohibit the voting of debentures "owned" (other terms of similar effect are also sometimes used) by the debtor.

Review the material on two-tier tender offers in Chapter 6, Section 2(B).

Katz v. Oak Industries, Inc.

508 A.2d 873 (Del.Ch.1986).

. . .

Plaintiff is the owner of long-term debt securities issued by Oak Industries, Inc. ("Oak"), a Delaware corporation; in this class action he seeks to enjoin the consummation of an exchange offer and consent solicitation made by Oak to holders of various classes of its long-term debt. As detailed below that offer is an integral part of a series of transactions that together would effect a major reorganization and recapitalization of Oak. The claim asserted is in essence, that the exchange offer is a coercive device and, in the circumstances, constitutes a breach of contract. This is the Court's opinion on plaintiff's pending application for a preliminary injunction.

I.

The background facts are involved even when set forth in the abbreviated form the decision within the time period currently available requires.

Through its domestic and foreign subsidiaries and affiliated entities, Oak manufactures and markets component equipment used in consumer, industrial and military products (the "Components Segment"); produces communications equipment for use in cable television systems and satellite television systems (the "Communications Segment"); and manufactures and markets laminates and other materials used in printed circuit board applications (the "Materials Segment"). During 1985, the Company has terminated certain other unrelated businesses. As detailed below, it has now entered into an agreement with Allied–Signal, Inc. for the sale of the Materials Segment of its business and is currently seeking a buyer for its Communications Segment.

Even a casual review of Oak's financial results over the last several years shows it unmistakably to be a company in deep trouble. During the period from January 1, 1982 through September 30, 1985, the Company has experienced unremitting losses from operations. . . . Financial markets, of course, reflected this gloomy history.[2]

Unless Oak can be made profitable within some reasonably short time it will not continue as an operating company. Oak's board of directors, comprised almost entirely of outside directors, has authorized steps to buy the company time. In February, 1985, in order to reduce a burdensome annual cash interest obligation on its $230 million of then outstanding debentures, the Company offered to exchange such debentures for a combination of notes, common stock and warrants. As a result, approximately $180 million principal amount of the then outstanding debentures were exchanged. Since interest on certain of the notes issued in that exchange offer is payable in common stock, the effect of the 1985 exchange offer was to reduce to some extent the cash drain on the Company caused by its significant debt.

About the same time that the 1985 exchange offer was made, the Company announced its intention to discontinue certain of its operations and sell certain of its properties. Taking these steps, while effective to stave off a default and to reduce to some extent the immediate cash drain, did not address Oak's longer-range problems. Therefore, also during 1985 representatives of the Company held informal discussions with several interested parties exploring the possibility of an investment from, combination with or acquisition by another company. As a result of these discussions, the Company and Allied–Signal, Inc. entered into two agreements. The first, the Acquisition Agreement, contemplates the sale to Allied–Signal of the Materials Segment for $160 million in cash. The second agreement, the Stock Purchase Agreement, provides for the purchase by Allied–Signal for $15 million cash of 10 million shares of the Company's common stock together with warrants to purchase additional common stock.

The Stock Purchase Agreement provides as a condition to Allied–Signal's obligation that at least 85% of the aggregate principal amount of all of the Company's debt securities shall have tendered and accepted the exchange offers that are the subject of this lawsuit. Oak has six classes of

---

2. The price of the company's common stock has fallen from over $30 per share on December 31, 1981 to approximately $2 per share recently. The debt securities that are the subject of the exchange offer here involved have traded at substantial discounts.

such long term debt. If less than 85% of the aggregate principal amount of such debt accepts the offer, Allied–Signal has an option, but no obligation, to purchase the common stock and warrants contemplated by the Stock Purchase Agreement. . . .

Thus, as part of the restructuring and recapitalization contemplated by the Acquisition Agreement and the Stock Purchase Agreement, the Company has extended an exchange offer to each of the holders of the six classes of its long-term debt securities. These pending exchange offers include a Common Stock Exchange Offer (available only to holders of the $9\frac{5}{8}\%$ convertible notes) and the Payment Certificate Exchange Offers (available to holders of all six classes of Oak's long-term debt securities). The Common Stock Exchange Offer currently provides for the payment to each tendering noteholder of 407 shares of the Company's common stock in exchange for each $1,000 $9\frac{5}{8}\%$ note accepted. The offer is limited to $38.6 million principal amount of notes (out of approximately $83.9 million outstanding).

The Payment Certificate Exchange Offer is an any and all offer. Under its terms, a payment certificate, payable in cash five days after the closing of the sale of the Materials Segment to Allied–Signal, is offered in exchange for debt securities. The cash value of the Payment Certificate will vary depending upon the particular security tendered. In each instance, however, that payment will be less than the face amount of the obligation. The cash payments range in amount, per $1,000 of principal, from $918 to $655. These cash values however appear to represent a premium over the market prices for the Company's debentures as of the time the terms of the transaction were set.

The Payment Certificate Exchange Offer is subject to certain important conditions before Oak has an obligation to accept tenders under it. First, it is necessary that a minimum amount ($38.6 million principal amount out of $83.9 total outstanding principal amount) of the $9\frac{5}{8}\%$ notes be tendered pursuant to the Common Stock Exchange Offer. Secondly, it is necessary that certain minimum amounts of each class of debt securities be tendered, together with consents to amendments to the underlying indentures. Indeed, under the offer one may not tender securities unless at the same time one consents to the proposed amendments to the relevant indentures.

The condition of the offer that tendering security holders must consent to amendments in the indentures governing the securities gives rise to plaintiff's claim of breach of contract in this case. Those amendments would, if implemented, have the effect of removing significant negotiated protections to holders of the Company's long-term debt including the deletion of all financial covenants. Such modification may have adverse consequences to debt holders who elect not to tender pursuant to either exchange offer.

Allied–Signal apparently was unwilling to commit to the $15 million cash infusion contemplated by the Stock Purchase Agreement, unless Oak's long-term debt is reduced by 85% (at least that is a condition of their obligation to close on that contract). . . . But existing indenture covenants prohibit the Company, so long as any of its long-term notes are outstanding, from issuing any obligation (including the Payment Certificates) in exchange for any of the debentures. Thus, in this respect, amendment to the indentures is required in order to close the Stock Purchase Agreement as presently structured.

. . .

II.

. . .

As amplified in briefing on the pending motion, plaintiff's claim is that no free choice is provided to bondholders by the exchange offer and consent solicitation. Under its terms, a rational bondholder is "forced" to tender and consent. Failure to do so would face a bondholder with the risk of owning a security stripped of all financial covenant protections and for which it is likely that there would be no ready market. A reasonable bondholder, it is suggested, cannot possibly accept those risks and thus such a bondholder is coerced to tender and thus to consent to the proposed indenture amendments.[6]

. . .

III.

. . .

I turn first to an evaluation of the probability of plaintiff's ultimate success on the merits of his claim. I begin that analysis with two preliminary points. The first concerns what is not involved in this case. To focus briefly on this clears away much of the corporation law case law of this jurisdiction upon which plaintiff in part relies. This case does not involve the measurement of corporate or directorial conduct against that high standard of fidelity required of fiduciaries when they act with respect to the interests of the beneficiaries of their trust. Under our law—and the law generally—the relationship between a corporation and the holders of its debt securities, even convertible debt securities, is contractual in nature. . . . Arrangements among a corporation, the underwriters of its debt, trustees under its indentures and sometimes ultimate investors are typically thoroughly negotiated and massively documented. The rights and obligations of the various parties are or should be spelled out in that documentation. The terms of the contractual relationship agreed to and

6. It is worthy of note that a very high percentage of the principal value of Oak's debt securities are owned in substantial amounts by a handful of large financial institutions. Almost 85% of the value of the 13.50% Notes is owned by four such institutions (one investment banker owns 55% of that issue); 69.1% of the 9⅝% Notes are owned by four financial institutions (the same investment banker owning 25% of that issue) and 85% of the 11⅞% Notes are owned by five such institutions. Of the debentures, 89% of the 13.65% debentures are owned by four large banks; and approximately 45% of the two remaining issues is owned by two banks.

not broad concepts such as fairness define the corporation's obligation to its bondholders.[7]

Thus, the first aspect of the pending Exchange Offers about which plaintiff complains—that "the purpose and effect of the Exchange Offers is to benefit Oak's common stockholders at the expense of the Holders of its debt"—does not itself appear to allege a cognizable legal wrong. It is the obligation of directors to attempt, within the law, to maximize the long-run interests of the corporation's stockholders; that they may sometimes do so "at the expense" of others (even assuming that a transaction which one may refuse to enter into can meaningfully be said to be at his expense) does not for that reason constitute a breach of duty. It seems likely that corporate restructurings designed to maximize shareholder values may in some instances have the effect of requiring bondholders to bear greater risk of loss and thus in effect transfer economic value from bondholders to stockholders.   . . . But if courts are to provide protection against such enhanced risk, they will require either legislative direction to do so or the negotiation of indenture provisions designed to afford such protection.

The second preliminary point concerns the limited analytical utility, at least in this context, of the word "coercive" which is central to plaintiff's own articulation of his theory of recovery.   . . . Clearly some "coercion" is legally unproblematic. Parents may "coerce" a child to study with the threat of withholding an allowance; employers may "coerce" regular attendance at work by either docking wages for time absent or by rewarding with a bonus such regular attendance. Other "coercion" so defined clearly would be legally relevant (to encourage regular attendance by corporal punishment, for example). Thus, for purposes of legal analysis, the term "coercion" itself—covering a multitude of situations—is not very meaningful. For the word to have much meaning for purposes of legal analysis, it is necessary in each case that a normative judgment be attached to the concept ("inappropriately coercive" or "wrongfully coercive", etc.). But, it is then readily seen that what is legally relevant is not the conclusory term "coercion" itself but rather the norm that leads to the adverb modifying it.

In this instance, assuming that the Exchange Offers and Consent Solicitation can meaningfully be regarded as "coercive" (in the sense that Oak has structured it in a way designed—and I assume effectively so—to "force" rational bondholders to tender), the relevant legal norm that will support the judgment whether such "coercion" is wrongful or not will, for the reasons mentioned above, be derived from the law of contracts. I turn then to that subject to determine the appropriate legal test or rule.

7. To say that the broad duty of loyalty that a director owes to his corporation and ultimately its shareholders is not implicated in this case is not to say, as the discussion below reflects, that as a matter of contract law a corporation owes no duty to bondholders of good faith and fair dealing. *See, Restatement of Law, Contracts 2d,* § 205 (1979). Such a duty, however, is quite different from the congeries of duties that are assumed by a fiduciary.   . . .

Modern contract law has generally recognized an implied covenant to the effect that each party to a contract will act with good faith towards the other with respect to the subject matter of the contract.   . . .

It is this obligation to act in good faith and to deal fairly that plaintiff claims is breached by the structure of Oak's coercive exchange offer. Because it is an implied *contractual* obligation that is asserted as the basis for the relief sought, the appropriate legal test is not difficult to deduce. It is this: is it clear from what was expressly agreed upon that the parties who negotiated the express terms of the contract would have agreed to proscribe the act later complained of as a breach of the implied covenant of good faith—had they thought to negotiate with respect to that matter. If the answer to this question is yes, then, in my opinion, a court is justified in concluding that such act constitutes a breach of the implied covenant of good faith.   . . .

With this test in mind, I turn now to a review of the specific provisions of the various indentures from which one may be best able to infer whether it is apparent that the contracting parties—had they negotiated with the exchange offer and consent solicitation in mind—would have expressly agreed to prohibit contractually the linking of the giving of consent with the purchase and sale of the security.

IV.

Applying the foregoing standard to the exchange offer and consent solicitation, I find first that there is nothing in the indenture provisions granting bondholders power to veto proposed modifications in the relevant indenture that implies that Oak may not offer an inducement to bondholders to consent to such amendments. Such an implication, at least where, as here, the inducement is offered on the same terms to each holder of an affected security, would be wholly inconsistent with the strictly commercial nature of the relationship.

Nor does the second pertinent contractual provision supply a ground to conclude that defendant's conduct violates the reasonable expectations of those who negotiated the indentures on behalf of the bondholders. Under that provision Oak may not vote debt securities held in its treasury. Plaintiff urges that Oak's conditioning of its offer to purchase debt on the giving of consents has the effect of subverting the purpose of that provision; it permits Oak to "dictate" the vote on securities which it could not itself vote.

The evident purpose of the restriction on the voting of treasury securities is to afford protection against the issuer voting as a bondholder in favor of modifications that would benefit it as issuer, even though such changes would be detrimental to bondholders. But the linking of the exchange offer and the consent solicitation does not involve the risk that bondholder interests will be affected by a vote involving anyone with a financial interest in the subject of the vote other than a bondholder's interest. That the consent is to be given concurrently with the transfer of the bond to the issuer does not in any sense create the kind of conflict of interest that the indenture's prohibition on voting treasury securities contemplates. Not only will the proposed consents be granted or withheld only by those with a financial interest to maximize the return on their investment in Oak's bonds, but the incentive to consent is equally available to all members of each class of bondholders. Thus the "vote" implied by the consent solicitation is not affected in any sense by those with a financial conflict of interest.

In these circumstances, while it is clear that Oak has fashioned the exchange offer and consent solicitation in a way designed to encourage consents, I cannot conclude that the offer violates the intendment of any of the express contractual provisions considered or, applying the test set out above, that its structure and timing breaches an implied obligation of good faith and fair dealing.

One further set of contractual provisions should be touched upon: Those granting to Oak a power to redeem the securities here treated at a price set by the relevant indentures. Plaintiff asserts that the attempt to force all bondholders to tender their securities at less than the redemption price constitutes, if not a breach of the redemption provision itself, at least a breach of an implied covenant of good faith and fair dealing associated with it. The flaw, or at least one fatal flaw, in this argument is that the present offer is not the functional equivalent of a redemption which is, of course, an act that the issuer may take unilaterally. In this instance it may happen that Oak will get tenders of a large percentage of its outstanding long-term debt securities. If it does, that fact will, in my judgment, be in major part a function of the merits of the offer (i.e., the price offered in light of the Company's financial position and the market value of its debt). To answer plaintiff's contention that the *structure* of the offer "forces" debt holders to tender, one only has to imagine what response this offer would receive if the price offered did not reflect a premium over market but rather was, for example, ten percent of market value. The exchange offer's success ultimately depends upon the ability and willingness of the issuer to extend an offer that will be a financially attractive alternative to holders. This process is hardly the functional equivalent of the unilateral election of redemption and thus cannot be said in any sense to constitute a subversion by Oak of the negotiated provisions dealing with redemption of its debt.

Accordingly, I conclude that plaintiff has failed to demonstrate a probability of ultimate success on the theory of liability asserted.

PROBLEM

Suppose that Sleeze Corp. has outstanding $10 million worth of debentures, in denominations of $1,000 each. These debentures are held by 500 separate individuals, no one of whom holds more than 50 of them. The debentures are infrequently traded so it is difficult to establish a market price. The most recent reported sale was at a price of $850. Sleeze Corp.

has the right to call the debentures for redemption at any time at a price of $1,050.

Sleeze Corp. has recently sold one of its divisions and wants to distribute the proceeds of that sale to its shareholders as a dividend. The payment of this extraordinary dividend is prohibited, however, by a covenant in the indenture for the debentures. Were it not for this covenant, there would be no legal objection to the payment of the dividend. The covenant may be eliminated by a vote of a majority of the debentures.

Sleeze Corp. makes a tender offer of $860 per debenture. It is conditioned on a tender of at least 51 percent of the debentures and on submission of an "exit consent," which would vote the tendered debentures in favor of an indenture amendment eliminating the covenant that restricts the payment of dividends. In the written materials accompanying the tender offer, Sleeze Corp. states that if the tender is successful it intends to pay the extraordinary dividend. It is reasonable to expect that if the dividend is paid, the value of the debentures will be $800.

(a) Suppose you hold 10 of the debentures and do not wish to file a law suit. You think the debentures are worth $900 or more but your broker tells you that he cannot find a buyer at any price above $850. Do you tender?

(b) Suppose you are retained by a group of debenture holders to seek an injunction against the Sleeze Corp. tender offer and that the relevant law is that of Delaware, as set forth in Katz v. Oak Industries, Inc. On what theory, or theories, would you rely and how would you distinguish that case?

ANALYSIS

In Katz v. Oak Industries, Inc. a procedure was adopted to bring about a redemption, at less than face value (or, in Wall Street lingo, with a "haircut"), of substantially all of the debt obligations. That procedure consisted of a tender offer conditioned on the holder of each obligation submitting an exit consent voting that obligation in favor of the elimination of certain restrictive covenants. Under an alternative approach, the debtor corporation could have made a tender offer conditioned on a tender of, say, eighty-five percent of the obligations and on a *prior* vote eliminating the restrictive covenants. In a situation like that in Katz v. Oak Industries, Inc., is it likely that the outcome of the tender would have been different under the alternative approach from what it was under the approach in fact adopted? Might the outcome be different under the two approaches in other situations? What do your answers to these questions suggest about drafting provisions relating to the indenture amendments?

Morgan Stanley & Co. v. Archer Daniels Midland Company

570 F.Supp. 1529 (S.D.N.Y.1983).

[This suit arose from the redemption by Archer Daniels Midland Company (ADM) of $125 million of debentures bearing an interest rate of 16 percent. The plaintiff, Morgan Stanley & Company, Inc. (Morgan Stanley), claimed that the redemption violated a contractual prohibition and that it violated certain securities laws, including § 10(b) of the '34 Act. The reported decision in this case includes an opinion in support of the court's denial of the plaintiff's request for a preliminary injunction, followed by an opinion on the parties' cross motions for summary judgment. The former opinion, which contains a substantial discussion of the plaintiff's claims under the securities laws, as well as a discussion of its contract-law claims, is omitted.]

. . .

FACTS

In May, 1981, Archer Daniels issued $125,000,000 of 16% Sinking Fund Debentures due May 15, 2011. . . . The Debentures state in relevant part:

The Debentures are subject to redemption upon not less than 30 nor more than 60 days' notice by mail, at any time, in whole or in part, at the election of the Company, at the following optional Redemption Price (expressed in percentages of the principal amount), together with accrued interest to the Redemption Date . . ., all as provided in the Indenture: If redeemed during the twelve-month period beginning May 15 of the years indicated:

Year	Percentage	Year	Percentage
1981	115.500 %	1991	107.750 %
1982	114.725	1992	106.975
1983	113.950	1993	106.200
1984	113.175	1994	105.425
1985	112.400	1995	104.650
1986	111.625	1996	103.875
1987	110.850	1997	103.100
1988	110.075	1998	102.325
1989	109.300	1999	101.550
1990	108.525	2000	100.775

and thereafter at 100%; provided, however, that prior to May 15, 1991, the Company may not redeem any of the Debentures pursuant to such option from the proceeds, or in anticipation, of the issuance of any indebtedness for money borrowed by or for the account of the Company or any Subsidiary (as defined in the Indenture) or from the proceeds, or in anticipation of a sale and leaseback transaction (as defined in Section 1008 of the Indenture), if, in either case, the interest cost or interest factor applicable thereto (calculated in accordance with generally accepted financial practice) shall be less than 16.08% per annum.

The May 12, 1981 Prospectus and the Indenture pursuant to which the Debentures were issued contain substantially similar language.[1] The Moody's Bond Survey of April 27, 1981, in reviewing its rating of the Debentures, described the redemption provision in the following manner:

"The 16% sinking fund debentures are nonrefundable with lower cost interest debt before April 15, 1991. Otherwise, they are callable in whole or in part at prices to be determined.

The proceeds of the Debenture offering were applied to the purchase of long-term government securities bearing rates of interest below 16.089%.

ADM raised money through public borrowing at interest rates less than 16.08% on at least two occasions subsequent to the issuance of the Debentures. On May 7, 1982, over a year before the announcement of the planned redemption, ADM borrowed $50,555,500 [at] an effective interest rate of less than 16.08%. On March 10, 1983, ADM raised an additional $86,400,000 [at] an effective interest rate of less than 16.08%. . . .

In the period since the issuance of the Debentures, ADM also raised money through two common stock offerings. Six million shares of common stock were issued by prospectus dated January 28, 1983, resulting in proceeds of $131,370,000. And by a prospectus supplement dated June 1, 1983, ADM raised an additional $15,450,000 by issuing 600,000 shares of common stock.

Morgan Stanley, the plaintiff in this action, bought $15,518,000 principal amount of the Debentures at $1,252.50 per $1,000 face amount on May

---

1. The May 12, 1981 Prospectus announcing the issuance of the Debentures provides, in relevant part:

The Sinking Fund Debentures will be subject to redemption, . . . provided, however, that the Company will not be entitled to redeem any of the Sinking Fund Debentures prior to May 15, 1991 *as part of a refunding or anticipated refunding operation by the application, directly or indirectly,* of the proceeds of indebtedness for money borrowed which shall have an interest cost of less than 16.03% per annum.

The Indenture provides, in relevant part:

The Debentures may be redeemed, . . . provided, however, that

prior to May 15, 1991, the Company may not redeem any of the Debentures pursuant to such option *from the proceeds, or in anticipation, of the issuance of any indebtedness* for money borrowed by or for the account of the Company or any Subsidiary or from the proceeds, or in anticipation, of a sale and leaseback transaction (as defined in Section 1008), if, in either case, the interest cost or interest factor applicable thereto (calculated in accordance with generally accepted financial practice) shall be less than 16.08% per annum.

[Emphasis supplied by editors.]

5, 1983, and $500,000 principal amount at $1,200 per $1,000 face amount on May 31, 1983. The next day, June 1, ADM announced that it was calling for the redemption of the 16% Sinking Fund Debentures, effective August 1, 1983. The direct source of funds was . . . the two ADM common stock offerings of January and June, 1983. . . .

Prior to the announcement of the call for redemption, the Debentures were trading at a price in excess of the $1,139.50 call price. At no time prior to the June 1 announcement did ADM indicate in any of its materials filed with the Securities and Exchange Commission or otherwise that it intended to exercise its redemption rights if it felt it was in its self-interest to do so. Nor did it express any contemporaneous opinion as to whether it was entitled under the terms of the Indenture to call the Debentures when it was borrowing funds at an interest rate less than 16.08% if the source of such redemption was other than the issuance of debt.

Plaintiff . . . contends that the proposed redemption is barred by the express terms of the call provisions of the Debenture and the Indenture Agreement, and that consummation of the plan would violate the Trust Indenture Act of 1939, 15 U.S.C. § 77aaa *et seq.* and common law principles of contract law. The plaintiff's claim is founded on the language contained in the Debenture and Trust Indenture that states that the company may not redeem the Debentures "from the proceeds, or in anticipation, of the issuance of any indebtedness . . . if . . . the interest cost or interest factor . . . [is] less than 16.08% per annum." Plaintiff points to the $86,400,000 raised by the . . . transaction within 90 days of the June 1 redemption announcement, and the $50,555,500 raised by the . . . trans-action in May, 1982—both at interest rates below 16.08%—as proof that the redemption is being funded, at least indirectly, from the proceeds of borrowing in violation of the Debentures and Indenture agreement. The fact that ADM raised sufficient funds to redeem the Debentures entirely through the issuance of common stock is, according to the plaintiffs, an irrelevant "juggling of funds" used to circumvent the protections afforded investors by the redemption provisions of the Debenture. Plaintiff would have the Court interpret the provision as barring redemption during any period when the issuer has borrowing at a rate lower than that prescribed by the Debentures, regardless of whether the direct source of the funds is the issuance of equity, the sale of assets, or merely cash on hand.

The defendant would have the Court construe the language more narrowly as barring redemption only where the direct or indirect source of the funds is a debt instrument issued at a rate lower than that it is paying on the outstanding Debentures. Where, as here, the defendant can point directly to a non-debt source of funds (the issuance of common stock), the defendant is of the view that the general redemption schedule applies.

. . .

According to Morgan Stanley, the fact that the Debentures were trading at levels above the call price prior to the redemption announcement bolsters the argument that the investing public thought it was protected against early redemption.   The plaintiff asserts that it would not have bought the Debentures without what it perceived to be protection against premature redemption.

ADM contends that plaintiff's allegations of securities fraud stem in the first instance from its strained and erroneous interpretation of the redemption language.   Defendant argues that the redemption language itself—a boilerplate provision found in numerous Indenture Agreements— was sufficient disclosure.   Moreover, defendant asserts that it had no plan or scheme at the time the Debentures were issued to exercise its call rights in conjunction with speculation in government securities or otherwise and that the provision existed solely to offer the issuer "financial flexibility." More important, defendant contends that its view of the Debenture language was the one commonly accepted by both bondholders and the investing public.   .   .   .

ON MOTION FOR SUMMARY JUDGMENT

Contract Claims

The plaintiff's contract claims arise out of alleged violations of state contract law.   Section 113 of the Indenture provides that the Indenture and the Debentures shall be governed by New York law.   Under New York law, the terms of the Debentures constitute a contract between ADM and the holders of the Debentures, including Morgan Stanley.   .   .   .

We note as an initial matter that where, as here, the contract language in dispute is a "boilerplate" provision found in numerous debentures and indenture agreements, the desire to give such language a consistent, uniform interpretation requires that the Court construe the language as a matter of law.   See Sharon Steel Corp. v. Chase Manhattan Bank, N.A., [supra page 722].

In Franklin Life Insurance Co. v. Commonwealth Edison Co., 451 F.Supp. 602 (S.D.Ill.1978), aff'd per curiam on the opinion below, 598 F.2d 1109 (7th Cir.), rehearing and rehearing en banc denied, id., cert. denied, 444 U.S. 900, 100 S.Ct. 210, 62 L.Ed.2d 136 (1979), the district court found, with respect to language nearly identical to that now before us, that an early redemption of preferred stock was lawful where funded directly from the proceeds of a common stock offering.

Morgan Stanley argues, however, that *Franklin* was incorrectly decided and should therefore be limited to its facts.   We find any attempt to distinguish *Franklin* on its facts to be wholly unpersuasive.   Commonwealth Edison, the defendant in *Franklin,* issued 9.44% Cumulative Preferred Stock in 1970.   The stock agreement contained a redemption provision virtually identical to that at issue in this litigation.   The prospectus announcing the preferred stock would be used primarily for interim financing of a long-term construction program.   The construction program required an estimated expenditure of approximately $2,250,000,000, of which $1,150,000,000 would have to be raised through the sale of additional securities of the company.   *Franklin, supra,* 451 F.Supp. at 605.   In accord with this estimate, Commonwealth Edison's long-term debt increased from $1.849 billion at the end of 1971 to an amount in excess of $3 billion by the time of trial in 1978. All of this debt was issued at interest rates below 9.44%. In January of 1972, Commonwealth Edison announced its intention to redeem the preferred stock with the proceeds of a common stock issue.

The Franklin Life Insurance Company brought suit, contending that the language of the redemption provision barred redemption where Commonwealth Edison had been borrowing at interest rates below 9.44%, and expected to continue borrowing at such rates in the near future. The district court rejected plaintiff's claims, and held that the redemption was lawful because the refunding was accomplished solely from the proceeds of the common stock issue. In adopting a rule that looked to the source of the proceeds for redemption, the court rejected a "net borrower" theory that would have examined the issuer's general corporate borrowing history. Thus, Edison's borrowing projections and the sizable anticipated increase in its long-term, lower-cost debt was irrelevant, given that the undisputed source of the redemption was the common stock issue.

. . .

Morgan Stanley contends . . . that *Franklin* was wrongly decided, as a matter of law, and that a fresh examination of the redemption language in light of the applicable New York cases would lead us to reject the "source" rule. In this regard, Morgan Stanley suggests a number of universal axioms of contract construction intended to guide us in construing the redemption language as a matter of first impression. For example, Morgan counsels that we should construe the contract terms in light of their "plain meaning," and should adopt the interpretation that best accords with all the terms of the contract. . . . Words are not to be construed as meaningless if they can be made significant by a reasonable construction of the contract. . . . Where several constructions are possible, the court may look to the surrounding facts and circumstances to determine the intent of the parties. Finally, Morgan Stanley urges that all ambiguities should be resolved against the party that drafted the agreement. . . .

We find these well-accepted and universal principles of contract construction singularly unhelpful in construing the contract language before us. Several factors lead us to this conclusion. First, there is simply no "plain meaning" suggested by the redemption language that would imbue all the contract terms with a significant meaning. Either party's interpretation of the redemption language would dilute the meaning of at least some of the words—either the "indirectly or directly," "in anticipation of" language, were we to adopt defendant's "source" rule, or the "from the proceeds," "as part of a refunding operation" language, were we to adopt the plaintiff's interpretation. Any attempt to divine the "plain meaning" of the redemption language would be disingenuous at best.

Equally fruitless would be an effort to discern the "intent of the parties" under the facts of this case. It may very well be that ADM rejected an absolute no-call provision in its negotiations with the underwriters in favor of language it viewed as providing "greater flexibility." It is also clear, however, that neither the underwriters nor ADM knew whether such "flexibility" encompassed redemption under the facts of this case. The deposition testimony of ADM officials suggesting that they believed at the time they negotiated the Indenture that they could redeem the Debentures at any time except through lower-cost debt merely begs the question. Had ADM management so clearly intended the Indenture to allow refunding under the circumstances of this case, it surely would have considered that option prior to the suggestions of Merrill Lynch, which appears to represent the first time the idea of early redemption funded directly by the proceeds of a stock issue was presented by any of ADM's investment advisors.

Finally, we view this as a most inappropriate case to construe ambiguous contract language against the drafter. The Indenture was negotiated by sophisticated bond counsel on both sides of the bargaining table. There is no suggestion of disparate bargaining power in the drafting of the Indenture, nor could there be. Moreover, even if we were to adopt this rule, it is not at all clear that ADM would be considered the drafter of the Indenture, given the active participation of the managing underwriter. Indeed, it is arguable that the ambiguous language should be construed in favor of ADM. See Broad v. Rockwell International Corp., [642 F.2d 929, 947 n. 20 (5th Cir.), cert. denied, 454 U.S. 965 (1981)] (purchaser of Debentures may stand in the shoes of the underwriters that originally negotiated and drafted the Debentures).

Not only do the rules of contract construction provide little aid on the facts before us, but we find the equities in this action to be more or less in equilibrium. Morgan Stanley now argues, no doubt in good faith, that the redemption is unlawful under the Indenture. Nevertheless, . . . Morgan Stanley employees were fully aware of the uncertain legal status of an early call at the time they purchased the ADM Debentures. To speak of upsetting Morgan's "settled expectations" would thus be rather misleading under the circumstances. By the same token, however, it is also clear that ADM had no expectations with respect to the availability of an early redemption call until the idea was first suggested by Merrill Lynch.

Because we find equitable rules of contract construction so unhelpful on the facts of this case, the decision in *Franklin* takes on added importance. While it is no doubt true that the decision in that case was a difficult one and in no sense compelled under existing law, we find the reasoning of the court thoroughly convincing given the obvious ambiguity of the language it was asked to construe. We also find the result to be a fair one . . . . Moreover, we note that the decision in *Franklin* preceded the drafting of the ADM Indenture by several years. We must assume, therefore, that the decision was readily available to bond counsel for all parties. That the parties may not in fact have been aware of the decision at the time the Indenture was negotiated is not dispositive, for the law in force at the time a contract is entered into becomes a part of the contract. . . . While *Franklin* was decided under Illinois law and is therefore not binding on the New York courts, we cannot ignore the fact that it was the single existing authority on this issue, and was decided on the basis of universal contract principles. Under these circumstances, it was predictable that *Franklin* would affect any subsequent decision under New York law. *Franklin* thus adds an unavoidable gloss to any interpretation of the redemption language.

Finally, we note that to cast aside the holding in *Franklin* would, in effect, result in the very situation the Second Circuit sought to avoid in *Sharon Steel,* supra. In that case, the Court warned that allowing juries to construe boilerplate language as they saw fit would likely result in intolerable uncertainty in the capital markets. To avoid such an outcome, the Court found that the interpretation of boilerplate should be left to the Court as a matter of law. *Sharon Steel,* supra, 691 F.2d at 1048. While the Court in *Sharon Steel* was addressing the issue of varying interpretations by juries rather than by the courts, this distinction does not diminish the uncertainty that would result were we to reject the holding in *Franklin.* Given the paramount interest in uniformly construing boilerplate provisions, and for all the other reasons stated above and in our prior Opinion, we chose to follow the holding in *Franklin.*[4]

Accordingly, we find that the ADM redemption was lawful under the terms of the Debentures and the Indenture, and that therefore defendant's motion for summary judgment on Counts VI and X through XII is hereby granted.

. . .

4. We note in this regard that the "source" rule adopted in *Franklin* in no sense constitutes a license to violate the refunding provision. The court is still required to make a finding of the true source of the proceeds for redemption. Where the facts indicate that the proposed redemption was indirectly funded by the proceeds of anticipated debt borrowed at a prohibited interest rate, such redemption would be barred regardless of the name of the account from which the funds were withdrawn. Thus, a different case would be before us if ADM, contemporaneously with the redemption, issued new, lower-cost debt and used the proceeds of such debt to repurchase the stock issued in the first instance to finance the original redemption. On those facts, the redemption could arguably be said to have been indirectly funded through the proceeds of anticipated lower-cost debt, since ADM would be in virtually the same financial posture after the transaction as it was before the redemption—except that the new debt would be carried at a lower interest rate. Here, by contrast, there is no allegation that ADM

intends to repurchase the common stock it issued to fund the redemption. The issuance of stock, with its concomitant effect on the company's debt/equity ratio, is exactly the type of substantive financial transaction the proceeds of which may be used for early redemption.

Moreover, we fail to see how, on the facts of this case, the redemption could be argued to be a refunding from the proceeds of lower-cost debt. The [$50.5 million] transaction occurred over a year before the redemption and appears completely unrelated to it. The proceeds of that transaction were used to purchase government securities that remain in ADM's portfolio. The [$86.4 million] transaction, while closer in time, similarly is not fairly viewed as the source of the redemption, given that the proceeds of that transaction were applied directly to reducing ADM's short-term debt. To view the redemption as having been funded *indirectly* "from the proceeds" of the [$86.4 million] transaction would require us to ignore the *direct* source of the refunding, the two ADM common stock issues.

AFTERMATH

A recent book on bonds, in discussing the ADM redemption, states, "Investors don't readily forget the times that they lost money, especially if they felt that they might have been 'bamboozled.'" ADM's next bond issue, in 1984, containing the same, standard refunding provision that gave rise to the litigation with Morgan Stanley, "was not well received." Over a year later, when ADM again sold debentures, the obligations were noncallable for life (20 years)[4]. And in 1986, when ADM sought to redeem high-interest bonds, it did so by a tender offer, at an above-market price. R. Wilson and F. Fabozzi, The New Corporate Bond Market 188 (1990).

PROBLEM

In 1986, X Corp. issued $10 million of 15 percent subordinated debentures due January 15, 2006, which contained a prohibition on lower-rate refunding, using language identical to that in the *Archer Daniels Midland* case. In 1988, X Corp. built a new manufacturing plant to replace one that it had used for many years and was no longer large enough for its operations. The cost of the new plant was $20 million. It borrowed $18 million short term from a bank to finance the construction. On January 10, 1989, X Corp. moved its manufacturing operations to the new plant. On January 20, it raised $18 million by a public sale of $18 million of 12 percent subordinated debentures due January 20, 2009. It deposited the proceeds of the loan in a special account and on January 21, 1989, used those proceeds to pay off the bank loan. On January 25, X Corp. sold its old plant for $10 million, deposited the proceeds in its general account, and used those proceeds to redeem the 15 percent debentures. Did X Corp. violate the refunding prohibition? What if it had sold the old plant two days before it issued the 12 percent debentures, deposited the proceeds of both transactions in its general account, then paid off the 12 percent debentures and, an hour later, paid off the bank loan?

PLANNING

1. What language could have been included in the ADM debenture to give Morgan Stanley the protection that it claimed it had?

2. How might the redemption price on debentures be set so as to eliminate the problem that arose in the *Archer Daniels Midland* case? In answering this question, bear in mind that the value of a debenture can rise because (a) the market rate of interest has fallen or because (b) the issuer's creditworthiness has improved.

---

4. Redemption provisions making a bond "noncallable," as opposed to "nonrefundable," had been familiar to issuers and lenders at the time ADM issued the bonds that gave rise to the litigation with Morgan Stanley.

*

INDEX

879